INTERNATIONAL LAW

INTERNATIONAL LAW

Contemporary Issues and Future Developments

Edited by
Sanford R. Silverburg
CATAWBA COLLEGE

WESTVIEW
PRESS
A Member of the Perseus Books Group

Westview Press was founded in 1975 in Boulder, Colorado, by notable publisher and intellectual Fred Praeger. Westview Press continues to publish scholarly titles and high-quality undergraduate- and graduate-level textbooks in core social science disciplines. With books developed, written, and edited with the needs of serious nonfiction readers, professors, and students in mind, Westview Press honors its long history of publishing books that matter.

Published by Westview Press,
A Member of the Perseus Books Group

Find us on the World Wide Web at www.westviewpress.com.

Every effort has been made to secure required permissions to use all images, maps, and other art included in this volume.

Westview Press books are available at special discounts for bulk purchases in the United States by corporations, institutions, and other organizations. For more information, please contact the Special Markets Department at the Perseus Books Group, 2300 Chestnut Street, Suite 200, Philadelphia, PA 19103, or call (800) 810-4145, ext. 5000, or e-mail special.markets@perseusbooks.com.

Library of Congress Cataloging-in-Publication Data
    International law : contemporary issues and future developments / edited by
Sanford R. Silverburg.
       p.   cm.
    Includes bibliographical references and index.
    ISBN 978-0-8133-4471-3 (paperback : alk. paper) — ISBN 978-0-8133-4523-9 (e-book)
    1. International law.   I. Silverburg, Sanford R.
    KZ3410.I5792 2011
    341—dc22
                                                                    2010045667

10 9 8 7 6 5 4 3 2 1

Olivia Francesca, the light of my life
Kristine, the beam of that light
Leanore, my life's aura of light

CONTENTS

PREFACE

International law texts abound for all levels of study along with a variety of interpretive approaches, each emphasizing one theme or another. Insofar as attention has been brought to supplemental instructional support for the many different academic audiences, it has been sparse. One of the better known contributions in this line of thought is the collection of course syllabi with accompanying commentary and material compiled by John King Gamble and Christopher Joyner.[1] There is also, of course, a currently available source on the Internet blogosphere that comes from the American Society of International Law in the form of an online database.[2] Having approached this subject with a concern, I should mention that the interest in presenting international law in creative ways has increased, as evidenced by two unpublished papers, one by Charles J. Beck[3] and the other by Robert Perry Barnidge.[4] There are also different approaches to the study of international law[5] as well as specialized treatments.[6] In truth, it should be mentioned that some attention has been directed to subjects included in this reader.[7] Outlets for scholars interested in the subjects presented here, it appears, continue to expand, even to include multiple themes.[8]

Therefore, when approached by Anthony Wahl, Westview's senior acquisitions editor, about authoring a text, my first reaction was to question why should more trees be sacrificed for still another text to sit on the shelf alongside so many others. However, I knew of but one international law text reader that has become a standard on which instructors could rely to augment their instructional efforts.[9] Of much interest to those in the academe is the relationship between the strategic placement of international law in nations' foreign policies and the administrative importance of international law courses in institutions' curricula. More importantly, from my experience in academia at a small, liberal arts college, where a premium is placed on the quality of the instructor's pedagogy, there was a need for a single repository of material from which an instructor could draw both information and also perspective on traditional elements as well as some of the more nuanced facets of a field, as differentiated from international legal research. There was also a need, in my opinion, to open the eyes of students in the West in particular to the views of non-Western analysts and specialists whose perspectives may be bounded by personal, cultural, and geographic exposure. For students who have had little opportunity to venture out to the vast reaches of the globe, the parochial view of global politics and its relationship to international law is as universal as their world will allow. If, then, they have not had the opportunity to garner ideas from the growing array of published sources of information and even from the electronic media, they might not be aware of some of the current developments in international politics and their international legal implications. Hopefully, this reader will fill a void for those at the undergraduate or graduate level of study in institutions of higher learning or in the professional schools of law in which a concentrated study of international law is even more pronounced. For American instructors of international law, their potential audiences have been limited somewhat by the U.S. Supreme Court.[10] The decision by the High Court most likely will not have widespread impact across the globe I suspect, save perhaps for academicians in Turkey and Sri Lanka.

I am truly grateful for the cooperation I have received from the assembly of scholars and practitioners, who represent at least five continents. Their efforts are indicative of the level of attention given to international law as well as the awareness of a set of concerns that have broad implications for all manner of political organizations and social communities.[11]

Sanford R. Silverburg
Salisbury, NC
July 2010

NOTES

1. TEACHING INTERNATIONAL LAW: APPROACHES AND PERSPECTIVES, no. 11 (American Society International Law, Nov. 1997).

2. *Available at* http://asila.org/teachingmaterial/review.html.

3. "Teaching International Law as a Hybrid/Blended Course," an unpublished paper presented at the 2009 annual meeting of the International Studies Association, New York, NY (Feb. 15, 2009). Appended, readers will find an extensive bibliography. *Available at* www.allacademic.com/meta/p310921_index.html.

4. "The Socratic Method in the Teaching of International Law" (Mar. 27, 2009). *Available from* SSRN, http://ssrn.com/abstract=1369278.

5. Richard B. Finnegan, *Three Models of Science in the Study of International Law*, 8 CAL. W. INT'L L. J. 274 (1978).

6. Ariel Dinar and Daene McKinney, *Realizing Conflict, Negotiation, and Cooperation Concepts in the Context of International Water Courses*, 6 J. POL. SCI. ED. 188–209 (2010).

7. Alison Duxbury, *Drawing Lines in the Sand—Characterizing Conflicts for the Purpose of Teaching International Humanitarian Law*, 8 MELB. J. INT'L L. 259–72 (2007).

8. I have in mind here items such as the JOURNAL OF HUMAN RIGHTS AND THE ENVIRONMENT, vol. 1, no. 1 (2010), ISSN 1759–7188.

9. INTERNATIONAL LAW: CLASSIC AND CONTEMPORARY READINGS (Charlotte Ku and Paul F. Diehl eds., 3d ed. 2009).

10. Roger Alford, "Supreme Court Upholds Criminal Ban on Teaching International Law," in the blog Opinio Juris, June 22, 2010, *available at* http://opiniojuris.org/. The referenced case is *Holder v. Humanitarian Law Project*, 561 US ___ (2010); *more specifically at* Slip op. at 9, 16, 22, *but see also* the dissent at Slip op. at 13. Relative to the Court's decision is AMERICAN CIVIL LIBERTIES UNION, BLOCKING FAITH, FREEZING CHARITY (2009).

11. Strongly recommended for an appreciation of the basic approaches to the study of international relations to which international law is attached would be PAUL SHARP, DIPLOMATIC THEORY OF INTERNATIONAL RELATIONS (2009).

ABOUT THE AUTHORS

Dave O. Benjamin is an associate professor of global development at the University of Bridgeport.

Raj Bhala is the Rice Distinguished Professor at the University of Kansas School of Law.

Igor Borba is a Brazilian attorney at law and a recipient of a master of arts degree in international affairs from Marquette University.

Sophie Cacciaguidi-Fahy is a former lecturer above the bar in law at the National University of Ireland, Galway. She is presently a researcher at the Responsible Investment Academy Australasia (RIAA).

Anthony J. Colangelo is an assistant professor of law at the Southern Methodist University, Dedman School of Law.

Jeffrey Davis is an assistant professor in the Department of Political Science at the University of Maryland in Baltimore County.

Giulherme M. Dias is a professor in the Department of International Relations at La Salle College in Manaus, Brazil.

Emeka Duruigbo is an associate professor at the Thurgold Marshall School of Law at Texas Southern University.

Steven Freeland is a professor of international law at the University of Western Sydney and a visiting professor of international law at the University of Copenhagen.

Joan MacLeod Heminway is the College of Law Distinguished Professor of Law at the University of Tennessee College of Law and a fellow of the University of Tennessee Corporate Governance Center, Center for Business and Economic Research, and Center for the Study of Social Justice.

Douglas Jobes is the president of the Space Settlement Institute.

Stefan Kirchner is an attorney at law in Frankfurt am Main and lecturer, research assistant, and programme director at the Faculty of Law of Georg-August-University in Göttingen.

Timo Koivurova is a research professor and the director of the Northern Institute for Environmental and Minority Law at the Arctic Centre of the University of Lapland.

Catherine Lotrionte is an associate director of the Institute for Law, Science and Global Security at Georgetown University.

Jackson Nyamuya Maogoto is a senior lecturer at the University of Manchester School of Law.

Jeffrey S. Morton is a professor in the Department of Political Science at Florida Atlantic University.

Michael A. Newton is a professor of the practice of law at the Vanderbilt University Law School.

Thomas R. O'Connor is the director of the Institute for Global Security and an associate professor of public management and criminal justice at the Austin Peay State University (Ft. Campbell Center).

Anna Oehmichen is a legal researcher at the law firm Jus Cogens in Brussels.

Sundhya Pahuja is an associate professor at the Melbourne Law School and a co-director of the Law and Development Research Program at the Institute for International Law in University of Melbourne.

Elena Pariotti is a professor of human rights and legal theory at the University of Padua.

Vincent-Joël Proulx is an associate legal officer in the Chamber of the Vice President of the International Court of Justice, The Hague, Netherlands.

Andrew A. Rosen is a principal of AAgave, LLC.

Sanford R. Silverburg is a professor of political science in the Department of History and Politics at Catawba College. He is the editor of *Palestine and International Law: Essays in Politics and Economics* (2002, 2008).

Prabhakar Singh is an assistant professor at the Jindal Global Law School, O. P. Jindal Global University in India. He has earned an LL.M. from the University of Barcelona) as well as a B.A. LL.B. (Hons.) from the National Law Institute University in Bhopal.

Bjorn C. Sorenson is a practicing attorney in New York City.

James Larry Taulbee is an associate professor in the Department of Political Science at Emory University.

Ramesh Thakur is a professor of international relations at the Asia-Pacific College of Diplomacy at Australian National University in Canberra.

Davor Vidas is the director of the Marine Affairs and Law of the Sea Programme at the Fridtjof Nansen Institute. He is also the editor of *Law, Technology and Science for Oceans in Globalisation* (2010).

Edward H. Warner is a graduate student in the Department of Intercultural Communications at the University of Maryland in Baltimore County.

Alan Wasser is the chairman of the Space Settlement Institute.

1

Introduction

SANFORD R. SILVERBURG

An interesting task that would also serve as a disciplinary indicator of where exactly the study of international law is today is to survey international law texts from the classics like J. L. Brierly and even Lassa Oppenheim and Hersch Lauterpacht to the most currently available, paying attention to the subjects covered.[1] Although the fact that the political environment is constantly undergoing change is easily observable, international law is frequently expected to evolve commensurately. Whether law guides global developments or the reverse is the case, it can and often is the topic of rigorous discussion and debate in academic circles as well as in judicial fora. But the question remains: How would Hugo Grotius, whose *Mare Liberum* was meant to be global in scope, treat the subject of the transit of nuclear submarines under the Arctic ice cap, or Emerich de Vatel and the emergence of nongovernmental organizations and multinational corporations? Blaise Pascal in his *Pensées*, of course, pondered the extent of man's understanding of the universe from the earth skyward, but he did not, for he could not, even contemplate the boundary between air and space. Although some topics will appear to some as basic, even with a different nomenclature or emphasis— that is, political violence or, as it would now be called, terrorism—there are issues that simply would never have crossed the mind of an international legal jurist or writer before the twenty-first century. Cyberspace[2] and the electronic media as well as bioterrorism[3] and concerns for the environment fill the space of books and journals, having never been anticipated before the Second World War. Indeed, following the human devastation of the world conflicts of the first half of the twentieth century, a concern for human dignity and life itself reached global proportions with the emergence of international humanitarian law and the challenges to a nation's sovereignty with the introduction of universal jurisdiction, amongst a myriad of others.[4] Having presented this perspective, a traditional understanding of the evolutionary development of international law, beginning with Roman law up to a universally-created rules system should, nevertheless, be appreciated along with their philosophical bases.[5]

But although the discipline is ever widening, we have focused on a set of impressive issues that can serve as models of discourse in the classroom. In doing so, we have artificially halted the transitory nature of events and human affairs. No doubt, others have a concentrated interest elsewhere on issues neglected here, regrettably because of editorial space allowance. Perhaps the most striking developmental perspectives around the world have been the integration of international law into national legislation,[6] thereby giving rise to a new generation of international legal rules. On the topics that are included here, our desire is that instructors make use of the materials included so as to augment their classroom presentations and by examining some of the citations in the Selected Bibliography section. This reader is meant to be user-friendly, in this instance the user being understood as the instructor and the class. Teaching international law, whether in an undergraduate or graduate curriculum, in institutions of higher learning or at the professional level in law school, is important if for no other reason than the ever-hovering and classic question that remains: Does international law exist because the cynicism continues to find adherents?[7]

In the initial chapter, we deal with the evolving foundations of international law, or what may be considered contemporary values, in which we examine the expansion of the concept of a "crime" and the need for prosecuting and punishing or sanctioning individuals found to violate the accepted standards set by the world community, branded as *hostis humani generis*. Here a comment from a professor of international law is impressive because it is a prescient statement that also introduces the initial essay in this collection. Professor Kenneth Anderson thus penned "The emergence of international criminal law ranks as perhaps the signal achievement in public international law since 1990 and the end of the Cold War."[8] Adding to this theme is Dave Benjamin, who introduces here the subject with a historical context and looks to continued developments. Ramesh Thakur, though an academician in the West, speaks with the perspective of a non-Westerner and offers ideas that allow for questions of norms and values entrenched in one cultural system that may not necessarily be acceptable outside that realm.

From a paternalistic rationalization for domination in order to secure domestic benefits, a responsibility to protect has emerged as a means to obtain and ensure global stability and equilibrium, using the capabilities of the more powerful political entities in the world to prop up those who have intent but less ability. The traditional notion of sovereignty was about to change anyway in the contemporary era, and

credit must go to those who announced the precursory indicators to that phenomenon. The acceptance of any limitation to national sovereignty was founded in the failure of the international community to engage the perpetrators of genocide in Rwanda in 1994 and the U.S.-NATO alliance to respond to the atrocities in the eastern Bosnian enclave of Srebrenica in the Former Republic of Yugoslavia in 1995. Here attention must be brought to former Secretary-General Kofi Annan, who early on before Responsibility to Protect (R2P) became recognized, sounded the clarion call.[9] In the United Nations in 2004 self-examination for the need for institutional reform highlighted the "emerging norm that there is a collective international responsibility to protect exercisable by the Security Council authorizing military intervention as a last resort."[10] The UN panel's conclusion was subsequently endorsed and reinforced by the then-Secretary-General Annan, who in March 2005 pronounced that "we must embrace the responsibility to protect, and, when necessary, we must act on it."[11] Annan's successor, Ban Ki-moon, continued to press the effort.[12] To examine this theme is Professor Giulherme Dias, a Brazilian international relations specialist who brings a middle-power perspective to the discussion of the developing theme of R2P.

If states external to where someone has faced harm of some sort have a responsibility to protect such victims, altering the traditional concept of sovereignty becomes necessary. The limiting character of international controls is then overridden by a growing sense of obligation to render justice whenever the occasion allows, albeit under incomplete rules. Those who act in a criminal manner, as determined by states, judicial bodies, or international organizations, become subject to criminal prosecution, regardless of whether they are pursued, rendered, or bound over to a political authority. Recently, universal jurisdiction has gained a recognition that is, perhaps, not entitled to an emergent appreciation. National sovereignty traditionally has entailed the ability of the state's governing process to control all activities within its territorial jurisdiction and areas under its domination. Once that quality is threatened, surrendered, or limited, a nation's sovereignty is affected to some degree. In the evolutionary development of global politics, criminality, as the connection made by states to the international legal order, has led to exaggerated national authority to hold non-nationals to account for behavior considered to be unwarranted according to the international legal rule of *nullum crimen sine leges*. Media technology in general and the blogosphere in particular has loosened government control over public diplomacy and the employment of plausible deniability or the claim of transparency. Even election outcomes, often the subject of extralegal manipulation, are less opportune to speculation for the purposes of analysis. But, importantly, governments' action, often operating covertly and taken outside national territorial jurisdictions, culminated in an undertaking of universal jurisdiction by many states affected by the political behavior of some others. This technical legal development is taken up by professor of law Anthony Colangelo, who provides the background to its emergence and explains how it plays out internationally. A novel alternative, employed by still another application of the traditional court system to disputes, is the (special) tribunal, which tries inapprehensible suspects *in abstentia*. In support of this approach is the comment by the respected jurist Antonio Cassese, who, as the president of the Special Tribunal for Lebanon (STL), said, "I don't believe in the acts of a sovereign state but I believe in the acts of civil society because it is through individuals and organizations that governments can be pressured into fulfilling their commitments."[13]

We move on to deal with new dimensions of political organization, different from that conceived of at Osnabrück and Münster. We know that international organizations began to appear in the latter half of the nineteenth century. Today we operate in the midst of intergovernmental (IGO)[14] and nongovernmental organizations (NGO)[15] and even nonrecognized political entities.[16] Whether these alterations of the international political system are innovative or an improvement on previous conditions must be subject to some sort of value index and authoritative evaluation. Elena Pariotti delves into the emergence of nonstate actors whose interaction with recognized states in traditionally considered political practices has been cemented into the global environment. She then examines the varied roles that these styles of organizations have accepted, including a discussion of the responsibilities they bear.

If there is anything that is real, it is oneself, nature, and the connection between those two, which is survival, understood here as economics and this serves as the useful foundation for any belief. Social and political interaction is soon given sustainability through the exchange of the necessary means of existence, which are frequently exhibited through the production of goods and services. We thus look at the contemporary instruments of global economic interchange. The complexity of the relationship between investment, capital accumulation, and trade is sometimes made even more complicated when one party has more complete information than the other. A condition that adds to this situation is insider trading, which many are aware of with regard to domestic fiscal affairs, but the subject may not be as similarly transparent in international economics. Distinguished Professor Joan Heminway brings to bear an analysis of this condition in order to appreciate one of the factors that hangs over the debate of free and fair trade. Raj Bhala, a law professor whose expertise is in international trade law, presents a picture of the Chinese policy of trade protectionism and the relevant application of World Trade Organization (WTO) rules. The emergence of the new corporate phenomenon of the multinational corporation (MNC), especially as it operates within the confines of international law, is covered by Emeka Duruigbo. He organizes his thought around the fact that politics and its relationship to economics has brought the world to a new and different level of interaction.

Conflict has long been understood to be resolved pacifically—if mutually beneficial—

through the operation of courts. From the establishment on the international level of the Permanent Court of Justice in 1922, we have witnessed a full circle, from the signing of the Rome Statute and the creation of the International Criminal Court[17] to the proposed establishment of a so-called international piracy court to deal with a specific issue arising off the Horn of Africa.[18] The emergence of postconflict, reconciliation tribunals as well as simply regional and international courts has brought a clearer focus on the nature of crime at the international level.[19] There can be little doubt that this occurrence has had an impact not only on international legal developments but on national political affairs as well.[20] The section dealing with international courts is introduced by reference to a local conflict. Central and Latin America have been rife with incessant political violence from the time of national independence. The causes for the turmoil most often have been attributed to the regions' culturally based class structure, conditioned by the introduction of Western religion and the addition of imported ideological conflicts. The sanguineous character of the social conflict has frequently led to overt human rights abuses. Jeffrey Davis and Edward Warner take up an attempt by a regional court, the Inter-American Court of Human Rights, to restore some sense of stability to the human condition in Guatemala. A broad survey of the regional court system is then presented by Igor Borba, a Brazilian international relations specialist and an attorney.

The high value attributed to human life can be found universally in all cultures, though it is applied differently to selected groups in different eras. The violent devastation that engulfed so many millions of people during the first half of the twentieth century led jurists to push and achieve a Universal Declaration of Human Rights.[21] This attempt to gain recognition for human dignity became a legal maieutic to cross cultural divides and achieve greater unanimity, and it has been relatively successful, as one can observe regions and states following suit. Human rights have now been extended beyond

the limits of the human race and social rights to include climate change[22] and the environment.[23] Introducing the reader to the field of human rights is a German attorney, Stefan Kirchner, who highlights the configuration of international humanitarian law as it exists today as international human rights law. The anarchic state of affairs on the Horn of Africa, where there is no established governing presence in Somalia, led the United Nations, with additional support from the United States, to become involved with a mission there, sent on the basis of humanitarian intervention. Bjorn Sorenson examines this attempt to introduce a modicum of stability, but this ultimately led to an unfortunate collapse.

Human existence is now recognized as more than mere material sustenance; it also includes the world around us, including the air we breathe, the essential components of the water we drink, and generally the overall quality of life.[24] Hence, international environmental law has awakened the consciousness of people around the globe, and the legal community soon followed.[25] Attention is thus brought here to air and space and the seas.

Not that long ago tales of space travel and extraterrestrial colonies were the trademark of science fiction. Today, however, those possibilities appear more realistic, as Alan Wasser and Douglas Jobes bring those prospects closer to our grasp, at least for the purposes of discussion. When and if the international legal community can reach an agreement on the dividing line between air and space, we will have made great progress.[26] Following this, Jackson Maogoto and Steven Freeland provide an overview of the issues with which those who work in these areas are confronted.

Grotius's demand for open seas was challenged not only by the Englishman Robert Selden but also by naval piracy, which has historically been considered an international crime subject to automatic prosecution, sentencing, and punishment wherever the culprit was apprehended. Indeed, U.S. codified law allowed American officials to imprison for life those apprehended for piracy.[27] The oceans of the globe offered ancient civilizations the means to connect with other known regions for purposes of conquest, trade, or sustenance. However, concerns over depletion of the resources within the ocean space as well as the surface of the ocean bottom and subsoil doesn't appear with any significance until the middle of the twentieth century, when, under the auspices of the United Nations, states saw fit to enter into a set of major multilateral conventions.[28] Capital investment, corporate expansion, and the continuously increasing need for sources of energy, precious metals, and an industrial fishing industry has led to exploration and a greater appreciation for what the oceans and its subsoil could offer. Davor Vidas, an authority on marine legal affairs, explores the implementation of the United Nations Convention on the Law of the Sea (UNCLOS) to the European Union in a case study of the Adriatic Sea coast. Timo Koivurova then notes that although states have generally complied with the instruments of the UNCLOS, the littoral states to the Arctic Ocean continental shelf serve as a challenge to the Arctic Council, an intergovernmental forum. Following this, presented as a lawyer and researcher, Sophie Cacciaguidi-Fahy is concerned about the relationship between human rights and the law of the sea, and by looking at what happens to those lost at sea and how vessels in distress are to be treated, she brings together the international legal instruments governing the sea and the whole idea of human rights. As noted above, albeit briefly, the resources found in the sea, the adjacent seabed, and below offer a rich resource of food and national mineral supply that could easily make life better for millions of people who are otherwise bereft of the necessities for basic existence.

Political violence that may appear to be oxymoronic since the origin of the concept of politics is civil dialogue. Nevertheless, political history has involved numerous episodic periods of violence. One characterization of a form of this phenomenon has focused on the effect on the public when fear or terror is created amongst those who are not officially integrated to a conflict. Terrorism per se has dotted the political landscape for more than two centuries but now has become the international scourge du jour. One of the most complicated aspects of asymmetrical warfare, contextualized by the overarching theme of terrorism, is how recognized states are authorized to respond to the nonstate actor–initiated violence.[29] Then there is the question of terminological status of those apprehended by a state's military or other police authorities, how to properly detain these subjects, and, finally, the best method to prosecute for alleged wrongful acts. These complications necessarily affect domestic legislation and test the limits of judicial activism.[30] Catherine Lotrionte steps into the fuzzy area of the appropriate use of what has been euphemistically referred to as "coerced interrogation," which is otherwise referred to in a more common manner as torture. When is this approach to counterterrorism an acceptable practice, and when this is found to be the case, what is the effect on the moral fiber of the state employing it? Vincent-Joël Proulx takes the position that in order to increase accountability for acts of transborder aggression, it will become necessary for states to create a sound counterterrorism strategy that prioritizes acceptance of liability over state sovereignty. The surprise attack by al-Qaeda, a transnational organization using civilian airliners to conduct a suicide terrorist attack on the Twin Towers in New York City and the Pentagon in the Virginia suburbs of Washington, DC—though targeting the White House, ultimately failed to reach it—established a hallmark for the study of terroristic violence. How states have responded along an international legal dimension is the subject of study by a German attorney, Anna Oehmichen.

The immediate post–World War II era brought about a structural reconfiguration of the political landscape of the globe. There certainly was no inclination or even opportunity to allow another Congress of Vienna or a Conference of Berlin. Former dependencies of the European Metropoles recognized that the once-powerful states of Europe were now depleted of the basis for dominating much of the world.[31] The age of empires passed and was replaced with democratic political aspirants, popular governments, and even a demand for national self-determination. Many people in Africa and Asia seized on the altered political environment to create an opportunity to regain control over their cultures and lifestyles, which had been repressed for close to a century, understood in contemporary political terms as irredentism. Comparative politics was guided by paradigms of "third world studies," North-South conflict, and lesser development and underdevelopment. Later, a more nuanced approach to the study with a comparative and international legal context became known as postcolonialism.[32]

The issue of the use of violence to make a claim in an era in which total satisfaction has not been achieved is contextualized uniquely by Thomas O'Connor. As a result of status deprivation *inter alia*, violence has been employed to accomplish what diplomatic practice would normally have appointed. The condition of terroristic violence is then placed in a philosophical context that is given a specific set of political conditions. Many borders of modern states have been subject to the demarcation or delimitation by western European diplomats at post–World War I and –World War II negotiation tables. The unintended consequences of these diplomatic maneuverings has been ethnic and armed political conflict. The observer need not look further than the Iraqi claim to Kuwait as the ancient province of Basra or the breakaway state of Biafra from Nigeria. Here Alan Rosen surveys border disputes in the contemporary era, applying the international legal principle of *uti possedetis*.[33] Then, Prabhakar Singh, clearly from a non-Western perspective, gives us a philosophical overview of international law as understood by both western and non-Western sources. Following this, Sundhya Pahuja, again as a spokesperson from the South,[34] then places postcolonialism alongside international law because, as he argues, much of it was formed from imperial impulses of Western states.

As ancient as international law is, politics among differently organized people preceded it. Once international law was established, however, it was necessarily married to international politics, a condition that exists up to this day. The alteration of the international political scene certainly occurs with greater alacrity than the most progressive movers among international legal agents. As the international political system has become more global in recognition, the exchange of goods and services similarly has expanded in both scope and form. Professor Jeffrey Morton brings us almost full circle with a foundational analysis of some of the basic principles that undergird international law and, therefore, necessarily affect the operation of the international political system. This is followed by a representative perspective on the nexus between the two studies of world politics and international law, something Professor J. Larry Taulbee has been involved with for most of his academic career. Professor Sanford Silverburg addresses the oft-assumed notion that law and justice are synonymous and applies this connection to the negotiating process of the Arab-Israeli conflict. The purpose is to dispose of the connection and, indeed, show that its lack of connectedness is the basis for the asymmetry of the conflict.

The reader will find here two distinct citation styles. Because the substance of this reader is law, the bulk of the materials will be referenced according to the Harvard Blue Book style. The Select Bibliography section provides more inclusive citation information for the use of the student and researcher.

NOTES

1. For a general examination, *see* Renée Jeffery, *Hersch Lauterpacht, the Realist Challenge and the "Grotian Tradition" in 20th Century International Relations,* 12 EUR. J. INT'L RELS. 223 (2006).

2. A term introduced via science fiction in 1984. *See* WILLIAM GIBSON, NEUROMANCER 5 (1984). *See, e.g.,* JAMES A. LEWIS, A NOTE ON THE LAWS OF WAR IN CYBERSPACE (Apr. 2010).

3. *See, e.g.,* JENNIFER MACKBY, STRATEGIC STUDIES ON BIOTERRORISM (Oct. 16, 2006).

4. One indication of the globalization of international law is the ruling from the U.S. Supreme Court on international family law in *Abbott v. Abbott*, 560 U.S. ___ (2010), upholding the Hague Convention on the Civil Aspects of Child Abduction, T.I.A.S. No. 11670, S. Treaty Doc. No. 99–11. With this decision, the American High Court accepted the use of foreign law to interpret treaties. Interestingly, in the same session, the Court employed foreign law to deal with capital punishment, *see also Graham v. Florida*, 560 U.S. ___ (2010), a further step to integrating global jurisprudence into national law.

5. The Philosophy of International Law (Samantha Besson & John Tasioulas eds., 2010).

6. Indeed, it was the well-respected Percy Corbett who noted the integration of state consensus on international law formation, but his realm was strictly Western, with no appreciation or mention of any source outside of Western Europe. Percy E. Corbett, From International to World Law (1969). The formal role of the legal adviser to foreign policy makers has, indeed, come under increased scrutiny. I Michael P. Scharf & Paul R. Williams, Shaping Foreign Policy in Times of Crisis: The Role of International Law and the State Department Legal Advisor (2010), and Richard Bilder, *The Office of the Legal Advisor: The State Department's Lawyer and Foreign Affairs*, 56 Am. J. Int'l L. 633 (1962), *available at* http://ssrn.com/abstract=1551956.

7. Eric Posner, *Think Again: International Law*, For. Pol'y, Sept. 17, 2009, *available at* www.foreignpolicy.com/articles/2009/09/17/think-again-international-law. The theme is also examined in an expanded format by Posner *in* The Perils of Global Legalism (2009).

8. Kenneth Anderson, *The Rise of International Criminal Law: Intended and Unintended Consequences*, 20 Eur. J. Int'l L. 331 (2009), *but see contra* Brad R. Roth, *Coming to Terms with Ruthlessness: Sovereign Equality, Global Pluralism and the Limits of International Criminal Justice*, 8 Santa Clara J. Int'l L. 231 (2010), and a series of commentaries in the EJIL: *Talk!* blog on May 3, 21, 27, and July 8, 2010, *available at* www.ejiltalk.org.

9. Kofi Annan, *Two Concepts of Sovereignty*, 352 The Economist 49–50 (Sept. 18, 1999).

10. United Nations, *Secretary General Report from a High-Level Panel on the Threats Challenged and Change. A More Secure World: Our Shared Responsibility*, at para. 66, U.N. Doc. A/59/565 (2004).

11. Kofi Anan, *In Larger Freedom: Towards Development, Security and Human Rights for All. Report of the Secretary-General to the U.N. Summit 21 March 2005*, at paras. 126 & 135, U.N. Doc. A/59/2005 (2006). The full text of the report is *available at* www.un.org/largerfreedom/. The United Nations' concern is analyzed in depth by Global Centre for the Responsibility

to Protect, Implementing the Responsibility to Protect: The 2009 General Assembly Debate: An Assessment (Aug. 2009), and International Coalition for the Responsibility to Protect, Report on the General Assembly Plenary Debate on the Responsibility to Protect (Sept. 15, 2009). For general background, *see* Gareth Evans & Mohamed Shanoun et al., The Responsibility to Protect (Report of the International Commission on Intervention and State Sovereignty) (2001).

12. *Secretary-General Defends, Clarifies "Responsibility to Protect" at Berlin Event on "Responsible Sovereignty: International Cooperation for a Changed World" Implementing the Responsibility to Protect*, U.N. Doc. SG/SM/11701 (Jul. 15, 2008). *See also Report of the Secretary General*, U.N. Doc. A/63/677 (Jan. 12, 2009), and Edward C. Luck, *The Responsible Sovereign and the Responsibility to Protect*, 1 Annual Rev. of UN Aff. xxiii–xliv (Joachim W. Müller & Karl P. Sauvant eds., 2008).

13. *STL Officials Explain Court's Use of Trials in Absentia*, The Daily Star (Beirut), May 14, 2010, *available at* www.dailystar.com.lb/printable.asp?art_ID=114844&cat_ID=1. It should be noted that the STL allows for "total" *in abstentia* proceedings while other U.N tribunals have permitted only "partial" *in abstentia* proceedings. For a more extensive analysis, *see* [Lt. Col.] Chris Jenks, "Notice Otherwise Given: Will in Abstentia at the Special Tribunal for Lebanon Violate Human Rights?" *available at* http://works.bepress.com/chris_jenks/3.

14. Nigel D. White, *Separate But Connected: Inter-Governmental Organizations and International Law*, 5 Int'l Org. L. Rev. 175 (2008).

15. Ludmila Galenskaya, *The International Institutional System and International Non-Governmental Organizations*, *in* Multiculturalism and International Law: Essays in Honour of Edward McWhinney 415–28 (Sienho Yee ed., 2009).

16. See, *e.g.*, Turkish Republic of Northern Cyprus, Iraqi Kurdistan, and Transnistria.

17. An intriguing development introduced by the Review Conference of the Rome Statute of the International Criminal Court, which took place in Kampala, Uganda (May 31–June 11, 2010), was to adopt an amendment making "aggression" a war crime. Resolution RC/Res. 6 is *available at* www.icc-cpi.int/ccdocs/asp_docs/Resolutions/RC-Res.6_ENG.pdf. *See also* Dapo Akande, *What Exactly Was Agreed in Kampala on the Crime of Aggression?* EJIL: *Talk!* June 21, 2010, *available at* www.ejiltalk.org/what-exactly-was-agreed-in-kampala-on-the-crime-of-aggression/, and Michael J. Glennon, *The Blank-Prose Crime of Aggression*, 35 Yale J. Int'l L. 71 (2010), *available at* ssrn.com/abstract=1526754. The ICC's Special Working Group also spelled out the elements of aggression as a crime in a "non-paper" by the Group's

Chairman on May 28, 2009, *available at* www.icc-cpi .int/iccdocs/asp_docs/SWGCA/Non-paper-Elements-of -theCoA-28May2009-ENG.pdf.

18. UN Security Council Resolution 1918 (2010) calls on states to "criminalize piracy under their domestic law and favourably consider the prosecution of suspected and imprisonment of convicted, pirates apprehended off the coast of Somalia, consistent with applicable international human rights law." U.N. S/RES/1918, at para. 2 (2010). For additional background, *see* Michael Passman, *Protections Afforded to Captured Pirates under the Law of War and International Law*, 33 TUL. MAR. L. J. 1 (2008), and Michael Bahar, *Attaining Optimal Deterrence at Sea: A Legal and Strategic Theory for Naval Anti-Piracy Operations*, 40 VAND. J. TRANSNAT'L L. 1 (2007).

19. David D. Caron, *Towards a Political Theory of International Courts and Tribunals*, 24 BERKELEY J. INT'L L. 401 (2006).

20. Jonathan I. Charney, *The Impact on the International Legal System of the Growth of International Courts and Tribunals*, 31 N.Y.U. J. INT'L L. & POL. 697 (1999); Angela Del Vecchio, *Globalisation and its Effect on International Courts and Tribunals*, 5 THE LAW & PRACTICE OF INT'L CTS. & TRIBUNALS 1 (2006).

21. G.A. Res. 217A, U.N. GAOR, 3d Sess., 1st plen. Mtg., U.N. Doc. A/810 (Dec. 12, 1948). The two primary binding treaties are the International Covenant on Civil and Political Rights, Dec. 16, 1966 (ICCPR), 999 U.N.T.S. 171 and the International Covenant on Economic, Social, and Cultural Rights, Dec. 16, 1966 (ICESCR), 993 U.N.T.S. 3. For the early evolutionary development, *see* Andrew Moravcsik, *The Origins of Human Rights Regimes: Democratic Delegation in Postwar Europe*, 54 INT'L ORG. 217 (2000), and Samuel Moyn, *Human Rights in History*, THE NATION, Aug. 11, 2010, available at www.thenationa.com/print/article/153993/ human-rights-history.

22. *Report of the Office of the U.N. Commissioner for Human Rights on the Relation Between Climate Change and Human Rights*, Human Rights Council Resolution 7/23, A/HRC/10/61 (Jan. 15, 2009).

23. *See* the related material in connection to the BIOT, *infra* note 32.

24. Professor Douglas Cassel has asked an important question in *Do We Have a Human Right to a Healthy Environment?* WORLDVIEW, Apr. 23, 2009, *available at* www.chicagopublicradio.org/content.aspx?audioID =33760#.

25. Modern environmental law is most often noted to begin with the United Nations Conference on the Human Environment, June 5–16, 1972 (Stockholm), *Declaration of the United Nations Conference on the Human Environment*, U.N. Doc. A/CONF.48/14 (June 16, 1972), and evolves to the 1992 United Nations Conference on Environment and Development, which adopted the *Rio Declaration on Environment and Development*, U.N. Doc. A/CONF.151/5/Rev.1 (June 13, 1992).

26. *See, e.g.,* UN General Assembly, Committee on the Peaceful Uses of Outer Space, *Historical Summary on the Consideration of the Question on the Definition and Delimitation of Outer Space*, U.N. Doc. A/AC.105/769 (2002); John A. Vosburgh, *Where Does Outer Space Begin?* 56 A.B.A. J. 134 (1970); Raymond J. Barrett, *Outer Space and Air Space: The Difficulty in Definition*, 24 AIR U. REV. 34 (1973); Stanley B. Rosenfield, *Where Air Space Ends and Outer Space Begins*, 7 J. SPACE L. 137 (1979).

27. 18 U.S.C. §165, interpreted by the U.S. Supreme Court in *United States v. Furlong*, 18 U.S. 184 (1820), following *United States v. Smith*, 18 U.S. 153 (1820), *but see United States v. Said*, ___ F. Supp. ___ (E.D. Va., Aug. 17, 2010). Practically speaking, when looking for a definition of piracy, consult the Convention for the Suppression of Unlawful Acts Against the Safety of Maritime Navigation, 1678 U.N.T.S. 221, 27 I.L.M. 668 (1988). For a digitized collection of pre-1923 piracy trials before the U.S. Supreme Court, *see* Law Library, Library of Congress, Piracy Trials, *available at* www .loc.gov/law/help/piracy/piracy_trials.php. For regional activities, *see* Regional Cooperation Agreement on Combating Piracy and Armed Robberies against Ships in Asia (ReCapp), 2398 U.N.T.S. 199; 44 I.L.M. 829 (2005), and International Maritime Organization, Resolution A.1025 (26), Jan. 28, 2010, The Code of Conduct Concerning the Repression of Piracy and Armed Robbery against Ships in the Western Indian Ocean and the Gulf of Aden.

28. It begins with the Conventions Adopted by the United Nations Conference on the Law of the Sea, April 29, 1958. U.N. Doc. A/Conf. 13/L.52-L.55; and Misc. No. 15 (1958). International Convention for the Prevention of Pollution from Ships, 1340 U.N.T.S. 61, 12 I.L.M. 1319 (Nov. 2, 1973); Convention for the Prevention of Marine Pollution from Land-Based Sources, 1546 U.N.T.S. 119; 13 I.L.M. 352 (Jun. 4, 1974); United Nations Convention on the Law of the Sea, Dec. 10, 1982, 1833 U.N.T.S. 3, 397, 21 I.L.M. 1261 (1982).

29. *See* NOAM LUBELL, EXTRATERRITORIAL USE OF FORCE AGAINST NON-STATE ACTORS (2010).

30. I have in mind here the notion of legal cosmopolitanism. *See e.g.,* *Boumediene v. Bush*, 553 U.S. 723 (2008), or what Eric Posner refers to as judicial cosmopolitanism. Eric Posner, *Boumediene and the Uncertain March of Judicial Cosmopolitanism*, CATO SUP. CT. REV. 23 (2007–2008), and *generally* Rainer Baubock, *Political Community Beyond the Sovereign State, Supranational Federalism, and Transnational Minorities*, in

Conceiving Cosmopolitanism: Theory, Context, and Practice 113 (Steven Vertovec & Robin Cohen eds., 2002).

31. Some, however, would argue that the struggle continues, as evidenced by the British Indian Ocean Territory (BIOT). Christian Nauvel, *A Return from Exile in Sight? The Chagoissians and Their Struggle*, 5 Northwest. J. Int'l Hum. Rts. 96 (2006).

32. This is a theme widely popular in critical literature as well. Our concern, however, is with an international legal perspective within a political context. *See, e.g.,* Postcolonialism and Political Theory (Andrew Vincent ed., 1997); Jasper Goss, *Postcolonialism: Subverting Whose Empire?* 17 Third World Q. 239 (1996).

33. This principle applied, in another context but explanatory nonetheless, can be found in Sanford R. Silverburg, Uti Possidetus *and a* Pax Palestiniana: *A Proposal,* 16 Duq. L. Rev. 757 (1977–1978).

34. The South here is the post–Cold War referent to the North-South economic conflict, where the North represented the industrialized sector of the world economy, whereas the South was the underdeveloped region.

PART ONE

INTERNATIONAL LAW FOUNDATIONS

2

Prosecuting Crimes Against Humanity

The Revolution in International Criminal Law

DAVE O. BENJAMIN

1. Introduction

Since the end of the Second World War, great strides have been made in international humanitarian law. The Nuremberg and Tokyo Tribunals prosecuted thousands of leaders of the Nazi Party and the Japanese state and military for crimes against humanity and war crimes. Although, ultimately, the heads of state were not prosecuted; instead, powerful leaders of the state and rank-and-file soldiers were prosecuted for crimes hitherto unacknowledged in the discourse on international humanitarian law. The prosecution of German and Japanese leaders rested on three principal bases: (1) they were ad hoc processes; (2) they were punished by the victorious powers, although with consent of successor regimes in those states; and (3) they were prosecuted chiefly for breaches of the peace and war crimes, with crimes against humanity coming in a distant third place. Only in later decades were surviving Nazis prosecuted for crimes against humanity and war crimes, and in that order.

The Nuremberg and Tokyo Tribunals paved the way for the multilateral negotiation of arrangements in international criminal and humanitarian law that were to have a long-term and far-reaching impact. First of all, at least two major international legal instruments resulted from the German and Japanese prosecutions: the UN Convention on the Prevention and Punishment of the Crime of Genocide (Genocide Convention) (1948)[1] and the four Geneva Conventions on the treatment of prisoners of war and civilians (1949).[2] The Genocide Convention has been subsumed into the Rome Statute of the International Criminal Court (2001), but the Geneva Conventions remain the standard in international humanitarian law regarding the treatment of prisoners of war and civilians during conflict. Although the Geneva Conventions are applicable to conflict exclusively, the Genocide Convention is broader in its scope, including the treatment of civilians in both conflict and nonconflict situations. Although the Geneva Conventions address the treatment of enemies in wartime, the Genocide Convention does not have a concept of enemies and is not limited in its application to conditions of war.

Furthermore, the Nuremberg Tribunals and the Tokyo War Crimes Trials, which were ad hoc processes, paved the way for the International Criminal Court to become a permanent court of international criminal law. This occurred through three mechanisms: first, the Nuremberg and Tokyo Tribunals as ad hoc processes;

second, the legislating of international conventions through the United Nations that sought to prevent mass killing; and third, the appointment of ad hoc tribunals in the 1990s by the UN Security Council. Thus, the International Criminal Court continues the work of the Nuremberg and Tokyo Tribunals by holding states' leaders responsible for how their own nationals are treated.

Although Nuremberg and Tokyo held leaders of Germany and Japan responsible primarily for the crime of breaching the peace and secondly for crimes against humanity, the revolution in international human rights and humanitarian law since 1946 has seen a reversal through a legislative and judicial process. UN General Assembly adopted conventions and the Security Council appointed ad hoc tribunals to bring crimes against humanity to the forefront—not as a feature of interstate war but instead to hold political and military leaders of states accountable for the manner in which they treat their nationals.

Ultimately, the process that began with Nuremberg and Tokyo, based on crimes that occurred in transnational wars and crimes against humanity within and across boundaries, has evolved into one that challenges the unparalleled power of the regime within the boundaries of the state. Contemporary international criminal law seeks to offer redress to civilians when intrastate conflict victimizes entire sections of the population on the basis of gender, religion, ethnicity, or political persuasion. It holds war lords equally accountable to heads of state and government and attempts to place the individual and community at the center of the legal process. Once the stepchild to Raphael Lemkin's crime of genocide, crimes against humanity have become the focus of investigation, leading to the prosecution of crimes against persons and communities. However, the Genocide Convention originally subsumed crimes against humanity into the concept of genocide, in which Lemkin's definition of genocide was the "intent to destroy, in whole or in part, a national, ethnical, racial or religious group."[3] Al-

though at the time some members of the United Nations recommended that genocide be incorporated into a broader structure of crimes against humanity, the Lemkin construct prevailed and, with it, the challenges of prosecuting leaders under the Nuremberg first principles. Many of the acts classified as genocide in the Genocide Convention have since been expanded as crimes against humanity and are now specified in the Rome Statute. These are

(a) murder;
(b) extermination;
(c) enslavement;
(d) deportation or forcible transfer of population;
(e) imprisonment or other severe deprivation of physical liberty in violation of fundamental rules of international law;
(f) torture;
(g) rape, sexual slavery, enforced prostitution, forced pregnancy, enforced sterilization, or any other form of sexual violence of comparable gravity; and
(h) persecution against any identifiable group or collectivity on political, racial, national, ethnic, cultural, religious, gender as defined in paragraph.

Crimes against humanity further include

(i) enforced disappearance of persons;
(j) the crime of apartheid; and
(k) other inhumane acts of a similar character that intentionally cause great suffering or serious injury to body or to mental or physical health.[4]

This chapter traces the evolution of international humanitarian law from the Nuremberg Tribunals and Tokyo Trials to the International Criminal Court and poses some awkward questions about the universality of application of conventions—the Rome Statute, in particular—in holding political leaders, especially the heads of state and governments, responsible for "mass atrocities" and other systematic crimes against humanity.[5] This chapter pays special attention to the comparison between special tribunals and the International Criminal Court, referral processes, practicalities of prosecuting heads of state and governments, and the further evolution of the ideal of universally applying international humanitarian law, especially in holding states and governments responsible for protecting their peoples.

2. The Myth of Sovereignty

For centuries, leaders and thinkers have generated many ideas about the meaning of sovereignty and its implications for the people in the state. The trajectory of these ideas reflect a progression in political discourse moving from a paternalistic view of state leadership and sovereignty[6] to the notion of the unchallenged authority and power of the leader of the state as the central authority who forges disparate communities together into a single nation-state.[7] The era immediately preceding the Enlightenment saw contemporaneous ideas about absolutism and the divine right to rule.[8] However, the Enlightenment then gave rise to the idea that the sovereign was more a symbol of authority than the executor of power—thinking that represented the autonomy of the state and people. On one hand, there was a call for limited monarchy; on the other, the idea of a constitution as a contract among citizens intended to restrict and constrain the sovereign and those who represented the people.[9] Although the Enlightenment did offer a revolutionary approach to conceptualizing sovereignty, Westphalian sovereignty, originating at the Peace of Westphalia, and the notion of the power of central authority dominated for centuries thereafter, thus establishing the nation-state system and replacing religious authority over people with political domination. As David Hamburg, M.D. put it: "In the foolish years before World War II, the concept of 'sovereignty' permitted autocrats and tyrants to treat their own people as they wished without serious question from outside. In this myopic context, what Hitler did to Jews and other unwanted groups, including dissidents, was his own business."[10]

Beyond the ideas of representative government, the centrality of the constitution, and the central authority of the state, Westphalia became the legal standard in recognizing the state as autonomous[11] and was enshrined in the Montevideo Convention of 1933, which defined the sovereign state as that which has met four conditions: internationally recognized territory; permanent population; central authority; and internationally recognized government authority.[12] Although Westphalia and Montevideo have remained the legal standard in defining the state and sovereignty, political thinking took a radical turn in the last decade of the twentieth century.

First, Francis Deng posited that sovereignty resides in the people, and given that states purport to be representing the sovereign people in imposing their power and authority, sovereignty really means responsibility of the state to and for its people.[13] Basing his thesis on decades of civil war and ethnic conflict in Africa that caused the deaths, displacement, and maiming of millions of civilians, Deng also contended that "Absolute sovereignty is clearly no longer defendable; it never was."[14] The scourge of ethnic and ideological conflict, which has brought death and misery to millions of civilians, especially in Africa, invariably leads to questioning the Eurocentric definition of sovereignty that has prevailed since the seventeenth century. Deng identified four features of sovereignty in the modern world:

i. "moral and material responsibilities for the population. It is from this that the legitimacy of a government derives, whatever the political system or the prevailing ideology."

ii. In countries in which "armed conflict and communal violence cause massive internal displacement, the country is so divided on fundamental issues that legitimacy, and indeed sovereignty, is sharply contested." In such circumstances "the validity of sovereignty must be judged using reasonable standards of how much of the population is represented."

iii. Sovereignty requires "a transcendent authority capable of holding the supposed sovereign accountable." External sovereignty—accountability to the international community—has long been integral to the recognition of the state.

iv. The "dominant authority or power leadership" has a duty to "transcend parochialism or exclusive national interests." Sovereignty implies a duty to the "collective interests of the human family."[15]

To Deng, therefore, sovereignty is the exercise of the responsibility of the state to protect its people and provide for their basic needs. Deviation from that fundamental responsibility leads to questions about the legitimacy of the state as representative of the sovereign people.

Following Deng's thesis, then-Secretary-General of the United Nations Kofi Annan developed a more refined thesis: that sovereignty resides in the individual. According to Annan:

> States are now widely understood to be instruments at the service of their peoples, and not vice versa. At the same time, individual sovereignty—by which I mean the fundamental freedom of each individual, enshrined in the charter of the UN and subsequent international treaties—has been enhanced by a renewed and spreading consciousness of individual rights. When we read the charter today, we are more than ever conscious that its aim is to protect individual human beings, not to protect those who abuse them.[16]

The International Commission on Intervention and State Sovereignty (ICISS) agreed with both Deng and Annan and, building on the sovereignty as responsibility thesis, concluded that

> Thinking of sovereignty as responsibility, in a way that is being increasingly recognized in state practice, has a threefold significance. First, it implies that the state authorities are responsible for the functions of protecting the safety and lives of citizens and promotion of their welfare. Secondly, it suggests that the national political authorities are responsible to the citizens internally and to the international community through the UN. And thirdly, it means that the agents of state are responsible for their actions; that is to say, they are accountable for their acts of commission and omission. The case for thinking of sovereignty in these terms is strengthened by the ever-increasing impact of international human rights norms, and the increasing impact in international discourse of the concept of human security.[17]

The ICISS definition of sovereignty implies that the authorities—both institutions and individuals—are responsible for the safety, well-being, and basic human rights of their people. They are also charged with the ultimate responsibility of ensuring that the apparatus of the state neither conspires nor colludes in harming or decimating the people.

Conversely, the Charter of the United Nations asserts that the sovereignty of the state cannot be impeded or interfered with by any other state or by the UN for that matter. According to Article 2(7): "Nothing contained in the present Charter shall authorize the United Nations to intervene in matters which are essentially within the domestic jurisdiction of any state."[18] By implication, neither the UN nor any other state has the right to interfere in any matter that is within the purview of the sovereign state. This rests on the basic assumption that the state has a right to make its own policies, create and adjudicate its own laws, and undertake to do what is required to ensure internal cohesion. This arcane interpretation of sovereignty makes the concept of international accountability and the responsibility of the state to its population problematic.[19] Although recognizing the state as the primary actor in international affairs, Article 2(7) imputes an assumption that all member states of the UN would act in the common interests of their peoples and the international community, an assumption that is far removed from the reality of the six decades since the organization was founded. The one caveat in Article 2(7) is that state sovereignty does not preclude or exclude the obligations of a state in which the UN has decided to apply enforcement measures.

It is important to examine the nuances of sovereignty for the following reasons:

1. The UN Charter addresses states as unit actors in international relations. Thus, the Charter protects state sovereignty and does not authorize intervention in the state.
2. The authors of the Charter did not foresee a world of ethnic and communal conflict within states and, for that matter, state collapse. Therefore, they had no reason to think the UN would debate intervention in states, even for humanitarian purposes.
3. The reality today is that with the prevalence of intrastate, ethnic, and communal conflict, civilians are at risk, not from marauding invaders from other states, but rather from those who rule in the name of the sovereign people but who abuse the apparatus of the state.
4. One of the critical contemporary questions is how to prosecute sitting heads of state and government, thereby preventing them from further violating their people and holding them ultimately accountable for their crimes against humanity.

Although the scholarship in political and international relations theory has progressed, the norm in international law has remained static. The Westphalia and Montevideo standard remains intact, with the possible exception that there is some greater emphasis on international accountability and external constraint on the state's exercise of power. However, that norm is largely influenced by the dynamics of power relations, ideology, and the orbit of a satellite state in the global power system.

The legal concept of sovereignty, supposedly derived from Westphalia, does not, however, adequately address either the responsibility of the state to its population or the constraints placed on states by the multilateral system, nor does it recognize the enormous contradictions between the legal standard and the realities of collapsed and quasi-states. Robert Jackson noted that sovereignty in many postcolonial states is based on "self-determination and development entitlements," with the consequence that "many Third World governments [are] classified as inadequate protectors of human rights."[20] The Jackson thesis raises a broader question: Is the Westphalian sovereignty legitimate in the first place? Andreas Osiander contended that it is not. According to Osiander, Westphalia is an erroneous assumption of sovereignty, in which the treaty merely affirmed the agreement among parties to cooperate with each other. Moreover, according to Osiander, state sovereignty is really a twentieth-century concept based more on belonging and the projection of power than on the nuances of Westphalia.[21]

Examining the evolution of sovereignty as a political idea and legal norm is critical to this discussion because of the intervention of international criminal law into the affairs of what have become nominal states. The reality of state collapse, as manifested in protracted internal wars, whether on ideological, ethnic, or economic grounds, has brought to the forefront the imperative of protecting the most vulnerable populations, especially women and children. The stark reality is that in Sierra Leone, gunmen representing the economic interests of warlords could ask civilians to choose between "short sleeves" and "long sleeves" prior to being amputated in the war for diamonds is indicative of the absolute failure of the state to protect its people, its most vulnerable, and minority ethnic groups.[22]

The issue, then, is not the state but rather governments or those who claim authority and power to govern, invariably in the name of the people but often not in the interest of the people. As Ramesh Thakur and Vesselin Popovski have pointed out, "Human rights can be violated most cruelly, pervasively and systematically by governments."[23] There is, therefore, an imperative to establish judicial institutions that protect civilians on an international level when their states and governments fail them.

3. Legislating Crimes Against Humanity After Nuremberg and Tokyo

The decades after Nuremberg and Tokyo saw the specter of internal conflict in which systematic violations of human rights, massacres, genocide, ethnic cleansing, and rape were not uncommon. From the Great Leap Forward and the Cultural Revolution in the People's Republic of China in the 1950s and 1960s through the Biafra conflict in the mid-1960s to the Cambodian genocide in the late 1970s, those in control of the state have not hesitated to use its full power against the civilian population.

It is important to note that the main focus of the Nuremberg Tribunals was not the crimes against humanity for which they have been given credit. Rather, as Michael Marrus has pointed out, crimes against humanity were classified as Count Four (after the Common Plan or conspiracy, crimes against peace, and war crimes).[24] This was based on Article 6 of the Charter of the International Military Tribunals, which prioritized the crimes "coming within the jurisdiction of the Tribunal" as, first, crimes against peace, then war crimes, and finally, crimes against humanity.[25] The Statement of the Offense contended that all the defendants committed crimes against humanity "in execution of a common plan and conspiracy to commit . . . War Crimes"; in other words, crimes against humanity were categorized as offenses committed as part of the common plan or conspiracy for which the Nazi Party was responsible.[26] During the Nuremberg Tribunals, crimes against humanity comprised, according to the Statement of the Offense, murder, extermination, enslavement, deportation, and other inhumane acts committed against the civilian populations before and during the war, as well as persecution on political, racial, and religious grounds in exe-

cution of and in connection with the Common Plan mentioned in Count One.[27]

In specific terms, there were three elements that made Nuremberg and Tokyo significant. First, the individual, acting as representative of the state, was held personally responsible for his or her actions in planning and/or executing international crimes.[28] Second, the classification of crimes against peace, war crimes, and crimes against humanity as international crimes meant that state sovereignty was superseded by such crimes and could not be used to avoid prosecution. Third, act of state could not be used as a defense by someone being prosecuted for international crimes, nor could status as a mere subordinate. Preeminent legal scholar Antonio Cassese has pointed out that the Nuremberg and Tokyo Tribunals "marked a crucial turning point" in international criminal law for two reasons. First, two new categories of crimes were established: crimes against peace and crimes against humanity. Second, until 1945 "senior state officials had never been held personally responsible for their wrongdoings."[29] In setting an important precedent, the Report of the Tribunal asserted that "the very essence of the Charter [of the International Military Tribunal at Nuremberg] is that individuals have international duties which transcend the national obligations of obedience imposed by the individual state."[30] This conclusion was based on the crucial and pivotal observation that "Crimes against international law are committed by men, not by abstract entities, and only by punishing individuals who commit such crimes can the provisions of international law be enforced."[31] Beyond this, as Michael Biddiss has pointed out, "there was a hope that the achievements of the IMT would help to lay the foundations for some form of permanent court capable of dealing effectively with violations of international criminal law and of being able to act promptly, irrespective of the specific location of the offences and of the particular national or other loyalties professed by those alleged to have perpetrated them."[32] Beyond this, the IMT, according to Martin and his colleagues, "marked a watershed in the conceptual and institutional development of international human rights and humanitarian law. The treaty law creating and governing the IMT wove together all the different and separate strands of the nascent international human rights and humanitarian law," including individual standing and liability, treatment of aliens, prohibition of discrimination against national minorities, the outlawing of slavery, and "even the use of natural law for recognizing international crimes where customary international law arguably had been less than clear."[33]

More broadly, the International Military Tribunals in Nuremberg and Tokyo established a moral imperative. The victorious powers demonstrated that they possessed the political will to prosecute crimes against humanity—crimes that had hitherto been committed but not prosecuted as international crimes. Beyond this, Nuremberg and Tokyo represented an effort to give substantive meaning to the mantra "Never Again"—that such inhumane acts committed on "political, racial or religious grounds" would never again be allowed to occur without penalty. At the same time, the victorious powers set themselves up as the arbiters of such international crimes, a position they essentially carried on as the Permanent Five Members of the UN Security Council. Although Nuremberg and Tokyo were successful in prosecuting and punishing many of those responsible for crimes against humanity, systematic crimes against humanity remained a feature of state control and state collapse over the next half-century. The dynamics of superpower geopolitics during the Cold War were powerful obstacles to both preventing and prosecuting crimes against humanity.

The achievements of Nuremberg and Tokyo were, however, short-lived. Although in the decades after World War II a number of international conventions and treaties were entered into under the auspices of the UN that proscribed acts and categories of acts as violations of human rights, little was done to prosecute the architects and executors of systematic crimes against civilians that had been outlawed by the

Genocide Convention 1948 or by the Geneva Conventions 1949. Louis Henkin has suggested that the significance of Nuremberg and Tokyo, as with the Genocide and Geneva Conventions that quickly followed, may have been that the great powers "agreed to outlaw only what no longer exists for them . . . or what they cannot conceive of as relevant to them."[34] Madoka Futamura was more optimistic when she noted that "While they had not been implemented internationally, principles derived from the Nuremberg Trial surely had some *normative* impact on post–Second World War international relations."[35] However, Futamura also observed that

The legacy of Nuremberg during the Cold War was rather ambiguous and ambivalent. While international humanitarian law and human rights law developed immensely based on principles set out by the Nuremberg Tribunal, states were reluctant to resort to the Nuremberg precedent; there was no international war crimes tribunal established thereafter to prosecute war crimes and crimes against humanity. The underlying belief was that strictly following the Nuremberg precedent would threaten state sovereignty and the non-intervention principle, on which international peace and security rested.[36]

4. The Role of the United Nations Genocide Convention

The postwar reality was that there was a great reluctance on the part of the United Nations, especially the Security Council, to intervene in countries in which there was evidence of systematic crimes against humanity, even genocide. Beyond this, according to Steven D. Roper and Lilian A. Barria, "the major problem with these and other human rights accords was the absence in the text of any specific obligation for states to prosecute and punish human rights violators."[37] In short, whereas Nuremberg and Tokyo were processes that punished leaders of states for egregious crimes against humanity, the legislative acts of the UN in the period immediately after the war omitted institutions that were authorized and competent to prosecute such crimes.

Consequently, the Genocide Convention, a product of the UN, was severely limited in five ways. First, it ceded prosecution of genocide and crimes against humanity to states. This meant that the very states responsible for genocide and other crimes against humanity were somehow expected to prosecute themselves for such crimes, which was rather unlikely given that arguably almost every state had engaged in crimes against humanity at some point. Even the United States—one of the sponsors of this new regime—could have been held responsible for crimes against humanity because of segregation, denial of the franchise, and other violations of basic human rights. As Jack A. Goldsmith and Eric A. Posner have noted, "No liberal democracy is beyond human rights reproach."[38] Second, the convention did not set out mechanisms for how to identify the committing of crimes, to investigate those crimes, or to prosecute such crimes. Third, there was no judicial apparatus, such as a permanent court, to prosecute crimes against humanity. Fourth, although Nuremberg and Tokyo issued sentences to those found guilty, the Genocide Convention did not develop in legislative or broader legal terms a framework for sentencing those found guilty of crimes against humanity, including genocide. Finally, although Nuremberg and Tokyo asserted the principle that individual leaders have responsibilities that transcend national interests, the vital political will to prosecute such leaders was clearly absent, as evidenced by events in Biafra in the 1960s and Cambodia in the 1970s.

The Cold War era was replete with protracted wars over sovereignty and governance that occurred to the detriment of nationals of the colonies or states. Throughout this era, the superpowers and their allies in Europe and Asia supported political organizations and military regimes that repeatedly violated the basic rights of human beings but did not violate the Genocide Convention to the letter. National liberation movements in Africa fought bitter protracted wars throughout the 1970s and 1980s for political and economic control that were fueled by the geostrategic ambitions of both the Soviet Union and the United States. China and the United States confronted each other through proxies in Indo-China during the 1960s and 1970s. Concurrently, the United States was wrapping up a bitter protracted war in Vietnam, in which they carpet bombed the north but ultimately lost the war. In the 1970s much of Latin America erupted with bloody coups and over a decade of "dirty wars." Vanguard movements in Angola and Mozambique fought against enemies backed by apartheid South Africa. Although throughout these struggles there were episodes of systematic crimes against humanity and war crimes, there was little political will to prosecute, and more important, the vital judicial institutions and procedures were not yet adequate or existent.

At the same time, European institutions of government in Africa disintegrated or failed to protect the sovereign people from governments themselves. Governments starved civilians to gain political power in defense of the sovereign state, as occurred in Biafra in the mid-1960s, which one scholar has termed "a noticeable omission."[39] Idi Amin, president of Uganda, unceremoniously expelled the entire population of Asians in 1972. The most dramatic episode during the Cold War was, arguably, the Cambodian genocide, during which over 1.6 million people were killed by the Khmer Rouge (although some sources estimate fatalities as high as 3.42 million).[40] The United States, United Kingdom, and the People's Republic of China supported the recognition of Pol Pot and sought to ensure that the Khmer Rouge retained Cambodia's seat at the United Nations, despite the mounting evidence of genocide.[41] Cambodia, therefore, illustrates the impact of the complexities of the Cold War on episodes of genocide.[42] At the same time, the stark reality was that genocide and other systematic crimes against humanity were prevalent, not in liberal democracies in the industrial world but rather in the former European colonies in Africa, Asia, and Latin America. Finally, the very fact that interest in prosecuting crimes against humanity, including genocide, was revived after the Cold War is indicative of the role played by the superpower standoff in preventing progress toward universal acceptance of criminal responsibility of political and military leaders for crimes directed at civilians.

There were also issues germane to the language of the Charter of the United Nations. The norm of nonintervention in Article 2(4) underscored not only the notion of state sovereignty but also the reality that the architects of the organization did not foresee intrastate war, genocide, and state collapse.[43] They proceeded on the assumption that the UN was a multilateral institution in which states represented their interests while working toward solving interstate issues, including conflict. As Erskine Childers and Brian Urquhart pointed out, the UN was "a blueprint for the post-war world" and the institutions which were to "save succeeding generations from the scourge of war."[44] The primacy of state sovereignty meant that even where regimes were clearly not representing their peoples and where they were complicit in systematic crimes against their own citizenry, such regimes were protected by the norm of state sovereignty, which violated the Nuremberg principles and contradicted "We The Peoples"—the Preamble to the Charter.

5. Reviving Prosecution Through Ad Hoc Tribunals

The Berlin Wall was not the only symbol of the chasm between East and West that was taken apart by the sovereign people at the end of the Cold War. The protections enjoyed by state leaders gradually eroded as civil society in rich and poor countries alike demanded some greater say in international political decision making. Paradoxically, as the Cold War came to an end, so did the artificiality of the nation-state in much of Eastern Europe. The Baltic states

quickly severed ties to Russia, as did the Central Asian states. Soon the movement spread to the Balkans, where the Yugoslav Republic was in its last days in the post-Tito era. By 1992 civil war was in progress, as Bosnia-Herzegovina declared independence from the former Yugoslav Republic, following Slovenia and Croatia. Massacres, "ethnic cleansing," and forced deportation were soon identified as hallmarks of the Serbo-Yugoslav-Croat effort to prevent ethnically diverse Bosnia from asserting state sovereignty. Concurrently, Somalia imploded into open civil war with warlords confronting each other for total political control. Shortly thereafter, the world was shocked by the massacres that occurred in Burundi and Rwanda in 1994. This chapter focuses on the responses of the international community in general and the United Nations in particular, not the ethnic and political causes of conflict in Bosnia and Rwanda because these are not germane to this discussion.

Since 1993 a number of special or ad hoc tribunals have been convened to prosecute political and military leaders for crimes against humanity and war crimes. These have been:

- the International Criminal Tribunal for the Former Yugoslavia (ICTY) 1993;
- the International Criminal Tribunal for Rwanda (ICTR) 1994;
- the Special Court for Sierra Leone (SCSL) 2002;
- the Extraordinary Chambers for Cambodia (ECCC) 2003;
- the Special Tribunal for Lebanon (STL) 2005; and
- the East Timor Commission for Reception, Truth and Reconciliation (CAVR) 2002.

Although all these have had an important impact on international humanitarian law, this chapter places greater emphasis on the contributions of the ICTY and ICTR, while briefly discussing the SCSL and ECCC.

The Security Council established the International Criminal Tribunal for the Former

Yugoslavia in 1993.[45] In setting up the ICTY, the Security Council expressed

> its grave alarm at continuing reports of widespread and flagrant violations of international humanitarian law occurring within the territory of the former Yugoslavia, and especially in the Republic of Bosnia and Herzegovina, including reports of mass killings, massive, organized and systematic detention and rape of women, and the continuance of the practice of "ethnic cleansing," including for the acquisition and the holding of territory.[46]

The Security Council resolved that the "sole" purpose of the ICTY was "prosecuting persons responsible for serious violations of international humanitarian law committed in the territory of the former Yugoslavia."[47] Critically, the Security Council recognized Bosnia-Herzegovina as part of the State of Yugoslavia and the conflict as an insurrectionary war, not as an independent state at war with the Yugoslav Republic.[48] The resolution called on all states "to fully cooperate" with the Tribunal, thereby invoking the principle of enforcement. The ICTY came about in part because there was the political will within the Clinton administration to demand prosecution of leaders in the Bosnia conflict for war crimes and other crimes against humanity. As Sabrina Ramet noted, "As early as 16 December 1992, Acting Secretary of State Lawrence Eagleburger called for the establishment of a war crimes tribunal to try war criminals in the Bosnian war, specifying, among others, Serbian President Milošević, Bosnian Serb President Karadzic, Bosnian Serb commander General Ratko Mladic, Serbian Radical leader Vojislav Seselj, and paramilitary leader Zeljko Raznjatovic ("Arkan")."[49] Ramet noted that "[a] specific feature of the Bosnian war [was] the incidence of organized systematic rape—or rather, forced impregnation, since pregnancy was a conscious goal of the Serbs."[50] The scope of crimes against humanity, then, was broadened to prosecute sexual violence that was intended to destroy a population, humiliate entire

families, and wreak a certain level of fear among citizens. Thus, the ICTY was intended to inquire into and prosecute crimes that extended beyond what were traditionally considered the essence of crimes against humanity.

Prosecuting the genocide in Rwanda posed a slightly different challenge for the United Nations.[51] As Michael Barnett has pointed out, the UN was faced with the embarrassment of its own culture, one that "could make nonintervention not merely pragmatic but also legitimate and proper—even in the face of crimes against humanity."[52] In adopting Security Council Resolution 955 (1994), which established the ICTR, the Council "expressed grave concern at the reports indicating that genocide and other systematic, widespread and flagrant violations of international humanitarian law have been committed in Rwanda" and classified the reports as a threat to international peace and security.[53] Based on a "request from the Government of Rwanda," the Security Council therefore resolved "to establish an international tribunal for the sole purpose of prosecuting persons responsible for genocide and other serious violations of international humanitarian law committed in the territory of Rwanda and Rwandan citizens responsible for genocide and other such violations committed in the territory of neighboring States."[54] The purpose was to prosecute genocide, recognizing that the Hutu government intended to destroy the Tutsi population. Moreover, the Security Council did not confine the work of the Tribunal to events in Rwanda; rather, it included events in neighboring states, thereby significantly expanding the domain of the ICTR. The point was not that non-Rwandans were complicit but that the Hutus responsible for the genocide had fled to neighboring countries, especially Eastern Zaire. There were two differences between the circumstances that gave rise to the ICTY and ICTR. One was that there was political will within both the Security Council and the European Union to monitor and enforce the embargo on Bosnia and Serbia. However, France, a permanent member of the Security Council, continued to ship weapons, including firearms, to the

Hutu Interahamwe—the militia responsible for carrying out the genocide—in Rwanda in violation of the Security Council embargo.[55] Another was that the UN Security Council moved rapidly to embargo Bosnia and authorize NATO to intervene, whereas in Rwanda the Security Council moved to withdraw much of the monitoring mission and thereby virtually condoning the genocide.

However, the Security Council moved decisively to establish the ad hoc tribunals needed to prosecute the crimes that occurred in both places and emphasized enforcement in resolving that all states were to "cooperate fully with the Tribunal." More recently, a UN Security Resolution[56] established special courts to prosecute crimes that have occurred since the Rome Statute came into effect in 2001. Arguably, the most notable is the Special Court for Sierra Leone, which at present is prosecuting Charles Taylor, former president of Liberia, for crimes against humanity.[57] Investigated by the Office of the Prosecutor at the ICC, the case against Taylor is based on his conduct of hostilities first as a warlord and then in his official capacity in Liberia, and it holds that he "is individually responsible" for crimes against humanity, including rape, slavery, terrorizing the civilian population, burning of private property, and the unlawful killing of civilians.[58] Some of the crimes were, according to the prosecutor, violations of the Rome Statute, whereas others were violations of the Geneva Conventions.

Then, in 2003 the UN General Assembly adopted two resolutions that authorized the establishment of the Extraordinary Chambers for Cambodia, which was charged with investigating and prosecuting the surviving leaders of the Khmer Rouge movement.[59] Financed by the United Nations, the purpose of the court is to investigate and bring to trial "senior leaders of Democratic Kampuchea and those who were most responsible for the crimes and serious violations of Cambodian penal law, international humanitarian law and custom, and international conventions recognized by Cambodia, that were committed during the period from 17 April 1975 to 6 January 1979."[60] This court began proceedings in 2009.[61]

The international tribunals are afforded significant latitude beyond cooperation with and service to the states in which crimes have occurred. They are able to request—and expect—the cooperation of states in identifying, locating, arresting, or detaining persons; gathering evidence; and surrendering or transferring the accused.[62] Although there is an implication of cooperation, the capability of tribunals to request and expect assistance from other states is at one level a return to the Nuremberg principles and, at another level, an assertion of a mandate from the international community that can have the effect of superseding the powers and authority of the state.

There are, however, limitations to the work of ad hoc and special tribunals. Foremost is that they are appointed by the UN Security Council or the UN General Assembly and are, as such, politically motivated. They are not the product of independent investigation and referral for the purpose of prosecution. As has been pointed out in the case of the ICTY, the United States advocated prosecution of the Bosnian-Serb and Serb leaders for crimes against humanity, including genocide and war crimes. Another limitation is that they are the product of a degree of selectiveness. As Thakur and Popovski pointed out, "The international criminal tribunals have been *ad hoc* and *ex post facto*, set up to try limited numbers of individuals for specific activities, in specific situations and specific regions. They therefore suffer from particularism."[63] However, the special tribunals have successfully hastened the removal from office of state leaders against whom charges have been laid. For example, the overthrow of Slobodan Milošević and Charles Taylor, respectively, was, arguably, triggered by the intent to prosecute them for crimes against humanity and war crimes.[64]

The ad hoc tribunals of the 1990s were interim measures while the international community, including nongovernmental organizations and other representatives of civil society, negotiated a permanent international court for investigating and prosecuting international crimes, including crimes against humanity.

6. The International Criminal Court

The signing of the Rome Statute that established the International Criminal Court in 1998 was a landmark event in international criminal and humanitarian law. The final vote that approved the Agreement and created the court was 120 states in favor, 7 opposed (the United States, Israel, China, Iraq, Sudan, Yemen, and Libya), with 21 states abstaining.[65] As of January 2007, 104 states had ratified the Rome Statute, including 26 of 29 members of NATO as well as Afghanistan, Australia, Colombia, Central African Republic, Democratic Republic of Congo, Georgia, Peru, and Uganda. Those not ratifying the treaty include Chile, China, India, Indonesia, Iran, Israel, Pakistan, Russia, Rwanda, Sudan, Syria, and Zimbabwe.[66] The negotiation process saw three groupings of states: the "like-minded states" (which included a wide array of states in the developing world, Scandinavia, and the European Union, and was led by Canada and Australia, supported by the United Kingdom and France, and aided by a number of nongovernmental organizations); other permanent members of the UN Security Council (the United States, Russia, and China); and the nonaligned group, which included Barbados, Dominica, Jamaica, and Trinidad and Tobago, and insisted on including the crime of aggression and drug trafficking.[67] The apparent convergence of positions of the states that oppose (and continue to oppose) the International Criminal Court says less about the credibility of the Court than about the role of geopolitics, international human rights, and humanitarian law in the foreign policies of those states.

The Preamble to the Rome Statute of the International Criminal Court (ICC) asserts that the signatories were determined "that the most serious crimes of concern to the international community as a whole must not go unpunished and that their effective prosecution must be ensured by taking measures at the national level and by enhancing international cooperation."[68] Although one is not certain about the broader intentions of the states that negotiated the Rome Statute in 1996 or the UN General Assembly, the president of the ICC, Judge Philippe Kirsch, told the UN General Assembly in 2007 that

> Throughout the course of history, genocide, crimes against humanity and other serious international crimes have not arisen spontaneously. Rather, these crimes have occurred—and continue to occur—in the context of complex political conflicts. More often than not, there were attempts to resolve such conflicts through expedient political compromises. More often than not, these compromises ignored the need for justice and accountability. And more often than not, expedient political solutions which ignored the need for justice unraveled, leading to more crimes, new conflicts and recurring threats to peace and security. The International Criminal Court was created to break this vicious cycle of crimes, impunity and conflict. It was set up to contribute to justice and the prevention of crimes, and therefore to peace and security.[69]

In a number of respects, the principles guiding the ICC resemble the precepts that underlay the IMT at Nuremberg and Tokyo, especially the notion that the individual is ultimately responsible for state policy. Thus, personal responsibility of state leaders was restored as a principle that transcended the constraints of state sovereignty. An individual could not offer as defense that he was either acting as a mere subordinate or representative of the interests of the state or sovereign. Article 27 of the Rome Statute asserts that "This Statute shall apply equally to all persons without any distinction based on official capacity. In particular, official capacity as a Head of State or Government, a member of a Government or parliament, an elected representative or a government official shall in no case exempt a person from criminal responsibility under this Statute, nor shall it, in and of itself, constitute a ground for reduction of sentence." Furthermore, Article

28 establishes the crime of omission, which is deemed to be as important as the crime of commission. The implication is that Article 27 makes the failure to act in defense of the vulnerable as much a crime as an act against the vulnerable. Morrison noted that

> there has been a defining and broadening of the concept of individual criminal responsibility so that anyone in a position of responsibility, military or civilian, may be liable for acts and, increasingly, omissions. The liability does not simply depend on rank and any chain of command [although it may well do] but devolves down to unjustified individual acts and can be applicable in instances of war crimes, crimes against humanity and genocide including conspiracies and attempts.[70]

Beyond this, the ICC represents a permanent independent international court charged with the responsibility of investigating and prosecuting genocide, crimes against humanity, war crimes, and crimes of aggression. Finally, the ICC represents the embodiment of legal positivism: that international human rights and humanitarian crimes are to be prosecuted because they are determined to be wrong by an international community whose evolution has arrived at a critical juncture at which it accepts a notion of universal application of legal principles, and even, perhaps, the application of *jus cogens* to prosecuting international human rights violations that are considered the most heinous crimes.

The Rome Statute, in seeking to establish the ICC as an independent judicial body, provides for four means by which matters can be referred to the court for investigation and or prosecution:

- A state "in which one or more crimes within the jurisdiction of the Court appear to have been committed" (Article 14);
- The Office of the Prosecutor based on evidence transmitted to the Prosecutor or authority from the Court (Article 15). The Office of the Prosecutor is also authorized

to "act independently as a separate organ of the Court" (Article 42);
- The UN Security Council (Article 53); and
- nongovernmental organizations and other groups representing civil society (Article 15).

Integral to the ICC is the principle of complementarity. According to the Preamble to the Rome Statute, the ICC "shall be complementary to national criminal jurisdictions."[71] Complementarity is laid out as a central feature of the administration of justice in the establishment of the ICC and is based on recognizing the state as the unit actor both in adjudicating its judicial issues and in international affairs. Thus, the state has primary responsibility for prosecuting its nationals for crimes against humanity and war crimes. Both the ICC and ad hoc tribunals will prosecute only when the judicial apparatus is absent from the state. Hence, the ICC does not seek to impose its judicial process and procedure on the sovereign state but rather holds it as an option when the apparatus of the state fails its people. The Rome Statute identifies four circumstances in which the ICC cannot admit a case:

(a) The case is being investigated or prosecuted by a state that has jurisdiction over it, unless the state is unwilling or unable to carry out the investigation or prosecution genuinely;

(b) The case has been investigated by a state that has jurisdiction over it and the state has decided not to prosecute the person concerned, unless the decision resulted from the unwillingness or inability of the state to prosecute genuinely;

(c) The person concerned has already been tried for conduct that is the subject of the complaint, and a trial by the Court is not permitted under article 20, paragraph 3;

(d) The case is not of sufficient gravity to justify further action by the Court.[72]

Lijun Yang noted that "One of the most important roles of the principle of complementarity is to encourage the State Party to implement the provisions of the Statute, strengthening the national jurisdiction over those serious crimes listed in the Statute."[73] Thus, one finds that the United States has prosecuted its nationals for war crimes during the invasion and occupation of Iraq, whereas the Special Court for Sierra Leone is prosecuting Charles Taylor, former president of Liberia, for war crimes and crimes against humanity.

The Rome Statute also imposes specific and definite penalties consistent with the classification of its domain as the most egregious crimes. According to Article 77, the maximum penalty is a life term not exceeding thirty years, and the minimum is either a fine or forfeiture of goods, property, and assets "derived directly or indirectly from the crime."[74]

Yet the ICC, like the goals of international human rights and humanitarian law, remains an ideal, and the broader referral process is filled with loopholes that diminish the power of the Court to actually prosecute political and military leaders who violate the vulnerable in their countries. First, the provision in the Rome Statute that states refer matters to the Court based on the principle of state sovereignty is almost futile. As has been shown in so many cases, it is near impossible for states and regimes to accept culpability even in the face of the most egregious crimes against humanity, including war crimes and, for that matter, genocide. The issue is really not the state but rather the actions of the regime. A regime that is intent on exploiting cultural cleavages to pursue its own manifesto will appropriate means by which to do so violently and to the detriment of its people. As Payam Akhavan put it in the context of Yugoslavia, the intent to destroy a population "is the consequence of a deliberate resort to incitement of ethnic hatred and violence as an expedient instrument by which elites arrogate power to themselves."[75] Furthermore, Mark Drumble argued that although "perpetrators of mass atrocity are not a uniform group," they are led by "conflict entrepreneurs: namely, those individuals who exacerbate discriminatory divisions, which they then commandeer. Among their goals is to ac-

quire and retain political power."[76] In short, mass atrocity is not the product of seething intercultural cleavages that erupt spontaneously; rather, based on the historical record, it is planned and executed by those who see a vested political and possibly economic interest in destroying a population to maintain or retain power.

Second, reliance on the UN Security Council for referring matters to the ICC is flawed. As has been seen recently in Zimbabwe and Sudan, the Security Council is very reluctant to refer matters to the ICC for investigation and prosecution. Great power politics continues to be pervasive in the central organ of the UN responsible for maintaining international peace and security. The notion that Russia and China are defending the sovereignty of Sudan is questionable when the issue is really the evidence of collusion between the regime and the Janjaweed in persecuting, raping, and mass murdering ethnic Darfuris.

Third is a temporal issue. So often (with the exceptions of Rwanda and the former Yugoslavia) prosecuting crimes against humanity occurs decades after the fact, by which point those responsible for such crimes are either dead, aged, or incapacitated. For instance, Pol Pot, the leader of the Khmer Rouge, died before prosecution. The prosecutor at the ICC withdrew charges against Foday Sankoh, the notorious leader of the Revolutionary United Front—despite the substantial evidence against him—upon his death and years after his crimes were committed against the people of Sierra Leone. Moreover, crimes have to be committed for indictments and prosecutions to occur, which means that millions of innocent people are killed, maimed, raped, and otherwise violated before the violators are either brought to trial or evade prosecution.

Fourth, it has been nearly impossible for the ad hoc tribunals or the ICC to prosecute sitting heads of state. Invariably, leaders first have to be removed from office before they can be summoned to appear before the Court. This was the case with Slobodan Milošević and Charles Taylor, and it is also the case with Omar al-Bashir. Whereas municipal law in the liberal democratic state assumes that the head of state or government is equal to all others under the law, international law assumes that the sovereign cannot be prosecuted due to his or her status as representative of the sovereign state.

Fifth, the United States, Russian Federation, and the People's Republic of China—three permanent members of the UN Security Council—have refused to ratify the Rome Statute. This makes incomprehensible the notion that states that are not parties to the Statute will refer matters to the Court. Moreover, the seeming division between the liberal democratic states of the West, which are more culturally diverse and more willing to engage in collective social introspection to remedy divisions of the past, and authoritarian states of the East and South is problematic. Finally, there remains division between those states that subscribe to positivism and those that hold on to realism in international law and politics. At one level of analysis, the "like-minded" states have relinquished their claim of sovereignty superseding international obligations in the interest of an international criminal regime that holds all states and leaders to a common standard based on Nuremberg principles. At another level of analysis, the global power play has the most powerful states defending dispensation in which their leaders were immune from prosecution. This constrains the ICC in universally applying international criminal law and the Nuremberg principles.

Of importance in discussing the role of the ICC in prosecuting crimes against humanity and defending the dispossessed is the central role played by nongovernmental organizations and other representatives of civil society in negotiating the Rome Statute. David Wippman pointed out that "most of the 300 or so NGOs present in Rome" regularly caucused with the "like-minded states."[77] The central role played by NGOs in negotiating the Rome Statute has become emblematic of their involvement in representing the dispossessed.[78] NGOs have become a transnational check on sovereign states, pressuring them to subscribe to human-rights norms and standards as well as actively and aggressively pursuing the prosecution of state leaders who violate their

peoples. NGOs are now integral to the establishment, working, and monitoring of the international judicial process, especially in furthering international human rights. They were instrumental in gathering evidence for the indictment of Omar al-Bashir, president of Sudan, and in the Rwanda trials. Their work is tangible, invaluable, and recognized in the trigger mechanism that the Rome Statute provides for investigation and prosecution

7. Current and Future Challenges

Current and future challenges are both legal and geopolitical. Although there is some overlap, an effort will be made to distinguish between them. At the center of the legal conundrum is the issue of prosecuting a sitting sovereign, head of state, or head of government. Often regarded as the symbol of sovereignty and normally immune from prosecution while in office, the head of state or government is now culpable under Article 27 of the Rome Statute, which makes one holding a public office no longer immune from criminal prosecution. That means that a head of state or government who enjoys the support of the majority of the population, as did Hitler, nonetheless has to be removed from office and has to be made available to the ICC by the state. This was the case with Slobodan Milošević in Serbia and is currently the case with Omar al-Bashir of Sudan. Milošević was removed from office by a public uprising, and the successor regime handed him over to the ICTY for prosecution. Furthermore, the procedure for referring matters for investigation and/or prosecution is also flawed. Relying on the UN Security Council for referral, arguably because of the power of enforcement, is optimistic at best. For instance, the response of the People's Republic of China and Russia when the Office of the Prosecutor at the ICC transmitted a warrant for the arrest of President al-Bashir to the Security Council was indicative of the power of divisions, not of consensus, in the Security Council.[79]

Political, especially geopolitical, issues are, arguably, the more critical for three main reasons.

First, there remain concerns among G-77 states about the intent and power of the ICC, especially as it seems to be more inclined to investigate and prosecute political and military leaders in Third World countries. This was, arguably, the reason why the African Union was willing to offer a shield to President al-Bashir in 2009 after the ICC issued an indictment of him and a warrant for his arrest.[80] Second, permanent members of the UN Security Council are determined to offer protection to proxy heads of state who are indicted by the ICC. Again, this was manifest in China's and Russia's decision to announce their intention to veto any draft resolution that would have referred prosecution of President al-Bashir by the ICC when he was indicted in 2008.[81] Third, three permanent members of the UN Security Council— the United States, the People's Republic of China, and the Russian Federation—continue to be reluctant to ratify the Rome Statute. Although this ambivalence does not undermine the integrity and effectiveness of the ICC, it does draw into question the commitment of these three powerful states, which claimed responsibility for maintaining international peace and security, including justice for all peoples, to the very principles that underlie the United Nations and the norm of international justice. Their reservations remain far from convincing in that, whereas they reserve a right to support and even initiate ad hoc tribunals that have the potential to be arbitrary in their scope, they reject a permanent international criminal court whose responsibility is to protect the most vulnerable people of the world, which is in total opposition to the idea that the UN Charter opens "We the Peoples."

8. Conclusions

International criminal law has come a long way since the end of World War II. The very idea that political leaders could be prosecuted for crimes against their citizens was unheard of before 1945 and came into being in the face of the most dramatic and intense episode of genocide the world had seen up to that point. The International Military Tribunal at Nuremberg made a bold state-

ment in asserting that leaders of the state have responsibilities and obligations to their peoples and the community of nations that supersede and transcend the laws of their states. After all, they have the power to make and adjudicate laws within their borders to the detriment of their populations (and to the absolute detriment of their populations in autocracies), especially toward the most vulnerable minorities. The significance of the IMT statement lay in its assertion that the international community has a responsibility to hold such leaders to standards set down in international law. In so doing, the IMT laid the groundwork for a legislative and prosecutorial approach to accountability for crimes against humanity. Moreover, the IMT established a foundation for transnational justice that was based on the notion of the absolute responsibility of political and military leaders for policies and laws made in the name of the people such that, when domestic judicial institutions fail to hold these leaders responsible, international institutions will do so based on international statutes adopted by the global community of states.

During the Cold War, systematic crimes against humanity were committed in the name of political ideology and without accountability. The bipolar system, which worked to the benefit of the permanent five members of the UN Security Council, afforded impunity to autocrats and military leaders in much of the postcolonial world, who sacrificed their peoples in pursuit of absolute political power. There was concurrently a conspicuous contradiction between the numerous human rights treaties entered into by states and regimes and the utter disregard for the lives and well-being of the most vulnerable civilians. As absolute power corrupted, the vital transnational legal and judicial institutions needed for accountability were conspicuous in their absence. The political will to investigate and prosecute was simply not there.

The post–Cold War era ushered in a new period of civil war, ethnic conflict, and state collapse that resulted in massive crimes against humanity in such countries as Sierra Leone and Liberia, Rwanda and the Former Yugoslav Republic. However, many responsible political actors across the globe were newly determined to hold both heads of state or government and warlords responsible for their crimes and persecuting their peoples. The UN Security Council authorized regional and ad hoc tribunals to investigate and prosecute to the full extent of international criminal law.

Concurrently, the international community negotiated and adopted a new set of legal norms and standards that essentially invoked the Nuremberg principles by, finally, establishing a permanent international court of criminal law. The resulting Rome Statute lent credence to the International Criminal Court and paved the way for systematic investigation and prosecution of political and military leaders for crimes against humanity. However, the Rome Statute and ICC are not without a measure of controversy. Three of the five permanent members of the UN Security Council have, to date, not ratified the Rome Statute, but that has not deterred the Court from pursuing its mission. The success of the Court lies in its will to aggressively prosecute officials of the state and warlords.

Holding heads of state or government, military leaders, and warlords responsible for crimes against humanity remains an ideal, but international criminal and humanitarian law has made significant strides in establishing norms, standards, and procedures for judicial activism. Founding the International Criminal Court represented a will to build on the Nuremberg first principle that an official of the state has duties that transcend state law, and immunity cannot be sought because of official office or military command when civilians are deliberate victims of crimes against humanity.

NOTES

1. U.N., Convention on the Prevention and Punishment of the Crime of Genocide 78 U.N.T.S. 277 (Jan. 12, 1951).

2. Geneva Convention for the Amelioration of the Condition of the Wounded and Sick in Armed Forces in the Field, Aug. 12, 1949, 6 U.S.T. 3114, T.I.A. S.

No3362, 75 U.N.T.S. 31; Geneva Convention for the Amelioration of the Condition of the Wounded and Sick, and Shipwrecked Members of the Armed Forces at Sea, Aug. 12, 1949, 6 U.S.T. 3217, T.I.A.S. No. 3363, 75 U.N.T.S. 85; Geneva Convention Relative to the Treatment of Prisoners of War, Aug. 12, 1949, 6 U.S.T.S. 3316, T.I.A.S. No. 3364, 75 U.N.T.S. 135; Geneva Convention Relative to the Protection of Civilian Persons in Time of War, Aug. 12, 1949, 6 U.S.T.S. 3516, T.I.A.S. No. 75, 75 U.N.T.S. 287.

3. *Supra* note 1. Raphael Lemkin was a Polish lawyer who, in 1943, employed the term "genocide" in his classic work, Axis Rule in Occupied Europe: Laws of Occupation—Analysis of Government—Proposals for Redress (1944). He was also instrumental in the drafting of the Genocide Convention.

4. Statute of the International Criminal Court, U.N. Doc. A/CONF. 183/9, art. 7 (1998) [hereinafter Rome Statute].

5. Gareth Evans, The Responsibility to Protect: Ending Mass Atrocity Crimes Once and For All (2008).

6. Aristotle, Politics and the Constitution of Athens (Stephen Everson ed., Cambridge Univ. Press, 1996).

7. Nicolò Machiavelli, The Prince 1–37 (Luigi Ricci trans., Signet Classic, 2008) (1515).

8. Jean Bodin, On Sovereignty (Julian H. Franklin ed., Cambridge University Press, 1992) (1583); Thomas Hobbes, Leviathan (Richard Tuck ed., Cambridge Univ. Press, 1992) (1651).

9. John Locke, Two Treatises of Government (Peter Laslett ed., Cambridge University Press, 1988) (1690); Charles de Secondat Montesquieu, The Spirit of the Laws (Anne M. Cohler, Basia Carolyn Miller, & Harold Samuel Stone eds., Cambridge Univ. Press, 1989) (1748).

10. David A. Hamburg, M.D., Preventing Genocide: Practical Steps Toward Early Detection and Effective Action 180 (2008).

11. Treaties/Peace of Westphalia, Munster, October 24, 1648, *available at* http://pax-westphalica.de. The classic analysis of this diplomatic event is found in Leo Gross, *The Peace of Westphalia: 1648–1948*, 42 Am. J. Int'l L. 20 (1948).

12. Montevideo Convention on Rights and Duties of States 165 L.N.T.S (Dec. 26, 1933), 165.

13. Francis M. Deng et al., Sovereignty as Responsibility: Conflict Management in Africa (1996).

14. Francis M. Deng, Protecting the Dispossessed: A Challenge for the International Community 18 (1993).

15. *Id.* at 18–19.

16. Kofi Annan, *Two Concepts of Sovereignty*, 352 The Economist 49–50 (Sept. 18, 1999).

17. INTERNATIONAL COMMISSION ON INTERVENTION AND STATE SOVEREIGNTY, THE RESPONSIBILITY TO PROTECT 13 (2001).

18. UN Charter.

19. CHRISTOPHER CLAPHAM, AFRICA AND THE INTERNATIONAL SYSTEM: THE POLITICS OF STATE SURVIVAL 11 (1996), referring to "the mythology of statehood."

20. ROBERT H. JACKSON, QUASI-STATES: SOVEREIGNTY, INTERNATIONAL RELATIONS AND THE THIRD WORLD 40 (1990).

21. Andreas Osiander, *Sovereignty, International Relations, and the Westphalian Myth*, 55 INT'L ORG. 251–87 (2001).

22. Special Court for Sierra Leone, "The Prosecutor Against Foday Saybana Sankoh also known as Popay also known as Papa also known as Pa, Indictment," SCSL-Case No. 2003–02-I, (March 7, 2003), *available at* www.sc-sl.org/LinkClick.aspx?fileticket=Aehotqx6lAA%3d&tabid=187. "The Prosecutor Against Charles Taylor: The Prosecutor's Second Amended Indictment," SCSL-03–01-PT-263 (May 29, 2007), *available at* www.sc-sl.org/LinkClick.aspx?fileticket=lrn0bAAMvYM%3d&tabid=107. *See generally* JOHN L. HIRSCH, SIERRA LEONE: DIAMONDS AND THE STRUGGLE FOR DEMOCRACY (2001), and Maheta M. Molango, *From "Blood Diamond" to "Blood Colton": Should International Corporations Pay the Price for Rape of the DR Congo?* 12 GONZ. J. INT'L L. (2008–2009), *available at* www.gonzagajil.org/content/view/191/26/.

23. Ramesh Thakur & Vesselin Popovski, *The Responsibility to Protect and Prosecute: The Parallel Erosion of Sovereignty and Impunity*, 1 GLOBAL COMMUNITY Y.B. INT'L L. & JURIS 45 (2007).

24. MICHAEL MARRUS, THE NUREMBERG WAR CRIMES TRIAL 1945–46: A DOCUMENTARY HISTORY 57–70 (1997).

25. Agreement by United Kingdom, United States of America, France, and U.S.S.R. for the Prosecution and Punishment of the Major War Criminals of the European Axis and Charter of the International Military Tribunal 82 U.N.T.S. 279, 286 (Aug. 8, 1945) [hereinafter Nuremberg]. Note the same terms were outlined in Article 5 of the Charter of the International Military Tribunal for the Far East, Tokyo (Jan. 19, 1946) [hereinafter Tokyo].

26. MARRUS, *supra* note 24, at 69.

27. *Id.* at 69–70.

28. DAVID ARMSTRONG ET AL., INTERNATIONAL LAW AND INTERNATIONAL RELATIONS 179 (2007).

29. ANTONIO CASSESE, INTERNATIONAL CRIMINAL LAW 31 (2d ed. 2008).

30. Trial of the Major War Criminals Before the International Military Tribunal, Nuremberg, 14 November 1945–1 October 1946, at 223 (Nuremberg: International Military Tribunal, 1947). This is also partially cited in *id.* at 31.

31. *France et al. v. Goering et al.*, 22 IMT 411, 466 (Int'l Mil. Trib. 1946), quoted in William A. Schabas, *State Policy as an Element of International Crimes*, 98 J. CRIM. L. & CRIMINOLOGY 953 (2008).

32. Michael D. Biddiss, *From the Nuremberg Charter to the Rome Statute: A Historical Analysis of the Limits of International Criminal Accountability*, in FROM SOVEREIGN IMPUNITY TO INTERNATIONAL ACCOUNTABILITY: THE SEARCH FOR JUSTICE IN A WORLD OF STATES 48 (Ramesh Thakur & Peter Malcontent eds., 2004).

33. FRANCISCO FORREST MARTIN ET AL., INTERNATIONAL HUMAN RIGHTS AND HUMAN LAW: TREATIES, CASES & ANALYSIS 5 (2006).

34. Louis Henkin, *The United Nations and Human Rights*, 19 INT'L ORG. 508 (1965).

35. MADOKA FUTAMURA, WAR CRIMES TRIBUNALS AND TRANSITIONAL JUSTICE: THE TOKYO TRIAL AND THE NUREMBERG LEGACY 39 (2008).

36. *Id.* at 50.

37. STEVEN D. ROPER & LILIAN A. BARRIA, DESIGNING CRIMINAL TRIBUNALS: SOVEREIGNTY AND INTERNATIONAL CONCERNS IN THE PROTECTION OF HUMAN RIGHTS 10 (2006).

38. JACK L. GOLDSMITH & ERIC A. POSNER, THE LIMITS OF INTERNATIONAL LAW 131 (2005).

39. Norman Mlambo, *Rethinking Economic Agendas in African Conflicts: A Critique of the Paul Collier Thesis*, in VIOLENT CONFLICTS, FRAGILE PEACE: PERSPECTIVES ON AFRICA'S SECURITY PROBLEMS 146 (Norman Mlambo ed., 2008).

40. BEN KIERNAN, THE POL POT REGIME: RACE, POWER, AND GENOCIDE IN CAMBODIA UNDER THE KHMER ROUGE, 1975–79 458 (1996); TOM FAWTHROP & HELEN JARVIS, GETTING AWAY WITH GENOCIDE: ELUSIVE JUSTICE AND THE KHMER ROUGE TRIBUNAL 3–4 (2004).

41. FAWTHROP & JARVIS, *supra* note, at 24–39; KENTON CLYMER, TROUBLED RELATIONS: THE U.S. AND CAMBODIA SINCE 1870 (2007).

42. Serge Thion, *Genocide as a Political Commodity*, in GENOCIDE AND DEMOCRACY IN CAMBODIA: THE KHMER ROUGE, THE U.N. AND THE INTERNATIONAL COMMUNITY 163–90 (Ben Kiernan ed., 1993).

43. UN Charter, Article 2(4): "All Members shall refrain in their international relations from the threat or use of force against the territorial integrity or political independence of any state, or in any other manner inconsistent with the Purposes of the United Nations."

44. Erskine Childers & Brian Urquhart, *Renewing the United Nations*, Special Issue DEV. DIALOGUE 11 (1994).

45. Statute of the International Criminal Tribunal for the Prosecution of Persons Responsible for Serious Vio-

lations of International Humanitarian Law Committed in the Territory of the Former Yugoslav Republic Since 1991 (ICTY), 32 I.L.M. 1192 (May 25, 1993). The Tribunal was established under the authority of UN Security Council Resolution 827 (1993).

46. U.N. Doc S/Res/827 (1993).

47. *Id.*

48. Sabrina Petra Ramet, Balkan Babel: The Disintegration of Yugoslavia from the Death of Tito to the War for Kosovo 217 (3rd ed. 1999).

49. *Id.*

50. *Id. See also* David Reiff, Slaughterhouse: Bosnia and the Failure of the West (1995).

51. The International Criminal Tribunal for Rwanda (ICTR), U.N. Doc S/Res/955 (1994) under Chapter VII of the UN Charter, 32 I.L.M. 1602 (Nov. 8, 1994). Established by the UN Security Council under authority of SC Resolution 977 (1995).

52. Michael Barnett, Eyewitness to a Genocide: The U.N. and Rwanda xi (2002).

53. UN Security Council, Resolution 955, U.N. Doc S/Res/955 (1994).

54. *Id.*

55. Mel McNulty, *French Small Arms and the Genocide in Rwanda*, 33 Crime, L. & Soc. Change 105–29 (2000).

56. S.C. Res. 995, U.N. SCOR, 3453d mtg (1994).

57. *Prosecutor v. Taylor*, SCSL, Case No. SCSL-03–01 (June 4, 2007), *available at* www.sc-sl.org/. *See generally* Statute of the Special Court for Sierra Leone, 2178 U.N.T.S. 137 (Jan. 16, 2003).

58. *Prosecutor v. Taylor, supra* note 57.

59. UN General Assembly Resolution 57/228 (2003) and UN General Assembly Resolution 57/228B (2003). *See generally* Law on the Establishment of Extraordinary Chambers in the Courts of Cambodia for the Prosecution of Crimes Committed During the Period of Democratic Kampuchea, Reach Kret No. NS/RKM/1004/006 (Oct. 27, 2004), *available at* www.eccc.gov.kh/english/cabinet/law/4/KR_Law_as_amended_27_Oct_2004_Eng.pdf, and Website of the Extraordinary Chambers in the Courts of Cambodia, *available at* www.eccc.gov.kh/english/default.aspex.

60. UN General Assembly Resolution 57/228B, "Khmer Rouge Trials B," Article 1 (May 22, 2003).

61. Seth Mydans, *Trial Begins for Khmer Rouge Leader*, Global Pol'y Forum, February 16, 2009, *available at* www.globalpolicy.org/component/content/article/163/28942.html.

62. Juan Carlos Ochoa, *The Settlement of Disputes Concerning States Arising from the Application of the Statute of the International Criminal Court: Balancing Sovereignty and the Need for an Effective and Independent ICC*, 7 Int'l Crim. L. Rev. 4 (2007).

63. Thakur & Popovski, *supra* note 23, at 55.

64. Declan O'Callaghan, *Is the International Criminal Court the Way Ahead?* 8 Int'l Crim. L. Rev. 542 (2008).

65. David Forsythe, Human Rights in International Relations 106 (2d ed. 2006); Rome Statute; *supra* note 2.

66. Henry J. Steiner et al., International Human Rights in Context: Law, Politics, Morals 1291 (3d ed. 2007).

67. Antonio Cassese, International Criminal Law 329–30 (2d ed. 2008); David Wippman, *The International Criminal Court*, in The Politics of International Law 151–88 (Christian Reus-Smit ed., 2004).

68. Rome Statute.

69. O'Callaghan, *supra* note 64, at 535.

70. Howard Morrison, *International Crimes and Trials*, 8 Int'l Crim. L. Rev. 397 (2008).

71. Rome Statute, Preamble, Para. 10, Article 1.

72. Rome Statute, Article 17(1).

73. Lijun Yang, *On the Principle of Complementarity in the Rome Statute of the International Criminal Court*, 4 Chinese J. Int'l L. 123 (2005).

74. Rome Statute, Article 77.

75. Payam Akhavan, *Justice in the Hague, Peace in the Former Yugoslavia, A Commentary on the United Nations War Crimes Tribunal*, 20 Hum. Rts. Q. 741 (1998).

76. Mark A. Drumbel, Atrocity, Punishment, and International Law 25 (2007).

77. David Wippman, *The International Criminal Court*, in The Politics of International Law 160 (Christian Reus-Smit ed., 2004).

78. Paul J. Nelson & Ellen Dorsey, New Rights Advocacy: Changing Strategies of Development and Human Rights NGOs (2008); James Bohman, Democracy Across Borders: From Dêmos to Dêmoi 110 (2007).

79. Dave Benjamin, *Sudan and the Resort to Regional Arrangements: Putting Effect to the Responsibility to Protect?* 14 Int'l J. Hum. Rts. (forthcoming June 2010); *Turkish authorities not to arrest Sudan President: Hurriyet*, ws.am (Nov. 6, 2009), *available at* http://news.am/en/news/8007.html.

80. *The Prosecutor v. Omar Hassan Ahmad Al Bashir*, ICC-02/05–01/09, Pre-Trial Chamber I, Warrant of Arrest for Omar Hassan Ahmad Al Bashir (Mar. 6, 2009). *See also* ICC Office of the Prosecutor, Press Release, "ICC Issues a Warrant of Arrest for Omar Al Bashir, President of Sudan" (Mar. 4, 2009) and Marko Milanovic, *ICC Prosecutor Charges the President of Sudan with Genocide, Crimes Against Humanity and War Crimes in Darfur*, 12 Am. Soc'y of Int'l L. Insights 15 (July 28, 2008). For the text of the indictment, *see* Santa Clara University School of Law, Legal Studies Research Paper Series, Working Paper No. 08–58, July 2008, *available at* http://ssrn.com/abstract=1160448.

81. Benjamin, *supra* note, at 79.

3

The Responsibility to Protect and the North-South Divide

RAMESH THAKUR

We had "a teachable moment" on July 17, 2009 when Sergeant James Crowley arrested Harvard Professor Henry Louis Gates in Boston. The incident showed how it is possible for both sides in a disputed sequence of events to be right. Intelligent and reasonable people who share a common experience can nonetheless interpret events differently and draw contradictory conclusions because we view events through the prism of our respective collective and individual historical narratives and life experiences. American police officers operate in a more hostile and life-threatening environment than their counterparts in other Western countries. For this reason, they are more heavily armed and operate with a different mind-set that prioritises securing compliance from a suspect over other considerations of politeness and nicety. Called to investigate a domestic break-in in progress, they will assume the worst until convinced otherwise and treat anyone on the premises as an offender. For their part, blacks, Hispanics, and other visible minorities have deeply ingrained memories and experiences of racial profiling. The racially differentiated statistics of those who have been stopped, charged, and convicted for all manner of offences—the popular phrase "driving while black" demonstrates the prevalence of this practice—are deeply disturbing as they illuminate the separate and unequal status of whites and nonwhites in the United States.

In responding to a concerned citizen calling the police about a suspected break-in, Crowley was doing his duty of protecting the property of a resident. For his part, Gates had just returned home from a long overseas trip, only to find his front door jammed. Annoyed and irritable, he entered through a back door and asked the driver to help him force the front door open. After having established that the person effecting forcible entry was indeed the legal owner and resident, Crowley was preparing to leave. There is no evidence he said anything racist or was discourteous to the professor. However, after having been accosted by a police officer demanding proof of identity, Gates was entitled to feel aggrieved at having to bow to white authority in his own home.

It is also possible for both parties to be part right and part wrong at the same time. This is why it is often said that the colour of truth is grey, not black and white. Gates was wrong to hurl charges of racial bias at the police officer in the absence of any evidence, seeing racial slights where none exist. In turn, Crowley was wrong to arrest Gates: Courtesy is a civic virtue, not a legal duty. Disrespecting the police is not "disorderly conduct" and does not warrant handcuffing and arresting a citizen; contempt of cop is not a crime.

Ascribing patterns of behaviour to groups based on assumptions of monolithic identity is risky. For example, many whites were critical of Crowley's behaviour and acknowledged the reality of racially segregated justice in the U.S. legal system and law enforcement practices. Conversely, several blacks criticised Gates for having overreacted against an officer doing his duty and also faulted President Barack Obama for rushing into judgment prematurely. Despite these individual variations, generalising at the group level is still possible. Proportionately, far more blacks and Hispanics than whites empathised and sympathised with Gates, for they share the same historical narrative and collective consciousness.[1]

Similarly, in world politics, at a certain level of analysis, it is possible to argue that in general, compared to the industrialised Western countries, developing countries are more suspicious of claims to a right of humanitarian intervention; more interested in justice among rather than within nations;[2] more concerned about the root causes of terrorism such as poverty, illiteracy, and territorial grievances; more interested in economic development than worried about nuclear proliferation; and more committed to defending national sovereignty than promoting human rights.[3]

The fact that there are individual differences within developing countries and among Westerners neither negates nor invalidates the generalisation. To the extent that developing country viewpoints rarely get an airing, let alone a respectful hearing, in Western mainstream media Western publics and governments typically have a seriously distorted understanding of many international issues. Responding to the agenda-setting discourse by Obama on March 18, 2008 on race and politics in modern America, Nicholas Kristof noted that "the Obama campaign has led many white Americans to listen in for the first time to some of the black conversation—and they are thunderstruck."[4] To those from developing countries or with knowledge of their worldview, a similar chasm exists between the industrialised Western and the developing countries—the so-called global North

and South—except the North has yet to listen in to the Southern conversation. At the 13th African Union summit of heads of government/state in July 2009, for example, Africa's leaders agreed to denounce the International Criminal Court (ICC) and refuse to arrest and extradite to the ICC Sudan's President Omar al-Bashir. Some of the leaders said that it was a signal to the West not to impose its ways on Africa.[5]

Furthermore, the nature of armed conflict has changed.[6] Until the Second World War, war was fought between huge mechanised armies as an institution of the states system, having distinctive rules, etiquette, norms, and stable patterns of practices. Today's wars, however, are mostly fought in poor countries with small arms and light weapons between weak government forces and ill-trained rebels. Disease and malnutrition resulting from warfare kill far more people today than missiles, bombs, and bullets.

For most Westerners, "war" has become a remote abstraction far removed from their daily experience. Not so for many developing countries, especially in Africa. The majority of armed conflicts involve challenges to national integration or to the government's authority. Westerners are incapable of comprehending the framework within which their developing country counterparts must cope with such challenges; most developing country leaders can empathise with one another on this point. Although to Western minds intervening to stop the bloodletting restores order around the periphery, to developing countries international intervention is a direct threat to territorial integrity. Related to this, it is a terrible moral hazard to encourage ethnonational groups everywhere to demand independence and back it with violence that provokes state retaliation, which then promotes external intervention.

In this paper, I want to examine the North-South divide with respect to the new global norm of the Responsibility to Protect (R2P) developed by the Canadian-sponsored but independent International Commission on Intervention and

State Sovereignty (ICISS) and unanimously endorsed at the world summit in 2005.[7] In an interview with *Time* magazine, Liberia's President Ellen Johnson Sirleaf, Africa's first elected woman president, said, "Look at how we have gone from [a stance] of non-interference in our internal affairs to respect for the principle of the responsibility to protect."[8] Is R2P well meaning enough to be attractive because it promises to make a difference, yet so vague that it potentially threatens by being open to abuse? Is it in danger of falling prey to the fatal organisational paradox syndrome, where the effort to preserve the fragile diplomatic consensus in the international community is privileged over the call to protect vulnerable populations that led to the consensus being forged in the first place? That is, can the North-South consensus on R2P, necessary for the world to be able to translate R2P from noble principle to actual deeds, be stopped from fraying only at the cost of the integrity of R2P that neuters the will to act? Alternatively, is R2P a norm in search of a self-justifying crisis?

Ironically, although aspects of sovereignty are being progressively pooled and superseded in Europe where they originated, in constructing a borderless continent, some of its most passionate defenders are to be found among developing countries. The Nonaligned Movement—with 113 members, the most representative group of countries outside the United Nations itself—three times rejected "the so-called 'right of humanitarian intervention'" after the Kosovo war in 1999 and the subsequent statements from UN Secretary-General Kofi Annan.[9]

This paper examines the normative contestation between North and South with respect to the so-called challenge of humanitarian intervention. It begins with a survey of views and opinions across the major developing regions in 2001 during the ICISS outreach exercise, describes the evolution and consolidation of the norm between 2001 and 2009, discusses some challenging test cases in Asia and the Middle East, and concludes with an analysis of the 2009 General Assembly debate on R2P.

The Divisiveness of "Humanitarian Intervention"

> General Bonaparte, following the footsteps of Alexander would have entered India not as a devastating conqueror . . . but as a liberator. He would have expelled the English forever from India so that not one of them would have remained and . . . would have restored independence, peace, and happiness to Asia, Europe, and to the whole world. . . . All the Princes in India were longing for French intervention.[10]

As the above quote shows, the practice of intervention and the belief that it is in the best interests of the natives who will warmly welcome and benefit from it has a long but not necessarily distinguished lineage. We no longer have wars, only "humanitarian interventions" that rest on assumptions of moral superiority. Some crises are privileged and securitised over others that are not, and this reflects the interests and perspectives of the powerful and the rich at the expense of the weak and the poor. The voiceless in the human rights "discourse" are the marginalised and powerless in the global power equation. In Europe, centralising states sought to bring order to their societies by claiming a monopoly on the legitimate use of force. Likewise, today, developing countries fear that in some sections of the West, the view that anyone *but* the legitimate authorities can use force has gained ground.

At one level, the developing countries' attachment to sovereignty is deeply emotional. The most important clue to understanding their concerns is the history of Europe's encounter with Arabs, Africans, and Asians. Even the deployment of moral arguments to justify imperialist actions in Iraq in 2003 had a direct structural counterpart in the British annexation of the Indian kingdom of Awadh (Oudh in its anglicized version) in the first half of the nineteenth century. As Partha Chatterjee noted,

> What is remarkable is how many of the same arguments, including the evangelical fervour, the

axiomatic assumption of the mantle of civilisation, the fig-leaf of legalism, the intelligence reports, the forgeries and subterfuges and the hard-headed calculations of national interest, remain exactly the same at the beginning of the 21st century . . . the liberal evangelical creed of taking democracy and human rights to backward cultures is still a potent ideological drive, and . . . the instrumental use of that ideological rhetoric for realist imperialist ends is . . . seen in Iraq.[11]

If I were to try to communicate and provide an explanation for the sense of passionate conviction behind some of the developing countries' positions on the major contemporary controversies regarding the use of force overseas by the major Western powers, I would use strong and forceful language along the following lines:

"They" (the European colonisers) came to liberate "us" (the colonised natives) from our local tyrants and stayed to rule as benevolent despots. In the name of enlightenment, they defiled our lands, plundered our resources, and expanded their empires. Some, like the Belgians in the Congo, left only ruin, devastation, and chaos, whose dark shadows continue to blight. Others, like the British in India, left behind ideas, ideals, and structures of good governance and the infrastructure of economic development alongside memories of national humiliation. Should they be surprised that their fine talk of humanitarian intervention translates in our consciousness into efforts to resurrect and perpetuate rule by foreigners? That we look for the ugly reality of geostrategic and commercial calculations camouflaged in lofty rhetoric? Should we be mute accomplices when they substitute their mythology of humanitarian intervention for our narratives of colonial oppression? Do they think we do not remember or do not care, or is it simply that they themselves do not care?

At another level, the commitment to sovereignty is functional. State sovereignty is the bedrock principle of the contemporary international system that provides order and stability. The most important task on the agenda of the international community, therefore, should be not to weaken states nor to undermine the doctrine of state sovereignty but rather to strengthen the institutions of state to make them legitimate, help them empower people, uphold respect, and protect people's rights.[12]

Asia

The Asia consultations were enriched by the many examples from within that formed the historical backdrop to the more abstract discussion, from Bangladesh and Cambodia in the 1970s to Sri Lanka and the Maldives in the 1980s and East Timor in the 1990s. The consultations were notable also for the sympathetic reception that we received for the reformulation of "humanitarian intervention" into the responsibility to protect, with the responsibilities to prevent and rebuild as integral components of it.

On balance, "the idea of humanitarian intervention has received a generally hostile response in Asia." However, the reformulation of "humanitarian intervention" as the "responsibility to protect . . . does not entirely succeed in separating the humanitarian imperative from the political and geopolitical constraints of a UN system that will remain dominated by the P-5."[13] Yet Asia could face demands from several potential cases of intervention for human protection purposes: state breakup, breakdown, incapacity, complicity, or perpetration. The Asia-Pacific also contains at least four countries with the military capacity to launch interventions: China, India, Australia, and Japan.[14]

The hardest line against intervention was taken at the roundtable discussions in New Delhi and Beijing in June 2001.[15] It was argued that humanitarianism is good, interventionism is bad, and "humanitarian intervention" is "tantamount to marrying evil to good." In such a shotgun marriage, far from humanitarianism burnishing meddlesome interventions, it will itself be tarnished by interventionism.

A number of reasons were advanced for rejecting "the doctrine of humanitarian intervention."

First, it was claimed that there is no basis for it in the UN Charter, which recognises only self-defence and the maintenance and restoration of international peace and security as legitimate grounds for the use of force. Second, the use of force for moral reasons is dangerous and counterproductive in its practical effects. On the one hand, it can encourage warring parties inside a country to be rigid and irresponsible in the hope of internationalising the conflict.[16] On the other hand, it can facilitate interventions by those exploiting the cloak of legality for their own purposes. Both can cause or prolong large-scale killings. Third, there is an inherent conceptual incoherence. The individualistic conception of human rights in Western discourse is somehow mystically transformed into collective rights (the protection of groups of people) at the same time as the collective rights of the entire nation are still denied legitimacy. Fourth and finally, the inconsistent practice, the double standards, and the sporadic nature of Western powers' interest in human rights protection—from the Middle East, Africa, Latin America, and Asia to Europe—shows that noble principles are convenient cloaks for hegemonic interests.

With respect to the agency for lawful authorisation, there was surprising consensus around the world on the central role of the UN. For China, as one of the five permanent members, self-interest restricts this to the paramount role of the Security Council. Elsewhere and especially in New Delhi, there was one additional argument made with some emphasis: If the Security Council was going to be making decisions on interventions as an evolutionary adaptation of the Charter, then the question of reforming its structure and procedures becomes vitally important. Otherwise, more frequent interventions launched by an unreconstructed Security Council would erode the global legitimacy of the UN rather than imbue the interventions with international legitimacy.

There was also general agreement that interventions cannot become the pretext for imposing external political preferences with regard to regimes and political and economic systems.

Consequently, even though sovereignty may be violated, the cases justifying such action must be tightly restricted to such heinous crimes as genocide and mass murders,[17] they must always be the option of last resort, they must be temporary, intervening forces must withdraw as soon as possible, their actions while inside the target country must be guided by considerations of political impartiality and neutrality between the domestic political contenders as well as strict fidelity to international humanitarian law, and, above all, they must respect and ensure the territorial integrity of the target state.[18]

Frequent and intensive interactions with Asian-Pacific analysts and officials from 2002–2004—at representative seminars that had several speakers on the podium[19] as well as conversations that I led as the sole or keynote speaker as an ICISS Commissioner—led me to conclude that the majority who had not read the ICISS report were reluctant to accept the principal conclusions of R2P based on an instinctive resistance to the very word "intervention." Conversely, among those who had read it, there was surprising sympathy and receptivity to its main thrusts and recommendations, with the sense that R2P was needed but ahead of its time.[20]

Middle East

The double standards criticism was raised most forcefully in the Middle East with regard to the Palestinians. Mohammed Ayoob has articulated the argument with characteristic forcefulness: "Israel's continued occupation and the continuing armed assault against the Palestinians is already a breach of international security that makes it obligatory for the Security Council to intervene under Chapter VII of the charter."[21] Ambassador Omran el-Shafie of the Egyptian Council for Foreign Affairs expressed the dominant Arab belief that the Palestinians' exercise of the right to self-determination had been met with "excessive and disproportionate force." Yet he also acknowledged that internal armed conflicts can compel the government to use excessive force, and it was difficult to establish the conditions under which this could justify international intervention.[22]

Others noted that the results of Western intervention had not always been beneficial and sometimes had aggravated the crises and created fresh problems. Many expressed reservations regarding the term "humanitarian," saying it should never be associated with war. There was considerable support for the involvement of regional and civil society organisations in close coordination with the UN, particularly with respect to early warning and conflict prevention.[23]

Africa

Article 4(h) of the Constitutive Act of the Africa Union, adopted in Lomé on July 11, 2000, explicitly spells out the principle of intervention: the "right of the Union to intervene in a Member State" with respect to the commission of "war crimes, genocide and crimes against humanity."[24] One analyst calls this a shift from "humanitarian" to "statutory" intervention, wherein African states "have themselves accepted sovereignty not as a shield but as a responsibility."[25]

There are many possible explanations for Africans' increased willingness to accept intervention. Their greatest fear is state failure leading to humanitarian crises, whereas their sensitivity to intervention is less than it is for other continents. Asia and Latin America have been more successful in state consolidation, and for them, the trigger to intervention is more likely to be alleged human rights violations, on which there is far more international disagreement. Sovereignty is elusive in the African context of tensions and the polarisation between state and society. In effect, sovereignty has been "alienated" from society and restricted to an international relational dimension (the negative conception of noninterference rather than the positive one of enabling attributes and assets). Also, many weak African states lack empirical sovereignty, being subject instead to warlords, robber barons, gun and drug runners, and so on.[26]

The greater African openness to interventions may be explained also by recent African history. Far too many regimes had used the shield of sovereignty for their abusive records, treating people as objects rather than actors. In response, civil society groups had concluded that in the midst of egregious and massive atrocities and abuses, sovereignty should be subordinate to international concerns and humanitarian assistance. But they, too, were uncomfortable with the association of the term "humanitarian" with "war" and appreciative of the shift in terminology from "humanitarian intervention" to the "responsibility to protect" with preventive and postconflict peace building as integral elements.[27]

The more challenging question was not whether sovereignty should be an absolute shield but instead who has the authority to speak and act on behalf of the people when their sovereign interests are no longer represented by their own governments, when there is no functioning government at all, or when the government subjects minorities to extreme oppression in the name of the majority community. The important points were to ensure that interventions result from the explicit authority of a mandated multilateral organisation and to link them to a political strategy that allows for a strategic engagement with the country subject to intervention.

Latin America

In the twentieth century, Latin America was the most frequent target of intervention by its great and powerful neighbour to the north. The continent also had its share of rogue regimes (often backed by Washington) that brutalised their own people as recently as the 1970s and 1980s. The dual experience has shaped its response to the tension between sovereignty and intervention more sharply than in Africa and Asia.[28]

Chilean Foreign Minister Maria Soledad Alvear acknowledged that "humanitarian intervention" is one of the most controversial and hotly disputed topics on the international agenda that highlights "a disturbing vacuum in our collective humanitarian system" in coping effectively with massacres and other tragedies. The fundamental ethical premise must be that solidarity unites human beings across borders. However, sovereignty is rooted in painful historical encounters, and many have understandable fears that generalising a supposed right to intervention could be abused by the great powers to launch unilateral interventions. The tension must be approached and resolved with sensitivity and caution. Soledad went on to state that "For Chile, the United Nations Charter constitutes the only possible legal framework, the condition sine qua non, governing humanitarian intervention." In turn, this ties the topic to UN practice, the role of the Security Council, and the use of the veto. "We must respect the prerogatives of the Security Council, but at the same time we must remember that our interests do not always coincide with those of the permanent members, and that international law and United Nations practice are not frozen in time," she concluded.[29]

Others noted that geography and history ensure that in Latin America, "the contrast between [U.S.] hard power and [UN] legitimacy is viewed in even more vivid colours than in other regions of the globe."[30] The UN reflected and depended on the interests of member states, was not organised to make quick decisions, and needs innovations to permit a global oversight system. Participants agreed that the Security Council is the most acceptable institution for authorising intervention, but they disagreed on what was permissible when circumstances called for intervention but the Council failed to act.

From 2001 to 2009

The Responsibility to Protect was published in late 2001. The agenda was kept alive by the UN Secretary-General's High-Level Panel in 2004,[31] followed by Kofi Annan's own report in 2005[32] before government leaders meeting at the UN's world summit endorsed R2P in autumn 2005. The summit's outcome document contained a clear, unambiguous, and unanimous acceptance of individual state responsibility to protect populations from genocide, war crimes, ethnic cleansing, and crimes against humanity. Leaders further declared that they "are prepared to take collective action, *in timely and decisive manner*, through the Security Council . . . and in cooperation with relevant regional organisations as appropriate, should peaceful means be inadequate and national authorities are manifestly failing to protect their populations."[33]

Drawing on Special Adviser Edward Luck's wide-ranging consultations and reflections, in January 2009 Ban Ki-moon published his report on implementing R2P, fleshing out in greater and clearer detail many of the original ICISS ideas.[34] His report notes explicitly that all peoples inside a state's territorial jurisdiction—not just citizens but also immigrants, foreign students, and visitors—must be protected by a state (para. 11.1). It clarifies and elaborates that just because force is the last resort does not mean that the international community has to go through a sequential or graduated set of responses before responding robustly to an urgent crisis (para. 50). Building on the 2005 outcome document, the report effectively packages R2P in the language of three pillars: the state's own responsibility to protect all peoples on its territory, international assistance to help build a state's capacity to deliver on its responsibility, and the international responsibility to protect.

Three actual test cases are worth discussing here to highlight the potential for North-South divisions over R2P: Myanmar, Gaza, and Sri Lanka. With Burma's deadly Cyclone Nargis in 2008, principles, politics, and practicality converged in counselling caution in invoking R2P. There is little moral or conceptual difference between soldiers firing into crowds and killing large numbers of people and comparable numbers of people being killed as a result of the government blocking help from being delivered to the victims of natural disasters. Politically, however, we cannot ignore the significance of the noninclusion of natural and environmental disasters in 2005. To attempt to reintroduce it by the back door today would strengthen suspicion of Western motivations and reinforce cynicism of Western tactics. Practically, there is no humanitarian crisis so grave that it cannot be made worse by military intervention. Unappealing as they might be, the generals were in effective control of Myanmar. The only way to get aid quickly to where it was most needed was with the cooperation of the authorities. If they refused, the militarily overstretched. Western powers had neither the capacity nor the stomach to fight a new war in the jungles of Southeast Asia. If foreign soldiers are involved, it does not take long for a war of liberation or humanitarian assistance to morph into a war of foreign occupation.

A related danger is seeking remedy in R2P when better or more appropriate tools and instruments are available. In 2009, when Israel launched a major offensive in Hamas-ruled Gaza, there were issues of international and UN Charter law: the well-established rights to self-defence against armed attack and to resist foreign occupation, the validity of these justifications for resorting to violence by Israel and Palestinians, and the limits to exercising these rights. There were issues of international humanitarian law: Regardless of whether the use of force itself is lawful or not, the conduct of hostilities is still governed by the Geneva laws with respect to proportionality, necessity, and distinction between combatants and civilians. There were charges and countercharges of possible war crimes.[35] In the midst of all this, the invocation of R2P did not seem to be the most pressing or the most relevant contribution to the solution. At the same time, the debate over Gaza also raised the further question of occupying powers' responsibility to protect all peoples living under their occupation, be they Palestinians or Iraqis or Afghans.

The Goldstone Report carefully marshalled evidence of wrongdoing by both Hamas and Israel during the Gaza war. It called on both Palestinian and Israeli authorities to conduct investigations in good faith in conformity with international standards. It called on the Security Council to monitor these, and, only if credible

inquiries were not carried out within six months, to refer them to the ICC. Both recommendations are in line with what European and U.S. governments advocate regularly elsewhere. Failure to follow them in the Gaza context will undermine the broader international legal principles and also "the Obama administration's ability to press for justice in places such as Kenya, the Congo and Darfur."[36]

Protecting civilians and prosecuting perpetrators are, thus, two sides of the same coin.[37] The interrelated twin tasks are to protect the victims and punish the perpetrators. Both require substantial derogations of sovereignty, the first with respect to the norm of nonintervention and the second with respect to sovereign impunity up to the level of heads of government and state. At the same time, both require sensitive judgment calls: Use of external military force to protect civilians inside sovereign jurisdiction should first and foremost satisfy legitimacy criteria rooted largely in just war theory, whereas prosecuting alleged atrocity criminals should be balanced against the consequences for the prospects and process of peace, the need for postconflict reconciliation, and the fragility of international as well as domestic institutions.

In May 2009, in the closing stages of the government's successful military campaign against the Liberation Tigers of Tamil Eelam (LTTE), there was debate over R2P's applicability to Sri Lanka. Colombo was waging a military offensive against a guerrilla army that had fought a brutal war against the legitimate state for twenty-six years, killed up to 80,000 people, and assassinated an Indian prime minister as well as a Sri Lankan president. Civilians were held against their will by the Tigers, not the army. Many who tried to flee were shot by the Tigers. There are no reports of civilians trying to flee from the Sri Lankan forces to the Tigers. A movement that began as the protector of the nation's oppressed Tamil minority had mutated into their killers. Along the road, the Tigers are the ones who fought for a solely military solution to the three decade–long conflict, spurning the few opportunities that were presented for a

political settlement through dialogue and negotiations, including through Indian and Norwegian mediation. They insisted on being the sole
representative of the Tamil population and
cause, liquidating all rival challengers, and they
lost international goodwill after 9/11 as the
global tolerance for terrorism as a tactic collapsed, regardless of the justice of the cause.

R2P places the responsibility first and foremost on the state itself. Given the Tigers' nature
and record, it was not unreasonable for the government to build the capacity and demonstrate
the determination to defeat the Tigers as part of
its responsibility to protect. There is also the
moral hazard of validating the tactic of taking
civilians hostage as human shields.

All this helps to explain the outcome of the
Human Rights Council deliberations. Switzerland, supported by twelve Western countries,
tabled a censorious resolution calling for unfettered access to 270,000 civilians detained in
government-run camps and an investigation of
alleged war crimes by both sides. China, Cuba,
Egypt, and India were among twenty-nine developing countries that supported a successful
Sri Lanka–sponsored resolution describing the
conflict as a domestic matter that did not warrant "outside interference," praising the defeat
of the Tigers, condemning the rebels for using
civilians as human shields, and accepting the
government's argument that aid groups should
be given access to the detainees only "as may be
appropriate." Although Colombo was jubilant,
Western diplomats and human rights officials
were said to be shocked by the outcome at the
end of the acrimonious two-day special session,
saying it called into question the whole purpose
of the Human Rights Council.[38]

The inapplicability of R2P does not, of
course, exempt the government or the Tigers
from the requirements of international humanitarian law (IHL) in the conduct of hostilities.
Where R2P does apply to the government is in
its preventive and rebuilding components. The
Tigers were the after-product of systematic and
institutionalised discrimination by the Sinhalese
majority against the Tamil minority that quickly

degenerated into oppression and then killings.
Calls for equal treatment were ignored, which
thus escalated into demands for autonomy and,
finally, a homeland. A military victory, though
necessary, will not guarantee a peaceful future
for a united Sri Lanka. The responsibility to reconstruct and rebuild, with international assistance, shows the way forward. The best time for
the state to adopt measures of accommodation
and power sharing within a federal framework
is in the flush of military victory, when no one
can accuse it of weakness. The Sri Lankan
Tamils as well as the international community
will mark the government's noble magnanimity.
Conversely, should there be vulgar triumphal-
ism, gloating, or an atavistic return to oppression and killings, Sri Lanka will suffer a reprise
of the brutal civil war.

The July 2009 General Assembly Debate

The General Assembly debate on R2P on July
23, 24, and 28, 2009 was addressed by ninety-
four speakers, almost two-thirds of them from
Africa, Asia, and Latin America. Almost all reaffirmed the 2005 consensus, expressed opposition to any effort to reopen it, and insisted that
its scope be restricted to the four crimes of genocide, crimes against humanity, war crimes, and
ethnic cleansing. Most speakers supported the
Secretary-General's three-pillar strategy based on
the 2005 document. Several expressed reservations about selectivity and double standards in
implementing R2P and criticised past Security
Council failures to act, with some urging voluntary self-restraint in the use of the veto when
faced with atrocity crimes. There was near-
unanimity in accepting state and international
responsibility to prevent atrocities by building
state capacity and will and also providing international assistance (pillars one and two) and in
grounding these fundamental obligations in the
UN Charter, human rights treaties, and IHL.
Most affirmed that, should other measures not
be adequate, timely and decisive coercive action,
including the use of force, is warranted to save
lives. Only a few speakers rejected the use of

force in any circumstance, and only Cuba, Nicaragua, Sudan, and Venezuela sought to roll back the 2005 consensus.[39] It is hard to describe the debate as anything other than a resounding success for the R2P principle and for advocates and victims working to prevent atrocity crimes by all means necessary within the Charter regime that governs international relations.

The debate was called for by General Assembly president Father Miguel D'Escoto Brockmann of Nicaragua, who in his background note described R2P as "redecorated colonialism."[40] He referred to "the consecrated cornerstones . . . enshrined in the UN Charter and in international law," including sovereignty and nonintervention, that should not be subverted. He warned of the risk of R2P, its "laudable motives" notwithstanding, being misused "to justify arbitrary and selective interventions against the weakest states"; of a lack of enforceable accountability for the abusers of R2P; and of double standards in its application.[41] He cited the case of Iraq as an example of R2P being abused—seemingly unaware of the irony that it took place more than two years before R2P was adopted. In response, Ed Luck has emphasised that R2P seeks to "discourage unilateralism, military adventurism and an over-dependence on military responses to humanitarian need."[42]

D'Escoto was followed by two known critics of R2P. Professor Jean Bricmont of Belgium, insisting that "the protection of the weak always depends on limitations of the power of the strong," argued that R2P would in effect relax those limitations.[43] The well-known U.S. Professor Noam Chomsky argued that "virtually every use of force in international affairs has been justified in terms of R2P," "the cousin of humanitarian intervention."[44] It fell to ICISS cochair Gareth Evans to place R2P in context and rebut mischaracterisations.[45] The fourth speaker was Ngugi wa Thiong'o, a Kenyan writer, who welcomed the development of R2P in response to crises like the Rwanda genocide.[46]

In the debate that followed,[47] several speakers from developing countries emphasised the need to stick closely to the 2005 Outcome Document. In this, they had been foreshadowed by China's Ambassador Liu Zhenmin in a Security Council debate on December 4, 2006, when he warned that the Outcome Document was "a very cautious representation of the responsibility to protect populations from genocide, war crimes, ethnic cleansing and crimes against humanity . . . it is not appropriate to expand, wilfully to interpret or even abuse this concept."[48] Yet that is precisely what was suggested in 2008 in the context of Cyclone Nargis and more recently by the London-based One World Trust.[49] Ban is surely right in warning that "it would be counterproductive, and possibly even destructive, to try to revisit the negotiations that led to the provisions of paragraphs 138 and 139 of the Summit Outcome."[50]

Several speakers expressed concerns about double standards and abuse. Most welcomed the attention paid to prevention and international assistance in capacity building. Several referred to such "root causes" as poverty and underdevelopment. Many talked of the need for a proper balance of responsibilities between the General Assembly and the Security Council in developing and implementing the new norm. Some speakers, for example the representatives of Japan and Singapore, pointed to a linkage between R2P and the agenda of international criminal prosecution. Yet several kept returning to the core of the R2P norm: that in extremis, something has to be done to avoid a shameful repeat of Rwanda-type inaction. Thus, Ghana's delegate pointedly noted that Chomsky, though recalling the tendency to abuse intervention, had failed to address the abuse of the principle of noninterference. R2P attempted to strike a balance between noninterference and what the African Union called nonindifference. Guinea-Bissau's delegate called for the "gap between what was said in 2005 and the ability to act now" to be closed. In a marked change from its strong opposition to R2P in 2001, even India's Ambassador Hardeep Singh Puri emphasised that "A State's responsibility to protect its citizens was among the foremost of its responsibilities."[51] The pro-R2P interventions by the delegates of East Timor and Rwanda were especially poignant. The latter said that "the 2005 World Summit Outcome, coupled with the Secretary-General's report and today's debate, made it much less likely that such horrific events [as the 1994 genocide] would be repeated anywhere in the future."[52]

Conclusion

The "transformation of human rights inverts the concept, from one premised on protecting people from the violence of states to one justifying the application of violence by the world's most powerful states against weaker ones. With this transformation, human rights betrays its own premises and thus becomes its own travesty."[53] "Cherry picking" norms and laws to suit the partisan interests of the powerful will undermine respect for the principle of world order founded on law. That is to say, the normative consensus on which law rests will begin to fray and the international order will risk collapse. Much of the twentieth century advances in globalising norms and international law were progressive and beneficial. However, their viability will be threatened if developing countries are not brought more attentively into the process of norm formation, promulgation, interpretation, and articulation—that is, made equal partners in the management of regimes in which international norms and laws are embedded. Otherwise, norms will become the major transmission mechanism for embedding structural inequality in international law, instruments, and regimes. In constructing the normative architecture of world order after the end of the Cold War, developing countries have been ringside observers, not members of the project design or implementation team.

It seems reasonable to conclude that the developing countries were reassured by most countries' refusal to broaden the 2005 crimes to cover natural disasters in Myanmar in 2008 and the broad support of Sri Lanka's right to defend the state against a violent secession by terrorist means in 2009. Had these cases gone in the opposite direction, the tenor and outcome of the July 2009 General Assembly debate might well have been totally different.

That said, it is also important that leaders of the global South examine their own policies and strategies critically. If the impetus for action in international affairs usually appears to come from the North, this is partly due to a failure of leadership from the South. Instead of forever opposing, complaining, and finding themselves on the losing side anyway, developing countries should learn how to master the so-called "New Diplomacy" to become norm entrepreneurs. Otherwise, in practice they risk simply being dismissed as the international "nattering nabobs of negativism."

Living in a fantasy world is a luxury we can ill afford. Our ability and tools to act beyond our borders have increased tremendously, thereby increasing demands and expectations "to do something." Consider an analogy from health policy. Rapid advances in medical technology have greatly expanded the range, accuracy, and number of medical interventions. With enhanced capacity and increased tools have come more choices that have to be made, often involving philosophical, ethical, political, and legal dilemmas. The idea of simply standing by and letting nature take its course has become less and less acceptable. As a result, parents can be charged in court for criminal negligence for refusing to seek timely medical help for ailing children.

Similarly, calls for military intervention happen. Because human nature is fallible, leaders can be weak and corruptible, and states can be frail and vulnerable to outbreaks of multiple and complex humanitarian crises.[54] The real choice is no longer between intervention and nonintervention but rather between different modes of intervention: ad hoc or rules-based, unilateral or multilateral, and consensual or deeply divisive. R2P will help the world to be better prepared normatively, organisationally, and operationally to meet the challenge, wherever and whenever it arises again—as assuredly it will. To interveners, R2P offers the prospect of more effective results. The question is not whether interventions should be forbidden under all circumstances but whether the powerful should respect procedural safeguards if interventions are to be justified.

To potential targets of intervention, R2P offers the option and comfort of a rules-based system instead of one based solely on might. It is rooted in human solidarity, not in exceptionalism of the virtuous West against the evil rest. It provides developing countries better protection through agreed upon and negotiated in advance rules and roadmaps for when outside intervention is justified and how it may be accomplished under UN authority rather than unilaterally. It will lead to the "Gulliverization" of the use of force by major global and regional powers, tying it with numerous threads of global norms and rules. Embedding international intervention within the constraining discipline of the principles and caution underlying R2P would be far better than risking the inherently more volatile nature of unilateral interventions. Without an agreed upon new set of rules, there will be nothing to stop the powerful from intervening "anywhere and everywhere." This is why during the General Assembly debate in July 2009, speaker after speaker, from both the global North and South, described the 2005 Outcome Document's endorsement of R2P as historic because it spoke to the fundamental purposes of the United Nations and responds to a fundamental and critical challenge of the twenty-first century.

All too often, supporters are trapped into providing ammunition to the critics by their failure to pay attention to politics. Steve Stedman, who had headed the high-level panel's secretariat and was then appointed senior adviser to Secretary-General Kofi Annan at the rank of Assistant Secretary-General, subsequently described R2P as "a new norm . . . to legalize humanitarian intervention."[55] Secretary-General Ban Ki-moon's choice to appoint an American special adviser, no matter how good he may be—and Ed Luck is very good indeed—was impolitic. Ban's own Asian identity is neutralised by the general perception that he was a former U.S. ambassa-

dor and UN-sceptic John Bolton's choice for Secretary-General. Western academics miss entirely the powerful sense of grievance and resentment when they read and cite one another to the near total exclusion of colleagues from developing countries. Agreement among Western scholars can neither hide nor overcome the deep divisions between Western and developing country diplomats.

At the end of the day, R2P is mainly about protecting at-risk populations largely in developing countries. These are the states that will face external involvement in their internal affairs, with the risk of military intervention at the far end of the spectrum of modes of international engagement. Because these states will be the primary victims and potential beneficiaries, the conversation on R2P should take place principally among their governments, scholars, and civil society representatives. Instead, however, they were asked, by one of their own, to be in the audience. General Assembly President Fr. D'Escoto did them a disservice by choosing three Westerners among his four experts as the lead speakers in the debate in July 2009. This all too easily allows opponents to reinforce dormant fears that R2P is a debate for and by Westerners in which developing countries are the objects, not authors, of policy and the exercise of Western power. Was this a subconscious deference to racial superiority, a devious but deliberate plot to plant R2P as a Western preoccupation, or merely an innocent slip with no malice or forethought?

The debate is also wrongly framed on substance. In the real world, we know there will be more atrocities, victims, and perpetrators—and interventions. They were common before R2P and are not guaranteed help with R2P. Navi Pillay, the South African High Commissioner for Human Rights, urged that "We should all undertake an honest assessment of our ability to save lives in extraordinary situations" like Rwanda in 1994.[56] It was good to have the likes of Rwanda, Sierra Leone, Bosnia-Herzegovina, East Timor, Indonesia, Nigeria, South Africa, India, and Japan speak in support of R2P.

By the same token, however, Westerners need to recognize and accommodate developing country sensitivities. Developing country viewpoints rarely get an airing in the dominant Western mainstream media, let alone a respectful hearing open to the possibility that they may be right. The crisis over "humanitarian intervention" arose because too many developing countries concluded that, intoxicated by its triumph in the Cold War, a newly aggressive West was trying to ram its values, priorities, and agenda down their throats. Even today, differences within both camps notwithstanding, the global North/South divide is the most significant point of contention for "the international community."[57] With regard to the use of force, for example, advocates of the right to non-UN authorised humanitarian intervention in essence insisted that a non-Western country's internal use of force would be held to international scrutiny, but the international use of force by the West could be free of UN scrutiny. For developing countries, the United Nations was a key instrument for protecting vulnerable nations from predatory major powers; for many Westerners, it was acting to thwart forceful action to forestall or stop the killing of vulnerable people.

In the meantime, there actually has been an example of a successful road testing of R2P. According to Kofi Annan, "I saw the crisis in the R2P prism with a Kenyan government unable to contain the situation or protect its people. . . . I knew that if the international community did not intervene, things would go hopelessly wrong. The problem is when we say 'intervention,' people think military, when in fact that's a last resort. Kenya is a successful example of R2P at work."[58]

R2P is much more fundamentally about building state capacity than undermining state sovereignty. The scope for military intervention under its provenance is narrow and tight. The instruments for implementing its prevention and reconstruction responsibilities on a broad front are plentiful. When postelection violence broke out in Kenya in December 2007–January 2008, Francis Deng urged the authorities to meet their responsibility to protect the civilian population.[59] Archbishop Emeritus Desmond Tutu interpreted the African and global reaction to the Kenyan violence as "action on a fundamental principle—the Responsibility to Protect."[60] Called in to mediate, Annan also saw the crisis in R2P terms. His successful mediation to produce a power-sharing deal is our only positive R2P marker to date.

The 2005 Outcome Document formulation of R2P meets the minimum requirement of the call to action of classical humanitarian intervention while protecting the bottom-line interests of the weaker developing countries and thereby assuaging their legitimate concerns. It navigates the treacherous shoals between the Scylla of callous indifference to the plight of victims and the Charybdis of self-righteous interference in others' internal affairs. As argued by Mohamed Sahnoun, the other cochair of the original international commission, in many ways R2P is a distinctly African contribution to global human rights.[61] Similarly, India's constitution imposes R2P-type responsibility on governments in its chapters on fundamental rights and directive principles of state policy.[62] Contrary to what many developing country governments might claim, a responsibility to protect is rooted more firmly in their own indigenous values and traditions than in abstract notions of sovereignty derived from European thought and practice. Many traditional Asian cultures stress the symbiotic link between duties owed by kings to subjects and loyalty of citizens to sovereigns—a point also made by civil society representatives who accordingly concluded that, far from abridging, R2P *enhances* sovereignty.[63]

The General Assembly debate showed how easy it is to mistake the volubility of the few for broad agreement among the many. Support for R2P in the global South may not yet be very deep, but it is broad. The General Assembly debate has sidelined the sceptics. Stephen Krasner famously described sovereignty as organised hypocrisy.[64] For 350 years, from the 1648 Treaty of Westphalia to 1998, sovereignty functioned as institutionalised indifference. In the final analysis, then, R2P mobilises the last resort of the world's will to act to prevent and halt mass atrocities. It is our normative instrument of choice to convert a shocked international conscience into timely and decisive collective action.

NOTES

1. In a CNN opinion poll shortly after the incident, 59 percent of blacks but only 29 percent of whites said Crowley acted stupidly; 58 percent of whites said that of Gates, with African Americans evenly split. *CNN Poll: Did Obama act stupidly in Gates arrest comments*, CNN, Aug. 4, 2009, *available at* http://politicalticker.blogs.cnn.com/2009/08/04/cnn-poll-did-obama-act-stupidly-in-gates-arrest-comments/.

2. Mohammed Ayoob, *Humanitarian Intervention and State Sovereignty*, 6 INT'L J. HUM. RTS. 98–99 (2002).

3. *See* RAMESH THAKUR, TOWARDS A LESS IMPERFECT STATE OF THE WORLD: THE GULF BETWEEN NORTH AND SOUTH, Dialogue on Globalisation Briefing Paper 4 (2008).

4. Nicholas D. Kristof, *Obama and Race*, NEW YORK TIMES, Mar. 20, 2008.

5. *African Nations Unite to Defend Sudanese Leaders*, ASSOCIATED PRESS, Independent (London), Jul. 4, 2009.

6. HUMAN SECURITY REPORT 2005: WAR AND PEACE IN THE 21ST CENTURY (Andrew Mack et al. eds., 2005).

7. INTERNATIONAL COMMISSION ON INTERVENTION AND STATE SOVEREIGNTY, THE RESPONSIBILITY TO PROTECT (2001); *2005 World Summit Outcome*, adopted by UN General Assembly, G.A. Res. A/RES/60/1, (Oct. 24 2005), at paras. 138–40.

8. *Look across Africa and see the major changes that are happening*, TIME, July 13, 2009, *available at* www.time.com/magazine/article/0,9171,1908312,00.html.

9. THOMAS WEISS & DON HUBERT ET AL., THE RESPONSIBILITY TO PROTECT: RESEARCH, BIBLIOGRAPHY, AND BACKGROUND, Supplementary volume to *supra* note 7, at 162, 357. *See also* Philip Nel, *South Africa: the demand for legitimate multilateralism*, in KOSOVO AND THE CHALLENGE OF HUMANITARIAN INTERVENTION: SELECTIVE INDIGNATION, COLLECTIVE ACTION AND INTERNATIONAL CITIZENSHIP 245–59 (Albrecht Schnabel & Ramesh Thakur eds., 2000).

10. Louis Bourquien, in an article published in 1923 on the failed effort by Napoleon Bonaparte to take India from the British toward the end of the eighteenth century; quoted *in* WILLIAM DALYRMPLE, THE WHITE MUGHALS: LOVE AND BETRAYAL IN EIGHTEENTH CENTURY INDIA 147–48 (2002).

11. Partha Chatterjee, *Empire after Globalisation*, 39 ECON. & POL. WEEKLY 4163 (2004).

12. *See* MAKING STATES WORK: STATE FAILURE AND THE CRISIS OF GOVERNANCE (Simon Chesterman, Michael Ignatieff, & Ramesh Thakur eds., 2005).

13. Amitav Acharya, *Redefining the Dilemmas of Humanitarian Intervention*, 56 AUSTL. J. INT'L AFF. 377, 378, 380 (2002).

14. *See* Ramesh Thakur, *Intervention Could Bring Safeguards in Asia*, DAILY YOMIURI, Jan. 3, 2003.

15. Sripapha Petcharamesree, "Rapporteur's Report, ICISS Round Table Consultation, New Delhi, June 10, 2001"; unattributed, "Rapporteur's Report, ICISS Round Table Consultation, Beijing, June 14, 2001." The reports from all the ICISS regional discussions are *available* on the Commission's website at www.iciss.gc.ca.

16. For a full-fledged discussion of the moral hazard argument, *see* Alan J. Kuperman, *The Moral Hazard of Humanitarian Intervention: Lessons from the Balkans*, 52 INT'L STUD. Q. 49–80 (2008).

17. Intriguingly, and presumably with the example of the Bamiyan statues in mind, although also perhaps the destruction of the mosque in Ayodhya in 1992, one person in New Delhi also suggested that the responsibility to protect extended to cultural heritage. *See also* Ramesh Thakur & Amin Saikal, *Vandalism in Afghanistan and No One to Stop It*, INT'L HERALD TRIB., Mar. 6, 2001.

18. At first glance, East Timor—an operation to which even China acquiesced—would appear to contradict this. But in fact, from a strictly technical point of view, East Timor was not a coercive intervention in the internal affairs of a member state. For one thing, the UN had never given formal consent to Indonesia's annexation of the territory and so the question of requiring Indonesian consent did not arise. For another, Indonesian consent was, in fact, secured.

19. Tokyo, Dec. 16, 2002; Bangkok, March 19, 2003; Singapore, Mar, 20, 2003; 17th Asia-Pacific Roundtable, Kuala Lumpur, Aug. 6–9, 2003; Jakarta, Feb. 23–25, 2004.

20. *See* Landry Subianto, "The Responsibility to Protect: An Indonesian View," and Mely Anthony, "The Responsibility to Protect: Southeast Asian Perspectives," papers delivered at the 17th Asia-Pacific Roundtable, Kuala Lumpur, Aug. 9, 2003.

21. Mohammed Ayoob, *Third World Perspectives on Humanitarian Intervention and International Administration*, 10 GLOBAL GOVERNANCE 112 (2004).

22. Omran el-Shafie, "Intervention and State Sovereignty," discussion paper for the ICISS Round Table consultation in Cairo, May 21, 2001.

23. *See* Ambassador (retired) Ahmed T. Khalil, "Rapporteur's Report, ICISS Round Table Consultation,

Cairo, May 21, 2001," *available* on the Commission's website at www.iciss.gc.ca.

24. The text of the Constitutive Act is *available at* www.africa-Union.org/home/Welcome.htm.

25. Dan Kuwali, *The End of Humanitarian Intervention: Evaluation of the African Union's Right of Intervention*, 9 AFR. J. CONFLICT RES. 41 (2009).

26. Adonia Ayebare, "Regional Perspectives on Sovereignty and Intervention," discussion paper prepared for the ICISS Round Table Consultation, Maputo, Mar. 10, 2001.

27. Emmanuel Kwesi Aning, "Rapporteur's Report, ICISS Round Table Consultation, Maputo, Mar. 10, 2001,"*available* on the Commission's website at www.iciss.gc.ca.

28. *See* Jorge Heine, *The Responsibility to Protect: Humanitarian Intervention and the Principle of Non-Intervention in the Americas, in* INTERNATIONAL COMMISSIONS AND THE POWER OF IDEAS 221–45 (Ramesh Thakur, Andrew F. Cooper, & John English eds., 2005).

29. Maria Soledad Alvear, "Humanitarian Intervention: How to Deal with Crises Effectively," introductory remarks at the ICISS Round Table Consultation, Santiago, May 4, 2001 (unofficial translation).

30. Luis Bitencourt, "Rapporteur's Report, ICISS Round Table Consultation, Santiago, May 4, 2001," *available* on the Commission's website at http://www.iciss.gc.ca.

31. High-Level Panel on Threats, Challenges and Change (HLP), "A More Secure World: Our Shared Responsibility," U.N. Doc. A/59/565 (2004).

32. Kofi A. Annan, "In Larger Freedom: Towards Development, Security and Human Rights for All: Report of the Secretary-General," U.N. Doc. A/59/2005 (2005), at paras. 122–35.

33. 2005 World Summit Outcome, adopted by U.N. G.A. Res. A/RES/60/1 (2005), at paras. 138–40 (emphasis added).

34. Ban Ki-moon, "Implementing the Responsibility to Protect: Report of the Secretary-General," U.N. Doc. A/63/677 (2009).

35. *See* the Goldstone Report, "Human Rights in Palestine and Other Occupied Arab Territories: Report of the United Nations Fact Finding Mission on the Gaza Conflict," U.N. Doc. A/HRC/12/48 (2009), *available at* www2.ohchr.org/english/bodies/hrcouncil/special session/9/docs/UNFFMGC_Report.pdf. *See also* Chris McGreal, *Demands Grow for Gaza War Crimes Investigation*, GUARDIAN, Jan. 13, 2009; Richard Falk (UN Special Rapporteur on Palestinian human rights), *Israel's War Crimes*, LE MONDE DIPLOMATIQUE (English edition) (Mar. 15, 2009, *available at* http://mondediplo.com/2009/03/03warcrimes.

36. Antonio Cassese (President of the Special Tribunal for Lebanon and past president of the International Criminal Tribunal for Former Yugoslavia), *We Must Stand Behind the UN Report on Gaza*, FIN. TIMES, Oct. 14, 2009. For discussions of R2P in relation to Darfur, *see* Cristina G. Badescu & Linnea Bergholm, *The Responsibility to Protect and the Conflict in Darfur: The Big Let-Down*, 40 SEC. DIALOGUE 287–309 (2009); Howard Adelman, *Refugees, IDPs and the Responsibility to Protect: The Case of Darfur*, J. ACAD. ETHICS (forthcoming); Richard W. Williamson, *Sudan and the Implications for Responsibility to Protect*, STANLEY FNDN. POL'Y ANAL. BRIEF (Oct. 2009).

37. *See* Ramesh Thakur & Vesselin Popovski, *The Responsibility to Protect and Prosecute: The Parallel Erosion of Sovereignty and Impunity, in* Y.B. INT'L L. AND JURISPRUDENCE 39–61 (2008).

38. This paragraph is based on Catherine Philp, *Sri Lanka Forces West to Retreat Over "War Crimes" with Victory at UN*, THE TIMES, May 28, 2009, *available at* www.timesonline.co.uk/tol/news/world/us_and_americas/article6375044.ece.

39. Helpful summaries have been provided by two civil society organisations: Global Centre for the Responsibility to Protect, "Implementing the Responsibility to Protect—The 2009 General Assembly Debate: An Assessment," GCR2P Report, Aug. 2009, *available at* www.GlobalR2P.org; and INTERNATIONAL COALITION FOR THE RESPONSIBILITY TO PROTECT, REPORT ON THE GENERAL ASSEMBLY PLENARY DEBATE ON THE RESPONSIBILITY TO PROTECT (2009), *available at* www.Responsibilitytoprotect.org.

40. *Quoted in* Neil MacFarquhar, *Memo from the United Nations: When to Step in to Stop War Crimes Causes Fissures*, NEW YORK TIMES, Jul. 22, 2009.

41. "At the Opening of the Thematic Dialogue of the General Assembly on the Responsibility to Protect," UN Headquarters, New York, Jul. 23, 2009, *available at* www.un.org/ga/president/63/statements/openingr2p230709.shtml.

42. Edward C. Luck, Special Adviser to the Secretary-General, "Remarks to the General Assembly on the Responsibility to Protect," Jul. 23, 2009, at 3, *available at* www.un.org/ga/president/63/interactive/protect/luck.pdf.

43. Jean Bricmont, "A More Just World and the Responsibility to Protect," statement to the Interactive Thematic Dialogue of the General Assembly on the Responsibility to Protect, United Nations, New York, Jul. 23, 2009, *available at* www.un.org/ga/president/63/interactive/protect/jean.pdf.

44. Noam Chomsky, "Statement to the UN General Assembly Thematic Dialogue on the Responsibility to Protect," United Nations, New York, Jul. 23, 2009, *available at* www.un.org/ga/president/63/interactive/protect/noam.pdf.

45. Gareth Evans, "Statement to United Nations General Assembly Informal Interactive Dialogue on the

Responsibility to Protect," New York, Jul. 23, 2009, *available at* www.un.org/ga/president/63/interactive/protect/evans.pdf.

46. Ngugi wa Thiong'o, "Uneven Development Is the Root of Many Crimes," statement to UN General Assembly Dialogue on the Responsibility to Protect, New York, Jul. 23, 2009, *available at* www.un.org/ga/president/63/interactive/protect/ngugi.pdf.

47. *See* "Delegates Seek to End Global Paralysis in Face of Atrocities as General Assembly Holds Interactive Dialogue on Responsibility to Protect," U.N.G.A. Doc. GA/10847 (2009), *available at* www.un.org/News/Press/docs/2009/ga10847.doc.htm; "More Than 40 Delegates Express Strong Scepticism, Full Support as General Assembly Continues Debate on Responsibility to Protect," U.N.G.A. Doc. GA/10849 (2009), *available at* www.un.org/News/Press/docs/2009/ga10849.doc.htm; and "Delegates Weigh Legal Merits of Responsibility to Protect Concept as General Assembly Concludes Debate," U.N.G.A. Doc. GA/10850 (2009), *available at* www.un.org/News/Press/docs/2009/ga10850.doc.htm.

48. U.N. Doc. S/PV.5577 (Dec. 4, 2006) at 8, *quoted in* Sarah Teitt, *Assessing Polemics, Principles and Practices: China and the Responsibility to Protect*, 1 GLOBAL RESPONSIBILITY TO PROTECT 216 (2009).

49. Elodie Aba & Michale Hammer, "Yes We Can? Options and Barriers to Broadening the Scope of the Responsibility to Protect to Include Cases of Economic, Social and Cultural Rights Abuse," One World Trust, Briefing Paper No. 116 (March 2009).

50. Ban, *supra* note 34, at para. 67.

51. "More than 40 delegates express strong scepticism, full support," *supra* note 47.

52. *Id.*

53. Robert M. Hayden, *Biased Justice: "Humanrightism" and the International Criminal Tribunal for the Former Yugoslavia, in* YUGOSLAVIA UNRAVELED: SOVEREIGNTY, SELF-DETERMINATION, INTERVENTION 280 (Raju G. C. Thomas ed., 2003).

54. Gareth Evans & Mohamed Sahnoun, *The Responsibility to Protect*, 81 FOR. AFF. 100 (2002).

55. Stephen John Stedman, *UN Transformation in an Era of Soft Balancing*, 83 INT'L AFF. 933, 938.

56. *Id.*

57. *See* Ramesh Thakur, "Towards a Less Imperfect State of the World: The Gulf Between North and South," Friedrich Ebert Stiftung, Dialogue on Globalisation Briefing Paper 4 (Apr. 2008). The most recent manifestation of this came when the majority of the African Union, the Arab League, and the Nonaligned Movement expressed reservations about the ICC indictment of the President of Sudan on Mar. 4, 2009. For an analysis of "international community" as a contested concept, *see* David C. Ellis, *On the Possibility of "International Community*,*"* 11 INT'L STUD. REV. 1–26 (2009).

58. Kofi Annan in an interview with Roger Cohen, *How Kofi Annan Rescued Kenya*, N.Y. REV. OF BOOKS 52 (Aug. 2008).

59. Daily Press Briefing by the Office of the Spokesperson for the Secretary-General, 28, Jan. 8, 2008, *available at* www.un.org/News/briefings.

60. Desmond Tutu, *Taking the Responsibility to Protect*, INT'L HERALD TRIB., Feb. 19, 2008.

61. Mohamed Sahnoun, *Africa: Uphold Continent's Contribution to Human Rights, Urges Top Diplomat*, ALLAFRICA.COM, Jul. 21, 2009, *available at* http://allafrica.com/stories/printable/200907210549.html. For another African perspective that also strongly supports R2P, *see* Samuel Atuobi, "The Responsibility to Protect: The Time to Act Is Now," KAIPTC Policy Brief, No. 1 (Jul. 2009).

62. I argued this in *The Responsibility to Protect Revisited*, DAILY YOMIURI, Apr. 12, 2007.

63. *See* World Federal Movement, "Global Consultative Roundtable on the Responsibility to Protect: Civil Society Perspectives and Recommendations for Action," Interim Report 8 (Jan. 2009): "At almost every roundtable, civil society emphasized how R2P principles already resonate with pre-existing cultural values."

64. STEPHEN KRASNER, SOVEREIGNTY: ORGANIZED HYPOCRISY (1999).

4

Responsibility to Protect

New Perspectives to an Old Dilemma

GIULHERME M. DIAS

Introduction

Humanitarian intervention raises debates in different segments of the academic community concerned with international relations. Since the last decade of the twentieth century, it was possible to observe how the topic led scholars, politicians, and think tanks to seek remedies to recurring issues such as the relation of humanitarian intervention to alleged violations of sovereignty and possible subtractions of rights that are enshrined in international law, among others.

This chapter begins by analyzing the origins and changes in the international system that now demand clearer rules on humanitarian intervention. Following this, it explains the structure and goals of the Responsibility to Protect (R2P) report as well as its priorities and foundations, balancing the document's elements with a critical view. Finally, this chapter discusses the impact of R2P among states, especially regarding the discussion at the 2005 World Summit, and outlines some perspectives that arise from the international community implementing the report.

Background: Why a Responsibility to Protect?

The bipolar world order, a hallmark of the Cold War period, can be considered an important element in terms of differentiating the political repercussions of humanitarian interventions and the prevalence of the principle of state sovereignty. The first years following the Human Rights Conference in Tehran (1968) marked the occurrence of multiple interventions that, though challenged at the time, now represent a milestone in the discussion of this subject. Taking this into consideration, Nicholas Wheeler has divided the humanitarian interventions into two phases: during and after the Cold War. Indeed, this approach seems the most appropriate way to analyze this phenomenon, as it is possible to notice exactly how the international community reacted differently during both periods. However, we also need to understand which factors have caused such differences.

Interventions During the Cold War

Wheeler picked three interventions implemented during the Cold War, all of which were carried out without the consent of the UN Security Council or regional organizations. The first case is India's intervention in what was then East Pakistan, now Bangladesh, which occurred in 1971. The Indians intervened to eradicate human rights violations that Bengali people suffered and to ensure the subsequent independence of East Pakistan. As soon as the intervention started, however, the Pakistani government called on the

UN Security Council, which saw the Indian action as a flagrant violation of the Charter and demanded the immediate ceasefire and withdrawal of the invading troops.[1] To prevent retaliation from the Pakistanis militarily or some combination of states externally and politically, the Indian government claimed that it had been attacked earlier by the Pakistani army and only exercised their right guaranteed by Article 51 of the Charter.[2]

That the Indian government did not claim a human rights violation in the Bengali case shows that during this period, despite the growing number of agreements in this legal area, sovereignty reigned above any other allegations. This would be confirmed in 1979, when India based other interventions on the same principle, which ultimately also prompted explanations of a similar sort.

The year 1979 was one of the most complex times of the Cold War. While the United States found themselves at odds with the Iranian Revolution and the crisis of the American embassy in Tehran, the Soviet Union exerted all its influence to avert a crisis in Afghanistan, which ultimately led the newly installed Afghan President Babrak Karmal to request military action from Western supporters. Around the same time, the world experienced a series of interventions aimed at eliminating recurring practices of human rights abuses in Asia and Africa. Among these, the cases least cited are France's interventions in Central African Republic, which culminated with the fall of Emperor Bokassa, and Spain's intervention in Equatorial Guinea to topple dictator Macias Nguema. When France and Spain have tried to justify their actions, they did not cite the history of disrespect for human rights in these African countries. In both cases, the intervening countries claimed that the African rulers had already been removed from power when European troops stepped into their territories. Neither military action was discussed before the UN Security Council, even though several countries protested these former colonial powers' actions.

Conversely, two cases of intervention that did attract the attention of the international community were the Vietnamese overthrow of the Pol Pot regime in Cambodia[3] and the military action of Tanzania, which ended the government of Idi Amin Dada in Uganda.[4] In the latter case, the discussion was restricted to within the African Union, which did not legitimate Tanzania's claim of humanitarian action, thereby leading the Tanzanian government to allege not only that Amin had attacked prior to Tanzania's military action but also that Uganda's dictatorial regime had already fallen before the foreign army arrived in Kampala.

In the case of Vietnam, even though the world community recognized that the Cambodian Khmer Rouge regime was one of the biggest violators of human rights, the Vietnamese government was nonetheless accused of disrespecting the UN Charter, especially at the General Assembly. The Security Council, blocked by the ideological struggle of the Cold War, has yet to approve any resolution, and the United States reinforced its opposition of Vietnam's intervention, with massive support from the lesser-developed countries (LDCs).

Despite the documented human rights violations committed in all the overthrown countries, none of the intervening countries stressed the humanitarian action when criticized internationally. This is a significant difference when comparing with interventions after the Cold War, when, in some cases, the call for humanitarian action has taken precedence over the principle of nonintervention in the internal affairs of a sovereign country.

Humanitarian Interventions After the Cold War

If, during the Cold War, the primacy of sovereignty was responsible for drastically limiting humanitarian intervention and even halting states' from claiming this as a means to legitimize their actions—especially when seeking approval of the United Nations—the emerging reality of the post–Cold War new world order and its multipolarity changed the international community's focus. Boutros Boutros Ghali, the UN Secretary-General during this last transitional phase in international politics, spoke passionately on the correlation between international security and human rights as a guarantor of international stability. For Ghali,

> We must leave false debates behind us, and reaffirm that it is not a question of considering human rights either from the point of view of absolute sovereignty or from that of political interference. By their very nature, human rights do away with the traditional distinction between national and international orders. . . . In this context, the state remains, indeed, the best guarantor of human rights, and it is to the state that the international community must delegate the primary role of ensuring the protection of individuals. . . . However, it is up to the international organizations, whether global or regional, to step in when states prove themselves unworthy of this task, when they contravene fundamental principles of the Charter, and when, failing in their duty as protectors of individuals, they become their persectors.[5]

Despite this incisiveness, this new phase in the international arena has also represented a problem, especially when crises occurred in regions under Soviet influence during the Cold War. The UN Security Council, working on issues like the Iraqi invasion in Kuwait, found itself blocked with the new lack of consensus—for example, when the crisis in the Balkans erupted. At the same time, the international community, most notably the permanent members of the Security Council, was largely disinterested in issues of human rights, particularly with respect to the problems in Africa. This led to situations already possessing a high degree of complexity to be aggravated to levels unimaginable until then, thereby culminating in genocide and other humanitarian disasters.

The first of these humanitarian disasters after the Cold War is related to Operation Desert Storm, approved by the United Nations in late 1990 and launched the following year, being led by the United States. Its main objective was to remove Iraqi troops from the territory of Kuwait. The scourge suffered by Kurds in northern Iraq led the permanent members to interpret a Security Council resolution in such a way as to establish a security zone and send humanitarian aid to these populations. This became known as Operation Provide Comfort.[6]

That this resolution was interpreted in this way is important because there is no reference in Security Council documents regarding the creation of these areas called humanitarian corridors that were used to ensure the Kurds' access to provisions. Even the Chinese and Russian representatives did not comment about the issue, stating that the resolution's efficacy in defending the principles of sovereignty and nonintervention would apply only to the conduct of Yugoslavia, which, at the time, was fragmenting from the Yugoslav Wars, discussed below.

This first case is one of the few instances of consensus on humanitarian action in recent times. Since then, there was also the Somali case, a state that became divided between hundreds of clans struggling for power, forcing the country into civil war. This situation further threatened a population already living with hunger and misery, thereby causing Somali refugees to flood into other states, prompting neighboring countries to demand a response from the Security Council. Despite the establishment of a peacekeeping operation[7] to stabilize the situation, the contributions of all UN members were insufficient to carry out the mission as planned. After UN peacekeepers faced many difficulties, the United States offered to help deliver humanitarian aid.

Following a request from the U.S. government, the United Nations established a new peacekeeping operation authorized to use force in order to fulfill its mandate in Somalia. Nevertheless, the mission members experienced constant attacks as well as internal criticism for allowing certain countries to participate in peacekeeping forces. Because of this, the U.S. government, along with France and Belgium, withdrew. As a result, the mission saw its work continue to weaken until the Security Council finally chose to not renew the mandate, thereby leaving the situation in Somalia unresolved and opening itself to criticisms for its ineffective intervention.

Meanwhile, as the crisis in the Horn of Africa continued to spread, the Balkans also began to experience a bloody civil war. The separatist movements erupted in Yugoslavia in 1991 with the Slovenian declaration of independence. Soon after, Croatia also announced that it would no longer be part of the Yugoslav Federation, which prompted the Belgrade government to send troops to the region. In response, in February 1992 the United Nations established its Protection Force (UNPROFOR) to try to stabilize the situation. The war in Croatia, however, lasted but a short time. Soon after, Bosnia-Herzegovina also declared its independence, and the conflict moved to Sarajevo and other major cities within the breakaway territory.

A unique feature of this conflict was the divisions among the ethnic populations. Particularly, in the case of Bosnia, significant portions of citizens were Orthodox (Serbs) or Christians (Croats), and the majority was Muslim (Bosnian). This characteristic established a threefold dispute in which the orthodox wanted to be linked to Serbia, the Christians were trying to annex part of Bosnian territory to Croatia, whereas the Muslims were fighting for their independence. Serbian and Croatian governments financed their respective ethnic groups living in Bosnia.

The diplomatic effort was exhausting and ultimately failed. As in Iraq, Security Council resolutions created several humanitarian corridors, but in Bosnia the attacks against them were constant. Furthermore, three sides of the dispute engaged in ethnic cleansing, especially the Serbs, who were responsible for the massacre in Srebrenica. Only with NATO's support of the UN Protection Force, three years after the start of the conflict, did the warring parties finally end hostilities. Although the Dayton Agreement marked the end of the war, it did not ease the tensions in the region. Furthermore, the international community once again criticized the

UN's role in the force's failed performance, especially its difficulties in adopting and implementing resolutions on the subject. In this case, most of the barriers were related to Russia's position of protecting Serbia, a historical ally.

Then, in 1994 the international community witnessed the biggest genocide since the Second World War. The Rwandan civil war between Tutsis and Hutus resulted in the deaths of about 800,000 Tutsis. In this case, the permanent members of the Security Council hesitated to act, which became a fundamental factor in the execution of the genocide. At the height of the crisis, the United Nations reduced its Assistance Mission quota by over 80 percent. Even France, the only country that engaged more effectively in the region, took a role in the conflict that centered on concerns that only contributed to the carnage.

However, the genocide in Rwanda can be considered the first milestone for humanitarian interventions after the Cold War. Because states were unable to act through the United Nations, the system of collective security and the safeguarding of human rights faced a justifiable challenge on a level not seen since the fall of the Soviet bloc.

A second key element to help us understand why most states reject claims of humanitarian intervention is the crisis in the Serbian province of Kosovo. This conflict holds many similarities to the Bosnian case but also presents a fundamental difference: the lack of consensus among members of the Security Council.

Kosovo is an autonomous Serbian province on the border with Albania. Because of this, much of the Kosovar population is composed of Albanians. As the former Yugoslavia underwent its successive separation processes, the Kosovar nationalists decided to tread the same path. However, unlike the new independent states, Kosovo was linked to Serbia even before Yugoslavia formed. Thus, the looming independence of Kosovo led the Serbian President Slobodan Milošević to intervene militarily in the region, chasing the Albanian population out of the country and violating their most basic human rights. The Security Council was called to seek a solution to the issue, but this time the threat of a Russian veto prevented any effective action against the Serbs.

In the face of Milošević's unwillingness to cooperate with the requests of the European Union and the United States, NATO intervened militarily in the region without the authorization of the Security Council. Although most international public opinion initially approved the action, this quickly changed. Because NATO used military force excessively, which resulted in the deaths of thousands of civilians, the intervention was the target of severe criticism, especially from China and Russia, which blocked the action of the Council.

The dubious result of NATO action in Kosovo prompted a new question: How should the international community act when the Council is blocked because of political divisions? This chapter continues with the remarks of former Secretary-General Kofi Annan, who, facing a very similar question, demanded the international community seek alternatives, among which emerged the Responsibility to Protect.

Interventions, Loss of Legitimacy, and Questioning

The genocide in Rwanda showed us how terrible the consequences of inaction can be in the face of mass murder. But this year's conflict in Kosovo raised equally important questions about the consequences of action without international consensus and clear legal authority.

It has cast in stark relief the dilemma of so-called "humanitarian intervention." On the one hand, is it legitimate for a regional organization to use force without a UN mandate? On the other, is it permissible to let gross and systematic violations of human rights, with grave humanitarian consequences, continue unchecked?[8]

Kofi Annan has raised a challenge to the international community. He has placed before the world's leaders the urgency of compromise between two basic factors necessary for successful international cooperation: the principle of sovereignty (especially nonintervention) and the

full respect for human rights. Surely the seasoned diplomat knew his proposal in itself carried controversial aspects regarding the global political agenda.

Military intervention in any situation that is not prompted by self-defense and is without the consent of the UN Security Council constitutes a flagrant disregard for international law. Likewise, practices of genocide, ethnic cleansing, and human rights violations are intolerable crimes to an international society increasingly integrated and aware of events, even those in more distant regions.

The regulation of a collective security system,[9] on the one hand, is often controversial, in that the permanent members of the Security Council hold differing opinions about its actions in critical situations such as humanitarian crises in Kosovo and Rwanda. On the other hand, there is growing consensus that respect for human rights is fundamentally necessary for stable relations among states. Not coincidentally, emphasizing the relationship between human rights and international security prompts a significant discussion in regard to humanitarian intervention and the limits of sovereignty.

Today, a new perception of sovereignty is gaining strength. In it, the rights of the state come after the rights of the citizens, without which the state itself would not exist. In the current debate, the role of humanitarian interventions is a challenge for those willing to defend a world order that does not threaten the rights of individuals. Such interventions, when conducted on the fringes of international norms, not only generate international instability, but may also lead to subjugating the rights of populations in order to privilege interests that are not theirs but rather of the foreign intervening nations.

Looking for answers to such questions, Kofi Annan, in a relatively ambiguous statement, reinforced the doubts that recur among many international relations analysts: "in the context of several challenges facing humanity today, the collective interest is the national interest."[10] It is possible to interpret his statement in a few different ways. For example, one must ask whether the goal is to direct all national demands toward the unique demands of the international community. In this chapter, it is assumed that Annan's demand cannot be other than compliance with the Charter in all its aspects, especially nonintervention, human rights, and maintaining international peace and security.

In late 2000 the Canadian government sponsored a meeting of a group of academics, politicians, and diplomats in an independent commission, the International Commission on Intervention and State Sovereignty (ICISS), in order to prepare responses to the challenge presented by the former UN Secretary-General. The point raised by Annan was the need to establish a consensus on how to address violations of human rights so as to ensure the full respect of humanitarian law. In fact, the main objective of ICISS was to establish mechanisms to reconcile two points that many analysts consider to be irreconcilable: sovereignty and intervention. This is a very controversial issue, as the key element of Westphalian sovereignty is precisely the nonintervention in internal affairs of other states.

Despite the difficulties, the commission submitted a proposal to consider the act of ratifying the UN Charter of assuming the responsibilities of the international community, chief among which are compliance with human rights, especially pertaining to human security. This type of binding, as pointed out earlier, had been regarded as plausible by some authors who tried to justify the practice of humanitarian intervention. Most member states, however, several times expressed opposition to the resolution, even following the aftermath of bloody conflicts, such as those in the Balkans and Rwanda.

Nonetheless, there had never been a mobilization for resolution of this magnitude before. The Canadian government's willingness to take the first step and the initiatives that have succeeded are representative of this, especially when considering the level of participation of other states in this effort in order to reconcile sovereignty with the faithful compliance of human rights.

The Responsibility to Protect: Structure and Critics of Structure

The Responsibility to Protect can be divided into its basic principles, foundations, specific responsibilities, and priorities. It also outlines the principles for military action, divided at the threshold of just cause and on the grounds of precaution and right authority. Each of these elements is described in detail below.

The Basic Principles of Responsibility to Protect

According to the document, state sovereignty comes from a liability to citizens. Resuming the Hobbesian thought, people give up their personal freedom, transferring it to the figure of Leviathan, the state, which would provide security and stabilize the relationships among individuals. From this line of thought we can infer that the source of state authority is its ability to meet its share of the tacit agreement established with its own nationals.

The basis of the report, therefore, involves the need to demystify the idea of absolute sovereignty. In fact, as seen in the above analysis of interventions during the Cold War, in gauging the relationship between intervention and state sovereignty, intervention was clearly subordinated to sovereignty when the international community did not consider whether the actions to safeguard the existence of certain regimes represented some kind of risk to individuals.

More recently, however, the perceived limits of state sovereignty as well as the adoption and recognition of humanitarian interventions along with their motivations, successes, and failures has caused the international community to clamor to review the debate. Now we can see that sovereignty cannot be realized if the state does not guarantee human protection. But contrary to what critics believe, the Responsibility to Protect's motto is not this challenge to sovereignty; rather, it holds the principle that the primary responsibility of human protection still belongs to the state.

The second basic principle of R2P is the need to complement this initiative so as to ensure that there is some kind of support for the growing need to protect individuals internationally. For this principle, in cases in which the state is unable or unwilling to meet their obligations mentioned above, then an international responsibility to protect threatened citizens would replace the hallowed principle of nonintervention.

These two principles are designed to fulfill two goals. First, replace the figure of the "right to intervene," much criticized during the Kosovo crisis in late 1990s and stigmatized by a subjective discussion in which humanitarianism succumbed to less important political issues. Secondly, from this change of approach, endorse NATO's response in the Balkans, so that the pattern of action of the Atlantic Alliance will serve as a reference for future practice and Uniting for Peace can be seen as an alternative to the lack of consensus in the UN Security Council.

Foundations

The Responsibility to Protect is guided by four important aspects of international law: obligations inherent in the concept of sovereignty; the responsibility of the Security Council to maintain international peace and security; treaties, agreements, and internal rules of human rights and international humanitarian law; and the practices of states, regional organizations, and the Security Council. Below we detail each of these aspects.

According to the report, the obligations attached to the concept of sovereignty are directly related to the idea of effectiveness: The state must fulfill its obligations toward its citizens, and if the state does not take responsibility, someone has to protect that population. In parallel, the responsibility of the Security Council to maintain international peace and security is a crucial element in the structure of collective security as established in 1945. However, a violation of human rights within a given state will not necessarily merit a threat at the UN level. Moreover, as the members of Council decide what constitutes a threat to in-

ternational peace and security, political relations may limit the Council's ability to focus effectively on a real threat, as we saw occur in the case of Rwanda, for example.

Treaties, agreements, and internal rules of human rights and international humanitarian law are important as guides of acceptable government practice, but their absence cannot serve as an excuse for certain political actors to commit acts against a particular population. Importantly, beyond any argument based on treaties, agreements, and established law, there is a recognition of universal standards of human rights and the UN's commitment to protecting individuals.

Finally, the practices—the political and military actions of states, regional organizations, and the Security Council—promote several different views. Examples of successful actions, infringement of the prerogatives of the collective security system, omission of specific norms, and neglect of those norms already established and accepted should suffice. Each of these possibilities can be pointed out to support the assertion. Thus, the need for such conduct so as to protect the rights of individuals is reiterated.

The Responsibilities in R2P

The effectiveness of the Responsibility to Protect is based on stages of past humanitarian crises, which were usually treated in different ways in interventions before R2P was established. Historical examples emphasize military action, thus disregarding the need for preventive measures and the search for reconciliation and understanding in order to stabilize threatened societies. In response to these past interventions, the tripartite division proposed in the report states that there are three responsibilities that form the combined structure and core of protecting individuals: the responsibility to prevent, the responsibility to react, and the responsibility to rebuild. Below we detail each of them.

The Responsibility to Prevent
The threats to which populations are subject are linked to the existence of conflicts. The logic of

prevention involves tackling the roots of possible conflicts before resorting to the use of force. A major challenge of prevention is determining whether relationships between certain political actors' actions are directed toward escalating tensions into conflict. At the same time, another question emerges: How does one convince the political actors that their decisions can have serious repercussions for the international and domestic order without having this "advice" interpreted as an intervention, which would constitute a violation of sovereignty? The density and difficulty posed by this question may be one reason why the report proposes such few practical alternatives: It seeks to emphasize that it considers prevention to be the primary responsibility of the international community. However, critics of the Responsibility to Protect normally agree that the report is too generic in its suggestions for how to prevent conflicts.

It is important to consider that the levels of authority are preserved in the report's subdivision of responsibilities; that is, the state has the task of preventing conflicts that could threaten its people. If it fails to comply with this defined objective, the international community would be responsible for taking preventive initiatives, preferably by Security Council. Furthermore, when the Council fails to act due to a lack of consensus among its members, other states would then have the prerogative to enforce such liability.

The Responsibility to React

If the preventive initiatives fail, the report indicates that the situations threatening the integrity of individuals must be emphatically repulsed. This, however, does not imply the automatic use of force. For the Responsibility to Protect, the resources of warfare apply only when other alternatives are exhausted completely.

Initiatives to address situations of risk are directly linked to coercion. The report presents economic, political, military, and diplomatic sanctions as alternatives to consider. Concerned countries can adopt any of these sanctions unilaterally and voluntarily or an action can be imposed through a Security Council resolution.

The Responsibility to Protect also presents the use of instruments of international law as another alternative in responding to practices that cause death and suffering to people. For instance, in the 1990s the Security Council used international tribunals to judge alleged criminals and restore order, and this led to the creation of the International Criminal Court, even though key states were absent during this means of maintaining the collective security system.

Finally, only when all other forms of response have been unable to bring order to situations that risk individual welfare is the alternative of using military force valid. The authors of R2P recognized that extreme cases may require such action, so they deferred to the Security Council to determine when it is a necessity and how it should be implemented. The report does not ignore or condone unilateral military action without the consent of the Council—one of its most controversial points, which we will discuss below.

The Responsibility to Rebuild

If military force has been used on behalf of protecting the rights of threatened populations, then the social and physical structure of the state has likely been compromised. Because of this, the Responsibility to Protect demands stakeholders to also extend the mission to assist into the process of recovery, reconstruction, and reconciliation in order to ensure a stable atmosphere in the region targeted by the intervention. The reconstruction process should focus on the causes that led to intervention in order to prevent those same threats being reactivated and, thus, leading to new conflict. In other words, initiatives to rebuild should be directed toward what the report defines as primary causes of the disputes and violations of people's rights.

Efforts to revise the structure of the United Nations, repeatedly cited as the institution holding the authority to act on the three fronts that embody the Responsibility to Protect, led to the creation of the Peacebuilding Commission, an agency that works to rebuild regions that suffered from the scourge of war and aims to regain the security of individuals whose rights were suppressed in the midst of conflicts. The work of the Peacebuilding Commission focuses on building solid foundations for peace consolidation. Based on the Secretary-General's report, quoted in the Responsibility to Protect, the initiatives should close cycles of conflict and human rights violations by preventing further armed conflicts.

Priorities

A crucial factor for the Responsibility to Protect is the role that prevention plays in solving the problem that motivates the report: ensuring the rights of threatened populations. According to the report, prevention is the largest consideration, and efforts and resources should concentrate on this responsibility in order to maximize chances of success. According to Alex Bellamy,[11] identifiable elements of the report demonstrate the framers' primary concern with prevention. For instance, it calls for research and debate on how to implement mechanisms and also mentions propositions, such as pointing out three areas that, if addressed, are capable of preventing elements that make possible conflicts with devastating effects: early warning, root causes, and direct prevention.

Since its founding in 1945, the mechanisms of early warning are part of the structure of the United Nations. In its article 99, the UN Charter gives the Secretary-General the authority to draw the attention of the Security Council to a given situation that poses a threat to international peace and security. However, despite the concern demonstrated by this authority, allowing the Secretary-General to take an effective step, the United Nations was not able to clearly define mechanisms of effective early warning. Humanitarian crises of the 1990s demonstrated the need for such instruments to be institutionalized, such as using other actors, not necessarily linked to the UN, to obtain information to help prevent invasive alternatives and the spread of conflict to other regions.

For Gareth Evans, there is a significant amount of early warning tools that can be coordinated, but the practical indicators of effectiveness are insufficient as the number of variables that contribute to the emergence and escalation of conflicts that threaten the civil population is immense.[12] Each case is unique, and although it is possible to monitor each potential conflict, the costs of such monitoring reduce the willingness of states to support such initiatives. In this way, Evans highlights the important role of institutions like the International Crisis Group in monitoring situations that could evolve into armed confrontation.

Beyond early warning mechanisms, the Responsibility to Protect points out that economic, political, and cultural issues play an important role in the occurrence of violent disputes. The disputes over such factors constitute the foundation and root causes of conflicts that need to be prevented to avoid human suffering. If those preventive actions are delayed, the ways for implementing prevention would be changed, requiring the use of what the report defines as the direct prevention toolbox.

It is important to understand that facing a problem's root causes is more than an ephemeral action; rather, it is a long process that individual states should control, but one that may be accompanied and supported by the international community, thereby giving legitimacy to those actions taken to stabilize a situation.

The means for such actions are outlined by four guidelines given in Responsibility to Protect: political-diplomatic, socioeconomic, legal, and military. The difficulty in pointing out all the substantive issues underlying a conflict does not mean that all four actions listed above should be involved in analyzing and addressing a conflict.

Political-diplomatic aspects are structural measures to promote good governance and invite the threatened state to take effective part in international organizations. Doing so highlights for the state the opportunities that such participation represents and, in parallel, it demonstrates the responsibilities and obligations the international community assumes as well as its ability to shape the behavior of states and lead them to a more cooperative attitude toward the norms of international law.

Concerning socioeconomic aspects, according to the report, the international community should support development initiatives and policies aimed at increasing states' economies. Furthermore, the profits a state's economic development should be investing in are educating citizens of the importance of social tolerance by emphasizing the benefits of maintaining good relationships between individuals and respecting differences.

In regard to legal mechanisms, defining clear constitutional rules that are accepted by the community is the first step in internal stabilization. What's more, these rules must promote respect for human rights. The principle of equality of all before the law establishes that the rule of law is the basis for relations between the state and its nationals, thereby strengthening, for example, the fight against corruption, which is nothing more than a form of privileging a minority at the expense of the rights and needs of the majority.

Finally, the security or military structural measures of security need to be reformed so that the citizenry of a state is confident in those individuals who undertake to protect and preserve the state. This trust is reaffirmed when democratic instruments are strengthened, with the military leaving the rule of the state in the hands of civilians. The report also highlights the importance of controlling the flow of small arms and light weapons, which are partially responsible for fueling conflict and causing suffering to individuals.

These four aspects are also valid when the time for need for preventing conflict is scarce. The direct preventive toolbox is necessary in order to avoid the need for invasive measures, which can resolve the issue but may also impact innocent civilians and delegitimize the intervention.

The political-diplomatic direct measures are directly linked to preventive diplomacy. At this stage of a situation, the imminence of the conflict is clear, but it has not erupted yet. To prevent disputes that might result in death and pain, diplomatic negotiations play a major role. The threat of political sanctions can substantiate the negotiation process by pointing out to potential belligerents that the costs of the conflict are greater than the initial prospects.

The direct measures related to socioeconomic aspects also involve using economic sanctions to demonstrate to the disputing parties that the suffering of innocents is unacceptable to the international community. In addition to restrictions, offering economic incentives in exchange for reducing tensions is also an alternative, as is being willing to grant and maintain financial aid for parties that engage in peaceful conduct.

The legal direct measures should provide less traumatic alternatives when it comes to resolving disputes. They should support the local courts and, when the domestic legal structure is unable or unwilling to fulfill its mandate, indicate the possibility of bringing possible violations of the rights of populations to the international courts for investigation and prosecution.

With respect to direct measures in military and security areas, the international community can assign a preventive deployment, which is not authorized to use force, as an alternative that also shows its concern and its willingness to take all reasonable steps to avoid bigger problems. Arms embargoes and suspending military cooperation agreements also represent options for preventing the outbreak of warfare.

Bellamy highlights actions taken by the international community, some even before the Responsibility to Protect was adopted, that related to conflict prevention. Among them we can underline the report,[13] presented in June 2001, of the UN Secretary-General on this issue. The document reaffirms the leading role of national governments but opens up some space in the domestic sphere for civil society, thus leaving the international organizations and the international community a kind of complementary ability that would be activated only in cases when states fail to undertake necessary preventive measures.

In "A More Secure World: Our Shared Responsibility," Kofi Annan and a group of experts mention the necessity of prevention, reinforcing that this issue should be prioritized in order to achieve better results in dealing with conflicts. The report was intended to be the first step in responding to calls for reform in the UN system. In its second part, the document approaches the relationship between collective security and conflict prevention. Every threat analyzed features a section discussing ways to meet the challenge of prevention. Once again, we are shown just how difficult the mission of addressing preventive actions is. The report uses conflict resolution as examples of preventive actions, thus prompting again the inescapable question: When does the responsibility to prevent turn into a responsibility to react?

R2P and Military Intervention

As stated before, the effective priority of Responsibility to Protect is to prevent humanitarian crisis. However, as preventive measures are prone to failure, the report does not reject the possibility of using coercive measures that have a greater impact, such as military intervention. In regard to this, R2P points out the need for adequate effective actions to determine the threshold of just cause.

For the Responsibility to Protect, the use of force is only justified when there is no alternative available to avoid a large-scale loss of life, either because of the deliberate actions of a state or by its inability or failure to act in response to events of this size. Furthermore, the use of force is justified in cases of ethnic cleansing, mass murder, forced displacement of populations, any acts designed to terrorize people, and rape as an instrument of war. The occurrence of such acts of villainy justifies the use of military instruments to prevent the suffering of threatened populations, requiring states that support such practices to review their positions and assisting states unable to meet their responsibilities to do so with the utmost readiness.

Amid the need for military intervention, the report identifies four Precautionary Principles that must be met in order to legitimize the use of force as a humanitarian action and ensure that doing so is contingent solely on the protection of individuals at risk. The first Precautionary Principle is the intention must be right, which means the real purpose of intervention must be humanitarian. The action must first and foremost effect to eliminate people's suffering and pain without taking into account the particular interests of intervening forces. In this sense, the report is clear in prioritizing the use of multilateral forces in such operations that are supported by regional institutions, as defined in the UN Charter's Chapter VIII.

The second Principle is that other alternatives must be exhausted before adopting coercive instruments. Military intervention should be the last resort to resolve a humanitarian crisis, thus preventing the possibility that, instead of a relief and hope, it would actually result in more deaths and violence in areas of conflagration.

The third Precautionary Principle is that the means for intervention must be proportional to the conflict at hand. The operation must be designed to use minimal military resources and last the shortest time possible in order to ensure the achievement of its objective: protecting human beings.

The last Precautionary Principle is that there must be reasonable prospects for military action. For the international community to intervene in a humanitarian crisis by using force, the possibility that such will be successful must be significant. If the result of the intervention can be worse than the result of not taking military action, its humanitarian character is negated and the mission will be delegitimized.

The Decision to Intervene

According to the Responsibility to Protect, the structure of the collective security system, based on the UN Security Council, should be supported. In this sense, even with the challenges faced when taking responsibility and ensuring international peace and security, the report recognizes that the best way to respond to humanitarian crises involves the consensus of the members of the Council.

According to the report, the Council must be aware and ready to act at any time, acting immediately in situations that could threaten the rights of populations. Concerning the role that the report gives the Security Council, consensus can be easily achieved if the permanent members voluntarily abdicate use of veto power in cases of humanitarian crises that do not involve vital interests of the five states. In this sense, it is interesting to note that the report takes a realistic approach in acknowledging that there is a limit to international humanitarian action.

Finally, the report presents alternatives if the Security Council is blocked and unable to deal with extreme situations. The first recalls 1950, when the UN General Assembly adopted Resolution 377, the Uniting For Peace. According to this resolution, in case the Council is blocked, the Assembly may meet in an emergency session and recommend the use of collective measures to ensure international peace and security. The main objective of this resolution is to find a prompt solution for a crisis and to ensure that this alternative would be adopted by a larger number of states and is, therefore, a more legitimate decision. In the latter case, the Responsibility to Protect recognizes that regional organizations can act in their jurisdiction, backed by the principles of the report, and then seek an endorsement *a posteriori* from the Security Council. Some scholars compare this possibility to what occurred in the Kosovo crisis in 1999, although the areas in which military action was taken were not part of NATO.

The report also brings some operating principles for when military force is adopted in response to a humanitarian crisis. According to the Responsibility to Protect, the objective must be clear that this is an extreme measure aimed solely at preventing people from suffering from the atrocities that threaten their rights. The chain of command shall establish a common approach for all participants of the intervention, and that approach will be related to the mission's humanitarian goal.

From these definitions, the report also highlights the need for military force to coordinate its efforts with humanitarian organizations that are present in the region as well as to understand the limits of its action, defined by the rules of international law and the principles of Responsibility to Protect.

If it is possible to find among analysts some that consider the report timid in its willingness to provide effective responses to humanitarian crises, then, conversely, many political leaders came to believe that legitimating after intervention was a way to restrict the prerogatives of sovereignty and nonintervention in the UN Charter. This dichotomy between political ideas will be expanded with the adoption of Responsibility to Protect in 2005. The debate and the varying positions of the states stress that different perceptions of the issue continue to hinder the construction of a consensual and definitive solution, as discussed below.

The R2P and the 2005 World Summit

Many countries have repeatedly demanded UN reform because they are not content with the power structure that the organization represents. The arguments about representativeness and legitimacy are present because the number of nonpermanent members of the Security Council was enlarged in 1965. The first Cold War, however, blocked more exacerbated demands.

After the Cuban Missile Crisis, a new international order began to be consolidated, marked by the logic of détente. During this period, the first signs of dissatisfaction with the power structure represented by the United Nations, in particular its Security Council, become visible. This claim for change was strengthened as decolonization progressed and the number of UN members increased significantly. In the late 1970s the superpowers resumed their tensions, and the possibilities for other states to manifest their discontent were restricted once again. The international agenda focused on security issues and global bipolarity, thereby deflating the reformist pretensions.

Then, the end of Cold War marked the emergence of new alternatives in international order. This brought about a new global reality, in which the Security Council was no longer subjected to bipolarity and its consequent blockade, as evidenced by the consensus for intervention in Iraq in 1991.

However, when the international community failed to define humanitarian responses to threats in Africa and the Balkans, reformists demanded a redistribution of world power through a UN reform. The issue then became part of the ongoing UN agenda, discussed especially during the General Assembly sessions on its fiftieth, fifty-fifth, and sixtieth anniversaries.

As stated earlier, the Responsibility to Protect was presented in 2001 and, supported particularly by the then Secretary-General Kofi Annan, became one of the issues discussed at the United Nations and was presented as an alternative to the dilemma the UN faced when responding to humanitarian crises.

In "A More Secure World," one of the main documents prepared by the UN to promote debate on its reform during its sixtieth anniversary, the term "responsibility to protect" appears thirteen times, almost always in reference to safeguarding the rights of individuals. It is important to remember that "A More Secure World" is a technical document—a set of proposals made by experts[14] on behalf of the organization and is meant to be used as a basis for negotiation that would take place in 2005.

A year later, the 2005 World Summit was held, aimed to adapt the structure of the United Nations to a new reality, one in which global threats are now issues, such as terrorism, climate change, intrastate conflicts, poverty, and violations of individual rights. The meeting participants approved several documents, most notably the 2005 World Summit Outcome, which presents the outcome of discussions set up by states. For supporters of the Responsibility to Protect, that it was indirectly mentioned in the World Summit Outcome report in paragraphs 138 and 139 means that it has been effectively recognized and adopted as a new tool with which to face humanitarian crises. However, the document is mentioned only three times throughout the entire UN report, which indicates that the Secretary-General's emphasis was not shared by member states. Below, the original paragraphs of the World Summit Outcome show how the Responsibility to Protect is recognized by states:

Responsibility to protect populations from genocide, war crimes, ethnic cleansing and crimes against humanity

138. Each individual State has the responsibility to protect its populations from genocide, war crimes, ethnic cleansing and crimes against humanity. This responsibility entails the prevention of such crimes, including their incitement, through appropriate and necessary means. We accept that responsibility and will act in accordance with it. The international community should, as appropriate, encourage and help States to exercise this responsibility and support the United Nations in establishing an early warning capability.

139. The international community, through the United Nations, also has the responsibility to use appropriate diplomatic, humanitarian and other peaceful means, in accordance with Chapters VI and VIII of the Charter, to help to protect populations from genocide, war crimes, ethnic cleansing and crimes against humanity. In this context, we are prepared to take collective action, in a timely and decisive manner, through the Security Council, in accordance with the Charter, including Chapter VII, on a case-by-case basis and in cooperation with relevant regional organizations as appropriate, should peaceful means be inadequate and national authorities are manifestly failing to protect their populations from genocide, war crimes, ethnic cleansing and crimes against humanity. We stress the need for the General Assembly to continue consideration of the responsibility to protect populations from genocide, war crimes, ethnic cleansing and crimes against humanity and its implications, bearing in mind the principles of the Charter and international law. We also intend to commit ourselves, as necessary and appropriate, to helping States build capacity to protect their populations from genocide, war crimes, ethnic cleansing and crimes against humanity and to assisting those which are under stress before crises and conflicts break out.[15]

With all the doubts surrounding the intensity and degree of states' commitment to R2P's principles, it is certain that the initiative of the Responsibility to Protect became part of the humanitarian intervention debate and would guide the actions of individual states and the United Nations. It was up to the Security Council to take the next step—adopting the assumptions of the report.

In April 2006 the Security Council held its 5,430th meeting, which adopted resolution 1674. The fourth paragraph of the document reaffirms support to Responsibility to Protect, clarifying provisions related to war crimes, genocide, ethnic cleansing, and crimes against humanity, but maintaining a lack of specificity regarding the measures that need to be taken when these occur.

Although the Security Council indicates its willingness to accept the suggestions of the ICISS report and endorse their proposals, the states continued to be skeptical about the real meaning of the Responsibility to Protect. For some states, the report represented a new tool to legitimize the intervention of external actors in their domestic issues. For these critics, the vagueness or lack of greater depth in R2P proposals is the first issue to contest, using the claim that more debate on the subject is needed until such a time that this debate is replaced by some other issue that is more relevant at the moment, thereby sending the Responsibility to Protect to the political wilderness where other initiatives have been relegated. However, when the Secretary-General sent to the UN General Assembly a document suggesting mechanisms for implementing the Responsibility to Protect, the debate over the effectiveness of the report was taken up more intensely. During six meetings of the General Assembly held in July 2009, a series of demonstrations on the subject showed that the states were still divided over the Responsibility to Protect.

The positions of the states vary along a range of options: waiving with explicit support the adoption of the document, relativizing its repercussions in terms of restricting the power of the Security Council on humanitarian issues involving threat or breach of the international peace and security, and acting without fear of sanction. In this group we can recognize the positions of the European Union, especially initiatives from France and the United Kingdom[16] as well as the sponsor of the report, Canada.

The idea of transferring powers from the Council to the General Assembly and the proposal to limit veto power on issues involving humanitarian emergencies prompted China and Russia to adopt a reticent position.[17] The NATO intervention in Kosovo still echoes in the memories of the two permanent members of the Security Council, who fear that the report will legitimize violations of sovereignty against their allies through human rights procedures that are culturally relativized, which means to position their diplomacy clearly within the initiating states' political culture. Its policy relevance, however, encourages these states to defend a more neutral stance, calling for more negotiation and the clarification of unclear points.

On the other extreme of the debate, states that have expressed opposition to adopting the report believe that effective accountability is linked to the state and that sovereignty cannot be restricted or relaxed without risking the destabilization of the international system. Pakistan, even before the 2005 World Summit, expressed opposition to the report. At 2009 meetings the position was less emphatic, but the Pakistani[18] government reiterated that adopting a document that does not clearly define its scope and its means of realization presents a problem.

Final Remarks

The Responsibility to Protect was a breath of fresh air to a discussion that had gone stale at the turn of the millennium. However, even though the attacks of 9/11 and the subsequent War on Terror attained a privileged position on the international agenda, which could have undermined the discussion of how to deal with humanitarian issues, the debate has not ended. On the contrary, it has continued amid controversy and disagreement.

Thus, it is important to recognize the role of former Secretary-General Kofi Annan and his successor, Ban Ki-moon, in managing and pushing the subject within the United Nations. The organization's past errors help explain why they continue to be concerned about the issue; the UN said "never again" in response to the Holocaust, but this needs to be said for the massive violations of rights of peoples.

In proposing measures, Gareth Evans (Australia), Mohamed Sahoun (Algeria), and the ICISS team contributed greatly to this discussion. The progress made by political actors in high-level meetings, the General Assembly, and the Security Council should also be mentioned. It is important to recognize that there exists a responsibility to human rights and humanitarian concerns and, more importantly, to realize that speech alone does not bring about much difference in actuality, despite the fact that political practice does not always match political rhetoric.

However, consider certain states' proposition that R2P's unwillingness to offer exhaustive explanations and directives is a mistake. If states sometimes seek loopholes in official documents in order to justify unethical postures, then this report's lack of clarity constitutes a real problem. The superficial aspect of the means of prevention, intervention principles, and the density of rebuilding initiatives do not necessarily prevent humanitarian arguments from being used for political means, namely their use to violate sovereignty and change political regimes.

Thus, the willingness of states to at least continue the debate on the Responsibility to Protect is salutary, even if they do so with the intention to postpone its implementation. Insofar as the international dynamics increasingly involve other actors beyond states, the influence of nonstate actors can help to prevent the implementation of this document, causing its principles to fall by the wayside but, at the same time, exercising a critical stance regarding the need for transparency when formulating rules for issues as sensitive as those treated here.

NOTES

1. S.C. Res. 307, U.N. Doc. S/RES/307 (1971).

2. Colin S. Gray, *The RMA and Intervention: A Sceptical View, in* DIMENSIONS OF WESTERN MILITARY INTERVENTION 55 (Colin McInnes & Nicholas J. Wheeler eds., 2002).

3. Cori E. Dauber, *Implications of the Weinberger Doctrine for American Military Intervention in a Post-Desert Storm, in* DIMENSIONS OF WESTERN MILITARY INTERVENTION, *supra* note 2, at 79.

4. Dominick Donald, *The Doctrine Gap: The Enduring Problem of Contemporary Peace Support Operations Thinking, in* DIMENSIONS OF WESTERN MILITARY INTERVENTION, *supra* note 2, at 111.

5. Boutros Boutros Ghali, General Secretary of the International Organization of la Francophonie Egypt, "Human Rights and Democratization," *available at* www.droitshumains.org/Forum/Unesco/DOCS/Boutros GhaliE.html.

6. OLIVER RAMSBOTHAM & TOM WOODHOUSE. HUMANITARIAN INTERVENTION IN CONTEMPORARY CONFLICT: A RECONCEPTUALIZATION 69–85 (1996).

7. The UNOSOM I was established in April 1992.

8. Kofi Annan, *Two Concepts of Sovereignty: International Intervention in Humanitarian Crises,* THE ECONOMIST 49–50 (Sept. 18, 1999).

9. Collective security is understood here to mean that if one member of the system is inadvertently attacked, the other members are not committed to come to the defense of the attacked state.

10. Kofi Annan, op. cit., p. 4.

11. Alex Bellamy, *Conflict Resolution and the Responsibility to Protect* (14) GLOBAL GOVERNANCE 135–56 (2008).

12. GARETH EVANS, THE RESPONSIBILITY TO PROTECT: ENDING MASS ATROCITY CRIMES ONCE AND FOR ALL 83 (2008).

13. The Secretary-General, "Report of the Secretary-General on Prevention of Armed Conflict," U.N. Doc. S/2001/574, A/55/985 (Jun. 7, 2001).

14. Among them, one of ICISS chairpersons, the former Australian Ministry of Foreign Affairs, Gareth Evans.

15. U.N. Resolution A/RES/60/1.

16. U.N. GAOR, 63d Sess., 97th plen. Mtg., U.N. Doc. A/63/PV.97 (Jul. 23, 2009).

17. U.N. GAOR, 63d Sess., 98th plen. Mtg., U.N. Doc. A/63/PV.98 (Jul. 24, 2009).

18. *Id.*

5

Universal Jurisdiction as an International "False Conflict" of Laws

ANTHONY J. COLANGELO

I. Evolving Norms of International Law

What makes universal jurisdiction so extraordinary—and extraordinarily controversial—is the way it authorizes and circumscribes a state's power to make and apply law or prescriptive jurisdiction.[1] Many people who like universal jurisdiction like it because they think it allows states to extend their laws without any limitation to activity anywhere on the globe involving anyone. Thus, tyrants and terrorists are not immune from prosecution just because their home states refuse to prosecute them. People who dislike universal jurisdiction tend to dislike it for these very same reasons: Because any state in the world can claim to exercise it over acts committed anywhere by anyone, universal jurisdiction invites easy manipulation for purely sensationalist or propagandist ends. Neither view is entirely correct.

This chapter proposes a framework for analyzing the concept of universal jurisdiction and evaluating its exercise by states in the international legal system. In brief, I argue that universal jurisdiction is unique among the bases of prescriptive jurisdiction in international law and that its unique character gives rise to unique—and underappreciated—limiting principles. The main analytical device I use to make this argument is the notion of a "false conflict," which I borrow from the private law field of conflict of laws, also known outside the United States as private international law.[2] I do not suggest that any particular permutation of false conflict (there are a few) [3] in the private law sense can or should be seamlessly grafted onto the international legal system. Rather, my aim is to explore some general themes captured by the idea of a false conflict of laws and to craft a species of false conflict for the international legal system that can helpfully structure legal and policy thinking about universal jurisdiction in ways that accommodate both prevailing state sovereignty and individual rights concerns.

Part I of the chapter argues that universal jurisdiction is different from all other bases of jurisdiction in international law. Other bases of jurisdiction derive from distinct national entitlements to make and apply law, like entitlements over national territory or persons. These bases of national jurisdiction grant states great freedom to regulate whatever conduct they deem deserving of regulation in essentially whatever regulatory terms they choose. In this respect, international law circumscribes the geographic range of situations to which states may apply their laws but without much restricting the content of the law a state seeks to apply once it has been determined that a situation falls within the state's recognized prescriptive range.

In contrast, universal jurisdiction derives from a state's shared entitlement—with all other states in the international legal system—to apply and enforce the international law against universal crimes. As a result, a state cannot unilaterally decide what conduct falls within its universal jurisdiction and cannot regulate that conduct in any terms it chooses (unlike when exercising national jurisdiction). Rather, the state exercising universal jurisdiction acts as a decentralized enforcer of international law on behalf of the international legal system. This is, in a sense, the opposite of the way national jurisdiction works. The geographic range is limitless, but international law places restrictions on the content of the law being applied. Part II shows how the uniqueness of universal jurisdiction presents a species of false conflict for the international legal system. It examines the notion of false conflicts and concludes that, properly exercised, universal jurisdiction by its nature creates no conflict of laws among states. Because the state exercising universal jurisdiction merely enforces shared normative and legal commitments of all, no conflict of laws exists since the law being applied is the same everywhere. And, because the universal jurisdiction state is enforcing an otherwise applicable international norm that necessarily governs within all other states, including states with national jurisdiction, the latter can claim no sovereign interference. That is, they have no "sovereignty claim" under international law that, for instance, genocide, torture, or war crimes are legal within their borders. Hence, put in conflict-of-laws terms, there is a "false conflict" both (1) because the universal jurisdiction state applies a norm that by force of international law applies within the jurisdictions of all other interested states, and (2) no other state can claim a legitimate sovereign interest in the choice of a domestic law contrary to that norm.

This is not to say, however, that territorial or national jurisdiction states have no legitimate interest in seeing the matter resolved at home in domestic courts rather than abroad in foreign courts through principles of jurisdictional primacy. But that jurisdictional ordering is more a question of adjudicative, as opposed to prescriptive, jurisdiction. Put another way, it relates more to choice of forum as opposed to choice of law. For the international law against, say, genocide, is in theory the same everywhere;[4] it thus axiomatically would erase any "true conflict" of laws among states.

Accordingly, and couched within the topic of the present symposium, I want to suggest that the prescriptive reach of universal jurisdiction is not really extraterritorial at all, but rather comprises a comprehensive territorial jurisdiction, originating in a universally applicable international law that covers the globe. Individual states may apply and enforce that law in domestic courts, to be sure, but its prescriptive scope encompasses all territory subject to international law, that is, the entire world.

Whereas Parts I and II set out to show that a false-conflict view of universal jurisdiction can provide a coherent account of the international legal concept, Parts III and IV use the false-conflict view to articulate some important and underrecognized limiting principles. First, states exercising universal jurisdiction must faithfully apply the international legal definitions of the crimes they seek to prosecute. There is both a state sovereignty and an individual rights dimension to this limiting principle. As to state sovereignty, if states do not faithfully apply the international law definitions of universal crimes, the exercise of jurisdiction contradicts the very international law upon which it purports to rely by arrogating to the state more jurisdiction than is authorized under international law. This can become especially problematic where the exercise of jurisdiction applies a law contrary to the law of the state with national jurisdiction; that is, in cases of "true conflicts" of laws among states. In this respect, the state claiming an exorbitant universal jurisdiction may well interfere with the sovereignty of other jurisdictionally involved states—most notably, territorial and national states—through the unauthorized projection of domestic law into their territories or over their nationals.

Of equal if not greater importance, the false-conflict view implies strong individual-rights limits that affect both victims and defendants. This key piece of the universal jurisdiction puzzle is often overshadowed by sovereignty concerns, yet its elaboration helps throw into sharper relief the contours and ramifications of the limiting principles inherent in the concept. To begin with, a false-conflict view protects the rights of victims to see justice done by extinguishing defendants' objections to expansive assertions of extraterritorial jurisdiction, whether such objections are styled ex post facto, legality, or due process. The accused cannot claim lack of notice of the illegality of his conduct or, indeed, of the applicable law—international law.

Yet correspondingly, the false-conflict view also protects the rights of defendants. If the state exercising universal jurisdiction departs from international law through an exorbitant claim of jurisdiction over activity that does not qualify as a universal crime under international law and that lacks a recognized jurisdictional link to the forum, the defendant's individual rights claims may have traction. Here the accused may well be subject to a law of which he had no notice, thus potentially violating principles of legality, due process, and nonretroactivity of the criminal law. This limiting principle is significant because the rights of defendants not to be unfairly subject to laws of which they had no notice too often go unmentioned or undertreated in conversations about universal jurisdiction and, indeed, about extraterritorial jurisdiction generally. Legal and policy debate that centers only on highly charged sovereignty clashes among governments while ignoring the rights of defendants is ironic because, as noted above, a major objective of universal jurisdiction is vindication of individual rights—those of victims. But anytime a state exaggerates the definition of a crime upon which it bases universal jurisdiction, it potentially exposes the defendant to a law of which he had no notice, thereby triggering strong individual rights objections.

Another potential limitation on universal jurisdiction is that, at present, international law precludes its exercise by states over certain public officials of other states through doctrines of immunity. In this circumstance, international law does grant states a form of "sovereignty claim," or recognized state interest, against the decentralized application of its prohibitions by other states through universal jurisdiction. However, once the accused leaves office, no immunity attaches for international crimes. Moreover, no rule of international law currently requires a state exercising universal jurisdiction to respect an amnesty granted by another state. Therefore, any claim against the exercise of universal jurisdiction based on such an amnesty is substantially weaker than an immunity claim, if not altogether nonexistent under international law.

Finally, and perhaps most controversially, I suggest that a state may not successively prosecute based on universal jurisdiction when another state already has prosecuted in good faith the crime in question. The first prosecution already would have enforced the international law against that crime, leaving the universal jurisdiction state seeking successive prosecution no law upon which to prosecute again. The chapter concludes that a false-conflict approach can provide a workable and desirable international legal framework for evaluating the exercise of universal jurisdiction.

II. The Uniqueness of Universal Jurisdiction

This part discerns two kinds of prescriptive jurisdiction in international law in order to demonstrate the uniqueness of universal jurisdiction. One kind I label "national jurisdiction," and the other I label "international jurisdiction."[5] National jurisdiction derives from what we typically think of as "sovereignty" in international law and relations. It springs from independent entitlements of each individual state vis-à-vis other states in the international system to make and apply its own law—principally, from entitlements over national territory and persons. We might think of national courts exercising national jurisdiction and applying national law in the international system as roughly analogous to U.S. state courts applying their own state's law in the U.S. federal system.

What I will refer to as international jurisdiction, on the other hand, derives from a state's shared entitlement—along with all other states as members of the international system—to enforce international law. At the risk of stretching an analogy beyond its natural breaking point, we might think of national courts exercising international jurisdiction, and thus applying and enforcing international law, as roughly analogous to U.S. federal courts geographically sitting in different U.S. states but applying and enforcing the same federal law.

A. National Jurisdiction

Under international law, certain "sovereign" or national interests authorize states to apply their national laws to activity affecting those interests. These national interests, in other words, underlie national bases of prescriptive jurisdiction, or what might be called national entitlements,[6] recognized by international law, to make and apply law. For example, principal among these entitlements is jurisdiction over a certain piece of geographic territory.[7] Thus, State A has prescriptive jurisdiction over State A's territory because of State A's national entitlement over its territory, as recognized by international law.

The list of national entitlements recognized by international law authorizing a state's prescriptive jurisdiction is fairly intuitive. As already mentioned, a state legitimately may claim jurisdiction over activity that occurs, even in part, within its territory.[8] This is called subjective territoriality.[9] A state also may claim jurisdiction over activity that does not occur but that has an effect within its territory, or what is called objective territoriality.[10] Furthermore, a state may claim jurisdiction over activity that involves its nationals.[11] Where the acts in question are committed by a state's nationals, the state may claim active personality jurisdiction. And where the acts victimize a state's nationals, the state may claim passive personality jurisdiction.[12] Ad-

ditionally, under the protective principle, a state may claim jurisdiction over activity that is directed against the state's security and/or its ability to carry out official state functions, such as its exclusive right to print state currency.[13]

All of these national entitlements relate distinctly back to the particular state claiming jurisdiction—whether to its territory, punishing or protecting its nationals, or affirming its very statehood.[14] And because international law recognizes multiple national entitlements, there may be multiple states with national jurisdiction over a given activity. Thus, Germany may claim jurisdiction over acts committed by a German national in the United States,[15] but clearly so, too, may the United States.[16] In such cases there are overlapping or concurrent national jurisdictions.[17]

Yet the list of national entitlements also circumscribes the jurisdiction of states. Although the entitlements authorize projecting one state's laws to activity taking place in other states (for example, where activity abroad affects the first state's territory or involves its nationals), such extraterritorial prescriptive jurisdiction still requires some measurable and objective nexus to the first state's national entitlements.[18] For instance, absent some nexus, Germany may not apply its racial hate speech laws to speech by U.S. nationals speaking only in the United States and having no connection to Germany. Thus, through the limited list of national entitlements, international law effectively limits the geographic range of situations to which states may make and apply their laws.

But although the geographic range of its national jurisdiction may be limited, within the parameters of that jurisdiction a state enjoys a relatively free hand under international law to exercise its law-giving power however it chooses. With the notable exception that it may not prescribe laws contrary to fundamental norms of international law[19] (for example, a state may not, under international law, legislatively endorse or permit genocide),[20] international law leaves states at great liberty to regulate whatever conduct they deem deserving of regulation in essentially whatever regulatory terms they like. Thus, the United States claims jurisdiction over acts that occur in the United States or involve U.S. nationals, and Germany claims jurisdiction over acts that occur in Germany or involve German nationals. And both the United States and Germany may pass whatever laws they like in largely whatever terms they like criminalizing largely whatever activity they like where that activity takes place within their geographic borders or involves their nationals. Consequently, although international law limits the geographic range of states' national jurisdiction, once a situation falls within that range, states enjoy great freedom to regulate the situation how they see fit. International law places few restrictions on the content of the state's law.

To sum up then, international law contains multiple bases of national jurisdiction. These bases of jurisdiction derive from a state's independent national entitlements as recognized by international law—namely, the state's entitlement over its territory, its entitlement to punish and protect its nationals, and its entitlement to secure itself as a state. Moreover, when states seek to regulate activity falling within the compass of their national jurisdiction, they largely are free to employ their domestic law-giving apparatus however they see fit by defining offenses according to their own individual—and independent—prescriptive prerogatives.

B. International Jurisdiction

Although each base of national jurisdiction just described relies upon some nexus to a national entitlement of the state claiming jurisdiction, which authorizes and circumscribes the range of that state's national prescriptive jurisdiction in relation to other states, there is another base of jurisdiction in international law that requires no nexus at all: universal jurisdiction. According to this doctrine, the very commission of certain crimes denominated universal under international law engenders jurisdiction for all states irrespective of where the crimes occur or which state's nationals are involved.[21] The category of

universal crime began long ago with piracy,[22] expanded in the wake of World War II, and is now generally considered to include serious international human rights and humanitarian law violations like genocide, crimes against humanity, war crimes, torture, and, most recently, certain crimes of terrorism.[23] Instead of deriving from a state's independent national entitlements, universal jurisdiction derives from the commission of the crime itself under international law. It is the international nature of the crime—its very substance and definition under international law—that gives rise to jurisdiction for all states. Thus, although a state may not, without a nexus to its national entitlements, extend its national prescriptive reach into the territories of other states, international law extends everywhere and without limitation the international prohibition on universal crimes.[24] Universal jurisdiction consequently has nothing to do with any particular state's independent national jurisdiction; rather, it is a base of international jurisdiction. It does not authorize states to enforce any distinctly national entitlement, but instead authorizes them to enforce a shared international entitlement to suppress universal crimes as prescribed by international law.[25] Recently, Spain's Constitutional Court made the point emphatically when it upheld universal jurisdiction over crimes committed in Guatemala by Guatemalans against Guatemalans: "the principle of universal jurisdiction . . . is based exclusively on the particular characteristics of the crimes covered thereby, whose harm (paradigmatically in the case of genocide) transcends the specific victims and affects the international community as a whole."[26] "Consequently," the Court explained,

the repression and punishment [of universal crimes] constitute not only a commitment, but also a shared interest among all states, whose legitimacy in consequence does not depend on the ulterior individual interests of each of them. In that regard, the concept of universal jurisdiction in current international law is not based on points of connection founded on the individual interests of a state . . . [but] on the particular nature of the crimes being prosecuted.[27]

Or, as a recent Joint Separate Opinion in the International Court of Justice put it, "those States . . . who claim the right . . . to assert a universal criminal jurisdiction . . . invoke the concept of acting as 'agents for the international community.'"[28]

States, through their common and coordinated practice, collectively contribute to international lawmaking, including the law of universal jurisdiction—whether that law is made through entrance into treaties affirming the serious nature of the crime under international law and every state's attendant obligation to prosecute it as such, even absent domestic links,[29] or through a practice of domestic legislation and judicial decision making that emphasize the universal nature of the crime under international law and the ensuing authority to act as an agent of the international legal system in exercising jurisdiction.[30] But the upshot is that a single state cannot unilaterally and subjectively determine what crimes are within its universal jurisdiction—that is a matter of international, not national, law.[31] For example, Germany cannot just decide on its own that racial hate speech is now a universal crime over which it might assert jurisdiction around the world, including racial hate speech in the United States involving U.S. nationals and having no connection to Germany. Of course states control whether and to what degree their courts may enforce universal jurisdiction. Depending on how their domestic laws view international law, states often must legislatively implement or "transform" this international legal power of universal jurisdiction into their national laws so that they might exercise it in domestic courts.[32] But what is important is that Germany, or any other state, cannot unilaterally define its universal jurisdiction in relation to other states, that is to say, the crimes giving rise to such jurisdiction—again, that is exclusively a matter of international law.

Furthermore, because the crime itself generates jurisdiction, courts must use the definition of that crime, as prescribed by international law, when prosecuting on universal jurisdiction grounds; otherwise there is no jurisdiction. Thus the exercise of universal adjudicative jurisdiction by states (through their courts) depends fundamentally on applying the substantive law of universal prescriptive jurisdiction. And this substantive law, or the definitions of universal crimes, is a matter of international law. In this respect, international law places restrictions on the content of the law being applied in situations of universal jurisdiction. Where courts invent or exaggerate the definition of the crime on which they claim universal jurisdiction, their jurisdiction conflicts with the very international law upon which it purports to rely.[33] Hence, the symbiotic relationship between universal prescriptive jurisdiction (the power to apply law to certain persons or things) and universal adjudicative jurisdiction (the power to subject certain persons or things to judicial process): the international legal definitions of universal crimes define not only the crimes themselves as a matter of states' prescriptive jurisdiction but also the judicial competence for all courts wishing to exercise universal jurisdiction.

I address below more concrete legal questions of how to tell whether a crime is universal under international law and whether a state faithfully applies that international law through its domestic legal apparatus.[34] The takeaway for now is that universal jurisdiction is foundationally different from national jurisdiction. Its jurisdictional anchor for states, or source of prescriptive authority, is distinctly international—that is, the international legal system's interest in suppressing certain international crimes no matter where they occur and whom they involve. And, when individual states wish to implement their universal jurisdiction through domestic legislation and enforce it in domestic courts, they are constrained to determine the crimes they adjudicate as the crimes are determined under international law. A state may not, as it may when exercising its national jurisdiction, criminalize essentially any activity it likes in any terms it likes according to its own independent prescriptive prerogative. In short, if the international legal definition and substance of a crime authorizes universal jurisdiction as states claim,[35] then states must base their exercise of jurisdiction in that international legal definition and substance.

III. Universal Jurisdiction as a False Conflict

The unique nature of universal jurisdiction yields an analytically helpful correspondence to the notion of false conflicts in the conflict of laws or private international law field. This part introduces two prominent conceptions of false conflict and recasts universal jurisdiction as a species of international false conflict of laws. The remainder of the chapter then maps the false-conflict model onto states' use of universal jurisdiction to discern some limiting principles inherent in the concept under the view presented so far.

Before getting into the meat of the false-conflict analysis, however, and because the project takes a decidedly prescriptive turn at that point, I would like to smooth the bridge between explaining what universal jurisdiction is and now prescribing how I think it should work based on that explanation. The false-conflict view I propose is not simply the top-down superimposition of a conceptual model onto the legally relevant bottom-up practice of states. Rather, it flows from that practice; indeed, it takes states at their word. If the international legal justification advanced for exercising universal jurisdiction is that the state acts as a decentralized enforcer of a predominant set of international norms on behalf of the system, then the false-conflict view follows from that justification. That is, states must then actually apply and enforce international law—and the result is the false-conflict view outlined immediately below and the set of limiting principles identified and elaborated in Part IV.

A. False Conflicts

The conflict of laws discipline addresses situations in which more than one state's laws potentially apply to the same set of facts; that is, cases of overlapping prescriptive jurisdictions.[36] "False conflicts" come in a variety of flavors,[37] with the meaning of the term in any given case often tied to the choice of law methodology adopted to resolve that case. As one commentator has noted, "The concept of 'false conflicts' enjoys protean facility for justifying everyman's choice-of-law theory. Members of the choice of law guild who discover a rational solution for a conflicts problem, tend to characterize the problem as a 'false conflict.'"[38]

The concept of false conflicts is generally regarded to have originated as part of Brainerd Currie's governmental interest approach to choice-of-law questions (though Currie himself referred to false conflicts situations as "false problems").[39] According to Currie, courts deciding choice of law questions "should first of all determine the governmental polic[ies]" expressed by the laws of the involved states and whether "the relationship of the . . . state to the case at bar . . . is such as to bring the case within the scope of the state's governmental concern, and to provide a legitimate basis for the assertion that the state has an interest in the application of its policy in this instance."[40] From this interest analysis, three main conflicts categories emerge: false conflicts, true conflicts, and unprovided-for cases.[41] False conflicts occur when only one involved state has an interest in applying its law.[42] Because only one state is interested in applying its law, there is no conflict of laws and the sole interested state's law applies.[43] True conflicts, by contrast, occur when more than one involved state has an interest in applying its law.[44] And unprovided-for cases occur when no involved state has an interest in applying its law.[45] Although questions of whether and when precisely governmental interests exist have generated much commentary,[46] "the concept of a false conflict . . . has become an integral part of all modern policy based [choice of law] analyses."[47] Another popular variety of false conflict in judicial decisions [48] and academic literature[49] occurs when the laws of the involved states are the same, such that there is effectively no conflict of laws. As Robert Leflar put it, "if the laws of [all involved] states, relevant to the set of facts, are the same . . . then there is no real conflict of laws at all, and the case ought to be decided under the law that is common to [the] states."[50]

These two permutations of false conflict—where only one state is interested in applying its laws and where the laws of all involved states are the same—can offer a heuristically rich foundation for crafting a false-conflict framework for exercises of universal jurisdiction in the international legal system. The anthropomorphized "interested state" can capture sovereignty concerns that continue to pervade and organize the system, although the notion of the "same law" across jurisdictions can capture the coercive harmonization of norms against certain crimes deemed universal by international custom.[51]

B. As Applied to Universal Jurisdiction

1. The Same Law

The second type of false conflict mentioned above presents obvious semblance to the concept of universal jurisdiction and probably offers a conceptually cleaner place to start than a governmental interest analysis. The idea of the "same law" across jurisdictions holds immediate appeal for universal jurisdiction because "Universal jurisdiction . . . is a result of universal condemnation" of the international crimes that generate it.[52] As explained above, when a state exercises universal jurisdiction, it acts as the adjudicative and enforcement mechanism for the international law against the universal crime at issue.[53] And that law is, in theory, the same everywhere. Thus, there is no conflict of laws as to, say, the international legal prohibition on genocide. In this respect, the exercise of universal jurisdiction always produces a species of international false conflict because, by definition, it leads to the application and enforcement of a law common to all states: international law.

2. State Interests

A governmental interest analysis of false conflicts poses a somewhat trickier yet perhaps more provocative tie to universal jurisdiction. We have already said that a state's universal jurisdiction springs not from any distinct national interest or entitlement in applying its national prescriptive jurisdiction to a dispute but rather from a shared entitlement and commitment—with all other states—to suppress certain international crimes deemed universal. In other words, universal jurisdiction stems from the nature and substance of the crime under international law as opposed to any national connecting link.

To illustrate, suppose a U.S. national is alleged to have committed torture in Egypt. Clearly Egypt may exercise prescriptive jurisdiction and may apply Egyptian law proscribing torture to activity committed in its territory.[54] Moreover, under international law, the United States also may exercise prescriptive jurisdiction and may apply U.S. law proscribing torture to activity committed by its national.[55] Thus, we have two states that potentially may claim jurisdiction, under international law, based on state interests. But that is not all. Spain, among other states,[56] has a universal jurisdiction law that allows Spanish courts to prosecute for torture wherever it occurs and whomever it involves.[57] So it, too, conceivably could exercise jurisdiction on these facts.[58]

But unlike the United States and Egypt, Spain's interest is not linked to any distinctly national jurisdictional entitlement. If the crime were instead an "ordinary" crime,[59] say a robbery in an Egyptian marketplace by a U.S. national, Spain could not apply and enforce Spanish national law over that crime. Rather, for Spain to prosecute, it must rely uniquely upon its international jurisdiction over the universal crime of torture. The Spanish national law used to prosecute is therefore really just a shell, with no self-supporting national jurisdictional basis, through which Spain applies and enforces international law. Yet Spain surely has an "interest" in exercising jurisdiction. It may not be an interest related distinctly to national entitlements like national territory and persons, but it is an interest nonetheless (and one that Spain shares with all other states): applying and enforcing international law against universal crimes.[60]

The real question for interest analysis, then, is whether any other jurisdictionally involved state can claim a contrary interest in its laws. And the answer here has to be no. Although Currie's approach frames false conflicts as multijurisdictional situations in which only one state has an interest in applying its laws,[61] and true conflicts as situations in which more than one state has an interest in applying its laws,[62] that analysis presupposes conflicting interests expressed in the laws of different states.[63] But when it comes to the application of international legal prohibitions on universal crimes, by force of international law no state has a legitimate contrary interest in its laws.

This argument conceivably can function on two distinguishable but related levels given the underlying international legal principle at play. The first is that, empirically speaking, states' laws publicly will not express interests contrary to international legal prohibitions on universal crimes. Indeed, such widespread consensus by states regarding the international prohibition on a crime presumably gave rise to universal jurisdiction over it in the first place as a matter of customary international law, which is composed of state practice and *opinio juris* (the belief or intent that the practice arises from a sense of legal obligation).[64] Thus, as a practical matter, when a state exercises universal jurisdiction, other states simply will not have laws expressing interests contrary to the international legal prohibitions expressed in the universal jurisdiction law, therefore mooting interest analysis and creating a false conflict.

Second, as a legal matter, there is a strong argument that even if they wanted to, other states cannot have laws expressing interests contrary to the international legal prohibitions on universal crimes. This is because crimes subject to universal jurisdiction generally are considered the most serious offenses under international law,[65] such that states cannot lawfully commit or sanction them through domestic law. Some experts have identified prohibitions on universal

crimes with *jus cogens*, or peremptory norms of international law, from which states may not derogate,[66] though approaches to this proposition vary.[67] But whatever else it may stand for,[68] a central justificatory tenet of modern universal jurisdiction is that states cannot, under international law, legitimately endorse or permit universal crimes through national legislation.

It may be worth taking a step back here. The basic rationale for the doctrine, as we know, is to provide a basis of jurisdiction over crimes that international law considers so harmful that, even absent a national link to the crime, all states may prosecute the perpetrators.[69] But one could ask why this should be. If universal crimes are in fact prohibited by all states, then there should be no need for the doctrine at all, except perhaps with regard to piracy—the original crime of universal jurisdiction—perpetrated on the high seas by stateless actors.[70] As to all other universal crimes, every state would prosecute them when committed within its territory or by its nationals; and consequently, creating such expansive jurisdiction in all other states would be nothing more than a needlessly dangerous recipe for sovereign interference contrary to the dictates of the UN Charter.[71]

Yet one reason such expansive jurisdiction is needed is precisely because authorities in territorial and national jurisdiction states may themselves be the perpetrators of universal crimes.[72] Universal jurisdiction thus functions as a mechanism for overriding national laws contrary to predominant international norms. This principle has been built into the international legal system since at least the prosecution of Nazi war criminals by the International Military Tribunal at Nuremberg (IMT), which, as Leila Sadat has explained, "clearly affirmed the primacy of international law over national law" with regard to serious international crimes.[73] Indeed, "The [London] Charter . . . was explicit in rejecting municipal law as a defense to an international crime."[74] And that principle holds irrespective of whether the adjudicatory organ applying international law is a multilateral tribunal like the IMT or a national court because, as the Tribunal itself noted, the signatories to the London Charter were merely "do[ing] together what any one of them might have done singly."[75]

But suppose there had been no World War II or IMT, and suppose further that the Nazi final solution had been implemented only inside Germany and only against Germans. No other state would have national jurisdiction on these facts. Thus, absent universal jurisdiction, those committing horrible atrocities under the color of German law at the time effectively could be insulated from the reach of international law because of jurisdictional principles bounded by national connecting links. This situation of impunity is remedied through the mechanism of universal jurisdiction, whereby international law empowers all states to apply and enforce its proscriptions. As I've stated elsewhere,

> [universal jurisdiction] purports to refuse states a degree of exclusivity in the prescriptive authority they generally enjoy within their territories. That is, under the doctrine, states cannot legislatively endorse universal crimes; where they do so, international law (often operating through the laws of other states) effectively reaches into the territory of the offending state to proscribe the acts as criminal irrespective of domestic law.[76]

All of this is to say that under an interest analysis, where one state exercises universal jurisdiction, no other state will have a legitimate contrary interest expressed in its laws. Either other states simply will not have laws contrary to the international norms proscribing universal crimes as a practical matter, or they cannot as a legal matter. The result, in either case, is a false conflict of laws.

3. Choice of Forum

Although states with territorial or national jurisdiction would have no legitimate choice-of-law objection under international law to other states exercising universal jurisdiction, they may have a choice of forum objection. That is, territorial or national states may claim an adjudica-tive jurisdictional primacy to prosecute in their own courts universal crimes committed in their territories or by their nationals. Because states have begun only recently to explore in earnest universal jurisdiction over activity occurring in the territories of other states,[77] it is probably premature to conclude that state practice and *opinio juris* already have combined to definitively establish that a state with territorial or national jurisdiction has adjudicative priority over states with only universal jurisdiction. Nonetheless, a legal trend appears to be developing in this direction.

I have conducted elsewhere an extensive empirical canvassing of state practice in this regard—including examining national judicial opinions, national legislation, and the use of prosecutorial discretion, all of which provides national jurisdiction states with adjudicative priority to prosecute universal crimes.[78] The survey also observes that this type of hierarchy finds support in jurisdictional provisions of the vast majority of recent multilateral treaties covering international crimes as well as in a Joint Separate Opinion from the International Court of Justice.[79] This chapter is not the place to recapitulate that wide-ranging study, but suffice it to say that with the increase of national legislation authorizing universal jurisdiction has emerged a trend of giving the courts of states with territorial or national links to the crimes priority to prosecute.

Yet that jurisdictional priority concerns not so much the law being applied and enforced over universal crimes—again, that is, in principle, the same everywhere—but rather the forum in which that law is applied and enforced. For any number of philosophical and practical reasons, giving states with closer links to universal crimes priority to adjudicate makes good sense.[80] Perhaps an appropriate model here, and the one that appears to be gaining traction in practice, is a complementary jurisdiction similar to that contained in the Rome Statute for the International Criminal Court,[81] which precludes jurisdiction by the ICC where states with territorial or national links to the crime prosecute in good faith.[82] I will return to this jurisdictional dynamic in Part IV when I discuss double jeopardy or *non bis in idem* rules governing the exercise of universal jurisdiction for successive prosecutions by different states.

IV. Limiting Principles

This part uncovers and explores three limiting principles inherent in the concept of universal jurisdiction as conceived by the false-conflict framework advanced so far. First, states must faithfully apply the international legal definitions of the crimes they seek to prosecute when exercising universal jurisdiction. Second, international law at present prevents exercising universal jurisdiction where the defendant's home state has a valid immunity claim. Third, a state may not prosecute on the basis of universal jurisdiction where the crime in question already has been prosecuted by another state.

A. Faithful Application of International Law

If universal jurisdiction presents no conflict of laws because at bottom it merely authorizes the application of a law that is "the same" around the globe—that is, the international law against universal crimes—and to which other states cannot legitimately object based on conflicting domestic laws, then a state exercising universal jurisdiction must apply that "same" law common to all: international law. If the state exercising universal jurisdiction does not, it risks a true conflict of laws with other states. Such a true conflict can have both troubling state sovereignty and individual rights consequences for the international legal system.

1. State Sovereignty
The state sovereignty argument is simple: By not applying faithfully the international law against the universal crime in question, the state claiming universal jurisdiction over that crime could interfere with the sovereignty of other states by arrogating to itself more prescriptive jurisdiction than what is authorized under international law.

For example, suppose State A claims universal jurisdiction over X, a national of State B, for committing the crime of torture in State B against other State B nationals. But imagine that instead of using the internationally agreed-upon definition of torture to prosecute,[83] State A defines torture as taking someone to Dallas Cowboys playoff games. However disturbing watching the Cowboys may be, it clearly does not constitute torture under international law. I use this example not to make light of the extreme gravity of universal crimes, but simply to highlight in the starkest possible terms the fundamental problem with exercises of universal jurisdiction based on idiosyncratically defined offenses masquerading as "universal" in national legislation through headings like "torture," "genocide," "war crimes," or, for that matter, "terrorism."[84] Namely, that by idiosyncratically defining universal crimes however it likes, a state theoretically could declare its entire body of national law applicable inside the territory of every other state in the world.

This becomes especially problematic where the state into whose territory or over whose nationals the universal jurisdiction is claimed has no law prohibiting the conduct in question— indeed, it may be explicitly protected by domestic law, perhaps even constitutionally protected. That is, it becomes problematic in cases of "true conflicts" of laws. Suppose for instance that the underlying substance of the crime involved speech or expression that is outlawed on human dignity or religious grounds in the state claiming jurisdiction but is protected under the first amendment to the U.S. Constitution. If the foreign state redefined "genocide" to include racially or religiously offensive speech so as to claim jurisdiction over U.S. nationals for remarks spoken in the United States to other U.S. nationals and having no effect in the forum state, the United States might well claim sovereign interference.

Now it should be understood that if the speech was uttered by one of the foreign state's own nationals or had a substantial effect in the foreign state, that state might have its own sovereignty claim, based in its own national entitlements over national persons and territory,[85] to extend its laws to the conduct in question. In that case, there would be overlapping national prescriptive jurisdictions, deriving from different states' recognized national entitlements, or "sovereignties" under international law.

But once again, that is not the basis of universal jurisdiction, which requires no link at all to a state's sovereign entitlements and, therefore, has no limitation grounded in the state's own sovereignty to extend its laws vis-à-vis other, co-equal sovereigns in the international system. Rather, the literally universal ambit of jurisdiction exists precisely because no state can claim a sovereign interest contrary to its applicable substantive prohibitions—as prescribed by international, not national, law. Divorcing the exercise of universal jurisdiction from the faithful application of the international law against the crime serving as the jurisdictional trigger not only contradicts the underlying legal principle but also effectively guts any restriction on a state's ability to project any law, anywhere, to anyone—and in this respect would stamp an open invitation to arbitrary and unchecked interference with the sovereignty of other states.

Yet one could imagine thornier questions with real-world plausibility involving harsh interrogation techniques, crackdowns on political dissent, or elastic concepts of terrorism that may not fall strictly within the international definitions of universal crimes but over which states nonetheless may claim universal jurisdiction. Further, any time the commission of a universal crime is measured by a standard—take for instance standards of proportionality and necessity governing military strikes that collaterally kill civilians and could, therefore, result in war crimes allegations—room for disagreement is large indeed. [86] The central challenge for the international legal system regarding universal jurisdiction is to devise a regime that allows states to exercise jurisdiction over serious international crimes but not to manipulate the definition and scope of those crimes to claim an unwarranted authority to project domestic law onto the sovereign entitlements of other states in what are often highly charged and politically sensitive situations.

What this regime will look like and how it actually will operate are epistemic questions to which we do not yet have the necessary data, though we might be able to infer some basic lines of inquiry. In my view,[87] the first would be to ask how states are to determine the international legal definitions of the universal crimes they seek to prosecute. Next would be to figure out a way for other states to evaluate whether the state claiming universal jurisdiction has departed from the international definition of the crime. Finally, we might ask how other interested states, that is, states on whose territories the crimes occurred and/or whose nationals are the subject of foreign universal jurisdiction proceedings, might enforce against definitional expansions of universal crimes by overzealous courts—courts that might even seek to exploit universal jurisdiction for purely political or sensationalist ends.

As to the first inquiry—how to determine the international legal definitions of universal crimes—I would submit that their core substantive elements are set forth quite explicitly in the various treaties and conventions prohibiting the crimes under positive international law. Because universal jurisdiction is a customary, not a treaty-based law,[88] treaties do not (and cannot) set forth definitively the customary definitions of the crimes; but they do provide the best evidence of what those definitions are.[89] The treaties represent a relatively broad consensus not only as to the prohibition on the crimes but also as to their substance.[90] Thus, although state practice and *opinio juris* will continue to fill in, refine, and modify aspects of the customary definitions, for present purposes states wishing to exercise universal jurisdiction have a fairly clear and workable catalog of core definitions handy, in the treaty provisions, with which to prosecute universal crimes. National legislation enabling universal jurisdiction in fact tends to draw from treaty law to define the relevant offense,[91] and courts consequently use that definition to prosecute universal crimes,[92] thus reinforcing the customary law definitions.

Because treaties largely evidence the core definitions of universal crimes, we might respond to the second inquiry—how to determine when states claiming universal jurisdiction deviate from the customary definitions—by initially distinguishing between "easy cases" and "hard cases."[93] Where a court claiming universal jurisdiction clearly departs from the subject crime's core definition (as evidenced by the treaty), absent a showing that customary law has evolved to justify such a departure, its jurisdictional overreach should be easily identifiable. Particularly subject to easy-case categorization are universal crimes with rule-based elements. A quick example is the Spanish Audiencia Nacional's expansion of the victim classes in the definition of genocide to include political groups, which purported to justify an early assertion of universal jurisdiction over former Chilean dictator Augusto Pinochet.[94] Had the case gone forward on these grounds, Chile—both the territorial and national state—would have had a strong legal objection to the exercise of Spain's jurisdiction because the definition employed was exorbitant against the existing state of customary law.[95]

But although treaties strongly evidence the core elements of universal crimes, there invariably will be aspects of the definitions that need to be ironed out further by state practice. Moreover, the decentralized and organic nature of the international legal system inevitably will result in variation among states on the precise definitions of universal crimes. At the same time, some definitional variation or flexibility in importing and enforcing international law is probably unavoidable,[96] given how decentralized enforcement of international law actually works: through states' national laws and procedures.[97] Consequently, objections to universal jurisdiction that are not based on a court's clear departure from the universal crime's core substantive definition might fall into the "hard-case" category. As indicated above, especially subject to hard-case classification would be crimes that depend on the application of standards. Examples

here might include whether a specific act constitutes a war crime under standards of proportionality and necessity contained in the Geneva Conventions[98] and their Additional Protocols,[99] or whether a particular interrogation technique constitutes torture under the Torture Convention's definition of that crime.[100] The decisions of international criminal tribunals, and of national courts exercising universal jurisdiction (which are not precedent on their own but nonetheless constitute state practice)[101] would be particularly helpful guides here. In the end, the more states purport to apply international law through the exercise of universal jurisdiction, the more hard data the international legal system will have regarding the accepted scope and definitions of those crimes. Even where states clash on the definitions, the resolution of those clashes will only further add to customary law—which brings us to our final line of inquiry.

Everything said so far threatens to do something deeply antithetical to the very concept of custom: freeze it. If states are constrained in their exercise of universal jurisdiction to use the customary definitions of the crimes as they presently exist, then how can state practice evolve those definitions? One easy solution would be for states to get together and simply change the definition of the crime through an amendment to the relevant treaty or to create a new instrument relating to that crime.[102] But what about the state that tries to spark a change in international law by modifying on its own the definition of the crime? It has long been thought that states can alter international law by breaching it where that breach then gains acceptance and comes to represent a new customary norm.[103] Indeed, to state that proposition is to go far toward answering our question. Namely, the first state to exercise universal jurisdiction on the basis of an expanded definition may breach international law, but customary law's recursive constitution may immediately reduce the illegality of that breach if other states acquiesce in or approve of the universal jurisdiction assertion.

The logical last question is, which states' reactions count most? In comparison to other areas of international law, where it may be hard to identify and measure the various interests of various states implicated by a given claim,[104] the universal jurisdiction scenario presents a relatively clear picture of the interested states and the degree of their interests. The most interested states are those whose sovereignty is most implicated—that is, states that would have national jurisdiction, based on national entitlements, over the crime in question. Consequently, the potential for evolving (or not) the definitions of universal crimes by the process of customary-law-violation-turned-new-custom rests not so much with the state claiming universal jurisdiction but rather with the states whose nationals are in the dock. Where interested states object to the universal jurisdiction claim by rejecting a definitional expansion of the crime that purports to justify the exercise of jurisdiction, the claim signifies an enduring breach of international law. However, if interested states approve of or acquiesce in the definitional expansion, such approval or acquiescence may signal a possible customary shift regarding the definition of the crime in line with the definition purporting to justify the exercise of universal jurisdiction.[105] As we shall see next, there still may be individual rights problems with post hoc acceptance of prosecutions that utilize definitions that stretch beyond the established proscriptions of customary law. But as far as state sovereignty goes, this section hopefully has exposed a basic limiting principle and sketched a constructive line of legal and policy inquiry for thinking about the questions it raises.

2. Individual Rights

Expanding definitions of universal crimes in order to claim jurisdiction over non-nationals for activity abroad can also lead to individual rights problems, mostly associated with the principle of legality, which is often expressed by the Latin maxim *nullum crimen sine lege, nulla poena sine lege* (no crime without law, no punishment without law). Paul Robinson has noted

that "The [legality] principle is not a legal rule, but rather a legal concept embodied in a series of legal doctrines."[106] In the United States, it incorporates doctrines like the constitutional bar on ex post facto laws, due process protection against retroactive application of the criminal law, and modern prohibitions on the common law creation of criminal offenses.[107] As Beth Van Schaack has recently and comprehensively examined, the principle also exists in international law and is "enshrined in a number of human rights declarations and treaties"[108] as well as international criminal tribunal statutes.[109] Van Schaack also has explained, however, that its protections tend to be more relaxed in the international context than in the domestic context, due in large part to the special character of a fairly young and evolving field of international criminal law.[110] As a result, international criminal tribunals, starting with the post–World War II tribunals at Nuremberg and Tokyo, have devised various ways to avoid invalidating criminal charges on legality grounds.[111]

The legality question of fair notice looms particularly large in cases of extraterritorial jurisdiction because the state asserting jurisdiction is by definition not one in which the defendant committed her allegedly criminal acts. Thus, assumptions about the territorial nature of criminal law and attendant presumptions that the defendant is on notice of that law in the territory in which she acts can quickly fall away.[112] Universal jurisdiction further cuts away at notice based on other connecting links, such as nationality. In this respect, the legality question in universal jurisdiction cases hovers at the intersection of criminal law and conflict of laws. Both fields protect the defendant against the unfair application of a law of which she had insufficient notice, whether because that law went into effect after the commission of the allegedly criminal activity or because it is applied by a sovereign to whose laws the defendant could not reasonably have known she was subject.

In the domestic conflict-of-laws arena, the U.S. Supreme Court has placed constitutional limits on a state's choice of law as a matter of

Fourteenth Amendment due process. For a state constitutionally to apply its laws to a dispute, "that [s]tate must have a significant contact or significant aggregation of contacts, creating state interests, such that choice of its law is neither arbitrary nor fundamentally unfair."[113] According to the Court, "When considering fairness in this context, an important element is the expectation of the parties."[114] More recently, U.S. Courts of Appeal have been evaluating extraterritorial claims of U.S. federal jurisdiction regarding foreigners abroad under limits imposed by the Fifth Amendment's Due Process Clause.[115] These limits, in turn, raise questions about the constitutionality of applying U.S. criminal laws to individuals who have no or only slight connections to the United States at the time they commit their acts abroad, but later find themselves in U.S. custody.[116] In the first ever prosecution under the U.S. Torture Convention Implementation Act,[117] Chuckie Taylor, former Liberian dictator Charles Taylor's son, leveled precisely this Fifth Amendment due process challenge at the application of U.S. law to him for alleged acts of torture in Liberia against non-U.S. nationals.[118]

This discussion of legality and choice-of-law fairness principles circles back to a false-conflict view of universal jurisdiction because if the false-conflict view is followed, it protects both victims' and defendants' rights under both sets of fairness principles. It protects victims' rights because defendants cannot avoid conviction by claiming lack of notice that their conduct was illegal, or even of the law being applied to them—that is, international law. Again, because the state exercising universal jurisdiction is not extending its own laws extraterritorially but is instead acting as the application and enforcement vehicle of an otherwise applicable and pre-existing international law that covers the globe, there is no legality problem.

This type of analysis can hold important lessons for those U.S. Courts of Appeal that model their Fifth Amendment due process tests for federal extraterritorial jurisdiction after the Supreme Court's Fourteenth Amendment due process test for state extraterritorial jurisdiction. A test that borrows unthinkingly from the domestic context, and that therefore requires some connection to the forum state—or "nexus," as Courts of Appeal are fond of saying[119]—fails to take account of universal prohibitions contained in international law that are capable of being applied and enforced in U.S. courts. Such a cramped view of U.S. jurisdiction at the international level, not only unduly constrains the United States' ability to prosecute serious human rights violators like torturers and war criminals, but it also ties prosecutors' hands in their struggle against transnational terrorism by erecting constitutional barriers to convicting those in U.S. custody for universal terrorist crimes outlawed in the U.S. code but that may have had no overt domestic connection; crimes including the bombing of public places,[120] infrastructure,[121] transportation systems,[122] airports[123] and aircraft,[124] as well as hijacking,[125] hostage taking,[126] and even financing foreign terrorist organizations.[127]

Why these crimes would qualify as universal has been elaborated in more detail elsewhere,[128] but a brief explanation can highlight legality issues for the present discussion. Each of the crimes listed above is the subject of a widely ratified international instrument not only criminalizing the act in question and requiring its criminalization at the national level but also providing extraterritorial and extranational jurisdiction for all States Parties with respect to the prosecution of the crime's perpetrators, even where the crime is committed in the territory of a non-party state.[129] Specifically, the treaties contain "prosecute or extradite" provisions mandating each State Party on whose territory offenders are "present" or "found" both (i) to "establish its jurisdiction over the offence" and (ii) either to prosecute or to extradite (to another State Party),[130] thus creating a comprehensive jurisdiction among States Parties. Moreover, because States Parties may establish jurisdiction and prosecute perpetrators of the crime absent any territorial or national connection—and even where the crime occurs in the territory of a non-party state—the prescriptive prohibition on the crime contained in the treaty effectively extends into all states, even non-parties. It would be strange to say the prohibition does so as a matter of the positive law of the treaty, because states are not bound by treaties to which they are not party.[131] Rather, the better view is that it does so as a result of the intent and practice of those States Parties to the treaty to create a generalizable customary norm of universal prescriptive jurisdiction over the crime in question. Said another way, because the prohibition may be applied to the perpetrators of the crimes even where those crimes are committed in the territories of non-party states, states parties have created through their entrance into the treaty a customary international legal prohibition that extends into the territories of all states, irrespective of their status under the positive law of the treaty.

This can be crucial to a legality analysis. For example, if the treaty did not establish universal jurisdiction as a matter of customary law, then the defendant from a nonparty state who commits an act in his home state that is (a) prohibited under the treaty, but (b) permissible in his home state, and (c) who is later prosecuted by a state party to the treaty, would seem to have a quite valid legality defense. To be sure, one reason the defendant's home state may have declined to enter into the treaty was because it had laws contrary to those contained in the treaty; in which case, there would be a "true conflict" of laws between the states parties on the one hand, and the non-party state on the other. Why should the defendant be "on notice" of a prohibition in a treaty to which his home state is not a party, where he is acting within his home state, and—let us stipulate because it makes no difference under the treaty regime—acts against other nationals of his home state under the color of his home state's laws? Unless the prohibition in the treaty is constitutive of a customary norm of universal jurisdiction against the crime, the treaty provisions allowing states parties to prosecute the defendant would seem unavoidably to raise legality issues.

Seen in this light, a distinction drawn by the Joint Separate Opinion of Judges Higgins, Kooijmans, and Buergenthal in the fairly recent Arrest Warrant case in the International Court of Justice[132] can be worrisome for legality purposes. The Opinion distinguishes between "a classical assertion of universal jurisdiction" exercised where the accused is not present on the state's territory[133] and the types of treaty provisions I have referred to above that, according to the Opinion, have "come to be referred to as 'universal jurisdiction,' though this is really an obligatory territorial jurisdiction over persons albeit in relation to acts committed elsewhere."[134]

That distinction may well hold for universal adjudicative, or *in personam*, jurisdiction: The presence of the accused on a state's territory gives that state's courts personal jurisdiction, under the treaty, irrespective of where the crime occurred. Yet the distinction becomes more difficult to sustain with respect to prescriptive jurisdiction, or the state's initial power to apply its laws to the conduct in question. The crime did not occur on the state's territory and, thus, as the Opinion concedes, it is not that the state is exercising territorial jurisdiction over the crime itself. Rather, the Opinion seems to be suggesting that once the defendant is in the state's territory, the state has jurisdiction to prescribe as to that defendant. But if the presence of the accused—at some later point—is all that is giving the state prescriptive power, the exercise of that power inevitably raises retroactivity problems if the state did not already have that power to begin with at the time the crime was committed (when the state had no link to the defendant). It could betray bedrock principles of legality to say, for instance, "we had no power to apply our law prohibiting Y to you at the time you committed Y; but now that you're in our territory we are empowered retroactively to apply our prohibition to you." Only if Y were already prohibited under a universal legal prohibition—that the state subsequently enforces once it obtains personal jurisdiction over the defendant—would the prescriptive jurisdiction stand. Again, this becomes especially troubling in the case of the international true conflict where, absent the customary norm extending into his home state, the defendant national of a non-party state would have no notice of the prohibition contained in the treaty.

As is probably evident by now, the flip side of the conceptual coin to protecting victims' rights by extinguishing legality defenses is that the false-conflict view requires that when states exercise universal jurisdiction the crimes are in fact universal under international law and the law used to prosecute faithfully reflects the crime's international legal definition.[135] Otherwise, the defendant with no connection to the state claiming jurisdiction might not be sufficiently on notice of the proscription the state is claiming to apply to him for purposes of prosecution and punishment.

Once again, the situation most susceptible to a legality defense is the true conflict where the defendant's acts are not prohibited in the state of their commission, but another state has unilaterally deemed them "universal" and thus subject to prosecution in its courts even though the state has no connection to either the defendant or his allegedly criminal activity. Similar to the sovereignty analysis in the previous section, proverbial "easy cases" for identifying such legality problems would occur where a state exercising universal jurisdiction manufactures a brand new universal offense on which it bases jurisdiction. In the not-totally-unlikely combination of these two situations—a true conflict with the defendant's domestic law and the manufacturing of a new universal crime on which jurisdiction is based in a foreign court—the defendant easily could be prosecuted under a law of which he had no notice.

By contrast, "hard cases" would be those in which the state exercising universal jurisdiction massages or expands the definition of a crime, perhaps one that regulates activity *malum in se* so that the defendant cannot claim lack of notice of the wrongfulness of his conduct, even though the definition of the crime used to prosecute is different than that generally recognized under the international law of which the defen-

dant is deemed on notice.[136] It is not my objective here to tackle the full extent of the legality principle in international criminal law, which may well be inherently flexible to allow for necessary jurisprudential innovation;[137] that task has been skillfully and effectively handled by others.[138] Neither is it to explore whether international tribunal statements on legality can or should be transposed to national courts exercising universal jurisdiction.[139] Rather, my goal is simply to demonstrate that exercises of universal jurisdiction that comport with the false-conflict view protect both victims' and defendants' rights: by erasing defendants' legality and due process defenses and by protecting the same from the arbitrary and unfair application of laws of which they had no notice.

B. Immunity and Amnesty

Through doctrines of immunity, international law grants states another type of "sovereignty claim" against the application of its proscriptions by other states claiming universal jurisdiction. International law is relatively clear, for instance, that "sitting heads of state, accredited diplomats, and other officials cannot be prosecuted while in office for acts committed in their official capacities."[140] The immunity that attaches to the holder of a protected state office or status is referred to as immunity *ratione personae*.[141] The most famous example here is probably the International Court of Justice's 2002 ruling, mentioned earlier, that a Belgian arrest warrant grounded in universal jurisdiction over the Democratic Republic of the Congo's acting Minister of Foreign Affairs, Abdoulaye Yerodia Ndombasi, contravened the international law of immunity and was therefore void.[142]

However, the Court went out of its way to emphasize that "the immunity from jurisdiction enjoyed by incumbent [officials] does not mean that they enjoy impunity in respect of crimes they might have committed."[143] Immunity, therefore, does not absolve the defendant of international criminal liability but instead merely shields him from prosecution in certain circumstances—and that shield is neither absolute nor an individual right but rather rests in the hands of the defendant's home state.[144] As the Court observed, the defendant's state could itself prosecute[145] or waive the immunity.[146] The Court further explained that the immunity would not stand in the way of a prosecution by an international tribunal with jurisdiction over the crime.[147] On this last point, it appears that in striking the balance between sovereignty and justice in the international system, international law prefers internationally constituted tribunals to administer justice over state sovereignty, but prefers state sovereignty over justice where such justice is to be administered by another, coequal sovereign state exercising universal jurisdiction.[148]

The Court also indicated that the immunity shield is weaker once the accused leaves office,[149] consequently watering down an objection to the exercise of universal jurisdiction. Former officials only enjoy immunity *ratione materiae* under international law, which "precludes domestic prosecutions of current and former foreign-state agents for acts that those agents committed . . . within the scope of their official functions."[150] Notably, "such immunity from foreign domestic criminal jurisdiction does not exist when the person is charged with an international crime."[151] This was, in fact, one of the knottier issues in the famous rulings by the British House of Lords in response to the Spanish extradition request based on universal jurisdiction over Pinochet for torture.[152] A majority of the British Law Lords held that Pinochet was not entitled to immunity with respect to the torture charges because of his status as former head of state.[153]

A related matter involves domestic amnesties. There is substantial literature addressing amnesties and their proper role in resolving tensions between peace and justice.[154] That debate is, naturally, well beyond the scope of this chapter. However, it does demonstrate broad agreement that international law currently does not require one state to respect another state's domestic amnesty for universal crimes. Eugene

Kontorovich, for example, has critiqued universal jurisdiction precisely because it poses obstacles to peacemaking because a single "holdout" state unconnected to a conflict can stand in the way of a complete amnesty favored by involved states, potentially defeating an optimally brokered peace by those with the highest stake in resolving the conflict.[155] In fact, amnesties themselves are often viewed with suspicion under international law. In this connection, Michael Scharf has noted many scholars' operating "assumption that the widespread state practice favoring amnesties constitutes a violation of, rather than a reflection of, international law in this area."[156] And Leila Sadat has recommended that a state exercising universal jurisdiction "should keep in mind that amnesties are disfavored, perhaps even illegal in international law"[157] and "to permit national amnesties to extinguish obligations imposed by international law would seem contrary to the foundational principles of international criminal law, and stand in opposition to the clear weight of authority and much of the state and international practice emerging in this field."[158] Thus, although states may have certain immunity claims against another state's exercise of universal jurisdiction, a claim based only on a domestic amnesty is substantially weaker if not nonexistent given the present state of international law.

C. Double Jeopardy or *Non Bis in Idem*

A final limiting principle inherent in the concept of universal jurisdiction is that a state may not prosecute on the basis of universal jurisdiction after a prior prosecution of the same individual for the same crime by another state. This is an exception to how double jeopardy or *non bis in idem* rules conventionally are thought to operate in systems of multiple sovereigns. The general rule in the international system, much like the dual sovereignty doctrine in the U.S. federal system,[159] is that each sovereign may prosecute for an offense against its own laws.[160]

This general rule largely explains modern international law and practice regarding double jeopardy protections. For example, human rights and humanitarian law instruments limit double jeopardy coverage to successive prosecutions by one state;[161] extradition treaties narrowly and self-consciously construe exceptions to a default rule permitting double jeopardy among states;[162] and no general principle of law has developed to prevent double jeopardy among states.[163] Double jeopardy protection therefore attaches only to successive prosecutions by the same sovereign—or, put another way, to successive prosecutions under the same law (deriving from the same sovereign's lawmaking power).

However, because universal jurisdiction does not provide states with an independent power to prescribe law, but only the power to apply via domestic process international law, a state has no separate law to apply and enforce in a successive prosecution where the crime already has been prosecuted by another state. Briefly put, because all states are members of the international lawmaking, -applying, and -enforcing collective, where one state applies the international norm through a good faith prosecution, that state effectively uses up the international law over that crime and consequently extinguishes jurisdiction for all other states wishing to exercise universal jurisdiction. In effect, universal jurisdiction functions as a kind of complementary or subsidiary jurisdiction: States with jurisdiction based on territorial or national entitlements may apply international law (because they, too, are members of the international legal system), and once they do, universal jurisdiction states have no law left upon which to prosecute again, thereby creating a double jeopardy bar.

To illustrate, suppose X, a national of State B, commits a crime in State A's territory. Both State A and State B successively may prosecute after an initial prosecution by the other state because each has a distinct national entitlement, based on nationality or territoriality, giving each national jurisdiction or independent lawgiving power over the crime, thus making each a separate "sovereign" for purposes of double jeopardy. Now imagine the crime is a universal crime

under international law. Both State A and State B still successively may prosecute after a prior prosecution by another state because each still has a distinct national entitlement, creating national jurisdiction and, hence, independent prescriptive power over the crime.

But what about State C, which only may prosecute on the basis of universal jurisdiction?[164] State C is in the same position as Spain in the hypothetical above in which the U.S. national is alleged to have committed torture in Egypt.[165] If instead of committing a universal crime under international law, X committed a garden-variety robbery in State A, State C would have no ordinary ability to apply State C national law to X. Rather, for State C to prosecute, it would need to rely uniquely upon its international jurisdiction over the universal crime in question. The State C national law used to prosecute therefore has no self-supporting national jurisdictional basis but is merely the vehicle through which State C applies and enforces international law. Because State C has no independent national jurisdiction to apply its national law but must rely uniquely on a shared international jurisdiction to apply international law, State C would be blocked from prosecuting by a prior prosecution for the universal crime in question.

The reasoning would be roughly as follows. Let's suppose State B, the national state, prosecutes X first for the universal crime. State B, like every state, is part of the international lawmaking collective. It is also part of the international law-applying and -enforcing collective. Thus when State B prosecutes X for a universal crime, State B applies and enforces international as well as its national law. There is, in other words, no independent "international sovereign" in the way that there would be an independent national sovereign in the government of State A (the territorial state with a national entitlement to exercise national jurisdiction—and apply its own national law—to activity within its borders). Rather, the "sovereignty" or lawgiving and -applying power of the international legal system is invariably bound up in the individual states that make and apply international law in decentralized fashion, of which State B is one.

Where State B applies the international prohibition in its courts, State C cannot then come along and claim itself to be the international law-enforcer if State B already has performed that function. It is conceptually no different than someone being prosecuted in the Second Circuit under a federal law, and then the same person being prosecuted in the Ninth Circuit for the same offense under the same federal law. Such a prosecution plainly would violate the prohibition on double jeopardy, and the doctrine of dual sovereignty cannot pretend to save it.

To sum up then, State B's initial application and enforcement of international law blocks a successive State C prosecution because State C is jurisdictionally constrained to apply and enforce that same law, that is, international law. State C has no alternative basis of jurisdiction or lawgiving power (unlike State A, which retains a national entitlement to apply its national law to acts within its borders). As a universal jurisdiction state, all State C can enforce is a shared international law, which State B already enforced. We are left, in turn, with the paradigmatic double jeopardy protection: You cannot be prosecuted for the same offense under the same law (here international law) twice.

This conceptual model explains why the one situation states overwhelmingly if not uniformly refrain from pursuing successive prosecutions is one in which their only basis of jurisdiction is the universal nature of the crime under international law.[166] In fact, as noted earlier, many states' universal jurisdiction laws incorporate directly principles of complementarity or subsidiarity, often because such laws implement obligations under the Rome Statute,[167] thus precluding the exercise of universal jurisdiction where a state with national jurisdiction has already prosecuted in good faith.

Moreover, this sort of national enforcement of international law appears to be exactly what the double jeopardy provisions of certain international tribunal statutes have in mind. The provisions in the ad hoc tribunals for both the former Yugoslavia and Rwanda protect an individual from a successive tribunal prosecution where that individual previously has been tried in good faith for the same criminal act in national court.[168] The prior national court prosecution already would have enforced international law over the act in question, thus precluding the tribunal from enforcing that same law again.

But there is an exception to this double jeopardy bar, and one that is very telling in light of the discussion above: The tribunal may well prosecute again where "the act for which [the individual] was tried was characterized as an ordinary crime"[169]—in other words, where the national prosecution did not use the international substance and definition of the crime and, thus, did not enforce international law.

For example, if Jane kills some people based on their ethnic identity with the intent to destroy that ethnic group in whole or in part, and a national court prosecutes Jane for the international crime of genocide,[170] the ad hoc tribunals may not then prosecute Jane a second time for genocide. But if the national court prosecutes Jane not for the international crime of genocide but instead for the "ordinary crime" of homicide, the international tribunal may still prosecute Jane for that same act under the international law proscribing genocide. Because the prior national court proceedings did not apply and enforce international law but prosecuted only for "ordinary crimes" under national law, the national court did not act as the decentralized "international sovereign." The international tribunal, therefore, could continue to represent a distinct lawgiver (the international legal system) applying and enforcing a distinct law (international law), in respect of a distinct crime (an international crime), resulting from acts for which an individual already was prosecuted in national court.[171] Finally, and perhaps most fascinatingly, these same rules of international double jeopardy seem to have been articulated in a U.S. Supreme Court opinion from 1820, the same year the Court began to develop the jurisdictional reasoning that underpins the dual sovereignty doctrine in the U.S. federal system today.[172] *United States v. Furlong* explained in *dicta* that if someone were prosecuted in U.S. courts for piracy, an offense against the "law of nations" and subject to a shared "universal jurisdiction" by all states,[173] that person would have a double jeopardy defense against a successive prosecution in the courts of any other "civilized State."[174] But the same would not hold regarding successive prosecutions for the parochial crime of murder. This is because murder was a crime within each state's national jurisdiction and was determined under each state's own national law, allowing each state independently to apply and enforce its own law where it had jurisdiction over the crime.[175] Hence, double jeopardy protection attaches to bar a successive prosecution based only on universal jurisdiction, not only because the law used to prosecute looks the same as that already used by a national jurisdiction state, but because it actually is the same.

V. Conclusion

Standing controversially but firmly in the crossroads of state sovereignty and human rights, universal jurisdiction raises vital questions for international lawyers and policy makers that cut to the very heart of the modern international legal system. The most basic is how to let it do its work combating serious international crimes and vindicating fundamental human rights while at the same time checking its potential to disrupt stability through interstate meddling in a system premised on the coequal sovereignties of its members. This question is far from simple; indeed, it is intriguingly multilayered. To conclude, I want to suggest that a false-conflict view of universal jurisdiction does a pretty good job of starting to answer it and that such a view can offer a solid conceptual framework with which to approach the issue as we move forward.

Under the false-conflict view, no conflict of laws exists among states because the state exercising universal jurisdiction does not extend ex-traterritorially its own national laws, but instead applies through domestic process a universally applicable international law that covers the globe. Consistent with this model, a state exercising universal jurisdiction must apply the international legal proscriptions on the universal crimes it seeks to prosecute. The incorporation and application of substantive international law through domestic procedures holds a number of significant implications and counter-implications.

First, it erases claims of sovereign interference by states unwilling or unable to prosecute universal crimes committed in their territories or by their nationals. Correspondingly, however, it provides states whose nationals are the subject of foreign universal jurisdiction proceedings that depart from established international law a basis on which to identify and object to jurisdictional overreaching by other states. Second, perpetrators of serious international crimes cannot avoid conviction by claiming that they were not on notice of the law being applied to them. But correspondingly, the false-conflict view protects defendants' rights not to be unfairly subject to laws of which they had no notice. Third, it provides states with recognized immunity claims under international law to object to potentially destabilizing universal jurisdiction assertions over public officials. And finally, because an exercise of universal jurisdiction fundamentally applies international law, once a good faith prosecution for a universal crime has already taken place in one state, universal jurisdiction is unavailable in other states because the first prosecution already would have applied the international law against that crime, thereby leaving the universal jurisdiction state no law upon which to prosecute again.

Each of these implications and counter-implications seeks to accommodate sovereignty and individual rights concerns in the international legal system. Yet there are many questions left unresolved—including questions about the precise definitions of universal crimes and the availability of certain forms of liability for those crimes under international law, due process, and fair procedures across jurisdictions, minimum thresholds for recognizing foreign judgments, and sentencing practices and policies—some of which can only be answered through the accumulation of hard data in the form of universal jurisdiction assertions by states and the reactions of other interested states. My purpose has been simply to offer a helpful way of thinking about them.

NOTES

1. RESTATEMENT (THIRD) OF THE FOREIGN RELATIONS LAW OF THE UNITED STATES §401(a) (1987).

2. SYMEON C. SYMEONIDES, AMERICAN PRIVATE INTERNATIONAL LAW 15 (2008).

3. *See infra* notes 48–50 and accompanying text.

4. I say "in theory" because I am working on a conceptual level here to frame the relevant empirical and epistemic questions about national implementation and enforcement of international law in the context of universal jurisdiction. I highlight those questions and suggest how I think they should be addressed in Part III.

5. The discussion of national versus international jurisdiction is taken substantially from my most recent article, *Double Jeopardy and Multiple Sovereigns: A Jurisdictional Theory*, 86 WASH. U. L. REV. 769, 791–97 (2009) [hereinafter Colangelo, *Double Jeopardy and Multiple Sovereigns*].

6. I borrow the "entitlement" terminology here from Anthony D'Amato. *See* Anthony D'Amato, *The Concept of Human Rights in International Law*, 82 COLUM. L. REV. 1110, 1113 (1982) [hereinafter D'Amato, *Human Rights*]; Anthony D'Amato, *Is International Law Really "Law"?* 79 NW. U. L. REV. 1293, 1308 (1984) [hereinafter D'Amato, *Is International Law Really "Law"?*]. For a recent interesting and persuasive discussion of the universal jurisdictional entitlement to prosecute, *see* Eugene Kontorovich, *The Inefficiency of Universal Jurisdiction*, 2008 U. ILL. L. REV. 389 (2008).

7. *See* D'Amato, *Is International Law Really "Law"? supra* note 6, at 1308.

8. *Supra* note 1, at §402(1)(a) (1987).

9. *Id.*

10. *Id.* at §402(1)(c).

11. *Id.* at §402(2).

12. *Id.* at §402(2), cmt. g.

13. *Id.* at §402(3).

14. *See* Anne-Marie Slaughter, *Defining the Limits: Universal Jurisdiction and National Courts, in* UNIVERSAL JURISDICTION: NATIONAL COURTS AND THE PROSECUTION OF SERIOUS CRIMES UNDER INTERNATIONAL LAW 94 (Stephen Macedo ed., 2004).

15. *See supra* note 1, at §402(2) (1987).

16. *Id.* at §402(1)(a).

17. *See, e.g.*, S.S. "Lotus" (Fr. v. Turk.), 1927 P.C.I.J. (ser. A) No. 10, at 30–31 (Sept. 7).

18. *See* Anthony J. Colangelo, *Constitutional Limits on Extraterritorial Jurisdiction: Terrorism and the Intersection of National and International Law*, 48 HARV. INT'L L. J. 121, 169–75 (2007) [hereinafter Colangelo, *Constitutional Limits on Extraterritorial Jurisdiction*].

19. *Cf.* Marcel Brus, *Bridging the Gap Between State Sovereignty and International Governance: The Authority of Law, in* STATE SOVEREIGNTY AND INTERNATIONAL GOVERNANCE 3, 4 (Gerard Kreijen ed., Oxford 2004) (discussing the concept of global governance).

20. Convention on the Prevention and Punishment of the Crime of Genocide, 102 Stat. 3045, 78 U.N.T.S. 277 (Dec. 9, 1948) [hereinafter Genocide Convention].

21. *See supra* note 1, at §404 (1987); Leila Nadya Sadat, *Redefining Universal Jurisdiction*, 35 NEW ENG. L. REV. 241, 246 (2001) [hereinafter Sadat, *Redefining Universal Jurisdiction*].

22. *See United States v. Furlong*, 18 U.S. 184, 197 (1820).

23. *See, e.g.*, *United States v. Yunis*, 924 F.2d 1086, 1091 (D.C. Cir. 1991) (citing *supra* note 1, at §§404, 423 (1987)); *see also* PRINCETON PROJECT ON UNIVERSAL JURISDICTION, THE PRINCETON PRINCIPLES ON UNIVERSAL JURISDICTION princ. 2(1) (Stephen Macedo ed., 2001) [hereinafter PRINCETON PRINCIPLES ON UNIVERSAL JURISDICTION].

24. This argument is spelled out in greater detail in Anthony J. Colangelo, *The Legal Limits of Universal Jurisdiction*, 47 VA. J. INT'L L. 149 (2007) [hereinafter Colangelo, *The Legal Limits of Universal Jurisdiction*].

25. Professor Sadat distinguished between "universal international jurisdiction," exercised by the international community through international tribunals, and "universal inter-state jurisdiction," exercised by individual states through national courts. *See* Leila Nadya Sadat, *Exile, Amnesty and International Law*, 81 NOTRE DAME L. REV. 955, 974–975 (2006) [hereinafter Sadat, *Exile, Amnesty and International Law*]; Sadat, *Redefining Universal Jurisdiction, supra* note 21, at 246–47; Leila Nadya Sadat & S. Richard Carden, *The New International Criminal Court: An Uneasy Revolution*, 88 GEO. L. J. 381, 412 (2000). This helpfully explains the difference between international adjudicative jurisdiction, created by international tribunal statutes, and national adjudicative jurisdiction, created by national law. My argument here is that, as a matter of prescriptive jurisdiction, individual states exercising universal jurisdiction are acting as decentralized enforcers of international law. By their very nature, universal prescriptions—whether adjudicated by international tribunals or national courts—derive from the same source of law-giving authority:

international law. The adjudicative bodies that apply this law may be creatures of either international treaty or national legislation, but they are both enforcing the same—international—law.

26. STC, Sept. 26, 2005 (S.T.C. No. 237, §II), *available and translated at* www.tribunalconstitucional.es/jurisprudencia/Stc_ing/STC2007-237-2005.html [hereinafter Guatemala Genocide Case].

27. *Id.*

28. Arrest Warrant of 11 April 2000 (*Dem. Rep. Congo v. Belg.*), 2002 I.C.J. 3, 78 (Feb. 14) (joint separate opinion of Judges Higgins, Kooijmans, and Buergenthal).

29. I address why I think treaty law can lead to universal jurisdiction as a matter of customary law in Part III.A.

30. *See supra* notes 26–28.

31. Colangelo, *The Legal Limits of Universal Jurisdiction, supra* note 24, at 161.

32. *See, e.g.*, Code de procédure pénale, titre préliminare, article 12 bis (Belg.); Colangelo, *Constitutional Limits on Extraterritorial Jurisdiction, supra* note 18, at 175–77. Such municipal legislative authorization for the exercise of universal jurisdiction also may reflect modern antipathy toward common law creation and the evolution of crimes.

33. Colangelo, *The Legal Limits of Universal Jurisdiction, supra* note 24, at 153.

34. *See infra* Part III.A.

35. *See, e.g., supra* notes 26–28.

36. *See generally* SYMEONIDES, *supra* note 2.

37. *See* DAVID F. CAVERS, THE CHOICE-OF-LAW PROCESS 64 (1965); *see also* Peter Kay Westen, *Comment, False Conflicts*, 55 CAL. L. REV. 74, 76–78 (1967) (enumerating seven types of false conflict).

38. Westen, *supra* note 37, at 78.

39. *Id.* at 76; *See also* Brainerd Currie, *Married Women's Contracts: A Study in Conflict-of-Laws Method*, 25 U. CHI. L. REV. 227 (1958); Brainerd Currie, *On the Displacement of the Law of the Forum*, 58 COLUM. L. REV. 964 (1958); Brainerd Currie, *Survival of Actions: Adjudication versus Automation in the Conflict of Laws*, 10 STAN. L. REV. 205 (1958).

40. Brainerd Currie, *The Constitution and the Choice of Law: Governmental Interests and the Judicial Function*, 26 U. CHI. L. REV. 9, 10 (1958) [hereinafter Currie, *The Constitution and the Choice of Law*].

41. *Id.* Also, "In his later work, Currie recognized a fourth category, what he called an 'apparent conflict,' which is something between a false and a true conflict." Symeon C. Symeonides, *The American Choice-of-Law Revolution in Courts: Today and Tomorrow*, 298 RECUEIL DES COURS 1, 44 (2002).

42. *See* Currie, *The Constitution and the Choice of Law, supra* note 40, at 10 ("When one of two states re-

lated to a case has a legitimate interest in the application of its law and policy and the other has none, there is no real problem; clearly the law of the interested state should be applied.").

43. *Id.*

44. EUGENE F. SCOLES ET AL., CONFLICT OF LAWS 28 (4th ed. 2004).

45. *Id.*

46. *See id.* at 25–38; Westen, *supra* note 37, at 80.

47. Scoles et al., *supra* note 44, at 29.

48. *See Phillips Petroleum Co. v. Shutts*, 472 U.S. 797, 838 n.20 (1985) (Stevens, J., concurring) ("'[F]alse conflict' really means 'no conflict of laws.' If the laws of both states relevant to the set of facts are the same, or would produce the same decision in the lawsuit, there is no real conflict between them" (quoting Robert Leflar, American Conflicts Law §93, 188 (3d ed. 1977))); Wachsman *ex rel, Wachsman v. Islamic Republic of Iran*, 537 F. Supp. 2d 85, 94 (D.D.C. 2008); *Gulf Group Holdings, Inc. v. Coast Asset Mgmt. Corp.*, 516 F. Supp. 2d 1253, 1271 (S.D. Fla. 2007); *Greaves v. State Farm Ins. Co.*, 984 F. Supp. 12, 14 (D.D.C. 1997); *Brenner v. Oppenheimer, Inc.*, 44 P.3d 364, 372 (Kan. 2002); 16 Am. Jur. 2d Conflict of Laws §85 (2008). *But cf. Hammersmith v. TIG Ins. Co.*, 480 F.3d 220, 229–30 (3d Cir. 2007) (noting, but ultimately rejecting, previous court decisions suggesting that instances where the laws of two states do not differ should be characterized as "false conflicts").

49. *See, e.g.*, Elizabeth T. Lear, *National Interests, Foreign Injuries, and Federal Forum Non Conveniens*, 41 U.C. DAVIS L. REV. 559, 583n. 116 (2007); Joel P. Trachtman, *International Regulatory Competition, Externalization, and Jurisdiction*, 34 HARV. INT'L L. J. 47, 70 (1993); Leigh Anne Miller, *Choice-of-Law Approaches in Tort Actions*, 16 AM. J. TRIAL ADVOC. 859, 866 (1993); *See also* Michael S. Gill, *Turbulent Times or Clear Skies Ahead?: Conflict of Laws in Aviation Delict and Tort*, 64 J. AIR L. & COM. 195, 227 (1998) (noting that prior to Currie's development of his notion of "false conflicts," the "conventional thinking was that a false conflict arose when the content of the substantive laws . . . were the same").

50. Robert A. Leflar, *Choice-Influencing Considerations in Conflicts Law*, 41 N.Y.U. L. REV. 267, 290 (1966). Leflar also suggested that false conflicts exist where different states' laws, although not the same, would produce the same result. *See id.* However, as Peter Westen has pointed out, this view of a false conflict runs into trouble when the court "splits" the case into separate issues and "the law of one contact state is invoked to resolve one issue . . . and the law of another state is applied to a different issue, so that combined they produce a result contrary to the common one which would obtain if the entire law of only one state were applied." Westen,

supra note 37, at 114. Along with Currie's version of a false conflict—that is, where only one state has an interest—these two versions of false conflicts—that is, where the laws are the same and where the laws would, although different, produce the same result—probably comprise the three most common varieties of false conflict in domestic conflict jurisprudence.

51. Again, I am not suggesting that a false-conflict analysis would work exactly the same way in the international system as in the U.S. interstate system (indeed, there is no such thing as universal jurisdiction in the latter), but rather that false conflicts provide a helpful and coherent way to structure thinking about the exercise of universal jurisdiction in the international system.

52. *Supra* note 1, at §404 cmt. a (1987).

53. *See supra* Part I.B.

54. *Supra* note 1, at §402(1)(a) (1987).

55. *See id.* at §402(2).

56. *See* Strafgestzbuch [StGB] [Penal Code] §64(1) (6) (Austria), *translated in* Luc Reydams, Universal Jurisdiction: International and Municipal Legal Perspectives 94 (2003); Code de procédure pénale, titre préliminaire, article 12 bis (Belg.), translated in Reydams, *supra*, at 105; Straffeloven [Strfl] [Penal Code] §8(1)(5) (Den.), translated in Reydams, *supra*, at 127; Strafgesetzbuch [StGB] [Penal Code] §6, translated in Reydams, *supra*, at 142; Wet Internationale Misdrijven (International Crimes Act), Staatsblad van het Koninkrijk der Nederlanden [Stb.] 270 (Neth.).

57. Ley Orgánica del Poder Judicial [L.O.P.J.] 6/1985, B.O.E. (1985), 157.

58. This was precisely Spain's jurisdictional justification for its famous extradition request for Pinochet.

59. *See* Statute of the International Criminal Tribunal for the Former Yugoslavia, S.C. Res. 827, art. 10, U.N. Doc. S/RES/827 (May 25, 1993) [hereinafter ICTY Statute]; Statute of the International Criminal Tribunal for Rwanda, S.C. Res. 955, art. 9, U.N. Doc. S/RES/955 (Nov. 8, 1994) [hereinafter ICTR Statute].

60. *See* Guatemala Genocide Case, *supra* note 26, §II. The Spanish Constitutional Court rejected the argument that universal jurisdiction existed in Spanish courts over genocide abroad only where the victims were Spanish because such a limitation "contradicts the very nature of the crime and the shared objective that it be combated universally." *Id.*

61. *See supra* notes 39–40. *See* Protocol No. 7 to the European Convention for the Protection of Human Rights and Fundamental Freedoms, art. 4, Europ. T.S. No. 117 (Nov. 22, 1984) (entered into force Nov. 1, 1988); International Covenant on Civil and Political Rights, art. 14(7), 999 U.N.T.S. 17 (Dec. 16, 1966).

62. *See supra* note 44.

63. *See* Brainerd Currie, Selected Essays on the Conflict of Laws 182 (1963) (explaining that in a true-conflict situation, courts should apply the forum's law because "assessment of the respective values of the competing legitimate interests of two sovereign states, in order to determine which is to prevail, is a political function of a very high order. This is a function that should not be committed to courts in a democracy."); *See also id.* at 184 ("If the court finds that the forum state has an interest in the application of its policy, it should apply the law of the forum, even though the foreign state also has an interest in the application of its contrary policy.").

64. *See infra* note 1, at §102(2) (1987).

65. Princeton Principles of Universal Jurisdiction, *supra* note 23, princ. 2; *See also* Sadat, *Exile, Amnesty and International Law*, *supra* note 25, at 970–74, 1025–26; Donald Francis Donovan & Anthea Roberts, *The Emerging Recognition of Universal Civil Jurisdiction*, 100 Am. J. Int'l L. 142, 159 (2006) ("By definition, universal jurisdiction applies to norms whose enforcement has been made imperative by the international community.").

66. For a good examination of this topic, *see* Sadat, *Exile, Amnesty and International Law*, *supra* note 25, at 970–74. The Vienna Convention on the Law of Treaties defines a *jus cogens* norm as a "peremptory norm of general international law [that] is a norm accepted and recognized by the international community of States as a whole as a norm from which no derogation is permitted and which can be modified only by a subsequent norm of general international law having the same character." Vienna Convention on the Law of Treaties, art. 53, opened for signature May 23, 1969, 1155 U.N.T.S. 331 [hereinafter Vienna Convention].

67. *See* Donovan & Roberts, *supra* note 65, at 145, who noted that "commentators often link the principle [of universal jurisdiction] with jus cogens norms and erga omnes obligations, though many express divergent views on their relationship. In one view, these concepts directly support one another, as jus cogens norms give rise to erga omnes obligations and also require or permit states to exercise universal jurisdiction. In another view, jus cogens norms and erga omnes obligations are primarily or exclusively concerned with state responsibility, while universal jurisdiction deals primarily or exclusively with individual responsibility, so that the former concepts provide analogous support for the latter. In yet another view, universal jurisdiction should extend to all serious crimes under international law, not just jus cogens norms."

68. For a thoughtful and compelling account of universal jurisdiction's normative underpinnings, *see* Adeno Addis, *Imagining the International Community: The Constitutive Dimension of Universal Jurisdiction*, 31 Hum. Rts. Q. 129, 132 (2009) (arguing that universal jurisdiction has a "constitutive function . . .

through which the international community imagines its identity").

69. *See supra* notes 21–23.

70. For a discussion of piracy and its relationship to modern doctrines of universal jurisdiction, *see* Eugene Kontorovich, *The Piracy Analogy: Modern Universal Jurisdiction's Hollow Foundation*, 45 HARV. INT'L L. J. 183, 210 (2004).

71. *See* U.N. Charter, art. 2, para. 1 ("The Organization is based on the principle of the sovereign equality of all its Members.").

72. However, this nonaccountability argument has trouble explaining on its own why certain crimes are subject to universal jurisdiction and others are not. *See* Addis, *supra* note 68, at 141 ("[A]s a descriptive matter, the likelihood of non-prosecution as a rationale for the kind of crimes we consider as properly subject to universal jurisdiction is under-inclusive. Many crimes go unpunished in a particular country, but that alone can never be the basis for asserting universal jurisdiction. If the purpose is to ensure against legal gaps (no 'law-free zones'), then one would have to show that dealing with these and not other offenses is the proper way to fill the gaps.").

73. Sadat, *Exile, Amnesty and International Law, supra* note 25, at 1025.

74. *Id.* at 1026.

75. International Military Tribunal (Nuremberg), Judgment and Sentences (Oct. 1, 1946), *reprinted in* 41 AM. J. INT'L L. 172, 216 (1947).

76. Colangelo, *Constitutional Limits on Extraterritorial Jurisdiction, supra* note 18, at 134.

77. *See* Reydams, *supra* note 56, at 1.

78. *See* Colangelo, *Double Jeopardy and Multiple Sovereigns, supra* note 5, at 830–32.

79. *Id.* at 832–35.

80. For example, the authors of the PRINCETON PRINCIPLES ON UNIVERSAL JURISDICTION note "the longstanding conviction that a criminal defendant should be tried by his 'natural judge.'" PRINCETON PRINCIPLES ON UNIVERSAL JURISDICTION, *supra* note 23, at 53. They further note that "societies that have been victimized by political crimes should have the opportunity to bring the perpetrators to justice," and "the exercise of territorial jurisdiction will often also satisfy several of the other factors . . . such as the convenience to the parties and witnesses, as well as the availability of evidence." *Id.*

81. To be sure, some States' universal jurisdiction laws specifically provide for only complementary jurisdiction precisely because the laws implement obligations under the ICC's Rome Statute. *See, e.g.,* Volkerstrafgesetzbuch [VStGB] [International Criminal Code]) June 30, 2002), Bundesgesetzblatt, Teil I [BGBl.I] 2254, *translated at* www.iuscomp.org/gla/statutes/VoeStGB.pdf.

82. Rome Statute of the International Criminal Court, art. 17, 2187 U.N.T.S. 90 (Jul. 17, 1998) [hereinafter ICC Statute].

83. *See, e.g.*, Convention Against Torture and Other Cruel, Inhuman or Degrading Treatment or Punishment, G.A. Res. 39/46, art. 1, U.N. GAOR, 39th Sess., Supp. No. 51, U.N. Doc. A/39/51 (Dec. 10, 1984) [hereinafter Convention Against Torture].

84. For a discussion of universal jurisdiction in relation to terrorism, *see* Colangelo, *Constitutional Limits on Extraterritorial Jurisdiction, supra* note 18.

85. *See supra* notes 6–18 and accompanying text.

86. I have argued against the broad use of universal jurisdiction over war crimes in part for this reason as well as for limiting its exercise only to grave breaches of the Geneva Conventions. *See* Colangelo, *The Legal Limits of Universal Jurisdiction, supra* note 24, at 191–95.

87. *See generally id.*

88. Like all bases of jurisdiction in international law, universal jurisdiction is a matter of customary law. *Id.* at 166. Indeed, otherwise it could not be truly universal (unless perhaps every state in the world was a party to the relevant treaty).

89. For the principle that treaties may embody customary norms, *See* North Sea Continental Shelf (*F.R.G. v. Den.; F.R.G. v. Neth.*), 1969 I.C.J. 3, 30 (Feb. 20); *See also supra* note 1, at §102(3) (1987) ("International agreements create law for the states [P]arties thereto and may lead to the creation of customary international law when such agreements are intended for adherence by states generally and are in fact widely accepted.").

90. For a catalogue of the relevant international treaties covering universal crimes and the number of states' parties, *see* Colangelo, *The Legal Limits of Universal Jurisdiction, supra* note 24, at 186–98.

91. Some legislation expressly declares its purpose in this regard. The since-tamed Belgian War Crimes Act, under which Belgian courts have prosecuted a number of Rwandan war criminals for acts committed in Rwanda against Rwandans, had as its purpose "to define three categories of grave breaches of humanitarian law and to integrate them into the Belgian domestic legal order." Stefaan Smis & Kim Van der Borght, *Introductory Note to Belgium: Act Concerning the Punishment of Grave Breaches of International Humanitarian Law*, 38 I.L.M. 918, 919 (1999). In fact, "to remain consistent with the definitions used in international law, the Act textually refers to the wording of the relevant provisions of the international conventions." Id. Furthermore, its definitional provisions even explicitly invoke the relevant conventions by name; for example, the Act sets forth the definition of genocide after stating that the crime is defined "In accordance with the Convention on the Prevention and Punishment of the Crime of

Genocide of 9 December 1948." *Belgium: Act Concerning the Punishment of Grave Breaches of International Humanitarian Law*, art. 1, §1, *translated and reprinted in* 38 I.L.M. 921 (1999). Although the Act formally adopts the definitions of the crimes from conventional law, like the Netherlands' International Crimes Act, *supra* note 56, it went beyond conventional law regarding the availability of universal jurisdiction over "grave breaches" by including within this category acts that were not committed as part of an international conflict, Smis & Van der Borght, *supra*, at 920.

92. To take one of the earliest and most well-known examples of universal jurisdiction, the definitions of "war crimes" and "crimes against humanity" contained in the Nazi and Nazi Collaborators (Punishment) Law, under which the Israeli Supreme Court convicted Nazi war criminal Adolf Eichmann for acts that—leaving no doubt as to the universal basis of the jurisdiction—were committed before Israel was even a state, embodied the definitions of the respective crimes in the Nuremberg Charter. *See* The Nazi and Nazi Collaborators (Punishment) Law, 5710–1950, 4 LSI 154 (1949–50) (Isr.), *translated and reprinted in* Human Rights in Israel, 1950 Y.B. Hum. Rts. 163, U.N. Sales No. 1952.XIV.1; Agreement for the Prosecution and Punishment of the Major War Criminals of the European Axis, arts. 6(b)–(c), E.A.S. No. 472, 82 U.N.T.S. 280 (Aug. 8, 1945).

93. Colangelo, *The Legal Limits of Universal Jurisdiction*, *supra* note 24, at 155.

94. The court upheld jurisdiction for genocide based on crimes allegedly committed against a "national group" by stretching this victim class designation beyond its customary definition to include "a national human group, a differentiated human group, characterized by some trait, and integrated into the larger collectivity." Audiencia Nacional, Nov. 5, 1998 (No. 173/98), reprinted and translated in THE PINOCHET PAPERS: THE CASE OF AUGUSTO PINOCHET IN SPAIN AND BRITAIN 103 (Reed Brody & Michael Ratner eds., 2000) [hereinafter PINOCHET PAPERS]. Finding that the acts alleged constituted genocide because they were designed "to destroy a differentiated national group" of political opponents irrespective of their nationalities, that is, "those who did not fit in [Pinochet's] project of national reorganization . . . [whether] Chileans or foreigners," *id.* at 103–04, the court effectively (and none-too-subtly) amended the victim groups within the definition of genocide. Genocide has been defined consistently since the 1948 Genocide Convention in the statutes of international courts and treaties to have as victim groups only a "national, ethnical, racial or religious group, as such." Genocide Convention, *supra* note 20, art. 2; ICTY Statute, *supra* note 59, art. 4; ICTR Statute, *supra* note 59, art. 2; ICC Statute, *supra* note 82, art. 6. Indeed, according to the International Criminal Tribunal for Rwanda, "a national group is defined as a collection of people who are perceived to share a legal bond based on common citizenship." *Prosecutor v. Akayesu*, Case No. ICTR-96–4-T, Judgment, P512 (Sept. 2, 1998). The Audiencia's sprawling construction de facto enlarges the class of victims to include potentially any group whatsoever—including, as in the case before it, political groups, which had been explicitly rejected as victims in the drafting of the Genocide Convention. *See* Beth Van Schaack, *The Crime of Political Genocide: Repairing the Genocide Convention's Blind Spot*, 106 YALE L. J. 2259, 2262–69 (1997). In short, the ruling clashes with one of the more recognizable legal demarcations of the crime of genocide under international law. For another example of an exorbitant definition of genocide, *see* Addis, *supra* note 68, at 153 n.99 (describing the Ethiopian Penal Code's "erroneous definition of . . . genocide and crimes against humanity" and prosecutions based on that definition).

95. *See* Van Schaack, *supra* note 94, at 2262–69.

96. Certain variations on language will inevitably result, for instance, from differences between general prescriptions of international treaties as compared to more state-specific prescriptions of national laws implementing those treaties. For example, Article 1 of the Montreal Convention for the Suppression of Unlawful Acts Against the Safety of Civil Aviation provides for the treaty equivalent of universal jurisdiction over anyone who "unlawfully and intentionally: . . . (c) places or causes to be placed on an aircraft in service, by any means whatsoever, a device or substance which is likely to destroy that aircraft, or to cause damage to it which renders it incapable of flight, or to cause damage to it which is likely to endanger its safety in flight." Montreal Convention for the Suppression of Unlawful Acts Against the Safety of Civil Aviation, art. 1, 24 U.S.T. 565, 974 U.N.T.S. 178 (Sept. 23, 1971).

The U.S. implementing legislation similarly provides for such jurisdiction over whomever "willfully: . . . (3) places or causes to be placed on a civil aircraft registered in a country other than the United States while such aircraft is in service, a device or substance which is likely to destroy that aircraft, or to cause damage to that aircraft which renders that aircraft incapable of flight or which is likely to endanger that aircraft's safety in flight." 18 U.S.C. §32(b)(3).

97. The field of conflict of laws can also provide guidance on how to deal with procedural versus substantive issues regarding the application of international law by national courts. According to longstanding conflict principles, the forum state uses its own procedural rules when applying foreign substantive law. *See* Restatement (Second) of Conflict of Laws §122 (1971); Restatement (First) of Conflict of Laws §585 (1934). Although international law is, of course, not "foreign" to any state,

states enforce its substantive rules through their own domestic processes. In this general vein, Leila Sadat has suggested that international law needs an Erie-type choice-of-law doctrine to aid in the treatment of international law in domestic courts. Sadat, *Exile, Amnesty and International Law, supra* note 25, at 1028.

98. *See, e.g.*, Geneva Convention Relative to the Treatment of Prisoners of War, 6 U.S.T. 3316, 75 U.N.T.S. 135 (Aug. 12, 1949).

99. *See* Protocol Additional to the Geneva Conventions of 12 August 1949, and Relating to the Protection of Victims of International Armed Conflicts, art. 75(4)(h), adopted June 8, 1977, 1125 U.N.T.S. 3 (entered into force Dec. 7, 1979).

100. Convention Against Torture, *supra* note 83, art. 1.

101. *Supra* note 1, at §103 cmts. a, b (1987).

102. This has taken place to some extent with respect to crimes spelled out in the statute for the newly established International Criminal Court and to a lesser degree (because they are not treaties, strictly speaking) in the statutes of various international tribunals created under the auspices of the United Nations. For example, the Charter of the International Military Tribunal under which the Nazis were prosecuted defined crimes against humanity as "murder, extermination, enslavement, deportation, and other inhumane acts committed against any civilian populations." Agreement for the Prosecution and Punishment of the Major War Criminals of the European Axis, art. 6(c), 59 Stat. 1544, 82 U.N.T.S. 279 (Aug. 8, 1945). Although acts such as torture, imprisonment, and rape could potentially fall into the "other inhumane acts" receptacle, they are not set forth explicitly in the Charter, and courts using its definitional provisions therefore would be on more precarious ground prosecuting these crimes as universal crimes against humanity than in prosecuting a listed offense such as "extermination" or "enslavement." Yet, by the end of the last century, international law evolved such that the statutes of the ICTY, ICTR, and ICC do affirmatively list torture, imprisonment, and rape as crimes against humanity, thus clarifying or perhaps adding to the customary definitions of crimes against humanity and, in any event, providing courts with firmer prosecutorial footing as to certain of these crimes. *See* ICTY Statute, *supra* note 59, art. 5; ICTR Statute, *supra* note 59, art. 3; ICC Statute, *supra* note 82, art. 7.

103. *See* ANTHONY A. D'AMATO, THE CONCEPT OF CUSTOM IN INTERNATIONAL LAW 97–98 (1971).

104. *See* Michael Akehurst, *Custom as a Source of International Law, in* THE BRIT. Y. B. OF INT'L L. 1974–1975, at 1, 40 (R. Y. Jennings & Ian Brownlie eds., 1977).

105. It should be noted that one territorial or national state's approval of or acquiescence in a definitional

expansion would not be enough to change the customary definition of the crime, especially against the backdrop of a widely ratified and longstanding treaty to the contrary. A basic definition of the hard-to-pin-down threshold for determining the existence of customary law appears in the Restatement, which states that "customary international law results from a general and consistent practice of states followed by them from a sense of legal obligation." *Supra* note 1, at §102(2) (1987). Whatever view one takes of how much practice achieves the threshold level of generality and consistency necessary to form customary law, one improper assertion of universal jurisdiction accepted as legitimate by an interested state and in the face of a treaty to the contrary would not meet that test.

106. Paul H. Robinson, *Fair Notice and Fair Adjudication: Two Kinds of Legality*, 154 U. PA. L. REV. 335, 336 (2005).

107. *Id.* at 337.

108. Beth Van Schaack, *Crimen Sine Lege: Judicial Lawmaking at the Intersection of Law and Morals*, 97 GEO. L. J. 119, 173 (2008).

109. *Id.* at 176 (discussing the ICC's legality provisions).

110. *See generally* Van Schaack, *supra* note 108.

111. *Id.* at 133–71.

112. *See, e.g.*, ROLAND J. STANGER, INTERNATIONAL LAW STUDIES 1957–1958: CRIMINAL JURISDICTION OVER VISITING ARMED FORCES 5 (1965) (noting that "charges of unfairness toward an alien on grounds of lack of notice are in part met by the consideration that, since he was aware that he was subject to the local law, he should have informed himself of its prohibitions.").

113. *Phillips Petroleum Co. v. Shutts*, 472 U.S. 797, 818 (1985) (quoting *Allstate Ins. Co. v. Hague*, 449 U.S. 302, 312–13 (1985)).

114. *Shutts*, 472 U.S. at 822.

115. *See United States v. Yousef*, 327 F.3d 56, 111–12 (2d Cir. 2003); *United States v. Moreno-Morillo*, 334 F.3d 819, 827–30 (9th Cir. 2003); *United States v. Quintero-Rendon*, 354 F.3d 1320, 1324–26 (11th Cir. 2003); *United States v. Perez-Oviedo*, 281 F.3d 400, 402–03 (3d Cir. 2002); *United States v. Suerte*, 291 F.3d 366, 369–75 (4th Cir. 2002); *United States v. Cardales*, 168 F.3d 548, 552–54 (1st Cir. 1999).

116. Particularly because the Supreme Court has also stated that "a postoccurrence change of residence to the forum [s]tate—standing alone—[is] insufficient to justify application of forum law." *Allstate*, 449 U.S. at 302.

117. 18 U.S.C. §§2340-2340A (2000).

118. *United States v. Emmanuel*, No. 06–20758-CR, 2007 WL 2002452, at 15 (S.D. Fla. July 5, 2007) (order on defendant's motion to dismiss the indictment). The District Court rejected the challenge, finding that Taylor was a presumptive U.S. citizen and,

therefore, a sufficient nexus existed so that the application of U.S. law was neither arbitrary nor fundamentally unfair. *Id.* at 16.

119. *See supra* note 115 and accompanying cases.

120. 18 U.S.C. §2332f (Supp. 2003).

121. *Id.*

122. *Id.*

123. *Id.* at §37.

124. *Id.* at §32.

125. 49 U.S.C. §46502 (2000).

126. 18 U.S.C. §1203 (2000).

127. 18 U.S.C. §2339C (2000).

128. Colangelo, *Constitutional Limits on Extraterritorial Jurisdiction, supra* note 18, at 176–88.

129. *See id.* at 189–201.

130. A famous example here is the Convention Against Torture. Article 5(2) of the Convention provides: "Each State Party shall . . . take such measures as may be necessary to establish jurisdiction over such offences in cases where the alleged offender is present in any territory under its jurisdiction and it does not extradite him." Convention Against Torture, *supra* note 83, art. 5(2). And Article 7(1) provides "The State Party in the territory under whose jurisdiction a person alleged to have committed any offence referred to in [the relevant provision] is found shall in the cases contemplated in article 5, if it does not extradite him, submit the case to its competent authorities for the purpose of prosecution." *Id.* at art. 7(1).

131. Article 34 of the Vienna Convention on the Law of Treaties provides that "a Treaty does not create either obligations or rights for a third State without its consent." Vienna Convention, *supra* note 66, art. 34. Article 35 provides that treaties are only binding on nonparties when the nonparty "State expressly accepts that obligation in writing." *Id.* at art 35. Moreover, "[a] treaty provision establishing standards for extraterritorial criminal liability must be read, in light of 'any relevant rules of international law applicable in the relations between the parties,' against the background doctrine of nullum crimen sine lege." Brad R. Roth, *Just Short of Torture: Abusive Treatment and the Limits of International Criminal Justice*, 6 J. INT'L CRIM. JUST. 215, 237 (2008).

132. Arrest Warrant of 11 April 2000 (Dem. Rep. Congo v. Belg.), 2002 I.C.J. 3, 63 (Feb. 14) (joint separate opinion of Judges Higgins, Kooijmans, and Buergenthal). For further discussion of the court's decision, *See infra* Part III.B.

133. *Id.* at 69.

134. *Id.* at 75.

135. For example, had the district court in the Chuckie Taylor case not determined that Taylor was a presumptive U.S. citizen, *see supra* note 118, the court would have had to address whether the U.S. Torture Act adequately reflected the international legal prohibition on torture so as to put Taylor on notice of the substantive law being applied to him for acts that, in and of themselves, had no connection to the United States at the time they were committed. For a discussion of this requirement regarding U.S. jurisdiction over terrorist crimes abroad, *see* Colangelo, *Constitutional Limits on Extraterritorial Jurisdiction, supra* note 18, at 176–88.

136. *See* Van Schaack, *supra* note 108, at 155–58.

137. *See id.* at 124. Van Schaack asserted that "higher-order principles underlying the [nullum crimen sine lege, nulla poena sine lege] prohibition" are not infringed where new standards are applied to past conduct because "defendants [are] on sufficient notice of the foreseeability of [international criminal law] jurisprudential innovations in light of extant domestic penal law, universal moral values expressed in international human rights law, developments in international humanitarian law and the circumstances in which this law has been invoked, and other dramatic changes to the international order and to international law brought about in the postwar period." *Id.*; *see also id.* at 183.

138. *See generally* Van Schaack, *supra* note 108.

139. This issue raises a host of interesting questions on its own. For example, even if we were to accept a more flexible international law version of legality, it nonetheless "may exert greater resistance in domestic prosecutions than it does in international ones, where domestic courts are bound by constitutional articulations of the principle and where courts may not be able to rely upon the varied sources of international law for applicable rules of decision." *Id.* at 190.

140. PRINCETON PRINCIPLES ON UNIVERSAL JURISDICTION, *supra* note 23, at 31.

141. Dapko Akande, *International Law Immunities and the International Criminal Court*, 98 AM. J. INT'L L. 407, 409–10 (2004).

142. Arrest Warrant of 11 April 2000 (*Dem. Rep. Congo v. Belg.*), 2002 I.C.J. 3, 22 (Feb. 14).

143. *Id.* at 25.

144. *See* Ruth Wedgewood, *International Criminal Law and Augusto Pinochet*, 40 VA. J. INT'L L. 829, 838 (2000); Curtis A. Bradley & Jack L. Goldsmith, *Pinochet and International Human Rights Litigation*, 97 MICH. L. REV. 2129, 2140 (1999).

145. Arrest Warrant of 11 April 2000, 2002 I.C.J. 3, 25–26.

146. *Id.*

147. *Id.*

148. For why this may be, *see* Sadat, *Exile, Amnesty and International Law, supra* note 25, at 975–76 (explaining that "The vertical relationship between international and national law, at least as regards jus cogens crimes, . . . is quite different from the horizontal perspective apparent in cases of universal inter-state juris-

diction.""). Dapo Akande drew a distinction between tribunals established by the UN Security Council and tribunals established by treaty and asserted that the former can override immunity ratione personae, but the latter cannot with regard to officials of nonparty states. *See* Akande, *supra* note 141, at 417 (footnotes omitted). Akande observed that "the possibility of relying on international law immunities (particularly immunity ratione personae) to avoid prosecutions by international tribunals depends on the nature of the tribunal: how it was established and whether the state of the official sought to be tried is bound by the instrument establishing the tribunal. In this regard, there is a distinction between those tribunals established by United Nations Security Council resolution (i.e., the International Criminal Tribunals for the Former Yugoslavia (ICTY) and Rwanda (ICTR)) and those established by treaty. Because of the universal membership of the United Nations and because decisions of the Council are binding on all UN members, the provisions of the ICTY and ICTR Statutes are capable of removing immunity with respect to practically all states. But this is only because those states are bound by and have indirectly consented (via the UN Charter) to the decision to remove immunity. On the other hand, since only parties to a treaty are bound by its provisions, a treaty establishing an international tribunal cannot remove immunities that international law grants to officials of states that are not party to the treaty. Those immunities are rights belonging to the nonparty states and those states may not be deprived of their rights by a treaty to which they are not party." *Id.*

149. Arrest Warrant of 11 April 2000, 2002 I.C.J. 3, 25–26 ("[A]fter a person ceases to hold the office . . . he or she will no longer enjoy all of the immunities accorded by international law in other States. Provided that it has jurisdiction under international law, a court of one State may try a former [official] of another State in respect of acts committed prior to or subsequent to his or her period of office, as well as in respect of acts committed during that period of office in a private capacity.").

150. Roth, *supra* note 131, at 218; *see also*, Akande, *supra* note 141, at 412–14.

151. Akande, *supra* note 141, at 413. Moreover, as Brad Roth pointed out, "it is possible for the nullem crimen defence to arise directly from immunity ratione materiae: where, in the name of redressing an international law violation that has not been established as an international crime, a domestic prosecution proceeds from extraterritorial penal legislation that somehow falls within the state's internationally-recognized jurisdiction to prescribe, immunity ratione materiae blocks the prosecuting state's jurisdiction to prescribe within the scope of the foreign-state agent's official capacity, thereby leaving no penal law that condemns the agent's conduct." Roth, *supra* note 131, at 223.

152. For a discussion of the complexities here, *see* Bradley & Goldsmith, *supra* note 144, at 2140–46.

153. *See Regina v. Bow Street Metropolitan Stipendiary Magistrate*, Ex parte Pinochet Ugarte (No. 3), [1999] UKHL 17, (1999) 2 W.L.R. 827, *reprinted in* Bartle ex parte Pinochet (1999) 38 I.L.M. 581 (Eng.). Some have argued that this absence of immunity ratione materie for international crimes stems in part from the fact that "international law has subsequently [to the development of immunity ratione materie] developed rules permitting domestic courts to exercise universal jurisdiction over certain international crimes and . . . [that] that those rules contemplate prosecution of crimes committed in an official capacity. . . . In those circumstances, immunity ratione materiae cannot logically coexist with such a grant of jurisdiction. Indeed, to apply in such cases, the prior rule according immunity would serve to deprive the subsequent jurisdictional rule of practically all meaning." Akande, *supra* note 141, at 415.

154. For recent commentary, see Kontorovich, *supra* note 6; Diane F. Orentlicher, *Settling Accounts: The Duty to Prosecute Human Rights Violations of A Prior Regime*, 100 YALE L.J. 2537 (1991); Sadat, *Exile, Amnesty and International Law*, *supra* note 25; Michael P. Scharf, *From the eXile Files: An Essay on Trading Justice for Peace*, 63 WASH. & LEE L. REV. 339 (2006); Ronald C. Slye, *The Legitimacy of Amnesties Under International Law and General Principles of Anglo-American Law: Is a Legitimate Amnesty Possible?* 43 VA. J. INT'L L. 173 (2002); Charles P. Trumbull IV, *Giving Amnesties a Second Chance*, 25 BERKELEY J. INT'L L. 283 (2007).

155. *See* Kontorovich, *supra* note 6, at 401.

156. Scharf, *supra* note 154, at 341.

157. Sadat, *Exile, Amnesty and International Law*, *supra* note 25, at 1027.

158. *Id.* at 1028.

159. *See Heath v. Alabama*, 474 U.S. 82, 88 (1985). The Supreme Court in Heath resolved the dual sovereignty issue in the context of U.S. federalism. The Court held that because "by one act [the defendant] has committed two offenses, for each of which he is justly punishable," no violation of the prohibition on double jeopardy results from successive prosecutions by different sovereigns. *Id.*

160. Colangelo, *Double Jeopardy and Multiple Sovereigns*, *supra* note 5.

161. *See* Protocol No. 7 to the European Convention for the Protection of Human Rights and Fundamental Freedoms, art. 4, Europ. T.S. No. 117 (Nov. 22, 1984) (entered into force Nov. 1, 1998); International Covenant on Civil and Political Rights, art. 14(7), 999 U.N.T.S. 17 (Dec. 1966).

162. *See* U.N. Model Treaty on Extradition, G.A. Res. 116, art. 3(d), U.N. GAOR, 45th Sess., Annex, U.N. Doc. A/RES/45/116 (1990); European Convention on Extradition, art. 9, Dec. 13, 1957, 359 U.N.T.S. 274.

163. *See* Colangelo, *Double Jeopardy and Multiple Sovereigns*, *supra* note 5, at 815–20.

164. *See supra* note 1, at §402(1)(a) (1987).

165. *See supra* Part II.B.2.

166. *See* Colangelo, *Double Jeopardy and Multiple Sovereigns*, *supra* note 5, at 827.

167. ICC Statute, *supra* note 82, at art. 17.

168. ICTY Statute, *supra* note 59, art. 10; ICTR Statute, *supra* note 59, at art. 9.

169. *Id.*

170. *See* Convention on the Prevention and Punishment of the Crime of Genocide, art. 6, 102 Stat. 3045, 78 U.N.T.S. 277 (Dec. 9, 1948); *see also* ICTY Statute, *supra* note 59, art. 4(2)(a)(2); ICTR Statute, *supra* note 59, art. 2(2)(a).

171. More broadly for successive international tribunal and universal jurisdiction prosecution purposes, the line between "ordinary" and international crimes may not always be clean. For instance, customary international law prohibitions arise out of state practice accompanied by *opinio juris*. Although most modern international crimes are the result of treaties, the state practice component of a customary prohibition could also take the form of national prohibitions on crimes whose suppression becomes a matter of international legal obligation either in its own right or through incorporation into a preexisting category of international crime like crimes against humanity. In that situation, a prosecution under national law for the crime could effectively apply the emergent international prohibition on the crime, making successive prosecution under a distinct international law unavailable. The best inquiry for determining the availability of such a successive international law prosecution is probably whether the substantive definition of the crime in the national law used to prosecute faithfully reflects the emergent international prohibition on the crime and whether the national law penalty sufficiently reflects the gravity of that international crime. Michele N. Morosin further pointed out that the argument for a successive international tribunal prosecution after a national prosecution for the same conduct "is strengthened if the country [in which the national court proceedings occur] has a statute addressing [the international crime] and did not charge the defendant with this crime." Michele N. Morosin, *Double Jeopardy and International Law: Obstacles to Formulating a General Principle*, 64 Nordic J. Int'l L. 261, 265 (1995).

172. *See Houston v. Moore*, 18 U.S. 1, 32–35 (1820); *United States v. Furlong*, 18 U.S. 184, 197 (1820).

173. *Furlong*, 18 U.S. at 184.

174. *Id.* at 197.

175. *Id.*

PART TWO

NON-TERRITORIALISM

6

Non-State Actors, International Law, and Human Rights

ELENA PARIOTTI

1. Introduction

The awareness that rights may be infringed not only by states but also by private actors, who very often are even in a position to protect and promote rights, is the basis of the increasing attention devoted to non-state entities by international law. The emergence of active roles played by non-state and nongovernmental entities is one of the features of current international law, which prompt the question of whether they can be regarded as subjects rather than only objects of international legal order. Of course, the list of non-state entities could be open-ended and even hard to define.[1] Nevertheless, in what follows, the non-state entities that without doubt have emerged as *actors* in international legal processes and with specific reference to human rights law will be addressed. According to the view that is here embraced, an entity can be said to become an *actor* when to some degree it is able to participate in building international order and is the direct addressee of rights and duties.

Such analysis is obviously related to the issue of the legal status of non-state actors (NSAs), but it does not necessarily require that we take a position on the possibility of defining them as *subjects* under international law. Rather, focusing (more in descriptive than in normative terms) on the new roles played by such entities

may give some arguments for reshaping the very debate on their legal status, thus resulting in giving the debate a lower relevance than it had in the past.[2] This kind of analysis can affect the general view of international law itself, thereby leading to a less state-centered perspective of it and contributing to giving human rights their proper place as tools at the direct disposal of individuals and groups or being able to directly regulate the relationships between private actors.[3]

Globalization, on the one hand, and the progress in criminal international law—namely the shaping of the notion of individual criminal responsibility for international crimes—on the other hand, are the main background for the emergence of new actors, besides states and international organizations, in international law making, law adjudication, and law enforcement.

Globalization is in many senses connected to the increasing role played by so-called global civil society as well as to the process of privatizing human rights. These processes are, in their turn, connected to the "retreat" of the state from political decisions, including from its role of human rights addressee and guarantor.

A terminological note needs to be made here. With respect to those who can be regarded as emerging actors on the scene of international protection and/or promotion of human rights, the term "non-state actors" is intended here to

95

stress two features: (1) the independence from institutions and political power for what concerns their establishment and working, and (2) the nonterritorial and transnational character of their activity.

Starting from the premise that, on the whole, norms related to human rights create obligations to respect, protect, and fulfill the content of those rights, what is becoming increasingly obvious is that, as a matter of fact, some private actors—and not only states—have the power to violate human rights. As a result, legal and quasi-legal means have been sought that can influence these actors to comply with human rights and even to help states protect and fulfill them. This is what is occurring with the role of transnational corporations in the human rights domain, to the extent that many soft law means (codes of conduct, international tools establishing principles and standards, certification systems) have been created in order to make TNCs accountable for human rights violations, protection, and promotion.

The question could be posed as to whether acknowledging the new role played by several NSAs in international law requires revising the conceptual framework, namely the liberal framework, of human rights as well.[4] In this sense, the attention on NSAs may (1) give more relevance to the content of rights and on the actual violations rather than to the form of rights and the legal status of the violator;[5] (2) emphasize the indivisibility and interdependence of human rights as well as weaken the importance of the differences among rights based on the structure—negative or positive—of correlative duties; and (3) help withdraw human rights from their ambiguous link with state sovereignty and give expression to their inner universality.

2. The "Voice" of Transnational Civil Society: Nongovernmental Organizations and Human Rights

In regard to human rights, transnational civil society tends to be reflected in nongovernmental organizations (NGOs) that are active at an international level. The term "nongovernmental organizations" emerged after World War II and has different and even contradicting interpretations. Sometimes the terms "civil society organizations," "transnational advocacy networks," "transnational" or "nongovernmental norm entrepreneurs," and "transnational moral entrepreneurs,"[6] "pressure groups," "interest groups" and "private voluntary organizations"[7] have been used as alternatives.

The very definition of NGOs is something controversial, and actually NGOs are very diverse in both their size and scope of activities as well as organizational status.[8] In this chapter, "NGOs" will refer to groups of persons or societies, freely created by private initiative (not established by governments or by intergovernmental agreements), that are active with regard to issues of public concern, and that pursue an interest in matters that cross or transcend national borders and are not profit seeking.[9] Moreover, a group may only take the label of "NGO" if it is nonviolent, and this is what mainly makes it different from some other groups that have become increasingly relevant for international law, such as armed non-state actors.[10]

To give a picture of the role played by NGOs with regard to human rights, two elements have to be taken into consideration. First, the overall impact of international NGOs' activity in international law, especially in the domain of human rights, has been leading "the states to see the international dimension of what was previously regarded as a purely domestic matter."[11] In this sense, as has been forcefully said, "NGOs act as a solvent against the strictures of sovereignty."[12] This is particularly true and important in the human rights field, which is conceptually oriented toward universality. Second, NGOs are widely regarded as the most genuine expression of transnational (or global) civil society. This is because of two main reasons: (1) NGOs are composed of individuals according to a relationship that is spontaneous and voluntary in character. In this sense, the "self-actuated" nature of NGOs distinguishes them from International Organizations (IOs). Thus, NGOs are a form in which the cosmopolitan standing of individuals in the global order may be organized; (2) NGOs "have more a moral authority than legal authority" (they are supposed to be the "voice of the people"[13]), and their influence stems from the attractiveness of their ideas and of the values they embrace.[14]

Although the term has been coined by the UN, the UN Charter does not provide either a definition or criteria for individuating which groups should be regarded as NGOs. In Resolution 1996/31 the UN established some requirements: To be regarded as an NGO, a group must have established headquarters, an organization (i.e., an executive organ and officer, a democratically adopted constitution, an authority to speak for its members) that gives them stability over time and financial independence from governmental bodies.[15] Moreover, NGOs are required "to have a recognized standing within the particular field of their competence, to be of representative character and to represent larger sections of the population."[16]

The normative starting point from which NGOs' activity in the international sphere has developed is Article 71 of the UN Charter, in which NGOs are given a consultation partner status toward the UN Economic and Social Council (ECOSOC). Such a role has been widely acknowledged, and the consultative role for NGOs became the usual practice throughout the UN system and even outside the UN.[17] By exercising this role, NGOs have contributed to the contemporary change of international law with regard both to its content as well as its range of competence, especially in humanitarian, human rights, and environmental law and with regard to procedural implementation. Furthermore, the *Declaration on the Rights and Responsibilities of Individuals, Groups and Organs of Society to Promote and Protect Universally Recognized Human Rights and Fundamental Freedoms*, approved by the UN General Assembly in 1999, provides that "everyone has the right, individually and in association with others, at the national and international levels . . . to commu-

nicate with non-governmental or intergovernmental organizations."

For what concerns the activity of human rights protection and promotion, the role of NGOs started with the drafting of the UN Charter and of the Universal Declaration of Human Rights, it continues, to different degrees, according to several directions. NGOs are vehicles of advocacy, in which they individuate issues and promote their solution through the language and mechanisms of human rights. They also monitor human rights (by gathering information on human rights abuses) as well as humanitarian and environmental law.[18] NGOs have contributed to advancing international standards and have put forward proposals for implementing human rights and environmental protection, with the aim of promoting state compliance with international obligations. They have undertaken field activities and provided services in the implementation of aid programs, and participation informally in treaty making. Such kinds of activities are well illustrated by the role played by some NGOs in shaping the Rome Treaty, which established the International Criminal Court. Michael Struett has pointed out how, in this case, NGOs "defined the issues, prioritized items on the negotiation agenda, advocated text for treaty provisions, and identified the grounds for political compromise more effectively than the delegation from any single state."[19] This was a clear example of how NGOs can contribute to the development and change of international law. With reference to this contribution, a distinction should nevertheless be made between the right to speak and the right to negotiate, as NGOs seem to hold only the former.[20] Other cases in which NGOs have informally participated in treaty law making are those of the UN Convention on the Rights of the Child[21] and the Treaty on Anti-Personnel Landmines in 1997.[22] They have also contributed to interpreting international law and participating in international adjudication by making *amicus curiae* submissions to tribunals. In the latter sense, major international tribunals have developed procedures enabling

NGOs to submit information or statements on pending cases."[23] The International Court of Justice remains closed to NGO participation, even if a change occurred in 2004, when this court adopted the Practice Direction XII, according to which, in an advisory proceeding, if an international NGO submits a statement or document on its own initiative, it will be placed in a designated place in the Peace Palace. The document should be regarded as a publication and states and International Organizations may refer to it. Moreover, since 2001 *amicus curiae* submissions have also started in investment arbitration.

So reconstructed, the contribution of NGOs to protecting and promoting human rights can be seen both as an activity *against* states, in which governments intentionally do not respect or do not guarantee human rights (the word "nongovernmental" has been sometimes understood as meaning "*against* the government") and as an activity *supporting* states "in carrying out those tasks which are inherent in the concept of statehood under modern international law."[24] NGOs "strengthen states by enhancing the 'rule of law' and democracy . . . in situations where state organs or agencies fail to fulfill their essential functions."[25]

3. Transnational Corporations and Human Rights

One of the most relevant effects of globalization on the law concerns the role played by private actors operating in the economic field.[26] In particular, transnational corporations (TNCs) have acquired not only increasing freedom of movement among legal orders but also the ability to influence the lawmaking process within the transnational law sphere. More generally, it has been widely recognized that corporations play a pervasive role in public national and international policy making.[27] This awareness has led the United Nations to search for ways of making transnational corporations responsible and accountable for human rights. That is why the literature has given increasing attention to situations in which private actors like TNCs may violate or even promote human rights.

Implicit in the notion and term of "TNCs" is their capacity to transcend national boundaries and the fact that they are usually limited liability companies.[28] Corporations become transnational in a way that can be relevant to human rights when their activity is able to affect individuals, communities, and the environment not only in their home country but also in other host countries, and when their economic and organizational size makes them interact with governments. Thus, this attention given to the relationship between TNCs and human rights is justified in two ways.

On the one hand, according to the traditional view, the state has an obligation to protect human rights and to prevent actors subject to state control from infringing the rights of others. For example, according to paragraph 18 of the *Maastricht Guidelines on Violations of Economic, Social and Cultural Rights*, "The obligation to protect includes the State's responsibility to ensure that private entities or individuals, including transnational corporations over which they exercise jurisdiction, do not deprive individuals of their economic, social and cultural rights. States are responsible for violations of economic, social and cultural rights that result from their failure to exercise due diligence in controlling the behavior of such non-State actors."

Nevertheless, further problems arise because the host states are often developing countries, where in many cases the government may not be interested in guaranteeing human rights or takes advantage of complicity with the conduct of TNCs. So the host states may be willing to apply domestic rules when the legal norms of the home states of TNCs are based on higher standards.[29] This is why it is relevant to establish whether indirect state responsibility can reach out to the overseas activity of TNCs. Up to now, the only effective system for transnational human rights claims against TNCs (before U.S. courts) is internal to the U.S. legal order and is provided by the application of the

Alien Tort Claims Act (ATCA) to the activities of TNCs abroad.[30]

On the other hand, according to a new perspective, at the international level a way is being sought for making TNCs directly responsible or accountable for human rights.[31] In this sense, specific problems dealing with the attribution of liability arise when firms form part of a large group structure with a holding company and subsidiaries, all of which may be characterized by limited liability. In this case, identifying and ascribing responsibilities among the parent firm and the subsidiaries can be difficult. Each firm of the group is, in front of third parties, a separate legal entity, and this maximizes the advantages (for the firm) of limited liability. In this context, limited liability not only limits the liability of the shareholder to the value of their share capital but also limits the responsibility of a parent firm for the conduct of its subsidiaries. As has been pointed out, "Each legally distinct entity is subject to the laws of the countries in which it operates, but the transnational corporate group or network as a whole is not governed directly by international law."[32] There is, therefore, a specific and high risk that any ostensibly illegal actions of TNCs that form part of a corporate group may go unpunished because the principle of limited liability also makes it very difficult, if not in some cases impossible, to sanction a firm's conduct both at domestic and at international levels.[33]

Given the theoretical and practical difficulties in ascribing legal responsibilities to TNCs, international law has developed alternative tools in order to prevent violations of and foster compliance with human rights that tend to directly address firms. Such instruments belong to the domain of soft law: They are not formally binding, and they mainly aim to diffuse sensitivity and regard for human rights as well as to promote the voluntary allegiance of influential actors in the relevant fields. Such soft law tools are mainly of three kinds.

The first kind is the guidelines and standard-setting tools of intergovernmental organizations, such as the *Guidelines for Multinational Enter-prises* promoted by the Organization for Economic Cooperation and Development (OECD), as an add-on to the *Declaration on International Investment and Multinational Enterprises.*[34] The *Guidelines* are addressed to TNCs operating in or from the adhering states of the OECD with regard to their worldwide business operations. This "globalization" of the OECD guidelines[35] rests on the idea that, when firms operate in states that do not give sufficient regard to human rights, the firms themselves more than the states have an interest—first of all for reasons of their reputation—to avoid being implicated in complaints procedures.

The second kind of soft law tool comprises the declarations of international organizations and nongovernmental organizations, such as the *International Labor Organization* (ILO) *Tripartite Declaration,*[36] the UN *Norms on Responsibilities of Transnational Corporations and Other Business Enterprises with Regard to Human Rights* (hereinafter UN Norms),[37] the *Business Charter for Sustainable Development* promoted by the International Chamber of Commerce (ICC),[38] and the International Finance Corporation's (IFC) *Environmental and Social Standards* (2006).[39] The *Global Compact*[40] may be included in this group of tools even if it is, strictly speaking, a personal initiative of the former UN Secretary-General, Kofi Annan. This soft law instrument puts obligations on TNCs regarding both principles (from the obligation to ensure equality of opportunity and treatment to environmental protection) and specific human rights, such as freedom of association and the right to collective bargaining, the elimination of all forms of forced or compulsory labor, the effective abolition of child labor, and the elimination of discrimination with respect to employment and occupation. They aim to prevent TNCs themselves from infringing human rights and to prevent their direct, beneficial, or silent complicity in violations. Direct complicity is regarded as occurring "when a company knowingly assists a state in violating human rights";[41] beneficial complicity "suggests that a company benefits directly from human rights abuses committed by someone else";[42] and silent complicity "describes the way human rights advocates see the failure by a company to raise the question of systematic or continuous human rights violations in its interaction with the appropriate authorities."[43]

The implementation process connected to this second kind of measure rests on three mechanisms: (1) corporations periodically report to the UN about their dissemination and internal implementation of rules in compliance with the UN *Norms*; (2) the UN independently monitors corporations' activities (through mechanisms already existent or to be created); and (3) governments ensure that corporations implement UN *Norms*.

The third kind of instruments belong to the domain of self-regulation and are mainly multistakeholder in form, with mechanisms based on certification systems or that involve partial legislation, often specific to particular economic sectors.

All these tools directly address corporations and seem to be the outcome of a convergence between the international law of human rights and the Corporate Social Responsibility (CSR) paradigm. The CSR paradigm is based on the idea that firms should not only maximize profit and shareholders' interests as well as control (and account for) their negative externalities and obey the law but they should also contribute to social development and the common welfare. In other words, firms are required to assume an idea of responsibility that goes beyond their strict legal duties and take into account the wider and broader interests of various "stakeholders." Stakeholders (i.e., those who are in some sense affected by a firm's activity)[44] may be internal (e.g., employees, suppliers, subcontractors, clients, etc.) or external (e.g., environment, community, members of the public, etc.). Social impact indicators are embedded, according to this view, in the very idea of profit. Obligations are stretched so that firms turn out to have simultaneous economic, legal, and moral duties.

It should be noted that soft law tools embracing this view tend to impose on TNCs not only negative obligations to respect human rights but also positive obligations concerning human rights protection (e.g., duties to control the conduct of their subsidiaries as well as suppliers and subcontractors) and promotion, even in the absence of a legal framework or governmental action.

It is obvious that the aims of the CSR paradigm change depending on whether corporations operate in states where human rights are supported by legal norms or in states where such support does not exist. In the first case, economic activities have a limit in legal norms and CSR can function as a valuable input for TNCs to go beyond the law. In the second case, because the host state may not be able to or be interested in ensuring compliance with human rights, CSR tools seemingly take on the function of replacing the law. Therefore, a set of means that originally should have led TNCs to go beyond the law are brought in instead of the law or to support it. As we have seen above, home states may also have problems in exercising extraterritorial control over TNCs and in making human rights justiciable. This is why convergence between the CSR paradigm and international law can play a strategic role in internationalizing human rights.[45] This ambition is well clarified in the very text of the UN *Norms*: "[The UN] Norms enlist transnational corporations as agents of international law implementation, even against states that have either refused to ratify certain international instruments or that have objected to the gloss advanced by international institutions."[46] Moreover, it is clear that in this kind of tool there is a trend to "implement current as well as aspirational international law standards through private law,"[47] and, therefore, to combine public and private regulatory frameworks. By imposing international law standards through private law—that is, resting on private and contractually binding behavior—UN *Norms*, for example, aim to build forms of consensus for the adoption of hard international law.[48] This is consistent with the weakening of the distinction between public and private international law that seems to result from the focus on globalization.

4. Armed Non-State Actors

With reference to the violation of civil and political human rights, armed conflicts are further contexts in which new actors have been addressed by international law. Such actors are identifiable on the basis of the idea that their behavior would be qualified as a violation of human rights if they were state actors.[49] Even in this case, the list may be very long and changeable. The actors that are relevant in this context are mainly qualified as (1) rebels, insurgents, and belligerents; and (2) national liberation movement groups. Furthermore, after the attacks of September 11, 2001, the term "NSAs" could be also associated with terrorist groups.

In discussing armed NSAs, it is also possible to talk about a trend toward the demise of the reference to state recognition and the possibility of seeing obligations stemming from international norms as directly addressing armed non-state actors. Again and also in this domain, the non-state actors have been addressed through both new interpretations of hard law and soft law tools as well as by the introduction of new accountability mechanisms.

The first kind of actors mentioned above can be regarded as subjects under international law if (1) "rebels should prove that they have effective control over some part of the territory"[50] or (2) "civil commotion should reach a certain degree of intensity and duration."[51] Theoretically, states can bestow rights and obligations on rebels by recognizing them as either insurgents or belligerents. Nevertheless, such recognition is quite unlikely, because, for example, it would amount to an acknowledgment that the government has lost control. Still, rebels may be regarded as addressees of international obligations under contemporary humanitarian law, especially according to the Common article 3 to the four Geneva Conventions of 1949, protocol II of 1977 to the Geneva Conventions, and Art. 19 of the Hague Convention on Cultural Prop-

erty of 1954. In the light of these norms, "international law imposes obligations on certain parties to an internal armed conflict irrespective of any recognition granted by the state they are fighting against or by any third state."[52] For what concerns national liberation movements, they "may be able to claim rights, and will be subject to international obligations, even in the absence of control of territory or express recognition by their adversaries,"[53] according to the terms of international humanitarian law treaties.

In the Resolution adopted in 1999 by the distinguished expert body, the Institute of International Law, it stated that all parties to armed conflicts involving non-state entities, regardless of their legal status, "have the obligation to respect international humanitarian law as well as fundamental human rights."[54] Furthermore, the protection of human rights in the context of armed conflicts has received an interesting development through the adoption of commitments, declarations, codes of conduct, and memoranda of understanding by the armed groups themselves; that is, through soft law measures.[55]

Geneva Call[56] has invited armed groups to sign a "Deed of Commitment for Adherence to a Total Ban on Anti-Personnel Mines and for Cooperation in Mine Action." According to the standard Deed, even though human rights are not the specific subject of the commitments, the Deed and its implementation/accountability mechanisms recognizes that armed groups have human rights obligations.[57] It has been maintained that "a partial effect of the Deed is to endow the non-state actor with some sort of enhanced moral status; by eclipsing the traditional legal approach, whereby the focus is on international recognition by governments and intergovernmental organizations, Geneva Call has opened the door to a new accountability mechanism for armed opposition groups."[58] Such a mechanism includes an obligation for the non-state actor to allow for monitoring as well as the publicity of noncompliance.[59]

Moreover, it should be noted that the state parties to the Ottawa Treaty seem willing to think that the norms contained in the treaty extend to non-state actors;[60] in general, "the commitments regime developed by Geneva Call has encouraged governments and inter-governmental organizations to incorporate such an approach into their own mission."[61]

5. Individuals

Individuals have gradually changed their position in international law. Looking at this change, the Kantian distinction between *jus cosmopoliticum* and international law seems to weaken. The gradual but increasing emergence of the individual in the international legal order is intrinsically linked to the positivization of human rights. Namely, this emergence is the premise for the achievement of the universality of human rights and of what is involved in Art. 28 of the Universal Declaration of Human Rights, which provides that "Everyone is entitled to a social and international order in which the rights and freedoms set forth in this Declaration can be fully realized."

In order to address this topic, the issue of whether individuals may be regarded as subjects of international law takes on a greater relevance than in the case of the other non-state actors. This is because what is at stake is not, of course, the participation of individuals as such in international processes but the possibility that they are directly given rights, duties, and the capacity to claim for them.

There are three main positions on the issue. First, according to the most traditional perspective, because in order to be a subject under a given legal order it is necessary both to be direct addressees of legal norms and to have a *locus* and *jus standi* before international courts, it should be concluded that individuals are only "objects" of international law. Second, according to a second perspective, either because to be subjects under a given legal order it suffices to be direct addressees of legal norms, or because it can be demonstrated that even individuals have the ability to bring international claims to assert their rights before international courts, it is

maintained that individuals are subjects of international law. This second position is based (1) on the establishment, at the international level, of the principle of individual criminal responsibility and of the International Criminal Court's (ICC's) jurisdiction, and (2) on the possibility for individuals to claim rights before regional human rights courts. The third view maintains that the very contraposition between the notions of *object* and *subject* is "an intellectual prison"[62] and that it should be replaced, in analysis and in debate, by the notion of *participant*. In this sense, individuals have to be addressed as participants in the international legal system.[63]

It could be maintained that, although the first perspective seems to neglect some important developments in human rights law as well as in humanitarian and international criminal law, which do involve a change in the legal status of individuals under international law, the second perspective tends to underestimate that such developments—due to the treaty nature of the rules and mechanisms to be applied—continue to be linked to the intermediary or direct involvement of the states. This means that the third position could be the most convincing one.

6. Theoretical Issues

The new roles played and envisioned by NSAs in current international law raises some issues, which basically concern two levels. The first level deals with the definition of the legal status of non-state entities and is common to the discourses that have been worked out about all the NSAs considered above. The second level deals with legitimacy issues and specifically concerns those NSAs that seem to play a role not only in respecting human rights but also in protecting and promoting them.

For what concerns the legal status level, international law continues to focus on the NGOs' status under national jurisdiction.[64] The *European Convention on the Recognition of the Legal Personality of International Non-Governmental*

Organizations (which came into force in 1991) makes a little change by providing for the general recognition of the legal personality of an NGO in any state party to the convention, in the sense that the national law of the respective state in which the NGO has its headquarters is recognized.[65] Therefore, it should be concluded that NGOs are subjects under national jurisdiction and not under international law. Furthermore with regard to legal capacity, NGOs have *locus standi* before the African Commission on Human and Peoples' Rights. An NGO may, moreover, bring a case before the European Court of Human Rights, but only if the NGO itself claims to be a victim.

Coming to the legitimacy issues, two main trends are likely to be faced. According to some scholars, the increasing participation of NGOs in international processes is a sign both of the pressure and of the feasibility of democracy in international order or even in global order.[66] This is because NGOs are thought of as the voice of transnational/global civil society and may "have authenticity, legitimacy and authority of the 'people' of the world in a way that states and international organizations do not."[67]

Nevertheless, from a different perspective, it is pointed out that NGOs cannot claim legitimacy and their activity should not be regarded as democratic solely on the basis that they express ideas or interests present in international/global civil society.[68] A legitimacy deficit is in this sense underlined, because "[NGOs] . . . are in no sense a substitute for some direct form of representation of people."[69] The possibility for NGOs to play a role not only in consultative action but also in negotiating activity is questioned just because of their deficit of formal representative power. Such deficit is not much relevant per se but rather because it reverberates on NGOs accountability and responsiveness— that is, "whether and how independently they formulate their working programmes; who their donors are, and whose interests they represent."[70] In fact, some critics of NGOs' activity maintain that their participation in international decision making "should be seen as a step in the de-velopment of global transnational elites at the expense of genuinely democratic but hence local, processes."[71]

A good answer to these criticisms addressing internal accountability—that is, the issue of how and how much NGOs represent and account for their own behavior to their members— stresses the importance of "competition" among NGOs: Several NGOs are active on the same issues and exiting from any NGO is quite easy.[72] This should lead NGOs to try to best represent the position and the interests embraced by their members, especially considering that "insofar as NGOs tend to be focused on a limited set of issues, their members will be in a better position to monitor and discipline leaderships than are voters with respect to governmental representation."[73] In this sense, the assessment of NGOs' legitimacy seems to be biased by the conceptual contraposition between government and NGOs; nevertheless, it should be noted that this premise rests on an idealization of the accountability of governments.[74]

On the contrary, the issue of external accountability concerning "how to keep NGOs accountable to the system in which they are exercising power"[75] seems to be more crucial. From this perspective, a paradox—named the "inclusion paradox"[76]—has been shown: Because participation in international decision making is informal, NGOs have no formal obligation to respect decisional outputs. Some scholars suggest that, instead of challenging NSAs' legitimacy, this very paradox may offer a good argument for giving NSAs a legal personality because in this way they would be formally given both rights and obligations.[77]

Regardless, such criticisms and debate make it clear that the role played by NGOs, especially in the human rights domain, challenges the notion of representative democracy and calls for a view of democracy that can accommodate participation with both global problems and the retreat of the state from many decisional arenas.

A useful way to discuss the issue of whether NGOs' participation in international processes fosters some form of democracy at the global level consists in distinguishing between inputs and outputs of international decision making. NGOs contribute to input legitimacy by promoting accountability in two ways: first, by monitoring governmental decisions in international contexts and informing people about such decisions, and second, by fostering communication from the people to decision makers and informing the latter about the people's interests. Of course, whether NGOs' activity actually makes decisions more democratic depends on the way each NGO construes its relationship with the part of civil society whose interests or views it aims to represent. Conversely, NGOs can contribute to output legitimacy by offering their specialized expertise for more informed decisions.[78]

A further issue to be addressed is how to reconcile, in the decisional process, competing interests not only within each NGO but also between different NGOs.[79] Indeed, the challenge, when the new roles played by NSAs in international processes and human rights law are acknowledged, is to find how to map and coordinate interests in the private sphere, on the one hand, but also to accommodate them into the public framework on the other hand.

Coming to TNCs, two main theoretical, doctrinal, and practical problems must be addressed in order to ground and strengthen the new role/status of TNCs under international law. Such issues deal with (1) the possibility of ascribing a legal personality to TNCs under international law and (2) the existence of the horizontal effect of human rights—that is, the applicability and the justiciability of norms containing human rights directly to relationships among private subjects.

What is the legal status of TNCs? As has been noted above, the conditions under which an entity may be regarded as a legal subject are (1) being the direct addressees of norms containing rights and duties and (2) having the *jus standi* (and *locus standi*)—that is, procedural competencies before international tribunals—on the basis of these norms. According to different doctrines, both of them or only one of them is required. However, in the case of TNCs, the picture becomes even more complicated because the relationship between legal personality and legal responsibility is also a topic under discussion. Of course, the lack of an explicit recognition of the legal personality of TNCs may prevent the construction of effective enforcement mechanisms for human rights when they are violated by TNCs. However, the relationship between the legal basis for TNCs' human rights responsibility and the possibility of ascribing a legal personality and legal subjectivity to TNCs are not univocally viewed. Nevertheless, a trend has emerged that is willing to ascribe legal personality to TNCs in a weaker sense than that of the state's legal personality. This perspective argues that TNCs have a legal personality, though to a limited degree,[80] to the extent that they are addressees of rights and duties and that in some cases they also have *jus standi* and are subject to at least an international jurisdiction—that is, the jurisdiction of the European Court of Human Rights (ECtHR). From this perspective, the role to be given to the notion of legal personality is weakened on the premise that "the whole notion of subjects and objects has no credible reality and . . . no functional purpose"[81] and that it would be better to speak of "participants instead of subjects."[82] It is, therefore, concluded that the contemporary structure of international order "requires that MNCs are included in the system of international law"[83] and that this is what really counts in order to approach the responsibility issues. Such an argument rests on a view of international law whereby the multiplication of relevant actors is taken seriously, regardless of their formal legal status according to the bipartition of subject vs. object and giving weight to their role as participants.[84]

Even so reshaped, legitimacy issues continue to arise with reference to justifying TNCs' role in protecting and promoting rights. For, as it has been underlined above, soft law means giving TNCs obligations not only to respect (abstaining from violation of rights) but also to protect (acting to make others respect human rights) and promote (acting to fulfill both civil and social human rights). In some sense, that TNCs may be direct addressees of obligations to not violate human rights is quite ascertained, to the extent that the horizontal effect of rights—though it should not be taken for granted and indeed is an open issue[85]—seems to be working in this case.[86] On the contrary, some view protection and promotion as undue tasks for non-state entities, and they view them thus for two reasons: first, because such obligations cannot rest on the horizontal effect of rights and therefore lack any legal basis, and second, because this way of depicting TNCs' role contributes to the retreat of the state and to the takeover of the state by corporations. Actually, as has been pointed out, "there is emerging a new dimension to corporate activity, one that puts corporations in the role of welfare providers and social engineers, environmentalists and mediators, in which corporations assume the traditional functions of the nation state."[87]

The first line of reasoning is well founded, and this is why, in order to ground private actors' positive obligations to protect and, specifically, to promote human rights, at the international level quasi-legal or ethical means and paths have been sought. In no sense does this necessarily mean that such solutions cannot be even more effective than legally binding ones. On the contrary, they might become highly effective; therefore, the above-mentioned second order of reasons should be addressed because it tends to reject not only the formal and legal ascription of proactive responsibility to TNCs but also their more informal and even ethical accountability for decisions and matters traditionally involved with governmental action. Among the alleged reasons is the possibility that corporate intervention in welfare and social issues may be unstable and may cause conflict among different local communities[88] or that private or sectorial interests bias the definition of the aims to be pursued.

In a different perspective, a proactive role for TNCs is defended according to the idea that there are situations in which "TNCs might be able to alleviate the conditions associated with burdened societies at a cost that is lower than that faced by governments and international cooperative organizations."[89] Generally speaking, this idea seems to be embraced and applied in international (soft) law regarding TNCs and human rights: Its aim is to shape new methods for encouraging compliance with human rights by resting on the principle that, regardless of their formal legal status, those who have the power to do something to protect and promote human rights should properly exercise such power.

The involvement of NSAs in human rights protection and promotion is part of a wider shift from a government-based to a governance-based approach that characterizes not only the domestic order but also the construction of the international and global order.[90] The model of governance rests greatly on the idea of diffused responsibility and accountability, including responsibility and accountability for human rights, which is expressed by the role international legal tools give to NGOs and TNCs.

NOTES

1. Philip Alston, *The "Not-a-Cat" Syndrome: Can the International Human Rights Regime Accommodate Non-State Actors?* in NON-STATE ACTORS AND HUMAN RIGHTS 14 (Philip Alston ed., 2005); Andrea Bianchi, *Introduction,* in NON-STATE ACTORS AND INTERNATIONAL LAW xix (Andrea Bianchi ed., 2009).

2. On this point, *see* Alston, *id.* at 19. The notion of *actor* is borrowed from political science.

3. August Reinisch, *The Changing International Legal Framework for Dealing with Non-State Actors,* in Andrea Bianchi, *Globalization of Human Rights: The Role of Non-State Actors,* in NON-STATE ACTORS AND INTERNATIONAL LAW, 375–408, at 412.

4. Michael Goodhart, *Human Rights and Non-State Actors: Theoretical Puzzles,* in NON-STATE ACTORS IN THE HUMAN RIGHTS UNIVERSE 23–41 (George Andreoploluos et al. eds., 2006).

5. *Id.* at 35–36. This view has been defined as a functionalist approach to human rights.

6. Steve Charnovitz, *Nongovernmental Organizations and International Law,* in Bianchi, *supra* note 1, at 161.

7. Kerstin Martens, *Mission Impossible? Defining Nongovernmental Organizations,* 11 VOLUNTAS 278 (2002).

8. *Id.* at 277.

9. Charnovitz, *supra* note 6, at 149. Charnovitz has pointed out that "although profit-seeking business entities are not NGOs, associations of business entities can be, such as the International Chamber of Commerce"; Daniel Thürer, *The Emergence of Non-Governmental Organizations and Transnational Enterprises in International Law and the Changing Role of the State*, in Bianchi *supra* note 1, at 43. On the definitional issue, *see also* Martens, *supra* note 7, at 282.

10. Martens, *supra* note 7, at 279.

11. Charnovitz, *supra* note 6, at 117.

12. *Id.*

13. Peter Willetts, *From Consultative Arrangements to Partnership: The Changing Status of NGOs in Diplomacy at the UN*, 6 GLOBAL GOVERNANCE 191–212 (2000).

14. Charnovitz, *supra* note 6, at 118.

15. Martens, *supra* note 7, at 274.

16. *Id.*

17. *See* Charnovitz, *supra* note 6, at 124, where it is underlined that the consultation norms contained in Article 71 have influenced institutional developments outside the UN, such as the Organization of American States and the African Union.

18. *See* on this Andrea Bianchi, *Globalization of Human Rights: The Role of Non-State Actors*, in NON-STATE ACTORS AND INTERNATIONAL LAW, 375–408, at 384–86.

19. Michael J. Struett, *NGOs, the International Criminal Court, and the Politics of Writing International Law*, in Bianchi, *supra* note 1, at 208–19, for the quotation, *id.* at 351. On this, *see also* Ruth Wedgwood, *Legal Personality and the Role of Non-Governmental Organizations and Non-State Political Entities in the United Nations System*, in NON-STATE ACTORS AS NEW SUBJECTS OF INTERNATIONAL LAW 25–26 (Rainer Hoffmann & Nils Geissler eds., 1999).

20. Willetts, *supra* note 13.

21. *See* Struett, *supra* note 19.

22. For some criticisms of the role played by NGOs in this treaty, *see* Kenneth Anderson, *The Ottawa Convention Banning Landmines: The Role of International Non-governmental Organizations and the Idea of International Civil Society*, in Bianchi, *supra* note 1, at 221–50.

23. Charnovitz, *supra* note 6, at 152.

24. Thürer, *supra* note 9, at 46.

25. *Id.*

26. ANDREW CLAPHAM, HUMAN RIGHTS IN THE PRIVATE SPHERE (1993); ANDREW CLAPHAM, HUMAN RIGHTS OBLIGATIONS OF NON-STATE ACTORS (2006).

27. Michael K. Addo, *Introduction, in* HUMAN RIGHTS STANDARDS AND THE RESPONSIBILITY OF TRANSNATIONAL CORPORATIONS 3 (Michael K. Addo ed., 1999).

28. For a detailed picture of definitional issues, *see* CINTHIA DAY WALLACE, THE MULTINATIONAL ENTERPRISE AND LEGAL CONTROL chaps. IV and V (2002). *See*

also François Rigaux, *Transnational Corporations, in* INTERNATIONAL LAW: ACHIEVEMENTS AND PROSPECTS 121–32 (Mohammed Bedjaoui ed., 1991); Clapham, *supra* note 26 (2006), at 199–201.

29. PETER T. MUCHLINSKI, MULTINATIONAL ENTERPRISES AND THE LAW 110 (1999).

30. Clapham, *supra* note 26 (2006), at 252–61.

31. *Id.*; Andrew Clapham, *Revisiting Human Rights in the Private Sphere: Using the European Convention on Human Rights to Protect the Right of Access to the Civil Courts*, in TORTURE AS TORT: COMPARATIVE PERSPECTIVES ON THE DEVELOPMENT OF TRANSNATIONAL HUMAN RIGHTS LITIGATION 513–16 (Craig Scott ed., 2001).

32. John Gerard Ruggie, *Business and Human Rights: The Evolving International Agenda,* 101 AM. J. INT'L L. 824 (2007).

33. Olivier De Schutter, *The Accountability of Multinationals for Human Rights Violations in European Law*, in Alston, *supra* note 1, at 227, 276–81.

34. ORGANISATION FOR ECONOMIC CO-OPERATION AND DEVELOPMENT, THE OECD GUIDELINES FOR MULTINATIONAL ENTERPRISES: TEXT, COMMENTARY AND CLARIFICATIONS, *available at* www.olis.oecd.org/olis/2000doc.nsf/LinkTo/NT00002F06/$FILE/JT00115758.PDF.

35. Some examples of how the globalization of the guidelines have started to work may be found in *supra* note 26 (2006), at 203–04.

36. *See* www.ilo.org/wcmsp5/groups/public/—-ed_emp/—-emp_ent/—-multi/documents/publication/wcms_094386.pdf.

37. Adopted by the Sub-commission on the Promotion and Protection of Human Rights in 2003, U.N. Doc E/CN.4/Sub.2/2003/12/Rev.2.

38. International Chamber of Commerce, The ICC's Commission on Environment and Energy, *available at* www.iccwbo.org/policy/environment/id1309/index.html.

39. International Finance Corporation, IFC Sustainability—Environmental and Social Standards, *available at* www.ifc.org/ifcext/sustainability.nsf/Content/EnvSoc Standards.

40. United Nations Global Compact, The Ten Principles, *available at* www.unglobalcompact.org/AbouttheGC/TheTENPrinciples/index.html.

41. Clapham, *supra* note 26 (2006), at 221.

42. *Id.*

43. *Id.,* at 222.

44. Bruce Langtry, *Stakeholders and the Moral Responsibility of Business,* 4 BUS. ETHICS Q. 432–33 (1994); Josep M. Lozano, *Towards the Relational Corporation: From Managing Stakeholder Relationships to Building Stakeholder Relationships (Waiting for Copernicus),* 5 CORP. GOVERNANCE 60–77 (2005); Robert Phillips, *Stakeholder Legitimacy,* 13 BUS. ETHICS 25–41 (2003).

45. Rory Sullivan & Des Hogan, *The Business Case for Human Rights: The Amnesty International Perspective, in* COMMERCIAL LAW AND HUMAN RIGHTS 70 (Stephen Bottomley & David Kenley eds., 2002).

46. U.N. Doc. E/CN.4/Sub.2/Res/1998/8, at 106.

47. *Id.*

48. Kenneth Paul Kinyua, *The Accountability of Multinational Corporations for Human Rights Violations: A Critical Analysis of Select Mechanisms and Their Potential to Protect Economic, Social and Cultural Rights in Developing Countries,* Sept. 30, 2009, *available at* http://ssrn.com/abstract=1599842.

49. Herbert F. Spirer & Louise Spirer, *Accounting for Human Rights Violations,* in George Andreoploluos et al., *supra* note 4, at 44.

50. ANTONIO CASSESE, INTERNATIONAL LAW 125 (2d ed. 2005).

51. *Id.*

52. Clapham, *supra* note 26 (2006), at 272.

53. *Id.* at 273.

54. The Application of International humanitarian Law and Fundamental Human Rights in Armed Conflict in which Non-State Entities are Parties, resolution adopted at the Berlin session, August 25, 1999, art. II.

55. Clapham, *supra* note 26 (2006), at 288–89.

56. Geneva Call is an international humanitarian organization dedicated to engaging armed non-state actors to respect and adhere to humanitarian law, starting with the ban on antipersonnel mines, because non-state actors are not entitled to sign the Ottawa Convention on the prohibition of the Use, Stockpiling, Production and Transfer of Anti-personnel Mines and on their Destruction.

57. Clapham, *supra* note 26 (2006), at 292–93.

58. *Id.* at 294.

59. *Id.* at 296.

60. *See* the Declaration of the Fourth Meeting of States Parties, adopted by the plenary meeting on September 20, 2002, at 10, para. 12.

61. Clapham, *supra* note 26 (2006), at 299.

62. ROSALYN HIGGINS, PROBLEMS AND PROCESS: INTERNATIONAL LAW AND HOW WE USE IT 49 (1994).

63. *Id.*

64. *Supra* note 7; Karsten Nowrot, *Legal Consequences of Globalization: The Status of Non-Governmental Organizations Under International Law,* 6 IND. J. GLOBAL STUD. 579–645 (1999); Menno T. Kamminga, *The Evolving Status of NGOs Under International Law: A Threat to the Inter-State System?* in Alston, *supra* note 1, at 93–111.

65. Martens, *supra* note 7, at 277.

66. RICHARD FALK, ON HUMAN GOVERNANCE: TOWARDS A NEW GLOBAL POLICY (1995).

67. Anderson, *supra* note 22, at 241.

68. Charnovitz, *supra* note 6, at 164; Kamminga, *supra* note 64, at 110; Anderson, *supra* note 22, at 249–50.

69. Thomas M. Franck, *Individuals and Groups of Individuals as Subjects of International Law,* in Hoffmann & Geissler, *supra* note 19, at 152, discussion.

70. Jayati Srivastava, *Non-Governmental Organizations as Negotiators at the World Trade Organization: A Perspective from the South,* 39 INT'L STUD. 257 (2002).

71. Anderson, *supra* note 22, at 221.

72. Peter J. Spiro, *Accounting for NGOs, in* THE GLOBALIZATION OF INTERNATIONAL LAW 551 (Paul S. Berman ed., 2005).

73. *Id.* at 553.

74. *Id.* at 552.

75. *Id.* at 554.

76. *Id.*

77. *Id.* at 555–56.

78. Charnovitz, *supra* note 6, at 166.

79. *Id.* at 171.

80. NICOLA M. C. P. JÄGERS, CORPORATE HUMAN RIGHTS OBLIGATIONS: IN SEARCH OF ACCOUNTABILITY 27–34 (2002); David Kinley and Junko Tadaki, *From Talk to Walk: The Emergence of Human Rights Responsibilities for Corporations at International Law,* 44 VA. J. INT'L L. 945–46 (2003).

81. HIGGINS, *supra* note 62, at 49–50; JÄGERS, *supra* note 80, at 266.

82. JÄGERS, *supra* note 80, at 267.

83. *Id.*

84. This notion has been introduced by WOLFGANG FRIEDMANN, THE CHANGING STRUCTURE OF INTERNATIONAL LAW 70–71 (1964). *See also* HIGGINS, *supra* note 62, at 50; JÄGERS, *supra* note 80, at 23.

85. *Supra* note 3, at 412.

86. Elena Pariotti, *International Soft Law: Human Rights and Non-State Actors: Towards the Accountability of Transnational Corporations?* 10 HUM. RTS. REV. 139–55 (2009).

87. NOREENA HERTZ, THE SILENT TAKEOVER: GLOBAL CAPITALISM AND THE DEATH OF DEMOCRACY 220, 157–58, and more widely chap. 6 (2001), *but see contra* Varun Gauri, *Social Rights and Economic Claims to Health Care and Education in Developing Countries, in* HUMAN RIGHTS AND DEVELOPMENT: TOWARDS MUTUAL REINFORCEMENT 72 (Philip Alston & Mary Robinson eds., 2005).

88. On this, *see* DAVID VOGEL, THE MARKET FOR VIRTUE: THE POTENTIAL AND LIMITS OF CORPORATE SOCIAL RESPONSIBILITY 148–49 (2005).

89. Nien-hê Hsieh, *The Obligations of Transnational Corporations: Rawlsian Justice and the Duty of Assistance,* 14 BUS. ETHICS Q. 651 (2004).

90. *See,* on such keys of understanding, Zoe Pearson, *NGOs and International Law: New Mechanisms for Governance,* AUST. Y.B. INT'L L. 73 (2004).

PART THREE
ECONOMIC INSTRUMENTS

7

Disparate Notions of Fairness

Comparative Insider Trading Regulation in an Evolving Global Landscape

JOAN MACLEOD HEMINWAY

Should it be legal for entities and individuals who possess important nonpublic information about a corporation, its management, or its securities to trade in the corporation's securities in the open market or with individuals who lack knowledge of the nonpublic information? If the answer to this question is *not* an unqualified "no," then under what circumstances should this kind of trading be permitted or prohibited? These questions are the essence of the law of insider trading, a body of law that has slowly proliferated and evolved from state to state as securities and other financial markets multiply and become more established and as international and cross-border securities trading has become more prevalent.

Given the relatively recent introduction of insider trading regulation in many states, the study of international and comparative insider trading (and other aspects of corporate governance and corporate finance) lags somewhat behind the study of more traditional areas of public international law. This lag is unfortunate given the increasingly international scope of business and, more specifically, corporate finance. Yet even with the comparatively recent advent of international and comparative scholarship in the area of insider trading regulation, one thing is quite clear: Different states regulate

insider trading in quite different ways and with quite different policy objectives and effects. Each of these systems of regulation has benefits and detriments. But the fact of their difference is, in itself, an important issue in international law and business. Without agreement across states on what, precisely, is *legally* objectionable about insider trading, cross-border investors who are trading while in possession of important nonpublic information cannot be sure whether their conduct is legal. This uncertainty is compounded by ambiguities associated with the boundaries of regulatory and enforcement jurisdiction. Differences in insider trading regulation from state to state may have undesirable effects on cross-border transactions as well as both developed and emerging markets, with those investors intent on extracting individual profit from nonpublic information fleeing certain securities markets and entering others.

The many facets of international and comparative insider trading regulation that contribute to its uncertain international regulatory status are too numerous to cover in one chapter. Accordingly, this chapter analyzes global insider trading regulation from one uniformly understood perspective—fairness. Although fairness is not the policy underpinning of insider trading law in all states that legally restrict insider trading (and, in the eyes of some, is not a legitimized objective in regulating insider trading[1]), it is commonly offered as a rationale for restricting trading for those possessing important nonpublic information. To understand insider trading from this angle requires that we first understand the concept of fairness. Once we have that fundamental understanding of fairness, we can look at basic principles of insider trading regulation in different states (here, I focus on the United States, Japan, and Germany), the divergent development of insider trading regulation in these states, and various aspects of insider trading regulation in different states through the lens of fairness. This description and analysis sheds light on the gaps among national regulatory frameworks that must be closed in order for effective international regulation to occur. Although the International Organization of Securities Commissions has undertaken efforts to standardize international securities regulation (including by fostering insider trading regulation among its members),[2] this chapter assumes that greater international coordination of insider trading regulation is a desirable objective.

Defining Fairness in the Context of Regulation

Fairness, as a first principle in international and other law, both serves as a filter (or test) for lawmakers in identifying, selecting, and combining legal prescriptions and proscriptions, and it then characterizes the result of that process. Yet fairness is somewhat difficult to precisely and uniformly define; in fact, multiple conceptions of fairness exist and are accepted.[3] Fairness may be coextensive with consensual agreement, untainted by duress or deception.[4] Fairness may be seen as synonymous with equity—but not with formal equality (although equal treatment may sometimes be fair).[5] According to the Merriam-Webster Online Dictionary, the root adjective "fair" means (in the relevant part) "marked by impartiality and honesty" or "free from self-interest, prejudice, or favoritism" or "conforming with

the established rules."[6] These basic, general definitional words are packed with meaning. What is impartial or honest about a particular type of regulation? What does it mean for regulation to be "free from self-interest, prejudice, or favoritism" or to conform to established rules?

The seminal philosophical work of John Rawls approaches and resolves these issues by describing a construct for societal development and maintenance. Specifically, in *Justice as Fairness*, Rawls defined fairness as the basis for a system of cooperation in pluralistic, democratic society, and in doing so, he equated fairness with reasonableness.[7] According to Rawls, fairness, as a basis for regulation and other societal decision making, constrains the individualism that is permitted in a society that incorporates freedom and equality for the greater good of the whole.[8] In a fair system of societal cooperation, people who are free and equal have two moral powers: "the capacity for a sense of justice" and "the capacity for a conception of the good."[9] These powers effectively describe human circumstance. The capacity for a sense of justice allows free and equal members of society "to understand, to apply, and to act from (and not merely in accordance with) the principles of political justice that specify the fair terms of social cooperation."[10] Without the capacity for a sense of justice, there can be no fair system of societal cooperation—no way of arbitrating among various individuals' conceptions of the good. The capacity for a conception of the good allows free and equal members of society "to have, to revise, and rationally to pursue . . . an ordered family of final ends and aims which specifies a person's conception of what is of value in human life or, alternatively, of what is regarded as a fully worthwhile life."[11] A person's conception of the good includes one or more things to which the person aspires in life. There is room in this Rawlsian vision of fairness for personal asset accumulation and prosperity: "Income and wealth are general all-purpose means required to achieve a wide range of (permissible) ends, whatever they may be, and in particular, the end of realizing the two moral powers and advancing the ends of the (complete) conceptions of the good that citizens affirm or adopt."

This philosophical conception of fairness is helpful, even if not completely transparent in its application. Rawls did, however, make at least one truly useful contribution in defining fairness as an applied first principle: decision making from the "original position" and, more precisely, from behind the "veil of ignorance":[12]

> the original position is a device of representation: it models, first, what we regard (here and now) as fair conditions for the terms of social cooperation to be agreed to (reflected in the symmetry of the parties' situation); and second, it models what we regard (here and now) as reasonable restrictions on reasons that may be used in arguing for principles of justice to regulate the basic structure. Various formal constraints of the concept of right are modeled in the original position by requiring the parties to evaluate principles of justice from a suitably general point of view. However rational it might be for parties to favor principles framed to promote the determinate and known interests of those they represent, should they have the opportunity, the constraints of right, joined with the limits on information (modeled by the veil of ignorance), make that impossible.

The veil of ignorance, as a key condition of the original position, specifies that societal decision makers approach their task with an ignorance of both their own position and that of others.[13] It "removes differences in bargaining advantages, so that in this and other respects the parties are similarly situated," and this, as a result, makes the original position fair.[14]

Specifically, from behind the veil of ignorance, societal decision makers can identify, adopt, and implement principles of justice in their decision making. Rawls articulated two principles of justice: that "Each person has the same indefeasible claim to a fully adequate scheme of equal basic liberties" and that "social and economic inequalities are to . . . be attached to offices and positions open to all under con-

ditions of fair equality of opportunity . . . and they are to be to the greatest benefit of the least-advantaged members of society (the difference principle)."[15] Regulators in a fair system of regulation would, therefore, determine the existence, nature, and extent of regulation not as a means of addressing the concerns or desires of a particular interest group or groups (as public choice theory posits) but rather by reference to and application of foundational, accepted principles of justice that take into account the interests of all constituents, from the most to the least advantaged. Specifically, Rawls stated that the second principle of justice "applies at the legislative stage and it bears on all kinds of social and economic legislation, and on the many kinds of issues arising at this point."[16] Regulation is fair, then, when it provides or fosters fair equality of opportunity and complies with the difference principle (the two aspects of the second principle of justice).

Others have posited alternative conceptions of fairness in a legal context. In one law review article, for example, the author described two different ways of looking at fairness in rulemaking:

> The term "fairness" has at least two possible meanings. In one sense, it means an action, decision, or state of affairs that reflects the best overall balance of competing values and interests. This is the sense one means when one refers to a regulation that reflects a compromise among conflicting interests as a "fair" resolution of the controversy. It is a fair resolution if it strikes a good balance among all the affected interests—those of consumers, regulated parties, and the public at large.
>
> "Fairness" also has a narrower and more precise meaning. In this second sense, the term denotes one set of values in the overall normative calculus: those, such as rights-protection and distributive justice, that focus on how individuals are treated rather than how everyone benefits in the aggregate. This is the sense of fairness one means when one contrasts fairness with efficiency or utilitarianism. In our regulation example, fairness in this second sense refers to

how the regulation affects each consumer and each regulated interest, apart from how it affects social costs and benefits overall.

More precisely, fairness in this second sense denotes a normative claim that can limit or constrain decisions aimed at maximizing aggregate welfare. Fairness is concerned with how persons are treated either individually or in relation to one another—whether their rights are respected, for example, or whether they are treated as equals in the distribution of social goods. For instance, an egalitarian might invoke fairness to object to an unequal distribution of wealth on the ground that the distribution is unjust even if it also increases total social wealth in the long run by allocating larger shares to more productive individuals.[17]

These two alternative, non-Rawlsian definitions of fairness both require the comparative analysis of societal actors in different positions; but each resolves inequalities in different ways— the first by balancing competing individual interests for the good of the whole and the second by focusing on the treatment of individual actors.

Yet these three conceptions of fairness are not exclusive, nor are they necessarily guidance for rule makers. Rule makers may not be (often are not) clear about whether fairness is the basis for a particular rule or in what conception of fairness a specific rule is rooted. Some or all notions of fairness may be flawed, but they each have proponents as well as detractors. Be this as it may, disparate notions of fairness may present a basis or explanation for some variations in legal rules among states, including variations in insider trading regulation.

Basic Principles of Insider Trading Regulation

Many states ostensibly use (or at least credit) U.S. insider trading doctrine under Rule 10b-5[18] as the model for their own regulation of insider trading.[19] This phenomenon has occurred in part because of historical and political factors and in part because the United States is seen as (and has wielded regulatory power as) a market leader—an early adopter of regulation with both (a) a well-established supervisory and policy-oriented regulatory and enforcement agency, and (b) a well-developed, disaggregated, public securities market. As a result, the laws of many countries now prohibit identified classes of persons from trading while in possession of material nonpublic information, which is the central focus of insider trading regulation under Rule 10b-5.[20]

Yet despite seemingly convergent beginnings and a general agreement on the nature of the regulated conduct, operative insider trading principles in the United States (as a rule originator) have evolved to protect different interests and regulate different specific market activities than insider trading rules have in other countries.[21] For example, because of its origins in the context of an antifraud rule prohibiting manipulation and deception in connection with the purchase or sale of securities, U.S. insider trading doctrine fosters, supports, and protects, first and foremost, a fiduciary or fiduciary-like duty (that of an agent to a principal) rather than affording primacy to informational fairness (whether in the form of equal access to information or strict informational parity).[22] Also, the definition of an "insider"—the person regulated in his or her trading activities—varies from country to country, with the United States defining the concept to include any individual having a specified duty of trust and confidence (the fiduciary or fiduciary-like duty referenced in the preceding sentence) rather than a specified person or entity affiliated or associated with the issuing corporation in a defined way.[23] Moreover, U.S. insider trading rules broadly protect investors against market and nonmarket risks (through an expansive definition of materiality), whereas regulation in other countries purports to protect investors against market risks only (by focusing on market-affecting information).[24] And finally, because unlawful insider trading in the United States involves deceptive conduct, U.S. insider trading violations require proof of scienter—an ill-defined state of mind requirement that, according to the U.S. Supreme Court, consists of "a mental state embracing intent to deceive, manipulate or defraud."[25]

This essay focuses on the insider trading laws of three developed states: the United States, Japan, and Germany. Their laws have a common doctrinal, policy, and enforcement foundation, owing in no small part to the fact that U.S. insider trading doctrine was transplanted into (first) Japan and (much more recently) Germany as part of an international effort to encourage insider trading regulation consistent with the predominant U.S. model. Each state's law prohibits people from trading on the basis of important nonpublic information. Yet those who are regulated and the nature of the protected information vary from state to state. Moreover, the law has been adopted and has developed in different ways in each state due to (among other things) common law/civil law distinctions between the United States, on the one hand, and Japan and Germany, on the other, as well as external pressures from the international community, in general, and from supranational governance structures, in particular—in this case, the European Community.

U.S. Insider Trading Regulation

In the United States, insider trading is principally regulated under Rule 10b-5, although the rule is not narrowly tailored to address insider trading alone.[26] Rather, it is a general antifraud prohibition that has been shaped, principally by judge-made law, to include insider trading, among other practices. Adopted in 1942, Rule 10b-5 makes it

> unlawful for any person, directly or indirectly, by the use of any means or instrumentality of interstate commerce, or of the mails or of any facility of any national securities exchange,
>
> (a) To employ any device, scheme, or artifice to defraud,

> (b) To make any untrue statement of a material fact or to omit to state a material fact necessary in order to make the statements made, in the light of the circumstances under which they were made, not misleading, or
>
> (c) To engage in any act, practice, or course of business which operates or would operate as a fraud or deceit upon any person, in connection with the purchase or sale of any security.[27]

Typically, unlawful insider trading is deemed to violate subparagraph (a) or subparagraph (c) of Rule 10b-5 because insider traders remain silent; they withhold, rather than make, statements, oftentimes in the absence of other statements that are then made misleading by the insider trader's lack of disclosure.[28] I parenthetically note here an important linguistic difference: in the United States, the term "insider trading" is used to describe only illegal trading by those deemed to be insiders for Rule 10b-5 purposes; in many other states, the term "unlawful" (or "illegal" or "prohibited" or the like) must be used to indicate trading by insiders that constitutes a violation of law.

The adoption of Rule 10b-5 by the Securities and Exchange Commission ("SEC") is authorized under Section 10(b) of the Securities Exchange Act of 1934, as amended ("Section 10(b)" and the "1934 Act," respectively).[29] Section 10(b), like Rule 10b-5, is broadly worded and applicable to securities fraud that includes, but is not limited to, insider trading. In particular, Section 10(b) prohibits "any person, directly or indirectly, by the use of any means or instrumentality of interstate commerce or of the mails, or of any facility of any national securities exchange" from using or employing

> in connection with the purchase or sale of any security registered on a national securities exchange or any security not so registered . . . any manipulative or deceptive device or contrivance in contravention of such rules and regulations as the Commission may prescribe as necessary or appropriate in the public interest or for the protection of investors.[30]

Specific restrictions developed in decisional law construing Section 10(b) and Rule 10b-5 legally prohibit (under certain circumstances) both securities trading transactions and tipping information in connection with securities transactions as unlawful deceptive activities. Early cases painted a general deception argument for applying Section 10(b) and Rule 10b-5 in this context—deception grounded in informational unfairness or inequity (though admittedly leaving parts of the relevant doctrine unclear and undecided). For example, in 1951 the U.S. District Court for the District of Delaware explained its application of Section 10(b) and Rule 10b-5 to facts involving insider trading:

> The rule is clear. It is unlawful for an insider, such as a majority stockholder, to purchase the stock of minority stockholders without disclosing material facts affecting the value of the stock, known to the majority stockholder by virtue of his inside position but not known to the selling minority stockholders, which information would have affected the judgment of the sellers. The duty of disclosure stems from the necessity of preventing a corporate insider from utilizing his position to take unfair advantage of the uninformed minority stockholders. It is an attempt to provide some degree of equalization of bargaining position in order that the minority may exercise an informed judgment in any such transaction. Some courts have called this a fiduciary duty while others state it is a duty imposed by the 'special circumstances'. One of the primary purposes of the Securities Exchange Act of 1934 . . . was to outlaw the use of inside information by corporate officers and principal stockholders for their own financial advantage to the detriment of uninformed public security holders. I gave approval to this view of the Act in an earlier opinion in the case at bar.[31]

Only with a 1961 SEC enforcement action, however, did modern U.S. insider trading law permanently and inextricably (at least to date) link itself to Rule 10b-5.[32] The SEC's decision in this action, In re *Cady, Roberts & Co.*, is cred-ited with establishing the "disclose or abstain" rule at the heart of current insider trading doctrine under Rule 10b-5.[33] Under the "disclose or abstain" rule, a corporate insider must either disclose all material nonpublic facts in his or her possession or refrain from trading the corporation's securities.

> We, and the courts, have consistently held that insiders must disclose material facts which are known to them by virtue of their position but which are not known to persons with whom they deal and which, if known, would affect their investment judgment. Failure to make disclosure in these circumstances constitutes a violation of the anti-fraud provisions. If, on the other hand, disclosure prior to effecting a purchase or sale would be improper or unrealistic under the circumstances, we believe the alternative is to forgo the transaction.[34]

As illuminated and defined in subsequent case law, a fact is material if there is a significant likelihood that a reasonable investor (1) would find it important in making a buy/sell decision or (2) would find that disclosure of the fact significantly alters the total mix of publicly available information;[35] a fact is public if it has been "effectively disclosed in a manner sufficient to insure its availibility [sic] to the investing public."[36]

Cady, Roberts was followed by a number of other cases in federal court, notably including *SEC v. Texas Gulf Sulphur*,[37] endorsing and applying the "disclose or abstain" rule. Like earlier court and SEC decisions on insider trading, *Cady, Roberts* and these other cases are expressly premised on the unfairness associated with an insider's beneficial use of undisclosed information obtained by the insider because of his, her, or its insider status.[38]

In the post–*Cady, Roberts* era, the basic tenets of U.S. insider trading doctrine under Section 10(b) and Rule 10b-5 have been shaped principally by opinions in three U.S. Supreme Court cases decided over a seventeen-year period. The first of these opinions, the Supreme Court's 1980 decision in *United States v. Chiarella*,[39] endorses and reinforces the "disclose or abstain" rule articulated in *Cady, Roberts*. Under *Chiarella*, public issuers of securities and their insiders—people with a fiduciary or fiduciary-like duty of trust and confidence to shareholders—cannot trade in the issuer's securities while in possession of material, nonpublic information.[40]

Three years later, in 1983, the Supreme Court decided *Dirks v. SEC*.[41] *Dirks* regulates tipping by an insider and trading by a tippee—a person who obtains information directly or indirectly from an insider for an inappropriate purpose.[42] Effectively, under *Dirks*, (1) a tipping insider is liable if he breaches his fiduciary duty to the corporation and its shareholders by improperly (i.e., in expectation of a personal benefit) disclosing material nonpublic information and (2) a tippee is liable if the tipping insider breaches his fiduciary duty by improperly disclosing material, nonpublic information to the tippee and the tippee knows or should know of the breach.[43] As long as these requirements for tipper or tippee liability are met, an insider tipper may be held liable for trading by a tippee who does not receive information directly from the insider, and a tippee may be held liable for a trade made while in possession of material, nonpublic information received only indirectly from an insider.[44]

Finally, in 1997 the Supreme Court decided the third case in the trilogy, *United States v. O'Hagan*.[45] The *O'Hagan* case prohibits securities trading by a person who is not an insider of the corporation who possesses material, nonpublic information obtained from a source (other than an insider) to whom or which the trader owes a duty of trust and confidence.[46] The insider trading liability in this context is based on the trader's "deception of those who entrusted him with access to confidential information."[47]

These three cases outline the basic principles of insider trading in the United States today. As a group, they prohibit at least four securities trading–related activities: trading by insiders in possession of material, nonpublic information (known as the "classical theory" of insider trading liability); improper insider disclosure of material, nonpublic information directly or indirectly to noninsiders who may trade on that information (known as "tipper liability"); trading by noninsiders who receive material, nonpublic information directly or indirectly from insider tippers who share that information improperly, if the noninsider knows that the information was shared improperly (known as "tippee liability"); and trading by those who possess material, nonpublic information and breach a duty of trust and confidence to the source of that information by engaging in the trade (known as the "misappropriation theory") of insider trading regulation. The SEC summarizes the overall insider trading proscription as follows:

> The "manipulative and deceptive devices" prohibited by Section 10(b) of the Act . . . and § 240.10b-5 thereunder include, among other things, the purchase or sale of a security of any issuer, on the basis of material nonpublic information about that security or issuer, in breach of a duty of trust or confidence that is owed directly, indirectly, or derivatively, to the issuer of that security or the shareholders of that issuer, or to any other person who is the source of the material nonpublic information.[48]

Actions for violation of these insider trading prohibitions can be criminal (brought by the Department of Justice, U.S. Attorney's office) or civil (brought by the SEC in federal court or in an administrative action or by private parties, including through class action litigation). Enforcement activity varies from year to year but is significant. For example, from 2001 to September 22, 2006, the SEC alone brought 300 cases primarily classified as insider trading cases.[49]

Japanese Insider Trading Regulation

Enacted in the shadows of World War II, the overall securities regulation regime in Japan is modeled after the U.S. securities laws.[50] Although the Japanese Securities and Exchange Law of 1948 (the *Shoken Torihikiho*, or "SEL," now known as the Financial Instruments and Exchange Act, or "FIEA") included a provision similar to U.S. Section 10(b), it was not and is not used to enforce insider trading prohibitions:[51]

Although it was never used in an insider trading case, old Article 58 carried a penalty of no more than three years in prison, or a fine of no more than three million Yen, or both. There are several reasons why this Article was never used. First, the Japanese public did not care who gained and who lost in an insider trading case. Until the 1980's few Japanese individuals bought securities on the market. Securities trading was thought to be "professional work"— a term which has a negative meaning, as in gambler, cheater, or gang member. An honest person would work hard, but not to buy shares—because share prices were controlled by professionals and you never could win. Only professionals played the game with professionals. . . . Second, politicans [sic] raise campaign funds through or take bribes from the securities market. . . . Politicians raise funds not only by manipulation but also by insider trading. Third, and most importantly, the Article 58 wording was too vague and its scope too broad to be used effectively against insider trading. This Article could be applied to any kind of securities, whether listed, traded on the over-the-counter (OTC) market, held privately, or issued by governments or foreigners. Anyone who did any kind of fraudulent act under the Article was liable.[52]

A more direct form of insider trading regulation was implemented in 1988 in response to pressure from the United States and other developed states.[53] Then-current facts indicating a significant instance of insider trading also acted as a catalyst for the 1988 changes:[54] "The 1988 amendments are premised on the concept that insider trading is unfair and violations rightfully should be punished."[55] Accordingly, Japanese insider trading law prohibits corporate insiders knowing material facts about the business of a listed company from making a sale, purchase, or assignment or acquisition for value of a security of the listed company until the material fact has been made public.[56] Interestingly, under Japanese law, although it is unlawful for a tippee receiving material facts about a listed company directly from an insider to trade in the securities of that listed company,[57] the statute does not provide for indirect tippee liability, tipper liability, or liability premised on misappropriation.[58]

Despite Japan's relatively early and comprehensive statutory regulation of securities transactions and insider trading, enforcement of insider trading prohibitions in the wake of the 1988 amendments to the SEL was not immediately forthcoming.[59] In the 1990s enforcement activity increased, although not by any measure to the level of enforcement activity in the United States.[60] This increase in enforcement, like the 1988 adoption of direct insider trading regulation in Japan, was in part a response to pressure from the United States.[61] However, factors inside Japan handicapped enforcement efforts, even as external pressures increased. One commentator offered that "a significant factor in the Japanese government's non-enforcement of its insider trading laws may be the 'widespread participation of Japanese politicians in insider trading.'"[62] Despite these factors, however, with the introduction of civil fines in 2005 amendments to the SEL, Japanese insider trading enforcement has continued to increase in the new millennium.[63] Assessments of these fines are made by an administrative order after an administrative investigation.[64] These orders, unchallenged by the alleged violators, represent significant progress in enforcing insider trading prohibitions in Japan.[65] Press reports indicate that insider trading fines have been doubled from previous rates, adding further retributive and deterrent value to insider trading enforcement in Japan.[66]

German Insider Trading Regulation

Until 1994 Germany had no law against insider trading. Instead, insider trading was regulated informally through nonbinding guidelines in place (adopted in 1970 and amended in 1976 and 1988) and stock exchange rules that prohibited insiders from engaging in certain trading transactions.[67] These informal pronouncements were wholly unsuccessful as a means of combating German insider trading.[68]

Then, in 1994 Germany criminalized insider trading.[69] Germany was the last EC member to pass insider trading regulation, having failed to enact legislation by the June 1, 1992 deadline set by the first EC Directive on insider trading, issued in 1989.[70] A second EC Directive was adopted in 2003, resulting in adjustments to the original regulatory framework.[71]

The United States, acting through the SEC, was an impetus behind both the EC Directive and, ultimately, Germany's law.[72] Other factors also "contributed to the . . . legislative drive to improve the Finanzplatz Deutschland, including increased pressures to compete internationally, harmonize European capital markets, assist international enforcement efforts, and adapt to technological developments."[73] Like Japan, Germany was dealing with capital market dislocations (attributable to various causes, including a then-current insider trading scandal) when it adopted legislative insider trading prohibitions.[74]

Under Germany's insider trading law,[75] "Insiders cannot buy or sell securities based on nonpublic information, cannot convey this information to another person, and cannot recommend that others trade in securities based upon such information. A third person who becomes aware of inside information is also prohibited from such actions."[76]

Enforcement is supervised by a federal agency organized under the German Ministry of Finance—initially, the Federal Supervisory Authority or Federal Supervisory Office ("FSA" or "FSO" or, from the original German, "*BAWe*"), and now the *Bundesanstalt für Finanzdienstleistungsaufsicht* (or "*BaFin*").[77] The law contemplates "a three-tiered surveillance structure on the federal, state (*Lander*), and exchange levels."[78]

In Sum

The United States was an early adopter of insider trading regulation and became the international leader in the diaspora of that regulation among states with developed public securities markets.[79] Not content to rest after achieving its regulatory objectives at home, the United States, through the SEC, has successfully promoted the adoption of its brand of insider trading regulation in other countries, including Japan and Germany:

> Apart from its interest in protecting U.S. investors from insider trading, irrespective of wherever such trading is effected, the SEC has executed its global crusade against insider trading on the assumption that such transactions are inimical to the development of other national markets, and hence the international market. However, no consensus exists among other national regulators and market participants that such transactions have an overall negative effect on their markets. This is most evident from the laxity with which insider trading laws have traditionally been enforced in many of these jurisdictions. Cases in point are Japan, where insider trading laws were instituted under U.S. influence after the Second World War, and Germany where such laws were grudgingly passed pursuant to a directive of the European Community.[80]

The insider trading laws adopted by Japan and Germany are, at their respective cores, built on the same "disclose or abstain" rule enunciated in the United States in the *Cady, Roberts* enforcement action in 1961. Moreover, although actual enforcement of insider trading laws has been inconsistent over time,[81] Japanese and German insider trading laws provide for enforcement through regulatory bodies modeled after the SEC.[82]

A number of commentators have noted these and other similarities in the regulatory frameworks of the three countries and, from this, have assumed regulatory convergence.[83] This assumption, however, proves to be flawed. The central commonalities of the three systems of insider trading regulation do not tell the whole story. A number of legal scholars have started to tell this more detailed version of the story,[84] and this chapter extends that literature.

Divergent Development of Insider Trading Regulation

Despite the common roots and substantial overall similarities of the prohibitions against insider trading in the United States, Japan, and Germany, insider trading doctrine has developed differently among the three countries in a number of important respects.[85] In this part of the chapter, I describe and explain the significance of four of these divergent aspects of insider trading law development: the increasingly central role that agency law—and particularly agency-based duty—has come to play in U.S. insider trading regulation (which has not been transplanted or otherwise replicated in Japan and Germany); the dissimilar ways in which the three countries define who an "insider" (or other regulated person) is; differences in defining the type of information that may trigger the application of the "disclose or abstain" rule; and the distinctive requirement of scienter in U.S. insider trading law. Each of these aspects of insider trading law is important in that the differences contribute meaningfully to an understanding of the interests regulated and protected through insider trading doctrine and to an understanding of the transaction costs associated with trading and communication decisions.

The Unique Requirement of a Breach of Duty in the United States

The regulation of insider trading can be justified along a number of different—but not wholly distinct—policy continuums, including safeguarding fiduciary duties relating to an agent's proper use of her principal's information, promoting fairness in the market for informa-

tion (whether through equal access to or a strict parity of information), and protecting property rights in information.[86] In the United States, despite the SEC's continued promotion of an informational fairness rationale[87] and pointed scholarly critiques urging policy justifications other than the promotion of fiduciary duties,[88] insider trading doctrine has developed as a specific type of securities fraud, primarily rooted in fiduciary and fiduciary-like duty principles that originate in agency law. "Agency law provides a . . . comprehensive and coherent basis for dealing with the problem of insider trading, which is, at bottom, the misuse by faithless agents of information that belongs to others."[89]

Under general principles of agency law, agents are fiduciaries:[90] "An agent has a fiduciary duty to act loyally for the principal's benefit in all matters connected with the agency relationship."[91] Accordingly, "An agent has a duty not to acquire a material benefit from a third party in connection with transactions conducted or other actions taken on behalf of the principal or otherwise through the agent's use of the agent's position."[92] As part of this duty, "An agent has a duty (1) not to use property of the principal for the agent's own purposes or those of a third party; and (2) not to use or communicate confidential information of the principal for the agent's own purposes or those of a third party."[93] Commentary on this last, two-part expression of an agent's fiduciary duty further clarifies the agency law basis for insider trading prohibitions:

> An agent's use of the principal's confidential information for the agent's own purposes breaches the agent's duty as stated in subsection (2) although the agent's use of the information does not necessitate revealing it. Thus, it is a breach of an agent's duty to use confidential information of the principal for the purpose of effecting trades in securities although the agent does not reveal the information in the course of trading.[94]

The agent is liable to the principal for a breach of these prescribed duties.[95] Possible remedies include avoidance of any related contract entered into by the agent, disgorgement to the principal of any benefit (or the value of or proceeds from the benefit) received by the agent, and related damages.[96]

In its opinion in the *O'Hagan* case (affirming the misappropriation theory),[97] the Supreme Court summarized the linkage between these agency law fiduciary duties and the U.S. law regarding insider trading:

> Under the "traditional" or "classical theory" of insider trading liability, § 10(b) and Rule 10b-5 are violated when a corporate insider trades in the securities of his corporation on the basis of material, nonpublic information. Trading on such information qualifies as a "deceptive device" under § 10(b), we have affirmed, because "a relationship of trust and confidence [exists] between the shareholders of a corporation and those insiders who have obtained confidential information by reason of their position with that corporation." That relationship, we recognized, "gives rise to a duty to disclose [or to abstain from trading] because of the 'necessity of preventing a corporate insider from . . . taking unfair advantage of . . . uninformed . . . stockholders.'" . . . The "misappropriation theory" holds that a person commits fraud "in connection with" a securities transaction, and thereby violates § 10(b) and Rule 10b-5, when he misappropriates confidential information for securities trading purposes, in breach of a duty owed to the source of the information. Under this theory, a fiduciary's undisclosed, self-serving use of a principal's information to purchase or sell securities, in breach of a duty of loyalty and confidentiality, defrauds the principal of the exclusive use of that information. In lieu of premising liability on a fiduciary relationship between company insider and purchaser or seller of the company's stock, the misappropriation theory premises liability on a fiduciary-turned-trader's deception of those who entrusted him with access to confidential information.[98]

Because, under U.S. insider trading law, a tippee effectively assumes the duty of the tipper if the tippee knows that the tipper had a duty of trust and confidence and breached that duty in making the tip, tipper and tippee liability also is premised on the breach of a fiduciary duty arising out of agency law.[99] Accordingly, based on Supreme Court doctrine, liability for insider trading in the United States is tied directly to the existence and breach of an agency law–based fiduciary or fiduciary-like duty.[100] As such, U.S. insider trading regulation under Rule 10b-5 is inextricably intertwined with agency law principles.[101]

Yet agency law does not perfectly sync with or fully explain insider trading regulation under Rule 10b-5. Notions of informational fairness—in the form of equal access, rather than information parity—and property right protections play a role (and arguably, based on recent lower court decisions and SEC activity, an increasing role) in regulating insider trading in the United States.[102]

Moreover, fiduciary duty principles do not well explain the law governing insider trading in other countries. Neither Japanese nor German law is rooted in securities fraud doctrine, and neither law ties insider trading liability to the existence and breach of a duty by a fiduciary or even the existence of a fiduciary or fiduciary-like relationship. Rather, these two states and "other jurisdictions soundly have rejected the U.S. fiduciary relationship (or relationship of trust and confidence) model to define the scope of illegal insider trading and tipping."[103] Instead, the insider trading doctrines in Japan, Germany, and elsewhere primarily serve informational fairness objectives. Specifically,

> Many countries opt for an insider trading proscription premised on the "access" doctrine. As a generalization, this standard prohibits insider trading by those who have unequal access to the material nonpublic information. This concept may extend the insider trading prohibition to tippees who receive the subject information from traditional insiders or others who, due to their office, employment, or profession, have access to such information.[104]

Although many in the United States do regard fairness as a significant policy consideration underlying insider trading regulation, the primary fiduciary duty emphasis of U.S. doctrine may compromise—and certainly eclipses—certain fairness considerations as a matter of law.[105]

These different policy emphases in insider trading regulation are significant in that they may be outcome-determinative as to questions of liability. Insider trading liability premised on a breach of fiduciary or fiduciary-like duty may be under- or overinclusive as compared to liability based on informational fairness. For example, a person who, as a result of her position or a personal or professional relationship with a corporate executive, comes to possess material, nonpublic information and trades on that information without any breach of a predicate fiduciary or fiduciary-like duty does not violate U.S. insider trading law under Rule 10b-5, but she is likely or sure to violate insider trading prohibitions under Japanese or German (or other similar) law. Conversely, a person possessing material nonpublic information who has and breaches a fiduciary or fiduciary-like duty by trading in securities violates U.S. insider trading law but may not violate the insider trading law of Japan, for example, if the trader's position does not make him a statutory insider (i.e., as defined under the law, afford him unequal access to inside information).

Disparate policy considerations also have meaning in terms of transaction and litigation planning. Specifically, reliance on nebulous and changing conceptions of fiduciary and fiduciary-like duty under U.S. insider trading law introduces transaction costs in the form of uncertainty and unpredictability into transaction and litigation decision making that are not present under Japanese and German insider trading law.[106] Over time, insider trading law in the United States has developed through SEC rule making and decisional law to incorporate and protect various different fiduciary or fiduciary-like relationships in which a person with knowledge of material, nonpublic information trades securities or tips others who then trade or pass on the tip to someone else. Because the existence and breach of a duty is often more difficult to discern in insider trading cases involving the misappropriation of material, nonpublic information, the SEC adopted a new rule under the 1934 Act in 2000, Rule 10b5–2, that sets forth (in paragraph (b) of the text) three nonexclusive circumstances in which a duty of trust and confidence is deemed to exist.[107] These circumstances include:

1. Whenever a person agrees to maintain information in confidence;
2. Whenever the person communicating the material, nonpublic information and the person to whom it is communicated have a history, pattern, or practice of sharing confidences, such that the recipient of the information knows or reasonably should know that the person communicating the material, nonpublic information expects that the recipient will maintain its confidentiality; or
3. Whenever a person receives or obtains material, nonpublic information from his or her spouse, parent, child, or sibling—provided, however, that the person receiving or obtaining the information may demonstrate that no duty of trust or confidence existed with respect to the information, by establishing that he or she neither knew nor reasonably should have known that the person who was the source of the information expected that the person would keep the information confidential because of the parties' history, pattern, or practice of sharing and maintaining confidences, and because there was no agreement or understanding to maintain the confidentiality of the information.[108]

This rule is at issue in a case that, at the time this chapter went to press, is being contended on appeal from a decision of the United States District Court for the Northern District of Texas, Dallas Division. The case, *SEC v. Cuban*,[109] involves trading in a corporation's securities by a noncontrolling shareholder who was given information about a planned securities offering—clearly material, nonpublic information—by the chief executive officer of the corporation for proper corporate purposes: to encourage further investment by the shareholder in the planned offering. In the action, the SEC asserts that the defendant, Mark Cuban (entrepreneur and owner of the Dallas Mavericks basketball team), had a duty of trust and confidence under Rule 10b5–2(b)(1) because he agreed to maintain the information given to him confidentially. The federal District Court dismissed the action, finding that the agreement referenced in Rule 10b5–2 must impose both duties of nondisclosure and nonuse in order for it to be deceptive and, therefore, consistent with the authority granted to the SEC by the Congress in Section 10(b).[110] Accordingly (and this is important to remember when applying any SEC rule or interpretive pronouncement), the list of circumstances set forth in Rule 10b5–2 may not be definitive on its face and must be read in the context of the authorizing statute—here, the law governing insider trading under Section 10(b).

Moreover, Rule 10b5–2 does not purport to define relationships of trust and confidence for all insider trading activity that is unlawful under Section 10(b) and Rule 10b-5. Although Rule 10b5–2 supplies a list of circumstances in which the requisite duty of trust and confidence exists in misappropriation cases, the list is nonexclusive. Moreover, there is no well-defined list of relationships in the statutes, administrative rules, or decisional law that identifies the liability-creating fiduciary or fiduciary-like duties in cases not involving misappropriation; apart from precedent and nonbinding guidance provided in federal court opinions, the law of agency, which in theory may evolve from case to case, provides the outer limits of a definition in those contexts.[111] Accordingly, it may not be easy for a transaction participant to know or understand in advance that he or she owes or is breaching a fiduciary or fiduciary-like duty that may subject him or her to insider trading liability under any of the existing theories. Similarly, enforcement agents and potential private plaintiffs may not find it easy to identify and prove the existence and breach of a fiduciary or fiduciary-like duty in

order to plead and prove a claim. Conversely, informational fairness principles in Japanese and German insider trading regulation are largely articulated in the relevant statutory provisions, thus enhancing certainty and predictability for transaction and litigation planners.

Policy-related uncertainty and unpredictability under U.S. insider trading doctrine is exacerbated by enforcement activities undertaken at the margins of allegedly proscribed activity. Over the years, criminal prosecutions brought by the U.S. Department of Justice as well as administrative or judicial enforcement actions brought by the SEC have attempted to expand the scope of potential liability by (among other things) adding to the fiduciary and fiduciary-like duties that may be culled from decisional law. The Department of Justice's prosecution of the *O'Hagan* case and the SEC's enforcement actions against Martha Stewart (as the purported tippee of an alleged misappropriator) and Mark Cuban are salient examples of these expansive interpretations of U.S. insider trading policy and doctrine.[112]

Defining Insiders and Others Whose Conduct Is Regulated

To achieve underlying national policy objectives, operative insider trading law in the United States, Japan, and Germany regulates a range of securities trading conduct in which specific types of people are engaged. The market participants whose conduct is regulated under each state's law are different, and they are identified with varying levels of specificity.

Under U.S. law, an insider (defined broadly to include classical insiders, tippers, tippees, and misappropriators—the last of these sometimes referred to as "outsiders") is a person with a direct or derivative duty of trust and confidence emanating from agency law.[113] The specific positions or relationships that create insider status are defined in Rule 10b5–2 and through judicial decisions in insider trading cases. It is widely acknowledged that key corporate executives, corporate directors, and controlling shareholders—

as well as corporate advisers (like lawyers and accountants) are insiders of the corporation they control or serve.[114] Because it is unclear under U.S. law whether U.S. government officials have a fiduciary or fiduciary-like duty that would be breached by trading or tipping, federal legislation was introduced in the United States to prohibit (a) trading while in possession of material, nonpublic information and tipping material, nonpublic information by members of the executive Branch, members of Congress, and congressional staff and (b) trading by tippees of material, nonpublic information obtained from the Executive Branch or Congress.[115]

Masanori Hayashi has noted that "Japanese law on insider trading, codified in the *Shoken Torihikiho*, follows the U.S. statutory and common law schemes in some respects."[116] Japanese insider trading law defines insiders to include corporate officers, employees, agents, and shareholders having access to corporate records; those with statutory authority over the corporation; and those who come to know material facts in contracting with the corporation (and the officers, employees, and agents of contracting parties that are entities).[117] This list of regulated individuals and entities includes potential traders who are not regulated under U.S. insider trading law. As Franklin A. Gevurtz explained,

> The traditional theory in the United States would not pick up individuals obtaining information through a government supervisory role, as does the Japanese prohibition. Moreover, individuals obtaining information by virtue of a contractual relationship with the corporation would not count as insiders of that corporation under *Dirks* unless there is an expectation that they will hold the information in confidence. By contrast, under Japanese law, a contractual relation giving access to non-public information evidently is enough regardless of the expectation of confidentiality.[118]

However, Japan's statutory list of insiders also may exclude potential traders who would be deemed insiders under U.S. law:

Japanese law does not prohibit trading by persons who gain information through professional relationships other than with the corporation whose stock they trade, or with a corporation making a tender offer for the stock they trade. Of course, in many instances—such as when attorneys and financial advisors obtain non-public information through working on the personal behalf of insiders—traders who obtain information through professional relationships could be liable as tippees under the Japanese statute.[119]

Japanese insider trading law does regulate trading by tippees—but only trades made by tippees who receive material, nonpublic information directly from insiders.[120] In both cases, these regulated persons (individuals and entities) are listed and described directly in the statute. Unlike U.S. law, the Japanese statute regulates neither tippers nor misappropriators.[121]

German insider trading law takes the broadest approach to this issue, prohibiting (1) the use of material, nonpublic information in trading, making trading recommendations, or inducing trading and (2) the tipping of material nonpublic information by any individual or entity.[122] Although prior versions of the German statute formally separated regulated insiders into primary and secondary insider groupings to the same (or a substantially similar) effect, the current statute is efficient and streamlined, relying merely on its definition of inside information and its articulation of proscribed actions to identify those whose conduct is regulated.[123] The German conception of insider status seemingly incorporates all those who are insiders under U.S. law and Japanese law.[124] Its breadth is a direct result of EC pronouncements[125] and may be a reaction to (among other things) concerns under the prior statute that government officials who leak material, nonpublic information to market participants may not have been liable for that conduct.[126]

The varied notions of an insider (or other person regulated as an insider) under the insider trading laws of the United States, Japan, and Germany, like insider trading policy distinctions among the three countries, have both substantive and process-oriented implications. In fact, because U.S. insider trading law protects an agency law fiduciary duty principally by defining insiders as persons who have that duty, the earlier noted significance of national policy differences plays out in part through each country's conception of the insider.

The differing bases for determining insider status under U.S., Japanese, and German law may be outcome-determinative; different people will be held liable for trading, tipping, and other related activities under each system of insider trading regulation. For example, government officials who trade while in possession of material, nonpublic information may not be liable under U.S. law but are liable under Japanese and German law.[127] In addition, tippers, remote tippees, and misappropriators who trade on the basis of material, nonpublic information are liable under U.S. insider trading law and under the German statute but are not liable under the Japanese statute.[128]

The different national conceptions of an insider also generate different transaction costs for transaction and litigation planners. Under U.S. insider trading law, transaction and litigation planners need to assess whether traders possessing material, nonpublic information or those disclosing material, nonpublic information to others are among the direct or indirect fiduciaries for whom trading and tipping is proscribed. The assessment of fiduciary status on the part of a potential insider is a predicate to recognizing a protected agency law fiduciary or fiduciary-like duty. Accordingly, the earlier-described transaction costs arising from the unpredictability and uncertainty associated with identifying the predicate fiduciary or fiduciary-like duty are similarly and equally applicable here.[129]

Materiality and Other Measures of the Level of Significance of Nonpublic Information

Under general principles of insider trading law, an insider or tippee must trade while in possession of material, nonpublic information or a tipper must selectively disclose material, nonpublic information in order to violate the law. Although there are sometimes questions about whether a specified type of information is a "fact" or whether particular facts are public,[130] more significant questions typically arise as to whether particular facts are material. Edmund W. Kitch noted that "In the insider-trading context, materiality has to do with the bar against insiders profiting from inside information. It deals with the question: When has enough information been disclosed so that insiders are free to trade?"[131] Or, conversely, when is nonpublic information possessed while trading with others or used in tipping others important or significant enough that it will subject the insider trader or tipper and any tippees to liability?

Under U.S. insider trading law, a fact is material if it is substantially likely that a reasonable investor would find the fact important in making an investment decision or if it is substantially likely that a reasonable investor would find that revealing the fact will significantly alter the total mix of publicly available information.[132] Material information may comprise historical and speculative, contingent, or other forward-looking facts and may be quantitatively or qualitatively important or significant:[133]

> To violate insider-trading laws, the corporate insider must use *material*, nonpublic information. Information is material if there is a "substantial likelihood that a reasonable investor would consider it important in making an investment decision." . . . While speculative or "soft" information is often immaterial, courts have been reluctant to find it per se immaterial. This court . . . found that an uncertain stock price increase was material, even though speculative, because "it would have been considered important in making investment decisions."[134]

The materiality of speculative or contingent forward-looking facts is assessed using a specialized test:[135] "information about future events is material if—taking into account both the probability of those events and their potential importance—a reasonable investor would regard the information as 'significantly' different from the information already made public."[136] Materiality is a mixed question of law and fact and is not generally deemed to be an appropriate subject for summary judgment.[137]

Japanese insider trading regulation approaches the subject of materiality in a somewhat more concrete fashion than U.S. law does, but the Japanese rule ends up being quite like the U.S. standard in substance. Specifically, the Japanese statute defines materiality (a "Material Fact Pertaining to Business or Other Matters") to include items on a listed set of facts, excluding any transaction or event (specified from among certain listed facts) "regarded under the criteria provided by a Cabinet Office Ordinance as one that may have only minor influence on investors' Investment Decisions."[138] Among the listed facts under the Japanese statutes are various transactions and events involving both the issuer and its subsidiaries, including certain expected categories of corporate finance transaction (e.g., securities offerings, business combination transactions, recapitalizations, buybacks, stock splits, dividends, dissolution), damages created by disaster, significant changes in shareholder composition, a change in position that could cause delisting or deregistration, significant changes in financial condition or results from operations, and "material facts concerning operation, business or property of the Listed Company, etc. that may have a significant influence on investors' Investment Decisions."[139] The list also may be enhanced in a certain limited respect by a Cabinet Order prescribing that certain occurrences are material.[140] Accordingly, contingent or speculative forward-looking information, for example, may be material under Japanese law even though the listed types of information generally reference an actual board decision to proceed with an action. As one legal scholar summarized,

Japanese law attempts much greater specificity. The Japanese insider trading statute contains a laundry list of important facts that can trigger the insider trading prohibition. These include: management decisions about issuing securities, reductions in capital, stock splits, alterations in dividends, mergers, purchases or sales in whole or in part of a business, dissolution, and marketing a new product; disasters or damages to the corporation; changes in principal shareholders; events causing delisting of a security; differences between actual and forecasted sales and profits; any other events listed by Cabinet Ordinance; and, finally, other important facts involving the management, business or assets of the corporation which would materially affect investment decisions.[141]

Although the greater specificity in the Japanese statute offers more certainty in making certain materiality determinations, the potential for exclusions under Cabinet Office Ordinance criteria and the catchall category for transactions and events that may influence investor decision making may mean that the facial appearance of certainty is illusory.

Interestingly, the statute does restrict the catchall category to facts "concerning operation, business or property of the Listed Company, etc." Conversely, the materiality formulation under U.S. insider trading law is not restricted to corporate or corporate-related facts. In fact, U.S. legal scholars and the media have paid significant attention to the possibility that personal facts concerning executive officers of public companies also may be deemed material under Rule 10b-5.[142] Few countries have embraced the all-encompassing "importance test" reflected in the materiality standard applicable in U.S. insider trading cases or, for that matter, the arguably narrower "significant influence" test applicable to unlisted events under Japan's insider trading statute.[143] However, German insider trading regulation is apparently converging toward these materiality formulations.

German insider trading law defines materiality in the context of an overall definition of "inside information" (which also encompasses a definition of the nonpublic nature of inside information). Specifically, the statute provides that

Inside information is any specific information about circumstances which are not public knowledge relating to one or more issuers of insider securities, or to the insider securities themselves, which, if it became publicly known, would likely have a significant effect on the stock exchange or market price of the insider security.[144]

The statute further offers that

Specifically, inside information refers to information about circumstances which are not public knowledge . . . , which
 1. is related to orders by third parties for the purchase or sale of financial instruments or
 2. is related to derivatives . . . relating to commodities and which market participants would expect to receive in accordance with the accepted practice of the markets in question.[145]

This statutory definition expressly relies on market price effects as a primary determinant of materiality. Curiously, however, the statute goes on to offer that "Such a likelihood is deemed to exist if a reasonable investor would take the information into account for investment decisions."[146] This latter formulation or guidance was not in earlier versions of the statute[147] and brings the German formulation closer to the U.S. standard. Moreover, German law incorporates the concept that forward-looking information can be material by providing that, under the definition quoted above, "The term circumstances . . . also applies to cases which may reasonably be expected to come into existence in the future."[148]

However, the German statute is narrower than the U.S. formulation (and more similar to the language in the Japanese materiality catchall) in an important respect: It restricts the content of the information at issue to that "relating to one or more issuers of insider securities, or to the insider securities themselves."[149] Accordingly, although the relevant terms may be susceptible to broad interpretations, it may be harder to argue that nonpublic personal facts, for example, are inside information under the German insider trading law than it is to make the same argument under U.S. law.[150]

Under the insider trading regimes in each country—the United States, Japan, and Germany—insiders are not liable for trading while in possession of insignificant nonpublic information. Approaches to the determination of the requisite threshold level of informational materiality vary from country to country; yet under current insider trading rules, the approaches taken in the United States, Japan, and Germany converge to some extent around an investor-oriented perspective of the importance of information possessed by an insider (or other regulated person) at the time of a trade or shared by an insider in a tip.

Still, as this descriptive comparative analysis of insider trading laws suggests, subtle but important differences in materiality exist or, based on enforcement activity, may exist. For example, as noted above, U.S., Japanese, and German approaches to materiality apparently differ in substance on whether or to what extent personal information about a corporate executive may be material. The United States has a one-tiered test for materiality in this context that is alternatively expressed in two ways. Under U.S. law, there must be a substantial likelihood that the personal information would be important to the reasonable investor in deciding whether to buy or sell the issuer's securities or, stated in the alternative, there must be a substantial likelihood that disclosure of the personal information would significantly alter the total mix of information in the market.[151] One can imagine circumstances where personal information about a public company executive officer is (at least arguably) material.[152]

By contrast, Japan and Germany both apply a two-tiered test for materiality in the context of personal facts: A threshold test restricts substantive content (although the restrictions now may be less significant under German law) and a secondary test gauges importance or significance. The Japanese approach is, perhaps, the most narrow in this regard, in that the personal information must constitute "material facts concerning operation, business or property of the Listed Company, etc. that may have a significant influence on investors' Investment Decisions."[153]

German law requires that the personal information relate "to one or more issuers of insider securities, or to the insider securities themselves" and that the personal information "would likely have a significant effect on the stock exchange or market price of the insider security," which the likely effect is deemed to exist if "a reasonable investor would take the information into account for investment decisions."[154] As a threshold issue in Japan and Germany, it may be difficult for a public enforcement agent or (as applicable) a private litigant to establish that a personal fact meets the applicable content restrictions. Even assuming proof of the requisite content connection, one must also then successfully argue that the personal facts satisfy either the "significant influence" test (in Japan) or the modified "price-effect" test (in Germany). It is unclear from the face of the respective Japanese and German statutes how easy or difficult it may be to successfully make that argument. However, it appears to be easier to make the argument in the United States under the one-tiered test.

Although transaction costs associated with materiality determinations involving personal facts are likely to be high in all three countries profiled here, under most other circumstances, the relatively "open architecture" of the materiality concept under U.S. insider trading laws is likely to generate more transaction costs than the more well-defined approaches to determining materiality under Japanese and German insider trading law.[155] The elements of materiality in the United States, as a combined issue of law and fact, evolve incrementally as a matter of federal common law in response to specific cases brought before the federal courts. As a result, materiality determinations under U.S. law are fraught with uncertainty and unpredictability.[156] Although similar determinations made under Japanese and German insider trading law may not be certain or predictable, the more detailed, tailored statutes in these civil law states provide more guidance in the form of anchoring concepts (in Japan, a list of material events and transactions, and in Germany, a focus on significant market price effects), thereby enhancing

the prospects for certain and predictable results and limiting transaction costs incurred by transaction and litigation planners.

The Distinctive Requirement of Scienter in the United States

Under U.S. insider trading law, an insider who breaches a fiduciary duty by trading in a corporation's securities while in possession of material, nonpublic information or by tipping material, nonpublic information is not violating the law unless the insider acts with scienter—a state of mind that involves an awareness of the propensity to deceive investors and at least a reckless (and certainly an intentional) disregard of the probability that the actions taken will result in investor deception.[157] Similarly, a tippee of material, nonpublic information is not liable absent scienter.[158] This element of unlawful insider trading in the United States emanates from the nature of insider trading regulation in the United States as a type of securities fraud. The deception necessary to find illegal insider trading as fraudulent conduct under Section 10(b) and Rule 10b-5 requires some level of intentional conduct, at least as construed by the U.S. Supreme Court.[159] Although the SEC adopted a rule in 2000—Rule 10b5-1[160]—that many believe changes the nature of the scienter requirement (making it a weaker requirement), this rule has not been tested at the margins at the Supreme Court level.[161] The meaning of Rule 10b5-1 is, in fact, quite unclear.[162]

Because insider trading regulation in Japan and Germany is not based in the law of fraud, there is no equivalent requirement for a state of mind in either state's statutes. Both Japanese and German law is violated if an insider who possessed material, nonpublic information trades or discloses that information before it is publicly disseminated, regardless of that insider's state of mind.[163]

The scienter requirement may be the largest difference among the three states' laws—and the biggest difference between U.S. insider trading regulation and insider trading regulation in the rest of the world. Substantively, the scienter requirement makes it less likely that an insider trader or tipper, or an insider's tippee, will be held liable for violating the insider trading prohibitions under Section 10(b) and Rule 10b-5. Scienter represents an additional requirement for the Department of Justice, SEC, and private plaintiffs to meet, and it is difficult to prove in the absence of a clear statement or clear conduct establishing the actor's intent (although perhaps less so after the adoption of Rule 10b5–1). Accordingly, the scienter requirement narrows the scope of potential liability under U.S. law in relation to the laws of Japan and Germany, where, absent scienter, facts would support liability under the laws of all three countries, whereas scienter may excuse an insider from liability in the United States.

Difficulties in defining and proving scienter increase uncertainty and unpredictability in insider trading enforcement in the United States. The definitional issues will be explored and, no doubt, settled through federal court decisions over time, but the proof issues will remain. In each case, however, the scienter requirement adds transaction costs to the U.S. insider trading compliance and enforcement systems. These costs are not present in the Japanese and German regulatory schemes.

Fairness as a Way of Understanding Insider Trading Regulation

Although there are common origins of and bases for insider trading regulation in different states, there also are significant differences among state insider trading prohibitions. It is one thing to describe these similarities and differences and how they operate; it is another thing altogether to understand them in a way that enables optimal regulation in a global market. This part of the chapter looks at comparative insider trading regulation through a fairness lens in an effort to better understand, and an attempt to bridge, the differences among state laws governing insider trading. As an outlier, the United States is our starting point and our comparative base.

The U.S. Supreme Court is credited with overruling fairness as a defining policy basis for U.S. insider trading regulation in the *Chiarella* and *Dirks* cases,[164] but it is possible to view the Court's decisions in *Chiarella* and *Dirks* as merely focusing on a different conception of fairness. A number of scholars have approached the analysis of U.S. insider trading principles from this angle. Professor Kimberly Krawiec, for example, cogently described current U.S. insider trading regulation from a fairness standpoint:

> Insider trading law currently attempts to draw the line between legal and illegal informational advantages by reference to breach of a fiduciary duty. Because the gathering of information through a fiduciary breach is not considered socially productive behavior, there is no identifiable romantic author whose diligence and effort must be rewarded through permission to profit from such informational advantages. Information gained through a fiduciary breach, therefore, is considered part of the public sphere and, along with other public sphere privileges, such as access to the criminal justice system or the right to vote, must be shared equally among marketplace participants. This egalitarian goal is accomplished by forcing those in possession of secret knowledge attained through a fiduciary breach to disclose that information prior to trading. By contrast, nonpublic information gained through means other than a fiduciary breach is considered socially useful research that must be rewarded by permitting the information possessor to profit from her superior trading knowledge. Such information, therefore, is subconsciously delegated to the private sphere where, along with other private sphere resources, such as wealth, experience, or education, equality is not expected. Consequently, those in possession of material nonpublic information attained through means other than a fiduciary breach are permitted to trade on that information without disclosure to their trading partners.[165]

We may say, then, that U.S. insider trading regulation attempts to be fair to both those trading in the market without the benefit of material, nonpublic information and to those who acquire material, nonpublic information in a socially productive way.

In legal scholarship, another, more egalitarian form of fairness in insider trading regulation has been termed "level playing field" fairness, and the equal access informational fairness at the root of most insider trading regulation may be described in those terms.[166] Japan's insider trading rules, for example, were designed to promote this type of fairness. The fairness of an equal access principle can be explained in a manner similar to that used to explain the fairness of the fiduciary duty rule in the United States:

equality of access advocates maintain that informational advantages that cannot be lawfully eroded through the expenditure of sufficient time and effort should be prohibited. . . . [i]nformational advantages that cannot be lawfully eroded through the expenditure of sufficient time and effort, such as, for example, the informational advantages possessed by a corporate insider or misappropriator, are not considered socially useful research. . . . Such information, therefore, is part of the public sphere and must be shared with other securities traders before the information possessor is permitted to exploit her informational advantage through securities trading. Consequently, trading based on informational advantages that cannot be lawfully eroded would be prohibited under an equality of access approach to insider trading regulation. Equality of access advocates contend with the informational advantages enjoyed by market professionals by arguing that, although every investor does not have the opportunity to become a corporate insider or misappropriator or a tippee of an insider or misappropriator, every investor could purchase the services of an investment analyst. Investment analysts, market makers, exchange members, and others who are assumed to provide socially useful research are thus romantic authors whose beneficial behavior must be rewarded though permission to profit from their informational advantages. In-

formation attained through the research of such parties, therefore, is considered part of the private sphere and can be freely exploited in the pursuit of trading profits.[167]

Japan's insider trading rules attempt to provide equal access by identifying and regulating the conduct of those who have advantaged access to material, nonpublic information. Japanese insider trading regulation does not, however, provide for comprehensive equal access, in that it (1) may not accurately and completely identify those with privileged access to material, nonpublic information, (2) allows insiders to personally benefit from tipping (punishing only the tippee), (3) permits misappropriators to trade for personal benefit, and (4) embodies a narrow definition of material, nonpublic information. Each of these aspects of the Japanese insider trading regime may enable traders or tippers with privileged informational access to benefit from that privilege at the expense of other market participants.

Although the fiduciary duty rationale that operates in the United States and the equal access rationale exemplified in Japan each express a different—but equally valid—conception of fairness in insider trading regulation, neither helps the investor who believes that she is being treated inequitably because others in the market have an information advantage over her.[168] Some analysts have noted that "A broader 'fairness' objection to insider trading . . . regards the trade as unfair—and dishonest—based upon the simple unavailability of inside information to all parties. . . . The other party's decision to consent arises from information of which he is aware, not from information that is merely available to him."[169] This fairness objection is known as the parity of information rationale and is the policy that underlies the German insider trading statute. It is the most helpful conception of fairness to the disadvantaged investor and the easiest type of fairness to explain. Here, equity is based not on an equal access to or availability of information but, rather, on an equal awareness of information. German insider trading law exemplifies this policy in that all possessors of material, nonpublic information are restricted from trading and tipping, regardless of whether they have preferential access to that information.

How do these three insider trading regimes correspond with larger, more universal notions of fairness, outside the realm of insider trading regulation? U.S. insider trading regulation and Japanese insider trading regulation do comport well with a Rawlsian conception of fairness. According to Rawls, insider trading regulation is fair if it (1) allows for equality of opportunity and (2) provides the greatest benefit to those least advantaged. These are the two components, as you will recall, of the second principle of justice.[170] Rawls admitted, however, that "Whether the aims of the second principle are realized is . . . difficult to ascertain. To some degree, these matters are always open to reasonable differences of opinion; they depend on inference and judgment in assessing complex social and economic information."[171]

Distinctions based on fiduciary or fiduciary-like duties (including the related definition of an insider) or based on advantaged access to information provide some foundation for a claim that the "disclose or abstain" rule provides equal opportunity. If a person with a duty of trust and confidence (in the United States) or a statutory insider (in Japan) possesses nonpublic information that is significantly likely to be important to a reasonable investor, then he must disclose it before trading (or uncomfortably rely on a lack of scienter as a defense); if anyone else possesses the same type of information, the information must have been available to all for the taking, even if only some are lucky or smart enough to have acquired it. Broad materiality standards like those operating under U.S. law accentuate equal opportunity by enlarging the scope of information that must be disclosed before trading may be undertaken. Yet, Rawls noted that it is not enough that opportunities are available to all; rather, it should also be true that "all should have a fair chance to attain them."[172] Fiduciary or fiduciary-like relation-

ships and corporate or other positions creating unequal access to information are not fairly attainable by all, evidencing a lack of equal opportunity.

Insider trading regulation based on a parity of information, by its very essence, provides investors with equal opportunity in the market. We can say that German insider trading regulation, which is based on information equality, affords equal opportunity to all potential market participants because each is treated in exactly the same way. Unless everyone in the market possesses the same material information that an individual trader has, the individual trader must abstain from trading or tipping others.

Assuming that equal opportunity exists, insider trading regulation may not always supply the greatest benefit to the least advantaged. Even if we view U.S. insider trading law as providing equal opportunity to those seeking material information, for example, allowing insiders without scienter to use material, nonpublic information in breach of a duty of trust and confidence appears to weight the regulatory system toward insiders—those advantaged by their informational access. Those who have greater access to material, nonpublic information are permitted under U.S. law to use it negligently to their own advantage. Moreover, U.S. and Japanese insider trading regulation may be faulted for not providing the greatest benefits to the least advantaged because both U.S. and Japanese law allow those who have advantaged access to information (but are not regulated as insiders, tippees, or misappropriators) to trade for personal benefit to the disadvantage of other traders in the market.[173] Japanese insider trading law is, however, on its face, better than U.S. insider trading law at allocating benefits to the least advantaged market participants in that its definition of insiders is specifically designed to include those who are advantaged in their access to material, nonpublic information. In defining insider status by reference to a duty of trust and confidence, U.S. insider trading regulation may be both over- and underinclusive as a measure of those who are advantaged in their access to material, nonpublic information. Yet in both the United States and Japan, investors without practical access to material, nonpublic information, as the least advantaged market participants in the insider trading analysis, may not be afforded the greatest benefit. Conversely, informationally disadvantaged investors who can, through effort or expense, obtain material, nonpublic information remain incentivized to do so, and trading through these entrepreneurial investors would increase available information in the market, thus making market prices more efficient.

Insider trading regulation based on equal information does appear to provide the greatest benefit to the least advantaged. By taking trading and tipping benefits away from those in the market with informational advantages, German insider trading law unambiguously reallocates inequities in the market toward those with no information. In doing so, however, German insider trading law removes any incentive on the part of informationally disadvantaged investors to increase their wealth and market efficiency by expending time and money to acquire material, nonpublic information and use it in trading. Because Rawls's framework does not demand formal equality and desires to preserve, to the extent possible, benefits inuring to those who work for them, this disincentive makes us think hard about the fairness of informational parity as a basis for insider trading regulation.

Nevertheless, German law most closely resembles the Rawlsian notion of fairness in regulation. It is the regulatory system that investors would most frequently choose from behind the veil of ignorance—without knowing whether they would be, in a particular circumstance, advantaged or disadvantaged (although Rawls does not apparently intend that legislative determinations, as opposed to agreement on principles applicable to those judgments, be made from behind the veil of ignorance). This is true notwithstanding potential informational efficiencies created through trades made by the best-informed investors. Fairness of price cannot be assessed in isolation or to the exclusion of fairness of position and outcome.

Recall now the two alternative non-Rawlsian notions of fairness mentioned earlier in the essay—one that assesses fairness based on a balancing of individual interests for the good of society as a whole and one that assesses fairness based on the equal or equitable treatment of individuals.[174] How do insider trading regimes stack up under these two notions of fairness?

As outlined in this essay and described by Professor Krawiec, U.S. insider trading regulation does attempt to balance individual interests—those of insiders (traders and tippers), tippees, and misappropriators (in each case, with and without scienter) as well as those of actual and prospective investors—for greater societal good. However, U.S. insider trading law does not provide for equal treatment of market participants. Among other things, U.S. insider trading law permits unequal access to and use of material, nonpublic information by nonfiduciaries that have privileged access to information, and it permits insiders, tippees, and misappropriators without scienter to trade or tip (as applicable) without having to publish and disseminate the material, nonpublic information they possess.

Japanese insider trading regulation has similar attributes in these respects. Japan's legal rules endeavor to balance the interests of multiple investor constituencies (statutory insiders and other actual and prospective investors), although we may question the judgments made in the failure of these rules to regulate, for example, tippers and misappropriators. Moreover, Japanese insider trading regulation does not achieve equal treatment. Noninsiders, tippers, and misappropriators are all free to reap personal benefits from their access to material, nonpublic information.

Conversely, German insider trading rules represent a less clear balancing of interests for the greater good of society. Little, if any, value appears to be placed on entrepreneurial efforts to acquire material, nonpublic information to enhance individual wealth and improve market price efficiencies. However, as previously observed, German law does come the closest to achieving equal treatment by valuing information equality in securities trading.

Conclusion

The insider trading rules of various states have both core similarities and important differences. A fairness analysis of these laws exposes the various implications of these extant similarities and differences. U.S., Japanese, and German insider trading regulation, as three exemplars, embody different conceptions of fairness, each likely emanating from both culture and context.[175]

Understanding these regulatory differences in a fairness context provides important information to those who desire to effectuate meaningful international insider trading regulation. Effective international insider trading regulation will require consensus around the type of fairness that the regulatory scheme should be designed to achieve as well as, for example, agreement on and implementation of effectual enforcement. This represents an enormous—perhaps even insurmountable—challenge for lawmakers with different cultural and contextual backgrounds.

Rawls's work is relevant here, too. In *The Law of Peoples*, Rawls posited that eight key principles, determined from the original position (behind the veil of ignorance), govern an international effort to achieve a fair cooperative society.[176] If there is agreement on these foundational principles among people with different cultures who have experienced life under different circumstances, then there is hope for an eventual agreement on a unifying conception of fairness that would enable the construction and implementation of international insider trading regulation.

NOTES

1. Notably, Henry Manne is among many law and economics scholars that decry fairness as a policy underpinning for insider trading regulation. *See, e.g.,* HENRY G. MANNE, INSIDER TRADING AND THE STOCK MARKET (1966). This essay does not engage the debate over fairness policy in insider trading regulation (although brief reference is made to market efficiencies); rather, it uses conceptions of fairness as a sorting device for the substantive outcomes of different insider trading regimes.

2. International Organization of Securities Commissions, *Objectives and Principles of Securities Regulation*, at 5 (May 2003), *available at* www.iosco.org/library/pubdocs/pdf/IOSCOPD154.pdf ("Investors should be protected from misleading, manipulative or fraudulent practices, including insider trading, front running or trading ahead of customers and the misuse of client assets.").

3. Jeffrey L. Dunoff, *Fairness in the World Economy: US Perspectives on International Trade Relations*, 101 AM. J. INT'L. L. 907, 908 (2007) (Book Review) ("Fairness is a multifaceted concept with many dimensions and many meanings."). Charles C. Cox & Kevin S. Fogarty, *Bases of Insider Trading Law*, 49 OHIO ST. L. J. 353, 360 (1988).

4. *Id.; see also* Judith G. Greenberg, *Insider Trading and Family Values*, 4 WM & MARY J. OF WOMEN & L. 303, 349 (1998) ("The legitimacy of market transactions depends on the assumption that the parties have freely and voluntarily agreed.").

5. *See* BLACK'S LAW DICTIONARY 560 (Bryan A. Garner ed., 7th ed. 1999) (defining "equity" as "fairness, impartiality," among other things).

6. Merriam-Webster Online Dictionary, May 18, 2010, *available at* www.merriam-webster.com/dictionary/fair.

7. *See, e.g.,* JOHN RAWLS, JUSTICE AS FAIRNESS 4–5 (Erin Kelly ed., 2001).

8. *See, e.g., id.* at 7–8.

9. *Id.* at 18–19.

10. *Id.* at 19.

11. *Id.*

12. *Id.* at 85–89.

13. *Id.* at 88 ("[T]he veil of ignorance prevents the parties from knowing the (comprehensive) doctrines and conceptions of the good of the persons they represent.").

14. *Id.* at 87.

15. *Id.* at 42–43. The principles are applied in an ordered fashion; "the first principle is prior to the second; also, in the second principle fair equality of opportunity is prior to the difference principle." *Id.* at. 43.

16. *Id.* at 48.

17. Robert G. Bone, *Agreeing to Fair Process: The Problem with Contractarian Theories of Procedural Fairness*, 83 B.U.L. REV. 485, 495 (2003).

18. 17 C.F.R. § 240.10b-5 (2010). Rule 10b-5 was adopted by the U.S. Securities and Exchange Commission under Section 10(b) of the Securities Exchange Act of 1934, as amended. 15 U.S.C. § 78j(b) (2007).

19. *See* Amir N. Licht, *International Diversity in Securities Regulation: Roadblocks on the Way to Convergence*, 20 CARDOZO L. REV. 227, 233 (1998) ("[A] growing number of countries have adopted laws which preclude insider trading, originally at the behest of the SEC and today largely under the auspices of IOSCO."); George C. Nnona, *International Insider Trading: Reassessing the*

Propriety and Feasibility of the U.S. Regulatory Approach, 27 N.C. J. INT'L L. & COM. REG. 185, 201 (2001) ("The SEC has . . . exported U.S. insider trading laws to other jurisdictions, as part of the crusade to stem insider trading globally.").

20. *Id.*; Robert A. Prentice, *The Inevitability of a Strong SEC*, 91 CORNELL L. REV. 775, 837 (2006) ("Within roughly the past fifteen years, EU members, Japan, China, and other countries have prohibited insider trading in similar circumstances and on substantially the same grounds as the United States.").

21. *E.g.*, Marc I. Steinberg, *Insider Trading, Selective Disclosure, and Prompt Disclosure: A Comparative Analysis*, 22 U. PA. J. INT'L ECON. L. 635, 666 (2001) ("Not surprisingly, other jurisdictions soundly have rejected the U.S. fiduciary relationship (or relationship of trust and confidence) model to define the scope of illegal insider trading and tipping."); *id.* at 664 ("[C]ontrary to the U.S. definition, the concept of materiality is connected to the information's impact on market price.").

22. *Chiarella v. United States*, 445 U.S. 222, 231–35 (1980); *see* Alexander F. Loke, *From the Fiduciary Theory to Information Abuse: The Changing Fabric of Insider Trading Law in the U.K., Australia and Singapore*, 54 AM. J. COMP. L. 123, 124 (2006) ("The fiduciary theory animates to a considerable degree the U.S. federal law against insider trading."); Dimity Kingsford Smith, *The Same Yet Different: Australian and United States Online Investing Regulation*, 37 U. TOL. L. REV. 461, 493 n.222 (2006) (noting Australia's deviation from the fiduciary rationale used in the United States in favor of "an information parity or market fairness approach").

23. *United States v. O'Hagan*, 521 U.S. 642, 652 (1997) (identifying those subject to misappropriation liability for insider trading by reference to "breach of a duty owed to the source of the information"—"a duty of loyalty and confidentiality"); *Dirks v. SEC*, 463 U.S. 646, 664 (1983) (noting that tippee liability depends on a predicate breach of duty by the tipper/insider); *Chiarella*, 445 U.S. at 230 (classifying those with "a relationship of trust and confidence"—those "who have an obligation to place the shareholder's welfare before their own"—as classical insiders); *see* Eric Engle, *The EU Means Business: A Survey of Legal Challenges and Opportunities in the New Europe*, 4 DEPAUL BUS. & COMM. L.J. 351, 370–71 (2006) (noting the more concrete, functional-role definition under the 1989 and 2003 European Union insider trading directives); Joan MacLeod Heminway, *Materiality Guidance in the Context of Insider Trading: A Call for Action*, 52 AM. U. L. REV. 1131, 1134 n.11 (2003) (summarizing the U.S. conception of an insider).

24. *Basic Inc. v. Levinson*, 485 U.S. 224, 231–32 (1988); *see* Heminway, *supra* note 23, at 1158–60 (describing the status of a "market effect" test under U.S. insider trading law).

25. *Ernst & Ernst v. Hochfelder*, 425 U.S. 185, 193 n.12 (1976). *See* Donald C. Langevoort, *Reflections on Scienter (and the Securities Fraud Case Against Martha Stewart That Never Happened)*, 10 LEWIS & CLARK L. REV. 1, 13 (2006) ("Defining scienter with respect to insider trading has been controversial, with courts and the SEC disagreeing about whether it must be shown that the defendant 'used' the inside information to profit (i.e., that he traded because of the information) or whether mere possession of the information is enough, without regard to motivation.").

26. Insider trading also is regulated by and under Section 16(b) of the 1934 Act. 15 U.S.C. § 78p(b) (2007). In addition, Rule 14e-3 regulates insider trading in connection with tender offers. 17 C.F.R. § 240.14e-3 (2010). Further, disclosures made to brokers, dealers, investment advisers, investment companies, and other specified potential securities traders are addressed under Regulation FD. 17 C.F.R. § 243.100–03 (2010). Although these regulatory provisions relate to the insider trading prohibitions under Section 10(b) and Rule 10b-5, the elements of each rule and the remedies provided, among other things, differ from those under Section 10(b) and Rule 10b-5. Accordingly, these other related rules are not addressed in this chapter.

27. 17 C.F.R. § 240.10b-5 (2010).

28. *See* Roberta S. Karmel, *Outsider Trading on Confidential Information—A Breach in Search of a Duty*, 20 CARDOZO L. REV. 83, 86 (1998) ("The complete failure to disclose that a buyer or seller of securities is in possession of material nonpublic information is not generally viewed as a violation of subsection (b) of Rule 10b-5, which relates only to the making of untrue or misleading statements. Rather, such inaction can be interpreted as 'a device, scheme or artifice to defraud' in violation of subsection (a) or as an 'act, practice or course of business which operates as a fraud or deceit' upon a third person in violation of subsection (c)."); *see also* Donna M. Nagy, *Insider Trading and the Gradual Demise of Fiduciary Principles*, 94 IOWA L. REV. 1315, 1323 (2009) (explaining how silence can constitute fraud by deception under Rule 10b-5).

29. 15 U.S.C. § 78j(b) (2007).

30. *Id.*

31. *Speed v. Transamerica Corp.*, 99 F. Supp. 808, 828–29 (D. Del. 1951) (footnote and citation omitted). In an earlier case, the U.S. District Court for the District of Pennsylvania found that, "Under any reasonably liberal construction, these provisions [Section 10(b) and Rule 10b-5] apply to directors and officers who, in purchasing the stock of the corporation from others, fail to disclose a fact coming to their knowledge by reason of their position, which would materially affect the judgment of the other party to the transaction." *Kardon v. National Gypsum Co.*, 73 F. Supp. 798, 800 (D. Pa.

1947). And in an even earlier administrative action, the SEC similarly concluded that "there was a clear necessity, in order not to take unfair advantage of shareholders, for the issuer and those in control to make timely disclosure of the identity of the purchaser, of improved financial and operating condition of the issuer, and of the full terms of the transfer to Salta of the Truck Corporation's business and of its liquidation. . . . It is our opinion that the purchase of the securities under the circumstances set forth herein unaccompanied by appropriate disclosure of material facts constituted a violation of Rule X-10B-5." *In re* The Purchase and Retirement of Ward La France Truck Corporation Class "A" and Class "B" Stocks, 13 S.E.C. 373, 381 (1943).

32. Franklin A. Gevurtz, *The Globalization of Insider Trading Prohibitions*, 15 TRANSNAT'L L. 63, 71 (2002) (noting that after the 1942 adoption of Rule 10b-5, "Nearly two decades passed before anyone applied Rule 10b-5 to trading on undisclosed inside information.").

33. *In re* Cady, Roberts & Co., 40 S.E.C. 907, 911 (1961).

34. *Id.*

35. *Basic Inc. v. Levinson*, 485 U.S. 224, 231–32 (1988) (endorsing these alternative standards for materiality).

36. *SEC v. Texas Gulf Sulphur*, 401 F.2d 833, 854 (2d Cir. 1968), *cert. denied*, 394 U.S. 976 (1969).

37. *Id.* at 848 ("[A]nyone in possession of material inside information must either disclose it to the investing public, or, if he is disabled from disclosing it in order to protect a corporate confidence, or he chooses not to do so, must abstain from trading in or recommending the securities concerned while such inside information remains undisclosed.").

38. *Id.*; *In re* Cady, Roberts & Co., 40 S.E.C. at 912; *see also supra* note 31.

39. *Chiarella v. United States*, 445 U.S. 222 (1980).

40. *Id.* at 228.

41. *Dirks v. SEC*, 463 U.S. 646 (1983).

42. *Id.* at 660.

43. *Id.* at 659–64; *see also* David T. Cohen, Note: *Old Rule, New Theory: Revising the Personal Benefit Requirement for Tipper/Tippee Liability under the Misappropriation Theory of Insider Trading*, 47 B.C. L. REV. 547, 549–50 (2006); Masanori Hayashi, Note: *Japanese Insider Trading Law at the Advent of the Digital Age: New Challenges Raised by Internet and Communication Technology*, 23 HASTINGS COMM. & ENT. L. J. 157, 165 (2000) ("Under U.S. law, an insider is liable for tipping material nonpublic information if he anticipates some personal benefit from the disclosure. Tippees can be held liable if the tipper breached a duty and the tippee knew that the tipper was breaching the duty." (footnote omitted)).

44. Kathleen Coles, *The Dilemma of the Remote Tippee*, 41 GONZ. L. REV. 181, 211–16 (2005/2006) (outlining the liability of "remote tippees" under U.S.

insider trading law); *id.* at 227 (noting that under the Insider Trading & Securities Enforcement Act of 1988, "primary tippers are liable for remote tippee trades in actions brought by the government, but are relieved of liability to private plaintiffs for remote tippee trades."); Hayashi, *supra* note 43, at 165 ("Presumably, the duty to abstain or disclose could be passed down a chain of tippees indefinitely, and individual liability could be attached to each who breached that duty.").

45. *United States v. O'Hagan*, 521 U.S. 642 (1997).

46. *Id.* at 652–53.

47. *Id.* at 652.

48. 17 C.F.R. § 240.10b5–1 (2010).

49. Linda Chatman Thomsen, Testimony Concerning Insider Trading, Sept. 26, 2006 (before the U.S. Senate Committee on the Judiciary), *available at* http://sec.gov/news/testimony/2006/ts092606lct.htm.

50. Shen-Shin Lu, *Are the 1988 Amendments to Japanese Securities Regulation Law Effective Deterrents to Insider Trading?* 1991 COLUM. BUS. L. REV. 179, 181–83 (tracing the pre-1988 development of the Japanese securities laws); Sadakazu Osaki, *The Evolution of Insider Trading Regulations in Japan*, in INSIDER TRADING: GLOBAL DEVELOPMENTS AND ANALYSIS 144 (Paul U. Ali & Greg N. Gregoriou eds., 2009); Larry Zoglin, *Insider Trading in Japan: A Challenge to the Integration of the Japanese Equity Market into the Global Securities Market*, 1987 COLUM. BUS. L. REV. 419, 420 (1987) ("Japan's securities law, adopted in 1948, was modeled upon American securities statutes.").

51. *See* Lu, *supra* note 50, at 186 ("Old Article 58 was a copy of Rule 10b-5 of the American Securities Exchange Act of 1934. Rule 10b-5 is a catchall fraud provision in federal securities regulations, and it has been widely used against insider trading in the United States. In contrast to Rule 10b-5, old Article 58 was rarely used in Japan and was never used in an insider trading case."); Osaki, *supra* note 50, at 145; Note: *The Regulation of Insider Trading in Japan: Introducing a Private Right of Action*, 73 WASH. U. L. Q. 1399, 1409 (1995) ("While the U.S. anti-fraud provision, section 10(b), became the most effective weapon against insider trading, the Ministry of Finance considered its equivalent, article 58, 'too vague' to apply.").

52. Lu, *supra* note 50, at 186–88.

53. Stephen J. Choi & Andrew T. Guzman, *National Laws, International Money: Regulation in a Global Capital Market*, 65 FORDHAM L. REV. 1855, 1890 (1997) ("The United States, for example, through the 1980s and into the 1990s, . . . pursued an active effort to obtain agreements from several different countries to impose an insider trading regime similar to the one in place in the United States. As a result of this pressure, several countries, including Japan have instituted similar regimes."); Lu, *supra* note 50, at 193–94 (describing the impetus for insider trading initiatives in a number of

countries in the late 1980s); Osaki, *supra* note 50, at 145–46; Ramzi Nasser, *The Morality of Insider Trading in the United States and Abroad*, 52 OKLA. L. REV. 377, 381 (1999) ("Based on domestic and foreign criticism of rampant unpunished insider trading, Japan amended its insider trading laws in 1988."); *see also* Lu, *supra* note 50, at 185 (noting and describing the 1988 amendments).

54. *See* Lu, *supra* note 50, at 195–97; Osaki, *supra* note 50, at 145.

55. James A. Kehoe, *Exporting Insider Trading Laws: The Enforcement of U.S. Insider Trading Laws Internationally*, 9 EMORY INT'L L. REV. 345, 355 (1995).

56. Financial Instruments and Exchange Act, art. 166(1), Apr. 1, 2008, *available at* www.fsa.go.jp/common/law/fie01.pdf.

57. Financial Instruments and Exchange Act, art. 166(3), Apr. 1, 2008, *available at* www.fsa.go.jp/common/law/fie01.pdf; *see also* Gevurtz, *supra* note 32, at 83–84 ("Under Japanese law, persons receiving non-public information directly from corporate related parties are subject to the prohibition on trading."); Hayashi, *supra* note 43, at 165 ("Under Japanese law, the tipping rule provides that no person to whom an insider has communicated a material fact may trade on that company's stock until the information has been publicly disclosed.").

58. *See* Coles, *supra* note 44, at 227 ("In Japan, for example, the prohibition on inside trading extends only to someone who receives nonpublic information directly from a party related to the corporation."); Gevurtz, *supra* note 32, at 84 ("[U]nlike the United States' law (or the EU Directive), the Japanese prohibition only extends to a person who receives information directly from a corporate related party, and not to remote tippees."); Hayashi, *supra* note 43, at 165–66 ("[T]he possibility that liability can be extended to those removed from the original 'source' of information under U.S. law can be contrasted with a mere 'direct communication' standard under Japanese law.").

59. Lu, *supra* note 50, at 185 ("There are numerous insider trading cases in the United States, while in Japan the figure is near zero."); *id.* at 193 (reporting in 1991 that "In the United States there are up to forty insider trading cases every year. But in Japan, although Tokyo has become the world's largest securities market, there have been practically no insider trading cases in forty years.").

60. Nasser, *supra* note 53, at 382 (summarizing Japanese enforcement of insider trading in the 1990s); Osaki, *supra* note 50, at 150–52; Richard G. Small, *Towards a Theory of Contextual Transplants*, 19 EMORY INT'L L. REV. 1431, 1455 n.5 (2005) ("Although in 1988, as a result of a domestic scandal and overseas pressure, the prohibition was amended, few cases were brought until the mid-1990s.").

61. Enrico Colombatto & Jonathan R. Macey, *A Public Choice Model of International Economic Coopera-*

tion and the Decline of the Nation State, 18 CARDOZO L. REV. 925, 952 (1996) ("Japan stepped up enforcement of its previously ignored insider trading regulations due to the United States's pressure.").

62. Kehoe, *supra* note 55, at 375.

63. *See* Osaki, *supra* note 50, at 152–54 (describing a recent case and the adoption and operation of the civil fine system).

64. *Id.* at 153.

65. *Id.* at 153–54.

66. *See Japan to double fines for insider trading*, JAPAN WEEKLY MONITOR, Jun. 9, 2008.

67. Joseph Blum, *The Regulation of Insider Trading in Germany: Who's Afraid of Self-Restraint?* 7 NW. J. INT'L L. & BUS. 507, 516 (1986) ("[T]the German authorities opted for a unique system mixing voluntary compliance with self-regulation."); James H. Freis, Jr., *An Outsider's Look into the Regulation of Insider Trading in Germany: A Guide to Securities, Banking, and Market Reform in Finanzplatz Deutschland*, 19 B.C. INT'L & COMP. L. REV. 1, 30 (1996); Stephen J. Leacock, *In Search of a Giant Leap: Curtailing Insider Trading in International Securities Markets by the Reform of Insider Trading Laws under European Union Council Directive 89/592*, 3 TULSA J. COMP. & INT'L L. 51, 61–62 (1995); Peter M. Memminger, *The New German Insider Law: Introduction and Discussion in Relation to United States Securities Law*, 11 FLA. J. INT'L L. 189, 192 (1996); Victor F. Calaba, Comment: *The Insiders: A Look at the Comprehensive and Potentially Unnecessary Regulatory Approaches to Insider Trading in Germany and the United States, Including the SEC's Newly Effective Rules 10b5–1 and 10b5–2*, 23 LOY. L.A. INT'L & COMP. L. REV. 457, 468–9 (2001); Ursula C. Pfeil, Note and Comment: *Finanzplatz Deutschland: Germany Enacts Insider Trading Legislation*, 11 AM. U. J. INT'L L. & POL'Y 137, 140–43 (1996).

68. Blum, *supra* note 67, at 524 ("In sum, the German Insider Trading Guidelines can be characterized, in the words of University of Munich Professor Doctor Michael Will, as a 'toothless device.'"); Roberta S. Karmel, *Transnational Takeover Talk—Regulations Relating to Tender Offers and Insider Trading in the United States, the United Kingdom, Germany, and Australia*, 66 U. CIN. L. REV. 1133, 1150 (1998) ("Germany had relied on a voluntary code of conduct which was wholly ineffective."); Memminger, *supra* note 67, at 192–93 ("The Guidelines were generally regarded as quite ineffective, since they neither had the legal authority of an enacted law, nor were they accepted by courts as trade practice.").

69. Susan-Jacqueline Butler, *Models of Modern Corporations: A Comparative Analysis of German and U.S. Corporate Structures*, 17 ARIZ. J. INT'L & COMP. LAW 555, 582–83 (2000) ("In 1994, Germany enacted a national law to deal with this problem known as the *Wertpapierhandelsgesetz* (Security Trading Act). Under this

act, insider trading is a criminal offense punishable by fines or imprisonment up to five years."); Colombatto & Macey, *supra* note 61, at 945 ("Even more striking is the fact that in June 1994 the German Parliament authorized legislation making insider trading a crime for the first time in that country's history."); Freis, *supra* note 67, at 4–5, 40 (noting the adoption and effectiveness of criminal insider trading legislation in Germany); Karmel, *supra* note 68, at 1149–50 ("On August 1, 1994, Germany took a step toward aggressively competing in the international financial arena when it finally outlawed insider trading."); Memminger, *supra* note 67, at 192 ("On July 26, 1994, the German parliament adopted the Second Financial Market Promotion Law (*Zweites Finanzmarktförderungsgesetz*). . . . With its enactment, the German legislature began to regulate insider trading for the first time in German history."); Pfiel, *supra* note 67, at 137, 152 (noting the adoption and effectiveness of German criminal insider trading sanctions).

70. Calaba, *supra* note 67, at 470; Karmel, *supra* note 68, at 1150; Pfiel, *supra* note 67, at 149.

71. Luca Enriques & Paolo Volpin, *Corporate Governance Reforms in Continental Europe*, 21 J. ECON. PERSPECTIVES 117, 136, 137 (2007).

72. Colombatto & Macey, *supra* note 61, at 952; Karmel, *supra* note 68, at 1167; Daniel James Standen, *Insider Trading Reforms Sweep across Germany: Bracing for the Cold Winds of Change*, 36 HARV. INT'L L. J. 177, 200 (1995).

73. Pfeil, *supra* note 67, at 144.

74. As one contemporaneous commentator summarized, "Germany . . . finally recognized the need for some form of insider-trading legislation in order to build a competitive international financial sector, despite its formerly vigorous opposition to EU proposals for banning insider trading by legal means. This recognition followed a relatively sharp decline in the German capital markets index. This accompanied a correspondingly significant decline in foreign investor confidence in the German market due to the highly publicized insider-trading scandal involving Germany's largest banking interest, Deutsche Bank. Foreign perceptions of the German economy had become the 'pivotal factor in the movement of share prices,' and apprehension over insider trading and interest rates had lowered the stock market index." Leacock, *supra* note 67, at 54 (footnotes omitted).

75. Securities Trading Act (*Gesetz über den Wertpapierhandel/ Wertpapierhandelsgesetz-WpHG*), Part 3, Section 14, Sept. 9, 1998 (last amended Jan. 5, 2007), *available at* www.BaFin.de/cln_171/nn_720786/SharedDocs/Aufsichtsrecht/EN/Gesetze/wphg_28neu_29__en.html#Start.

76. *Id.*; *see also* Freis, *supra* note 67, at 41; Karmel, *supra* note 68, at 1150–51 (explaining prohibited conduct); Memminger, *supra* note 67, at 215–26 (same).

77. Securities Trading Act (*Gesetz über den Wertpapierhandel/ Wertpapierhandelsgesetz-WpHG*), Part 3, Section 14, Sept. 9, 1998 (last amended Jan. 1, 2007), *available at* www.BaFin.de/cln_171/nn_720786/SharedDocs/Aufsichtsrecht/EN/Gesetze/wphg_28neu_29__en.html#Start; *see also* Freis, *supra* note 67, at 42 ("The duty to carry out these provisions rests upon the Federal Securities Trading Supervisory Authority. This entity is an independent federal superior agency within the competence of the Federal Ministry of Finance."); Gary L. Gassman & Perry S. Granof, *Global Issues Affecting Securities Claims at the Beginning of the Twenty-First Century*, 43 TORT & INS. L. J. 85 ("Germany formed the *Bundesanstalt fur Finanzdienstleistungsaufsicht (BaFin)* in 2002 to regulate and oversee banking, securities, and insurance services. By instituting proceedings as 'administrative matters,' BaFin enforces German statutes and regulations regarding insider trading, market and price manipulation, corporate disclosures, directors' conduct, and the like."); Karmel, *supra* note 68, at 1150 ("The newly created Federal Supervisory Authority for Securities Trading (FSA), is somewhat similar to the SEC. It is a federal agency under the Federal Ministry of Finance."); Pfiel, *supra* note 67, at 165 ("The German Parliament delegated the principal power for enforcing Germany's Insider Trading Law to the newly-created Federal Supervisory Office for Securities Trading (Federal Supervisory Office). The Federal Supervisory Office is a self-funding, independent government agency within the jurisdiction of the Federal Ministry of Finance." (footnotes omitted)); Anupama J. Naidu, Comment: *Was Its Bite Worse Than Its Bark? The Costs Sarbanes-Oxley Imposes On German Issuers May Translate into Costs to the United States*, 18 EMORY INT'L L. REV. 271, 299 (2004) ("Currently, regulation at the federal level is conducted by the Federal Securities Trading Supervisory Office, known in Germany as the BAWe. The BAWe is responsible for investigations of insider trading, protection of investors, improvements to market transparency, and cooperation on the international level." (footnotes omitted)).

78. Pfiel, *supra* note 67, at 164 (footnote omitted); *see also* Securities Trading Act (Gesetz über den *Wertpapierhandel/ Wertpapierhandelsgesetz-WpHG*), Part 3, Section 14, Sept. 9, 1998 (last amended Jan. 1, 2007), *available at* www.BaFin.de/cln_171/nn_720786/SharedDocs/Aufsichtsrecht/EN/Gesetze/wphg_28neu_29__en.html#Start; Freis, *supra* note 67, at 42–43 ("Additionally, a Securities Council (*Wertpapierrat*), composed of representatives of the *Lander* and other federal agencies, shall assist the Securities Trading Supervisory Authority in its supervision. The Authority shall work together with other German regulatory agencies responsible for banking and insurance regulation, the German Bundesbank, and the stock exchange supervisory authorities of

the *Lander*"); Pfiel, *supra* note 67, at 173 (describing the operation of the components of the regulatory structure).

79. Robert A. Prentice, *The Inevitability of a Strong SEC*, 91 CORNELL L. REV. 775, 837 (2006) ("By the turn of the millennium, virtually all developed nations had enacted U.S.-style insider trading laws and enforcement actions in the United Kingdom, France, Germany, China, Japan, South Korea, and elsewhere were no longer rare.").

80. George C. Nnona, *International Insider Trading: Reassessing the Propriety and Feasibility of the U.S. Regulatory Approach*, 27 N.C.J. INT'L L. & COM. REG. 185, 214–15 (2001); *see also* Kal Raustiala, *The Architecture of International Cooperation: Transgovernmental Networks and the Future of International Law*, 43 VA. J. INT'L L. 1, 33 (2002) ("The SEC has pressured Japan and Switzerland, for instance, to develop insider-trading regimes similar to that in place in the U.S. Similarly, the SEC 'made its disapproval of [Germany's] current system known both directly and indirectly through the prosecution of high-profile cases that violate United States insider trading laws.'" (footnote omitted)).

81. Colombatto & Macey, *supra* note 61, at 945 ("As recently as the mid-1980s, actual enforcement of insider trading regulations was largely confined to the United States. Most other major financial center nations either did not have insider trading regulation (e.g., Germany) or, if they did, did not actively enforce the regulations (e.g., Japan).").

82. Prentice, *supra* note 79, at 834.

83. *See also* Licht, *supra* note 19, at 233 ("Insider trading is another area where one observes a convergence trend towards a common rule. . . . These laws may differ in the scope of liability they impose and in other aspects. Nonetheless, they represent a growing acceptance among regulators of the need to regulate this conduct."); Amir N. Licht, *The Mother of All Path Dependencies Toward a Cross-Cultural Theory of Corporate Governance Systems*, 26 DEL. J. CORP. L. 147, 195 (2001) ("Insider trading regulation is among the prominent subjects, which underwent a strong convergence process as part of the internationalization of securities markets. As a result, one is likely to find laws, which prohibit insider trading in many countries in quite similar language."); Robert A. Prentice, *The Internet and its Challenges for the Future of Insider Trading Regulation*, 12 HARV. J. LAW & TECH. 263, 349–50 (1999) ("[I]n no field has the SEC been more successful at producing . . . convergence than in insider trading. It is now possible to speak of an 'emerging global consensus favoring punishment [of insider trading] activity because it undermines the integrity of the marketplace and threatens the market's efficiency.'").

84. *See* Stephen M. Bainbridge, *Insider Trading Regulation: The Path Dependent Choice Between Property Rights and Securities Fraud*, 52 SMU L. REV. 1589 (1999) (de-

scribing the metaphoric "path dependency" of U.S. insider trading law); Gevurtz, *supra* note 32, at 68 ("[I]nsider trading prohibitions around the world differ as to when it is illegal for a party in possession of information unknown to the other side to buy or sell stock without first disclosing the information."); Steinberg, *supra* note 21, at 635 (noting, with respect to both insider trading and issuer affirmative disclosure requirements, that "a survey of the securities laws of developed markets reveals that these countries have rejected the U.S. approach.").

85. *See generally* Gevurtz, *supra* note 32, at 68–89 (comparing insider trading prohibitions in the United States, under the EU Directive, in Australia, and in Japan); Steinberg, *supra* note 21, at 662–72 (describing various similarities and differences in insider trading laws in developed countries). When I began researching the laws of Japan and Germany in 2004, there were no English translations of the relevant statutes available on the Web. I am deeply indebted to Hilary Foulkes and Bob Wray, two of my former colleagues at Skadden, Arps, Slate, Meagher & Flom LLP, and Stefan Koch, also of Skadden, Arps, Slate, Meagher & Flom LLP, for their assistance in getting me English translations of each statute. I also will take this opportunity to thank Lauren Medley Gunnels (J.D., 2006, The University of Tennessee College of Law), who provided assistance in the early stages of my research.

86. *See* Shelby D. Green, *To Disclose or Not to Disclose? That Is the Question for the Corporate Fiduciary Who Is Also a Pension Plan Fiduciary Under ERISA: Resolving the Conflict of Duty*, 9 U. PA. J. LAB. & EMP. L. 831, 841 (2007) (setting forth these three justifications); Roberta S. Karmel, *The Relationship Between Mandatory Disclosure and Prohibitions Against Insider Trading: Why a Property Rights Theory of Inside Information Is Untenable*, 59 BROOKLYN L. REV. 149 (1993) (book review) (describing all three justifications and critiquing the property law basis for insider trading regulation); *see also* Ray J. Grzebielski, *Why Martha Stewart Did Not Violate Rule 10b-5: On Tipping, Piggybacking, Front-Running and the Fiduciary Duties of Securities Brokers*, 40 AKRON L. REV. 55, 72 (2007) ("A significant policy reason to prohibit insider trading is to protect the corporation's property rights in the information."); Loke, *supra* note 22, at 170–71 (describing the fiduciary duty and parity of information justifications); Nnona, *supra* note 80, at 207–10 (noting four broad justifications for insider trading regulation); Bryan C. Smith, Comment: *Possession Versus Use: Reconciling the Letter and the Spirit of Insider Trading Regulation Under Rule 10b-5*, 35 CAL. W. L. REV. 371, 381 (1999) ("[T]hree considerations routinely pointed to as reasons to prohibit insider trading are: (1) Equity or Fairness, (2) Property Rights, and (3) Efficiency.").

87. Bainbridge, *supra* note 84, at 1598 ("The equality of access principle admittedly has some intuitive ap-

peal. . . . [T]he SEC consistently has tried to maintain it as the basis of insider trading liability."); Coles, *supra* note 44, at 184 ("Through its enforcement policies and legal positions advocated in judicial proceedings, the SEC is constantly pushing the boundaries of the law in an attempt to bring insider trading restrictions quietly and indirectly back to a fairness-based system—a system that has ostensibly been rejected by the Supreme Court.").

88. *See, e.g.*, Bainbridge, *supra* note 84, at 1644–50 (arguing that insider trading should be based on property right protections rather than securities fraud); Jill E. Fisch, *Start Making Sense: An Analysis and Proposal for Insider Trading Regulation*, 26 GA. L. REV. 179 (1991) (providing a critique and suggesting an alternative).

89. A. C. Pritchard, United States v. O'Hagan: *Agency Law and Justice Powell's Legacy for the Law of Insider Trading*, 78 B.U.L. REV. 13, 17 (1998).

90. *Id.* ("The relationship between a principal and an agent is a fiduciary relationship."); *see also* Restatement (Third) of Agency § 1.01 (including especially cmt. e).

91. Restatement (Third) of Agency § 8.01 (2006). As noted in the comments to this rule, "Unless the principal consents, the general fiduciary principle, as elaborated by the more specific duties of loyalty stated in §§ 8.02 to 8.05, also requires that an agent refrain from using the agent's position or the principal's property to benefit the agent or a third party." *Id.* at cmt b.

92. *Id.* at § 8.02.

93. *Id.* at § 8.05.

94. *Id.* at cmt. c.

95. *See, e.g., id.* at § 8.01 cmt. d(1) ("The law of restitution and unjust enrichment . . . creates a basis for an agent's liability to a principal when the agent breaches a fiduciary duty. . . . If through the breach the agent has realized a material benefit, the agent has a duty to account to the principal for the benefit, its value, or its proceeds. The agent is subject to liability to deliver the benefit, its proceeds, or its value to the principal."); *see also Diamond v. Oreamuno*, 248 N.E.2d 910, 914 (N.Y. 1969).

96. Restatement (Third) of Agency § 8.02 cmt e.

97. *See supra* note 45–47 and accompanying text.

98. *United States v. O'Hagan*, 521 U.S. 642, 652 (1997) (citation omitted).

99. *See supra* notes 41–44 and accompanying text.

100. *See* Nagy, *supra* note 28, at 1323–24 ("The classical and misappropriation theories of insider trading liability establish the circumstances under which such a disclosure duty arises and . . . under either of the Supreme Court's theories, the existence of a fiduciary-like relationship is essential.").

101. *See* Pritchard, *supra* note 89.

102. Nagy, *supra* note 28, at 1319 ("Despite the fact that fiduciary principles underlie the offense of insider

trading, there have been recent repeated instances in which lower federal courts and the Securities and Exchange Commission . . . have disregarded these principles.").

103. Steinberg, *supra* note 21, at 666.

104. *Id.* at 667 (footnotes omitted).

105. *Id.* at 666–67 ("[A]s a matter of fairness, the U.S. framework has significant loopholes. . . . By adhering to a fiduciary relationship like-model . . . , the U.S. insider trading approach unduly complicates an already complex area and at times smacks of unfairness among similarly situated market participants." (footnotes omitted)).

106. A student commentator noted that "the misappropriation theory makes potential liability less predictable under section 10(b), and the *O'Hagan* decision does nothing to alleviate the problem. When addressed with this problem in the past, the Supreme Court has emphasized that the securities market "demands certainty and predictability," and that it is "essential . . . to have a guiding principle for those whose daily activities must be limited and instructed by the SEC's insider-trading rules." . . . "[I]n several cases where courts have imposed liability under the misappropriation theory, the breach has not been . . . clear." Amy E. Fahey, Note: United States V. O'Hagan: *The Supreme Court Abandons Textualism to Adopt the Misappropriation Theory*, 25 FORDHAM URB. L. J. 507, 538–39 (1998).

107. 17 C.F.R. § 240.10b5–2(b) (2010).

108. *Id.*

109. *SEC v. Cuban*, 634 F. Supp. 2d 713 (N.D. Tex. 2009).

110. *Id.* at 724–27.

111. *See* Richard W. Painter et al., *Don't Ask, Just Tell: Insider Trading after* United States v. O'Hagan, 84 VA. L. REV. 153, 208 (1998) ("[W]e can anticipate that the types of relationships ultimately subject to the *O'Hagan* insider trading regime will continue to expand. Relationships of confidence often arise without being designated as such by the persons entering into them, and in most circumstances persons in a fiduciary relationship cannot simply choose to characterize their relationship as nonfiduciary.").

112. *See* Joan MacLeod Heminway, *Save Martha Stewart? Observations about Equal Justice in U.S. Insider Trading Regulation*, 12 TEX. J. WOMEN & L. 247, 285 n.31 (2003) (noting that allegations in the SEC's complaint against Martha Stewart "appear to suggest that the SEC desires to extend tippee liability to tippees of third-party brokers who misappropriate personal trading information from insiders"); David A. Skeel Jr. & William J. Stuntz, *Christianity and the (Modest) Rule of Law*, 8 U. PA. J. CONST. L. 809, 827 (2006) (describing the expansiveness of the SEC's breach of duty theory in its insider trading case against Martha Stewart); Lawrence M. Solan, *Statutory Inflation and Institutional*

Choice, 44 WM. & MARY L. REV. 2209, 2243 (2003) ("[B]y the time *O'Hagan* was decided, both the Justice Department and the SEC for many years had been attempting to expand liability for insider trading. They had failed twice before the Supreme Court, and had won an affirmance by an equally divided Court. *O'Hagan*, the government's fourth effort, was a success."); Dave Michaels & Brendan Case, *Legal Stars Defend Cuban: Team of Professors from Top Law Schools Attacks SEC Authority*, DALLAS MORNING NEWS, Feb. 3, 2009, at D1 (describing a challenge to the SEC's insider trading case against Mark Cuban on the basis of a lack of duty).

113. *See supra* notes 98 & 99 and accompanying text; *see also* Gevurtz, *supra* note 32, at 80–81.

114. *United States v. O'Hagan*, 521 U.S. 642, 652 (1997) ("The classical theory applies not only to officers, directors, and other permanent insiders of a corporation, but also to attorneys, accountants, consultants, and others who temporarily become fiduciaries of a corporation.").

115. *See* H.R. 682, 111th Cong., 1st Sess. (2009); *Brian Introduces Legislation to Prohibit Insider Trading on Capitol Hill*, Jan. 27, 2009, *available at* http://insidertrading.procon.org/sourcefiles/BairdPressRelease09.pdf.

116. Masanori Hayashi, Note: *Japanese Insider Trading Law at the Advent of the Digital Age: New Challenges Raised by Internet and Communication Technology*, 23 HASTINGS COMM. & ENT. L. J. 157, 161–62 (2000).

117. Financial Instruments and Exchange Act, art. 166(1), Apr. 1, 2008, *available at* www.fsa.go.jp/common/law/fie01.pdf; *see also* Gevurtz, *supra* note 32, at 83 ("The Japanese prohibition reaches so-called corporate related parties. This includes directors, officers, employees, shareholders, as well as persons associated with a corporation through either a contract or a government supervisory role, who obtain material non-public information by virtue of their relationship with the company.").

118. Gevurtz, *supra* note 32, at 83.

119. *Id.* at 84.

120. Financial Instruments and Exchange Act, art. 166(3), Apr. 1, 2008, *available at* www.fsa.go.jp/common/law/fie01.pdf; *see also* Gevurtz, *supra* note 32, at 83–84 ("Under Japanese law, persons receiving non-public information directly from corporate related parties are subject to the prohibition on trading. . . . [U]nlike the United States' law . . . , the Japanese prohibition only extends to a person who receives information directly from a corporate related party, and not to remote tippees."); *id.* at 86 ("[T]he . . . way in which the Japanese law deals with the problem is by punishing first-tier recipients of information who trade.").

121. *See* Gevurtz, *supra* note 32, at 84 (noting "Japan's failure to adopt the equivalent of . . . the United States' misappropriation theory" and, by way of explanation, "that at the time the Japanese enacted their in-

sider trading provisions in 1988, the United States Supreme Court had not accepted the misappropriation theory—at least in the context of a securities law violation."); *id.* at 86 ("Japan has the narrowest law. The Japanese statute does not prohibit tipping.").

122. Securities Trading Act (*Gesetz über den Wertpapierhandel/ Wertpapierhandelsgesetz-WpHG*), Part 3, Sections 13 & 14, Sept. 9, 1998 (last amended Jan. 5, 2007), *available at* www.BaFin.de/cln_171/nn_720786/SharedDocs/Aufsichtsrecht/EN/Gesetze/wphg_28neu_29__en.html#Start; *see also* Memminger, *supra* note 67, at 205 ("The broad formulation of Section 13 of the German Securities Trading Act, however, qualifies every person or legal entity that has knowledge of inside information as an insider.").

123. *Id.*; *see also* Karmel, *supra* note 68, at 1150–51 (describing primary and secondary insiders under the prior German statutory scheme); Memminger, *supra* note 67, at 205–12 (same); Calaba, *supra* note 67, at 470 (same).

124. *Cf. id.* at 211–12 (making this point under Germany's prior statute).

125. Council Directive 2003/6/EC, 2003 O.J. (L 96) 16; *see also* Council Directive 2003/124/EC, 2003 O.J. (L 339) 70. I am extremely grateful for the assistance in this area that I received from Prof. Dr. Gerhard Wegen, LL.M. and Dr. Felix Born of Gleiss Lutz in Hootz Hirsch Partnerschaftsgesellschaft von Rechtsanwälten, Steuerberatern (AG Stuttgart PR 136) in Stuttgart, Germany, for their assistance with these and related materials.

126. Pfeil, *supra* note 67, at 176–77.

127. *See supra* notes 115, 117, 120, and 126 and accompanying text.

128. *See supra* notes 113, 120, 121 & 124 and accompanying text.

129. *See supra* notes 106–12 and accompanying text.

130. *See, e.g.*, *SEC v. Mayhew*, 121 F.3d 44, 50–51 (2d Cir. 1997) (discussing the meaning of nonpublic information); *SEC v. Conaway*, 2010 U.S. Dist. LEXIS 4254, at *145-*163 (E.D. Mich. Jan. 20, 2010) (discussing implied misrepresentations as facts). Under German insider trading law, facts include forward-looking information. Securities Trading Act (*Gesetz über den Wertpapierhandel/ Wertpapierhandelsgesetz-WpHG*), Part 3, Section 13, Sept. 9, 1998 (last amended Jan. 5, 2007), *available at* www.BaFin.de/cln_171/nn_720786/SharedDocs/Aufsichtsrecht/EN/Gesetze/wphg_28neu_29__en.html#Start (noting that circumstances forming the basis of inside information include "cases which may reasonably be expected to come into existence in the future").

131. Edmund W. Kitch, *The Theory and Practice of Securities Disclosure*, 61 BROOKLYN L. REV. 763, 824 (1995).

132. *Basic Inc. v. Levinson*, 485 U.S. 224, 231–32 (1988) (*citing to TSC Indus., Inc. v. Northway, Inc.*, 426

U.S. 438, 449 (1976)); *see also* Heminway, *supra* note 23, at 1137–38.

133. *Basic*, 485 U.S. at 232 (noting the potential materiality of contingent or speculative information); SEC SAB No. 99, 64 Fed. Reg. 45,150 (Aug. 19, 1999) (referenced at 17 C.F.R. pt. 211) (providing materiality guidance in the context of accounting disclosures); Heminway, *supra* note 132, at 1200–01, 1160 n.114 (describing the task of balancing quantitative and qualitative materiality and the materiality of contingent, speculative, and forward-looking information).

134. *United States v. Anderson*, 533 F.3d 623, 629 (8th Cir. 2008) (citations omitted).

135. *Basic*, 485 U.S. at 232–41.

136. *United States v. Nacchio*, 519 F.3d 1140, 1158 (10th Cir. 2008).

137. *Endo v. Albertine*, 863 F. Supp. 708, 717 (N.D. Ill. 1994) ("'The Issue [sic] of materiality may be characterized as a mixed question of law and fact, involving as it does the application of a legal standard to a particular set of facts.' . . . Only if the established misrepresentations or omissions are so obviously important or so obviously unimportant to an investor, that reasonable minds cannot differ on the question of materiality, can the ultimate issue of materiality be appropriately resolved as a matter of law at the summary judgment stage." (citation omitted)).

138. Financial Instruments and Exchange Act, art. 166(2), Apr. 1, 2008, *available at* www.fsa.go.jp/common/law/fie01.pdf.

139. *Id.*

140. *See, e.g., id.* art. 166(2)(i)(o), 166(2)(ii)(d), and 166(2)(iii)(h).

141. Gevurtz, *supra* note 32, at 73–74 (footnotes omitted).

142. *See generally* Joan MacLeod Heminway, *Personal Facts About Executive Officers: A Proposal for Tailored Disclosures to Encourage Reasonable Investor Behavior,* 42 WAKE FOREST L. REV. 749 (2007); Allan Horwich, *When the Corporate Luminary Becomes Seriously Ill: When Is a Corporation Obligated to Disclose That Illness and Should the Securities and Exchange Commission Adopt a Rule Requiring Disclosure?* 5 N.Y.U. J. L. & BUS. 827 (2009); Jeff Poor, *Gore, Other Apple Directors Face Possible Suit over CEO Jobs' Health,* BUS. & MEDIA INSTIT., Jan. 17, 2009, *available at* www.businessandmedia.org/articles/2009/20090117125945.aspx; Dunstan Prial, *Can We Trust What CEOs Say?* FOXBUSINESS, March 9, 2009, *available at* www.foxbusiness.com/story/markets/trust-ceos-say/.

143. Steinberg, *supra* note 21, at 664 (footnotes omitted) ("The U.S. standard, focusing on whether the subject information would assume importance to the mythical 'reasonable' investor in making his investment decision, has not been adopted with great frequency elsewhere.").

144. Securities Trading Act (*Gesetz über den Wertpapierhandel/ Wertpapierhandelsgesetz-WpHG*), Part 3, Section 13, Sept. 9, 1998 (last amended Jan. 5, 2007), *available at* www.BaFin.de/cln_171/nn_720786/Shared Docs/Aufsichtsrecht/EN/Gesetze/wphg_28neu_29__en .html#Start.

145. *Id.*

146. *Id.*

147. *See* Securities Trading Act (*Gesetz über den Wertpapierhandel/ Wertpapierhandelsgesetz-WpHG*), Part 3, Section 13, Sept. 9, 1998, *available at* www.iuscomp .org/gla/statutes/WpHG.htm#13; *see also* Karmel, *supra* note 68, at 1151 (describing the price-effect standard under a prior version of the German statute); Steinberg, *supra* note 21, at 664–65 (same); Calaba, *supra* note 67, at 472 (same).

148. Securities Trading Act (*Gesetz über den Wertpapierhandel/ Wertpapierhandelsgesetz-WpHG*), Part 3, Section 13, Sept. 9, 1998 (last amended Jan. 5, 2007), *available at* www.BaFin.de/cln_171/nn_720786/Shared Docs/Aufsichtsrecht/EN/Gesetze/wphg_28neu_29__en .html#Start.

149. *Id.*; *see also* Securities Trading Act (*Gesetz über den Wertpapierhandel/ Wertpapierhandelsgesetz-WpHG*), Part 3, Section 15(1), Sept. 9, 1998 (last amended Jan. 5, 2007), *available at* www.BaFin.de/cln_171/nn_720 786/SharedDocs/Aufsichtsrecht/EN/Gesetze/wphg _28neu_29__en.html#Start ("[I]nside information directly concerns an issuer if it relates to developments within the issuer's sphere of activity."); *see also* Memminger, *supra* note 67, at 201 (mentioning and explaining, under a prior version of the German statute, this aspect of the definition of inside information).

150. *See supra* note 142 and accompanying text.

151. *See supra* notes 132–37 and accompanying text.

152. *See, e.g.,* Heminway, *supra* note 142, at 759 ("Although personal facts about an executive are less likely to be material than corporate facts, a court may find that it is substantially likely that a reasonable investor would consider certain personal facts important in making an investment decision relating to the corporation's securities. Moreover, a court may find it substantially likely that a reasonable investor would have viewed disclosure of an omitted personal fact about an executive officer as a significant alteration of the total mix of available information." (footnotes omitted)).

153. *See supra* notes 138–42 and accompanying text.

154. *See supra* notes 144–50 and accompanying text.

155. *Cf.* Heminway, *supra* note 23, at 1174–82 (describing transaction costs associated with materiality determinations in an insider trading context).

156. *See id.* at 1138–39 ("The interpretation and application of the materiality standard are highly fact-dependent and do not always produce predictable or certain planning options or judicial results.").

157. *See* 17 C.F.R. § 240.10b5–1 (2010) ("a purchase or sale of a security of an issuer is 'on the basis of' material nonpublic information about that security or issuer if the person making the purchase or sale was aware of the material nonpublic information when the person made the purchase or sale"); Langevoort, *supra* note 25, at 13 (noting that an awareness standard is applicable after the adoption of Rule 10b5–1); Elena Marty-Nelson, *Securities Laws in Soap Operas and Telenovelas: Are All My Children Engaged in Securities Fraud?* 18 S. CAL. INTERDIS. L. J. 329, 351 (2009) ("The Third Circuit has found that recklessness amounts to scienter.").

158. *See* Marty-Nelson, *supra* note 157, at 351 ("Generally, when dealing with tippee liability, the requisite mental state may be found when the tippee 'knew,' or 'should have known,' or perhaps even 'consciously avoided' knowing that she was trading on improperly divulged nonpublic information." (footnote omitted)).

159. *Ernst & Ernst v. Hochfelder*, 425 U.S. 185, 197 (1976) ("The words 'manipulative or deceptive' used in conjunction with 'device or contrivance' strongly suggest that § 10 (b) was intended to proscribe knowing or intentional misconduct.").

160. 17 C.F.R. § 240.10b5–1 (2010).

161. *See* Carol B. Swanson, *Insider Trading Madness: Rule 10b5–1 and the Death of Scienter*, 52 KAN. L. REV. 147, 193–96 (2003).

162. *Id.* at 196–200.

163. *See supra* notes 53–58 and accompanying text (regarding the Japanese law); *supra* notes 75 & 76 and accompanying text (regarding the German law).

164. *See, e.g.*, Greenberg, *supra* note 4, at 307. In *Chiarella*, the Court stated that "not every instance of financial unfairness constitutes fraudulent activity under § 10 (b)." *Chiarella v. United States*, 445 U.S. 222, 232 (1980).

165. Kimberly D. Krawiec, *Fairness, Efficiency, and Insider Trading: Deconstructing the Coin of the Realm in the Information Age*, 95 NW. U.L. REV. 443, 474–75 (2001) (footnotes omitted).

166. Dunoff, *supra* note 3, at 908 (describing one author's conception of "level playing field" fairness and noting its connection to equal access principles); Thomas A. McGrath III, Note: *The Rise and Fall (and Rise?) of Information-Based Insider Trading Enforcement*, 61 FORDHAM L. REV. 127, 129 (1993) ("The original theory of insider trading—the equal access theory—was premised on considerations of fairness and the public

interest in market participants having equal access to corporate information—'the level playing field.'").

167. *Id.* at 476–77 (footnotes omitted); *see also* Cox & Fogarty, *supra* note 3, at 360 ("Fairness as equal access to information may be seen, then, . . . as an attempt to prevent exploitation of unearned informational advantages, to promote equality of opportunity in the securities markets, or, more starkly, to transfer wealth from the informed to the uninformed. In this respect, insider trading is unfair much in the sense that inheritances, or even good luck, are unfair; and an insider trading prohibition is not so much an antifraud rule as a law against easy money.").

168. To this point, Professor Krawiec noted, "An investor's sense of the unfairness of securities markets is . . . unlikely to be assuaged by reassurances that the material information possessed by her trading partner and not by her is technically public and that if she cares to quit her job and instead spend all day monitoring courtroom trials, searching for obscure public reports or loitering at corporate offices she is likely to discover this same information. Rather, investors are likely to feel that such transactions are unfair regardless of whether the unshared information was acquired through breach of a fiduciary duty, through theft, from a disclosure made to analysts in a closed session, or from information that, while public in theory, is simply beyond the reach of the average investor." Krawiec, *supra* note 165, at 479.

169. Cox & Fogarty, *supra* note 3, at 359.

170. *See supra* notes 15 & 16 and accompanying text.

171. Rawls, *supra* note 7, at 48.

172. Rawls, *supra* note 7, at 43.

173. One commentator on U.S. insider trading regulation wrote, "The current fraud-based law of insider trading does not promote the policies of fairness and equal access to information underlying the federal securities laws. The fiduciary principle narrows the scope of insider trading liability to such an extent that many traders, unfairly using their privileged access to information, are beyond the reach of the statute. As a result, present law is inadequate to curtail widely condemned activity." Jeffrey P. Strickler, *Inside Information and Outside Traders: Corporate Recovery of the Outsider's Unfair Gain*, 73 CALIF. L. REV. 483, 496 (1985).

174. *See supra* note 17 and accompanying text.

175. Small, *supra* note 60, at 1455 ("Law is a product of its context as well as its culture.").

176. JOHN RAWLS, THE LAW OF PEOPLES 37 (1999).

8

China's First Loss

RAJ BHALA

I. China's Development and the Historic Case

A. Introduction

It was a fight over cars and car parts that marked the end of China's honeymoon period in the World Trade Organisation (WTO), those blissful few years when China's major trading partners were willing to forgive its trespasses because this largest of developing countries had just joined the club. The United States was not alone in bringing the *Auto Parts* case against China, the first WTO litigation brought against China since it acceded to the WTO on December 11, 2005 (previous Chinese involvement was limited to a third-party role).[1] Canada and the European Communities (EC) also filed suit against China. No longer was China a voluntary third-party participant; now, it was compelled to defend its trade rules and policies before an independent international adjudicator.

More than history was at stake. Commercially, China is the third largest economy in the world (measured by Gross Domestic Product (GDP)), after the United States and Japan, and besting Germany in 2007.[2] After the United States, China boasts the second largest consumer auto market in the world.[3] Likewise, following America, China is the second largest producer of autos and auto parts in the world.[4] Yet in these two countries, the fortunes of this strategic sector are headed in opposite directions.

Car sales of new passenger vehicles in the United States (both total and retail) have trended downward since 2000 (from just under 18 to below 12 million vehicles per year between 2000 and 2009, respectively).[5] Job loss and wage decline in the American auto industry are a decades-long phenomenon. Conversely, the auto industry has been an engine of Chinese economic development. The market share of Chinese-owned vehicle producers (such as Chery) has risen relative to that of joint ventures between Chinese and foreign companies, and imported cars account for less than 5 percent of all auto sales in China.[6] China aims to win 10 percent of the global car market by about 2016.[7] (A worrying sign for China is the effect of recession on its prized auto industry; in early 2009, the market for used cars was growing faster than for new cars, adding to protectionist pressures within the country.[8]) These commercial facts have their own political ramifications—that is, the *Auto Parts* case is an historic one set in the broad context of China's political economy and development.

This chapter explores China's first loss in the WTO. And lose it did, at both the Panel and Appellate Body stage, on all the claims that mattered. The 25 percent charge China imposed on imported auto parts ran afoul of the Golden Rule of international trade law: national treatment. Part II sets out the facts of the case. Part III examines the Panel rulings. Part IV surveys the key issues on appeal and the holdings of the Appellate Body. Parts V and VI analyze the appellate arguments China made and lost.

Part VII puts the case in the wider context of China's legal and political development. This Part offers three perspectives. First, China can take heart from a small victory it achieved in the case, namely, in proving it did not violate the promises it made when acceding to the WTO. Second, the case is a useful tutorial for China about the Golden Rule of trade, which stems from Article III of the General Agreement on Tariffs and Trade (GATT). Third, and perhaps most importantly, the case plays only a small role in a much grander drama on stage in China concerning the grip on political power held by the Chinese Communist Party (CCP).

B. The Broad Context

As intimated above, the *Auto Parts* case ought not to be viewed narrowly as a one-off technical legal event. Rather, it ought to be seen in a broad context. Development is the underlying narrative in the story of China's first defeat in the WTO. A common feature of developing countries (and, *a fortiori*, the least-developed countries) is that they lack the legal capacity to participate fully and effectively in the international trade arena. As the world's largest developing country, China is a land of pockets of garish wealth and stunning skylines amidst a desert of mild to extreme poverty and life-threatening pollution. Its legal capacity in international trade is a microcosm of this macrocosm.

China has a small but growing cadre of brilliant trade lawyers, typically educated outside China and now working in Beijing and Shanghai. The vast majority of lawyers and, worryingly, judges have precious little appreciation for the policies, much less intricacies, of the GATT–WTO regime. Thus, the *Auto Parts* dispute provides the first case study in the development of China's legal capacity to bring and defend claims on the world stage. Why did China not settle the case after it failed to give a convincing justification for its controversial measures?[9] Why did it press on with an appeal after the widely reported preliminary and final panel rulings that clearly condemned its controversial trade measures?[10] How did China argue the case, given that it was aware of the strong claims against it since 2004?[11] Why were China's arguments largely unpersuasive? What legal lessons are there for China as it develops in the area of international trade adjudication? These and related topics will be asked and debated for generations to come, and rightly so if China aspires to develop its trade law capacity. Assuming China indeed has this aspiration, it might also be queried as to why (despite the requests of the complainants) it refused to allow public access to the WTO proceedings?[12]

Not surprisingly, *The Economist* summarized the wide context and repercussions of China's first loss not only for China but also for foreign countries and their industries:

> on a symbolic and practical level, the case could be a turning-point for many industries in China: the start of a new era in which they are attacked by litigation. . . .
>
> The WTO decision also draws attention to China's increasingly fractious trade relationships, which are the source of a growing number of anti-dumping actions. . . . Most importantly, it shows China's potential vulnerability before the WTO.
>
> . . . [T]he Chinese government has not just intervened on behalf of partsmakers. It has erected barriers to protect many other industries, for example by imposing elaborate registration and certification requirements for imported food, cosmetics, chemicals, and pharmaceuticals. These do not apply to local firms, which is just the kind of preferential treatment that could fall foul of WTO rules.
>
> China was eager to join the WTO on the basis that membership of a large, multilateral organisation would enhance its ability to compete with other big countries. But its odd, state-dominated economy makes it particularly sensitive to verdicts of this kind.[13]

A related matter is the role exports play in Chinese economic growth, which, in two words, is "huge" and "unsustainable."

As even China's Premier, Wen Jiabao, has admitted, its growth is "unstable, unbalanced, uncoordinated, and unsustainable" for China to continue to rely on exports rather than domestic consumption as the dominant component of its growth in Gross Domestic Product (GDP).[14] In the United States personal consumption was 67 percent of GDP for the last quarter of the twentieth century, and 72 percent between 2000 and 2008. In China, however, domestic consumption has fallen from 45 percent of the GDP in the mid-1990s to 35 percent in 2009. If China hopes to boost this percentage, it must increase its wage levels so that its citizens have more disposable income to spend. (Wages in China account for 40 percent of GDP, whereas in the Group of Seven (G-7) industrialized nations, the comparable figure is 52 percent.) But how can China boost wage levels without damaging its international competitive advantage by driving up its own labor costs? Even if wage levels rise, why would average Chinese citizens spend on consumer items when they must save for their and their children's education and health care as well as for their pensions, as the state no longer provides a comprehensive safety net? Amidst these challenges, how can China continue to privatize state-owned enterprises (SOEs), end export subsidies, allow its currency to float freely in foreign exchange markets, and open major sectors, like autos and auto parts, to free trade?

In sum, the historic *Auto Parts* case is a multilayered story in an environment of colossal challenges for China and the world. The case is about the development of legal capacity in the one developing country about which every other country cares. It is about a sector on which the fortunes of tens of millions of Chinese and foreigners ride. It is about the structure of the Chinese economy and the role the CCP plays in directing domestic and foreign factors of production. The *Auto Parts* case may even be about—in a tiny way—the beginning of the end of CCP's six decades of political dominance.

II. China's 2004 Automobile Policy[15]

Underlying the actions brought against China by the United States, Canada, and the EC was the same factual predicate. China imposed measures that adversely affected exports of automobile parts into the Chinese market.[16] In controversy were three legal instruments issued by the CCP government:

(1) Policy Order 8
   Policy on Development of the Automotive Industry, Order Number 8 of the National Development and Reform Commission, effective May 21, 2004.
(2) Decree 125–
   Administrative Rules on Importation of Automobile Parts Characterized as Complete Vehicles, Decree Number 125 of the People's Republic of China, effective April 1, 2005.
(3) Announcement 4
   Rules on Verification of Imported Automobile Parts Characterized as Complete Vehicles, Public Announcement Number 4 of 2005 of the Customs General Administration of the People's Republic of China, effective April 1, 2005.

Policy Order 8 establishes the legal basis for Decree 125 and Announcement 4. Under that Order, the Customs General Administration (CGA) works with other relevant Chinese governmental departments, such as the Ministries of Commerce and Finance, the National Development and Reform Commission (NDRC), and the Verification Centre, to promulgate specific rules about the imports of autos and auto parts. Decree 125 implemented those rules. Essentially, the rules deal with the supervision and administration of parts that are imported and subsequently assembled into certain models of cars. The rules also set the criteria to characterize whether imported auto parts should be treated as a complete vehicle. Announcement 4 gives further details on the procedures and criteria set out in Decree 125.

Taken together, the measures may be referred to as "China's 2004 Automobile Policy."[17]

Briefly stated, the Policy imposes a 25 percent charge on imported auto parts used in the manufacture or assembly of certain models of motor vehicles in China that are sold in the Chinese domestic market. But the imposition occurs only if those imported parts are characterized as—or, stated differently, if they have the essential character of—a completed vehicle based on criteria prescribed in the Policy.[18] Further, the charge is levied only after the parts are imported and assembled in China into a finished vehicle. The criteria are a set of thresholds concerning the type or value of imported auto parts used to produce specific models of vehicles. More precisely, as the Appellate Body explained,

The measures set out . . . the criteria that determine when imported parts used in a particular vehicle model must be deemed to have the "essential character" of complete vehicles and are thus subject to the 25 per cent charge. These criteria are expressed in terms of particular combinations or configurations of imported auto parts or the value of imported parts used in the production of a particular vehicle model. The use in the production of a vehicle model of specified combinations of "major parts" or "assemblies" that are imported requires characterization of *all* parts imported for use in that vehicle model as complete vehicles. [Note that the noun "assembly" as a synonym for "major part" should not be confused with the verb "assemble" in the sense of putting together parts to make a finished car.] Various combinations of assemblies will meet the criteria, for example: a vehicle body (including cabin) assembly and an engine assembly; or five or more assemblies other than the vehicle body (including cabin) and engine assemblies. The use, in a specific vehicle model, of imported parts with a total price that accounts for at least 60 per cent of the total price of the complete vehicle also requires characterization of *all* imported parts for use in that vehicle model as complete vehicles. Imports of CKD and SKD kits [completely knocked down vehicle kits and semi-knocked down vehicle

kits, respectively, discussed below] are also characterized as complete vehicles.[19]

Broadly speaking, this passage reveals two thresholds that will lead to characterizing imported auto parts as a completed vehicle:

(1) Volume threshold
    Employing certain key imported major parts (i.e., assemblies), or a designated combination of imported major parts, to make a vehicle, which effectively summed to 60 percent or more of the content of the vehicle.[20]
(2) Value threshold
    Employing imported parts in a vehicle that account for 60 percent or more of the total price of that vehicle.[21]

If the imported parts used in a particular vehicle meet or exceed the relevant threshold, then all of the imported parts used to assemble that model of vehicle are characterized as complete vehicles. As the Appellate Body explained,

When the imported parts used in the production of a specific vehicle model meet the criteria under the measures at issue, then the 25 per cent charge and the requirements under the measures apply in respect of *all* imported parts assembled into the relevant vehicle model. [That is, the charge affects every imported part assembled into a completed vehicle, even a part that was not considered when determining whether the vehicle model in question met the volume or value threshold.] It is immaterial whether the auto parts that are "characterized as complete vehicles" were imported in multiple shipments—that is at various times, in various shipments, from various suppliers and/or from various countries—or in a single shipment. It is also immaterial whether the automobile manufacturer imported the parts itself or obtained the imported parts in the domestic market through a third party supplier such as an auto part manufacturer or other auto part supplier. However, if the automobile manufacturer purchases imported parts from such an independent third party supplier, the automobile manufacturer may deduct from the 25 per cent charge that is due the value of any customs duties that the third party supplier paid on the importation of those parts, provided that the automobile manufacturer can furnish proof of the payment of such import duties. If optional parts that are imported are installed on a relevant vehicle model, the manufacturer must report those optional parts to the Verification Centre, make declarations at the time of the actual installation of the optional parts and pay the 25 per cent charge on such optional parts.[22]

In sum, under the 2004 Automobile Policy, imported automobile parts used in the production in China of a vehicle for sale in China are subject to a charge. That charge equals the tariff for a completed imported vehicle, namely, 25 percent, and the automobile parts manufacturer (not the importer) is legally liable for paying the charge.[23] In effect, China rolls up all imported parts together, and presumes irrebutably the imported parts impart the essential character of a completed vehicle. In turn, all imported parts used for the vehicle model are subject to the 25 percent charge. China imposes the charge after the vehicles have been assembled.

The 25 percent figure is no accident. It equals the average applied and bound tariff rate China lists in its Schedule of Concessions as applicable to complete motor vehicles.[24] The 25 percent most-favoured nation (MFN) duty rate is higher than the average rate China applies to auto parts, and has bound, which is 10 percent. As for imported auto parts that China does not characterize as complete vehicles, they are subject to the duty rate in China's Schedule for parts—that is, an average of 10 percent. Manifestly, China's 2004 Automobile Policy was an effort, *inter alia*, "to discourage foreign car makers from importing vehicles in large parts to circumvent the higher tariff."[25]

In sum, under the 2004 Automobile Policy, the imported automobile parts production charge is levied only if those parts are imported and used in the production and assembly of a vehicle in excess of certain thresholds. The thresholds, which are based on volume and value criteria the Policy lays out, define whether imported parts used in a particular vehicle model have the essential character of, and thus qualify as, a completed vehicle. If the imported parts have the essential character of a completed vehicle, then China slaps a 25 percent tariff on those parts and, indeed, all imported parts used to make that model of vehicle.

China also applies the 25 percent charge—that is, the tariff for a complete vehicle—on a CKD and SKD kit.[26] These kits are a subset of all the products covered by China's 2004 Automobile Policy.[27] Yet its Policy does not provide any definition of a "CKD" or "SKD" kit. Filling this definitional void, the Panel stated it considered these kits to refer to all, or nearly all, of the auto parts necessary to assemble a complete vehicle, which must be packaged and shipped in a single shipment and, following importation, must go through a process of assembly to become a completed vehicle.[28] The distinction between the two kits concerns assembly. A CKD kit contains auto parts imported together in an unassembled state. Subsequently, the parts are assembled to make a complete vehicle. An SKD kit also has auto parts imported together, but some of the components in an SKD kit have been assembled prior to importation.

The auto parts subject to the 25 percent charge fall into four categories of the Harmonized Commodity Description and Coding System (Harmonized System, or HS):

(1) Complete motor vehicles (headings 87.02–87.04).[29]
(2) Certain intermediate categories of auto parts, specifically chassis fitted with engines (heading 87.06) and bodies for motor vehicles (heading 87.07).
(3) Other intermediate categories of auto parts, specifically parts and components of motor vehicles that fall under a particular HS heading (heading 87.08).[30]

(4) Parts and accessories of motor vehicles that fall under a variety of HS Chapters other than Chapter 87, such as engines (Chapter 84) (specifically, parts under headings 84.07–84.09, 84.83, 85.01, 85.03, 85.06, 85.11–85.12, and 85.39).

Thus, for example, suppose imported parts exceed the applicable volume or value threshold. When this occurs, the Chinese government imposes on all imported parts used in the relevant vehicle model a charge amounting to 25 percent *ad valorem*, which is in addition to the normal MFN rate applicable to the parts. The Chinese government does not impose the same charge on domestically produced parts. Thus, the 2004 Automobile Policy imposes different charges on vehicles made in China depending on the domestic content of the parts used in the production process. The Policy penalizes a Chinese vehicle manufacturer for using imported auto parts in a vehicle destined for sale in China. Conversely, it gives producers an advantage if they use domestically made parts.

In sum, under the 2004 Automobile Policy, China bound its tariff on auto parts at most-favoured nation (MFN) rates considerably lower than its tariff bindings for complete vehicles— 10 versus 25 percent. Yet if an imported part is incorporated into a vehicle made and sold in China, and that vehicle contains imported parts in excess of a government-defined threshold, then the tariff imposed on the part is at the higher level—that is, that of a finished vehicle. In effect, China bumped up the tariff on the imported part to the level of a finished good.

Note, then, China's Schedule displays tariff escalation—the bound tariff rates are higher for complete motor vehicles than for components. The typical purpose of tariff escalation is to encourage the location of high value-added economic activity within the territory of the importing country. Further, the bump up is a way for China to discourage vehicle producers located in that country from using too many imported parts and encourage them to source their inputs from suppliers in China. That is be-

cause China's 2004 Automobile Policy specifies domestic content thresholds (using value or volume metrics).

This kind of encouragement is a prohibited subsidy, a Red Light import-substitution subsidy, under Article 3:1(b) of the WTO *Agreement on Subsidies and Countervailing Measures (SCM Agreement)*. That is, the "subsidy" (under Article 1) is government revenue China foregoes by imposing a lesser tariff on imported auto parts if a final, assembled vehicle contains the requisite amounts of local content. The subsidy is "specific" (under Article 2) to the auto industry. This specific subsidy is for import-substitution under Article 3:1(b). Avoidance of the extra charges is contingent on the use of domestic over imported goods. That, in turn, helps keep Chinese factories in business and workers employed—all at the expense of Canadian, European, and American car parts companies and their workforces.

The 2004 Automobile Policy also biases the pattern of foreign direct investment (FDI) into China, raising concerns among the complainants that China ran afoul of the WTO *Agreement on Trade-Related Investment Measures (TRIMs)*. The Policy confers an advantage on enterprises that use domestic rather than imported parts in the production of vehicles. This advantage may induce firms to establish parts manufacturing operations in China. By locating their plants in China rather than importing auto parts from outside China, they avoid imposition on the parts of the full vehicle duty rate.

III. China's Defeat at the Panel Stage[31]

In their separate actions before the Panel, the EC, Canada, and the United States made a large number of claims. Each complainant averred that China's 2004 Automobile Policy violated all or some of the following multilateral trade obligations:

- GATT Articles II:1(a)-(b) (concerning tariff bindings), III:1–2 and III:4 (concerning national treatment for fiscal and nonfiscal measures, respectively), III:5 (concerning domestic content requirements), and XI:1 (concerning quantitative restrictions).[32]

- Articles 2:1–2:2 of the WTO *TRIMs Agreement* (concerning national treatment and quantitative restrictions and referring to GATT Articles III and XI), along with the related Illustrative List (in Annex 1 thereto, particularly Paragraphs 1(a) and 2(a), concerning domestic sourcing and import-substitution, and referencing GATT Articles III:4 and XI:1).[33]

- Articles 3:1(b) and 3:2 of the WTO *SCM Agreement* (concerning prohibited or "Red Light," specifically import-substitution, subsidies).[34]

- Certain provisions in the WTO accession documents agreed to by China that lay out commitments China made to join the WTO, particularly Part I, Paragraphs 7.2–3 of the *Protocol of Accession*, and Paragraphs 93, 203, and 342 of the *Working Party Report on the Accession of China* (in conjunction with Part I, Paragraph 1.2 of the *Accession Protocol*).[35]

The complaining WTO members also asserted that the Automobile Policy nullified or impaired benefits accruing to them under the aforementioned agreements.

In the first decision by any WTO adjudicatory body against China, the *Auto Parts* Panel rendered a strong verdict against China's Automobile Policy on the most potent arguments of the complainants. In particular,[36]

- *National Treatment (Fiscal Measures) Violation*
  The complainants alleged that the 25 percent levy imposed under China's 2004 Automobile Policy was an "internal charge" incongruous with GATT Article III:2 (first sentence). China applied the internal charge to imported auto parts, but not to like domestic auto parts. That is, the internal charge China imposed on imported parts was in excess of that imposed on

domestic parts. China's response was that the 25 percent levy was an ordinary customs duty (OCD) within the meaning of Article II:1(b) (first sentence), not an internal charge subject to Article III:2 (first sentence). The Panel agreed with the complainants.

- *National Treatment (Non-Fiscal Measures) Violation*
  The complainants argued that by imposing the 25 percent levy, China violated GATT Article III:4 because it treated imported auto parts less favourably than like domestic auto parts. The less favourable treatment arose because China imposed additional administrative requirements and additional charges on automobile manufacturers that used imported auto parts in excess of thresholds specified in the 2004 Automobile Policy. The result was a disincentive for producers to use imported parts. China's response again was that the 25 percent levy was an OCD under Article II:1(b) (first sentence), not an internal measure governed by Article III:4. The Panel agreed with the complainants.

- *Alternative Tariff Bindings Violation*
  As an alternative contention, the complainants said China breached GATT Article II:1(a)-(b). The charge on imported auto parts imposed under China's 2004 Automobile Policy—if considered an OCD—exceeded the bound tariff rates set out in China's Schedule of Concessions. That Schedule is annexed to its *Protocol of Accession*, hence there was a violation of it and the *Accession Working Party Report*. China countered that the Policy did not run afoul of Article II but rather gave effect to the proper interpretation of the term "motor vehicles" in its Schedule. As an alternative to its findings under Article III:1–2, the Panel held that the Policy established an OCD within the scope of Article II:1(b) (first sentence). Under its Policy, China imposed duties in excess of the relevant tariff bindings in China's

Schedule, which were incongruous with Article II:1(a)-(b).

• *Special Finding on Auto Kits*

On the assumption the 25 percent charge is characterized as an OCD, the complainants charged China violated GATT Article II:1(b) (first sentence) in its treatment of the CKD and SKD kits. The Panel disagreed, handing China its only substantive victory in the case. That is, the Panel said China legitimately could classify a CKD and SKD kit as a completed "motor vehicle" under its Schedule of Concessions, impose a 25 percent charge, and not breach its Article II:1(b) (first sentence) tariff binding for finished cars.[37] However, the Panel held that Chinese treatment of these kits was inconsistent with Paragraph 93 of China's *Accession Working Party Report*. In that Paragraph, China pledged not to apply a tariff rate above 10 percent to imports of CKD and SKD kits. This Paragraph states,

Certain members of the Working Party expressed particular concerns about tariff treatment in the auto sector. In response to questions about the tariff treatment for kits for motor vehicles, the representative of China confirmed that China had no tariff lines for completely knocked-down kits for motor vehicles or semi-knocked down kits for motor vehicles. *If China created such tariff lines, the tariff rates would be no more than 10 per cent.* The Working Party took note of this commitment.[38]

To reach its conclusion, the Panel held that by implementing the 2004 Automobile Policy, China had created new tariff lines for CKD and SKD kits at the HS-10 digit level.

• *Failure of the Administrative Necessity Defense*

The complainants urged that the violation of Article III:4, or in the alternative Article II:1(a)-(b), could not be excused under the administrative necessity exception of Article XX(d), which China had invoked.

China invoked this exception because it said 2004 Automobile Policy ensures "substance over form" in its administration of customs law. That is because the Policy allows Chinese customs officials to classify as a complete motor vehicle those groups of auto parts that have the essential character of a complete vehicle, regardless of how an importer structures importation of the parts. In other words, the Policy prevents the circumvention of China's tariff headings for complete motor vehicles. (This argument, of course, is about substantial completeness, a problem dealt with in United States customs law by the five-factor *Daisy Heddon* Test in U.S. customs law and under World Customs Organisation (WCO) standards by the *General Rule of Interpretation* (*GRI*) 2(a), known as the "Doctrine of the Entireties."[39] China's point was that it properly applied *GRI* 2(a) by treating a dissembled set of parts that has the essential character of a car—that is, is a substantially complete car—as a complete vehicle. Indeed, if it did not do so, said China, then importers would be able to circumvent its 25 percent MFN tariff on cars.) However, the Panel rejected China's argument about tariff circumvention, partially because of the increasing standardization of auto parts, which means that many parts can be used interchangeably among different car models, allowing manufacturers to realize economies of scale by making families of vehicle models that share platforms and components, and for which 60–70 percent of parts are common to the models. The Panel agreed China failed to prove that its violations of its GATT obligations satisfied the two-step test under the Article XX(d) exception.

Still other major claims against China arose under GATT Articles III:5 and XI:1; Article 2 of the *TRIMs Agreement* (including Paragraph 1(a) of Annex 1 thereto); Article 3:1(b) and 3:2 of the *SCM Agreement*; Part I, Paragraphs 7:2–3 of China's *Accession Protocol*; and Paragraph 203 of its *Accession Working Party Report*. On all these claims, the Panel exercised judicial economy.

IV. The Unsuccessful Appeal[40]

A. Issues and Holdings

Not surprisingly, but perhaps not wisely, China appealed the verdicts of the Panel. For the Appellate Body, the key issues were as follows:[41]

- *Internal Charge or OCD?*
  Is the 25 percent charge an internal charge under GATT Article III:2 (first sentence) rather than an OCD under Article II:1(b) (first sentence)?[42] China argued that the Panel erred in ruling that this charge is properly characterized as an internal charge and is thus subject to the national treatment rule rather than an OCD governed by the tariff binding rule. Briefly, the Appellate Body upheld the Panel finding; that is, the Appellate Body agreed the charge is an internal charge under Article III:2 (first sentence), not an OCD under Article II:1(b) (first sentence).[43]
- *National Treatment (Fiscal Measures) Violation?*
  Is the 25 percent charge illegal under GATT Article III:2 (first sentence)?[44] China urged the Panel was wrong in holding that the charge exceeded impositions levied on like domestic products. Briefly, the Appellate Body upheld the Panel. In respect to imported auto parts in general, China's 2004 Automobile Policy violates Article III:2 (first sentence) because it subjects imported parts to an internal charge not applied to like domestic auto parts.[45]
- *National Treatment (Non-Fiscal Measures) Violation?*
  Is the 2004 Automobile Policy through which China imposes the 25 percent charge illegal under GATT Article III:4?[46] China claimed the Panel was mistaken in finding that its Policy treated imported auto parts less favourably than like domes-

tic merchandise. The Appellate Body thought China was mistaken, ruling with respect to auto parts in general that the Policy accords less favourable treatment to imported parts than to like domestic parts and, thus, violates Article III:4.[47]
- *Tariff Bindings Violation?*
  Is the 2004 Automobile Policy through which China imposes the 25 percent charge illegal under GATT Article II:1(a)-(b)?[48] That is, assuming *arguendo* the Appellate Body reverses the finding of the Panel that the charge is an internal charge under Article III:2 (first sentence) and classifies it as an OCD under Article II:1(b) (first sentence), then was the Panel wrong in its alternative ruling that the Policy violates the Article II:1(a)-(b) tariff binding provisions? China faulted this alternative ruling. The Appellate Body exercised judicial economy, finding it unnecessary to issue a ruling on the question.[49]
- *Accession Commitment Violation?*
  Is the 2004 Automobile Policy inconsistent with the conditional commitment China made in Paragraph 93 of its *Accession Working Party Report* not to apply a tariff rate above 10 percent to imports of CKD and SKD kits?[50] Specifically, did the Panel err in construing the Policy as imposing a charge on CKD and SKD kits, and was it mistaken to rule that China did not meet its Paragraph 93 commitment? This holding rested on two other findings, namely, that the Policy (1) was deemed to have created tariff lines for CKD and SKD kits, and (2) established separate tariff lines at the HS-10 digit level for these kits. Accordingly, these findings were at issue on appeal. Briefly, the Appellate Body sided with China, holding that the Policy did not impose a charge on CKD and SKD kits, and China did meet its accession commitments with respect to the kits.[51]

On all but the final issue, which itself was at the periphery of the case, China lost its appeal.

Given the meticulous work of the Panel, premised on a considerable amount of GATT Panel and Appellate Body jurisprudence, the loss was predictable. It was all the more predictable because of China's appellate argumentation. China overwhelmingly relied, not on well-grounded in facts, but instead on the claim that the 25 percent charge was governed by GATT Article II, not Article III. Put differently, China gambled that the same argument it made and lost at the Panel stage would somehow persuade the Appellate Body.

China did not appeal the finding of the Panel that its 2004 Automobile Policy failed to qualify for administrative necessity under GATT Article XX(d).[52] That decision is mildly puzzling. With the gamble China took on its argument-in-chief, it raised the stakes on itself when it removed its only viable fallback position, namely, the administrative necessity defense.

B. The Key Threshold Question[53]

A trade measure cannot simultaneously qualify as an internal charge under GATT Article III and an OCD under Article II. The measure either is imposed after the border (i.e., post-entry), in which case it is in the first category and governed by the national treatment rules, or it is imposed at the border (i.e., pre-entry), in which case it is in the second category and governed by the tariff binding rules. Put simply, a measure is either an internal tax or a tariff, but not both. Even China accepted this elementary distinction.[54]

Thus, logically, the Appellate Body started with the question of what the 25 percent charge is and thereby what rules of GATT govern it. Indeed, it spent considerable time and effort doing so. Why did the Appellate Body agree with the Panel and hold that the 25 percent charge is best characterized as a internal charge under GATT Article III:2 (first sentence)?[55]

The answer, in brief, is that the Panel performed its task of defining and delineating carefully. Following the dictates on treaty interpretation in Articles 31–32 of the *Vienna Convention on the Law of Treaties*, the Panel looked to the ordinary meaning of the terms "internal charge" and "OCD." It also looked to the context in which each term is situated. For internal charge, that context is the phrase "imported into the territory" in Article III:2 (first sentence) and the Interpretative Note, *Ad Article III, Paragraph 2* (also called the "*Ad Note*"). For "OCD," the context was the phrase "on their importation" in the first sentence of Article II:1(b) and the phrase "on or in connection with the importation" in the second sentence of Article II:1(b). Also informing the meaning of the two terms was the accretion of GATT and WTO jurisprudence, starting as far back as 1952 with the GATT Panel Report, *Belgium—Family Allowances*,[56] and the 1990 GATT Panel Report in *EEC—Parts and Components*.[57]

On these bases, in respect of "OCD," the Panel concluded logically as follows:

the ordinary meaning of "on their importation" in Article II:1(b), first sentence, of the GATT 1994, considered in its context and in light of the object and purpose of the GATT 1994, contains a *strict and precise temporal element* which cannot be ignored. This means that the obligation to pay ordinary customs duties is linked to the product at the moment it enters the territory of another Member. . . . It is at this moment, and this moment only, that the obligation to pay such charge accrues. . . . And it is based on the condition of the good at this moment that any contemporaneous or subsequent act by the importing country to enforce, assess or reassess, impose or collect ordinary customs duties should be carried out.

In contrast to ordinary customs duties, the obligation to pay internal charges does not accrue because of the importation of the product at the very moment it enters the territory of another Member but because of the internal factors (*e.g.,* because the product was re-sold internally or because the product was used internally), which occurs once the product has been *imported* into the territory of another member. The status of the *imported* good, which does not necessarily correspond to its status at the moment of *importation*, seems to be the relevant basis to assess this internal charge.[58]

Succinctly put, the Panel said,

if the obligation to pay a charge does not accrue based on the product at the moment of its importation, it cannot be an "ordinary customs duty" within the meaning of Article II:1(b), first sentence of the GATT 1994: it is, instead, an "internal charge" under Article III:2 of the GATT 1994, which obligation to pay accrues based on internal factors.[59]

In contrast, in respect to the internal charge, the Appellate Body summarized the Panel understanding as follows:

161. Like the Panel, we consider that the adjectives "internal" and "imported" suggest that the charges falling within the scope of Article III are charges that are imposed on goods that have already been "imported," and that the obligation to pay them is triggered by an "internal" factor, something that takes place *within* the customs territory. Further, the second sentence of Article III:2 expressly refers to the principles set forth in Article III:1. The Appellate Body has stated that Article III:1 articulates a general principle, that informs all of Article III, that internal measures should not be applied so as to afford protection to domestic production.[60]

162. . . . in examining the scope of application of Article III:2, in relation to Article II:1(b), first sentence, the time at which a charge is collected or paid is not decisive. In the case of Article III:2, this is explicitly stated in the GATT 1994 itself, where the *Ad* Note to Article III specifies that when an internal charge is "collected or enforced in the case of the imported product at the time or point of importation," such a charge "is nevertheless to be regarded" as an internal charge. What is important, however, is that the *obligation* to pay a charge must accrue due to an internal event,

such as the distribution, sale, use or transportation of the imported product.

163. This leads us, like the Panel, to the view that a key indicator of whether a charge constitutes an "internal charge" within the meaning of Article III:2 of the GATT 1994 is "whether the obligation to pay such charge accrues because of an *internal* factor (*e.g.*, because the product was *re-sold* internally or because the product was *used* internally), in the sense that such 'internal factor' occurs *after the importation* of the product of one Member into the territory of another Member."[61]

The work of the Panel serves as an excellent tutorial—not only for China but also all WTO Members—on the different scope of application between the tariff binding and national treatment obligations in GATT, and it is no surprise the Appellate Body admired the Panel's analytical approach.

The boundaries between these obligations must be respected if their distinct objects and purposes are to be served.[62] Binding tariffs under Article II preserves the value of negotiated reductions in duties. Nondiscriminatory treatment, with respect to both internal taxes and regulatory measures, under Article III is essential in order to avoid the devilish protectionist temptation to favour like domestic products over imported merchandise. Together, the distinct disciplines promote the objective of the *Agreement Establishing the World Trade Organisation* (*WTO Agreement*), namely, to promote the security and predictability of reciprocal, mutually advantageous trade-liberalizing arrangements.

In lawyerlike fashion, the Panel then turned to the task of applying these GATT principles to the facts of the case. Briefly, the Panel was struck by four key facts about the operation of China's 2004 Automobile Policy:

- The obligation to pay the charge becomes ripe internally, that is, after the auto parts have entered the customs territory of China and been assembled into motor vehicles in China.

- The 25 percent charge is imposed on automobile parts manufacturers, not on importers.
- The charge is not levied on specific imported parts at the moment of importation. Rather, it is levied on specific imports based on what other imported or domestic parts are used together with those specific imports in assembling a vehicle model.
- Identical imported parts, which are imported simultaneously in the same container and vessel, can be subject to a different charge rate, depending on whether the vehicle model into which these parts are subsequently assembled satisfies the thresholds in the criteria set out in the Policy.

These four facts (supplemented by others, as explained below) led the Panel inexorably to the conclusion that the 25 percent charge is an internal one under GATT Article III:2 (first sentence).

Notably, China misunderstood or obscured what the Panel did and did not infer from these facts, particularly the first one. China suggested the Panel held that

the mere fact that the assembly of parts into a completed vehicle will necessarily occur *after* the parts have entered the customs territory means that a charge assessed on this basis is an internal charge.[63]

Not so, said the Appellate Body.[64] The Panel simply looked at when and where the obligation to pay the charge accrues and then weighed that with other facts. The small comfort for China was that the Panel excluded from this finding the charge on CKS and SKD kits and found that the charge on the kits was an OCD under the first sentence of Article II:1(b).

V. China's Three Unsuccessful Claims of Panel Error

China's appellate argument was that the Panel failed to take into account *GRI* 2(a)—the Doctrine of the Entireties, as it is known in U.S. customs law—which states,

Any reference in a heading to an article shall be taken to include a reference to that article incomplete or unfinished, provided that, as presented, the incomplete or unfinished article has the essential character of the complete or finished article. It shall also be taken to include a reference to that article complete or finished (or falling to be classified as complete or finished by virtue of this Rule), presented unassembled or disassembled.[65]

China asserted that this Rule enables customs authorities to classify unassembled auto parts as a complete motor vehicle, even in the situation in which the parts arrive in multiple shipments and the parts are assembled after importation.[66] As for the text of Article II:1(b) (first sentence), China said it requires customs authorities to determine what the "product" in question is, and then, following HS Rules, classify the product and apply the correct OCD to it.

Specifically, China accused the Panel of three mistakes. First, the Panel ought not to have separated (1) the threshold question of whether the 25 percent charge is an OCD from (2) the question of whether China is authorized to apply *GRI* 2(a) to multiple entries of auto parts. The 25 percent charge is inextricably linked to valid classification procedures under HS Rules. The Panel should have examined the two questions simultaneously, not sequentially.

Second, the Panel wrongly refused to characterize the 25 percent charge as an OCD under Article II:1(b) (first sentence). China urged that it is impossible to decide whether its charge is an OCD without taking proper account of the term "product" in that Article, in light of the classification rules of the HS, like *GRI* 2(a). China conceded Article II:1(b) (first sentence) emphasizes the moment of importation as pertinent to ascertaining whether a charge is an OCD, but, no less relevant is the "condition," or "status," of the product at the moment it enters the importing country. *GRI* 2(a) is needed to determine whether or not the condition of status of a completely unassembled motor vehicle at that moment permits the parts to be classified as a complete vehicle. In essence, the Panel erred by neglecting to use the HS Rule to interpret the significant GATT terms.

Third, said China, the Panel erroneously dubbed the 25 percent charge an internal charge under GATT Article III:2 (first sentence). China insisted that the fact that auto parts are assembled into a completed vehicle after importation does not mean the 25 percent charge is governed by that provision. In other words, China faulted the Panel for making too much of the time and place of assembly—after importation, postborder. All three claims of Panel error were related, and to some degree China's style of argumentation—as recounted by the Appellate Body—lacked the clarity and precision expected of a sophisticated presentation.

A. Wrongful Separation of Issues

China's argument about the first error it contended the Panel made was a *post hoc* rationalization for the 25 percent charge as well as an argument with no factual basis. Conceptually, its argument made no sense. As the United States, Canada, and the EU all rightly pointed out, to accept China's position would be to "blur," or "confuse," the threshold issue of what provision of GATT governs the controversial 25 percent charge with the distinct question of whether the charge is consistent with that provision.[67] China put the "cart before the horse" when it presumed the charge is an OCD, especially when that is the first question in need of analysis.[68]

Unsurprisingly, the Appellate Body sided with the Panel and complainants:

> In its appeal, China challenges the Panel's decision to analyze the threshold issue separately from the issue of the consistency of the measures with Article II:1(b) of the GATT 1994. Yet, as the Appellate Body has previously observed, the "fundamental structure and logic" of

a covered agreement may require panels to determine *whether* a measure falls within the scope of a particular provision or covered agreement *before* proceeding to assess the consistency of the measure with the substantive obligations imposed under that provision or covered agreement. We consider this to be just such a case, particularly in the light of the Panel's observation—with which China expressly agrees—that "a charge cannot be at the same time an 'ordinary customs duty' under Article II:1(b) of the GATT 1994 and an 'internal tax or other internal charge' under Article III:2 of the GATT." If, as the Panel considered, the charge imposed on automobile manufacturers could fall within the scope of either the first sentence of Article II:1(b) *or* Article III:2, then the Panel had to begin its analysis by ascertaining *which* of these provisions applied in the circumstances of this dispute.[69]

In sum, the Appellate Body approved of the sequential methodology of the Panel to treat the threshold issue of "what GATT rule applies?" before considering "did the 25 percent charge violate the rule?"[70]

B. Using the *GRI* as Context to Interpret GATT

As to the second error China contended the Panel made, here, too, the Appellate Body looked approvingly at the work of the Panel and quoted generously from it. There is a strict, precise temporal element to Article II:1(b) (first sentence). That is clear from the terms surrounding OCD that indicate an OCD is imposed on "products, on their importation."[71] If a charge does not accrue at the moment of importation, it is not an OCD. China cited an Appellate Body precedent, *EC—Chicken Cuts*, in which the Appellate Body agreed it is permissible to examine the HS as context for interpreting a GATT–WTO text, even though the HS is not technically part of the accords annexed to the *WTO Agreement* (i.e., it is not a covered agreement).[72]

In *EC—Chicken Cuts,* the Appellate Body considered the issue of whether the Harmonized

System could constitute context for the interpretation of a term in the European Communities' Schedule of Concessions. The Appellate Body pointed out that although the Harmonized System is not formally part of the *WTO Agreement*, there is nonetheless a close link between that System and the covered agreements. The Appellate Body explained that

> . . . prior to, during, as well as after the Uruguay Round negotiations, there was broad consensus among the GATT Contracting Parties to *use* the Harmonized System as the basis for their WTO Schedules, notably with respect to agricultural products. In our view, this consensus constitutes an "agreement" between WTO Members "relating to" the *WTO Agreement* that was "made in connection with the conclusion of" that *Agreement*, within the meaning of Article 31(2)(a) of the *Vienna Convention*. As such, this agreement is "context" under Article 31(2)(a) for the purpose of interpreting the WTO agreements, of which the EC Schedule is an integral part. In this light, we consider that the Harmonized System is relevant for purposes of interpreting tariff commitments in the WTO Members' Schedules.[73]

However, the complainants astutely observed that China made too much of this precedent. It relates to the use of the HS only to interpret a term in a Schedule of Concessions, not a term in a GATT–WTO rule.

The Appellate Body agreed with the view of the complainants on *EC—Chicken Cuts*:

> The negotiators of the *WTO Agreement* used the Harmonized System as the basis for negotiating Members' Schedules of Concessions, and included express references to the Harmonized System in certain covered agreements for purposes of defining product coverage of those agreements or specific provisions thereof. It follows that the Harmonized System is context for purposes of interpreting the covered agreements, in particular for the classification of products under Schedules of Concessions and

for defining the product coverage of certain covered agreements. This is what the Appellate Body found in *EC—Chicken Cuts*. Yet this does not answer the question of whether the Harmonized System is context that is relevant to the determination of whether a charge is an ordinary customs duty or an internal charge.[74]

As to the latter question, the Appellate Body looked to the direction of Article 31(2) of the *Vienna Convention*, which states,

> The context for the purpose of the interpretation of a treaty shall comprise, in addition to the text, including its preamble and annexes:
>
> (a) any agreement relating to the treaty which was made between all the parties in connection with the conclusion of the treaty;
>
> (b) any instrument which was made by one or more parties in connection with the conclusion of the treaty and accepted by the other parties as an instrument related to the treaty.[75]

The Appellate Body explained that context must be relevant to the interpretative question at issue.

Because the Schedule of Concessions of every WTO Member is constructed using the HS, the rules of the HS are relevant context for discerning the meaning of a term in a Schedule. Thus, if the question in the case at bar was whether China could classify auto parts as complete motor vehicles, then it would be necessary to interpret China's Schedule. Yet, that is not the question. The key matter—to which the HS rules are not pertinent—is defining "OCD" and "internal charge" under GATT Articles II:(1)(b) and III:2 (first sentence), respectively.

> 155. . . . The Harmonized System categorizes products, and the characteristics of particular products are relevant to how they are categorized. We recognize, as China argues, that classification, and hence the tariff rate applied, might, in some circumstances, vary depending on the condition of goods at the moment of importation. Since different categories of products are subject to different bound and applied tariff

rates, the classification of a given product may affect the amount of the duty imposed. Accordingly, classification issues have some bearing on the question of whether a Member applying such a duty is in conformity with its obligation, under Article II:1(b), not to impose duties in excess of the bound rate set out in the Member's Schedule for the product concerned. Yet this issue (whether a duty applied to a *product* by virtue of its classification is consistent with Article II:1(b)) is separate from the issue of whether a *charge* falls under the first sentence of Article II:1(b) at all (as opposed to under Article III:2). It is not evident to us how classification rules are relevant to the latter issue. While it is true, as China argues, that the "classification of the product necessarily precedes the determination of which 'ordinary customs duty' applies," it is not the case that classification of the product (even if properly done) necessarily precedes a determination of *whether* the charge that applies is an ordinary customs duty. . . .

158. Yet we fail to see how the Panel erred in not relying on GIR 2(a) in resolving the threshold issue of whether the charge imposed under the measures at issue is an ordinary customs duty or an internal charge. The *right* of a WTO Member to impose a customs duty, and the *obligation* of an importer to pay such a duty, accrue at the very moment the product enters the customs territory of that Member and by virtue of the event of importation. In contrast, the classification rules according to which customs authorities determine under which tariff heading the "product" concerned falls, depending on its "status" or "condition," are not relevant to the nature of the "duty" itself because they do not determine the *moment* at which the *obligation* to pay accrues, but only the *amount* of that duty. Similarly, as all of the participants agree, the moment at which a charge is *collected* or *paid* is not determinative of whether it is an ordinary customs duty or an internal charge. Ordinary customs duties may be collected *after* the moment of importation, and internal charges may be collected at the moment of importation. For a charge to constitute an ordinary customs

duty, however, the *obligation* to pay it must accrue at the moment and by virtue of or, in the words of Article II:1(b), "on," importation. . . .

163. . . . We also observe that the Harmonized System does not serve as relevant context for the interpretation of the term "internal charges" in Article III:2.

164. In sum, we see the Harmonized System as context that is most relevant to issues of classification of products. The Harmonized System complements Members' Schedules and confirms the general principle that [as the Appellate Body stated in *EC—Chicken Cuts*] it is "the 'objective characteristics' of the product in question when presented for classification at the border" that determine their classification and, consequently, the applicable customs duty. The Harmonized System, and the product categories that it contains, cannot trump the criteria contained in Article II:1(b) and Article III:2, which distinguish a border measure from an internal charge under the GATT 1994. Among WTO Members, it is these GATT provisions that prevail, and that define the relevant characteristics of ordinary customs duties for WTO purposes. Thus, even if the Harmonized System and GIR 2(a) would allow auto parts imported in multiple shipments to be classified as complete vehicles based on subsequent common assembly, as China suggests, this would not *per se* affect the criteria that define an ordinary customs duty under Article II:1(b). . . .

166. . . . [A] determination of whether a particular charge falls under Article II:1(b) or Article III:2 of the GATT 1994 must be based on a proper interpretation of these two provisions. The Harmonized System does not provide context that is relevant to the threshold question or to the assessment of the respective scope of application of "ordinary customs duties" in the first sentence of Article II:1(b) and "internal charges" in Article III:2 of the GATT 1994 that must be undertaken in answering that question. It follows that the Panel did not err in interpreting the term "ordinary customs duties" in the first sentence of Article II:1(b) of the GATT 1994 without relying on the rules of the Harmonized System, in general, or GIR 2(a), in particular.[76]

The above-quoted paragraphs may be distilled as follows: The essence of China's appellate argument was that China correctly classified the "product"—a completed vehicle—under *GRI* 2(a), thus its 25 percent charge must be an OCD under Article II:1(b) (first sentence). But, "must be" and "is" are not the same. It is specious to conflate tariff classification under HS Rules with the related matter of respect for tariff bindings under Article II:1(b) (first sentence), with the characterization of a charge as an OCD under that Article. Just because classification is done properly (a completed vehicle despite dissembled parts) and a charge has been imposed (25 percent) does not make that charge an OCD. As for the HS Rules, they are context most relevant to product classification, but they are not context that supersedes the language of GATT.

To this finding and rationale the Appellate Body added a consequential justification, one suggested by the Panel.[77] Suppose China's argument was accepted: A 25 percent charge imposed on auto parts following and as a result of their assembly into a completed vehicle constitutes an OCD. The consequence would be that whether any charge is an OCD would depend on circumstances that transpire after the border rather than solely on the moment of (and by virtue of) importation. The distinction between border and postborder would collapse because what happens after importation would affect the characterization of a charge at the border. Stated differently, the scope of OCD and Article II:1(b) (first sentence) would expand, but the scope of internal charges and Article III:2 (first sentence) would contract. The latter consequence would enervate the highly important national treatment discipline and upset the balanced structure that has been so carefully arranged by the GATT drafters and elaborated on through GATT and WTO adjudication.

C. Not Really an Internal Charge

Obviously, with the Appellate Body upholding the decision of the Panel that China's 25 percent levy was not an OCD under GATT Article II:1(b) (first sentence), the proper categorization was an internal charge under Article III:2 (first sentence). That categorization, according to China, was the third error made by the Panel. The Appellate Body did not agree and found no fault with the work of the Panel.

The Panel rightly scrutinized all relevant characteristics of the 25 percent charge, particularly its design and operation. That scrutiny enabled the Panel to identify the "center of gravity" of the charge based on its "core" or "leading" features—an essential task because some aspects may point to a conclusion that this charge is an OCD whereas others suggest it is an internal charge. The Panel also correctly examined the circumstances under which China imposed the 25 percent charge. In brief, the Panel correctly followed the teaching of the Appellate Body in *India—Additional Import Duties*, a case concerning whether a measure was governed by Article II:2(a) or the *Ad Note* to Article III.[78]

As summarized by the Appellate Body, the characteristics of the 25 percent charge that impressed the Panel and persuaded it that the charge was not an OCD governed by Article II:1(b) (first sentence) were as follows:

> 172. . . . The Panel identified the following characteristics of the charge as having particular significance for legal characterization purposes: (i) the obligation to pay the charge accrues internally after auto parts have entered the customs territory of China and have been assembled/produced into motor vehicles; (ii) the charge is imposed on automobile manufacturers rather than on importers in general; (iii) the charge is imposed based on how the imported auto parts are *used*, that is, *not* based on the auto parts as they enter, but instead based on what other parts from other countries and/or other importers and/or domestic parts are subsequently used, together with those imported parts, in assembling a vehicle model; and (iv) the fact that identical auto parts imported at the same time in the same container or vessel can be subject to different charge rates depending on which vehicle model they are assembled into.

173. We agree with the Panel as to the legal significance of these features of the measures at issue. Furthermore, there are additional characteristics of the charge imposed under the measures that the Panel recognized, and that support its characterization of that charge as an internal charge falling within the scope of Article III:2 of the GATT 1994. Foremost among these is the fact that it is not the declaration made at the time of importation, but rather the declaration of duty payment made subsequent to the assembly/production of complete motor vehicles, that determines whether the charge will be applied.

174. That the declaration made at the time of importation does not control or necessarily affect whether the charge under the measures will ultimately be applied to specific imported parts is illustrated most prominently in the scenario where an automobile manufacturer does not import parts directly, but instead purchases them from an independent third party supplier within China. In such circumstances, the third party supplier imports and declares those auto parts at the border and pays a 10 per cent duty. Yet those same parts may subsequently be subject to the 25 per cent charge—imposed after assembly—if they are sold to an automobile manufacturer and assembled into a vehicle model that meets the thresholds set out in the measures at issue.

175. In addition, there are at least two circumstances in which imported auto parts that are not characterized as complete vehicles or declared as such at the moment of importation will nonetheless be subject to the charge under the measures at issue following vehicle assembly: (i) when imported auto parts are installed on a vehicle as *options* (that is, such parts were not mentioned in the self-evaluation or Verification Report because they are not installed on the baseline models of the particular vehicle model in question), the manufacturer must report the options to the Verification Centre and make declarations for purposes of paying the charge at the time of the actual installation of the optional parts; and (ii) when, following re-verification due to an increase in the combinations or value of imported parts vis-à-vis

domestic parts, a vehicle model that previously did not meet the criteria under the measures at issue is determined to meet those criteria, the imported parts used in the production/assembly of that model must be declared after assembly, and will then be subject to the charge.

176. There are also at least two circumstances in which auto parts that are characterized as complete vehicles and declared as such at the time of importation will *not* attract the 25 per cent charge under the measures at issue, namely: (i) when imported parts that are characterized as complete vehicles in the declaration made at the time of importation are not assembled/produced into complete vehicles within 12 months, they must be declared within 30 days of the expiration of the 12-month period and will be subject to a 10 per cent charge, rather than the 25 per cent charge that would otherwise apply under the measures at issue; and (ii) when, following re-verification due to a decrease in the combinations or value of imported parts vis-à-vis domestic parts, a vehicle model that previously met the criteria under the measures at issue is determined no longer to meet those criteria, the imported parts used in the assembly/production of that model will not be subject to the charge under the measures at issue.[79]

Even a quick read of these characteristics indicates that the facts weighed heavily against China's argument of Panel error. Were there any countervailing facts supporting China's proposition that the 25 percent charge was an OCD? Indeed, China stressed four characteristics:

(i) the measures at issue use language typically reserved for references to "ordinary customs duties"; (ii) China's explanation of the policy purpose of the measures, and that the charge imposed thereunder "objectively relate[s] to the administration and enforcement of China's tariff provisions for motor vehicles"; (iii) China's view that parts imported directly by an automobile manufacturer remain subject to customs control until after assembly/production of the relevant vehicle model; and (iv) the measures at issue and the charge imposed thereunder are administered primarily by China's customs authorities.[80]

Here, again, even a glance at these characteristics reveals the weakness of China's argument. None of the premises individually, or taken in aggregate, are persuasive enough to offset the features pointing toward classifying the 25 percent charge under Article III:2 (first sentence).

The first feature is a matter of labeling by China. A WTO member can manipulate rubrics to suit its ends, but the job of a panel or the Appellate Body is to see through formalistic labels and look to underlying substantive reality. That is clear from Appellate Body precedent in *Softwood Lumber IV*.[81] The second feature is China's perspective. Legislative intent is difficult to discern, especially by external adjudicators, and it is not conclusive. That is apparent from the Appellate Body decision in the *Byrd Amendment* case.[82] The third feature actually cuts against China's argument. Imported auto parts are not physically confined or otherwise restricted by customs authorities and can be used freely in China's internal market. That is, importing these parts under the financial guarantee of a bond hardly amounts to "ongoing customs control." The fourth feature is a matter of China's internal administrative edifice. Decisive weight about interpreting a provision of GATT cannot be given to a point, like governmental structure, which is wholly under the control of a WTO Member. That is manifest in the 1990 *EEC— Parts and Components* GATT Panel Report.[83] The fourth feature cited by China also is not the whole truth. Other organs of the CCP—the Ministries of Commerce and Finance, and the NDRC, and the Verification Centre—have official roles in administering the 25 percent charge.

VI. What China Got Wrong

A. National Treatment

With the 25 percent charge clearly characterized as an internal charge, the next question concerned its consistency with the governing provision, GATT Article III:2 (first sentence). China made the job of the Appellate Body easy.[84] At no point in the case did China contend that the imported and domestic auto parts were not like products. Further, China admitted that if the charge was an internal one, then it violated Article III:2 (first sentence). Indubitably, the 25 percent charge was in excess of levies imposed on like domestic products. In other words, once China lost the debate to slot the charge as an OCD under Article II:1(b) (first sentence), it lost the debate about compliance with national treatment and fiscal measures.[85]

There is, of course, a second national treatment obligation. GATT Article III:4 covers all nonfiscal measures. The United States, Canada, and EU all successfully persuaded the Panel that China's 2004 Automobile Policy was an internal one within the ambit of this obligation and that it was incongruous with that obligation. That success carried through to the Appellate Body. The focus of this debate was on the regulatory requirements in the Policy that require all vehicle manufacturers in China to register and provide a listing and detailed records to Chinese customs authorities if they use imported auto parts.

China's losing argument on Article III:4 was essentially the same as on Article III:2 (first sentence): The 2004 Auto Policy imposes an OCD, so the correct rule to apply is Article II:1(b) (first sentence). Additionally, the administrative procedures for implementing the Policy are associated with imposing an OCD and should be viewed as customs measures to implement the classification rules of the HS, not internal rules governed by Article III:4. Not surprisingly, with little effort, the Appellate Body rejected the Chinese argument in the Article III:4 context, as it had in the Article III:2 (first sentence) context.[86] Manifestly, China had too much confidence in its characterization that the 25 percent charge, and the measures by which China administered the charge, were governed by Article II:1(b) (first sentence). Once China lost that debate, most of its case crumbled.

To be sure, however, China put up one argument on which the Appellate Body paused.[87]

China said the Panel was wrong to find that the 2004 Automobile Policy influences the choice by an automobile manufacturer between domestic and imported auto parts and, thus, affects the internal use of imported parts. China said the influence is created by the differential tariff structure—namely, a 10 percent bound duty on parts and a 25 percent bound rate for completed vehicles. The Panel wrongly premised an Article III:4 violation on an inherent feature of China's Schedule of Concessions. There is nothing illegal about discriminating against imported auto parts merely through the imposition of a customs duty validly imposed under GATT rules, that is, that those rules countenance one kind of discrimination—tariffs.

Unfortunately for China, it again misunderstood or obfuscated what the Panel had ruled.[88] The difference in bound rates for auto parts and completed vehicles in China's Schedule was not the discrimination concerning the internal use of imported auto parts on which the Panel relied to find a violation of GATT Article III:4. Rather, the Panel looked to the measures at issue, especially the incentives created for car manufacturers by the volume thresholds (i.e., the use of designated assemblies or combinations of assemblies) and value thresholds (i.e., the 60 percent test). Those thresholds determine whether China characterizes imported auto parts as complete vehicles. For an automobile manufacturer to avoid the 25 percent charge for a completed vehicle (and instead qualify for a 10 percent duty on parts), it must ensure that the imported parts it uses to assemble a vehicle model are below the thresholds. Moreover, if a manufacturer exceeds the thresholds, then the 25 percent charge applies to all imported parts it uses in the vehicle model in question. Further, if a manufacturer does exceed the thresholds, then it is subject to tracking and reporting requirements, and their attendant delays, concerning auto parts imported in multiple shipments.

Quite obviously, these realities are incentives for a manufacturer to limit its use of imported relative to domestic parts, and they "'affect' the *conditions of competition* for imported auto parts

on the Chinese internal market."[89] The Panel was on solid ground, citing the *U.S.—FSC (Article 21:5—EC)* decision of the Appellate Body, which explained that an incentive for a manufacturer not to use imported inputs affects the internal use of imported products, and thus violates Article III:4. That decision, plus long-standing jurisprudence under this Article, emphasizes the importance of not tilting the competitive playing field against foreign products vis-à-vis like domestic products. That lesson may be especially important for a Communist country like China when it is claiming that it is no longer a nonmarket economy (NME).

B. The Alternative

The United States, Canada, and EC convinced the Panel to reach an alternative finding; namely, if the 25 percent charge were an OCD, then China violated GATT Article II:1(a)-(b) by exceeding the bound rates for auto parts in its Schedule of Concessions.[90] Why did the Panel agree to embark on the alternative analysis in the first place? It looked out to the demands of the parties and up to the Appellate Body. The complainants and China disagreed on whether the charge violated this Article, so an issue was joined. There was the specter (perhaps remote) that the Appellate Body might overturn its finding under Article III:2 (first sentence), as the line between an OCD and an internal charge is not always bright.[91]

The Panel sided with the complainants, stating,

> the tariff provisions for motor vehicles (87.02–87.05) of China's Schedule of Concessions do not include in their scope auto parts imported in multiple shipments based on their assembly into a motor vehicle. Accordingly, to the extent the measures could be considered as falling within the scope of Article II of the GATT 1994, China's measures have the effect of imposing ordinary customs duties on imported auto parts in excess of the concessions contained in the tariff headings for auto parts under its

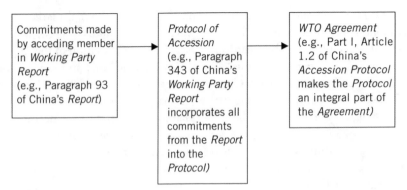

FIGURE 8.1 Legal linkages among WTO accession commitments and WTO Agreement

Schedule, inconsistently with its obligations under Article II:1(a) and (b) of the GATT 1994.[92]

The Panel premised this alternative finding on more than just the interpretation of "motor vehicles" in China's Schedule of Concessions. The criteria China applied to determine whether imported parts have the essential character of a completed vehicle also indicate China accords less favourable treatment to imported auto parts than it promises in its Schedule.

China's appeal raised serious systemic concerns, and the United States and EC expressly stated as much.[93] These two complainants sought the Appellate Body to perform a complete examination of the alternative finding of the Panel so as to leave no doubt about the inconsistency of China's 25 percent charge under GATT Article II. China posited two different scenarios. First, trotting out its old argument, China urged the Appellate Body to reverse the Panel and hold the 25 percent charge as an OCD under GATT Article II:1(b) (first sentence). If the Appellate Body does so, then it would see that the charge is based on a valid classification of imported auto parts under *GRI* 2(a) as a completed vehicle—hence, the charge is not a duty and is not in excess of China's tariff binding. This scenario, of course, did not materialize. Second, on the assumption that the Appellate Body upheld the conclusion of the Panel that the 25 percent charge was an internal one

governed by Article III:2 (first sentence), China called on the Appellate Body to declare the alternative finding of the Panel to be moot and of no legal effect. Seeing no reason to do so, the Appellate Body rejected that call.[94] In sum, leaving the Panel's alternative finding alone, the Appellate Body did the bidding of neither the complainants nor China.

VII. Legal Development and More

A. Keeping an Accession Promise

Promises made by a country in order to gain membership into the WTO are not political campaign promises; rather, they have legal consequences. They create an obligation enforceable under GATT–WTO law, specifically through the *DSU*.[95] That is true for a pledge set out in the *Working Party Report* on the accession of that member and for one set out in the *Protocol of Accession*. As the Diagram below indicates, the *Accession Protocol* itself states it is an integral part of the *WTO Agreement*. For example, this link is made in Part I, Article 1.2, of China's *Accession Protocol*. In turn, a *Working Party Report* incorporates into the *Accession Protocol* any commitment an acceding country makes in that *Report*. In China's case, Paragraph 342 of the *Working Party Report* incorporates China's promises in that *Report*, including Paragraph 93 concerning the 10 percent tariff on CKS and SKD kits.

Consequently, when faced with the issue of whether a member has broken a promise it made when joining the WTO, a WTO adjudicator can—indeed, must—apply the Article 31–32 *Vienna Convention* rules on treaty interpretation to *Working Party Reports* and *Accession Protocols*. That is exactly what the Panel and Appellate Body did in the *Auto Parts* case. The Panel held that China broke its promise not to apply a tariff rate in excess of 10 percent on CKD and SKD units.[96] China appealed on three grounds.

First, China said the Panel was wrong to characterize its 2004 Automobile Policy as imposing a "charge" or "duty" on an automobile manufacturer importing a CKS or SKD unit that declares the kit and pays subsequent duties at the border.[97] In fact, the Policy excludes the kits from both administrative procedures (e.g., declarations, bonding requirements, tracking, reporting, and verifications) and the 25 percent charge. True, the kits attract a 25 percent duty, but that is the MFN rate in China's Schedule of Concessions for completed vehicles, not the 25 percent charge under the Policy. In brief, the Policy entirely excludes the kits, and the basis for imposing the duty is Chinese customs law. So it was illogical for the Panel to say China's Policy as applied to the kits violated its accession commitments.

The Panel ruled that China misread or misunderstood its own Policy. The Panel examined carefully the relevant language in it (especially Articles 2(1)-(2) and 21 of Decree 125). An auto manufacturer importing a CKD or SKD kit has the option to exclude them from the administrative procedures attendant with the Policy, declare the kit at the border, and pay a 25 percent charge on the kit as a completed vehicle. A manufacturer exercising this option is relieved not from the obligation to pay the charge but rather the red-tape associated with paying the charge later, after it assembles the vehicle at a postborder location. This option is why the Panel excluded CKD and SKD kits from its ruling under GATT Article III:2 (first sentence). If an importer chooses to declare and pays duties on a kit at the border, then the 25 percent

charge it pays is a result of the operation of the Policy, not an internal charge subject to the national treatment rule. Additionally, held the Panel, the Chinese Policy created new tariff lines at the HS 10-digit level for CKD and SKD kits. The 25 percent charge on the kits is associated with those new lines.

The logical consequence of this reasoning was that China violated its Paragraph 93 accession commitment. Under its 2004 Automobile Policy, China imposed a tariff on CKD and SKD units higher than 10 percent. Existing WTO members negotiating with China for its accession specifically anticipated that China, once it joined the WTO, might try to treat the kits as completed vehicles. Doing so, they feared, would impede access to China's internal market; the 15 percentage point differential is a hefty cost for automobile manufacturers importing the kits. Thus, China was asked—and agreed—to hold the line at 10 percent.

The Appellate Body did not accept the finding and rationale of the Panel.[98] Reviewing the same language in the 2004 Automobile Policy, the Appellate Body said China had established (especially in Decree 125) a special, seamless regime of administrative procedures and the 25 percent charge covering imported auto parts characterized as a complete vehicle. The procedures and the charge were inseparable. A CKD and SKD kit that is declared for and paid at the border is exempt from that regime. The 25 percent tariff China levies on the kit is, as China argued, a consequence not of the special regime but rather arises under normal customs law. That is the MFN tariff on a finished car under China's Schedule governed by GATT Article II:1(b). The Appellate Body also faulted the Panel for not properly scrutinizing the key characteristics of the 25 percent charge in the context of CKD and SKD imports.[99] That failure was an asymmetry in the Panel Report. The Panel did study these characteristics in its threshold analysis under GATT Articles II:1(b) (first sentence) and III:2(b) (first sentence).

The bottom line was that China did not violate its Paragraph 93 accession commitment about a 10 percent cap on tariffs applied to SKD and CKD kits. The finding of the Panel that China broke its promise rested on an erroneous reading by the Panel that the 25 percent charge on imported kits arose under China's 2004 Automobile Policy. It did not. China's Policy is a seamless web. A declaration of a kit as a complete vehicle at the border exempts the declarer from both the administrative procedures and 25 percent charge arising under the Policy. The declaration subjects the kits to payment of a 25 percent duty under China's Schedule. In effect, Paragraph 93 is irrelevant to such kits. The charge on the kits is nothing more than an OCD—the MFN duty—governed by Article II:1(b) (first sentence). Here, China kept its promise.[100]

B. Applying the Golden Rule

The drafters of GATT showed considerable foresight in making as a pillar of their document the national treatment principle. They knew well that if a government is prone to discriminate, then it is highly likely to prefer its domestic producers over foreign competitors. GATT Article III is nothing less than the international trade law equivalent of the Golden Rule. One version, in the Judeo-Christian tradition, is found in the Old Testament:

> *Do to no one what you yourself dislike.* Give to the *hungry* some of your bread, and to the *naked* some of your clothing. *Seek counsel* from *every wise* man. At all times bless the Lord God, and ask him to make all your paths *straight* and to grant success to all your *endeavors and plans.*[101]

The New Testament expression is in the Gospel according to Matthew:

> When the Pharisees heard that he [Jesus] had silenced the Sadducees, they gathered together, and one of them [a scholar of the law] tested him by asking, "Teacher, which commandment in the law is the greatest?" He said to him, "You shall have the Lord, your God, with all your heart, with all your soul, and with all your mind.

This is the greatest and the first commandment. The second is like it: *You shall love your neighbour as yourself.* The whole law and the prophets depend on these two commandments."[102]

By no means, of course, is the Golden Rule uniquely Christian. It is expressed (directly or indirectly) in the sacred texts of other religions and philosophies.

The advocates for including China in the WTO urged that by making China a member, the international rule of law would circumscribe China's trade behavior. The GATT Golden Rule would be an international legal obligation incumbent on China to eschew viewing its domestically produced merchandise better than foreign competitors. That shift might help China emerge from a Middle Kingdom mentality, in a Maoist-era semi-isolationist sense, into a responsible stakeholder on the world stage.[103]

The *Auto Parts* case was China's first lesson via adverse litigation as to what the Golden Rule of trade means in practice as well as theory. No doubt an elite cadre of CCP trade professionals in Beijing knew the logic and details of GATT Article III even before China acceded to the WTO on December 11, 2005. No doubt, too, this cadre is slowly increasing as China develops, spreading beyond the roughly 63 million CCP members and Beijing to non-Party members and other major cities. But, even in a small country, let alone the most populous nation, appreciation for why national treatment matters is not (and probably never will be) universal. Moreover, even advanced developed countries make mistakes on national treatment. The loss that the United States suffered in the *Section 337* case is just one example.

That said, was China smart to fight the *Auto Parts* case? The facts and the law were against it from the outset. In fact, then-U.S. Trade Representative (USTR) Rob Portman said exactly that when the case was launched:

> It's a classic example of discrimination. China maintains regulatory policies that impose discriminatory tariffs and encourage its automak-

ers to use Chinese parts, at the expense of auto parts from the United States and other countries. These regulations discourage U.S. exports and create an incentive for auto parts makers to relocate to China.[104]

Hence, it was a case China was nearly destined to lose. Thus, the answer to the above question is "yes" only if China secretly hoped to lose and then use the Appellate Body Report to bludgeon recalcitrant hard-liners to change their ways and begin treating foreign auto imports fairly. This response—though privately admitted by trade officials from time to time representing other countries—is sheer conjecture in the Chinese context. The point, then, may be that China ought to review carefully the cases it chooses to defend versus settle if it hopes to avoid running up a string of losses. After all, there is no shortage of potential cases China may find itself defending in the years to come.[105]

C. Politics and Human Rights

The *China Auto Parts* case is a minor part in a far larger drama at play inside China. The context in which China's 2004 Automobile Policy is set, which is obviously not a WTO matter, is the grip—dare it be dubbed "iron" or "tenacious"—on political power that certain elements within the CCP insist on keeping.[106] A sagging economy amidst global recession, significant wage declines and job losses, and consequent industrial unrest would undermine the claim (again, made by some—not all—CCP members) that the CCP alone can guide China to higher heights of economic prosperity and social peace. Thus, the *Financial Times* wrote,

> Beijing is feeling defensive: concerned above all else to ensure that a sharp slump in growth does not trigger regime-threatening unrest. *All Chinese policies can almost always be traced back to this primal fear.*[107]

The CCP is scared in part because it is well aware of what most average Chinese understand intu-

itively: Despite the large absolute size of China's GDP, in *per capita* purchasing power parity terms, China ranks a pathetic 122nd in the world, behind Egypt, El Salvador, and Armenia.[108]

Yet in the long run, what the CCP is not mindful of—whether through willful blindness or intentional suppression—is what will doom its monopoly on power. Thousands of Chinese intellectuals and distinguished leaders like the Dalai Lama have signed *Charter '08*, which (*inter alia*) calls for nonviolent regime change toward modern democratic institutions and practices that safeguard basic human dignity and fundamental freedoms, including the freedom of conscience and speech.[109] To some elements within the CCP, the drafters and signatories of the *Charter* are enemies of the state who are to be ignored or, better yet, quashed rather than Chinese patriots seeking peaceful change toward an economic, political, and social climate that is enjoyed in every other major country except China.

Do the signatories of *Charter '08* speak for the people, including the 20 million rural migrant Chinese laborers (15 percent of the total of that cohort) who have lost their jobs in the coastal manufacturing centers and returned to the interior?[110] The short answer is "yes." Based on its erroneous Marxist premise about human nature—that man is fundamentally an economic creature—the official ideology of the CCP holds that as long as the CCP can provide the conditions for rapid growth in per capita GDP, reduce poverty, and rectify rural-urban imbalances, no rational Chinese citizen would want anything more out of life. Throughout history, poor people have shown themselves to be more than *homo economicus*. China need look no further than its southern neighbor and no further back than sixty years. Mahatma Gandhi led a movement that, at its root, was about the dignity of every person—no matter how destitute or socially outcast. Thus, without doubt, regarding the points raised in *Charter '08*, the CCP ideology is on the wrong side of history. This echoes a point made by U.S. President Barack H. Obama in his Inaugural Address, when he stated,

To the Muslim world, we seek a new way forward, based on mutual interest and mutual respect. To those leaders around the globe who seek to sow conflict, or blame their society's ills on the West—know that your people will judge you on what you can build, not what you destroy. *To those who cling to power through corruption and deceit and the silencing of dissent, know that you are on the wrong side of history; but that we will extend a hand if you are willing to unclench your fist.*[111]

Regrettably, the CCP actually censored parts of the new president's speech, particularly in Chinese-language translations.[112] Trade protectionism through measures in key sectors like autos might extend the rule of the CCP—but not forever.

Likewise, no amount of fiscal stimulation will extend in perpetuity the CCP's monopoly on power. In 2008 China's auto sector posted the lowest growth rate in a decade—6.7 percent. Thus, in November 2008 the CCP announced a US$586 billion economic stimulus package, which contained three components to assist China's auto industry:[113]

(1) A cut in the sales tax on small cars (vehicles with engines of 1.6 liters or less) from 10 to 5 percent.

(2) Investment of US$1.5 billion to upgrade technology.

(3) Expenditures of US$750,000 to help farmers shift away from three-wheeled gas-powered vehicles that pollute heavily.

All three initiatives are laudable, and all three are environmentally friendly, as they will help boost fuel efficiency and reduce pollution. To give China the benefit of the doubt, these initiatives are the result of dedicated CCP officials sincerely concerned about the present and future livelihoods of their people. But neither these kinds of initiatives nor the legal record the CCP achieves in WTO adjudication really matters in proportion to the ideals of *Charter '08*—and, in all probability, the CCP knows that.

NOTES

1. The formal citation to the case is *China—Measures Affecting Imports of Automobile Parts* (complaints by European Communities, United States, and Canada), WT/DS/339/AB/R, WT/DS/340/R, and WT/DS/342/AB/R (adopted January 12, 2009).

Argentina, Australia, Brazil, Japan, Mexico, Thailand, and, notably, Taiwan (Chinese Taipei) participated as third parties in all three Panel proceedings and at the Appellate Body stage. Taiwan attended the oral hearing and provided no written submission. There is no coverage in the Appellate Body report of what Taiwan thought about the case. Some of the third parties have major auto and auto parts interests in respect to China, as exporters to China, foreign direct investors in China, or both.

At the request of all three complainants, the same Panel heard all three cases, and at the request of the United States, this Panel issued a single report with slightly different conclusions and recommendations for each complainant. Also at the request of the United States, the Appellate Body set out its conclusions and recommendations separately for each complainant (in paras. 253–54), thus issuing three reports, although the main body (paras. 1–252) is presented as a unity. *See China Auto Parts* Appellate Body Report, *infra*, at paras. 1 fn. 1, 9, 12; *China Auto Parts* Panel Report, *infra*, at para. 2.7. Canada, the European Communities, and the United States also participated as third parties in the actions brought by the other members. Given the significant interests of all three in the Chinese auto market, their collaboration is not surprising. For example, car manufacturers from Europe account for 20–25 percent of all auto production in China. *See China Probed Over Car Parts Tariffs*, FINANCIAL TIMES, Oct. 27, 2006, at 2.

Interestingly, the Appellate Body received an unsolicited *amicus curiae* brief, but (after giving the complainants, respondent, and third parties the chance to express their opinion) did not find it necessary to rely on it to decide the case. *See China Auto Parts* Appellate Body Report, *infra*, at para. 11.

2. *See* Geoff Dyer, *Chinese Data Put Economy in Third Place*, FINANCIAL TIMES, Jan. 15, 2009, at 1. Of course, some healthy skepticism is appropriate in respect to statistics put out by the Chinese Communist Party. *See* Geoff Dyer, *Economists at Odds Over Reliability of Beijing Data*, FINANCIAL TIMES, Jan. 15, 2009, at 3.

3. *See* John Reed & Bernard Simon, *The Thrill is Gone*, FINANCIAL TIMES, February 3, 2009, at 9; Jonathan Lynn, *UPDATE 2—China Loses WTO Appeal in Car Parts Dispute*, REUTERS, Dec. 15, 2008, *posted at* www.reuters.com. *See also* Kathleen E. McLaughlin, *China Poised to Be 2nd Largest Car Market by End of 2006, Government Economist Says*, 23 INTERNATIONAL TRADE REPORTER (BNA) 1566 (Nov. 2, 2006) (*quoting*

Xu Changming, Senior Economist, State Information Center, State Council of China, stating "The era of common household car ownership in China is drawing near.").

4. *See China Probed Over Car Parts Tariffs*, *supra* note 1, at 2.

5. *See* John Reed & Bernard Simon, *supra* note 3, at 9.

6. *See* Daniel Pruzin, *WTO Panel Upholds U.S., EU, Canada in Final Ruling in China Auto Parts Case*, 25 INTERNATIONAL TRADE REPORTER (BNA) 448–49 (Mar. 27, 2008) (reporting on 2006 data).

7. *See China Probed Over Car Parts Tariffs*, *supra* note 1, at 2.

8. *See* Patti Waldmeir & John Reed, *China Used-Car Dealers in Top Gear*, FINANCIAL TIMES, Feb. 5, 2009, at 6.

9. *See* Daniel Pruzin, *WTO Talks with China on Auto Parts Dispute Ends with No Sign of Resolution*, 23 INTERNATIONAL TRADE REPORTER (BNA) 762 (May 18, 2006). The United States brought the first WTO action against China, contending that China taxed imported semiconductors in a discriminatory fashion. China settled that action by agreeing to end the discriminatory treatment. *See id.* In the *Auto Parts* case, China's cut on auto tariffs to 10 percent (from a range with a high point of 16.4 percent) and its cut on autos to 25 percent (from 28 percent), effective Jul. 1, 2006, seemed a clumsy effort to solve the case that failed to address the underlying claims of discriminatory treatment, and in any event were necessary for China to fulfill its WTO accession commitments. *See* Kathleen E. McLaughlin & Christopher S. Rugaber, *China to Reduce Import Tariffs on Autos, Some Parts Effective July 1*, 23 INTERNATIONAL TRADE REPORTER (BNA) 947 (Jun. 22, 2006); *China to Cut Car Import Duties*, FINANCIAL TIMES, Jun. 16, 2006, at 5; Daniel Pruzin & Christopher S. Rugaber, *U.S., EU Initiate WTO Dispute Complaints Against Chinese Restrictions on Auto Parts*, 23 INTERNATIONAL TRADE REPORTER (BNA) 530–31 (Apr. 6, 2006).

China also blocked the first request for establishing a panel in the *Auto Parts* case, did not accept the slate of panelists (requiring WTO Director-General Pascal Lamy to appoint them), and reacted angrily to the eventual formation of a panel—all signs, perhaps, adducing a pugnacious approach, in contrast to the semiconductor case. *See* Daniel Pruzin, *U.S., EU, Canada Ask Lamy to Appoint Panel Members in China Auto Parts Case*, 24 INTERNATIONAL TRADE REPORTER (BNA) 134 (Jan. 25, 2007); Kathleen E. McLaughlin, *China Ministry Complains About WTO Case on Auto Part Tariffs, Cites Shrinking Duties*, 23 INTERNATIONAL TRADE REPORTER (BNA) 1566–67 (Nov. 2, 2006); Daniel Pruzin, *U.S., EU, Canada to Renew Requests at WTO for Panels to Rule on China Car Parts Tariffs*, 23 INTERNATIONAL TRADE REPORTER (BNA) 1507 (Oct. 19, 2006); Daniel Pruzin, *China Blocks U.S., EU, Canadian Requests for WTO Panel Review of Auto Parts Tariffs*, 23 INTERNATIONAL TRADE REPORTER (BNA) 1436–37 (Oct. 5, 2006).

10. *See* Frances Williams, *WTO Panel Finds Against China in Import Tariff Dispute*, FINANCIAL TIMES, Jul. 19–20, 2008, at 2; Rossella Brevetti, *WTO Panel Issues Ruling Upholding U.S. Complaint on China Auto Part Import Duties*, 25 INTERNATIONAL TRADE REPORTER (BNA) 1100 (Jul. 24, 2008); Daniel Pruzin, *WTO Panel Upholds U.S., EU, Canada in Final Ruling in China Auto Parts Case*, 25 INTERNATIONAL TRADE REPORTER (BNA) 448–49 (Mar. 27, 2008); Daniel Pruzin, *WTO Issues Preliminary Ruling Condemning China on Auto Parts Tariffs in U.S., EU Case*, 25 INTERNATIONAL TRADE REPORTER (BNA) 270 (Feb. 21, 2008).

11. Daniel Pruzin & Christopher S. Rugaber, *U.S., EU Initiate WTO Dispute Complaints Against Chinese Restrictions on Auto Parts*, 23 INTERNATIONAL TRADE REPORTER (BNA) 530–31 (Apr. 6, 2006).

12. *See* Daniel Pruzin, *WTO Panel Chairman Sets Dates for Decision on China Auto Tariffs*, 24 INTERNATIONAL TRADE REPORTER (BNA) 308 (Mar. 1, 2007) (noting the contrast between the policy of the complainants to make WTO adjudication more transparent, hence their request to open the panel proceedings in the *Auto Parts* case, and the political sensitivity of China about its first case).

The transparency of China's international trade law regime—like that of many developing countries—has been a long-standing concern of the United States and other developed countries. The ostensibly straightforward task of obtaining accurate information about Chinese laws—what they are and how they are applied—often proves not to be simple. *See, e.g.*, Daniel Pruzin, *U.S. to Press China for Answers on Alleged Barriers to Goods Trade*, 23 INTERNATIONAL TRADE REPORTER (BNA) 1636–37 (Nov. 16, 2006) (reporting on the difficulty in obtaining data from China on barriers to trading rights of foreign firms, export quotas and export duties on coking coal (used to make steel), value added tax (VAT) rebates for steel, investment incentives for the purchase of domestic industrial machinery, and policies on SOEs).

13. *Inevitable Collision*, THE ECONOMIST, Feb. 23, 2008, at 82–83 (commenting on the impact of the Panel decision).

14. *Quoted in* David Pilling, *China Should Raise Wages to Stimulate Demand*, FINANCIAL TIMES, Feb. 5, 2009, at 9. The statistics in this paragraph are taken from this source.

15. This discussion is drawn from Appellate Body Report, *China—Measures Affecting Imports of Automobile Parts* (complaints by EC, U.S., Canada), WT/DS/339/AB/R, WT/DS/340/R, and WT/DS/342/AB/R (adopted Jan. 12, 2009) paras. 1–13, 109–26 [hereinafter, *China Auto Parts* Appellate Body Report]; Panel Report, *China—Measures Affecting Imports of Automobile Parts*

(complaints by EC, US, Canada), WT/DS/339/AB/R, WT/DS/340/R, and WT/DS/342/AB/R paras. 1.1–2.7 (adopted as modified by the Appellate Body, Jan. 12, 2009) [hereinafter, *China Auto Parts* Panel]; World Trade Organisation, *Update of WTO Dispute Settlement Cases*, WT/DS/OV/33 (Jun. 3, 2008), at 54–56.

16. Among the Chinese auto component makers are Weichai Power Co. Ltd. and Changchun FAW–Sihuan Automobile Co. Ltd. Some American component makers, like Delphi Corp. and Visteon Corp., also produce parts in China. Insofar as car manufacturers import some components, rather than purchase from domestic suppliers, these firms are among the ones potentially affected by the Appellate Body decision discussed herein. *See* Jonathan Lynn, *UPDATE 2—China Loses WTO Appeal in Car Parts Dispute*, REUTERS, Dec. 15, 2008, *posted at* www.reuters.com. Without doubt, exporters of autos and auto parts in the complainant countries are affected, and their representatives at the meeting of the WTO Dispute Settlement Body (DSB) urged China to implement the Appellate Body decision as quickly as possible given the "current perilous state of the automobile industry." Daniel Pruzin, *Citing Carmaker's Woes, U.S., EU Urge China to Implement Quickly WTO Auto Parts Ruling*, 26 INTERNATIONAL TRADE REPORTER (BNA) 77 (Jan. 15, 2009).

To be sure, several foreign car manufacturers (e.g., Honda, General Motors, Toyota, and Volkswagen AG) are wont to rely on components produced in China (and they account for 80 percent or more of the value of the models the foreign firms build in China) because the local parts are cheaper than imports (and the quality of local parts has improved), notwithstanding the added tariff cost associated with imports. In other words, these companies do not all complain about high Chinese tariffs, which leads to the inference that the *Auto Parts* dispute is perhaps more political than economic in nature. *See UPDATE 1—China Commerce Ministry Regrets WTO Car Parts Ruling*, REUTERS, Dec. 16, 2008, *posted at* www.reuters.com; Richard McGregor & Geoff Dyer, *Trade Friction Puts Heat on China*, FINANCIAL TIMES, Apr. 1–2, 2006, at 4.

17. *See* Amy Tsui, *WTO Affirms Chinese Measures, Treatment of Imports of Auto Parts Violate Obligations*, 25 INTERNATIONAL TRADE REPORTER (BNA) 1779 (Dec. 18, 2008).

18. Both the Panel and Appellate Body intentionally used the term "charge" rather than "duty" or "tariff." China's 2004 Automobile Policy employs the latter two terms, but the Panel and Appellate Body preferred the word "charge" because it was neutral as to whether the "charge" fell under Article II or Article III of the General Agreement on Tariffs and Trade (GATT). *See China Auto Parts* Appellate Body Report, para. 109 fn. 127.

19. *China Auto Parts* Appellate Body Report, para. 114 (citations omitted, emphasis original). In a footnote,

the Appellate Body explained that the term "assembly" under Decree 125 included "the vehicle body (including cabin) assembly, the engine assembly, the transmission assembly, the driving axle assembly, the driven axle assembly, the frame assembly, the steering system, and the braking system." As indicated, the term corresponds loosely to the major parts of a vehicle. In a separate footnote, the Appellate Body summarized Decree 125 as containing "The following combinations of "assemblies" . . . : (i) imports of a vehicle body (including cabin) assembly and an engine assembly for the purpose of assembling vehicles; (ii) imports of a vehicle body (including cabin) assembly or an engine assembly, plus at least three other assemblies, for the purpose of assembling vehicles; and (iii) imports of at least five assemblies other than the body (including cabin) and engine assemblies for the purpose of assembling vehicles. . . . In turn, the determination of whether auto parts used to produce an assembly will be deemed an "imported assembly" and therefore count towards the thresholds . . . is made based on criteria specified in . . . Decree 125. These criteria include: (i) a complete set of parts imported to assemble the assembly; (ii) "key parts" or "sub-assemblies" that reach or exceed specified quantities referred to in Annexes 1 and 2 to Decree 125; and (iii) the total price of the imported parts accounts for at least 60 per cent of the total price of that assembly." *China Auto Parts* Appellate Body Report, para. 114 fn. 147.

20. *See* Daniel Pruzin & Christopher S. Rugaber, *U.S., EU Initiate WTO Dispute Complaints Against Chinese Restrictions on Auto Parts*, 23 INTERNATIONAL TRADE REPORTER (BNA) 530–31 (Apr. 6, 2006). This account states the volume threshold is in excess of 60 percent.

21. The value threshold, originally scheduled to take effect on July 1, 2006, entered into force on Jul. 1, 2008, because of the administrative complexity in implementing it. *See China Auto Parts*, Appellate Body Report, para. 195 fn. 275.

22. *China Auto Parts* Appellate Body Report, para. 121 (citations omitted, emphasis original).

23. If a manufacturer buys imported parts from an independent supplier, then the manufacturer may deduct from the 25 percent charge it owed the value of any customs duties the supplier paid on those parts (as long as the manufacturer has proof of such payment). *See China Auto Parts* Appellate Body Report, para. 174 fn. 235.

24. This document is Schedule CLII—People's Republic of China (Part I—Schedule of Concessions and Commitments on Goods), attached as Annex 8 to China's *Accession Protocol*, WT/ACC/CHN/49/Add.1.

25. *UPDATE 1—China Commerce Ministry Regrets WTO Car Parts Ruling*, REUTERS, Dec. 16, 2008, *posted at* www.reuters.com. *See also* Daniel Pruzin, *China Outlines Defense in WTO Dispute Over Auto Parts Tariffs*, 24

INTERNATIONAL TRADE REPORTER (BNA) 621 (May 3, 2007) (summarizing China's argument about preventing circumvention by treating dissembled auto parts that have the essential character of a car as a complete vehicle and thereby subjecting the shipment to the 25 percent vehicle tariff, not the 10 percent parts tariff).

26. *See China Auto Parts* Appellate Body Report, para. 4 fn. 19.

27. *See China Auto Parts* Appellate Body Report, para. 210.

28. The Appellate Body explained in further detail the procedural steps an automobile manufacturer must follow. In summary, before beginning production of a new vehicle model that will incorporate imported parts and be sold in the Chinese market, the manufacturer performs a self-evaluation as to whether the imported parts to be used in that model have the essential character of a complete vehicle and thus qualify as such and trigger the 25 percent charge. It submits the results to the NDRC and Ministry of Commerce. If the self-evaluation yields an affirmative result, then the manufacturer arranges for the Chinese government to list the vehicle model in question in a Public Bulletin. If the result is negative, then the Chinese government—specifically, the Verification Centre—conducts a verification examination to ensure the proposed vehicle model meets the thresholds established by the criteria in the 2004 Automobile Policy. If the Centre verifies the self-evaluation results, then the manufacturer is not subject to the 25 percent charge.

Once listed in the Public Bulletin, the manufacturer applies to the CGA to register the vehicle model. Assuming approval of the registration application, CGA requires the manufacturer to post a duty bond (a financial guarantee that final duties ultimately assessed will be paid) that corresponds to the 10 percent tariff rate on auto parts multiplied by the projected monthly importations of auto parts. At this point, the manufacturer may start importing parts for use in its new vehicle model. When the manufacturer imports the parts that are characterized as complete vehicles, it must specify on the relevant customs documentation that the parts are "characterized as complete vehicles." Thereafter, the manufacturer is free to use the parts, though it must submit information (according to prescribed deadlines) to the CGA about all completed vehicles it made so that a "Verification Report" can be issued (by the Verification Centre).

Once that Report is issued, the relevant district customs office classifies the auto parts as complete vehicles and assesses the 25 percent charge. The manufacturer makes a duty declaration on the tenth working day of each month for all complete vehicles of the relevant model that it assembled during the preceding month. The office collects the charge.

There are four principal qualifications to these procedures. First, an automobile manufacturer may apply for a reverification of a vehicle model if it changes the configuration or combination of imported parts it uses to manufacture that model and it believes the change will affect the determination that the vehicle meets the essential character criteria. The Verification Centre is responsible for Re-Verification Reports. Second, if an automobile manufacturer does not use imported auto parts that it had declared as a complete vehicle, then it is eligible for the 10 percent auto parts duty rate. Third, if a Chinese auto or auto parts manufacturer substantially processes imported auto parts (other than an entire imported assembly or subassembly—that is, it incorporates imported parts into an assembly or subassembly—then the imported parts are treated as domestic parts and are not subject to the 25 percent charge. Fourth, an automobile manufacturer importing a CKD or SKD may declare and pay duties on the kits at the time of importation and thereby obtain an exemption from certain aspects of the 2004 Automobile Policy that establish the 25 percent charge. *See China Auto Parts* Appellate Body Report paras. 114–26.

29. This category is the one to which the average applied Chinese tariff is 25 percent. There are variations at the HS 8 digit level, but the 25 percent figure is the average.

30. This and the fourth categories are the ones for which China has an average applied tariff rate of 10 percent.

31. This discussion is drawn from *China Auto Parts* Appellate Body Report paras. 1–13, 108–26; World Trade Organisation, *Update of WTO Dispute Settlement Cases*, WT/DS/OV/33 (Jun. 3, 2008), at 54–56.

32. These provisions are discussed in RAJ BHALA, MODERN GATT LAW chs. 4–6 (national treatment) and 11 (tariff bindings) (2005), as well as RAJ BHALA, INTERNATIONAL TRADE LAW: INTERDISCIPLINARY THEORY AND PRACTICE chs. 12 (tariff bindings) and 13 (national treatment) (3rd ed. 2008).

33. The *TRIMs Agreement* is treated in BHALA, INTERNATIONAL TRADE LAW, *supra* note 32, ch. 13, pt. II.C.

34. The *SCM Agreement* is treated in BHALA, INTERNATIONAL TRADE LAW, *supra* note 32, at ch. 34.

35. Canada pled an additional violation, namely, Article 2(b)-(d) of the WTO *Agreement on Rules of Origin*. *See generally* Raj Bhala, *Enter the Dragon: An Essay on China's WTO Accession Saga*, 15 AMERICAN UNIVERSITY INTERNATIONAL LAW REVIEW 1469–1538 (2000) (assessing China's accession commitments based on the November 15, 1999, bilateral agreement between the United States and China).

36. *See China Auto Parts* Appellate Body Report, paras. 3–5, 7, 128–33, 183–84, 187.

37. This specific conclusion was not appealed. The application of *GRI* 2(a), discussed *infra* note 65, to the

term "motor vehicles" in China's Schedule of Concessions, provided China with the legal basis for its classification of the kits.

38. *Quoted in China Auto Parts* Appellate Body Report, para. 212 (emphasis added).

39. *See* RAJ BHALA, INTERNATIONAL TRADE LAW, *supra* note 32, at 534. The *Daisy-Heddon* test was developed in *Daisy-Heddon, Div. Victor Comptometer Corp. v. United States*, 600 F.2d 799 (CCPA 1979) and is summarized and applied in *Simod America Corp. v. United States*, 872 F.2d 1572 (1989). *See* BHALA, INTERNATIONAL TRADE LAW, *supra*, at 538–44.

40. This discussion is drawn from *China Auto Parts* Appellate Body Report, paras. 1–13, 108–26, 253; World Trade Organisation, *Update of WTO Dispute Settlement Cases*, WT/DS/OV/33 (Jun. 3, 2008), at 54–56.

41. *China Auto Parts* Appellate Body Report, para. 108. Also at issue on appeal was whether the Panel violated Article 11 of the WTO *Understanding on Rules and Procedures Governing the Settlement of Disputes* (*Dispute Settlement Understanding*, or *DSU*) concerning its ruling about the United States and Canada mounting a *prima facie* case. The Appellate Body exercised judicial economy on this issue. *See China Auto Parts* Appellate Body Report, para. 108(d)(ii), 246. At the Panel Stage, China unsuccessfully argued that its 2004 Automobile Policy does not itself impose a duty or fee but rather defines the circumstances under which China classifies imported parts under a different tariff provision. The Panel held that the Policy does establish a charge, and China did not appeal the finding.

42. *See China Auto Parts* Appellate Body Report, para. 108(a).

43. *See China Auto Parts* Appellate Body Report, Findings and Conclusions in the Appellate Body Report WT/DS339/AB/R (European Communities), para. 253(a); *China Auto Parts* Appellate Body Report, Findings and Conclusions in the Appellate Body Report WT/DS340/AB/R (United States), para. 253(a); *China Auto Parts* Appellate Body Report, Findings and Conclusions in the Appellate Body Report WT/DS342/AB/R (Canada), para. 253(a).

44. *See China Auto Parts* Appellate Body Report, para. 108(b)(i).

45. *See China Auto Parts* Appellate Body Report, Findings and Conclusions in the Appellate Body Report WT/DS339/AB/R (European Communities), para. 253(b); *China Auto Parts* Appellate Body Report, Findings and Conclusions in the Appellate Body Report WT/DS340/AB/R (United States), para. 253(b); *China Auto Parts* Appellate Body Report, Findings and Conclusions in the Appellate Body Report WT/DS342/AB/R (Canada), para. 253(b).

46. *See China Auto Parts* Appellate Body Report, para. 108(b)(ii).

47. *See China Auto Parts* Appellate Body Report, Findings and Conclusions in the Appellate Body Report WT/DS339/AB/R (European Communities), para. 253(c); *China Auto Parts* Appellate Body Report, Findings and Conclusions in the Appellate Body Report WT/DS340/AB/R (United States), para. 253(c); *China Auto Parts* Appellate Body Report, Findings and Conclusions in the Appellate Body Report WT/DS342/AB/R (Canada), para. 253(c).

48. *See China Auto Parts* Appellate Body Report, para. 108(c).

49. *See China Auto Parts* Appellate Body Report, Findings and Conclusions in the Appellate Body Report WT/DS339/AB/R (European Communities), para. 253(d); *China Auto Parts* Appellate Body Report, Findings and Conclusions in the Appellate Body Report WT/DS340/AB/R (United States), para. 253(d); *China Auto Parts* Appellate Body Report, Findings and Conclusions in the Appellate Body Report WT/DS342/AB/R (Canada), para. 253(d).

50. The complainants did not appeal the finding of the Panel that China acted consistently with GATT Article II:1(b) in classifying the kits as a complete motor vehicle and imposing a 25 percent charge on them. *See China Auto Parts* Appellate Body Report, para. 211.

51. *See China Auto Parts* Appellate Body Report, Findings and Conclusions in the Appellate Body Report WT/DS340/AB/R (United States), para. 253(e); *China Auto Parts* Appellate Body Report, Findings and Conclusions in the Appellate Body Report WT/DS342/AB/R (Canada), para. 253(e).

52. *See China Auto Parts* Appellate Body Report, para. 198 fn. 282.

53. This discussion is drawn from *China Auto Parts* Appellate Body Report, paras. 127–82.

54. *See China Auto Parts* Appellate Body Report, para. 184.

55. *See China Auto Parts* Appellate Body Report, paras. 181–82.

56. *See* GATT Panel Report, *Belgium—Family Allowances (Allocations Familiales)*, II B.I.S.D. (1st Supp.) 59 (1953, adopted Nov. 7, 1952). This case is excerpted and discussed in BHALA, INTERNATIONAL TRADE LAW, *supra* note 32, at ch. 11.

57. *See* GATT Panel Report, *European Economic Community—Regulation on Imports of Parts and Components*, B.I.S.D. (37th Supp.) 132 (adopted May 16, 1990).

58. *China Auto Parts* Panel Report, paras. 7.184–7.185, *quoted in China Auto Parts* Appellate Body Report, para. 129 (original emphasis, footnotes omitted).

59. *China Auto Parts* Panel Report, paras. 7.204, *quoted in China Auto Parts* Appellate Body Report, para. 131.

60. The Appellate Body cited its Report in *Japan—Taxes on Alcoholic Beverages*, WT/DS8/AB/R, WT/

DS10/AB/R, WT/DS11/AB/R, 18 (adopted November 1, 1996) (*Japan—Alcoholic Beverages II*. This case is excerpted and discussed in BHALA, INTERNATIONAL TRADE LAW, *supra* note 32, at ch. 13.

61. *China Auto Parts* Appellate Body Report, paras. 161–63 (citations omitted, emphases original).

62. *See China Auto Parts* Appellate Body Report, para. 130 fn. 190.

63. *China Auto Parts* Appellate Body Report, para. 179 (emphasis original).

64. *See id.*

65. *Quoted in China Auto Parts* Appellate Body Report, para. 134 fn.197.

66. *See China Auto Parts* Appellate Body Report, paras. 134–35.

67. *China Auto Parts* Appellate Body Report, para. 136.

68. *China Auto Parts* Appellate Body Report, para. 136.

69. *China Auto Parts* Appellate Body Report, para. 139 (emphasis original).

70. Neither side in the case, at either the Panel or Appellate stage, argued the 25 percent charge qualified for the phrase of GATT Article II:1(b) (second sentence) as "all other duties and charges [ODC] of any kind imposed on or in connection with the importation" of the product in question. In other words, the dispute was over whether the 25 percent charge fell within the first sentence of Article II:1(b) as an OCD, not whether it was an ODC under the second sentence. Likewise, there was no dispute as to the delineation between an OCD and ODC. The Appellate Body said that in deciding whether a particular charge falls under Article III:2 as an "internal charge" or under Article II:1(b) (first sentence) as an "OCD," it would be helpful to examine the meaning of "ODC." That would produce a complete understanding of the architecture of Articles II and III. But the Panel's choice not to study ODC neither affected the outcome of the case (because China said no products at issue in the case were affected by an ODC) nor was it a reversible error. *See China Auto Parts* Appellate Body Report, para. 140.

71. *See China Auto Parts* Appellate Body Report, para. 153 (*quoting* GATT Article II:1(b)).

72. *See* Appellate Body Report, *European Communities—Customs Classification of Frozen Boneless Chicken Cuts*, WT/DS269/AB/R, WT/DS286/AB/R (adopted September 27, 2005). This case is discussed in Raj Bhala & David Gantz, *WTO Case Review 2005*, 23 ARIZ. J. INT'L & COMP. L. 107–345 (2006).

73. *China Auto Parts* Appellate Body Report, para. 146 (original emphasis).

74. *China Auto Parts* Appellate Body Report, para. 148 (citation omitted).

75. *Quoted in China Auto Parts* Appellate Body Report, para. 150.

76. *China Auto Parts* Appellate Body Report, paras. 155, 158, 163–64, 166 (citations omitted, emphases original).

77. *See China Auto Parts* Appellate Body Report, para. 165.

78. *See* Appellate Body Report, *India—Additional Import and Extra-Additional Duties on Imports from the United States*, WT/DS360/AB/R (adopted November 17, 2008). This case is reviewed in Raj Bhala & David Gantz, *WTO Case Review 2008*, 26 ARIZ. J. INT'L & COMP. L. 113, 119–135 (2009).

79. *China Auto Parts* Appellate Body Report, paras. 172–76.

80. *China Auto Parts* Appellate Body Report, para. 177.

81. *See* Appellate Body Report, *United States—Final Countervailing Duty Determination with Respect to Certain Softwood Lumber from Canada*, WT/DS257/AB/R para. 56 (adopted Feb. 17, 2004). This decision is reviewed in Raj Bhala & David Gantz, *WTO Case Review 2004*, 22 ARIZ. J. INT'L & COMP. L. 99–249 (2005).

82. *See United States—Continued Dumping and Subsidy Offset Act of 2000*, WT/DS217/AB/R, WT/DS/234/AB/R para. 259 (adopted Jan. 27, 2003). This decision is reviewed in BHALA, MODERN GATT LAW, *supra* note 32, at ch. 29 sec. X, and in Raj Bhala & David Gantz, *WTO Case Review 2003*, 21 ARIZ. J. INT'L & COMP. L. 317–439 (2004).

83. The key relevant parts of the decision are paras. 5.6–5.7, and the case is cited *supra* note 57.

84. *See China Auto Parts* Appellate Body Report, paras. 183–86.

85. As explained below, the Article III:2 finding of the Appellate Body, like that of the Panel, excluded the imposition of the 25 percent charge on CKD and SKD kits. See *China Auto Parts* Appellate Body Report, para. 186 fn. 259.

86. *See China Auto Parts* Appellate Body Report, para. 189.

87. *See China Auto Parts* Appellate Body Report, paras. 190–97.

88. *See China Auto Parts* Appellate Body Report, para. 192.

89. *China Auto Parts* Appellate Body Report, para. 195 (emphasis added).

90. *See China Auto Parts* Appellate Body Report, para. 198.

91. *See China Auto Parts* Appellate Body Report, para. 198 fn. 283.

92. *Quoted in China Auto Parts* Appellate Body Report, para. 199.

93. *See China Auto Parts* Appellate Body Report, paras. 204–08.

94. *See China Auto Parts* Appellate Body Report, paras. 203, 209.

95. *See China Auto Parts* Appellate Body Report, paras. 213–14.

96. *See China Auto Parts* Appellate Body Report, para. 215.

97. *See China Auto Parts* Appellate Body Report, paras. 216–45.

98. *See China Auto Parts* Appellate Body Report, paras. 235–45. Interestingly, the Appellate Body rejected an American argument that construction by a WTO panel of municipal law is a factual determination that is not subject to review under *DSU* Article 17:6. Citing its Reports in *U.S.—Section 211 Omnibus Appropriations Act of 1998*, WT/DS176/AB/R para. 105 (adopted Feb. 1, 2002), and *India—Patent Protection for Pharmaceutical and Agricultural Chemical Products*, WT/DS50/AB/R paras. 65–66, 68 (adopted Jan. 16, 1998), the Appellate Body pointed out municipal law is not only evidence of facts, but also of compliance (or the lack thereof) with international legal obligations. Thus, if a panel interprets municipal law to determine whether a member has complied with its WTO obligations, then the finding of the Panel is a legal one, subject to Appellate Body review. *See id.* paras. 224–26. The *Section 211* case is discussed in Raj Bhala & David Gantz, *WTO Case Review 2002*, 20 ARIZ. J. INT'L & COMP. L. 143–289 (2003). The *India Patent* case is excerpted and discussed in BHALA, INTERNATIONAL TRADE LAW, *supra* note 32, at ch. 49.

99. *See China Auto Parts* Appellate Body Report, para. 243.

100. The Appellate Body exercised judicial economy as to whether China's 2004 Automobile Policy created new tariff lines, at the HS 10-digit level, for those kits or could be deemed as having done so. *See China Auto Parts* Appellate Body Report, para. 252.

101. BOOK OF TOBIT, Chapter 4:15a-19 (emphasis added).

102. THE GOSPEL ACCORDING TO MATTHEW, 23:34–40 (emphasis added). *See also* CATECHISM OF THE CATHOLIC CHURCH, para. 2055, at 499 (Washington, DC: United States Catholic Conference, Inc.—Libreria Editrice Vaticana, 2d ed. 1997) (*quoting* the two Great Commandments from Matthew 22:37–40 and discussing them in relation to the Ten Commandments).

103. Although U.S. Deputy Secretary of State, Robert Zoellick coined this appellation in a speech he delivered in New York on Sept. 21, 2005. His remark was that the United States should "step up efforts to make China a responsible stakeholder in the international system." Thus, in the context of Doha Round talks, Chinese Foreign Ministry spokesman Liu Jianchao declared in December 2008 that "China will continue to play a constructive and active role as a responsible country, and work with all sides to promote the negotiations to achieve a comprehensive and balanced result on the basis of existing achievements." *Foreign Ministry: China to "Actively" Join Doha Round*, XINHUA (ENGLISH), Dec. 4, 2008, *posted at* http://english.sina.com.

104. *Quoted in* Daniel Pruzin & Christopher S. Rugaber, *U.S., EU Initiate WTO Dispute Complaints Against Chinese Restrictions on Auto Parts*, 23 INTERNATIONAL TRADE REPORTER (BNA) 530–31 (Apr. 6, 2006).

105. *See, e.g.*, UNITED STATES TRADE REPRESENTATIVE, 2008 REPORT TO CONGRESS ON CHINA'S WTO COMPLIANCE (Dec. 2008), *posted at* www.ustr.gov (chronicling many areas of apparent noncompliance, as summarized in Table II, at 11–14).

106. Lest this comment be wrongly misread as premised on a disposition hostile toward China or the CCP rather than as being offered in the spirit of friendly, constructive suggestions, it may be worth referring to Raj Bhala, *Virtues, the Chinese Yuan, and the American Trade Empire*, 38 HONG KONG L. J. part I, 183–253 (May 2008). As the late Professor Edward Said rightly remarked, it is the job of the scholar to speak the truth to power. *See* EDWARD W. SAID, REPRESENTATIONS OF THE INTELLECTUAL xvi (1994).

107. *Chinese Leadership Besieged by Caution*, FINANCIAL TIMES, Feb. 3, 2009, at 10 (emphasis added).

108. *See* Geoff Dyer, *Chinese Data Put Economy in Third Place*, FINANCIAL TIMES, Jan. 15, 2009, at 1.

109. *China's Charter '08* is published in a variety of sources, including 56 NEW YORK REVIEW OF BOOKS issue 1 (Jan. 15, 2008), *available at* www.nybooks.com/articles/22210 (Perry Link trans.).

110. *See* David Pilling, *China Should Raise Wages to Stimulate Demand*, FINANCIAL TIMES, Feb. 5, 2009, at 9; Jamil Anderlini & Geoff Dyer, *Downturn Has Sent 20m Rural Chinese Home*, FINANCIAL TIMES, Feb. 3, 2009, at 1.

111. Inaugural Address, President Barack H. Obama, Jan. 20, 2009, *available at* http://news.bbc.co.uk (emphasis added).

112. *See* Michael Bristow, *Obama Speech Censored in China*, BBC NEWS, Jan. 21, 2009, *available at* http://news.bbc.co.uk. *See also It Never Stays Long*, THE ECONOMIST, Jan. 17, 2009, at 60 (remarking "the failure of the Beijing Olympics to bring any of the promised (or more accurately, hoped-for) changes in China's policy was probably the biggest disappointment of 2008).

113. *See* Kathleen E. McLaughlin, *Chinese Government Announces Auto Industry Aid Under Stimulus*, 26 INTERNATIONAL TRADE REPORTER (BNA) 99 (Jan. 22, 2009).

9

Corporations and International Law

EMEKA DURUIGBO

Traditionally, international law was concerned with providing a legal foundation for the orderly management of international relations or, more precisely, interstate relations.[1] Accordingly, the international legal system reserved little room for nonstate actors, including private corporations. The basis of this treatment was the position that only states possessed international legal personality and were subjects of international law. Nonstate actors interacted with the international legal system but were not its subjects.[2]

Over the past several decades, the legal landscape has started witnessing a major shift, corresponding to corporations' rise in importance, especially the multinational variety.[3] Today, multinational corporations (MNCs) are major actors and important players on the international plane, playing a key role as the leading drivers of international trade and investment.[4] Though not glossing over the positive aspects of multinational corporate activity, such as creating jobs and introducing new technologies, there is mounting concern over the negative consequences of economic globalization.[5] Corporations have been associated with violating human rights, degrading the environment, escalating poverty, and increasing social vices in their foreign operations. At the same time, many believe that multinational corporate power and influence could be harnessed for the greater good. These developments have engendered a loud clamor for corporate accountability and international regulation.[6]

The discussion here focuses primarily on international business (with a tangential look at other business entities), particularly the phenomenal rise of MNCs from barely noticed business associations to a major global force with enormous influence on social, economic, political, and legal developments nationally and internationally, the various private and public initiatives to control their activities, and the current state of international law regarding their regulation.[7] As one commentator has astutely observed, "The regulation of multinational corporations looms as one of the major challenges facing the international legal system at the start of the 21st century."[8]

I. Evolution and Growth of Multinational Corporations

"Multinational Corporation" is a term that admits of no easy definition but is often used interchangeably with other similar terms such as "transnational corporation" and "multinational enterprise."[9] A simple definition of the MNC is a firm that partially or completely owns, controls, and manages income-generating assets simultaneously in more than one country.[10] Other commentators have stated that "A more complicated definition would add that an MNC has productive facilities in several countries on at least two continents with employees stationed worldwide and financial investments scattered across the globe."[11]

The first known use of the term "multinational corporation" was by David Lilienthal, at a conference at Carnegie Mellon University in 1960.[12] This fact, of course, says nothing about the age of the MNC, an entity whose origin has been traced back several centuries.[13] Some classical scholars and economic and business historians assert that MNCs came into existence more than 2,000 years ago. They posit that "the businesses operated by the ancient Assyrian colonists [in the second millennium BC] constituted the first genuine multinational enterprises in recorded history."[14] Some other scholars do not go as far back as this period but nonetheless hold that many European businesses involved in such diverse sectors as banking, mining, and manufacturing had investments and operations across political borders between the thirteenth and the sixteenth centuries, so conceivably they could be categorized as transnational or multinational.[15] The above contentions, however, have been forcefully rejected by another school of thought that argues that the MNC could not have existed in earlier epochs. This school notes that although trading groups whose operations were transnational existed about two thousand years ago, the fact that nation-states did not exist at that time gives a different meaning to the notion of multinational.[16] In addition, the concept of corporations is even a much later creation.[17] Scholars of this persuasion are rather comfortable linking the emergence of the modern MNC to the seventeenth century, when corporations in the shape of the Dutch and British East India companies entered the scene and flourished.[18]

Yet, some other scholars believe that MNCs did not emerge until the second half of the nineteenth century.[19] As one legal scholar asserted, "Although business enterprises probably have had some type of foreign operations since the Middle Ages, multinational corporations as we now know them did not appear until the mid-nineteenth century, when advances in technol-ogy, manufacturing, and management processes made possible the international division of a firm's production."[20]

The disagreements on the exact date of the entrance of the MNC does not obscure consensus on some related matters, notably the fact that the MNC has undergone a metamorphosis over the course of time that make today's MNCs substantially different from the transnational companies of even a century ago, particularly when viewed from the prisms of size, scope, and operational sophistication.[21] Further, until the period following the end of the Second World War, the presence of the MNC in the global scene was hardly noticeable and its influence was infinitesimal.[22] The substantial changes in the MNC have been accompanied by a multiplication of measures to regulate them at both the domestic and international levels. Some of these measures take the form of voluntary initiatives devised by the private and public sectors.

II. Corporate Regulation Through Voluntary Initiatives

A variety of voluntary initiatives exist to regulate corporate behavior and make it more amenable to societal interests and expectations.[23] Some of these initiatives emanate from individual companies or are generated by external governmental and nongovernmental interests. This part discusses self-regulation, intergovernmental approaches, and multi-stakeholder initiatives.

A. Self-Regulation

The idea of self-regulation has been in existence since the earliest days of the corporation. Indeed, prior to the emergence of the corporation, its forerunners—merchant and craft guilds—provided a measure of regulation over the members' conduct.[24] Some modern corporations, such as JC Penney, which introduced the "Penney Idea" in 1913, put in place a set of principles to guide their conduct even in the early part of the twentieth century.[25] The primary self-regulatory tool employed by many corporations is the code of conduct. The genesis of codes of conduct for corporations engaged in international business is traceable to the "Sullivan Principles" that were introduced in the 1970s.[26] The Sullivan Principles were designed to steer American companies doing business in South Africa toward taking an active role in dismantling the notorious and inhumane system of apartheid.[27] Businesses that subscribed to the principles were expected to eschew discrimination at the workplace, thereby providing a catalyst for dismantling discriminatory barriers in the larger society.

The past few years have witnessed an explosion in the number of corporate codes, as corporations, industry and other groups, and public authorities enlist them to address certain issues of global importance, including protecting human rights and preserving the environment. Explanations abound for this development. Consumer pressure precipitates code formulation as corporations sometimes adopt codes as a reaction to or in a bid to prevent consumer backlash or adverse public opinion.[28] Corporations also introduce codes ostensibly as a means of preempting governmental regulation. One analyst stated, "In the world of politics, voluntary action can deter more onerous forms of regulation. That is an important incentive for industry to design codes of conduct with which member firms can live."[29] Codes have also grown in appeal because of recent significant developments in the global order—including the resurgence of capitalism, growing power of the multinational corporation, increasing complexity of the international business arena, and effects of international business activities on different segments of the society—and the exposure of the limitations of existing institutions and structures to deal with these changes.[30]

B. Intergovernmental Approaches

Beginning in the 1970s, the United Nations expended enormous energy, resources, and time trying to develop a "Code of Conduct for Transnational Corporations." Unfortunately, notwithstanding the immensity of the investment, the UN efforts did not result in an acceptable code.[31] The process was dropped in 1993, succumbing to the pressure of vehement opposition from multinational corporations and western governments, who disfavored a code that would impose onerous burdens on international investment.[32] Interestingly, at the time the UN commenced the draft process, its goals were primarily to regulate multinational corporations in order to prevent their interference with the internal politics of the host countries and curtail the negative impact of their activities on national economic objectives.[33] Over the years, there has been a perceptible shift, with a growing tendency to insist on mandating corporations to influence internal political relations so as to advance human rights and environmental protection. The relationship between multinational corporations and host countries that was often cantankerous in the past has also undergone a metamorphosis, with many developing country governments dropping their hostility and courting foreign investors, while the developed countries are gradually recognizing the social responsibilities associated with their corporations investing abroad.[34]

The Organisation for Economic Cooperation and Development (OECD) introduced its own code of conduct, known as the "Guidelines for Multinational Enterprises" in 1976. The Guidelines were revised in 1991 and further revised in 2000. The Guidelines, which apply to MNCs that operate from or within the thirty member countries of the OECD as well as six nonmember "adhering countries," represent the firm expectations that the participating countries have for the behavior of multinational enterprises, including parent companies, local subsidiaries, and intermediary levels of the organization.[35] Multinational enterprises are expected to take into account policies in the countries of operation as well as the views of other stakeholders. They should also abide by national laws and policies and work toward achieving sustainable development by contributing to economic, social, and environmental progress. The enterprises should also accord respect to the human rights of those who live in areas where they operate and act consistently with the host government's obligations and commitments in international law. One of the key elements of the new OECD Guidelines is an enhanced procedure for implementing the provisions. Member and adhering countries are required to set up National Contact Points to implement the Guidelines and further their effectiveness. There is also a reporting procedure to the Committee on International Investment and Multinational Enterprise (CIME), the OECD body charged with the responsibility of overseeing the implementation of the Guidelines.

On January 31, 1999, at the World Economic Forum in Davos, then UN Secretary-General Kofi Annan challenged world business leaders to demonstrate global citizenship by adopting a number of universally agreed principles in their individual corporate practices and supporting appropriate public policies in that direction. The UN Global Compact, based on that challenge, was created in July 2000 as a voluntary coalition to promote human rights, labor, and environmental standards in business. Initially focused on nine principles drawn from the Universal Declaration of Human Rights, the International Labor Organization's Fundamental Principles on Rights at Work, and the Rio Principles on Environment and Development, the Compact added corruption as a tenth principle in 2004.

According to its leading architect, Professor John Ruggie, the Global Compact is "Focused on norm diffusion and the dissemination of practical know-how and tools."[36] Encouraging principled investment,[37] the initiative's core objective, seeks to ensure the smooth conduct of international business transactions in a manner that accounts for the costs and concerns that flow from them.[38] This objective is accomplished when corporations pledge to and practicalize the Compact's ten principles, namely supporting and respecting the protection of international human rights within a business's sphere of influence; avoiding complicity in human rights abuses; upholding freedom of association and

recognizing the right to collective bargaining; upholding the elimination of all forms of forced and compulsory labor, child labor, and discrimination in employment and occupation; supporting a precautionary approach to environmental challenges; undertaking initiatives to promote greater environmental responsibility; encouraging the development and diffusion of environmentally friendly technologies; and working against corruption in all its forms.[39]

Participation in the Global Compact has grown considerably over the years from the initial 50 corporations that made a commitment at inception to more than 4,700 businesses operating in 120 countries as of 2009.[40] This makes the compact the world's largest corporate social responsibility initiative.[41] Participating companies are expected to integrate the Compact and its principles in their business strategy, day-to-day operations, and organizational culture; incorporate the principles in the highest level of decision-making processes; and document annually progress made in implementing the principles.[42] Recently, the Compact added a complaint mechanism, the Global Compact Office, which receives complaints and forwards them to corporations accused of wrongdoing.[43] A corporation that fails to engage in a dialogue on a registered complaint may be delisted.

The major strengths of the Compact are its utility in providing a process in which the efforts of responsible corporations may be rewarded while hoping to modify the behavior of others through shaming.[44] Conversely, the primary weakness of the Compact is the fact that it is voluntary and "relies upon public accountability, transparency, and the self-interest of participants to achieve compliance."[45] Some believe that structuring the compact in voluntary terms illustrates a submission to the reality that voluntariness was a necessary condition to securing the business sector's participation.[46] In fact, some scholars see the Compact as "reflect[ing] the increased influence of corporations in international lawmaking."[47] Nevertheless, some commentators contend that the Compact should insist on "a minimum social compliance threshold for participation."[48]

C. Multi-Stakeholder Initiatives

In some cases, different stakeholders, including national governments, corporations, and nongovernmental organizations, have teamed up to formulate voluntary initiatives aimed at guiding corporate behavior, particularly in specific issue areas such as human rights and armed conflicts. Three of the most prominent stakeholder initiatives are the Voluntary Security Principles, Extractive Industries Transparency Initiative (EITI), and the Kimberley Process.

Announced in December 2000 by the U.S. State Department and the British Foreign Office, the Voluntary Principles on Security and Human Rights is a pact specifically designed for companies in the oil and mining sectors and aimed at protecting human rights and providing security in the international operations of these businesses. The Principles are the outcome of collaborative efforts of leading companies in the extractive industry, major human rights and labor organizations, and the U.K. and U.S. governments.[49] The governments of the Netherlands and Norway joined the arrangement shortly afterward.

The Voluntary Principles address the difficult security constraints under which international business operations are conducted in some parts of the world. To assure unhindered access to resource extraction facilities, security agents acting on behalf or for the benefit of corporations have been known to adopt abusive practices. Oil companies like Chevron in the Niger Delta region of Nigeria, Exxon Mobil in the Aceh Province of Indonesia, and BP in Colombia came under incessant attacks for relationships they had forged with security forces that engaged in human rights abuses. In Aceh and the Niger Delta, security forces used company equipment to perpetrate their atrocities. In Colombia, BP hired security forces known for nefarious practices. Moreover, the Nigerian government, without due process, had executed a

human rights and environmental campaigner, Ken Saro-Wiwa, along with eight other activists, who had voiced real concerns and lodged serious complaints about Shell's operations in their community. Shell was widely assailed for not employing its influence with the Nigerian government to stop the executions.[50]

These incidents formed the springboard that propelled the American and British governments to adopt a more proactive stance on the issues of security and human rights. According to Harold Koh, then Assistant Secretary of State, whose Bureau of Democracy, Human Rights and Labor (DRL) led U.S. efforts to develop the pact, the Voluntary Principles set out to provide companies with "practical guidance on how to prevent human rights violations in dangerous environments, while meeting legitimate corporate security requirements."[51] The Voluntary Principles incorporate and build on existing standards while also highlighting and crystallizing emerging best practices.[52] Indeed, the accord's preamble proclaims that it was guided by the principles set forth in the Universal Declaration of Human Rights and contained in international humanitarian law.[53] Under the accord, companies are expected to conduct a study of democratic and human rights conditions as part of their risk assessment. They should also ensure that the security measures they undertake to protect their installations comply with international law and do not violate human rights. The companies are also responsible for monitoring human rights violations committed by state security forces engaged to protect their facilities and installations.[54]

The Principles have received high marks for "the significant level of detail" and the distinctive "emphasis on providing how-to guidelines rather than taking a more aspirational approach. Such guidelines enable participating companies to operationalize their commitments more readily."[55] The agreement is an ambitious one that seeks to lay the foundation for global standards on these issues.[56] Corporations in various places are increasingly utilizing the Voluntary Principles.[57] Some analysts view the Principles as providing legitimacy to states' and private actors' use of private military firms.[58] Others are concerned that the Principles contain "only opaque enforcement mechanisms."[59]

The Extractive Industries Transparency Initiative was initiated by then British Prime Minister Tony Blair, who announced its establishment at the World Summit on Sustainable Development in Johannesburg in September 2002. Aimed at increasing transparency at both the corporate and governmental levels, EITI promotes transparency of payments made by energy and mining companies to host country governments and government-linked entities as well as of revenues received by these governments from the development and sale of their natural resources.[60] The EITI's principal purpose is to replace the "lose-lose" situation in which all the major participants in the extractive process suffer reputational, pecuniary, and other losses as a result of the opacity that has characterized payments. The designers noted that although the revenues ordinarily should aid economic growth and social development in the host countries, the lack of transparency and accountability has frustrated such result and instead has exacerbated poor governance and led to corruption, conflict, and poverty.[61]

The idea behind the EITI is that the provision of financial information will empower the citizens to demand accountability from their governments, thus ensuring that the benefits spread to the people.[62] Governments that disclose revenue automatically face the pressure to be more responsible. As U.S. Supreme Court Justice Brandeis observed almost a century ago, "Sunshine is said to be the best of disinfectants; electric light the most efficient policeman."[63] EITI has generated substantial support from a host of institutions, including the World Bank Group, the International Monetary Fund (IMF), national governments and major nongovernmental organizations.[64] However, skepticism abounds as to the EITI's ability to accomplish its framers' objectives. Some commentators have noted that the EITI "is not necessarily a blueprint for good governance" in the targeted resource-rich countries.[65] They note that the EITI by itself "is incapable of facilitating reduced corruption, prudent management of [resource] revenues, or mobilizing citizens to hold corrupt government officials accountable for embezzling profits from extractive industry operations."[66] More specifically, transparency is of limited potency where there is no "strong civil society to hold the government accountable for misappropriations that are brought to light."[67]

The Kimberley Process Certification Scheme (KPCS) came into effect on January 1, 2003, after a few years of negotiations involving governments, the diamond industry, and nongovernmental organizations.[68] It arose out of concerns that the illegal involvement of paramilitary and guerilla groups was fuelling or prolonging civil conflicts in several countries, including Sierra Leone, Angola, and the Democratic Republic of the Congo (DRC).[69] The KPCS is principally an intergovernmental regime that contains a set of common standards that are politically binding and domesticated in national legislation, but this regime also functions alongside a complementary self-regulatory system that the diamond industry established and adopted.[70]

Overall, the KPCS is a system of certifying that diamonds emanate from conflict-free areas, and it does so to prevent rebel groups in unstable countries from financing their operations through the sale of "blood diamonds."[71] Accordingly, participating countries institute internal controls on the import and export of diamonds. Countries' involvement is not limited to certification but also includes establishing a chain of custody scheme that covers the movement of diamonds from the point of mining to the point of export.[72] They are also required to provide transparent information regarding trade in diamonds. Participating countries cannot legally trade with those who have not met the minimum requirements of the scheme.[73] Viewing the Scheme "as a valuable contribution against trafficking in conflict diamonds," the UN Security Council gave the KPCS its blessing in 2003.[74]

Many criticize the KPCS because it lacks a proper enforcement mechanism.[75] A 2006 assessment of the United States' 2003 implementation of the KPCS through the Clean Diamond Act raised questions about the initial inspection process upon the entry of the diamonds into the country and the reporting system for the receipt of rough diamonds with other participants.[76] The U.S. Treasury Department's Office of Foreign Assets Control issued new regulations in May 2008 targeted at strengthening U.S. oversight of the diamond trade.[77] Describing the Kimberley Process as a "meager effort" by the diamond industry to improve its human rights record after the terrible tragedies in Sierra Leone and Liberia, one commentator assailed the process as "far too ineffective, relying on voluntary self-regulation."[78] One notorious example that reinforces the weakness of the KPCS is that the Republic of Congo (ROC) was expelled from the Kimberley Process because of its role as an indirect facilitator of and primary destination for conflict diamonds smuggled from the neighboring DRC. Yet this expulsion did not make a huge dent on the ROC's illegal activities in relation to rough diamonds.[79] Proposals for improvement include the suggestion that individuals should be given the right to institute suits against violators.[80]

Nevertheless, the KPCS is not without considerable merit. It was precisely in recognition of its value that the world's largest diamond trader, De Beers, decided to back efforts to establish the Scheme as a way of escaping consumer backlash from negative publicity surrounding conflict diamonds and any attendant effect on the cartel.[81] Indeed, the Kimberley Process was led by the industry itself, further providing the process additional legitimacy that may be lacking in other efforts to address armed conflicts, such as international arms embargoes or sanctions, which are typically orchestrated and designed by states without the express involvement of the arms industry.[82]

A collective criticism leveled at the EITI, the Voluntary Principles, and the Kimberley Process is that they seek to focus on "flashpoint" or "headline-making" corporate responsibility issues, including corruption, abuse of human rights by security personnel, and armed conflict, "but do not address the underlying root causes of community opposition to extractive industry projects, including communities' lack of control over their own destinies and the natural resources they consider their own."[83]

D. Evaluation of Voluntary Initiatives

Both from economic and philosophical perspectives, the business sector favors voluntary initiatives over intrusive and more cumbersome government regulations. The cost of compliance with expensive regulatory requirements aligns industry with the attractive alternative of voluntary initiatives. In addition, industry holds an "ideological resistance to regulation."[84] One legal scholar has observed that corporate actors have a far greater likelihood "to adhere to laws that in their eyes are legitimate, particularly when compliance is expensive," adding that "There is no question that many businesses remain philosophically opposed to some substantial portion of the current regime of environmental regulation, and indeed, consider it illegitimate."[85] Although this observation was made in the domestic environmental arena, it appears to be pertinent and equally applicable to international regulation of corporate activities, thus explaining the relevance of voluntary mechanisms and arrangements.

The immense utility of voluntary arrangements is particularly evident in places where host country laws are weak or marked by inadequate enforcement of applicable standards. As the UN Centre on Transnational Corporations has noted, "In some cases, self-regulation may be more effective than national regulations themselves, especially in those countries in which enforcement mechanisms are weak."[86] In fact, enormous social change has occurred in various places, driven in large measure by voluntary efforts.[87] The Sullivan Principles served as a catalyst for the growth of a black trade union movement in South Africa, which contributed ultimately to improving both the well-being of workers and industrial relations in that country.[88] The MacBride Principles served as a veritable instrument for reducing employment discrimination on the basis of religion and advancing equitable job opportunities in Northern Ireland.[89]

Voluntary initiatives also serve a critical function of laying the foundation for future public initiatives at domestic and international levels. One lesson from history is that the solution to many social or economic problems has often followed a familiar trajectory: self-regulation as a way to fend off public regulation, dissatisfaction with voluntary efforts, clamor for public regulation, and the ultimate enactment and enforcement of laws to deal with the problem.[90] As a matter of fact, some commentators and activists believe that either voluntary initiatives will become widespread or corporate excesses will become intolerable before binding obligations can firmly and finally emerge.[91] One can also contemplate situations, similar to the approach adopted with promises made in company handbooks, where "common law courts could construe the codes of conduct as contracts and make them enforceable."[92]

However, private initiatives also harbor some drawbacks. Some commentators have noted that many of these voluntary arrangements "declare laudable goals that, if implemented as advertised, would indeed better protect people and their resources."[93] Unfortunately, there seems to be a wide gap between their rhetoric and reality. The fact that the initiatives are neither binding nor contain any meaningful enforcement mechanism has drawn a lot of criticism.[94] It should be pointed out that voluntariness is not an incurable impediment to effectiveness and that binding obligations are not coterminous with successful ones.[95] Yet one would be remiss to ignore the pitfalls of voluntary arrangements, including the point that they tend to foster a free-rider problem, as many actors are able to take advantage of any benefits conferred by the arrangement without sharing in the obligations. Because voluntary arrangements have the po-

tential to breed opportunism, as illustrated by free riding, critics argue that effective countermeasures, such as binding obligations and institutions, are necessary.[96]

Incorporating monitoring mechanisms can, at minimum, further strengthen codes.[97] Monitoring may be internal (by the corporation itself), external (by an outside monitor hired by the corporation), or independent (by individuals or institutions without financial ties to the corporation).[98] Independent monitoring is considered the most effective, yet many companies opt for internal monitoring. Internal monitoring is assailed because it "smells of the fox minding the chicken coop, and serious questions arise regarding the extent to which code violations will be disclosed."[99] External monitoring has shown some weaknesses, too,[100] and independent monitoring has not always delivered the expected results, further amplifying the dissenting voices.[101] Furthermore, voluntary measures scarcely afford any remedies to victims in the event of violation, and they largely fail to include locally affected communities, the presumed beneficiaries of the initiatives, at the design stage or carve out any meaningful role for them in enforcing the standards and norms.[102]

In a nutshell, voluntary initiatives have proven inadequate in addressing the negative externalities of global commerce, thereby disappointing, in the process, the aspirations of their originators and supporters.[103] Indeed, they have been dismissed as "meaningless generalities, unreliable guidances, unenforceable promises, and inadequate substitutes for regulation."[104] Accordingly, the clamor for public international regulation has received significant attention in recent years.

III. Regulation of Corporations Under International Law

A. Rationale

The primary explanation for articulating legal obligations to bind MNCs is that they have transformed from mere business organizations into behemoths that are beyond the legal reach of many nation-states. Some commentators have put it succinctly when they stated, "As a matter of logic, global corporations can only be adequately regulated at a global level."[105] The growth of MNC business operations has been accompanied by an increase in activities that occasion harm to individuals and communities or frustrate the realization of international legal objectives. Corporations have been able to perpetrate these wrongs without being called to account because they have often acted in partnership with the governments of the countries in which they operate—the same governments that are expected to protect the citizens.

Without doubt, these problems occur because many of the political leaders are irresponsible and do not care about the well-being of the citizens. In some cases, they even employ corporate relationships as a device for consolidating their hold on power.[106] Yet the fact cannot be discounted that political and economic realities sometimes constrain these leaders to turn a blind eye to the nefarious and multifarious activities of MNCs. If history is any guide, not giving MNCs a free rein could lead to the violent overthrow of the uncooperative government.[107] A need to attract foreign investment may also dictate lax regulation of corporate operations.[108] Many developing countries also lack the technical and legal expertise needed to monitor and effectively regulate such complex activities as environmental pollution.[109] Bringing MNCs within the control of the international legal system is, therefore, a logical consequence of these developments.

Because of their growth in size and influence, MNCs are also viewed as possessing an enormous capacity to do good, providing an additional impetus for calls to incorporate them into the core of international law.[110] MNCs have acquired the kind of power that recently was reserved for governments, thus opening them up to correspondingly assume the type of responsibilities that international law already assigns to states.[111] The argument is that because MNCs have enormous power to shape the realization of human rights, this power should come with corresponding responsibility.[112]

The campaign to regulate corporations under international law has also been informed by the perception that voluntary initiatives have failed to adequately address the social, economic, environmental, and political consequences of corporate activity in many countries.[113] Finally, and flowing from the foregoing, international regulation of harmful business activities is justified by the bedrock jurisprudential principle that the breach of a right should be accompanied by a remedy, as encapsulated in the maxim, *ubi ius ibi remedium.*[114] The argument therefore, is that to the extent that MNCs play a role, through complicity with national governments, in violating the rights guaranteed individuals and indigenous communities under international law, a remedy under international law is called for, especially when the domestic legal system offers none. Indeed, even where sound national regulations exist and are adequately enforced, international regulation may still be preferred because national officials' ability to "actually control the behavior of corporations operating within their borders has been substantially diminished by the global dispersion of assets," thus exposing the glaring reality that no single state has been able to effectively control MNCs.[115] International regulation is, therefore, warranted to close the lacunae and forestall corporate impunity.[116] It would also emphasize the importance of collective action in addressing globally relevant current issues, including human rights, the environment, public health, poverty, and security.

An effective international regulatory arrangement for corporations should incorporate a number of vital components, including the prescription of international regulations to govern corporate activity and, at minimum, an international complaint mechanism to receive and review allegations of violations from any part of the world. An adjudicatory mechanism may also be added at the international level or the rules may solely be enforced at the domestic level in the countries where the infractions occurred, in the country where the parent corporation is headquartered, or in any other country willing to make its judicial institutions and resources available.

The absence of these elements coupled with a frustration with existing initiatives may have been the galvanizing influence behind resorting to international civil litigation that utilizes foreign judicial systems to address and redress corporate human rights abuses.[117] The most prominent effort in this connection is litigation under the Alien Tort Statute, a nineteenth-century piece of legislation in the United States that provides that federal district courts shall have original jurisdiction for civil actions brought by aliens for torts committed in violation of the law of nations or a treaty of the United States.[118] Although human rights advocates see the statute as a veritable tool in vindicating the rights of those for whom hardly any other remedy exists—especially in their native countries where the alleged abuses occur[119]—skeptics doubt its utility and question the approach of conferring the role of the "World's Judiciary" on U.S. courts.[120]

B. Recent Developments

A major response to corporate human rights abuse was drafting and adopting in August 2003 a set of norms to govern business conduct. Drafted by the UN Sub-commission for the Protection and Promotion of Human Rights, the Norms were enthusiastically embraced by human rights, labor, and environmental groups, but they were widely rejected by governments and the business community.[121] To strike a compromise, the U.N. Secretary-General, at the request of the Human Rights Commission appointed a Special Representative (SRSG) on Business and Human Rights in July 2005, naming Professor John Ruggie to the post. The SRSG has a broad five-part mandate, including an assignment to "identify and clarify standards of corporate responsibility and accountability for transnational corporations and other business enterprises with regard to human rights" as well as to "elaborate on the role

of states in effectively regulating and adjudicating the role of transnational corporations and other business enterprises with regard to human rights, including through international cooperation."[122] The mandate was for an initial two-year period but was extended for another year at the SRSG's request. In 2008 the Human Rights Council extended the mandate by another three years until 2011.[123]

In his interim report in 2006, Ruggie noted that "it may be desirable in some circumstances for corporations to become direct bearers of international human rights obligations, especially where host governments cannot or will not enforce their obligations and where the classical international human rights regime, therefore, cannot possibly be expected to function as intended."[124] He added that "Under customary international law, emerging practice and expert opinion increasingly do suggest that corporations may be held liable for committing, or complicity in, the most heinous human rights violations amounting to international crimes, including genocide, slavery, human trafficking, forced labor, torture, and some crimes against humanity."[125] Further surveying the extant landscape, Ruggie, in his 2007 Report to the UN Human Rights Council, stated that although noticeable changes have occurred regarding the international legal status of corporations, these changes do not extend to most international human rights obligations.[126] In his 2008 Report, Ruggie focused on a tripartite framework of "protect, respect and remedy."[127] States are obligated to protect human rights, including forestalling efforts by nonstate actors within their domain to infringe on these rights. Corporations are obligated to respect human rights, but this is not a legal duty; instead, it is an obligation that stems from "social expectations—as part of what is sometimes called a company's social licence to operate."[128] The remedy prong examines various judicial and nonjudicial mechanisms that aggrieved individuals could utilize to seek redress for corporate human rights abuse. The SRSG also submitted a companion report addressing the concepts of "sphere of influence" and corporate complicity, in which corporations are not directly involved in human rights violations but an imposition of liability is nevertheless sought for aiding and abetting violations perpetrated by public or private security forces, other government agents, armed factions in civil conflicts, or other similar actors.[129] Ruggie submitted his fourth report in 2009, in which he reiterated and focused on operationalizing the three-pillar framework.[130]

Ruggie is also examining the role of extraterritorial jurisdiction as a tool that home states of MNCs may utilize to oversee their operation overseas. Some observers have noted that this tool is of immense utility if there is any real hope of overcoming the weak institutional framework in host states that militate against corporate accountability.[131] Questions, however, remain as to whether, in the absence of international legal requirement, home states would be willing to police and punish their corporations for activities abroad that do not affect their nationals or whether host states would be disinclined to view such exercise of jurisdiction as an intrusion into their domestic matters and an exercise verging on legal or cultural imperialism.[132] These questions are only a snapshot of the numerous challenges that confront any substantial change to the rights and obligations of corporations in international law.

C. Challenges to Change

The first set of challenges to changing the international legal status of corporations is conceptual or philosophical.[133] Traditionalists insist that the international legal system is reserved for states and intergovernmental organizations; that is, they are the only subjects of international law.[134] In more recent years, especially since the period following the end of the Second World War, individuals have been recognized as selective subjects of international (humanitarian) law. The argument today is that corporations should, or already do, enjoy a similar status. One commentator forcefully contended, "To the extent that individuals have rights and duties under customary international law and international humanitarian law, MNCs as legal persons have the same set of rights and duties."[135] Another commentator summed up the controversy with an acknowledgment that "jurists have argued that the relations of states and foreign corporations as such should be treated on the international plane and not as an aspect of the normal rules governing the position of aliens and their assets on the territory of a state," but concludes contrarily that "In principle, corporations of municipal law do not have international legal personality. Thus, a concession or contract between a state and a foreign corporation is not governed by the law of treaties."[136] The SRSG believes that the old doctrinal battle is fading and that experience from international investment and environmental law suggests that corporations have certain rights or duties, thus making it easier to argue that corporate responsibility should be extended to international crimes.[137]

Another conceptual obstacle relates to the nature of human rights. Purists believe that human rights emerged as a concept to constrain state power vis-à-vis the citizens and should remain so, and it should not, therefore, be extended to interactions between citizens, including corporations. Not only do they believe that such an extension would amount to trivializing the notion of human rights, but they foresee additional problems, especially considering that we are still wrestling with the implementation of states' human rights obligations.[138] As a result, in trying to include corporations into the human rights system, we risk collapse of the whole edifice. Some scholars dismiss the objection, noting that the system is strong enough to handle the needed reconceptualization and that we should begin to see these rights as the entitlement of everybody in the society, deserving of respect from everybody else.[139]

An additional (partly) conceptual obstacle is the near-universal opposition to corporate integration into the international legal system based on ideological and other unrelated considerations. MNCs face political opposition from socialist countries and suspicion from a majority of developing countries, thereby ensuring that "both groups will never allow them to play an autonomous role in international affairs. Even Western countries are reluctant to grant them international standing; they prefer to keep them under their control—of course, to the extent that this is possible."[140] This is further accentuated by the fact that corporations do not seem eager to be accorded enhanced international legal status, as their current nonstatus seems to favor them, allowing them to access international processes while not burdened by clearly defined international obligations.[141] Viewed from the perspective that crafting effective solutions to the problem of negative corporate behavior demands a collaborative undertaking of the key stakeholders, including the corporations themselves, figuring out a way to get them adequately on board is imperative.[142]

Moreover, states' opposition seems to be succumbing to the practical realities of the need to attract investment and the risk to economic globalization that abusive conduct poses because it could lead to a withdrawal of the "social license" to operate in some places, with significant consequences to all interested parties. The corporations themselves would also likely make a strategic shift if presented a real choice between international duties without rights or duties accompanied by rights, predictably opting for the latter.

Apart from the conceptual challenges, there are formidable practical objections to regulating corporations internationally. Corporate regulation may limit international private investment in developing countries that have been able to attract otherwise unavailable corporate involvement in key sectors of the economy. Leveling the playing field on human rights, environmental, and other obligations may reduce the incentive and thereby invite corporate hesitancy to invest in these countries. Although nobody disputes the long-term benefits of a strong framework for protecting rights in these countries, the short-term consequences of reducing the com-

petitiveness of developing countries are quite substantial.[143]

There is also the concern that any international complaints or adjudicatory system established to handle cases of international human rights and humanitarian law breaches by corporations would suffer from an overload. It is one thing to do so with states when you are dealing with two hundred countries, only a few of whom are targets of such complaints, but an entirely different matter to run a similar system for multinational corporations running into the tens of thousands.[144] Moreover, only a limited number of victims would be able to muster the resources or assistance needed to vindicate their claims at a distant international tribunal. Thus, there have been calls for more feasible alternatives, such as using domestic courts and private arbitral bodies.[145] Along similar lines, the SRSG has evinced amenity toward strengthening domestic legal systems as the best way to guarantee human rights.[146] Considering the weak judicial apparatuses and related institutions in many countries where violations of international human rights and humanitarian law take place continually as well as the enormous time and resource commitments needed to create or strengthen these institutions, it is still likely that a role will be created for an international process. Accordingly, a prominent network of nongovernmental organizations have cautioned that "While building the capacity of national governments to provide protection by 'regulating and adjudicating' the role of transnational corporations and other business enterprises is important, the SRSG should recognize that in reality in conflict-prone countries or in countries with a poor human rights record this is not something that is achievable in the short-term."[147] The network suggests that "In the interim there is an urgent need for the international community to offer some means to protect the rights of the victims of corporate malpractice."[148]

Another problem is that although some people favor imposing international obligations on corporations, they are not enamored of the fact that "with international corporate obligations come international corporate rights."[149] Corporations may be endowed with substantive human rights as well as procedural rights to make claims when they believe that they are human rights victims. States with questionable human rights records and antiglobalization activists are likely to mount significant opposition to an international system of corporate rights, even when obligations are imposed on the same corporations. How successful the opposition will continue to be is open to serious question.[150] In any case, corporate procedural rights will likely emerge as corporations begin to defend themselves at criminal or civil proceedings founded on allegations of breaches of international law.[151]

It may be concluded that although challenges abound, the status quo is unacceptable. The history of international law is inexorably intertwined with a constant recognition of the need to adapt to changing realities, understanding that its continued viability is inextricably tied to such adaptation. It is rightly expected that such will be the case with corporations and international law.

NOTES

1. Philip C. Jessup, *The Subjects of a Modern Law of Nations*, 45 MICH. L. REV. 383, 384 (1947).

2. For a useful discussion, *see* Andrew Clapham, *Extending International Criminal Law Beyond the Individual to Corporations and Armed Opposition Groups*, 6 J. INT'L CRIM. JUST. 899 (2008). This legal lacuna is not limited to corporations engaged in commercial transactions, but extends to private military companies providing services in conflict and transition zones and even in stable societies. *See* Oliver R. Jones, *Implausible Deniability: State Responsibility for the Actions of Private Military Firms*, 24 CONN. J. INT'L L. 239, 252 (2009); James Cockayne, *Regulating Private Military and Security Companies: The Content, Negotiation, Weaknesses and Promise of the Montreux Document*, 13 J. CONFLICT & SECURITY L. 401 (2008).

3. *See Developments in the Law—Corporate Liability for Violations of International Human Rights Law*, 114 HARV. L. REV. 2025, 2030–31 (2001); Andrew Clapham, *The Question of Jurisdiction Under International Criminal Law Over Legal Persons: Lessons from the Rome Conference on an International Criminal Court*, in LIABILITY OF MULTINATIONAL CORPORATIONS UNDER INTERNATIONAL LAW 139, 191 (Menno T. Kamminga & Saman Zia-Zarifi eds., 2000).

4. MICHELLE LEIGHTON ET AL., BEYOND GOOD DEEDS: CASE STUDIES AND A NEW POLICY AGENDA FOR CORPORATE ACCOUNTABILITY 2–3 (2002).

5. EMEKA A. DURUIGBO, MULTINATIONAL CORPORATIONS AND INTERNATIONAL LAW: ACCOUNTABILITY AND COMPLIANCE ISSUES IN THE PETROLEUM INDUSTRY 105 (2003).

6. For the contention, however, that a new era of decline in corporate power began in September 2008 with the demise of Lehman Brothers, *see* Herman F. Greene, *Hot, Crowded, and Not-So-Flat: The Changing Climate for Corporations*, 44 WAKE FOREST L. REV. 799, 811 (2009).

7. This issue of regulating international business is gaining increased interest. *See* Kenneth W. Abbott & Duncan Snidal, *Strengthening International Regulation Through Transnational New Governance: Overcoming the Orchestration Deficit*, 42 VAND. J. TRANSNAT'L L. 501, 503 (2009) ("Regulation of transnational business has become a dynamic area of international governance.").

8. Beth Stephens, *Corporate Accountability: International Human Rights Litigation Against Corporations in US Courts*, in LIABILITY OF MULTINATIONAL CORPORATIONS, *supra* note 3, at 209.

9. *See* WILLIAM MEADE FLETCHER, FLETCHER CYCLOPEDIA OF THE LAW OF PRIVATE CORPORATIONS § 8926.10 (Sept. 2007).

10. Alfred D. Chandler Jr. & Bruce Mazlish, *Introduction*, in LEVIATHANS: MULTINATIONAL CORPORATIONS AND THE NEW GLOBAL HISTORY 1, 3 (Alfred D. Chandler Jr. & Bruce Mazlish eds., 2005) [hereinafter LEVIATHANS]; PETER MUCHLINSKI, MULTINATIONAL ENTERPRISES AND THE LAW 12 (1995).

11. Chandler & Mazlish, *supra* note 10, at 3. *See further* David Weissbrodt & Maria Kruger, *Norms on the Responsibilities of Transnational Corporations and Other Business Enterprises with Regard to Human Rights*, 97 AM. J. INT'L L. 901, 907–10 (2003) (providing various definitions of the terms multinational corporations, transnational corporations, and multinational enterprises).

12. Stephen J. Kobrin, *Multinational Corporations, the Protest Movement, and the Future of Global Governance*, in LEVIATHANS, *supra* note 10, at 219, 222; *Bulova Watch Company, Inc. v. K. Hattori & Co.*, 508 F. Supp. 1322, 1335 (E.D.N.Y. 1981).

13. For useful historical accounts of the evolution of multinational enterprises, *see inter alia*, JAMES W. VAUPEL & JOAN P. CURHAN, THE MAKING OF MULTINATIONAL ENTERPRISE (1969); MIRA WILKINS, THE EMERGENCE OF MULTINATIONAL ENTERPRISE: AMERICAN BUSINESS ABROAD FROM THE COLONIAL ERA TO 1914 (1970); JAMES VAUPEL & JOAN P. CURHAN, THE

WORLD'S MULTINATIONAL ENTERPRISE (1973); MIRA WILKINS, THE MATURING OF MULTINATIONAL ENTERPRISE: AMERICAN BUSINESS ABROAD FROM 1914 TO 1970 (1974); JOAN CURHAN ET AL., TRACING THE MULTINATIONALS (1977); GEOFFREY JONES, THE EVOLUTION OF INTERNATIONAL BUSINESS: AN INTRODUCTION (1996); John H. Dunning, *Changes in the Level and Structure of International Production: The Last One Hundred Years*, in THE GROWTH OF INTERNATIONAL BUSINESS 84 (Mark Casson ed., 1983).

14. KARL MOORE & DAVID A. LEWIS, BIRTH OF THE MULTINATIONAL: 2000 YEARS OF ANCIENT BUSINESS HISTORY—FROM ASHUR TO AUGUSTUS 27 (1999).

15. *See* Mira Wilkins, *Multinational Enterprise to 1930: Discontinuities and Continuities*, in LEVIATHANS, *supra* note 10, at 45, 47–49; Yitzhak Hadari, *The Structure of the Private Multinational Enterprise*, 71 MICH. L. REV. 729, 735 (1973); Mark B. Baker, *Private Codes of Corporate Conduct: Should the Fox Guard the Henhouse?* 24 U. MIAMI INTER-AM. L. REV. 399, 401 (1993); KWAMENA ACQUAAH, INTERNATIONAL REGULATION OF TRANSNATIONAL CORPORATIONS: THE NEW REALITY 45 (1986) ("Some intellectual archaeologists have traced the origins of TNCs to the fifteenth century Fuggers merchant family which was based in Augsburg [Germany] and operated various economic activities throughout Europe.").

16. Bruce Mazlish, *A Tour of Globalization*, 7 IND. J. GLOBAL LEGAL STUD. 5, 11 (1999). *See further*, Sigmund Timberg, *The Corporation as a Technique of International Administration*, 19 U. CHI. L. REV. 739, 739 (1952).

17. Mazlish, *id.*, at 11.

18. *Id.*

19. *See* MUCHLINSKI, *supra* note 10, at 20; Natasha Rossell Jaffe & Jordan D. Weiss, *The Self-Regulating Corporation: How Corporate Codes Can Save Our Children*, 11 FORDHAM J. CORP. & FIN. L. 893, 897 (2006).

20. Linda A. Mabry, *Multinational Corporations and U.S. Technology Policy: Rethinking the Concept of Corporate Nationality*, 87 GEO. L. J. 563, 569 (1999) (citation omitted).

21. *See* Wilkins, *supra* note 15, at 51.

22. *See* Bulova Watch, *supra* note 12, at 1335 (stating that "it was not until after World War II that the phenomenon of the multinational enterprise, as we know it, became a major factor in the world scene."); PETER J. BUCKLEY & MARK CASSON, THE FUTURE OF THE MULTINATIONAL ENTERPRISE 1 (25th Anniv. ed. 2002) ("One of the most remarkable economic phenomena of the postwar period has been the rise of the multinational enterprise (MNE).").

23. These initiatives go by such names as "corporate codes of conduct," "corporate directives," "administrative practices," "standards of business conduct," "code of best practice," "corporate compliance programs," "corporate compliance policies," "guiding principles," "code of ethics and business conduct," and "code of worldwide business conduct." *See generally*, BLACKWELL ENCYCLOPEDIC DICTIONARY OF BUSINESS ETHICS 114 (Patricia H. Werhone & R. Edward Freeman eds., 1997).

24. Mark B. Baker, *Private Codes of Corporate Conduct: Should the Fox Guard the Henhouse?* 24 U. MIAMI INTER-AM. L. REV. 399, 401 (1993).

25. Patrick E. Murphy, *Corporate Ethics Statements: An Update*, in GLOBAL CODES OF CONDUCT: AN IDEA WHOSE TIME HAS COME 295 (Oliver F. Williams ed., 2000).

26. Ariadne K. Sacharoff, *Multinationals in Host Countries: Can They be Held Liable Under the Alien Tort Claims Act for Human Rights Violations?* 23 BROOKLYN J. INT'L L. 927, 935 (1998).

27. *See* Richard L. Herz, *The Liberalizing Effects of Tort: How Corporate Complicity Liability Under the Alien Tort Statute Advances Constructive Engagement*, 21 HARV. HUM. RTS. J. 207, 224 (2008).

28. Elizabeth Macek, *Scratching the Corporate Back: Why Corporations Have No Incentive to Define Human Rights*, 11 MINN. J. GLOB. TRADE 101, 110 n.64 (2002).

29. James E. Post, *Global Codes of Conduct: Activists, Lawyers, and Managers in Search of a Solution*, in GLOBAL CODES OF CONDUCT, *supra* note 25, at 103, 108.

30. *Id.* at 105–8; S. Sethi, *Gaps in Research in the Formulation, Implementation, and Effectiveness Measurement of International Codes of Conduct*, in GLOBAL CODES OF CONDUCT, *supra* note 25, at 117–18; Robert Kinloch Massie, *Effective Codes of Conduct: Lessons from the Sullivan and CERES Principles*, in GLOBAL CODES OF CONDUCT, *supra* note 25, at 281.

31. Garth Meintjes, *An International Human Rights Perspective on Corporate Codes*, in GLOBAL CODES OF CONDUCT, *supra* note 25, at 83, 91.

32. *See generally*, David M. Schilling, *Making Codes of Conduct Credible: The Role of Independent Monitoring*, in GLOBAL CODES OF CONDUCT, *supra* note 25, at 221, 222; Pia Z. Thadhani, *Regulating Human Rights Abuses: Is Unocal the Answer?* 42 WM. & MARY L. REV. 619, 640 (2000).

33. Barbara A. Frey, *The Legal and Ethical Responsibilities of Transnational Corporations in the Protection of International Human Rights*, 6 MINN. J. GLOB. TRADE 153, 158 (1997).

34. *Id.* at 167; Cai Congyan, *China-US BIT Negotiations and the Future of Investment Treaty Regime: A Grand Bilateral Bargain with Multilateral Implications*, 12 J. INT'L ECON. L. 457, 502 (2009).

35. THE OECD GUIDELINES FOR MULTINATIONAL ENTERPRISES: TEXT, COMMENTARY AND CLARIFICATIONS (Oct. 31, 2001).

36. John Gerard Ruggie, *Business and Human Rights: The Evolving International Agenda*, 101 AM. J. INT'L L. 819, 820 (2007) [hereinafter Ruggie, *Evolving International Agenda*]. *See also* Christen Broecker, *"Better the Devil You Know": Home State Approaches to Transnational Corporate Accountability*, 41 N.Y.U. J. INT'L L & POL. 159, 176 (2008) (referring to John Ruggie as the "primary architect" of the compact).

37. Mac Darrow & Louise Arbour, *The Pillar of Glass: Human Rights in the Development Operations of the United Nations*, 103 AM. J. INT'L L. 446, 479 (2009).

38. *See* Shira Pridan-Frank, *Human-Genomics: A Challenge to the Rules of the Game of International Law*, 40 COLUM. J. TRANSNAT'L L. 619, 669 (2002).

39. U.N. Global Compact, The Ten Principles of the Global Compact, *available at* www.unglobalcompact .org/AbouttheGC/TheTENPrinciples/index.html.

40. *See* U.N. Global Compact Participants, *available at* www.unglobalcompact.org/ParticipantsAndStakeholders/index.html. There are ongoing efforts to recruit additional participants. *See* Perry S. Bechky, *Darfur, Divestment, and Dialogue*, 30 U. PA. J. INT'L L. 823, 846 n. 111 (2009) (stating that "52 investors representing about $4.4 trillion in assets under management recently wrote a letter to the chief executive officers of 9000 companies listed on major indices worldwide urging them to join the U.N. Global Compact.").

41. Ruggie, *Evolving International Agenda*, *supra* note 36, at 820.

42. UN Global Compact, Corporate Citizenship in the World Economy (Oct. 2008), at 4; *available at* www.unglobalcompact.org/doc/news_events/8.1/GC_brochure_FINAL.pdf.

43. *See* Global Compact: Note on Integrity Measures 2–4, *available at* www.unglobalcompact.org/AboutTheGC/gc_integrity_measures.pdf.

44. *See* William H. Meyer & Boyka Stefanova, *Human Rights, the U.N. Global Compact, and Global Governance*, 34 CORNELL INT'L L. J. 501, 504 (2001).

45. Mark E. A. Danielson, *Economic Espionage: A Framework for a Workable Solution*, 10 MINN. J.L. SCI. & TECH. 503, 528 (2009) (citation omitted).

46. *See* Beth Stephens, *The Amorality of Profit: Transnational Corporations and Human Rights*, 20 BERKELEY J. INT'L L. 45, 81 (2002); Meaghan Shaughnessy, *The United Nations Global Compact and the Continuing Debate About the Effectiveness of Corporate Voluntary Codes of Conduct*, 2000 COLO. J. INT'L ENVTL. L. & POL'Y 159 (2000).

47. Kendra Magraw, *Universally Liable? Corporate-Complicity Liability Under the Principle of Universal Jurisdiction*, 18 MINN. J. INT'L L. 458, 484 n.168 (2009).

48. Evaristus Oshionebo, *The U.N. Global Compact and Accountability of Transnational Corporations: Separating Myth from Realities*, 19 FLA. J. INT'L L. 1, 38 (2007).

49. Participating oil companies were Texaco, Chevron (both of whom are now part of Chevron), BP, Conoco (now Conoco-Philips), and Royal Dutch/Shell. Freeport McMoran and Rio Tinto represented the mining sector. Representing the human rights groups were Amnesty International, Human Rights Watch, the Lawyers' Committee for Human Rights, and International Alert, and the International Federation of Chemical, Energy, Mine, and General Workers' Unions represented trade unions. Participating business organizations were the Prince of Wales Business Leaders Forum and Business for Social Responsibility.

50. Paul Lewis, *Rights Groups Say Shell Oil Shares Blame*, NEW YORK TIMES (Nov. 11, 1995).

51. Harold Hongju Koh, *A United States Human Rights Policy for the 21st Century*, 46 ST. LOUIS L. J. 293, 321 (2002) (citation omitted).

52. Bennett Freeman et al., *A New Approach to Corporate Responsibility: The Voluntary Principles on Security and Human Rights*, 24 HASTINGS INT'L & COMP. L. REV. 423, 435 (2001).

53. The Voluntary Principles on Security and Human Rights, *available at* www.voluntaryprinciples.org/files/voluntary_principles.pdf. Sean D. Murphy, *Voluntary Human Rights Principles for Extractive and Energy Companies*, 95 AM. J. INT'L L. 626 (2001).

54. *See* Voluntary Principles on Security and Human Rights, Participants + Companies, *available at* www .voluntaryprinciples.org/participants/companies.php. *See further* Cynthia A. Williams, *A Tale of Two Trajectories*, 75 FORDHAM L. REV. 1629, 1639 (2006) (stating that under the Principles, "companies agree to incorporate UN human rights standards in their relationships with public and private security forces, and to establish procedures for training security personnel to avoid human rights infractions, for monitoring their activities, and for responding to complaints.").

55. Note, *Organizational Irrationality and Corporate Human Rights Violations*, 122 HARV. L. REV. 1931, 1944 (2009) (citations omitted).

56. Bennett Freeman, *Drilling for Common Ground*, FOREIGN POL'Y (Jul. 1, 2001).

57. *See* Caroline Kaeb, *Emerging Issues of Human Rights Responsibility in the Extractive and Manufacturing Industries: Patterns and Liability Risks*, 6 N.W. U. J. INT'L HUM. RTS. 327 (2008) (discussing the use of the Principles by French oil corporation, Total, in implementing a two-pronged policy that includes conducting human rights training sessions for its security staff and formalizing relations between the corporation's subsidiaries and governments on security matters); Seher Khawaja, *Corporate Free Market Responsibility: Addressing Human Rights Violations with a Fiduciary Duty Approach*

to *Natural Resource Extractions in Weak Governance Zones*, 3 BROOK. J. CORP. FIN. & COM. L. 185 n.185 (2008) (discussing Chevron's participation).

58. *See* Jones, *supra* note 2, at 259 n.173.

59. Christiana Ochoa, *From Odious Debt to Odious Finance: Avoiding the Externalities of a Functional Odious Debt Doctrine*, 49 HARV. INT'L L. J. 109, 137 n.146 (2008).

60. *See generally*, Extractive Industries Transparency Initiative, EITI Summary, *available at* www.eitransparency.org/eiti/summary.

61. *See* Emeka Duruigbo, *The World Bank, Multinational Oil Corporations, and the Resource Curse in Africa*, 26 U. PENN. J. INT'L ECON. L. 1, 48 (2005).

62. *See* Matthew Genasci & Sarah Pray, *Extracting Accountability: The Implications of the Resource Curse for CSR Theory and Practice*, 11 YALE HUM. RTS. & DEV. L. J. 37, 51 (2008) (stating that the EITI does place a significant amount of information in the hands of citizens, which holds great promise for the creation of a meaningful social contract).

63. LOUIS D. BRANDEIS, OTHER PEOPLE'S MONEY 92 (1914). *See also* Mary Graham, *Is Sunshine the Best Disinfectant? The Promise and Problems of Environmental Disclosure*, BROOKINGS REV. 18 (Spring 2002) (discussing Louis D. Brandeis's statement that "Publicity is justly commended as a remedy for social and industrial diseases. Sunlight is said to be the best of disinfectants." (alteration in original)).

64. In addition, the EITI is expected to play an important role in investment relations between China and African countries, especially in curbing the crippling corruption that has bedeviled the continent. *See* Uche Ewelukwa Ofodile, *Trade, Empires, and Subjects—China-Africa Trade: A New Fair Trade Arrangement, or the Third Scramble for Africa?* 41 VAND. J. TRANSNAT'L L. 505, 556 (2008).

65. Gavin Hilson & Roy Maconachie, *The Extractive Industries Transparency Initiative: Panacea or White Elephant for Sub-Saharan Africa?* in MINING, SOCIETY AND A SUSTAINABLE WORLD 469 (J. P. Richards ed., 2009).

66. *Id. See also* Gavin Hilson & Roy Maconachie, *"Good Governance" and Extractive Industries in Sub-Saharan Africa*, 30 MIN. PROC. & EXTRACTIVE METALLURGY. REV. 52 (2009).

67. Alex Kardon, Matthew Genasci, & Sarah Pray, *Extracting Accountability: Implications of the Resource Curse for CSR Theory and Practice*, 11 YALE HUM. RTS. & DEV. L. J. 59, 63 (2008).

68. Carola Kantz, *The Power of Socialization: Engaging the Diamond Industry in the Kimberly Process*, 9 BUS. & POLITICS 1 (2007).

69. *Id.* at 2. *See also* www.kimberleyprocess.com.

70. Kantz, *supra* note 68, at 3.

71. John R. Crook, *Contemporary Practice of the United States Relating to International Law*, 102 AM. J. INT'L L. 894, 900 (2008) (citation omitted).

72. *See* Luke A. Whittemore, *Intervention and Post-Conflict Natural Resource Governance: Lessons from Liberia*, 17 MINN. J. INT'L L. 387, 428 (2008).

73. *See* www.kimberleyprocess.com.

74. S.C. Res. 1459, para. 1, U.N. Doc. S/RES/1459/58 (Jan. 28, 2003).

75. *See* Kori Kelley, *Are Mined Diamonds Forever? The Emergence of Lab Diamonds and the Suppression of Conflict Diamonds*, 20 GEO. INT'L ENVTL. L. REV. 451, 460 (2008) (discussing scholars' claim that "the KPCS's language is 'vague' because the internal controls required for participation lack an effective monitoring and enforcement mechanism").

76. *See* Peter White, *It's Greek to Me: The Case for Creating an International Agency to Enforce International Accounting Standards to Promote Harmonization and International Business Transactions*, 27 WISC. INT'L L. J. 195, 213–14 (2009).

77. *See* Crook, *supra* note 71, at 900.

78. M. Cherif Bassiouni, *The New Wars and the Crisis of Compliance with the Law of Armed Conflict by Non-State Actors*, 98 J. CRIM. L. & CRIMINOLOGY 711, 776 n.262 (2008).

79. *See* Haley Blaire Goldman, *Between a ROC and a Hard Place: The Republic of Congo's Illicit Trade in Diamonds and Efforts to Break the Cycle of Corruption*, 30 U. PA. J. INT'L L. 359, 359 (2008).

80. *See* Julie L. Fishman, *Is Diamond Smuggling Forever? The Kimberley Process Certification Scheme: The First Step Down the Long Road to Solving the Blood Diamond Trade Problem*, 13 U. MIAMI BUS. L. REV. 217, 235 (2005).

81. Diane L. Fahey, *Can Tax Policy Stop Human Trafficking?* 40 GEO. J. INT'L L. 345, 379 (2009).

82. Alexandra R. Harrington, *Faceting the Future: The Need for and Proposal of the Adoption of a Kimberley Process–Styled Legitimacy Certification System for the Global Gemstone Market*, 18 TRANSNAT'L & CONTEMP. PROBS. 353, 361 (2009).

83. Lisa J. Laplante & Suzanne A. Spears, *Out of the Conflict Zone: The Case for Community Consent Processes in the Extractive Sector*, 11 YALE HUM. RTS. & DEV. L. J. 69, 83 (2008).

84. Clifford Rechtschaffen, *Competing Visions: EPA and the States Battle for the Future of Environmental Enforcement*, 30 ENVTL. L. REP. 10,803 (2000).

85. *Id.*

86. JOSHUA KARLINER, THE CORPORATE PLANET: ECOLOGY AND POLITICS IN THE AGE OF GLOBALIZATION 48 (1997) (quoting UNTCMD, WORLD INVESTMENT REPORT 1992: TRANSNATIONAL CORPORATIONS AS ENGINES OF GROWTH 90–91 (1992)).

87. *See* Marisa B. Van Saanen, *Paul Collier, Laws and Codes for the 'Resource Curse'*, 11 YALE HUM. RTS. & DEV. L. J. 29, 29–30 (2008) (stating that voluntary codes have been effective on some issues but may not be as effective in other matters).

88. Jorge F. Perez-Lopez, *Promoting International Respect for Worker Rights Through Business Codes of Conduct*, 17 FORDHAM INT'L L. J. 1, 47 (1993).

89. *Id.* at 44–45. *See also* Heidi S. Bloomfield, *"Sweating" the International Garment Industry: A Critique of the Presidential Task Force's Workplace Codes of Conduct and Monitoring System*, 22 HASTINGS INT'L & COMP. L. REV. 567, 590 (1999).

90. *See generally*, Robert J. Liubicic, *Corporate Codes of Conduct and Product Labeling Schemes: The Limits and Possibilities of Promoting International Labor Rights Through Private Initiatives*, 30 LAW & POL'Y INT'L BUS. 111, 157 (1998); Lance Compa & Tashia Hincliffe-Darricarrere, *Enforcing International Labor Rights Through Corporate Codes of Conduct*, 33 COLUM. J. TRANSNAT'L L. 663, 687 (1995); Donna Lee Van Cott, *Regional Environmental Law in the Americas: Assessing the Contractual Environment*, 26 U. MIAMI INTER-AM. L. REV. 489, 515 (1995); Steven R. Salbu, *True Codes Versus Voluntary Codes of Ethics in International Markets: Towards the Preservation of Colloquy in Emerging Global Communities*, 15 U. PA. J. INT'L BUS. L. 327 (1994).

91. *See* Bill Baue, *Ruggie Report Says Voluntary Human Rights Initiatives Set Stage for Binding Global Standards*, SOCIALFUNDS.COM, Mar. 19, 2007, *available at* www.socialfunds.com/news/article.cgi/2253.html (quoting the views of Mort Winston, former Chair of Amnesty International USA).

92. Katherine van Wezel Stone, *To the Yukon and Beyond: Local Laborers in a Global Labor Market*, 3 J. SMALL & EMERGING BUS. L. 93, 127 (1999).

93. LEIGHTON ET AL., *supra* note 4, at 50.

94. *See* Meintjes, *supra* note 31, at 83.

95. *See* Sir Geoffrey Chandler, *John Ruggie: Compelling Corporate Action on Human Rights*, ETHICAL CORPORATION (Apr. 4, 2007), *available at* www.ethicalcorp.com/content.asp?ContentID=4995 ("The debate has long been mired in controversy between the proponents of voluntary and mandatory measures, though history shows that voluntarism has never worked and that the law on its own is inadequate to control so protean an activity as business."). *See also* Paul Collier, *Laws and Codes for the Resource Curse*, 11 YALE HUM. RTS. & DEV. L. J. 9 (2008) (discussing reasons behind the power held by voluntary codes but also reserving a role for international regulation).

96. *See* Jeffrey L. Dunoff & Joel P. Trachtman, *Economic Analysis of International Law*, 24 YALE J. INT'L L. 1, 41 (1999) ("Asset specificity . . . gives rise to potential opportunism. In turn, this gives rise to the need for binding mechanisms or institutions.").

97. Laura Ho et al., *(Dis)Assembling Rights of Women Workers Along the Global Assembly Line: Human Rights and the Garment Industry*, 31 HARV. C.R.-C.L. L. REV. 383, 401 (1996).

98. *See* Ruth Rosenblum, *In Whose Interest? A Global Code of Conduct for Corporations*, in GLOBAL CODES OF CONDUCT, *supra* note 25, at 211, 215.

99. Sarah Cleveland, *Global Labor Rights and the Alien Tort Claims Act*, 76 TEX. L. REV. 1533 (1998) (reviewing HUMAN RIGHTS, LABOR RIGHTS, AND INTERNATIONAL TRADE (Lance A. Compa & Stephen F. Diamond eds., 1996)).

100. *See Watching the Sweatshops,* NEW YORK TIMES, Editorial (Aug. 20, 1997) (criticizing Andrew Young's monitoring of Nike).

101. *See* Douglass Cassel, *Corporate Initiatives: A Second Human Rights Revolution?* 19 FORDHAM INT'L L. J. 1963, 1971 (1996) (discussing the failure of the Sullivan Principles, an initiative that enjoyed extensive independent monitoring).

102. Natalie L. Bridgeman & David B. Hunter, *Narrowing the Accountability Gap: Toward a Foreign Investor Accountability Mechanism*, 20 GEO. INT'L ENVTL. L. REV. 187, 190 (2008).

103. *See, e.g.*, Douglas S. Morrin, *People Before Profits: Pursuing Corporate Accountability for Labor Rights Violations Abroad Through the Alien Tort Claims Act*, 20 B.C. THIRD WORLD L. J. 427, 429 (2000) (stating that "while codes of conduct may seem impressive, they have been largely ineffective at realizing the goals they purport to pursue") (citation omitted). *See also* RUSSELL MOKHIBER & ROBERT WEISMAN, CORPORATE PREDATORS: THE HUNT FOR MEGA-PROFITS AND THE ATTACK ON DEMOCRACY 84 (1999).

104. Michael S. Baram, *Multinational Corporations, Private Codes, and Technology Transfer for Sustainable Development*, 24 ENVTL. L. 33, 42 (1994) (citation omitted).

105. LEIGHTON ET AL., *supra* note 4, at 158.

106. For a discussion by this author of the "leadership curse" that has plagued many resource-rich developing countries, *see* Emeka Duruigbo, *Permanent Sovereignty and People's Ownership of Natural Resources in International Law*, 38 GEO. WASH. INT'L L. REV. 33 (2006).

107. The United Fruit Company (UFC) (now known as Chiquita Corporation), a U.S. multinational, seriously concerned that land reforms then going on in Guatemala would jeopardize its interests, orchestrated a coup in that country in 1954. *See* Ariadne K. Sacharoff, *Multinationals in Host Countries: Can They Be Held Liable Under the Alien Tort Claims Act for Human Rights Violations?* 23 BROOKLYN J. INT'L L. 927, 927 (1998). UFC also engineered an armed invasion of Honduras. *See* THOMAS DONALDSON, THE ETHICS OF INTERNATIONAL BUSINESS 9 (1989). Similarly, International

Telephone & Telegraph (ITT) played a prominent role in the overthrow of the Allende government in Chile in 1973. *See* Celia Wells & Juanita Elias, *Catching the Conscience of the King: Corporate Players on the International Stage*, in NONSTATE ACTORS AND HUMAN RIGHTS, 141, 143–44 (Philip Alston ed., 2005); O. E. Udofia, *Imperialism in Africa: A Case of Multinational Corporations*, 14 J. BLACK STUD. 353, 360 (1984); Olivier de Schutter, *Transnational Corporations as Instruments of Human Development*, in HUMAN RIGHTS AND DEVELOPMENT: TOWARDS MUTUAL REINFORCEMENT 403, 406 (Philip Alston & Mary Robinson eds., 2005) (discussing "Well-known historical episodes, such as the influence of the U.S.-based corporations ITT, Pepsi-Cola and the Chase Manhattan Bank in the *coup d'état* which put Pinochet into power in Chile or the role of the Union Miniere in the secession of Katanga from Congo" that demonstrate MNC interference in internal affairs of states in which they operate).

108. *See* Matthew Lippman, *Transnational Corporations and Repressive Regimes: The Ethical Dilemma*, 15 CAL. W. INT'L L. J. 542, 545 (1985).

109. *Id.* For a litany of reasons behind inadequate legal provisions and weak enforcement in many developing countries, including absence of political will, lack of technical and financial capacity, presence of corruption, and disproportionate negotiating power, *see* Bridgeman & Hunter, *supra* note 102, at 196–97.

110. *See* Karsten Nowrot, *Reconceptualising International Legal Personality of Influential Non-State Actors: Toward a Rebuttable Presumption of Normative Responsibilities*, 79 PHIL. L. J. 563 (2004) ("The increasingly important role of multinational corporations as economic and political actors on the international scene results in chances for, but especially also risks to, the promotion of community interests, also known as global public goods, such as, for example, the protection of human rights and the environment, as well as the enforcement of core labour and social standards.") (citations omitted). For an earlier articulation of this point, *see* Sigmund Timberg, *Corporate Fictions: Logical, Social and International Implications*, 46 COLUM. L. REV. 533, 580 (1946) ("Particularly in the international sphere, corporations . . . should be regarded as not only the carriers of their own private interests, but instrumentalities for effectuating social and economic interests which the national and international community regards as paramount.").

111. *See* Meintjes, *supra* note 31, at 86.

112. Weissbrodt & Kruger, *supra* note 11, at 901.

113. International Federation for Human Rights, Position Paper, *Comments to the Interim Report of the Special Representative of the Secretary-General on the Issue of Human Rights and Transnational Corporations and Other Business Enterprises, Feb. 22, 2006*, at 7 (Mar. 15, 2006), *available at* www.fidh.org/IMG/pdf/business442a.pdf (stating that "the move toward a binding framework has grown out of the gross failure of voluntary mechanisms").

114. *See* 3 WILLIAM BLACKSTONE, COMMENTARIES 109 (1765); *see also Marbury v. Madison*, 5 U.S. 137, 163 (1803) ("[F]or it is a settled and invariable principle . . . that every right, when withheld, must have a remedy, and every injury its proper redress."); Richard A. Epstein, *Standing and Spending—The Role of Legal and Equitable Principles*, 4 CHAP. L. REV. 1, 13 (2001); Reinhard Zimmermann, *Roman-Dutch Jurisprudence and its Contribution to European Private Law*, 66 TUL. L. REV. 1685, 1696 (1992).

115. Plenary Theme Panel, *The Challenge of Non-State Actors*, 92 AM. SOC'Y INT'L L. PROC. 20, 33 (1998) (remarks of Linda Mabry). *See also* Michael K. Addo, *Human Rights and Transnational Corporations–an Introduction*, in HUMAN RIGHTS STANDARDS AND THE RESPONSIBILITY OF TRANSNATIONAL CORPORATIONS 3, 11 (Michael K. Addo ed., 1999) [hereinafter Addo, *Human Rights*]. ("In the era of the global economy and the reduction of trading and investment barriers, the laws of one particular country will be inadequate in controlling corporate behavior."); Adam Mcbeth, *Every Organ of Society: The Responsibility of Non-State Actors for the Realization of Human Rights*, 30 HAMLINE J. PUB. L. & POL'Y 33, 34 (2008) (including multinational corporations among the "many powerful actors that transcend the regulatory capacity of any one state").

116. *See generally*, Saman Zia-Zarifi, *Suing Multinational Corporations in the U.S. for Violating International Law*, 4 UCLA J. INT'L L. & FOREIGN AFF. 81, 84–86 (1999). *See also* Claudio Grossman & Daniel Bradlow, *Are We Being Propelled Towards a People-Centered Transnational Legal Order?* 9 AM. U. J. INT'L L. & POL'Y 1, 8–9 (1993); Martin A. Geer, *Foreigners in Their Own Land: Cultural Land and Transnational Corporations—Emergent International Rights and Wrongs* 38 VA J. INT'L L. 331, 335–36 (1998); Robert J. Fowler, *International Environmental Standards for Transnational Corporations*, 25 ENVTL. L. 1, 2 (1995).

117. For a discussion of recent human rights litigation under the Alien Tort Statute and elsewhere, including the United Kingdom, the Netherlands, and France, *see* Sarah A. Altschuller & Amy Lehr, *Corporate Social Responsibility*, 43 INT'L LAW 577, 580–86 (2009).

118. 28 U.S.C. § 1350 (2008). The original version was in Judiciary Act, ch. 20, §9, I Stat. 73, 77 (1789).

119. For more detailed discussions of the arguments in favor of, or in opposition to, alien tort litigation, *see* Emeka Duruigbo, *The Economic Cost of Alien Tort Litigation: A Response to Awakening Monster: The Alien Tort Statute of 1789*, 14 MINN. J. GLOB. TRADE 1 (2004); Emeka Duruigbo, *Exhaustion of Local Reme-*

dies and Alien Tort Litigation: Implications for International Human Rights Protection, 29 FORDHAM INT'L L. J. 1245 (2006).

120. For these contrasting views, *see, e.g.*, Beth Stephens, *Judicial Deference and the Unreasonable Views of the Bush Administration*, 33 BROOKLYN J. INT'L L. 773 (2008), and John B. Bellinger III, *Enforcing Human Rights in U.S. Courts and Abroad: The Alien Tort Statute and Other Approaches*, 42 VAND. J. TRANSNAT'L L. 1 (2009).

121. *See generally*, Melina Williams, *Privatization and the Human Right to Water: Challenges for the New Century*, 28 MICH J. INT'L L. 469, 489–91 (2007); *See* Upendra Baxi, *Market Fundamentalisms: Business Ethics at the Altar of Human Rights*, 5 HUM. RTS. L. REV. 1, 3 (2005) (stating that the *Norms* encountered a "silhouette of global corporate resistance") (citation omitted).

122. *See* Office of High Commissioner for Human Rights, *Human Rights and Transnational Corporations and other Business Enterprises*, Human Rights Resolution 2005/69, (Apr. 20, 2005), *available at* http://ap.ohchr .org/documents/E/CHR/resolutions/E-CN_4-RES -2005–69.doc.

123. Nicholas Lusiani & Tricia Feeney, *Advocacy Guide on Business and Human Rights in the United Nations, Part I: The Mandate of the Special Representative*, International Network for Economic, Social and Cultural Rights (Escr-Net), Corporate Accountability Working Group (Oct. 2009), at 11–12.

124. The Special Representative of the Secretary-General, *Interim Report of the Special Representative of the Secretary-General on the Issue of Human Rights and Transnational Corporations and Other Business Enterprises*, delivered to the Commission on Human Rights, U.N. Doc. E/CN.4/2006/97 (Feb. 22, 2006), at para. 65 [hereinafter *Interim Report*].

125. *Interim Report*, *supra* note 124, at para. 61.

126. The Special Representative of the Secretary-General, *Report of the Special Representative of the Secretary-General on the Issue of Human Rights and Transnational Corporations and Other Business Enterprises, John Ruggie: Business and Human Rights: Mapping International Standards of Responsibility and Accountability for Corporate Acts*, delivered to the Human Rights Council, U.N. Doc. A/HRC/4/35 (Feb. 9, 2007), at para. 20 [hereinafter *Mapping International Standards*]; HENRY J. STEINER, PHILIP ALSTON, & RYAN GOODMAN, INTERNATIONAL HUMAN RIGHTS IN CONTEXT: LAW, POLITICS, MORALS 1405 (3d ed. 2008) ("In 2007, Ruggie provided his own assessment of the existing legal and other landscape.").

127. John Ruggie, *Report of the Special Representative of the Secretary-General on the Issue of Human Rights and Transnational Corporations and Other Business Enterprises, Protect, Respect and Remedy: A Framework for Business and Human Rights*, U.N. Doc. A/HRC/8/5 (Apr. 7, 2008).

128. *Id.* at para. 54.

129. Special Representative of the Secretary-General, *Report of the Special Representative of the Secretary-General on the Issue of Human Rights and Transnational Corporations and Other Business Enterprises*, U.N. Doc. A/HRC/8/16 (May 15, 2008), *available at* www2.ohchr .org/english/bodies/hrcouncil/8session/reports.htm.

130. Special Representative of the Secretary-General, Business and Human Rights: *Towards Operationalizing the Protect, Respect and Remedy Framework*, A/HRC/11/13 (Apr. 22, 2009), *available at* www2.ohchr.org/english/ bodies/hrcouncil/docs/11session/A.HRC.11.13.pdf.

131. *See* International Federation of Human Rights, *Human Rights and Business: Upholding Human Rights and Ensuring Coherence, Submission to the Special Representative of the Secretary-General on the issue of Human Rights and Transnational Corporations and other Business Enterprises* (Oct. 2009), at 5. *See also* Sara L. Seck, *Unilateral Home State Regulation: Imperialism or Tool for Subaltern Resistance?* 46 OSGOODE HALL L. J. 565 (2008); Sara L. Seck, *Home State Responsibility and Local Communities: The Case of Global Mining*, 11 YALE HUM. RTS. & DEV. L. J. 177 (2008).

132. *See* Carlos M. Vazquez, *Direct vs. Indirect Obligations of Corporations Under International Law*, 43 COLUM. J. TRANSNAT'L L. 927, 931 n.14 (2005); Rory Sullivan, *Legislating for Responsible Corporate Behavior: Domestic Law Approaches to an International Issue*, in GLOBAL GOVERNANCE AND THE QUEST FOR JUSTICE, VOL. 2: CORPORATE GOVERNANCE, 183, 195 (Sorcha MacLeod ed., 2006).

133. For a more elaborate discussion of the recent changes and challenges, *see* Emeka Duruigbo, *Corporate Accountability and Liability for International Human Rights Abuses: Recent Changes and Recurring Challenges*, 6 N.W. J. INT'L HUM. RTS. 222 (2008).

134. S. JAMES ANAYA, INTERNATIONAL HUMAN RIGHTS AND INDIGENOUS PEOPLES 44 (2009) (discussing the positivist view that "international law is concerned only with the rights and duties of states"); Beth Stephens, *Individuals Enforcing International Law: The Comparative and Historical Context*, 52 DEPAUL L. REV. 433, 448 (2002) (noting that under the positivist conception, states are "the only actors recognized as subjects of international law").

135. Anita Ramasastry, *Corporate Complicity: From Nuremberg to Rangoon, An Examination of Forced Labor Cases and Their Impact on the Liability of Multinational Corporations*, 20 BERKELEY J. INT'L L. 91, 96 (2002); Michael Reiterer, Book Review, 81 AM. J. INT'L L. 970, 970 (1987) (reviewing RUTH DONNER, THE REGULATION OF NATIONALITY IN INTERNATIONAL LAW (1983) (challenging the proposition that only states are the subject of international law and positing that nongovernmental organizations (NGOs), transnational

corporations and individuals are "new (at least partly) subjects of international law").

136. IAN BROWNLIE, PRINCIPLES OF PUBLIC INTERNATIONAL LAW 65 (6th ed. 2003) (citation omitted).

137. *Mapping International Standards, supra* note 126, at para. 20.

138. *See* Hurst Hannum, Book Review, 101 AM. J. INT'L L. 514, 519 (2007) (reviewing ANDREW CLAPHAM, HUMAN RIGHTS OBLIGATIONS OF NON-STATE ACTORS (2006)).

139. Christine Chinkin, *International Law and Human Rights*, in HUMAN RIGHTS FIFTY YEARS ON: A REAPPRAISAL 105, 115 (Tony Evans ed., 1998); ANDREW CLAPHAM, HUMAN RIGHTS OBLIGATIONS OF NON-STATE ACTORS 58 (2006) (stating that "we can legitimately reverse the presumption that human rights are inevitably a contract between individuals and the state; we can presume that human rights are entitlements enjoyed by everyone to be respected by everyone"). *See also* Addo, *Human Rights, supra* note 115, at 27 ("The view that human rights affect all sectors of society by conferring entitlements and imposing obligations on everyone is a powerful one in defining the relationship between human rights standards and corporate policy."); Sigrun I. Skogly, *Economic and Social Human Rights, Private Actors and International Obligations*, in HUMAN RIGHTS STANDARDS, *supra* note 115, at 239 (providing justification for the reconceptualization).

140. ANTONIO CASSESE, INTERNATIONAL LAW IN A DIVIDED WORLD (1986).

141. *See* Jonathan I. Charney, *Transnational Corporations and Developing Public International Law*, 1983 DUKE L. J. 748, 767 (noting that corporations are the beneficiaries of their international nonstatus); Duncan Hollis, *Private Actors in Public International Law: Amicus Curiae and the Case for the Retention of State Sovereignty*, 25 B.C. INT'L & COMP. L. REV. 235, 236 (2002) (discussing the growing influence of MNCs in the making and implementation of international law); International Chamber of Commerce & International Organisation of Employers, *Joint Views of the IOE And ICC on the Draft "Norms on the Responsibilities of Transnational Corporations and Other Business Enterprises with Regard to Human Rights"* (Mar. 2004), *available at* www.reports-and-materials.org/IOE-ICC-views-UN-norms-March-2004.doc (outlining the opposition of the business sector to the imposition of direct obligations on corporations).

142. *See* Chandler, *supra* note 95; Steven R. Ratner, *Corporations and Human Rights: A Theory of Legal Responsibility*, 111 YALE L. J. 443, 530 (2001).

143. *See* Richard Falk, *Human Rights*, FOREIGN POL'Y (Mar./Apr. 2004), at 18, 22 (stating that "given the clear benefits of foreign investment in mitigating poverty, imposing international standards that reduce the attractiveness of countries with minimal regulation would, in the short term at least, likely accentuate human suffering").

144. *See* Laura A. Dickinson, *Public Law Values in a Privatized World*, 31 YALE J. INT'L L. 382, 388 (2006). There are up to 77,000 transnational firms operating in the global economy, in addition to 770,000 subsidiaries and millions of suppliers. *See* UNCTAD, WORLD INVESTMENT REPORT 2006, UN Sales No.E.06.II.D.11 (2006), *available at* www.unctad.org/en/docs/wir2006_en.pdf.

145. *See* Dickinson, *supra* note 144 (advocating the use of contracts with private actors, incorporating public international law norms and enforceable in domestic courts); *see also* Laura A. Dickinson, *Government for Hire: Privatizing Foreign Affairs and the Problem of Accountability Under International Law*, 47 WM & MARY L. REV. 135 (2005).

146. John Ruggie, Opening Statement to United Nations Human Rights Council (Sept. 25, 2006).

147. INTERNATIONAL NETWORK FOR ECONOMIC, SOCIAL & CULTURAL RIGHTS, JOINT NGO SUBMISSION ON HUMAN RIGHTS & THE EXTRACTIVE INDUSTRY-2005 28 (2005), *available at* www.escrnet. org/actions_more/actions_more_show.htm?doc_id=430968.

148. *Id.*

149. Patrick Macklem, *Corporate Accountability under International Law: The Misguided Quest for Universal Jurisdiction*, 7 INT'L L. FORUM 281 (2005).

150. *See* Michael K. Addo, *The Corporation as a Victim of Human Rights Violations*, in HUMAN RIGHTS STANDARDS, *supra* note 115, at 187 (decrying the lack of appreciation of the suggestion that corporations can also be human rights victims and discussing the value of recognizing the rights of corporations in the overall objective of human rights protection).

151. *See* Macklem, *supra* note 149 (stating that such rights, in the context of universal jurisdiction, "would emerge incrementally as corporations seek to defend themselves from criminal prosecution").

PART FOUR

COURTS

10

Reaching Beyond the State

Judicial Independence, the Inter-American Court of Human Rights, and Accountability in Guatemala

JEFFREY DAVIS AND EDWARD H. WARNER

1. Introduction

Guatemalan security forces killed an estimated 200,000 people during that country's thirty-year internal conflict. Most of those responsible for these crimes remain hidden behind a stubborn wall of impunity. In one episode, on July 18, 1982, Guatemalan military and paramilitary personnel slaughtered 268 civilians. The massacre took place in Plan de Sánchez and surrounding communities where "soldiers randomly picked their victims, raping and torturing young women before rounding up villagers in a house, throwing in hand grenades and firing machine guns."[1] Most of the 268 victims were Mayan. For more than twenty years, Guatemala blocked all attempts to punish those responsible for this massacre.

As nations work to democratize and liberalize after periods of intense conflict, how can they confront this history of brutal human rights atrocities? How can their recurrence be prevented? Although traditional Anglo-American democratic theory suggests that an independent judiciary is the institution ideally suited to hold the government accountable to the law, in this chapter we will consider whether international courts are necessary to help postconflict nations confront their past and

democratize. By looking at the Inter-American Court of Human Rights (IACHR), we examine whether international courts can effectively promote human rights accountability and protection, and if so, to what extent. Human rights scholarship is perhaps at its most revealing when the analysis is coupled with the human stories from which the legal and political issues arise. Therefore, our analysis will orbit around the case studies of Guatemala's *Mack*, *Carpio*, and *Plan de Sánchez* trials.[2] Guatemala is an ideal subject of analysis for this chapter because it is emerging from thirty years of political violence. It has suffered some of the most horrific human rights violations in the region, and it is now struggling to reconcile this past and embrace liberal democracy. It has one of the worst human rights records in Latin America, according to observers like Amnesty International and the U.S. State Department, and thus it is a monumentally challenging case.[3]

To uncover answers to our questions, we first provide a brief history of Guatemala. We then consider the role of courts in the struggle for human rights, demonstrating the need for international judicial action. Accompanying this section, we include a discussion of the purpose of international courts. Then, after a brief introduction to the Inter-American human rights system and our three case studies, we examine whether and how the IACHR accomplishes the purpose of an international human rights tribunal. Finally, drawing on lessons from the analysis, we conclude that international courts, and specifically the Inter-American Court, can indeed promote human rights. We base our analysis on interviews with lawyers and activists working in the area, on our observation of proceedings before the IACHR, and on the content analysis of IACHR decisions.[4]

2. Historical Background

Guatemala has a deeply tragic history of political violence and widespread human rights violations with causes traceable to its colonial roots. In an effort to break with years of repression, stratification, and exploitation by the colonial and postcolonial regimes, Guatemala elected populist presidents in the two elections following World War II. Dr. Juan José Arévalo and his successor Colonel Jacobo Árbenz Guzmán embraced land reform and encouraged broader political participation. In 1954, however, when President Árbenz's reform efforts were perceived as harming U.S. interests, the U.S. Central Intelligence Agency helped Colonel Carlos Castillo Armas overthrow Árbenz. In order to consolidate power and reverse the political opening of the Arévalo and Árbenz regimes, the Armas government strengthened the state security apparatus and extended it to the rural areas. For more than forty years this security apparatus has been brutally repressing opposition in whatever form it appears—supporters of land reform, the labor movement, and the rural insurgency. When General Romeo Lucas García became president in 1978, he first targeted political opposition in the urban centers and later the labor movement and insurgency in the countryside. Then, after taking power in a coup in 1982, General Efraín Ríos Montt launched a bloody, scorched–earth, anti-insurgency campaign. Most of the male peasants were conscripted into civil patrols and tens of thousands of innocent Guatemalans and combatants were killed.[5]

In 1983 General Óscar Mejía Victores overthrew Ríos Montt and began a painstakingly slow process of democratization. However, this promising step did not coincide with the cessation of violence, as the military continued its bloody anti-insurgency campaign. Despite a relatively successful democratic power transition in 1986, the civilian governments were unable to wrest meaningful authority from the military.[6]

Jorge Serrano Elías was elected president of Guatemala in 1990, defeating the National Center Party led by Jorge Carpio Nicolle. However, Serrano's legislative coalition dissolved in 1993, causing him to lose control of his legislative agenda. On May 25, 1993, Serrano executed a "self-coup," in which he dismissed Congress, the Supreme Court, the Constitutional Court, and the Procurator of Human Rights. He suspended fundamental liberties and took control of radio and television broadcasting.[7] On June 1, 1993, the Guatemalan Constitutional Court declared Serrano's administration illegal and Serrano fled to El Salvador amidst rising opposition. Five days later the Congress appointed the Procurator of Human Rights, Ramiro de León Carpio, Jorge Carpio Nicolle's cousin, President of Guatemala.[8] Serrano's failed coup signaled the first, albeit small, step away from military dominance. Then, in 1996 Álvaro Arzú was elected president and the Guatemalan Peace Accords were signed later that year.

Even with the Peace Accords and the transition to democratically elected civilian governments, Guatemalans continued to suffer brutal human rights violations. For example, when the war ended in 1996, the Peace Accords required Guatemala to reform its justice system. However, the UN agency established to monitor compliance with the peace accords, MINUGUA, reported continued impunity and the persistent lack of due process. In its 2000 Special Report, MINUGUA concluded that "With regard to the allegations of threats, harassment and intimidation of judges, the Special Rapporteur finds that these concerns are real [and that t]he Government ha[s] failed to provide the requisite protection or assistance to those who have complained."[9] In addition, "the large number of unsolved violent murders and the high incidence of impediments to investigations and prosecutions in these murders and human rights-related crimes . . . should give an indication of the very high rate of impunity."[10] The MINUGUA report in 2001 states that "Harassment and threats to justice operators continue to be of serious concern [and that] rather than declining, these incidents have actually increased."[11] This report finds that "impunity is still widespread."[12] In 2004, Óscar Berger was sworn in as Guatemala's latest president. President Berger emphasized improving Guatemala's human rights protections as a central feature of his campaign. As we discuss below, the Berger administration took some steps to fulfill that promise. However, there are still monumental obstacles to improving human rights conditions and to achieving justice for human rights violations that were committed.

3. The Role of Courts

A. Legal Accountability

In the face of the legacy of catastrophic political violence, victims frequently look to the courts to reconstruct the rule of law and provide justice. According to many human rights activists and scholars, courts *must* act to consolidate democratic reform based on the rule of law in postconflict or postauthoritarian settings.[13] As Laurel Fletcher and Harvey Weinstein argued, "Accountability provides a direct, moral, and ethical response to victims on behalf of society that demonstrates that the state is validating their innocence and their lack of culpability in the deeds."[14] By punishing those responsible, the state recognizes the suffering of the victims and issues a moral condemnation of the actions committed.[15] As Jamie Mayerfeld wrote, punishment "communicates society's condemnation of [the] violation, and helps actual and potential aggressors to absorb the lesson that such violation is morally wrong."[16] Courts address the victims' desire for retribution by punishing individual defendants and, in so doing, may also serve to protect against future violations.[17] Mayerfeld argued that "the obligation to deter constitutes the core rationale for punishing human rights violations."[18] Yet another scholar, Jennifer Widner, pointed out that by punishing violators, courts can provide a credible threat that future violations will be punished as well.[19] In order to guarantee human rights in the present, past threats to punish must be carried out.[20]

Indeed, according to Mayerfeld, effective judicial dispute resolution systems "encourage social reconciliation by modeling a fair procedure for the just disposition of violent conflicts fueled by bitter political and ideological divisions."[21] Judicial action against human rights violators may also prevent future abuses by reestablishing norms such as respect for the rule of law and basic human rights.[22] Ruti Teitel stated that "When criminal justice denounces these crimes, such prosecutions have a systemic impact transcending the implicated individual . . . [and to] society, such trials express the normative value of equality under the law, a threshold value in the transformation to liberal democratic systems."[23] Teitel also argued that "establishing knowledge of past actions committed under color of law and its public construction as wrongdoing is the necessary threshold to prospective normative uses of the criminal law."[24] Martha Minow agreed with this assertion when she wrote, "To respond to mass atrocity with legal prosecutions is to embrace the rule of law."[25] Human rights trials, according to Minow, transform individual desires for vengeance to the state, and this "transfer cools vengeance into retribution, slows judgment with procedure and interrupts, with documents, cross-examinations and the presumption of innocence, the vicious cycle of blame and feud."[26]

B. Judicial Independence and Accountability

Scholars and activists frequently urge judicial independence and reform in order to establish a domestic institution capable of holding government accountable to the rule of law.[27] The result, in theory, is an independent court system at home that can check tyranny from the other political institutions. Judicial independence can be defined as the extent to which the members of a court may adjudicate free from controls, incentives, and impediments imposed by other political institutions or forces.[28] In *Federalist 78*, Alexander Hamilton stated that "the courts were designed to be an intermediate body between the people and the legislature, in order, among other things, to keep the latter within the limits assigned to their authority."[29] According to Hamilton, the independence of the judiciary operates as a "safeguard against the effects of occasional ill humors in the society."[30] As Charles Epp stated in his comparative study, "the judicial system's structural independence . . . is widely recognized as a necessary condition for any significant judicial check on arbitrary power."[31]

Independence would seem to be especially important if courts are to hold government officials accountable for past or ongoing violations of human rights. In a comparison of the U.S. and Canadian high courts, Mark Miller discovered that the U.S. Supreme Court was more likely to challenge other branches because it possessed more autonomy than its Canadian counterpart.[32] Comparative scholars have consistently recognized the importance of judicial independence in democratization, protecting individual rights, and promoting the rule of law.[33] Michael Dodson and Donald Jackson linked the impotence of the judiciary directly to human rights violations in Guatemala and El Salvador.[34]

Thomas Jefferson differed with Hamilton's view of judicial independence, however, arguing that judges "should be submitted to some practical and impartial control."[35] He observed that "All know the influence of interest on the mind of man, and how unconsciously his judgment is warped by that influence."[36] Critics of absolute judicial autonomy "object to what they consider to be an inordinate and constitutionally unjustifiable grant of power to the branch of government which is least likely to accurately represent the genuine will of the people."[37] Mark

Tushnet argued that granting judges independence encourages them to follow their political will and not necessarily their legal judgment,[38] and Michael Collins pointed out that an independent court "could itself engage in acts of constitutional usurpation that might be difficult to remedy."[39]

It is possible, then, that the traditional pillar of judicial independence could, in some circumstances, impede human rights accountability. Steven Ratner and Jason Abrams argued that "Accountability cannot be isolated from the political dynamic in which competing factions within states seek to manipulate the past in order to justify both their prior activities and the current programs."[40] In repressive states, judges abetting tyranny could continue to do so unencumbered by the constraints of democratic accountability. Independence can only free courts from unwanted influence; it cannot grant judges the will to confront decades of impunity, nor can it anoint them with the wisdom to overcome legislatively or constitutionally rooted opposition to accountability. Judges will, after all, always be bound to the political elite at least to some degree and, as Ratner and Abrams articulated, "the most critical reason for the lack of prosecutions . . . is that serious violations of international human rights or humanitarian law are usually committed on behalf of or with the complicity of the state."[41] In addition to judicial ties to state actors, the barriers maintaining impunity include doctrines of sovereign immunity and amnesty laws, both of which are raised and maintained by the state.

In new and unstable democracies, prosecuting human rights cases can actually destabilize the democratic government and harm the cause of accountability. Ratner and Abrams pointed out that "if a nation's leaders allow the prosecutions to become a pawn in the competition for power, the trials will lack credibility and damage the foundations of democracy."[42] These authors cited the Argentine experience, in which prosecuting human rights cases motivated the military "to challenge the young and insecure civilian government, thereby putting an end to the prosecutorial process." Similar dangers exist in Guatemala. Conversely, Ratner and Abrams recognized that "outside actors—states, international organizations, and NGOs—can often help strengthen regimes seeking accountability and defuse threats from the opponents of prosecutions."[43]

To summarize, judicial independence allows courts to provide some measure of accountability for human rights violations. However, because domestic courts are part of the state, they are constrained by state-constructed barriers. The level of accountability they can provide, therefore, is severely limited. To overcome these barriers and to reach greater levels of accountability, victims must reach beyond the state. As we will demonstrate further below, doing so not only affords victims with a forum beyond state control but it can also strengthen the independence of local judicial processes.

C. Deep Wounds and Shallow Justice— Domestic Prosecutions in the *Carpio*, *Plan de Sánchez*, and *Mack* Cases

There is support for these assertions from the trenches of human rights litigation in Guatemala. In the spring of 1993, politician, reform activist, and newspaper-owner Jorge Carpio Nicolle opposed the Serrano self-coup and the subsequent proposals to grant amnesty to those who orchestrated the coup. Within a month of this outspoken opposition, a state-sponsored civil patrol intercepted and murdered Carpio and several of his associates.[44] The families sought justice for the killings in Guatemala, but judge after judge refused to hear the case. Guatemalan trial and appellate courts twisted the law to block all efforts to hold accountable those responsible for the killings.[45] Throughout the more than ten years of investigation, numerous crucial pieces of evidence have been lost, mislabeled, or otherwise destroyed.[46] Despite a report prepared by a chief prosecutor implicating eleven members of a civil defense patrol in the murders, only four of these men were tried and only one, Juan Patzan, was convicted of the

crime. Moreover, this conviction came in 1996 after three years of dilatory tactics by the defense and by the trial courts. In an additional blow, the trial court refused to consider the role of the civil defense patrol and foreclosed any investigation of the intellectual authors of the attack. Then, in 1998, in a shocking ruling, the Guatemalan Court of Appeals absolved Patzan of any responsibility for the murder and ordered his immediate release. The Court cited numerous evidentiary irregularities, including the broken chain of custody of the alleged murder weapon. The Guatemalan Supreme Court upheld this result and, although the investigation remains open, no notable progress has occurred since that time.[47]

The result was an utter destruction of any belief in justice emanating from the democratizing state. As the wife of one of the victims, Silvia Villacorta testified before the Inter-American Court, "Guatemala is a country of deep wounds and shallow justice."[48] The wife of Jorge Carpio, Mrs. Arrivillaga de Carpio, recounted the utter failure of the justice system in Guatemala and told the Inter-American Court that, as a result, she lived each day in fear.[49] "I felt unprotected," she testified.[50]

The state obstructed all efforts to pursue truth and justice in the *Plan de Sánchez* massacre case as well. During the period in which the massacre occurred, the military was terrorizing the Mayan peasant countryside as part of its scorched-earth counterinsurgency campaign. These onslaughts came in the form of murders, violent intimidation, displacement, and the destruction of houses, farms, and livestock. Thus, in the decade that followed the 1982 massacre, the state was almost completely successful in blocking attempts to investigate those responsible. One of the victims, Juan Manuel Jerónimo, testified, "The first years after the massacre we didn't do anything to seek justice because we were not even allowed to talk about what happened never mind what we wanted to do."[51] Finally, in 1993 victims represented by the Center for Human Rights Legal Action (CALDH) brought charges. After exhumations and an investigation began in 1994, the process quickly ran into state-erected road blocks. Evidence, such as ammunition cartridges and ballistics reports disappeared, and exhumations slowed to a stop. As one of the victims, Buenaventura Manuel Jerónimo, testified before the Inter-American Court:

> After a long time, a report of the incident was filed by the Center for Human Rights Legal Action [in Guatemala]. Nevertheless, until today there has been neither justice nor any results of that process. The violence, the corruption, and the discrimination against the indigenous peoples and farmers impede justice. Until this day there are still threats against any judge involved in the case.[52]

On September 11, 1990, Myrna Mack Chang, an anthropologist studying the displacement of thousands of indigenous Guatemalans, was assassinated by members of a military death squad. Authorities originally informed Myrna Mack's sister, Helen, that Myrna perished in an auto accident. Skeptical of the claim, Helen eventually discovered the true cause of her sister's death: She had been stabbed twenty-seven times outside her Guatemala City office. For Helen Mack, the path to justice has been an insufferable ordeal. The state actively blocked her efforts to hold those responsible for the murder accountable under Guatemalan law. As in the *Carpio* and *Plan de Sánchez* cases, the mechanisms of impunity were first deployed during the initial investigation. Investigators neglected to take fingerprints, photographs, or blood samples from the crime scene. Although Myrna Mack's clothing and fingernail samples were initially retained, they were discarded before any laboratory analysis was conducted on them. A report drafted by investigators suggesting that Guatemalan security forces planned and carried out the murder was destroyed. When one of these investigators testified about this report, he was assassinated.[53]

In addition to legal and procedural obstructions, those wishing to preserve impunity launched a violent campaign against anyone working on the *Mack* case. In April 1994 the president of Guatemala's Constitutional Court, Epaminondas González Dubón, was shot and killed. At the time of the murder the Court was considering several controversial human rights cases, including preliminary rulings on Myrna Mack's case.[54] Throughout the more than ten years of judicial proceedings, death threats have driven more than ten judges to drop the case. Several judges, prosecutors, and witnesses have fled the country after receiving death threats. In July 1994 Helen Mack was forced to leave Guatemala after a plan to murder her was exposed. The next month Roberto Romero, a Myrna Mack Foundation lawyer, fled the country after assailants fired at him.[55] In an interview, an activist working in Guatemala reported that she has personal knowledge of judges and prosecutors who suffer "harassment, threats . . . in a lot of cases their families have been threatened, they're harassed, some of them have suffered attacks and some have suffered pressure from within the system."[56]

D. The Need for International Court Involvement

Both governmental agencies and nongovernmental organizations (NGOs) monitoring the judiciary in Guatemala during and after the war have unanimously found that Guatemala's courts not only failed to offer citizens adequate judicial remedies but actually aided human rights violations and perpetrated impunity. For example, the Historical Clarification Commission for Guatemala concluded, "The justice system, non-existent in large areas of the country before the armed confrontation, was further weakened when the judicial branch submitted to the requirements of the dominant national security model." The Historical Clarification Commission went even further, finding that

> by tolerating or participating directly in impunity, which concealed the most fundamental violations of human rights, the judiciary became functionally inoperative with respect to its role

of protecting the individual from the State, and lost all credibility as guarantor of an effective legal system. This allowed impunity to become one of the most important mechanisms for generating and maintaining a climate of terror.[57]

Even after the Peace Accords were signed in 1996, justice was simply not available to human rights victims. Few cases were prosecuted, and the intimidation of complainants, judges, prosecutors, and witnesses obstructed the judicial process. With the *Mack*, *Carpio*, and *Plan de Sánchez* cases, we see a fundamental justification for international courts. When a domestic system so completely fails in its duty to uphold the rule of law, it is incumbent on the international system to fill the void. According to Ruti Teitel, international human rights "jurisprudence evinces the clear delimiting of state power on the basis of individual rights norms."[58] Extranational rulings against former officials shatter the view that these officials are immune from prosecution and inspire local attempts to penetrate the shield of impunity. Prosecutions in international courts, therefore, can send a powerful message to the legal and human rights communities in postconflict nations. Ratner and Abrams pointed out that international courts can "put pressure on governments to comply with their international obligations (including their duties to prosecute offenders."[59] They also recognize that these institutions can "establish an authoritative factual record" and "serve the cause of developing human rights and humanitarian law."[60] Minow argued that when a crime against humanity is "prosecuted outside the affected territory, in the absence of regime change, it is perhaps the purest illustration of the potential of law to effect normative transition . . . [i]ndeed, the very response to the crime against humanity instantiates its core value of transcendent justice."[61] Furthermore, extranational convictions can aid local prosecutions by communicating legal strategies and even precedent by embracing a broad concept of international law. As Minow observed, "Especially when framed in terms of universality, the language of

rights and the vision of trials following their violation equip people to call for accountability even where it is not achievable."[62]

4. Cases Before the IACHR

A. Introduction to the Inter-American System

The Organization of American States (OAS) established the Inter-American Commission on Human Rights (Commission) in 1959 to monitor compliance with the American Declaration of the Rights and Duties of Man. Then in 1965 the OAS gave the Commission the power to hear individual human rights cases and recommend solutions. In 1969 the OAS recast its human rights principles by passing the American Convention on Human Rights. The Convention not only sets out the basic human rights standards for member states but it also establishes the Inter-American Court of Human Rights (IACHR). Of the thirty-five OAS member nations, twenty-four have accepted the binding jurisdiction of the IACHR.[63] Guatemala signed the Inter-American Convention on Human Rights on May 25, 1978, and accepted the jurisdiction of the Court on March 9, 1987.

Under the Convention, the primary functions of the Commission are to consider individual complaints and impose conciliatory remedies, monitor human rights compliance in the region, conduct on-site studies of human rights conditions, and impose "precautionary measures" to prevent potential human rights violations. In this capacity, the Commission has frequently involved itself in Guatemala's human rights affairs. For example, after an on-site visit in 2001, the Commission concluded that

profound systemic deficiencies continue to subvert justice, and have yet to be effectively addressed. These include serious problems in the systems and procedures for delivering justice, as well as the paralyzing effect of attempts to coerce those involved in the pursuit and administration of justice through threats and corruption. Given the central role of the judiciary in safeguarding all individual rights, the challenge of redressing these problems is both urgent and paramount.[64]

To pursue a human rights claim in the Inter-American system, victims must first file a complaint with the Commission. The Commission then seeks a response from the nation alleged to have committed the violation. Once a response is received, the Commission must decide if the case is admissible—meaning within the Commission's jurisdiction. Furthermore, for the petition to be admissible, it must allege violations of rights protected by one of the several instruments recognized by the OAS and it must demonstrate that the petitioners exhausted their domestic remedies.[65] The Commission can hear complaints against any member nation of the OAS.[66]

If the Commission determines a case is admissible, it then considers evidence presented by each of the parties and frequently encourages a negotiated settlement. If negotiations fail, the Commission issues a ruling on culpability. If it finds the nation culpable, it issues recommendations and prescribes remedies. These rulings are confidential at this stage and designed to encourage violating nations to comply with the mandated human rights instruments. If a nation fails to comply with the orders of the Commission, the Commission brings the case before the IACHR. Here the Commission prosecutes the case against the nation in question. Evidence is presented and a formal decision is issued by the court that contains a ruling on culpability as well as remedies if appropriate. The victims may be represented by counsel before the Commission and IACHR.

B. The *Carpio* Case

With all efforts to pursue justice at home blocked, Carpio's wife, Martha Arrivillaga de Carpio, and daughter-in-law, Karen Fischer, looked beyond Guatemala to the Inter-American Commission of Human Rights. With the help of the Human Rights Office of the Archbishop of Guatemala, the Center for Justice and International Law (CEJIL), Human Rights Watch, and the International Human Rights Law Group, these women filed a petition with the Commission on July 12, 1994. Instead of pleading that they had exhausted local remedies, the *Carpio* petitioners argued that the state actively obstructed their attempts to seek justice domestically and that domestic remedies were, therefore, unobtainable.[67] The Commission agreed that the state had completely obstructed justice in Guatemala.

The Commission typically makes the decision on admissibility at the outset, as it did in the *Plan de Sánchez* case discussed below. However, if more information is needed to make the determination—as it was in the *Carpio* case—the Commission can reserve this decision until it has heard from the parties and considered the facts. At this early stage the Commission sets out to find a conciliatory solution by receiving evidence and negotiating with the parties. After doing so in the *Carpio* case, the Commission finally ruled that the case was admissible. It then ordered Guatemala to investigate the murders thoroughly in order to punish those responsible for planning and carrying out the attack.[68] The Commission's order also included provisions recommending reparations for the families of the victims.[69] On June 10, 2003, when Guatemala failed to reply within the time required, the Commission took the case to the Inter-American Court.[70] It alleged that Guatemala violated the victims' rights to life, personal integrity, judicial protection, freedom of expression, and the rights of the child under the Inter-American Convention. While the Commission prosecuted cases, recent changes in the IACHR's rules allowed the victims and survivors to be represented by counsel at the proceedings as well. CEJIL represented the *Carpio* parties.[71]

As the *Carpio* hearing began on July 5 and 6, 2004, the president of the Guatemalan Presidential Commission of Human Rights announced that his government accepted Guatemala's international responsibility for the attack on Carpio and his associates.[72] Guatemala acknowledged that Carpio was murdered to chill opposition to the amnesty provisions. Because the state accepted responsibility, neither the Commission nor CEJIL were required to prove the elements of each of the alleged violations. However, CEJIL stressed the importance of allowing the victims and families to tell their stories in open court and the state voiced no opposition to allowing them to do so.[73]

The Court ruled that the state, acting through paramilitaries, murdered Carpio for political reasons and that it erected obstructions to justice that resulted in "total impunity."[74] It went beyond a simple judgment that Carpio's rights were violated and ruled that the rights of all those threatened and attacked in their pursuit of justice in the case were also violated.[75] The reparations assigned by the Court in both cases reflect a desire to extend beyond compensation and take steps to remedy conditions in Guatemala. For example, in addition to money damages totaling US$1,360,000 for the victims' families, the Court ordered the state to enact concrete measures to prevent similar violations and continued impunity.[76]

C. The *Plan de Sánchez* Case

Blocked by the same infrastructure of impunity in Guatemala, the victims of the Plan de Sánchez massacre filed their claim with the Inter-American Commission on May 11, 1999. As in the *Carpio* case, the petitioners argued and the Commission agreed that local remedies were unobtainable due to the wall of impunity erected by the state. CALDH represented the victims and families before the Commission and the IACHR.

In August 2000 President Alfonso Portillo admitted "institutional responsibility" for the Plan de Sánchez massacre during conciliation discussions between the state, the petitioners, and the Commission.[77] On February 28, 2002, the Commission, after analyzing the positions of both sides, made a series of recommendations to the state, including a demand that the state

conduct an investigation to identify and sanction those responsible for the massacre.[78] The Commission also required Guatemala to pay both material and nonmaterial compensation to the survivors of the massacre and to take measures to ensure that such an atrocity would never recur. Despite Portillo's acceptance of responsibility, Guatemala failed to take the steps required by the Commission.[79]

Therefore, the Commission presented the case before the IACHR on July 31, 2002. At this stage, Commission lawyers took on new roles and prosecuted the case against the state before the Inter-American Court. They alleged that the state of Guatemala violated the rights to personal integrity, judicial protection, judicial guarantees, equality before the law, property, and freedom of religion embodied in Articles 5, 8, 25, 24, 12, 21, and 1.1 of the American Convention of Human Rights.[80] In addition to prosecuting the rights of those killed and wounded during the attacks and the rights of those who suffered losses, the Commission alleged violations based on Guatemala's resistance to truth and justice in the case.

The *Plan de Sánchez* hearing took place before the IACHR in San José, Costa Rica, on April 23 and 24, 2004. In addition to depositions and affidavits, the Commission and CALDH called family members of those killed in the massacre and experts on the effects of the attack. After the Commission concluded its case, Guatemala announced that it was retracting its exceptions to the complaint and accepting full international responsibility for the massacre and subsequent violations.[81] Doing so constituted complete acceptance of the Commission's complaint and an admission that Guatemala committed the violations therein alleged. The Court accepted Guatemala's admissions and shifted the proceeding to the reparations phase.[82]

The Inter-American Court of Human Rights ruled that the *Plan de Sánchez* victims were denied their rights to personal integrity, judicial protection, equality before the law, freedom of religion, and property.[83] Moreover, the state's efforts to preserve impunity after the massacre violated the petitioners' rights to judicial protection.[84] The Court awarded US$20,000 per beneficiary in pecuniary damages, totaling almost US$7 million.[85] Moreover, the Court ordered Guatemala to construct health care and mental health facilities in the Plan de Sánchez community as well as road, water, and sewer systems.[86]

D. The *Myrna Mack* Case

Immediately after Myrna Mack's murder, Helen Mack approached the Inter-American Commission. On Helen's behalf, on September 12, 1990, the Guatemalan Human Rights Commission filed a complaint against Guatemala in the Commission. The Commission reserved its determination of admissibility while it observed the domestic process. However, on March 5, 1996, after seeing the ineffectiveness of the domestic proceedings, the Commission ruled that the *Mack* case was admissible. At a hearing before the Commission, the state accepted institutional responsibility for the extrajudicial killing of Myrna Mack. This step facilitated a compromise agreement on the remedies to be prescribed. In this agreement, Guatemala promised to reinitiate the domestic case against the alleged intellectual authors of the killing and to protect the integrity of those proceedings.[87]

The Inter-American Commission sent a delegation to Guatemala to ensure the state complied with the agreement, and in two separate reports the delegation found that Guatemala failed to do so. In light of these findings, on March 8, 2001, the Commission issued a decision finding Guatemala responsible for violating Myrna Mack's right to life and Helen Mack's right to justice. It assessed damages and required Guatemala to investigate and prosecute those responsible for orchestrating the murder. In response, Guatemala revoked its admission of institutional responsibility. The Commission ruled that Guatemala showed no indication that it would follow the Commission's recommendations and filed the case in the IACHR on July

26, 2001. Guatemala objected, arguing that neither the Commission nor the Court had jurisdiction because the domestic prosecution was ongoing. The IACHR agreed with the Commission's ruling that the domestic prosecution was a façade, disrupted by obstructions orchestrated by the state.[88]

The IACHR heard the *Mack* case from February 18–20, 2003. CEJIL represented the victims, and along with the Commission, they presented evidence of the state's responsibility for the murder, the repeated state efforts to obstruct the domestic proceedings, and the tremendous toll Myrna Mack's death had on the lives of her family members. Myrna Mack's daughter, who was sixteen years old when her mother was killed, testified that she "thinks of her mother every day, especially of the way she was murdered, of the pain of the 27 knife wounds she suffered, and of how she must have felt lying alone on the street."[89]

On November 25, 2003, the Court issued its judgment, in which it ruled that the Presidential General Staff had ordered Guatemalan security forces to murder Myrna Mack and that this murder violated the right to life protected in the American Convention.[90] The IACHR ruled that the murder was planned and executed for political purposes as part of a campaign to silence those who would expose Guatemalan human rights violations.[91] The Court also found that Guatemala had denied the Mack family the right to justice by covering up the crime and obstructing the judicial process through legal and violent means.[92] Finally, the Court ruled that Guatemala violated the Mack family's rights to humane treatment by committing the murder and by using threats and coercion to impede the family's attempts to pursue justice.[93] In addition to more than $600,000 in pecuniary damages divided among three family members, the Court required Guatemala to remove all obstacles to the domestic prosecution, to name a street after Myrna Mack, and to create a permanent anthropology scholarship in Myrna Mack's name.

These three cases present a typical formula for Guatemala. In each, the state orchestrated a brutal human rights violation. In each, the state deployed a multifaceted campaign to cover up the crime and obstruct all efforts to attain justice. And in each, the litigants reached beyond the state, to the Inter-American Court, to escape the Guatemalan formula of injustice.

5. The IACHR and Human Rights Accountability

A. The Function of the IACHR

In their study of international courts, Eric Posner and John Yoo argued that the IACHR is ineffective because it hears few cases and compliance rates are low.[94] In their effort to compare a wide variety of international courts, these authors necessarily simplify their criteria for effectiveness by concentrating on the number of cases heard and the rate of compliance. This assessment may not fully reflect the effectiveness of an institution like the IACHR. For example, when comparing the IACHR to the European Court of Human Rights (ECHR), Posner and Yoo find the IACHR to be less effective. However, these institutions are in completely different political universes, serving radically different purposes. The ECHR is the pinnacle tribunal created and supported by predominantly established democracies. Although it considers cases from transitional democracies, some of which are dealing with political violence, many of its rulings address nonviolent violations. The ECHR, and European courts in general, have comparatively high levels of legitimacy.[95] Importantly, the European Union provides significant material incentives to submit to and comply with the authority of the ECHR. In this environment the goal of the ECHR is to constrain member states under the conventions— member states that, for the most part, have established records of compliance with the rule of law. Conversely, the IACHR is striving to solidify its institutional legitimacy in a sea of new and developing democracies. Many of these democracies are experiencing or emerging from drastic political violence. The cases before the IACHR often arise from the political violence that preceded democratization or that is part of the transition struggle. The purpose and setting of the IACHR is fundamentally different, therefore, than that of the ECHR.

In this piece we focus our assessment on whether the IACHR improves human rights conditions in the Americas, concentrating on one of the toughest challenges: Guatemala. Drawing from the scholarship discussed above we identify four purposes of an international court that hears human rights cases from post-conflict democracies. (See table 10.1). First, it should operate to deter future violations with rulings that "equip people to call for accountability."[96] Second, it should facilitate the legal and moral condemnation of human rights violations.[97] Third, its jurisprudence should transcend the parties in the case in order to express the normative value of justice and equality under the law to broad classes of victims.[98] Fourth, it should establish "knowledge of past actions committed under color of law" and create a historical record.[99] An overview of the IACHR's jurisprudence demonstrates that, given the tribunal's authority and resources, it has had some success.

B. Facilitating Accountability— Equipping Victims to Seek Justice

There are numerous examples of the IACHR overriding state efforts to erect institutional barriers to human rights accountability. In 2001 the IACHR ruled that Peruvian amnesty laws protecting military personnel from prosecution for a 1991 massacre violated the American Convention on Human Rights.[100] After this decision the Peruvian government filed charges against security forces allegedly responsible for this and other human rights crimes.[101] In 1999 the IACHR ruled that El Salvador was responsible for the 1989 murder of six Jesuit priests and two others. In doing so, the Court struck down El Salvador's amnesty law, holding that the state had unlawfully denied citizens the right to justice by granting amnesty to those convicted for the murder.[102]

TABLE 10.1 Standard for assessing the Inter-American Court of Human Rights

Purpose of international court	Source	Contribution of the Inter-American Court of Human Rights
Facilitating accountability—equipping victims to seek justice	Minow Roht-Arriaza	• Circumventing institutional barriers to accountability • Innovating international human rights law • Protecting litigants, victims, and witnesses
Condemning human rights violations	Minow Mayerfeld Widner Roht-Arriaza	• Holding states accountable for violations • Communicating societal condemnation of the violations • Upholding the rule of law
Addressing a broad class of victims with individual cases	Teitel Minow	• Hearing cases that are emblematic of widespread violations • Tailoring remedies to address systemic problems • Issuing sanctions to aid a broad class of victims
Establishing a historical record	Teitel Minow Ratner and Abrams	• Allowing victims to testify often for the first time • Recording events based on evidence • Overcoming state denials and obfuscations • Enshrining the truth in the Court's judgments

Pursuant to IACHR decisions, Chilean courts ruled that a 1978 amnesty law could not supersede international law. Because Chile had signed the Inter-American treaties prohibiting torture and other human rights violations, the amnesty law as applied to these crimes violated Chile's international obligations.[103] By circumventing these barriers to accountability, the IACHR equips litigants with the legal tools to pursue justice domestically. These rulings poke holes in the wall of impunity that the state erects.

The most illustrative example of this phenomenon in Guatemala may be the *Myrna Mack* case—as the IACHR revived the case on at least two occasions. After Myrna Mack was killed by security forces, prosecutors and the Myrna Mack Foundation tried for more than ten years to convict the intellectual authors of the attack. Guatemala had an interest in keeping the domestic case going in order to argue that domestic remedies had not been exhausted and

that the Commission case was inadmissible. Then in March 2000, faced with an imminent IACHR trial, the government offered to take responsibility for the murder. The stalled domestic trial of the senior officers accused in the case suddenly resumed and, armed with IACHR rulings, prosecutors won guilty verdicts against two officers who planned the murder. In another setback, however, these verdicts were overturned on appeal. Once again, the IACHR stepped in. In December 2003 the IACHR unanimously ruled that Guatemala had violated the right to life and the right to judicial guarantees and protection. The tribunal ordered Guatemala to, among other things, "remove all obstacles to justice in the case."[104] Just one month later, the Guatemalan Supreme Court reinstated the guilty verdicts against the officers who orchestrated Myrna Mack's murder.

It is clear from the Guatemala cases that the IACHR sees its role as a mechanism to circumvent the systemic impunity in oppressive nations. Throughout the *Carpio* trial, IACHR judges asked witnesses and counsel what the Court could order to remedy impunity, push human rights cases through the Guatemalan courts, and prevent future judicial stonewalling.[105] For example, Judge Garcia Sayan asked several witnesses "what ingredients might be necessary to conduct an effective investigation" in the *Carpio* case and in similar cases. Judge Jackman asked the lawyers in the case, "What formal steps are needed to reopen the [*Carpio*] case on Guatemala?"[106]

Another way the IACHR helps advocates seek accountability is through the publicity accompanying international cases. Human rights NGOs use the Inter-American process to call attention to the mechanisms fostering impunity domestically. The Washington Office for Latin America (WOLA) worked with the lawyers in the *Mack* case to conduct a public relations campaign so that the case would have a significant impact both in Guatemala and globally. As Adrianna Beltran, the head of this campaign, stated in an interview, "we used the *Mack* case as a way of highlighting the inefficiencies of the judicial system."[107] The purpose of the media campaign, according to Beltran, was to "illustrat[e] the impunity that the military enjoyed, the weaknesses and the failures of the judicial system, the human rights situation and the fact that so many witnesses, lawyers, judges were being threatened, harassed, murdered."[108] Based on the IACHR case, this group orchestrated a campaign to use the case to bring pressure to bear on Guatemala from members of the U.S. government. Beltran recalled that "if the [domestic] case was stalling—or if security was necessary—we would organize a campaign involving 'dear colleague' letters or remarks on the floor, [we] would then circulate it to U.S. and International media."[109]

As Jo Pasqualucci observed, the Inter-American Court has liberally settled several controversial questions of international human rights law, thereby giving advocates legal tools in their campaign for accountability.[110] For example, the Court rejects the contention that rights are "culturally relative" and instead holds them to be universal.[111] The IACHR fundamentally altered rights jurisprudence in the region when it held that human rights law was part of international law but that, unlike traditional international law, it did not merely grant rights to states.[112] Moreover, early in its history, the IACHR held that international law obligated states and granted to individuals the authority to hold states to compliance.[113] In doing so, the Court struck down state efforts to circumvent this obligation. According to Pasqualucci, the Court allowed fundamental human rights to develop and expand over time. Instead of interpreting rights as they existed when the Court was established, it considered rights within the legal framework at the time of interpretation.[114] Another crucial element of the Court's jurisprudence, according to Pasqualucci, is that it has held that certain fundamental human rights are nonderogable, even in times of emergency. The Court has refused to allow states to reserve recognition of these fundamental rights.[115]

A CEJIL lawyer, Roxanna Altholz, observed in an interview that the Court is increasingly recognizing impunity and failure to provide justice as distinct human rights violations. Its remedies in the Guatemalan cases are direct attempts to address these violations. IACHR rulings have mandated new and revived prosecutions and even the reinterpretation of amnesty and limitations laws. Along these lines, Ratner and Abrams noted generally that "Certain trends in the international legal process suggest these somewhat vaguely worded provisions are evolving into obligations by states to take specific action against offenders."[116] According to these scholars, "Among the most significant developments" moving this trend, "was a 1988 decision of the Inter-American Court of Human Rights, which interpreted the American Convention of Human Rights to require states to investigate seriously, identify and punish offenders as well as compensate victims."[117]

The Court also equips victims to seek justice by protecting their safety while they are in litigation.

This occurs both directly and indirectly. In the direct approach, litigants can ask the IACHR for "provisional measures" if they believe they are in danger or that witnesses are being threatened.[118] The Court will often issue these "provisional measures" ordering, for example, the state to provide armed security to litigants. The indirect element of safety that comes from litigating before the IACHR arises as a result of the publicity surrounding these cases. Defendants are less likely to attack or threaten a litigant if they are known internationally. NGOs working within the system foster this. For example, Adrianna Beltran, introduced earlier, coordinated the public relations effort during the *Mack* case. In an interview, she explained that "when [the Mack family's] lawyer was receiving a number of threats—right before the case actually went to trial—[Helen] called me and said we're receiving threats and everybody was on the phone with the state department, with the embassy, with members of congress or their staff, saying please call and tell them that you're really concerned."[119] In this effort, Beltran observed, "we were sending the message that she was not alone."[120]

C. Condemning Human Rights Violations

For more than twenty years Guatemala blocked all attempts to punish those responsible for the Plan de Sánchez massacre of 268 Mayan Guatemalans (see above). Then in 2004 the IACHR ruled that Guatemala was responsible not only for the massacre but for denying justice to the victims and families for these many years. In addition to financial compensation, Guatemala was ordered to conduct a public apology. On July 18, 2005, exactly twenty-three years after the massacre, Guatemalan Vice President Eduardo Stein traveled to Plan de Sánchez to formally apologize for the killings before the families and survivors of the victims. In his remarks, Stein conceded that the army had "unleashed bloodshed and fire to wipe out an entire community."[121] He observed that the "people want moments that commemorate their victims,

but more than anything, they don't want what happened to keep being denied officially."[122]

The IACHR recognizes the significance of its rulings as the sole voice of justice after years of impunity. In its judgments, therefore, the IACHR goes beyond traditional reparations and includes provisions to amplify the impact of its decisions. Often this takes the form of a mandated, public apology, such as the event described above. In one of his first official acts as President, Óscar Berger publicly apologized for the murder of Myrna Mack pursuant to an IACHR demand. President Berger apologized to Myrna Mack's sister and daughter and to the Guatemalan people in a ceremony broadcast on national television and held in front of the military and other dignitaries.

As the IACHR hearing began in the *Carpio* case, the president of the Guatemalan Human Rights Commission asked to address the Court. He stood, faced the families of the victims, admitted that the state was responsible for the murder of Carpio and his associates, and asked for forgiveness. When each family member testified, counsel for the state opened his remarks by apologizing for the state's actions.[123] Soraya Long, the CEJIL lawyer representing the families, commented in an interview that "It is extremely important that the state has recognized its responsibility—this is a very significant step—it is a very important gesture that the state asked for pardon from the victims."[124] Long explained, "For more than ten years the families of the victims have said the murder of my husband, my father, was political—and the state said no, no . . . and now finally they have said you were right, you were right."[125]

D. Addressing a Broad Class of Victims with Individual Cases

A primary critique of the IACHR levied by Posner and Yoo is that the Court resolves very few cases. Although this critique certainly has merit and the IACHR would have a broader effect if it decided more cases, it is a somewhat misleading measure by which to assess this Court. The

IACHR must, after all, preserve its precarious legitimacy in a political sea with currents often hostile to judicial review. If the IACHR were to review large numbers of human rights cases while many national judiciaries in the region are struggling, support for the institution would almost certainly be withdrawn. Instead, the IACHR and the parties that litigate in the Inter-American system seek to make the most of the limited resources available to them. For the most part, litigants pursue and the Court decides cases that reflect a widespread human rights violation or that have symbolic importance to the nation and region.

NGOs operating in the Inter-American system seek out cases and victims whose injuries reflect wounds carried by a broader class of victims. CEJIL represents the victims and survivors in most cases heard before the IACHR. Roxanna Altholz, the CEJIL lawyer who served as lead counsel in the *Myrna Mack* case, explained that the organization seeks cases that are "emblematic of a wider set of violations."[126] And certainly the *Myrna Mack* case carried this weight. When Myrna Mack was murdered on September 11, 1990, she was studying the displacement of thousands of indigenous Guatemalans. As an anthropologist with international notoriety, Mack's findings were embarrassing to those in power, many of whom were complicit in the disappearances. The case, therefore, is symbolic of several of the deepest wounds inflicted during the thirty-year civil war. Because of Myrna Mack's work, the case also symbolized the effort to reveal the truth about the thousands of Mayan Guatemalans killed and displaced during the war. Moreover, because the state made every effort to block justice in the case, the result was a victory over the rampant impunity plaguing Guatemala. Myrna Mack's sister Helen testified before the IACHR that the "case is a paradigmatic one not only for her family but also for many Guatemalans who see themselves reflected in it" and that by litigating it, she was "representing, with dignity, the thousands of victims who had no chance."[127]

The *Plan de Sánchez* case clearly had these broad implications. During the civil war the Guatemalan military and civil patrols frequently attacked Mayan villages, murdering and causing thousands of indigenous Guatemalans to disappear. The Plan de Sánchez massacre, therefore, represented one of the most common and most horrific practices of the repressive regimes. As one of the victims testified before the IACHR, "During the 15 years after the death of our loved ones, there has been repression on the part of the authorities in the area—they try to stop us from performing our cultural practices and or from celebrating our religious ceremonies."[128] Representatives and victims have been attempting to hold accountable the powerful figures responsible for these killings for more than twenty years.

Similar cases benefit from the *Plan de Sánchez* IACHR litigation. For example, the *Tuluché* massacre case involves indigenous villagers who were also labeled as subversives during the civil war and were extrajudicially executed. Infrastructure of impunity entrenched in the Guatemalan judicial system repeatedly blocked attempts to hold accountable those who planned and participated in the massacre.[129] Much like *Plan de Sánchez*, the *Tuluché* case in Guatemala was plagued by death threats, the dismissal of important evidence, and arbitrary acquittals of those accused. The results of the *Plan de Sánchez* case in the IACHR, and other cases like it, have the ability to bring justice for Mayans by creating a domino effect of legal accountability for thousands accused of similar human rights violations in Guatemala.

As discussed above, the Court required public apologies not only to the victims and their families but also to the affected communities and the Guatemalan people. In the *Plan de Sánchez* case, the Court further demonstrated the importance of public recognition in that it ordered the state to publicize key sections of the Court's judgments in its official gazette and in a major national newspaper in both Spanish language and Achi Maya.[130] The Court ordered the state to enact efforts to support the growth and welfare of the Maya in the Plan de Sánchez Municipality with measures to promote the Achi Maya language and culture.[131]

The *Carpio* case had similarly broad implications. Jorge Carpio Nicolle was murdered because of his opposition to an amnesty provision that would have prevented legal accountability for thousands accused of human rights violations. He was a reform activist and a journalist who frequently spoke out against the Guatemalan military state and efforts to preserve impunity. His wife, Martha Arrivillaga de Carpio, testified during the trial before the IACHR that the Carpio case was "emblematic of the injustice in Guatemala."[132]

Indeed, it was clear that the IACHR realized these implications in handling these cases. Instead of merely awarding reparations, the Court frequently requires the state to take concrete steps to address the broad class of victims not included in the case. It sets out to attack broad problems through individual cases. CEJIL lawyer Soraya Long argued in an interview that "the court uses its judgments to break systemic and structural failings and solve the macro problems" facing nations under its jurisdiction.[133]

In the *Carpio* case, the Court also assessed remedies designed to address weaknesses in Guatemala. For example, in addition to traditional compensatory damages, the Court ordered the state to take concrete steps to prevent similar violations.[134] In its ruling, the Court targeted the widespread, systematic impunity by ordering a full investigation to identify and punish those responsible for planning and carrying out the attack and the subsequent obstruction of justice.[135] For example, the Court ordered the state to remove all "obstacles and mechanisms . . . that maintain impunity" and to provide security for all witnesses, judges, and prosecutors.[136] According to the order, all information discovered in the investigation must be made public because the victims, their families, and the Guatemalan people, the Court stressed, have "a right to the truth."[137] The Court stretched its authority even further and ruled that to the extent that legislation may have granted the attackers amnesty, that legislation is invalid because such laws violate the victims' rights to justice and the truth.[138]

E. Creating a Historical Record

Recognizing the victims' story and enshrining it in the judicial record are essential parts of achieving justice for human rights violations.[139] In these cases, the state denied responsibility and obstructed any effort to find the truth. To the victims, therefore, the official recognition of the truth is invaluable. In its judgment in the *Myrna Mack* case, the IACHR ordered Guatemala to publicize a full account of its violations because "This right to the truth . . . constitutes an important means of reparation."[140]

When the *Myrna Mack* case reached the IACHR, Guatemala offered to accept responsibility for the killing, but the state was not willing to allow witnesses to testify.[141] CEJIL's Altholz, the lead counsel representing the Mack family, opposed Guatemala's offer. In an interview Altholz stated that they refused Guatemala's offer because "we didn't want a sentence that just recognized responsibility and went on to reparations."[142] She pointed out that "we wanted, and it was very important for [Myrna Mack's sister] Helen, to have all these pages of *hechos probados* [proven facts]."[143] More than that, Altholz stated, "what was so important for us was to have the *hechos probados* include an indication that the state security forces were responsible— that was fundamental for us."[144] Not only did the IACHR include in its decision an exhaustive account of these *hechos probados*, but it also ordered Guatemala to publish them in the "official gazette" and another daily newspaper with national circulation.[145] In all its cases, CEJIL stresses the importance of allowing the victims and families to tell their stories in open court. Altholz pointed out that allowing victims an opportunity to create a historical record and to express their suffering is an essential element of seeking justice. She stated that "the more you can let the victims' voices come through the better your litigation is—the legal theories ring truer, your case is stronger."[146]

This interest can be seen in the *Carpio* case as well. Even after Guatemala accepted responsibility for the violations, CEJIL lawyers encouraged their witnesses—the families of the victims—to testify extensively on their experiences, their suffering, and their loss. CEJIL lawyers asked the court to "establish that the attack was a politically motivated execution."[147] They asked the court to set out an official version of the truth by determining the specific acts and omissions that amounted to violations of the Convention and by assigning institutional responsibility.[148] The representative of the state did not object to allowing this testimony, "recogniz[ing] the right of the victims to testify and tell their truth."[149] The victims' counsel, Soraya Long, pointed out in an interview that for "the Carpio family . . . it was very significant to come here to [the Inter-American Court] because with the internal proceeding they felt thwarted . . . and to come to this court and say what occurred, to establish a record and to demonstrate that they had overcome."[150]

Never has the importance of creating an historical record been more evident than in the *Plan de Sánchez* case. The IACHR recognized the injury inflicted by the state's repeated denials and obstruction. It held that "the impunity in this case keeps the memory of these acts fresh and impedes social reconciliation."[151] An expert on the rights of indigenous peoples, Augusto Willemsen-Diaz testified that "To end the discrimination and racism of the indigenous people in Guatemala I recommend that the most important things are the acknowledgment of what occurred and that the people take notice of the enormous amount of abuses that have occurred."[152] The anguish in the victims' stories was memorialized in the Court's opinion. In the testimony of a family member, Juan Manuel Jerónimo, "the following day the bodies of our loved ones were still decomposing when the military commissioners from Chipuerta arrived. . . . They did the most savage of burials and we were no longer able to recognize our relatives."[153] The decision also included testimony regarding the impunity entrenched in the Guatemalan legal system. Another family member, Buenaventura Manuel Jerónimo, stated that "the violence, the corruption, and the discrimination against the

indigenous peoples and farmers impeded justice." He continued, "Until this day there are threats against the judges" who hear these cases against the state.[154] Through this testimony in front of the IACHR, Guatemala's violent past and present were finally given a voice.

The IACHR is effective in setting out these histories. In its decisions, the *hechos probados* sections are extensive, memorializing the victims' stories, the violations, and the impunity. For example, in the *Carpio* case, the IACHR included an account of Mr. Carpio's work for Guatemalan democracy through his government service, political activism, and leadership of the newspaper *El Grafico*.[155] CEJIL's Soraya Long stressed the importance of establishing a historical record, commenting in an interview that "Carpio's work exists in the fabric of Guatemala—in acts of the assembly, in articles of the constitution—his family demands that their father—their husband—be included in the history of his country."[156]

6. Conclusions—Impact of the Inter-American Court

Our analysis demonstrates that the Inter-American Court is a valuable factor promoting human rights accountability and reconciliation in Latin America. (See table 10.1). It is a powerful voice of accountability in a region struggling to fully democratize. By holding states accountable, it demonstrates to citizens that overcoming impunity is possible. Thus, the Court's jurisprudence, to use Teitel's language, "evinces the clear delimiting of state power on the basis of individual rights norms."[157] Lawyers, judges, and activists then seek human rights protections in domestic institutions armed with the principles of law established by the Court. This positive impact is accentuated when the activists pursue and the Court hears cases that are emblematic of broader human rights problems. Finally, in each case the Court enshrines the victims' stories of suffering into a historical record. After years of official denial, the Inter-American Court represents an official acceptance of the truth.

There are several critiques that may be levied at the Inter-American system. Posner and Yoo correctly pointed out that the IACHR hears very few cases and that compliance rates are questionable.[158] Victor Rodriguez Rescia and Marc David Seitles argued that the delay in processing cases, along with procedural deficiencies and normative problems, are significant failings of the system.[159] One can see support for this in the *Carpio* case, which was filed in 1994 and resolved in 2004. Indeed, these critiques have some merit and this essay is not intended to refute them. On the contrary, we conclude that even with these weaknesses, the IACHR is still indispensable in aiding reconciliation and democratization for the postconflict democracies in Latin America. The system would be even more effective if it addressed many of the concerns voiced by critics.

In postconflict democracies, domestic courts struggle for legitimacy, resources, and a meaningful role in their state's political discourse. However, as arms of the state, they often share the state's interest in quieting efforts to uncover past atrocities. Moreover, they are frequently subject to influence from the other political powers.[160] When litigants are able to reach beyond the state for justice, they escape this institutional deck that is heavily stacked against them.

Human rights observers often note the effect of the IACHR's work. For example, in its 2005 Report, Human Rights Watch observed that the "Inter-American human rights system has provided an important venue for human rights advocates seeking to press the state to accept responsibility for abuses."[161] Similarly, after the *Carpio*, *Mack*, and *Plan de Sánchez* cases, Amnesty International recognized that, although Guatemala is still suffering serious human rights violations, it has achieved "minor progress in trying past cases of genocide or crimes against humanity."[162] Moreover, Amnesty International pointed out that after these cases, the Berger administration "took some positive measures including modernization of the army and establishing a National Reparations Commission."[163] Similar effects can be seen in other nations appearing before the Court. For example, Helio Bicudo credited the Court's rulings with helping Peru restore democracy and the integrity of its judiciary after President Fujimori's attempt to circumvent constitutional constraints.[164]

During the *Carpio* hearing, Silvia Villacorta, the wife of one of the victims, told the Court that "in Guatemala there is no justice so we must look to international justice." "We want," she told the judges, "a precedent that future generations can look to."[165] Although the institutions and procedures of the Inter-American Court do need strengthening, it is a positive—and necessary—force for human rights accountability in the region. It offers victims like Villacorta the justice she deserved.

NOTES

1. Guatemala Human Rights Commission, *Ruling Against Government in Plan de Sanchez Massacre*, 16 GUATEMALA HUM. RTS. UPDATE (2004).

2. *Carpio v. Guatemala case*, Inter-Am. Ct.H.R. (Ser. C) No. 117 (2004); *Mack Chang v. Guatemala case*, Inter-Am. Ct.H.R. (Ser. C) No. 101 (2003); *Plan de Sanchez v. Guatemala case*, Inter-Am. Ct.H.R. (Ser. C) No. 105 (2004).

3. AMNESTY INTERNATIONAL, ANNUAL REPORT— COLUMBIA (1995–2005); U.S. STATE DEPARTMENT, COUNTRY REPORT ON HUMAN RIGHTS PRACTICES—EL SALVADOR (1995–2004).

4. All transcriptions and translations from interviews and from the Carpio hearing were conducted by the authors.

5. Stephen C. Ropp & Kathryn Sikkink, *International Norms and Domestic Politics in Chile and Guatemala*, in THE POWER OF HUMAN RIGHTS: INTERNATIONAL NORMS AND DOMESTIC CHANGE (Thomas Risse, Stephen C. Ropp, & Kathryn Sikkink eds., 2003).

6. *Id.*

7. *Carpio v. Guatemala case*, Inter-Am. Ct.H.R. (ser. C) No. 117, at paras. 76.9–76.10 (2004).

8. *Id.* at paras. 76.11–76.14, 76.16.

9. MINUGUA Special Report, at 30 (2000), *available at* www.minugua.guate.net/Informes/OTROS%20INF/ Informe%20del%20Sr%20Cumaraswamy%201.pdf.

10. *Id.* at 31.

11. MINUGUA, at 24 (2001), *available at* www .minugua.guate.net/Informes/OTROS%20INF/Informe %20del%20Sr%20Cumaraswamy%202.pdf.

12. *Id.*

13. Michael J. Dodson & Donald W. Jackson, *Judicial Independence in Central America*, in JUDICIAL INDEPENDENCE IN THE AGE OF DEMOCRACY (Peter H. Russell & David M. O'Brien eds., 2001); RACHEL SIEDER, CENTRAL AMERICA: FRAGILE TRANSITION (1996); Neil J. Kritz, *The Rule of Law in the Post-Conflict Phase: Building a Stable Peace*, in MANAGING GLOBAL CONFLICT (Chester Crocker, Fen Osler Hampson, with Pamela Aall eds., 1997).

14. Laurel E. Fletcher and Harvey M. Weinstein, *Violence and Social Repair: Rethinking the Contribution of Justice to Reconciliation*, 24 HUM. RTS. Q. 573, at 590 (2002).

15. MARTHA MINOW, BETWEEN VENGEANCE AND FORGIVENESS (1998).

16. Jamie Mayerfeld, *Who Shall Be Judge?: The United States, the International Criminal Court, and the Global Enforcement of Human Rights*, 25 HUM. RTS. Q. 93, 100 (2002).

17. Julie Mertus, *Only a War Crimes Tribunal: Triumph of the International Community, Pain of the Survivors*, in WAR CRIMES: THE LEGACY OF NUREMBERG (1999).

18. Mayerfeld, *supra* note 16, at 99.

19. Jennifer Widner, *Courts and Democracy in Post-Conflict Transitions: A Social Scientist's Perspective on the Africa Case*, 95 AMER. J. INT'L L. 64–75 (1998).

20. *See id.* and *supra* note 16.

21. Mayerfeld, *supra* note 16, at 100.

22. Naomi Roht-Arriaza, *Punishment, Redress, and Pardon: Theoretical and Psychological Approaches*, in IMPUNITY AND HUMAN RIGHTS: INTERNATIONAL LAW PRACTICE (Naomi Roht-Arriaza ed., 1995); Jaime Malamund-goti, *Transitional Governments in the Breach: Why Punish State Criminals?* 12 HUM. RTS. Q. 1, 11–13 (1990).

23. Ruti Teitel, *Transitional Jurisprudence: The Role of Law in Political Transformation*, 106 YALE L. J. 2047–48 (1997).

24. *Id.* at 2050–51.

25. Minow, *supra* note 15, at 25.

26. *Id.* at 26; *see also* Widner *supra* note 19.

27. WILLIAM C. PRILLAMAN, THE JUDICIARY AND THE DEMOCRATIC DECAY IN LATIN AMERICA: DECLINING CONFIDENCE IN THE RULE OF LAW (2000).

28. THEODORE L. BECKER, COMPARATIVE JUDICIAL POLITICS: THE POLITICAL FUNCTIONINGS OF COURTS (1970).

29. ALEXANDER HAMILTON, JAMES MADISON, & JOHN JAY, THE FEDERALIST PAPERS 457 (Clinton Rossiter ed., American Library 1961).

30. *Id.* at 470.

31. CHARLES R. EPP, THE RIGHTS REVOLUTION 11 (1998).

32. Mark C. Miller, *A Comparison of the Judicial Role in the United States and in Canada*, 22 SUFFOLK TRANSNAT'L REV. 1–26 (1998).

33. JUDICIAL INDEPENDENCE IN THE AGE OF DEMOCRACY (Peter H. Russell & David M. O'Brien eds., 2001); Epp, *supra* note 31; Prillaman, *supra* note 27; and Dodson & Jackson, *supra* note 13.

34. Dodson & Jackson, *supra* note 13.

35. Thomas Jefferson, *Autobiography*, in THE WRITINGS OF THOMAS JEFFERSON 121 (Andrew A. Lipscomb ed., 1903).

36. *Id.*

37. Mihui Pak, *The Counter-Majoritarian Difficulty in Focus: Judicial Review of Initiatives*, 32 COLUM. J. L. & SOC. PROBS. 237 (1999).

38. Mark Tushnet, *Constitutional Interpretation and Judicial Selection: A View from the Federalist Papers*, 61 U. SOUTH. CAL. L. REV. 1669 (1988).

39. Michael G. Collins, *Judicial Independence and the Scope of Article III—A View from the Federalist*, 38 U. RICH. L. REV. 675, 676 (2004).

40. STEVEN R. RATNER & JASON S. ABRAMS, ACCOUNTABILITY FOR HUMAN RIGHTS ATROCITIES IN INTERNATIONAL LAW—BEYOND THE NUREMBERG LEGACY 157 (2001).

41. *Id.* at 183.

42. *Id.*

43. *Id.*

44. *Carpio, supra* note 7, at paras. 76.21–76.22.

45. Jeffrey Davis, *Struggling Through the Web of Impunity—The Jorge Carpio Nicolle Case*, 8 HUM. RTS. REV. 53–67 (2006).

46. *Carpio, supra* note 7, at paras. 76.27–76.33.

47. *Id.* at paras. 76.55–76.59.

48. Martha Arrivillaga de Carpio, Testimony before the Inter-American Court of Human Rights, San José, Costa Rica (July 5, 2004), translated and transcribed by the authors.

49. *Id.* at para. 69(a).

50. *Id.*

51. *Supra* note 1, at para. 38(a).

52. *Id.* at para. 38(b).

53. David Baluarte & Erin Chlopak, *The Case of Myrna Mack Chang: Overcoming Institutional Impunity in Guatemala*, 10 HUM. RTS. BRIEF 3, 11–14 (2003).

54. HUMAN RIGHTS WATCH, WORLD REPORT—GUATEMALA (2003), *available at* www.hrw.org/reports/world/reports/.

55. HUMAN RIGHTS WATCH, WORLD REPORT—GUATEMALA (2005), *available at* www.hrw.org/reports/world/reports/; Human Rights First (formerly Lawyers Committee for Human Rights), Human Rights Defenders—Myrna Mack (2003), *available at* www.lchr.org/defenders/hrd_guatemala/hrd_mack/hrd_mack.htm.

56. Interview with Adriana Beltran, Associate for Washington Office for Latin America, in Washington, DC (June 4, 2004).

57. Guatemalan Historical Clarification Commission Report (1998), *available at* http://shr.aaas.org/guatemala/ceh/report/english.

58. Teitel, *supra* note 23, at 2054.

59. Ratner and Abrams, *supra* note 40, at 226.

60. *Id.*

61. Minow, *supra* note 15, at 48.

62. *Id.*

63. JO M. PASQUALUCCI, THE PRACTICE AND PROCEDURE OF THE INTER-AMERICAN COURT OF HUMAN RIGHTS (2003).

64. Fifth Report on the Situation of Human Rights in Guatemala, Chapter IV, (2001), *available at* www.cidh.oas.org/countryrep/Guate01eng/chap.4htm.

65. Rules of Procedure of the Inter-American Commission on Human Rights, ch. II, art. 30–34.

66. *Id.* at art. 27.

67. *Id.* at art. 31.

68. *Supra* note 68, at para. 9.

69. *Id.*

70. *Id.* at paras. 5–11.

71. *Id.* at para. 22.

72. Frank La Rue, President of the Guatemalan Presidential Commission of Human Rights, Statement before the Inter-American Court of Human Rights, San José, Costa Rica (Jul. 5, 2004).

73. Soraya Long, Statement before the IACHR, Jul. 5, 2004.

74. *Supra* note 68, at paras. 77–78.

75. *Id.* at para. 82(b).

76. *Id.* at para. 84.

77. *Supra* note 1, at para. 8.

78. *Id.* at para. 9.

79. *Id.* at Judgment, paras. 8, 9.1–9.3.

80. *Id.* at Reparations, para. 2.

81. *Id.* at Judgment, para. 30.

82. *Id.* at para. 31.

83. *Id.* at para. 52.

84. *Id.*

85. *Id.* at Reparations, para. 90.

86. *Id.* at para. 89.

87. *Mack v. Guatemala case*, Inter-Am. Ct.H.R. (Ser. C) No. 101, paras. 6–17 (2003); *see also* David Baluarte and Erin Chlopak, *supra* note 53, at 11–14.

88. *Id.*

89. *Id.* at Judgment para. 127 (c).

90. *Id.* at para. 158.

91. *Id.*

92. *Id.* at 218.

93. *Id.* at 233.

94. Eric A. Posner & John C. Yoo, *Judicial Independence in International Tribunals*, 93 CAL. L. REV. 3–73 (2005).

95. Gregory Caldeira & James Gibson, *The Legitimacy of the Court of Justice in the European Union Models of Institutional Support*, 89 AM. POL. SCI. REV. 356–76 (1995); Gregory Caldeira & James Gibson, *Democracy and Legitimacy in the European Union: The Court of Justice and Its Constituents*, 152 INT'L SOC. SCI. J. 209–24 (1997).

96. Minow, *supra* note 15, at 48.

97. Mayerfeld, *supra* note 16.

98. Minow, *supra* note 15, at 48.

99. Teitel, *supra* note 23, at 2050–51.

100. U.S. STATE DEPARTMENT, COUNTRY REPORT ON HUMAN RIGHTS PRACTICES—PERU (2002), *available at* www.state.gov/www/global/human_rights/.

101. *Id.*

102. U.S. STATE DEPARTMENT, COUNTRY REPORT ON HUMAN RIGHTS PRACTICES—EL SALVADOR (2000), *available at* www.state.gov/www/global/human_rights/.

103. HUMAN RIGHTS WATCH, WORLD REPORT—CHILE (1995), *available at* www.hrw.org/reports/world/reports/.

104. Mack, *supra* note 2.

105. Jeffrey Davis, 2003. Notes from the Carpio trial, *supra* note 7.

106. Testimony and proceedings transcribed by the author.

107. Interview with Adrianna Beltran, Associate for Washington Office for Latin America, Washington, DC (Jun. 4, 2004).

108. *Id.*

109. *Id.*

110. *Supra* note 63.

111. *Other Treaties Subject to the Consultive Jurisdiction of the Court*, Inter-Am. Ct HR. Advisory Opinion OC-1/82, of Sept. 24, 1982, Ser. A, No. 1, para. 40 (1982).

112. Pasqualucci, *supra* note 63.

113. *Effect of Reservations on Entry into Force of the American Convention on Human Rights*, Inter-Am. Ct HR. Advisory Opinion OC-2/82 of Sept. 24, 1982, Ser. A, No. 2, para. 29 (1982).

114. Pasqualucci, *supra* note 63.

115. *Habeas Corpus in Emergency Situations*, Inter-Am. Ct HR. Advisory Opinion OC-8/87, of Jan. 30, 1987, Ser. A, No. 8, para 11 (1987); *Judicial Guarantees in States of Emergency*, Inter-Am. Ct HR. Advisory Opinion OC-9/87, of Oct. 6, 1987, Ser. A, No. 9, para 35 (1987).

116. *Supra* note 40, at 152.

117. *Id.* citing Velasquez Rodriguez Case, Inter-Am. Ct. Hum. Rts. (Ser. C), No. 4 (judgment), para. 174 (1988).

118. Article 63(2) of the American Convention on Human Rights, Nov. 22, 1969, 9 I.L.M. 673 (entered into force Jul. 18, 1978), establishes that in cases of extreme gravity and urgency, and when necessary to avoid irreparable damages to persons, the Court shall adopt

such provisional measures as it deems pertinent in matters it has under consideration. With respect to a case not yet submitted to the Court, it may act at the request of the Commission.

119. Interview with Adrianna Beltran, *supra* note 107.

120. *Id.*

121. Associated Press, *Guatemala Acknowledges, Apologizes for Government-Directed Massacre in 1982* (2005).

122. *Id.*

123. Jeffrey Davis, 2003. Notes from Carpio trial, *supra* note 7.

124. Interview with Soraya Long, Counsel for the Center for Justice and Accountability, San José, Costa Rica (Jul. 5, 2004).

125. *Id.*

126. Interview with Roxanna Altholz, Attorney, Center for Justice and Accountability, Washington, DC (May 11, 2004).

127. Mack, Judgment, *supra* note 2, at para. 127(d).

128. Plan de Sanchez, *supra* note 2, Reparations, at para. 38(a).

129. Edward H. Warner, *Guatemalan National Culture and Power* (2005) (unpublished manuscript).

130. Associated Press 2005, *supra* note 121.

131. *Id.*

132. Carpio, *supra* note 48.

133. Interview with Soraya Long, *supra* note 124.

134. Carpio, *supra* note 7, at para. 84.

135. *Id.* at paras. 125–26, 129, 132.

136. *Id.* at para. 134.

137. *Id.* at para. 128.

138. *Id.* at para. 130.

139. Teitel, *supra* note 23; Minow, *supra* note 15.

140. Mack, Judgment *supra* note 2, at para. 274.

141. Roxanna Altholz, *supra* note 126.

142. *Id.*

143. *Id.*

144. *Id.*

145. Mack, Judgment, *supra* note 2, at para. 280.

146. *Id.*

147. *Id.*

148. Viviana Krsticevic, Executive Director of the Center for Justice and Accountability, Statement before the Inter-American Court of Human Rights, San José, Costa Rica (Jul. 5, 2004).

149. La Rue, *supra* note 72.

150. Interview with Soraya Long, *supra* note 124.

151. Plan de Sanchez *supra* note 1, Reparations, at para. 49.18.

152. *Id.* at para. 38(d).

153. *Id.*

154. *Id.* at para. 38(b).

155. Carpio *supra* note 7, at para. 76.15–76.16.

156. Interview with Soraya Long, *supra* note 124.

157. Teitel, *supra* note 23, at 2054.

158. Posner & Yoo, *supra* note 94.

159. Victor Rodriguez Rescia & Marc David Seitles, *The Development of the Inter-American Human Rights System: A Historical Perspective and a Modern-Day Critique*, 16 N.Y.L. SCHL. J. HUM. RTS. 593–632 (2000).

160. Dodson & Jackson, *supra* note 13; Davis, *supra* note 45.

161. *Supra* note 55.

162. *Id.*

163. *Id.*

164. Helio Bicudo, *The Inter-American Commission on Human Rights and the Process of Democratization in Peru*, trans. Alison A. Hillman, 9 HUM. RTS. BRIEF 18 (2002).

165. Silvia Villacorta, Testimony before the Inter-American Court of Human Rights (July 6, 2004), transcribed by the author.

11

The Upsurge in International Courts After the Establishment of the ICJ

IGOR BORBA

Introduction

Since the beginning of human civilization, the nature of human beings has been to disagree and have disputes. In archaic societies, those disputes would often be settled in cruel ways. The will of the strongest party typically would be imposed on the weaker party instead of having a just settlement. With the development of sovereign states, however, court houses were created, where a judge would decide a dispute and fair outcomes became more common. At first, the court houses operated with a fairly simple legal system, and as states further developed, the legal system that guides the decisions made in courthouses became more complex.[1] The increasing complexity of legal systems is a consequence of the cases that were brought to state courthouses.

In latter times, the disputes that were brought to courthouses began to have parties located in different jurisdictions and international cases became a reality. As a consequence of this, international courthouses were created. These courts are permanent institutions composed of judges that adjudicate disputes between two or more parties. At least one of the parties is a state or an international institution. The decisions of these courts are based on predetermined rules and are binding.[2]

In this chapter, I am going to analyze international courts that were created after the end of World War II. There is a larger number of international courts playing an ever-bigger role in society, thus this subject needs to be further studied. I will look carefully at the International Court of Justice (ICJ), European Court of Justice (ECJ), and the International Criminal Court (ICC) because these are the most important international courts. I will also analyze smaller and more recent courts, such as the International Tribunal for the Law of the Sea (ITLS), Appellate Body of the World Trade Center, and the Central American Court of Justice, among others.[3] The increase of globalization is causing a greater necessity for international courts, so the number of these institutions is likely to increase over time.[4]

International Courts Before World War II

The development of international courts and international law boomed after the end of World War II (WWII). The panic and destruction caused by conflict from 1939 to 1945 led nations around the world to cooperate to find ways to foster international peace. However, court rulings regarding international law cases have been registered as early as the thirteenth century.

In 1268 the Duke of Swabia, Conradin von Hohenstaufen, was tried for starting an unjust war.[5] In the following century another case was registered as what today would be considered a war crime. Sir William Wallace was tried in England in 1305 for committing violence against English citizens,[6] and in the fifteenth century, Peter Von Hagenbach was tried for crimes against humanity.[7] Regular state courthouses tried all these cases based on domestic laws.

In the nineteenth century, military courts began to prosecute and try these types of crimes as courts started incorporating international criminal laws into their statutes.[8] However, the creation of international courts did not in fact happen until after the First World War ended. In the beginning of the twentieth century, the military tribunals became more specialized in international law cases, but they were still essentially military courthouses.[9]

In 1920 the League of Nations fostered the Permanent Court of International Justice (PCIJ), which can be considered the first modern international tribunal. This court aimed to provide a reasonable service to the international community and prevent the outbreak of a new international war. Just like the League of the Nations, however, this institution ceased after the end of World War II and was superseded by the International Court of Justice.[10]

The International Court of Justice (ICJ)

Based in The Hague, Netherlands, the ICJ is the most important international court today.[11] Since its creation in 1945 (in April 1946 this court was installed and had its first session),[12] this court has already ruled on 144 cases.[13] Although compared to a domestic court this number may not seem impressive, for an international court, this is a considerable number. This institution is one of the six principal bodies of the United Nations and is the only one not located in New York. The importance of this institution is pointed out in the words of Judge Lachs, who said when ruling a case that

"The ICJ is the guardian of legality for the international community as a whole, both within and without the United Nations."[14]

This court is composed of fifteen judges, each from a different country.[15] These justices, who have diplomatic privileges when working for the ICJ,[16] are elected by the General Assembly of the UN Security Council[17] for a term of nine years and can be reelected.[18] The elections occur every three years; thus, there are always experienced judges on the court. Once the judges are elected they cannot be dismissed unless all other judges of the court unanimously agree that he or she has failed to fulfill the requirements of a member of that court.[19] This is an important rule that enables the judges to perform their duties without fear of dismissal for political reasons. Although the judges are not obligated to reside in The Hague (except for the president), most of them do. The requirements to be elected a judge of the court are the same ones to be chosen a judge in the highest judicial office in the home country of the candidate. Furthermore, once a judge is a member of the ICJ, he/she cannot preside in cases that they may have heard in their home country.

The statute of the ICJ contains all the rules that guide this institution. This statute is annexed to the Charter of the United Nations and has been amended twice since its creation in 1945. Articles were added and revised in 1972 and 1978, albeit no major change happened in the system. The court has the power to create the rules it needs to regulate its statute and operate properly.[20] Thus, the statute of 1945 can be considered the upper law that regulates the ICJ, whereas the rules of the court, adopted in 1978, are the detailed body of rules that regulate the functioning of the court. Thus, the statute of the ICJ is equivalent to the constitution of that court, and the rules of the ICJ are comparable to the procedural law applied by The Hague-based institution.

There are four types of chambers that form the court: summary procedure, summary proceedings, for a particular category of crimes, for a particular crime. The summary procedure chamber has not yet been used and, according to article 29 of the statute, it would be composed of five judges and would deal with cases that are less complex, at the request of the parties. The chamber for categories of cases has not yet been used, although a chamber for environmental cases has been created. One example of a chamber created for dealing with a particular case is the chamber for the Gulf of Maine case, in which the United States and Canada were involved in the creation of the committee. Besides this case, five others were heard by ad hoc chambers.[21] It seems to be a good decision to use those chambers, as long as all the parties involved request so. The fact that a chamber will be created to deal only with one case implies that the ICJ will give it more attention because there will be only the one case analyzed by the chamber (composed of five judges).

The ICJ performs two functions when it is involved in a case. It will either settle a case brought to its judges or express an opinion in advisory proceedings brought either by the United Nations or any of its specialized agencies. The main difference between these functions is that the litigation cases have a binding decision, whereas in the advisory procedures the court delivers an opinion that is not binding. Thus, the ICJ does not act only as a dispute settler because it also provides legal opinions in international law cases. All the states involved in a dispute in the ICJ need to accept the jurisdiction of that court. Signing an agreement in order to have the dispute settled by the ICJ is one procedure that is similar to an arbitration agreement. Through this method, the parties sign an agreement according to which the dispute among them will be submitted to the ICJ and the court's decision will be respected. The ICJ also has jurisdiction when an international treaty states that a dispute regarding that treaty will be decided by the ICJ. Thus, any international treaty can contain a clause according to which a dispute regarding that treaty will be settled by The Hague-based court.[22]

There are three sources of laws that can be used in the decisions of the ICJ: international conventions that have been recognized by the contesting states, international custom, and general principles of law (deciding *ex aequo et bono*). There has not yet been a decision based solely on *ex aequo et bono*. For example, in the advisory case "The legality of the threat or use of nuclear weapons," the court was dealing with the issue of threatening the use of nuclear weapons, and they concluded that there was no law on which to base a definitive opinion of the court.[23]

The parties involved in cases discussed by the ICJ are states that either accepted the jurisprudence of the ICJ or belong to the United Nations.[24] As Dinah Shelton analyzed, the main focus of the ICJ is to have states as parties in its cases: "The ability of a nongovernmental organization to initiate an international case or intervene as a party is limited because in many international courts only states may be parties to proceedings." She then continued, "The jurisdiction of the International Court of Justice is similarly restricted."[25] Other international tribunals to be discussed later in this article have a different perspective and can accept an individual as a party in a claim. With the current level of globalization, in the opinion of the author, not allowing individuals to be part of claims is a poor legal standpoint. Today individuals have cases against states that would be better judged in an international court such as the ICJ instead of being brought to a domestic court.

It is also possible for states that do not belong to the United Nations to be a party in a case in the ICJ. In this situation, they need to sign another treaty that specifically allows their case to be tried by the ICJ.[26] A few cases have been decided by the court based on arbitration agreements: *Belgium v. Netherlands*, *Tunisia v. Libya*, and *Libya v. Chad*. Although the vast majority of countries in the world are members of the UN, there are some exceptions, and article 35 allows them to use the ICJ. Currently, all the states that signed the statute of the ICJ are members of the UN. However, five nations—Japan, Liechtenstein, San Marino, Nauru, and

Switzerland—were members of the statute of the ICJ before they entered the UN.[27]

One interesting feature of the ICJ is how its decisions are enforced. Because this court is not like a domestic court that can order the police and military of a country to take the physical action necessary to enforce a decision, the ICJ needs to use different mechanisms to enforce its decisions. Once given, the ICJ's decisions are final and cannot be appealed. If the party that lost does not want to comply with the decision, what can be done? Because The Hague-based court does not have a physical force, there is no way the ICJ can compel the state to comply with its decisions. However, states that do not comply will have their reputations damaged in the international scenario, which may cause serious repercussions for those states. Thus, putting one's reputation at stake in the international arena is an efficient way to make sure that states comply with ICJ decisions. The court assumes that compliance will occur. In the *Nuclear Test* case, the court so attested: "Once the court has found that a state has entered into a commitment concerning its future conduct it is not the court's function to contemplate that it will not comply with it."[28]

Provisional measures can be taken by the ICJ as long as they are necessary in order to preserve the rights of the party.[29] This is an important measure for the success of this court because in many cases taking a provisional measure early in the procedure is necessary in order to avoid risking these rights. While discussing a recent case between Argentina and Uruguay, Roy Tyson asserted, "In addition to properly maintaining its high evidentiary standard for imposition of provisional measures, the court also emphasized the obligation of each party to refrain from any action which might hinder the court from effectively resolving the dispute."[30] The court may decide at a later point, after granting a provisional measure, that it does not have jurisdiction in the case, after which the court should cancel the provisional measure.[31] The requirement of urgency is necessary for any provisional measure to be granted.[32]

The ICJ does have two notable limitations. First, it cannot perform judicial review over the acts of the UN, even though this is the main legal institution of the UN. Second, individuals are not allowed as parties in this court. Nevertheless, the range of cases decided by the ICJ is broad, and this is the oldest and most respected international court currently operating. International law and globalization are among the main reasons for the rising success of this institution. The role that the court plays today in the international scenario was unimaginable a few decades ago, and this court will likely continue to be more and more important in the future.

The European Court of Justice (ECJ)

The European Union is the most successful economic bloc in the world. There are several factors that indicate this success, including that the number of member states has risen from the original six to the current twenty-seven and that there are now more eastern European countries seeking admission;[33] that the volume of trade within those states has risen most years; and that the legislation in this bloc is more complete and advanced each year. Above all, however, the European Court of Justice is vital for the EU's success. Europe is so integrated that an efficient system to settle legal issues in this bloc is essential, as Mark Kesselman and his associates stated, "Today European law is superior to, and supersedes, member state law. The European Court of Justice (ECJ), born in the European Coal and Steel Community Treaty, has been the major institutional actor in making this happen, and ECJ rulings have provided for the new Europe."[34]

Originally created in 1952 by the Treaty of Paris, the Luxembourg-based court had only seven judges, one appointed by each of the six member states of the European Coal and Steel Community, and the seventh appointed by one of the three wealthier nations. An odd number of judges was necessary to guarantee that there would be no tie decisions. Today this court is regulated by the European Community Treaty, signed in 1992,[35] and it was also profoundly modified by the Amsterdam treaty in 1997.[36] It has two levels of jurisdiction: The lower one is composed of twelve judges[37] and the higher is composed of fifteen judges.[38]

All the judges are selected for terms of six years[39] and are replaced in alternate years.[40] Each of the now twenty-seven judges is appointed by a member state of the European Union. Each judge should have the same qualifications necessary for being appointed to the highest judicial office of their respective countries.[41] Unlike in the United States, where the president nominates justices to the Supreme Court, in the ECJ there is little evidence of political appointments. When judges are nominated to this court, the member states are usually naming their country's well-known lawyers rather than their top judges. Thus, these appointments should not be considered political because the nations are nominating attorneys with a vast amount of knowledge, and the lawyers have rarely been known to pressure the leaders of their countries to nominate them. Besides the judges, the ECJ is also composed of six advocates-general, who advise the judges.[42] Thus, an advocate-general does not participate in the judgment but does express his or her opinion of the best decision for the case.

The influence of the Luxembourg-based court has been growing since its creation. As the number of international treaties and regulations in the European Union grew, so did the number of cases in the ECJ. In 1954 only 10 cases were lodged to the ECJ. Six years later there were 27. In 2008 the number was 586 and, in 2009, 554.[43] Furthermore, the European Court of Justice can refuse to hear a case if its judges believe they have no competence in its subject matter. In this situation, the national court of the nation where the case originated will decide it. Despite the creation of the first jurisdiction level, the large increase in the number of cases being lodged in this court has created a long backlog, and as a result, the idea of creating regional courts in the European Union, similar to the circuit courts in the United States, is becoming more popular.

The competence of the ECJ is quite large. Each one of the EU member states can bring another state to the court when it believes that the other state is not complying with their obligations related to EU treaties.[44] The European Court of Justice can also impose penalties on the states that are not complying with the Maastricht or other EU treaties.[45] Performing judicial review, an essential mechanism in democratic societies, is also a function of the ECJ.[46] Regarding judicial review, Simon Hix has noted that "the ECJ can review the legality of acts (other than recommendations and opinions) adopted by the Council, the EP, the Commission and the European Central Bank, and acts of the EP intended to produce legal effects on third parties."[47]

Interpreting the European Community treaty is one of the most important functions of the ECJ due to the treaty's importance and size. In addition to this treaty, there are several other EU treaties and legislation that the ECJ also analyzes. ECJ may also decide any question raised by any other member state court.[48] For example, if a case is filed in a court in France and that court assumes that its decision pertains to the entire or part of the EU bloc then the French court can request the ECJ to rule on that case. This is important because if a plaintiff prefers to file a claim in a national court, thereby trying to avoid the ECJ, the national court will have the authority to transfer that case to the European Court of Justice.

A review of the cases that the ECJ has decided demonstrates just how important this court has been in Europe and how an international court created only half a century ago has been dealing with important issues in Europe. For instance, in *Van Gend in Loos v. Nederlandse Administratie der Belastingen*,[49] the court decided that national courts can apply European Law in national cases, just like any other domestic law. In this case, a company tried to use European law in the Netherlands court. The Netherlands court brought the case to the ECJ, inquiring if it was good to use European statutes or laws in a state court. This ruling caused several new cases to be taken to the ECJ.

In *Costa v. E.N.E.L.*, the court decided that when there is the possibility to apply either European law or domestic law to rule on an issue, if these laws are contradictory, then European legislation must prevail: "By creating a community of unlimited duration, having its own institutions, its own personality, its own legal capacity and capacity of representation on the international plane and, more particularly, real powers stemming from a limitation of sovereignty or a transfer or powers from the states to the community, the member states have limited their sovereign rights and have thus created a body of law which binds their nationals and themselves."[50]

Through its decisions, the ECJ has fostered the economic development of the European Union as well as created better conditions for strengthening the EU. In the *Dassonville* case,[51] decided in 1974, the court concluded that the national laws of EU member states cannot create burdens or difficulties to discourage the European Union. With that decision, any kind of quotas and restrictions in imports within the bloc were prohibited. The ECJ has also made important decisions in other areas, such as environmental preservation and social policy (ensuring equal treatment for everybody in the EU). Regarding the environmental cases, Jacob Werksman has stated, "There can be little doubt that without the Court's jurisprudence, environmental law in the Community legal order would be less well developed and there would probably be a lower degree of support for environmental objectives in other Community institutions, and in the Community more generally."[52]

Furthermore, in 1998 there was an especially important ruling regarding social policy. In *Kohll*,[53] the court decided that European citizens have the right to health care anywhere in the bloc, regardless of whether or not they are in the country where they officially reside and pay their taxes. That case arose after a Luxembourg citizen needed emergency medical care when she was visiting Germany. That same year, the court delivered a similar decision in *Decker*.[54] Although these decisions were heavily criticized at the time, they marked important strides for the EU's progress.

The European Court of Justice is playing an essential role for the success and integration of the European Union. An independent, well developed judicial power is as important for the European Union as a like institution would be in any country. The rulings of the ECJ have clearly been in favor of European integration, as discussed above. It is important to note that although this court is neutral, it has been applying European legislation that supports integrating the European Union.

The International Criminal Court (ICC)

The International Criminal Court was established in July 2002 by the Roman Statute, which was signed in July 1998 and entered into force after 60 states ratified it.[55] As of December 2009 110 countries are members of the Roman Statute.[56] Among these countries are most of the European and South American nations and about half of the African nations. This institution is not a member of the United Nations (like the ICJ), although it is related to it.[57] The intention to create an international tribunal to try criminal cases goes back to the end of WWII, when, after the end of the war, the Nuremberg and Tokyo ad hoc tribunals prompted the discussion of creating an international criminal court so ad hoc tribunals no longer have to be specially created in order to judge war crimes. Although based in The Hague,[58] Netherlands, the court can meet anywhere.[59]

The Hague-based court is competent only when ruling on the crimes of genocide, crimes against humanity, war crimes, and the crimes of aggression,[60] all of which would not be likely to be tried in a fair way within the borders of the country where they happened; for this reason, having an international tribunal to judge these crimes is imperative. Furthermore, the UN has provided a detailed definition of these crimes in order to make them clearly understood and to avoid doubts about the tribunal's competence. Although the crime of genocide was not difficult to define in article 6, crimes against humanity required more discussion so as to define and specify their scope. As such, the second and third paragraphs of article 7 further explain the terms used in the first paragraph to define crimes against humanity. The Statute of Rome gives even more attention to the term "war crime," devoting several paragraphs and subparts to further defining this term. Although there are only four crimes that the court is competent to try, these crimes can happen in a variety of ways and there can certainly be a large number of these crimes happening in the signatory countries of the Rome Statute.

Whatever crime the ICC is investigating, there is one mandatory *ratione temporis* required for the ICC to have competency: The crime must have happened after the Roman Statute entered force[61]—thus, after July 2002. Whatever crime happened before this date cannot be tried in this court. This is a fair requirement, because ICC was not created to be an ad hoc tribunal. In fact, one of the reasons to create this court was to avoid creating ad hoc courts. If a country signed and ratified the statute after it was already in force, the ICC will have competence to judge crimes that happened only after the statute was valid for that country,[62] unless the state declares that the ICC can exercise jurisprudence for crimes that happened before the Statute was in force for that country. I argue that this is an unfair option: the Rome Statute should not be allowed because there may be individuals who can be tried for a crime that happened before the statute was adopted, which would configure an ad hoc tribunal. Furthermore, there are two additional requisites needed for the ICC to have competence: First, the accused must either be a national from a signatory of this Rome Statute, or, second, the crime must have happened within the borders of one of the signatory countries.[63] One more possibility is if the Security Council of the United Nations referred the situation to the ICC prosecutor, regardless of the nationality of the accused or the place where the crime may have happened.[64]

The ICC is composed of four bodies: presidency, judicial chambers, office of the prosecutor, and the registry.[65] There are eighteen judges composing the court[66] who, as in the ECJ, should have the same qualifications necessary to be members of the highest court in their home country.[67] However, the ICC judge candidates must have proven high achievements in criminal and international law, which are certainly important areas for members of this court.[68] The terms are for nine years, the judges are eligible for reelection,[69] and there may not be more than one judge from the same member state.[70]

The presidency of the ICC, composed of a president and vice president, is responsible for the administration of the court, except for the administration of the prosecutor's office, which operates independently of the court.[71] The judicial chamber is the most important body of the ICC, and is subdivided into three parts: a pretrial division, a trial division, and an appeal division.[72] Thus, when a legal action takes place in the ICC, it starts in the pretrial division, moves on to the trial stage if appropriate, and it ends in the appeal level if there is an appeal. The pretrial and trial divisions have at least six judges, whereas the appeal division is composed of the president plus a minimum of four judges.[73] The prosecutor's office is independent of the rest of the court. The prosecutor receives all the crime referrals and investigates them independently from the court itself.[74] This is important in order to guarantee the impartiality of the court because the independent prosecutor's office is the one performing the investigation. Agreeing with that, Roy Lee wrote, "The creation of the office of an independent prosecutor responsible for initiating investigations represents a major step in the enforcement of international law."[75] As for the registry, this office is responsible for running all the aspects of the court.[76] The expenses of the court shall be paid from a fund to which member states must contribute.[77]

From its creation in 2002 until today, only four cases were initiated in the ICC.[78] The situation of Uganda is currently being heard on pretrial. One of the defendants has died, but the procedure continues against the four remaining defendants. For the situation in the Congo, the prosecutor filed three charges, two of which are in the pretrial stage and one is in the trial stage. For the Darfur situation, there are three cases, all of which are in the pretrial stage. The United States, although not a member of the ICC, is one of the nations that claims genocide has been happening in Darfur, regarding which John Crook stated, "U.S. concerns regarding the conflict in Darfur continue to contribute to an apparent softening of U.S. opposition to the International Criminal Court (ICC)."[79] As for the Central African Republic, the case is in the pretrial stage.

Although the ICC has improved international law and has certainly contributed to international justice, major countries did not sign this treaty. Although 110 countries have signed it,[80] most of the world's population lives in countries that have not signed it, such as the United States, China, and India. These nations, besides being major economic powers, play a huge role in the international scene. Although the United States and China hold a permanent seat on the UN Security Council, they have not yet signed this treaty. In order for this court to be more successful, nations that have not signed this treaty need to do so.

Human Rights Courts

Some international courts specialize in human rights. The European Court of Human Rights and the Inter-American Court of Human Rights are important institutions that ensure that human rights are protected around the world. Because these courts deal exclusively with human rights, the most basic rights for human beings, gaining a better understanding of those rights is essential.

The European Convention of Human Rights (ECHR), signed in Rome in 1950 and began operating in 1959, established the European Court of Human Rights (ECtHR).[81] In 1998 all the forty-seven member-states of the Council of Europe adopted the "protocol 11" of that statute, and this court then changed significantly following a considerable increase in its caseload. From 1959 to 1988 this court judged 837 cases, and from that time forward, the number increased to more than 1,500 cases per year since 2006.[82]

The court, based in Strasbourg (France), is composed of one member for each contracting party,[83] which currently is forty-seven, covering virtually all of Europe (all of them adopted protocol 11). The judges hold six-year terms and can be reelected no more than one time.[84] When the "protocol 11" was adopted in 1998, the major change was that any person can file a case in this court, which made the number of cases soar. Most of the cases are brought against three countries: Russia, Romania, and Turkey.[85] The most common violations of human rights were the right to a fair trial,[86] the right to liberty and security,[87] and property-related rights.

One of the problems regarding decisions of the ECtHR is that some countries do not always enforce the decisions of the European Court of Human Rights. Yulia Dernovsky has noted that "Russia's poor record at the ECtHR reflects years of isolationist and repressive politics during the tsarist and Soviet periods. This Note reasoned that the reluctance by Russia's judiciary to effectively implement ECtHR judgments and Convention norms in domestic court judgments is a result of the weakened position of the judiciary within the Russian government."[88] Thus, pressuring countries to enforce the decisions of the ECtHR is important; otherwise, those decisions are pointless. Although there are occasions when the decisions of this court are not enforced, this institution is nonetheless internationally respected for fostering human rights.

The Inter-American Court of Human Rights (IACHR) is regulated by the Statute of the Inter-American Court of Human-Rights (SIACHR) and it sits in San José, Costa Rica.[89] This court is composed of seven judges,[90] each elected for six-year terms,[91] and was established in 1979 when the SIACHR was adopted in La Paz, Bolivia. The judges are nationals of the countries that belong to the Organization of American States (OAS), and the IACHR cannot have more than one judge from each state.[92]

Any victim of a violation of human rights can present a claim to the Human Rights Commission, and if that institution concludes the case is admissible, it will begin the procedure at the IACHR.[93] In order to be deemed admissible, a prosecutor must show that the victim tried to use the domestic legal remedies in the country where the violation happened.[94] This is one reason why the number of cases at this court is lower than at its European counterpart. The number of complaints that the IACHR received per year from 2005–2009 ranged between 1,323 and 1,456.[95] The countries that received the most complaints were Peru, Colombia, Mexico, and Argentina.[96]

Despite the fact that citizens cannot file cases directly with the IACHR, this court has been protecting fundamental rights on the American continent, as Steven Keener and Javier Vasquez have commented, "the Inter-American Court of Human Rights began enforcing the right to life, traditionally considered a 'negative' right, in a way that closely resembles enforcement of the right to health, traditionally viewed as a 'positive' right."[97] IACHR decisions have been influencing some national courts to further defend human rights, as Angel Oquendo explained, "It has taken an increasingly progressive, as well as assertive role, and has impressively developed its prestige over the last decades."[98] Oquendo uses the Argentine Supreme Court case of *Miguel Angel Ekmekdjian v. Gerardo Sofovich* as an example of this, in which the Argentine court used decisions of the IACHR to back up its ruling. Although the European Court is overall more respected and known, the Inter-American Court has been steadily gaining a better reputation.

There are other regional charters that ensure human rights. For instance, the Human Rights Chamber of Bosnia and Herzegovina[99] analyzes cases of human rights in the Bosnia and Herze-

govina area. Other examples are the Banjul Charter on Human and People's Rights[100] and the Arab Charter on Human Rights.[101] The increase in the number of covenants that recognize and enforce human rights reflects the growing international concern to ensure these rights.

International Courts Created After the End of the Cold War and Arbitration Courts

As globalization has advanced, there has been an ever-greater need for international law, and as a result, the number of international courts has risen significantly. In the 1990s at least five new international courts were created: the International Tribunal for the Law of the Sea (ITLOS), the Appellate Body of the World Trade Organization dispute-settlement system (WTO-AB), the Court of the European Economic Area (EFTA), the Central America Court of Justice (CCJ), and the Economic Court of Justice of the Common Market of Eastern and Southern Africa (COMESA).

In 1982 the Law of the Sea Convention (LOS) created the ITLOS.[102] This court, based in Hamburg, Germany, is composed of twenty-one members,[103] each elected for nine-year terms.[104] States that signed the Law of the Sea Convention can participate in this tribunal, as can international organizations.[105] The decisions of this tribunal are final and binding,[106] and each party should bear its own costs.[107] This tribunal is one of only three dispute resolution methods mentioned in the LOS, the others being the ICJ and arbitration.

The Appellate Body of the World Trade Organization dispute-settlement system is composed of seven judges appointed for four-year terms,[108] according to the Uruguay Round Agreement (URA). The Geneva-based court hears appeals of panel cases decided by the World Trade Organization (WTO).[109] Only parties that were previously involved in the panel dispute can appeal to the appellate body, and the proceedings in this court should not exceed sixty days.[110] Since its creation in 1996, this court has received ninety-six cases (as of August 2009).[111]

The other courts created in the 1990s (EFTA, CCJ, and COMESA) are examples of how international courts have spread around the world—not only in the most developed countries. In the last decade, the Court of Justice of the Economic Community of West African States (ECOWAS CCJ) was created in 2002 to settle disputes in the west African states. In the same year the ICC became a reality. In South America the Mercado Comun Del Sur (Mercosur) court of review has been operating since 2004. The Olivos protocol established Mercosur to settle disputes related to the South Common Market. In 2005 the Caribbean Court of Justice started operating.

The rise of international courts after the end of the Cold War is mentioned by C. Leah Grunger: "With the proliferation and reinvigoration of international tribunals since the end of the Cold War, states and organizations have developed a number of special purpose institutions that perform similar functions to traditional tribunals."[112] In fact, international tribunals that have been created in the last two decades rule on cases in a similar way to traditional courts, though they are generally more efficient and tend to be fairer.

Besides binding international courts, there has also been a notable development in the establishment of arbitration bodies in the last decade. There is not always an international court for international cases, which may lead parties to seek international arbitration. Other advantages of international arbitration are confidentiality, faster speed to settle the dispute, and the cost, which is generally lower than litigation in state-operated courts.

There are many international arbitration courts, and the number of cases received in these courts increases every year.[113] The two most important arbitration bodies are the International Chamber of Commerce (ICC) arbitration court and the American Arbitration Association (AAA). Other important international arbitration bodies are the London Court of International Arbitration (LCIA), the Stockholm Chamber of Commerce (SCC), and the Swiss Chambers of International Arbitration (SCIA). There are also numerous other regional arbitration courts that deal with international disputes, such as the Mongolian Arbitration Court, the Japan Commercial Arbitration Court, and the Australian Centre for International Commercial Arbitration.

However, this proliferation of international courts can lead to some problems in the international arena. For instance, some disputes can be brought to more than one international binding court. One example is the *Swordfish Stocks* case, which Chile brought to the ITLOS court, but in its defense, the European Union claimed that the case should be discussed in the ICJ, not the ITLOS. Regardless, the ITLOS court has so far considered itself competent to judge this case, and a decision is expected in 2010.[114]

Another problem regarding the proliferation of international courts is that there could be divergent jurisprudence because different courts could be deciding similar cases. Regarding this, Luis Barrionueva Arélo stated, "The multiplication of international judicial bodies over the last few decades has given rise to a series of problems, such as jurisdictional overlapping, forum shopping and inconsistent interpretation of rules of law that should not be underestimated for they may endanger the integrity and cohesiveness of international law."[115] However, the growing number of international tribunals is a consequence of globalization, and this growth leads to an improvement in international law.

Conclusion

The international courts have been increasingly present in the international scene and will continue to have a growing importance as the world continues to be more globalized and national borders become less important. The larger numbers of international agreements and a stronger belief in international law have fostered conditions that encourage this upsurge in the number of international courts created in the second half of the twentieth century and continue to increase to this day. Furthermore, national courts are not the proper place to discuss international issues because there is a higher tendency for a state to influence a case there than in an international court.

Finally, the problems created by the multiplication of international judicial bodies should be controlled so they do not cause burdens to international society. It is important that the international courts work in harmony so there is consistency in the decisions, which will prevent the parties from "shopping" for the most convenient court to file their case. However, the large number of international bodies nonetheless contributes to a fairer and more peaceful world, which should be a goal for all mankind.

NOTES

1. YUVAL SHANY, THE COMPETING JURISDICTIONS OF INTERNATIONAL COURTS AND TRIBUNALS 3 (2003).

2. Karen Alter, *The Law and Politics of International Delegation: Delegating to International Courts: Self-binding v. Other-binding Delegation,* 71 L. & CONTEMP. PROBLEMS J. 37 (2008).

3. *Supra* note 1, at 4.

4. *Id.* at 1.

5. RICHARD J. GOLDSTONE & ADAM M. SMITH, INTERNATIONAL JUDICIAL INSTITUTIONS 31 (2009).

6. *Id.*

7. *Id.* at 6.

8. *Supra* note 5, at 18.

9. The "Military Bureau of Investigation of Violations of the Law of War" was created in 1914.

10. The History of the ICJ, *available at* www.unesco.org/archives/sio/Eng/presentation_print.php?idOrg=1016.

11. MALCOLM SHAW, INTERNATIONAL LAW 960 (5th ed. 2006).

12. ICJ website, *available at* www.icj-cij.org/court/index.php?p1=1&p2=1.

13. ICJ website, *available at* www.icj-cij.org/docket/index.php?p1=3&PHPSESSID=ecf4c8ff77babf1216db6ddc524b6a6a.

14. JOHN P. GRANT, THE LOCKERBIE TRIAL: A DOCUMENTARY HISTORY (2004).

15. Statute of the International Court of Justice, 3 Bevans 1179; 59 Stat. 1031; T.S. No. 993, art. 3.

16. *Id.* at art. 19.

17. *Id.* at art. 13.

18. *Id.* at art. 16.

19. *Id.* at art. 18.

20. *Id.* at art. 30.

21. ICJ website, *available at* www.icj-cij.org/court/index.php?p1=1&p2=4.

22. *Supra* note 15, at art. 35.

23. ICJ report 1996, *available at* www.icj-cij.org.

24. *Supra* note 15, at art. 34.

25. Dinah Shelton, *The Participation of Nongovernmental Organizations in International Judicial Proceedings,* 88 AM. J. INT'L L. 616 (1994).

26. *Supra* note 15, at art. 35.

27. ICJ website, *available at* www.icj-cij.org/jurisdiction/index.php?p1=5&p2=1&p3=1&sp3=b&PHPSESSID=6a42db463838d7d7d2769dd355efd48a.

28. ICJ Nuclear Tests, *available* at www.icj-cij.org/docket/index.php?p1=3&p2=3&code=af&case=58&k=78.

29. *Supra* note 15, at art. 41.

30. Roy Tyson, *Case Comment: International Law—I.C.J. Maintains High Evidentiary Standard in Granting Requests for Indication of Provisional Measures: Argentina v. Uruguay: Request for the Indication of Provisional Measures,* 32 SUFFOLK TRANSNAT'L L. REV. 219, 229 (2008).

31. Arbitral award, July 1989, *Guinea-Bissau v. Senegal* (1991) ICJ Rep. 53, 31 I.L.M. 32 (1992), *available at* www.icj-cij.org/docket/index.php?p1=3&p2=2&PHPSESSID=dae597472858758c3862cca6bc599f6c.

32. Great Belt case, *Finland v. Denmark* (1992) ICJ Rep. 3, 37 I.L.M. 468 (1998) *available at* www.icj-cij.org/docket/index.php?p1=3&p2=2&PHPSESSID=dae597472858758c3862cca6bc599f6c.

33. European Union website, *available at* http://europa.eu/abc/european_countries/index_en.htm.

34. MARK KESSELMAN ET AL., EUROPEAN POLITICS IN TRANSITION 86 (5th ed. 2006).

35. Treaty on European Union (Maastricht Treaty), Feb. 7, 1992, 1992 O.J. (C191) 1; 31 I.L.M. 253 (1992).

36. Treaty of Amsterdam Amending the Treaty on European Union, the Treaties Establishing the European Communities and Certain Related Acts, Oct. 2, 1997, 1997 O.J. (C340) 1; 37 I.L.M 56 (1998).

37. Consolidated Versions of the Treaty on European Union and of the Treaty Establishing the European Community (2002), 2002 O.J. (C325) 1, art. 168a.2.

38. *Id.* at art. 165.

39. *Id.* at art. 167.

40. *Id.* at art. 168a.3.

41. *Id.* at art. 168a.3.

42. *Id.* at art. 166.

43. ECJ website, *available at* http://curia.europa.eu/en/content/juris/index.htm.

44. *Supra* note 35, at art. 177.

45. *Id.* at art. 172.

46. *Id.* at art. 173.

47. SIMON HIX, THE POLITICAL SYSTEM OF THE EUROPEAN UNION 106 (1999).

48. *Supra* note 35, at art. 182.

49. Case 26/62, *Van Gend & Loos v. Nederlandse administratie der Belastingen*, 1963 E.C.R. 1.

50. Case 6/64, *Costa v. E.N.E.L.*, 1964 E.C.R. 585.

51. Case 8/74, *Procureur du Roi v. Benoît and Gustave Dassonville*, 1974 E.C.R. 837.

52. JACOB WEKSMAN, GREENING INTERNATIONAL INSTITUTIONS 234 (1996).

53. Case 158/96, *Kohll v. Union des Caisses de Maladie*, 1998 E.C.R. I-1931.

54. Case 120/95, *Decker v. Caisse de Maladie des employés privés*, 1998 E.C.R. I-1831.

55. Rome Statute of the International Criminal Court, 2187 U.N.T.S. 90; 37 I.L.M. 1002 (1998), art. 126.1.

56. ICC website, *available at* www.icc-cpi.int/Menus/ICC/About+the+Court/ICC+at+a+glance/.

57. *Supra* note 55, at art. 2.

58. *Id.* at art. 3.1.

59. *Id.* at art. 3.3.

60. *Id.* at art. 5.

61. *Id.* at art. 11.1.

62. *Id.* at art. 11.2.

63. *Id.* at art. 12.2.

64. *Id.* at art. 13.2.

65. *Id.* at art. 34.

66. *Id.* at art. 36.1.

67. *Id.* at art. 36.3.

68. *Id.* at art. 36.3.b.

69. *Id.* at art. 36.9.

70. *Id.* at art. 36.7.

71. *Id.* at art. 38.3.

72. *Id.* at art. 34.b.

73. *Id.* at art. 39.1.

74. *Id.* at art. 42.

75. ROY LEE, THE INTERNATIONAL CRIMINAL COURT 34 (1999).

76. *Supra* note 55, at art. 43.

77. *Id.* at art. 115.

78. ICC website, *available at* www.icc-cpi.int/Menus/ICC/Situations+and+Cases/.

79. John Crook, *Contemporary Practice of the United States Relating to International Law: International Criminal Law: United States Eases Opposition to International Criminal Court, Opposes Efforts to Thwart ICC Proceedings Involving Darfur*, 103 AMER. J. INT'L L. 152 (2009).

80. ICC website, *available at* www.icc-cpi.int/Menus/ASP/states+parties/The+States+Parties+to+the+Rome+Statute.htm.

81. European Convention for the Protection of Human Rights and Fundamental Freedoms, 213 U.N.T.S. 222, Nov. 4, 1950, art. 19.

82. ECHR website, www.echr.coe.int/ECHR/EN/Header/The+Court/Introduction/Information+documents/.

83. *Supra* note 81, at art. 20.

84. *Id.* at art. 23.

85. *Id.* at art. 78.

86. *Id.* at art. 6.

87. *Id.* at art. 5.

88. Yulia Dernovsky, *Overcoming Soviet Legacy: Non-Enforcement of the Judgments of the European Court of Human Rights by the Russian Judiciary*, 17 CARDOZO J. INT'L & COMP. L. 471, 512 (2009).

89. Statute of the Inter-American Court on Human Rights, O.A.S. Res. 448 (IX-0/79), O.A.S. Off. Rec. OEA/Ser.P/IX.0.2./80, vol. 1, at 98, entered into force Jan. 1, 1989, Article 3. *See also* American Convention on Human Rights, Nov. 22, 1969, 1144 U.N.T.S. 123, O.A.S.T.S. No. 36, at 1, OEA/Ser.L/V/II.23 doc. Rev. 2, entered into force July 18, 1978 [hereinafter Convention].

90. *Id.* at art. 4.1

91. *Id.* at art. 5.

92. *Id.* at art. 4.2.

93. American Convention on Human Rights, Nov. 22, 1969, 1144 U.N.T.S. 123, O.A.S.T.S. No. 36, at 1, OEA/Ser.L/V/II.23, doc. Rev. 2, entered into force Jul. 18, 1978 [hereinafter Convention], art. 61.

94. *Id.* at art. 46.1.a

95. IACHR 2008 Report, *available at* www.cidh.org/annualrep/2009eng/Chap.III.eng.html.

96. *Id. supra.*

97. Steven Keener & Javier Vazquez, *A Life Worth Living: Enforcement of the Right to Health Through the Right to Life in the Inter-American Court of Human Rights*, 40 COLUM. HUM. RTS. L. REV. 595, 597 (2009).

98. Angel R. Oquendo, *The Solitude of Latin America: The Struggle for Rights South of the Border*, 43 TEX. INT'L. L. J. 185, 230 (2008).

99. The General Framework Agreement for Peace in Bosnia and Herzegovina (known as the "Dayton" Agreement), initiated on Nov. 21, 1995 and signed in Paris on Dec. 14, 1995, *available at* www.state.gov/www/regions/eur/bosnia/bosagree.html, Annex 6.

100. Banjul Charter on Human and Peoples Rights, Jun. 24–27, 1981, 21 I.L.M. 58.

101. Council of the League of Arab States, Arab Charter on Human Rights, Sept. 15, 1994, *reprinted in* 18 HUM. RTS. L. J. 151 (1997). *See also* The Casablanca Declaration of the Arab Human Rights Movement, adopted by the First International Conference of the Arab Human Rights Movement, Apr. 23–25,

1999, Casablanca, *available at* www.cihrs.org/activities/Conference/Conference.htm.

102. UN Convention on the Law of the Sea, Dec. 10, 1982, UN Doc. A/Conf. 62/121. 21 I.L.M. 1261, art. 286 and annex VI.

103. *Id.* at art. 2.

104. *Id.* at art. 5.

105. *Id.* at art. 20.

106. *Id.* at art. 33.

107. *Id.* at art. 34.

108. Understanding on Rules and Procedures Governing the Settlement of Disputes arts 17.1–2, Apr. 15, 1994, Marrakesh Agreement Establishing the World Trade Organization, Annex 2, Legal Instruments—Results of the Uruguay Round, 33 I.L.M. 1226, art. 17.2.

109. *Id.*

110. *Id.* at art. 17.5.

111. WTO-AB website, *available at* www.wto.org/english/tratop_e/dispu_e/stats_e.htm.

112. C. Leah Granger, *The Role of International Tribunals in Natural Resource Disputes in Latin America,* 34 ECOL. L. Q. 1297, 1298 (2007).

113. PriceWater House International Arbitration Study, *available at* www.pwc.co.uk/pdf/PwC_International_Arbitration_2008.pdf.

114. Press release 1/29/08, *available at* www.itlos.org/cgi-bin/cases/case_detail.pl?id=6&lang=en.

115. Luis Barrionueva Arélo, *The Multiplication of International Jurisdictions and the Integrity of International Law,* 15 ILSA J. INT'L & COMP. L. 49, 59 (2008).

PART FIVE

INTERNATIONAL HUMANITARIAN LAW

12

Modern International Humanitarian Law

STEFAN KIRCHNER

A. Fundamentals of International Humanitarian Law

I. Introduction

The prohibition of the use of armed force is not only codified in Art. 2 (4) of the Charter of the United Nations[1] but it is also a rule of *jus cogens*. If it is broken, however, a separate set of rules starts to apply, regulating the behavior of those who participate in an armed conflict. This international law of war, or *ius in bello*, is commonly referred to as international humanitarian law. Unlike the *ius ad bellum*, the *ius in bello* does not distinguish regarding the causes for the conflict. In the words of Roberta Arnold, international humanitarian law applies equally to "the 'good' and the 'bad' guys."[2]

II. The Development of International Humanitarian Law[3]

The first rules regulating the "how" of combat can be found in antiquity. Sun Tzu held that "the worst policy is to attack cities,"[4] Hindu rules—the Laws of Manu—prohibited the use of poisoned arrows,[5] Romans and Greeks "customarily observed a prohibition against using poison or poisoned weapons,"[6] and the Catholic Church declared the crossbow and the arbalest illegal during the 1132 Lateran Council.[7] This approach of reacting to new technological developments through more regulation continues to this very day and is bound to continue as military technology develops.

1. Codification Efforts[8]

Large parts of international humanitarian law only began to be codified in the late nineteenth and the twentieth century.[9] Of particular importance are the Hague rules, which derived from a total of fourteen international conventions that were adopted in 1899 and 1907, respectively.[10] The second major set of rules is usually referred to as the Geneva rules, consisting primarily of the 1949 Geneva Conventions and the Additional Protocols thereto.[11] Some argue that the Hague law is more concerned with means and methods of warfare and that the Geneva law is more humanitarian in nature, but this distinction does do justice to the considerations underlying both sets of rules,[12] as the Hague law is also based on considerations of humanity.[13] In addition, the material distinction between both sets of rules has become increasingly blurred, which is why a categorization of the existing international conventions in the field of International Humanitarian Law, if one insists on categorizing them in the first place, is best done by looking at the chronological development of the law and the particular issues and challenges that were meant to be addressed by the conventions in question.

231

In modern times, four major eras of treaty making can be identified: before World War I, in the interbellum era, in reaction to World War II, and in reaction to the conflicts after the end of the Cold War. Among the early modern norms are the 1856 Paris Declaration Respecting Maritime Law;[14] the 1868 St. Petersburg Declaration Renouncing the Use, in Time of War, of Explosive Projectiles Under 400 Grammes Weight;[15] and the Hague Declarations concerning Asphyxiating Gases[16] and concerning Expanding Bullets[17] (both dating from 1899). The year 1907 saw a large number of new treaties, such as the Hague Convention IV Respecting the Laws and Customs of War on Land[18] and its well-known Annex, the Regulations Respecting the Laws and Customs of War on Land;[19] the Hague Convention V Respecting the Rights and Duties of Neutral Powers and Persons in Case of War on Land;[20] and the Hague Convention VIII Relative to the Laying of Automatic Submarine Contact Mines.[21] In response to World War I and the new technological developments that emerged during this conflict, new weapons became regulated, for example, in the 1923 Hague Rules of Aerial Warfare;[22] the 1925 Geneva Protocol for the Prohibition of the Use in War of Asphyxicating, Poisonous or Other Gases, and of Bacteriological Methods of Warfare;[23] and the 1936 London Procès-Verbal Relating to the Rules of Submarine Warfare set forth in part IV of the Treaty of London of 1930.[24]

More important developments took place in response to the horrors of World War II. The Geneva Conventions of 1949 now form the core of the modern law of armed conflict. They include the Geneva Convention I for the Amelioration of the Condition of the Wounded and Sick in Armed Forces in the Field (GC I); the Geneva Convention II for the Amelioration of the Condition of the Wounded, Sick and Shipwrecked Members of Armed Forces at Sea (GC II);[25] the Geneva Convention III Relative to the Treatment of Prisoners of War (GC III);[26] and the Geneva Convention IV Relative to the Protection of Civilian Persons in Time of War (GC IV).[27] When the Geneva Conventions turned out to be inadequate to cover all conflicts,[28] they were supplemented by the 1977 Additional Protocols relation to the Protection of Victims of International (Additional Protocol I–AP I)[29] and Non-international (Additional Protocol II–AP II)[30] Armed Conflicts. In 2005 a third Additional Protocol (AP III)[31] was created, which adopted an additional distinctive emblem, the red crystal, along with the red cross and the red crescent.

Although the Hague law is more focused on the means of warfare, the Geneva rules address methods of warfare. As we will see later, this strict separation is no longer without exceptions, and in recent years new rules have been created to deal with new technological developments, such as the 1980 UN Convention on Prohibitions or Restrictions on the Use of Certain Conventional Weapons Which May be Deemed to be Excessively Injurious or to Have Indiscriminate Effects[32] and the 1997 Ottawa Convention on the Prohibition of the Use, Stockpiling, Production and Transfer of Anti-Personnel Mines and their Destruction.[33] That these conventions are informed by the humanitarian concerns that are evident in the Geneva rules is also evidenced by the fact that the effects on the victims are at the center of the considerations concerning which weapons are to be banned per se. Accordingly, the 1980 UN Convention on Prohibitions or Restrictions on the Use of Certain Conventional Weapons Which May be Deemed to be Excessively Injurious or to Have Indiscriminate Effects is supplemented by a number of protocols that regulate nondetectable fragments,[34] booby traps (1980[35] and 1996[36]), incendiary weapons,[37] blinding laser weapons,[38] and the explosive remnants of war.[39] In addition, the humanitarian considerations of the Geneva law have translated into more general rules aimed not at protecting participants in armed conflicts but rather the general good as a whole. For instance, this is the case in the 1976 UN Convention on the Prohibition of Military or Any Other Hostile Use of Environmental Modification Techniques (ENMOD);[40] the

1954 Hague Convention,[41] Regulation,[42] and Protocol;[43] and the 1999 Second Hague Protocol for the Protection of Cultural Property in the Event of Armed Conflict.[44] Finally, in response to the atrocities in Rwanda and the former Yugoslavia, enforcing international humanitarian law has taken a greater role due to the significant strengthening of international criminal law, particularly through the creation of the International Criminal Tribunal for Rwanda (ICTR)[45] or for the former Yugoslavia (ICTY);[46] the creation of hybrid courts, special courts, or special chambers in Sierra Leone,[47] Bosnia,[48] or Cambodia;[49] and, most prominently, through the Rome Statute, which established the permanent International Criminal Court in The Hague.[50]

In the last decades, international armed conflicts—that is, classical interstate wars—have not completely disappeared, though they have taken a backseat in absolute numbers when compared with noninternational armed conflicts and as the distinction between international and noninternational conflicts has become increasingly unclear.[51] Due to the fact that the laws of war were tailored to international conflicts, this required new rules as well, which led to the creation of two Additional Protocols in the 1970s.

The two Additional Protocols adopted in 1977 had become necessary, as both dogmatic and technical issues had shown the inadequacy or at least incompleteness of the 1949 Geneva Conventions.[52] The most important feature of the Additional Protocols is the extension of the term "international armed conflict" in Art. 1 (4) AP I.[53] According to this rule, international armed conflicts within the meaning of international law also include conflicts in which people fight against colonial rule, foreign occupation, or racist regimes in the course of exercising their right to self-determination, which is codified in the Friendly Relations Declaration in conformity with the Charter of the United Nations. The natural consequence of widening the scope of the term "international armed conflict" was that those conflicts that were still not covered under the wider definition needed to be regulated as

well, which is what was achieved with AP II. The third major feature of the Additional Protocols is the strengthening of the prohibition of indiscriminatory attacks, Art. 51 (4) AP I, which was further clarified in Art. 52 (1) AP I, that clearly prohibits attacks against civilians or civilian populations.[54]

The Geneva law has not replaced the Hague law but instead has supplemented and clarified it,[55] and although the Geneva law has not completely abandoned the classical understanding of armed conflict,[56] the rise of human rights law after World War II has significantly influenced it. The Geneva law is characterized by an increasing focus on the human person and has moved away from considerations of military necessity.[57] This military perspective was reflected in the fact that states upheld the laws of war because they wanted to protect their own soldiers against violations of the laws of war by other states. Although this consideration is still valid, it is increasingly supplemented by human rights concerns regarding all potential victims of war.[58] This approach is highlighted by the fact that abstract human rights considerations have entered the realm of international humanitarian law. Although rules aimed at protecting individuals are concrete considerations, abstract human rights considerations leave the question open as to who exactly is protected. It is in this sense that we can understand how environmental law and international humanitarian law have begun to overlap in recent decades, notably since the decision of the International Court of Justice in the Advisory Opinion on the Legality of the Threat or Use of Nuclear Weapons,[59] in which the ICJ held that there is "a general obligation to protect the natural environment against widespread, long-term and severe environmental damage"[60] with the Convention on the Prohibition of Military or Any Other Hostile Use of Environmental Modification Techniques (ENMOD).

2. Customary Law

Customary law continues to play a key role in international humanitarian law because not all great military powers nor all states commonly involved in armed conflicts have ratified all relevant international conventions in the field. Nonetheless, nonparties to the existing conventions are bound by customary international law.[61] Customary law requires state practice and an accompanying *opinio juris*. In particular, the latter is sometimes hard to determine in the field of international humanitarian law because state behavior during an armed conflict is often influenced by military considerations, including the expectation of reciprocity, rather than by the sense of obligation that is required to establish *opinio juris*. In fact, often international humanitarian law treaty obligations will only be observed due to an expectation of reciprocity rather than because of the binding nature of the treaty in question.[62] The reciprocity aspect also explains why in conflicts in which only one party to the conflict is party to a certain convention, the other side often declares its willingness to adhere to the same rules.[63]

Despite all the changes the law of armed conflict has seen, in particular in the wake of World War II and in response to the conflicts in the former Yugoslavia, we must keep in mind that the key rule of the law of armed conflict remains the same: the distinction between valid and invalid targets.

III. Key Rules of International Humanitarian Law

A few rules have emerged as key principles of the laws of war, most notably the requirement to discriminate between civilians and combatants as well as considerations of necessity and proportionality.

1. Distinction

The most central rule of international humanitarian law is the need to discriminate between civilians and combatants. Only combatants may participate in an armed conflict and only combatants may be attacked.[64] Civilians may not be attacked.[65] Therefore, parties to an armed conflict "must at all times distinguish between civil-

ian objects and military objectives. Attacks may only be directed against military objectives. Attacks must not be directed against civilian objects."[66] The notion that civilians were fair game and that occupation troops were expected to live off the land started to change during the sixteenth to eighteenth centuries.[67] Today the distinction principle is a rule of customary international law and is codified in Art. 48 AP I, which requires that

in order to ensure respect for and protection of the civilian population and civilian objects, the Parties to the conflict shall at all times distinguish between the civilian population and combatants and between civilian objects and military objectives and accordingly shall direct their operations only against military objectives.

In the words of Knut Dörmann, a "civilian is any person who does not belong to one of the categories of persons referred to in Article 4A (1), (2), (3) and (6) of GC III and Article 43 of [A]P I."[68] Specifically,

Prisoners of war, in the sense of the present Convention, are persons belonging to one of the following categories, who have fallen into the power of the enemy: (1) Members of the armed forces of a Party to the conflict, as well as members of militias or volunteer corps forming part of such armed forces. (2) Members of other militias and members of other volunteer corps, including those of organized resistance movements, belonging to a Party to the conflict and operating in or outside their own territory, even if this territory is occupied, provided that such militias or volunteer corps, including such organized resistance movements, fulfil the following conditions: (a) that of being commanded by a person responsible for his subordinates; (b) that of having a fixed distinctive sign recognizable at a distance; (c) that of carrying arms openly; (d) that of conducting their operations in accordance with the laws and customs of war. (3) Members of regular armed forces who profess allegiance to a government or an authority not recognized by the Detaining Power. (4) Persons who accompany the armed forces without actually being members thereof, such as civilian members of military aircraft crews, war correspondents, supply contractors, members of labour units or of services responsible for the welfare of the armed forces, provided that they have received authorization, from the armed forces which they accompany, who shall provide them for that purpose with an identity card similar to the annexed model. (5) Members of crews, including masters, pilots and apprentices, of the merchant marine and the crews of civil aircraft of the Parties to the conflict, who do not benefit by more favourable treatment under any other provisions of international law. (6) Inhabitants of a non-occupied territory, who on the approach of the enemy spontaneously take up arms to resist the invading forces, without having had time to form themselves into regular armed units, provided they carry arms openly and respect the laws and customs of war. (Art. 4A GC III)

Even if they contribute to the enemy's war effort, for example by working as a secretary in the ministry of defense, civilians may not be targeted.[69]

The protection of civilians also extends to civilian objects. Art. 48 AP I contains the basic rule that

> In order to ensure respect for and protection of the civilian population and civilian objects, the Parties to the conflict shall at all times distinguish between the civilian population and combatants and between civilian objects and military objectives and accordingly shall direct their operations only against military objectives.

This basic rule is elaborated further in the following articles of the First Additional Protocol. Because "civilian objects cannot be positively defined,"[70] in case of doubt as to the nature of an object, that is, if it is used for civilian or for military purposes, according to Art. 52 (3) AP I, "an object which is normally dedicated to civilian purposes, such as a place of worship, a house

of other dwelling or a school, is being used to make an effective contribution to military action, it shall be presumed not to be so used"[71] This rule, however, is thought to have not yet grown into a rule of customary international humanitarian law.[72] The dual use problem, that is, the problem that an object may be used for both civilian and military purposes, highlights the need to give additional protection to certain objects.

2. Necessity

Just like the *ius ad bellum*,[73] the *ius in bello* requires that the use of force is a last resort, dictated by necessity. This is the basic reason why, for example, wartime rape has to be illegal under all circumstances.[74] Military necessity does not serve to justify any military action but rather provides a limit to military attacks, in particular to the means and the amount of force that may be employed.[75] No measures may be taken that are not necessary from a military perspective.[76] Art. 35 (2) AP I clarifies that "It is prohibited to employ weapons, projectiles and material and methods of warfare of a nature to cause superfluous injury or unnecessary suffering."

Furthermore, military necessity may not be invoked to justify violations of international humanitarian law.[77] No considerations of military necessity justify direct attacks against civilians or civilian objects.[78] That said, international humanitarian law not only regulates who may participate in an armed conflict or who or what may be targeted but also which weapons may be employed. In the longstanding tradition of the laws of war, weapons have been banned when they were perceived to cause excessive suffering or to violate established ideas of chivalry.[79] Among these weapon-specific conventions are the 1899 Declaration Prohibiting the Launching of Projectiles and Explosives from Balloons;[80] the Declaration Concerning Asphyxiating Gases;[81] the Declaration Concerning Expanding Bullets[82] (commonly referred to as Dum Dum Bullets after the location of the weapons depot in India where they were invented) from the same year; the

1910 Convention Relative to the Laying of Automatic Submarine Contact Mines;[83] the 1925 Protocol for the Prohibition of the Use of Asphyxiating, Poisonous or Other Gases, and of Bacteriological Methods of Warfare;[84] the 1971 Treaty on the Prohibition of the Emplacement of Nuclear Weapons and Other Weapons of Mass Destruction on the Seabed and the Ocean Floor and the Subsoil Thereof;[85] the Agreement on Measures to Reduce the Risk of Outbreak of Nuclear War Between the United States of America and the Union of Soviet Socialist Republics from the same year;[86] the 1972 Convention on the Prohibition of the Development, Production and Stockpiling of Bacteriological (Biological) and Toxin Weapons and Their Destruction;[87] the 1976 ENMOD Convention;[88] the 1980 Convention on Prohibitions or Restrictions on the Use of Certain Conventional Weapons Which May be Deemed to be Excessively Injurious or to Have Indiscriminate Effects[89] as well as its Protocols on Non-Detectable Fragments,[90] on Prohibitions or Restrictions on the Use of Mines, Booby-Traps and Other Devices,[91] and on the Use of Incendiary Weapons[92] as well as the Protocols on Blinding Laser Weapons[93] and on Explosive Remnants of War.[94] Chemical Weapons were prohibited in a 1993 Convention,[95] and in 1997 the Convention on the Prohibition of the Use, Stockpiling, Production and Transfer of Anti-Personnel Mines and on Their Destruction[96] was adopted. Particular attention needs to be given also to the International Court of Justice's 1996 landmark advisory opinion on the legality of the threat or use of nuclear weapons,[97] which still leaves some open questions.[98]

3. Proportionality

In fact, the amount of force used has to be proportionate to the expected benefits of the attack.[99] The idea of proportionality is part of the Christian heritage of the laws of war,[100] just as the idea that war should be just eventually lead to the development of the *ius ad bellum*. Art. 51 (5) lit. b AP I clarifies the concept of proportionality (which will be more familiar to readers from continental European legal systems than to readers from Common Law systems[101]) to the effect that attacks are forbidden if they "may be expected to cause incidental loss of civilian life, injury to civilians, damage to civilian objects, or a combination thereof, which would be excessive in relation to the concrete and direct military advantage anticipated."[102] Furthermore, the attacker has to take the necessary precautions to prevent that an attack becomes disproportionate.[103] If necessary, the proportionality and distinction principles require that an attack, even if it has already been initiated, has to be stopped to prevent excessive harm "in relation to the concrete and direct military advantage anticipated," Art. 57 (2) lit. b AP I.[104]

The principle of proportionality was accepted as a rule of customary international law in *Nicaragua v. United States of America*[105] and is codified in Art. 51 (5) lit. b) and Art. 57 (2) lit. a) (iii) AP I. The *Nicaragua* judgment is a good source to better understand customary international humanitarian law. In addition, this decision is noteworthy for the Court's approach to establishing the existence of customary international law: In *Nicaragua v. United States of America,* the International Court of Justice "found *opinio juris* in verbal statements of governmental representatives to international organizations, in the content of resolutions, declarations and other normative instruments adopted by such organizations, and in the consent of states to such instruments."[106] This approach—reminiscent of the *South West Africa*[107] and *Western Sahara*[108] cases[109] as well as of decisions of national courts[110]—might distract from the necessary focus on state practice, which has to be the point of departure in any search for customary international law.[111] Although certainly well intentioned, this approach might also serve to blur the line between the *lex lata* and the *lex ferenda*, which is particularly unfortunate in the field of international humanitarian law because doing so might cause confusion regarding the obligations on the battlefield. At the same time, that the ICJ has a hard time finding customary international law is understandable, and the underlying causes for this are welcome: Determining rules of customary international humanitarian law is becoming harder because more and more states become parties to treaty law in this field. However, as the number of states that are parties to relevant conventions increases (not only in absolute but, more importantly, in relative terms), there are less states (i.e., states that are not parties to the conventions in question) from which we can make conclusions regarding the state of customary international law.[112] This phenomenon, which is commonly referred to as the Baxter paradox,[113] highlights a problem that by no means is restricted to the international law of war. The reluctance of a few key military powers to ratify all conventions on international humanitarian law, however, means that customary international humanitarian law continues to remain important even as determining its rules becomes more difficult.

The concepts of distinction and proportionality are particularly important in attacks that affect a large number of people, such as aerial attacks.[114] Although AP II does not make an explicit reference to the proportionality requirement,[115] it has grown into a rule of customary international law.[116]

These principles also add to our understanding of the legality of collateral damage. Civilians may not be targeted as such, but they might be accidentally injured: "the immunity of noncombatants from the effects of warfare is not, and has never been regarded as, absolute. Some civilian casualties have always been tolerated as a consequence of military action."[117] Even though such injuries or even deaths have to be prevented as far as possible, international humanitarian law accepts that there is no such thing as a perfectly "clean" war. Nevertheless, the parties to an armed conflict need to aim to minimize the number of civilian casualties. Hugo Grotius wrote that those who participate in an armed conflict "must take care, so far as it is possible, to prevent the death of innocent persons, even by accident."[118] This rule still applies today. Accordingly, participants in an armed conflict with highly accurate weapons systems at their disposal, such as GPS-guided ammunitions, are obligated to use them.[119] Sooner or later, "intelligent" ammunitions, such as laser- or GPS-guided bombs, will be no longer be "a targeting choice but an armed combat requirement of customary international law and, in time, the subject of treaty-made law."[120]

IV. Legitimate and Illegitimate Actors

What has been said so far mainly serves to determine what may be done during an armed conflict and who may be targeted. Similarly important and linked to the question of who may become the object of an attack is the question of who may participate in an armed conflict in the first place. This is important because the laws of war permit a behavior that under normal circumstances would be punishable in practically every society, specifically killing or injuring other humans and destroying property. It is, therefore, necessary to establish clear rules that allow societies to draw a line between criminal conduct and conduct that is permitted because it occurs in an armed conflict. Not only are certain wartime behaviors prohibited as war crimes, international humanitarian law also regulates who is covered by the privilege afforded to legitimate participants in an armed conflict as opposed to peacetime rules of domestic criminal law.

1. Combatants

To be termed combatant means to be entitled to participate in an armed conflict (Art. 43 (2) AP I).[121] If one combatant kills another during an armed conflict, he is—assuming no violation of international humanitarian law occurred—not punishable. Were he to kill the same person in peacetime, however, he would be punished. This combatant privilege is limited in two directions: by limiting what the combatant may legitimately do during an armed conflict (which is the bulk of the issues with which international humanitarian law is concerned) and by limiting who actually is a combatant and may take the actions in question.

2. Unlawful Participants in Armed Conflicts[122]

In general, international humanitarian law differentiates between combatants and civilians. Previously, according to the Lieber Code,[123] no criminal protection was given to fighters who were not part of an official army.[124] Only legitimate combatants may participate in international armed conflicts, though the distinction does not apply in noninternational armed conflicts.[125] But this distinction can at times be difficult to uphold, in particular as the term "unlawful combatant," which has been used frequently during Operation Enduring Freedom, has no basis in international humanitarian law and does not appear in the conventions on international humanitarian law.[126] We can only assume that it refers to persons who participate in an armed conflict without being entitled to do so.

An unlawful participant in an armed conflict cannot be granted POW status and loses many of the protections afforded to civilians, but the preamble of the Martens Clause of 1899, which today has its place in Art. 1 (2) AP II, "intended to establish a legal 'safety net' for [illegal participants in an armed conflict]"[127] It goes on to state that "This Protocol shall not apply to situations of internal disturbances and tensions, such as riots, isolated and sporadic acts of violence and other acts of a similar nature, as not being armed conflicts." However, in the context of the war on terror whether a person captured during the course of operations is a lawful combatant or an unlawful fighter is often unclear. Rather than creating an artificial category such as "unlawful combatants," the law provides for a mechanism to deal with persons of unclear legal status captured on the battlefield:

> 1. A person who takes part in hostilities and falls into the power of an adverse Party shall be presumed to be a prisoner of war, and therefore shall be protected by the Third Convention, if he claims the status of prisoner of war, or if he appears to be entitled to such status, or if the Party on which he depends claims such status on his behalf by notification to the detaining Power or to the Protecting Power. Should any doubt arise as to whether any such person is entitled to the status of prisoner of war, he shall continue to have such status and, therefore, to be protected by the Third Convention and this Protocol until such time as his status has been determined by a competent tribunal. 2. If a person who has fallen into the power of an adverse Party is not held as a prisoner of war and is to be tried by that Party for an offence arising out of the hostilities, he shall have the right to assert his entitlement to prisoner-of-war status before a judicial tribunal and to have that question adjudicated. Whenever possible under the applicable procedure, this adjudication shall occur before the trial for the offence. The representatives of the Protecting Power shall be entitled to attend the proceedings in which that question is adjudicated, unless, exceptionally, the proceedings are held in camera in the interest of State security. In such a case the detaining Power shall advise the Protecting Power accordingly. 3. Any person who has taken part in hostilities, who is not entitled to prisoner-of-war status and who does not benefit from more favourable treatment in accordance with the Fourth Convention shall have the right at all times to the protection of Article 75 of this Protocol. In occupied territory, any such person, unless he is held as a spy, shall also be entitled, notwithstanding Article 5 of the Fourth Convention, to his rights of communication under that Convention. (Art. 45 AP I)

Furthermore, removing one's uniform or fixed distinctive sign, though not a war crime, does deprive the fighter of his legitimacy and, consequently, of the rights afforded to combatants, such as POW status upon capture.[128]

Unlawful fighters are not protected by GC III[129] but only by GC IV, which aims to protect those who are not protected by GC I-III, as is stated in Art. 4 (4) GC IV, in accordance with Art. 5 GC IV:

> Where in the territory of a Party to the conflict, the latter is satisfied that an individual protected

person is definitely suspected of or engaged in activities hostile to the security of the State, such individual person shall not be entitled to claim such rights and privileges under the present Convention as would, if exercised in the favour of such individual person, be prejudicial to the security of such State. Where in occupied territory an individual protected person is detained as a spy or saboteur, or as a person under definite suspicion of activity hostile to the security of the Occupying Power, such person shall, in those cases where absolute military security so requires, be regarded as having forfeited rights of communication under the present Convention. In each case, such persons shall nevertheless be treated with humanity and, in case of trial, shall not be deprived of the rights of fair and regular trial prescribed by the present Convention. They shall also be granted the full rights and privileges of a protected person under the present Convention at the earliest date consistent with the security of the State or Occupying Power, as the case may be.

It has to be taken into account, though, that applying *ratione personae* of GC IV is limited by Art. 4 (2) GC IV, which can exclude some persons who otherwise would be protected: "Nationals of a State which is not bound by the Convention are not protected by it. Nationals of a neutral State who find themselves in the territory of a belligerent State, and nationals of a co-belligerent State, shall not be regarded as protected persons while the State of which they are nationals has normal diplomatic representation in the State in whose hands they are." Moreover, the view that illegal participants in an armed conflict are protected by GC IV is controversial.[130] At the very least, apart from the common Article 3, Art. 75 AP I protects persons who have participated in an armed conflict without (by virtue of Art. 45 (3) AP I) being a legitimate combatant or otherwise permitted to do so. Art. 45 (3) AP I states that[131]

Any person who has taken part in hostilities, who is not entitled to prisoner-of-war status and

who does not benefit from more favourable treatment in accordance with the Fourth Convention shall have the right at all times to the protection of Article 75 of this Protocol. In occupied territory, any such person, unless he is held as a spy, shall also be entitled, notwithstanding Article 5 of the Fourth Convention, to his rights of communication under that Convention.

But the words "and who does not benefit from more favourable treatment in accordance with the Fourth Convention" indicate that illegal fighters "are protected persons under GC IV if they fulfil the above-mentioned nationality criteria"[132] of Art. 4 GC IV[133] but are still subject to derogations[134] in accordance with Art. 5 GC IV.

In any case, Art. 3 GC I-IV applies. This article, which is usually referred to as the "common Art. 3," is often thought to provide an absolute minimum standard. In the case of armed conflict not of an international character occurring in the territory of one of the High Contracting Parties, each Party to the conflict shall be bound to apply, as a minimum, the provisions included in this article:

Persons taking no active part in the hostilities, including members of armed forces who have laid down their arms and those placed hors de combat by sickness, wounds, detention, or any other cause, shall in all circumstances be treated humanely, without any adverse distinction founded on race, colour, religion or faith, sex, birth or wealth, or any other similar criteria. To this end the following acts are and shall remain prohibited at any time and in any place whatsoever with respect to the above-mentioned persons: (a) violence to life and person, in particular murder of all kinds, mutilation, cruel treatment and torture; (b) taking of hostages; (c) outrages upon personal dignity, in particular humiliating and degrading treatment; (d) the passing of sentences and the carrying out of executions without previous judgment pronounced by a regularly constituted court, affording all the judicial guarantees which are recognized as indispensable by civilized peoples. (2) The wounded and sick shall be collected and cared for. An impartial humanitarian body, such as the International Committee of the Red Cross, may offer its services to the Parties to the conflict. The Parties to the conflict should further endeavour to bring into force, by means of special agreements, all or part of the other provisions of the present Convention. The application of the preceding provisions shall not affect the legal status of the Parties to the conflict.

However, whether this article applies to resistance fighters, terrorists, or freedom fighters is not immediately clear. This is not surprising as states are the ones that drafted the Conventions (prior to decolonialization), and they have little interest in legally strengthening nonstate actors who might take up arms against them. Also in the Additional Protocols, "the states responsible for the final text made sure they left themselves a bit of leeway."[135] Fortunately, the ICTY's decision in *Delalic* now provides us with a precedent to the effect that a minimum of organization[136] is sufficient for nonstate forces to be recognized. *Delalic*, also referred to as the *Celebici* case, which dealt with the conduct of nonstate forces in the former Yugoslavia—although it is technically speaking not binding on other courts and tribunals—will remain significant as it provides a clear statement on the *lex lata* by a competent judicial authority. Despite some uncertainties, key parts of the Conventions are sufficiently clear, making it even harder to ignore *Delalic* in the future, which established today's wider understanding of the applicability of the laws of war to nonstate actors.[137]

Through the planned closing of the detention facilities at Guantánamo Bay Naval Station (Cuba), the United States will force itself to release the detainees or to opt for either criminal proceedings (with all procedural rights due under U.S. law) or POW status for the detainees, thereby potentially adding to the customary law rights of detained foreign fighters who are not afforded POW rights.

3. Partisans

Partisans have an official role in international humanitarian law due to Art. 4A (2) GC III, which states,

> Members of other militias and members of other volunteer corps, including those of organized resistance movements, belonging to a Party to the conflict and operating in or outside their own territory, even if this territory is occupied [upon capture become prisoners of war], provided that such militias or volunteer corps, including such organized resistance movements, fulfil the following conditions: (a) that of being commanded by a person responsible for his subordinates; (b) that of having a fixed distinctive sign recognizable at a distance; (c) that of carrying arms openly; (d) that of conducting their operations in accordance with the laws and customs of war.

Thus, armed resistance by locals who defend their homeland against invasion by a hostile force is privileged in that the requirements of organization placed upon an armed force are relaxed compared to state-run armies. What's more, this article allows civilians to play a role in defending their homeland while it also protects all participants in an armed conflict, though especially those civilians who do not take up arms. However, the article does require that civilians who take up arms to be distinguishable from the rest of the civilian population, who continues to benefit from the full protection afforded to civilians.

4. Guerilla Fighters

Although partisans played a particular role in occupied areas during World War II, since then guerilla fighters has taken an important role on the stage of combat. The term guerilla literally means "little wars," and these wars are fought by irregular fighters—that is, usually not members of a state's armed force—against a technologically and militarily superior adversary by resorting to unusual means such as not wearing a uniform, blending in with the civilian population, surprise attacks, and so forth. In particular, the conflicts in Southeast Asia, including the U.S. experience with guerilla warfare in the Vietnam War, led to many discussions when the Additional Protocols to the Geneva Conventions were being drafted or up for ratification. Specifically, this issue received a lot of attention during the Geneva Conference of 1974 until 1977,[138] and its development was reflected in Article 44 AP II:

1. Any combatant, as defined in Article 43, who falls into the power of an adverse Party shall be a prisoner of war. 2. While all combatants are obliged to comply with the rules of international law applicable in armed conflict, violations of these rules shall not deprive a combatant of his right to be a combatant or, if he falls into the power of an adverse Party, of his right to be a prisoner of war, except as provided in paragraphs 3 and 4. 3. In order to promote the protection of the civilian population from the effects of hostilities, combatants are obliged to distinguish themselves from the civilian population while they are engaged in an attack or in a military operation preparatory to an attack. Recognizing, however, that there are situations in armed conflicts where, owing to the nature of the hostilities an armed combatant cannot so distinguish himself, he shall retain his status as a combatant, provided that, in such situations, he carries his arms openly: (a) during each military engagement, and (b) during such time as he is visible to the adversary while he is engaged in a military deployment preceding the launching of an attack in which he is to participate. Acts which comply with the requirements of this paragraph shall not be considered as perfidious within the meaning of Article 37, paragraph 1 (c). 4. A combatant who falls into the power of an adverse Party while failing to meet the requirements set forth in the second sentence of paragraph 3 shall forfeit his right to be a prisoner of war, but he shall, nevertheless, be given protections equivalent in all respects to those accorded to prisoners of war by the Third Convention and by this Protocol. This protection

includes protections equivalent to those accorded to prisoners of war by the Third Convention in the case where such a person is tried and punished for any offences he has committed. 5. Any combatant who falls into the power of an adverse Party while not engaged in an attack or in a military operation preparatory to an attack shall not forfeit his rights to be a combatant and a prisoner of war by virtue of his prior activities. 6. This Article is without prejudice to the right of any person to be a prisoner of war pursuant to Article 4 of the Third Convention. 7. This Article is not intended to change the generally accepted practice of States with respect to the wearing of the uniform by combatants assigned to the regular, uniformed armed units of a Party to the conflict. 8. In addition to the categories of persons mentioned in Article 13 of the First and Second Conventions, all members of the armed forces of a Party to the conflict, as defined in Article 43 of this Protocol, shall be entitled to protection under those Conventions if they are wounded or sick or, in the case of the Second Convention, shipwrecked at sea or in other waters.

5. *Levée en Masse*

Another notable exception to the fundamental distinction between combatants and civilians is the *levée en masse*, which entered a codified form in Art. 2 Hague Regulations War on Land, although the concept is much older. A *levée en masse* is said to occur when the population is called to take up arms to dispel an enemy attack on the homeland while lacking the time to organize properly in the manner described in the norms cited above.[139] Civilians who participate in an armed conflict in this manner are considered to be combatants "so long as they carry their arms openly and comply with the laws and customs of war."[140]

The criterion to carry arms openly is, like the fixed distinctive sign required for militias by Art. 4 (1) (ii) GC III, simply another way to ensure that civilians and combatants can be distinguished. The moment a fighter who participates in a *levée en masse* hides his weapon, he is no longer protected, either as a combatant or as a civilian.

The privilege afforded to the participants in a *levée en masse*, who are essentially drafted into armed service by the governments, does not apply to those members of the civilian population who take up arms *after* their homeland has already been occupied.[141] In addition, non-governmental troops who are not sufficiently organized to meet the criteria established for resistance forces "are regarded as marauders or bandits and may be tried as such if captured by the adverse party."[142] This legal situation is summed up in Art. 1 and 2 of the 1907 Hague Regulations respecting the Laws and Customs of War on Land:

> Art. 1. The laws, rights, and duties of war apply not only to armies, but also to militia and volunteer corps fulfilling the following conditions: 1. To be commanded by a person responsible for his subordinates; 2. To have a fixed distinctive emblem recognizable at a distance; 3. To carry arms openly; and 4. To conduct their operations in accordance with the laws and customs of war. In countries where militia or volunteer corps constitute the army, or form part of it, they are included under the denomination "army." Art. 2. The inhabitants of a territory which has not been occupied, who, on the approach of the enemy, spontaneously take up arms to resist the invading troops without having had time to organize themselves in accordance with Article 1, shall be regarded as belligerents if they carry arms openly and if they respect the laws and customs of war.

6. Mercenaries

Mercenaries, similar to spies,[143] have also traditionally been looked down upon as the outcasts of the law of war. Most important, Art. 47 (1) AP I prevents mercenaries from becoming prisoners of war if they are captured. This view has its roots in what is perceived as a lack of loyalty to a state. In international laws of war, the connection to one's state makes the moral difference between murder and killing in combat, but it is exactly

this connection that is lacking if a participant in an armed conflict does so for material gain rather than out of loyalty to one's nation. Mercenaries are by no means a phenomenon of the past. Rather, the conflicts in Africa in the 1960s[144] and the conflicts in the former Yugoslavia in the 1990s saw a significant influx of foreign mercenaries. According to Article 47 (2) AP I,

> A mercenary is any person who: (a) is specially recruited locally or abroad in order to fight in an armed conflict; (b) does, in fact, take a direct part in the hostilities; (c) is motivated to take part in the hostilities essentially by the desire for private gain and, in fact, is promised, by or on behalf of a Party to the conflict, material compensation substantially in excess of that promised or paid to combatants of similar ranks and functions in the armed forces of that Party; (d) is neither a national of a Party to the conflict nor a resident of territory controlled by a Party to the conflict; (e) is not a member of the armed forces of a Party to the conflict; and (f) has not been sent by a State which is not a Party to the conflict on official duty as a member of its armed forces.

The problem of mercenaries has received renewed attention, when, after 9/11, the United States relied heavily on private contractors to take over security roles in Afghanistan and Iraq.

7. Human Shields and Hiding in the Civilian Population

Blending in with the civilian population is a common tactic of guerilla warfare, which raises a number of legal issues. These issues have, at times, been exploited by participants in an armed conflict, in particular in asymmetric conflicts. It already follows from the prohibition of attacks against civilians that it is illegal to abuse civilians as human shields.

V. Rules for Civil Wars

Originally, international humanitarian law only applied to wars between states[145]—a fact that is still evident in Art. 2 GC I-IV, which does not require a declaration of war but simply that the conflict is a factual situation between states that are parties to the Conventions.[146] For domestic political reasons, then, governments will at times refrain from using the term "war" to describe an armed conflict in which their troops are engaged. This does not, however, affect the applicability of the laws of war because an armed conflict within the definition of the Geneva Conventions includes any difference between states.[147] As a matter of fact, "Contrary to popular belief, most conflicts did not start with a declaration of war even in the [eighteenth] and [nineteenth] centuries."[148] In fact, "[a] report prepared in 1883 for a Board of Trade committee examining the defence implications of a Channel Tunnel [between Britain and France] stated that out of 117 conflicts between 1700 and 1870, only 10 had begun with a declaration of war."[149] This is codified in Art. 2 GC I-IV:

> In addition to the provisions which shall be implemented in peace-time, the present Convention shall apply to all cases of declared war or of any other armed conflict which may arise between two or more of the High Contracting Parties, even if the state of war is not recognized by one of them. The Convention shall also apply to all cases of partial or total occupation of the territory of a High Contracting Party, even if the said occupation meets with no armed resistance. Although one of the Powers in conflict may not be a party to the present Convention, the Powers who are parties thereto shall remain bound by it in their mutual relations. They shall furthermore be bound by the Convention in relation to the said Power, if the latter accepts and applies the provisions thereof.

In principle, then, the laws of war have been developed with interstate conflicts, rather than with domestic conflicts, in mind. In fact, states have traditionally resisted the idea of regulating noninternational armed conflicts[150] and these states continue to be the key players on the international legal stage. This resistance was due

to their desire to not have others intervene in the internal affairs of states,[151] which has long been a principle of public international law and has been codified in Art. 2 (7) of the Charter of the United Nations. Since the creation of the UN Charter, however, this principle has been weakened significantly due to the increasing importance of international human rights law, which grew in reaction to the horrors of World War II and of the Shoa. Accordingly, human rights have become a foreign policy concern since 1945, culminating (from a legal perspective[152]) in the adoption not only of international human rights documents but also of AP II in 1977. It needs to be noted, though, that the principle of nonintervention continues to play an important role even in cases in which AP II applies: The fact that a nonstate actor has, by virtue of AP II, certain rights in its conflict with a state, the sovereignty of the state is not diminished by the rights of their nonstate opponents.[153] In fact, this state has the right to defend its national integrity,[154] and it is generally accepted that the right to self-determination does not automatically lead to a right to secede.

Furthermore, the emphasis on the sovereignty of the state reflects the customary law prohibiting recognizing prematurely the independence of a part of a state.[155] On a more fundamental level, the fact that nonstate groups can have rights under AP II though not necessarily being entitled, for example, to secede, is a reminder of the basic rule of the *ius in bello*—that is, its applicability to the parties of a conflict regardless of the legality of their actions under the *ius ad bello*.

AP II was the "first major attempt to introduce international legal control of non-international legal control of non-international conflicts by way of a statement of black-letter law."[156] Noninternational armed conflicts within the meaning of AP II do not include those domestic conflicts that are covered by Art. 1 AP I—that is, armed conflicts conducted in the name of self-determination. Such conflicts, as well as those noninternational armed conflicts that are covered under AP II, are often characterized in large part by ideologies, as is also the case in the global war on terror. At the same time, the persons involved are less likely to be trained in the laws of war. Both factors can contribute to a higher probability that international humanitarian law will be violated. Article 3, which is common to all four Geneva Conventions, extends the protection of international humanitarian law to noninternational armed conflicts and provides for a minimum set of rules to be applied in any case.[157]

Common Art. 3 is intended to apply also to domestic armed groups.[158] Unlike in other conventions, Art. 3 GC I-IV also applies even if the nonstate actors have not made a declaration to that effect.[159] In that sense, common Art. 3 truly provides a globally applicable minimum standard of protection in an armed conflict. Despite that,

> There is no provision in Article 3 concerning breaches or enforcement. Further, Art. 85 [AP I] does not include Article [3] as one the noncompliance with which would amount to a grave breach [of the laws of war, that is, a violation of international humanitarian law, which is particularly severe]. However, since the Conventions are binding, and have been held by the [ICTY] to amount to customary law[160] and since common Article 3 forbids a variety of activities, it may be presumed that it is the intention to ensure that its provisions are in fact observed. It may be possible to argue, therefore, that breach of any of the provisions of this Article, all of which are humanitarian in character, are enforceable in the same manner as are other breaches, even though they do not qualify as grave.[161]

In practice, however, the existing law needs to be developed further to help it adapt better to the realities of noninternational armed conflicts,[162] and like many other international humanitarian law rules, these rules are violated during armed conflicts.[163] The fact that knowledge of the laws of war is often not disseminated among the fighters of such nonstate groups, whereas states are obligated to disseminate knowledge of international humanitarian law and secure their enforcement domestically, increases the risk that armed forces that are not part of the regular forces of a state will violate the laws of war.

VI. Enforcing International Humanitarian Law[164]

If states fail to enforce international humanitarian law, or if those who have violated the laws of war[165] do not answer to a state and their military commanders fail to ensure compliance with international humanitarian law, then the problem of how to enforce the laws of war arises. Enforcement is already a problematic issue in a legal system as archaic as the current public international law, which lacks relative strength as well as generally accepted organs that could enforce the law against all states—a task the UN Security Council is not up to addressing due to the veto powers of its five permanent members. Furthermore, the (short-term) military gain that could be achieved by violating international humanitarian law contributes to the risk of violating the law,[166] and this is one of the reasons why enforcement, not the need for new rules, is the most important problem facing the contemporary law of armed conflict.[167]

Unlike in other fields of law, enforcing international humanitarian law is not restricted to one specific method or manner of enforcement; rather, it relies on a multitude of enforcement opportunities,[168] the most noticeable, of course, being the use of courts and tribunals on an international as well as on a national level in order to assign individual criminal responsibility for violations of the laws of war and to punish individual perpetrators rather than merely the abstract entity of the state. Without delving too far into the field of international criminal law, which has evolved into a self-contained regime within the overall context of public international law, we can differentiate between two types of enforcement mechanisms. However, the distinction will—as is often the case in international humanitarian law—not always be as clear as one would want it to be for such a field of law dealing literally with issues of life and death. This basic distinction separates measures to be taken in times of war from those to be taken in times of peace.[169] The fact that international tribunals might start their work during the course of an ongoing conflict indicates that this distinction has its limits. It becomes clearer, though, when we start to distinguish between enforcement mechanisms that are directed against individuals on one hand and those that are directed against parties to a conflict as such on the other. Although criminal law aims at the individual soldier, commander, or decision maker, classical enforcement actions aim at the other party to a conflict, classically but now more rarely: another state. These classical enforcement mechanisms are more usefully separated in terms of wartime and peacetime measures.

1. Retorsions

Retorsions are the peaceful and lawful but unfriendly response by one state toward another state in reaction to an unfriendly act committed by that state, such as expelling diplomats. In an armed conflict between two states, retorsions will most likely be not effective enough to provide an adequate reaction by a state to the breach of the laws of war by the adversary because they are *per se* limited to measures that have to be peaceful and that were lawful in any case, thus limiting the damage that can be inflicted on the adversary by means of retorsions.

2. Reprisals

A reprisal is the action by one state against another in retaliation for a violation of international law by the latter that otherwise would be illegal. According to the Friendly Relations Declaration,[170] however, armed reprisals are illegal under customary international law.[171] In addition, no party to an armed conflict is allowed to violate international humanitarian law in response to the other state's violation of international humanitarian law. Reprisals, therefore, are

not a permitted means of enforcing rights under the international law of war. Armed reprisals are not permitted because they do not comply with the *ius ad bellum* nor with the *ius in bello*,[172] which renders traditional interstate mechanisms for the bilateral enforcement of international legal claims practically useless when it comes to international humanitarian law.

3. Other Means of Enforcement

Other means of enforcement, apart from recourse to the UN Security Council, are the important roles played by the public conscience (Art. 1 (2) AP I), the protective powers (Art. 8 GC I-III and Art. 9 GC IV), and the International Fact Finding Commission. The Fact Finding Commission,[173] which was established in 1991 under Art. 90 AP I, has so far not lived up to international community's expectations with regard to the norm.

4. Compensation

The issue of compensation for violating the laws of war remains unsatisfactory. Although more than a century ago, Art. 3 HC IV demanded the violator state pay some compensation to the victim state, in practice, states have neither demanded nor given compensation, which raises the question of whether this article has fallen victim to *desuetudo*. In recent years, however, some *ex gratia* payments have been made to individual victims. For example, U.S. forces have offered compensation in Iraq and Afghanistan, and the UN Security Council established a Claims Commission (UNCC)[174] in the context of the Iraqi occupation of Kuwait,[175] though the *lex lata* still leaves much to be desired.

5. International Criminal Law

The most effective way to enforce the laws of war is through international criminal law, which relies on the responsibility of the individual perpetrator rather than on apportioning blame to the state. This has the benefit of achieving publicity and, thus, a deterrent effect on individuals, though the fact that many perpetrators go unpunished seriously threatens the latter. By now international criminal law, although it is still very closely related to international humanitarian law, has evolved into a legal regime of its own—an extensive treatment of which would go beyond the limitations of this chapter.[176]

B. Terrorism as a Challenge to International Humanitarian Law[177]

Asymmetrical warfare is warfare between fundamentally differently equipped opponents, in which the party to the conflict that is lacking in military capacity resorts to nontraditional methods that often are at odds with the laws of war. Chief among those methods are hiding in civilian populations as well as targeting civilians or resorting to perfidy. The fight against high-level international terrorism is currently the key example of asymmetrical warfare,[178] and although interstate wars are not completely out of the picture (as has been evidenced in recent years by the wars between the United States and Iraq, Russia and Georgia, or Ethiopia and Eritrea), noninternational conflicts are more important practically than international wars in a classic sense. Such noninternational conflicts, however, will often see an insurgent force pitted against militarily much better-equipped and -trained government forces. This imbalance provides an incentive for nonstate forces to resort to asymmetrical methods, which in turn increases the risk that government forces will, in turn, also violate the laws of war in retaliation.[179] In particular, the ongoing fight against terrorism as well as the continued terrorism—for example, by Hamas and Hezbollah against Israel—the effects of which are akin to the effects of war, make it necessary to look more closely at terrorism from the perspective of international humanitarian law.

I. General Principles

One scholar has noted that "The intentional use of terror violence for strategic purposes has long been considered by many authors to be prohibited by the customary law of war"[180] as well as a

violation of Art. 33 GC IV,[181] Art. 48 AP I[182] and even a crime against humanity[183] or, if committed during an armed conflict, a war crime.[184] We need to differentiate according to the circumstances in which a terrorist act occurs, whether in peacetime or in wartime, and if it occurs during an armed conflict and whether or not it occurs in the theater of operations.[185] Terrorist acts against civilians in times of war and in the theater of operations are usually war crimes punishable under both domestic and international law, whereas other terrorist acts are punishable under domestic law. From an international criminal law perspective, however, unlike in Nürnberg (Art. 6 of the Charter of the International Military Tribunal),[186] "crimes against humanity no longer need a nexus to . . . war,"[187] and this is due to Art. 7 of the Rome-Statute.[188]

II. Terrorism as a Challenge to Contemporary International Humanitarian Law

But this is not all there is to terrorism in the context of international humanitarian law.[189] Terrorist acts not only raise the question of what rules are violated, which already is a key issue in itself because terrorism has many facets,[190] but the use of terrorism for strategic purposes also provides a new challenge to the laws of war. Unlike earlier challenges, such as the development of new weapons, which could be dealt with through a regulatory approach, terrorism touches the core of the idea of the laws of war and raises more fundamental questions.

As we have seen earlier, civilians who take up arms lose the protection afforded to them under international humanitarian law without, some exceptions aside, becoming legitimate combatants. The same applies to terrorists. Terrorists are former civilians who have lost the protections afforded to them under the laws of war.

Although an attempt to include terrorism in the Rome Statute establishing the International Criminal Court failed,[191] terrorist acts are crimes that are punishable at least by domestic and often also under international law[192] and that might even amount to crimes against humanity.[193] Despite the fact that terrorist acts directed against the civilian population are prohibited by both treaty and customary law as being violations of international humanitarian law, states engaged in fighting terrorism have not given international humanitarian law much attention as a tool for fighting terrorism.[194] To the contrary, the laws of war are instead seen as an obstacle to counter-terrorism operations involving the armed forces.[195] This is unfortunate because if states fighting terrorists rely on military means and thereby de facto give terrorists a certain degree of standing as military adversaries rather than as mere criminals, then the illegality of terrorist acts is at risk of being obscured. Nevertheless, terrorist attacks against civilians are fundamentally criminal in nature.

III. Terrorist Attacks Against Civilians

Terrorist attacks against civilians violate the most fundamental rule of the laws of war: the prohibition of attacks against civilians. However, we must remember that an attack directed against a legitimate military target that happens to claim civilian casualties is not illegal per se,[196] although of course those who employ armed force are obliged to take measures to limit the number of civilian casualties under the principles of necessity and proportionality.[197] Furthermore, international humanitarian law does not prohibit all terrorist acts.[198] For example, terrorist attacks that only target legitimate military installations might not necessarily violate the laws of war.[199] Nevertheless, international humanitarian law is very clear in condemning terrorist attacks against civilians.[200]

Attacks on civilians and civilian objects are expressly prohibited under Art. 51 (2) and Art. 52 AP I as well as under Art. 13 AP II:[201]

1. The civilian population and individual civilians shall enjoy general protection against the dangers arising from military operations. To give effect to this protection, the following rules shall be observed in all circumstances. 2. The civilian population as such, as well as individual civilians, shall not be the object of attack. Acts or threats of violence the primary purpose of which is to spread terror among the civilian population are prohibited. 3. Civilians shall enjoy the protection afforded by this part, unless and for such time as they take a direct part in hostilities.

More specific rules that are likely to be violated in a terrorist attack include the common Art. 3 GC I-IV, Art. 53 AP I, Art. 16 AP II, Art. 56 AP I, Art. 15 AP II, Art. 75 AP I, Art. 4 (2) AP II, and Art. 37 AP I.[202] Particularly noteworthy is Art. 33 GC IV that prohibits collective punishments: "No protected person may be punished for an offence he or she has not personally committed. Collective penalties and likewise all measures of intimidation or of terrorism are prohibited. Pillage is prohibited. Reprisals against protected persons and their property are prohibited." This rule had already been included in Art. 50 of the 1907 Hague Regulations and is a norm of customary international law.[203] In addition, Art. 51 (2) AP I and the identical Art. 13 (2) AP II state that "The civilian population as such, as well as individual civilians, shall not be the object of attack. Acts or threats of violence the primary purpose of which is to spread terror among the civilian population are prohibited."

Art. 51 (2) AP I and Art. 13 (2) AP II specifically prohibit acts of terrorism "within the general customary prohibition of attack[s] on civilians."[204] Given that the laws of war were initially developed for international armed conflicts, Art. 33 GC IV, Art. 51 (2) AP I, and Art. 13 (2) AP II "are more likely to be applicable to acts of terrorism committed by the armed forces of States than by non-state actors."[205] Attacks by nonstate actors can fall under Art. 33 GC IV, Art. 51 (2) AP I, and Art. 13 (2) AP II—for example, in the case of an armed liberation movement that has accepted the applicability of said rules.[206] In addition, under Art. 1 (1) AP II, the groups in question would need a certain degree of organization because they would need a responsible command, and they are also required to exercise control over a certain territory of the state against which they fight.[207] This requirement indicates that the liberation and decolonialization struggles of the decades since the creation of the Geneva Conventions very much influenced the drafting of the Additional Protocols. Furthermore, such groups, required to carry out sustained and concerted military attacks, are to be given their desired recognition.[208] As is also the case with the applicability of the laws of war as a whole, according to Art. 1 (2) AP II, isolated incidents such as unrests, riots, or sporadic attacks are insufficient to trigger the applicability of AP II.[209] The latter limitation, however, has to be taken with more than a grain of salt. Take into account, for example, the frequent border skirmishes between India and Pakistan over control in Kashmir. Trading shots across the border might not yet trigger an actual war, but that does not mean that the prohibition against targeting civilians and the prohibition of perfidy do not apply in such circumstances. It has to be kept in mind that international humanitarian law applies to the first shot fired in an armed conflict.[210] In addition, in such cases it will often be impossible for the authorities of the targeted state to prosecute the shooter, who is abroad and usually inaccessible for prosecution, although individual criminal responsibility under the domestic law of the targeted state would be the logical consequence if one were to deny the applicability of the laws of war to border skirmishes.

Finally, the group in question has to implement AP II.[211] Although the requirements of AP II are met more easily than those of AP I or of GC I–IV,[212] it seems that few terrorist groups will be able to meet these criteria. Certainly this is the case with the Fuerzas Armadas Revolucionarios de Colombia (FARC) and once was the case with the Liberation Tigers of Tamil Eelam (LTTE) during the war in Sri Lanka, though it is not the case with al-Qaeda. This in turn means that the existing customary law rule prohibiting attacks against civilians continues to play a major role in assessing the legality of terrorist organizations' activities. Art. 4 AP II is of concern here because it guarantees that

1. All persons who do not take a direct part or who have ceased to take part in hostilities, whether or not their liberty has been restricted, are entitled to respect for their person, honour and convictions and religious practices. They shall in all circumstances be treated humanely, without any adverse distinction. It is prohibited to order that there shall be no survivors. 2. Without prejudice to the generality of the foregoing, the following acts against the persons referred to in paragraph I are and shall remain prohibited at any time and in any place whatsoever: (a) violence to the life, health and physical or mental well-being of persons, in particular murder as well as cruel treatment such as torture, mutilation or any form of corporal punishment; (b) collective punishments; (c) taking of hostages; (d) acts of terrorism; (e) outrages upon personal dignity, in particular humiliating and degrading treatment, rape, enforced prostitution and any form or indecent assault; (f) slavery and the slave trade in all their forms; (g) pillage; (h) threats to commit any of the foregoing acts. 3. Children shall be provided with the care and aid they require, and in particular: (a) they shall receive an education, including religious and moral education, in keeping with the wishes of their parents, or in the absence of parents, of those responsible for their care; (b) all appropriate steps shall be taken to facilitate the reunion of families temporarily separated; (c) children who have not attained the age of fifteen years shall neither be recruited in the armed forces or groups nor allowed to take part in hostilities; (d) the special protection provided by this Article to children who have not attained the age of fifteen years shall remain applicable to them if they take a direct part in hostilities despite the provisions of subparagraph (c) and are captured; (e) measures shall be taken, if necessary, and whenever possible with the consent of their parents or persons who by law or custom are primarily responsible for their care, to remove children temporarily from the

area in which hostilities are taking place to a safer area within the country and ensure that they are accompanied by persons responsible for their safety and well-being.

IV. "Enemy Combatants"?
The Legal Status of Terrorists Under International Humanitarian Law

Terrorists are not combatants and, therefore, do not enjoy the protections of international humanitarian law. However, members of armed forces, even of nonstate forces such as the FARC or the LTTE, can enjoy the benefits given to combatants under international humanitarian law, provided they fulfill the necessary requirements such as wearing a uniform or distinctive symbol and carry their weapons openly. Upon capture, terrorists, therefore, do not need to be treated as prisoners of war but can be brought to trial as criminals. This differentiation is key for understanding the nature of the laws of war. If one were to travel to another country in peacetime and were to kill somebody there, one would, of course, be put on trial. If one does so in the course of an armed conflict in one's role as a soldier in the regular forces of one's home state, then international humanitarian law and international criminal law privileges the soldier because the taking of a human life under these circumstances is not punishable unless certain requirements are met, such as the membership of the killed person in a protected group or other violations of the laws of war. International humanitarian law does not operate like "normal"—that is to say, peacetime—laws because it is *lex specialis* to international human rights law,[213] which of course prohibits the taking of human lives in principle.

As a general rule, people who participate in an armed conflict without being legitimized to do so can be punished for merely participating in the armed conflict, even if they do not violate the laws of war.[214] In addition, if they violate the laws of war, for example, by deliberately attacking civilians, they can be punished for war crimes.[215]

V. Targeted Killings

After 9/11 much attention has been given to the issue of so-called targeted killings of terrorists. In particular, the United States and Israel have explicitly targeted high-ranking terrorists. As we have seen earlier, illegitimate fighters are per se less protected than civilians or combatants, and terrorists can be prosecuted as criminals. The question that arises in the context of targeted killings is whether terrorists can be killed as illegal fighters or if they need to be tried before a court. The answer to this question depends on the context. In peacetime, they will have to be afforded the usual fair trial rights; in the context of an armed conflict, however, they may be treated as illegal fighters (provided that the state in question has derogated from the relevant international conventions[216]).

Acts of terrorism aimed at the civilian population are violations of the laws of war or—if international humanitarian law does not apply because there has not been an armed conflict and provided the terrorist act in itself does not trigger the applicability of the laws of war (which is the more likely scenario)—are subject to the provisions of criminal law, in particular the domestic criminal law of the country in which the terrorist act took place. Even if committed in a context in which international humanitarian law applies, the terrorist, who until the moment he started his attack was to be considered a civilian, has forfeited the protections afforded to civilians under international humanitarian law. He is, therefore, no longer immune from attack.

Furthermore, if criminal law applies, targeted killings are not permissible because the suspect of a crime has to be given a certain minimum standard of human rights, such as the presumption of innocence, the right to an attorney, and so forth. In most countries, these human rights flow from both domestic law and international human rights obligations.

If the terrorist act occurs during an armed conflict, for example, between Israel and Hamas or Israel and Hezbollah, the terrorist who has abandoned the protection of the laws of war has become a legitimate target. He who has not become a combatant who would be entitled to participate in an armed conflict has become an unlawful fighter. The term "unlawful combatant" is very unfortunate in this context because it implies that a terrorist is a legitimate combatant who merely happened to violate some rules, which is not the case. A terrorist is not a combatant but rather a mere criminal. In peacetime his place is in a courtroom, and during an armed conflict he has become a valid target.

The question, therefore, is whether an armed conflict exists or not. In the case of the United States and al-Qaeda operators located in Pakistan, this is at times uncertain, whereas the conflict between Western forces and the Taliban in Afghanistan amounts to an armed conflict. More specifically, it is a noninternational armed conflict (noninternational because, since the fall of the Taliban, the United States and their allies no longer fight against the government of Afghanistan) in which foreign forces from the United States, the United Kingdom, Germany, Canada, and other countries support Afghan forces in the fight against an armed group (the Taliban) that challenges the authority of the Karzai government in Kabul. Al-Qaeda operatives who are active in the context of this armed conflict between the Taliban and the Afghan government are unlawful fighters who do not enjoy combatant status. On the other side of the border, however, it becomes much less clear whether it should be considered an armed conflict between al-Qaeda or the Pakistani Taliban and the United States. Of course, the border between Afghanistan and Pakistan is highly porous, difficult to monitor, and dominated by a predominantly Pashtun population on both sides of the border.

When compared to Israel's targeted killings of Hamas or Hezbollah terrorists—killings that are permitted due to the state or armed conflict that de facto exists there and that is evidenced by frequent terrorist attacks and counter-terrorism operations—the legality of U.S. air strikes in Pakistan, which often lead to civilian victims as well, stands on a much less solid legal basis.

This conclusion cannot be satisfactory for the United States, but the war on terror poses challenges that might prove to be an incentive for the United States to get more involved with developing the international laws of war.

VI. Extraordinary Rendition

Among the different responses to international terrorism, extraordinary renditions are among the more controversial.[217] "Rendition is the transfer of an individual outside the jurisdiction. It is a generic term used to describe transfers for various purposes, such as to face justice in another state."[218] The regular rendition from one state to another is commonly referred to as extradition. Extraordinary rendition, however, refers to renditions "in circumstances that make it more likely than not that the individual [who is extradited] be subjected to torture or cruel, inhuman or degrading treatment."[219] The key difference between extraordinary and ordinary renditions is the lack of legal procedures.[220] Extraordinary renditions not only raise concerns regarding human rights but also of international humanitarian law.

The extradition of prisoners of war who are suspected of war crimes is permitted under Art. 45 GC IV if it occurs in pursuance of extradition treaties. Other prisoners of war can only be transferred under the conditions set by Art. 12 (2) GC III:

> Prisoners of war may only be transferred by the Detaining Power to a Power which is a party to the Convention and after the Detaining Power has satisfied itself of the willingness and ability of such transferee Power to apply the Convention. When prisoners of war are transferred under such circumstances, responsibility for the application of the Convention rests on the Power accepting them while they are in its custody.

Because, as we have seen earlier, many suspected terrorists will not be afforded POW status, Art. 31 GC IV will often have to be taken into account as well: "No physical or moral coercion shall be exercised against protected persons, in particular to obtain information from them or from third parties." This provision severely limits the possibilities of states concerning extraditions. In particular extraditions to states in which a suspect is likely to be tortured to obtain information are prohibited by Art. 31 GC IV. In addition, Art. 49 GC IV clearly forbids forced transfers: "Individual or mass forcible transfers, as well as deportations of protected persons from occupied territory to the territory of the Occupying Power or to that of any other country, occupied or not, are prohibited, regardless of their motive." Despite this article's wording, the norm has to be interpreted restrictively due to the historic context based on which it was created, specifically the mass deportations under the Nazi regime and during World War II.[221] Therefore, extraordinary renditions for the purpose of torture are prohibited, whereas other transfers may be permitted depending on the circumstances of the case.

C. The Privatization of War: Private Military and Security Companies (PMSCs)[222]

The privatization of war and the growing importance of PMSCs raise issues beyond those already discussed earlier regarding mercenaries. Like other states, states in which PMSCs are incorporated, states in which they operate, and states in which the citizens work for PMSCs have an obligation to disseminate knowledge of the laws of war. This obligation contrasts with a particular reluctance on the part of states that are incorporated to monitor PMSC behavior,[223] though it already follows from Art. 47 GC I, Art. 48 GC II, Art. 127 GC III, Art. 144 GC IV, and other conventions.[224]

D. Cyberwar[225]

Recent conflicts, for example in East Asia,[226] the Middle East[227] or Georgia,[228] have seen methods of cyberwarfare used either separately or in anticipation of or during an armed conflict. In an armed conflict, it is irrelevant under international humanitarian law, whether damage is done by a bomb or by a computer virus. The potential damage done through cyberwarfare, which can include serious damage to infrastructure such as the electricity grid, is in its severity already comparable to the use of armed force. If methods of cyberwar are applied during an armed conflict, their employment is subject to the limitations of the laws of war. But it is still unclear whether a cyberattack is sufficient to trigger the application of international humanitarian law in the first place. If the act triggering an armed conflict amounts to a war crime, it is already punishable as such. Furthermore, cyberattacks can amount to war crimes if all necessary requirements are met. Therefore, one might conclude that cyberattacks can trigger the applicability of the laws of war; however, this is not the case because Art. 2 (1) GC I, which insofar codifies the existing customary law, requires an armed conflict to exist beforehand. Thus, this situation is less than perfect and highlights the need to regulate this new technology, just as new military technologies have been regulated for centuries.

E. Conclusions

The nature of armed conflict has changed dramatically since the adoption of the Geneva Conventions, but the key rules of the laws of war are as important today as they were in the past. In addition, for centuries the laws of war have adapted to new challenges. Therefore, despite the emergence of the systematic violation of the laws of war as a strategy in asymmetric conflicts, international human rights law continues to remain relevant in times of armed conflict.[229] The most important development of the last decade certainly is the emergence of international criminal law as a separate regime that serves to enforce the laws of war. This trend is a key notion of today's public international law. Traditionally, enforcement has been a rather problematic aspect of public international law, and this is even more so in the case of international humanitarian law. International criminal law now allows the enforcement of international humanitarian law both on a domestic and an international level and, therefore, has contributed significantly to its effectiveness. States may rarely commit genocide[230] or crimes against humanity,[231] but this is not to say that the law of war is not important. To the contrary, the severity of such crimes as well as of other violations of the laws of war makes it necessary to maintain a clear stance regarding their illegality[232] and to ensure the continued dissemination of knowledge concerning international humanitarian law. At the same time, it is necessary to ensure that the laws of war receive the necessary attention beyond the context of concrete conflicts, and to do so, knowledge of them has to be disseminated. Although the Red Cross—that is, the International Committee of the Red Cross (ICRC), the national Red Cross, the Red Crescent societies, and the Magen David Adom—are already doing a great job disseminating knowledge of international humanitarian law, this effort needs to be increased due to the increasing role played by nonstate actors in armed conflicts who are far less likely to receive any training in international humanitarian law than their counterparts in the armed forces of states.

NOTES

1. 1 U.N.T.S. 15.
2. Roberta Arnold, *The New War on Terror: Legal Implications under International Humanitarian Law*, in TESTING THE BOUNDARIES OF INTERNATIONAL HUMANITARIAN LAW 87 (Susan C. Breau & Agnieszka Jackhec-Neale eds., 2006).
3. *See also* George H. Aldrich, *Progressive Development of the Laws of War*, 26 VA. J. INT'L L. 693 (1986).
4. Sun Tzu, *quoted by* LESLIE C. GREEN, THE CONTEMPORARY LAW OF ARMED CONFLICT 21 (2d ed. 2000).
5. GARY D. SOLIS, THE LAW OF ARMED CONFLICT: INTERNATIONAL HUMANITARIAN LAW IN WAR 49 (2010).
6. *Id.*
7. *Id.*
8. A more extensive overview of the codification of the international laws of war is provided by MICHAEL

HAAS, INTERNATIONAL HUMAN RIGHTS: A COMPREHENSIVE INTRODUCTION 145 (2008). *See also* GEOFFREY BEST, WAR AND LAW SINCE 1945 (1994).
9. *See* STEPHAN HOBE & OTTO KIMMINICH, EINFÜHRUNG IN DAS VÖLKERRECHT 505 (8th ed. 2004).
10. *Id.* at 506.
11. *Id.*
12. *Id.* at 506.
13. *Id.* at 507.
14. DOCUMENTS ON THE LAWS OF WAR 47 (Adam Roberts & Richard Guelff eds., 3d ed. 2000).
15. *Id.* at 53.
16. *Id.* at 59.
17. *Id.* at 63.
18. *Id.* at 67.
19. *Id.* at 73.
20. *Id.* at 85.
21. *Id.* at 103.
22. *Id.* at 139.
23. *Id.* at 155.
24. *Id.* at 169.
25. *Id.* at 221.
26. *Id.* at 243.
27. *Id.* at 299.
28. KNUT IPSEN, VÖLKERRECHT 1209 (5th ed. 2004).
29. *Supra* note 14, at 419.
30. *Id.* at 481.
31. *Available at* www.icrc.org/ihl.nsf/FULL/615?OpenDocument.
32. *Supra* note 14, at 515.
33. *Id.* at 645.
34. *Id.* at 527.
35. *Id.* at 528.
36. *Id.* at 536.
37. *Id.* at 533.
38. *Id.* at 535.
39. *Available at* www.icrc.org/ihl.nsf/FULL/610?OpenDocument.
40. *Supra* note 14, at 407; *see also* Philippe Antoine, *International Humanitarian Law and the Protection of the Environment in Time of Armed Conflict*, 32 INT'L REV. RED CROSS 517 (1992); Igor P. Blishchenko & Vladimir P. Shavrov, *The Legal Basis of Claims for Damage to the Environment Resulting from Military Action*, 39 ÖSTERREICHISCHE ZEITSCHRIFT FÜR ÖFFENTLICHES RECHT UND VÖLKERRECHT 29 (1988/89).
41. *Id.* at 371.
42. *Id.* at 387.
43. *Id.* at 397.
44. *Id.* at 667.
45. *Available at* www.unictr.org.
46. *Available at* www.icty.org.
47. *Available at* www.sc-sl.org.
48. *Available at* www.sudbih.gov.ba.
49. *Available at* www.eccc.gov.kh.

50. *Supra* note 28, at 667.

51. Antonio Cassese, International Law 344 (2001).

52. *Supra* note 9, at 508.

53. *Id.* at 509.

54. *Id.* at 510.

55. *Id.* at 330.

56. *Id.*

57. *Id.*

58. *Id*; ICTY—*Prosecutor v. Tadić*, Case No. IT-94-1-T, Decision of Oct. 2, 1995, para. 97.

59. ICJ—*Legality of the Threat or Use of Nuclear Weapons*, Adv. Op., ICJ Reports 1996, at 234.

60. *Id.* at para. 31.

61. *Supra* note 4, at 57.

62. *Id.* at 57.

63. *Id.*

64. Jean-Marie Henckaerts & Louise Doswald-Beck, 1 Customary International Law: Rules 3 (2005); *supra* note 5, at 251.

65. *Id.*

66. *Id.* at 25.

67. *Supra* note 5, at 251; Commentary on the Additional Protocols 585 (Yves Sandoz, Christophe Swinaski, & Bruno Zimmermann eds., 1987).

68. Knut Dörmann, *The Legal Situation of "Unlawful/Unprivileged Combatants*, 85 Int'l Rev. Red Cross 46 (2003).

69. *Supra* note 5, at 253.

70. Marco Sassoli & Lindsey Cameron, *The Protection of Civilian Objects—Current State of the Law and Issues de lege ferenda*, in The Law of Air Warfare: Contemporary Issues 36 (Natalino Ronzitti & Gabriella Ventunini eds., 2006).

71. Christopher Greenwood, *The Law of War (International Humanitarian Law)*, in International Law 792 (Malcom D. Evans ed., 2d ed. 2006).

72. *Id.*

73. *See* Theodor Meron, *Rape as a Crime Under International Humanitarian Law*, 87 Am. J. Int'l L. 424 (1993); Stefan Kirchner, Human Rights and International Security: Humanitarian Intervention and International Law 68 (2008).

74. *See* Stefan Kirchner Wartime Rape: Sexual Terrorism in the Eastern Province of the Democratic Republic of Congo: International Law and Human Rights 29 (2008).

75. *Supra* note 5, at 269.

76. *Id.*

77. *Id.* at 273.

78. *Id.* at 253; Guénaël Mettraux, International Crimes and the Ad Hoc Tribunals 120 (2005).

79. *See supra* note 71, at 795.

80. *Available at* www.icrc.org/ihl.nsf/FULL/160?OpenDocument.

81. *Supra* note 16.

82. *Supra* note 17.

83. *Supra* note 21.

84. *Supra* note 23.

85. *Available at* www.un-documents.net/seabed.htm.

86. *Available at* http://avalon.law.yale.edu/20th_century/sov001.asp.

87. *Available at* www.mpil.de/shared/data/pdf/convention_on_the_prohibition_of_the_development_production_bacteriological.pdf.

88. *Supra* note 40.

89. *Supra* note 32.

90. *Supra* note 34.

91. *Supra* notes 35 and 36.

92. *Supra* note 37.

93. *Supra* note 38.

94. *Supra* note 39.

95. *Available at* www.opcw.org/chemical-weapons-convention/.

96. *Available at* www.un.org/Depts/mine/UNDocs/ban_trty.htm.

97. ICJ—*Legality of the Threat or Use of Nuclear Weapons*, Adv. Op., ICJ Reports 1996, at 234.

98. *See also* Ove E. Bring & Heinrich Bernhard Reimann, *Redressing a Wrong Question: The 1977 Protocols Additional to the 1949 Geneva Conventions and the Issue of Nuclear Weapons*, 33 Neth. Int'l L. Rev. 99 (1989).

99. *Supra* note 5, at 273.

100. *See* Pastoral Constitution on the Church in the Modern World, para. 80.

101. On Common Law concerns regarding the concept of proportionality, *see supra* note 5, at 273.

102. *Id.*

103. *Supra* note 70, at 35 and 68.

104. *Supra* note 5, at 273.

105. Judith Gail Gardam, *Proportionality and Force in International Law*, 87 Am. J. Int'l L. 391 (1993); ICJ—*Nicaragua v. United States of America*, 1986 ICJ Reports 94, para. 176.

106. Theodor Meron, *The Geneva Conventions as Customary Law*, 81 Am. J. Int'l L. 362 (1987).

107. ICJ—*Legal Consequences for States of the Continued Presence of South Africa in Namibia*, Adv. Op., 1971 ICJ Reports 31.

108. ICJ—*Western Sahara*, 1975 ICJ Reports 12 and 30.

109. *Supra* note 106, at 348, 362 n.47.

110. *Id.*

111. *Id.* at 363.

112. *Id.* at 365.

113. *See* Richard Reeve Baxter, *Treaties and Customs*, 129 Recueil Des Cours 73 (1970/II).

114. On the rules of war at sea, *see* Robin Rolf Churchill & Alan Vaughan, The Law of the Sea 421 (1999).

115. *Supra* note 5, at 275.

116. ICTY—*Prosecutor v. Kupreškic and others*, Case No. IT-95-16-T, Judgment of January 14, 2000, para. 524; *supra* note 5, at 275; *supra* note 65, at 48.

117. *Supra* note 105, at 398.

118. Hugo de Groot (a.k.a. Grotius), 2 De Jure Belli Ac Pacis, Book III, Chapter XI, viii, at 733 (trans. Francis W. Kelsey, William Hein, Buffalo, 1995); *see also supra* note 5, at 275.

119. On high-tech weapons, *see* Herfried Münkler, *The Wars of the 21st Century*, 85 Int'l Rev. Red Cross 9 (2003).

120. *Supra* note 5, at 13.

121. *Supra* note 68, at 45 and 46, n.4.

122. *See also* George H. Aldrich, *The Taliban, al Qaeda, and the Determination of Illegal Combatants*, in 15 Humanitäres Völkerrecht-Informationsschriften 202 (2002).

123. Instructions for the Government of Armies of the United States in the Field, art. 85, also Art. 82, *available at* www.icrc.org/ihl.nsf/73cb71d18dc437274125 6739003e6372/a25aa5871a04919bc12563cd002d65c5 ?OpenDocument.

124. Jan Klabbers, *Rebel With a Cause? Terrorists and Humanitarian Law*, 14 Eur. J. Int'l L. 302 (2003).

125. *Supra* note 68, at 47; Inter-American Commission on Human Rights—Report on Terrorism and Human Rights, OEA/Ser.L/-V/II.116 Doc. 5 rev. 1 corr., Oct. 22, 2002, para. 70.

126. *Id.* at 46.

127. Hans-Peter Gasser, *International Humanitarian Law, the Prohibition of Terrorist Acts and the Fight against Terrorism*, 4 Y.B. Int'l Hum. L. 330 (2001).

128. *Supra* note 5, at 163.

129. *Supra* note 68, at 48.

130. An overview of the existing opinions is offered by Dörmann, *id.* at 68; *see also* The Handbook of Humanitarian Law in Armed Conflicts 301 (Dieter Fleck ed., 2nd ed. 2008); Gerald Irving A. Dare, *The Status of Combatants and the Question of Guerilla Warfare*, 45 Brit. Y.B. Int'l L. 197 (1971).

131. *See also supra* note 68, at 67.

132. *Id.* at 50.

133. *Id.* at 50.

134. *Id.* at 64.

135. *Supra* note 124, at 304.

136. *See already* Dietrich Schindler, *The Different Types of Armed Conflicts According to the Geneva Conventions and Protocols*, 136 Rd C. 121 et seq., 147 (1979–II).

137. *Cf.*, *also* with references to the later ICTR judgment in *Bagilishema*, Robert Heinisch, Die Weiterentwicklung des humanitären Völkerrechts durch die Strafgerichtshöfe für das ehemalige Jugoslawien und Ruanda—Zur Bedeutung von

internationalen Gerichtsentscheidungen als Rechtsquelle des Völkerstrafrechts 88 (1st ed. 2007).

138. *Supra* note 51, at 332.

139. *Supra* note 4, at 107.

140. *Id.*

141. *Id.* at 106.

142. *Id.* at 108.

143. *See* Art. 46 (1) AP I.

144. *Supra* note 51, at 333.

145. *Supra* note 71, at 785.

146. *Id.*

147. *See id.* at 786.

148. *Id.* at 785.

149. *Id.*, there n.8, citing J. Maurice, Hostilities Without Declaration of War (1883).

150. *Supra* note 4, at 317.

151. *Id.*

152. From a military perspective, this development might have culminated in NATO's 1999 Kosovo war, the legality of which was discussed at the time. The 9/11 terrorist attacks essentially cut this discussion short and shifted attention to the issue of terrorism. For a post-9/11 discussion of the issue of humanitarian intervention, *see supra* note 73.

153. *Supra* note 4, at 322.

154. *Id.*

155. *Id.*

156. *Id.* at 320.

157. *See* Peter Malanczuk, Akehurst's Modern Introduction to International Law 352 (7th ed. 1997).

158. *Supra* note 4, at 319.

159. *Id.*

160. *Supra* note 58, at para. 577.

161. *Supra* note 4, at 320.

162. *Supra* note 4, at 353.

163. *Id.*

164. *See* Gerald Irving A. Dare Draper, *The Implementation and Enforcement of the Geneva Conventions of 1949 and of the Two Additional Protocols of 1978*, 164 Recueil des Cours 1 (1979/III).

165. On responsibility for violations of the laws of war, *see* Mark Gibney, International Human Rights Law: Returning to Universal Principles 21 (2008).

166. *Supra* note 9, at 540.

167. *Supra* note 4, at 363.

168. *Supra* note 9, at 540.

169. *Id.*

170. G.A. Res. 2625 (XXV), Oct. 24, 1970.

171. Martin Dixon, Textbook on International Law, 6th ed., at 322. *See also* Derek W. Bowett, *Reprisals Involving Recourse to Armed Force*, 66 Am. J. Int'l L. 1 (1972).

172. *See* note 9, at 542.

173. *Available at* www.ihffc.org.

174. *Available at* www.uncc.ch.

175. S.C. Res. 674, U.N. Doc. S/RES/ S/0674 (1990), and S.C. Res. 687, U.N. Doc. S/RES/687 (1991).

176. On International Criminal Law, *see* the instructive introductions by ALEXANDER ZAHAR & GÖRAN, INTERNATIONAL CRIMINAL LAW (2008); *supra* note 51; and WILLIAM A. SCHABAS, AN INTRODUCTION TO THE INTERNATIONAL CRIMINAL COURT (3d ed. 2007).

177. On terrorism and International Humanitarian Law, *see* Stefan Oeter, *Terrorism and "Wars of National Liberation" from a Law of War Perspective—Traditional Patterns and Recent Trends*, 49 ZEITSCHRIFT FÜR AUSLÄNDISCHES ÖFENTLICHES RECHT UND VÖLKERRECHT 445 (1989); *see also* Gilbert Guillaume, *Terrorism and International Law*, 53 INT'L & COMP. L. Q. 537 (2004).

178. *See also* Toni Pfanner, *Asymmetrical Warfare from the Perspective of Humanitarian Law and Humanitarian Action*, 87 INT'L REV. RED CROSS 154 (2005).

179. *Id.* at 160.

180. Sébastien Jodoin, *Terrorism as a War Crime*, 7 INT'L CRIM. L. REV. 80 (2007). An early overview of the existing opinions is provided by Jordan Paust, *Terrorism and the International Law of War*, 64 MIL. L. REV. 11 (1974).

181. *Supra* note 178, at 96.

182. *Id.*

183. Roberta Arnold, *The New War on Terror: Legal Implications under International Humanitarian Law*, in *supra* note 2, at 105; *see id.* at 101, that there is also the instructive overview from the perspective of International Criminal Law.

184. *Supra* note 178, at 100.

185. Roberta Arnold, *The New War on Terror: Legal Implications under International Humanitarian Law*, in *supra* note 2, at 87.

186. *Id.* at 101.

187. *Id.*

188. *Id.*

189. On terrorism and the *ius ad bellum*, *see* MARTIN DIXON & ROBERT MCCORQUODALE, CASES AND MATERIALS ON INTERNATIONAL LAW 539 (4th ed. 2003).

190. *Supra* note 178, at 78.

191. Mahnoush H. Arsanjani, *The Rome Statute of the International Criminal Court*, 93 AM. J. INT'L L. 31 (1999); *supra* note 178, at 79.

192. ANTONIO CASSESE, INTERNATIONAL CRIMINAL LAW 120 (2003); *supra* note 178, at 78; Yoram Dinstein, *Terrorism as an International Crime*, 18 ISRAEL Y.B. HUM. RTS. 55 (1989).

193. *Supra* note 178, at 79.

194. *Id.*

195. *Id.*; Rona Gabor, *Interesting Times for International Humanitarian Law: Challenges from the War on Terror*, 27 FLETCHER FOR. WORLD AFF. 55 (2003); Luigi Condorelli & Yasmin Navqui, *The War Against Terrorism and Jus in Bello: Are the Geneva Conventions Out of Date?* in ENFORCING INTERNATIONAL LAW: NORMS AGAINST TERRORISM 25 (Andrea Bianchi ed., 2001).

196. *Supra* note 178, at 92; Official Record of the Diplomatic Conference on the Reaffirmation and Development of International Humanitarian Law Applicable in Armed Conflicts, Geneva (1974–1977), *available at* www.loc.gov/rr/frd/Military_Law/RC-dipl-conference-records.html.

197. *Supra* note 178, at 94.

198. *Id.* at 96.

199. *Id.* Such terrorist attacks, though, might be in violation of the prohibition of perfidy, as was the case with many attacks in Iraq while the attackers wore Iraqi police uniforms, *id.*

200. *Id.*

201. *Id.* at 80.

202. *Id.* at 81.

203. *Id.* at 91.

204. ICTY—*Prosecutor v. Galic*, Case No. IT-98–29-T, Trial Chamber, Judgment of December 5, 2003, para. 97; *supra* note 178, at 86.

205. *Supra* note 178, at 89; on the international legal responsibility for state-sponsored terrorism, *see* Stefan Kirchner, *Third Party Liability for Hezbollah Attacks against Israel*, 7 GERMAN L. J. 777 (2006); Luigi Condorelli, *The Imputability to States of Acts of International Terrorism*, 19 ISRAEL Y.B. HUM. RTS. 233 (1989); on the responsibility of states for harboring terrorists, *see supra* note 5, at 162. A good start into the law of state responsibility is provided by Dixon, *supra* note 171, at 403.

206. *Supra* note 178, at 89.

207. *Id.* The requirement to control some territory is one of AP II but not of AP I, *supra* note 4, at 321.

208. *Supra* note 178, at 89.

209. *Supra* note 4, at 321.

210. *Supra* note 28, at 1224.

211. *Supra* note 178, at 89.

212. *Id.*

213. *Supra* note 2, at 25.

214. *Supra* note 68, at 70.

215. *Id.*; *see also* Arnold, *supra* note 2, at 344; William A. Schabas, *Punishment of Non-State Actors in Non-International Armed Conflict*, 26 FORDHAM INT'L L. J. 907 (2002–2003).

216. For a European perspective, *see* Stefan Kirchner, *Human Rights Guarantees During States of Emergency: The European Convention on Human Rights*, 3 BALTIC J. L. & POL. (forthcoming).

217. Jane Mayer, *Outsourcing Torture. The Secret History of America's* Extraordinary Rendition *Program*, THE NEW YORKER, Feb. 14, 2007, *available at* www

.newyorker.com/fact/content/articles/050214fa_fact6 ?050214fa_fact6; Laura Barnett, Extraordinary Rendition: International Law and the Prohibition of Torture (Library of Parliament (Canada), PRB 07–48E) 8 (2008); Fernancdo Val-Garijo, Extraordinary Rendition: Illegal Limbos, Legal Safeguards and International Responsibility (Presentation at the Centre for Human rights in Conflict, London), June 10, 2008, *available at* www.uel.ac.uk/chrc/documents/FernandoValExtraordinaryRendition OralPresentation.pdf; Simon Koschut, *Germany and the USA in the "War against Terror": Is Extraordinary Rendition Putting Transatlantic Cooperation under Strain?* 3 Internationale Politic und Gesellschaft 36 (2007).

218. Extraordinary Rendition (A Summary of the Chatham House International Law Discussion), *available at* www.chathamhouse.org.uk/files/11390_il270 308.pdf, at 2.

219. Center for Human Rights and Global Justice, Torture by Proxy: International Law Applicable to Extraordinary Rendition 6 (2005).

220. *Id.*

221. The Supreme Court [of Israel] sitting as High Court—*Abd al Nasser al Aziz Abd al Aziz Abd al Affo et al. v. Commander of I.D.F. Forces in the West Bank; Abd al Aziz Abd Alrachman Ude Rafia et al. v. Commander of I.D.F. Forces in the Gaza Strip; J'mal Shaat Hindi v. Commander of I.D.F. Forces in the Judea and Samaria Region*, Joined Cases H.C. 785/87, H.C. 845/87 and H.C. 27/88, at 28.

222. For an overview of the privatization of armed conflict, *see supra* note 119, at 13.

223. Benjamin Perrin, *Promoting Compliance of Private Security and Military Companies with International Humanitarian Law*, 88 Rev. Int'l Red Cross 616 (2006).

224. *See also* International Community of the Red Cross Advisory Service on International Humanitarian Law, The Obligation to Disseminate International Humanitarian Law, *available at* www.icrc.org/Web/Eng/siteeng0.nsf/htmlall/5JYLTB/$ File/Obligation_to_disseminate.pdf.

225. Stefan Kirchner, *Distributed Denial-of-Service Attacks under Public International Law: State Responsibility in Cyberwar*, 8 ICFAI U. J. Cyber L. 10 (2009).

226. Dan Raywood, "North Korea blamed for DDoS attacks on United States and South Korea," *available at* www.scmagazineuk.com/north-korea-blamed-for-ddos -attacks-on-united-states-and-south-korea/article/139764/.

227. "DDoS on Israel/Gaza Cyberwar," *available at* http://belsec.skynetblogs.be/post/6597046/ddos-in -israelgaza-cyberwar-.

228. Jose Nazario, "Georgia DDoS Attacks—A Quick Summary of Observations," *available at* http://asert.arbornetworks.com/2008/08/georgia-ddos-attacks -a-quick-summary-of-observations/.

229. *Supra* note 183, at 25.

230. On the Genocide Convention, *see supra* note 163, at 104.

231. Jack L. Goldsmith & Eric A. Posner, The Limits of International Law 111 (2005).

232. On the shortcomings of the international community's response to genocide, *see* Richard Falk, *The Challenge of Genocide and Genocidal Politics in an Era of Globalization*, in Human Rights in Global Politics 183 (Tim Dunne & Nicholas J. Wheeler eds.,1999).

13

Peace Unkempt

How Ambiguities in Public International Law and International Humanitarian Law Contributed to the Failed U.N. Intervention in Somalia

BJORN C. SORENSON

Three interrelated ambiguities in the relations between Somalia, the United Nations, and the United States directly precipitated the collapse of the U.N. mission in Somalia. First, armed U.N. intervention in a failed state presented complex issues regarding the relation between Somalia and the United Nations, functional distinctions between international armed conflict and non-international armed conflict, and the applicability of international humanitarian law to U.N. military forces and belligerents in a failed state. Second, the Security Council's approval of humanitarian intervention in Somalia provided U.N. forces with a conflicting mandate: to establish a "caretaker" government, effectively overriding Somalia's sovereignty, while also conducting a "peacekeeping" operation that deferred to the sovereign will of Somalia's internal, domestic peace process. Finally, limited rules of engagement hampered UNOSOM missions that ostensibly acted under a banner of U.N. neutrality while they attempted to enforce a Security Council-issued "warrant" for the arrest of Aideed.

These ambiguities will be examined in five sections. Section I provides the background to the conflict in Somalia. Section II examines the

applicability of international humanitarian law to failed states and to U.N. forces. Section III addresses the justification for intervention in Somalia. Section IV examines the mandates and rules of engagement of U.N. forces. Section V concludes.

I. Background

The people of Somalia are an amalgamation of five clan families that share a common language and ethnicity.[1] Before colonization, "Somalia's inter-clan relations had local ethical rules but lacked an overarching concept of law essential to a modern centralized nation."[2] The Somali clans were spread—inconveniently for colonizers—throughout the Horn of Africa, from what is now northern Kenya through Somalia, Ethiopia, Djibouti, and Eritrea. European colonial powers primarily sought control of the kingdom of Ethiopia.[3] Even after colonial lines were drawn, Ethiopia and Somalia were at war over the Ogaden territory—a province of Ethiopia still inhabited by Somali clans.[4]

On July 1, 1960, the former Italian trusteeship in the south and British Somaliland were unified into the Somali Republic.[5] In the democratic years of the 1960s, an economy developed and Somalia grew as a Cold War proxy of the Soviet Union. Then, in October 1969 a bodyguard assassinated Somali President Abdi Rashid Ali Shermarke, which paved the way for a military coup led by Siad Barre.[6] Siad governed Somalia as a military dictator by authoritarian force and by manipulating differences between and among the clans.[7] Opposition to Siad grew over the course of twenty years and a decade of outright civil war. During this time, General Mohamed Farah Aideed controlled the military branch of the United Somali Congress. In 1991–92 Aideed and Siad battled throughout Mogadishu and the countryside. In May 1992, Aideed defeated Siad Barre's forces, and Siad fled the country.[8] What little central governance there was of a sovereign Somalia vanished, and the country descended fully into rule by warlords such as Aideed.

The armed conflict during the period of civil war, and particularly during engagements between Aideed and Siad, inhibited the fruitful cultivation of farm land. Years of fighting and untilled soil led to famine and a humanitarian food crisis. A report by the Secretary-General of the United Nations, Boutros Boutros-Ghali, declared that almost five million Somalis, including a million children, were "in urgent need of food assistance."[9] As the United Nations and international NGOs attempted to deliver much needed food aid to millions of starving Somalis, fighting raged between warlord factions for control over Mogadishu.[10]

On April 24, 1992, the Security Council authorized the United Nations Operation in Somalia (UNOSOM).[11] The initial delegation of fifty observers was supplemented with a small military presence, which the Security Council expanded under Resolution 775.[12] Despite emergency airlifts of aid into Somalia, relief efforts were often frustrated by continued fighting and the United Nations' dependence on warlords to protect and distribute such aid.

Recognizing the paradox of relying on notoriously factional warlords to provide security and facilitate humanitarian distribution, the Security Council unanimously passed Resolution 794 of December 3, 1992, authorizing "all necessary means to establish as soon as possible a secure environment for relief operations in Somalia."[13] The United States, as the main supplier of forces for the mission, declined to take disarmament of the population as a mission objective,[14] and also declined to adopt a general policing role.[15] The strategy, according to George H. W. Bush, was "feed and leave."[16]

Employing the euphemism "all necessary means"—code for the use of force—the Security Council established UNOSOM as a Chapter VII force. As discussed below, however, a resolution under Chapter VII of the Charter does not automatically provide troops full discretion to use force.

The U.N. forces sought to provide a more secure environment in Somalia and were somewhat successful. During "Operation Provide Relief," 28,000 tons of relief supplies were airlifted into Somalia, and the country was relatively stable for six months.[17] As a result of the success of UNOSOM, the Security Council authorized a permanent peacekeeping force—UNOSOM II.

On June 5, 1993, however, Aideed's militia attacked Pakistani forces of UNOSOM II while performing a weapons inspection. The attack killed twenty-four Pakistanis and wounded fifty-six other UNOSOM troops. Aideed's militia mutilated the bodies of the Pakistanis in public and kept them on display.[18] Soon after, Admiral Howe, the military head of the United Nations in Somalia, and Boutros-Ghali declared Aideed the "number one enemy and demonized him as the obstacle preventing peace."[19] The Security Council, "expressing outrage" at the "criminal attacks" on U.N. forces, passed Resolution 837, which effectively dismissed its previous position as a neutral force and mandated a police operation to capture Aideed.[20]

The resolution facilitated the "rapid and accelerated deployment" of the authorized forces. Most telling to the loss of neutrality, 837 authorized UNOSOM II to "establish the effective authority of UNOSOM II through

Somalia" and pressed for the "arrest and detention for prosecution, trial and punishment" of "those responsible" for the attacks on the Pakistani forces—an oblique but undeniable reference to Aideed.[21] This explicit mandate to take effective authority over Somalia contradicted the previous neutral mandate and the desire of the forces not to engage in policing or disarmament. The U.N. forces effectively became a belligerent in the chaos of an armed conflict within a failed state.

If the stresses of peacekeeping were not enough, peace enforcement proved ever more baffling for the troops. The entire population of Somalia was heavily armed, and the distinction between a civilian armed only for personal protection and the various factions of feuding and heavily armed warlords was practically impossible to make.[22] With no consistent and clear rules of engagement, troops struggled with the ability to keep the peace and even to defend themselves against raids by Somalis on U.N. supplies. Aideed continued to resist U.N. forces.

On October 3, 1993, Task Force Ranger attempted to raid a hotel at which Aideed's commanders were meeting. The sting, for various reasons, went terribly wrong.[23] The operation's plan was short in duration, but the fighting continued through the night as U.S. troops met heavy resistance and artillery from Aideed's forces in the streets of Mogadishu. U.S. forces captured twenty-four leaders of Aideed's faction. Eighteen U.S. troops and one Malaysian were killed during the fighting. An additional ninety were wounded, and Aideed claimed one U.S. pilot as a "prisoner of war."[24] Estimates "of Somalis killed and wounded, both civilians and factional fighters, ranged between 300 and 1000."[25] As video of Somalis dragging American soldiers through the streets of Mogadishu spread on television, President Clinton announced on October 7 that U.S. forces would withdraw "regardless of the situation on the ground."[26] This signaled the beginning of the end of the grand theory of humanitarian intervention.

The Security Council suspended its call for Aideed's arrest,[27] and on February 4, 1994, the Security Council recalled the UNOSOM II mission effective no later than March 1995. In doing so, it also seemed to concede that it had overstepped proper bounds with the mandate. In part, Resolution 897, authorizing the gradual reduction of the UNOSOM II mission: "Bear[s] in mind respect for the sovereignty and territorial integrity of Somalia in accordance with the Charter of the United Nations and recogniz[es] that the people of Somalia bear the ultimate responsibility for setting up viable national political institutions and for reconstructing their country."[28] Under military cover, the final Pakistani and Bangladeshi troops withdrew from Somalia by March 3, 1995.

II. The United Nations, State Sovereignty, and International Humanitarian Law

Armed conflicts, as examined from the perspective of international humanitarian law, are typically classified as either international armed conflict or non-international armed conflict. Conflicts may also be "internationalized" or "other." In all cases, the characterization of the conflict is tied to and reflective of the notion of state sovereignty. Two sovereigns at war with each other are likely in an international armed conflict. A conflict in which a sovereign is at conflict with an internal rebellion that rises to a certain level is a non-international armed conflict.[29] A conflict where one sovereign intervenes on behalf of a rebellion against a sovereign is said to be "internationalized." However, one sovereign, X, can act with the permission of another sovereign, Z, to help quell rebellion against Z in Z's territory.

In all cases, the sovereign retains the exclusive right to wage war. Where a state in an international armed conflict asks citizens to engage in combat on behalf of the sovereign, those soldiers have combatant's privilege, which effectively immunizes soldiers from prosecution for killing because it is done on behalf of the state. Non-privileged combatants, such as those in rebellions against their own sovereign, are not, by definition, immune from prosecution for murder or other crimes. Privileged combatants are to be given POW status upon capture,[30] whereas non-privileged combatants are, in the eyes of the state, criminals.[31]

A. State Failure and International Humanitarian Law in Somalia

Somalia was clearly a failed state—and remains so today. The failure of statehood in Somalia leads to ambiguity of sovereignty and thus of duties and privileges concomitant to sovereignty under international humanitarian law. International law provides for statehood for groups that meet four criteria. As codified in the Montevideo convention, "the state, as a person of international law should possess the following qualifications: a) a permanent population; b) a defined territory; c) a government; and d) a capacity to enter into relations with the other states."[32] Some scholars distinguish between an objective reading of the convention—that the four criteria constitute statehood regardless of other states' recognition—and a subjective reading of the convention—that the criteria provide means by which other states can evaluate whether or not to recognize another state as such.[33]

Somalia did not meet the criteria under any reading.[34] Although Somalia may have continued as a state in terms of relatively secure geographic integrity and a continued economy, the population was consistently in flux due to refugee movements.[35] Any semblance of central government effectively ceased to exist after the ouster of Siad Barre. At no point were the warring factions capable of entering into relations with another state on behalf of Somalia.

However, as some have observed, "the fact that there is no government does not mean that there is no state."[36] All Security Council resolutions refer to "the state" of Somalia and despite intervention on humanitarian grounds, recognized some integrity of Somalia. The United States did not want to disarm Somalis or police the streets and sought to enable Somalia to establish democratic institutions on its own terms, not to interfere with sovereignty or "state-build."

If there was some ambiguous modicum of sovereignty left in Somalia,[37] how does a failed state act under international humanitarian law? Daniel Thürer of the International Committee of the Red Cross pointed out that "international humanitarian law relies heavily on the hierarchical structures of the State—and above all the military command—both for dissemination and for implementation."[38] However, the state cannot be held responsible for allowing violations of international humanitarian law when there are no longer institutions or authorities authorized to act on behalf of the state. No matter the characterization of the conflict, Thürer asserted, "requirements are to be understood in a broad sense when it comes to practical application. In general, the international humanitarian law treaties are to be interpreted and handled in such a way as to fulfill their aim and spirit, namely assistance and protection for the victims of armed conflicts."[39]

As the ICRC insists on the application of international humanitarian law even to failed states,[40] how does the failure affect combatant's privilege as it pertains to the conflict? No warlord was sovereign in Somalia in the early 1990s. Even though Aideed controlled much of Mogadishu, he was not a legitimate government representative of the people as the head of state under the Montevideo Convention criteria. Within the context of an anarchical conflict among Somali factions, combatant's privilege would be quaint, if not completely absurd. State failure renders irrelevant any notion of propriety of law. The way to ensure immunity from prosecution would be to win the war and establish victor's justice under victor's rule. However, international humanitarian law is not merely a legalistic formulation of musts in armed conflict, it is also a codification of centuries of practical and, indeed, humanitarian considerations of the art of war.

Abiding by the rules of international humanitarian law can certainly encourage the perception of sovereign activity, if not actually help to establish sovereignty. During the failed raid of October 3, 1993, Aideed's forces captured Chief

Warrant Officer Michael Durant, a U.S. pilot, as a "prisoner of war." Although Aideed was a quintessential non-state actor, he exercised a grant of sovereign respect to the pilot by recognizing his POW status. Though the ICRC encourages all militants to abide at all times by rules of international humanitarian law, there is no grant of recognition or gain of status by doing so. In fact, the Geneva Conventions explicitly provide otherwise.[41] Aideed may have thought this act of "benevolence" would reinforce his position as "leader" of Somalia. However, it is also unlawful under the Geneva Conventions to display a POW by dragging such a prisoner through the streets in front of international media coverage.[42]

Under no circumstances were U.N. forces prepared to recognize combatant's privilege for any Somali forces. In fact, Security Council Resolution 837 explicitly refers to attacks on the Pakistani forces as "crimes," not as an encounter between two sovereign equals. If the Somali warlords had no sovereignty and no combatant's privilege, what then, is the status of the United Nations in relation to international humanitarian law?

B. The United Nations as an Actor in International Humanitarian Law

Because international humanitarian law developed from the conduct of states as actors and applies to states as actors, there is confusion over whether international humanitarian law applies to the United Nations as an actor, and if so, how.[43] It is settled that the United Nations has legal personality,[44] although it is not a sovereign in the sense of a Montevideo sovereign. In examining whether international humanitarian law applies to the United Nations, some have argued that "acceptance of the Charter by Member States meant acceptance by them of the superior legal position of the United Nations as regards the use of force and that, consequently, the United Nations may apply such rules as it wishes."[45] This special report of the "Committee on the Study of the Legal Problems of the United Nations" assumes that the United Nations would act via its own independent military force "rather than the national contingents contemplated in the Charter."[46] This "unitary" theory would disaggregate the sovereign responsibility of the national commitments made by the sovereigns that contribute troops to the U.N. unitary force. Such a force, then, "should not feel bound by all the laws of war, but should select such of the laws of war as may seem to fit its purposes."[47] The Committee argued that despite the ambiguities of war, the United Nations is an amalgamation of all sovereignty and, therefore, not obligated under international humanitarian law as the offending party may be. One scholar stated that "Whatever the definition of war may be, this much of it would be generally accepted, that war is conflict between states, between units of equal legal status; whereas the United Nations, acting on behalf of the organized community of nations against an offender, has a superior legal and moral position as compared with the other party to the conflict."[48]

In theory, the Security Council manages the military forces deployed pursuant to Security Council resolutions through the Military Staff Committee.[49] However, in practices developed well after the Committee's 1952 opinion, operations and direct oversight have been outsourced to states who willingly contribute forces and operational expertise.[50] Under the theoretical application of the Military Staff Committee and a hypothetical military force comprised of dedicated U.N. troops, the burden would fall on the Security Council to oversee the application of international humanitarian law during U.N. operations involving the use of force. In this unitary view of U.N. military operations, the United Nations acts as sovereign in regard to international humanitarian law commitments. In practice, U.N. forces are aggregated by contributions from states, and there is no binding oversight, thus the United Nations has no binding responsibility to manage the applicability of international humanitarian law in sanctioned operations. This responsibility falls on the commanders of the aggregated sovereign forces, respectively.

In *Prosecutor v. Tadić*, the ICTY Appeals chamber ruled that Article 1 common to the four Geneva Conventions is a peremptory norm that applies not only to states but also to "international entities including the United Nations."[51] Common Article 1 states that "The High Contracting Parties undertake to respect and to ensure respect for the present Convention in all circumstances." Even though the United Nations is incapable of contracting directly to the Geneva Conventions due to its lack of statehood, the peremptory norm status of Article 1 nonetheless binds U.N. missions to the practice of customary international humanitarian law. However, member forces act in aggregate and are held to domestic standards of international humanitarian law and respective rules of engagement. An analysis of the UNOSOM mission also suggests that the Fourth Geneva Convention applies in situations of state collapse.[52]

Though it seems that opinions have developed to apply international humanitarian law to U.N. forces, this view is not without dissent. A decision in the Supreme Court of Judicature Court of Appeal[53] in the United Kingdom seems to affirm the overarching superiority of the United Nations as presented by the Committee. U.N. Security Council resolutions may qualify individual rights.[54] Because the Security Council is the only legitimate source for the use of force[55] and because resolutions supersede other obligations under international law,[56] the United Nations and forces under its control—whether unitary or aggregated in theory—are only obliged to abide by international humanitarian law if the United Nations so chooses.[57]

C. Characterization of the Armed Conflict

Somalia floats in a quasi-sovereign state with warring factions, none of which have combatant status nor are sovereign enough to take prisoners of war under the Geneva Conventions. U.N. peacekeepers are either absolutely obligated at a minimum to abide by Article 3 common to the Geneva Conventions or are not at all obligated under *any* international agreement unless the Security Council opts to place such restrictions in a resolution.

The armed encounters between Somali warlords and U.N. peacekeepers do not fit squarely into any characterization of armed conflict. It was an über-internationalized non-international armed conflict. The conflict began as a non-international armed conflict between Siad Barre and those seeking to overthrow the government. After Siad Barre fled into exile, Somalia descended into civil war, removing the essential framework of sovereignty and combatant's privilege. When UNOSOM first arrived in Somalia as a neutral—though heavily armed—humanitarian provider, the conflict essentially remained the same: a state of civil war. However, when the Security Council passed Resolution 837, it chose sides, effectively becoming yet another belligerent in the conflict.

The United Nations, aggregated by design, is the most internationalized of all actors. Even though the peacekeepers did not fight *on behalf of* a particular sect in Somalia, they were certainly *against* Aideed. The United Nations came with a "superior legal and moral position"[58] under international law. This status was clearly not recognized by Aideed or other warlords, who saw them as aggressors into sovereign land, regardless of binding Security Council resolutions. Aideed sought to gain legitimacy by taking the U.S. pilot as a prisoner of war. However, the United Nations continued to treat the mission to capture Aideed as criminal enforcement under a U.N. mandate rather than an objective of armed conflict. Regarding the rest of Somalia, the United Nations purported to maintain neutrality even as it exercised a mandate to establish UNOSOM control throughout the country, acting more as an occupier than as a neutral peacekeeper.

These ambiguities in international law and international humanitarian law are not simply academic distractions. They directly affected both the mandate of the UNOSOM missions and the rules of engagement promulgated and followed by the constituent national forces.[59] Before delving into the complexities of *jus in bello*, it is worth examining the justification for the Security Council to authorize a mission in Somalia. In terms of *jus ad bellum*, the justness of the cause to initiate a war, the UNOSOM mission was the first time that the Security Council authorized an intervention on humanitarian grounds.

III. *Jus ad Bellum*: U.N. Authority and Humanitarian Intervention

Jus ad bellum is a measure and threshold of justification for going to war. Also known as "just war theory," the concept is a growth from and application of Catholic theological principles. The primary consideration is whether a cause is just and sufficient to authorize killing.[60] *Jus ad bellum* is, therefore, not simply an examination of the legality of the use of force; it is an inquiry into the underlying *morality* of the cause.[61] Military intervention in the Balkans and Iraq, for example, which have been condemned as "unlawful" by some legal scholars, have nonetheless been blessed by theologians as morally justifiable. The Security Council, in passing Resolution 794, took unprecedented steps in both moral and legal justification under the banner of humanitarian intervention.

A. United Nations Authority

After the global plague of conflict and slaughter of the first two world wars, the United Nations was formed "to save succeeding generations from the scourge of war."[62] The Charter strictly curtailed the legality of the use of force by members, obliging states to settle international disputes peacefully[63] and refrain from "threat or use of force,"[64] at least in terms of relations between states.[65] The Charter further "confer[s] on the Security Council primary responsibility for the maintenance of international peace and security."[66] Acting under Chapter VII,[67] the Security Council has the sole legitimate decision to authorize use of force, can take military force necessary to restore international peace and security, and may condone measures of Member States doing so.[68]

Examining the dire situation of chaos, famine, and rampant disregard for human rights, the international community via the Security Council felt *morally* compelled to intervene. However, there was no clear breach of *international* peace and security that would allow *legal* justification under the Charter. Somalia's problems were mostly an internal domestic matter, and even though Somalia was a failure as a state, it maintained geographic integrity. Even if Somalia was at "war,"[69] it was a civil war that threatened no other state. After much diplomacy and efforts under Chapter VI[70] in the preceding months, the Security Council authorized military force under Chapter VII, "determining that the magnitude of the human tragedy caused by the conflict in Somalia, further exacerbated by the obstacles being created to the distribution of humanitarian assistance, *constitutes a threat to international peace and security*."[71]

B. Justification of Humanitarian Intervention

The concept of justifiable humanitarian intervention[72] is tied to concepts of state sovereignty, politics, morality, and hegemony. Ian Brownlie, in his examination of use of force in international law, described humanitarian intervention in a chapter of "justifications for resort to force of doubtful validity."[73] His historical analysis concludes that humanitarian intervention "did not conspicuously enhance state relations and was applied only against weak states. It belongs to an era of unequal relations."[74]

This concern reinforces the political equality of sovereigns, if not sovereign states as institutions themselves. Even though Somalia was a failed state, some may argue, it is up to Somalis to form their own political processes, even amid civil war and humanitarian disaster.[75] Intervention, to the critics, is a political act[76] more than a legal act, and one that is steeped in moral judgment.[77] Rather than caring for peace and security, the Security Council is in danger of becoming the arbiter of viable and acceptable governments.[78]

Others have objected that "humanitarian concerns supersede sovereignty."[79] Tom Farer would place the burden on the intervener to justify the action using a cost-benefit analysis of the likelihood of success: "In order to meet their ethical obligations, advocates of military measures are peculiarly obligated to persuade us that the intervention they propose will not violate non-derogable rights and on balance is likely to enhance, rather than to diminish, the well being of the determinate people."[80]

Although Farer argued that this standard should apply in matters of self-determination, the standard is useful to analogize to situations such as the failed state in Somalia where the populace struggles not for independence, per se, but for popular government. The intervention does not transgress a particular sovereign person in a failed state situation like that of Somalia. The transgression is against the concept of an equal state. Further, there is an emerging norm for humanitarian intervention to "enforce" human rights, including the "Responsibility to Protect."[81] In the end, the Security Council avoided, at least textually, the debate of humanitarian intervention, citing in Resolution 794 a threat to "international peace and security,"[82] which is squarely within the Council's mandate.

These considerations of *jus ad bellum* reflect the ambiguities of international law and emerging norms of humanitarian intervention. They were also informed by and contributed to the complexities of the political and security situation in Somalia. As the Security Council set aside traditional comity of state sovereignty to intervene in Somalia, at the end of the conflict the Security Council seemed to rediscover the need for indigenous political solutions and self-governance.[83]

This respect for domestic relations came from the experience of U.N. peacekeepers who coped as best they could with the conflicting mandates provided by the Security Council. The effect of the mandates and the rules of engagement pro-vided to the troops are discussed in the context of *jus in bello*.

IV. *Jus in Bello*: U.N. Mandates and Rules of Engagement

As *jus ad bellum* relates to the propriety of initiating armed conflict, *jus in bello* governs the means and methods of warfare,[84] the treatment of prisoners and victims of conflict, and the protection of those not engaged in military activity as codified in the Geneva Conventions.[85] U.N. peacekeeping missions are typically characterized by neutrality and the use of force as a last resort. Tom Farer characterized this "old-fashioned" peacekeeping as a "trinity of (a) consent from all local armed factions, (b) neutrality, and (c) self-defense as the only occasion for the use of force."[86]

At no time did the Security Council have consent from the warring factions. The mission was a forcible humanitarian *intervention*, not a consensual security arrangement. Neutrality is both subjective and objective. Although the mandates from the Security Council objectively declared the mission neutral as to the parties, it is the subjective perception that makes the mission on the ground. After the passage of Resolution 837, the U.N. forces could not even claim objective neutrality: Aideed was clearly the enemy. It is unclear what status the U.N. forces had after this resolution. Although they still maintained neutrality as to the intra-factional conflict in Somalia, they were belligerent as toward Aideed, and thus changed to some unknown status under international humanitarian law.[87]

A report on "Lessons Learned" from UNO-SOM by the Department of Peacekeeping Operations at the United Nations provides a grim post-mortem of the mandate:

> Evaluation of UNOSOM at all levels has concluded that the Operation's mandate was vague, changed frequently during the process and was open to myriad interpretations. The mandate changed from protecting the delivery of hu-

manitarian assistance, to encouraging and assisting in political reconciliation, to establishing and maintaining a "secure environment,"
to capturing a leader of one of the factions at
one stage and, later, to encouraging negotiations with that same leader. These mandates
were, in many respects, contradictory, and
most often the changes were decided upon
with little explanation to Member States,
troop-contributing countries, the humanitarian community operating in Somalia or the
Somali people. As a consequence, UNOSOM
was bedeviled with disagreements among the
various players—between troop-contributing
countries and the Secretariat, contingents and
NGOs, senior UNOSOM officials and the humanitarian community, UNOSOM and UN
agencies—which, in the end, even led to clashes
between UNOSOM and some elements of the
Somali community. [88]

The report also states that the mission was
"hampered by the lack of a clearly defined
common goal."[89] This final analytical section
examines the paradox between neutrality and
militancy for the peacekeepers in Somalia in
terms of the mandate as well as how rules of
engagement—or the lack thereof—placed peacekeepers in a quandary.

A. Conflicting *U.N.* Mandates: Neutrality or Belligerency?

Acting under a Chapter VII mandate abrogates
the need for consent from the "host" nation to
place peacekeepers on the ground. Indeed, as
discussed above, there was no sovereign government in Somalia to provide consent. Regardless,
due to the influence of the Security Council on
the international diplomatic stage, even the act
of *requesting* consent may be seen as conclusive
and coercive. One skeptic noted "even where
consent is claimed . . . often it is constructive,
even fictive: acquiescence rather than vocal
agreement, consent by a de jure leader who lacks
local control, or a de facto warlord who lacks
any representative legitimacy."[90] This was cer-

tainly the case in Somalia. As warlords pointed
fingers around a circle, claiming that they alone
were acting in the interests of the people by
"managing" food distribution and providing "security," each diplomatically lobbied the international community to intercede on their behalf.

The peacekeepers, under the first UNOSOM
mandate, were strictly to provide food aid and
were ostensibly neutral in relation to the warring factions. However, in the hostile climate
pervading Somalia, even the provision of humanitarian food aid was not a neutral act. Aid
could be diverted to strengthen partisan and
weaken combatants or sold for weapons. As one
writer noted, "Aid was not a neutral act in a nation at war with itself."[91]

The issue of neutrality,[92] particularly the Somalis' *perception* of neutrality, was critical to the
initial success and subsequent failure of the UN-
OSOM mission. An official in the U.N. Department of Peace Keeping Operations has
stated that "the only way peacekeepers can work
is by being trusted by both sides, being clear and
transparent in their dealings and keeping lines
of communication open."[93] If this impartiality
is abandoned or is *perceived* to be abandoned,
the peacekeepers may *de facto* or *de jure* become
the enemy of one or more parties and, thus, a
belligerent in the conflict.[94]

Even as the Security Council authorized
forcible intervention into the civil war in Somalia, the Council also "expressly reaffirmed that
it was not its task to dictate a solution to internal differences."[95] Resolution 794 supported the
concept of popular sovereignty.[96] Although on
the international diplomatic stage the Security
Council seemed magnanimous statesmen feeding the people while the leaders sat down to a
cup of tea, the reality on the ground was strikingly different.

From the beginning of the peacekeepers' efforts to disarm and secure territory, they met resistance from warlords. Some saw attacks on U.N.
troops as a battle for self-determination and
against neocolonialism.[97] This pushback was
not limited to the warlords. The civilian population was also skeptical of this humanitarian

intervention or saw raids on peacekeepers as a way to procure supplies. Warlords would kill thieves attempting to steal food or supplies on sight. The peacekeepers were not as liberal with their use of force. The United Nations never had the popular support on the ground that would have made their mission achievable, and during some encounters, the mission seemed like a guerilla war: "The willingness of the population to support the insurgent 'is not necessarily related to the ultimate goals of the guerilla leadership. . . . The population will support the guerrillas if it is convinced that the guerrillas are operating effectively against the enemies of the people.'"[98] Though the warlords were no benevolent friend of the people, at least they were a familiar enemy, unlike the blue helmets.

Particularly after the brutal attacks on the Pakistani troops and the subsequent "declaration of war" on Aideed, the peacekeepers effectively became another belligerent in the fray of factional fighting. Even if they retained their "neutral" badge under international law, on the ground they were clearly biased, and the perception of neutrality vanished.

During the many skirmishes, peacekeepers apprehended many belligerent Somalis. However, because of limited resources and the difficulty of ascertaining the Somalis' status under rules of international humanitarian law, most often detainees were "disarmed, questioned and quickly released."[99] Given the various interpretations of the applicability of international humanitarian law in U.N. operations, it is no wonder that the soldiers themselves were confused.[100] Attempting to decipher the status of irregular combatants and POW status was all but impossible.[101]

B. Ambiguous Rules of Engagement

There is little wonder that the peacekeepers were not greeted with open arms by a Somali society that had been cowed by civil war for the better part of two decades. The Somali media were adept at managing Somali perception of the U.N. peacekeepers, and Aideed's control over a prominent radio station in Mogadishu consistently irked UNOSOM commanders. Throughout the UNOSOM missions, peacekeepers committed various crimes and human rights abuses. The media, both Somali and Western, quickly reported some of these incidents. One allegation was that U.N. troops assassinated a pregnant woman. Belgian troops were tried in 1997 for torture and attempting to roast Somali children on a spit.[102] Human rights groups meticulously documented abuses that could be verified, including violations of both human rights and international humanitarian law.[103]

In addition to the contradictory mandate of the mission, the command structure of the operation and the diversity of the rules of engagement between national contingents to the mission hampered the uniformity and consistency of the engagement of the troops with the Somalis. Just as the Security Council embraced vague references to direct military hostilities in resolutions,[104] so, too, did it passively endorse guidelines for the use of force. Resolutions, according to one U.S. military critic, "usually fail to mention the specific type of operation envisaged or the broad guidelines for the use of force under which it should operate."[105] The United Nations maintained fiscal control over military operations.[106] Although the United Nations ostensibly provided oversight for the entire mission, each national contingent was obligated to act under a joint command structure,[107] thereby causing a need to reconcile multiple sets of obligations.[108]

As a result of the confusion of mandates and rules of engagement as well as the media-savvy Somalis' grasp on the limits of the peacekeepers potential engagement,[109] the peacekeepers lost most of their deterrent effect, even though they were far better trained and equipped than most Somali factions. The effectiveness of a deterrent threat is proportional to the "deterred" party's belief that severe consequences will ensue. As Trevor Findlay put it, "The ability to deter successfully relies on clearly communicating the objective and the threat and demonstrating both capability and will."[110] There must be a uniformity of understanding both among the U.N. forces and among the general population that force can and will be used if a threat of force is to be successful. In Somalia, this policy failed. The various contingents had differing—though uniformly weak—rules of engagement, and the population knew it.

The Joint Task Force Rules of Engagement did not mention obligations under international humanitarian law. The rules for soldiers under U.S. command stated clearly that "the United States is not at war."[111] Even though "the UN has always insisted on the fact that during the exercise of their mandate these troops are under the sole authority of the organization and not that of their respective States,"[112] the ICRC has protested that "since the UN, as such, is not party to the [Geneva] Conventions, the ICRC considers that each State remains individually responsible for the application of these treaties whenever it provides a contingent for a [peace-keeping force]."[113] The obligations to address grievances of international humanitarian law violations are thus the responsibility of the national contingent, even while acting under U.N. supervision and Chapter VII authorization by the Security Council.[114]

For the U.S. troops, the military provided guidance under rules for Military Operations Other Than War (MOOTW). The purpose of the rules was to "preclude indiscriminate use of deadly force while simultaneously allowing soldiers sufficient latitude to defend themselves."[115] Training in MOOTW is "essential in developing soldiers' skills on how to respond to a variety of situations, when to use deadly force, and when and how to apply non-deadly force."[116]

As described, no soldier or national contingent was authorized to act consistently with their internal mandates, even though each soldier and national contingent is held accountable to their national standards under MOOTW. As Somalis raided U.N. weapons storage sites, for example, peacekeepers could not use deadly force unless such force was applied against them, even though the weapons stolen could then be turned on the peacekeepers at a later time.

Just as the Department of Peacekeeping Operations had a grim assessment of the mandate, a report by the Naval War College concluded that the principles of MOOTW were not applied properly. The objectives of the mission "were not well defined at the outset, resulting in an interpretation that led commanders to focus solely on military solutions, with goals skewed toward what were perceived as achievable."[117] Lieutenant Commander Lee S. Gingery, the author of the report, concluded that the failure of the mission was the result of a lack of "legitimacy."[118]

Findlay, in his thorough examination of the use of force during U.N. peace operations, suggested that rules of engagement provided by the United Nations "need to be drafted in consultation with all troop-contributing countries and take into account the special needs of peace operations in balancing restrictiveness with permissiveness and conciseness with comprehensiveness."[119] As the United Nations continues to deploy peacekeeping missions, the rules of engagement should be modified to address the legal and ethical ambiguities at the international level in terms of the application of international humanitarian law, the justness of humanitarian intervention under Chapter VII. Further, while promulgating the rules of engagement, the mission commanders should be clear in their mandate regarding how the complexities of joint-command and the application of international humanitarian law at the contingent-sovereign level will affect the engagement of the mission as a whole.[120]

V. Conclusion

Since the withdrawal of U.N. troops, Somalia has continued factional fighting and tribe-based governance and warfare. Despite the establishment of an internationally recognized Transitional Federal Government, no security or real government has been established in an effective way. The rise of Islamic courts through the late

1990s and early twenty-first century brought limited federal stability and adjudicatory structure. However, as the courts are infiltrated by extremists from al-Qaeda and other terrorist organizations, the interests of Kenya, Ethiopia, and the United States have been piqued. As this paper concludes, the Horn of Africa is tilting toward a regional war—the United States patrols from Djibouti, Kenya seeks to secure its borders, and Ethiopia and Eritrea are engaging in a proxy war in Somalia that mirrors the colonial games played in the Horn a century earlier.

Though the future of U.N. backed intervention under Chapter VII mandates—humanitarian or otherwise—remains in legal and political limbo, the ambiguities examined in this paper still apply to current U.N. deployments. The ambiguity of the applicability of international law and international humanitarian law did not disappear with the final airlift out of Somalia. These ambiguities will continue to develop unless there is considerable development of custom in terms of U.N. authority, failed states, and non-state actors.[121]

NOTES

1. *See* Terrence Lyons & Ahmed I. Samatar, Somalia: State Collapse, Multilateral Intervention, and Strategies for Political Reconstruction, 7–24 (1995); *see also* John L. Hirsch & Robert B. Oakley, Somalia and Operation Restore Hope: Reflections on Peacemaking and Peacekeeping, 3–16 (1995).

2. Lester H. Brune, The United States and Post-Cold War Interventions: Bush and Clinton in Somalia, Haiti, and Bosnia, 1992–1998 14 (1999).

3. Hirsch & Oakley, *supra* note 1, at 4.

4. Brune, *supra* note 2, at 14. *See also* Hirsch & Oakley, *supra* note 1, at 4–5.

5. Lyons & Samatar, *supra* note 1, at 5.

6. *Id.*

7. *See id.* at 6–9.

8. *See id.* at 10–13.

9. *Quoted in* Hirsch & Oakley, *supra* note 1, at 23.

10. This period of war and starvation has been characterized as "*Dad Cunkii*"—"the era of cannibalism." Abdi Ismail Samatar, *Destruction of State and Society in Somalia: Beyond the Tribal Convention*, 30, 4 J. Modern African Studies 625 (1992).

11. S.C. Res 751 U.N. Doc. S/RES/751 (Apr. 24, 1992).

12. S.C. Res 775 U.N. Doc. S/RES/775 (Aug. 28, 1992).

13. S.C. Res 794 U.N. Doc. S/RES/794 (Dec. 3, 1992).

14. *See* Trevor Findlay, The Use of Force in UN Peace Operations 167 (2002) (discussing the exchanges between Boutros-Ghali and Bush regarding the mission).

15. *Id.* at 175 (citing "the danger of becoming enmeshed in intra-Somali conflicts").

16. Tom Farer, *Intervention in Unnatural Humanitarian Emergencies: Lessons of the First Phase*, 18 Hum. Rts. Q. 1, 7 (1996).

17. Major Clifford E. Day, Critical Analysis on the Defeat of Task Force Ranger 2–3 (1997).

18. *See* Tom Farer, *Report Pursuant to Paragraph 5 of Security Council Resolution 837 (1993) on the Investigation into the 5 June 1993 Attack on the United Nations Forces in Somalia*, U.N. Doc. S/26351 (Aug. 24, 1993) (declaring "No act could by its very character more perfectly exemplify an international crime than the use of force against United Nations soldiers to prevent them from carrying out their responsibilities"). *Id.* at para. 7. *See also* Kenneth S. Freeman, *Recent Developments: Punishing Attacks on United Nations Peacekeepers: A Case Study of Somalia*, 8 Emory Int'l L. Rev. 845 (examining possible sources of international law to prosecute Aideed for his attack on U.N. Peacekeepers).

19. Brune, *supra* note 2, at 30.

20. S.C. Res 837 U.N. Doc. S/RES/837 (Jun. 6, 1993).

21. *Id.*

22. *See* discussion, *infra*, Section IV.

23. For detailed descriptions of the "mission failure" of the task force sent to capture Aideed's cohort, see Major Roger N. Sangvic, Battle of Mogadishu: Anatomy of a Failure (1998) and Day, *supra* note 17. *See also* Mark Bowden, *Black Hawk Down*, *available at* http://inquirer.philly.com/packages/somalia/sitemap.asp.

24. *See* discussion, *infra*, Section II (describing the status of the prisoner in this unique context of armed conflict).

25. Findlay, *supra* note 14. Day, *supra* note 17.

26. Findlay, *supra* note 14, at 201.

27. S.C. Res 885 U.N. Doc. S/RES/885 (Nov. 16, 1993).

28. S.C. Res 897 U.N. Doc. S/RES/897 (Feb. 4, 1994).

29. *See Juan Carlos Abella v. Argentina*, Case No. 11.137, Annual Report 1997, OEA/Ser.L/V/II.98, Doc. 7 rev (Apr. 13, 1998, ("La Tablada" Case), pp. 271–72, 303–16) (drawing distinctions between "internal disturbances" and non-international armed conflict).

30. Geneva Convention Relative to the Treatment of Prisoners of War, *opened for signature* Aug. 12, 1949, 6 U.S.T. 3316, 75 U.N.T.S. 287. Art. 4 of the convention lists those categories of persons who qualify for treatment as a POW.

31. *See* Robert K. Goldman & Brian D. Tittemore, *Unprivileged Combatants and the Hostilities in Afghanistan: Their Status and Rights Under International Humanitarian and Human Rights Law*, ASIL Task Force on Terrorism, December 2002.

32. Convention on Rights and Duties of States (inter-American), "Montevideo Convention," Dec. 26, 1933, art. I, 49 Stat. 3097.

33. Even though the Montevideo Convention provides that "the political existence of the state is independent of recognition by the other states." *Id.* at art. 3. *See* James Crawford, *The Criteria for Statehood in International Law*, 48 Brit. Y.B. Int'l L. 93 (1978) (providing a thorough examination of the history and complexities of "the State" in international law).

34. *But see* Rosa Ehrenreich Brooks, *Failed States, or the State as Failure?* 72 U. Chi. L. Rev. 1159 (2005) (contending that contemporary international legal frameworks premised on the state "stands in the way of developing effective responses to state failure"). *Id.*

35. *See* Peter D. Little, Somalia: Economy Without State (2003).

36. Fernando R. Teson, *Changing Perceptions of Domestic Jurisdiction and Intervention, in* Beyond Sovereignty: Collectively Defending Democracy in the Americas 29, 44 (Tom Farer ed., 1996).

37. "Somalia was persistently regarded as a sovereign state in international law, despite the loss of such critical criterion as a legitimate and effective government." Jarat Chopra, *Achilles' Heel in Somalia: Learning from a Conceptual Failure*, 31 Tex. Int'l L. J. 495, 513 (1996).

38. Daniel Thürer, *The "Failed State" and International Law*, 836 Int'l Rev. Red Cross 731, *available at* http://www.icrc.org/web/eng/siteeng0.nsf/html/57jq6u (discussing the inherent difficulty of applicability of international humanitarian law in conflicts involving or on the territory of failed states).

39. *Id.*

40. In addition to problems of attribution of obligations under international humanitarian law to failed states as sovereign entities, considerable importance should be placed on failed states as havens for non-state actors. *See* Ben N. Dunlap, *State Failure and the Use of Force in the Age of Global Terror*, 27 B.C. Int'l & Comp. L. Rev. 453 (2004) (arguing that military action against actors in failed states will only increase during the "war on terror").

41. Article 3 common to the Geneva Conventions states, "The application of the preceding provisions shall not affect the legal status of the Parties to the conflict."

42. *See* Geneva Convention Relative to the Treatment of Prisoners of War, *supra* note 30.

43. *See generally* James D. Fry, *The UN Security Council and the Law of Armed Conflict: Amity or Enmity?* 38 Geo. Wash. Int'l L. Rev. 327 (2006) (examining both the theoretical relationship between international humanitarian law and the Security Council, as well as how the Security Council "consistently falls short of authorizing a force that is expressly limited by all of [international humanitarian law's] general strictures"). *Id.* at 328.

44. *See, e.g., Reparation for Injuries Suffered in the Service of the United Nations* (the Bernadotte case) 1949 I.C.J. 174 (Apr. 11) *reprinted in* Louis Henkin et al., International Law 352 (3d ed. 1993) (holding that the United Nations has legal status and standing to bring a claim for damages upon the death of a U.N. representative).

45. William J. Bivens et. al., *Report of Committee on the Study of the Legal Problems of the United Nations, Should the Laws of War Apply to United Nations Enforcement Action?* 46 Am. Soc'y Int'l L. Proc 216, 217 (1952).

46. *Id.* at 218. *See also* U.N. Charter, art. 43 "All Members of the United Nations, in order to contribute to the maintenance of international peace and security, undertake to make available to the Security Council, on its call and in accordance with a special agreement or agreements, armed forces, assistance, and facilities, including rights of passage, necessary for the purpose of maintaining international peace and security." *Id.*

47. Bivens et al., *supra* note 45, at 220.

48. *Id.* at 217.

49. Findlay, *supra* note 14, at 9. The U.N. Military Staff Committee has never functioned as designed, and in practice, oversight of operations has fallen on the U.N. Secretary-General. *Id.* at 10.

50. Findlay, *supra* note 14, at 9.

51. *Prosecutor v. Tadić*, Decision on the Defense Motion for Interlocutory Appeal on Jurisdiction, Oct. 2, 1995, Case No. IT-94-1-AR 72, para. 93.

52. United Nations Department of Peacekeeping Operations, The Comprehensive Report on Lessons Learned from United Nations Operation in Somalia (UNOSOM): April 1992–March 1995 [hereinafter "UNOSOM Lessons Learned"], para. 57. "In an environment of state collapse, the Fourth Geneva Convention could supply adequate guidelines for regulating relations between peacekeeping troops and the local population." *Id.*

53. *The Queen (on the application of Hilal Abdul-Razzaq Ali Al-Jedda v. Secretary of State for Defence*, [Al-Jedda] (2006) EWCA Civ 327, Case No C1/2005/2251.

54. *See id.* at paras. 55 *et. seq.*

55. *See* discussion, *infra*, Section III.

56. "In the event of a conflict between the obligations of the Members of the United Nations under the present Charter and their obligations under any other international agreement, their obligations under the present Charter shall prevail." U.N. Charter, art. 103. Because the text places member obligations to the United Nations over member obligations to "other international agreement[s]," this would qualify, for example, even Article 3 common to the Geneva Conventions, only if these minimum standards of treatment conflicted with the U.N. mandate. *See* Geneva Convention Relative to the Treatment of Prisoners of War, *opened for signature* Aug. 12, 1949, 6 U.S.T. 3316, 75 U.N.T.S. 287. It seems exceedingly unlikely that the Security Council, itself an authority aggregated of Member States, would authorize action under the U.N. Charter that explicitly qualify or abrogate their obligations as individual states—even when acting under the theory of a unitary U.N. military force.

57. This "choice" is much less clear for troops acting on the ground. Even if international humanitarian law does not apply to U.N. troops, no soldier serving on the ground would see themselves as primarily a U.N. Peacekeeper and secondarily a U.S. Army Ranger, for example. They would still be obligated under domestic law or a particular military code to follow the rules of engagement, lest they be subject to court-martial. Practically speaking, a soldier is likely to perform as trained regardless of the ethereal cogitations of scholars on whether or not international humanitarian law applies to U.N. troops, and if so, how.

58. *See* Bivens et al., *supra* note 45 and accompanying text.

59. *See* Brian D. Tittemore, *Belligerents in Blue Helmets: Applying International Humanitarian Law to United Nations Peace Operations*, 33 STAN. J. INT'L L. 61 (1997) (providing recommendations for how to reconcile international humanitarian law with the unique challenges presented by a deployment of a U.N. military force).

60. According to Augustine, "Just wars are usually defined as those which avenge injuries, when the nation or city against which warlike action is to be directed has neglected to punish wrongs committed by its own citizens or to restore what has been unjustly taken by it." QUAESTIONES IN HEPTATEUCHEM (419), vi.10.

61. *See* Ralph B. Potter, *The Moral Logic of War*, OCCASIONAL PAPERS ON THE CHURCH AND CONFLICT no. 5, (1970) *reprinted in* XXIII, 4 MCCORMICK Q. 203 (on file with author) (providing a theological and ethical examination of the justifiable causes of war and the moral limits of warfare).

62. U.N. Charter, preamble.

63. U.N. Charter, art. 2.3.

64. U.N. Charter, art. 2.4.

65. U.N. Charter, art. 2.7 limits the United Nations from intervening "in matters which are essentially within the domestic jurisdiction" of a member state. Similarly, article 2.4 specifically protects the "territorial integrity or political independence of any state."

66. U.N. Charter, art. 24.

67. Covering "Action with Respect to Threats to the Peace, Breaches of the Peace, and Acts of Aggression."

68. *See* U.N. Charter, art. 42. A jaded view of the relation between Just War and the Security Council notes the circularity of the legality of Security Council authorization as the only legitimate declaration of force in international law, in which a war is just because the Security Council "said so." Although this is still subject to political, moral, and theological critique, there is no effective oversight of Security Council decisions.

69. *See* John Alan Cohan, *Legal War: When Does It Exist, and When Does It End?* 27 HASTINGS INT'L & COMP. L. REV. 221 (offering a legal and philosophical examination of the state and temporal distinctions of war by contrasting powers of the president as Commander in Chief and Congress's power to formally declare war).

70. Covering "Pacific Settlement of Disputes" in the U.N. Charter.

71. S.C. Res 794 U.N. Doc. S/RES/794 (Dec. 3, 1992) (emphasis added).

72. *See* Teson, *supra* note 36, at 30–31 (describing three types of intervention, "according to the degree of coercion utilized in the attempts to influence other states." "Soft" intervention is "discussion, examination, and recommendatory action" regarding the affairs of a state. "Hard" intervention is coercive measures that do not utilize force. "Forcible" intervention utilizes force "subject to independent legal constraints." All three forms of intervention are "aimed at influencing a government on an issue where the target state has legal discretion." *Id.*

73. IAN BROWNLIE, INTERNATIONAL LAW AND THE USE OF FORCE BY STATES 338 (1991).

74. *Id.* at 340–41.

75. For the argument that the Security Council may not authorize the use of force to enforce human rights, *see* Teson, *supra* note 36, at 37 (explaining an argument that even serious human rights deprivations do not rise to threats of peace, breaches of the peace, or acts of aggression as defined under Article 39 on the United Nations Charter). *See also* Ved P. Nanda et al., *Tragedies in Somalia, Yugoslavia, Haiti, Rwanda and Liberia—Revisiting the Validity of Humanitarian Intervention Under International Law—Part II*, 26 DENV. J. INT'L L & POL'Y 827 (1998) (assessing the validity of the title interventions according to a framework of justification to intervene on humanitarian grounds).

76. For a description of "The Political Dimensions of Peace Enforcement," see LYONS & SAMATAR, *supra* note 1 at 36–62 (1995).

77. "What sounds so utterly benign as peacekeeping can devolve into a kind of multilateral condescension." Ruth Wedgwood, *The Evolution of United Nations Peacekeeping*, 28 CORNELL INT'L L. J. 631, 636 (1995).

78. *See* Mark R. Hutchinson, *Recent Development: Restoring Hope: The U.N. Security Council Resolutions for Somalia and an Expanded Doctrine of Humanitarian Intervention*, 34 HARV. INT'L L. J. 624 (1993).

79. Nancy D. Arinson, *International Law and Non-Intervention: When do Humanitarian Concerns Supersede Sovereignty?* FLETCHER FORUM OF WORLD AFFAIRS 199, Summer 2003.

80. Tom J. Farer, *The Ethics of Intervention in Self-Determination Struggles*, 25 HUM. RTS. Q. 382, 383 (2003).

81. *See* Wayne Sandholtz, *Humanitarian Intervention: Global Enforcement of Human Rights? in* GLOBALIZATION AND HUMAN RIGHTS (Alison Brysk ed., 2002) (arguing that "global society has developed a set of rules that permit, but do not require, forcible intervention to stop gross violations of basic security rights"). *Id.* at 201. *But see* Teson, *supra* note 36.

82. S.C. Res 794 U.N. Doc. S/RES/794 (Dec. 3, 1992).

83. *See* S.C. Res 897 U.N. Doc. S/RES/897 (Feb. 4, 1994).

84. Largely codified in the Hague Conventions. *See, e.g.*, Convention with Respect to the Laws and Customs of War on Land (Hague, II) (July 29, 1899), 32 Stat. 1803.

85. The Geneva Convention for the Amelioration of the Condition of the Wounded and Sick in Armed Forces in the Field, Aug. 12, 1949, 6 U.S.T. 3114, 3116, T.I.A.S. No.3362, at 3, 75 U.N.T.S. 31, 32; Geneva Convention for the Amelioration of the Condition of the Wounded, Sick and Shipwrecked Members of the Armed Forces at Sea, Aug. 12, 1949, 6 U.S.T. 3217, 3220, T.I.A.S. No.3363, at 4, 75 U.N.T.S. 85, 86; Geneva Convention Relative to the Treatment to Prisoners of War, Aug. 12, 1949, 6 U.S.T. 3316, 3318, T.I.A.S. No. 3364. at 3, 75 U.N.T.S. 135, 136; Geneva Convention Relative to the Protection of Civilian Persons in Time of War, Aug. 12, 1949, 6 U.S.T. 3516, 3518, T.I.A.S. No.3365, at 3, 75 U.N.T.S. 287, 288.

86. Farer, *supra* note 16, at 6.

87. *See* Tittemore, *supra* note 59.

88. UNOSOM Lessons Learned, *supra* note 52, at para. 10.

89. *Id.* at para. 31.

90. Wedgwood, *supra* note 77, at 636.

91. *See* FREDERICK H. FLEITZ, PEACEKEEPING FIASCOES OF THE 1990S: CAUSES, SOLUTIONS, AND U.S. INTERESTS 133 (2002).

92. *See* Wedgwood, *supra* note 77, at 633 (citing minimal use of force, consent, and neutrality as "tenets of classical peacekeeping"). *Id. See also* GEERT-JAN ALEXANDER KNOOPS, THE PROSECUTION AND DEFENSE OF PEACEKEEPERS UNDER INTERNATIONAL CRIMINAL LAW 36–37 (2004).

93. *Quoted in* FINDLAY, *supra* note 14, at 4.

94. FINDLAY, *supra* note 14, at 4.

95. Teson, *supra* note 36, at 43.

96. Resolution 794 states that Somalis continue to "bear ultimate responsibility for the reconstruction of their own country."

97. *See, e.g.*, Nehal Bhuta, *The Antinomies of Transformative Occupation*, 16 EUR. J. INT'L L. 721, 739 (2005) (discussing subordination and legitimacy of the U.S. mission in Iraq).

98. *Id.* at 739 (quoting Chalmers Johnson, *Civilian Loyalties and Guerilla Conflict*, 14 WORLD POL. 646 (1962)).

99. Timothy P. Bulman, *A Dangerous Guessing Game Disguised as Enlightened Policy: United States Law of War Obligations During Military Operations Other Than War*, 159 MIL. L. REV. 152, 168 (1999).

100. "The existence and application of International Humanitarian Law in the conduct of military operations involving the use of force was not fully understood by some military forces deployed to Somalia. Troops must be made aware, in advance, of International Humanitarian Law and abide by these provisions during the exercise of their duty." UNOSOM Lessons Learned, *supra* note 52, at para. 58. Although some may dispute the extent of application of international humanitarian law in various engagement scenarios, it is troubling that "the existence" of international humanitarian law should ever be in doubt by U.N. peacekeepers engaged in military operations.

101. See Goldman & Tittemore, *supra* note 31, for an analysis of how irregular combatants may qualify or forfeit their entitlement to prisoner of war status as applied to the conflict in Afghanistan.

102. FLEITZ, *supra* note 91, at 121.

103. *See generally* Alex de Waal, *US War Crimes in Somalia*, 230 NEW LEFT REV. 131–44 (July–Aug. 1998) (describing a policy of excessive force, helicopter attacks on civilians, and general brutality by U.S. forces in violation of international law); *and* African Rights, *Somalia: Human Rights Abuses by the United Nations Forces* (July 1993) (detailing particular instances in which U.N. forces violated customary international humanitarian law and human rights law, including an attack on Digfer hospital on June 17, 1993, attacks on civilian demonstrators on June 12, 1993, and various instances of

unlawful killings, demolitions, and detentions in the first half of 1993).

104. *See* FINDLAY, *supra* note 14, at 8 (examining the implicit endorsement of direct military engagement in the term "all necessary means").

105. *See id.* at 13.

106. *See generally*, Major Louis A. Chiarella, *United Nations Operations: Problems Encountered by United States Forces When Subject to a "Blue Purse,"* 154 MIL. L. REV. 53 (discussing political and operational constraints and conundrums of funding during U.N. sponsored military operations).

107. *See* C. Kenneth Allard, *Lessons Unlearned: Somalia and Joint Doctrine* 9 JOINT FORCE Q. 105 (1995) (examining the difficulties of joint U.S.-U.N. command over forces in Somalia).

108. *See* F. M. Lorenz, USMC, *Rules of Engagement in Somalia: Were they Effective?* 42 NAVAL L. REV. 62 (1995) (examining the rules of engagement for the 13th Marine Expeditionary Unit); UNOSOM Lessons Learned, *supra* note 52, at paras. 44–46 (lamenting the difficulties of managing command structure of a multinational force as well as the uniformity of the rules of engagement propagated by various commanders of "their contingents' missions"). *Id.* at para. 46.

109. *See, e.g.*, ROMEO DALLAIRE, SHAKE HANDS WITH THE DEVIL: THE FAILURE OF HUMANITY IN RWANDA 240 (2003) ("The extremists had taken their cure from the grim farces of Bosnia and Somalia. They knew that the Western nations do not have the stomach or the will to sustain casualties in peace support operations. When confronted with casualties, as the United States was in Somalia or the Belgians in Rwanda, they will run, regardless of the consequences to the abandoned population."); *see also* SAMANTHA POWER, "A PROBLEM FROM HELL": AMERICA AND THE AGE OF GENOCIDE 316–18, 366–67, 374–75 (2002) (discussing the impact of the failed U.N. mission in Somalia on the operations of Bosnia and Rwanda).

110. FINDLAY, *supra* note 14, at 18.

111. Bulman, *supra* note 99, at n.92.

112. Umesh Palwankar, *Applicability of International Humanitarian Law to United Nations Peace-keeping Forces,* 294 INT'L REV. RED CROSS 227, para. 11 (1993).

113. *Id.*

114. *Id.*

115. Chairman of the Joint Chiefs of Staff, *Tactics, Techniques and Procedures (TTP) in Support of Operations Other Than War.*

116. *Id.*

117. LEE S. GINGERY, PRINCIPLES OF MILITARY OPERATIONS OTHER THAN WAR AS APPLIED TO THE UNITED NATIONS OPERATION IN SOMALIA II 15 (1997).

118. *Id.*

119. FINDLAY, *supra* note 14, at 371.

120. Findlay lists five categories for the United Nations to consider: (1) the United Nation's political, military, and legal purposes; (2) proportionality and restraint; (3) clarity; (4) simplicity versus detail; and (5) flexibility. *Id.* at 372–73.

121. *See* Dunlap, *supra* note 40.

PART SIX

THE ENVIRONMENT

14

Space Settlements, Property Rights, and International Law

Could a Lunar Settlement Claim the Lunar Real Estate It Needs to Survive?*

ALAN WASSER AND DOUGLAS JOBES

I. Introduction

Humanity's survival depends on moving out into the cosmos while the window of opportunity for doing so still exists. Besides helping to ensure the survival of humankind, the settling of space—including the establishment of permanent human settlements on the moon and Mars—will bring incalculable economic and social benefits to all nations. The settlement of space would benefit all of humanity. It would open a new frontier, provide resources and room for growth of the human race without despoiling the Earth, energize our society, and, as Dr. Stephen Hawking has pointed out, create a lifeboat so that humanity could survive even a planetwide catastrophe.[1] But, as Dr. Lawrence Risley pointed out, "Exploration is not suicidal and it is usually not altruistic, rather it is a means to obtain wealth. There must be rewards for the risks being taken."[2]

Unfortunately, neither private enterprise nor government currently has a sufficient incentive to invest the billions of dollars necessary to make space settlement happen. In the private sector, even the recent accomplishments of space entrepreneurs such as Richard Branson and Robert Bigelow are but tiny steps toward settlement.[3] These billionaires may be able to get a few passengers to low Earth orbit, but it is very unlikely that they will finance technology for people to live in space, especially on the moon or Mars.[4] They may be wealthy, but they are not that wealthy. And the U.S. government's current "Return to the Moon" plan[5] has numerous hurdles, not the least of which is whether financing will be sustained over the next decades by future administrations. In any case, the goal of the program is not a thriving settlement on the moon but rather a limited, government-run moon base.[6] The government space programs of other countries are even farther behind with regard to space settlement.[7]

There appears to be one incentive, however, that could spark massive private investment leading to the establishment of permanent space

---

*This chapter was originally published in the *Journal of Air Law and Commerce*, vol. 73, no 1 (Winter 2008). A Publication of Southern Methodist University School of Law (www.smu.edu/lra).

settlements on the moon and beyond with an immediate payback to investors. The concept of "land claims recognition" (developed by author Alan Wasser and others over the last twenty years) seems to be the most powerful economic incentive, much more so than all the other incentives, such as government-funded prizes and corporate tax holidays combined.[8]

If and when the moon and Mars are settled in the future through other incentives, the nations of Earth will eventually have to recognize these settlements' authority over their own land. But to create an incentive now, governments would need to commit to recognizing that ownership in advance, rather than long after the fact.

Land claims recognition legislation would commit the Earth's nations, in advance, to allowing a true private lunar settlement to claim and sell (to people back on Earth) a reasonable amount of lunar real estate in the area around the base, thus giving the founders of the moon settlement a way to earn back the investment they made to establish the settlement.[9] Appropriate conditions could be set in the law, such as the establishment of an Earth-moon space line open to all paying passengers regardless of nationality.[10]

The many other aspects of the land claims recognition concept are discussed in detail elsewhere,[11] but a major point of related debate involves what international law has to say about the legality of a private entity, such as a space settlement owned by a corporation or individual, claiming ownership of land on a celestial body like the moon on the basis of "occupation and use."[12] The following discussion lays out the argument that current international law, and especially "the Outer Space Treaty," does appear to permit private property ownership in space and to permit nations on Earth to recognize land ownership claims made by private space settlements, without these nations being guilty of national appropriation or any other legal violation.

II. A Tale of Two Treaties

The 1967 Treaty on Principles Governing the Activities of States in the Exploration and Use of Outer Space, Including the Moon and Other Celestial Bodies,[13] generally called the Outer Space Treaty, is the primary basis for most international space law. The treaty was negotiated by the United States and the Soviet Union in order to end the costly space race between them.[14]

There were, of course, a great many differences between the United States and the Soviet Union, which had to be compromised or papered over in order to get a treaty agreement.[15] For example, the Soviet Union wanted to ban all private enterprise space activity, but the United States refused.[16]

In many cases, the solution was to insert vague language that could be interpreted whichever way the reader wanted but would defer the enactment of any real rules to a future discussion. At the U.S. Senate ratification hearings for the treaty, Arthur Goldberg, who led the U.S. negotiating team, was asked about Article I of the treaty, and he told the senators that "the article [was] a 'broad general declaration of purposes' that would have no specific impact until its intent was detailed in subsequent, detailed agreements."[17]

About a decade later, there was a serious attempt to produce such a detailed agreement, the 1979 Agreement on the Activities of States on the Moon and Other Celestial Bodies,[18] generally referred to as the 1979 Moon Treaty.[19] The agreement would have banned all private property in space, and for that reason, among others, the U.S. Senate refused to ratify it.[20] No other spacefaring nation ratified it either.[21] Therefore, it is generally agreed today that the Moon Treaty is nonbinding and not a part of international law.[22] As Kurt Anderson Baca noted,

The Moon Treaty outlaws property rights in any celestial body absent the establishment of an international regime. The Moon Treaty also aims at closing the avenue toward property and quasi-sovereignty left by the Outer Space Treaty. The Moon Treaty, however, has yet not been ratified by any major space power and has been signed by very few states. It is not binding as a treaty on the non-party states and the claim that it represents customary law is probably not credible.[23]

It has also been pointed out that the very fact that the framers of the Moon Treaty felt the need to write a new specific ban on private property indicates that they did not feel that the earlier Outer Space Treaty had already accomplished such a prohibition.[24]

III. Expert Opinions on the Outer Space Treaty

So the question is whether it would be an exercise of sovereignty, and therefore a violation of the Outer Space Treaty (especially Article II),[25] for the United States to pass legislation agreeing to recognize the right of privately funded, permanent lunar or Martian settlements, regardless of nationality, to claim land around their base. Most experts now seem to agree that the Outer Space Treaty does not ban private property. The following are several examples:

1) As law Professor Glenn Reynolds and *National Review* columnist Dave Kopel said,

It is widely agreed by space-law scholars that the Outer Space Treaty forbids only national sovereignty—not private property rights. If, later this century, Americans settle Mars, they will acquire property rights to the land they settle. . . .

The American government may choose to respect the Martian settlers' property rights, and even defend them, without violating the treaty's terms, so long as the government doesn't proclaim its own sovereignty over portions of Mars. . . .

As independent settlers, they would not be bound by the Outer Space Treaty, which only restricts the Earth-based governments that have signed it.[26]

2) Joanne Gabrynowicz, a professor of law and the Director of the National Remote Sensing and Space Law Center, said, "As regards to property rights per se, the Outer Space Treaty is silent. It contains no prohibition."[27]

3) Writing for the *Fordham Law Review*, Professor Stephen Gorove, former Chairman of the Graduate Program of the School of Law and professor of law at the University of Mississippi School of Law, said,

the [Outer Space] Treaty in its present form appears to contain no prohibition regarding individual appropriation or acquisition by a private association or an international organization. . . . Thus, at present, an individual acting on his own behalf or on behalf of another individual or a private association or an international organization could lawfully appropriate any part of outer space, including the moon and other celestial bodies.[28]

Professor Gorove went on to say,

the establishment of a permanent settlement or the carrying out of commercial activities by nationals of a country on a celestial body may constitute national appropriation if the activities take place under tie [sic] supreme authority (sovereignty) of the state. Short of this, if the state wields no exclusive authority or jurisdiction in relation to the area in question, the answer would seem to be in the negative, unless, the nationals also use their individual appropriations as cover-ups for their state's activities.[29]

4) At the 50th International Astronautical Congress, National Space Society ("NSS") representatives Pat Dasch, Michael Martin-Smith, and Anne Pierce presented a report on space property rights. The presentation concluded that "Several important principles have been established by customary law and treaty. First, national sovereignty stops where outer space begins. . . . Second, that national appropriation of the Moon, other planets, asteroids, etc., is forbidden. And third, that private property rights are not forbidden."[30]

Dasch, Martin-Smith, and Pierce noted that the third point had been controversial for some time.[31] But, they said, it is now agreed that "The 1967 Outer Space Treaty forbids 'national appropriation' of the Moon and other celestial bodies. . . . It does not forbid private property rights on these bodies."[32]

5) Even attorney and space law consultant Wayne White, who opposes the "Space Settlement Initiative" (U.S. proposed legislation to utilize lunar land claims recognition as the financial incentive to impel private industry to finance settlements on the moon),[33] said, "Some interpret Article II narrowly to prohibit only national appropriation. Many others interpret the clause broadly to prohibit all forms of appropriation, including private and international appropriation. When Article II is compared to similar provisions in other documents, however, it becomes clear that the narrow interpretation is correct."[34]

Before the Space Treaty was drafted by the U.N. Committee on the Peaceful Uses of Outer Space (COPUOS), four other international legal organizations prepared draft resolutions. All of these documents recommended nonappropriation clauses that are broader than Article II.[35] The terminology in these clauses suggests that at the time the Space Treaty was drafted, international lawyers did not consider "national appropriation" to be an all-inclusive phrase.

For example, a resolution of the International Institute of Space Law specifically distinguished between national and private appropriation: "Celestial bodies or regions on them shall not be subject to national or private appropriation, by claim of sovereignty, by means of use or occupation or by any other means."[36]

6) A. F. van Ballegoyen said simply, "Article 2 of the treaty . . . needs to be interpreted in a restrictive, literal meaning, namely as just the prohibition of national appropriation. This interpretation would allow other entities like private companies and non-governmental organizations to appropriate territory."[37]

7) And, in the *Connecticut Law Review*, environment and energy lawyer Lynn M. Fountain notes that, "Without assurance of property rights, private industry will not invest in the development of outer space. The right of continued use does not have to mean a declaration of national sovereignty."[38] Fountain further acknowledged that

> The Outer Space Treaty only bans national appropriation of celestial bodies. It does not specifically mention resources removed from such bodies, nor does it specifically mention or prohibit appropriation by private industry. The Moon Treaty is more specific on both elements and thus has not been signed or ratified by any of the space powers.[39]

These experts and many others agree that the Outer Space Treaty does not ban private property on the moon, Mars, or other celestial bodies.

IV. Recognition of Property Ownership

If private property claims in space are legitimate under the Outer Space Treaty, must the nations of the world pretend that they are not, or could they publicly acknowledge that they are? White pointed out that "under international law states may do whatever is not expressly forbidden. Restrictions upon the independence of States cannot . . . be presumed."[40]

Clearly, if the Outer Space Treaty does not ban private property ownership, it certainly does not contain a separate, special provision expressly forbidding nations from recognizing that fact. The long-accepted legal doctrine *expressio unius est exclusio alterius* says that, when interpreting statutes, we should presume things not mentioned were excluded by deliberate choice, not inadvertence.[41]

So what motivates those who proclaim that the treaty does ban such recognition of private property? Some of those who make that claim "believe only governments and government employees belong in space at all, ever, as a matter of principle and safety."[42] Others are trying to justify their own competing approaches to space development. For example, some scientists want the moon reserved for research alone and everyone else kept away.[43] Some fear that developing competitive space settlements might lead to armed conflict.[44] And there are even people who believe that private property itself, especially all land ownership, is an abomination and should be made illegal in the new world of space.[45] For these advocates, whether or not the Outer Space Treaty actually bans private property claims, it should—and for them, that is the same thing. As a result of such conflicting viewpoints, little progress toward space settlement has been made in the thirty years since the Apollo program.

V. Differing Legal Systems: Common Law vs. Civil Law

Some critics of private ownership of extraterrestrial land only take into consideration the provisions of English common law.[46] With common law, ever since William the Conqueror confiscated the old nobility's lands after 1066, all property rights have derived ultimately from the King or sovereign. So these critics feel that a ban on private ownership is automatically implied by the Outer Space Treaty's ban on national appropriation.[47]

Some even say that private property in space would be impossible because it would need national sovereignty in space.[48] However, in countries like France, which follow civil law, property rights have never been based on territorial sovereignty.[49] Instead, they are based on the natural law principle of *pedis possessio* or "use and occupation"—that individuals mix their labor with the soil and create property rights independent of government.[50] Government merely recognizes those rights.[51] Wayne White explained this point well:

> The relationship between property and sovereignty differs under common law and civil law systems. The common law theory of title has its roots in feudal law. Under this theory the Crown holds the ultimate title to all lands, and the proprietary rights of the subject are explained in terms of vassalage. Civil law, on the other hand, is derived from Roman law, which distinguishes between property and sovereignty.

Under this theory, it is possible for property to exist in the absence of sovereignty.[52]

This is why "In the discussions leading to the conclusion of the [Outer Space] treaty, France [a civil law country] indicated more than once that she was not altogether satisfied with the wording of Article II. . . ." France's representative was "thinking in particular of the risks of ambiguity between the principle of non-sovereignty—which falls under public law—and that of non-appropriation, flowing from private law."[53]

A key realization is that the common law standard cannot be applied on the moon, where sovereignty itself is barred by international treaty. As John Locke wrote, "As much land as a man tills, plants, improves, cultivates, and can use the product of, so much is his property."[54] In other words, ownership can flow from the use of the land. A. F. van Ballegoyen pointed out that

> Before the emergence of the nation-state it was both normal and self-explanatory for non-state actors to own territory. Contemporary emphasis on the state as sole organizer and regulator of both domestic and world affairs ignores the enormous potential of non-state actors to efficiently organize affairs up to a certain point.[55]

In sum, there appears to be no explicit ban on private property claims in the Outer Space Treaty as there was in the Moon Treaty. In addition, there is no explicit ban on nations recognizing such private property in good faith, and what is not explicitly prohibited in international law is generally permitted.

VI. Confusion with Invalid Attempts to Claim

Others who feel that land claims recognition would violate international law are confusing recognition of a settlement's land claim with what Dennis Hope, a seller of novelty lunar land deeds, does[56] or are confusing it with a covert

U.S. seizure of the land for itself. In fact, the Space Settlement Prize Act[57] legislation, proposed by Alan Wasser, as an example of one way such legislation could be formed shows how a land claims recognition law could be structured so that claims would only be based on true occupation and use of the land, with the United States not seizing or claiming the land in any way.

The only claims recognized would be those made by permanently inhabited settlements—made by people who are, by then, inhabitants of the moon and are no longer "Earthlings."[58] If residents of Earth want to own an acre of lunar land, they would have to pay the residents of the moon for it, thus rewarding these "Lunarians" for risking their lives and fortunes to open the space frontier for all mankind.[59]

When the International Institute of Space Law (IISL) recently issued a statement aimed at discrediting claims like Dennis Hope's claims to the moon (i.e., claims with no legal basis, such as use and occupation), some of those who confuse the Space Settlement Initiative[60] with Hope's "Lunar Embassy" claims tried to pretend that the IISL statement applied to both.[61] Wasser contacted the Board of the IISL to ask if the statement did, in fact, apply to both.

Dr. Nandasiri Jasentuliyana replied personally to say that it certainly did not. He wrote "the Statement was without prejudice to any future regime which might or should be developed. The statement indeed implies that there is a need for further work to be done to cover the future developments relating to activities on the Moon and other celestial bodies."[62]

Noted space lawyer Declan J. O'Donnell states that the legal basis for lunar land claims recognition, as described in the Space Settlement Prize Act, is "a valid approach to real property rights in space resources." He further stated that "compared to most of the proposals out there, [the] basic assumptions are not radical at all."[63] Passing land claims recognition legislation now would mark the beginning of a new legal regime that would fill the current vacuum of enabling legislation. This regime would base property rights outside of this planet on natural and civil law.

VII. Not a U.S. Land Grab

Some of those who have written on this subject recognize the need for property rights as an incentive for space development and the ambiguity of the Outer Space Treaty, but they are still mired in the concept that space development can only be achieved as it was during the Cold War—by nations and for parochial national interests. For example, in his *Seton Hall Law Review* article, lawyer Brandon Gruner portrayed the question of whether the Outer Space Treaty permits private property solely in terms of whether a nation, presumably the United States, could use that permission to cheat the no-sovereignty rules.[64] What Gruner did not mention is the possibility of good faith claims made by genuine private enterprise settlements, rather than citizens of any single nation and not acting as a front for any nation trying to slip national appropriation past the rest of the world. But such good faith property claims are the only kind that should be encouraged and allowed.

Any effort to establish a human space settlement is almost certainly going to be a multinational effort. No U.S. company could alone build a lunar settlement.[65] Participation by international companies will be a requirement in practice and could be made part of the law.[66] Financially, building a settlement will be so expensive that it will have to be financed and owned by stockholders from many different countries.[67] The settlement would have to use rockets and other components built in many countries, be inhabited by the citizens of many other countries, and would almost certainly launch from someplace outside the United States, such as Kazakhstan or the Kourou launch pad in French Guiana.[68] As Fountain described it:

> Given the high cost of space development, the formation of international partnerships among private entities will be crucial in any future de-

velopment of outer space. Such cooperation has the added benefit of ensuring that no one state monopolizes too many of the resources. Additionally, partnerships would provide developing states the opportunity to participate in ventures on a modest scale. . . . Such states could provide scientists, engineers, and/or a smaller percent of investment capital in exchange for a smaller percent of the profits.[69]

Therefore, there is no reason at all for a settlement company to place itself on the U.S. registry or choose to be under U.S. jurisdiction, and there are good reasons for not doing so. Today, few, if any, ocean-going ships choose U.S. registry rather than a "flag of convenience."[70] Therefore, the fact that the United States chooses to recognize the land claims of Kazakh or Guyanese companies, for example, could in no way be considered a U.S. attempt to appropriate the moon.[71]

VIII. "Recognize" vs. "Confer"

There are other critics of lunar land claims recognition who, although they admit that the Outer Space Treaty does not prohibit a settlement from claiming private property, nevertheless claim it would be an act of "national appropriation," and hence a violation of the treaty, for any nation to publicly recognize that fact.[72] Their position boils down to the following: It is acceptable for a private entity to claim property, but it is a crime for a nation to recognize such a claim publicly. The reason these individuals fall into a "do not ask, do not tell" approach appears to be a misunderstanding or a confusion between the terms "recognize" and "confer."

"To recognize" means to "acknowledge the existence, validity, or legality of,"[73] or "accepts, acquiesces to, decides not to contest."[74] In contrast, "to confer" means to "grant (a title, degree, benefit, or right)."[75] If a nation claims the right to confer, give, or grant title to lunar land, then it could be violating the ban on national appropriation. But if a settlement is established and

the settlers claim private ownership of land around their settlement and then a dozen of Earth's nations recognize the settlers' claim, it is not reasonable to say that all dozen nations are trying to appropriate the land and thus are violating the Outer Space Treaty.[76] As the proposed Space Settlement Prize Act points out,

> U.S. courts already recognize, certify, and defend private ownership and sale of land which is not subject to U.S. national appropriation or sovereignty, such as a U.S. citizen's ownership (and right to sell to another U.S. citizen, both of whom are within the U.S.) a deed to land which is actually located in another nation. U.S. issuance of a document of recognition of a settlement's claim to land on the moon, Mars, etc., can be done on a basis analogous to that situation.[77]

IX. Articles VI, VII, and VIII of the Outer Space Treaty

Other critics attempt to construct a ban on private property claims in space from various provisions of Articles VI through VIII of the Outer Space Treaty.[78] Articles VI and VII make states responsible to other states if, for example, a privately owned rocket launched from their country lands in another country and causes damage.[79] Article VII says, "The State [Party to the Treaty] on whose registry an object launched into outer space is carried shall retain jurisdiction and control over such object, and over any personnel thereon," and Article V says that the appropriate State Party to the Treaty must authorize and supervise its nongovernmental entities to assure "that national activities are carried out in conformity with the principles set forth in the present Declaration."[80]

But the treaty clearly does not contain any language explicitly saying that states may not authorize their citizens to do anything that they themselves cannot do, contrary to what some authors appear to assume. The treaty does not say that what is prohibited to states is therefore prohibited to private entities nor that what is prohibited to the regulator is therefore always prohibited to the regulated. A baseball coach gives "authorization and continuing supervision" to his players. Does the fact that the coach is not allowed to run onto the field to catch a fly ball mean the players he supervises cannot either? There are plenty of longstanding precedents demonstrating actions that the United States itself cannot perform legally but that it can authorize its citizens to do and can recognize when they have done so, such as adopting a particular religion, numerous trade and commercial activities, getting married—or claiming land on the moon on the basis of use and occupation.

Private citizens do not suddenly become mere legal parts, "creatures," or branches of the state because the state authorizes and supervises their space activities;[81] rather, citizens retain their independent existence as separate legal entities.[82] Therefore, if the framers of the Outer Space Treaty had intended to mean that states may not authorize their citizens to do anything that they themselves cannot do, they would have written such language into the treaty explicitly. However, the framers did not do this.[83] They deliberately required only undefined "authorization and continuing supervision" and compliance with the treaty.[84] Declassified U.S. State Department records of the treaty negotiations between the delegations headed by Arthur Goldberg of the United States and Platon D. Morozov of the Soviet Union show how these articles came to impose only that nominal burden on private enterprise in space.[85] The Americans, adamantly opposed to the Communist proposal to ban all private enterprise space activity, stood fast until the Soviet Union agreed to those substantially meaningless face-saving formulations.[86] A. F. van Ballegoyen said of the Outer Space Treaty:

> it concerns only obligations and rights of states. The link between states and non-state actors comes in the form of the principle of responsibility. States would be, as they are now, responsible for activities of their nationals or companies founded under its law. It would be simple for the U.S. to insert rules of behavior into licenses required by companies before they can venture into space.[87]

The phrase "carried out in conformity with the provisions set forth in the present Treaty" means just what it says. It requires that nongovernmental entities abide by what is in the rest of the treaty. Other than this phrase, the treaty does not add any new provisions. If the remainder of the Outer Space Treaty does not contain any provision that bans private property in space, and in this chapter the authors have attempted to show it does not, then "carried out in conformity with the provisions set forth in the present Treaty" cannot be reinterpreted as a ban on private property either.[88]

Some experts argue that the very obligation to regulate private space activities authorizes and requires states like the United States to establish reasonable interim regulations for private property ownership in space until a new treaty is negotiated that resolves the current ambiguities.[89] Professor Gabrynowicz proposed that the treaty could be modified by establishing

> national laws that fill in or clarify legal gaps in the international regime. Like the development of the maritime law that preceded it, the national laws of spacefaring and space-using nations can develop space law. This approach has been taken in numerous space activities: launches, telecommunications, commercial remote sensing, Earth observations and astronaut codes of conduct, among others.[90]

And, she added, "Now this is a particularly relevant time for this particular route."[91] Furthermore, Robert P. Merges and Glenn H. Reynolds suggested that

> some purely national law will emerge as a standard, or at least as a model for other countries to follow. In other legal areas, national leaders have effectively established patterns that have been followed by other countries: commercial law in the United States (as seen in the United Nations

Convention on the International Sale of Goods) and patent law in Great Britain come to mind. Similarly, in the space context, other countries could adopt the basic framework devised in the pioneer country. Alternatively, private entities could specifically "opt into" coverage under the pioneer country's laws—for example, by choice of law provisions in private contracts.[92]

Thus, they argue a jurisdictionally limited legal regime could emerge as the de facto international standard.[93]

X. What to Do About Ambiguities

Regardless of their views on the questions raised so far, the one observation on which nearly every expert agrees is that, as space lawyer Ezra Reinstein stated,

> The Outer Space treaty is riddled with ambiguities. It is silent, outside of affirming freedom of "exploration and use," as to what sort of rights parties can claim in celestial bodies. It is silent as to the circumstances under which these unspecified property rights might vest, that is, what a person must do to gain whatever property rights are available.[94]

In fact, the framers of the Outer Space Treaty were deliberately ambiguous about private property, as opposed to nationally owned property, so as to allow ratification of the treaty by both the United States, which wanted to encourage private enterprise in space, and the Soviet Union, which did not.[95]

The UN's Dr. Ogunsola Ogunbanwo, a space lawyer, is one of those who declares that the ambiguities were not only deliberate but also the right thing for the time: "This was not a pressing concern in 1967, when the Outer Space Treaty was ratified. It was perfectly acceptable at the time to consign a deeper discussion of property rights to future negotiation, as the United Nations did."[96]

As prominent space lawyer Rosanna Sattler wrote in the *University of Chicago Law Review*,

"The provision of the Outer Space Treaty which has caused the greatest controversy and discussion is found in Article II. . . . The appropriation provision of the treaty is arguably unclear and undefined and therefore unworkable."[97] There is even some argument that this provision conflicts with the requirements of other multilateral treaties.[98]

Kurt Anderson Baca went even further. He pointed out that Article II's provision on use and appropriation conflicts with other multilateral treaties, contradicts other parts of the Outer Space Treaty, and is so vague and ambiguous that it can only be considered an expression of a wish rather than a binding rule on anyone.[99] The most obvious of those self-contradictions is that the very first words of the Outer Space Treaty are "[The States Parties to this Treaty], Inspired by the great prospects opening up before mankind as a result of man's entry into outer space, Recognizing the common interest of all mankind in the progress of the exploration and use of outer space for peaceful purposes."[100] Yet by confusing the question of private property and thereby discouraging private investment, the treaty itself has blocked that "common interest of all mankind" for more than three decades now. Unfortunately, in this kind of international law, unlike normal domestic law, there is no judge nor court with the authority to provide a binding ruling, so the difference of opinion and ambiguity will persist.[101]

When a treaty is ambiguous, each signatory must interpret for itself what its obligations are.[102] Therefore, regarding the question of whether the United States should recognize a settlement's claims, the opinion of the U.S. government matters most. If the government decides doing so would not be an exercise of sovereignty, then it would not be an exercise of sovereignty.

White pointed out that the Law of Treaties states, "A treaty shall be interpreted in good faith in accordance with the ordinary meaning to be given to the terms of the treaty in their context and in the light of its object and purpose."[103] Clearly, the ordinary meaning of the term "national appropriation" is appropriation by a nation.

XI. A Precedent: The Deep Seabed Hard Mineral Resources Act

An excellent precedent illustrating how ambiguities of international law are and should be handled is the Deep Seabed Hard Mineral Resources Act,[104] which has been on the books in the United States since the mid-1980s, and it has been renewed and reaffirmed several times since then. Many have argued that it would be an exercise of sovereignty for the United States to award its citizens exclusive licenses to mine the deep ocean floor under the high seas of international waters.[105] Many in the UN likewise thought it would be an exercise of sovereignty, and they thus drafted a Law of the Sea Treaty trying to make the resources below international waters "the common heritage of mankind."[106]

The U.S. Congress disagreed. Excerpts from the Deep Seabed Hard Mineral Resources Act illustrate that the United States explicitly renounced its sovereignty:

§ 1401. Congressional findings and declaration of purpose

12) it is the legal opinion of the United States that exploration for and commercial recovery of hard mineral resources of the deep seabed are freedoms of the high seas subject to a duty of reasonable regard to the interests of other states in their exercise of those and other freedoms recognized by general principles of international law;

(13) pending a Law of the Sea Treaty, and in the absence of agreement among states on applicable principles of international law, the uncertainty among potential investors as to the future legal regime is likely to discourage or prevent the investments necessary to develop deep seabed mining technology;

(16) legislation is required to establish an interim legal regime under which technology can be developed and the exploration and recovery of the hard mineral resources of the deep seabed can take place until such time as a Law of the Sea Treaty enters into force with respect to the United States.[107]

§ 1402. International objectives

(a) Disclaimer of extraterritorial sovereignty

By the enactment of this chapter, the United States—

(1) exercises its jurisdiction over United States citizens and vessels, and foreign persons and vessels otherwise subject to its jurisdiction, in the exercise of the high seas freedom to engage in exploration for, and commercial recovery of, hard mineral resources of the deep seabed in accordance with generally accepted principles of international law recognized by the United States; but

(2) does not thereby assert sovereignty or sovereign or exclusive rights or jurisdiction over, or the ownership of, any areas or resources in the deep seabed.[108]

This is just the sort of thing the Congress could do—and just the wording it could use—to create that tremendous prize for the first true private space settlement. The United States could "recognize" (acquiesce to or decide not to contest) the legitimacy of a land claim made by the settlement that is using and occupying the land itself, acting as a *de facto* but not *de jure* sovereign. At the same time, the United States could say that it does not thereby assert sovereignty or exclusive rights or jurisdiction over or the ownership of any areas or resources in space—just exactly as it does under the high seas.

The analogy between private ownership rights without national sovereignty as conferred by the Deep Seabed Hard Mineral Resources Act and a land claims recognition law for celestial bodies is customary and accepted legal reasoning. For example, General Counsel for NASA, Edward A. Frankle, in a 2001 letter denying Gregory Nemitz's quixotic claim to ownership of the asteroid 433 Eros, said,

Your [Nemitz's] individual claim of appropriation of a celestial body (the asteroid 433 Eros) appears to have no foundation in law. It is unlike an individual's claim for seabed minerals, which was considered and debated by the U.S. Congress that subsequently enacted a statute, The Deep Seabed Hard Mineral Resource Act, P.L. 96–283, 94 Stat. 553 (1980), expressly authorizing such claims. There is no similar statute related in outer space.[109]

Frankle clearly implied that, if Congress did enact a statute like the Deep Seabed Hard Mineral Resource Act for space, it would be a valid basis for an ownership claim under the law. Most importantly, unlike the Nemitz claim to Eros, the claimant's actual occupation and use of the land on the celestial body would be an essential requirement.[110] Julie Jiru added,

> The fact that the United States would use its own initiative to invent a system with which it could live, rather than be subject to the control of non-mining states and be forced to share profits, is important to understanding the current position that the United States takes in relation to space and space law. The United States' reaction to the III LOS [Third Law of the Sea Convention] may be a good indication of the likely reaction to its questionable obligations under the Outer Space Treaty.[111]

XII. Another Precedent: Ownership of Lunar Minerals

When the experts discuss the ambiguities of the Outer Space Treaty, they usually mention two in particular: 1) the ownership of minerals removed from the land, and 2) the ownership of the land itself.[112] The U.S. and Soviet governments resolved the first ambiguity by simply taking moon rocks and declaring ownership of them.[113] As Thomas Gangale and Marilyn Dudley-Rowley, who oppose lunar land claims recognition, say in their AIAA paper,

> Has there ever been a serious challenge to the US or Soviet/Russian governments over their ownership (or at least their control) of the material they brought back from the Moon? These precedents established a principle of customary

law that "if you take it, it's yours." Essentially, this derives from the Roman legal principle of *uti possidetis*: "as you possess," so you may continue to possess.[114]

An international private settlement simply landing on and taking possession of a hunk of lunar land could similarly resolve the second ambiguity.[115] The settlers could then offer to sell pieces of their land to anyone on Earth in order to recoup the cost of setting up the settlement and running a space line open to all paying passengers, regardless of nationality.[116] All any nation of the world would have to do is not contest the settlement's right to sell lunar land deeds to its citizens.[117]

XIII. A Third Precedent: Flexibility (U.S.-Iran Treaty of 1957)

Article VI of the U.S. Constitution says all treaties made under the authority of the United States shall be "the supreme Law of the Land."[118] Those who demand the strictest possible interpretation of the Outer Space Treaty sometimes cite that phrase, rejecting any flexible interpretation.[119] In practice, however, the U.S. government reserves to itself extreme flexibility to decide what it can and cannot do under treaties,[120] providing flexibility far, far greater than the authors are suggesting in the case of the Outer Space Treaty.

For one of many examples of that flexibility, consider the Treaty of Amity, Economic Relations, and Consular Rights Between the United States of America and Iran (the U.S.-Iran Treaty of 1957), signed into law by President Eisenhower in 1957.[121] Because it is a self-executing treaty, was approved by a two-thirds majority of the Senate, and, despite ample provocation, was never amended or withdrawn, the Constitution dictates that this treaty is still the "supreme Law of the Land."[122]

In Article VIII and elsewhere, the U.S.-Iran Treaty guarantees that the United States will give Iran as favorable trade rules as it gives any other nation.[123] But in 1987 President Reagan, in reaction to the Iran-Contra scandal, reportedly ordered a ban on trade with Iran.[124] For the past twenty years, in spite of the U.S.-Iran Treaty, the U.S. government has prohibited commercial trade with Iran.[125] Although challenged in federal courts several times, judges have always avoided this apparent conflict between the theoretical supreme law of the land and the actual law as it is enforced by the United States.[126]

XIV. Purpose and Limitations

Some critics assume that the purpose of lunar (and similarly Martian) land claims recognition is to protect lunar residents from claim jumping (stealing someone else's claim after it is staked out but before it is recorded) and to allow them to completely exclude others from their lunar land.[127] This assumption is incorrect on three different counts.

First, the sole purpose of land claims recognition is to generate an incentive for privately funded space development and settlement by creating the only product that a successful space settlement could sell to the public back on Earth for sufficient profit to justify the tremendous cost of establishing the space line and settlement.[128] This product is hundreds of millions of paper deeds that are recognized by the U.S. government as bona fide deeds to acres of lunar or Martian land, printed on Earth for pennies apiece, but sold to Americans and anyone else on Earth for investment or speculation, for perhaps hundreds of U.S. dollars each.

A claim for a circle of land with a radius of about 437 miles around a settlement's initial base would contain about 600,000 square miles, which is about the size of Alaska and approximately 4 percent of the moon's surface.[129] That 384 million acres would be worth almost US$100 billion dollars at only US$260 an acre. At US$500 an acre it would be worth US$192 billion. Even at the very conservative average price of US$100 an acre it would be worth nearly US$40 billion.[130] That is the purpose of lunar land claims recognition.

Second, unlike a gold rush mining camp, claim jumping is not going to be a problem in early lunar settlements. The settlement and space line control access to the moon, as well as everyone's oxygen and food supply and ability to ship anything back to Earth.[131] The value of the land, at least in the early years, is in the ability to sell deeds to speculators and investors on Earth, and no one would buy stolen land from someone who is not the recognized owner.[132] Because the settlement will be eager to sell land and/or provide transportation to and from the moon at reasonable prices, spending billions building one's own space line and then wasting it by stealing already claimed land would make no sense.[133]

Third, the Outer Space Treaty will limit the ability to exclude all others from one's land. Article XII states,

> All stations, installations, equipment and space vehicles on the moon and other celestial bodies shall be open to representatives of other States Parties to the Treaty on a basis of reciprocity. Such representatives shall give reasonable advance notice of a projected visit, in order that appropriate consultations may be held and that maximum precautions may be taken to assure safety and to avoid interference with normal operations in the facility to be visited.[134]

All settlements and property owners will have to accept this rule until and unless the treaty is ever changed. Of course, even on Earth, most private property is subject to such visits by officials of local, regional, and national governments, especially if they obtain the appropriate court orders.[135]

The "benefit of all" requirement in the Outer Space Treaty's very first article imposes another limitation, which says, "The exploration and use of outer space, including the moon and other celestial bodies, shall be carried out for the benefit and in the interests of all countries."[136] This is what would require the space line and settlement to be open to all paying passengers, regardless of nationality, as long as they are peaceful and abide by the rules.

XV. *Reductio Ad Absurdum*[137]

The falsehood of the proposition that the Outer Space Treaty prohibits ownership of private property on the moon[138] can be further demonstrated by carrying it to its logical conclusion. Imagine the moon has been settled for a century. Hundreds of thousands of people live there. Ships to and from various parts of the Earth and Mars come and go from the main lunar space port every hour.

Will those hundreds of thousands of lunar citizens still do without any private property rights because of the two-century-old Outer Space Treaty? Will no one own the land where they—or their grandfathers—built their homes and factories? Will no one ever own the land where that space port's giant terminal buildings stand?

Even if that restrictive view of the Outer Space Treaty were to prevail, sooner or later, and probably as soon as possible, lunar colonists would most certainly decide to scrap it and start claiming ownership of the land they occupy.[139] Whether or not the settlement is recognized as a government, it will certainly acquire many of the attributes of a government, like deciding which of its citizens owns what.

At that point, the governments of the Earth will have to decide what to do. Go to war against the lunar colonists over it? Of course not. They will spend endless hours in legal wrangling about it, but in the end, they will have no choice but to acquiesce to some sort of reasonable lunar property regime. The United States, and every other nation on Earth, will eventually have to agree to accept and/or recognize the settlement's claims.

XVI. How Much Is Too Much Land for a Space Settlement to Claim?

Some critics ask whether an Alaska-size claim on the moon would not be more land than a settlement could use, thus invalidating a land claim based on "use and occupation" under natural law.[140] The answer is that the amount of land that a settlement can—and must—use depends on what the land is being used for and how much land the settlement will need to survive.

Everyone remembers "forty acres and a mule," but a cattle ranch or modern agribusiness farm could not survive on that. When settling North America, French and Russian fur traders in the North needed vast territories in order to survive, much more than English farmers in Massachusetts needed.[141] Space settlements will need to be able to claim sufficient land to yield enough of the only "product" that the settlement can sell profitably enough to guarantee its survival.

Space settlements cannot pay their bills by farming, fur trading, mining, or anything else that requires transporting a physical product back to the Earth. The only product identified so far that a settlement could sell back on Earth profitably enough to justify the settlement's creation is a recognized land deed.[142] When your livelihood depends on selling speculative lunar land that has been surveyed for subdivision but is otherwise unimproved, you can, and must, use a lot more land than an 1800s dirt farmer could use.[143]

The ideal size for such a claim would be enough to justify a competition to develop safe, affordable, reliable space transport and establish a settlement, yet small enough to leave room for future settlements. The authors calculate that a potential, reasonable amount could be about 600,000 square miles, or 4 percent of the lunar surface—a circle of land about 437 miles around the initial base, roughly the area of Alaska.[144]

The next questions are how large a permanent settlement has to be to claim such a piece of land, and would there need to be at least one human being occupying each acre of land in the claim from the very beginning? Wayne White, whose own plan for lunar property rights is strictly limited to such little land in a "safety zone" that it would not constitute any particular incentive for settlement, charged that lunar land claims recognition fails the "use and occupation" test.[145] He claimed, "[natural law] requires that claimants 'mix their labor with the soil' in order to establish property rights, but the Space Settlement Prize Act does not require actual occupation or physical improvement of an area before title is granted."[146]

White went on to say that "there is no precedent in terrestrial law for granting or recognizing property rights without a physical presence."[147] Although physical presence certainly must be required, historical legal precedence, in fact, very much agrees with the standard described in the Space Settlement Prize Act concerning how much land can be claimed around a base.

For example, the Russian claim to what is now Alaska was based on the first permanent settlement established by Gregor Shelikhov on Kodiak Island in 1784.[148] He was a Russian private entrepreneur, and the fur-trading settlement established by his Shelikhov-Golikov Company was strictly a commercial venture.[149] Despite efforts to involve the Russian government, almost all they received from the state were ceremonial swords and gold medals with the Empress's portrait.[150]

Even after eighteen months, the entire settlement consisted of only seven or eight individual dwellings, a number of bunkhouses, a counting house, barns, storage buildings, a smithy, a carpenter shop, and a ropewalk.[151] Its permanent Russian inhabitants could not have numbered even one hundred men, all clustered in one spot.[152] This was enough to claim about 600,000 square miles of Alaska and have the world accept it, and in 1867 the U.S. government paid the then-huge sum of US$7.2 million for that claim.[153]

Even today, thousands of square miles of Alaska do not actually have a human being on them.[154] In fact, if you have ever flown over Alaska, you know how much of the state still, two centuries later, does not meet White's standard of actual occupation or physical improvement; regardless, Alaska is universally considered "occupied" and "in use."[155] Alaska is an excellent precedent for ownership of land on the moon.

Farmers are not the only ones who "mix their labor with the soil." The pioneers who risk their lives and fortunes to establish the first lunar settlement, surveying the land for sale to pay the settlement's bills, will have mixed their labor—and maybe their blood—with the soil, and, therefore, they have every right to claim it.

XVII. "Chicken or the Egg" Problem #1: Property Rights Will Evolve Naturally

Another possible argument, based on the "inevitable" future, is that there is no need to push the legal envelope by passing lunar land claims recognition now because once a space settlement is established, a property rights regime will evolve naturally. It certainly is true that if a permanent space settlement was established without prior legislation, there would be claims of property ownership in space that would have to be litigated at length in the courts of the United States and other countries. In fact, if no advance legislation has been passed, there will be outrageous property claims based on much lesser bases than actual settlement.[156] This legal uncertainty scares off space developers who fear that, after they have spent a fortune developing space, they will only win the right to spend another fortune on legal bills.[157] Worse, it would force unqualified judges to legislate in haste from the bench, possibly producing very bad rules.

Reinstein said, "A legal system that is unclear as to the rights of developers in the land they develop is almost as prohibitive of positive development as a system forbidding development altogether."[158] Antitrust and Trade Regulation lawyer David Everett Marko added, "Free enterprise institutions simply cannot make significant investments in space while they are under the threat of lawsuits over the meaning of treaty terms."[159] Therefore, it is not at all surprising that, without the incentive that advanced legal certainty would provide, space settlement is not currently happening and it probably never will.

A few space lawyers like Jim Dunstan argued that firm property rights are unnecessary for space development,[160] although this belies the fact that space settlement seems no closer today than it did twenty years ago when David Anderman said the same thing. That is why lunar land claims recognition legislation is needed now in order to create an incentive to make space settlement happen at all.

Even the president's 2004 Commission on Implementation of United States Space Exploration Policy recognized this need, in which he said,

> The issue of private property rights in space is a complex one involving national and international legal issues. However, it is imperative that these issues be recognized and addressed at an early stage in the implementation of the vision, otherwise there will be little significant private sector activity associated with the development of space resources, one of our key goals.[161]

Furthermore, Fountain said, "Another crucial element in attracting private industry to the development of outer space is the protection of property—both real and intellectual. Private industry will not invest in outer space unless there is a significant return on the investment."[162] Adding to this, Ty S. Twibell stated, "Although a viable and lucrative space industry exists, only a minute fraction of the industry's potential is reached as a result of uncertainty created by space law."[163] Rosanna Sattler noted about the security produced by a clear property rights protocol that

> The establishment of a reliable property rights regime will remove impediments to business activities on these bodies and inspire the commercial confidence necessary to attract the enormous investments needed for tourism, settlement, construction, and business development, and for the extraction and utilization of resources.[164]

Jiru agreed:

> By not providing clear legal guidelines concerning the possible property rights and rewards that make commercialization a venture at least

worth trying, the repercussions of this treaty are confusion, resulting in ill-will between the space-faring and non space-faring nations, along with discouraging commercialization and resource development in outer space.[165]

Congressman Tom Feeney (R-FL) also pointed out that the lack of a private property regime is stifling investment in space:

> The current international legal scheme covering space resembles that governing the vastness of Antarctica. Similar results occur—a human presence limited to scientific outposts. Contrast this dearth of economic activity to that found in Alaska's harsh conditions.
>
> [The reason for the difference is] this legal regime creates great uncertainty about private property rights in space. Accordingly, no private enterprise will undertake the high risk venture of exploring for mineral or energy sources on celestial bodies or any other proposal to obtain economic gain from space activities.[166]

Still, some refuse to recognize this point. For example, Henry Herzfeld and Frans von der Dunk proclaimed,

> Corporations exist to make profits, and property rights only matter to the extent that they are necessary to fulfill the objective of maximizing profit. Popular literature and the statements of corporate executives gives the impression that unless companies can obtain ownership to space territory, they will not be able to invest in space activities profitably. But in the reasonably near future, no company operating in space will likely need outright ownership of space territory, including land on the moon.[167]

Of course, in the reasonably near future, no company is going to operate beyond low-Earth orbit at all because there is no potential profit in it as things now stand. Herzfeld and von der Dunk overlook the fact that the only possible way that a legitimate space settlement might make a profit is by being allowed to legitimately claim, own, and sell recognized lunar real estate around the settlement. They fail to recognize that, if the sellers of even ersatz claims (such as Dennis Hope) can make so much money, any settlement that could sell real land ownership could make a lot of money. Failing to pass a land claims recognition statute now is effectively forfeiting the chance to create an absolutely necessary incentive for space development.

As space businessman Gregory Bennett, then President of the Artemis Society International, said in 2003, "[Land claims recognition] clears the legal path for everything we want to do in the realm beyond the sky. This may be the most realistic and achievable way to accomplish our goal of establishing permanent human settlements on the moon. It is certainly a necessary step."[168]

Another paper that shows a fundamental misunderstanding of the economics involved is by Thomas Gangale and Marilyn Dudley-Rowley. It asks,

> if it were profitable for a company to go to the Moon and pick up rocks, it would. But it is not profitable at this time. So, how does it make it any more profitable if the company can claim title to the land for miles around the rocks that are too unprofitable for it to pick up, land that contains yet more unprofitable rocks?[169]

The simple, vital point these authors overlook is that net profit comes from sales price less expenses—revenues less expenditures.[170] Because of the astronomical expense of transporting rocks back to Earth for sale, it is impossible to make a profit selling rocks. But people on Earth would pay approximately the same price for a lunar land deed as they do for lunar rocks sold en masse once the settlement is established,[171] and the cost of printing millions of those deeds and delivering them to the customers is pennies apiece. Thus, even though picking up rocks is nowhere near profitable enough for an established settlement, the ability to sell legitimate, recognized ownership of the land the rocks are on would produce revenues in the scores of bil-

lions of dollars and earn billions of dollars worth of profit. Those billions of dollars of potential profit could be a powerful incentive to develop space settlements.

A similar economic fallacy is the notion that land, in and of itself, is somehow worthless until one either extracts valuable materials or builds something valuable on it. If investors will pay millions of dollars for it even if no physical use of the land has yet been made, how can anyone say the land is "worthless"? Anything, by definition, is "worth" what people will pay for it. In other words, the value is what the market will bear.[172] It has already been demonstrated that investors and the general public are willing to pay millions for lunar land from which nothing has been extracted, on which nothing valuable has yet been built and nothing will be built for many years.[173]

People will line up to pay money for recognized titles to acres of speculative lunar real estate just because they are part of mankind's first permanent space settlement, which offers regular transportation back and forth, so the land could someday be developed, and, theoretically, they could visit it someday.

It is amazing how many people have not yet adapted mentally to the changes in the American economy in the last century. These individuals still think that the only honest way to earn money is in basic industries like farming or mining. These people still have great difficulty believing that money earned selling intangibles (entertainment, advertising, securities, and, yes, speculative real estate) is just as real as money earned picking up rocks—and is a lot more profitable. If the customers get what they paid for, it is just as honest and legitimate a way to make a profit.

Jeffrey Kargel, a planetary scientist at the U.S. Geological Survey, has written, "if you want to cross the bridge into the 21st century of space [development], then space must pay its way and give private investors a handsome early return on investment."[174] The only way to do that is to pass legislation now, setting the rules for property claims and legitimate land sales.

XVIII. "Chicken or the Egg" Problem #2: Replacing or Revising the 1967 Outer Space Treaty

Some experts suggest that, rather than trying to work with and around the Outer Space Treaty, the solution is to amend the treaty, withdraw from it, or replace it with a new treaty.[175] Many propose specific provisions for a new international property rights regime for space, and some of these proposals are quite good.[176] The development of an international legal regime for recognizing and protecting extraterrestrial property rights, if it were set up to encourage rather than discourage privately funded space settlement, would probably provide an important stimulus for space development and settlement.

The problem is that there is no way to get the United Nations, the U.S. State Department, or the world's foreign affairs departments to even consider such a thing. Many have written about what the new treaties should say, but to the authors' knowledge, not one has proposed a realistic way to "get there from here"—to make a new treaty actually happen.

As far as the world's diplomats are concerned, there are far too many problems in international relations to "waste" time arguing about space property rights just to promote space development.[177] The last thing they want to do is to add to their already huge workload by opening what will certainly be a proverbial can of worms when they see no pressing reason to do so at this time. They also know that any attempt to get the United Nations to negotiate an effective new treaty offering huge financial rewards for space development could easily backfire and result in another effort by greedy leaders of many non-spacefaring nations to extort money or other personal benefits for themselves from those who want to promote human space settlement.[178]

There is too much affection for the good parts of the Outer Space Treaty, especially its ban on weapons of mass destruction in space, to expect the U.S. Congress to ever just pull out of the whole treaty.[179] The UN could only take up the subject of revising the treaty or drafting a new one at the formal request of member states,[180] and there does not even seem to be much prospect of getting any state to do that. Why should they? In fact, it would probably be even more difficult to get the U.S. Congress to call for the UN to draft a new treaty on the subject of space property rights—or worse, withdraw unilaterally from the Outer Space Treaty—than it would be to get Congress to pass lunar land claims recognition legislation.

But if the U.S. Congress passed such land claims recognition legislation—if it even looked like there was a serious possibility—then that, in itself, would force the world's diplomats to consider the subject. Suddenly they would be forced to choose between coming up with a good new multinational treaty or continuing to do nothing and thus leave the United States and whatever nations decided to join it in bilateral agreements to act independently.

The United States would have charted a clear alternative path that the spacefaring nations could follow if a useful treaty cannot be negotiated. There would be much less likelihood of a bad treaty emerging because the spacefaring nations could so easily refuse to ratify it. Therefore, the best, and possibly the only, way to make a new multinational treaty actually happen is for the U.S. Congress to start the ball rolling by passing something like "The Space Settlement Prize Act."

XIX. Conclusion

Despite certain conventional wisdom, the Outer Space Treaty does not in fact appear to ban private property in space. Nations could recognize land ownership claims made by private space settlements without being guilty of national appropriation or any other violation of the treaty. Land claims recognition legislation would, therefore, be perfectly legal under existing international laws. Such legislation would be the best way to promote privately funded space settlement and, in fact, may be the *sine qua non* for expanding the habitat of humanity beyond the Earth.

This is not an arcane discussion of legal theory but rather a call for immediate action—a single enabling act that will cost nothing but will serve to lever the opening of the new frontier. The U.S. Congress should, in its next session, consider a bill like the Space Settlement Prize Act[181] to legitimize the property rights of individuals in space and create the financial reward system (at no cost to the government) that will make true space settlement actually happen.[182]

NOTES

1. Sylvia Hui, *Hawking Says Humans Must Colonize Space*, SPACE.COM, Jun. 13, 2006, *available at* www.space.com/news/060613_ap_hawking_space.html . In Hawking's words, "It is important for the human race to spread out into space for the survival of the species. . . . Life on Earth is at the ever-increasing risk of being wiped out by a disaster, such as sudden global warming, nuclear war, a genetically engineered virus or other dangers we have not yet thought of." *Id.*

2. Lawrence L. Risley, *An Examination of the Need to Amend Space Law to Protect the Private Explorer in Outer Space*, 26 W. ST. U. L. REV. 47, 47–48 (1998–1999).

3. Cathy B. Thomas, *The Space Cowboys*, TIME, Feb. 22, 2007, *available at* www.time.com/time/printout/0,8816,1592834,00.html.

4. *See id.*

5. *See* Guy Gugliotta, *NASA Unveils $104 Billion Plan to Return to Moon by 2018*, WASHINGTON POST, Sept. 20, 2005, at A03.

6. *See* Warren E. Leary, *NASA Plans Permanent Moon Base*, NEW YORK TIMES, Dec. 5, 2006, *available at* www.nytimes.com/2006/12/05/science/space/05nasa .html.

7. *See Spurred by NASA, Russia Plans Its Own Moon Base*, Canadian Broadcast Centre, *available at* www .cbc.ca/technology/story/2007/08/31/science-russia -moon.html.

8. Douglas O. Jobes & Alan B. Wasser, *Land Claims Recognition (LCR) Analysis: Leveraging the Inherent Value of Lunar Land For Billions in Private Sector Investment*, Space Settlement Inst., Aug. 18, 2004, *available at* www.space-settlement-institute.org/Articles/LCRbrief text.htm.

9. It cannot be stressed enough that the reason for land claims recognition legislation is not to establish a good property rights regime for its own sake, nor is it to protect lunar residents from claim jumping, which will not in fact be a problem, as will be shown later. *See* The

Space Settlement Initiative, www.spacesettlement.org. The sole reason is to create the only product that a privately funded space settlement could sell to the public back on Earth for sufficient profit to justify the tremendous cost of establishing a space settlement. *Id.* This product is hundreds of millions of paper deeds that are recognized by the U.S. government and other governments as *bona fide* deeds to acres of lunar or Martian land, printed on Earth for pennies apiece, and sold to investors on Earth for perhaps hundreds of U.S. dollars each. *Id.*

The chain of reasoning is as follows: The objective is to promote the settlement of space—the day when ordinary people will live and work in thriving communities on the moon and Mars. We do not want the moon and Mars to be permanent wastelands like Antarctica, but instead we want them developed like Alaska. This goal would require an enormous upfront investment, but government has proven unwilling or unable to make this investment. *Id.* Private enterprise could make this investment, but only if there were a prospect of a quick, enormous profit upon success. *Id.* For this, there needs to be a very profitable product that a privately funded space settlement could sell to the public back on Earth. *Id.* It would be ideal if every nation of the world allowed the sale and acknowledged the validity of the deeds but, because the biggest pool of money is concentrated in the United States, which tends to lead the way in economic matters, it is U.S. recognition that is by far the most important. A claim of 600,000 square miles—around 4 percent of the moon's surface and roughly the size of Alaska—would contain 384 million acres. That would be worth almost US$100 billion dollars at only US$260 an acre. At US$500 an acre it would be worth US$192 billion. Even at the very conservative average price of US$100 an acre it would be worth nearly US$40 billion. *Id.*

10. *See* Space Settlement Initiative, *supra* note 9, at 13.

11. *See, e.g.*, Douglas Jobes, *Lunar Land Claims Recognition: Designing the Ultimate Incentive for Space Infrastructure Development*, SPACE TIMES 4 (May/Jun. 2005); *see also* Wasser, *supra* note 9.

12. Thomas Gangale, *A Limited International Agreement on Property Rights*, AM. INST. AERONAUTICS & ASTRONAUTICS, Sept. 18–20, 2004.

13. Treaty on Principles Governing the Activities of States in the Exploration and Use of Outer Space, Including the Moon and Other Celestial Bodies, art. 11, Jan. 27, 1967, T.I.A.S. No. 6347 [hereinafter Outer Space Treaty].

14. U.S. State Department, Space Goals After the Lunar Landing, 13–16 (1966) *available at* www.space -settlement-institute.org/Articles/research_library/Space

Goals1966.pdf (this document was declassified pursuant to a Freedom of Information Act request by one of the authors of this chapter).

15. *See generally* U.S. Delegation on Negotiations with the Soviets on the Legal Problems of Outer Space, Position Paper, Sept. 24, 1963 (on file with author) [hereinafter Position Paper] (describing the U.S. government's position regarding the Soviet draft of the Outer Space Treaty).

16. *Id.* at 7. The U.S. negotiators were not sure whether this was "an attempt to extend Communist principles to outer space" or just a negotiating tactic. *Id.* That is, the Americans thought the U.S.S.R. might just want to trade "a Soviet concession on private companies in outer space" for U.S. concessions on issues such as banning the use of satellites for war propaganda or the Soviet proposal that "the use of artificial satellites for the collection of intelligence information in the territory of a foreign state is incompatible with the objectives of mankind in its conquest of outer space." *Id.* at 7, 9; Laura Grego, *A History of Anti-Satellite Weapons Programs*, Space Weapons Basics (Union of Concerned Scientists, Cambridge, MA), at n.3, *available at* www.ucsusa.org/global_security/space_weapons/a-history-of-asat-programs.html (quoting the 1962 draft proposal given to the UN legal subcommittee by the Soviets). The U.S. compromise proposal "insures that each national government accepts responsibility for its activities and those of its nationals, and is internationally liable for them." Position Paper, *supra* note 15, at 7 (this Position Paper was declassified Oct. 3, 1990 and was obtained from the LBJ Library in Austin, Texas).

17. John W. Finney, *Space Treaty Called "Fuzzy" at Senate Hearings: Rusk and Goldberg Dispute Unexpected Objections by Gore and Fulbright*, NEW YORK TIMES, Mar. 8, 1967, at 20.

18. Agreement Governing the Activities on the Moon and Other Celestial Bodies, Dec. 5, 1979, 1984 U.N.T.S. 22 [hereinafter Moon Treaty].

19. Wayne N. White Jr., Presentation at the 40th Colloquium on the Law of Space of the American Institute of Aeronautics and Astronautics: Real Property in Outer Space 1 (Oct. 6–10, 1997), *available at* www.space-settlement-institute.org/Articles/research_library/WayneWhite98–2.pdf. The 1979 Moon Treaty contains a nonappropriation clause that is more inclusive than Article II [of the 1967 Outer Space Treaty]. Although Article 11, paragraph 2 of the Moon Treaty reiterates the language of Article II of the Outer Space Treaty, Article 11, paragraph 3 further provides that "neither the surface nor subsurface of the moon . . . shall become property of any state, international inter-governmental or non-governmental organization, national organization or non-governmental entity or of any natural person"

(references to "the moon" in the Moon Treaty refer to all celestial bodies and areas of outer space other than Earth and Earth orbits): "The [Moon] treaty also says, in Article 11, paragraph 1, that 'the moon and its natural resources are the common heritage of mankind.' Opponents of the treaty note that the developing nations often interpret 'common heritage' to mean 'common property' of mankind. As a result, the Moon Treaty has encountered resistance from countries with free market economies." *Id.* at 5; *see also* Moon Treaty, *supra* note 18, at art. 11.

20. *See* White, *supra* note 19.

21. *Id.*

22. *See* Lotta Vikari, *Time Is of the Essence: Making Space Law More Effective*, SPACE POLICY 1–5 (Feb. 2005).

23. Kurt Anderson Baca, *Property Rights in Outer Space*, 58 J. AIR L. & COM. 1041, 1069 (1993). The Moon Treaty introduces the concept of the common heritage of mankind to considerations of space property law. The obligations incurred by states under this principle and the Moon Treaty itself are unclear and have been the subject of much commentary. *Id.* at 1068–69. That view was endorsed in an official review of the space treaties by the Netherlands, one of the few nations that ratified the Moon Treaty: "Contrary to the other treaties, the almost complete lack of ratification of the [Moon Treaty] Agreement by the world's States will preclude any conclusion that the Moon Agreement would be endowed with some measure of customary legal force as an elaboration of the Outer Space Treaty with respect to a particular area (or number of areas) within outer space as a whole." U.N. Comm. on the Peaceful Uses of Outer Space, *Review of the Status of the Five International Legal Instruments Governing Outer Space*, at 21, U.N. Doc. A/AC.105/C.2/L.210 (Mar. 2, 1998).

24. Alan Wasser, *The Law That Could Make Privately Funded Space Settlement Profitable*, SPACE GOVERNANCE 56 (Jan. 1998).

25. Outer Space Treaty, *supra* note 13, at art. II.

26. Glenn Reynolds & Dave Kopel, *The New Frontier: Preparing the Law for Settling on Mars*, NAT'L REV. ONLINE, Jun. 4, 2002, *available at* www.nationalreview.com/kopel/kopel060402.asp.

27. Joanne Irene Gabrynowicz, *The International Space Treaty Regime in the Globalization Era*, AD ASTRA 30 (Fall 2005), *available at* www.space-settlement-institute.org/Articles/IntlSpaceTreatyGabryno.pdf.

28. Stephen Gorove, *Interpreting Article II of the Outer Space Treaty*, 37 FORDHAM L. REV. 349, 351 (1969).

29. *Id.* at 352.

30. Pat Dasch, Michael Martin-Smith, & Anne Pierce, Nat'l Space Society, Presentation at the 50th

International Astronautical Congress: Conference on Space Property Rights: Next Steps (Oct. 4–8, 1999).

31. *Id.*

32. *Id.*

33. *See* Space Settlement Initiative, *supra* note 9.

34. White, *supra* note 19.

35. *Draft Resolution of the International Institute of Space Law Concerning the Legal Status of Celestial Bodies*, in PROCEEDINGS OF THE EIGHTH COLLOQUIUM ON THE LAW OF OUTER SPACE 467–69 (Andrew G. Haley & Mortimer D. Schwartz eds., 1966); *Institute de Droit International, Resolution on the Legal Regime of Outer Space*, in SPACE LAW 416 (C. W. Jenks ed., 1965) (adopted unanimously Sept. 11, 1963); *David Davies Memorial Institute of International Studies, Draft Code on the Exploration and Uses of Outer Space*, in SPACE LAW, *supra*, at 419; International Law Association, *Resolution on Air Sovereignty and the Legal Status of Outer Space, in* SPACE LAW, *supra*, at 167.

36. Draft Resolution of the International Institute of Space Law Concerning the Legal Status of Celestial Bodies, *supra* note 35, at 468; White, *supra* note 19.

37. A. F. van Ballegoyen, *Ownership of the Moon and Mars: The Land-Grant Act as Means of Stimulating Human Settlement of Celestial Bodies*, AD ASTRA 37 (Jan./Feb. 2000), *available at* www.space-settlement-institute.org/Articles/research_library/BallegoyenOwn.pdf

38. Lynn M. Fountain, *Creating Momentum in Space: Ending the Paralysis Produced by the "Common Heritage of Mankind" Doctrine*, 35 CONN. L. REV. 1753, 1777 (2003).

39. *Id.* at 1777 n.156.

40. Case of the S.S. Lotus (*Fr. v. Turk.*), 1927 P.C.I.J. (ser. A) No. 10, at 18 (Sept. 7); White, *supra* note 19, at 4.

41. *Expressio unius est exclusio alterius* is defined as "A cannon of construction holding that to express or include one thing implies the exclusion of the other, or of the alternative"; also called "*inclusio unius est exclusio alterius.*" BLACK'S LAW DICTIONARY 620 (8th ed. 2004); IAN BROWNLIE, PRINCIPLES OF PUBLIC INTERNATIONAL LAW 602, 604 (6th ed. 2003).

42. *See* Space Settlement Initiative, *supra* note 9; *see also* Hickman & Simberg, *Why Is NASA the Only Game in Space?* LOS ANGELES TIMES, Oct. 1, 2007, *available at* http://latimes.com/news/opinion/la-op-dustup1oct01,0,3687593,print.story?coll=la-home-commentary; Press Release, Space Frontier Foundation, *NASA Can Fix Its Budget Problems by Buying from Private Industry Instead of Competing with It* (Feb. 5, 2007).

43. *See, e.g., Scientists Are Split on Whether Lunar Base Is Too Ambitious*, REDORBIT, Jan. 7, 2007, *available at* www.redorbit.com/news/space/791549/scientists_are_split_on_whether_lunar_base_is_too_ambitious/index.html.

44. For example, Patricia M. Sterns, G. Harry Stine, and Leslie I. Tennen say that "clearly, international peace and security would be served by the prevention of conflict over competing terran [sic] claims to portions of the cosmos. The resolution of this issue, therefore, was a universal prohibition of national appropriation in space." Patricia M. Sterns, G. Harry Stine, & Leslie I. Tennen, *Preliminary Jurisprudential Observations Concerning Property Rights on the Moon and Other Celestial Bodies in the Commercial Space Age, in* PROCEEDINGS OF THE THIRTY-NINTH COLLOQUIUM ON THE LAW OF OUTER SPACE 53 (1997). By extension, states could not license private parties to appropriate privately that which cannot be appropriated publicly because "wars of conquest also could result." *See id.* at 54. To the authors it seems most unlikely that a settlement established by, for example, a consortium led by Boeing and Energia would end up settling a dispute with the Mitsubishi/Aerospatiale settlement by means of a "war of conquest." It should be noted that Sterns, Stine, and Tennen advocate an international agreement recognizing a true permanent settlement's "autonomy . . . like unto another state" and "capacity as a legal regime," "an *exinde civitas politicae*, a political city-state in space." *Id.* at 60. But, somehow, they don't mention whether that "city-state" should have the right to claim even the land it stands on.

45. Space activist Paul Beich wrote a denunciation of lunar land claims recognition, saying, "capitalism is instead the primary obstacle to the . . . goal of a spacefaring civilization." Paul Beich, *Letters: Will Capitalism Work?* AD ASTRA 3 (May/Jun. 1998). Beich further wrote, "Capitalism is a disincentive for any activity that does not directly or indirectly result in the production of wealth for the elite. The profit motive is capitalism's euphemism for greed, and greed is a poor motivation for anything, especially the noble and exciting human endeavor of moving into the universe." *Id.*

46. *See* THOMAS GANGALE & MARILYN DUDLEY-ROWLEY, AMERICAN INSTITUTE OF AERONAUTICS & ASTRONAUTICS, TO BUILD BIFROST: DEVELOPING SPACE PROPERTY RIGHTS AND INFRASTRUCTURE 1 (2005), *available at* www.astrosociology.com/Library/PDF/Submissions/To%20Build%20Bifrost.pdf.

47. *See* Ray T. Black, *The Historical Background of Some Modern Real Estate Principles*, 34 REAL EST. L. J. 327, 333–34 (2005); *see also* Gangale & Dudley-Rowley, *supra* note 46, at 1; Richard Epstein, *International News Service v. Associated Press: Custom and Law as Sources of Property Rights in News*, 78 VA. L. REV. 85, 88 (1992).

48. *See* GANGALE & DUDLEY-ROWLEY, *supra* note 46, at 1; *see also* Henry R. Herzfeld & Frans G. von der

Dunk, *Bringing Space Law into the Commercial World: Property Rights Without Sovereignty*, 6 CHI. J. INT'L L. 81, 81 (2005).

49. *See* O. Lee Reed, *What is Property?* 41 AM. BUS. L. J. 459, 501 n.30 (2004).

50. "*[P]edis possessio* [Latin] A foothold; an actual possession of real property, implying either actual occupancy or enclosure or use." BLACK'S LAW DICTIONARY 1201 (8th ed. 2004). Similarly, "*pedis positio* [Latin] A putting or placing of the foot. This term denoted possession of land by actual entry." BLACK'S LAW DICTIONARY 1167 (8th ed. 2004).

51. *See* Epstein, *supra* note 47, at 85.

52. *See* White, *supra* note 19, at 6.

53. *Id.*; *see also* U.N. Commission on the Peaceful Uses of Outer Space, Legal Sub-Committee, *Summary of the Record of the Seventeenth Meeting*, at 14, U.N. Doc. A/AC.105/C.2/SR.70 (Oct. 21, 1966).

54. JOHN LOCKE, TWO TREATISES OF GOVERNMENT 290 (Peter Laslett ed., Cambridge University Press, 1988) (1690).

55. van Ballegoyen, *supra* note 37, at 37. Similarly, Seneca, in *De Beneficiis*, said "to kings belongs authority over all; to private persons, property." CHARLES M. MCILWAIN, THE GROWTH OF POLITICAL THOUGHT IN THE WEST: FROM THE GREEKS TO THE END OF THE MIDDLE AGES 394 (1932).

56. Dennis Hope, The Lunar Embassy Website, *available at* www.lunarembassy.com.

57. Alan Wasser, Space Settlement Institute, Draft of an Act Proposed, *available at* www.spacesettlement.org/law [hereinafter The Space Settlement Prize Act].

58. *See id.*

59. *See id.* at § 4(7). Before the Outer Space Treaty, it was always assumed, and almost common knowledge, that the people who first settled on the moon would own it. For example, in Robert Heinlein's 1961 science fiction classic *Stranger in a Strange Land*, the Federation High Court rules the moon, which is owned by a group of men who were sent on the second ship to land there, by a private, American-controlled Swiss corporation an island leased from Ecuador. *See generally* ROBERT A. HEINLEIN, STRANGER IN A STRANGE LAND (1961). Heinlein's court ruled that, although another ship, sent by the United States and Canada, had been to the moon first, it hadn't left anyone behind, and so "the real owners were the flesh-and-blood men who had maintained the occupation—Larkin and associates. So they recognized them as a sovereign nation and took them into the Federation." *Id.* at 43.

60. *See* Space Settlement Initiative, *supra* note 9.

61. Wayne White argued that the Space Settlement Prize Act would violate the Outer Space Treaty, citing the IISL Statement. Wayne White, *Homesteading the High Frontier*, AD ASTRA 34–35 (Fall 2005).

62. E-mail from Nandasiri Jasentuliyana, President, International Institute of Space Law, to Alan Wasser, Chairman, The Space Settlement Institute (Oct. 26, 2004, 08:54 p.m.) (on file with author). Dr. Nandasiri Jasentuliyana is the President of the International Institute for Space Law, which can be *accessed at* www.iafastro-iisl.com/.

63. E-mail from Declan J. O'Donnell, Esq., to Alan Wasser, Chairman, The Space Settlement Institute (Jan. 10, 2005, 01:24 p.m.) (on file with author): "Yes, the Space Settlement Institute has a valid approach to real property rights in space resources. In fact, compared to most of the proposals out there, your basic assumptions are not radical at all. Remember, until there is an answer there is no answer. Only time and effort and our working in the vineyard of space governance will solve the riddle. Technically, space resources appear to be public property. That is my starting place. Then research it and discover that individuals can get property rights in public properties, (but not in monuments). How to effect that is the open issue." *Id.*

64. Brandon Gruner, Comment, *A New Hope for International Space Law: Incorporating 19th Century First Possession Principles into the 1967 Space Treaty for the Colonization of Outer Space in the 21st Century*, 35 SETON HALL L. REV. 299, 332–33 (2004).

65. *See* HARRISON H. SCHMITT, BUSINESS APPROACH TO LUNAR BASE ACTIVATION 1–2, 4–5 (2002).

66. The Space Settlement Prize Act, *supra* note 57, at § 9 (1–3).

67. *See* Schmitt, *supra* note 65, at 6.

68. A new Boeing airliner these days has to use components and whole sections built in many different countries, and of course a lunar settlement would be much more complex and expensive. The International Space Station is another example of the need to use components and personnel from many different countries for big projects, and again, a lunar settlement would be much more complex and expensive. No one company, no matter how large, has—or wants to have—enough manufacturing capacity to do the whole job itself. Besides that, the cost of manufacturing, especially labor, can be significantly reduced by doing most of the work in multiple non-U.S. factories. Even more important, the financing of really big projects requires raising money all over the world (often from sovereign wealth funds), and to please those international sources of funding and their governments, the expenditure of funds must also be spread around. Similarly, international investors and their governments would certainly insist that the settlement's crews include citizens from their countries. As to where to launch from, commercial space launches from the United States are difficult, expensive, and involve a huge amount of red tape. Other countries are likely to be much more eager for

the business and, therefore, much more accommodating. Some might well offer significant financial incentives to use their space port. Onerous U.S. regulations force almost all U.S.-owned ocean-going ships to register under a flag of convenience, like Panama and Liberia—and that reasoning will apply even more in the case of big commercial space launches. Finally, the Kourou launch pad in French Guiana, being closer to the equator than any U.S. launch site can be, would probably be the most practical, efficient site from which to launch.

69. Fountain, *supra* note 38, at 1778, 1787 n.161.

70. *Vessel Operations Under Flags of Convenience and Their Implications on National Security: Hearing Before the Special Oversight Panel on the Merchant Marine of the H. Comm. on Armed Services*, 107th Cong. 6 (2002) (statement of Rep. Hunter, Chairman, House Commission on Armed Services).

71. As Henry R. Herzfeld & Frans G. von der Dunk pointed out, "States are liable if they qualify as 'launching State(s)' under Art I(c) of the [Convention on International Liability for Damage Caused by Space Objects, usually called] the Liability Convention, which provides the following definition '(i) A State which launches or procures the launching of a space object; (ii) A State from whose territory or facility a space object is launched.' Whether '[a] State which launches or procures the launching of a space object' includes a state whose citizens undertake an action in space depends critically on the circumstances; the mere fact of a citizen being active in space and thereby causing damage does not attach liability to the state of which that individual is a citizen, at least according to the Liability Convention." Hertzfeld & von der Dunk, *supra* note 48, at n.11 (citations omitted). Of course, no state would be launching or procuring the launch of a private settlement's ship, so the "launching state" would be the state from whose territory the space craft is launched.

72. *See, e.g.*, Jijo George Cherian & Job Abraham, *Concept of Private Property in Space—An Analysis*, 2 J. INT'L COM. L. & TECH. 211, 213 (2007); Lawrence D. Roberts, *Ensuring the Best of All Possible Worlds: Environmental Regulation of the Solar System*, 6 N.Y.U. ENVTL. L. J. 126, 140–41 (1997).

73. COMPACT OXFORD ENGLISH DICTIONARY (3d ed. 2005), *available at* www.askoxford.com/concise_oed/recognize?view=uk. Similarly, *Black's Law Dictionary* defines "recognition" as "1. Confirmation that an act done by another person was authorized. . . . 2. The formal admission that a person, entity, or thing has a particular status." BLACK'S LAW DICTIONARY 1299 (8th ed. 2004).

74. Space Settlement Initiative, *supra* note 9.

75. COMPACT OXFORD ENGLISH DICTIONARY (3d ed. 2005), *available at* www.askoxford.com/concise_oed/confer?view=uk. Similarly, *Black's* defines "Grant" as "1.

To give or confer (something) with or without compensation. . . . 2. To formally transfer (real property) by deed or other writing." BLACK'S LAW DICTIONARY 720 (8th ed. 2004).

76. Sometimes it is hard to tell whether writers are confusing "recognizing" and "granting a claim" deliberately, or just through semantic carelessness. For example, author Bill Carswell claimed that Vigilu Pop said, "for a private appropriation of land to survive it must be endorsed by a state, but that state endorsement of a private appropriation is interpreted legally as a form of state appropriation and is therefore disallowed by the Outer Space Treaty." Bill Carswell, *The Outer Space and Moon Treaties and the Coming Moon Rush*, SPACE DAILY, Apr. 18, 2002, *available at* www.spacedaily.com/news/oped-02c.html. But he gives no hint of whether he is using "endorse" here, to mean "recognize" or "grant." *See id.* If a genuine permanent human settlement was established on the moon, with a space line shuttling between it and Earth, and it (as opposed to a Dennis Hope) made a claim to private ownership of a reasonable amount of land around its base, the authors of this chapter and many others would heartily "endorse" the settlers claim. Would that "endorsement" be interpreted legally as a form of state appropriation—by us or the nations we are citizens of? The answer is no. That "endorsement" would obviously mean "recognizing," not "granting," the claim. So why couldn't every nation on Earth "endorse" the claim in exactly the same "recognition" meaning of "endorse" without violating the OST (as they would have if "endorse" meant "granting" a claim)?

77. The Space Settlement Prize Act, *supra* note 57, at § 2 (13).

78. Outer Space Treaty, *supra* note 13, at art. VI–VIII.

79. *See id.* at art. VI–VIII.

80. *See id.* at art. VII, V.

81. *See* John C. Yoo, *Laws as Treaties? The Constitutionality of Congressional Executive Agreements*, 99 MICH. L. REV. 757, 794–95 (2001).

82. *Id.*

83. *See* Outer Space Treaty, *supra* note 13.

84. *See Id.* at art. V.

85. *See generally*, Position Paper, *supra* note 15.

86. *Id.*

87. van Ballegoyen, *supra* note 37, at 37.

88. It is also worth remembering that, as mentioned earlier, there is no reason at all for a multinational settlement company to put itself on the U.S. registry or to choose to be under U.S. jurisdiction, and there are good reasons for it not to do so. If it is a problem, the United States need not be "the appropriate State Party to the Treaty" to authorize and supervise a ship owned by, for example, a Swiss-registered company, owned by stock-

holders from all over the world (even if a majority of them are American), crewed by citizens of a dozen countries, or launched from Kazakhstan or Guyana and flying a flag of convenience. (*See* discussion *infra* Part VII).

89. *See* Gabrynowicz, *supra* note 27, at 31.

90. *Id.*

91. *Id.*

92. Robert P. Merges & Glenn H. Reynolds, *Space Resources, Common Property, and the Collective Action Problem*, 6 N.Y.U. ENVTL. L. J. 107, 112 (1997).

93. *Id.*

94. Ezra J. Reinstein, *Owning Outer Space*, 20 Nw. J. INT'L L. & BUS. 59, 71 (1999). A different expert, Milton L. Smith, who disagrees with us about private property, nonetheless comes to the same conclusion about the Outer Space Treaty's ambiguity. Milton L. Smith, *The Commercial Exploitation of Mineral Resources in Outer Space*, *in* SPACE LAW: VIEWS OF THE FUTURE 47 (Tania L. Zwaan et al. eds., 1988). Smith expressed his personal opinion that authorities who adopt the "literal interpretation of the non-appropriation clause" and consider that the nonappropriation clause applies only to nations that go too far. *Id.* at 47. Then he debated whether the Outer Space Treaty also bans taking exclusive possession of minerals mined on the moon, but concludes it does not. *Id.* at 48–50. So, he said, "In summary, mining is a permissible exercise of the freedom of use guaranteed by the Outer Space Treaty. Both the non-appropriation and the freedom of use provisions, however, raise potential problems for exclusive claims in outer space. The language of the Outer Space Treaty is so broad and general that these provisions are susceptible to varying interpretations. Since disagreement on these issues exists, the Outer Space Treaty, of itself, cannot provide a satisfactory legal regime." *Id.* at 50. He also said that there are two ways to create a "commercially suitable legal regime": a new UN agreement, which he considered unlikely, or a private agreement among the spacefaring nations, reached outside of the UN, which he said "would be fully compatible with the Outer Space Treaty." *Id.* at 54.

95. *See* Position Paper, *supra* note 15, at 7.

96. Ezra J. Reinstein, *Owning Outer Space*, 20 Nw. J. INT'L L. & BUS. 59, 71 (1999) (citing Ogunsola O. Ogunbanwo, INTERNATIONAL LAW AND OUTER SPACE ACTIVITIES 70–71 (1975)).

97. Rosanna Sattler, *Transporting a Legal System for Property Rights: From the Earth to the Stars*, 6 CHI. J. INT'L L. 23, 28–29 (2005).

98. Baca, *supra* note 23, at 1066.

99. *Id.* at 1068. The interpretation of the Outer Space Treaty that allows property holding in space and quasi-sovereignty must, by inference, allow for some form of reasonable first use method of allocation. Because the Outer Space Treaty envisions use of space but does not establish any regulatory regime to oversee allocations of outer space, first use is the only possible form of allocation. This could take the form of occupation and reasonable use. But it is still difficult to distinguish this private appropriation with national sanction under national jurisdiction from a form of national appropriation at some level. The Outer Space Treaty may simply be vague, and hence merely precatory, on the issues of use and appropriation. The consequence of this could be to make the treaty nonbinding as creating no specific rule on these issues by analogy to the treatment of Article I. *Id.* at 1067–68.

100. Outer Space Treaty, *supra* note 13, at pmbl.

101. *See* Gruner, *supra* note 64, at 340–41.

102. *Id.* at 351. Gruner pointed out many advantages of U.S. withdrawal from the Outer Space Treaty but then added, "Yet, unilateral withdrawal from the 1967 Space Treaty by the United States is not the only way to implement a model of first possession; rather, any State might incorporate principles of first possession into an interpretation of the 1967 Space Treaty that retains the Treaty's broader philosophical ideals." *Id.*

103. Vienna Convention on the Law of Treaties art. 31, May 23, 1969, 1155 U.N.T.S. 331.

104. Deep Seabed Hard Mineral Resources Act, Pub. L. No. 96–283, 94 Stat. 553 (codified as amended at 30 U.S.C.A., §§ 1401–73 (West 2007).

105. *See* Lea Brilmayer & Natalie Klein, *Land and Sea: Two Sovereignty Regimes in Search of a Common Denominator*, 33 N.Y.U. J. INT'L L. & POL. 703, 736–37 (2001).

106. *Id.* at 736.

107. 30 U.S.C.A. § 1401.

108. 30 U.S.C.A. § 1402.

109. Letter from Edward Frankle, Gen. Counsel, NASA, to Gregory Nemitz, Chief Executive Officer, Orbital Development (Apr. 9, 2001), *available at* www .orbdev.com/010409.html.

110. *See id.*

111. Julie A. Jiru, *Star Wars and Space Malls: When the Paint Chips Off a Treaty's Golden Handcuffs*, 42 S. TEX. L. REV. 155, 161 (2000).

112. Sattler, *supra* note 97, at 28–29.

113. GANGALE & DUDLEY-ROWLEY, *supra* note 46, at 1.

114. *Id.*; BLACK'S LAW DICTIONARY 1582 (8th ed. 2004) ("*uti possidetis* = [Latin] 1. Int'l Law. The doctrine that colonial administrative boundaries will become international boundaries when a political subdivision or colony achieves independence."). Obviously, that doctrine may have a further role to play in the future of the moon and Mars.

115. Planets for Sale! Dave Wasser, Alan Wasser, and Tom Gangale in Conversation, http://pweb.jps.net/ ~gangale/opsa/spaceEx/PlanetsForSale2.htm.

116. Jobes, *supra* note 11, at 6.

117. *See id.* at 9.

118. U.S. Constitution, art. VI, cl. 2.

119. *See, e.g.*, Kenneth Silber, *A Little Piece of Heaven*, REASON, Nov. 1998, *available at* www.reason.com/news/show/30796.html.

120. *See* Lawrence J. Block et al., *Arms Control Treaty Reinterpretation: Commentary: the Senate's Pie-In-the-Sky Treaty Interpretation: Power and the Quest for Legislative Supremacy*, 137 U. PA. L. REV. 1481, 1506–07 (1989).

121. Treaty of Amity, Economic Relations, and Consular Rights Between the United States of America and Iran, U.S.–Iran, Aug. 15, 1955, 8 U.S.T. 899 [hereinafter Treaty of Amity].

122. *See* U.S. Const., art. VI, cl. 2.

123. Treaty of Amity, *supra* note 121, art. II.

124. Elaine Sciolino, *Reagan Bans All Iran Imports and Curbs Exports*, NEW YORK TIMES, Oct. 27, 1987, at A12.

125. *See* Akbar E. Torbat, *Impacts of the U.S. Trade and Financial Sanctions on Iran*, 28 THE WORLD ECONOMY 407, 410–11 (2005).

126. *See* U.S. Const., art VI, cl. 2; *see also* Lawsuits Against the U.S. Government, www.soudavar.com/index_files/Page431.htm.

127. *See* Leonard David, *NEAR Landing Sparks Claim-Jumping Dispute*, SPACE, Feb. 14, 2001, *available at* www.space.com/missionlaunches/missions/near_claim_010214.html.

128. Jobes, *supra* note 11, at 9.

129. *Id.* at 7.

130. *Id.* at 8.

131. *See* Narayanan Komerath, James Nally, & Elizabeth Zilin Tang, *Policy Model for Space Economy Infrastructure* 8, *available at* www.adl.gatech.edu/archives/adlp05101701.pdf; *see also* Space Settlement Initiative, *supra* note 9.

132. Jobes, *supra* note 11, at 7.

133. *See id.*

134. Outer Space Treaty, *supra* note 13, at art. XII.

135. U.S. Const. amend. IV; Los Angeles County, *California v. Rettele*, 127 S. Ct. 1989, 1993–94 (2007).

136. Outer Space Treaty, *supra* note 13, at art. I.

137. In logic, disproof of an argument by showing that it leads to a ridiculous conclusion. BLACK'S LAW DICTIONARY 1305 (8th ed. 2004).

138. *See* Carswell, *supra* note 76.

139. *See Homesteading the High Frontier*, *supra* note 61.

140. *See id.*

141. *See generally* Peter A. Thomas, *The Fur Trade, Indian Land and the Need to Define Adequate "Environmental" Parameters*, 28 ETHNOHISTORY 359, 373 (1981). *See also* Powell County Museum & Arts Foundation, *The Fur Trade*, *available at* www.pcmaf.org/fur_trade.htm.

142. Jobes, *supra* note 11, at 5–6.

143. It should be noted that the sale of speculative land deeds is intended to repay the huge initial costs of developing safe, affordable, reliable human transport to and from the moon and Mars and of using it to establish a space settlement and space line. It will also support the space settlement in its early days. Eventually, however, the existence of the space settlement and space line will make possible the development of many other more sustainable revenue producing activities. Some are predictable now, from astronomical observatories to televised low-gravity sports, but surely there will be many that we cannot yet predict.

144. Space Settlement Initiative, *supra* note 9.

145. *Homesteading the High Frontier*, *supra* note 61.

146. *Id.*

147. *Id.*

148. *See* Athanasius Schaefer, *Fort Ross*, *available at* www.athanasius.com/camission/ft_ross.htm.

149. *See id.*

150. *See id.*

151. *See id.*

152. *See* Sonoma.net, History of the Russian Settlement at Ft. Ross, California, *available at* www.parks.sonoma.net/rosshist.html.

153. U.S. Department of State, Purchase of Alaska, 1867, *available at* www.state.gov/r/pa/ho/time/gp/17662.htm.

154. *See* James A. Miller & R. L. Whitehead, Ground Water Atlas of the United States—Alaska, Hawaii, Puerto Rico and the U.S. Virgin Islands (1999), *available at* http://capp.water.usgs.gov/gwa/ch_n/N-AKtext1.html.

155. *See Homesteading the High Frontier*, *supra* note 61.

156. *See* Risley, *supra* note 2, at 59–61, 68–69.

157. *See* Reinstein, *supra* note 96, at 71.

158. *Id.* at 71.

159. David Everett Marko, *A Kinder Gentler Moon Treaty: A Critical Review of the Current Moon Treaty and a Proposed Alternative*, 8 J. NAT. RESOURCES & ENVTL. L. 293, 315 (1993).

160. James E. Dunstan, Garvey, Schubert & Barer, Presentation to the National Academies: Space Settlement: Homesteading on the Moon? Can I Own That "Back Forty" on the Moon? SLIDE 16 (Oct. 26, 2006). "If I can own *pieces* of space, and I can effectively own *places* in space, and I can own *intellectual property* in space. . . . Do I really need a formal property rights regime? It is NOT the lack of firm property rights that has stopped space development, it is something else. . . . It is *expectations and perceptions* that are the problem." *Id.*

161. PRESIDENT'S COMMISSION ON IMPLEMENTATION OF U.S. SPACE EXPLORATION POLICY, A JOURNEY TO INSPIRE, INNOVATE AND DISCOVER 34 (2004), *available at* www.nasa.gov/pdf/60736main_M2M_report_small.pdf
.

162. Fountain, *supra* note 38, at 1777.

163. Ty S. Twibell, *Space Law: Legal Restraints on Commercialization and Development of Outer Space*, 65 UMKC L. REV. 589, 610 (1997).

164. Sattler, *supra* note 97, at 27.

165. Jiru, *supra* note 111, at 156.

166. Tom Feeney, *Private Property and a Spacefaring People*, CPR Newsletter (Coalition for Property Rights, Orlando, FL), July 22, 2004, *available at* www.proprights.com/newsviews/.

167. Herzfeld & von der Dunk, *supra* note 48, at 91.

168. *Moon Society and Artemis Society Endorse Space Settlement Initiative*, SPACEDAILY.COM, Apr. 30, 2003, *available at* www.spacedaily.com/news/mars-base-03b.html.

169. Gangale & Dudley-Rowley, *supra* note 46, at 5.

170. BLACK'S LAW DICTIONARY 1246 (8th ed. 2004) (defining "profit" as "The excess of revenues over expenditures in a business transaction").

171. Space Settlement Initiative, *supra* note 9.

172. BLACK'S LAW DICTIONARY 1639 (8th ed. 2004) (defining "worth" as "The monetary value of a thing"); *Id.* at 1586 (defining "value" as "The monetary worth or price of something; the amount of goods, services, or money that something will command in an exchange").

173. *See* Jobes, *supra* note 11, at 7. It isn't necessary to guess what the rock-bottom value for lunar land would be, either. Over the last twenty-five years, an entrepreneur named Dennis Hope unwittingly conducted an experiment that indicates the potential market for lunar deeds: "A nationally recognized real estate expert. Dr. Jeffrey D. Fisher, believes Hope's sales of novelty deeds represent a fair comparison with the real lunar deeds that may one day exist. As the director of the Center for Real Estate Studies at the Indiana University School of Business and professor of real estate, Fisher is an expert in the science of property valuation. . . . He notes, 'One way appraisers estimate value is the comparable sales approach. That Mr. Hope has been able to sell novelty deeds for lunar land at this price [$19.95 per acre] may be an indication of the actual novelty value per acre. If an entity were selling land sanctioned by the U.S. government, which would make the ownership rights more official, then I can see the value being even greater.'" *Id.*

174. Reinstein, *supra* note 96, at 72 (citing Jeffrey S. Kargel, *Digging for Gold: U.S. National Aeronautics and Space Administration's Plans for Mining Extraterrestrial Resources*, ASTRONOMY 48 (Dec. 1997).

175. *See generally* Risley, *supra* note 2.

176. Reinstein, *supra* note 96, at 72 (stating "What is needed is an amendment to the Outer Space Treaty, one that both clarifies and expands property rights in space."); *see also* Risley, *supra* note 2, at 56, 66 (stating "the United Nations or a body with authority to govern the activities in outer space . . . must amend the space law to allow nations and individuals to recover the costs of missions to space, and even acquire wealth from space"). Heidi Keefe suggested a global organization that represents all the people of the Earth be created to lease out land in space. Heidi Keefe, *Making the Final Frontier Feasible: A Critical Look at the Current Body of Outer Space Law*, 11 SANTA CLARA COMPUTER & HIGH TECH. L. J. 345, 367 (1995). Fountain proposed a "Regulatory Agency" to create an equitable, efficient, and stable legal environment for the commercial development of outer space . . . promote cooperation and opportunity for all interested states, as well as for private industry . . . to promote productivity, investment, and the development of expertise; to protect property and profits; to promote international cooperation; to develop a set of affirmative duties; and to provide a forum for dispute resolution. Fountain, *supra* note 38, at 1776. But Fountain had no practical suggestion as to just how to make this agency actually come into being. None of the others deal with that problem either.

177. *See, e.g.*, Merges & Reynolds, *supra* note 92, at 107–08; Douglas O. Jobes, Space Settlement Institute, *After Apollo Why Didn't Space Settlement Happen?*, *available at* www.space-settlement-institute.org/30years.htm.

178. *See* Fountain, *supra* note 38, at 1758–60.

179. *See* Jayantha Dhanapala, Under-Secretary-General for Disarmament Affairs, United Nations, Opening Remarks at The Outer Space Treaty at Thirty-Five (Oct. 14, 2002), *available at* http://disarmament.un.org/speech/14oct2002.htm.

180. Outer Space Treaty, *supra* note 13, at art. XIV.

181. The Space Settlement Prize Act, *supra* note 57.

182. In September 2007, during a NASA-sponsored discussion of space property rights policy in Washington DC, a NASA official raised the interesting question of whether a Presidential Executive Order could be used, instead of Congressional legislation, to establish land claims recognition as a national policy. This would certainly appear to be an idea worth further study.

15

A Contemporary Review of the Air Space and Outer Space Regimes

The Thin Lines Between Law, Policy, and Emergent Challenges

JACKSON NYAMUYA MAOGOTO AND
STEVEN FREELAND

Introduction

The skies have always held a fascination for humankind, fanning our centuries-long quest to conquer and master them. Air balloons were the first to take humans to the skies in the eighteenth century. The first aircraft to make routine controlled flights were nonrigid airships-blimps at the turn of the twentieth century. At the start of that century, the Wright brothers made history when they successfully launched the first sustained, controlled, and powered heavier-than-air manned flight at Kitty Hawk, North Carolina, on December 17, 1903. Within a decade, various aircraft were being actively deployed for an array of purposes, ranging from commercial to military, although military and strategic imperatives primarily led the impetus.

In the course of the first four decades of the twentieth century, humankind continued its quest to master the skies with a series of technological and engineering breakthroughs fast-tracking these ambitions, while scientists increasingly cast their eyes even further afield to the heavens. By 1919 the first international treaty governing aviation—Paris Convention for the Regulation of Aerial Navigation—was opened for signature.[1] The era of air travel had arrived, and with hindsight, only technological challenges stood in the way of developments allowing for travel to even more ambitious destinations. Indeed, in the same year, Robert H Goddard demonstrated in laboratory conditions that spaceflight was an engineering possibility and that rockets would work in the vacuum of space; although not all the scientists of the day believed they would. In 1944 twenty-five years after the first international treaty on Air Law and Goddard's groundbreaking work, the first rocket, the German V-2 Rocket, reached space, although this was a suborbital flight.

With the end of the Second World War, scientists and governments focused their attention more singularly on outer space, with the then-only world superpowers—the United States and the Union of Soviet Socialist Republics (Soviet Union)—leading the way. During the course of the 1950s both of these states embarked on a series of initiatives that included satellite launches, manned spacecraft, and nuclear detonations. In

1957 humankind ascended into space with the Soviet Union's launch of Sputnik I, followed shortly thereafter by a series of successful nuclear detonations in space by the United States.[2]

In 1961 the Soviet Union launched the first manned spaceflight when it placed Yuri Gagarin into earth orbit. The United States followed suit in 1962. This marked the start of a new dimension in space activities. The earliest satellite programs focused on communications, weather intelligence, and navigation aids; however, almost simultaneously and indeed as an outgrowth of these technological advances, the military advantages that outer space offered were hard to resist once the United States and Soviet Union succeeded in placing satellites in orbit, and manned flights now also had become a possibility.

Shortly after the significant milestone of manned space flight, the development of a legal regime to govern outer space began when, in 1963, the UN General Assembly adopted the Declaration of Legal Principles Governing State Activity in the Exploration and Use of Outer Space.[3] This was described as the "first significant step in the development of space law;"[4] such was the import of the rules that were elaborated in that resolution at that time.

In the same year that the Declaration on Legal Principles was adopted, the Treaty Banning Nuclear Weapons in the Atmosphere, in Outer Space and Under Water[5] entered into force to address the contested and controversial issue of nuclear detonations in space.[6] Even before then, however, rules relating to the use and exploration of outer space had begun to evolve. A fundamental principle regulating outer space is that it is not open to claims of sovereignty. This reflects a customary law principle evidenced by the practice of states as early as the launch of Sputnik I. As Judge Manfred Lachs of the International Court of Justice observed in a decision handed down only a matter of months before humans first reached the moon:[7]

The first instruments that men sent into outer space traversed the air space of States and cir-

cled above them in outer space, yet the launching States sought no permission nor did the other States protest. This is how the freedom of movement into outer space, and in it, came to be established and recognized as law within a remarkably short period of time.

Currently, both air and space law represent increasingly important areas of international law and impact a wide range of governmental and private commercial activities. Many activities in space affect everyday life, including telecommunications, direct satellite broadcasts, weather forecasting, agricultural planning, mapping, remote sensing, surveillance and other military activities, exploration, and scientific experimentation.

This chapter examines the fundamental legal principles that underpin both air and space law but more significantly those that specifically regulate the use, exploration, and exploitation of outer space. It also raises and addresses several key issues and challenges posed by human activities in outer space, particularly relating to commercial use and its effects, emerging environmental concerns, and the militarization of outer space. Commencing in part 1, the chapter explores the prickly and as yet unsettled legal issue of the delimitation of air and outer space and offers a suggestion for resolving the matter. It then moves in part 2 to sketch out the main treaties that underpin the outer space law regime. The sketch here, though appearing rudimentary, is deliberately so. This is in light of the fact that in the subsequent parts (3, 4, and 5), the chapter fleshes out further the provisions of the various treaties within the framework of the themes. Parts 3 and 4 actively engage with extant uses of outer space, emerging uses, and the co-relation of legal provisions with engineering and technological breakthroughs.

Part 1: Air Law and Outer Space Law: Legal and Policy Dynamics

The international law of outer space is "a [relative] newcomer to the family of legal disciplines."[8]

The law of outer space has developed as a discrete body of law within international law. Since the launch of Sputnik I, this process of evolution has been remarkably rapid, largely driven by the realization of the international community of the need to agree on rules to regulate activities in this new "frontier." There is now a substantial body of international and domestic law principles dealing with many—but not all—aspects of the use and exploration of outer space. The principles are mainly contained in a series of UN-sponsored multilateral treaties, UN General Assembly Resolutions, a wide range of national legislation, decisions by national courts, bilateral arrangements (particularly, but not only, between the United States and the Soviet Union), and determinations by Intergovernmental Organizations. Of all of these, the most important elements of the legal regime of outer space as it now exists are the five principal UN treaties on outer space.[9] These treaties themselves largely evolved from a series of UN General Assembly Resolutions and declarations, which followed from the UN General Assembly's creation of the Committee on the Peaceful Uses of Outer Space (COPUOS) to study the regulation of governing outer space.[10]

With the space race between the superpowers continuing in earnest and the new regime covered only by general and nonbinding principles, in 1967 the considerable authority of the pronouncements of the 1963 Declaration of Legal Principles were cemented into a binding legal instrument with the adoption of the Outer Space Treaty. This treaty, referred to as "the constitution of outer space,"[11] represents "the primary basis for legal order in the space environment."[12] Drawn principally from previous UN General Assembly Resolutions,[13] the Outer Space Treaty has sometimes been termed as the "Magna Carta of outer space law."[14]

History has demonstrated that as technology has evolved and states have increasingly recognized the potential of outer space, the range of activities planned for outer space has proliferated. In addition, the commercial prospects offered by outer space have led private enterprises

to participate significantly. As these activities have emerged, the international community has adopted further regulatory procedures, largely on an ad hoc and reactive basis. These are mainly found in five sets of principles adopted by the UN General Assembly.[15] By definition, resolutions of the General Assembly are nonbinding and these principles have largely been considered as constituting "soft law," although a number of their provisions may now represent customary international law.[16]

As a consequence, despite providing a framework of fundamental principles and some very important specific guidelines, the existing international legal regime that currently regulates outer space has not kept pace with much of the remarkable technological and commercial progress of space activities since 1957. This represents a major challenge, and all the more so in view of the strategic, military, and commercial potential of outer space.

1.1. Air Space Law Vis-À-Vis Outer Space Law

This section raises important aspects of the space law regime and, in particular, the instruments that underpin this international legal framework. However, before analyzing pertinent treaties, it provides a preliminary discussion of the interrelationship between the air space and outer space legal regimes, which involves a discussion of the as yet still-undetermined matter of the delimitation between air space and outer space. That the matter of delimitation is, remarkably, still an active debate, despite the existence of distinct legal regimes and principles governing the use of air space on the one hand, and outer space on the other, itself represents a growing challenge given the increasingly diverse range of activities people have undertaken in both arenas.

1.1.1. Two Different Regimes, Different Dynamics

Few issues in the field of space law have been raised as often or elicited as much diversity of opinion and theorization as the delimitation between air space and outer space. The matter is put in a much more forceful perspective when one considers that, more than five decades after humankind's ascent into space and against the backdrop of the development of a substantial body of space law and the evolution of many customary principles, there is still no broad-based consensus on the demarcation between air space and outer space.

The question of delimitation is particularly important because the legal regimes applicable to both spheres are diametrically opposed. In terms of air space, national sovereignty is total and exclusive. By the time Sputnik I had begun its orbit of earth, there was in place a well-established body of international law dealing with commercial air travel. These principles are primarily reflected in a number of widely accepted multilateral treaties, the most important of which include the Convention for the Unification of Certain Rules Relating to International Carriage by Air,[17] which deals with the liability of air carriers, and the Convention on International Civil Aviation,[18] which sets out the legal categorization of air space.

Although it is beyond the scope of this chapter to describe the fundamentals of the international law of air space, it is important to note that this law is based on the legal assumption that, to a large degree, air space constitutes the "territory" of the underlying state. Indeed, mirroring the terms of the Paris Convention,[19] the Chicago Convention provides that "every State has complete and exclusive sovereignty over the airspace above its territory."[20] This is also reflected in customary international law.[21] As a consequence, civil and commercial aircraft only have certain limited rights to enter the air space of another state.[22] In direct contrast, claims of exclusive national sovereignty in outer space are expressly prohibited by international agreement. The Outer Space Treaty provides that "Outer space . . . is not subject to national appropriation by claim of sovereignty, by means of use or occupation, or by any other means."[23]

The delimitation of outer space is one that has (and continues to) taxed scholars, practitioners, as well as the broader international community. To date, this matter still remains unresolved, with a slew of theories actively on the table. Over the years, many suggested methodologies have been proffered to resolve this uncertainty, though none of these have been accepted as a legal definition by the international community through the COPUOS process, partially in response to the advancing technology in relation to conventional aircraft but also due to an apprehension that to agree to such a demarcation may formalize the surrendering of "future valuable sovereign rights."[24]

One of the main principles that have evolved is the right to launch satellites or space objects that orbit over the subjacent territory of other sovereign countries without prior permission or authorization. In essence, outer space is "free" for use; activities that take place in outer space are (generally) not subject to prior consent on the part of any sovereign state. In space law this international right is well entrenched both through treaty law and customary principles. The right is encapsulated in treaty form in articles I and II of the Outer Space Treaty, which reflect the consensus that outer space is the "province of mankind" and not "subject to national appropriation by claim of sovereignty."[25] This encapsulation forms the basis of the customary principle. Both the treaty and customary positions are backed by strong state practice and *opinio juris*. This customary law position is evident from the reality that, since the first launching of satellites into outer space, there have not been any significant objections regarding the right of Earth-orbiting satellites to pass over the territories of other nations without their consent.

However, the wide acceptance of the norm in relation to outer space is completely at odds with well-recognized and -established principles of air law referred to above. This spatial exclusivity has seen military and civilian aircraft frequently shot down for allegedly unauthorized aerial intrusion in the air space of foreign states.[26] Jurisdiction for such conduct stems from the clearly recognized international air law principle that countries enjoy exclusive sovereignty and control of the air space over their territory.

The various theories relating to space law fall broadly in two dominant schools of thought (each of which has several subtheories tucked into it): the functionalist and spatialist schools. The functionalist approach examines the nature of the activities pursued as a means of definition, whereas the spatialist approach defers to examining various atmospheric layers or zones. The section now turns to consider these schools in more detail.

1.1.1.1. The Functionalist School

The basic premise associated with the functionalist approach is predicated on the purpose of the activity conducted in space rather than the physical location of its occurrence, thereby leading to a distinction between purely aeronautical activities and astronautical activities.[27] At first glance, the functionalist approach appears to provide a clear and unambiguous standard for determining what is to be considered air space or outer space. However, a functional approach still requires a definition of "aeronautical activities" in order to differentiate between air space and outer space. This in turn would require defining the purposes of various missions on an ad hoc basis. It is the ad hoc, piecemeal nature of this school that hobbles its utility as a legal standard. No firm or certain calibration can be made on the basis of the fluidity of the school's central premise.

1.1.1.2. The Spatialist School

The notion of dividing the atmosphere into layers or zones lies at the heart of the spatialist approach. Considering that this school generally seems to be more ascendant than the functionalist school (although by no means is it accepted unanimously), we set out below a more detailed enunciation. Spatialist theories include demarcation based on the equation of the upper limit of the atmosphere, the division of the atmosphere into layers, the maximum altitude of an aircraft, the aerodynamic characteristics of flight instrumentalities, the lowest perigee of an orbiting satellite, and the Earth's gravitational effects.[28]

Predominant in this school is the aerodynamic lift theory, based on the Council of the International Civil Aviation Organization's (ICAO) definition of an aircraft as "any machine that can derive support in the atmosphere from the reactions of the air other than the reactions of the air against the earth's surface."[29] the ICAO Secretariat presently estimates the maximum altitude at which a machine can derive support from the reactions of the air to be about 35 kilometers. This position provides the basis of one of the most widely discussed proposals for a demarcation between air space and outer space—the so-called "Von Kármán line."[30] This line, though hostage to technological progress, is nonetheless a valuable reference boundary, and its utility is bolstered by the fact that the United States, a leading space power, designates people who travel above an altitude of 80 kilometers as astronauts.

A second basis for demarcation under the spatialist school is based on the lowest perigee of an orbiting satellite. In the present practice, the lowest limit of satellite orbits is approximately at 150–160 kilometers in height.[31] Underpinning this approach is the fact that, at a certain altitude, the Earth's atmosphere is too dense for an artificial satellite to stay in orbit. The lowest perigee approach has the advantage of being in accord with existing practices in orbiting satellites and with countries' attitudes toward objects in Earth orbit. Although the perigee of a durable satellite orbit may be a fluid measure in light of ongoing improvements in space flight technology,[32] this delimitation offers a robust and relatively stable reference boundary when compared with other positions in a pool of varying and often divergent theories. Importantly, the conclusion of an extensive and comprehensive survey by Professor Robert F. A. Goedhart, a leading international space scholar, also supports this measure.[33]

1.1.2. A Third Path?

More recently, there have been examples of a randomly chosen altitude as a demarcation for the purposes of particular regulatory regimes.

There has, for example, recently been an interesting development in the context of Australian domestic space legislation that may herald the move toward a more widely recognized demarcation point.[34]

Of even greater significance is the suggestion in a major draft international treaty that the 100-kilometre mark be used as the point to define the meaning of outer space. In February 2008 the Minister of Foreign Affairs of the Russian Federation, Sergey Lavrov, presented a draft document headed Treaty on the Prevention of the Placement of Weapons in Outer Space, the Threat or Use of Force Against Outer Space Objects (PPWT) to the sixty-five members attending the Plenary Meeting of the UN Conference on Disarmament (CD) in Geneva.[35] Two of the major space superpowers in the world, Russia and China, developed the PPWT. An earlier draft had been informally circulated the previous June, resulting in comments from a number of other countries.[36]

Article I (a) of the PPWT defines "outer space" as "space beyond the elevation of approximately 100 km above ocean level of the Earth." Apart from the curious use of the word "approximately"—in what circumstances would it *not* be 100 kilometers?—this represents a rather revolutionary suggestion by two major superpowers, which, along with the United States, have tended to stifle previous attempts to designate a formal demarcation, primarily for strategic and political reasons. Indeed, it was only a few years ago that a Chinese Foreign Ministry spokesperson referred to outer space as the "Fourth Territory."

It remains to be seen both whether and to what extent these examples are copied elsewhere and also if a clear customary international law principle incorporating a 100-kilometre demarcation will ultimately emerge.

Part 2: The International Legal Regime and Outer Space in a Nutshell

Outer space activity is regulated by both national and international law. As noted above, the international legal regime is based on five major treaties negotiated primarily under the auspices of COPUOS. They are as follows:

2.1. Treaty on Principles Governing the Activities of States in the Exploration and Use of Outer Space, Including the Moon and Other Celestial Bodies

The major principles governing activities in space are presented in articles I, II, and III of the Outer Space Treaty.[37] Article I states that activities in outer space, including the moon and other celestial bodies, shall be conducted for the benefit of all countries and that outer space shall be the province of humankind.[38] It also provides for freedom of scientific investigation in outer space and for international cooperation in such investigation.[39] Article II provides that nations cannot appropriate outer space by claim of sovereignty.[40] Article III provides that states parties to the treaty will conduct their activities in space in accordance with international law, the UN Charter, and in the interest of international peace, security, cooperation, and understanding.[41]

2.2. Agreement on the Rescue of Astronauts, the Return of Astronauts, and the Return of Objects Launched into Outer Space

The second major space treaty to emerge from COPUOS is the Agreement on the Rescue of Astronauts, the Return of Astronauts, and the Return of Objects Launched into Outer Space. It focuses primarily on the relief of distressed space travelers. However, article 5 of this agreement requires a state to assist in recovering space objects of other states that land on its territory.

2.3. Convention on International Liability for Damage Caused by Space Objects

The Convention on International Liability for Damage Caused by Space Objects (Liability Convention) is probably the most "legal" of the space treaties. Essentially, this convention gives vitality to article VII of the Outer Space Treaty.[42] The Liability Convention imposes strict liability on states that launch space objects for damage caused by those objects "on the surface of the Earth or to aircraft in flight." Liability according to fault is imposed for damage in outer space caused by one state's space object to persons or property on board a space object of another state. The Liability Convention establishes joint and several liability for accidents caused by two or more launching states and provides for indemnity and apportionment agreements between launching states. Most importantly, the Liability Convention sets up procedures by which a state damaged (either directly or indirectly) by a space object may present a claim for the damage to the launching state. The parties first try to settle claims through diplomatic negotiations. If negotiations fail, the parties will establish a Claims Commission to make an award, which may be binding or advisory as determined by the parties themselves.[43]

2.4. Convention on Registration of Objects Launched into Outer Space

Just as the Liability Convention fleshed out article VII of the Outer Space Treaty, the Convention on Registration of Objects Launched into Outer Space (Registration Convention) gives meaning to provisions in the Outer Space Treaty that refer to the registration of space objects (principally article VIII). The Registration Convention provides for two types of registration: national and international.

2.5. Agreement Governing the Activities of States on the Moon and Other Celestial Bodies

The final of the space treaties is the Agreement Governing Activities of States on the Moon and Other Celestial Bodies—the so-called Moon Treaty. Like the Outer Space Treaty, it provides that the moon shall be used exclusively for peaceful purposes, that there shall be freedom of scientific investigation on the moon, that weapons of mass destruction and military bases are forbidden on the moon, and that states exploring and using the moon are obligated to prevent harmful contamination of the moon's environment. Article III of the Moon Agreement repeats much of article IV of the Outer Space Treaty's.[44] It states that the moon shall be used exclusively for "peaceful purposes" and prohibits placing nuclear weapons or any other kinds of weapons of mass destruction in the moon's orbit or trajectory. It also forbids establishing military bases, installations, or fortifications; testing weapons; or conducting military maneuvers on the moon, but it does allow the use of military personnel for scientific purposes or for any other peaceful purposes. Article III further prohibits the threat or use of force or any other hostile act on the moon as well as using the moon to commit such an act in relation to the Earth or to manufactured space objects.

Part 3: The Nature and Scope of Commercial Activities in Outer Space

3.1. Telecommunications

Telecommunications was the first aspect of outer space activity to be commercialized. It remains the most lucrative sector of space commerce. Space-based commerce began early in the Age of Space Exploration. Beginning in 1962 space-based commerce was propelled when the U.S. government established the first for-profit space-related company, the Communications Satellite Corporation (COMSAT).[45] Not surprisingly, entrepreneurial uptake was slow, partly owing to the expense of technology and partly to the significant risks and lack of underwriting available from private insurers. In the 1980s, however, these two main obstacles had largely diminished. Private finance and ventures raced into the field as the potential for space commerce beyond telecommunications became apparent.

By the 1990s revenues from international, regional, state, and private satellite systems had annual revenues of billions of dollars.[46] The dominant two global players are the International Telecommunications Satellite Organization (INTELSAT) and the International Maritime Satellite Organization (INMARSAT), which began as international organizations; they have both since been privatized, primarily serving the needs of the international community of states and, as an aside, commercial players. As early as 1965 INTELSAT was the first commercial supplier of satellite communications services.[47] INTELSAT satellites have two functions. First, the primary satellite in each ocean region provides basic connectivity to all nations in the region. Second, other satellites provide specialized services, such as bundling major path communications so as to alleviate traffic on the primary satellite, business communications to small antennas, cable restoration, and domestic leased services.[48]

INMARSAT is an international organization that provides global satellite telecommunications services, primarily to the maritime community. Although maritime services are its biggest revenue source, it also offers land mobile and aeronautical services. INMARSAT operates through a system of land, coastal, and ground Earth stations supplemented with a dozen or so satellites that deliver almost complete global coverage.

In addition to INTELSAT and INMARSAT, there are a number of regional satellite communications organizations, including the European Telecommunications Satellite Organization (EUTELSAT), the International Organization of Space Communications (INTERSPUTNIK), the Asia Satellite Telecommunications Company (ASIASAT), the Association of Telecommunication Undertakings of the Andean Sub-Regional Agreement (ASETA), the Arab Satellite Communications Organization (ARABSAT), and the Regional African Satellite Communications Organization (RASCOM). EUTELSAT is the largest global, international telecommunications satellite system after INTELSAT and INMARSAT. Like INTELSAT and INMARSAT, EUTELSAT is governed by multilateral agreement.

At the turn of the millennium, at least fifty countries used satellites they own for some or all of their telecommunications and broadcasting needs.[49] In addition, there are now dozens of satellites deployed, owned, and managed by private enterprises. The list of private commercial satellite service providers includes but is not limited to American Mobile Satellite Corp, Alascom, Globalstar, PanAmSat, Shinawatra Sat. Co., APT Sat. Co. Ltd., Hughes Galaxy, Embratel, Columbia Communications, COMSAT, GE Americom, AT&T Communications, GTE Spacenet, American Satellite Corporation, Orion Satellite Corporation, Qualcomm, and Loral Systems.

3.2. Transportation

The transportation sector of space commerce delivers payloads into space but extends to also include the service activities that support launches. These activities consist mainly of constructing, operating, and maintaining space launch facilities. In the United States, the first commercial launch by a private company took place in 1982.[50] After that, problems with NASA's space shuttle and a subsequent ban on commercial payload launches on the shuttle[51] created a market that attracted a rush of small entrepreneurial firms as well as several established aerospace concerns, such as McDonnell Douglas and Martin Marietta. The transportation sector of space commerce experienced the greatest growth during the mid- to late 1980s. On March 29, 1989, Space Services, Inc. (Space Services) launched Starfire One, the first commercially licensed spacecraft launch in the United States. In the same year the private space industry achieved a further milestone with the launch in August of a communications satellite by McDonnell Douglas Space Systems Company.[52]

For years the U.S. government and private companies were the dominant players. By the mid-1980s, however, the European Space Agency had become a strong participant in the commercial launch market through its launch services contractor, France-based Arianespace.[53] However, as more and more states and private enterprises built and/or acquired satellites, the field morphed into one of the competitive sectors, with China's Great Wall Industrial Corporation increasingly seeking to gain a share of the emerging new satellite powers through competitive pricing,[54] as well as with Glavkosmos, the Soviet civil space organization and Japan's National Space Development Agency making aggressive overtures into the market.[55]

3.3. Remote Sensing

Remote sensing is the phrase commonly used to describe the gathering of data about the Earth and its environment by means of satellite retrieval using electromagnetic and other means to perceive objects and features on the Earth's surface.[56] The information from this satellite electronic surveillance has proved of immense value to many fields and professionals, ranging from geologists and land use planners to meteorologists, environmentalists, and journalists.

However, the political, international, and legal implications have intensified with the widening use of remote sensing data. All nations are affected by this activity, either as operators, users, or objects of remote sensing applications. Most nations are sensitive to the operation of foreign surveillance satellites over their own territory, thereby leading to controversy as to the permissible range and detail of this activity and how the collected data may be used. Nations have disagreed as to who has the right to retrieve such data by satellite, who owns such data, who may distribute it, and whether the sensed state has any priority to access the derived data.

Many states (and that is the majority) that depend on the sophisticated facilities of a handful of major players are concerned that remote sensing amounts to a form of "sovereignty invasion," with concomitant concerns relating to commercial and national security issues. In 1986, after years of highly volatile discussions regarding developing a framework to govern this sensitive field, the UN General Assembly adopted principles on remote sensing that require sensing states to notify the Secretary-General of the United Nations of their activities and to make data available to sensed states "on a non-discriminatory basis and on reasonable cost terms."[57]

3.4. Space Tourism

In spring 2001 U.S. citizen Dennis Tito journeyed into outer space as the first paying tourist, alongside two cosmonauts from the Russian Space Agency. Tito's eight-day space vacation cost him US$20 million and gained him international recognition for his dream ride. Tito's journey as a tourist in outer space excited and interested those concerned with the future of space exploration as well as those with hopes of becoming the next civilian space traveler. Buoyed by Tito's journey, recreational travel is among one of the rising branches of commercial space activity, with both private and public entities expanding their uses of space. The Outer Space Treaty and the Moon Agreement are the most important international treaties relevant to the continuing developments within the space industry of space tourism as an evolving commercial endeavor. These two treaties govern space exploration, travel, and use, but they do not address the specific legal implications of tourist space travel in the twenty-first century.

Part 4: Space as a Theatre of War? The Militarization of Outer Space

Recent leaps in space technologies have put the development of space weapons within the realm of possibility for several different countries. As "New World Vistas: Air and Space Power for the 21st Century," a USAF board report, states, "In the next two decades, new technologies will allow the fielding of space-based weapons of devastating effectiveness to be used to deliver energy and mass as force projection in tactical and strategic conflict. These advances will enable lasers with reasonable mass and cost to affect very many kills." While the United States continues its relentless drive to place weapons in outer space, the other major space-faring powers are not sitting idly by on the sidelines. China has embarked on an ambitious space program, part of which is also driven by military considerations.

The emerging bid by the United States and other major military powers to gain and maintain space superiority is anchored in the convergence of air and space power functions. The development of offensive counter space capabilities seeks to provide combatant commanders with new tools for counter space operations. The net result has been to spur the United States to aggressively pursue research and development of innovative space weapons and, in particular, develop Space Operated Vehicles (SOVs) with the capability of delivering and deploying ordnances from space through low-earth orbit, geo-synchronous orbit, or sun-synchronous orbit. The SOV is a multipurpose rugged low-earth orbit–capable vehicle designed to conduct multiple sorties for military purposes, including space-based reconnaissance and deployment of ordnances through boosting a Combat Aero Vehicle (CAV). All these developments demonstrate that space warfare is not mere talk but, unfortunately, appears to be unfolding into potent reality.

4.1. Direct Physical Military Force in Space: Kinetic/Hypervelocity Weaponry

In light of the various spectrums of space militarization and weaponization, two cleavages are evident: (1) direct military force—physical space devices that make actual proximate contact with their targets; and (2) indirect force—the use of space weaponry that makes contact with space assets by using shock waves, electromagnetic pulses, radiation belts, or laser beams.

4.1.1. The Use or Threat of Force Paradigm

The UN Charter forbids the "threat or use of force against the territorial integrity or political independence of any State, or in any other manner inconsistent with the Purposes of the United Nations."[58] To some commentators at least, the

meaning of this prohibition remains hotly contested. The prevailing view is that this provision absolutely bars the use of force, with the sole exceptions being self-defense and UN Security Council authorization. Under the Outer Space Treaty, although the principle of self-defense remains intact, the method of that defense is limited. However, a wide range of military activity can still fit under the self-defense umbrella. Article III of the Outer Space Treaty provides that parties to the treaty will conduct their activities in space in accordance with international law, the UN Charter, and in the interest of international peace, security, cooperation, and understanding.[59] Of significance with regard to the use of force is article III's reference to article 51 of the UN Charter and, in particular, its express preservation of the right of states to use space in self-defense.

The most relevant provisions regarding weaponization of space are articles IV and IX of the Outer Space Treaty. Major Douglas Anderson noted that "Article IV (1) is viewed by most commentators as only a limited disarmament provision."[60] Evidence supporting the view that the drafters only intended article IV (1) to ban orbiting nuclear-type weapons can be found in the drafters' understanding that the treaty does not prohibit stationing land-based ICBMs even though their flight trajectory would take them through outer space.[61] It is well established that the only specific limitation placed on the use of the "outer void space" for military purposes is that found in article IV (1).[62] Professor Bin Cheng asserted that "the outer void space as such can be used for any military activity that is compatible with general international law and the Charter of the United Nations," so long as no "nuclear weapons or any other kind of weapons of mass destruction are stationed there."[63]

Alongside the specific reference to the restriction of only particular weapons, article IV is the setting for much greater controversy. It provides for "two separate legal regimes for military activity in outer space: (1) activity conducted on the moon and other celestial bodies, and (2) activity conducted in outer space itself."[64] Article IV divides the extraterrestrial universe into three parts: the Earth's orbit, celestial bodies, and outer space. This then means that the Outer Space Treaty does not completely free all of outer space from military use.

From the foregoing paragraphs, it can be deduced that article IV of the Outer Space Treaty contemplates the military use of space for scientific research and grants a (virtual) carte blanche to civilian scientific applications. The reality is that civilian applications of space capabilities, such as weather, navigation, communications, and remote sensing, are equally significant for military purposes. In addition, as a technical matter, there is no absolutely clear line between military "missiles" and civilian "space launch vehicles." Technologies used to build sophisticated weaponry are often similar or even identical to the technologies required for civilian space programs.[65]

The tacit acceptance of military usages coupled with the express permission to civilian endeavors provides a strong argument that weaponization of space through the placement of non-nuclear and other weapons of destruction is in and of itself permissible under the space law regime. Richard A. Morgan argued that most experts agree that the Outer Space Treaty does not prohibit "military use" of space.[66] He went on to note that there is a "consensus, within the United Nations that 'peaceful' more specifically equates to 'non-aggressive.'"[67] However, the general stance by commentators Morgan cited is at odds with the Conference on Disarmament's observation in 1986 that "No country should develop, test or deploy space weapons in any form."[68]

4.1.2. The Armed Attack Paradigm

A key issue is the matter of the use or threat of force. It is inconceivable that deploying Anti-Satellite (ASAT) weaponry or SOVs would be seen as a benign activity considering that they are offensive in character. Thus, under the regime on the use of force, deployment of this weaponry can amount to the threat of the use of force, particularly where space weaponry is hoisted to the same orbital plane as another state's space assets. This is even more poignant if it occurs in circumstances where the states are on a war footing or a militarily volatile situation. Compounding the matter would be testing the weapons or military maneuvers under these circumstances. Major Anderson offered the sobering observation that

> All forms of military, and not only "warlike," uses of outer space, including defensive activities, are in conflict with the clearly established principle set forth in Article I(1) of the Space Treaty. Nonaggressive, or defensive, uses of outer space cannot be lawful since most all existing States have agreed on that principle.[69]

4.2. Indirect Military Force in Space: Electromagnetic/Laser/Radiation Weaponry

4.2.1. The Use or Threat of Force Paradigm

In 1995 a study for the USAF analyzing the future of air and space power reported that a combination of high-radio-frequency power and large antenna technology would make projecting extremely high power densities and electromagnetic radiation possible.[70] The report suggested that such a weapon in geo-synchronous orbit could create a six-mile footprint on a battlefield that would "blank out" all radar receivers and damage all unprotected communication sets within that area.[71] As the USAF Report shows, there are activities in outer space that have the potential to meet the threshold of a threat of force. Consider, for example, the use of space assets to jam military communication and electronic gathering facilities. To what extent can generating "an electronic footprint" that jams radar and other communication facilities crucial to military command systems be considered a use or threat of use of force? The matter is clear-cut in the context of hostilities, but it is far from clear in nonhostile situations.

Could a country consider the "blacking out" of its communication systems as a tactical military strategy to test its command systems and, thus, a threat of use of force that would provide the basis for defensive actions such as deploying an ASAT, laser, or other electromagnetic weaponry? These are crucial questions, and more so when one considers that USSPACE-COM's Long Range Plan encompasses space control, which is articulated thus: "the ability to ensure un-interrupted access to space for U.S. forces and our allies, freedom of operations within the space medium and an ability to deny others the use of space, if required."[72] Translated into legal terms, "attempts to ensure un-interrupted access to space and to maintain an ability to deny others the use of space,"[73] will no doubt encompass active interference with the space assets of third states.

4.2.2. The Armed Attack Paradigm

Perhaps the biggest question with respect to the self-defense principle embodied in article 51 relates to the meaning of the phrase "if an armed attack occurs." This seems to preclude the right to defend with arms until an actual armed attack has triggered the right. Article 51 of the UN Charter provides that the inherent right of self-defense is expressly linked to an armed attack.[74] Yet as the International Court of Justice noted in the case of *Nicaragua v. United States*, "a definition of the 'armed attack' which, if found to exist, authorises the exercise of the 'inherent right' of self-defence, is not provided in the Charter, and is not part of treaty law."[75] Consequently, it is necessary to look elsewhere to determine whether a cyber attack constitutes an "armed attack," thereby justifying self-defense within the framework of article 51. At first glance, a cyber attack can be objectively likened to "armed force." This necessitates some textual interpretation in line with the UN Charter to see whether this actually fits within the international regime on the use of force.

Let us consider whether a cyber attack constitutes an "armed attack" justifying self-defense within the framework of article 51. Armed attack clearly implies the use of arms or military force and has an offensive, destructive, and illegal nature.[76] Significant in this regard is the

"Definition of Aggression" adopted by the UN General Assembly through Resolution 3314.[77] Article 1 defines aggression as the "use of armed force by a State against the sovereignty, territorial integrity or political independence of another State, or in any other manner inconsistent with the Charter of the United Nations, as set out in this Definition."[78] To the extent that "nonpeaceful" means the aggressive use of force, such uses are prohibited by the UN Charter's provision to the contrary. Article 3 of Resolution 3314 enumerates specific acts that amount to acts of aggression "regardless of a declaration of war."

The text of Resolution 3314 makes clear the fact that it is intended to serve as a guide to the UN Security Council to determine the existence of aggression under article 39 and not as a definition of "armed attack."[79] Nevertheless, if armed attack is understood to be a type of aggression that justifies self-defense under article 51 of the Charter, that is, "*une agression armée*" (or "aggression which is armed"),[80] then the resolution's definition of aggression and the specific acts of aggression enumerated in article 3 are at least illustrative of the types of circumstances wherein recourse to self-defense is vindicated.[81]

It is significant that the space law regime provides that states have a right to deploy satellites and proscribes any interference. In this regard, using ASATs or Direct Energy Weapons—primarily lasers—on a state's satellites would be commensurate with a state using armed force against the sovereignty of another state or, perhaps, would be equated with a state using weapons against the territory of another state. It is clear, then, that the cyber attack cannot be justified as self-defense in the absence of any prior action by the victim state targeting a state's satellites. Any action absent a prior action by another state can thus be inferred to constitute an "armed attack" within the meaning of article 51. This would, at the very least, involve laser blinding of satellites and, at the very most, deploying hyper-velocity kinetic weapons—this would clearly amount to an attack. However, the finer points would be whether detonations in an orbital plane that generate an Electro-Magnetic Pulse (EMP) or Van Allen radiation belts that impair the operation of satellites of a third state constitute an armed attack.

Despite the provisions of the Outer Space Treaty prescribing the "peaceful" use and exploration of space, the Liability Convention appears to recognize the distinct possibility that States may engage in intentional damage to space objects.[82] The Liability Convention takes as its goal to elaborate "effective international rules and procedures concerning liability for damage caused by space objects and to ensure, in particular, the prompt payment under the terms of [the] Convention of a full and equitable measure of compensation to victims of such damage."[83]

Part 5: Some Environmental Issues/Concerns Associated with Activities in Outer Space

Environmental damage in space can be categorized as either "forward" pollution or "back" pollution:[84]

> Forward pollution is pollution that occurs in outer space as the result of human activity. Back pollution, on the other hand, is pollution that occurs on the Earth as a result of extraterrestrial matter entering the Earth's environment. Both types of pollution can result from commercial activities in outer space. Either type may be caused by one of five types of waste: solid, hazardous, radioactive, biological, or electromagnetic.[85]

5.1. Forward Pollution

There currently exist in space thousands of man-made objects.[86] Of this, less than 50 percent are "trackable."[87] Of great concern is the estimated hundreds of thousands of pieces of space debris that represent the most serious threat to space activities because, unlike trackable objects that can be avoided by the maneuvering capabilities of satellites, these cannot.[88] As Christopher D.

Williams noted, "Estimates of the current untrackable debris population range up to 3,500,000 objects. An additional danger posed by space debris is the more than forty-eight active or inactive satellites which carry over a ton of highly radioactive material in orbit around the planet."[89]

Generally, space debris falls into various identifiable categories, which include inactive payloads, operational debris, and fragmentation debris.[90] This represents a long-term threat to orbital activities because satellites have an orbital lifetime of several hundred years.[91] Operational debris is closely associated with inactive payloads. This category includes objects used in various space activities that, for a variety of reasons, remain in orbit.[92] Although the launch of space vehicles produces most of the operational debris (such as rocket stages, motors, or nose cones), humankind has left behind a variety of other material.[93]

The most common form of pollution from commercial space activities is forward pollution by solid waste. In simple terms, space is full of junk, the remains of derelict satellites and thousands of other objects, discarded deliberately or otherwise.[94] Importantly, space assets (whether based in space or traversing space) emit a great deal of electromagnetic waste coming from the millions of electromagnetic transmissions associated with space commerce. The problem is that after the commercial lifespan of space devices, they remain indefinitely in the universe, not being readily biodegradable. Thus, there is the real potential to clog telecommunications channels, coupled with the fallout effect of space assets interfering with each other or with collecting often vital civilian and military information.

5.2. Back Pollution

Space debris sometimes falls to Earth as its orbit decays, creating solid-waste back pollution. Thousands of pieces of debris have fallen from orbit since humankind first put things into space.[95] The greatest danger debris poses with regard to back pollution is the dozens of active or inactive satellites, many of which carry up to a ton of highly radioactive material—the increasingly preferred power source for many satellites.

There have been several incidents involving the return to Earth of nuclear-powered objects.[96] However, the most widely reported radioactive back pollution resulted from a Soviet satellite re-entry in 1978. Cosmos 954 was launched in September 1977 with a reactor containing Uranium-235. Within weeks of its launch it began to malfunction and re-entered the atmosphere over Canada on January 24, 1978 with debris hitting the ground and spreading over an area of about 124,000 square kilometers. Fortunately, the area the satellite landed on was the largely frozen and scarcely populated areas of Canada's Northwest Territories.

5.2.1. The International Legal Regime in Outer Space

Regarding the international regime on outer space and the environmental concerns, no specific treaty exists that addresses the matter, but extant treaties discussed above contain provisions that conceivably might be invoked in the effort to control space pollution. Although the Outer Space Treaty is largely hortative, it contains language that might provide the basis for practical international action to protect against the environmental effects of space activity. Central to the notion of environmental protection in outer space is the principle that a state is responsible for activity in outer space that originates in its territory or that is conducted by its nationals. Space activity that results in "harmful contamination" of outer space or celestial bodies or in "adverse changes in the environment of the Earth," therefore, breaches international obligations for which the launching state is responsible. The Outer Space Treaty,[97] for example, makes clear that states are responsible for activities in outer space carried on by their nationals, whether governmental or nongovernmental.[98] Furthermore, a state is liable for damage caused *inter alia* by space ob-

jects launched from its territory.[99] In article IX, environmental protection is expressly mentioned among the principles, with states conducting space activities agreeing to conduct such activities "so as to avoid . . . harmful contamination [an admonition against forward pollution] and also adverse changes in the environment of the Earth [back pollution]."[100]

The Liability Convention[101] is the more practically and legally assertive. Essentially, this convention gives vitality to article VII of the Outer Space Treaty. The Liability Convention imposes strict liability on states that launch space objects for damage caused by those objects "on the surface of the Earth or to aircraft in flight."[102] Liability according to fault is imposed for damage in outer space caused by one state's space object to persons or property on board a space object of another state.[103] The Liability Convention establishes joint and several liability for accidents caused by two or more launching states and provides for indemnity and apportionment agreements between launching states.[104]

It is of note that remote sensing offers a great opportunity for environmental planning and protection and, in fact, offers the technology to assess the environmental effects of other space activities. Indeed, the UN principles state that remote sensing shall "promote the protection of the Earth's natural environment" and "promote the protection of mankind from natural disasters."[105] However, the environmental issues that outer space activities raise still need to develop a more comprehensive formal legal and policy framework.

Conclusion

In practical terms, the space law regime has a somewhat schizophrenic quality, which exposes a number of significant internal and external legal and policy contradictions in the face of rapid commercialization and militarization. As space technology develops into more sophisticated areas, such as low-earth systems, space planes, and a variety of space-based platforms carrying a variety of systems, the issue of finally settling definitively the delimitation of the outer space area district from national airspace is important and, hopefully, nigh. As noted in the discussion above, the extant space law regime finds itself stretched when dealing with the main spectrums of humankind's ever-increasing presence, from commercial uses to militarization, as the race to space supremacy is played out among governments and, at times, private entities.

Because of its uniquely commanding height, outer space has gained even greater strategic and commercial value in the post–Cold War international strategic environment. The use of satellites for undertakings in communication, navigation, space flight, meteorology, remote sensing, disaster reduction, and other fields of science and technology are indispensable for peaceful scientific and exploration endeavors. Though achieving notable progress in the peaceful uses of outer space, humanity is faced, nevertheless, with space's ever-expanding use. International security and stability requires that peaceful capabilities be sustained and advanced within an internationalized context.

The space-faring powers have repeatedly expressed a commitment to all nations' ability to explore and use outer space for peaceful purposes and for the benefit of all humanity. States should pursue greater levels of partnership and cooperation in national and international space activities and work together to ensure outer space's continued exploration and use strictly for peaceful purposes—more so in light of the unique qualities of its atmosphere and its increasing interrelationship with the Earth.

NOTES

1. *Paris Convention for the Regulation of Aerial Navigation,* opened for signature Oct. 13, 1919, 11 LNTS [hereinafter *Paris Convention*].

2. A Tass news agency announcement of Aug. 27 1957 that reported the successful test of the Soviet ICBM also included reference to "a series of explosions of nuclear and thermonuclear (hydrogen) weapons . . . set off at great altitudes." MYRES MCDOUGAL ET AL., LAW AND PUBLIC ORDER IN SPACE 389 (1963).

3. *Declaration of Legal Principles Governing the Activities of States in the Exploration and Use of Outer Space,*

GA Res 1962, U.N. GAOR, 18th sess, 1280th plen mtg, U.N. Doc A/RES/1962 (1963).

4. [Maj.] Robert A. Ramey, *Armed Conflict on the Final Frontier: The Law of War in Space,* 48 A.F. L. REV. 1, 110 (2000).

5. *Treaty Banning Nuclear Weapon Tests in the Atmosphere, in Outer Space and Under Water,* opened for signature Aug. 15, 1963, 480 U.N.T.S. 43 (entered into force Oct. 10, 1963) (*Limited Test Ban Treaty*).

6. The declaration primarily aimed to limit nuclear weapons testing but was also a reaction to Soviet pleas that nuclear detonations posed a danger to the safety of its cosmonauts. *See* Ramey, *supra* note 4, at 12–13.

7. *North Sea Continental Shelf Cases* (*Germany v. Denmark; Germany v. Netherlands*), 1969 ICJ 3, 230 (Feb. 20, 1969) (separate opinion of Judge Lachs).

8. Ramey, *supra* note 4.

9. *Treaty on Principles Governing the Activities of States in the Exploration and Use of Outer Space, Including the Moon and Other Celestial Bodies,* opened for signature Jan. 27, 1967, 610 UNTS 205 (entered into force Oct. 10, 1967) [hereinafter *Outer Space Treaty*]; *Agreement on the Rescue of Astronauts, the Return of Astronauts and the Return of Objects Launched into Outer Space,* opened for signature April 22, 1968, 672 UNTS 119 (entered into force Dec. 3, 1968); *Convention on International Liability for Damage Caused by Space Objects,* opened for signature Mar. 29, 1972, 961 UNTS 187 (entered into force Sept. 1, 1972) [hereinafter *Convention on Liability*]; *Convention on Registration of Objects Launched into Outer Space,* opened for signature Jan. 14, 1975, 1023 UNTS 15 (entered into force Sept. 15, 1976); *Agreement Governing the Activities of States on the Moon and Other Celestial Bodies,* opened for signature Dec. 18, 1979, 1363 U.N.T.S. 21 (entered into force Jul. 11, 1984) [hereinafter *Moon Agreement*].

10. Question of the Peaceful Use of Outer Space, GA Res 1348, U.N. GAOR, 13th sess, 792nd plen mtg, U.N. Doc A/RES/1348 (1958). For an examination of COPUOS' working procedures, *see* Margot Bourély, *The Contributions Made by International Organizations to the Formation of Space Law,* 10 J. SPACE L. 143 (1982).

11. Ivan Vlasic, *[The Outer Space Treaty] Represents de facto and de jure the Constitution of Outer Space: Some Thoughts on Negotiating and Drafting Arms Control and Disarmament Agreements Relating to Outer Space,* 4 ARMS CONTROL AND DISARMAMENT IN OUTER SPACE: TOWARDS A NEW WORLD ORDER OF SURVIVAL, 203, 212 (N. M. Matte ed., 1991).

12. CARL CHRISTOL, THE MODERN INTERNATIONAL LAW OF OUTER SPACE 20 (1982).

13. Namely, *International Co-operation in the Peaceful Uses of Outer Space,* GA Res 1802, U.N. GAOR, 17th sess, 1192nd plen mtg, U.N. Doc A/RES/1802 (1962); *Declaration of Legal Principles Governing the Activities of*

States in the Exploration and Use of Outer Space, GA Res 1962, U.N. GAOR, 18th sess, 1280th plen mtg, U.N. Doc A/RES/1962 (1963); and *International Co-operation in the Peaceful Uses of Outer Space*, GA Res 1963, U.N. GAOR, 18th sess, 1280th plen mtg, U.N. Doc A/RES/1963 (1963).

14. Nandasiri Jasentuliyana, *The Role of Developing Countries in the Formation of Space Law*, 20 ANNALS AIR & SPACE L. 95, 97 (1995).

15. These are (i) Declaration of Legal Principles Governing the Activities of States in the Exploration and Use of Outer Space, General Assembly Res No 1962, U.N. Doc No A/RES/1962 (1963); (ii) Principles Governing the Use by States of Artificial Earth Satellites for International Direct Television Broadcasting, General Assembly Res No 37/92, U.N. Doc No A/RES/37/92 (1982); (iii) Principles Relating to Remote Sensing of the Earth from Outer Space, General Assembly Res No 41/65, U.N. Doc No A/RES/41/65 (1986) [hereinafter Principles Relating to Remote Sensing] ; (iv) Principles Relevant to the Use of Nuclear Power Sources in Outer Space, General Assembly Res No 47/68, U.N. Doc No A/RES/47/68 (1992); and (v) Declaration on International Cooperation in the Exploration and Use of Outer Space for the Benefit and in the Interest of All States, Taking into Particular Account the Needs of Developing Countries, General Assembly Res No 51/122, U.N. Doc No A/RES/51/122 (1996).

16. *See* Ricky J. Lee & Steven Freeland, *The Crystallisation of General Assembly Space Declarations into Customary International Law*, 46 PROCEEDINGS OF THE COLLOQUIUM ON THE LAW OF OUTER SPACE 122 (2004).

17. 49 Stat 3000 (1929) [hereinafter *Warsaw Convention*]. The Warsaw Convention rules were modified by the *Convention for the Unification of Certain Rules for International Carriage by Air*, S Treaty Doc No 106–45 (1999) [hereinafter *Montreal Convention*].

18. 59 Stat 1693 (1947) [hereinafter *Chicago Convention*].

19. Art. 1 of the *Paris Convention*, *supra* note 1, provides that "The High Contracting Parties recognise that every Power has complete and exclusive sovereignty over the air space above its territory."

20. *Chicago Convention*, *supra* note 18, at art. 1.

21. In *Case Concerning Military and Paramilitary Activities in and against Nicaragua (Nicaragua v. U.S.) (merits)* [hereinafter "*The Nicaragua Case*"], the International Court of Justice noted that "The principle of respect for territorial sovereignty is also directly infringed by the unauthorised over flight of a state's territory by aircraft belonging to or under the control of the government of another state," ICJ 14, 128 (1986).

22. *See Chicago Convention*, *supra* note, at arts. 5 and 6.

23. *Outer Space Treaty*, *supra* note 9, at art. II.

24. MALCOLM N. SHAW, INTERNATIONAL LAW 480 (5th ed. 2003).

25. See *Outer Space Treaty*, *supra* note 9.

26. *See, e.g.,* Oliver J. Lissitzyn, *Some Legal Implications of the U-2 and RB-47 Incidents*, 56 AM. J. INT'L L. 135 (1962) (discussing the incident in 1960 when a U.S. U-2 reconnaissance aircraft was shot down while flying over the then Soviet Union, with the United States choosing diplomatic negotiations rather than attempting to justify or criticize the subsequent trial of the pilot. An additional example is the tragedy of Korean Airlines Flight 007 in 1983, when the civilian airliner carrying 269 passengers strayed into Soviet airspace and was shot down, killing all on board. Subsequent statements from both governments expressed regret rather than full-scale, legally based accusations.).

27. *See* N. M. MATTE, SPACE ACTIVITIES AND EMERGING INTERNATIONAL LAW 380 (1984).

28. *The Question of the Definition and/or the Delimitation of Outer Space*, U.N. Doc A/AC.105/C 2/7 and U.N. Doc A/AC.105/C.2/7 Add 1 (1970).

29. To accomplish aerial flight, weight equals aerodynamic lift plus centrifugal force. Aerodynamic lift decreases with altitude because of the decreasing density of the air. Beyond zero airlift, centrifugal force takes over.

30. This approach, however, involves several difficulties that seem to preclude a uniform and constant boundary, including technological and engineering breakthroughs as well as the fluctuation of the atmosphere itself.

31. Vladimír Kopal., *What Is "Outer Space" in Astronautics and Space Law?* PROCEEDINGS. OF THE 10TH COLLOQUIUM ON THE LAW OF OUTER SPACE 275, 277–78 (1967).

32. However, improvements in space flight technology, such as orbiting with continuing rocket thrust, may lower this perigee to seventy to seventy-five miles.

33. Robert F. A. Goedhart, *The Never Ending Dispute: Delimitation of Air Space and Outer Space*, in 4 FORUM FOR AIR AND SPACE LAW 59–60 (Marietta Benkö & Willem de Graaff eds., 1996).

34. *The Australian Space Activities Act 1998* (Cth) (No. 123 of 1998), as amended by the Space *Activities Amendment Act 2002* (Cth) (No. 100 of 2002), incorporates into the definition of a "launch," a "launch vehicle," a "return," and a "space object" for the purposes of the legislation a reference to "the distance of 100 [kilometers] above mean sea level." For a discussion of the Australian legislation and its relationship to Australia's current space engagement policy, *see* Steven Freeland, *When Laws Are not Enough—The Stalled Development of an Australian Space Launch Industry* 8 U. W. SYDNEY L. REV. 79–95 (2004).

35. The UN Conference on Disarmament was established in 1979 as the single multilateral disarmament negotiating forum of the international community, following the first Special Session on Disarmament (SSOD I) of the United Nations General Assembly held in 1978, The United Nations Office at Geneva (UNOG), "Disarmament," *available at* www.unog.ch/80256EE600585943/(httpHome pages)/ 6A03113D1857348E80256F04006755F6?Open Document.

36. For a detailed discussion of the PPWT, *see* Steven Freeland, *The 2008 Russia/China Proposal for a Treaty to Ban Weapons in Space: A Missed Opportunity or an Opening Gambit?* 51 PROCEEDINGS OF THE COLLOQUIUM ON THE LAW OF OUTER SPACE 261–71 (2008).

37. *Outer Space Treaty, supra* note 9.

38. *Id.* at art I.

39. *Id.*

40. *Id.* at art II.

41. *Id.* at art III.

42. Art. VII of the *Outer Space Treaty, supra* note 9, provides that "Each State Party to the Treaty that launches or procures the launching of an object into outer space, including the moon and other celestial bodies, and each State Party from whose territory or facility an object is launched, is internationally liable for damage to another State Party to the Treaty or to its natural or juridical persons by such object or its component parts on the Earth, in air or in outer space, including the moon and other celestial bodies."

43. For a detailed analysis of the Liability Convention, Steven Freeland, *There's a Satellite in My Backyard—MIR and the Convention on International Liability for Damage Caused by Space Objects*, 24 U. NEW S. WALES L. J. 462–84 (2001).

44. Art. III of the *Moon Agreement, supra* note 9, provides as follows:

"1. The moon shall be used by all States Parties exclusively for peaceful purposes.

2. Any threat or use of force or any other hostile act or threat of hostile act on the moon is prohibited. It is likewise prohibited to use the moon in order to commit any such act or to engage in any such threat in relation to the earth, the moon, spacecraft, the personnel of spacecraft or man-made space objects.

3. States Parties shall not place in orbit around or other trajectory to or around the moon objects carrying nuclear weapons or any other kinds of weapons of mass destruction or place or use such weapons on or in the moon.

4. The establishment of military bases, installations and fortifications, the testing of any type of weapons and the conduct of military maneuvers on the moon shall be forbidden. The use of military personnel for scientific research or for any other peaceful purposes shall

not be prohibited. The use of any equipment or facility necessary for peaceful exploration and use of the moon shall also not be prohibited."

45. H. C. Manson, *The Impact of International Outer Space Commerce on the Environment*, 26 TEX. INT'L L. J. 541, 543 (1991).

46. *See* Elizabeth Corcoran & Tim Beardsley, *The New Space Race*, SCI. AM. 72, 76–84 (Jul. 1990).

47. DAVID W. E. REES, SATELLITE COMMUNICATIONS: THE FIRST QUARTER CENTURY OF SERVICE 267 (1989).

48. DAVID H. MARTIN, COMMUNICATIONS SATELLITES 1958–1992 214, 277 (1991).

49. The United States, Russia, Canada, Argentina, Indonesia, U.K., France, Italy, Japan, India, China, Brazil, and so forth.

50. *See* White House Press Office, Fact Sheet: Presidential Directive on National Space Policy 9 (Feb. 11, 1988).

51. *Id.*

52. *America's Private Road to Heaven*, U.S. NEWS & WORLD REPORT 11–12 (Sept. 11, 1989).

53. *See e.g.*, J. M. Lenorovitz, *Air and Space Plans 1989 Launches to Clear Backlog of Payloads*, AVIATION WK. & SPACE TECH. 28 (Jan. 30, 1989).

54. Corcoran and Beardsley, *supra* note 46, at 73.

55. *Id.* at 76–77.

56. LEGAL IMPLICATIONS OF REMOTE SENSING FROM OUTER SPACE xi (Nicolas Matessco Matte & Hamilton DeSaussure eds., 1976).

57. Principles Relating to Remote Sensing of the Earth from Space, G.A.Res. 41/65, 41 U.S.GAOR Supp. (No. 53), at 115, U.N. Doc. A/Res/41/65 Annex (1986).

58. *Charter of the United Nations*, art. 2(4).

59. *Outer Space Treaty, supra* note 9, at art III.

60. [Maj.] Douglas S. Anderson, *A Military Look into Space: The Ultimate High Ground*, ARMY LAW 19, 23 (Nov. 1995).

61. Other weapons of mass destruction not relevant to the issue of planetary defense would be biological and chemical weapons. [Capt.] Michael G. Gallagher, *Legal Aspects of the Strategic Defense Initiative*, 111 MIL. L. REV. 11, 41 (1986).

62. BIN CHENG, STUDIES IN INTERNATIONAL SPACE LAW 529 (1997).

63. *Id.*

64. Jackson N. Maogoto, *The Military Ascent into Space: From Playground to Battleground: The New Uncertain Game in the Heavens*, 52 NETH. INT'L L. REV. 461, 477–78 (2005).

65. "The differences relate to intentions, not capabilities." Barry J. Hurewitz, *Non-Proliferation and Free Access to Outer Space: The Dual-Use Dilemma of the Outer Space Treaty and the Missile Technology*

Control Regime, 9 BERKELEY TECH. L. J. 211, 228 (1994).

66. Robert A. Morgan, *Military Use of Commercial Communication Satellites: A New Look at the Outer Space Treaty and "Peaceful Purposes*," 60 J. AIR L. & COMM. 237, 288 (1994).

67. *Id.*

68. *Conference on Disarmament, Final Record of the 350th Plenary Meeting*, U.N. Doc CD/PV.350 (1986).

69. Major Anderson noted, "The SDI provided a measure of legitimacy to many ideas that were formerly seen as impossible." Anderson, *supra* note 60, at 26.

70. Ivan Bekey, *Force Projection from Space in Air Force Scientific Advisory Board*, 83 NEW WORLD VISTAS: AIR AND SPACE POWER FOR THE 21ST CENTURY: SPACE APPLICATIONS 84 (1995).

71. *Id.* at 84–85. With respect to information warfare, the report gives a number of examples: network viruses, disinformation, memory erasures, and false signals—for a brief discussion of information warfare and its relation to space combat.

72. U.S. SPACE COMMAND, LONG RANGE PLAN: IMPLEMENTING USSPACECOM VISION FOR 2020, at 21 (1998).

73. *Id.*

74. *See* UN Charter, at art 51.

75. *The Nicaragua Case, supra* note 21, at 94.

76. *See* J. N. SINGH, USE OF FORCE UNDER INTERNATIONAL LAW 15 (1984).

77. *Definition of Aggression*, GA Res 3314, UN GAOR, 29th sess, 2319th plen. mtg, U.N. Doc A/RES/3314 (1974).

78. *Id.*

79. *Id.* at Preamble, art 6.

80. *See* YORAM DINSTEIN, WAR, AGGRESSION, AND SELF-DEFENCE 166 (2d ed. 1994) (describing the Kellogg-Briand Pact as "a watershed . . . in the history of the regulation of the use of inter-States force").

81. THE CHARTER OF THE UNITED NATIONS: A COMMENTARY 668 (Bruno Simma ed., 1994) (asserting that "aggression" as defined in Resolution 3314 does not coincide with the notion of "armed attack" under art 51 of the Charter).

82. *Convention on Liability, supra* note 9.

83. *Id.*

84. *See* Stephen Gorove, *Pollution and Outer Space: A Legal Analysis and Appraisal*, 5 N.Y.U. J. INT'L L. & POL'Y 53, 54–55 (1972).

85. Manson, *supra* note 45, at 546.

86. J. P Lampertius, *The Need for an Effective Liability Regime for Damage Caused by Debris in Outer Space*, 13 MICH. J. INT'L L. 447, 449 (1992).

87. *Id.*

88. Christopher D. Williams, *Space: The Cluttered Frontier*, 60 J. AIR L. & COMM. 1139, 1141 (1995).

89. *Id.* at 1141–42.

90. HOWARD A. BAKER. SPACE DEBRIS: LEGAL AND POLICY IMPLICATIONS 3 (1989).

91. Williams, *supra* note 88, at 1142.

92. Baker, *supra* note 90, at 4.

93. *Id.*

94. *See* Christol, *supra* note 12, at 130–31.

95. *See* B. K. Schafer, *Solid, Hazardous, and Radioactive Wastes in Outer Space: Present Controls and Suggested Changes*, 1 CAL. W. INT'L L. J. 5–6 (1988–89).

96. Manson, *supra* note 45, at 547–48.

97. *Outer Space Treaty, supra* note 9.

98. *Id.* at art. VI.

99. *Id.* at art. VII.

100. *Id.* at art. IX.

101. *Convention on Liability, supra* note 9.

102. *Id.* at art. II.

103. *Id.* at art. III.

104. *Id.* at art. IV.

105. Principles Relating to Remote Sensing, *supra* note 15.

16

The UN Convention on the Law of the Sea, the European Union, and the Rule of Law

*What Is Going on in the Adriatic Sea?**

DAVOR VIDAS

> *The Union is founded on . . . the rule of law*
> —Treaty on European Union

1. Introduction

On December 10, 2007, the "Constitution for the Oceans," as the UN Convention on the Law of the Sea (LOS Convention) is sometimes called, marked its twenty-fifth anniversary.[1] On that same day the Council of the European Union (EU) called on Croatia "not to apply any aspect of the Zone [in the Adriatic Sea] to the EU Member States until a common agreement in the EU spirit is found."[2]

Why would the European Council use such an occasion—the unique anniversary of one of the most important international treaties of our time—to call on an Adriatic Sea coastal state to refrain from implementing its maritime zone based on the Exclusive Economic Zone (EEZ) provisions, which contain some of the fundamental rights and duties of a coastal state under the LOS Convention? In 2002 the UN Secretary-General had reported, "twenty years after the adoption of the Convention, there is almost a universal acceptance of maritime zones as established by UNCLOS."[3] What is going on in the Adriatic Sea, then, five years later, that could have prompted the European Council to require a "common agreement in the EU spirit" before an EEZ, a part of international customary and treaty law, can be applied to EU Member States?

That something must indeed be going on is evident from several recent annual reports of the UN Secretary-General on "Oceans and the Law of the Sea." Since the August 2003 addendum to the Annual Report, there has been regular mention of Adriatic Sea developments in the section on "Maritime claims and the delimitation of maritime zones."[4] Moreover, there is

*This chapter was published as an article under the same title in THE INTERNATIONAL JOURNAL OF MARINE AND COASTAL LAW, Vol. 24, No. 1, 2009, at 1–66 (Martinus Nijhoff Publishers, an imprint of Koninklijke Brill NV). Permission granted for publishing it in this book is gratefully acknowledged.

hardly any issue of the UN *Law of the Sea Bulletin* published since No. 53 in 2004 that does not contain some exchange of diplomatic notes or translation into "world languages" of new and amended national legislation by some of the Adriatic Sea states. Before late 2003/early 2004 those publications rarely made any mention of the Adriatic Sea, let alone of maritime disputes there. In the past few years, however, maritime issues in the Adriatic Sea, in addition to diplomatic exchanges, have become a frequent subject of statements made by high-level politicians, documents adopted by various EU bodies, and heated debates in domestic political fora, including the national parliaments of some eastern Adriatic countries, which have been accompanied by considerable media attention as well.

In this chapter we first briefly look at some key features of the Adriatic Sea as a region, including aspects and trends in uses of Adriatic Sea living resources and maritime space as well as resource conservation and marine pollution concerns. A review of developments leading to recently adopted national legislation and positions on maritime jurisdiction by the Adriatic Sea states of Croatia, Italy, and Slovenia is presented in the following sections. These regulations, positions, and developments are assessed from the perspective of the law of the sea as well as from relevant policy perspectives, including aspects of EU membership. Developments in and underlying reasons for the changing jurisdictional picture in that marine region are examined so as to enable a documented response to the basic question: What is going on in the Adriatic Sea?

2. The Adriatic Sea: Coastal States, Key Maritime Uses, Conservation and Environmental Concerns

The Adriatic Sea, although a part of the wider Mediterranean region, has its own specific features and is considered a distinct marine subregion.[5] It is a narrow, semi-enclosed sea, formed as a gulf deeply incised into the European mainland and connected to the rest of the Mediterranean only by the Strait of Otranto.

Prior to 1991 there were only three coastal states on the Adriatic Sea north of the Strait of Otranto: Albania, Italy, and Yugoslavia. Today, there are six: in addition to Albania and Italy, also Bosnia and Herzegovina, Croatia, Montenegro, and Slovenia. Except for Italy, all these states are situated on the eastern coast of the Adriatic Sea.

The share of the Adriatic Sea coast of each of those countries differs greatly. Croatia has by far the longest coastline of all. Including the coasts of its numerous islands,[6] Croatia's coastline extends over 6,200 kilometers—approximately 75 percent of the length of all the Adriatic Sea coastlines together (which is around 8300 km).

Italy, situated on the western coast, has an Adriatic Sea coastline of some 1,300 kilometers, that is, around 15 percent of the total. However, Italy has by far the largest share of maritime traffic and trade in the region: Italian ports annually receive around 75 percent of all commercial ship traffic in the Adriatic Sea. Also in some other economic aspects, such as fisheries, Italy is by far the biggest user of the Adriatic Sea, as will be further discussed below. The proportions are diametrically reversed in that respect as well: Although Italy has the dominant fishing fleet, most of the fishing grounds lie in waters closer to the Croatian island chain.

Thus, it should be noted that there exist great regional imbalances, even diametrically opposed situations, as illustrated by the share of coastline, on the one hand, and the extent of key maritime uses of the Adriatic Sea, on the other. As a result, whereas some overall interests in the Adriatic Sea remain shared, other, more specific ones are quite different.

Some of the remaining eastern Adriatic states have very short coastlines: Slovenia has around 45 kilometers; Bosnia and Herzegovina has even less than half of that, only some 20 kilometers. The unusual positions of those coasts are but one indication of the complex and generally

MAP 16.1 The Adriatic Sea: coastal ports and main ports

troubled past of the region, where boundaries have been subject to the vagaries of history.

2.1. The Adriatic Sea as a Maritime Transport Route: Key Aspects and Trends

Deeply incised into the European mainland, the Adriatic Sea has long been an important transport route. The reason is obvious from its geographical, and indeed geopolitical, placement. On its west-

ern coast is a highly industrially developed country, Italy. As to the eastern coast, although coastal states there are less industrially developed, various developed mid-European countries (several of which are landlocked) gravitate naturally to the Adriatic Sea. Some of these are heavily dependent on that maritime route for their energy imports: Austria, for instance, receives 75 percent of its oil imports through Adriatic ports, and Bavaria in Germany even 100 percent.

In the foreseeable future the Adriatic region may see major changes. The Eurasian space today is in a process of tremendous restructuring due to the changes in energy export/import flows. As to future oil transport routes, several large-scale visions clash when it comes to projections for the next decade. Although this chapter is not the place to enter into further details of that highly complex matter,[7] it is important to note that maritime transport patterns in the Adriatic Sea are likely to be undergoing change in the near future in terms of the use intensity of existing routes and due to the introduction of new ones.

The eastern Adriatic coast, due to its geological composition, has several deep-water ports, especially along the Croatian coast (thus also closer to mid-Europe). These can accommodate supertankers, and this, under various scenarios, could be part of the future solution for today's bottlenecks in oil export routes in Eurasia. In addition, plans are underway for large liquefied natural gas (LNG) import terminals to help diversify mid-European gas imports and lessen the dependence on Russia. The Croatian coast, due to its placement and natural features, is central in several such energy transport plans and projects. In addition to industrial interests, the geopolitical interests of main players on the Eurasian scene—Russia, the United States, and some key EU countries—are at stake here and should be taken into account when explaining overall Adriatic Sea developments.[8]

2.2. Maritime Uses of the Adriatic Sea: Conservation and Environmental Concerns

By the early 2000s scientific and monitoring projects had already documented the worrisome effects and risks of current maritime uses of the Adriatic Sea—both shipping and fishing—on the state of its living resources and the marine environment. Due to its special features and the slow exchange of water with the rest of the Mediterranean through the Strait of Otranto, the Adriatic is a particularly sensitive sea, highly vulnerable to marine pollution.[9]

As to maritime transport and shipping in general, the current levels of traffic in the Adriatic Sea, apart from accident risks, raise serious concerns for the coastal states. That especially relates to *operational* oil discharges from large ships, mainly on international shipping routes that traverse the Adriatic. The extent and frequency of that type of pollution in the Adriatic Sea have been confirmed by an analysis performed from 1999 onwards by the Sensors, Radar Technologies and Cybersecurity Unit, DG Joint Research Centre of the European Commission. Analysis of images obtained through special satellite technology (satellites equipped with Synthetic Aperture Radar, SAR) has demonstrated the occurrence of enhanced spill concentrations along major maritime routes. An analysis made specifically for the Adriatic Sea detected an average of between 200 and 250 possible illegal oil spills from ships each year for the period from 1999 to 2002.[10] These studies, carried out under the auspices of the European Commission, have provided the first accurate statistical mapping of oil discharges from ships in the Adriatic Sea. The studies also proved that such activity is underway on a large scale here, despite the Special Area status of the entire Mediterranean Sea, including the Adriatic, under MARPOL Annex I, whereby the discharge of oil and oily waste is prohibited.[11]

Another major concern relates to the marine living resources and their conservation and management. Due to its specific characteristics, the Adriatic Sea contains some of the highest fish-producing areas in the entire Mediterranean.[12] This is especially the case in the northern Adriatic as well as in several other localities along the Croatian coast. Overall, however, the Adriatic ichthyofauna is characterized by high diversity, with numerous species but low abundance. Exploitation pressure has not been proportional to the productivity of many important species and stocks, resulting in a key problem for the sustainability of the Adriatic Sea fisheries.

Historically, there has been only one strong fishing fleet in the Adriatic Sea—Italy.[13] A comparison of total catches of the three Adriatic coastal states whose legal and policy positions are discussed further in this paper—Croatia, Italy, and Slovenia—shows their highly unequal involvement in Adriatic Sea fisheries. In the early 2000s total Italian marine capture fisheries for all areas stood at around 300,000 tons (and at least half of that came from the Adriatic Sea); the Croatian catch in the Adriatic Sea was for several years at around 20,000 tons (gradually returning to pre-1990 levels of over 30,000–40,000 tons from 2004 onward); and the Slovenian catch remained at around 1,500 tons per year.[14] Among the coastal states of the Adriatic, Italy has always been the undisputed fishing superpower. The disproportion is especially obvious in bottom-trawl fishery, with the Croatian catch at around 5,000 tons and the Italian catch exceeding 50,000 tons.

From the commercial perspective, the most interesting species are demersal (benthic, bottom-dwelling) ones because of their market price. In the Adriatic Sea, the profitability and accessibility of demersal resources, due also to the wide and mostly shallow shelf, have contributed to their depletion.[15] At the same time, the abundance of typical prey species has increased. Especially disturbing findings were revealed in 2000/2001 based on data comparison of two research survey cruises monitoring the state of demersal fish stocks over a span of fifty years: the results of the HVAR cruise in 1948 and those of the MEDITS cruise in 1998.[16] The comparison revealed several major negative changes in the composition and distribution of demersal fish resources, clearly indicating their overexploitation (decrease of elasmobranch diversity and occurrence, considerably lower biomass indices, etc.). Some species, such as rays, have been especially affected by the intensity of trawl fishery and were disappearing; moreover, various indicators of the poor state of demersal Adriatic fish stocks have been documented.

Despite serious concerns for the sustainability of Adriatic Sea fisheries as well as frequent incidents of illegal oil spills from vessels, most of the Adriatic Sea remained under the legal status of the high seas until the autumn of 2003 because no state had proclaimed an EEZ there. It was, therefore, not possible for coastal states to exercise their sovereign rights and jurisdiction as guaranteed under the LOS Convention, neither for the purposes of living resource management and conservation nor in respect of marine environmental protection regarding pollution from vessels.

3. Croatia and Its Adriatic Sea Zone

3.1. The Long Road Toward an EEZ

In 1994 Croatia adopted its Maritime Code, according to which the "[exclusive] economic zone of the Republic of Croatia comprises the maritime spaces from the outer limit of the territorial sea in the direction of the open sea up to its outer limit permitted by general international law."[17] However, the 1994 code also stipulated that its provisions on the EEZ (Articles 33 to 42) are to apply only after the Parliament has decided to declare such a zone.[18]

For years Croatian scientists and experts had argued for an EEZ to be implemented in the Adriatic Sea, in vain presenting increasingly alarming scientific findings about the state of fish stocks as well as the need for improved resource conservation and marine environmental protection, all supported by legal arguments. Indeed, soon after the conclusion of the Third UN Conference on the Law of the Sea (UNCLOS III, 1973–1982), several (Croatian) experts and members of the Yugoslav delegation to that conference proposed to the federal (Yugoslav) governmental bodies to establish an EEZ. Nevertheless, from the mid-1980s (in the final years of Yugoslavia) and likewise in the 1990s (in the first years of an independent Croatian state), no ruling policies favored such a move. The official explanation was that Yugoslavia (later also Croatia) lacked the facilities necessary to control an EEZ in the Adriatic Sea.[19] The real reason behind that hesitant policy was the concern not to challenge Italy—the biggest user of and indeed the major regional power on the Adriatic Sea coasts. In the final years before its dissolution, Yugoslavia had quite different priorities than establishing an EEZ; as did Croatia, especially in the years following the 1991–1995 war, when the country faced other pressing problems in both its domestic and foreign politics.

The first political move for declaring a Croatian EEZ was made in 2001, when the Parliament opened a debate on a proposal submitted by an opposition party.[20] That was met with reservations by the parliamentary majority and the government, and the decision on the substance of the proposal was postponed until the next year (and then not reverted to).

In February 2003 Croatia submitted its application for membership in the EU. In the spring of the same year, the Croatian government established an interministerial Working Group on the Common European Fisheries Policy in the Mediterranean (hereinafter Working Group). EU fisheries policy was then undergoing a process of review, and a Ministerial Conference on the sustainable development of fisheries in the Mediterranean, scheduled to be held in Venice in November 2003, was in preparation. In that context, the European Commission initiated discussions on the need to consider extending the jurisdiction of coastal EU Member States beyond the territorial sea in the Mediterranean, possibly by establishing fisheries protection zones.[21] That in turn triggered the consideration of a Croatian EEZ within the coalition government. Concerns about the state of the living resources of the Adriatic Sea were rising. Moreover, prompted by oil transport projects discussed for the Adriatic Sea, fears of marine pollution incidents were voiced in public, not least in the aftermath of the disaster of the tanker *Prestige*. Parliamentary elections scheduled for the autumn of 2003 were approaching, and sentiments among the Croatian public for preserving the Adriatic Sea environment were growing. Indeed, the country was increasingly gaining international recognition for the beauty of its coastal areas and its preserved marine environment, attracting tourists from many countries and gradually replacing the war

images that had dominated perceptions of the region throughout most of the 1990s.

3.2. Preparing the Ground for the Extension of Maritime Jurisdiction

The Working Group was tasked with presenting Croatia's intention to extend its maritime jurisdiction beyond the territorial sea and exploring the positions of the neighboring countries, other Mediterranean countries, and the European Commission. As later documented in a report adopted by the Croatian government,[22] in the period from late spring to early autumn 2003, representatives of the Working Group engaged in a series of bilateral and multilateral meetings.[23]

At the multilateral level, the Croatian position was initially outlined at the first preparatory meeting (Athens, June 2003) for the Venice ministerial conference on fisheries in the Mediterranean, and elaborated in Croatia's position paper for the second preparatory meeting (Brussels, September 2003), where a meeting of the Adriatic Sea countries was arranged by Croatia.[24] As to bilateral contacts with Adriatic neighbors, of special concern for Croatia were reactions by Italy as well as Slovenia, while it also engaged in talks with Montenegro. Bilateral consultations with Italy, on the deputy-foreign-minister level, commenced in June 2003, and in July it was agreed that a Joint Croatian/Italian working group should be formed to coordinate the activities. Italy's initial reactions were not perceived as negative, although Italy expressed its preference for a protected fishing zone instead of an EEZ.[25] Slovenia, soon (on May 1, 2004) to become another Adriatic Sea EU Member State, was, however, "not interested in bilateral talks on a political level so as not to provide Croatia with the argument to consume the process of consultations," and it only agreed to a meeting at the level of heads of legal departments at foreign ministries.[26] Croatia also sought reactions from the European Commission.

Croatian diplomacy initially received ambivalent responses that, though not challenging the legal or scientific foundations of the intended extension of the country's jurisdiction, referred to political aspects, including the timing, as unfortunate. In addition, some argued that an EEZ would, among other undesirable effects, emphasize "exclusion" (as involved in the very notion of an "Exclusive" Economic Zone), which was perceived as not being inclusive or in an "EU spirit."

Croatia, which had submitted its application for EU membership earlier in 2003, proved sensitive to reactions of this type. Regarded as a goal ever since the inception of the Republic of Croatia, future EU membership has been highly desired (and equally uncertain). Croatian policy makers thus took care not to obstruct the country's road toward the EU. At the same time, they wanted to use the legitimate means available to protect Croatia's marine resources and the Adriatic Sea environment in accordance with international law. This episode took place during Italy's EU presidency (July–December 2003). Moreover, the President of the European Commission was a prominent Italian politician, Romano Prodi, who before then, as well as later, served as Italian Prime Minister.

The rapid shift from quiet diplomacy to a political show in public was triggered on August 1, 2003 by a memo published on the Web pages of the Croatian Ministry of Agriculture (also in charge of fisheries), unambiguously arguing for the declaration of Croatia's EEZ.[27] That announcement was followed by two months of intense pressure on Croatia not to proclaim an EEZ or any similar zone in the Adriatic Sea. Although the main criticism of Croatia's intentions came from a range of sources, including top political leaders of Italy, Slovenia, and the European Commission, the heart of the debate is encapsulated in a passage in the 2003 Croatian Government Report, stating, "He warned that if the Government of Croatia was to pass the decision on the extension of jurisdiction this could affect the pace of its approaching the EU, *notwithstanding Croatia's reasons.*"[28]

That coincided with European Commission President Prodi's letter to Croatian Prime Minister Ivica Račan, who referred to it as "another warning that, with regard to our intention of joining the EU, we need to accept behaviour according to European criteria."[29] As later reported by the Croatian Government, President Prodi's letter expressed concerns about Slovenian/Croatian relations and suggested refraining from unilateral decisions.[30] Slovenia was then indeed by far the most outspoken critic of Croatia's intended extension of jurisdiction (see further discussion below); Italy, though less in evidence in media headlines, was the most convincing and persistent one.

At that stage, Italy was already advocating the idea of a single joint fishing zone for the Adriatic states as well as the inclusion of Slovenia in further talks.[31] Although Croatia did not accept the idea of a joint zone, it was to re-emerge in the spring of 2004 as a proposal presented by Slovenia.

3.3. Declaring the "Ecological and Fisheries Protection Zone"

The Croatian government, faced with both intense international pressure to refrain from declaring an EEZ and a domestic public that largely supported such a move, eventually opted to propose extending Croatia's jurisdiction, albeit in a somewhat milder form, labeled the "Ecological and Fisheries Protection Zone." There were several reasons for choosing that option. Presentationally, the concept of a zone being "exclusive" was not expressly included in the notion. Also, it suggested that Croatia was not venturing beyond the practice of some other EU Member States that had already declared their zones in the Mediterranean: Spain had declared a fisheries protection zone in 1997, and France had adopted regulation on an ecological protection zone earlier in 2003 and implemented it in January 2004.[32] Croatia's proposed zone implied that it only combined the two European concepts into one and, thus, refrained from setting a precedent.

As to the substance, under the notion of an "Ecological and Fisheries Protection Zone" (hereinafter Zone), the Croatian Parliament proclaimed on October 3, 2003 only certain functions, or parts of the full "content," of an

EEZ under the LOS Convention.[33] Those functions related to three sets of rights that were the minimum acceptable to Croatia:

- sovereign rights for the purpose of exploring and exploiting, conserving and managing living resources;
- jurisdiction with regard to protecting and preserving the marine environment; and
- jurisdiction with regard to marine scientific research.

Croatia declared the Zone, but it initially postponed its implementation for one year. According to paragraph 3 of the 2003 Decision, that period was to be used for "preparing the implementation mechanisms and for possible signing of agreements or making arrangements with interested States and the European Communities."

Furthermore, according to the 2003 Decision (paras. 5 and 6), the outer limit of the Zone shall be as allowed under general international law and "shall be determined through delimitation agreements" with the neighboring states. Pending the conclusion of these delimitation agreements, the outer limits of the Zone temporarily follow those of the relevant delimitation agreements in the Adriatic Sea—most importantly, the delimitation line established under the 1968 Agreement on the delimitation of the continental shelf with Italy.[34]

A comment by the Croatian deputy minister of foreign affairs, who headed the Working Group, captured the essence of how Croatian diplomacy and politicians of the governing majority at first perceived the outcome: "time will show that we can be very satisfied with what we have accomplished—we have protected our interest *without unnecessary irritation of others*."[35] Time can indeed be a tough test of how durable political decisions are.

3.4. Croatia's Zone as an Expression of Unilateralism

Although avoiding the direct use of the notion of an EEZ and instead drawing nominally on the recent practice of two EU countries (Spain and France) in the Mediterranean Sea as well as expressly opening opportunities for additional arrangements with the states concerned and allowing a period of one year of postponed implementation of the Zone, Croatia's decision was met with strong criticism from the neighboring Adriatic Sea countries, Italy and Slovenia. The keyword of that criticism was that Croatia's decision was a "unilateral" measure. That label could hardly be understood to imply criticism of the unilateral proclamation of an EEZ in its technical legal meaning, because how else (bilaterally? multilaterally?) could one declare an EEZ?[36]

Also, the content of the Zone was strictly within the confines of the LOS Convention and thus based on a multilaterally agreed framework to which all the states concerned were parties. The label of unilateralism was, thus, a political one, implying that Croatia, due to its decision on the Zone, was not viewed as sufficiently cooperative. That its decision was regarded as "unilateral" was swiftly echoed by some leading European policy makers and soon by documents adopted by EU bodies. However, denying that Croatia's proclamation of the Zone was indeed in accordance with international law was difficult. For instance, when meeting Croatian Prime Minister Račan immediately after Croatia's proclamation, EU High Representative for the Common Foreign and Security Policy Javier Solana spoke of the recent "unilateral decision by Croatia" on the Zone, yet added that its legitimacy under international law was not in question.[37] In a similar vein, a document adopted thereafter by the European Council "noted with regret that the Croatian Parliament decided to declare a protected ecological and fishing zone in the Adriatic Sea without appropriate dialogue and co-ordination with the other countries concerned," yet went on to state that this was noted "without prejudice to sovereign rights of States deriving from the relevant international law."[38] In other words, though attributed the mark of unilateralism, Croatia's proclaimed Zone in the Adriatic Sea had to be, hesitantly or not, accepted as a legal fact.

3.5. From Bilateral, Regional, and EU— To Trilateral Adriatic Dialogue

Following on the European Council's call on Croatia "to urgently pursue a constructive dialogue with its neighbours to meet the concerns of all the parties involved,"[39] Croatia entered into further consultations with Italy and Slovenia.[40] That course had in fact been envisaged in Croatia's own 2003 Decision on the proclamation of the Zone, where a one-year span of postponed implementation had been set aside for that purpose.

However, due to substantially different sets of issues to be addressed with each of the neighboring countries in question, Croatia had originally intended to engage in a bilateral dialogue with each of these separately. Moreover, because key aspects of fisheries lay within the European Community's exclusive competence regarding its Member States, Croatia aimed at discussing with the European Commission a possible provisional regime, pending its future EU membership.[41] A year ahead of when Croatia adopted its decision on the Zone, the European Commission suggested in its Action Plan for fisheries in the Mediterranean that bilateral fisheries agreements could be concluded with non-EU countries (such as Croatia) who followed by establishing their own zones.[42] Finally, Croatia offered to host a subregional conference of all Adriatic Sea countries in March 2004;[43] this was also announced to all countries at the Venice Conference in November 2003.[44]

Yet instead of those intended bilateral and multilateral avenues to complement its national measure, Croatia eventually pursued a third option. Following the change of government in Croatia at the end of 2003, in early 2004 Croatia entered into trilateral—political, not technical—meetings with Italy and Slovenia (at a later stage also facilitated by the European Commission), held at the deputy-foreign-minister (state secretary) level.[45]

During those meetings, the other two countries proposed three options to Croatia. The key proposal, now put forward by Slovenia and supported by Italy, involved establishing a joint zone of the three countries in the Adriatic Sea. Although understandably favored by Italy (which had by far the dominant fishing fleet) and Slovenia (without any major fishing interest, but a geographically disadvantaged coastal state because it cannot lawfully claim an EEZ of its own),[46] this proposal was not acceptable to Croatia, which was in a favorable geographical position and had the major share of Adriatic Sea living resources closer to its own coasts. The disparities in rights under international law, interests, and capabilities among the three states proved so great that the proposal of a joint zone could not be a realistic solution.

The two other options proposed to Croatia basically involved maintaining the status quo in the Adriatic Sea, either by postponing implementing the Zone until Croatia became an EU Member State (at an uncertain date) or by not applying the Zone to EU countries. Neither of these proposals was in fact related to conserving fish stocks or protecting the marine environment. Croatia, which did not regard a joint zone as a feasible solution, felt that agreements among the Adriatic states, pursuant to establishing their own zones, might enable a more equitable distribution of fish resources, subject to fisheries conservation and management decisions based on scientific knowledge. Within such a framework, Croatia was prepared to make regionally (or bilaterally) agreed concessions. Bearing in mind the exclusive competence of the European Community in fisheries, Croatia aimed at negotiating a fisheries partnership agreement with the European Commission.

Soon after the third trilateral meeting was held in Pula, the European Commission adopted its Opinion on Croatia's application for EU membership.[47] The opinion in many respects gave a favorable assessment of conditions in Croatia and concluded by recommending that negotiations for accession to the EU should be opened, pending certain requirements. Among critical remarks, the opinion linked Croatia's declaration of the Zone to the outstanding delimitation dispute with Slovenia over the Bay of Piran and concluded that "Croatia's unilateral decision . . . has provoked considerable tensions with neighboring countries."[48] The opinion further stated that the "unilateral declaration" of the Zone "was an initiative not in line with the European principle of regional co-operation" and that it was "regrettable that Croatia decided to declare . . . [the Zone] . . . without appropriate dialogue and co-ordination with the other countries concerned."[49] Concluding on the "Political criteria" for Croatia's EU membership, the European Commission stated the need for Croatia to resolve issues arising from its unilateral declaration of the Zone.[50]

3.6. Postponing Implementation of the Zone to EU Countries

A European Council meeting of prime ministers was soon to follow (in mid-June 2004), and here the EU candidate status of Croatia was scheduled to be decided (as well as, possibly, the date for commencing negotiations on EU accession). Croatia's aspirations of becoming a candidate for EU membership, which the country openly expressed as its key foreign policy strategic objective, soon proved to be closely related to the future of its Adriatic Sea Zone.

The leader of Croatia's main opposition party (SDP), Ivica Račan, confirmed in an interview that earlier in June he had been informed by the Prime Minister Ivo Sanader that "Croatia may face a veto by Slovenia and Italy" at the upcoming European Council meeting.[51]

Rushing ahead of the June trilateral meeting to be held in Brussels, the Croatian government sent a proposal to the Parliament to amend and modify the 2003 Decision on the Zone, to be dealt with as a matter of urgency. After strong polarization of political parties on the issue, the Parliament modified its only eight-months-old Decision on the Zone. A new paragraph was added that provided that, with regard to the EU Member States, "implementation of the legal regime [of the Zone] shall commence after the conclusion of the fisheries partnership agreement between the European Community and the Republic of Croatia."[52]

This was adopted on June 3, 2004, only one day before the trilateral meeting in Brussels was scheduled to take place. It is difficult to see why nonapplication to the EU Member States of Croatia's jurisdiction regarding protection of the marine environment (namely, the ecological component of the Zone) would be linked with and made directly conditional on reaching a fisheries partnership agreement. Although fisheries were a chapter to negotiate with the EU, and the one in which the European Community has exclusive competence, marine environmental protection was not. However, within the European Commission, the handling of the issue was already the matter in which its External Relations Directorate-General (DG) was involved, rather than the DG for Fisheries and Maritime Affairs, under whose competence the substance of the matter would belong. By that time, indeed, the involvement of the European Commission in the issue of the Croatian Zone had crystallized. It was left to the political aspects—and thus the involvement of DG External Relations—and, later in the process, also the DG for Enlargement.

The scheduled trilateral meeting of deputy ministers of foreign affairs of Croatia, Italy, and Slovenia was held in Brussels on June 4, 2004. The deputy director-general of the European Commission's DG on External Relations, Michael Leigh, took part as "facilitator of the discussion." A record of that meeting was written in the form of "agreed minutes" and signed by the three deputy ministers and the European Commission's deputy director-general Leigh.

3.7. Agreed Minutes: Record of the Meeting, or an Agreement?

It is beyond doubt that the agreed minutes represented a record of the meeting held in Brussels. However, the issue was raised whether the minutes were more than a meeting record only. Because the agreed minutes were later attributed key weight in developments on the Zone, they need to be examined in some detail. As written in these minutes:

[The] State Secretary from Croatia informed the parties about the Decision taken on 3 June 2004 by the Croatian Parliament . . . which states that the implementation of the [Zone] with respect to the [EU countries] shall start after the conclusion of the Fisheries Partnership Agreement between [Croatia] and the European Community, and expressed Croatia's readiness to enter into talks to this end.

Croatia confirmed that during that period there will be no changes in the present regime for the [EU countries] in the area of the Adriatic Sea concerned.

The Italian and Slovenian State Secretaries took note of the decision of the Croatian Parliament. They welcomed suspension of all aspects of the [Zone] to [EU countries]. They *expressed the view* that this *should* apply *until a common agreement in the EU spirit is found* taking into account the interests of the neighboring EU states.

The participants at the meeting expressed their readiness to *continue to work* together . . . *until* a common *agreement is reached.*[53]

Following the Brussels meeting, in the evening of the same day, Slovenia's Prime Minister Anton Rop publicly stated that an "agreement" had been reached at that meeting.[54] Moreover, the Slovenian Ministry of Foreign Affairs issued a statement according to which, at the Brussels meeting, "Those present *agreed* that Croatia would postpone the implementation of the zone in respect of EU Member States *until a consensual solution* in a European spirit is reached, one that will take into account the *interests* of EU neighboring countries."[55] However, the next day Croatia's Foreign Minister Miomir Žužul stated that an understanding with Slovenia had not yet been achieved on all the elements in connection with the Zone and expressed hope that clarifications could soon be achieved.[56] Moreover, after the Brussels meeting, the Italian State Secretary for Foreign Affairs, Roberto Antonione, stated that in the agreed minutes from the meeting Croatia confirmed in writing that during that period (until the Fish-

eries Partnership Agreement is concluded) there will be no changes in the present regime for the EU countries.[57]

Soon afterward, at its meeting on June 17–18, 2004, the Presidency of the European Council adopted Conclusions by which it "notes the *Croatian decision* not to apply to EU Member States *any aspect* of the [Zone]. In this context, it welcomes the *agreement reached* by Italy, Slovenia and Croatia at the Trilateral meeting in Brussels on 4 June 2004."[58]

Thus, instead of "agreed minutes" from that meeting, an "agreement" was referred to. Other than its possible political perceptions, the name of the document is rather irrelevant as to its possible legal effect. As, for instance, stated by the International Court of Justice when deciding on jurisdiction and admissibility in the case concerning maritime delimitation and territorial questions between Qatar and Bahrain:

> Contrary to the contentions of Bahrain, the Minutes are not a simple record of a meeting, similar to those drawn up within the framework of the Tripartite Committee; they do not merely give an account of discussions and summarize points of agreement and disagreement. They enumerate the commitments to which the Parties have consented. They thus create rights and obligations in international law for the Parties. They constitute an international agreement.[59]

The Qatar/Bahrain minutes indeed started with the clause "the following was agreed" and proceeded with enumerating the agreed points. The Brussels minutes of June 4, 2004, however, only contained a reference to the readiness of the participants to continue working with a view to reaching an agreement. Moreover, they contained the views presented by *two parties* at the meeting—not all—that suspending (application of) all aspects of the Zone to the EU countries should apply until a common agreement in the EU spirit is found. What would be the exact effect of an "agreement," which the conclusions welcomed as already being reached, was also left open. However, additional specifications were later to follow (see discussion below and in section on the "Outcome"), in which the views presented by only some of the parties were gradually becoming presented as the content of a trilateral agreement reached.

At that point, though, the focus of Croatian policy makers was elsewhere. By the same conclusions, the Presidency of the EU Council decided that Croatia had become a candidate country for EU membership—a milestone long desired by Croatia.[60] Yet the exact date for opening negotiations on Croatian accession remained unspecified, although the Council had indicated that this should take place "early in 2005."[61] Croatian policy makers saw this as a political "victory" due to an alternative version in earlier drafts that had envisaged the opening of negotiations "in the course of 2005."[62] In fact, negotiations did not start until October 2005.

Further specifications of understanding the terms of the Brussels document followed. In a diplomatic note of August 30, 2004, Slovenia claimed that, at the trilateral meeting of state secretaries in Brussels, "agreement was reached that Croatia would postpone the implementation of the regime of the [Zone] for European Union Member States until a joint, consensual solution is found, which would take into account interests of Croatia's neighboring countries."[63] But there had been no tacit consent by Croatia to such an interpretation. In a diplomatic note of January 11, 2005, sent to the UN Secretary-General, Croatia stressed that

no agreement has ever been reached to the effect that Croatia would postpone the legal regime of the zone *until a consensual solution is found*. At the meeting of State Secretaries . . . [on June 4, 2004] . . . Croatia communicated the already adopted decision of the Croatian Parliament by which the regime of the [Zone] will not be implemented with regard to the European Union Member States *until the partnership agreement on fisheries is concluded* with the European Commission. The Agreed Minutes of the said meeting provide the record of the meeting at which the participants gave their

statements and expressed their views and readiness to continue to work together in the EU spirit.[64]

In fact, there already existed an unambiguous agreement of all states concerned on the regime of the EEZ (or a zone based on it), including the exercise of states' rights and duties in such a zone: This is the LOS Convention. All the states whose state secretaries participated in the June 4 Brussels meeting and signed the agreed minutes from that meeting are parties to the LOS Convention and are bound by it. Should the parties wish to conclude agreements modifying or suspending the operation of the LOS Convention applicable solely to relations between them, they may do so under certain conditions.[65] Moreover, the LOS Convention is explicit on the requirement that states parties *intending* to conclude such an agreement "*shall* notify other States Parties through the depositary of this Convention of their intention to conclude the agreement and of the modification or suspension for which it provides."[66]

No such notification of intention had been made by the states parties concerned; quite the contrary, there were contradictory "notifications" made to the UN Secretary-General, and both came *after* the trilateral meeting. Slovenia claimed that an agreement had been concluded, whereas Croatia argued that there was none because it considered that the only binding instrument remained the one adopted by the Croatian Parliament on June 3, 2004 (which can thus also be altered only by the Parliament itself). Croatia argued that the substance of the matter (a fisheries partnership agreement) should be resolved, whereas Slovenia argued that political aspects were the key ones (consensual solution in an EU spirit). Both those notes were made after—not prior to—the trilateral meeting of June 4, 2004, and the LOS Convention requirement on notification of the "intention to conclude an agreement" had not been followed. There was, therefore, no indication of the intention of the LOS Convention parties to conclude an agreement, at least not in accordance with the LOS Convention to which they all are parties.

However, the agreed minutes, though controversial among their "signatories" as to the real intentions and effects, remained written on paper—and the signature of the Croatian state secretary of foreign affairs was on it. From that moment, the Croatian Zone, earlier criticized as being politically "unilateral," albeit formally in accordance with international law, gained a new dimension. Now a signed document (meeting minutes) became available to enable a question mark to be posed also regarding the formal legal validity of the Zone should it be made applicable to the EU Member States (in reality, Italy and Slovenia) "without their consent."

That was to become a crucial element in further developments (as discussed below in section 6, "Outcome"). At this point, however, we should first see what the "interests of the neighboring EU states" referred to in the agreed minutes were.

4. Slovenia: The High Seas Too Far Away

Soon after the trilateral Brussels meeting, Slovenia expressed its view that, until a final consensual solution is found and an agreement reached between Croatia and its neighboring EU countries (Italy and Slovenia), the high seas regime should continue to apply to (all twenty-seven) EU countries in the area of the Zone.[67] Otherwise, according to Slovenia, Croatia would be unilaterally infringing on the area of the high seas and denying the rights of Slovenia.[68] Ever since Croatia proclaimed the Zone in 2003, Slovenia argued that this decision "prejudices the border at sea" between the two countries and "encroaches on the area in which [Slovenia] exercises its sovereignty and sovereign rights."[69] The key question is, therefore, whether the Croatia's proclaimed Zone falls, in any of its parts, within the area where Slovenia exercises sovereignty or sovereign rights—or may exercise these in accordance with international law.

That is an important matter to examine because the linking of the Croatian Zone to the maritime delimitation dispute with Slovenia was not left as a bilateral issue between the two countries only but instead emerged as a crucial problem attributed to the Zone in documents adopted by EU bodies. As stated by the European Commission in its Opinion on Croatia's application for EU membership: "*As [a] consequence of* this outstanding border issue [the border dispute between Croatia and Slovenia over the Bay of Piran], Croatia's unilateral decision of October 2003 . . . *has provoked* considerable tensions with neighboring countries."[70] The question, then, is whether such a causal relationship is based on international law or rather on the political perceptions created. Several aspects need to be considered before a conclusion based on international law can be reached.

4.1. Baselines and Breadth of the Territorial Sea of Slovenia

The law of the sea is unambiguous on the right of a coastal state to establish the breadth of its territorial sea up to a limit not exceeding 12 nautical miles (nm).[71] The 12-nm breadth is to be measured from baselines determined in accordance with the LOS Convention.

Currently, the distance of the Slovenian coast, and any related baseline, from the nearest point of the Croatian Zone (i.e., the nearest high seas, before the Zone was proclaimed in 2003) *exceeds* 12 nm.[72] In fact, the distance is 15.5 nm as measured between Point 5 at sea and the nearest point on the Slovenian coast (Cape Madona, close to Piran; see map 16.2).[73]

Nevertheless, Slovenia argues that Point 5, which "marks the *beginning* of the high seas in the Adriatic," is "the point of Slovenia's territorial exit to the high seas."[74]

The breadth of the Slovenian territorial sea in the direction of the high seas is not only limited by the LOS Convention but is also pending until a solution of the maritime delimitation dispute with Croatia is reached. In 1975 Yugoslavia and Italy delimited their territorial seas by the Treaty of Osimo. After Yugoslavia dissolved, however, a dispute emerged between the

MAP 16.2 Agreed maritime boundaries in the north Adriatic Sea

two newly independent states, Croatia and Slovenia, on the territorial sea delimitation in the maritime area situated between their coasts and the Osimo delimitation line with Italy.

As shown on map 16.2, the coasts of the two states lie opposite each other in the Bay of Piran (hereinafter the Bay)[75] and meet at the foot of the Bay. It is, therefore, that area within the Bay where the endpoint of the land frontier between Croatia and Slovenia meets the sea. Yet the two countries are in profound disagreement as to the exact point from which to draw their maritime delimitation line, and how it is to be drawn.

Croatia argues that, pending final delimitation *within* the Bay, neither of the two states is entitled to extend its territorial sea beyond the median line. Slovenia, on the contrary, argues, and has recently also stated in its domestic regulations, that the *entire* Bay is internal waters of Slovenia, notwithstanding the fact (which it does not dispute) that Croatia also has part of the coast within the Bay.[76]

It is not necessary for the present analysis to enter into any further details of that segment of the delimitation dispute, confined to the area of the Bay.[77] The key conclusion here remains unaffected by any possible final solution to that question. No matter how the Bay is eventually delimited, the resulting Slovenian baselines will remain more than 12 nm away from Point 5 (be it the high seas or the Croatian Zone that "begins" from that point). This is so even if the entire Bay is, hypothetically, regarded as internal waters of Slovenia and a closing line at the mouth of the Bay is thus determined as a straight baseline.

In order to arrive at a 12-nm distance from Point 5, Slovenia would need to extend its baseline considerably outside the mouth of the Bay, but such a baseline would not be related to the Bay nor to its own coast. The closest point on the coast located at a distance of 12 nm from Point 5 is in fact well beyond the area of dispute: all the way around Cape Savudrija, where the northernmost Croatian lighthouse is situated (see map 16.2). To be valid, however, baselines need to be determined in accordance with the LOS Convention—and must be related to one's own coast, not the coast of a neighboring country.

Moreover, delimitation of the territorial seas between Croatia and Slovenia is still pending, and this question cannot be resolved merely by extending Slovenia's territorial sea in the direction of the high seas. However, it is important to clarify that, independent of Croatia's territorial sea in the area, Slovenia would remain cut off from the high seas already due to the distance from Point 5 because this exceeds the breadth of the territorial sea allowed under the LOS Convention. Neither is it within the rights of Croatia and Slovenia to agree on a breadth of the territorial sea in excess of the 12-nm limit between themselves.

The conclusion at this stage is clear: There neither is nor can there be any impact of the Croatian Zone on Slovenian sovereignty or sovereign rights at sea. The reason is found in basic geographic circumstances and relevant international law. Bluntly stated, it is not Croatia's territorial sea (or the Zone) that is cutting Slovenia off from the high seas; it is the high seas that are too far away from Slovenia for it to be able to "territorially" access them.

4.2. The Croatian Zone as Prejudicing the Border at Sea with Slovenia

There is to date no agreement in force between Croatia and Slovenia on their maritime delimitation. However, in 2001 negotiators from the two countries initialed a "final working adjustment" for the text of an agreement on the state border.[78] There is no disagreement between Croatia and Slovenia that the text was neither signed nor ratified and that it is legally not in force. Where they differ is in interpretations as to whether the initialed text was just a phase in the treaty negotiation process or an agreement (record of the agreement reached).[79] Slovenia has since presented it as an "agreement," whereas Croatia referred to it as a "draft agreement." We hereinafter refer to it as the "final working adjustment" because that is how both negotiating parties designated the text that they initialed in 2001.

In Slovenia's view, by declaring the Zone, Croatia has prejudiced the final enforcement of a consensual solution to the issue of the maritime boundary and encroached on the area in which Slovenia exercises its sovereignty and sovereign rights. Slovenia has held that Croatia's decision on the Zone "hinders the final enforcement of an agreed solution concerning the border at sea between the two States."[80]

Here we need to examine two aspects of the 2001 "final working adjustment." First, does the area to which it related in any part overlap with the area in which the Croatian Zone is proclaimed? That is not the case because the respective areas of application are each on a different side of Point 5.

Second, would Slovenia's territorial sea, under the "final working adjustment" and the chart attached to it,[81] extend to Point 5? That, too, is not the case because the territorial sea of Slovenia would not extend to Point 5 but rather would remain separated from it by several nautical miles (and only the territorial sea of Croatia would remain in contact with Point 5).

To date, the solutions contained in the "final working adjustment" have clearly been abandoned by both countries; Slovenia, for instance, has since passed regulations for the entire Bay as its internal waters and has also extended its territorial sea to Point 5 (thereby well exceeding the 12-nm limit). However, the relevant conclusion here is that, even under the hypothesis that the "final working adjustment" would become a treaty in force, Croatia's proclaimed Zone would in no way hinder its final enforcement because it is located in an area beyond and without any direct effect on either the sovereignty or sovereign rights of Slovenia that can be based on the LOS Convention.

4.3. The Right of Slovenia to a "Territorial Exit to the High Seas"

Slovenia nevertheless claims that it is entitled to a "territorial exit to the high seas," and has specified Point 5 as the point of that territorial "exit."[82] So far, Slovenia has put forth various arguments to support its claim; those arguments have evolved and changed over time. In its 1993 Memorandum, Slovenia stated its "specific situation" as well as that it "belongs to the group of so-called geographically disadvantaged states, which due to their geographical situation can claim no exclusive economic zone of their own."[83] On those grounds, Slovenia explained its need for an "exit to the high seas," arguing that it is "in accordance with the principle of equity and taking into account special circumstances, to draw the boundary with [Croatia] so as to enable, at least in a narrow section, the *contact* of the territorial sea of [Slovenia] with the high seas in the Adriatic."[84] Several years later, the "need" to enable contact of Slovenia's *territorial sea* with the high seas was expressed as the "right" to a direct territorial "exit" to the high seas, but was now based on different grounds. In 1999 Slovenia stated that it had, just like Croatia, in the former joint state of Yugoslavia, "exercised all rights based on that *territory*, including the direct *territorial* exit to the high seas, and thus has inherited that sovereignty as a successor of the former [Yugoslavia]."[85] Consequently, Slovenia now claims

that it has "a direct territorial exit to the high seas *and has the right to declare its own exclusive economic or ecological and fisheries protection zone.* Slovenia has already exercised this right as one of the coastal Republics of the former [Yugoslavia] ever since its dissolution, and consequently has the same right also at present."[86]

In 2006 Slovenia went a step further in an attempt to affirm the basis of its "preserved territorial exit to the high seas." It argued that Italy had recognized Slovenia's succession to the 1968 Agreement on the continental shelf, "consequently 'admitting' that Slovenia has the continental shelf. . . . Since Slovenia has the continental shelf, it also has territorial exit to the high seas."[87] According to Slovenia, "all this leads to a very simple conclusion: The Slovenian territorial sea extends to [Point 5] where the Slovenian continental shelf starts."[88]

It is, indeed, not possible to acquire territorial sea rights by logical deduction. Rather, sovereignty over the coast and the application of the relevant rules of the LOS Convention to that situation are the key requirements under the law of the sea. Moreover, the main Slovenian thesis, placing its "territorial exit to the high seas" in the context of state succession, requires a brief comment. The territorial sea in Yugoslavia was not delimited between the various republics, in contrast to their land territories, where administrative borders did exist between the republics within the federation. In Slovenia's view, the "joint," once-Yugoslav sea is yet to be divided, and as long as there is no agreed division, Slovenia preserves all the rights it had as a Yugoslav republic, including the right of a territorial exit to the high seas.[89] However, a "territorial exit" to the high sea is not found in the LOS Convention—there is only the territorial sea *through* which such an "exit" can be practiced. A territorial sea, in turn, is acquired *ratione territorii* and not through a division of the sea as a "succession mass." In other words, upon becoming an independent state, Slovenia did not "inherit" an ideal, undivided part of the sea (and all various rights appertaining to it) as a unit separate and independent of its coast, but rather only got that part of the sea and those rights appertaining to it that can be related to its own coast. Today, when Yugoslavia no longer exists, that coast is the basis for determining Slovenia's rights on the adjacent sea. As stated by the International Court of Justice, it is "the terrestrial territorial situation that must be taken as [a] starting point for the determination of the maritime rights of a coastal State."[90]

Apart from the fundamental legal aspects under the law of the sea discussed above, there is, however, another aspect not to be underestimated: the interest of a coastal state in having unimpeded *access* to the high seas.[91] It is of considerable importance for Slovenia not to be cut off from such access to the high seas, and that point in itself should not be controversial. Where the controversy arises is whether such access must be *territorial* or not.

Croatia did propose, already in the mid-1990s, that a navigational "way" be determined *within* the territorial sea of Croatia to connect the territorial sea of Slovenia with the high seas.[92] Within that area, not innocent passage but instead a regime more liberal than a transit passage and "almost identical to the high seas regime" would be established for ships of all flags.[93] That proposal, however, was not accepted by Slovenia[94]—so the countries were back to a deadlock.

The key obstacle to resolving this north Adriatic Croatian/Slovenian "Rubik's cube" puzzle lies in the mixing, within a single set of solutions, of maritime delimitation between the two countries, on the one hand, and Slovenia's legitimate concern for unimpeded *access* to the high seas as possible, on the other. If the problem remains confined to one set of solutions only, that can lead to no solution at all. It is important to realize that maritime delimitation between Slovenia and Croatia is one issue to be solved, whereas Slovenia's access to the high seas is yet another one—and is only partly related to the first. Just like access to the sea by landlocked states, access, or "exit," to the high seas by a geographically disadvantaged coastal state is not a function of (maritime) delimitation

only. As observed by the UN Secretary-General: "UNCLOS was not negotiated to correct geographical circumstances. To compensate partially for the latter, the Convention provides adequate remedies for situations where States are at a disadvantage."[95]

As to the maritime delimitation line between Croatia and Slovenia, it will have to be drawn in the area of the previously Yugoslav side of the Osimo delimitation line; that is certainly an open bilateral issue between Croatia and Slovenia—and those two states alone. Regarding Slovenia's access to the high seas, a solution in harmony with existing navigation rules and established practice in the area of the Gulf of Trieste ought to be considered. That access, though legally as unimpeded as possible under international law, must be as safe as possible for navigation as well. A solution for the latter cannot be found on one side of the Osimo delimitation line only because a meaningful and practical solution must include *both* sides, and thus *three* countries—Italy, Croatia, and Slovenia—rather than only two.

As of December 1, 2004, a set of new traffic separation schemes adopted by the Maritime Safety Committee of the International Maritime Organization (IMO) applies to all ships in the north Adriatic, including approaches to the Gulf of Trieste and to/from Slovenia's sole international commercial port, Koper.[96] That routing system was jointly proposed by the Adriatic Sea countries, including Slovenia, Italy, and Croatia, with the objective of enhancing the safety of navigation, protecting the marine environment, and facilitating the efficiency of vessel traffic in the area.[97] This IMO traffic regulation relates to the Gulf of Trieste, which is among maritime areas with the highest density of Adriatic Sea commercial traffic. Over 40 million tons of oil are transported on tankers every year in this small area, as well as various other forms of hazardous cargo. In practical navigation terms, the "exit" (i.e., the direction for outgoing traffic) as regulated by the IMO is not where the Slovenian politicians argue that it should be, and this is because the "entrance" (the direction for in-

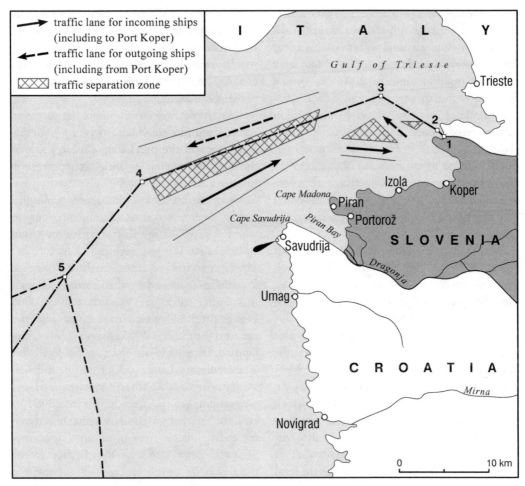

MAP 16.3 IMO traffice separation scheme in the north Adriatic Sea

coming traffic) is in the sea along the Croatian coast of Istria, or for that matter in that area of the former Yugoslav side of the Osimo delimitation line. To have a "corridor" enabling direct "exit" to the high seas (and thus traffic in both directions) in the same area, or on that side of the Osimo line only, would be contradictory to the IMO regulation and the established practice of navigation there. The "exit" for ships is indeed regulated in an area different from where the "entrance" is—on the Italian side of the Osimo delimitation line. It is the territorial seas of both Italy and (once the limits are drawn) Croatia that have enclosed the territorial sea of Slovenia upon its emergence as an independent state. Aspects of Slovenia's access to the high seas

should be resolved with those two countries while taking into account the existing IMO traffic regulation and established navigation practice in the area. This should not be difficult to achieve as long as the access (or "exit") to the high seas is not viewed as synonymous with territorial sea gains beyond what is permitted under international law.

Slovenia has expressed concerns for the "exercise of its right of communication with the rest of the world"[98] and stated that a "territorial exit to the high seas is also important because of maritime transport to and from the Port of Koper (which, in turn, is important for Slovenia's economic development)."[99] However, facts and figures so far do not support these views. In

1990, when Slovenia was still a Yugoslav republic and thus allegedly with a "direct territorial exit to the high seas," its single international commercial port, Koper, had an annual throughput of only 5 million tons. By 2007 the annual throughput in that port had tripled to 15 million tons (increasing on average by one million tons every year since 2003, when Croatia proclaimed the Zone).[100] These figures may indicate that access to and from the high seas in the area is functioning well in practice, and any remaining practical, political, or legal issues could best be resolved by building on the existing regulation and practice of navigation.

As it stands, therefore, it is apparent that Slovenia's desired "territorial exit" to the high seas is not prejudiced by Croatia's Zone. Rather, the basic provisions of the LOS Convention confine the exercise of Slovenia's territorial rights at sea. Moreover, geographic circumstances prevent the "territorial exit" because between the Slovenian coast (and/or any conceivable baseline), on the one hand, and Point 5 at sea, on the other, lies the Peninsula of Savudrija, which is indisputably under the sovereignty of Croatia. In order for Slovenia to gain, even theoretically, a "territorial" contact with the high seas at Point 5, either the LOS Convention or the legal status of the Savudrija Peninsula would need to be changed.

4.4. Asserting Claims to Sovereign Rights in the Maritime Area South of Point 5

Notwithstanding political claims, Slovenian legislation and regulations long remained in line with the statement contained in the 1993 Memorandum, according to which Slovenia "belongs to the group of so-called geographically disadvantaged states, which due to their geographical situation *can claim no exclusive economic zones of their own*" (emphasis added). Accordingly, its 2001 Maritime Code regulated Slovenia's maritime "sovereignty" (as well as its "jurisdiction" and "control") in the territorial sea and the internal waters, but not "sovereign rights" in maritime areas beyond these.[101]

However, in December 2003, soon after Croatia proclaimed its Zone, Slovenia followed by amending its own Maritime Code.[102] The words "sovereign rights" were inserted after "sovereignty" in Article 1 of the Code, and a new paragraph was added to Article 4, which now states that Slovenia "may exercise its sovereign rights, jurisdiction and control over the sea surface, water column, sea bed and subsoil beyond the limits of state *sovereignty* in accordance with international law."[103]

Two years later, Slovenia adopted additional legislation and passed regulations specifying to where it exercises sovereignty at sea and from where it exercises sovereign rights. Its October 2005 Act on the Proclamation of the Ecological Protection Zone and on the Continental Shelf (hereinafter 2005 Act)[104] and the January 2006 Decree on the Determination of the Fisheries Sea Area (hereinafter 2006 Decree),[105] when juxtaposed, largely explain the national legislative and regulatory patchwork of marine areas to which Slovenia has asserted sovereignty and sovereign rights claims. According to the 2006 Decree, the internal waters of Slovenia lie between the coast and the line connecting Cape Savudrija and Cape Madona—thus in fact closing the Bay at its mouth and actually serving as a straight baseline (see map 16.2).[106] From Cape Savudrija (which, incidentally, is the coast of Croatia), the territorial sea of Slovenia extends in the direction of the high seas,[107] to the point from where sovereign rights of Slovenia are asserted under the 2005 Act. The relevant points are Point 5 (presented also as point "T5" in the 2005 Act) and, temporarily, until final agreement on maritime delimitation with Croatia is reached, Point T6 (2006 Decree).[108] Both Points 5 and T6 lie at a distance well exceeding 12 nm from even the nearest point of the line closing the Bay. Even if measured from Cape Savudrija, which the 2006 Decree explicitly uses as the relevant point (although that Cape is on the Croatian coast),[109] the closest distance to Point T6 is still 13 nm, whereas the distance between Point T6 and the nearest Slovenian coast (Cape Madona) is 15.8 nm. In addition, the maritime delimitation dispute with Croatia is pending both within and outside the Bay.

Slovenia extended its sovereign rights to apply in, *inter alia*, its "Ecological Protection Zone." The provisional "external border" of that zone follows the continental shelf delimitation line of Yugoslavia/Italy under the 1968 Agreement and extends along that line from Point 5 southward as far as the parallel 45°10' N. That parallel, according to the 2005 Act, also forms the provisional "external border" of the ecological zone in the south, and the southern boundary of the zone runs along this parallel.[110] In other words, Slovenia's proclaimed zone of sovereign rights extends at sea southward from Point 5, running parallel to the Croatian coast of Istria, (provisionally) to the latitude just under Cape Grgetov—close to the town of Vrsar on the western Istrian coast of Croatia (see map 16.2). Indeed, the continental shelf that Slovenia claims to have in that area is *not* a natural prolongation of its own land territory but rather of the land territory of Croatia in front of its western Istrian coast.[111]

Moreover, calling the proclaimed zone "ecological" might have been a "name of convenience" because rights in the zone are not limited to jurisdiction with regard to protecting and preserving the marine environment[112] but comprise also Slovenia's "sovereign rights relating to research and sustainable use, preservation and management of marine wealth" (2005 Act, Article 3).[113]

So far there have been no official or public reactions from the EU bodies or other EU Member States to Slovenia's evidently excessive territorial sea claim, nor to further extension of its sovereign rights based on that claim, although both are clearly in violation of the LOS Convention. No state except Croatia has publicly protested.[114] However, as observed by the UN Secretary-General when commenting on the universal applicability of the provisions of the LOS Convention regarding the regime of maritime zones: "no international recognition must be given to maritime claims in excess of the limits allowed by these provisions and . . . the regime of maritime zones and jurisdiction established under national legislation must fall within their scope."[115]

Thus, the Slovenian "ecological zone," although a paper tiger only, remains formally in effect under its national legislation and with no distinction made as to whether or not it applies to the EU Member States.

4.5. Toward a Consensual Solution– "In the EU Spirit"

Several main observations on the trend of development follow from the above discussion. First, Slovenia managed to link its bilateral delimitation dispute with Croatia to the issue of the Zone, although there exists no international law basis for that connection whatsoever. Various documents adopted by EU bodies have confirmed and strengthened the thesis of a causal link between the boundary dispute of the two countries, Slovenia's "exit" to the high seas, and Croatia's Zone. That thesis has become broadly accepted not only in political decisions but also in the media—including some leading international ones—regardless of the basically local character of the dispute at hand.[116]

Second, neither rules of international law nor evidently needed environmental, conservation, and management aspects of the Croatian Zone have been decisive in the process that developed within the EU, which has been dominated by political aspects. This made it possible to maintain the thesis of a causal relationship between the Croatian-Slovenian boundary dispute and Croatia's Zone—as long as the matter was left to political perceptions only.

Third, although negotiations on maritime delimitation failed to progress after the 2001 "final working adjustment" (which both parties abandoned in the meantime), Slovenia, since becoming an EU Member State in spring 2004, has become positioned such that it will ultimately take part in approving whatever final solution may be found for applying the Croatian Zone to EU countries. That should be a joint, consensual solution, as first argued by Slovenia (in 2004) and then gradually adopted by the EU decision makers and bodies in their documents (between 2004 and 2007), ultimately requiring a common agreement "in the EU spirit."[117]

As commented by the Economist Intelligence Unit already in mid-August 2003: "for Croatia there is plenty of reason to stay *within the rules.* . . . On the diplomatic front, indeed, this represents Croatia's best chance to show that it can be a team player inclined to compromise in the manner expected of an EU member."[118]

In protesting against Croatia's Zone, Slovenia stated that this had been proclaimed "contrary to the European way."[119] However, Slovenia's own ecological zone has been proclaimed contrary to international law. Because in its very fundamentals the EU is based on the rule of law, the "European way" and international law (in this case, the LOS Convention, to which all the EU Member States are parties) should indeed correspond.[120]

Placing the entire issue of the Zone in the context of Croatia's accession process for EU membership facilitated an outcome that would certainly have been more difficult to achieve without having a "convincing" issue to relate to, such as an unresolved territorial delimitation dispute.[121] Whether that was the main reason for opposing the Croatian Zone or simply an optimal justification to put forth remains to be seen. That leads us to the next section.

5. Italy: Not Yet Ready for Delimitation of Adriatic Sea Zones?

According to one Italian author, Italy's "interests in fishing may be compared to the typical interests of a distant water State."[122] However, there is an important difference as well. Although fishermen of that country mostly fish outside the territorial sea limits, due to the poor state of fish stocks within the Italian territorial sea, this activity does not take place far away from Italian coasts—especially not in the narrow Adriatic Sea. Thus, in contrast to distant-water fishing fleets, the activities and fishing practices of Italian fishermen have an impact on resources in the relative vicinity of Italy's own coasts. As explained above (in the section on maritime uses

of the Adriatic Sea), the sustainability of the Adriatic fisheries today is facing serious problems. In that respect, and given the largely subregional nature of the Italian fishery here, Italy would presumably have dual interests: the exploitation interest of a "distant water"–like fishing state and the rational management and conservation interest of an Adriatic coastal state.

In public statements, Italian politicians have related the prospects of a Croatian Zone to the negative economic effects this might have on Italian fisheries in the Adriatic Sea; however, the political implications have been mentioned as well. According to reports, the Italian State Secretary responsible for fisheries, Paolo Scarpa, has stated that Italian fishers, who currently fish in the Adriatic Sea in high sea waters up to the limits of the territorial seas of other countries, would be denied such access should limits of zones of sovereign rights be introduced in the middle of the Adriatic Sea.[123] On that point, the Croatian Governmental Report concluded, "The recent statements of State Secretary Scarpa clearly show that the interests of Italian fishermen are the basis of [the] Italian position on the extension of jurisdiction in the Adriatic, and it is as yet uncertain which means Italy will employ to implement its policy."[124]

However, on October 2, 2003, one day prior to the Croatian proclamation of the Zone, the Italian press published excerpts from a letter sent on October 1, 2003 by State Secretary Scarpa to the European Commission President Romano Prodi and the Commissioner responsible for fisheries, Franz Fischler.[125] The letter, along with arguments for EU involvement in the issue, contained explanations about the special circumstances of the Adriatic Sea, where, allegedly, unilateral proclamation of an EEZ would have serious economic and political consequences. In that context, State Secretary Scarpa was cited as stating, "Due to geomorphologic features of the [Croatian] Dalmatian coast, characterised by numerous islands, affecting baseline determination and the related criteria for maritime delimitation of EEZ, Croatia could [through its Zone] gain exclusive fisheries rights over some 3/5 of the Adriatic Sea."[126]

Moreover, the need for cooperation in and coordination of coastal state activities on the semi-enclosed Adriatic Sea was emphasized, and reference was made to the LOS Convention. At present, three important documents, issued or adopted by Italy in the period from 2004 to 2006, are the key for understanding its position regarding the extension of jurisdiction in the Adriatic Sea.

5.1. The Italian Note of April 2004

On April 16, 2004, Italy sent a note to the UN Secretary-General,[127] in which two main arguments were stated against the lawfulness of the Croatian Zone under international law. Firstly, Italy pointed to Article 123 of the LOS Convention and also argued that Croatia had failed to fulfill the obligation to cooperate when it issued the unilateral declaration of the Zone because "this obligation to cooperate does not cease if a coastal State bordering an enclosed or semi-enclosed basin decides *to establish* reserved zones of functional jurisdiction" (emphasis added). According to the Italian note, for coastal states bordering on enclosed or semi-enclosed seas, there is the specific obligation to cooperate to determine the limits of the zone of functional jurisdiction. This obligation, as argued by Italy, is even more evident in enclosed or semi-enclosed basins that are particularly narrow, such as the Adriatic Sea, where the circumstances are such that "coordination in determining the zone of functional jurisdiction is even indispensable."

Second, Italy argued in its 2004 note that the determination, in a temporary manner, of the limit of the Croatian Zone coinciding with the delimitation line agreed for the continental shelf under the 1968 Agreement is "against Italian interests." In support of that argument, Italy put forth the following reasons:

- the automatic extension of the continental shelf delimitation line agreed in 1968, to serve as the provisional outer limit of the Croatian Zone, is legally not well founded because that limit was agreed on the basis of special circumstances that differ from

those to be considered in the determination of superjacent waters;

- the 1968 delimitation was agreed at a time when the notion of [an] EEZ was not well defined in the international law of the sea; and

- a change of relevant geographical circumstances took place after the conclusion of the 1968 Agreement, implying a consequential change of the objective parameter of the median line.

5.2. Law on the Italian Ecological Protection Zone, February 2006

On February 8, 2006, Italy adopted Law 61 on the establishment of an ecological protection zone beyond the outer limit of the territorial sea (hereinafter the 2006 Law).[128] It authorizes the establishment of ecological protection zones on the basis of a decree by the President of the Republic. This is related to achieving delimitation agreements with the "states involved," that is, those whose territory is adjacent to or facing Italian territory. Until the date when said agreements enter into effect, the outer limits of the ecological protection zones follow the outline of the median line, each point of which is equidistant from the closest points on the baselines of the Italian territorial sea and of the states involved.

Within the zone, Italy exercises its jurisdiction in the area of protection and conservation of the marine environment, including the archaeological and historic heritage. Norms of Italian and EU law as well as international treaties apply to foreign ships and persons in the zone regarding marine pollution, including from ships, ballast water, and dumping of garbage as well as pollution from seabed exploration and exploitation activities and also of atmospheric origin. According to an explicit provision (Article 2(3)), the 2006 Law does *not* apply to fishing activities.

5.3. The Italian Note of March 2006

On March 15, 2006, Italy sent a second note to the UN Secretary-General,[129] now prompted by

Croatia's submission of the list of geographical coordinates defining the outer limit of its Zone.[130] In this Note, Italy stated that the provisional limit of the Croatian Zone appeared "harmful to Italian interests" not only in procedural terms but also in substance.

As to procedural terms, Italy argued that Croatia, in violation of Article 74 of the LOS Convention, had failed to involve Italy in setting the provisional limit of the Zone, despite the provision on the need for cooperation contained in that Article. There was no reference to Article 123 in the 2006 Note.

As to provisional limits of the Croatian Zone being "harmful to Italian interests" in substance, Italy put forth the following reasons in the 2006 Note:

- the 1968 Agreement had been concluded when the Italian system of baselines was profoundly different because the method of straight baselines was introduced only later (in 1977)[131];
- the flow of detritus from the Po River from 1968 to the present has led to a further lengthening of the Italian coastline toward the open sea; and
- the constant jurisprudence of the International Court of Justice has consistently recognized that the delimitation of sea areas invokes special circumstances that differ for the continental shelf and for superjacent waters—such as, for example, *historic fishing rights*—which in turn leads to different delimitation methods and that, consequently, in this specific case there is no legal foundation, however provisional, for automatically extending the 1968 seabed line to superjacent waters.

5.4. Assessment

The Italian position, as presented in those two diplomatic notes (of 2004 and 2006), along with the provisions of the 2006 Law, has introduced several complex issues regarding extending jurisdiction in the Adriatic Sea, especially as to delimitation aspects between the Italian and Croatian zones.

First, in its 2004 Note, Italy argued that Croatia's "obligation to cooperate," already when declaring the Zone, consisted "in the specific obligation to cooperate in determining the limits of the zone . . . i.e., in agreeing on those limits with other interested States" and that Croatia did not fulfill that obligation when it unilaterally declared the Zone. Both Croatian and Italian leading experts on the international law of the sea have commented on this statement. According to Vukas, such a reaction misinterprets the LOS Convention (Article 123 in particular) because any state is free to establish unilaterally its EEZ; however, "*after* having undertaken such a decision, it may be necessary to adjust the cooperation with neighboring States to the new situation."[132] Similarly, as observed by Scovazzi,

> If the note meant that a State bordering an enclosed or semi-enclosed sea cannot proceed to establish its exclusive economic zone (or other *sui generis* zones) without the agreement of its neighboring States, this would be wrong. It would be contrary to both the spirit and letter of Article 123 UNCLOS and the UNCLOS provisions on the exclusive economic zone (Part V), which do not distinguish among different categories of seas.[133]

Besides, it is difficult to see how this alleged "obligation to cooperate" on agreeing, or even negotiating, on (provisional) limits of the zone ahead of its actual proclamation could be implemented by Croatia given the fact that Italy has, already as of September 2003, argued for the establishment of a joint zone in the Adriatic Sea,[134] which by itself excludes any prospect of delimitation. In fact, once the Croatian intention to declare an EEZ became public (on August 1, 2003), further negotiations with Italy were headed in only one direction: Italian political disapproval of Croatia's "unilateral" Zone proclamation.

Second, already in its 2004 Note (with additional views formulated in the 2006 Note), Italy

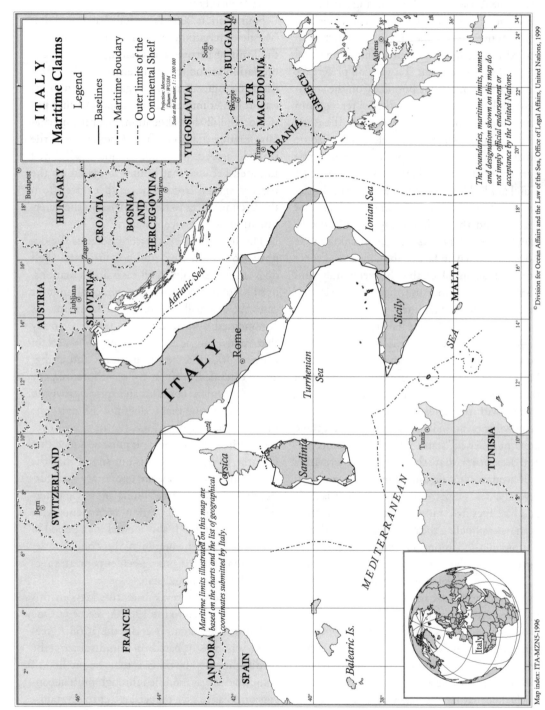

Map index: ITA-MZN5-1996

MAP 16.4

clearly argued against a single maritime boundary in the Adriatic Sea, thus favoring a delimitation line between the Croatian Zone and the (prospective future) Italian zone distinct from the existing continental shelf delimitation based on the 1968 Agreement. This Italian preference for a different maritime boundary on the continental shelf from that in the water column above it does not relate exclusively to the Adriatic Sea; it is of particular relevance to some other maritime delimitations that may be on the horizon for Italy in other seas surrounding its mainland.[135] However, when it comes to the delimitation of water-column zones (ecological or similar) and their relationship to the existing continental shelf boundaries, the situation in the Adriatic Sea may in fact be the converse of some other situations, like that between Italy and Tunisia, as to the zone in which to argue for the priority of the median line.

Third, in its 2006 Law, Italy relies on the median line, that is, equidistance from the closest points of the baselines, as the temporary outer limits of its ecological protection zone until these limits are determined on the basis of agreements "with the states involved." Due to Italy's geographic position in the Mediterranean, there are a number of "states involved," and on several seas other than the Adriatic where Italy will need to agree on outer limits of its zone. In several cases—especially due to Italian islands and baselines determined with reliance on these islands—upholding the median line is the delimitation method more advantageous for Italy. Given the configuration of Italian and Croatian coasts in the Adriatic Sea, the situation here is different due to the Croatian island chain along the coast and the straight baselines determined with reliance to this island chain following the general direction of the coast.[136] In such a situation, and with its 2006 Law explicitly relying on the median line until a final agreement is reached, it may be reasonably expected that Italy would place priority, through negotiations toward agreements with the "states involved," on the determination of those limits of its zone—or segments of it (i.e., "zones")[137]—where stricter

reliance on the median line can be advocated more favorably for Italy.

Fourth, in its 2004 Note Italy had stated that "the determination, in a temporary manner" of the limit of the Zone coinciding with the delimitation line of the continental shelf based on the 1968 Agreement was "against Italian interests in the Adriatic Sea." In support of that position, the 2004 Note went on to say that "automatic extension of the delimitation of the seabed, agreed in 1968, is not legally well founded because that limit was agreed on the basis of special circumstances that differ from the circumstances to be considered in the determination of superjacent waters."

The Italian view is correct insofar as the delimitation of an EEZ and a continental shelf does not necessarily, in all cases and situations, need to follow the same line—although in most cases these actually do follow the same line. As commented by Scovazzi, "the point is simply that, where an agreement refers to a certain zone . . . it cannot be automatically and unilaterally extended to other zones." Moreover, the 1968 Agreement contains an explicit provision (Article 4) stating that it does not influence the juridical state of the waters (or air space) over the continental shelf. Here it must be added that Croatia, in its 2003 Decision, stated that the outer limits of its Zone are temporary and, furthermore, that the final limits are to be determined through delimitation agreements with neighboring states. It also allowed for a period of postponed implementation of the Zone in order to facilitate arriving at agreements or arrangements with interested states.

There are two key substantive facts in this context, as related to the 1968 Agreement. One is that the delimitation under the 1968 Agreement was mostly based on equidistance—the median line.[138] The other is that the method of equidistance was modified through mutual concession so as to give reduced effect to several islands situated significantly far offshore (and thus not following the general trend of the coastline), and due to that, Italy, in total, actually received a sizeable concession through the 1968 Agreement as compared to what would have been the case with a strict application of the median line. Some authors have estimated the total size of the concession in Italy's favor at 2,664 square kilometers.[139] Although the exact surface area of that concession may still need to be determined precisely, there is no doubt that, as observed by Scovazzi, the 1968 Agreement "provides for a boundary line which is more favorable to Italy with respect to what would result from the application of a strict equidistance method."[140]

Directly related to this aspect are several circumstances that must be borne in mind regarding the situation existing when Croatia proclaimed its Zone in October 2003. No Italian zone had as yet been proclaimed nor had any Italian law to that effect been adopted, and the outer limit of the Croatian Zone was to meet with the high seas. The Croatian Zone was, however, not intended to exceed the line at which Italian interests, based on international law, might be affected—should Italy decide to venture into establishing its own zone. The practice of the Mediterranean states in establishing unilaterally the outer limit of their jurisdictional zones vis-à-vis states that have no such zones has recently been assessed by Irini Papanicolopulu, who concluded that those states "generally have not exceeded the median line, thus implicitly recognizing the entitlement of the opposite or adjacent state to a future claim of a similar jurisdictional zone."[141] If, however, in the situation as of October 2003, Croatia were to rely on the "outline of the median line" (as, e.g., provided by the 2006 Law on the ecological zone by Italy), this would in effect mean *exceeding* the projection of the existing continental shelf delimitation line of 1968. Provisional reliance (until agreement is reached) on the latter delimitation line can thus also be seen as a rather cautious move on Croatia's part. As commented by Blake et al., "it would be extremely difficult to maintain any claim, for example to an EEZ, *beyond* [this] well-established and accepted maritime [boundary] in the Adriatic."[142]

Fifth, although its 2006 Law explicitly provided for the outline of the median line as a pro-

visional outer limit of its ecological zone, Italy, through its 2004 and 2006 Notes, in fact protested against relying on a median line with sizeable adjustments in the Adriatic Sea, thereby considerably correcting a strict median line to its advantage. In its 2004 Note, Italy stated that automatically extending the 1968 delimitation line was "against Italian interests" because it failed to take into account a "change of relevant *geographical circumstances* that took place after the conclusion of the 1968 Agreement, which implies a consequential change of the objective parameter of the median line" (emphasis added). However, since 1968 there had been no major changes in the geography of the region that would have had an impact on the median line between Italy and Croatia.[143] It has thus been commented that the "unclear reference to geography probably refers to political geography, and not to physical geography."[144] Italy probably did not want to point out that, after the dissolution of Yugoslavia, there is a considerably smaller state, Croatia, that now has sovereignty over most of the eastern Adriatic coastline. However, the additional explanations offered by Italy in the 2006 Note, referring to the flow of detritus from the River Po from 1968 to the present and leading to a lengthening of the Italian coastline to the open sea, would not appear particularly relevant either.

Sixth, in its 2006 Note, Italy pointed to the example of "historic fishing rights" as being among the special circumstances "consistently recognized" in "constant jurisprudence" of the International Court of Justice, leading to different delimitation methods for the continental shelf and the superjacent waters. However, maritime zone delimitation in the Adriatic Sea in the present situation would be between the Croatian Zone and the Italian ecological zone. In its 2006 Law Italy stated that the law "does not apply to fishing activity." Fisheries' rights are thus an element expressly excluded from the content of the Italian ecological zone. Therefore, even without further discussion of that subject—given the 2006 Law excluding fishing activity from its application—"historic fishing rights" remain irrelevant when determining the outer limit of the Italian ecological zone.

In sum, there may be many complex reasons—not only economic and political but, in the current situation, also legal—for Italy to prefer the status quo in the Adriatic Sea. It might have been all too tempting to present the issue of Croatia's Zone as an Adriatic "East Side Story"—yet another "Balkan niggle," as *The Economist* put it[145]—where two small countries, Croatia and Slovenia, were shown as involved in a fierce but basically irrational dispute over a small area of sea. Although their maritime delimitation dispute is a real and unresolved one, we have seen in the preceding section that there is no basis in international law for relating that delimitation dispute to Croatia's proclaimed Zone.

In fact, the implications of the Croatian Zone for the longitudinal Adriatic maritime delimitation with Italy, though essentially a bilateral issue—and entirely beyond a territorial one[146]—may represent the single most serious impediment to the application of that Zone to the EU Member States. An agreement on the substance of the rights of the neighboring EU Member States in that Zone presupposes the need for entering into negotiations between Croatia and Italy on the limits of their respective zones in the Adriatic Sea.

If, however, the Croatian Zone were to be made nonapplicable to EU Member States, that might be a solution that could enable open access to the high seas resources to be maintained (and with the by-product of excluding non-EU states) while at the same time postponing the related delimitation implications along most of the Adriatic Sea.

From here, two avenues may be possible. One is to maintain the status quo as long as Croatia does not become a Member State of the EU; this would until that time also allow for the continuation of current fishing practices in the Adriatic Sea, including the consequences these have been shown to have for the sustainability of the Adriatic fisheries and status of fish stocks so far. The other avenue may be to continue trying to persuade Croatia to accept the establishment of a joint zone in the Adriatic Sea, regardless of its entitlement under international law to implement its own EEZ.

6. Outcome

The outcome developed in two phases. First, in December 2006 the Croatian Parliament adopted a decision to implement the Zone—also with regard to EU Member States—from January 1, 2008. From that date the Zone was, at least formally, in full implementation—yet for seventy-five days only. Croatia then decided to discontinue application of the Zone to the EU countries from March 15, 2008. How and why could that turnabout be possible in such a short period of time?

6.1. Deciding to Implement the Zone Fully

By the autumn of 2006, over two years had elapsed since Croatia amended its Decision on the Zone (on June 3, 2004) and since (on June 4, 2004) the trilateral meeting was held in Brussels. In the meantime, some important circumstances had changed, whereas others remained in stalemate.

On the one hand, the two Adriatic EU Member States, Slovenia (in October 2005 and January 2006) and Italy (in February 2006) had adopted their legislation and regulations on "ecological protection" zones or aspects of extended maritime jurisdiction. On the other hand, it became evident that no fisheries partnership agreement would ever be concluded. In accordance with the 2004 Decision, implementation of Croatia's Zone with regard to the EU countries was to commence only after the conclusion of a fisheries partnership agreement with the European Union. Croatia invited the European Commission to initiate negotiations on the agreement; however, Croatia's calls to conclude such a fisheries partnership agreement remained unanswered after the Brussels trilateral meeting.[147] It was argued that the European Commission does not negotiate that kind of agreement with a candidate for EU membership with which the accession negotiations were opened (for Croatia, in October 2005). It thus became evident that no fisheries partnership agreement would ever be reached. Instead, fisheries issues were to be discussed under a separate chapter of the accession negotiations. However, progress toward opening negotiations on the fisheries chapter has remained deadlocked since autumn 2006 and remains blocked at the time of writing (June 30, 2008). Croatian officials have pointed out that "one Member State" (Slovenia) in effect blocked further procedures in the European Council, which requires unanimity by EU Member States for a Council decision on preparedness for the opening of negotiations on individual chapters.[148] In this way, progress toward opening of the negotiations on Chapter 13 (Fisheries) has been prevented, and in that context any discussion of the fisheries segment of the issues related to the implementation of the Zone has been disabled.[149]

The stalemate on the Zone was increasingly becoming the subject of a renewed domestic political debate in Croatia. The government had long been reluctant to propose a new amendment of the decision on the Zone, though it had no doubts as to the international legal basis for Croatia to change a previous decision adopted by its own Parliament; rather, it perceived maintenance of its position as self-restraint due to policy considerations. The deadlock in the process toward opening the fisheries chapter in Croatia's EU accession negotiations, however, may have had a triggering effect for the government's change of position. Here it should be borne in mind that the question of the Zone, which by that time had remained unresolved for over three years, was already a dominant political issue in Croatia and that calls by the main parliamentary opposition parties for full implementation of the Zone echoed those put forth by environmental nongovernmental organizations (NGOs), fishers' associations, marine scientists, and prevailing expert views, meeting a broad consensus in general public opinion.

In October 2006 Croatian Prime Minister Ivo Sanader announced that the conditions had been met for proposing an amendment of the 2004 Decision to the Parliament, and he invited a consensual proposal by all the parliamentary parties. It initially appeared that an amendment decision might result from following such a course.[150]

A key change, however, had been introduced since November 30, 2006, when the European Commissioner for Enlargement, Olli Rehn, visited Croatia and attended a meeting of the government. On that occasion Rehn had commented that a unilaterally decided application of the Zone to the EU Member States would be contrary to the agreement of June 2004, adding that this agreement had facilitated the EU membership candidate status for Croatia.[151] Reference to an international agreement, instead of a 2004 Decision by the Croatian Parliament, as the legal basis for the nonapplication of the Zone to the EU countries, marked a substantial difference. On this point, Croatian Prime Minister Sanader indicated that Commissioner Rehn might have been misinformed by his advisers regarding the existence of such an agreement.[152] The Delegation of the European Commission in Croatia then issued a Communiqué, stating,

> The document to which Commissioner Rehn was referring to, are agreed minutes of a trilateral meeting Italy/Slovenia/Croatia which took place in Brussels on 4 June 2004. . . . The agreed minutes set out a *jointly agreed procedure* and do include a *specific commitment* on the application of the Zone. In this respect, it would be detrimental to Croatia's credibility as a reliable partner in the region if it came out now with a unilateral move by activating the Zone. We believe that the reference to the European Council from June 2004 which conferred candidate status to Croatia is the key one for clear understanding.[153]

The day after, the Croatian Prime Minister reiterated that no such agreement existed.[154]

Moreover, the Croatian Ministry of Foreign Affairs pointed out that "interpretations stating that the Minutes might be taken as a legally binding document are completely groundless" and that any interpretations that could imply attempts to limit the rights of Croatian institutions to pass sovereign decisions would be unacceptable.[155] Indeed, also the European Commission's Screening Report for Chapter 13 (Fisheries) stated, "*Pursuant to the Decision of the Croatian Parliament* of 3 June 2004, the Ecological and Fisheries Protection Zone is not applied to EU vessels. This decision was *noted* by the trilateral meeting between Croatia, Italy and Slovenia, facilitated by the Commission, of 4 June 2004."[156]

Moreover, in its 2005 Progress Report on Croatia, the European Commission, under the "Political Criteria" section, included a reference to the Decision of the Croatian Parliament of June 3, 2004, according to which implementation of the Zone to EU countries would start after the conclusion of an agreement on partnership in fisheries. Yet under the section "Chapter 13: Fisheries" of the Report, it stated that "in line with the trilateral agreement between Croatia, Italy and Slovenia of June 2004, [the Zone] is not applied to EU vessels."[157]

Nevertheless, it immediately became clear that the issue was not one of possible misinterpretation of a document ("agreed minutes" or "agreement") made by the European Commission Delegation in Zagreb or accidental misinformation of Commissioner Rehn by his advisers. The President of the European Commission, José Manuel Barroso, stated after the meeting held in Brussels on December 6, 2006 with the President of Croatia, Stjepan Mesić, that the European Commission expected Croatia, as a credible candidate country, to commit to its obligations assumed at the start of (accession) negotiations and not to take unilateral measures regarding the Zone.[158] At that point, the issue of the Croatian Zone, although still being handled by the European Commission as a political one, was no longer left to its DG for External Relations but instead to the DG Enlargement. Although the Directorates were different, there was in fact a personal continuity because the facilitator of the discussion at the June 4, 2004 Brussels meeting and a "signatory" of the resultant agreed minutes on behalf of the European Commission, then deputy director-general of DG External Relations, had in the meantime become director-general of DG Enlargement.[159]

Croatian diplomacy intensified its activity on the issue of the Zone while the government formed a working group tasked with preparing the proposal on the rules for applying the Zone.[160] Differences surfaced between the government's approach (possibly resulting from enhanced diplomatic consultations) and the major opposition parties. Although still arguing to apply the Zone, the government was now also proposing a new one-year period of postponement. Key parliamentary opposition parties, however, argued for instant application of Croatia's jurisdiction on marine environmental protection within the Zone while allowing for additional negotiations on the exercise of sovereign rights related to fisheries—yet within a predetermined time limit of six months. In addition to sovereign rights related to living resources, Croatia's Zone notably related to jurisdiction with regard to protecting and preserving the marine environment and with regard to marine scientific research—thus not *all* aspects of applying the Zone to the EU countries could (and should) have been negotiated either through a fisheries partnership agreement or within the fisheries chapter of the accession negotiations.

In line with the proposal made by the government, on December 15, 2006, the Croatian Parliament adopted a third decision on the Zone.[161] This modified paragraph 3(2) of the 2004 Decision by providing that "For the Member States of the European Union the implementation of the legal regime of the [Zone] shall start no later than 1 January 2008, whereof, fisheries and ecological regulations of the Republic of Croatia shall be applied to fishing and other European Community vessels."

Moreover, an amendment added to the same paragraph emphasized Croatia's orientation toward its future EU membership and underlined awareness of its current candidate status. The provision also contained a rather declaratory political slant:

> Croatia will, through a partnership relation with the Member States of the European Union and the European Commission, in accordance with its status of a candidate country which negotiates on accession to full membership to the European Union and the importance of promoting good neighbourly relations, continue dialogue on measures that ensure sustainable fisheries and protection of the Adriatic marine environment, taking into account fundamental principles of the Common Fisheries Policy of the European Community, scientific data collected through national and international projects . . . and the regulations of the Republic of Croatia and interested parties.

The 2006 Decision, in fact, provided for a new postponement of the application of the Zone and enabled an additional (but now temporally defined) one-year span for further negotiations with neighboring countries and the European Commission. With that decision, a period of more than four years altogether—since the adoption of the October 2003 Decision until December 31, 2007—has been provided for such negotiations.

6.2. Discontinuing the Application to EU Member States

In the first half of 2007 several rounds of technical consultations were held between Croatia, Italy, and Slovenia in the presence of the European Commission.[162] Croatia was ready to cooperate on aspects of implementation of the Zone in accordance with EU common fisheries policy and practice. However, certain issues remained controversial, including that of Croatian control over (Italian) fishing vessels in the Zone. No final solution on such issues emerged from those technical consultations.

With the date for full implementation of the Croatian Zone approaching, pressure on Croatia to suspend its decision was increasing. There were also two important political aspects of the timing, as embodied in the 2006 Decision. First, implementation of the Zone as of January 1, 2008 would follow immediately after the parliamentary elections in Croatia (scheduled for late November 2007). Second, beginning the implementation of the Zone on January 1, 2008 would coincide with the first day of Slovenia's six-month EU presidency. It has been an unwritten rule that the EU Presidency does not use that position to promote the political agenda of its own country, as in bilateral issues.

In early November 2007 the Commission issued its annual report on Croatia's progress in preparing for EU membership.[163] Although the previous annual progress report did not include any direct reference to the Croatian Zone,[164] the 2007 report dealt with the Zone in the context of "Political Criteria" for EU membership. Under the heading "Regional issues and international obligations," the 2007 report stated that the 2006 Decision by Croatia "deviates from the *political* agreement reached between the countries concerned in June 2004, referred to in the European Council conclusions of June 16–17 2004."[165]

The Commission simultaneously issued a draft for the revised Accession Partnership for Croatia in order to update the 2005 Accession Partnership.[166] Compared to the 2005 Partnership document, major changes as related to the issue of the Zone were now introduced. In the 2005 Accession Partnership, the Zone was not mentioned under "Key Priorities" or among the "Regional issues and international obligations"; the only reference was under the heading on "Fisheries."[167] In the 2007 Accession Partnership for Croatia, however, the situation was reversed. There was no longer any mention of the Zone under the heading on "Fisheries," but references to the Zone were now included under "Key Priorities" identified for Croatia and "Political Criteria" defined for it. In that context, the Zone was ranked first in the listing of issues under

"Regional issues and international obligations": "Fully respect the 4 June 2004 agreement concerning the Ecological and Fisheries Protected Zone referred to in the June 2004 European Council conclusions *and the Negotiating Framework* and do not apply any aspect of the Zone to the EU Member States until a common agreement in the EU spirit is found."[168]

As commented by Christian Danielsson, director of the Directorate B (in charge of, *inter alia*, Croatia) in the DG Enlargement: "We are making clear that it is important for Croatia to address this issue and address it before the January 1. We should be aware that there was an agreement in 2004 on how this issue should be addressed and that agreement was *in force* for long time."[169]

At that point, it was highly unlikely that Croatia would address the issue of the Zone. Parliamentary elections were scheduled for November 25, 2007, and a move by the government toward changing the decision on the Zone could make winning the elections a "mission impossible" for the governing party. However, January 1, 2008, was quickly approaching. Two weeks after the Croatian elections, on December 10, 2007, the European Council adopted conclusions on enlarging the EU. These actually restated the wording already contained in the 2007 Accession Partnership draft: for Croatia to "fully respect the June 4, 2004 agreement" and "not to apply any aspect of the Zone to the EU Member States until a common agreement in the EU spirit is found."[170] Although carrying political weight, these conclusions by the Council came after the elections but at a time when no government had been formed in Croatia, and the new Parliament had not been constituted as yet—so it was in fact technically impossible for any amendment to the existing decision to be adopted. Moreover, in order to form the government, the party that won the relative majority (the Croatian Democratic Party, HDZ) was negotiating with the Croatian Peasant Party (HSS) as its main prospective coalition partner. For the HSS, maintaining full application of the Zone was a key political issue.

Political messages to Croatia were at that stage increasingly referring to the prospect of blocking accession negotiations with the EU should it persist with the scheduled implementation of the Zone. The Italian Minister of Agricultural, Food, and Forestry Policies (responsible also for fisheries), Paolo de Castro, reportedly stated that four to five accession negotiation chapters might be "frozen."[171] Prior to that, Slovenian Foreign Minister Dimitrij Rupel already indicated that blocking negotiations in "five to six" chapters may be a possible scenario.[172] The key thesis put forward by Slovenian politicians was that the issue of the Zone was not a bilateral one but rather the matter of the relationship between Croatia and the EU. The European Commission, in turn, was calling on Croatia to deal with the issue of the Zone as a matter of urgency in order to avoid negative consequences for the accession process to EU membership.[173]

With no Parliament formed in Croatia by December 31, 2007, the implementation of the Zone, also with regard to EU countries, formally commenced on January 1, 2008, in accordance with the earlier Decision. Once a Croatian government was formed, its Prime Minister Sanader proposed quadrilateral talks (between Croatia, Italy, Slovenia, and the European Commission) to discuss and find a solution for the reasons for Italian and Slovenian opposition to the Croatian Zone. Slovenia, however, repeatedly stated that it would be prepared for such talks only after Croatia had fulfilled its obligation under the "Brussels agreement" (June 4, 2004) and suspended application of the Zone to the EU countries.[174] Although, in contrast to Slovenia, Italy seldom expressed official views on the issue of the Zone publicly, its politicians were now indicating that Croatia should "freeze" or "not apply" the Zone to EU countries as long as a solution was not found.[175] However, days later, the Prodi government fell and Italy was left with a technical government, which further complicated handling the matter of the Zone.

Dramatic confirmation of the need for implementing coastal state jurisdiction, also beyond the territorial sea in the Adriatic, came on February 6, 2008, when the Turkish-flagged Ro-Ro freighter, *Und Adriyatik*, carrying hazardous cargo, caught fire 13 nm off Croatia's Istrian coast, near Rovinj.[176] An environmental disaster was prevented through an action that involved both Croatian jurisdiction and international cooperation, in accordance with international law.

Nonetheless, ten days later, the European Council, presided over by Slovene Foreign Minister Rupel, repeated its call to Croatia not to apply any aspect of the Zone to the EU countries until a common agreement in the EU spirit is found.[177] The European Council invited the European Commission to continue dialogue with Croatia on the issue and to report back.

The turning point came when European Commissioner for Enlargement Ollie Rehn visited Croatia on March 6, 2008.[178] It also became clear that no quadrilateral meeting, which Croatian Prime Minister Sanader had expected might take place on March 13 or14, alongside the European Council meeting,[179] would be held.

Instead, on March 13, 2008, the Croatian Parliament adopted yet another amendment of its Decision on the Zone—the third in a row. Paragraph 3(2) of the 2004 Decision had been modified once again. It now provides that the Zone "shall provisionally not apply to Member States of the European Union, as of March 15, 2008, until a common agreement in the EU spirit is reached."[180] On the same day, the president of the European Commission, José Manuel Barroso, listed several conditions for the European Commission's presenting an "indicative timetable for the technical conclusion" of the accession negotiations with Croatia in 2009. These included "last but not least, Croatia must suspend all aspects of the Ecological and Fisheries Protection Zone, with respect to EU vessels. I consider this now done."[181]

Indirectly confirming that Croatia's accession negotiations had in effect been blocked prior to the March 13 Decision of its Parliament, Commissioner Rehn commented, "Removal of this obstacle by Croatia should now allow for chapters to be unblocked and negotiations to resume

again at [a] normal pace."[182] In other words, this outcome means further maintenance of the status quo regarding the Croatian Zone's application to EU countries in the Adriatic Sea as long as the (Adriatic) EU Member States do not accept a change in that situation. The roots of that outcome can be traced back to the spring of 2004, with the series of (political) trilateral meetings of state secretaries, first as a proposed option made by Italy and Slovenia.[183] Then, on June 4, 2004, the view was expressed by the same two parties at the trilateral meeting held in Brussels that suspending all aspects of the Zone should apply until a common agreement in the EU spirit is found.[184] Thereupon, the outcome of that meeting was interpreted as an agreement[185] and its content specified as an alleged undertaking by Croatia to postpone implementing the Zone until a consensual solution is found.[186] Full respect for this, in turn, became formulated by the European Commission as a political criterion in the 2007 Accession Partnership for Croatia[187] and was then restated in the Conclusions by the European Council on December 10, 2007.[188] When, on March 13, 2008, the Croatian Parliament finally came to adopt a decision in exactly the same wording, the four-year circle was closed.

In that same four-year period, no progress was made regarding management and conservation measures for the heavily depleted Adriatic fish stocks. Quite the contrary, the status quo was maintained: The same harmful fishing practices in the Zone continued without any legal possibility of control by the coastal state. Due to political considerations, advances in measures to combat marine pollution were also limited, even though research projects conducted under the auspices of the European Commission itself had proven frequent incidents of illegal oil spills. This is not the place to discuss but only to remind of the EU's proclaimed policies and numerous measures adopted with a view to securing sustainable fisheries in general and deterring devastating fishing practices—for example, illegal, unregulated, and unreported (IUU) fishing—in particular. Over the past decade, the

EU has also been especially active in developing measures to counter marine pollution from vessels (whether resulting from accidents or from operational oil pollution). The application of coastal state jurisdiction has regularly played a key role in making such proclamations and measures a reality. The Adriatic Sea, however, demonstrates a profoundly different situation.

6.3. Credibility and the Rule of Law

Whether the European Commission, and indeed the Adriatic EU Member States, were referring to the "agreed minutes" as constituting a legal or a political agreement remains vague. Either interpretation presents a fundamental problem in relation to the LOS Convention. If the agreed minutes were regarded as a political agreement, how could they derogate from the rights and duties of the parties under the LOS Convention? If, however, the meeting record was understood as a legal agreement, how could it be reconciled with the rights and duties of the parties under the LOS Convention? The key legal principle of *pacta sunt servanda* creates a fundamental problem regardless of which way the "agreed minutes" may be understood, due to the LOS Convention.

Another aspect has been the state practice so far. A quarter of a century has passed since the LOS Convention was adopted. So far, over 130 states have proclaimed EEZs (or derivates, like fisheries and other zones) in the world's oceans and seas. Regarding the EU Member States, the current status fully confirms the general trend. As to the two Adriatic Sea EU countries, Italy and Slovenia, their legislation has been described and discussed above. Out of the remaining twenty-five EU countries, twenty are coastal states. Among those, nineteen have an EEZ or a similar ("ecological" or "fisheries") zone. The single exception is Greece. Some EU countries have recently undertaken changes in the content of their zones: For example, Finland in 2005 expanded its earlier Fisheries Zone in the semi-enclosed Baltic Sea into an EEZ.[189] There is nothing in EU law that would prevent a coastal state—an EU Member State, a country aspiring to EU candidacy (like Croatia in 2003), or a membership candidate country (like Croatia since 2004)—from exercising the right to proclaim and accordingly apply an EEZ, fully in accordance with its EU membership rights and duties, once it became an EU Member State.

Unlike the case in most other countries, however, the Croatian Zone was not a technical issue or a matter of regular, routine procedure. Quite the contrary, due to external political pressure it evolved into a top domestic political issue and has, as such, become a prime media target for almost five years. The facts—that the Croatian Zone (or for that matter an EEZ) is solidly based on international law, that the practice of establishing such zones by EU countries is widespread, and that there are real resource conservation and marine environmental concerns in the Adriatic Sea—had an important impact in shaping Croatian public opinion. The Zone has been recognized as a necessary legal and legitimate measure.

The importance of a well-preserved coastal and marine Adriatic area for Croatia—a young, small country that owes its worldwide image largely to those features—and the country's maritime profile were additional important factors informing the sentiments of the public. Discontinuing the application of the Zone in March 2008, though formally Croatia's own decision, in fact meant yielding to external political pressure. That resulted in widespread perceptions among the general public of unequal treatment and deeply unfair conduct—and a conduct that was contrary to the rule of law.

One could argue (as indeed it has been argued in public debates) that, although Croatia may have the right to an EEZ, no state is legally entitled to join the EU membership nor is the EU obligated to accept any given state as a member. From such a perspective, it could be argued that the EU may deny Croatia an asset—EU membership status—that the Union controls just as legitimately and legally as Croatia controls its decision on an EEZ. There is, however, a fundamental question here: Would it be legitimate for the EU to hamper or even deny access to EU membership to a candidate country because the latter had applied international law, such as provisions of the UN Law of the Sea Convention, binding on all EU Member States and the European Community alike? The EU is based on the rule of law—that is one of the main values on which its very foundation rests.[190] The EU's international actions are to be guided by the principles that have inspired its own creation, development, and enlargement and that it seeks to advance in the wider world—and these include the rule of law, the principle of equality, and respect for the principles of international law.[191]

Respect for the rule of law, including in this case the LOS Convention—a "Constitution for the Oceans"—is far from being a formal requirement only, devoid of real-life substance. Among the (proclaimed, at least) key purposes of the EU membership for countries in the so-called "Western Balkans" region—the countries that have emerged from the recent war and disintegration of Yugoslavia (minus Slovenia in the north, plus Albania in the south)—is to facilitate the rule of law and political stability.[192] Seeing the developments regarding the Croatian Zone in that light is difficult. Quite the contrary, by nurturing widespread disapproval among the domestic population over the conduct of the neighboring Adriatic EU countries, supported by some key EU policy makers and facilitated by senior European Commission bureaucrats, the current outcome of the Croatian Zone issue may contain a nucleus of instability. For many, it may be seen as a litmus test, leading to disillusion on such basic EU values as the rule of law and equal treatment. And that may become a major, long-term loss for the role the EU can play in the region—all on account of relatively minor, short-term individual gains by a few of its Member States in their exclusively bilateral relations with Croatia.

7. Concluding Remarks

The entire "episode" of the Croatian Zone raises some fundamental questions far beyond re-gional or national confines. EU policy makers and bodies have increasingly been favoring the political avenue for handling matters of international law, which is what the application of an EEZ regime amounts to. In order for Croatia's Adriatic Sea Zone to become applicable to the EU countries (and in practice to neighboring Italy and Slovenia), an additional "common agreement in the EU spirit" has been sought. That trend, though perhaps not quite crystallized in the early phase (before and immediately following the proclamation of the Zone in 2003), has become evident since the spring of 2004 onward. Indeed, as the European Commission clearly stated in its Opinion of April 2004, the purpose of the trilateral meetings was to find a political agreement.[193]

However, the international law framework cannot be dismissed as entirely irrelevant. Moreover, as to political aspects, it should be noted that a political agreement on the EEZ regime had already been reached by all the countries involved and expressed in legal form a full twenty-five years ago—today contained in the provisions of the LOS Convention. This does not contradict EU law. Quite the contrary, all the current twenty-seven EU Member States as well as the European Community itself are also parties to the LOS Convention. A related important consideration has been formulated by the UN Secretary-General:

> Views have been expressed that in some regions, the proclamation of certain maritime zones foreseen by UNCLOS would be contrary to certain general obligations under international law. It is the Secretary-General's belief that the rights and obligations under UNCLOS should not be region-dependent and that *no additional conditions* on the enjoyment by States parties of rights provided by UNCLOS should be imposed.[194]

In addition to the right of any coastal state that can lawfully proclaim an EEZ to apply that regime in accordance with the Convention, some core principles of the law of the sea have been undergoing testing in the Adriatic Sea. Most importantly, these include the basic axiom that the land dominates the sea in determining maritime areas under sovereignty and the sovereign rights of coastal states. Reasons for this principle, based on an objective geographic criterion and sovereignty over the coast, relate to the core functions of international law. By enabling a good measure of predictability, such objective criteria facilitate the stability of the international order. Disregarding such an important principle of international law of the sea may, in the context of maritime delimitation, seriously hamper the potential for settling international disputes peacefully. Although related to a rather regional, if not local, case only, the matter thus deserves far broader attention.

The vicissitudes of Croatia's Zone raise considerations not only of legality under international law but also those of legitimacy. Problems surrounding the Zone seem deeply rooted in the imbalances that today characterize the Adriatic Sea. A coastal state of a relatively small political strength (re-emerged in that space after the dissolution of a larger state, Yugoslavia, yet retaining most of the former Yugoslavia's coastline) is geographically placed so as to be entitled, by the current rules of international law, to govern a considerable share of the Adriatic marine area and resources. Notwithstanding the rules of international law, such a division may appear at odds with the decidedly asymmetric bargaining power of the nations involved. Some important stakeholders probably oppose the EEZ as a step toward consolidating this imbalance between law and political might.

The need to conserve the marine resources and prevent environmental degradation of the Adriatic Sea speaks strongly in favor of adopting and implementing all measures available, including an EEZ. There is, however, no more than international law to support this line of action. Powerful economic and political interests, both on the Adriatic regional and the broader Eurasian strategic level, seem to favor maintaining the status quo in the overall picture of Adriatic Sea jurisdiction.

To achieve that, only two avenues remain open. One is to change the current law of the sea, as codified in the LOS Convention, which is hardly a feasible or desirable option, at least in the short run. The other is to persuade Croatia, a country that became renowned primarily due to its well-preserved Adriatic coastal and maritime area, *not* to use its rights based on the LOS Convention.

And that brings us back to the beginning of our story when, on December 10, 2007, the European Council opted to mark the twenty-fifth anniversary of the LOS Convention in a very special way.

NOTES

1. *See* Tommy Koh, *A Constitution for the Oceans*, in THE LAW OF THE SEA, UNITED NATIONS CONVENTION ON THE LAW OF THE SEA xxii, U.N. Pub. Sales No. E.83V.5 (1983), at xxiii. UN Convention on the Law of the Sea, opened for signature Dec. 10, 1982, in force Nov. 16, 1994. 1833 U.N.T.S. 396, 21 I.L.M. 1261 [hereafter the LOS Convention]. The Convention marked the culmination of over fourteen years of work, preceding and during the Third UN Conference on the Law of the Sea (1973–1982) involving participation by more than 150 countries representing all regions of the world. There are (as of June 30, 2008) 155 parties to the Convention, including all 27 EU Member States, as well as the European Community.

2. Council of the European Union, *2839th Council Meeting, General Affairs and External Relations*, Brussels, Dec. 10, 2007, 16326/07 (Presse 288), at 10.

3. The Secretary General, *Report of the Secretary General on Oceans and the Law of the Seal*, U.N. Doc. A/57/57, para. 51 (Mar. 2002).

4. The Secretary General, *Report of the Secretary General on Oceans and the Law of the Sea*, U.N. Doc. A/58/65/Add.1, para. 30 (Aug. 29, 2003), U.N. Doc. A/59/62, paras. 30–31 (Mar. 4, 2004); U.N. Doc. A/59/62/Add.1, para. 39–44 (Aug. 18, 2004); U.N. Doc. A/60/63, para. 12 (Mar. 4, 2005); U.N. Doc. A/60/63/Add.2, para. 22 (Aug. 15, 2005); U.N. Doc. A/61/63, paras. 7, 9, 11 (Mar. 9, 2006); U.N. Doc. A/61/63/Add.1, paras. 18–20 (Aug. 17, 2006); and U.N. Doc. A/62/66/Add.1, paras. 25, 27–28 (Aug. 31, 2007).

5. *See also* Art. 4(2)(b) of the EU Marine Strategy Framework Directive (Directive 2008/56/EC of the European Parliament and of the Council, of June 17, 2008, establishing a framework for community action in the

field of marine environmental policy), EUROPEAN UNION, Jun. 25, 2008, O.J. (L 164), 19.

6. For recent research on the exact number of islands along the Croatian coast and coastal length measurements, *see* Tea Duplačić-Leder, Tin Ujević, & Mendi Čala, *Coastline Lengths and Areas of Islands in the Croatian Part of the Adriatic Sea Determined from the Topographic Maps at the Scale of 1 : 25000*, 9 GEOADRIA 5–32 (2004). Although Croatia's mainland coastline extends over 1,880 km, its island chain (with 4,398 km coastline length) has important international law implications for the drawing of straight baselines, from which the breadth of the territorial sea (as well as the EEZ) is measured; *see* Art. 7 of the LOS Convention.

7. For an overview, *see* Davor Vidas, *Particularly Sensitive Sea Areas: The Need for Regional Cooperation in the Adriatic Sea*, in CROATIAN ACCESSION TO THE EUROPEAN UNION: THE CHALLENGES OF PARTICIPATION 354–58, 361–63 (Katrina Ott ed., 2006), *available at* www.ijf .hr/eng/EU4/vidas.pdf.

8. *See* Davor Vidas, *Global Trends in Use of the Seas and the Legitimacy of Croatia's Extension of Jurisdiction in the Adriatic Sea*, 9 CROATIAN INT'L RELS. REV. 4–10 (2003).

9. *See also* discussion in Vidas, *Particularly Sensitive Sea Areas*, *supra* note 7, at 359–65.

10. *See* EUROPEAN COMMISSION, DG JOINT RES. CENTRE, ATLANTE DELL'INQUINAMENTO DA IDROCARBURI NEL MARE ADRIATICO 10 (2005). According to that report, 257 oil spills from ships were detected in the Adriatic Sea (area north of latitude 39° N) in 1999, 263 spills in 2000, 184 in 2001, and 244 spills in 2002. A special campaign for the Adriatic Sea during only two-and-a-half summer months in 2004 (Jul. 16–Sept. 30) revealed 77 possible oil spills there; *see id.* at 9–10 and 49–53.

11. The International Convention for the Prevention of Pollution from Ships, 1973, as modified by the Protocol of 1978 relating thereto; for the Convention with Annexes, including unified interpretations and amendments, *see* INTERNATIONAL MARITIME ORGANIZATION, MARPOL 73/78 (Consolidated ed. 2002).

12. On this and other features of the Mediterranean fisheries, *see Mediterranean Fisheries, in* DEVELOPMENT AND AGRI-FOOD POLICIES IN THE MEDITERRANEAN REGION 151–229 (2002).

13. In addition, the involvement of (mostly seasonal) extraregional fishing vessels has been observed in the Adriatic Sea, targeting large pelagic species such as tuna. Neither has the Adriatic Sea been spared the phenomenon of IUU (illegal, unregulated, and unreported) fishing. On problems in deterring IUU fishing and the law of the sea aspects, *see* Davor Vidas, *IUU Fishing or IUU Operations? Some Observations on Diagnosis and Current*

Treatment, in BRINGING NEW LAW TO OCEAN WATERS 125–44 (David D. Caron & Harry N. Scheiber eds., 2004).

14. *See* FAO Yearbooks of Fishery Statistics and FAO Fishery Country Profiles, at www.fao.org. As for Adriatic fisheries, *see* especially FAO AdriaMed at www.faoadri amed.org. Statistics on marine capture fisheries of other Adriatic states do not change the picture to any significant degree: Albania's annual catch in the Adriatic Sea in the same period was at around 2,500 tons, whereas Montenegro's marine capture fisheries was under 1,000 tons per year. However, the problem of reliability of statistics on Adriatic Sea fisheries has often been noted; *see, e.g.*, Ivan Katavić & Neda Skakelja, *Status and Future of Croatian Marine Fisheries*, 9 CROATIAN INT'L RELS. REV. 28–32 (2003).

15. *See also* Katavić & Skakelja, *Status and Future*, *supra* note 14, at 29.

16. *See* S. Jukić-Peladić, N. Vrgoč, S. Krstulović-Sifner, C. Piccinetti, G. Piccinetti-Manfrin, G. Marano and N. Ungaro, *Long-term Changes in Demersal Resources of the Adriatic Sea: Comparison Between Two Trawl Surveys Carried Out in 1948 and 1998*, 53 FISHERIES RES. 95–104 (2001).

17. Art. 33, The Maritime Code of January 27, 1994, Narodne novine–Službeni list Republike Hrvatske (Official Journal of Croatia) No. 75, 1994; English translation in LAW OF THE SEA BULLETIN, nos. 42 and 43, 2000; emphasis on the word "exclusive" added. Although the English translation in the *Bulletin* uses the term "exclusive economic zone," in the original Croatian text of the Code published in *Narodne novine* that term is not found: "economic zone" (*gospodarski pojas*) is the wording employed. Drafters of the Code omitted the word "exclusive" from the notion, perhaps seeking not to overemphasize that aspect of the EEZ. *See also* comment by Budislav Vukas, *Croatia and the Law of the Sea*, in ESSAYS ON THE NEW LAWS OF THE SEA 19 (Budislav Vucas ed., 1996).

18. *Id.* at art. 1042, The Maritime Code.

19. The Adriatic Sea is rather narrow (on average 86 nm in width), and the size of an EEZ is thus limited (Croatia's Zone would hence comprise around 23,500 sq. km). Compared to many other EEZs, that is a relatively small area, and is also close to many ports. Although not a legal requirement for establishing an EEZ, controlling an area with such features should not present a major challenge either.

20. The proposal for the adoption of a "Decision on the declaration of the exclusive economic zone of the Republic of Croatia in the Adriatic Sea" was made by the Croatian Party of Rights, which at that time held only four seats in the Croatian Parliament, *Sabor. See Izvješća Hrvatskoga sabora* (Reports of the Croatian Parliament), No. 304, at 38–44 (Jul. 23, 2001).

21. *See Communication from the Commission on the Reform of the Common Fisheries Policy ("Roadmap")*, at 8, COM(2002) 181 final (May 28, 2002).

22. Government of the Republic of Croatia, *Izvješće o mogućnostima i učincima širenja jurisdikcije Republike Hrvatske na Jadranu* (Government Report on the possibilities and effects of the extension of jurisdiction of the Republic of Croatia in the Adriatic Sea), Oct. 2, 2003. English translation published in 9 CROATIAN INT'L RELS. REV. 50–60 (2003) [hereinafter Government Report 2003].

23. *Id.* at 56–59.

24. *Id.* at 58. *See also* GOVERNMENT OF THE REPUBLIC OF CROATIA, WORKING GROUP ON THE EUROPEAN FISHERIES POLICY IN THE MEDITERRANEAN, POSITION OF THE REPUBLIC OF CROATIA ON THE FISHERIES POLICY IN THE ADRIATIC (2003).

25. Government Report 2003, *supra* note 22, at 56–57.

26. *Id.* at 57.

27. Ministry of Agriculture and Forestry, Croatia, "Isključivi gospodarski pojas (IGP) u Jadranu" (An exclusive economic zone (EEZ) in the Adriatic Sea), *published at* www.mps.hr on August 1, 2003, coinciding with the first day of the summer recess for most public institutions in Croatia (and Italy). The Ministry was under the second coalition party, the Croatian Peasant Party, the main proponent of an EEZ declaration within the governing coalition.

28. Government Report 2003, *supra* note 22, at 58 (summarizing the reactions at the meeting held on September 23, 2003, with Eneko Landaburu, Director-General, DG External Relations, the European Commission) (emphasis added).

29. "Premijer Račan o pismu Romana Prodija" (Prime Minister Račan on the letter of Romano Prodi), Zagreb, Sept. 26, 2003, on the website of the Croatian Government, *available at* www.vlada.hr.

30. Government Report 2003, *supra* note 22, at 58.

31. *Id.* at 57.

32. As for Spain, *see* R. D. 1997, 1315, establishing a Fisheries Protection Zone in the Mediterranean Sea; English translation in LAW OF THE SEA BULLETIN, No. 36, 1998, at 47–48. As to the French Ecological Protection Zone ("zone de protection écologique") in the Mediterranean, *see* Law No. 2003–346 of Apr. 15, 2003, implemented by Decree No. 2004–33 of Jan. 8, 2004; published in the JOURNAL OFFICIEL DE LA RÉPUBLIQUE FRANÇAISE [J.O.] [Official Gazette of France], Apr. 16, 2003 and Jan. 10, 2004, respectively.

33. Decision on the Extension of Jurisdiction of the Republic of Croatia in the Adriatic Sea, published in NARODNE NOVINE (Official Gazette), No. 157, of Oct. 6, 2003; English *translation in* LAW OF THE SEA BULLETIN, No. 53, 2004, at 68–69. [hereinafter the 2003 Decision]. The Parliament reserved the right to proclaim other elements of the EEZ when it deems appropriate; para. 2 of the 2003 Decision.

34. Published in *Službeni list SFRJ, Dodatak: Međunarodni ugovori i drugi sporazumi* (Official Gazette of the SFR Yugoslavia, Annex: International Treaties and Other Agreements), No. 28, 1970; English translation in 7 I.L.M. (1968).

35. Ivan Šimonovic, *Concluding Remarks at the Round Table on Fisheries Policy in the Mediterranean and the Extension of Jurisdiction in the Adriatic Sea, Zagreb, 14 October 2003*, 9 CROATIAN INT'L REL. REV. 48 (2003) (emphasis added).

36. *See also* Vladimir Ibler, *Legal Foundations of the Economic Zone in the Framework of International Legal Regimes at Sea*, 9 CROATIAN INT'L RELS. REV. 3 (2003). Some authors, however, questioned the compatibility with the LOS Convention; *see*, for instance, Peter Sand, *"Green" Enclosure of Ocean Space—Déjà Vu?* 54 MARINE POLLUTION BULL. 374–76 (2007), who commented on Croatia's (and several other) zones as having a common feature of "unabashed unilateralism ('enclose now, negotiate later')" and "a hidden neo-Seldenian agenda," at 375. The legal basis for that comment remains vague.

37. Press Release, European Union, Javier Solana, EU High Representative for the CFSP, met today with Ivica Račan, Prime Minister of the Republic of Croatia, S0202/03 (Oct. 9, 2003).

38. *Council conclusions on Western Balkans*, in EUROPEAN COUNCIL, 2533RD COUNCIL MEETING, EXTERNAL RELATIONS (2003), *available at* http://ue.eu.int/. On the same day the Council meeting on Agriculture and Fisheries was held, noting that in respect to the Mediterranean, the European Commission identified overexploited fishery areas in the Adriatic Sea as well as a significant fall in some important fish stocks; *see* EUROPEAN COUNCIL 2534TH COUNCIL MEETING, AQUACULTURE AND FISHERIES (2003), *available at* http://ue.eu.int/.

39. Council conclusions on Western Balkans, *supra* note 38.

40. Those consultations were, however, postponed by both Italy and Slovenia until *after* the conclusion of the Venice Conference on sustainable fisheries in the Mediterranean, held Nov. 25–26, 2003. In practice, that also meant after the elections (Nov. 23, 2003) and formation of the new government in Croatia (end Dec. 2003).

41. According to the former Croatian Minister of Foreign Affairs, Tonino Picula, the European Commission, by a letter of its Director-General for Fisheries, Jörgen Holmquist, had on December 15, 2003 invited Croatia to enter into expert consultations on arrangements regarding the fisheries aspects of the Zone, with a

view to future Croatian membership in the EU; *see* Izvješća Hrvatskoga sabora (Reports of the Croatian Parliament), No. 393, at 45 (July 8, 2004). Picula was, in mid-December 2003, still Croatian Foreign Minister; however, in a "technical" government only, following the defeat of the then-governing SDP at the November 2003 parliamentary elections and in anticipation of the new, HDZ-led coalition government, confirmed by the Parliament on December 23, 2003.

42. *Communication from the Commission to the Council and the European Parliament Laying Down a Community Action Plan for the Conservation and Sustainable Exploitation of Fisheries Resources in the Mediterranean Sea under the Common Fisheries Policy*, at 14, COM(2002) 535 final (Oct. 9, 2002).

43. *See* Press Release 343/03, Ministry of Foreign Affairs and European Integration, Croatia (Nov. 5, 2003) *available at* the website of the Ministry, www.mvpei.hr.

44. Croatia maintained that an effective protection of the Adriatic Sea was possible only through complementary national, bilateral, and multilateral measures; *See id.* For the Croatian proposal on regional cooperation toward designating a PSSA in the Adriatic Sea, *see* Vidas, *Particularly Sensitive Sea Areas, supra* note 7, at 369–71.

45. The first trilateral meeting of state secretaries was held in Trieste, Italy, on February 12, 2004; the second in Portorož, Slovenia, on March 11, 2004; and the third in Pula, Croatia, on April 7, 2004. The fourth and last meeting was held at the European Commission's headquarters in Brussels, on June 4, 2004, as further discussed in the text.

46. *See* the Slovenian "Memorandum o Piranskem zalivu" (Memorandum on the Bay of Piran) Apr. 7, 1993 [hereinafter: 1993 Memorandum], which stated that "Slovenia belongs to the group of so-called geographically disadvantaged states, which due to their geographical situation can claim no exclusive economic zones of their own." Document on file with the author. The Croatian language translation of the 1993 Memorandum is reproduced in VLADIMIR IBLER, MEĐUNARODNO PRAVO MORA I HRVATSKA (International Law of the Sea and Croatia) 553–54 (2001). Several commentators indicate that the 1993 Memorandum by the Government was also discussed and approved by the Slovenian Parliament; for the analyses of the Memorandum, *see* Ibler, *id.* at 136–67; also Iztok Simoniti & Marko Sotlar, *The Land Boundary Between the Republic of Slovenia and the Republic of Croatia and the Negotiations on the Maritime Boundary Delimitation*, 3 J. INT'L RELS. 85–91 (1996). *See also* a commentary on the origins of that governmental Memorandum and a special session of the Slovenian Parliament on relations with Croatia (May 25–26, 1993), in IGOR MEKINA, MLADINA, Oct. 15, 2003.

47. *Communication from the Commission: Opinion on Croatia's Application for Membership of the European Union*, COM(2004) 257 final (Apr. 20, 2004).

48. *Id.* at 35. Although referring only to the delimitation dispute with Slovenia, it should be noted that in the Communication the plural form was used of the "countries" with whom tensions had been provoked.

49. *Id.* at 37 and 75.

50. *Id.* at 118.

51. Interview with Ivica Račan, President of the SDP (Social-Democratic Party), in Novi list, Jun. 5, 2004.

52. Decision on Amending the Decision on the Extension of the Jurisdiction of the Republic of Croatia in the Adriatic Sea, *Narodne novine* (Official Gazette), No. 157, 2004; English translation *published in* LAW OF THE SEA BULLETIN, No. 55, 2004, at 31. [hereinafter 2004 Decision].

53. *See* text of the Agreed Minutes *in* Press Release 160/04, Ministry of Foreign Affairs and European Integration (Jun. 4, 2004) (*available in* English and Croatian at the website of the Ministry: *www.mvpei.hr*) (emphasis added).

54. Slovenian PM Rop to POP-TV and TV Slovenia (emission "Odmevi") on the evening of Jun. 4, also reported by STA (Slovenian News Agency) and HINA (Croatian News Agency) on Jun. 4–5, 2004.

55. Press Release, Ministry of Foreign Affairs, Slovenia (Jun. 2004), *available at* the website of the Ministry, www.mzz.gov.si/nc/en/tools/news/cns/news/article/141/9046/ (emphasis added).

56. Statement of the Foreign Minister Žužul to HINA on Jun. 5, after the meeting of foreign ministers of Austria, Croatia, and Slovenia held on the margins of the European forum "Wachau 2004" at Goettweig, Austria, Jun. 5, 2004.

57. Statement by the State Secretary Roberto Antonione as reported by ANSA (Italian Press Agency), Jun. 4, 2004; also by HINA, Jun. 4, 2004.

58. Council of the European Union, *Presidency Conclusions (June 17–18, 2004)*, 10679/2/04 Rev. 2, at para. 38 (Jul. 19, 2004) (emphasis added), *available at* www.consilium.europa.eu. Slovenia at that time had recently become an EU Member State (May 1, 2004) and was involved in the decision-making process.

59. Maritime Delimitation and Territorial Questions between Qatar and Bahrain, Jurisdiction and Admissibility, Judgment, 1994 I.C.J. 12, para. 25.

60. Council of the European Union, *Presidency Conclusions, op. cit., supra* note 58, at para. 33.

61. *Id.* at para. 34.

62. Report by HINA, Jun. 4, 2004.

63. *See note verbale* by Slovenia, dated Aug. 30, 2004, addressed to the UN Secretary-General, published in LAW OF THE SEA BULLETIN, No. 56, 2005, at 139–42.

64. *See note verbale* by Croatia, dated Jan. 11, 2005 addressed to the UN Secretary-General, published in LAW OF THE SEA BULLETIN, No. 57, 2005, at 125–28 (emphasis added).

65. *See* LOS Convention, Art. 311(3).

66. *Id.* at art. 311(4) (emphasis added).

67. *See note verbale* by Slovenia, dated Aug. 30, 2004, *supra* note 63, at 140.

68. *Id.*

69. *See note verbale* by Slovenia, dated Nov. 7, 2003 addressed to the UN Secretary-General, *published in* LAW OF THE SEA BULLETIN, No. 53, 2004, at 70.

70. Commission of the European Communities, *Opinion on Croatia's Application for Membership of the European Union*, Apr. 20, 2004, *supra* note 47, at 35 (emphasis added).

71. Breadth of the territorial sea, as codified in Art. 3 of the LOS Convention.

72. As stated in Art. 13(2) of the 2001 Maritime Code of Slovenia: "The baseline shall be the hydrographic zero line running along the coast, or a straight line enclosing the entrance to a bay." The Maritime Code, as amended by the 2006 Act Amending the Maritime Code, provides in its Art. 5: "The internal waters of the Republic of Slovenia shall encompass all ports, bays and the anchorage of the Port of Koper circumscribed by meridian 13°40' east and latitude 45°35' north." For an English translation of the Maritime Code and Acts amending it, *see* LAW OF THE SEA BULLETIN, No. 60, 2006, at 58–126; No. 61, 2006, at 22–95; No. 62, 2007, at 16–51; and No. 63, 2007, at 59–71. The English translation is in many places imprecise or incomplete, occasionally confusing the meaning of the original, Slovene-language text of the Code, as published in *Uradni list Republike Slovenije* (Official Gazette of the Republic of Slovenia), No. 26, 2001 and No. 120, 2006 (consolidated text). *See also infra* notes 101, 103, 104, and 113.

73. The position of "Point 5" is of utmost importance for north Adriatic maritime delimitations. This is both the *final* point for territorial sea delimitation with Italy under the 1975 Treaty of Osimo (published in *Službeni list SFRJ, Dodatak: Međunarodni ugovori i drugi sporazumi* (Official Gazette of the SFR Yugoslavia, Annex: International Treaties and Other Agreements), No. 1, 1977), and, as "Point 1," the *first* point of delimitation of the continental shelf with Italy under the 1968 Agreement, *supra* note 34.

74. MINISTRY OF FOREIGN AFFAIRS, REPUBLIC OF SLOVENIA, WHITE PAPER ON THE BORDER BETWEEN THE REPUBLIC OF SLOVENIA AND THE REPUBLIC OF CROATIA 11 (2006) (English translation) (emphasis added).

75. In Croatia, some call it *also* Savudrija Bay. Slovenia protested against the usage of any other name but the "Bay of Piran," arguing that Croatia "unilaterally changed the historic and internationally recognised name of the Bay of Piran (Piranski zaliv) into the Bay of Savudrija (Savudrijska vala)"; *id.* at 25.

76. On the Bay as internal waters of Slovenia, *see* the 1993 Memorandum, as reproduced in Ibler, *supra* note 46, at 553–54, and the Slovenian Decree passed in Jan. 2006 (*see* further discussion below, as well as *infra* note 105).

77. For informed analyses of that delimitation dispute, *see, e.g.*, *The Maritime Boundaries of the Adriatic Sea*, 1 MARITIME BRIEFING 1–12, 19–33 (Gerald H. Blake & Duško Topalović with Clive Schofield & Mladen Klemenčić eds., 1996); Simoniti & Sotlar, *supra* note 46; Ibler, *supra* note 46, at 136–84; KRISTIAN TURKALJ, PIRANSKI ZALJEV, RAZGRANIČENJE TERITORIJALNOG MORA IZMEĐU HRVATSKE I SLOVENIJE ("The Bay of Piran: Territorial Sea Delimitation between Croatia and Slovenia") (2001); Budislav Vukas, *Maritime Delimitation in a Semi-enclosed Sea: The Case of the Adriatic Sea*, in MARITIME DELIMITATION 209–15 (Rainer Lagoni & Daniel Vignes eds., 2006); Vladimir-Djuro Degan, *Consolidation of Legal Principles on Maritime Delimitation: Implications for the Dispute between Slovenia and Croatia in the North Adriatic*, 6 CHINESE J. INT'L L. 601–34 (2007).

78. The initialed text has often been called the "Drnovšek-Račan Agreement" after the surnames of the then Prime Ministers of the two countries, although it was in fact designated as the "final working adjustment" ("končna delovna uskladitev" in the Slovene language; "konačno radno usklađenje," in the Croatian language), and as such was initialed by the two officials involved in actual negotiations, attached to the ministries of foreign affairs of Croatia and Slovenia—and not by the Prime Ministers.

79. *See especially* the exchange of diplomatic notes by Slovenia and Croatia on that matter: *note verbale* by Slovenia, dated Aug. 30, 2004, *supra* note 63, at 139; and *note verbale* by Croatia, dated Jan. 11, 2005, *supra* note 64, at 125. *See also note verbale* by Slovenia, dated Apr. 15, 2005, published in LAW OF THE SEA BULLETIN, No. 58, 2005, at 20–22. The two countries agree that heads of the negotiating delegations initialed the text. Slovenia, however, argues that the text was "then also endorsed" by both governments on July 20, 2001. Croatia points out that "no treaty on land and maritime boundary has either been signed or concluded."

80. *See* note by Slovenia to Croatia dated Oct. 3, 2003, published also as an Annex to the *note verbale* by Slovenia, dated Nov. 7, 2003, *supra* note 69, at 71.

81. For a chart based on the "final working adjustment," *see* Annex to the *note verbale* by Slovenia, dated Aug. 30, 2004, *supra* note 63, at 142.

82. *See, e.g.*, MINISTRY OF FOREIGN AFFAIRS OF SLOVENIA, *White Paper 2006*, *supra* note 74, at 11.

83. The 1993 Memorandum, as reproduced in Ibler, *supra* note 46, at 554.

84. *Id.* (emphasis added).

85. "Odgovor Republike Slovenije na Odgovor Republike Hrvaške na Stališča Republike Slovenije o določitvi meje na morju med Republiko Slovenijo in Republiko Hrvaško" ("Response of the Republic of Slovenia on the Response of the Republic of Croatia on the Positions of the Republic of Slovenia on the Delimitation of the Maritime Boundary between the Republic of Slovenia and the Republic of Croatia"), Nov. 8, 1999 [hereinafter 1999 Response]. For a detailed discussion of that document, *see* Ibler, *supra* note 46, at 167–84.

86. *See note verbale* by Slovenia, dated Nov. 7, 2003, *supra* note 69, at 70 (emphasis added). *See also note verbale* by Slovenia, dated Apr. 15, 2005, *supra* note 79, at 20.

87. MINISTRY OF FOREIGN AFFAIRS OF SLOVENIA, *White Paper 2006*, *supra* note 74, at 11.

88. *Id.* at 13. For a comment on the effect under international law of such an interpretation of Italian "recognition," *see* Degan, *supra* note 77, at 623–24.

89. Slovenian arguments according to the 1999 Response, *supra* note 85.

90. Maritime Delimitation and Territorial Questions between Qatar and Bahrain (*Qatar v. Bahrain*), Merits, Judgment, 2001 I.C.J. 97, para. 185, at 97. In its numerous judgments the International Court of Justice has indeed emphasized the fundamental law of the sea axiom, that "the land dominates the sea."

91. The LOS Convention does not include the notion of *access to the high seas* as such, which is guaranteed by various rights and freedoms, and accordingly duties, under the Convention. The term "access" is used by the Convention in the context of the right of landlocked countries of *access to and from the sea*, for the purpose of exercising the rights under the Convention, including those relating to the freedom of the high seas. Because those countries do not have a direct territorial contact with the sea, they enjoy freedom of transit, by all means of transport, *through the territory of states situated between* their territory and the sea ("transit states"). The terms and modalities for exercising freedom of transit are agreed upon through bilateral, subregional, or regional agreements. *See* Art. 125 of the LOS Convention.

92. *See* "Non-paper by Croatia," *reprinted in* Ibler, *supra* note 46, at 555. *See also note verbale* by Croatia, dated Jan. 11, 2005, *supra* note 64, at 127.

93. Ibler, *supra* note 46, at 555.

94. In its 1999 Response, *supra* note 85, Slovenia stated, *inter alia*, that "it cannot accept that its exit to the high seas would lead through a sovereign territory of another state."

95. The Secretary General, *Report of the Secretary General on Oceans and the Law of the Sea,* para. 41, U.N. Doc. A/59/62 (Mar. 4, 2004).

96. *See* "Report of the Maritime Safety Committee on its Seventy-Eighth Session," IMO Doc. MSC 78/26 of May 28, 2004, at 86, and Annex 21; and "New and Amended Traffic Separation Schemes," IMO Doc. COLREG.2/Circ. 54 of May 28, 2004.

97. *See* Albania, Croatia, Italy, Slovenia, and Serbia and Montenegro, "Establishment of new recommended Traffic Separation Schemes and other new Routing Measures in the Adriatic Sea," IMO Doc. NAV 49/3/7, of Mar. 23, 2003.

98. The 1993 Memorandum, as reproduced in Ibler, *supra* note 46, at 554.

99. MINISTRY OF FOREIGN AFFAIRS OF SLOVENIA, *White Paper 2006*, *supra* note 74, at 12.

100. *See* statistics on the website of the Port of Koper, *available at* www.luka-katsi.

101. Art. 1 of the 2001 Maritime Code, *supra* note 72. The English translation in the LAW OF THE SEA BULLETIN uses the word "supervision" instead of control, which is the legal term as used in the Slovenian language text ("nadzor").

102. *See* Act Amending the Maritime Code (PZ-B) of Dec. 19, 2003; *published in Uradni list* (Official Gazette), No. 2, 2004; English translation in LAW OF THE SEA BULLETIN, No. 60, 2006, at 126.

103. *Id.* at art. 2(1); emphasis is added to the word "sovereignty" because the English translation in the LAW OF THE SEA BULLETIN contains the word "jurisdiction" at that place, whereas the Act in its original Slovenian-language text published in *Uradni list* uses the word sovereignty ("suverenosti").

104. Adopted by the Slovenian Parliament, *Državni zbor*, on Oct. 4, 2005 and *published in Uradni list* (Official Gazette), No. 93, 2005 (2005 Act). English translation *in* LAW OF THE SEA BULLETIN, No. 60, 2006, at 56–57; that translation, however, does not contain the word "proclamation" in the title of the Act, which is otherwise contained in the title of the Act in its original Slovenian language-version: "Zakon o razglasitvi" (Act on the Proclamation).

105. The Government of Slovenia passed the Decree on Jan. 5, 2006, and *published in Uradni list* (Official Gazette), No. 2, 2006 (2006 Decree).

106. Art. 2 of the 2006 Decree. *See also* Arts. 5 and 13(2) of the 2001 Maritime Code, with amendments.

107. *See* Art. 3 of the 2006 Decree.

108. *See id.* Coordinates of "Point T6" are determined as 45°25' N and 13°13'42.9" E.

109. Arts. 2 and 3 of the 2006 Decree both refer to Cape Savudrija as the key point for determining *Slovenian* internal waters and territorial sea, respectively.

110. Art. 4 of the 2005 Act.

111. *See* Art 76(1) of the LOS Convention.

112. *See* Art. 56(1)(b)(iii) of the LOS Convention.

113. Terms as used in the English language translation of the 2005 Act *published in* the LAW OF THE SEA BULLETIN. In the LOS Convention terminology, that is actually "sovereign rights for the purpose of exploring and exploiting, conserving and managing the natural resources." (Art. 56(1)(a) of the Convention).

114. *See note verbale* by Croatia, dated May 31, 2007, in LAW OF THE SEA BULLETIN, No. 64, 2007, at 40–42.

115. *Oceans and the Law of the Sea: Report of the Secretary-General, op. cit., supra* note 95, at para. 40.

116. *See, e.g., Dispute festers in Slovenia, or is it Croatia?* INT'L HERALD TRIBUNE, July 18, 2006, *available at* www.iht.com/articles/2006/07/18/news/croatia.php; *A Balkan Border Dispute Is Nonviolent but Nettlesome*, NEW YORK TIMES, Jul. 18, 2006, *available at* www.nytimes.com/2006/07/18/world/europe/18customs.html; *Slovenia and Croatia: Hey, That's My Bit of the Sea*, ECONOMIST 22 (Aug. 30, 2003). An analysis by the Economist Intelligence Unit ("Eastern Europe Marine: Calming the Waves," *available at* www.eiu.com), used that line of argument already on August 19, 2003, some weeks after Croatia publicly announced its intention to declare the Zone.

117. The European Council in its document adopted on December 10, 2007, *supra* note 82. Compare the wording in the *note verbale* by Slovenia, dated Apr. 15, 2005, *supra* note 79, underlining postponement of application of the Zone to the EU countries "until a common, consensual solution is reached in the European spirit, that would take into account the interests of the neighboring countries."

118. Economist Intelligence Unit, *supra* note 116 (emphasis on "rules" added).

119. *See* note by Slovenia, dated Oct. 3, 2003, *supra* note 80.

120. On the Convention and the rule of law, *see* Bernard H. Oxman, *The Rule of Law and the United Nations Convention on the Law of the Sea*, 7 EUR. J. INT'L L. 353–71 (1996).

121. Incidentally, Slovenia recently became an EU Member State despite that same open territorial dispute with its neighboring country, then an EU candidate applicant, Croatia. The 2001 "final working adjustment" might have sufficed for that purpose. Be that as it may, the unresolved delimitation issue with Croatia proved to be a rather low-key one in Slovenia's accession process for EU membership.

122. Gemma Andreone, *The Legal Regime of Fisheries in the Mediterranean: Some Issues Concerning Italy*, 11 ITALIAN Y.B. INT'L L. 231 (2001). Another Italian author introduced an important distinction and described perceived Italian interests as "those of a State fishing outside its territorial sea." *See* Tullio Treves, *Italy and the Law of the Sea*, *in* THE LAW OF THE SEA: THE EUROPEAN UNION AND ITS MEMBER STATES 327 (Tullio Treves and Laura Pineschi eds., 1997), at 327–63.

123. Statement by Italian State Secretary for Agricultural and Forestry Policy, Paolo Scarpa Bonazza Buora, on Slovenian television on Sept. 24, 2003, as reported by STA (Sept. 24, 2003) and HINA (Sept. 25, 2003). The establishment of an EEZ or similar zone by Croatia would, in the Adriatic Sea circumstances, of course not result in denying access to Italian fishermen, but rather in regulating activities in accordance with the relevant LOS Convention provisions as well as Croatian legislation based on this. Importantly, Croatia has often emphasized that it intends to employ nondiscriminatory measures in its Zone.

124. Government Report 2003, *supra* note 22, at 57.

125. Mauro Manzin, IL PICCOLO, Oct. 2, 2003, at 7.

126. *Id.*

127. Note No. 1681 by Italy, dated Apr. 16, 2004, concerning the declaration of an ecological and fisheries protection zone in the Adriatic Sea by the Republic of Croatia of Oct. 3, 2003; published in LAW OF THE SEA BULLETIN, No. 54, 2004, at 129–30.

128. Published in Gazz. Uff. (Official Gazette of the Italian Republic), No. 52, March 3, 2006; English translation as provided by Italy in LAW OF THE SEA BULLETIN, No. 61, 2006, at 98.

129. *Note verbale* by Italy, dated Mar. 15, 2006, published in LAW OF THE SEA BULLETIN, No. 60, 2006, at 127–28.

130. *Note verbale* (No. 840/05) by Croatia, dated Sept. 2, 2005, addressed to the UN Secretary-General, published in LAW OF THE SEA BULLETIN, No. 59, 2005, at 28–29. In the note, Croatia stated that, in accordance with its 2003 Decision on the Zone, the coordinates are "provisional, pending the conclusion of the delimitation agreements with the States whose coasts are opposite or adjacent to the Croatian coast, once they extend their jurisdiction beyond their territorial sea in accordance with international law."

131. Decree No. 816, Apr. 26, 1977, published in Gazz. Uff., No. 306, Nov. 9, 1977.

132. *See* Budislav Vukas, *State Practice in the Aftermath of the UN Convention on the Law of the Sea: The Exclusive Economic Zone and the Mediterranean Sea*, in UNRESOLVED ISSUES AND NEW CHALLENGES TO THE LAW OF THE SEA 256 (Anastasia Strati, Maria Gavouneli, & Nikos Skourtos eds., 2006) (emphasis added).

133. Tullio Scovazzi, *Recent Developments as Regards Maritime Delimitation in the Adriatic Sea*, in MARITIME DELIMITATION 195–96 (Rainer Lagoni & Daniel Vignes eds., 2006).

134. *See* Government Report 2003, *supra* note 22, at 57.

135. *See also* Andreone, *The Legal Regime of Fisheries in the Mediterranean, supra* note 122, at 243–48; Irini Papanicolopulu, *A Note on Maritime Delimitation in a Multizonal Context: The Case of the Mediterranean*, 38 OCEAN DEV. & INT'L L. 381–98 (2007).

136. As commented by Blake et al., *supra* note 77, at 10, those baselines, which are based on Yugoslavia's straight baseline claims, "have attracted praise from commentators as an example of modest and appropriate application of straight baselines" and were cited as a "model against which other baselines connecting fringing islands could be tested."

137. In the original Italian language version of the 2006 Law, the word "zone" is also used in the plural.

138. At that time, Italian straight baseline system had not yet been introduced, and it is yet to be estimated to what extent this would have an impact on a different median line determination in the Adriatic Sea. However, some segments of the Italian straight baselines, as established by Decree No. 816, Apr. 1977, have been qualified as "open to challenge under the provisions of Article 7 of the LOS Convention, particularly the use of Termiti as a basepoint"; Blake *et al.*, *supra* note 77, at 13.

139. Blake *et al.*, *supra* note 77, at 15–16. *See also* Vukas, *supra* note 77, at 207, citing the same figure.

140. Scovazzi, *Recent Developments, supra* note 133, at 200–01.

141. Papanicolopulu, *supra* note 135, at 387.

142. Blake et al., *supra* note 77, at 13.

143. *See also note verbale* by Croatia, dated May 31, 2007, addressed to the UN Secretary-General, published in LAW OF THE SEA BULLETIN, No. 64, 2007, at 39–40.

144. Vukas, *supra* note 77, at 209.

145. *Slovenia and Croatia, supra* note 116, at 22.

146. Italy, an EU Member State, is yet to delimit a number of maritime zones with its neighbors, including with EU Member States, such as France, Spain, and Malta.

147. Explicit confirmation is found in "Address by Ambassador Vladimir Drobnjak, Chief Negotiator for Croatia, to the Committee on Foreign Affairs of the European Parliament," given in Brussels on Jan. 29, 2008; document on file with the author. *See also* Croatian Ministry of Foreign Affairs and European Integration, Press Release 289/06, Dec. 6, 2006, *available at* the website of the Ministry, www.mvpei.hr.

148. Memo by Croatia ("Non-paper"), Feb. 1, 2008, distributed to EU Member States; also Address, *supra* note 147 (documents on file with the author); and statement by Croatian Prime Minister Ivo Sanader, HINA, Feb. 4, 2008. *See also Union Tightens Conditions for Zagreb's Membership*, EUROPOL., No. 3469, Feb. 13, 2008, at 13. In the Memo by Croatia, it was pointed out that "Slovenia's position concerning Chapter 13 deviates from the EC's Screening Report recommendations and has not been supported by any other Member State." Slovenian Prime Minister Janez Janša, on February 5, 2008, confirmed Slovenia's reservation for the opening of Croatia's accession negotiations with the EU on the fisheries chapter, arguing that this was due to Croatia's failure to meet the conditions; *see* "Slovenia expresses reservations about Croatia's fisheries policy," SE TIMES, Feb. 6, 2008, *available at* www.csees.net/?page=news &news_id=65760&country_id=7.

149. Still to date (Jun. 30, 2008), in respect of the fisheries Chapter, there is no unanimity required for the Council's decision on Croatia's preparedness for the opening of negotiations (or on opening benchmarks). The "Negotiating Framework" for Croatia, of Oct. 3, 2005, set the negotiating procedure to involve "the Council [who], acting by unanimity on a proposal by the Commission, will lay down benchmarks for the provisional closure and, where appropriate, for the opening of each chapter" (para. 26 of the Negotiating Framework).

150. At a joint meeting of the government and opposition parliamentary parties, held Oct. 9, 2006, conclusions were adopted by consensus; *see* Croatian government, "Note on the meeting in the Government of the Republic of Croatia regarding issues of the Environmental and Fisheries Protection Zone," Oct. 12, 2006 (Croatian-language original *available at* the website of the Croatian government, www.vlada.hr). That was in contrast with the sharp polarization of Croatian parliamentary parties in the processes that led to both the 2003 and 2004 Decisions.

151. *See* Delo, Nov. 30, 2006; Jutarnji list, Dec. 1, 2006; Poslovni dnevnik, Dec. 1, 2006; Novi list, Dec.1, 2006; Glas Istre, Dec. 1, 2006; Slobodna Dalmacija, Dec. 2, 2006; Croatian radiotelevision, Dec. 4, 2006.

152. Statement by Prime Minister Ivo Sanader, as recorded on videotape of the Croatian radiotelevision, HRT-1, evening news, Dec. 4, 2006, *available at* the website of the Croatian radiotelevision, http://vijesti.hrt.hr.

153. Delegation of the European Commission to the Republic of Croatia, "Communiqué," Zagreb, Dec. 5, 2006, *available at* the website of the Delegation, www.delhrv.cec.eu.int (emphasis added). Reference to the European Council was made in respect of the Presidency Conclusions (Jun. 17–18, 2004), in which an "agreement" from the June 4, 2004 trilateral meeting was referred to, instead of "agreed minutes"; *see supra* note 58 and the related text.

154. *See* PM Ivo Sanader Protests against Degert's Statement about Fisheries Protection Zone, Dec. 6, 2006, *available at* the website of the Croatian government, www.vlada.hr.

155. Press Release 289/06, Ministry of Foreign Affairs and European Integration, Croatia (2006), *available at* the website of the Ministry, www.mvpei.hr.

156. Commission of the European Communities, *Screening Report Croatia, Chapter 13–Fisheries*, Brussels, Jul. 18, 2006 (emphasis added), *available at* the European Commission website, http://ec.europa.eu/ enlargement/pdf/croatia/screening_reports/screening _report_13_hr_internet_en.pdf. However, on the relevant website page of the Commission, where all other screening reports (32) are listed, the only missing report (as per Jun. 30, 2008) was precisely the cited one, on the Fisheries chapter 13; *see* http://ec.europa.eu/ enlargement/candidate-countries/croatia/screening _reports_en.htm.

157. European Commission, "Croatia 2005 Progress Report," SEC (2005) 1424, Nov. 9, 2005, at 32 and 68.

158. *See* "Barroso warns Croatia against unilateral moves regarding EFPZ," HINA, Dec. 6, 2006, reproduced at the website of the Office of the President of the Republic of Croatia: www.predsjednik.hr.

159. Dr. Michael Leigh, a political scientist from Oxford, has been director-general of the DG Enlargement since 2006; *see* further information at http://ec.europa .eu/civil_service/docs/directors_general/leigh_en.pdf.

160. *See* "Prime Minister: State Leadership with Party Leaders on the Proposal by the Government for the Rules of Application of the Zone," HINA, Dec. 7, 2006, *available at* the website of the Croatian Government, www.vlada.hr.

161. Decision on Modifying and Amending the Decision on the Extension of the Jurisdiction of the Republic of Croatia in the Adriatic Sea, *Narodne Novine* (Official Gazette), No. 138, 2006 [hereinafter: 2006 Decision].

162. Memo *supra* note 148; statement by Jan Truszczynsky, deputy director-general, DG Enlargement, HINA, Oct. 1, 2007; Ivan Katavić, interview in *Glas Istre*, Dec. 7, 2007; and Davorin Rudolf, Novi list, Jan.12, 2008 (citing dates of the meetings held regarding the Zone in Rome and Brussels in 2007: Jan. 12, Mar. 6, Mar. 15, Mar. 20, Apr. 17, Apr. 25, May 10, and Jun. 27).

163. European Commission, "Croatia 2007 Progress Report," SEC(2007) 1431, Nov. 6, 2007.

164. European Commission, "Croatia 2006 Progress Report," SEC(2006) 1385, Nov. 8, 2006.

165. Croatia 2007 Progress Report, *supra* note 163, para. 2.3, at 16 (emphasis on the term "political" added).

166. For the 2005 Accession Partnership for Croatia, *see* Annex to the Council Decision 2006/145/EC of Feb. 20, 2006, on the principles, priorities, and conditions contained in the Accession Partnership with Croatia and repealing Decision 2004/648/EC, O.J. (EU) (L 55) 30 (2006). For the final 2007 Accession Partnership for Croatia, *see* Annex to the Council Decision 2008/ 119/EC of Feb. 12, 2008, on the principles, priorities,

and conditions contained in the Accession Partnership with Croatia and repealing Decision 2006/145/EC, O.J. (EU)(L 42) 51 (2008).

167. The 2005 reference read, "With regard to the protected ecological and fishing zone, unilaterally declared by Croatia, continue the implementation of the trilateral agreement reached in June 2004."

168. Emphasis on the "Negotiating Framework" added. No explicit reference to the Zone is found in the Negotiating Framework—only a general reference to take account of, *inter alia*, the European Council conclusions of June 17–18, 2004. One direct reference in the Negotiating Framework that can be related to the Adriatic Sea issues, including the Zone, is "Croatia's undertaking to resolve any border disputes in conformity with the peaceful settlement of disputes in accordance with the United Nations Charter, including if necessary *compulsory jurisdiction of the International Court of Justice*" (emphasis added). Another such reference is to "international agreements concluded by the Communities, the Communities jointly with their Member States, the Union, and those concluded by the Member States among themselves with regard to Union activities." Rather than relating to agreed minutes from a meeting, that reference would, in the context of the debate on the Croatian Zone, relate primarily to the LOS Convention, to which the European Community, and all the EU Member States, are parties.

169. *Interview with Christian Danielsson, European Commission DG Enlargement* (full transcript of interview), in SOUTH EASTERN EUROPE TV EXCHANGES, Nov. 9, 2007 (emphasis added), *available at* www.seetv -exchanges.com.

170. *See supra* notes 2 and 168, and the accompanying text.

171. "Minister de Castro: 4 to 5 chapters could be blocked due to the Zone," HINA, Dec. 19, 2007.

172. "EU Calls on Croatia not to enforce Ecological Zone," Slovenian Government Communication Office, Dec. 10, 2007, *available at* Government's website www.ukom.gov.si.

173. *See, e.g.*, "Head of Delegation Degert meets President Mesić," Dec. 19, 2007, *available at* the website of the Delegation of the EC in Croatia, www.delhrv .ec.europa.eu; *Degert to Mesić: 'Worrisome Clouds' over Croatia's Accession Negotiations with EU*, HINA, Jan.31, 2008; and "Statement by Enlargement Commissioner Olli Rehn on Croatia and its Respect for the June 4, 2004 Agreement Concerning the Ecological and Fisheries Zone," *available at* http://ec.europa.eu/commission _barroso/rehn/press_corner/statements/statements _2007_en.htm.

174. *See* statements by the Slovenian Ministry of Foreign Affairs Jan. 15, 2008 ("Slovenia is not threatening but warning") and of Jan. 22, 2008 ("No consultations

ongoing in connection with the Zone"), *available at* the website of the Ministry, www.mzz.gov.si.

175. For a statement by Italian Foreign Minister D'Alema, *see* STA, Jan. 17, 2008; DELO, Jan. 17, 2008; and HINA, Jan.18, 2008. For a statement by the Italian Minister of Agricultural, Food and Forestry Policies, De Castro, *see* HINA, Jan. 21, 2008.

176. *Blazing Freighter Threatens Oil Spill Off Croatia*, REUTERS, Feb. 6, 2008, *available at* www.reuters.com/article/latestCrisis/idUSL06803310.

177. COUNCIL OF THE EUROPEAN UNION, COUNCIL MEETING, GENERAL AFFAIRS AND EXTERNAL RELATIONS 12 (2008), 6495/08 (Presse 40).

178. *See* "Resolution of the Zone key for continuation of accession negotiations" ("Rješenje ZERP-a ključno za nastavak pregovora s EU-om"), *Vjesnik*, Mar. 7, 2008, at 3.

179. *See* "Swoboda Says Good Talks on Croatia's Fishing Zone Under Way," Feb. 27, 2008, *available at* the website of the Croatian Mission to the European Union, http://eu.mfa.hr.

180. Decision on Modifying the Decision on the Extension of the Jurisdiction of the Republic of Croatia in the Adriatic Sea, *Narodne Novine* (Official Gazette), No. 31, 2008. The decision was adopted by a narrow majority, with 77 votes in favor, 56 abstentions, and 5 against. Because there are 153 seats in the current Croatian Parliament, 77 votes are needed to secure a majority decision. HSS, a governing coalition party, voted against.

181. "Speaking points of Commission President José Manuel Barroso Following Meeting with Croatian PM Sanader," Mar. 13, 2008, *available at* http://ec.europa.eu/commission_barroso/president/archives/2008/index_en.htm.

182. Olli Rehn, "2008 a Year of Benchmarks for Croatia and the Former Yugoslav Republic of Macedonia," speech to the European Parliament Plenary Session, Apr. 9, 2008 (Speech/08/186), *available at* ec.europa.eu/commission_barroso/rehn/press_corner/speeches/index_en.htm.

183. *See supra*, note 45 and the accompanying text on the trilateral meetings held in spring 2004.

184. *See supra*, note 53 and the accompanying text on the agreed minutes from the Brussels meeting.

185. *See supra*, note 58 and the accompanying text on the European Council Conclusions, June 17–18, 2004.

186. *See, e.g., supra* note 63 and the accompanying text discussing a *note verbale* by Slovenia, August 30, 2004.

187. *See supra* notes 166 and 168 and the accompanying text.

188. *See supra* notes 2 and 170 and the accompanying text.

189. *See* Act on the Exclusive Economic Zone of Finland, Nov. 26, 2004, in force as of Feb. 1, 2005, English translation in LAW OF THE SEA BULLETIN, No. 57, 2005, at 106–15.

190. *See also* Article 2 of the Treaty on European Union. Consolidated version published at 13, 2008 O.J. (C 115) (EU).

191. *Id.* at art. 21(1).

192. *See also* Art. 2 ("General principles") of the Stabilisation and Association Agreement between the European Communities and their Member States, of the one part, and the Republic of Croatia, of the other part (signed in Luxembourg, Oct. 29, 2001), published in 2005 O.J. (L 26) (EU), stating: "Respect for . . . international law principles and the rule of law . . . shall form the basis of the domestic and external policies of the Parties and constitute essential elements of this Agreement."

193. Commission of the European Communities, *Opinion on Croatia's Application for Membership of the European Union, supra* note 47, at 36.

194. *Oceans and the Law of the Sea: Report of the Secretary-General, supra* note 95, at para. 41 (emphasis added).

17

Power Politics or Orderly Development?

*Why Are States "Claiming" Large Areas of
the Arctic Seabed?*

TIMO KOIVUROVA

In recent times the media have given vast attention to the Arctic, especially the perceived competition as to which of the Arctic states is able to claim the biggest stake of the continental shelf and, thereby, be able to exploit the plentiful hydrocarbon resources lying underneath the seabed. The story line here is built on the idea that because climate change is opening this previously inaccessible region to natural resource development—resources that are plentiful—the states are engaging in their typical power politics to determine who gets to these resources first. Even though this story line seems very appealing, the argument in this chapter is that this is a fundamentally flawed account of what is taking place in the Arctic. In fact, the argument is that at least so far, the continental shelf developments in the Arctic can be explained by states observing their law of the sea duties. Another issue, however, is what will happen when the Arctic coastal states extend their presence farther onto the seabed of the Central Arctic Ocean. Will this development challenge the prevailing position of the Arctic intergovernmental forum, the Arctic Council, as the main platform for Arctic governance?

The chapter will proceed in two steps. First, it is important to take the "race to resources" story line seriously because it is not only media that perceives that such development is going on in the Arctic but also researchers as well. The chapter, therefore, makes the attempt to understand why this story line has become so popular in explaining the continental shelf claims in the region. Before explaining to the reader why we perceive the continental shelf claim development as an orderly process, it is useful to familiarise the reader with some basic concepts related to the seabed from a geophysical point of view in order to grasp how the law of the sea regulates the seabed and its resources. Thereafter, a brief overview of how the seabed law has evolved in the law of the sea is in order, after which we will demonstrate why, indeed, the law of the sea can be seen as the best explanation for these continental shelf developments in the Arctic.

Second, it is also important to examine the international political and legal consequences of Arctic coastal states further penetrating into the Arctic Ocean seabed. What is interesting is whether this development will challenge the present intergovernmental forum in charge of Arctic affairs, the Arctic Council. Before studying this question, however, it is useful to introduce the reader to what type of cooperation the eight Arctic states (the Russian Federation,

Canada, the United States, Denmark (Greenland), Iceland, Norway, Sweden, and Finland) have practised within the Arctic Council. It is important to examine what type of regional international political and legal dynamic the continental shelf development has engendered and whether this dynamic can be seen to challenge the Arctic Council as the predominant intergovernmental forum for Arctic affairs. An analysis on both of these questions will be drawn in the conclusion.

1. Is There a "Race to Resources" or Orderly Development Going on in the Arctic?

For many persons thinking along a rationalist or realist approach in international relations, it must seem only a matter of time before the natural resources of the Arctic would be exploited. Indeed, given that few humans live in the Arctic, and thus few who may try to fight against developing natural resources by claiming "not in my backyard," these areas would seem to be tempting places for natural resources exploitation. Only the inaccessibility of the region, according to this line of thinking, prevented the vast natural resources from being exploited; as soon as technology were developed to harness these resources, companies and states would enter the region.

Then came the awareness that climate change was hitting the Arctic hardest, especially evinced by the Arctic Council who sponsored the Arctic Climate Impact Assessment.[1] Because ice and snow are the first physical forums to react to global warming, it has been estimated that climate change has already impacted the Arctic and that the change in the region will be more intense than in other regions of the world. Indeed, climate change seems to open this previously inaccessible region for resource development, and there certainly are several reasons to make use of the hydrocarbons from the seabed of the Arctic waters.

First of all, fossil fuels seem to have a future in the energy markets. The International Energy Agency (IEA) has recently estimated that despite the efforts by the climate regime to convert our energy use toward renewables, with the present energy development scenarios our dependence on fossil fuels will actually grow by 2030.[2] Additionally, Arctic hydrocarbon resources seem tempting from two perspectives. They are estimated to be plentiful as exhibited by British Petroleum (BP, which recently estimated them to constitute 25–50 percent of the unfound reserves of hydrocarbons).[3] They are also generally considered to be safe because they are located in areas with no ongoing conflicts. It can thus be concluded that the combined effect of climate change and interests to exploit hydrocarbons in the Arctic might be behind the recent efforts by states to stake seabed areas in the Arctic.

This state activity began in the Arctic with the Russian Federation's vast claim in 2001, covering almost half of the Arctic Ocean seabed.[4] All the other Arctic Ocean coastal states, especially by the United States, reacted to the Russian claim, criticising many aspects of the claim, especially its attempt to claim the Lomonosov Ridge that runs through the Central Arctic Ocean Basin, which, according to the United States, "is oceanic part of the Arctic Ocean basin and not a natural component of the continental margins of either Russia or of any State."[5] In August 2007 the Russians planted their flag underneath the North Pole in the Lomonosov Ridge, thereby provoking heavy protests from the other Arctic coastal states. As reported by the Guardian newspaper,

> Russia symbolically staked its claim to billions of dollars worth of oil and gas reserves in the Arctic Ocean today when two mini submarines reached the seabed more than two and a half miles beneath the North Pole. In a record-breaking dive, the two craft planted a one metre–high titanium Russian flag on the underwater Lomonosov ridge, which Moscow claims is directly connected to its continental shelf. However, the dangerous mission prompted ridicule and scepticism among other contenders

for the Arctic's energy wealth, with Canada comparing it to a 15th century colonial land grab.[6]

BBC News then provided the following account:

Russian explorers have planted their country's flag on the seabed 4,200m (14,000ft) below the North Pole to further Moscow's claims to the Arctic. The rust-proof titanium metal flag was brought by explorers travelling in two mini-submarines, in what is believed to be the first expedition of its kind. Both vessels have now rejoined the expedition's ships, completing their risky return journey to the surface. Canada, which also claims territory in the Arctic, has criticised the mission. "This isn't the 15th Century," Canadian Foreign Minister Peter MacKay told the CTV channel. "You can't go around the world and just plant flags and say 'We're claiming this territory,'" he said. Melting polar ice has led to competing claims over access to Arctic resources. Russia's claim to a vast swathe of territory in the Arctic, thought to contain oil, gas and mineral reserves, has been challenged by several other powers, including the U.S.[7]

In the recent *Foreign Affairs* article, Scott G. Borgerson, International Affairs Fellow at the Council on Foreign Relations and a former Lieutenant Commander in the U.S. Coast Guard, argued that even military conflict of some sort may be possible:

the situation is especially dangerous because there are currently no overarching political or legal structures that can provide for the orderly development of the region or mediate political disagreements over Arctic resources or sea-lanes. The Arctic has always been frozen; as ice turns to water, it is not clear which rules should apply. The rapid melt is also rekindling numerous interstate rivalries and attracting energy-hungry newcomers, such as China, to the region. The Arctic powers are fast approaching diplomatic gridlock, and that could eventually lead to the sort of armed brinkmanship that

plagues other territories, such as the desolate but resource-rich Spratly Islands, where multiple states claim sovereignty but no clear picture of ownership exists.[8]

Overall, therefore, it does seem to make a sense to claim that the story line we're calling the "race to resources" explains the states' behaviour. In this story line, the climate change opens the regions for power politics over who is able to stake the hydrocarbon resources of the Arctic sea bed first. Yet, the present author perceives this as a flawed account of what is taking place. Why?

1.1. The Rights of States over the Seabed and Its Resources

Before moving to study closely how the present law of the sea regulates the ownership and use of the seabed and its resources, it is useful to clarify the difference between the terms used in geophysics and international law over the various portions of the seabed and provide a short account of how the law relating to seabed has evolved. Because geophysics tries to examine the reality of the seabed, it offers much more nuanced concepts for it: The continental shelf proper adjacent to the coast dives down to the average depth of 180 metres, which then gives way to steep slope averaging up to 2,500 metres deep and continues with the less steep continental rise, which then transforms into the ocean floor. Geophysics understands the concepts of the continental margin covering continental shelf, continental slope, and the rise. The present law of the sea, as mostly codified in the 1982 UN Convention on the Law of the Sea (UNCLOS),[9] grants the coastal state sovereign rights over the resources of the legal continental shelf, which can in most cases be equated with geophysical continental margin (not the geophysical continental shelf).

Before World War II, the coastal states enjoyed sovereignty only over a narrow three to four nautical miles of territorial sea. This was dramatically changed after the war, with the 1945 Truman Proclamation by the United

States declaring the following: "Having concern for the urgency of conserving and prudently utilizing its natural resources, the Government of the United States regards the natural resources of the subsoil and sea bed of the continental shelf beneath the high seas but contiguous to the coasts of the United States as appertaining to the United States, subject to its jurisdiction and control."[10] This started the era of creeping coastal state jurisdiction, especially in regard to the seabed, the outer limit of which was defined in Article 1 of the 1958 Continental Shelf Convention as follows:

> For the purpose of these articles, the term "continental shelf" is used as referring (a) to the seabed and subsoil of the submarine areas adjacent to the coast but outside the area of the territorial sea, to a depth of 200 metres or, beyond that limit, to where the depth of the super-adjacent waters admits of the exploitation of the natural resources of the said areas; (b) to the seabed and subsoil of similar submarine areas adjacent to the coasts of islands.[11]

The problem with this definition was that it effectively permitted the possibility of coastal states claiming larger seabed resources with the development of technology, to the extent that even ocean floors could have been divided between the coastal states. Yet because states all around the world continued to extend their sovereign rights over the resources of the continental shelf, the entitlement to these resources fairly quickly matured into a principle of customary international law. Consequently, all coastal states of the world came to possess entitlement to resources in the seabed adjacent to their coasts.

From an international law perspective, the seabed is a natural prolongation of the land territory into the sea, and thus the coastal state is not even legally obligated to claim it; it is automatically under the sovereign rights of the nearest coastal state. The main legal question to be resolved is related to where the outer limits of the continental shelf lie, which, on the basis of the 1958 Continental Shelf Convention, could

have meant that coastal states divided the resources of the ocean floor between themselves.

A counter-force for this trajectory came from Maltese ambassador Arvid Pardo, who, in 1967, proposed in the UN General Assembly that the ocean floor should be designated as "A common Heritage of Humankind" and governed by an international governance mechanism, whereby the economic benefits of the ocean floor riches could be shared equitably between developing and developed states. Pardo's proposal acted also as one major reason for convening the Third UN Conference on the Law of the Sea, with the aim to produce a comprehensive "constitution" of the oceans, which became the UNCLOS.[12]

The Convention was negotiated over an extended period of time, from 1973 to 1982, as a package deal, permitting no reservations to the Convention.[13] UNCLOS was able to achieve a compromise between various groupings of states having differing kinds of interests related to the seabed. For instance, broad continental margin states were able to have rules accepted, which allowed the whole continental margin to be subjected to the sovereign rights of coastal states, whereas the geologically disadvantaged states (those whose continental margin was minimal) managed to push for a rule that entitles all states to a minimum of 200 nautical miles of continental shelf (meaning that these states effectively exercise powers over ocean floor as well). UNCLOS was also successful in defining more clearly the outer limit of the continental shelf[14] than its 1958 predecessor convention and in designating the ocean floor as part of the common heritage of mankind and under the governance of International Sea-Bed Authority (ISBA).[15]

Even though broad continental margin states were able to extend the outer limit of the continental shelf to cover the whole geophysical continental margin (and in some exceptional cases beyond) during the negotiations, they had to make concessions as well. For example, they had to submit to rules requiring them to transfer some of the revenues from the offshore hydrocarbon exploitation in their extended continental shelf to developing states via the ISBA,[16] and more importantly, they had to scientifically prove the extent of their continental shelf in the Commission on the Limits of Continental Shelf (CLCS, or Commission), a scientific body with twenty-one members.[17] A coastal state must make the submission if it perceives that its continental margin exceeds 200 nautical miles within ten years from the date when it became a party to the UNCLOS.[18] Although the Commission can only make recommendations, these recommendations are legally influential because the continental shelf's outer limits become final and binding only when they have been enacted on the basis of the recommendations.[19] The deadline for such submissions is fairly tight given that states need to provide the Commission with vast amounts of scientific and technical data. Why? Doing so was seen as necessary in order to define the outer limits of continental shelves as quickly as possible given that only after knowing these limits is it possible to know where the boundary between states' continental shelves and the Area, which is under the jurisdiction of the ISBA, lies.

1.2. Which Explains Better the Continental Shelf Activity—"Rush to Resources" or UNCLOS?

Even though the "rush to resources" story line appears to be the more popular explanation for why states are engaged in staking continental shelf areas, I argue that this is a flawed account, and there are two good means to prove this.

States are themselves arguing that they are just following their UNCLOS duties. Can this be backed up with any reliable evidence? Indeed, because, at least for the time being, states have followed their duties under UNCLOS in an ideal manner. Russia was the first country to make the submission to the CLCS, and it was also the first country to which the Commission issued recommendations, requiring it to revise its submission in the Central Arctic Ocean Basin.[20] Whatever symbolic importance the Russian-flag planting had for the domestic policy of Russia, Russia has not argued that this

would have any legal effect,[21] and they have informed the CLCS that they will make the revised submission to the Commission within the new deadline. Norway made a submission in 2006 to three separate areas in its Northeast Atlantic and Arctic continental shelves, which invoked some reactions from other states as to the status of the seabed around Svalbard Islands.[22] Yet, as explained by the Norwegian foreign ministry, this is an issue unrelated to the outer limits of the continental shelf.[23] Now the CLCS has made recommendations to Norway for drawing the outermost limits of its continental shelf.[24] Deadlines for making submissions to Denmark (Greenland) and Canada are due in 2014 and 2013 respectively, and both states are cooperating to try to collect the necessary information within the tight deadline. According to news sources, the United States has also started to develop its continental shelf submission.[25] Even though not a party to the UNCLOS, the previous Bush Administration attempted to become a party, and the current Obama administration will likely continue these efforts.[26]

Finally, let's make a thought rehearsal. What if there was no climate change taking place at all? At least the UNCLOS was negotiated during a time period when there was little awareness of climate change. Would the states behave in the same way if the Arctic waters were as inaccessible as ever when considering whether to submit a claim to the CLCS? We argue that any rational state would make its submission exactly as large as it can on the basis of UNCLOS, and they would need to do it now because the UNCLOS entered into force in 1994 (and the first deadline for a submission was, thus, in 2004). If the whole state community accepts very generous rules regarding how the outer limits of the continental shelves are to be drawn, why would states not take full benefit of those rules? Moreover, because we cannot predict how fast and to which direction technology will develop, it would be only rational for a state to make as large as possible a submission to the CLCS because advancements in technology might have opened these regions for resource development even without climate change. With this in mind, it is difficult to envisage that the present and future consequences of climate change would have triggered this competition over hydrocarbon resources.

2. What Kind of Impact May the Continental Shelf Developments in the Arctic Have for Arctic Governance?

Even though we can conclude that, so far, the continental shelf developments are proceeding in the Arctic on the basis of the UNCLOS, it is clear that there are international legal and political consequences from the Arctic Ocean coastal states enlarging their presence in the high Arctic. It is also true that the perceived competition over hydrocarbon reserves in the region has triggered a new type of policy discussion over how the Arctic, in particular its ocean, should be governed. It is thus important to examine whether this continental shelf development can be one factor in challenging the prevailing intergovernmental forum dedicated to the Arctic governance, the Arctic Council. This condition relates especially to the recent Ilulissat meeting in Greenland between the five Arctic Ocean coastal states, which was largely organized to show to the rest of the world that there is no scramble for resources going on in the Arctic. The coastal states laid a regional agenda for cooperation, which challenged the prevailing structures of governance in the region, in particular the Arctic Council.

We now proceed in the following manner. First, it is useful to study how the intergovernmental cooperation in the Arctic commenced and investigate the dynamics of the Arctic Council body. Then it is important to examine the policy dynamics brought about by the five-coastal state meeting in Ilulissat, which provides a good basis for drawing conclusions as to whether the continental shelf developments in the region are indeed one factor pushing for an Arctic Council regime change toward more focused cooperation in the Arctic Ocean.

2.1. The Emergence of the Arctic Council

The initial idea of Arctic-wide cooperation was launched in 1987 in Murmansk by former Soviet Secretary-General Michail Gorbachev. The Soviet leader proposed that the Arctic states could initiate cooperation in various fields, one being protecting the Arctic environment.[27] This idea was developed further when Finland convened a conference of the eight Arctic states in Rovaniemi in 1989 to discuss the issue. After two additional preparatory meetings in Yellowknife, Canada, and Kiruna, Sweden, the eight Arctic states as along with other actors met again in Rovaniemi in 1991 to sign the Rovaniemi Declaration, by which they adopted the Arctic Environmental Protection Strategy (AEPS).[28]

The AEPS identified six priority environmental problems facing the Arctic: persistent organic contaminants, radioactivity, heavy metals, noise, acidification, and oil pollution. It also outlined the international environmental protection treaties that apply in the region and, finally, specified actions to counter the environmental threats. The eight Arctic states established four environmental protection working groups: Conservation of Arctic Flora and Fauna (CAFF), Protection of the Arctic Marine Environment (PAME), Emergency Prevention, Preparedness and Response (EPPR), and the Arctic Monitoring and Assessment Programme (AMAP). Three ministerial meetings (after the signing of the Rovaniemi Declaration and the AEPS) were held in this first phase of Arctic cooperation, generally referred to as the AEPS process. The meetings were held in 1993 (in Nuuk, Greenland), 1996 (in Inuvik, Canada), and 1997 (in Alta, Norway). Between the ministerial meetings, Senior Arctic Officials guided cooperation—officials who were typically from the foreign and environmental ministries of the eight Arctic states. The last AEPS ministerial was held after establishing the Arctic Council and focused on integrating the AEPS into the structure of the Council.

The Arctic Council was established in September 1996 in Ottawa, Canada, with the Arctic states signing the Declaration Establishing the Arctic Council and issuing a joint communiqué to explain the newly created body.[29] With the founding of the Council came changes in the form of Arctic cooperation that had been based on the AEPS document—changes that extended the terms of reference beyond the previous focus on environmental protection. The Council was empowered to deal with "common Arctic issues, in particular issues of sustainable development and environmental protection in the Arctic."[30] This yielded a very broad mandate because "common issues" can include almost any international policy issue; however, the Declaration provides in a footnote that "the Arctic Council should not deal with matters related to military security."[31] Environmental cooperation is now included as a principal focus within the mandate of the Council,[32] with the four environmental protection working groups that started as part of AEPS cooperation continuing under the umbrella of the Council.[33] The second "pillar" of the Council's mandate is cooperation on sustainable development,[34] whose terms of reference were adopted in the second ministerial meeting of the Council, held in 2000 in Barrow, Alaska, and that is managed by the Arctic Council Sustainable Development Working Group (SDWG).[35]

The Declaration amends and elaborates the rules on participation set out in the AEPS. It provides for three categories of participants: members, permanent participants, and observers. The eight Arctic states are members, and the three organisations representing the indigenous peoples of the Arctic are permanent participants.[36] The Declaration also lays down the criteria for acquiring the status of observer[37] and permanent participant as well as the decision-making procedure for determining those statuses.[38]

The decision-making procedure of the Arctic Council, which had developed with AEPS cooperation, was made more explicit in the Declaration. For example, Article 7 provides that "Decisions of the Arctic Council are to be by consensus of the Members." In Article 2, "member" is defined as including only the eight Arctic

states. Decision making by consensus is to be undertaken only after "full consultation"[39] with the permanent participants, that is, the organisations of the Arctic indigenous peoples. Although the permanent participants do not have formal decision-making power, they are clearly in a position to greatly influence in practice the decision making of the Council.[40]

The work of the Arctic Council is strongly controlled by its chair states. The first was Canada (1996–1998), followed by the United States (1998–2000), Finland (2000–2002), Iceland (2002–2004), Russia (2004–2006), and Norway (2006–2009);[41] the current chair is Denmark. Because the Council has no permanent secretariat, the chair state has a great deal of freedom to choose its priorities during its tenure, which hinders the formation of long-term policies (although the three Scandinavian states have created a semipermanent secretariat to function in Tromsø, Norway, until 2012).[42] The Arctic Council has also created certain programs of its own, such as the Arctic Council Action Plan to Eliminate Pollution in the Arctic (ACAP), which recently became the sixth working group, and the Arctic Climate Impact Assessment (ACIA). The Council has carried out many ambitious scientific assessments in addition to the ACIA, the most recent being the oil and gas assessment released in 2008 and the 2009 Arctic Marine Shipping Assessment.[43] Both the AEPS and the Arctic Council have been established by declarations, and, thus, Arctic-wide cooperation has been based on soft law from its very inception. Moreover, the Council's funding is still based on ad hoc contributions, and the Council has not yet engaged in any sensitive policy areas, retaining its basic focus on scientific assessments.[44]

2.2. Do the Continental Shelf Developments Constitute a Challenge to the Arctic Council?

The Ilulissat meeting in Greenland by the five coastal states of the Arctic Ocean flamed the discussion on future Arctic governance. This meeting was mostly designed to explain to the rest of the world that there is no scramble for resources going on in the Arctic, but rather an orderly development. Even though this might have been the original intention, it provoked many reactions among various Arctic "constituencies."

According to the Ilulissat Declaration, the coastal states found that the Arctic Ocean is at a threshold of significant changes due to climate change and melting sea ice, and because of this, "By virtue of their sovereignty, sovereign rights and jurisdiction in large areas of the Arctic Ocean the five coastal states are in a unique position to address these possibilities and challenges."[45] They also presented themselves as protecting the environment as well as indigenous and other local inhabitants in the Arctic Ocean in the following way:

> Climate change and the melting of ice have a potential impact on vulnerable ecosystems, the livelihoods of local inhabitants and indigenous communities. . . . By virtue of their sovereignty, sovereign rights and jurisdiction in large areas of the Arctic Ocean the five coastal states are in a unique position to address these possibilities and challenges. . . . The Arctic Ocean is a unique ecosystem, which the five coastal states have a stewardship role in protecting. Experience has shown how shipping disasters and subsequent pollution of the marine environment may cause irreversible disturbance of the ecological balance and major harm to the livelihoods of local inhabitants and indigenous communities.

The Arctic Ocean coastal states perceived that there is "no need to develop a new comprehensive international legal regime to govern the Arctic Ocean" because

> Notably, the law of the sea provides for important rights and obligations concerning the delineation of the outer limits of the continental shelf, the protection of the marine environment, including ice-covered areas, freedom of navigation, marine scientific research, and other uses of the sea. We remain committed to this legal

framework and to the orderly settlement of any possible overlapping claims. This framework provides a solid foundation for responsible management by the five coastal States and other users of this Ocean through national implementation and application of relevant provisions.

Even though Denmark insisted in the 2007 Narvik Senior Arctic Official (SAO) meeting prior to this Greenland meeting that the coastal state cooperation would not compete with the Arctic Council, the meeting caused friction among the Council members.[46] Iceland has been the most concerned of the three states (the others are Finland and Sweden) left out of this meeting. It expressed its concern in the Narvik SAO meeting[47] and also in the August 2008 Conference of the Arctic parliamentarians;[48] this is, of course, no surprise. The Ilulissat Declaration seems to outline an agenda for cooperation between the littoral states of the Arctic Ocean regarding high-level ocean policy issues, thus it is potentially challenging the Arctic Council, with its eight members, broad circumwide focus, and soft work on environmental protection and sustainable development. The coastal states committed themselves in the Ilulissat meeting to work in various international forums, organizations, and existing treaties to, among other things, improve shipping safety, prevent and reduce ship-based pollution in the Arctic Ocean, protect the marine environment, strengthen search and rescue capabilities, and improve accident response mechanisms in general. Moreover, they agreed to cooperate to collect scientific data on the continental shelf and especially to settle in an orderly manner any overlapping continental shelf entitlements.[49]

The Greenland meeting also provoked a reaction from one of the strongest Arctic Council permanent participants, the Inuit Circumpolar Council (ICC) and national Inuit leaders, who, in their "Statement issued by Inuit Leaders at the Inuit Leaders' Summit on Arctic Sovereignty,"[50] outlined their concerns over the five coastal state meeting:

Concern was expressed among us leaders gathered in Kuujjuaq that governments were entering into Arctic sovereignty discussions without the meaningful involvement of Inuit, such as the May, 2008 meeting of five Arctic ministers in Ilulissat, Greenland. The Kuujjuaq summit noted that while the Ilulissat Declaration asserts that it is the coastal nation states that have sovereignty and jurisdiction over the Arctic Ocean, it completely ignores the rights Inuit have gained through international law, land claims and self-government processes. Further, while the ministers strongly supported the use of international mechanisms and international law to resolve sovereignty disputes, it makes no reference to those international instruments that promote and protect the rights of indigenous peoples.

However, the ICC and the Inuit leaders were also critical of the present Arctic governance:

> We recognized the value of the work of the Arctic Council and asked ICC, through its permanent participant status on the Council, . . . We further noted the meaningful and direct role that indigenous peoples have at the Arctic Council, while at the same time expressing concern that the Council leaves many issues considered sensitive by member states off the table, including security, sovereignty, national legislation relating to marine mammal protection, and commercial fishing.

They also identified their own justification for being strongly involved in Arctic governance:

> We took note of various declarations and statements made by governments and industry regarding overlapping claims and assertions of Arctic sovereignty without full regard to Inuit concerns and rights. We further asserted that any claim of sovereignty that nation states may make is derived through the use and occupancy by Inuit of lands and seas in the Arctic. . . . Various aspects of what sovereignty means for Inuit were discussed. There was agreement among us that the foundation of Inuit sovereignty begins

at home, and that only through Inuit well-being and the development of healthy and sustainable communities can meaningful sovereignty be achieved. To achieve these goals, we called upon Arctic governments to be active partners in creating such a foundation.

Thereafter, they clarify their position in the event that a new governance arrangement is to be negotiated:

> We called upon Arctic governments to include Inuit as equal partners in any future talks regarding Arctic sovereignty. We insisted that in these talks, Inuit be included in a manner that equals or surpasses the participatory role Inuit play at the Arctic Council through ICC's permanent participant status.

Because they target serious criticism of the Council's inability to tackle sensitive issues, the Inuit can thus be interpreted as favoring a stronger governance arrangement than the present Arctic Council. Even though they naturally make their own case for why Inuits should be included in any future talks of Arctic governance, they also refer to indigenous peoples' rights in general and the Arctic Council's permanent participant status in particular. One possible view that emerges from their statement is that any future governance arrangement should include the present permanent participants of the Council as equal partners with the eight Arctic Council member states.

The EU Parliament on October 9, 2008[51] adopted a Resolution in which the Parliament first took note of the Greenland meeting (paragraph I) and then established its Arctic agency in the following words:

> whereas three of the EU's Member States, and a further two of the EU's closely-related neighbours participating in the internal market through the EEA Agreement, are Arctic nations, meaning that the EU and its associated states comprise more than half the numeric membership of the Arctic Council.

For the EU Parliament, the ultimate governance solution should involve a broader group of countries and the region's indigenous peoples. The EU Parliament

> Suggests that the Commission should be prepared to pursue the opening of international negotiations designed to lead to the adoption of an international treaty for the protection of the Arctic, having as its inspiration the Antarctic Treaty, as supplemented by the Madrid Protocol signed in 1991, but respecting the fundamental difference represented by the populated nature of the Arctic and the consequent rights and needs of the peoples and nations of the Arctic region; believes, however, that as a minimum starting-point such a treaty could at least cover the unpopulated and unclaimed area at the centre of the Arctic Ocean (paragraph 15).[52]

Given that the EU has no Arctic coastline but instead potentially significant navigational and fisheries interests in the region, the alternative of establishing a more inclusive governance arrangement for the Arctic would suit the interests of the EU better than the law of the sea approach pursued by the five Arctic coastal states or even the Arctic Council, which is built on the difference between Arctic and non-Arctic states. Parliament's strategic choice to pursue an inclusive governance arrangement for the Arctic is well reflected in the resolution: It suggests the Antarctic Treaty system (ATS) as a model for the Arctic—a system that is a very inclusive governance arrangement, as it is, in principal, open to all states who conduct scientific research in Antarctica.[53] As a minimum requirement, the Parliament outlines an idea of a treaty covering the unpopulated and unclaimed area at the centre of the Arctic Ocean. Even though it is worded in a legally incorrect manner,[54] this suggestion also takes an inclusive approach to Arctic governance because all states possess rights and interests in the high seas and deep seabed of the Arctic Ocean under the law of the sea.

Even though the European Parliament made the above-mentioned suggestion to the European Commission, the latter, in its November 2008 Communication, did not respond to this call. The Commission's Communication did, however, provide an interesting starting point for its Arctic policy by first diagnosing the problem: "The main problems relating to Arctic governance include the fragmentation of the legal framework, the lack of effective instruments, the absence of an overall policy-setting process and gaps in participation, implementation and geographic scope."[55] One remedy for tackling such problems is, according to the Commission, to "Explore the possibility of establishing new, multi-sector frameworks for integrated ecosystem management. This could include the establishment of a network of marine protected areas, navigational measures and rules for ensuring the sustainable exploitation of minerals." The non-Arctic coastal states have also expressed their willingness to become part of the established Arctic intergovernmental forum, currently via applying observer status from the Arctic Council (China, South Korea, and even Japan). For the time being, however, the Council did not approve in its last ministerial meeting in April 2009 in Norway permanent observer status to China or the European Commission.

Even though there clearly is a new dynamic in Arctic governance, the Arctic coastal states have not reacted to these new interests with enthusiasm, as shown by their rejection of the observership status for China and the European Commission. The recent Arctic policy documents of the United States and Russia have been very much in line with the Ilulissat Declaration, perceiving the current Arctic Council and the law of the sea as an adequate solution for the Arctic even though they are willing to engage in proactive regulation, for example, from the U.S. Arctic policy document. In this, the U.S. policy considers that the Arctic Council "should remain a high-level forum devoted to issues within its current mandate,"[56] but it should also promote ways to enhance governance in the changing Arctic:

> Consider, as appropriate, new or enhanced international arrangements for the Arctic to address

issues likely to arise from expected increases in human activity in that region, including shipping, local development and subsistence, exploitation of living marine resources, development of energy and other resources, and tourism.[57]

3. Evaluation

A reasonable assessment at the time of this writing is that the UNCLOS is able to contain the challenges that the continental shelf activity in the Arctic poses. This conclusion, however, can only be drawn cautiously because some of the Arctic submissions will in all likelihood overlap and Russia's vast submission may face challenges in the Commission procedure. Yet given that the Arctic Ocean coastal states are already preparing for the eventual delimitation of the boundaries of their continental shelves and that at least so far Russia has abided by the CLCS procedures, it can be presumed that the submissions will not prompt any serious conflicts in the Arctic. This does not mean that the process will progress in an orderly fashion to its conclusion; it only means that the development so far has been orderly and fully in line with international law, whereby there is no reason to presume that the process naturally engenders conflict.

The media and even some researchers try to claim that the melting brought on by climate change has made previously inaccessible Arctic waters targets for power politics and that the race is on among states to be the first to grab the resources, which could possibly provoke military conflicts. However, that this story line is more of a story than an account of the realities in the regions is clear. One reason for this misconception may be that it has taken such a long time for the UNCLOS continental shelf process to unfurl. The UNCLOS was negotiated for a long period of time—1973 to 1982—and it did not enter into force until 1994. The first deadline for a state party to the UNCLOS to make a submission concerning an extended continental shelf to the CLCS was 2004, and thus the process has started to operate only very recently.

It is exactly now that the submissions for extended continental shelves need to be made—and increasingly are being made.[58]

It is probably difficult for a nonlawyer to imagine that a process that started in 1973 is the main cause of the present continental shelf activity, but this is in fact the case. Yet, as shown above, this activity in the Arctic has clear politico-legal consequences even though it seems reasonable to surmise that no conflicts will arise from these. Overall, the reality of continental shelf activity in the Arctic testifies to the power of rules, rather than political considerations, in guiding state behaviour—at least thus far.

As discussed above, even though states have conducted continental shelf activity within the letter of the UNCLOS, these developments pose a possible challenge to the Arctic Council: They change the politico-legal setting in the Arctic simply by extending the presence of Arctic states farther onto the Arctic Ocean seabed. The politico-legal setting in the Arctic will change further when all the current continental shelf submissions are processed by the Commission and the Arctic coastal states have agreed (or not) on the boundaries of any overlapping entitlements.

The gradual penetration of the five littoral states further into the Arctic Ocean through their continental shelf submissions may be part of an overall challenge to the Arctic Council as the main intergovernmental forum managing the Arctic issues. Over time the coastal states may find it more reasonable to conclude multilateral treaties focusing on the Arctic Ocean rather than the entire Arctic, which has been the traditional focus of the Arctic Council. Moreover, the states may find it important to confront the difficult management problems caused by the melting sea ice (such as increased navigation and offshore hydrocarbon exploitation) through a more focused Arctic Ocean cooperation rather than a soft-cooperation platform such as the Arctic Council. Such a development would leave Finland, Sweden, and Iceland, all members of the Arctic Council, out of the core of the cooperation, which has already caused some friction.

Conversely, the Arctic Council has also evolved incrementally from the AEPS to the present Arctic Council. Gradually, the institutional formation of the Council and its deliverables have become more ambitious and an increasing number of states (China, South Korea, Japan) as well as the European Commission want to join the Council as observers. Of much importance is, therefore, whether the Arctic Council can transform itself to become a real governance body of the region or whether it will retain its current ambition of producing scientific assessments and nonbinding guidelines, especially given the vast challenges ahead. If the Council cannot renew its operating format, it is likely to be overrun by more focused and ambitious cooperation by the five coastal states of the Arctic Ocean.[59]

NOTES

1. Impacts of a Warming Arctic, ACIA Overview Report (2004) [ACIA Synthesis Report]; *see generally* the Arctic Climate Impact Assessment Final Scientific Report (2005), *available at* www.acia.uaf.edu/.

2. *See* the press reports from the IEA's World Energy Outlook website, *available at* www.iea.org/Textbase/publications/free_new_Desc.asp?PUBS_ID=2025.

3. *See* www.bloomberg.com/apps/news?pid=2060 1102&sid=ajnhJCcmv8pU. The U.S. Geological Survey has earlier estimated that these are plentiful. *See* http://geology.com/U.S.gs/arctic-oil-and-gas-report .shtml.

4. *See* www.un.org/depts/los/clcs_new/submissions _files/submission_rU.S.htm.

5. *See* the reaction, *available at* www.un.org/depts/los/clcs_new/submissions_files/rU.S.01/CLCS_01_200 1_LOS__U.S.Atext.pdf.

6. *See* www.guardian.co.uk/world/2007/aug/02/Russia.arctic.

7. *See* http://news.bbc.co.uk/2/hi/europe/6927395 .stm.

8. *See* www.foreignaffairs.org/20080301faessay87206 -p20/scott-g-borgerson/arctic-meltdown.html.

9. *See* www.un.org/depts/los/convention_agreements/texts/unclos/UNCLOS-TOC.htm.

10. *See* www.presidency.ucsb.edu/ws/index.php?pid =12332.

11. *See* http://sedac.ciesin.org/entri/texts/continental .shelf.1958.html.

12. The earlier attempts produced four separate laws of the sea conventions (I of 1958) and the second was a failure (1960).

13. *See* Article 309.

14. Article 76 contains fairly complex criteria for drawing the outer limit in its paragraphs 4 to 6. International Law Association (its outer continental shelf committee) has made an important contribution in its Toronto 2006 Conference Report, *available at* www .ila-hq.org/en/committees/index.cfm/cid/33.

15. As stated on the ISBA homepage, the ISBA is "an autonomous international organization established under the 1982 United Nations Convention on the Law of the Sea and the 1994 Agreement relating to the Implementation of Part XI of the United Nations Convention on the Law of the Sea. The Authority is the organization through which States Parties to the Convention shall, in accordance with the regime for the seabed and ocean floor and subsoil thereof beyond the limits of national jurisdiction (the Area) established in Part XI and the Agreement, organize and control activities in the Area, particularly with a view to administering the resources of the Area and subsoil thereof beyond the limits of national jurisdiction (the Area) established in Part XI and the Agreement, organize and control activities in the Area, particularly with a view to administering the resources of the Area." *See* www.isa.org .jm/en/about.

16. Article 82.

17. Article 76 and Annex II.

18. This date was postponed by the parties to the Convention to those states that had become parties before May 1999, thus extending their submission deadline to May 2009. *See* Annex II to the Convention, Article 4. A recent 2008 decision by the states parties to the Law of the Sea Convention (SPLOS) will further mitigate this deadline. In Decision SPLOS/183 regarding the workload of the Commission on the Limits of the Continental Shelf and the ability of states, particularly developing states, to fulfill the requirements of article 4 of annex II to the UN Convention on the Law of the Sea as well as the decision contained in SPLOS/72, paragraph (a), it was provided: [The Meeting of States Parties] "1. [The Meeting of States Parties] [d]ecides that: (a) It is understood that the time period referred to in article 4 of annex II to the Convention and the decision contained in SPLOS/72, paragraph (a), may be satisfied by submitting to the Secretary-General preliminary information indicative of the outer limits of the continental shelf beyond 200 nautical miles and a description of the status of preparation and intended date of making a submission in accordance with the requirements of article 76 of the Convention and with the

Rules of Procedure2 and the Scientific and Technical Guidelines of the Commission on the Limits of the Continental Shelf." *See* www.un.org/Depts/los/meeting_states_parties/eighteenthmeetingstatesparties.htm.

19. Article 76 (8).

20. *See* short summary of these recommendations, *available at* http://daccessdds.un.org/doc/UNDOC/GEN/N02/629/28/PDF/N0262928.pdf?OpenElement. According to paragraph 41, "As regards the Central Arctic Ocean, the Commission recommended that the Russian Federation make a revised submission in respect of its extended continental shelf in that area based on the findings contained in the recommendations."

21. Article 77 (3) of the Convention.

22. *See* www.un.org/depts/los/clcs_new/submissions_files/submission_nor.htm (11.6.2008). *See, e.g,.* Spain's reaction, *available at* www.un.org/depts/los/clcs_new/submissions_files/nor06/esp_0700348.pdf.

23. The Norwegian Ministry for Foreign Affairs responded to the author's e-mail question as follows: "It is clear that Svalbard is part of the Kingdom of Norway. According to the law of the sea, only states have continental shelf. Accordingly all continental shelf areas that originate from Norwegian territory are Norwegian in the sense that they are subject to Norwegian jurisdiction. It is also clear from all maps of the seabed that a continuous continental shelf extends north from mainland Norway and around and past Svalbard." E-mail response, April 8, 2008, from the official of the Ministry (on file with the author).

24. *See* www.un.org/Depts/los/clcs_new/submissions_files/nor06/nor_rec_summ.pdf.

25. *See* www.sciencedaily.com/releases/2008/02/080211134449.htm.

26. As of October 31, 2007, the U.S. Senate Foreign Relations Committee approved the Law of the Sea Convention, sending it to the full Senate for ratification. *See* "Law of the Sea Clears Committee," *at* http://lugar.senate.gov/sfrc/sea.html. The United States has now tried to become party to the UNCLOS under both Clinton and Bush Administrations, but in both cases the Senate was able to block its approval.

27. Gorbachev proposed that a nuclear-weapon-free zone be declared in northern Europe, naval activity be limited in the seas adjacent to northern Europe, peaceful cooperation be the basis for utilizing the resources of the Arctic, scientific study of the Arctic has great significance for all humankind, the countries of the North cooperate in matters of environmental protection, and the Northern Sea Route be opened by the Soviet Union to ice-breaker-escorted passage.

28. The history of the negotiation process is studied in MONICA TENNBERG, THE ARCTIC COUNCIL: A STUDY IN GOVERNMENTALITY 53–61 (1998). The AEPS is reproduced in 30 ILM 1624 (1991).

29. The 1996 Declaration on the Establishment of the Arctic Council. The Declaration is *reprinted* in 35 ILM 1385–90 (1996).

30. *Id.* at art. 1 (a) of the Declaration.

31. *Id.* at 3.

32. *Id.* at art. 1 (b).

33. *Id.* Article 1 (b) reads, "The Arctic Council is established as a high level forum to . . . b. oversee and coordinate the programs established under the AEPS on the Arctic Monitoring and Assessment Program (AMAP); Conservation of Arctic Flora and Fauna (CAFF); Protection of the Arctic Marine Environment (PAME); and Emergency Prevention, Preparedness and Response (EPPR)."

34. *Id.* Article 1 (c) reads, "The Arctic Council is established as a high level forum to . . . c. adopt terms of reference for, and oversee and coordinate a sustainable development program."

35. The home page of the SDWG is *at* http://portal.sdwg.org/.

36. Article 2 of the Declaration enumerates the following as permanent participants: "The Inuit Circumpolar Conference, the Saami Council and the Association of Indigenous Minorities of the North, Siberia and the Far East of the Russian Federation." Three organisations have since been accepted as permanent participants: the Aleut International Association, the Gwich'in Council International and the Arctic Athabascan Council.

37. *Id.* Article 3 of the Declaration reads, "Observer status in the Arctic Council is open to: a) non-Arctic states; b) inter-governmental and inter-parliamentary organisations, global and regional; and c) non-governmental organisations that the Council determines can contribute to its work."

38. *Id.* Article 2 (2) reads, "Permanent participation is equally open to other Arctic organisations of indigenous peoples with majority Arctic indigenous constituency, representing: a. a single indigenous people resident in more than one Arctic State; or b. more than one Arctic indigenous people resident in a single Arctic state." Decisions by the Arctic states on whether this criterion is fulfilled must be unanimous. Article 2 also states, "the number of Permanent Participants should at any time be less than the number of members."

39. *Id.* at art. 2.

40. Timo Koivurova & Leena Heinämäki, *The Participation of Indigenous Peoples in International Norm-making in the Arctic*, 42 POLAR RECORD (221) 101–9 (2006).

41. In the Scandinavian chair-period, with Norway, Denmark, and Sweden drawing up their own Action Plan, the ministerial meetings are organised during the spring rather than fall, as previously.

42. *See* http://arctic-council.org/article/2007/11/common_priorities.

43. *See* http://arctic-council.org/filearchive/amsa2009 report.pdf.

44. For a comprehensive account of the evolution of the Arctic Council, *see* Timo Koivurova & David VanderZwaag, *The Arctic Council at 10 Years: Retrospect and Prospects*, 40 U. Brit. Colum. L. Rev. 121–94 (2007).

45. Ilulissat Declaration 2008, *at* http://arctic-council .org/filearchive/Ilulissat-declaration.pdf.

46. Narvik SAO meeting 2007 (November 28–29, Final Report), *available at* http://arctic-council.org/ filearchive/Narvik%20-FINAL%20Report-%2023 Apr08.doc.

47. In the discussion in the Narvik SAO meeting (18.1.), "Iceland expressed concerns that separate meetings of the five Arctic states, Denmark, Norway, U.S., Russia and Canada, on Arctic issues without the participation of the members of the Arctic Council, Sweden, Finland and Iceland, could create a new process that competes with the objectives of the Arctic Council. If issues of broad concern to all of the Arctic Council Member States, including the effect of climate change, shipping in the Arctic, etc. are to be discussed, Iceland requested that Denmark invite the other Arctic Council states to participate in the ministerial meeting. Permanent participants also requested to participate in the meeting. Denmark responded that the capacity of the venue may be an issue."

48. The Conference statement in its paragraph 39 "Notes the information from the Danish delegation concerning the Ilulissat Declaration, and the concerns of the Icelandic delegation regarding full participation of all states of the Arctic Council." Conference Report 2008, *available at* www.arcticparl.org/_res/site/file/ files%20from%208th%20conference/Conference_Report _Fairbanks_final.pdf.

49. *See* the Ilulissat Declaration, *available at* http:// arctic-council.org/filearchive/Ilulissat-declaration.pdf.

50. Statement 2008 issued by Inuit Leaders at the Inuit Leaders' Summit on Arctic Sovereignty (Nov. 6–7, 2008), *available at* www.sikunews.com/art.html?artid =5711&catid=2.

51. European Parliament resolution of Oct. 9, 2008 on Arctic governance, *available at* www.europarl.europa .eu/sides/getDoc.do?pubRef=-//EP//TEXT+TA+P6 -TA-2008–0474+0+DOC+XML+V0//EN.

52. The Commission did not follow this suggestion by the EU Parliament but provided that "The full implementation of already existing obligations, rather than proposing new legal instruments should be advocated. This however should not preclude work on further developing some of the frameworks, adapting them to new conditions or Arctic specificities." Arctic Communication 2008: 4.

53. *See* the provision on membership in article IX.2 of the Antarctic Treaty, 72 UNTS (1961) 5778.

54. The EU Parliament spoke of the "unclaimed area at the centre of the Arctic Ocean," by which it can refer to types of areas beyond national jurisdiction, the deep seabed (the Area) and the high seas. First, if the Parliament refers to the deep seabed, this cannot be said to be an unclaimed area because the coastal states do not claim their continental shelf, for it is a natural prolongation of the land mass into the sea. Hence, the deep seabed is a result of what remains after the coastal states have drawn the outer limits of their continental shelves. Second, high seas cannot be subjected to sovereignty claims under the law of the sea. It would thus have been legally correct to speak, for instance, of "areas beyond national jurisdiction at the centre of the Arctic Ocean." It is also a bit odd why the Parliament spoke of this area as "unpopulated," given that it is referring to the core of an ice-covered ocean.

55. Arctic Communication 2008 (Nov. 20, 2008). Communication from the Commission to the European Parliament and the Council, The European Union and the Arctic Region. Brussels, COM(2008) 763, *available at* http://ec.europa.eu/ maritimeaffairs/pdf/com08_763_en.pdf.

56. U.S. Arctic Region Policy 2009. National Security Presidential Directive/Nspd–66, Homeland Security Presidential Directive/Hspd–25 (January 9, 2009), Arctic Region Policy. On file with the authors.

57. *Id.* at C 5b.

58. There was a vast amount of submissions made by coastal states of the world just before the revised deadline for these submissions, which was May 13, 2009. Currently, there are fifty-one submissions, either unilateral or joint.

59. For a forthcoming account, *see* Timo Koivurova, *Limits and Possibilities of the Arctic Council in a Rapidly Changing Scene of Arctic Governance,* Polar Record, forthcoming.

18

The Law of the Sea and Human Rights*

SOPHIE CACCIAGUIDI-FAHY

Introduction

Many scholars trace the origin of modern international law to Grotius's *Mare Liberum,* which itself defines "the law of the sea as one of the 'original' fields of international law."[1] The law of the sea, including admiralty law, is "as old as humanity's use of the sea," and yet little attention has been devoted to the human rights aspects its international treaties and customary law articulate.[2] Over the last three decades, many important human rights issues and humanitarian crises have been played out at sea, as it is the main conduit for people trafficking and the scene of some of the most appalling human tragedies. Cases such as the *Tampa* (involving a standoff between Australia and Norway over the responsibility for 433 Afghan asylum seekers), the *M/S Joola* (a Senegalese ferry carrying illegal migrants that capsized, resulting in the loss of 970 of her 1,034 passengers), and the *SIEV X* (of the 400 passengers it carried, 353 persons drowned, including 150 children)[3] have led to calls to increase protection and human rights initiatives, particularly with respect to the 1951 Refugee Convention.[4] Yet it would be wrong to embark on initiating changes in refugee law without first exploring the protection that in-

struments of the law of the sea may already afford. As observed by Bernard Oxman, "the law of the sea, its instruments and institutions has not only a direct contribution to make to human rights law but in some instances are sufficient to protect individual human rights."[5]

This chapter examines the law of the sea and some of the human rights considerations that it addresses, specifically the protection of life at sea expressed directly or indirectly in the various legal instruments of the law of the sea. It starts by examining the origins of humanitarian obligations at sea and the legal framework of the law of the sea, which aims to protect life at sea. In this context, the chapter addresses the duties of a shipmaster to protect life at sea by providing assistance to persons in distress along with the obligation of flag states and coastal states to likewise protect life at sea by providing rescue. It also briefly explores the long-standing maritime tradition of the concept of place of safety or refuge and their implications for the question of innocent passage and disembarkation as well as the role the IMO plays with regard to protecting life at sea. The chapter concludes by providing an overview of international and European jurisprudence with respect to the interaction between the law of the sea and human rights in

*This chapter is a revised version of Sophie Cacciaguidi, *The Law of the Sea and Human Rights*, 19 SRI LANKA J. INT'L L. 85 (2007). The author wishes to express her gratitude to Dr. Ronan Long (School of Law, NUI, Galway) for his comments and suggestions on an earlier version of this chapter.

general, with a view to show that neither the law of the sea nor human rights law are separate and self-contained legal regimes.

The Origins of Humanitarian Obligations at Sea

The obligation of rendering assistance to those in peril or lost at sea is one of the oldest and most deep-rooted maritime traditions.[6] For centuries, seafarers have considered it their duty to assist fellow mariners in peril on the high seas. Today, however, it has become more than just a moral obligation. It is now codified in international treaty law and is considered to form part of customary law.[7] In the mid-nineteenth century, one British mariner in five died at sea. Mortality among sailors was higher than in any other occupation, and between 1861 and 1870, 5,826 ships were wrecked off the British coast, with the loss of 8,105 lives.[8] It was against this background that the legal obligation of rendering assistance at sea was recognized in 1880 in the *Scaramanga v. Stamp* case: "to all who have to trust themselves to the sea it is of the utmost importance that the promptings of humanity in this respect should not be checked or interfered with the by prudential considerations which may result to a ship or cargo from the rendering of the needed aid."[9] This basic precept of British common law was subsequently codified in a number of international conventions, which well preceded any of the more modern human rights instruments.

The General Legal Framework of the Law of the Sea Protecting Life at Sea

The principle of humanitarian assistance at sea, which aims at saving lives, uses basic human rights principles as its foundation, in particular protecting the right to life and the right to dignity and humane treatment. The first law of the sea instrument to acknowledge the principle of rendering assistance at sea was the 1910 Brussels Convention on Salvage.[10] The present normative framework applying to states and the seafaring communities[11] is provided for by the 1982 United Nations Convention on the Law of the Sea,[12] the 1974 International Convention for the Safety of Life at Sea,[13] the 1979 International Convention on Maritime Search and Rescue,[14] and the 1989 International Convention on Salvage.[15] These conventions are regarded by most experts in the law of the sea as the "expression to the general tradition and practice of all seafarers and of maritime law regarding the rendering of assistance to persons or ships in distress at sea, and the elementary conditions of humanity."[16]

The 1982 LOS Convention

Many legal commentators argue that, although "the LOS Convention is not a 'human rights instruments' per se,"[17] several of its provisions articulate human rights principles that the human rights community, to date, still does not use effectively and to their full potential.[18] As discussed by Oxman, the primary purpose of the Convention is to uphold the universal rule of law[19] and provide effective governance at sea.[20] It allocates authority to govern and imposes qualifications on that authority. It mandates the rights and duties of states in a precise codified form, converting those rules into binding treaty obligations ratified by governments pursuant to their constitutional procedures.[21] Governance is clearly codified with respect to flag states of ships and coastal states. Yet as Oxman so pointedly argued,

> the Convention as a whole seeks to advance the interests of humanity by establishing a "legal order for the seas and oceans which will facilitate international communication, and will promote the peaceful uses of the seas and oceans, the equitable and efficient utilization of their resources, the conservation of their resources, and the study, protection and preservation of the marine environment" and by contributing "to the realization of just and equitable international

economic order which takes into account the interest and needs of mankind as a whole."[22]

Oxman further contended that the Convention not only acknowledges but actively "seeks to advance certain specific community interests" that have been associated with "affirmative human rights."[23] These rights are complex and somewhat difficult to identify. They mostly concern the relationship between human rights and the underlying concepts of community rights in general, common cultural rights or environmental rights, and the notion of the common heritage of mankind under international law that, in turn, gives rise to what may be appropriately referred to as the right of an individual. Their distinction is not easy to make. These rights are not generally enforceable by or against individuals under the Convention, but are in fact articulated as duties to be respected and enforced by states and other parties to the Convention.

One of these affirmative human rights principles—expressed in the Convention as a duty—is to be found in one of its most elaborate provisions, Article 98:

> Article 98. Duty to render assistance
> 1. Every State shall require the master of a ship flying its flag, in so far as he can do so without serious danger to the ship, the crew or the passengers;
> (a) to render assistance to any person found at sea in danger of being lost;
> (b) to proceed with all possible speed to the rescue of persons in distress, if informed of their need of assistance, in so far as such action may reasonably be expected of him;
> (c) after a collision, to render assistance to the other ship, its crew and its passengers and, where possible, to inform the other ship of the name of his own ship, its port of registry and the nearest port at which it will call.
> 2. Every coastal State shall promote the establishment, operation and maintenance of an adequate and effective search and rescue service regarding safety on and over the sea and, where circumstances so require, by way of mutual regional arrangements co-operate with neighbouring States for this purpose.

Article 98 thus addresses ships' obligation to assist vessels in distress or shipwrecked persons. It aims to implement the concept of the safety of life at sea—in other words to protect life at sea. The duty it refers to is known as the duty to render assistance. This duty purports to provide humanitarian assistance to any person in danger at sea regardless of their legal status, in whatever circumstances, whether in time of war or peace and in whatever parts of the world.[24] It is a well-established legal principle of the law of the sea. Its legal basis has deep roots in customary and humanitarian law principle in the history of the law of the sea.

Other International Treaties Establishing the Duty to Render Assistance

Other than the LOS Convention, several international treaties adopted under the auspices of the IMO impose a duty to rescue persons that are in distress, using similar language, albeit anticipating different types of responsibilities for the shipmaster, flag states, and coastal states. These include:

- Chapter V, Regulations 10(a) and (33) of the SOLAS Convention provides for "assistance, on receiving a signal from any source that persons are in distress at sea, is bound to proceed with all speed to their assistance";
- Article 10 of the SALVAGE Convention requires an obligation to "render assistance to any person in danger of being lost at sea";
- Regulation (2)(1)(10) of the SAR Convention Annex further stipulates that "Parties shall ensure that assistance be provided to any person in distress at sea. They shall do so regardless of the nationalities or status of such a person or the circumstances in which that person is found."

All the above provisions expressly articulate an unqualified duty to render assistance to "persons" or "any persons" "in distress" or "in danger of being lost at sea." This duty is clearly unaffected by the nationality, status of the persons, the mode of transport, the numbers involved, or the maritime zone in which they are found in distress.[25] But the scope of the assistance itself is not defined in any of the conventions. It is on that basis that the IMO in 1985 called on all states parties to the conventions to intensify their efforts in providing assistance to boat people during the Vietnamese refugee crisis.[26]

Legal Obligations to Provide Assistance and Rescue

One of the crucial points, albeit ambiguous, the above instruments and in particular article 98 of the LOS Convention raised is the extent to which states have an obligation to rescue and provide assistance. This essential consideration is often lost in the meandering debates that have taken place thus far in international *fora* on the right to humanitarian assistance at sea, disembarkation, and the delivery to a place of safety.[27] Indeed, specific rules in the law of the sea can be conveniently blurred and confused with other questions derived from other branches of international law and domestic legislation so as to facilitate a convenient oversight of basic humanitarian principles.[28] These are, as argued by Stuart Kaye, probably the most important issues to be considered because they are, in the first instance, what created, for example, the diplomatic crisis over the *Tampa* affair.[29] To address this consideration, a distinction must be made between the duty to provide "assistance," which is applicable to shipmasters, and the duty of rescue, which is imposed on flag and coastal states.[30] It is an important distinction because the latter extends to delivery to a place of safety where coastal states are concerned. Although rescuees can be brought on board, they must be allowed to disembark for the rescue to be considered fulfilled. We now propose to explore these duties a little further.

The Duties of the Master— The Obligation to Provide Assistance

Masters are legally bound by the provisions of the above conventions to respond with all possible speed to assist and rescue persons in distress with due regard for the safety of their own crew and ship. However, the duty placed on the master is only a duty to render assistance. Customary law has evolved in a manner that now differentiates between the obligation to assist and the obligation to rescue, which falls on states.[31] International maritime law considers that once the master has provided assistance, the rescue is effected.[32]

The scope of the duty to assist is not defined in any of the conventions. Most scholars argue that the language adopted was deliberately ambiguous so as to allow masters to fulfill their obligation with due regard for the safety of their own crew and ship, taking into consideration the various hazards of the high seas when answering a call for distress—mostly because distress is not clearly defined in the law of the sea. Debates on what constitute distress are still ongoing.[33] This constructive ambiguity exists so that masters are able to exercise moral and operational decisions when assessing the sort of assistance that can be provided. There are a variety of acts that may constitute "assistance," such as towing a boat, unloading crew, providing food and supplies, and so forth.

The Duties of Flag States— The Obligation to Rescue

Under article 98(1) of the LOS Convention and Chapter V, Regulations 7, 10(a), and 33 of the SOLAS Convention, flag states have an obligation to rescue insofar as they must adopt domestic legislation that establishes penalties for shipmasters who violate the duty to rescue or fail to provide assistance.[34] Yet while this obligation is widely accepted, it is often only partially incorporated into domestic law,[35] if not altogether absent. As a result, the fact that enforcement is problematic, if not impossible, further weakens the scope of the duty to assist imposed on masters. Shipmasters are known to have deliberately ignored persons in distress simply because of time delays and commercial pressures. This is particularly the case for those masters who sail under a flag of convenience.[36]

The Duties of Coastal States— The Obligation to Rescue

Coastal states, however, have a positive duty to rescue—that is, to coordinate search-and-rescue operations—under article 98(2) of the LOS Convention, which "promotes the establishment, operation and maintenance of an adequate and effective search and rescue service." Although some have argued that this provision is limited to the high seas and the EEZ by virtue of articles 86 and 58(2), it is quite clear that the provisions on innocent passage in the territorial seas reflect implicitly the duty to render assistance.[37] Chapter V, Regulation 15 of the SAR Convention also requires states to maintain adequate search-and-rescue assets and equipment along their coast,[38] and Regulation 2(1)(10) of the Annex expressly mandates assistance to any persons regardless of their status. Chapter V, Regulation 7 of the SOLAS Convention promotes the concept of cooperation and rescue zones, and Regulation 15(a) requires that states "undertake any necessary arrangements . . . for the rescue of persons in distress at sea round its coasts and . . . afford adequate means of locating and rescuing such persons." Finally, article 11 of the SALVAGE Convention "ensures the efficient and successful performance of salvage operations for the purpose of saving life or property in danger."

The SAR Convention defines the scope of the duty to rescue as "an operation to retrieve persons in distress, provide for their initial medical and other needs and deliver them to a place of safety."[39] However, neither the SAR Convention nor any other international instruments of the law of the sea clearly define or elaborate the normative criteria of a place of safety. In effect this means that none of the above conventions

specifically provide for the disembarkation of the rescuees, which in essence represents the final phase of the rescue process.[40] The "right to land" at sea relied primarily on coastal states' law.[41] The international legal right of innocent passage, as codified in the LOS Convention, also has a bearing on the wide margin of discretion afforded to states when it comes to fulfilling their obligation to rescue seaborne refugees.

Rights of Innocent Passage— Access to Port—Place of Safety or Refuge

The LOS Convention addresses both directly and indirectly the right to refuge or place of safety, innocent passage, and access to ports. Based on humanitarian considerations, the right to refuge is first and foremost, resulting from flag ships in situations of distress seeking or taking refuge in internal or territorial waters of other sovereign states.[42] The legal principle allows ships certain humanitarian considerations and jurisdictional exemptions, and it arises both in peace and war time and commands universal acceptance.[43] It requires a coastal state to avoid any risk to human life and to afford persons in distress any assistance that they may need.[44] This right is examined in several of the classical works on public international law.[45] Recent state practice, however, has imposed important limitations on the right of refuge by making a clear distinction between the humanitarian right to save life and action to save the ship and its cargo.[46] The Irish High Court of Admiralty particularly highlighted this limitation in the *MV Toledo* case, which held that the right to refuge, although no longer an absolute right, should be there when human life is at stake.[47] The articulation of the right by Barr J.[48] is now considered a classical exposition of the law on this point.

The law concerning the right of entry into port by a ship in distress is firmly rooted in treaty law.[49] Although the right of coastal states to regulate access to its ports, harbors, and internal waters is not disputable, when a ship is in distress, customary law again clearly allows entry to port.[50] The right to innocent passage is composed of two elements: the physical act of passage and the innocent mode of the act.[51] The IJC first defined the meaning of innocent passage in the *Corfu Channel* case (*United Kingdom v. Albania*).[52] Subsequently, article 18 of the 1958 Convention on the Territorial Sea and Contiguous Zone codified the right,[53] which is now comprehensively addressed in articles 17 to 19 of the LOS Convention.[54]

The Role of the IMO

The debate on the substantive nature of the right to rescue and provide assistance came to the forefront of the world stage during the *Tampa* incident, when Australia refused entry into its territorial waters, denying the right to innocent passage and access to port for the purpose of disembarkation, to a Norwegian commercial ship following the rescue, requested by the Australian Search and Rescue Services, of 433 people seeking asylum. The confrontation between Australia and Norway raised concerns in many coastal nations, shipping companies, and the commercial shipping world at large. It also prompted the IMO to become involved with the case within a day of its occurrence in order to facilitate a solution.

The *notes verbales* exchanged between Norway and Australia during the diplomatic negotiations clearly distinguished between the obligation to assist rendered by the *Tampa* and the obligation to rescue.[55] One of the disputed facts was that Australia saw the rescue as completed once the rescuees boarded the *Tampa*, notwithstanding the fact that the master had twice signaled to the authorities that his ship was in distress due to overloading and lack of supplies.[56] Norway argued that Australia had created "a most unwelcome obstacle to prevent seafarers from being rescued when they are in distress or shipwrecked."[57] The *notes* confirmed the varied interpretations of the word "rescue," which indicated Australia's unwillingness to cooperate, preventing a speedy resolution of the case. It is this impasse that prompted the Secretary-General of the IMO to advise the UN

High Commissioner for Human Rights and other UN agencies[58] that he would now intervene and order a review of the relevant IMO instruments, as the consequences of this rather significant incident could have serious repercussions for the integrity of the search-and-rescue system and assisting those found in distress at sea.[59] The IMO was now set to push the issue of seaborne refugees to the forefront of the international stage and portray it as a multifaceted challenge for all policy makers.[60] The IMO needed to clarify and elaborate on the interpretation of the terms "place of safety" and "disembarkation" within the meaning of the SOLAS and SAR Conventions.

At its November 2001 session, the IMO Assembly adopted Resolution A.920 (22) involving a Review of Safety Measures and Procedures for the Treatment of Persons Rescued at Sea. Its mandate was to instruct the IMO Maritime Safety Committee, the Legal Committee, and the Facilitation Committee to review all IMO instruments in order to "identify any existing gaps, inconsistencies, duplications or overlaps in that legislation."[61] As pointed out by Rolf Einar Fife, the purpose of the review was to ensure that three basic humanitarian principles expressed by the law of the sea instruments would be met, namely:

1. Persons in distress at sea will be provided assistance regardless of nationality, status, or the circumstances in which they are found;
2. Vessels that recover persons in distress at sea will be allowed to deliver the rescuees to a place of safety; and
3. Rescuees, regardless of their nationality, status, or the circumstances in which they are found, including undocumented migrants, asylum seekers, refugees, and stowaways, will be treated on board in the manner prescribed by the relevant IMO instruments and in accordance with international law and human rights law as well as longstanding humanitarian maritime traditions.[62]

As a result of Resolution A.920 (22), the IMO Maritime and Safety Committee, during its 77th session in 2003, approved draft amendments to Chapter V of the SOLAS and the SAR Conventions. The purpose of these amendments was to clarify how state parties and seafarers would cooperate to assist any persons rescued at sea regardless of their status. The amendments were then formally adopted one year later with a view to enter into force on July 1, 2006. In the meantime, to ensure that persons in distress at sea are assisted and to safeguard the integrity of the SAR Convention, the MSC Committee adopted Guidelines on the Treatment of Persons Rescued at Sea,[63] which aimed to assist state parties and ships masters in fulfilling their legal and humanitarian obligations toward persons rescued at sea under the relevant international law instruments. The Guidelines confirm that the obligation of a master to render assistance should be complemented by the corresponding obligation of states parties to rescue. In other words, to coordinate and cooperate in assisting the master toward the prompt delivery of persons rescued at sea to a place of safety and thereby relieving the master of the responsibility to provide ongoing assistance to those rescuees.

In the 2006 Report on Oceans and Law of the Sea, the Secretary-General reported that the General Assembly urged

> states to take all necessary measures to ensure the effective implementation of the amendments to the International Convention on Maritime Search and Rescue (*S.A.R.*) and to the International Convention for the Safety of Life at Sea relating to the delivery of persons rescued at sea to a place of safety (*SOLAS*) upon their entry into force, as well as of the associated Guidelines on the Treatment of Persons Rescued at Sea.[64]

On July 1, 2006, the amendments to the SOLAS and SAR Conventions concerning the treatment of persons rescued at sea entered into force. The amendments to Chapter V—Safety of Navigation—of the SOLAS Convention provide a definition of search-and-rescue services. They further clarify the existing longstanding obligation to provide assistance, adding a wording similar to that of Rule 2(1)(10) of the Annex to the SAR Convention: "This obligation to provide assistance applies regardless of the nationality or status of such persons or the circumstances in which they are found." They also set down coordination and cooperation requirements between states to assist masters in delivering persons rescued at sea to a place of safety. This is the first time that such an obligation has been placed on states. The amendments also added a new regulation emphasizing a shipmaster's discretion when assessing the safety of life at sea: "the owner, the charterer, the company operating the ship . . . , or any other person shall not prevent or restrict the master of the ship from taking or executing any decision which, in the master's professional judgment, is necessary for safety of life at sea." Amendments to the Annex of the SAR Convention are even more explicit. They add one new paragraph in Chapter 2—Organization and Coordination, clarifying the definition of persons in distress; several new paragraphs in Chapter 3—Cooperation between States, relating to assistance to the master in delivering persons rescued at sea to a place of safety; and one new paragraph in Chapter 4—Operating Procedures, concerning rescue coordination centers initiating the process of identifying the most appropriate places for disembarking persons found in distress at sea.

Overall, the new and amended provisions make it clear that states parties are to resolve any international conflicts arising out of a search-and-rescue mission and are not the responsibility of the master and crew. Governments are responsible for coordinating their actions and cooperating so that rescuees are disembarked from the assisting ship and delivered to a place of safety.[65] In today's commercial environment, where ships' captains are relentlessly requested to improve efficiency and cut costs, it is critical that they continue to assist those in distress at sea without regard to their nationality or status.

Their sole duty is to render assistance to persons in danger at sea. Their primary responsibility remains the protection and safety of life at sea. The entry into force of these amendments constitutes a significant milestone in applying basic humanitarian standards at sea.

The Interaction Between the Law of the Sea and Human Rights—An Overview of International and European Jurisprudence

The International Tribunal for the Law of the Sea, as part of the international institutional framework, first considered the protection of human rights in the *SAIGA (no. 2)* judgment, when ruling that "considerations of humanity must apply in the law of the sea, as they do in other areas of international law."[66] This clearly indicates that, like any other areas of international law, the law of the sea is applicable when taking into consideration international human rights law principles. The previous judgment of the International Court of Justice in the *Corfu Channel* case had already reflected the relevance of elementary conditions and considerations of humanity as a general principle of international law and, therefore, as a source of law in its own rights.[67] Since then, the International Tribunal of the Sea has considered other cases relating, in particular, to prompt release[68] and the protection of the individual,[69] taking into account "elementary considerations of humanity and due process of law."[70]

As pointed out by Richard Barnes, certain human rights are considered to be intrinsic.[71] The recognition of their existence and application does not depend on the geographic location of a person, including the oceans and the seas. Accordingly, international human rights law affords fundamental standards in relation to those in distress and rescued at sea as well as imposing on all states the responsibility to ensure basic human rights to all persons within their jurisdiction. In this respect, "the safe and humane treatment of anyone rescued at sea regardless of their legal status or the circumstances in which they were rescued is of paramount importance and is acknowledged explicitly in many human rights instruments."[72] Hence, basic human rights standards, such as protecting the right to life, are self-evident. Freedom from cruel, inhuman, and degrading treatment, security and protection, access to due legal process, respect for the inherent dignity of aliens and for family unity[73] are also quite obvious, simply by virtue of one's status as a human being rather than as a citizen of a particular state.[74]

The European Convention of Human Rights[75] makes no direct references to the law of the sea or maritime law. Yet the European Court of Human Rights (ECtHR) and previously the Commission have on several occasions considered cases concerning both the law of the sea and maritime law. Two types of cases have been heard by the ECtHR. The first type involves cases relating to state jurisdiction in maritime zones with respect to the European Convention of Human Rights and, more specifically, interpreting article 1 of the Convention—in other words, how the Convention can be applied in a maritime context.[76]

State jurisdiction is an essential concept of the law of the sea.[77] It is generally used to define the competences, duties, and rights of a state in the various maritime zones projected from its land territory.[78] The LOS Convention differentiates between the jurisdiction of sovereign rights and sovereignty because jurisdiction is sometimes qualified as exclusive, such in the case of the EEZ. The ECtHR has, on the contrary, following the *Loizidou* case[79] and subsequently the *Bankovic* case,[80] largely interpreted the notion of territoriality and extraterritoriality contained in article 1[81]—more precisely states' jurisdiction with respect to the specificity and traditional principles of human rights in maritime zones. This has allowed the court to consider all sorts of circumstances in which the law of the sea provides a state party with territorial competences in maritime zones that may at times be quite far in terms of distance from the actual territorial landmass of the state. In this respect the court's position is aligned with the many decisions rendered by the Human Rights

Committee when it affirmed that human rights obligations cannot be avoided by extraterritorial exercises of jurisdiction.[82] The jurisprudence here specifically relates to the jurisdictional competence of state parties in ports or its territorial sea[83] or, alternatively, involves situations in which a state's liability is engaged under article 1.[84]

The second type of case concerns a procedural or a substantial violation of the applicant's human rights within the context of the law of the sea.[85] When it comes to rule on an applicant's claiming a specific violation of their human rights, the court has been exceedingly cautious. Relying on the rules of international law and the law of the sea in particular, it is inclined to simply adopt solutions that conform to the customary or codified rules of the law of the sea and, in some cases, of the 1958 Convention insofar as they are applicable. To date, there are no contradictions between the protections of human rights as defined in the Convention and norms of the law of the sea. In fact, the court appears to be quite reluctant to depart from international law rules and the law of the sea.[86] It has consistently interpreted the ECHR Convention in harmony with and taking into account the existing law of the sea. As noted by Paul Tavernier, the reason for this is that the Convention cannot operate in a vacuum and must be interpreted harmoniously with other existing bodies of international law,[87] a point expressed in article 311(2) of the LOS Convention.

With regard to the examination of the duty to assist and the duty to rescue, applicants have never directly raised the duties defined in article 98 of the LOS Convention. One decision only briefly and quite indirectly refers to the normative content of article 98 when citing a violation of article 2 of the ECHR Convention. In *Viron Xhavara and 15 others v. Italy and Albania*,[88] the court rejected the defendants' application that a naval blockade imposed by Italy and Albania in the Albanian territorial waters and the international waters to prevent illegal immigration violated article 2, thus endangering the right to life and physical integrity of the

illegal immigrants. The case hit the headlines in March 1998, after an Italian naval corvette collided with and sank an Albanian boat transporting illegal immigrants while attempting to stop the Albanian vessel thirty-five nautical miles off the Italian coast in international waters. This resulted in the loss of eighty-six people. In rejecting the application, the court ruled that the applicants were under the Italian territorial jurisdiction as stipulated by article 1 of the Convention,[89] and although it felt that the applicants were unable to prove that the sinking was intentional, it reminded the parties of the extensive application it provides to article 2: States have a negative obligation to abstain from provoking the voluntary death of a person but equally have a positive duty to take all necessary and precautionary measures to protect the life of a person under its jurisdiction—a point that is reminiscent of the content of article 98.

Conclusion

Although many believe that the law of the sea and human rights law have developed in isolation from one another, it is clear that in some instances, they not only interact but have also produced an interesting dynamic forged by events, reactive to different political policies and legal needs.[90] And this, as recently pointed out by Tullio Treves, does not constitute "a fragmentation of international law, [it represents more a] recognition of the complexity of the law."[91]

This chapter has highlighted the relative success of the normative framework of the law of the sea and maritime law in establishing a comprehensive regime protecting the life and rights of those traveling the seas, notwithstanding ambiguities introduced by the interpretation and practices of coastal states with respect to disembarkation, the rights of innocent passage, and access to ports. If these ambiguities are to be resolved, coastal states must change their attitude to reflect a more genuine balance between security interests and the need to assist ships masters who have gone out of their way to fulfill their humanitarian obligation to assist and rescue persons in distress at sea.

The IMO framework is probably by far the best implementation of the duty to render assistance with respect to the humane treatment of persons in distress at sea and the respect of their human rights.[92] Its action driven by the IMO following the *Tampa* crisis has shown that a prompt and comprehensive multi-agencies approach provides a pragmatic example of how existing international instruments can be used to address the challenges of human rights with respect to persons rescued at sea. In particular, it highlighted the need for a more proactive multidimensional approach underpinned by a human rights framework and the important role that sanctions for a breach of regulation play. Success appears to come from embracing the longstanding underlying humanity principles and formulating frameworks that embrace principles of humanity rather than narrow international legal prescriptions. It brought to the forefront the importance of maintaining the basic humanitarian principles provided for in the law of the sea instruments while still respecting the rights and dignity of the persons rescued at sea regardless of their status.

As suggested by Oxman, like universal jurisdiction, a universal duty to rescue is a practical response to protecting the right to life. As it stands, this duty is duly confirmed in many law-of-the-sea instruments, which, without exception, all stress that it applies to "any person" found at sea in danger of being lost. Thus, as suggested by Oxman, if one were to take a Hohfeldian approach, one might conclude that international law establishes or at least implies a right to be rescued at sea. In terms of legal principles, this means that human rights law has an essential role to play in the law of the sea in order to sustain the applicability of the duty to assist and reinforce the duty to rescue by stressing that the protection of life be respected regardless of the status of the rescuees. This also means that the duty to assist persons in danger, to which shipmasters and states are bound to under the law of the sea, should be viewed as the ultimate, universal criteria—protecting another's person's right to life at sea. It should not be impeded by any other duties or rights arising out of other international instruments, and its scope should be broadened as suggested by the IMO to include the right to disembark to the nearest port or place of refuge, as this would allow for a better application of the human rights of those found in distress at sea.

Hence, when it comes to the law of the sea to protect or at least recognize human rights, we need to focus on the humanitarian elements that customary law already affords and then assess whether or not they meet the requirements of basic principles of human rights law—and how can we ensure that these humanitarian elements continue to be upheld and further strengthened within a human rights framework. In this context, there is no doubt that the law of the sea, and in particular the duty to assist and to rescue, provides an added value to protecting human rights for those at sea. And last but not least, we must remember that central to the concept of the duty to rescue is an ideal of maritime ethics based on the respect for human life and its dignity.

NOTES

1. Bernard H. Oxman, *Human Rights and the United Nations Convention on the Law of the Sea*, in POLITICS, VALUES AND FUNCTIONS, INTERNATIONAL LAW IN THE 21ST CENTURY, ESSAYS IN HONOR OF PROFESSOR LOUIS HENKIN 377 (Jonathan I. Charney, Donald K. Anton, & Mary Ellen O'Connell eds., 1997).

2. *Id.*

3. In that respect, *see* TONY KEVIN, A CERTAIN MARITIME INCIDENT: THE SINKING OF SIEV X (2004).

4. Convention Relating to the Status of Refugees, 189 U.N.T.S. 137 (Jul. 28, 1951).

5. Oxman, *supra* note 1, at 377.

6. Bernard Oxman, *Human Rights and the United Nations Convention on the Law of the Sea*, 36 COL JTL 399, 414 (1997); Craig H. Allen, *The Maritime Law Forum: Australia's Tampa Incident: The Convergence of International and Domestic Refugee and Maritime Law in the Pacific Rim: The Tampa Incident: IMO Perspectives and Responses on the Treatment of Persons Rescued at Sea*, 12 PAC. RIM L. & POL'Y J. 143, 148 (2003).

7. ROBIN CHURCHILL & VAUGHAN LOWE, THE LAW OF THE SEA 7–12 (3d ed. 1999).

8. Nicollette Jones, The Plimsoll Sensation: The Great Campaign to Save Lives at Sea (2006).

9. *Scaramanga v. Stamp*, [1880] 5 C.P.D. 295, 304.

10. Brussels Convention on Salvage, 1913, U.K.T.S. 4, Cd 6677; for a detailed history of the Brussels Convention on Salvage, which then became the 1989 International Convention on Salvage, *see* Allen, *supra* note 6, 148.

11. This includes ship owners, commercial insurers, national and international maritime organizations, and maritime unions.

12. (United Nations) Law of the Sea Convention, Dec. 10, 1982, 21 I.L.M. 1261 [hereinafter LOS Convention].

13. International Convention for the Safety of Life at Sea, Nov. 1, 1974, 1980 U.K.T.S. 46 [hereinafter SOLAS Convention].

14. International Convention on Maritime Search and Rescue, Nov. 1, 1979, 1986 U.K.T.S. 59 271 [hereinafter SAR Convention].

15. International Convention on Salvage, Apr. 28, 1989, 1996 U.K.T.S. 93 [hereinafter SALVAGE Convention].

16. 3 Myron H. Nordquist, The United Nations Convention on the Law of the Sea 1982: A Commentary 171 (1995).

17. Tullio Treves, *Human Rights and the Law of the Sea*, 28 Berkeley J. Int'l L. 1, 3 (2010).

18. *See id.*; *see also* Geneviève Bastid-Burdeau, *Migrations clandestines et droit de la mer*, in La Mer et Son Droit: Melanges Offerts a Laurent Lucchini et Jean-Pierre Queneudec 57–66 (Daniel-Heywood Anderson, Vincent P. Bantz, Geneviève Bastid-Burdeau, Mohammed Bedjaoui, & Josette Beer-Gabel eds., 2003); and *especially*, Paul Tavernier, *La Cour européenne des droits de l'homme et la mer*, in *id.* at 575–89.

19. The law of piracy is perhaps the best example of extending the rule of law at sea as it seeks to create universal jurisdiction—in particular in the high seas—to respond to acts of violence, such as piracy and terrorism for example, while respecting freedom of navigation.

20. Oxman, *supra* note 1.

21. *Id.* at 380.

22. *Id.* at 381–82.

23. *Id.* at 382.

24. The duty to provide assistance at sea is also required during wartime. *See* article 18 of the Geneva Convention for the Amelioration of the Condition of Wounded, Sick and Shipwrecked Members of Armed Forces at Sea, Aug. 12, 1949, 6 U.S.T. 3217.

25. In citing article 98 of the LSO Convention, Oxman insisted that "any persons" does not exclude any category of persons. *See* Oxman, *supra* note 6, at 414–15.

26. *See* IMO Circular decision C 54/17(d) (1985); Report of the UNCHR to the General Assembly, U.N. GAOR, 40th sess., Supp. No. 12, U.N. doc. A/40/12 (1985), as cited by Rolf Einar Fife, *The Duty to Render Assistance at Sea: Some Reflections After Tampa*, in Nordic Cosmopolitanism: Essays in International Law for Martti Koskenniemi 475 (Jarna Petman & Jan Klabbers eds., 2003).

27. Delivery to a place of safety or refuge involves further rights such as the rights of innocent passage and access to port. *See infra* pp. 380–83.

28. Fife, *supra* note 26, at 469–70.

29. Stuart Kaye, *Tampering with Border Protection: The Legal and Policy Implications of the Voyage of the MV Tampa*, in Protecting Australia's Maritime Borders: The MV Tampa and Beyond 68–72 (Martin Tsamenyi & Chris Rahman eds., 2002).

30. Frederick J. Kenney & Vasilios Tasikas, *The Tampa Incident: IMO Perspectives and Responses on the Treatment of Persons Rescued at Sea*, 12 Pac. Rim L. & Pol'y J. 143 (2003).

31. *Id.*; *see also* Martin Davies, *Obligations and Implications for Ships Encountering Persons in Need of Assistance at Sea*, 12 Pac. Rim L. & Pol'y J. 109 (2003); and Allen *supra* note 6.

32. Allen, *supra* note 6, at 61.

33. In the past it was often feared that fake distress calls could be used by pirates. Today, distress is linked to the concept of place of refuge and innocent passage. *See also* Donald Rothwell, *The Law of the Sea and the MV Tampa Incident: Reconciling Maritime Principles with Coastal State Sovereignty*, 13 Pub. L. Rev. 2 123 (2002); Michael Pugh, *Drowning Not Waving: Boat People and Humanitarianism at Sea*, 17 J. Refugees Stud. 1, 59 (2004).

34. *See also* SAR Convention, ch. 2, para. 2.1.10; Martin A. Harry, *Failure to Render Aid (USS Dubuque and Vietnamese Refugees in June 1988)*, 166 Proceedings 2, 65–68 (1990); Pugh, *supra* note 33, at 58; Kaye, *supra* note 29, at 68. Norway has given effect to this obligation in its Maritime Code 1994, ss 135, 164; Penal Code 1902, s 314; and Penal Code, ss 12, 387.

35. The Australian provision contained in the *Navigation Act 1912 (Cth)*, s 317A is not an absolute obligation as it is not fully translated into domestic law, *see* Davies, *supra* note 31, at 128–33.

36. *See* Mary Coombs, *Jurisdiction—Constitutionality of the U.S. State's Jurisdiction over Criminal Acts Occurring on the High Seas—Consistency of Such Jurisdiction with International Law—Effects Doctrine*, 95 AJIL 2, 438, 442 (2001).

37. Oxman, *supra* note 1, at 391; Richard Barnes, *Refugee Law at Sea*, 53 ICLQ 1, 52 (2004).

38. Para. 2.1.1. In 1998 amendments to SAR provided definitions for the terms "search" and "rescue," which in turn clarified the responsibilities of coastal states.

39. SAR., para 1.3.2. The *International Aeronautical and Maritime Search and Rescue Manual* also requires that "survivors must be delivered to a place of safety as quickly as possible." *See* vol. II, s 2.

40. Since the *Tampa*, the concepts of disembarkation and a place of refuge or safety have been explicitly linked. *See* Kenney and Tasikas, *supra* note 30. The matter has now been clarified by the IMO's amendments to the SAR and SOLAS Conventions. *See* chapter 5.

41. Rothwell, *supra* note 33, at 120.

42. Vattel recognized that humanitarian considerations were to be extended to ships that entered territorial seas as a result of weather or necessity. *See* EMMERICH DE VATTEL, THE LAW OF NATIONS, bk. 2, ch. 7, sec. 94, 170 (Joseph Chitty trans., 1869).

43. Ortolan highlighted the extent of that principle in the case of the *Elisabeth*, an English war ship that reached Havana as a port of refuge after a hurricane in the Gulf of Mexico in 1746. Ortolan stressed the fact that imminent and irresistible danger forced the ship to seek asylum in an enemy port. *See* 4d, 2 THEODORE ORTOLAN, REGLES INTERNATIONALES ET DIPLOMATIE DE LA MER 322–23 (1864).

44. Article III(e), International Convention Relating to Intervention on the High Seas in Cases of Oil Pollution Casualties, Nov. 29, 1975, U.K.T.S. 77.

45. JOHN. C. COLOMBOS, THE INTERNATIONAL LAW OF THE SEA 160, para. 181 (1962); I, Peace Parts 2–4 ROBERT JENNINGS & ARTHUR WATTS, OPPENHEIM'S INTERNATIONAL LAW 624, para. 204 (9th ed. 1996); PAUL REUTER, DROIT INTERNATIONAL PUBLIC 265 (1973). For further analyses, *see* 2 DANIEL P. O'CONNELL, THE INTERNATIONAL LAW OF THE SEA 853–58 (1984); IAN BROWNLIE, PRINCIPLES OF PUBLIC INTERNATIONAL LAW 315 (2003); RICHARD K. GARDINER, INTERNATIONAL LAW 408 (2003); TIMOTHY HILLIER, PRINCIPLES OF PUBLIC INTERNATIONAL LAW (1999). Vattel had already pointed out that a state had the right to refuse foreigners access to the territory of the state: "pourvu que l'on ne refusât point les secours de l'humanité à ceux que la tempête ou quelque nécessité contraignait de se présenter à la frontière." *See* 1 EMMERICH DE VATTEL, LE DROIT DES GENS 381 (1835).

46. Aldo Chircop, *Ships in Distress, Environmental Threats to Coastal States, and Places of Refuge: New Directions for an Ancient Regime?* 33 OCEAN DEV. & INT'L L. 2, 215 (2002).

47. *ACT Shipping (OTE) Ltd v. Minister for Marine, Ireland and the Attorney General (M/V Toledo)*, [1995] 2.I.L.R.M. 30.

48. *Id.* at 48–49.

49. For commentary, *see* O'Connell, *supra* note 45, at 857.

50. *Concerning Military and Paramilitary Activities in and Against Nicaragua (Nicaragua v. U.S.)* [1986] ICJ 14 [1986].

51. Rothwell, *supra* note 33, at 124.

52. ICJ Reports 4 [1949] (Merits).

53. Convention on the Territorial Sea and Contiguous Zone, Apr. 29, 1958, 516 U.N.T.S. 205.

54. Articles 18(2) (as well as article 39(1)(c) of the LOS Convention on innocent passage in the territorial seas) reflect implicitly the duty to render assistance. Cavaré made the following commentary on the corresponding article 14(3) of the Convention on the Territorial Sea and Contiguous Zone, *supra* note 53: "C'est un incident technique qui le motive (réparation à une machine), ou bien c'est une raison d'humanité qui le rend licite." *See* 2 LOUIS CAVARÉ, LE DROIT INTERNATIONAL PUBLIC POSITIF 757 (1969).

55. The IMO received copies of the *notes verbales* and circulated them to all IMO members.

56. IMO Circular Letter No. 2345, 2 (Oct. 15, 2001), containing the *notes verbales* between the Embassy of Australia, Copenhagen, Denmark, and the Royal Ministry of Foreign Affairs of the kingdom of Norway, Oslo.

57. IMO Circular Letter No. 2363 2 (Feb. 1, 2002), containing the *notes verbales* dated Sept. 1, 2001 and Jan. 29, 2002 from the Royal Ministry of Foreign Affairs of the kingdom of Norway to the Embassy of Australia, Oslo, Norway.

58. The UN Division for Ocean Affairs and the Law of the Sea has since included the issue of the rescue of persons at sea in the schedules of its annual report. *See, e.g,* Report of the Secretary-General, Oceans and the Law of the Sea, paras. 43–45, A/56/58 (March 9, 2001). The UNHCR High Commissioner also participated in discussions at the seventy-fifth and seventy-sixth MSC sessions, which focused on the meaning of the phrase "delivery to a place of safety." *See* Report of the Secretary General Oceans and Law of the Sea, para. 94, A/58/65 (3 Mar. 2003).

59. Opening address to the Twenty-Second Regular Session of the Assembly, Speech given by Mr. W. A. O'Neil, Secretary-General of IMO Headquarters, London (Nov. 19, 2001).

60. At its meeting on December 12, 2002, the General Assembly passed Resolution A57/141, Oceans and Law of the Sea, which acknowledged the IMO initiatives with regard to the treatment of persons rescued at sea. *See* para. 34, A/RES/57/141 (Feb. 21, 2003).

61. Review of safety measures and procedures for the treatment of persons rescued at sea, 22nd session, Agenda Item 8, IMO Assembly resolution A.920(22) (Nov. 2001).

62. Fife, *supra* note 26, at 477.

63. IMO Related Guidelines on the Treatment of Persons Rescued at Sea, also adopted in May 2004.

64. Report of the Secretary General Oceans and Law of the Sea. A/61/63 (Mar. 9, 2006).

65. *Report of the Secretary General Oceans and Law of the Sea*, para. 314, A/59/62/Add.1 (Aug. 18, 2004).

66. *The M/V 'SAIGA' (No. 2) Case (Saint Vincent and the Grenadines* v. *Guinea)* [1999], para. 155; *See also* Tavernier, *supra* note 19, at 575–83; Philippe Chrestia, *Chronique de jurisprudence international*, 104 RGDIP 2, 514–522 (2000).

67. *See Corfu Channel Case (United Kingdom v Albania)*, ICJ Reports 4 [1949], para. 22. Here the court stated that general and well-recognized principles include "elementary considerations of humanity, even more exacting in peace than in war." *See* Fife, *supra* note 26, at 484.

68. *See Camouco (Panama v. France)*, ITLOS Reports 2000, 10, 125 I.L.R. 164 (INT'L TRIB. L. SEA 2000), and *Monte Confurco (Seychelles v. France)*, ITLOS Reports 2000, 86, 125 I.L.R. 220 (INT'L TRIB. L. SEA 2000).

69. *Juno Trader (Saint Vincent and the Grenadines v. Guinea Bissau)*, ITLOS, Reports 2004, 17, 128 I.L.R. 267 (INT'L TRIB. L. SEA 2004), and *Hoshinmaru (Japan v. Russian Federation)*, Order of Jul. 9, 2007, ITLOS Reports 2005–2007, 18, para. 12 (INT'L TRIB. L. SEA 2007).

70. *Juno Trader, id.* at para. 77.

71. Barnes, *supra* note 37, at 61. The human rights involved are defined in article 14 of the Universal Declaration of Human Rights, Dec. 10, 1948, General Assembly Resolution 217A (III) GAOR, 3rd Sess., part I, Res., 71, which guarantees the right to seek and enjoy asylum [hereinafter UDHR]. There are also several articles of the International Covenant on Civil and Political Rights, Dec. 19, 1966, 999 U.N.T.S. 171, which respectively guarantee the right not to be deprived of one's liberty albeit certain conditions (article 9); the right to nondiscrimination (article 2(1)); the right to life (article 6); the basic requirement to respect the inherent dignity of the human person (article 7), and the right to an effective remedy (articles 2(3), 10(1)) [hereinafter ICCPR]. The Convention against Torture and Other Cruel, Inhuman or Degrading Treatment or Punishment, Dec. 10, 1984, 213 U.N.T.S. 221; the International Covenant on Economic and Social Rights, Dec. 16, 1966, 993 U.N.T.S. 14531 [hereinafter ICESCR]; the Convention on the Rights of the Child, Nov. 20, 1989, 1577 U.N.T.S. 27531 [hereinafter ICERD]; the International Convention on the Protection of the Rights of All Migrant Workers and Members of Their Families, Dec. 18. 1990, 2220 U.N.T.S. 39481; The UN Convention against Transnational Organised Crime, adopted Nov. 15, 2000, G. Res. 55/25; the Recommended Principles on Human Rights and Human Trafficking, May 20, 2002 E/2002/68/Add.1; the Protocol Against the Smuggling of Migrants by Land, Sea and Air, supplementing the UN Convention Against Transnational Organized Crime, adopted Nov. 15, 2000, G.A. Res. 55/25; the Protocol to Prevent, Suppress and Punish Trafficking in Persons especially Women and Children, supplementing the UN Convention against Transnational Organized Crime, adopted Nov. 15, 2000, G.A. Res. 55/25; and finally Human Rights Committee, General Comment, Mar. 29, 2004, 31 CCPR.C.21.Rev.1.Add.13, also comes into play when dealing with the human rights of seaborne refugees.

72. *See* UNCHR, Background Note on the Protection of Asylum-Seekers and Refugees Rescued at Sea, para. 32 (2002). The intrinsic rights involved here are defined in article 1 of the UDHR; the preambles of the ICCPR, the ICESCR, and the International Convention on the Elimination of All Forms of Racial Discrimination, Dec. 21, 1965, 60 U.N.T.S. 195. Note also that the Human Rights Committee has on numerous instances reiterated that human rights obligations cannot be avoided by extraterritorial exercises of jurisdiction. *See* MANFRED NOWAK, UN COVENANT ON CIVIL AND POLITICAL RIGHTS: CCPR COMMENTARY OF JURISDICTION 41–43 (1993), as cited in Barnes, *supra* note 37, at 61.

73. *See* David Fisher, Susan Martin, & Andrew Schoenholtz, *Migration and Security in International Law*, in MIGRATION AND INTERNATIONAL LEGAL NORMS 87–122, 185 (Thomas A. Aleinikoff & Vincent Chetail eds., 2003).

74. *See* General Comment 15, para. 7 (1986).

75. European Convention for the Protection of Human Rights and Fundamental Freedoms, Nov. 4, 1950, E.T.S. 5 [hereinafter ECHR Convention].

76. *See Gunnar and Annika Bendréus v. Sweden*, ECHR, Application No. 31653 /96; *Lennart Berglund and 92 others v. Sweden,* Application 34825/97 (Apr. 16, 1998). *See* also the recent chapter of Irini Papanicolopulu, I. *La nozione di giurisdizione ai sensi dell'art. 1 della Convenzione europea dei diritti umani nella recente giurisprudenza della Corte Europea dei Diritti Umani*, in DIRITTI UMANI DI FRONTE AL GIUDICE INTERNATIONALE 83–130, 120–24 (Tullio Scovazzi, Irini Papanicolopulu, & Sabrina Urbinati eds., 2009).

77. Tavernier, *supra* note 18.

78. The LOS Convention contains several provisions pertaining to the concept of jurisdiction: articles 27, 34, 55, and 60 (jurisdiction of a coastal State), articles 92 and 94 (jurisdiction of pavilion), article 194 (2) specifically refers to jurisdiction and pollution prevention measures, and so forth.

79. *Loizidou v. Turkey*, 23 EHRR 513 [1997].

80. *Bankovic and Others v. Belgium and 16 Other Contracting States*, Application No. 52207/99 (Dec. 12, 2001).

81. For reasons of space, the debates concerning the interpretation of territorial jurisdiction by the court,

which has sparked various controversial opinions among legal practitioners and academics, cannot be discussed here. *See, e.g.,* Gérard Cohen-Jonathan, *La territorialisation de la jurisdiction de la Cour européenne des droits de l'homme, observation sous la décision Bankovic et autres,* 52 RTDH 1069–82 (2002); and Scovazzi, Papanicolopulu, & Urbinati, *supra* note 76.

82. *See* Nowak, *supra* note 72, at 41–43. It is worth noting here that the ECHR also follows previous decisions it has rendered with respect to states' responsibility for the treatment of persons within their jurisdiction. As an example, *see Soering v. United Kingdom* 98 I.L.R., para. 88.

83. *Consorts D. v. France,* Aug. 31, 1994, ECtHR; *Antonsen v. Norway,* Jan. 15, 1997, ECHR. As such, these cases do not cause difficulty of interpretation because they concern zones where states already exercise sovereignty, so all the court had to do was to combine the rules of the Convention with those of the law of the sea.

84. *Gunnar and Annika Bendréus v. Sweden,* Sept. 8, 1997, ECHR; *Leray and Others v. France,* Application No. 44617/98 (2001) ECHR 880 (Dec. 20, 2001); *Angelos Rigopoulos v. Spain,* Application No. 37388/97, ECHR16

(Apr. 1998 and Jan. 12, 1999); *L.H.T.C. and G.C. v. France,* Application No. 15454/89, ECHR (Mar. 29, 1993). These types of cases often concern shipwrecks close to the high seas, boarding of ships in the high seas to arrest members of the crew, jurisdictional competences of a state in the EEZ, or the continental shelf.

85. These types of cases concern, for the most part, a violation of article 6 ECHR (Right to fair trial). *See Leray and Others;* art. 5 (Right to liberty and security of person). *See Rigopoulos, supra* note 84; and article 2 (Right to life). *See Xhavara and Others v. Italy and Albania,* Application No. 39473/98, ECHR (Jan. 11, 2001).

86. Tavernier, *supra* note 18, at 583.

87. *Id.*

88. *Xhavara, supra* note 85.

89. *Id.* at para. 1.

90. *See* Michael White, *M/V Tampa Incident: Shipping, International and Maritime Legal Issues,* 78 ALJ 101, 101–13 (2004).

91. Treves, *supra* note 17, at 12.

92. Ximena Hinrichs, *Measures Against Smuggling of Migrants at Sea: A Law of the Sea Perspective,* 36 Revue Belge de Droit Int'l 2, 448 (2003).

PART SEVEN

FORCE QUA TERRORISM

19

Moral Knowledge's Potential for Reducing the Restraint of Law

The Risk of Moral Education

CATHERINE LOTRIONTE

What Followed 9/11

After the terrorist attacks against the United States on 9/11, the U.S. government developed new operational and legal plans to fight the terrorists who attacked the country. In order to effectively counter an enemy who choses not to follow the laws of war, some in the U.S. government argued that the United States needed new and innovative methods for fighting the enemy. The operational plans that were authorized went beyond any prior authorities of the U.S. military and intelligence organizations. According to press reports, the Secretary of Defense authorized the use of enhanced interrogation techniques, such as prolonged stress positions with "hands chained to the ceiling and their feet shackled," sensory and sleep deprivation, hooding, exposure to cold and heat, removal of clothing, the exploitation of prisoners' individual phobias, and the withholding of pain killers for Abu Zubaydah, a high-level al Qaeda member who was shot several times during his capture.[1] As reports of prisoner abuse surfaced, many wondered whether the new authorities went too far. In fighting an enemy who chose abhorrent tactics and killed innocent people, did the United States itself cross the line by engaging in equally abhorrent, unethical, and immoral behavior? And if so, were the U.S. actions justified?

As the armed conflict against al Qaeda continued and the United States captured and detained al Qaeda members and other terrorists, a debate sparked in the United States and across the globe about whether torture could be used during the interrogations of terrorists. The Convention Against Torture and Other Cruel, Inhumane, or Degrading Treatment or Punishment, which the United States ratified in 1994, prohibits the torture of any person for any reason by any government at any time. The treaty states explicitly that torture is never justified— "no exceptional circumstances whatsoever . . . may be invoked as a justification for torture."[2] The Convention applies to everyone including terrorists and enemy combatants. This international legal ban on torture, a ban incorporated into U.S. law, is absolute. Before 9/11 few Americans would have argued that it should be any other way. After September 11, 2001, however, the Bush administration put aside certain international laws and developed policy plans for interrorgating al Qaeda members. Many Americans came to believe that "extreme circumstances," often called the "ticking time bomb scenario" dictated that the United States start to rethink its prohibition against using torture.

By 2004 evidence of U.S. interrogation techniques began to surface from as far away and distant places as Guantanamo Bay, Cuba; Bagram, Afghanistan; and Baghdad, Iraq. The revelations of these interrogation methods ignited an international debate about whether torture could ever be justified morally. The ongoing debate raised questions about what, if any, ethical rules or limitations exist that bind states in their actions against terrorists during conflict. Do these ethical standards of conduct apply in conflicts against terrorists? Are these standards different from those that are applicable during traditional armed conflicts between states? Most pointedly, although in general there may exist a prohibition against torturing combatants, is there an exception to that legal prohibition for certain individuals like al Qaeda members? In other words, can one be morally justified in torturing an al Qaeda member? When can a moral principle trump a legal obligation? Academics, journalists, human rights advocates, religious leaders, and average citizens alike have struggled with these questions.

As the international condemnation of the U.S. interrogations methods grew and the debate among many in the United States continued, government officials took steps to control the negative backlash and review the decisions behind interrogation policies. While the investigations proceeded, some sought justifications for the specific policies. The analysis about possible justifications for the harsh treatment of terrorists centered largely on a discussion of moral principles. Some involved in these deliberations called for educating the American people and those in battle fighting the terrorists on the ethical and moral justifications for the use of torture. Throughout these discussions, however, government attorneys within the Office of Legal Counsel at the Department of Justice largely ignored the legal obligations related to torture. When some within the government and the public, once the goverment legal memos were made public, raised legal principles, they were

typically addressed in one of two ways: first, how the specific interrogation techniques fell outside the strict legal definition of torture as codified in international treaties and U.S. law or, second, how moral principles can trump legal obligations. Some argued that under certain circumstances the act of torturing another human could be morally justified irrespective of what the law states. But this leads us to ask: What are the relevant moral principles? And what are the factual circumstances that could justify torture in accordance with these principles? Signficantly, the focus on the ethical and moral justifications for torture diverted attention away from the central issue of the nation's international and domestic legal obligations with regard to the treatment of prisoners. Furthermore, this focus led the U.S. government to develop a framework for analyzing the question of torture based on subjective understandings of what is "right" or "wrong" behavior related to torture, thereby raising questions about the role of the law and potentially minimizing the force of law.

This chapter focuses on the way academics, ethicists, activists, military and intelligence practitioners, and even the public has chosen to use moral principles to discuss the justification for torture. Not long ago I was asked to write a review for a new book on the ethics of intelligence and military operations. My background in the intelligence field and my academic work in the areas of international law and intelligence activities seemed to fit the topic of the book. The book, *Partly Cloudy: Ethics in War, Espionage, Covert Action, and Interrogation* by David Perry, focuses on the many ethical challenges involved in military and intelligence activities. It covers a broad range of specific topics from just war analysis of Shakespeare's *Henry V* to employing enemies to penetrate hostile regimes, covert political influence, coups, and targeted killings as well as anticipating and preventing atrocities in war. In this chapter I discuss the efficacy of Perry's analysis of the moral question of torturing prisoners and explore the analysis of torture based on concepts such as absolute duties versus prima facie obligations. Furthermore, I discuss the role of international law in prohibiting torture and argue that this prohibition ought to be followed by the United States under all circumstances. Although I defend an absolute prohibition on torture as required by law, I also recognize that the ticking-time-bomb scenario ought not be ignored or treated as a mere hypothetical. This scenario, however, should also not be the centerpiece for invoking moral justifications for violating the law or sanctioning torture. Rather, I suggest that the law needs to be followed and that prior moral justifications for torture serve only to delegitimize one's actions and create greater confusion among those responsible for fighting terrorists. Pointedly, I dissent from Perry's view that it is useful to educate soldiers and spies on moral knowledge in the classroom so that they can make critical decisions in battle, weighing the different moral principles at stake in their actions to determine which moral principles carry more weight given the circumstances. Rather, I argue that we must train and educate our military and intelligence officers on legal obligations in order to cultivate "legal wisdom" to better serve them and this country. Finally, I offer some practical, ethical, and legal reasons why torture should not ever be accepted as an appropriate policy tool to use in war or peace.

In his book *Partly Cloudy*, David Perry writes about ethics as "moral philosophy," that is, the "discipline of critical analysis of the meaning and justification of moral beliefs and arguments."[3] In his book, the author sought to teach moral philosophy to U.S. military and intelligence officers so that they can make good decisions in the field. For Perry, the good decisions would be the ones that are morally justified and, therefore, "right." He argued that teaching soldiers and spies moral philosophy will provide them with wisdom to judge in battle which moral views are the best given the circumstances and will guide their behavior in choosing the right actions.

The case Perry used in his analysis is the situation of an interrogator who must decide whether to torture a captive prisoner in order to get information from him that could save innocent lives. In this scenario the interrogator must balance the harm to the prisoner who will be tortured against the harm to innocent civilians who may die if the prisoner does not reveal the information he knows that could save those lives. Perry argued that "moral knowledge" will provide the interrogator with wisdom about the right balance between the potential harms. This chapter explores how the act of making moral judgments about torture is complicated, subjective, and lacks a clear and precise answer. In identifying the troubling aspects of Perry's analysis, this chapter concludes that asking soldiers to engage in this exercise while in battle under the most challenging of circumstances is to open the potential for extremely dangerous consequences for the interrogators and the American public in particular and this country's legitimacy more generally.

One could argue that on 9/11 the United States found itself in a state of "supreme emergency." Al Qaeda had been responsible for numerous attacks against U.S. soldiers as well as citizens abroad and at home for decades, and on 9/11 they had executed the most devastating attack against the homeland. In an essay entitled "Emergency Ethics," the well-known just war scholar Michael Walzer acknowledged that "supreme emergencies put morality itself at risk." According to Walzer, "'Supreme emergency' describes those rare moments when the negative value that we assign—that we can't help assigning—to the disaster that looms before us devalues morality itself and leaves us free to do whatever is militarily necessary to avoid the disaster, so long as what we do does not produce an even worse disaster."[4] For Walzer, then, it is the threat to "our deepest values and collective survival" that triggers a supreme emergency. For U.S. policy makers and most Americans living in the United States at the time, al Qaeda's attacks on 9/11 were devastating, evoking fear that more attacks were coming and the very survival of our nation was at risk. If one accepts the circumstances of 9/11 as a "supreme emergency," then, according to Walzer, the principle of military necessity would justify any U.S. action to stop the al Qaeda threat, "so long as what we do does not produce an even worse disaster."[5]

One of the main questions raised by the United States' treatment of al Qaeda detainees centered on whether "military necessity" justified the abhorrent treatment of prisoners and, therefore, trumped the international legal principle of humane treatment. According to international legal scholar Hugo Grotius, those who have captured prisoners in combat are obligated to treat those prisoners in a humane manner. The prisoner's position creates a fiduciary duty on the captors to ensure that the individual is treated humanely. But do these same conditions apply during a time of extreme military necessity? Could one compare Walzer's "supreme emergency" to the conflict that the United States is fighting against al Qaeda and justify the torture of al Qaeda? In fact, it is precisely this perceived notion of military necessity in the war against al Qaeda that has driven the discussion of the need to torture individuals in U.S. custody when fighting terrorists.

The basis of this argument lies at the heart of the often-proffered example of the "ticking time bomb," in which a captured terrorist knows information about the location of a bomb that is to explode shortly, killing millions of innocent people. The premise is that the prisoner can be made to reveal this information only through torture. Noted scholars, such as Alan Dershowitz of Harvard Law School, have used this example to advocate for a newly constituted judicial process for issuing warrants by federal judges sanctioning the torture of particular prisoners depending on the specifics of the circumstances (i.e., circumstances of a "ticking time bomb"). In his book, *Why Terrorism Works*, Dershowitz argued that under the ticking-time-bomb circumstances it would be permissible to torture if one first obtains a judicial or executive warrant. For Dershowitz, a warrant would dissolve the prohibition against torture. Putting aside the issue of a judicial warrant for torture, the premise of the ticking-time-bomb scenario is

that the interrogator would balance the harms that are at issue—the harm to the prisoner who will be tortured and the harm to the civilian victims if the bomb kills them—to determine the right balance between the potential harms involved. The decisions about the military-necessity justification for torture, therefore, involves assessing the moral justifications involved in balancing harms and taking specific actions.

International Law's Prohibition Against Torture

Interrogating prisoners and killing enemy combatants is nothing new to military organizations and intelligence agencies. For centuries, states have engaged in armed conflict and have operated according to the laws and customs of war as defined by international law. The prohibition against torture is deeply rooted in customary international law, international agreements, and U.S. domestic law. Of the first order of importance, however, is the fact that the prohibition against the ill treatment of persons under interrogation is rooted in the respect for human dignity and the inviolability of the human body and mind. According to the International Red Cross, "Certain human rights are never derogable. Among them are the right to life, prohibition of torture or cruel, inhumane or degrading treatment."[6] This prohibition against torture is considered a *jus cogens* under international law.

In 1998, in the *Furundžija* case, the International Criminal Tribunal for the Former Yugoslovia held that the laws of armed conflict prohibiting torture constituted a preemptory norm of customary international law, *jus cogens*. Few international rules obtain preeminent status of *jus cogens* under international law, that is, preemptory norms—rules that are recognized by the international community permitting no derogation. The prohibition on torture is *jus cogens* and, therefore, no other international norm can trump that prohibition for any reason under any circumstances, including the norm of self-defense. Even if states were to agree in a treaty that torture is allowed under certain circumstances, the fact that the prohibition on torture is a *jus cogens* norm means that the treaty would be void. When a given norm of international law has the status of *jus cogens*, modifying it through treaty or custom is difficult to accomplish. Furthermore, anyone who violates a *jus cogen* can be held criminally responsible by any state in any court.

In fighting conflict, including against terrorists, international law imposes substantive legal restraints on the conduct of the hostilities. The specific restrictions of *jus ad bellum* regulate when a state may resort to international armed force. The restraints of *jus in bello* restrict the means by which the hostilities are conducted and provide certain basic humanitarian protections to those who are involved in the conflict, innocent civilians, and combatants. Therefore, both the right to conduct war and the means by which it is conducted are subject to important substantive restraints. With respect to the treatment of terrorists who are prisoners during a conflict, the *jus in bellow* restraints are relevant. Article 3 common to the Geneva Conventions embodies the absolute and minimum rule against torture. According to Article 3, individuals in the hands of the party must "in all circumstances be treated humanely, without any adverse distinction founded on race, colour, religion or faith, sex, birth or wealth, or any other similar criteria," and "to this end, the following acts are and shall remain prohibited at any time and in any place whatsoever . . . violence to life and person, in particular . . . mutilation, cruel treatment and torture . . . outrages upon personal dignity, in particular humiliating and degrading treatment."

In addition to Article 3, the prohibition of torture is also codified in the grave breach provisions of Articles 50, 51, 130 and 147 of the four Geneva Conventions. The Fourth Geneva Convention, Article 31, specifically prohibits the use of force to obtain information: "No physical or moral coercion shall be exercised against protected persons, in particular to obtain information from them or from third par-

ties." In 1948, following the atrocities of World War II, the UN General Assembly inserted the prohibition against torture in the Universal Declaration of Human Rights. Article 5 of that Declaration states, "No one shall be subjected to torture or to cruel, inhuman or degrading treatment or punishment." The torture ban has also been included in Article 7 of the International Covenant on Civil and Political Rights and in the Convention Against Torture or Other Cruel, Inhuman or Degrading Treatment of Punishment.

For centuries, states have been engaged in hostilities, and the laws of armed conflict have allowed those parties to the conflict to conduct their conflict in both fierce and relentless fashions. These rules, however, are based on one important premise: According to the Hague Convention (II) of 1899 and the Hague Convention (IV) of 1907, "The right of belligerents to adopt means of injuring the enemy is not unlimited." According to the rules of armed conflict, both the method and means of warfare are limited. Importantly, not only are certain arms and armaments prohibited but particular forms of behavior by those involved in the hostilities are also limited. In essence, the international law of armed conflict balances the need to take action under the principle of military necessity against humanitarian considerations. These legal obligations have managed this tension between the need for parties to wage deadly wars and the requirements of humanity. In doing this, the rules have allowed for gruesome deaths, even of civilian victims of lawful collateral damage, while at the same time curbing specific freedoms of action. It is an approach that is very pragmatic, allowing parties to use means and methods necessary to achieve their goal—to win—while at the same time preserving the basic tenets of humanity.

In sum, according to international law, what is allowed is whatever is required by military necessity as long as it is not excluded on the ground of humanitarianism. The law allows certain actions that would otherwise be prohibited to be justified by a military necessity. For example, the destruction of property would normally be considered unlawful; however, the Hague Convention allows for the destruction of property when "such destruction or seizure be imperatively demanded by the necessities of war."[7] Conversely, when the law prohibits an action and does not expressly describe an exception based on military necessity, the norm must be obeyed and no justification of military necessity will suffice to overcome the illegality of the action.

The torture of prisoners is a primary example of the laws of armed conflict rejecting a military necessity exception in favor of humanitarian considerations. Under the laws of armed conflict and all major international human rights conventions against torture, the ban on torture is nonderogable. That is, torture cannot be abrogated or derogated no matter what the surrounding circumstances may be. Under the Covenant on Civil and Political Rights, there are some ordinary peacetime human rights that may be derogated during the time that the armed conflict exists. Importantly, however, not all human rights are derogated during a time of conflict, and there are specific rights that are listed within the Covenant as those that cannot be derogated during a time of conflict. For our purposes here, Article 4(2) of the Convenant forbids derogating the freedom from torture or cruel, inhuman, or degrading treatment or punishment, along with others. Furthermore, torture is prohibited in other treaties of the laws of armed conflict, including Additional Protocol I of the Geneva Conventions of August 12, 1949, Article 12 of Geneva Convention I, Article 17 of Geneva Convention III, and Article 32 of Geneva Convention IV. Therefore, no argument of "extreme emergencies" or military necessity can justify or excuse deviating from the prohibition against torture. The legally binding compromise between the military necessity to get information from a prisoner and the humanitarian interests of the prisoner in not being tortured was resolved in the law: No prisoners (prisoners of war or unlawful combatants) would be tortured. Furthermore, the law stated that individuals who engage in acts of torture implicate their government in violating the nation's international obligations and could expose it to a number of possible remedies, including criminal prosecution.

Moral Justifications for Torture

In Perry's book, *Partly Cloudy*, the author drew from the ethical theory of British philosopher W. David Ross, who argued that no absolute moral principles exist.[8] Instead, there exist only prima facie duties, each of which have moral significance. According to Ross, with no one duty having a higher controlling authority over the others, the individual must "simply wrestle with every duty relevant to a particular situation and determine which is most weighty, that is, which prima facie duty is our *actual* duty then and there."[9] Unlike Ross, Perry reserved the possibility of the existence of some absolute moral rules. Interestingly, however, Perry's description of an absolute rule is one in which you cannot imagine "any credible exceptions to those rules, where they could justifiably be overridden by more important duties."[10] This raises serious confusion about what constitues an absolute moral rule for Perry. Certainly, at a time of war, one could envision some "credible exceptions" during armed conflict to an apparent moral rule. In fact, the law of armed conflict incorporates those exceptions under military necessity exceptions for actions that would otherwise be immoral but are allowable because of the nature of warfare and the military need to obtain their objectives (i.e., killing another human).

In his book Perry fails to provide guidance for determining when one rule might override another rule. For example, he provides a list of what he states are "objective ethical principles." The principles listed range from being concerned for the well-being of others, treating people the way they deserve to be treated, respecting individual autonomy, and being honest, to name just a few. Perry acknowledged that at times some of these principles may conflict with each other. So how can we be sure that Perry's list is correct? And, how can we know which of these "prima facie" principles take priority? Furthermore, the author never provided a hierarchy of these principles and failed to explain how someone determines which principle takes precedence and under what specific factual circumstances. Perry and Ross concluded that the exercise of determining which is the actual duty at a specific time is not limited to the classroom. Rather, they argue that the soldiers in the field who face challenging, stressful, and ambiguous situations will wrestle with these principles and be able to determine which principle they should follow. But, in reality, it is very difficult for those in battle to make these types of decisions without some clear rules to guide them. Perry, unfortunately, did not provide any clear answers.

To the question of whether the torture of a human being can be morally just, Perry responded that there are times that torture in interrogation is moral.[11] He argued the right not to be tortured is not absolute; rather, it is a "prima facie right," one "that is clearly established and usually ought to be upheld but that can be trumped by other moral considerations under certain circumstances."[12] Based on the reasoning of the moral philosophy of utilitarianism, considerations of the greatest good for the greatest number led Perry to conclude that torture under certain circumstances is just. The argument is that an individual who may be responsible for the mass murder of others ought not be allowed to claim that he has absolute rights. And if innocent lives can be saved by torturing a prisoner, then torture is justified. For Perry, the captive al Qaeda members' prima facie moral rights not to be tortured is qualified in two possible ways: The right can be overridden by the rights of innocent people not to be murdered or the right can be forfeited. In the case of a captured al Qaeda leader, Perry argued that the right is forfeited.[13] He implied that the right is forfeited because of the al Qaeda leader's horrible actions. The presumption is that an al Qaeda leader is responsible for the murders of innocent people. What is lost in this argument,

however, is that the right to be free from torture is not based upon the individual's actions; rather, it is based on the fact that the individual is a human being with certain rights that come from being a human. Principles of humanity dictate that all humans have these rights that cannot be taken away. The very purpose of torture is to degrade the individual, to seek to make him less than human, depriving him of human dignity in order to get information from him. Given that a member of al Qaeda may be resonsible for horrible atrocities againt innocent victims, treating him as a human may be difficult. His horrible acts, however, do not make him any less human. Principles of humanity codified in law require that those basic rights be given to all humans in combat no matter what they have done.

There are other deficiences in Perry's argument that the right not to be tortured can be forfeited. Aside from stating that an al Qaeda leader could forfeit this right, Perry did not provide any specific facts about the prisoner that would trigger the forfeiture. He failed to illustrate how an al Qaeda leader would forfeit the prima facie right not to be tortured. Would a forfeiture occur because the leader personally killed innocent people? What if he did not personally order or plan the killings? Or is it enough that he might one day plan to kill innocent people? Would it suffice that he supported someone else who was responsible for killing innocent people? Does mere membership in al Qaeda constitute a forfeiture of the right not to be tortured? By stating that forfeiture would occur in the case of a captured al Qaeda leader, the author implied that membership, and possibly rank within the group, would result in the forfeiture of the right. There is no explanation, however, of who qualifies as a "leader" of al Qaeda. Furthermore, Perry did not offer an explanation to determine what level of certainty about the facts related to the specific prisoner the interrogator must have in order to justify torture based on the forfeiture reasoning.

The author drew a parallel between a captured prisoner who forfeits his right not to be tortured and the convicted murderer who forfeits his right to life and is put to death. This analogy between a captured al Qaeda leader and a convicted murderer, however, is a false one. Unlike the al Qaeda leader, the convicted murderer has had the opportunity to challenge the government's claims against him in an adversial judicial process in which he is represented by counsel and provided the full due process rights under the U.S. Constitution. Alleged murderers must be found guilty of murder "beyond a reasonable doubt" after the government presents the evidence against him in court. Furthermore, when the state does put a convicted murderer to death, it is done in a "humane" way that would not constitute torture. Even convicted mass murderers have the right not to be tortured while in prison. Captive terrorists who are tortured are not afforded the same judicial process, arguably because they are not entitled to that same due process during armed conflict before being interrogated. This parallel, however, is fundamentally flawed because the rights compared— the right not to be killed versus the right not to be tortured—are very different.

People, even human rights advocates, generally accept that there are circumstances such as armed conflict when the right not to be killed can be abrogated. According to the laws of armed conflict, combatants and civilians who join the armed conflict do not have any absolute right not to be killed. Those who are part of armed conflict may be killed, and such killing would be morally justified. In customary and international laws that were created based on ideas of human rights, however, there are long standing limitations placed on the means and methods by which combatants can be killed. Furthermore, the principles of noncombatant immunity provide protections for those who are not involved in the conflict in addition to those who are no longer a threat, such as those who have suffered or have been captured. In this respect, torturing a captive is not analogous to killing an enemy in battle. In combat, the killing of the other is because he is still a threat and he is killed in order to protect oneself. The torturer,

however, inflicts pain on the prisoner, who by virtue of being captive, is no longer a threat while captive. In combat, even under circumstances in which someone could be morally and legally justified in killing, they can never use torture against prisoners who are no longer combatants who pose a threat to the other's survival. These two rights, the right not to be killed and the right not to be tortured, are indeed fundamentally different. Killing can be done in a humane way that does not take away the human dignity of an individual. Torture, by definition, however, is an act intended to reduce the individual to something less than human. It strips away his human dignity. On practical, legal, or moral grounds, the act of killing is fundamentally different from the act of torture. The analogies used to explain the arguments for justifying torture are specious, unconvincing, and misleading.

Perry drew another false analogy when he compared the principle of collateral damage in armed conflict, that is, the accidental killing of innocent civilians during conflict, with the principle of the accidental torture of an innocent person. Under the laws of armed conflict it is recognized that during conflict innocent victims may be killed. As long as the noncombatants were not intentionally targeted, the law tolerates these deaths as collateral damage, and although tragic, it does not violate the law. Perry counseled against intentionally torturing innocent people even if it is to save other innocent lives, arguing that we would be no better than the terrorists if we did such acts. However, he supported the torture of prisoners who forfeit their rights not to be tortured. Perry wanted to limit the risk of torture of an innocent prisoner while not conceding a blanket prohibition on torture of prisoners. However, first and foremost, the difficulties in knowing whether a prisoner is innocent or not are the same difficulties faced when determining whether he actually forfeited the right not to be tortured. Perry implied that a member of al Qaeda is not innocent by his membership in the group, and, therefore, he has forfeited his right not to be tortured. How far would this reasoning go to justify others that could be tortured? What about a bystander who witnesses a terorrist attack? He might be innocent or he might be a member of al Qaeda who was watching the attack. How is an interrorgator to know for certain?

The author himself conceded that it is likely impossible to eliminate the chance of accidentally torturing the innocent. But he asked, "would it be possible to limit that risk significantly, short of a blanket prohibition? And if so, would that be morally acceptable?" Here he drew the parallel between the *jus in bello* principle of collateral damage of noncombatants. Under *jus in bello*, those in hostilities are prohibited from intentionally targeting noncombatants who are not legitimate military targets. One can only target combatants. If, however, while targeting combatants, innocent people are killed (collateral damage) that would not violate *jus in bello* because the target was a lawful one. The author compared the innocent civilian victim who was not a target with the possibly innocent prisoner who is the target. Although the end result may be the same—an innocent person is harmed—the author failed to identify the relevant point that in the case of collateral damage, the victim was never intentionally targeted. However, in the case of torture, the innocent victim (alleged al Qaeda member) is intentionally targeted. Furthermore, under *jus in bello* principles, the target must always be a legitimate military target and never an innocent person. Captive prisoners are never legitimate military targets: They stop being targets when they are captured.

Perry acknowledged there might be some absolute moral rules that, when evident, would resolve any moral dilemma where ethical principles were in conflict. For Perry, an absolute moral rule would be one that has no apparent exceptions, no overriding duties that would justify the rule being overridden. Perry agreed with Ross, however, that there are "no absolute moral *principles*; rather there is a cluster of prima facie duties, each of which has moral weight and may take precedence over others in different situa-

tions." Without telling the reader how he differentiates between "principles" and "rules," he provided two examples of what he proposed as possible absolute moral rules: "Don't rape" and "Don't torture children or animals."[14] No definitions are offered for rape, torture, or children. Perry, however, concluded that because it appears that there would be no credible exceptions to those rules and no other more important duty overridding them, they are, therefore, absolute moral rules. What if, however, the member of al Qaeda in custody is under the age of twenty-one? Even assuming there can be some agreement on whether someone of twenty-one years is a child or not, would the absolute moral rule apply under these circumstances or would there be some overriding duty (to save innocent lives) that would create an exception to that rule? Would Perry's absolute moral rule against torturing children apply or does the reasoning based on the ticking-time-bomb scenario and his assessment of a terrorist's forfeiture of their prima facie rights apply? Could a child who was a member of al Qaeda be tortured under this analysis if the child has forfeited his prima facie right not to be tortured? Here Perry seems to contradict himself because if the facts justified overridding the child's rights because of some other "more important duties," like saving innocent lives, then, according to Perry, a child could be tortured. How does one make such determinations? In sum, for Perry, there may never be any truly absolute rules because one might be able to imagine circumstances in which there is always the possibility for a "credible exception to the rule."

Can Teaching Moral Knowledge Be Dangerous?

In his book, Perry identified how the origins of intelligence activities have historical roots in war and diplomacy throughout the history of the United States. By examining aspects of how the United States has waged war in the past and conducted intelligence operations such as espionage (recruiting foreign) and covert actions (political actions, assassinations, and propaganda activities), the book illustrates the different dimensions of U.S. military and intelligence activities and their place in the nation's history, concentrating on some of the most controversial and morally questionable aspects of these activities. According to Perry, ethics, or "moral philosophy," is an exercise in analyzing the meaning and justification of moral beliefs and arguments. He stated that he intends to use moral philosophy in the book "to inform the ethical deliberations of U.S. military and intelligence officers, as well as relevant policy-makers and lawmakers in our executive and legislative branches."[15] In other words, the book is meant to assist those who practice the tradecraft of war, intelligence, and diplomacy to make decisions about some of the most ethically sensitive actions of the nation, such as the torture of those imprisoned by the state. Notably, Perry argued that the book can help educate and train these individuals working on behalf of the state to make moral decisions when they are on the battlefield under the fog of war, when time to think and deliberate about ethical choices is not an available luxury and "split-second decisions will not permit sophisicated analysis."

Although raising important moral questions, Perry's book provides little concrete guidance for those who will be interrogators. What value is created in teaching soldiers that torture may be moral when, in fact, the long-established and accepted laws of war prohibit torture? By discussing elaborate justifications for torture and the intricacies of how one moral rule may overcome another one, Perry's work makes it appear as if moral dilemmas can be resolved by going down a checklist and, as long as enough items are checked off, there is leave to commit torture. Nor should the act of torture become so routinized that it would seem like a checklist of justifications is all one needs. Moral dilemmas are just that—dilemmas. Dilemmas are not easily resolved. Soldiers should not have to grapple with these dilemmas in the field but be able to rely on established laws that have already incorporated the balancing of harms that others

have previously done in the process of drafting the law.

By this position that I am taking, it may seem that I am advocating moral laziness for our soldiers. They simply revert to a law rather than grapple with a terrible moral dilemma. Such grappling, however, ought not be done by soldiers and others in the field. Rather, such considerations should be examined and studied by those responsible for making the laws and drafting policy. Importantly, if those in the field were expected to regularly wrestle with such dilemmas and decide appropriate action, the laws themselves would lose their controlling power over the actions of soldiers. There are reasons that the rules of engagement exist for soldiers and intelligence officers facing these stressful circumstances. To require that each time they face a situation in which different interests are at stake that balance the moral dilemmas themselves would be unfair, impractical, and potentially dangerous for them as well as others. Rather, the lawmakers and policy makers are tasked with doing the job of weighing the different interests at stake and setting out the law for others to follow. Furthermore, if each soldier thought they could individually weigh the harms involved for each of their actions and determine what the prevailing moral rule was in each case, there would be little role for the law in restraining the soldiers' actions. As a result, the legal system in general may break down, as the ethos of obedience to law may be seriousuly shaken by challenges emerging with respect to the reasonableness of following the norms set out in law. In his book, Perry asked the reader to "imagine, hypothetically, what if the law were silent on torture?" But for soldiers and spies responsible for interrogating prisoners, what is real—not hypothetical—is what matters. The laws prohibiting torture exist in reality and can serve to help these soldiers perform their duties.

Those operating in battle—where uncertainty exists, facts are difficult to know at times, and a thick fog pervades all action—deserve as much clarity as possible in their training in hopes that it may assist them when facing the difficulties in battle. Teaching them about consequentialist considerations based on moral ideas with respect to torturing prisoners will not provide the clarity that will help them. The men and women carrying out these activities on behalf of the American people deserve better guidance and instruction. Raising moral questions without providing any clear answers only undermines the very international laws at issue without providing any alternative guidance. The danger is that such unanswered questions contribute to developing moral doubt in the minds of those in the battlefield. This doubt in turn could lead to an increased likelihood that international norms related to the treatment of prisoners will be violated.

Perry argued that he would not support legalizing torture because of the concern that innocent people might be tortured. At the beginning of the book, he asked the reader to put aside the law and think only about moral choices. At the end of the book, however, Perry ultimately advised interrogators to "stay clear of any methods that even contradict the spirit of those treaties."[16] In sum, Perry argued that torturing an al Qaeda leader during interrogations might be morally justified while also instructing future interrogators to follow the law (at least until it is changed by the U.S. government). Although not explicitly advocating that U.S. and international law be changed to allow for torture, he implied that the prohibition on torture might be restricting behavior that would be morally just under some circumstances. I fail to see how this is helpful to anyone who is involved in interrogating al Qaeda prisoners except to raise doubts about the legitimacy of the law.

Philosophers and ethicists did not invent morality but merely theorize on the nature of the phenomenon. Some argue that morality is merely a tool to further human interests. Others believe that the truths of morality are truths of reason that are perceived by reason. Still others simply believe that morality is a basic awareness that some things are just "right" to do and other things are just "wrong." There may be value in

asking, as Perry did, "why" certain acts are considered "right" or "wrong," seeking a justification for our justifications, without ultimately providing an understanding. In the end, however, there are dangers associated with such ruminations. They can be used to justify policies that the international community has prohibited, and they can cause doubt and moral dilemmas for government agents who carry the heavy responsibility of finding the ticking time bomb and saving the country from disaster.

By 2005 atrocities of prisoners tortured by U.S. personnel were well known and undeniable. Even President Bush recognized that certain rights are nonderogable and fundamental to human life. In a speech in June of that year, he stated that "Freedom from torture is an inalienable human right, and we are committed to building a world where human rights are respected and protected by the rule of law."[17] Only time will tell whether David Perry reverses course and finds that torture is an absolute moral wrong that all soldiers and spies should be prohibited from conducting. In thinking about what soldiers and spies ought to know, there are a few reasons that can be listed for arguing against torturing prisoners. Even if torturing the prisoner provides the nation with information it needs, here are a few thoughts on why torturing prisoners should never be sanctioned by this nation.

First, because torture is unambiguously illegal—under international legal covenants that the United States has ratified, under federal law, and under protocols of civilizations dating back to the Magna Carta.

Second, because torture can be unreliable at times. Many people will say anything in order to avert pain and suffering. These prisoners will provide false information in order to stop the torture. Conversely, there are those prisoners who will sometimes provide vital intelligence information under torture that could be used to save innocent lives. In sum, torture can, on the one hand, result in gaining vital information and, on the other hand, may result in false leads and misinformation.

Third, there is no way of ensuring that the torture used will be applied to only those who are true terrorists guilty of killing innocent civilians. There exists the possibility that an innocent person will be tortured. For those like Perry, their premise for using tactics such as waterboarding and other more inhumane techniques of torture is that those who are subject to torture are known terrorists who have murdered innocent people. In the fog of war, however, how much accurate information exists about the true identity of individual prisoners? Under circumstances in which third parties such as the Northern Alliance in Afghanistan, who have a vested interest in helping the United States find "terrorists," provide many prisoners to the U.S. military or intelligence personnel, the rush to provide the United States with what they are asking for may very well lead to innocent people being handed over. Some of these prisoners who ultimately are tortured may have simply been at the wrong place at the wrong time. Those who are doing the torturing often cannot determine the innocence of the prisoner. So those who support Perry's approach, based on a premise that those who are tortured are terrorists guilty of killing innocent victims, base their conclusions on a faulty premise that, particularly at a time of combat, cannot be proven.

Fourth, the practice of torture is just that: a practice. And it is a practice with a slippery slope based on the particular techniques that will have to be authorized as acceptable to use while torturing another human. If slapping and threatening a prisoner does not provide the needed information from the prisoners, will electric shock be justified to use if it is believed doing so will result in the prisoner providing information to prevent another 9/11? What if the electric shock does not result in the desired result? Would raping the prisoner's wife or daughter in his presence be justified? Would raping a terrorists family member violate an absolute moral rule (as Perry discussed) or would it only violate a terrorist's prima facie right to be treated humanely? Perry's qualifications result in confusion about the appropriate test to use under the

circumstances. If this is what will prevent the "ticking time bomb" from exploding, would rape be justified? A nation that constructs a framework for such a practice will, in effect, create a custom within our military and intelligence organizations for the use of torture. An exception created by any justification will become practice that is routinized within a culture. The result will be that a national culture will develop that accepts torture as a legitimate tool to fight terrorism. Such an acceptance of torture will destroy the social fabric of this country.

As international relations theorists have long recognized, one state's practice may not in and of itself create a universal acceptance of a custom. However, a custom based on the practice by one state, depending on the particular state, can influence the practice of other states, which can ultimately develop an emerging or new universal custom. If the global community believes that the United States accepts torture as a proper means of fighting the war on terrorists, then why should any other country refrain from using torture? The significance of the United States engaging in torture cannot be understated. The United States' primary role in establishing the long-accepted prohibitions against torture through both domestic and international law establishes it as an authoritative actor on the treatment of prisoners. Because of this status, other states may follow the U.S. custom of torture (if accepted in the United States), thereby accepting it as legitimate.

Every new conflict, whether involving terrorism or not, leaves its mark on international law as well as the culture of those nations involved. Each time the community of nations has to contend with acts of aggression from terrorists and others, states' responses will leave normative footprints in its wake. Like all major conflicts, 9/11 and the continuing armed conflict against the perpetrators of 9/11 are events in which principles of *jus in bello* are tested and forged. For those principles of *jus in bello* related to the treatment of prisoners, the United States and the international community must remain committed to prohibiting and condemning all torture and not seek to justify (morally or otherwise) it in any way. In doing this, the United States must ensure that our soldiers and spies have a clear understanding that torture in battle is unacceptable. If we as a nation give these individuals any less clear guidance or, even worse, confuse them with complex ruminations about what rights trump others, we are doing them and this country a grave disservice.

A U.S. culture of torture in response to 9/11 or terrorism in general would fundamentally contradict past U.S. practice, go against the basic principles on which the nation was founded, and could lead to a dangerous precedence for a worldwide practice of torture. Such a culture is unacceptable. Some practices are never worth doing. There are some things this nation should never do—not because torturing terrorists does not work, not because the terrorists do not "deserve" it, not because all human rights are of equal value—but because to torture says that we as a nation will devalue other humans and, thus, we corrupt our own value as humans and Americans. Torturing terrorists is less about them and more about us as humans and Americans. When we stop condemning torture and seek to find ways to justify it (even based on moral and ethical arguments), we stop being human beings. In order to find any justification, one has to see those who are tortured as not human. However, recognizing the humanness of others is core to being human. In sum, that is why torture is a crime against humanity.

Rather than trying to teach military and intelligence officers about difficult-to-apply exceptions to the torture prohibitions or about varying degrees of moral behavior, there should be an absolute rule against such practice as it has long been established in international and U.S.

domestic law. Otherwise, to teach and institutionalize an understanding that certain circumstances may make torture legitimate—and even moral—serves only to sanction individuals to act more violently than they otherwise would—a dangerous precedent the United States should consider carefully.

NOTES

1. Raymond Bonner, *Questioning Terror Suspects in a Dark and Surreal World*, New York Times, Mar. 9, 2003, at 1.

2. Convention Against Torture and Other Cruel, Inhuman, or Degrading Treatment or Punishment, adopted and opened for signature Dec. 10, 1984, 1465 U.N.T.S. 112.

3. David L. Perry, Partly Cloudy: Ethics in War, Espionage, Covert Action, and Interrogation 2 (2009).

4. Michael Walzer, Arguing About War 33–50 (2004).

5. *Id.* at 41.

6. ICRC, International Humanitarian Law and International Human Rights Law: Similarities and Differences (Jan. 2003), *available at* www.icrcorg/Web/Eng/siteeng).nsf/htmlall/57JR8L/$FILE/IHL_and_IHRL.pdf?OpenElement.

7. The Hague Conventions and Declarations of 1899 and 1907 66, 73 (James Brown Scott ed., 1918).

8. W. David Ross, The Right and the Good (1930).

9. *Supra* note 3, at 18.

10. *Id.*

11. *Id.* at 211.

12. *Id.* at 212.

13. *Id.*

14. *Id.*

15. *Id.* at xii.

16. *Id.* at 226.

17. Press Release, The White House, President's Statement on the UN International Day in Support of Victims of Torture (Jun. 26, 2005), *available at* www.whitehouse.gov/news/releases/2005/06/20050626.html.

20

Babysitting Terrorists

Should States Be Strictly Liable for Failing to
Prevent Transborder Attacks?

VINCENT-JOËL PROULX

I. Introduction

Of all the current challenges facing the international community, the question of state responsibility is certainly a source for concern. In fact, it has been described as the "most ambitious and most difficult topic of the codification work of the International Law Commission."[1] In the days of the famous *Caroline* incident, things seemed a lot simpler.[2] Whenever armed hostilities arose, the "tit for tat" principle reverberated as the guiding hymn. Self-defense appeared to be a reliable concept, imbued with rationality. In fact, an eloquently crafted three-part test was developed following the *Caroline* affair. From that point onward, any retaliatory recourse to force[3] would be governed by a standard involving the imminent threat of an attack, necessity, and proportionality.[4] This statement of the doctrine[5] was a law student's dream and an undeniable legacy to the international system for the century to come, leading up to the inception of Article 2(4) of the UN Charter. It is fair to say that some tenets of the *Caroline* doctrine, namely the concepts of proportionality and necessity, have remained central debate topics in the international arena, whether in the 1968 Beirut raid or in the 2001 military campaign in Afghanistan. Still, this doctrine of self-defense

fails to elucidate the question of state responsibility. Given the current state of modern warfare[6] and ideology-motivated violence, it appears that the simple days are long over.

To say that the events surrounding 9/11 changed the world forever has become cliché. It is nonetheless true with regard to international law and, more specifically, state responsibility. Many factors are now extending the debate beyond simply assigning blame to negligent or "willfully blind" governments. Whether obscured by intricate information networks, new technologies like the Internet, the sophisticated cellular structure of organizations like al Qaeda, complex financial systems, convoluted political realities, or other factors, the level of government involvement in terrorist activities is no longer readily discernible in all instances. We now live in an era dominated by security concerns, so the parameters of state responsibility need to be revamped accordingly. It is common knowledge that some countries are used as frequent launch pads or training grounds for terrorist organizations. If the events following 9/11 have taught us anything, it is that we must avoid attributing responsibility to those states indiscriminately and, rather, engage in a serious and methodical analysis of the conduct of the governments involved. In doing so, Professor Derek

W. Bowett's work on Israeli reprisals and the use of force in the 1960s should be considered as a starting point.

In his seminal article, *Reprisals Involving Recourse to Armed Force*,[7] Professor Bowett provides useful insights into the question of a host state's responsibility with regard to attacks launched from its territory. Although written in the aftermath of the 1968 Beirut raid and presented from the perspective of armed reprisals, as opposed to the analytically different angle of establishing state responsibility alone, the paper contributed tremendously to the debate and remains authoritative to this day. Of course, many subsequent and contemporaneous changes have come to complicate the equation of state responsibility.

Of particular importance to the discussion of state responsibility are the jurisprudential developments that have occurred over the last thirty years. For instance, one might invoke the influential *Nicaragua*[8] decision and then the *Tadić*[9] judgment, which tempered it. In the same spirit, the *Tehran*[10] case is also instrumental in this area and, in many ways, marks the starting point of the modern concept of indirect state responsibility. Needless to say, many terrorist attacks have punctuated our collective history and stirred the discussion since the Beirut raid days, be they the 1982 events between Israel and Lebanon or the 1998 bombing of U.S. embassies in Africa. Some of these accounts must be revisited in order to shed light on the level of responsibility of the host states involved.

In 2001 the International Law Commission (ILC) adopted the Draft Articles on the Responsibility of States for Internationally Wrongful Acts (Draft Articles),[11] a monumental portion of the legal mosaic on state responsibility. That same year, al Qaeda terrorists carried out unprecedented attacks on U.S. soil, events that are remembered as "9/11." Following the attacks, the United States staged a military campaign in Afghanistan that subverted the *Nicaragua* and *Tadić* legacy[12] and somewhat crystallized the move toward implementing indirect state responsibility in international law. These events, coupled with today's soaring technological possibilities and the far-reaching effects of terrorist structures, constitute a larger reality that undoubtedly falls within the ambit of Professor Bowett's work.

However, as time passes, international law evolves and, with it, the literature and jurisprudence should follow suit. Many unforeseen elements impacted the equation of indirect state responsibility and, as if confronted with a complex algorithm, we must now break down the pieces of this legal puzzle. Because the literature is far from dispositive on the issue, I propose to reopen the debate on indirect state responsibility and weigh different arguments in order to shed light on the law that governs this politically charged area. In doing so, I first draw a distinction between direct and indirect responsibility and argue that the international community has, in fact, moved toward a model of indirect responsibility. Second, I advocate a two-tiered model of strict liability vis-à-vis terrorism in order to address the new and polymorphic threats. Finally, I attempt to identify significant considerations in delineating the parameters of the obligation to prevent terrorist attacks.

II. Direct Responsibility vs. Indirect Responsibility

A. The Concept of Attribution

It is well documented in international law that a state will usually not answer for the acts of private or nonstate actors or, at the very least, that the conduct will not be attributable to the host state.[13] In other words, only the conduct of the host state's organs will be imputable to it. However, international law also recognizes that the actions of private persons may bind the host state should those actors or groups qualify as "agents" of the state.[14]

Since the publication of Professor Bowett's *Reprisals Involving Recourse to Armed Force*, international courts have formally adopted this concept of attribution. The International Court of Justice (ICJ) crafted the classical formulation in 1986.[15] In the *Nicaragua* decision, the ICJ was confronted with the United States' involvement in the funding and training of *contra* rebels in the Nicaragua–El Salvador conflict. Although the United States was found to have provided various forms of assistance to the rebels and the guerrillas were at times completely dependent on U.S. support, the ICJ refused to pronounce the *contra* rebels de facto U.S. agents:

> The Court has taken the view . . . that United States participation, even if preponderant or decisive, in the financing, organizing, training, supplying and equipping of the *contras*, the selection of its military or paramilitary targets, and the planning of the whole of its operation, is still insufficient in itself, on the basis of the evidence in the possession of the Court, for the purpose of attributing to the United States the acts committed by the *contras* in the course of their military or paramilitary operations in Nicaragua.[16]

The court then proceeded to elaborate a test for establishing state responsibility, a standard that would quickly gain international notoriety as the "effective control test." In short, the ICJ opined that in order to find the United States legally responsible for the activities of the Nicaragua *contras*, it would "have to be proved that that State had effective control of the military or paramilitary operations in the course of which the alleged violations were committed."[17] From this decision onward, it became common practice to analyze the degree of effective control exercised by a state over nonstate actors in order to determine the level of involvement of that state and, as a necessary corollary, its level of responsibility.

Thirteen years later the Appeals Chamber of the International Criminal Tribunal for the former Yugoslavia (ICTY) revisited the "effective control test" in *Tadić*. The court found that, when private individuals carry out acts contrary to international law, the only way to attribute such acts to the host state is to demonstrate "that the State exercises control over the individuals."[18] The court also pointed out that the degree of control might vary according to the circumstances and that the analysis should be guided by a flexible approach.[19] The court then purported to draw a distinction between an individual and an organized group. In the latter case, it was now necessary to demonstrate that the host state exercised "overall control" over the group in question, a legal inquiry that marked a significant relaxation of the "effective control test":

> Plainly, an organised group differs from an individual in that the former normally has a structure, a chain of command and a set of rules as well as the outward symbols of authority. Normally a member of the group does not act on his own but conforms to the standards prevailing in the group and is subject to the authority of the head of the group. Consequently, for attribution to a State of acts of these groups it is sufficient to require that the groups as a whole be under the overall control of the State.[20]

The ICTY pursued the analysis by making a crucial distinction between groups that are militarily organized and groups that are not.[21] For the former, it would have to be proved that the host state "wields overall control over the group, not only by equipping and financing the group, but also by coordinating or helping in the general planning of its military activity."[22] For nonmilitary groups, the threshold was higher, as overall control was deemed insufficient, and specific instructions[23] flowing from the host state to the group in question were required.[24] Alternatively, the threshold could be satisfied if the host state had publicly endorsed or approved the acts *ex post facto*.[25] The ICTY greatly advanced the debate on state responsibility by expanding the analysis to include not only a group's relationship to the host state but also the group's organizational structure.[26] *Tadić*'s legacy has come to be known as the "overall control test" and, in the post-*Nicaragua* era, it governs debates on the question of a state's involvement in funding and training insurgents or terrorists.[27]

Following these jurisprudential developments, the adoption of the ILC Draft Articles in 2001 constituted another crucial international effort to define state responsibility.[28] This landmark document ultimately codified the law to read: "Every internationally wrongful act of a State entails the international responsibility of that State."[29] Under the ILC framework, an act is wrongful if it amounts to a breach of a host state's international obligations, whether derived from treaty law,[30] customary law,[31] general rules of international law,[32] or *jus cogens*.[33] This principle, now codified in Article 2 of the Draft Articles, has also received wide support in international jurisprudence.[34] In tandem, these provisions operate on the premise that if a state has violated a primary rule of international law, whether through an act or omission,[35] the secondary rules of state responsibility contained in the Draft Articles will apply.[36]

B. The Direct/Indirect Dichotomy

An overarching dichotomy guides the law of state responsibility for internationally wrongful acts. On the one hand, a state may be held accountable if its direct act or omission led to harm. Cases such as *Nicaragua* and *Tadić* as well as the Draft Articles focused on this sort of direct responsibility. Such responsibility can attach where a terrorist group acts as a state agent or de facto state agent[37] or where the state subsequently approves of the terrorist act. It is now fair to say that a state that overtly and directly supports,[38] endorses,[39] authorizes,[40] or condones a terrorist attack on another state will presumably be held to have violated international law.[41] Hence, from both a conceptual and practical point of view, the issues surrounding direct state responsibility are relatively clear and require no further discussion here.[42]

On the other hand, there exists a subtler type of responsibility, one that hinges on the indirect involvement of a state in a wrongful act. Indirect responsibility usually arises when there is no causal link between the wrongdoer and the host state.[43] For instance, it is difficult to impute liability for an attack to a state when the state has no knowledge of or ties to terrorist activities arising from within its borders. At that juncture, the analysis focuses on the state's duty to prevent terrorist attacks and whether the state failed to thwart a given terrorist strike emanating from its territory. Not unlike the inquiry under direct responsibility, the focus here is on the host state's breach of an international obligation. However, a breach under indirect responsibility will likely translate into an omission, whether deliberate or innocent, rather than an act. Hence, a state's passiveness or indifference toward terrorist agendas within its own territory might trigger its responsibility, possibly on the same scale as though it had actively participated in the planning. As Mark Baker stated in the aftermath of the 1986 bombings of Libyan terrorist camps,

terrorism involves indirect aggression. Indirect aggression occurs when the state, without committing any aggressive acts, operates through its nationals or other foreigners who appear to be acting on their own. This appears to be the situation in Libya. The Libyan government is in violation of international law and can be held responsible for the terrorist actions of its nationals. The question is whether or not state responsibility is equivalent to a state sponsored armed attack and becomes even more sensitive when the state's responsibility results from mere toleration of the terrorist groups instead of active support of the groups.[44]

Some scholars have rejected the direct/indirect dichotomy because direct and indirect responsibility can be conceptually difficult to distinguish, and the delineation between both paradigms has blurred on occasion.[45] In fact, the post-9/11 U.S. military campaign in Afghanistan has exacerbated the confusion surrounding this legal distinction. The decision to take action against the Taliban government[46] has collapsed both branches of state responsibility into one confused framework.[47] I examine below how the military campaign in Afghanistan has created a new precedent in international law along with a significant shift in the law of state responsibility. In other words, I attempt to re-establish and delineate the significant boundary between direct and indirect responsibility while devoting careful analysis to the question of indirect state responsibility in preventing terrorist attacks.

We may start from the premise that most scholars acknowledge that 9/11 created a significant shift in international law or, at least, made combating international terrorism a priority.[48] The events of 9/11 created incentives for governments, policy makers, and judiciaries around the globe to revisit and revamp their domestic laws dealing with national security,[49] funding of terrorist organizations,[50] and immigration.[51] International law should be no exception. On September 12, 2001, Ambassador Valeriy Kuchinsky, the Ukrainian Representative to the United Nations, declared: "The magnitude of yesterday's acts goes beyond terrorism as we have known it so far. . . . We therefore think that new definitions, terms and strategies have to be developed for the new realities."[52] More than four years after 9/11, this need, highlighted by the March 2004 terrorist attack in Madrid and recent bombings in London, has only gained relevance and urgency. More importantly, international law seems to be progressively following the path Ambassador Kuchinsky set for it, despite some notable shortcomings in the global legal order.[53]

III. A Paradigm Shift: Toward a Law of Indirect Responsibility or Strict Liability?

A. The Evolution of Indirect Responsibility in International Law

The old paradigm of direct state responsibility, codified in Article 2 of the Draft Articles, indicated that the conduct underlying an internationally wrongful act must be attributed to a state's act or omission if the state is to be held

responsible.[54] That logic was founded on a concept of terrorist action that, as with *Nicaragua* and *Tadić*, involved actors that shared an intimate link with the host state or that became de facto state actors through the mechanisms of control and attribution.[55] However, those cases did not foresee modern terrorism.[56] The world is now faced with new and significant threats, sophisticated terrorist organizations, and complex financial structures. Modern technology provides terrorists with increased means and methods of inspiring fear and carrying out attacks.[57] There are cases in which host states have no knowledge of and wield no control over terrorist organizations operating within their territory. The only causal link between such a state and the organization is the fact that both coexist in the same geographically and politically delineated area. In such instances, it is imperative to establish new parameters for indirect responsibility. Before embarking on such an endeavor, however, it is helpful to briefly review important developments in the law of indirect state responsibility.

The *Tellini* case of 1923 provides a useful starting point. Following the assassination on Greek territory of several members of an international commission overseeing the delimitation of the Greek-Albanian border, the League of Nations organized a special committee[58] to address the legal issues raised by the incident.[59] Although the committee clearly rejected the possible attribution of the assassination to Greece, it opined that a host state could be held responsible in like circumstances if it "neglected to take all reasonable measures for the prevention of the crime and pursuit, arrest and bringing to justice of the criminal."[60] This language clearly foreshadowed a move from the more traditional analysis of the connection between state actors and the host state to a rigorous examination of the conduct of the host state itself vis-à-vis the wrongful act authored by private persons.

These considerations are even more relevant when contrasted with the findings in the *Tehran* case, which was instrumental in advancing the law of indirect state responsibility further. In

1979 a student militant group took over a U.S. embassy and its consulates in Iran, leading to serious vandalism, destruction of property, and the capture and detention of fifty American citizens, mostly diplomatic and consular personnel.[61] In light of these facts, the ICJ had to establish whether the takeover, ransacking of the embassy, and hostage taking—an operation that lasted approximately three hours— was attributable to the Iranian state. The court first considered whether Iran was directly responsible. Somewhat foreshadowing the reasoning in *Tadić*, the court asked whether "the militants acted on behalf of the State, having been charged by some competent organ of the Iranian State to carry out a specific operation."[62] The ICJ found no direct involvement on the facts given.[63]

The court then proceeded to analyze whether Iran was indirectly responsible for the attacks in that it failed to fulfill its duty to protect foreign diplomatic missions from assault. The court held that, even though the attacks could not be attributed directly to the state, Iran was not "free of any responsibility in regard to those attacks; *for its own conduct was in conflict with its international obligations.*"[64] By virtue of several treaty provisions and principles of international law, the court noted that Iran had a "categorical duty" to protect the victims of the attack along with the embassy.[65] In an excerpt that would mark the real starting point of the modern law of indirect responsibility and that can be applied today to the obligation to prevent terrorist attacks, the ICJ opined that "the Iranian Government failed altogether to take any 'appropriate steps' to protect the premises, staff and archives of the United States' mission against attack by the militants, and to take any steps either to prevent this attack or to stop it before it reached its completion."[66]

A more limpid boundary between direct responsibility and indirect responsibility was finally drawn in the *Tehran* decision. It is now clear that, under the direct responsibility paradigm, the initial focus of the inquiry hinges on the conduct of an extraneous person or group

and not on the actions of the host state itself. The overarching objective is to establish whether the wrongful action or omission, as engendered by the person or group, is directly attributable to the state. Interestingly enough, through the lens of *Nicaragua* and *Tadić*, this primary objective becomes somewhat ancillary to the question of whether the host state exercised control and direction over the person or group that committed the wrongful act. In fact, the question of control, as exercised by the host state, has become a sort of touchstone in modern scholarly attempts to reconcile both judgments.[67]

The final analysis culminates in three possible scenarios: The acts of state agents are binding on the host state; nonstate actors are deemed to be de facto government agents; or the acts of terrorist groups or insurgents are directly attributable to the host state without labeling them formal instrumentalities or agents of the state per se. When considering the events of 9/11, it seems improbable that the attacks could, in fact, be attributed to the Taliban government, even if analyzed through the lens of subsequent endorsement. The public record indicates that al Qaeda benefited from a large margin of autonomy within Afghanistan. Furthermore, although there is no evidence that the Taliban regime endorsed the attacks,[68] it is nonetheless possible to conclude that in some circumstances, the actions of a nonstate actor amount to the acts of the government itself, as though committed through a prolongation of the state. For instance, several scholars opined that the finding of direct responsibility against the Taliban government in the events of 9/11 would probably justify a military campaign in Afghanistan.[69]

It logically follows from the foregoing considerations that contrary to direct responsibility, which focuses on the wrongful act in itself, indirect responsibility is concerned with the conduct of the host state, namely its failure to fulfill an international obligation rather than committing some positive act. It should be noted that this type of indirect responsibility has sometimes been referred to as "vicarious responsibility."[70]

The parallel between the *Tellini* and *Tehran* cases is striking, even though they were decided nearly sixty years apart. In both instances, the inquiry hinged on a rationale of indirect state responsibility, with particular emphasis placed on the host state's failure to bring its conduct within the realm of its international obligation to prevent the given event from occurring: "For example a receiving State is not responsible, as such, for the acts of private individuals in seizing an embassy, but it will be responsible if it fails to take all necessary steps to protect the embassy from seizure, or to regain control over it."[71] Based on this reasoning, and bearing in mind that modern terrorism poses a significant and sometimes polymorphic threat, it is apparent that the inaction of host states will be thoroughly scrutinized when a given terrorist strike could have been avoided or even partially thwarted. The analysis will ineluctably shift toward establishing the duty of host states to forestall attacks rather than on their involvement in funding, supporting, or directing terrorist activities. In addition, a paradigm shift toward indirect responsibility signals the imposition of a greater burden of precaution or prevention on host states.[72]

Thus, the contents of the 1970 UN Declaration on Friendly Relations required every state to "refrain from organizing, instigating, assisting or participating in acts of civil strife or terrorist acts in another state *or acquiescing in organized activities within its territory* directed towards the commission of such acts."[73] From this, it is apparent that the UN General Assembly was concerned not only with host states directly orchestrating attacks on other states but also with the possibility of passive or willfully blind governments not exercising any degree of control over terrorist organizations.

B. The Shift Toward Indirect Responsibility

1. The Law Before 9/11

The attitude of the UN Security Council toward the repression of international terrorism has been, at best, confused or fact specific.[74] In some instances, the Council has allowed a state to enter a host state and eliminate the bases of terrorist operations there. The 1995–1996 entry of Turkish forces onto Iraqi soil in pursuit of Kurdish irregulars is one example.[75] Iran shortly followed suit, resorting to aerial attacks on Kurdish bases from which insurgent troops had launched excursions.[76] Senegal set foot in Guinea-Bissau both in 1992 and 1995 "to strike at safe havens used as bases by opposition forces";[77] "Tajikistan pursued irregulars into Afghanistan";[78] and the United States bombed parts of the Sudan and Afghanistan following the 1998 attacks on U.S. embassies in Tanzania and Kenya.[79] In these instances the Council recognized an injured state's right to pursue terrorists into a neighboring country: "It is becoming clear that a victim-state may invoke Article 51 [of the UN Charter] to take armed countermeasures . . . *against any territory harboring, supporting or tolerating* activities that culminate in, or are likely to give rise to, insurgent infiltrations or terrorist attack."[80]

In other instances, the Security Council remained unmoved by a host state's plea of territorial infringement when a neighboring state invaded the host state's territory in pursuit of terrorists. For instance, "in September 2000, the Security Council specifically rejected the Rwandan authorities' claim to a right to attack Hutu insurgents operating out of neighboring territory"[81] on the grounds that it would violate the host state's territorial integrity.[82]

The Security Council's unpredictability has been most extreme in the context of the ongoing Arab-Israeli hostilities.[83] One notable case was the Beirut raid of 1968. Following an attack on an El Al Boeing 707 at Athens airport, Israel sought to establish the responsibility of two members of the Popular Front of the Liberation of Palestine as well as that of Lebanon.[84] In fact, a flight from Beirut to Athens constituted the only territorial link between the two perpetrators and Lebanon.[85] In language reminiscent of the new paradigm of indirect responsibility, Israel accused Lebanon of "assisting and abetting acts of warfare, violence, and terror by irregular forces and organizations."[86] The argument did not, however, convince the Security Council.[87] The Security Council's decision not to endorse the reprisal was met with great disapproval by Israel, which stated that the Council was one-sided in its finding of responsibility and emphasized the fact that Lebanon's role had not been thoroughly scrutinized.[88]

A similar case was the 1982 Israel-Lebanon conflict, which stemmed from the 1956 Sinai incident between Israel and Egypt.[89] Since the Sinai incident, it had become common practice for Palestinians to launch strikes from Lebanon into Israel.[90] After Israel invaded a large part of the Lebanese territory in 1982, it contended that the Palestinian Liberation Organization (PLO) had effectively turned the southern part of Lebanon into a launchpad for terrorist attacks[91] and that Lebanon had failed to fulfill its "duty to prevent its territory from being used for terrorist attacks against other States."[92] Lebanon denied responsibility, alleging that the bases from which the attacks were launched evaded its own control.[93] The Security Council unanimously called on Israel to withdraw from Lebanon.[94] In the following days Israel made several vivid arguments in support of its decision to take military action after years of incursions perpetrated by PLO members against Israelis.[95] In its plea, Israel referred to Lebanon as a "logistic centre and refuge for members of the terrorist internationale from all over the world."[96] The Security Council remained undeterred in its objective to restore peace in the region and demanded the cessation of hostilities.[97]

Despite this inconsistent precedent, the concept of "harboring and supporting" terrorists has achieved international precedence over the general concept of attribution. This change is particularly significant considering that both *Nicaragua*[98] and *Tadić*[99] rejected financial and military assistance as a basis for imputing direct responsibility to a host state, even when such aid proved preponderant or decisive. Thus, given that terrorists need assets to operate and that governments across the globe have been trying to forestall their financial autonomy,[100] it be-

comes obvious that the international community has abandoned the reasoning of *Nicaragua* and *Tadić*, which imposed a stringent burden on the attacked state to establish direct responsibility, in favor of an expansive rule of indirect responsibility, which alleviates the injured state's onus exponentially. Based on that logic, the mere provision of logistical support to or the sheltering of terrorists within a given territory will supplant any inquiry into the level of control a host state exercises over a given attack. This shift in international law, which still requires a few adjustments,[101] now centers completely on a host state's failure to prevent an excursion by terrorists from its territory into that of another.

2. The Impact of 9/11

The pivotal point of reference in the modern development of indirect state responsibility is the events of 9/11. Following the attacks carried out by al Qaeda on the World Trade Center, the Pentagon, and in Pennsylvania, the United States and its allies launched a military campaign in Afghanistan.[102] Some commentators have questioned the legality of that retaliation,[103] whereas others have condoned or, at least, found it justified under the existing scheme of *jus ad bellum*.[104] Other commentators opine that Operation Enduring Freedom has relaxed international legal standards by loosening use-of-force principles[105] and contorting the self-defense standard.[106] Regardless of which interpretation one prefers, the U.S. action in Afghanistan has significantly impacted international law, especially in the realm of state responsibility.

International law could not endorse a U.S.-led war in Afghanistan solely against bin Laden and high-ranking members of al Qaeda, as a terrorist organization is simply not tantamount to a state.[107] Consequently, the United States could not simply pin responsibility on al Qaeda alone but "sought to impute al Qaeda's conduct to Afghanistan simply because the Taliban had harbored and supported the group."[108] As the stage was being set for the retaliatory strikes, President Bush accused the Taliban of murder, declaring that its members had supported and harbored the al Qaeda terrorists responsible for 9/11.[109] These remarks were eventually substantiated by a congressional authorization to "use all necessary and appropriate force" against Afghanistan and any other state or organization that aided or harbored the terrorists involved in the 9/11 attacks.[110] As the war on terrorism transitioned into a full-fledged military operation, it became clear that the United States would not differentiate between host states and terrorists[111] and would attempt to extirpate 9/11 perpetrators from any territory that offered them shelter.[112]

Publicly available facts tend to demonstrate that the Taliban harbored terrorists and, at best, provided them with limited logistical support. However, it is difficult to contend that the Taliban government did in fact exercise effective or overall control over al Qaeda, as al Qaeda had a complex structure and much organizational and operational autonomy from the Taliban.[113] The Taliban probably did not know of the 9/11 attacks beforehand and never endorsed them.[114] Further, it does not appear that al Qaeda was acting as a de facto agent of the Taliban.[115] Thus, under the *Nicaragua* and *Tadić* line of reasoning, these facts would not support a finding that the Taliban, and thus Afghanistan, was responsible for the 9/11 attacks.

The U.S. strike in Afghanistan has, therefore, subverted, or at least "lowered substantially,"[116] the classical direct responsibility threshold for attribution. Although the United States argued that the Taliban was directly responsible for the 9/11 attacks,[117] it also justified its response by declaring that the Taliban harbored and supported al Qaeda. Thus, through a conceptually nebulous application of international law, the United States seems to have collapsed direct and indirect state responsibility into one approach.[118] Some suggest the existence of a varying scale under the *Nicaragua* framework in characterizing acts of terrorism as "armed attacks" by referencing Article 51 of the UN Charter.[119] However, it is more appropriate to describe the U.S. strikes on Afghanistan as having signaled a monumental shift in international

law from direct to indirect state responsibility.[120] Indirect responsibility is no longer a second-best option when direct responsibility cannot be established; rather, it has supplanted direct responsibility as the dominant theme in the field of attribution.

3. The Law After 9/11

On September 12, 2001, the UN General Assembly adopted a resolution calling for "international cooperation to prevent and eradicate acts of terrorism" and stressing that "those responsible for *aiding, supporting or harbouring* the perpetrators, organizers and sponsors of such acts will be held accountable."[121] On the same day, the Security Council adopted Resolution 1368, emphatically prompting all states "to work together urgently to bring to justice the perpetrators, organizers and sponsors of these terrorist attacks . . . that those responsible for *aiding, supporting or harbouring* the perpetrators, organizers and sponsors will be held accountable."[122] Sixteen days later, the Security Council adopted Resolution 1373,[123] a landmark document in the modern counter-terrorism campaign. Although Resolution 1368 recognized the inherent right to individual or collective self-defense, Resolution 1373 additionally reaffirmed "the need to combat *by all means*, in accordance with the Charter [of the United Nations], threats to international peace and security caused by terrorist acts."[124] These resolutions signaled a departure from previous Security Council practice[125] and consecrated the international community's newfound obdurate will in combating terrorism.

The strongest case that can be made against the Taliban is that it failed to prevent a terrorist attack emanating from its territory and it refused to stop harboring al Qaeda members.[126] The UN Security Council had frequently deplored the continuing use of Afghan territory for the "sheltering" and "training" of terrorists and accused the Taliban of perpetrating egregious violations of international law.[127] In Resolution 1267, the Council insisted that the Taliban "cease the provision of sanctuary and training for international terrorists and their organizations."[128] In Resolution 1373,[129] the Council decided that all states must "Refrain from providing any form of support, *active or passive*," to terrorists and must "Deny safe haven to those who finance, plan, support, or commit terrorist acts, or provide safe havens."[130] These claims had also been made in other contexts, especially for the purpose of justifying retaliatory use of force or self-defense against a host state. Consequently, commentators have recognized the right to use force in such instances: "This clearly confirms the right of a victim state to treat terrorism as an armed attack and those that facilitate or harbor terrorists as armed attackers against whom . . . military force may be used in self-defense."[131]

It is inherently difficult to compare a collective history of terrorism and reprisals, such as the Arab-Israeli situation, to isolated events such as the 9/11 attacks or the recent train bombing in Madrid.[132] However, both the Beirut and the Sinai incidents can be compared to the U.S.-Afghanistan situation because in each case the attacks were instigated by irregular forces and launched from a third-party host state.[133] The Security Council rejected Israel's plea of self-defense[134] and Lebanon eventually relocated the PLO irregulars to Tunis.[135] In contrast, the Security Council permitted U.S. action in Afghanistan.[136] This difference in applying international law is difficult to explain,[137] but it illustrates the shift within the international community from a model of direct state responsibility, focused on "effective" or "overall" control, to one of indirect responsibility. In other words, Israel's arguments in 1982 did not resonate well with the international community. In 2001, however, when the Taliban provided safe haven to members of al Qaeda, a very similar factual situation engendered an unprecedented level of approval for retaliatory recourse to force. Operation Enduring Freedom not only gathered significant support from the Security Council but also from other high-profile international bodies. For instance, the North Atlantic Treaty Organization (NATO) supported the right to collective self-defense[138] and found that the Taliban had indeed harbored Osama bin Laden and al Qaeda.[139] The Organization of American States followed suit, recognizing the United States' inherent right to self-defense and referring to the appropriate provisions in the Inter-American Treaty of Reciprocal Assistance.[140] The United States also received vast support from other prominent intergovernmental bodies.[141]

One could also seek to explain the Security Council's different attitude to the United States' 9/11 response on the grounds of state sovereignty.[142] At the heart of this dilemma is the question whether a host state that cannot effectively thwart terrorist activities emanating from its own territory or that has lost control over the region where bases of operation are located should be required to allow foreign forces to enter its territory and repress the terrorist threat.[143] In 1982, when the attacks were based in the Middle East, far from UN headquarters, and the response was perhaps disproportionate, the Security Council allotted more weight to questions of Lebanese sovereignty. "Clearly, even under traditional law, the target of any reprisal had to be shown to have committed a prior delict so that, without proof of delictual conduct *by the Lebanon*, the Council was disinclined to accept Israel's plea of justification."[144] But with the 9/11 attacks, the situation was different: The world had come to recognize the need to change old legal notions to deal with the new threats of terrorism.[145] It is perhaps fair to say that the underlying legal tests found in *Nicaragua* and *Tadić* are now obliterated from the equation, save in clear cases of direct state involvement in terrorist activities. Thus, even with sovereignty as a factor, the Council's acquiescence in the U.S. strike on Afghanistan can best be explained as a concrete affirmation of the indirect responsibility paradigm in response to a changing global order. Indeed, it is now an accepted practice for an injured state to accuse a host state of not preventing excursions into the former state's territory. Most importantly, as a direct consequence of finding another state responsible for terrorism, the aggrieved state can use force to restore peace and security in most cases: "Although traditionally addressed as a law enforcement problem, it is now clear that international terrorism will often necessitate some sort of military response."[146]

The new paradigm, however, is not without problems of its own. In the past the Security Council had often rejected the idea of "collective guilt,"[147] the lumping together of terrorists and the states in which they base their operations, along with a finding of responsibility based solely on a state's harboring of terrorists. In the cases in which the Council found a host state responsible on that basis, it often condemned the reaction of the aggrieved state as disproportionate. Professor Bowett implied that this may have been due, in part, to the Council's reluctance to assume "that the territorial state assumed responsibility because it had the power to prevent these activities."[148] Bowett claimed that it is probably unrealistic, based on arguments of size and capacity of host states, to expect countries like Jordan and Lebanon to effectively thwart all terrorist operations within their territory.[149] These concerns demonstrate the complexity of the new legal paradigm, which somewhat ignores them, and evoke the above-mentioned tension[150] between respecting territorial integrity and sovereignty, and combating terrorism. For instance, if we accept that Lebanon cannot effectively thwart terrorist activities within its own territory because of widespread guerrilla activities, what exactly do we expect it to do? Based on the logic of Resolution 1373, we would have to require it to forego its sovereignty and allow foreign forces into its territory to suppress the terrorist threat.

An effective antiterrorism campaign will require a substantial strengthening of the international regime of state responsibility or a significant degradation of state sovereignty. The latter option would probably prove temporarily adequate to address Professor Bowett's concerns with regard to ineffective states, as the harboring of terrorists by a host state has sometimes been equated with relinquishing sovereignty or, at least, with exercising a state function that is deeply incompatible with the cardinal principles of sovereignty.[151] However, an increase in state responsibility seems far better suited to the current state of international law and is the most effective way to empower a global counter-terrorism campaign while upholding some fundamental values of the international legal order.

C. Doing Away with Attribution: Toward a Model of Strict Liability?

Given the international community's will to eradicate terrorism coupled with the Security Council's emphatic condemnation of terrorist acts and its resolve to eliminate threats to peace and security "by all necessary means," it is imperative to rethink the underlying tenets of indirect responsibility.[152] Although it is important to address the substantiality of a host state's obligation to prevent terrorist attacks, the trans-substantive rules of state responsibility must also be revisited in light of the paradigm shift. The thrust of my policy argument is that the interests and priorities of the international community, especially with regard to combating terrorism, would be better achieved by circumventing certain trans-substantive rules, namely attribution.[153]

Both before and after 9/11, several commentators highlighted the inadequacy of the current scheme of state responsibility in dealing with terrorism while also placing significant emphasis on the shortcomings of the *Nicaragua* and *Tadić* formulation of attribution.[154] Following 9/11, most of the criticism pertaining to the shift in the law of state responsibility deplored the revision of trans-substantive over the primary rules of international law. In other words, some critics believed that revisiting secondary rules of state responsibility, such as attribution, was ineffective and that the policy objectives of the international community would be better vindicated through reaffirming the primary obligations of host states.[155] This debate generated some academic writing, but to my knowledge, the validity of attribution as a concept has not been called into question. This is not to say that the ILC's treatment of attribution has not generated controversy in the past. For instance, before 2001 there had been significant concern over the distinction between the mechanism of imputation and whether there should be fault on behalf of a state to trigger its international responsibility vis-à-vis an internationally wrongful act.[156]

1. Revisiting Trans-Substantive Rules

I take issue with the claim that revising trans-substantive rules, especially attribution, would not yield effective results. The global effort against terrorism is an exercise in risk assessment. The war on terror definitely has Kantian roots and lends itself to several ethical, social, and philosophical considerations. Kant's theory that a human being should not be used as a means toward the collective well-being comes to mind—namely, that we should not balance human lives in the name of collective security.[157] Starting from that premise, there are no ideal scenarios or perfect solutions. Hence, mitigating the disparity in political and economic power between states, coupled with the essential goal of protecting civilians, remains a noble objective.

Indirect responsibility is now the rule of thumb in terms of counter-terrorism and will often supplant a course of action involving direct responsibility, given the inherent difficulty in substantiating such a claim. In other words, the response to 9/11 has provided aggrieved states with the opportunity to elect indirect responsibility over direct responsibility as the preferred mechanism in establishing the host state's liability.[158] Thus, given the recent paradigm shift toward a law of indirect responsibility, Article 2 of the Draft Articles is somewhat superfluous in the context of counter-terrorism. In light of recent state and Security Council practice, maintaining a rationale of attribution via indirect responsibility appears to rely predominantly on poor semantics. One only has to look at the precedent set in *Nicaragua* to infer that the notions of control and attribution should be, in

most circumstances, excised altogether from the equation of indirect state responsibility. For instance, the ICJ clearly associated attribution with direct state involvement when it stated that it had to investigate "not the complaints relating to alleged violations of humanitarian law by the *contras*, regarded by Nicaragua as imputable to the United States, but rather unlawful acts for which the United States *may be responsible directly in connection with the activities of the contras*."[159]

If the objective is truly, as the Security Council declared it, to eradicate terrorism using "all necessary steps," international mechanisms should remain unfettered by secondary rules, and the case for a responsibility-expanding regime should be more radical. In fact, several commentators also argue that the war on terror should attract new rules.[160] With this in mind, the recent trend in state responsibility should be governed solely by Article 12 of the Draft Articles as a matter of hermeneutics alone: "There is a breach of an international obligation by a State when an act of that State is not in conformity with what is required of it by that obligation, regardless of its origin or character."[161]

Although the traditional approach has been to attribute an internationally wrongful act to a host state when that state failed to prevent a given attack, this method should be revisited. Contrary to what certain commentators might anticipate, the idea of circumventing attribution altogether may prove efficient in the war on terror and elude the main criticisms aimed at preventing the revision of international trans-substantive rules. The main argument against revisiting attribution is that the international community should instead focus on delineating and defining primary rules of international law more clearly.

It is obvious that the language surrounding attribution is somewhat dissonant with the new paradigm shift toward indirect responsibility. For example, Article 8 of the Draft Articles characterizes the conduct of private persons as an "act of state" as long as the nonstate individuals act "on the instructions" or "under the direction or control" of the host state.[162] Hence, prior to 9/11 the debate ineluctably reverted back to the question of control in a circuitous fashion, as found in *Nicaragua* and *Tadić*.[163] By its delivery of the Draft Articles, the ILC seems to have narrowed the language of attribution to a more traditional model of state-condoned or state-sponsored insurgency, thereby eluding isolated attacks or massive one-time strikes such as 9/11. For example, the commentary on Article 8 of the Draft Articles is a salient example of the narrow application of the concept of attribution before 9/11. On this question, ILC Special Rapporteur James Crawford noted that in certain circumstances, "a specific factual relationship [exists] between the person or entity engaged in [terrorism] and the State."[164] These circumstances include "private persons acting on the instructions of the State" and "private persons act[ing] under the State's direction or control."[165] When transposed to the current war on terror, the commentaries appear to make attribution dependent on some level of control by the host state over a terrorist organization or on a factual nexus between the host state and the terrorist organization. It is clear that the provision does not extend to situations in which terrorist organizations are acting independently or autonomously from the state organs, as was the case in Afghanistan.

In this light, it is fair to assume that attribution will likely be an appropriate mechanism "only if the nonstate actor was in fact acting on the instructions of, or under the direction or control of, that State in carrying out the [wrongful] conduct."[166] Furthermore, based on the *Tehran* logic, attribution can also be triggered by the state subsequently acknowledging and adopting the wrongful conduct as its own. In fact, this legal device has been expressly incorporated in Article 11 of the Draft Articles.[167] Thus, the logic of attribution is to be understood in conjunction with the notion of control, and as semantically adjacent to the host state directly participating in the attack in some way, shape, or form. In other words, the work of the ILC prior to 9/11 expounded that con-

trol exerted by a host state constituted the linchpin, or catalytic device, of the mechanism of attribution.[168]

It is now recognized that all states have an obligation to prevent terrorist attacks emanating from their territory and injurious to other states. In terms of legal language, though, it should be noted that there is still no consensus within the international community as to a definition of terrorism.[169] Yet the concept is sufficiently circumscribed to entail international responsibility when coupled with the well-established principle that states will have to answer for attacks emanating from their territory. This legal scheme clearly evidences that the shortcomings of the international community will not preclude applying overriding principles of law, such as the prohibition on the use of force and the obligation to prevent injuries to neighboring states.

With regard to the legal characterization of terrorist attacks, the question of retaliation against a host state has always been difficult, especially when attempting to label the original act wrongful. In short, before 9/11 an aggrieved state would often run into legal and diplomatic problems in characterizing the original attack so as to justify a reprisal against the host state. As Professor Bowett explained, "Even a policy of reprisal which might seek to avoid condemnation because of its 'reasonableness' encounters the initial difficulty of demonstrating the illegality of the activities against which it is directed. . . . Apart from using emotive terms such as 'terrorists,' Israel has sought to have the guerilla activities condemned as illegal . . . on a variety of grounds."[170] The international response to 9/11 seems to have done away with these evidentiary problems. In sum, once a terrorist attack is carried out, we must look at it in the abstract—namely, as an attack emanating from another territory—and focus on how the host state could have limited or avoided altogether its responsibility.

Furthermore, the obligation to prevent terrorist attacks can be derived from several international texts, rules, and principles.[171] The only margin for polemic with regard to this duty pertains to the actual content of the obligation, especially when contemplating the vast range or shades of state passiveness, inaction, or "willful blindness" vis-à-vis terrorist activities taking root within a given territory. It follows from this proposition that the trans-substantive rules must also be revamped accordingly; the international community must decide whether to lower the threshold for imputation or to forego attribution altogether in the context of modern terrorism. As evidenced by the above-mentioned considerations, the latter scenario seems better tailored to fit within the current international framework.

2. The Temporal Element of the Breach of an International Obligation

The case for circumventing attribution is particularly compelling when one considers the temporal component of breaches of international obligations. The central theme behind Article 14 of the Draft Articles lies in the distinction "between a breach which is continuing and one which has already been completed."[172] The distinction between instantaneous and continuing breaches was explored in the *Rainbow Warrior* arbitration.[173] In that case the Arbitral Tribunal was confronted with France's failure to detain two individuals pursuant to an agreement between both parties. In finding that the breach at hand had a continuous character, the Tribunal delivered an important statement on the nature of the continuous breach, stating that "this classification is not purely theoretical, but, on the contrary, it has practical consequences, since the seriousness of the breach and its prolongation in time cannot fail to have considerable bearing on the establishment of the reparation which is adequate for a violation presenting these two features."[174] However, the distinction between instantaneous and continuing breaches has not, so far, been thoroughly applied to international terrorism per se. In fact, it has only been the central question in cases involving such matters as contracts,[175] forced or involuntary disappearances,[176] expropriation or wrongful taking of

property,[177] treaty obligations,[178] jurisdictional issues,[179] and the loss of social status.[180]

The portion of Article 14 dealing with continuing breaches of international obligations, which is premised on a state's obligation to prevent a given event,[181] can possibly extend to situations of repeated cross-border attacks and reprisals. This argument, however, does not insinuate that a single terrorist attack, such as the one perpetrated on 9/11, would not engender long-lasting consequences or ripple effects.[182] Nevertheless, such attacks would likely fall within the realm of instantaneous breaches, as the one-time failure to prevent the terrorist act itself indicates a breach by the host state without having a continuing effect. All of the surrounding repercussions, whether characterized by collateral damage to civilians and property or the ensuing deaths of targeted individuals, fall within the ambit of the consequences of a terrorist attack without confirming, per se, that the failure to prevent the attack has a continuing character.

Conversely, it is also interesting to note that the *in fine* portion of the same provision is couched in negative terms, which does not preclude applying the Draft Articles to a series of terrorist attacks, such as the aggregate acts of al Qaeda, including the 1993 World Trade Center bombing, the bombing of the United States' African embassies, the bombing of the *USS Cole*, and the events of 9/11. When seen through this lens and compared to the situation in the Middle East, these accounts appear to fit within Bowett's "overall relationship" theory. However, setting aside the Arab-Israeli context for a moment, the duty of a host state to prevent terrorist attacks may entail analyzing a different temporal dimension.

Unlike situations of contractual breaches or continued disappearances, the objective of the duty to prevent attacks is to actually stop them from occurring. Such scenarios do not primarily entail economic loss, such as contractual breaches do, but rather focus on protecting innocent civilians from widespread and systematic annihilation or loss of limb. For example, transferring the contractual notion of "efficient breach"[183] to the obligation of preventing terrorism would yield perverse results, as host states could engage in balancing human lives in deciding whether or not to breach their obligation. For example, a state could decide not to inject significant funds into law enforcement or border security measures if its intelligence concluded that a possible attack would only jeopardize a few human lives. Such a result is unpalatable. Therefore, in the context of international terrorism, the stakes are inherently greater and should justify a stricter regime of state responsibility.

Furthermore, given the international community's involvement and obvious resolve in combating international terrorism, one could argue that every state has an interest in preventing terrorist attacks. In fact, terrorism strikes at the very core of human dignity and security, and it would prove illusory to assert that a state has no interest in preventing a terrorist attack involving other states. Based on that logic, the obligation to prevent terrorism might, perhaps, qualify as an obligation *erga omnes*. Should this characterization of the obligation hold, it would entail a significant consequence under the Draft Articles: Third-party states could raise the failure to fulfill an obligation to prevent a terrorist attack when an excursion is launched from a host state against another state.[184] The confirmation of this characterization will depend largely on the evolution of international law in the upcoming years. Until that time, a single argument remains immutable: To expect the international legal order to countenance a claim that preventing terrorist attacks does not constitute a concern for the international community, as a whole, is unrealistic.

An obligation such as the one faced by Afghanistan on September 11, 2001, belongs to the realm of instantaneous breaches. This is not to say, however, that the Draft Articles preclude the breach of an obligation to prevent a given event from having a continuing character.[185] Once an attack is successfully launched from a host state, the threat has not been thwarted and

the object of the obligation is defeated. It is imperative to remember that this context is very different from transboundary environmental damage, for example. Here, the international community is not just concerned with containing the threat if the initial harm is unavoidable; rather, the objective is to forestall the initial wrongful act before it occurs. Furthermore, the failure to prevent terrorism entails far more serious consequences than the mere emission of toxic pollutants. ILC Special Rapporteur James Crawford spoke to this point:

> For example, the obligation to prevent transboundary damage by air pollution, dealt with in the *Trail Smelter* arbitration, was breached for as long as the pollution continued to be emitted. Indeed, in such cases the breach may be progressively aggravated by the failure to suppress it. However, *not all obligations directed to preventing an act from occurring will be of this kind. If the obligation in question was only concerned to prevent the happening of the event in the first place (as distinct from its continuation), there will be no continuing wrongful act.*[186]

Hence, a more stringent regime of state responsibility should be imposed, as we are sometimes confronted with situations that signal a departure from the Arab-Israeli relationship and, consequently, preclude the application of Article 14(3) of the Draft Articles. In sum, if we adopt the consensus that "one attack is too much," which generally aligns with the philosophy of the laws of war[187] and international law, we must necessarily impose a heavier burden of precaution on host states.

Once a host state fails to fulfill its obligation of prevention, thereby defeating the very purpose for which the obligation existed in the first place,[188] that state should not be able to escape scrutiny for not having acted on the right incentives, save in specific circumstances. If we want the war on terror to have a preventive rather than curative character, we must tackle the problem at its roots and provide the right impetus to governments. The objective here is to efficiently forestall terrorist attacks using, as the Security Council termed it, "all necessary steps" while also preventing an abusive application of state responsibility. Based on this objective, coupled with the above-mentioned considerations and the paradigm shift toward indirect responsibility, it would be helpful to forego attribution altogether in the context of modern terrorism. Besides, it is clear that the mechanism of indirect state responsibility has become a sort of "safety net" to pin responsibility on a host state should an aggrieved state endeavor to establish direct responsibility but fail to do so. With this in mind, a regime of state responsibility underpinned by a rationale of strict liability would better serve the interests of the international community. Even though much has been written on the notion of fault in international state responsibility, it should be cautioned that conventional wisdom does not preclude implementing a mechanism of strict liability in this area of the law.[189]

3. Domestic Law Analogies: The Products Liability Paradigm

Although not directly transposable to international law per se, we can consider domestic products liability law[190] as a philosophically similar phenomenon to the war on terrorism.[191] In the broader context of national tort law, it is sometimes more efficient to opt for a rule of strict liability over a negligence or fault-based rule.[192] Strict liability happens to be the course the United States follows in products liability litigation. For instance, in the exploding Coke bottle cases, the manufacturer was found strictly liable because public policy demands that manufacturers be responsible for the quality of their products.[193] This pro-consumer approach can easily be compared to terrorist attacks emanating from a given territory, namely through a pro-civilian posture vis-à-vis terrorism. Governments are obviously better positioned to thwart terrorist attacks than civilians, just as a goods manufacturer is more aware of the potential hazardous effects of a product than the unsuspecting consumer: "The purpose of such liability is

to insure that the costs of injuries resulting from defective products are borne by the manufacturers that put such products on the market rather than by the injured persons who are powerless to protect themselves."[194] In the post-Beirut raid days, state responsibility seemed more akin to the tort concept of negligence, or at least, it was governed by principles of due diligence and reasonableness.[195] The underlying reasonableness of the use of force vis-à-vis the original wrongful act guided much of the Security Council's attitude toward the legitimacy of reprisals against host states. This certainly entailed a rigorous evaluation of the host state's failure[196] to prevent a cross-border attack along with the severity of the terrorist strike.

It is clear that we are not dealing with a typical Law and Economics paradigm, as when addressing products liability litigation. However, products liability regulation and the war on terror do converge in one crucial aspect: They both constitute an exercise in risk assessment.[197] The driving force behind my reform is to provide the right incentives to governments in combating international terrorism. This type of regime could be tantamount to a compromise between sacrificing a host state's territorial integrity and sovereignty, and upholding its dignity on the international scene. Such a model clearly does not suit all areas within the realm of international state responsibility, which coexist on a continuum. Contractual breaches between states rest at one end of the spectrum and could never attract a rule of strict liability. The obligation to prevent terrorist attacks resides at the other end because, unlike with contract law, the international community engages in the objective of saving lives and protecting civilians. In addition, international terrorism is a crime so intrinsically repugnant to humanity[198] that it undoubtedly warrants a stringent scheme of state responsibility. It is needless to say that should the obligation of preventing terrorist attacks be construed as a rule of *jus cogens*, it would necessarily entail a stricter regime of responsibility.[199] It inevitably follows from this proposition that the international community will justifiably impose a higher burden of precaution on host states. Hence, it seems that the goals of the UN Charter, along with the relevant Security Council Resolutions, would be better served by transferring the onus onto the host state.

Under the new paradigm, the Security Council has considerably distanced itself from this earlier posture of reasonableness and could ultimately move toward a more radical concept such as strict liability. The objectives of Resolutions 1368 and 1373 would be better served by short-circuiting the concept of attribution altogether. My proposed framework of strict liability is, however, subject to a few caveats motivated by policy considerations.

4. Mitigating Tensions: Implementing a Model of Strict Liability

In tort law, the concept of strict liability has sometimes been construed as absolute liability. For example, under this approach a manufacturer cannot escape liability to the buyer once the harm is done, save in circumstances where causation cannot be established. Generally, defenses are not available under a rationale of absolute liability.[200] There has been some tendency within the legal community to impose an obligation of result[201] on host states, indicating that once a terrorist attack is successfully launched, the object of the obligation has been frustrated and responsibility should automatically follow. Otherwise, host states will elude responsibility and the obligation to prevent will be pointless. However, there exists a second and influential school of thought on the subject, which purports to demonstrate that several defenses do exist against a claim of strict liability[202] and that the pivotal device in such litigation resides in the onus shift from plaintiff to defendant. This school, concerned about weapons of mass destruction, argues that a collective duty to prevent terrorism would legitimize infringing sovereignty should host states fail to eliminate terrorist threats.[203]

Regardless of the approach espoused by the international community, it is fair to say that an obligation to prevent based on producing a specific outcome is not feasible, let alone reasonable.[204] Thus, the second conception of strict liability somewhat influences my model, although it likely rests on some middle ground between the two categorical positions. Given the serious nature of terrorist activity and the objective to protect civilians, this context provides us with more leeway in imposing stricter rules of state responsibility. Hence, more moderate views construe the obligation to prevent terrorist attacks as requiring an *ex post facto*[205] exercise of factual evaluation, to be performed on a case-by-case basis.

The most convincing argument for implementing strict liability vis-à-vis international terrorism resides in the evidentiary problems related to attribution.[206] When faced with the breach of an obligation to prevent a given event—namely, a terrorist attack—an aggrieved state is at somewhat of a legal impasse in establishing the international responsibility of the host state. As with the Coke bottle manufacturer who has exclusive knowledge over the manufacturing process, the host state is better positioned than the injured state to know, for example, what logistical, intelligence, police, and military means are at its disposal to eliminate the threat.[207] Furthermore, as the sole sovereign and legal guardian of its national borders, the host state simply has the most insight and reach into terrorist activities conducted within its territory. Establishing attribution based on very limited publicly available facts would pose a significant obstacle for aggrieved states, especially in light of the fact that the content of the obligation to prevent terrorism is far from being settled law. Because failing to prevent a given event from occurring is an inherently nebulous and difficult concept, the objectives of efficiency and legitimacy of international law would be better vindicated through a shift in onus to the host state.

5. A Two-Tiered Strict Liability Mechanism

The objective in a shift in onus to the host state is not only to transfer the burden of proof but also to shift the incentives to the host state. This could be achieved through a two-tiered strict liability mechanism—namely, through eliminating attribution and recognizing that once a terrorist attack has been launched from a host state, that state is automatically indirectly responsible for the attack. In other words, a successful cross-border terrorist strike establishes a prima facie case of responsibility against the host state. It is important to clarify that the idea is not to encourage or promote the creation of totalitarian states,[208] nor to implement a system of absolute liability[209] where host states are deprived of the opportunity to exculpate themselves *ex post facto*. If poorly conceived, this framework would be ripe for abuse against weaker states, especially developing countries that may not have the same means as industrialized countries to combat terrorism. Hence, we must correspondingly develop safeguards in order to avoid indiscriminate condemnation of host states, as it is not likely that the international community will accept a rationale of absolute liability and automatic reprisals against ineffective states.[210]

It logically follows that the host state will be able to refute the initial prima facie finding of responsibility. In other words, once responsibility has been established and the onus has shifted, the host state will have an opportunity to demonstrate how it exercised due care and exhausted all available options to thwart the terrorist attack. Considerations pertaining to the distinction between obligations of means and result,[211] such as the logistical capacity of the host state and the state's loss of control over its territory should only be invoked in this second step of the strict liability approach as an integral part of the defense against the prima facie finding of responsibility. The strict liability approach promotes fairness[212] among states and somewhat levels out the disparity in economic and political power. In sum, this proposed approach would place all host states on equal footing, irrespective of their economic or social status. In addition, this model would dissipate the direct responsibility paradigm in all cases except those rare circumstances in which an aggrieved state

can clearly establish direct involvement by the host state.

6. Other Advantages of a Strict Liability Model

This proposed system would also instill some legitimacy into the Security Council's decision making. Although different situations warrant different levels of response, the involvement of the Security Council in assessing state responsibility has, until now, been far too fact oriented. It is imperative to define clear rules of state responsibility, as the Council will likely sit as the final arbitrator in legitimizing responses involving force. Shifting the onus to the host state offers several advantages, including an overhaul of the Council's fact-finding function in establishing responsibility. In demonstrating that it fulfilled its obligation of prevention, a host state could convince the Security Council to authorize less invasive peacekeeping arrangements rather than full-scale military invasion. Based on the evidence adduced from the host state's case, the Security Council might consider that a given course of action is disproportionate and, therefore, gauge the adequate levels of response *ex ante*. More importantly, this type of structure will hopefully strive to eliminate the pursuit of retaliation inspired by retribution alone.

Aside from enhancing the legitimacy of international efforts to combat terrorism and delineating the ambit of state responsibility, this model would also foster states' comparative policy-making and collaborative efforts. Several commentators expound that multilateral collaboration should be preferred over unilateral state action in instilling a preventive character to the war on terrorism.[213] In this spirit, states could engage in significant risk control[214] and risk assessment of possible terrorist threats and, hopefully, encourage multilateral exchanges of information and intelligence along with financial "red flagging" of terrorist assets.[215] In addition to sending a message of deterrence to complacent governments, this approach would also provide states with a forum to voice and test out their counter-terrorism policies. We must remember that the objective is to make the war on terror a preventive rather than a curative effort, and thus the imposition of strict liability for failing to prevent a terrorist attack would be resorted to only after a preventable terrorist attack occurs. Beforehand, we must contemplate all reasonable steps to prevent it.

One final argument must be dealt with. Some might argue that a new law of strict liability would impugn the dignity of host states that honestly do their best to stop terrorism. Even though they would not be held directly responsible for the attack, they would nonetheless face the social stigma of having violated international law.[216] In response to this argument, it is imperative to recall that there are no ideal solutions to preventing international terrorism: Mitigating the tensions between sovereignty and reputation remains a noble objective in making the world a safer place. In addition, this approach seems to be a reasonable ground between the zeal of imposing unreasonable obligations on host states—namely, obligations of result—and envisioning a regime too loosely suited for modern warfare where states can easily elude responsibility. From that perspective, it would seem desirable and more efficient to slightly sacrifice "saving face," so to speak, rather than infringe territorial sovereignty and fail to prevent massive deaths and widespread terror. Finally, the social stigma argument can also be interpreted as a positive force, generating realistic incentives and expectations within the international community.

Based on the foregoing reasons and the precedence achieved by indirect responsibility, international law could countenance a regime of strict liability, albeit predicated on the opportunity for host states to raise defenses or justifications vis-à-vis their duty to prevent terrorist attacks. It is important to briefly explore the second tier of the strict liability approach, namely the possible considerations raised by host states against a prima facie presumption of indirect responsibility. This exercise starts with a brief overview of the obligation of prevention, which constitutes the focal point of my strict liability inquiry and the cornerstone of modern indirect state responsibility.

IV. The Obligation of Prevention in International Law

A. The Emergence of the Obligation of Prevention

It is now established that a state will be responsible for "noxious fumes" emanating from its territory, whether caused by a smelter or a terrorist organization.[217] The obligation of a host state to prevent terrorist attacks emanating from its territory is so widely recognized[218] that it should not fuel a debate. Many of the pertinent and modern sources of the obligation, such as Security Council Resolutions 1368 and 1373, have already been discussed above. In addition, there are several documents[219] adopted under the aegis of the UN, including other Security Council resolutions[220] and multilateral treaties,[221] which impose an affirmative duty on states to prevent acts of terrorism.[222]

This obligation stems from the basic principle of sovereignty, which entails both rights and obligations.[223] Under universal neighboring principles, it is well established that the rights of one state end where the territory of another state begins.[224] An obvious source of this obligation lies in Article 2(4) of the UN Charter, which reflects customary law in expressly prohibiting states from using or threatening to use force against another state.[225] Based on that logic, a host state that has the capability to prevent a terrorist attack but fails to do so will inherently fail to fulfill its duty under Article 2(4) because terrorism amounts to force by definition. This proposition is reinforced when the host state openly supports or endorses the terrorist attack on another state's territory.[226]

B. The Meaning of the Obligation of Prevention

The second tier of my strict liability approach centers on a host state's attempt to refute or, at least, dissipate the prima facie finding of indirect responsibility against it. Most of the usual considerations surrounding the failure to prevent a terrorist attack—be they the level of knowledge of the host state, the size of the territory and its police/military capacity, the nature of the circumstances and history of terrorism within the country, and so forth—should be invoked during this second step.

Although the distinction between obligations of conduct and result has been instrumental at times in the context of the Draft Articles,[227] obligations of prevention "are usually construed as best efforts obligations, requiring States to take all reasonable or necessary measures to prevent a given event from occurring, but without warranting that the event will not occur."[228] This distinction remains somewhat relevant for applying the Draft Articles, in that it "may assist in ascertaining when a breach has occurred,"[229] but it does not constitute the pivotal point. In terms of enforcing an obligation of result via the judiciary, courts will be more inclined to proceed on a case-by-case basis[230] rather than try to fit all similar obligations into a single legal matrix. In addition, the above-mentioned distinction has not been a determinative factor in guiding courts when adjudicating breaches of international obligations.[231]

The controversy over the distinction between obligations of conduct and result, along with their scope and content, is far from resolved.[232] Nevertheless, incorporating this distinction in international law is sound and desirable. As a general rule, it is fair to say that an obligation of result in preventing terrorist activities will not be reasonable, let alone realistic. The dispositive factor will lie, rather, in the conduct of the host state itself in addressing the potential threat and in attaining a realistic result in light of the factual circumstances.

The best way to conceptualize the obligation of prevention is to visualize a sliding element on a vertical bipolar continuum representing the conduct of the host state. At one end of the spectrum lies the expected (and specific) result dictated by the obligation to prevent terrorist attacks, namely, to thwart the attack completely.

At the other extremity of the continuum rests the utmost negligent and careless conduct a state can adopt in preventing terrorism. All along the way, various degrees of state efficiency in preventing attacks are delimited, increment by increment. This scale covers an exhaustive set of possibilities, ranging from the near prevention of a given attack to inaction.[233] The sliding element represents the host state's conduct and is positioned at the angle that better represents that state's action to prevent the given attack. The circumstances of the particular attack will affect the sliding element: Should they be favorable to the host state, the element will slide up, closer to the expected result. However, if they are construed against the host state, they will burden the element and bring it down toward negligent or careless conduct.

For example, if a state had the logistical capacity to crack down on terrorist cells that perpetrated an attack but failed to do so, for example, by not acting on intelligence reports or failing to properly manage them,[234] the element will descend. The same is true if the host state failed to freeze terrorist assets within its jurisdiction, if it endorsed or promoted the terrorists' cause,[235] or if it knowingly harbored or supported members of a terrorist organization within its territory[236] when the organization overtly perpetrates egregious violations of international law.[237]

Conversely, if a host state does not completely fulfill its obligation or does not attain its potential in preventing the attack because doing so would generate more social unrest and terror,[238] the element will slide up the continuum; if there is a significant disparity or disproportion between the size of the host state's territory and its military capacity relative to the expanse of terrorist activity within the territory, the onus of the state will decrease and the element will ascend. Similarly, the element will rise if a portion of the territory of the host state has been taken over, so that the legitimate government does not wield any kind of tangible control over the region[239] or if the host state is logistically incapable of preventing an attack but considers the panoply of options offered to it, including allowing foreign forces into its territory to combat the threat,[240] its burden will be lowered considerably, as it will have sacrificed sovereignty in favor of combating terrorism in a multilateral setting.[241] In short, the examination turns on an *ex post facto* analysis of whether the state could have put more effort into preventing the terrorist attack.[242]

Now visualize a second sliding element mounted on another bipolar continuum representing the obligation of prevention, placed in a parallel and proximate position to the first polar continuum. At the top of this continuum, and facing the expected (and specific) result pole on the other spectrum, one can find *jus cogens* obligations.[243] At the other end of the continuum rests the minimal standard of conduct prescribed by international law, this time sitting across from the pole of the utmost negligent conduct. Similarly to the other continuum, various degrees of international obligations are scattered between both poles, ranging from obligations to endeavor to obligations *erga omnes*. The gap between obligations of conduct and result, albeit a sliding concept as well, is dissimulated somewhere in the continuum of international obligations. On the second continuum, the element represents the international community's formal characterization of the specific obligation under study.

Consider that both elements are connected by an elastic band and that the ideal objective is to maintain the elastic in a horizontal position, such that the elements are aligned. As soon as a slight increase is felt in either continuum, the elastic will stretch, thereby creating a gap between the elements. In order for the host state to demonstrate that it used all "necessary means" to prevent the terrorist attack, there should be as small a gap as possible between the expected obligation and the conduct in question. Should such a cavity widen, it will undoubtedly inform the analysis of state responsibility: The liability of the host state should be proportional to that gap.

In theory, the distinction between obligations of conduct and result will slide along the second continuum and adapt to the circumstances of the case, namely, the conduct of the host state represented by the position of the element on the first continuum. In other words, reasonableness will exert an influence in guiding the elements toward what constitutes an acceptable threshold for the host state. Should the circumstances indicate that, within reason, more could have been done by the host state, the element will ineluctably fall lower on the first continuum, in which case the gap between elements will widen and, as a result, the elastic will elongate.

To complicate the equation, the international community's formal characterization of the obligation to prevent will also interact with the elements. For instance, should the obligation to prevent terrorist attacks be characterized as an obligation *erga omnes*, it will correspondingly attract a stricter regime of responsibility. Consequently, there will be a significant upward movement of the second element along with the gap between obligations of conduct and result; should the actual conduct of the host state on the first continuum fall below what is required by the obligation *erga omnes*, this will engender a considerable gap between the elements.

The most ostentatious upward thrust would result from the international community's characterization of the obligation to prevent as a *jus cogens* obligation.[244] This conclusion would inexorably turn on the development of a legal duty to prevent terrorist attacks—whether through a more confined or regional radius of operation or through a generalized and universally accepted rule—as mirrored by customary international law.[245] The higher the obligation to prevent, the more onerous and incumbent the burden of refuting indirect responsibility will be on the host state. Irrespective of where the elements may fall, there will often be a constant sliding gap, not only between how the obligation and the actual conduct of the state are characterized, but also between the obligation of conduct/result dichotomy and all the interpolar degrees on both axes.

This area of the law is far from settled. Although largely fact driven, these dimensions of state responsibility require the international community to develop the system further.[246] However, to require that all obligations of prevention be categorized into a single legal matrix is unrealistic. One inference becomes self-apparent: Regardless of the approach adopted by the international community, this area of indirect state responsibility should be governed by a variable threshold model. To impose an obligation of result to prevent terrorist attacks in all cases would prove unreasonable and inefficient. However, this does not preclude applying an obligation of result when the facts of the case warrant it, such as when the host state holds all the information and means to prevent a given attack but decides not to thwart the excursion. In such exceptional cases, namely where the misalignment between both axes is so astronomical and the regime of responsibility is akin to a bright-line rule, breaches of international obligations are easily cognizable. Finally, it seems that the international community must redefine some primary rules of international law after all, as the obligation itself is clear: A state has an affirmative duty to forestall transborder excursions emanating from its territory and injurious to other states.[247] Defining the contours of that rule, namely whether it should impose a specific result on states or belong to the realm of *jus cogens*, could send the international community back to the drawing board for quite some time.

V. Conclusion

The world now faces new threats and needs to rethink international mechanisms. The events of 9/11 mark perhaps the most pivotal point in recent memory with regard to international law. It changed the way states protect their borders, the way immigration flows in most Western countries, the way modern states conceive terrorism and counter-terrorism, and so forth. The importance of the response to 9/11 cannot be overemphasized, as it marked a clear departure from prior practice in several areas of international law, state responsibility being central. Not only did the response to 9/11 considerably alter the application of *jus ad bellum*, it also initiated an important shift in the law of indirect state responsibility. With the advent of important milestones in the field of state responsibility, such as the *Tehran* decision and the Draft Articles, the transition from a model of attribution and direct responsibility to a model of indirect responsibility was natural and logical. From this perspective, and also considering the Security Council's resolve to eradicate terrorism, the move toward a mechanism of strict liability does not seem so improbable, provided it is endowed with significant safeguards for host states. The objective here is to instill life and rigor into a truly global counter-terrorism campaign.

The strict liability model has great propensity for change, progress, and efficiency at the international level. Not only does it promote fairness among host states, but it also provides governments with the right incentives: Combating terrorism can only be successfully accomplished on a multilateral level through the mutual exchange of information and policies. The pursuit of egregious and blind self-interests will harmfully affect the efficacy of the regime of international responsibility. Although certain archetypal social elements such as crime and violence will never be completely obliterated, the objective remains to design a scheme of state responsibility that is the most conducive to international peace and security. Conversely, this model also poses problems and is potentially ripe for abuse by economically stronger states. Efficient international state responsibility can be encapsulated in one word: compromise. This notion has pervaded my discussion. Situations like the 1982 Israel-Lebanon incident illustrate the inherent tensions in establishing the parameters of indirect responsibility. Throughout most episodes of transborder aggression, the principles of sovereignty and territorial integrity have been opposed by the crucial and often time-sensitive need to prevent terrorist attacks. If members of the international community hope to empower the global counter-terrorism campaign, they will have to relinquish or, at least, concede some parts of the fundamental values found in the modern system of nation-states. In all likelihood, the choice will ultimately require some sacrifice of state sovereignty and dignity.

The international community is now seriously concerned with preventing attacks and deterring terrorist organizations. Forestalling the proliferation of terrorist activity through the channel of host states can be a judicious strategy, if well orchestrated. However, logistical considerations abound, and we must take stock of the realities facing developing countries and ineffective states. For example, it is unrealistic to ask a small country like Lebanon to effectively thwart PLO terrorists when it has already surrendered a considerable region of its own territory to them.

The "harboring and supporting" principle has essentially taken over as the linchpin of modern state responsibility vis-à-vis terrorism. Based on the new paradigm, host states can be found responsible for wrongful acts, as would the babysitter who fails to prevent the children under his or her guard from burning down the neighbor's house. The debates pertaining to attribution seem somewhat distant, and the question of direct state involvement does not hold the same relevance it once did. However, this new paradigm of indirect responsibility carries with it new and sometimes nebulous legal challenges, such as the difference between obligations of conduct and result, the definition of the obligation of prevention, and the applicable legal standard for ineffective states in combating terrorist activity. Given the current legal climate and lack of consensus on these issues, it is difficult to clearly establish a legal regime governing these politically volatile situations. In the meantime, we can only hope that our extant scheme of state responsibility, paired with vigilant law enforcement, will be able to contain the most serious threats. Indeed, the simple days are long over.

NOTES

1. PETER MALANCZUK, AKEHURST'S MODERN INTRODUCTION TO INTERNATIONAL LAW 254 (7th ed. 1997); see also ROSALYN HIGGINS, PROBLEMS AND PROCESS: INTERNATIONAL LAW AND HOW WE USE IT 148 (1994) (noting the inherent difficulty of codifying the law of state responsibility).

2. On a possible application of the *Caroline* doctrine to states that provide refuge to terrorists, see Michael Reisman, *International Legal Responses to International Terrorism*, 22 HOUS. J. INT'L L. 3, 42–50 (1999).

3. It is interesting to note that anticipatory self-defense is also governed by the requirements of necessity, imminence, and proportionality. See Robert Y. Jennings, *The Caroline and McLeod Cases*, 72 AM. J. INT'L L. 32, 82 (1978); see also Michael Byers, *Letting the Exception Prove the Rule*, at www.carnegiecouncil.org/viewMedia .php/prmTemplateID/8/prmID/852; Jutta Brunée & Stephen J. Toope, *Canada and the Use of Force: Reclaiming Human Security*, 59 INT'L J. 247, 251–52 (2004).

4. As Thomas Franck pointed out, some scholars contest the modern relevance of the *Caroline* elements. THOMAS FRANCK, RECOURSE TO FORCE: STATE ACTION AGAINST THREATS AND ARMED ATTACKS 67 n.82 (2002); see also CHRISTINE GRAY, INTERNATIONAL LAW AND THE USE OF FORCE 105–06 (2000); I OPPENHEIM'S INTERNATIONAL LAW 420 (Sir Robert Jennings & Sir Arthur Watts eds., 9th ed. 1992); MALCOLM SHAW, INTERNATIONAL LAW 691–92 (3d ed. 1991); Tawia Ansah, *War: Rhetoric and Norm-Creation in Response to Terror*, 43 VA. J. INT'L L. 797, 841, n.143 (discussing "the doctrine of self-defense beyond the customary law's ontological elements").

5. It is interesting to note that Thomas Franck took issue with what seems to be a prevailing interpretation of the *Caroline* case: "The assertion that self-defense requires 'immediate' action comes from a misunderstanding of the Caroline decision, which deals only with *anticipatory* self-defense." Thomas Franck, *Terrorism and the Right of Self-Defense*, 95 AM. J. INT'L L. 839, 840 (2001) (emphasis in original).

6. On the fundamentals of modern terrorism and warfare, generally, see Matthew Lippman, *The New Terrorism and International Law*, 10 TULSA J. COMP. & INT'L L. 297 (2003).

7. Derek W. Bowett, *Reprisals Involving Recourse to Armed Force*, 66 AM. J. INT'L L. 1 (1972). Given that Professor Bowett's article addresses the question of armed reprisals and not state responsibility per se, I will only invoke and analyze certain elements of his work. It should be mentioned, at the outset, that there has been some thought-provoking scholarly output on specific issues dealing with state responsibility and terrorism after 9/11. Interesting accounts on the issue include Giovanni Battaglini, *War Against Terrorism Extra Moenia, Self-Defence and Responsibility: A Pure Judicial Approach*, in INTERNATIONAL RESPONSIBILITY TODAY: ESSAYS IN MEMORY OF OSCAR SCHACHTER 137–50 (Maurizio

Ragazzi ed., Martinus Nijhoff Publishers, 2005); Alison Elizabeth Chase, *Legal Mechanisms of the International Community and the United States Concerning State Sponsorship of Terrorism*, 45 VA. J. INT'L L. 41–137 (2004); John Alan Cohan, *Formulation of a State's Response to Terrorism and State-Sponsored Terrorism*, 14 PACE INT'L L. REV. 77–119 (2002); Mark A. Drumbl, *Terrorist Crime, Taliban Guilt, Western Victims, and International Law*, 31 DENV. J. INT'L L. & POL'Y 69–79 (2002); Pierre-Marie Dupuy, *State Sponsors of Terrorism: Issues of International Responsibility*, in ENFORCING INTERNATIONAL LAW NORMS AGAINST TERRORISM 3–16 (Andrea Bianchi ed., Hart Publishing, 2004); Barry Kellman, *State Responsibility for Preventing Bioterrorism*, 36 INT'L L. 29–38 (2002); Michael J. Kelly, *Understanding September 11th—An International Legal Perspective on the War in Afghanistan*, 35 CREIGHTON L. REV. 283–93 (2002); Scott M. Malzahn, *State Sponsorship and Support of International Terrorism: Customary Norms of State Responsibility*, 26 HASTINGS INT'L & COMP. L. REV. 83–114 (2002); Sarah E. Smith, *International Law: Blaming Big Brother: Holding States Accountable for the Devastation of Terrorism*, 56 OKLA. L. REV. 735–75 (2003).

8. Military and Paramilitary Activities in and Against Nicaragua (*Nicar. v. U.S.*), 1986 I.C.J. 14 (Jun. 27) [hereinafter *Nicaragua*].

9. *Prosecutor v. Dusko Tadić*, Case No. IT-94-1-A, I.C.T.Y. App. Ch., 15 Jul. 1999 [hereinafter *Tadić*].

10. Tehran Hostages Case (*U.S. v. Iran*), 1980 I.C.J. 64 (May 24) [hereinafter *Tehran*].

11. State Responsibility: Titles and text of the draft articles on Responsibility of States for international wrongful acts adopted by the Drafting Committee on second reading. U.N. Doc. A/CN.4/L.602/Rev.1 (2001) [hereinafter *Draft Articles*].

12. For example, several commentators agree that the military campaign in Afghanistan has, for all intents and purposes, disabled the effective control test. *See, e.g.*, Carsten Stahn, *Terrorist Acts as "Armed Attack": The Right to Self-Defense, Article 51 (1/2) of the UN Charter, and International Terrorism*, 27 FLETCHER F. WORLD AFF. 35, 37 (2003) ("If there is one certainty after September 11, it is that the 'effective control test' articulated in the International Court of Justice's (ICJ) decision in Nicaragua has been over-turned."). *See also* Carsten Stahn, *"Nicaragua Is Dead, Long Live Nicaragua": The Right to Self-Defense Under Art. 51 UN Charter and International Terrorism*, in TERRORISM AS A CHALLENGE FOR NATIONAL AND INTERNATIONAL LAW: SECURITY VERSUS LIBERTY? 827–77 (Christian Walter et al. eds., Springer, 2004); Rüdiger Wolfrum, *The Attack of September 11, 2001, the Wars Against the Taliban and Iraq: Is There a Need to Reconsider International Law on the Recourse to Force and the Rules in Armed Conflict?* 7 MAX PLANCK

Y.B. UN L. 1–78 (2003); J. Wouters & F. Naert, *Shockwaves Through International Law After 11 September: Finding the Right Responses to the Challenges of International Terrorism*, in LEGAL INSTRUMENTS IN THE FIGHT AGAINST INTERNATIONAL TERRORISM: A TRANSATLANTIC DIALOGUE 411–546 (C. Fijnaut, J. Wouters, & F. Naert eds., Martinus Nijhoff Publishers, 2004). Others generally conclude that Operation Enduring Freedom has fundamentally challenged international law. *See* Asli Bâli, *Stretching the Limits of International Law: The Challenge of Terrorism*, 8 ILSA J. INT'L & COMP. L. 403–16 (2002); Richard A. Falk, *Rediscovering International Law After September 11th*, 16 TEMP. INT'L & COMP. L. J. 359–69 (2002); Christine Gray, *A New War for a New Century?: The Use of Force Against Terrorism After September 11, 2001*, in SEPTEMBER 11, 2001: A TURNING POINT IN INTERNATIONAL AND DOMESTIC LAW 97–126 (P. Eden & T. O'Donnell eds., Transnational Publishers, 2005); Laurence R. Helfer, *Transforming International Law After the September 11 Attacks?: Three Evolving Paradigms for Regulating International Terrorism*, in SEPTEMBER 11 IN HISTORY: A WATERSHED MOMENT? 180–93 (M. L. Dudziak ed., Duke University Press, 2003); John F. Murphy, *International Law and the War on Terrorism: The Road Ahead*, 32 ISRAEL Y.B. HUM. RTS. 117–63 (2003); Nico J. Schrijver, *Responding to International Terrorism: Moving the Frontiers of International Law for "Enduring Freedom"?* 48 NETHERLANDS INT'L L. REV. 271–91 (2001); Nico J. Schrijver, *September 11 and Challenges to International Law*, in TERRORISM AND THE UN: BEFORE AND AFTER SEPTEMBER 11 55–73 (J. Boulden & T. G. Weiss eds., Indiana University Press, 2004).

13. *See* Malanczuk, *supra* note 1, at 259. For a thoughtful and recent account on the issue, *see* Rüdiger Wolfrum, *State Responsibility for Private Actors: An Old Problem of Renewed Relevance*, in INTERNATIONAL RESPONSIBILITY TODAY: ESSAYS IN MEMORY OF OSCAR SCHACHTER 423–34 (Maurizio Ragazzi ed., Martinus Nijhoff Publishers, 2005).

14. *See* IAN BROWNLIE, SYSTEM OF THE LAW OF NATIONS: STATE RESPONSIBILITY (Part i) 132–66 (1983); David D. Caron, *The Basis of Responsibility: Attribution and Other Trans-Substantive Rules*, in THE IRAN–UNITED STATES CLAIMS TRIBUNAL: ITS CONTRIBUTION TO THE LAW OF STATE RESPONSIBILITY 109 (Richard B. Lillich & Daniel B. Magraw eds., 1998). On the specific question of Osama bin Laden's status as an agent of the state, *see* John Quigley, *International Law Violations by the United States in the Middle East as a Factor Behind Anti-American Terrorism*, 63 U. PITT L. REV. 815, 826 (2002).

15. It is also interesting to note that the Definition of Aggression, Annex to G.A. Res. 3314 (XXIX), U.N. GAOR, 29th Sess., Supp. No. 31, at 143, U.N. Doc.

A/9631 (1974), also alludes to the question of attribution to states of the acts of their agents. Article 3(g) of the Definition defines "aggression" as the "sending by or on behalf of a State of armed bands, groups, irregulars or mercenaries, which carry out acts of armed force of such gravity as to amount to the acts listed [in the preceding paragraphs]." With regard to this definition of aggression, Thomas Franck pointed out: "The prohibition does not specify what 'sending' means. Does it include 'permitting,' or 'tolerating'?" Frank, *supra* note 4, at 65. These considerations will be extremely relevant in the subsequent portions of this chapter, as I will discuss the shift toward indirect state responsibility at international law along with the importance of the "harboring terrorists" rule. *See also* Davis Brown, *Use of Force Against Terrorism After September 11th: State Responsibility, Self-Defense and Other Responses*, 11 CARDOZO J. INT'L & COMP. L. 1, 8 (2003).

16. *Nicaragua, supra* note 8, at 64–65. For more background on the issue of state responsibility for the acts of de facto agents, see Gregory Townsend, *State Responsibility for Acts of De Facto Agents*, 14 ARIZ. J. INT'L & COMP. L. 635–78 (1997).

17. *Id.*

18. *Tadić, supra* note 9, at 47.

19. *Id.* The court also identified various situations in which the threshold of control would vary.

20. *Id.* at 49. For support of the proposition that *Tadić* significantly relaxed the *Nicaragua* standard, see Ahmed S. Younis, *Imputing War Crimes in the War on Terrorism: The U.S., Northern Alliance, and "Container Crimes,"* 9 WASH. & LEE RACE & ETHNICITY J. 109, 114–15 (2003) (arguing that *Tadić* strengthened the effective control test by excepting organized armed forces).

21. *Tadić, supra* note 9, at 58.

22. *Id.* at 56, 58.

23. The *Tadić* decision essentially did away with the requirement of having specific orders issued from host states to militarily organized groups. *See, e.g.*, Stahn, *Terrorist Acts as "Armed Attack," supra* note 12, at 47; *see also* Mikael Nabati, *International Law at a Crossroads: Self-Defense, Global Terrorism, and Preemption (a Call to Rethink the Self-Defense Normative Framework)*, 13 TRANSNAT'L L. & CONTEMP. PROBS. 771, 781 (2003).

24. *Tadić, supra* note 9, at 56, 58.

25. *Id.* It is also interesting to note that in the *Tehran* case, Iranian responsibility for an attack carried out by militants on a U.S. embassy was predicated, in part, on the state authorities' subsequent approval of the attack. *Tehran, supra* note 10, at 33–35. Following the Ayatollah Khomeini's endorsement of the continuing occupation of the embassy and hostage taking, the Tribunal equated them to state acts. However, it did not attribute the attack and takeover of the embassy to Iran. On the topic of responsibility by endorsement, see Brown, *supra*

note 15, at 10–12. On the possibility of imputing responsibility to the Taliban for endorsing the 9/11 attacks, Brown argued that "the publicly available facts are insufficient to impute the September 11th attack to Afghanistan. They do not establish that Al-Qa'ida acted as an agent or instrumentality of the 'Afghan state,' but rather that Al-Qa'ida acted autonomously within Afghanistan." *Id.* at 11.

26. A case could be made that an organization like al Qaeda resembles a military group, given its organization, training, complex yet independent cellular structure, and efficient financial structures. *See, e.g.*, Jeffrey F. Addicott, *Legal and Policy Implications for a New Era: The "War on Terror,"* 4 SCHOLAR 209, 218 (2002) (referring to al Qaeda as a "sophisticated para-military" terrorist network); ROHAN GUNARATNA, INSIDE AL QAEDA: GLOBAL NETWORK OF TERROR 93–112 (2002).

27. Although there is still no consensus in international law on a universal definition of "terrorism," most states share a similar conception of the requisite elements of this crime. Whether through legislation, state treatment of terrorism, or multilateral instruments on the subject, it seems that the international community has sufficiently circumscribed the concept and identified two necessary elements: the *targeting of civilians* and *the ideological/political purpose*. Hence, an attack will be tantamount to an act of terrorism when it targets civilians and is inspired by an ideological purpose, namely, an intent that transcends the ordinary criminal standard. These considerations are consistent with the position I defended in an earlier article. *See* Vincent-Joël Proulx, *Rethinking the Jurisdiction of the International Criminal Court in the Post-September 11th Era: Should Acts of Terrorism Qualify As Crimes Against Humanity?* 19 AM. U. INT'L L. REV. 1009, 1030–41 (2004).

In this article, I construe "terrorism" as having an international character. For example, one might think of a terrorist organization that trains its forces, engages in fund-raising, and orchestrates an attack from the territory of Ruritania against the territory and civilians of State B. The aim of this article is to elucidate the elements surrounding the responsibility of Ruritania in the attack. Thus, I do not discuss cases such as the Timothy McVeigh situation, in which a terrorist attack is organized, planned, and carried out within the same national boundaries. In such scenarios, the accused are charged, tried, and convicted in conformity with national criminal law. Therefore, terrorist strikes lacking an extraterritorial component fall beyond the scope of this paper. Consequently, legal scholars have often differentiated between "domestic terrorists" and "international terrorists." *See, e.g.*, Lawrence Azubuike, *Status of Taliban and Al Qaeda Soldiers: Another Viewpoint*, 19 CONN. J. INT'L L. 127, 136 n.69 (2003); Mark A. Drumbl, *Victimhood in Our Neighborhood: Terrorist Crime, Taliban Guilt, and the Asymmetries of the International Legal Order*, 81 N.C. L. REV. 1, 65 (2002).

28. On the enormous challenges posed by the codification of the law of state responsibility, see Malanczuk, *supra* note 1, at 254.

29. *Draft Articles*, *supra* note 11, art. 1. As ILC Special Rapporteur James Crawford pointed out, the principle stated in Article 1—that once a wrongful act is committed, supplementary legal obligations are juxtaposed to existing state obligations—has been recognized prior to the Commission's adoption of that provision. JAMES CRAWFORD, THE INTERNATIONAL LAW COMMISSION'S ARTICLES ON STATE RESPONSIBILITY: INTRODUCTION, TEXT AND COMMENTARIES 78, 110 (2002); *see also* Mark B. Baker, *Terrorism and the Inherent Right of Self-Defense (A Call to Amend Article 51 of the United Nations Charter)*, 10 HOUS. J. INT'L L. 25, 26–27 (1987) (providing instances in which the principle contained in Article 1 was recognized after its formulation by the ILC).

30. For example, *see* North Sea Continental Shelf (F.R.G.-Den.), 1969 I.C.J. Rep. 3, 38–39 (Feb. 20); *Nicaragua*, *supra* note 8, at 95.

31. *Nicaragua*, *supra* note 8, at 95.

32. *See* Crawford, *supra* note 29, at 126.

33. *See* Vienna Convention on the Law of Treaties, May 23, 1969, 1155 U.N.T.S. 331; Crawford, *supra* note 29, at 127; *see also* Article 12 of the *Draft Articles*, *supra* note 11 (establishing that the "origin and character" of an international obligation is irrelevant in demonstrating a breach of that obligation).

34. Article 2 of the *Draft Articles*, *supra* note 11, reads as follows: "There is an internationally wrongful act of a State when conduct consisting of an action or omission: Is attributable to the State under international law; and Constitutes a breach of an international obligation of the State." This principle is also recognized in jurisprudence, albeit sometimes by different terminology. *See, e.g.*, *Nicaragua*, *supra* note 8, at 23; Phosphates in Morocco, Preliminary Objections, 1938 P.C.I.J. (ser. A/B) No. 74 (Jun. 14), at 10, 28; *Tehran*, *supra* note 10, at 28–29, 41–42; Gabčíkovo-Nagymaros Project (Hung.-Slovk.), 1997 I.C.J. Rep. 7 (Sept. 25) [hereinafter *Gabčíkovo-Nagymaros*]; Dickson Car Wheel Company (U.S.-Mex.), 4 U.N.R.I.A.A. 669, 679 (1931).

35. The *Draft Articles* make clear that both an act and an omission can constitute an internationally wrongful act. *See Tehran*, *supra* note 10, at 63, 67; Corfu Channel (U.K.-Alb.), 1949 I.C.J. 4, 22–23 (Apr. 9); Affaire relative à l'acquisition de la nationalité polonaise (Fr.-Pol.), 1 R.I.A.A. 26, 425 (Jul. 10, 1924); Velásquez Rodrìguez, Inter-Am. Ct. H.R., Ser. C, No. 4, at 154 (Jul. 29, 1988) ("under international law a State is responsible for the acts of its agents undertaken in their official capacity and for their omissions"). Yet it is probably erroneous

to contend that a host state is inherently responsible for a terrorist attack on account of omission simply because the attack is launched from the host state against another state. In fact, I discuss below scenarios in which states are actively attempting to thwart terrorist threats emanating from their territory. For now, it is fair to say that internationally responsible host states are not always complacent, inactive, or willfully blind to terrorist activities within their territory.

36. The significance of establishing the parameters of secondary rules of state responsibility in international law cannot be overemphasized. For a quintessential appreciation of the importance of the ILC's work in this area, *see* UNITED NATIONS CODIFICATION OF STATE RESPONSIBILITY (Marina Spinedi & Bruno Simma eds., 1987). On the distinction between and philosophy behind primary and secondary rules of state responsibility, *see* Roberto Ago, Report of the Sub-Committee on State Responsibility, U.N. Doc. A/CN.4/152 (1963), *reprinted in* 2 Y.B. INT'L L. COMM'N 227, 22; J. Combacau & D. Alland, *"Primary" and "Secondary" Rules in the Law of State Responsibility: Categorizing International Obligations*, 16 NETH. Y.B. INT'L L. 81–109 (1985).

37. *See* Crawford, *supra* note 29, at 110 (describing groups that, though not officially arms of the state, the state sends out to accomplish particular missions).

38. Some commentators express that this type of state support for terrorist activities could be addressed by the UN Security Council and punished through, for example, sanctions. *See, e.g.*, Baker, *supra* note 29, at 26–27.

39. On the question of responsibility by endorsement, see Brown, *supra* note 15, at 12 ("Thus, a state that endorses a terrorist attack and adopts it as its own will be responsible to the injured state for the continuing threat posed by the attackers, just as if the continuing threat came from the state itself.").

40. Many important international decisions recognize that conduct authorized by a host state may be attributed to it. *See, e.g.*, Earnshaw (U.K.-U.S.), 6 R.I.A.A. 160 (Nov. 30, 1925) (the "Zafiro Case"); Stephens (U.S.-Mex.), 4 R.I.A.A. 265, 267 (Jul. 15, 1927); Lehigh Valley R.R. Co. (U.S.-Ger.) (the "Sabotage Cases"); The Black Tom (U.S.-Ger.), 8 R.I.A.A. 84 (1930); The Kingsland (U.S.-Ger.), 8 R.I.A.A. 225, 458 (1939).

41. However, based on the theory of the *Nicaragua* and *Tadić* decisions, a finding of direct responsibility would require more than this, namely an effective or overall control by the host state.

42. *See* Baker, *supra* note 29, at 36 ("Of course, where the state itself is directly behind the terrorist attacks, its responsibility is clear.").

43. The concept of indirect responsibility, as I construe it, is compatible with the notion of "vicarious responsibility" described by others. *See* I OPPENHEIM'S

INTERNATIONAL LAW, *supra* note 4, at 502–3. Using similar terminology, Brown described the difference between direct responsibility (or original responsibility) and indirect responsibility so: "The difference between original responsibility and vicarious responsibility is that in the former, responsibility flows from the injurious acts, and in the latter, responsibility flows from the failure to take measures to prevent or punish the act." Brown, *supra* note 15, at 13.

44. Baker, *supra* note 29, at 41. For more background on the Libyan incident, *see* David Turndorf, *The U.S. Raid on Libya: A Forceful Response to Terrorism*, 14 BROOKLYN J. INT'L L. 187–221 (1988).

45. Some jurists opine that the direct/indirect dichotomy is erroneous. For instance, Judge Ago, in his separate judgment in *Nicaragua*, equates indirect responsibility with the transfer of responsibility flowing from one state to another, when the latter exercises control over the former. 1986 I.C.J. at 189–90 (separate opinion of Judge Ago). In the same spirit, *see* Gordon A. Christenson, *Attributing Acts of Omission to the State*, 12 MICH. J. INT'L L. 312, 350, 360–64 (1991). As I discuss below, my conception of indirect responsibility has sometimes been labeled "vicarious responsibility," much to the dismay of Ian Brownlie. Brownlie, *supra* note 14, at 136. Nevertheless, the concept of indirect responsibility, as I construe it, has been invoked by the ICJ in *Nicaragua* and by the Israeli Commission in THE BEIRUT MASSACRE: THE COMPLETE KAHAN COMMISSION REPORT 50–63 (1983).

46. Some of the legal rhetoric following 9/11 has been careful in characterizing the U.S. intervention in Afghanistan. *See, e.g.*, John Yoo, *Transferring Terrorists*, 79 NOTRE DAME L. REV. 1183, 1186 (2004) (terming it a "military campaign").

47. The Iraq conflict has also extended the confusion by merging other conceptually separate legal principles. *See* Brunnée & Toope, *supra* note 3, at 250 (noting the confusion created by the United States' justifications for the Iraq War, which have collapsed several distinct legal concepts, including human rights, refugee protection, and threats to international peace and security, into one overarching doctrine of preemption).

48. *Id.* at 247 ("The events of 11 September 2001 propelled the issue of global terrorism to the top of the international agenda, and prompted dramatic shifts in international political dynamics."); *see also supra* note 12.

49. *See, e.g.*, Uniting and Strengthening America by Providing Appropriate Tools Required to Intercept and Obstruct Terrorism ("USA PATRIOT") Act of 2001, Pub. L. No. 107–56, 115 Stat. 272.

50. On the U.S. government's attempt to suppress terrorist funding, see Montgomery E. Engel, *Donating "Blood Money": Fundraising for International Terrorism*

by United States and the Government's Efforts to Constrict the Flow, 12 CARDOZO J. INT'L & COMP. L. 251 (2004).

51. On the question of the United States' changes to immigration policies post-9/11, see Lawrence Lebowitz & Ira Podheiser, *A Summary of the Changes in Immigration Policies and Practices After the Terrorist Attacks of September 11, 2001: The USA Patriot Act and Other Measures*, 63 U. PITT. L. REV. 873–88; Karen C. Tumlin, *Suspect First: How Terrorism Policy Is Reshaping Immigration Policy*, 92 CAL. L. REV. 1173 (2004).

52. Statement of Valeriy Kuchinsky, Permanent Representative of Ukraine to the United Nations, U.N. SCOR, 56th Sess., 4370th mtg., at 3, U.N. Doc. S/PV.4370 (2001).

53. Some commentators argue that international law is inadequate or, at best, inefficiently tailored to address the phenomenon of modern terrorism. *See, e.g.*, M. Cherif Bassiouni, *Legal Control of International Terrorism: A Policy-Oriented Assessment*, 43 HARV. INT'L L. J. 83 (2002).

54. *See* Crawford, *supra* note 29, at 82 (arguing that there is no real difference between acts and omissions in such a context).

55. *See, e.g.*, Derek Jinks, *State Responsibility for the Acts of Private Armed Groups*, 4 CHI. J. INT'L L. 83, 89 (2003) ("Although the 'overall control' test applied in *Tadić* did indeed lower the threshold for imputing private acts to states when compared to the ICJ rule, the touchstone of both approaches is that states must direct or control—rather than simply support, encourage, or even condone—the private actor.").

56. *See generally* Lippman, *supra* note 6.

57. *See, e.g.*, Reisman, *supra* note 2, at 4 (noting how modern transportation and weaponry makes terrorism easier to engage in and more deadly).

58. Twenty & Twenty-First Meetings, 11 LEAGUE OF NATIONS O.J. 1338, 1349 (1923) (discussing proper jurisdiction for such matters under article 15 of the League of Nations Covenant).

59. *See* Crawford, *supra* note 29, at 91.

60. 4 LEAGUE OF NATIONS O.J. 524 (1924); *see also* Crawford, *supra* note 29, at n.99.

61. *See Tehran*, *supra* note 10, at 8–9.

62. *Id.* at 29 (emphasis added). *See also* Brown, *supra* note 15, at 10–11 (noting that a finding of direct responsibility in this scenario "would have required that the attackers act as agents or organs of the Iranian government, but no evidence indicated that to be the case").

63. *See Tehran*, *supra* note 10, at 29 (concluding that, in light of the evidence before it, the court could not establish the requisite nexus between the state and the militant group).

64. *Id.* at 30 (emphasis added).

65. *Id.* at 30–31 (noting how the Vienna Conventions required Iran to "ensure the protection of" the

U.S. embassy and consulates as well as their staff, belongings, and freedom of movement).

66. *Id.* at 31. The ICJ added that "the failure of the Iranian Government to take such steps was due to more than mere negligence or lack of appropriate means." *Id.* It is also interesting to note that, among several factors that the court considered in this case, the question of the state's inaction on that specific day bears special consideration. In fact, the ICJ mentioned several other similar instances in which Iranian authorities reacted proactively to thwart hostage situations. In light of previous efforts of the state to combat insurrectional conduct, the court found that Iran's passiveness in the *Tehran* case was inconsistent with that line of precedents.

67. *See supra* note 55.

68. *See infra* note 113.

69. *See infra* note 117.

70. *See supra* note 43.

71. Crawford, *supra* note 29, at 92.

72. Below I attempt to analogize the U.S. products liability paradigm to the law of indirect state responsibility. It is interesting to note, in passing, that the cost of preventing terrorist acts is acute in the context of landowner liability. *See, e.g.,* Melinda L. Reynolds, *Landowner Liability for Terrorist Acts,* 47 CASE W. RES. L. REV. 155, 175 (1996) ("Further, while the cost of safer alternatives may be generally low for ordinary criminal acts (e.g., safer locks, more lighting), the costs of preventing terrorism are generally significant.").

73. 1970 Declaration on Principles of International Law concerning Friendly Relations and Co-Operation among States in Accordance with the Charter of the United Nations, G.A. Res. 2625, U.N. GAOR, 25th Sess., Supp. No. 28, at 76, U.N. Doc. A/8028 (1971) [hereinafter Declaration on Friendly Relations] (emphasis added); *see also* Baker, *supra* note 29, at 38 ("Therefore, under international law, as interpreted by the United Nations, even if a government does not specifically support or approve a particular act of terrorism, if such activities are generally tolerated or encouraged, they become the responsibility of that government").

74. On the incongruities found in post-*Tehran* practice, see Franck, *supra* note 4, at 64–68.

75. *See infra* note 143.

76. *See* U.N. Doc. S/25843; U.N. Doc. S/1996/602 (1996); *see also* 1996 U.N.Y.B. 268–69.

77. Franck, *supra* note 4, at 65; *see also* Gray, *supra* note 4, at 103.

78. Franck, *supra* note 4, at 64.

79. As Thomas Franck noted in RECOURSE TO FORCE, this action was met by criticism in non-UN forums. *Id.* at 66. Franck added that "a year later, the Security Council condemned the sheltering and training of terrorists by the Taliban [through Resolution 1267,

and] . . . in May 2000, Russian President Vladimir Putin warned the Taliban authorities of his intent to take 'preventive measures if necessary' to stop support for Islamic militants fighting in Chechnya and the former Soviet Republics of Central Asia." *Id.* It is also interesting to contrast the Russian initiative with the recently adopted Bush Doctrine. *See* The National Security Strategy of the United States of America (2002), *available at* www.whitehouse.gov/nsc/nss.pdf. The Bush Doctrine devolves vast powers to the U.S. administration, namely the ability to engage in preemptive counter-terrorism activities. In the same spirit, Christopher Clark Posteraro argued that the tenets of self-defense are inadequate and that, in certain circumstances, preemptive counter-terrorism is preferable. Christopher Clark Posteraro, *Intervention in Iraq: Towards a Doctrine of Anticipatory Counter-Terrorism, Counter-Proliferation Intervention,* 15 FLA. J. INT'L L. 151–213 (2002). Whenever addressing the concept of preemptive strikes, it is imperative to reference Security Council Resolution 487 regarding Israel's preemptive attack on the Iraqi nuclear facility at Osiraq. S.C. Res. 487, U.N. SCOR, 2288th mtg., U.N. Doc. S/RES/487 (1981). On the problem of applying a clear concept of preemptive self-defense, see KRIANGSAK KITTICHAISAREE, INTERNATIONAL CRIMINAL LAW 210–11 (2001). On applying preemptive strikes against terrorist activities, see Reisman, *supra* note 2, at 17–20.

80. Franck, *supra* note 4, at 67 (emphasis added).

81. *Id.* at 66.

82. *See* S.C. Res. 1304, U.N. SCOR, 4159th mtg., U.N. Doc. S/RES/1304 (2000) (speaking of the "violation of the sovereignty and territorial integrity of the Democratic Republic of Congo").

83. In the Arab-Israeli context, the Armistice Agreements recognized the responsibility of the territorial state for "non-regular" forces: "No element of the land, sea or air, military or para-military forces of either Party, *including non-regular forces,* shall commit any war-like or hostile acts against" the other Party. Bowett, *supra* note 7, at 17 (citing the Armistice Agreement) (emphasis added). This development was crucial for the sustainability of international law, as it indicated the will of the parties to empower a mechanism of indirect state responsibility. It should be noted, however, that this agreement did not withstand the test of time and was quickly violated. Nonetheless, in a subsequent resolution dealing with the truce, the Security Council unequivocally brought back the terms of the agreements within the ambit of the "effective/overall" control scheme. *See* S.C. Res. 56, U.N. SCOR, 354th mtg., U.N. Doc. S/RES/56 (1948) (stating that "(a) Each party is responsible for the actions of both regular and irregular forces operating under its authority or in territory under its control; (b) Each party has the obligation to use all means at it disposal to prevent action violating

the Truce by individuals or groups who are subject to its authority or who are in territory under its control.").

84. For more details of the account, see Bowett, *supra* note 7, at 14 n.53.

85. For a more detailed account of the facts surrounding the Beirut raid, *see* Baker, *supra* note 29, at 34–35.

86. Letter dated December 29, 1968, from Israel to the President of the Security Council, U.N. SCOR, 23d Sess., U.N. Doc. S/8946 (1968).

87. U.N. Doc. S/PV.1460, at 28–30. The Beirut raid is not the only course of action of its kind, as countries have used recourse to force to retaliate against terrorist attacks. Israel's raid of Entebbe in 1976 and the United States' bombing of Libyan terrorist camps in 1986 come to mind. For a detailed account of the facts surrounding both incidents, *see* Baker, *supra* note 29, at 39 n.76, 43 n.94.

88. *See* Richard A. Falk, *The Beirut Raid and the International Law of Retaliation*, 63 AM. J. INT'L L. 415 (1969).

89. After sending troops across the 1949 cease-fire line into the Sinai, Israel invoked precedents of transborder excursions by Palestinian *fedayeen* as a basis for its resort to self-defense. *See* Provisional Agenda 748, U.N. SCOR, 11th Sess., U.N. Doc. S/Agenda/748 (1956). The argument was not well received by the UN Security Council, but the ensuing draft resolution implicitly recognized a link between the Palestinian excursions and Israel's use of force by calling upon Israel to withdraw from the Egyptian territory. Draft S.C. Res. 3710, U.N. SCOR, 11th Sess., U.N. Doc. S/3710 (1956). This implicit message was later substantiated through Security Council Resolution 1125, which approved of allowing the UN Emergency Force to prevent further Palestinian excursions into Israel as part of its peace-keeping mandate. G.A. Res. 1125, U.N. GAOR, 1st Emerg. Sess. (1957) (considering that, "after full withdrawal of Israel from the Sharm el Sheikh and Gaza areas, *the scrupulous maintenance of the Armistice Agreement requires the placing of the United Nations Emergency Force on the Egyptian-Israel demarcation line* and the implementation of other measures") (emphasis added).

90. Letter dated Mar. 13, 1978, from Representative of Israel to UN Secretary-General, U.N. Doc. A/33/64 (1978).

91. *See* Franck, *supra* note 4, at 57; DESMOND MC-FORAN, THE WORLD HELD HOSTAGE: THE WAR WAGED BY INTERNATIONAL TERRORISM 46–47 (1987) (stating that the PLO operated as a "state within a state").

92. Letter dated May 27, 1982, from the Representative of Israel to the UN Secretary-General, U.N. SCOR, 37th Sess., 2375th mtg., at 119, U.N. Doc S/15132 (1982).

93. Franck, *supra* note 4, at 57.

94. S.C. Res. 509, U.N. SCOR, 2375th mtg., U.N. Doc. S/RES/509 (1982).

95. *See, e.g.*, Letter from the Ambassador from Israel to the UN, U.N. SCOR, 37th Sess., 2375th mtg., at 4 (1982) [hereinafter 1982 Letter].

96. *Id.* at 5. *See also* McForan, *supra* note 91, at 45–46 (stating that the "Lebanese Government's inability to rectify the situation, resulted in Lebanon sacrificing its sovereignty to the Palestinian terrorists").

97. *See* S.C. Res. 508, U.N. SCOR, 2374th mtg., U.N. Doc. S/RES/508 (1982); S.C. Res. 509, *supra* note 94. Professor Bowett has even speculated that other instances of Israeli reprisal would have encountered the same reaction from the Security Council. For example, in 1969 Israel proceeded with aerial assaults on foreign terrorist camps belonging to the Popular Front for the Liberation of Palestine. Bowett, *supra* note 7, at 14. Israel believed that the organization was responsible for terrorist attacks against an Israeli aircraft and supermarket, but a rival terrorist organization known as Al Fatah claimed responsibility for the incidents. *Id.* As Professor Bowett emphasized, the Security Council would likely not have been convinced of the legitimacy of Israel's retaliation, and much of the analysis would have hinged on whether the guerilla bands actually fell under the host state's "unified command." *Id.* at 15. Once again, the legal discussion would have reverted back to the question of control over terrorist organizations rather than establishing the host state's responsibility for harboring terrorists.

98. The ICJ also added in *Nicaragua* that participation by the host state, "even if preponderant or decisive, in the financing, organizing, training, supplying and equipping of the *contras*, the selection of its military or paramilitary targets, and the planning of the whole of its operation, is still insufficient in itself . . . for the purpose of attributing to the United States the acts committed by the *contras*." 1986 I.C.J., at 62, 64–65.

99. 1986 I.C.J., at 72 ("[I]t is not sufficient for the group to be financially or even militarily assisted by a State.").

100. Much has been written on the United States' efforts to freeze terrorist assets and to obstruct fundraising channels of organizations such as al Qaeda. *See, e.g.*, Engel, *supra* note 50; Fletcher N. Baldwin, *The Rule of Law, Terrorism and Countermeasures Including the USA Patriot Act of 2001*, 16 FLA. J. INT'L L. 43 (2004); Nina J. Crimm, *High Alert: The Government's War on the Financing of Terrorism and Its Implications for Donors, Domestic Charitable Organizations, and Global Philanthropy*, 45 WM. & MARY L. REV. 1341 (2004); Eric J. Gouvin, *Bringing Out the Big Guns: The USA Patriot Act, Money Laundering, and the War on Terrorism*, 55 BAYLOR L. REV. 955 (2003).

101. Some commentators also argue that Operation Enduring Freedom may have engendered a shift in the law of state responsibility. *See, e.g.*, Jinks, *supra* note 55, at 83–84 ("The legal response to the terrorist attacks (and other recent developments) strongly suggest that the scope of state liability for private conduct has expanded. . . . [T]he response to the September 11 attacks may signal an important shift in the law of state responsibility"); Brown, *supra* note 15, at 2 ("The attack of September 11th and the American response represent a new paradigm in the international law relating to the use of force."). I will follow a different route in this chapter by arguing a more radical paradigm shift. *See also generally* Yutaka Arai-Takahashi, *Shifting Boundaries of the Right of Self-Defence—Appraising the Impact of the September 11 Attacks on Jus Ad Bellum*, 36 INT'L L. 1081–1102 (2002); Erin L. Guruli, *The Terrorism Era: Should the International Community Redefine Its Legal Standards on Use of Force in Self-Defense?* 12 WILLAMETTE J. INT'L L. & DISP. RES. 100–23 (2004); Lauri Hannikainen, *The World After 11 September 2001: Is the Prohibition of the Use of Force Disintegrating?* in NORDIC COSMOPOLITANISM: ESSAYS IN INTERNATIONAL LAW FOR MARTTI KOSKENNIEMI 445–68 (J. Petman & J. Klabbers eds., Martinus Nijhoff Publishers, 2003).

102. With regard to the considerations underlying the U.S. decision to attack Afghanistan, including self-defense concerns and alternative routes contemplated by the United States before launching the military campaign, *see* David Abramowitz, *The President, Congress, and Use of Force: Legal and Political Considerations in Authorizing Use of Force Against International Terrorism*, 43 HARV. INT'L L. J. 71–81 (2002).

103. *See, e.g.*, John Quigley, *The Afghanistan War and Self-Defense*, 37 VAL. U. L. REV. 541–62 (2003); Franck, *supra* note 4. *See generally* Steven Becker, *"Mirror, Mirror on the Wall . . . ": Assessing the Aftermath of September 11th*, 37 VAL. U. L. REV. 563–626 (2003). For thoughtful commentaries on the legality of the war on terror, *see* Stacie D. Gorman, *In the Wake of Tragedy: The Citizens Cry Out for War, but Can the United States Legally Declare War on Terrorism?* 21 PENN. S. INT'L L. REV. 669 (2003); Emanuel Gross, *The Laws of War Waged Between Democratic States and Terrorist Organizations: Real or Illusive?* 15 FLA. J. INT'L L. 389, 394–405 (2003); Matthew Scott King, *The Legality of the United States War on Terror: Is Article 51 a Legitimate Vehicle for the War in Afghanistan or Just a Blanket to Cover-Up International War Crimes?* 9 ILSA J. INT'L & COMP. L. 457 (2003); Karl M. Meessen, *Unilateral Recourse to Military Force Against Terrorist Attacks*, 28 YALE J. INT'L L. 341 (2003); Mary Ellen O'Connell, *American Exceptionalism and the International Law of Self-Defense*, 31 DENVER J. INT'L L. & POL'Y 43 (2002); and Jordan J. Paust, *Terrorism: The Legal Implications of the Response to Sep-*

tember 11, 2001, 35 CORNELL INT'L L. J. 533, 533–41 (2002). For different views on this debate, *see* Mary Ellen O'Connell, *Lawful and Unlawful Wars Against Terrorism*, in LAW IN THE WAR ON INTERNATIONAL TERRORISM 79–96 (Ved P. Nanda ed., Transnational Publishers, 2005); Jordan J. Paust, *Use of Armed Force Against Terrorists in Afghanistan, Iraq, and Beyond*, 35 CORNELL INT'L L. J. 533–57 (2002). For an American-centric view of this issue, *see* Ruth Wedgwood, *Al-Qaida, Military Commissions, and American Self-Defence*, in LEGAL INSTRUMENTS IN THE FIGHT AGAINST INTERNATIONAL TERRORISM: A TRANSATLANTIC DIALOGUE 547–66 (C. Fijnaut, J. Wouters, & F. Naert eds., Martinus Nijhoff Publishers, 2004); Ruth Wedgwood, *Countering Catastrophic Terrorism: An American View*, in ENFORCING INTERNATIONAL LAW NORMS AGAINST TERRORISM 103–18 (Andrea Bianchi ed., Hart Publishing, 2004); Ruth Wedgwood, *Responding to Terrorism: The Strikes Against Bin Laden*, 24 YALE J. INT'L L. 559–76 (1999).

104. *See, e.g.*, Brown, *supra* note 15; Gorman, *supra* note 103; Sean Murphy, *Terrorism and the Concept of "Armed Attack" in Article 51 of the U.N. Charter*, 43 HARV. INT'L L. J. 41–51 (2002); Mary Ellen O'Connell, *Lawful Self-Defense to Terrorism*, 63 U. PITT. L. REV. 889–909 (2002); Jordan J. Paust, *Post-9/11 Overreaction and Fallacies Regarding War and Defense, Guantanamo, the Status of Persons, Treatment, Judicial Review of Detention, and Due Process in Military Commissions*, 79 NOTRE DAME L. REV. 1335, 1344 (2004); George Walker, *The Lawfulness of Operation Enduring Freedom's Self-Defense Responses*, 37 VAL. U. L. REV. 489–540 (2003).

105. *See* Michael Byers, *Terrorism, the Use of Force, and International Law After 11 September*, 51 INT'L & COMP. L. Q. 401, 405–10 (2002).

106. It is interesting to note that some scholars, like Brown, argue that the principles of *jus ad bellum* and state responsibility are sufficiently tailored to respond to terrorism as long as they are viewed in a different light. *See* Brown, *supra* note 15. Other commentators, such as Franck, counterargue that the facts relied upon by the United States to describe its Afghanistan military campaign as self-defense should not be distorted to "fit" under the principles of lawful use of force. Franck, *supra* note 5. On the difficulties related to the evidentiary burden required to invoke self-defense against terrorist attacks, *see* Jonathan I. Charney, *Use of Force Against Terrorism and International Law*, 95 AM. J. INT'L L. 835–39 (2001).

107. Some commentators claim that the United States cannot wage war against nonstate actors such as members of al Qaeda. *See, e.g.*, Byers, *supra* note 105; Paust, *supra* note 104, at 1344 (arguing that, although the United States could fight al Qaeda members on its own soil, doing so in Afghanistan without that nation's

consent was illegal); Jordan J. Paust, *War and Enemy Status After 9/11: Attacks on the Laws of War*, 28 YALE J. INT'L L. 325, 326 (2003).

108. Jinks, *supra* note 55, at 89.

109. *See, e.g.*, *Bush's Remarks on U.S. Military Strikes in Afghanistan*, NEW YORK TIMES, Oct. 8, 2001, at B6; President Bush, Remarks to the UN General Assembly (Nov. 10, 2001), *available at* www.whitehouse.gov/news/releases/2001/11/20011110–3.html [hereinafter November 10 Speech]; Letter from President Bush to Congress on American Response to Terror (Oct. 9, 2001), *available at* www.whitehouse.gov/news/releases/2001/10/20011009–6.html ("U.S. Armed Forces began combat action in Afghanistan against Al Qaida terrorists and their *Taliban supporters*. This military action is a part of our campaign against terrorism and is designed to disrupt the use of *Afghanistan as a terrorist base of operations*.") (emphasis added).

110. Authorization for Use of Military Force, Pub. L. No. 107–40, 115 Stat. 224 (2001). It must be noted that the United States and the international community never recognized the Taliban as the legitimate government of Afghanistan. *See* S.C. Res. 1193, U.N. SCOR, 3921st mtg., U.N. Doc. S/RES/1193 (1998); S.C. Res. 1214, U.N. SCOR, 3952d mtg., U.N. Doc. S/RES/1214 (1998); S.C. Res. 1267, U.N. SCOR, 4051st mtg., U.N. Doc. S/RES/1267 (1999); S/RES/1333 (2000); S.C. Res. 1363, U.N. SCOR, 5113th mtg., U.N. Doc. S/RES/1363 (2001). Thus, it might be hard to justify the U.S. strikes in Afghanistan. Some commentators have resolved this discrepancy by asserting that the Taliban was the de facto government in Afghanistan, irrespective of the views of the United States or other nations. *See, e.g.*, Brown, *supra* note 15, at 6. It is also important to mention that not having been recognized as an official government did not, in any way, relieve the Taliban from its obligations toward the state of Afghanistan. *See id.* at 6, n.24.

111. *See* Jinks, *supra* note 55, at 84–85.

112. *See also* Nov. 10 Speech, *supra* note 109 ("The allies of terror are equally guilty of murder and equally accountable to justice. The Taliban are now learning this lesson—that regime and the terrorists who support it are now virtually indistinguishable.").

113. *See* Brown, *supra* note 15, at 11 (arguing that, under *Tehran*, al Qaeda's acts cannot be imputed to the Taliban government of Afghanistan); Gunaratna, *supra* note 26, at 72–112. In fact, it appears that al Qaeda operated independently from the Taliban regime within Afghanistan. *See, e.g.*, Manooher Mofidi & Amy E. Eckert, *"Unlawful Combatants" or "Prisoners of War": The Law and Politics of Labels*, 36 CORNELL INT'L L. J. 59, 75 (2003). It is interesting to note that the United States' position in justifying self-defense against Afghanistan was premised on a two-prong approach.

First, the United States characterized the acts of 9/11 as an "armed attack" under Article 51 of the *UN Charter*. Second, it predicated its right to use force on the fact that the Taliban had "supported" and "harbored" members of al Qaeda. *See* Charney, *supra* note 106; Jinks, *supra* note 55.

114. *See* Jinks, *supra* note 55, at 89; Brown, *supra* note 15, at 11.

115. Although difficult to substantiate, such a claim is not novel. For example, the possibility of a host state waging war against the United States through a terrorist organization has been raised very recently in the context of Iraq. *See, e.g.*, Jason Pedigo, *Rogue States, Weapons of Mass Destruction, and Terrorism: Was Security Council Approval Necessary for the Invasion of Iraq?* 32 GA. J. INT'L & COMP. L. 199, 217 (2004).

116. Jinks, *supra* note 55, at 89.

117. Several scholars have argued that, were the Taliban directly responsible for the 9/11 attacks, that responsibility would have justified the U.S. invasion. *See, e.g.*, Anne-Marie Slaughter & William Burke-White, *An International Constitutional Moment*, 43 HARV. INT'L L. J. 1, 19–21 (2002); Byers, *supra* note 105, at 405–10; Drumbl, *supra* note 27, at 34–35; Marco Sassòli, *State Responsibility for Violations of International Humanitarian Law*, 84 INT'L REV. RED CROSS 401, 406–09 (2002); Mary Ellen O'Connell, *Evidence of Terror*, 7 J. CONFLICT & SECURITY L. 19, 28–32 (2002); Helen Duffy, *Responding to September 11: The Framework of International Law*, Parts I-IV, at 20–23, *available at* www.interights.org/doc/Sept11,%20Section%201.pdf.

118. *See, e.g.*, Brunnée & Toope, *supra* note 3, at 248 ("Around the globe, the debate over responses to global terrorism has raised hard issues concerning the interplay of security concerns, human rights, democratic governance and the use of force. Within the U.S., influential voices are articulating a merging of these concerns in a way that fundamentally challenges the concepts of state sovereignty, non-intervention and political independence.").

119. *See* Murphy, *supra* note 104. Similarly, it is widely accepted that international responsibility also entails varying degrees of actual liability. *See* Gaetano Arangio-Ruiz, *State Fault and the Forms and Degrees of International Responsibility: Questions of Attribution and Relevance, in* LE DROIT INTERNATIONAL AU SERVICE DE LA PAIX, DE LA JUSTICE ET DU DÉVELOPPEMENT: MÉLANGES MICHEL VIRALLY 25–42 (Michel Virally ed., Pedone, 1991); Willem Riphagen, *Second Report on the Content, Forms and Degrees of International Responsibility*, U.N. GAOR., U.N. Doc. A/CN.4/344 (1981), *reprinted in* [1981] 2 Y.B. INT'L L' COMM. 79, U.N. Doc. A/CN.4/SER.A/1981/Add.1 (Part I).

120. *See* Franck, *supra* note 4, at 54, 66–67.

121. G.A. Res. 56/1, U.N. GAOR, 56th Sess., 1st mtg. U.N. Doc. A/Res/56/1 (2001) (emphasis added).

122. S.C. Res. 1368, U.N. SCOR, 4370th mtg., U.N. Doc. S/RES/1368 (2001) (emphasis added).

123. S.C. Res. 1373, U.N. SCOR, 4385th mtg., U.N. Doc. S/RES/1373 (2001). For a detailed discussion on Resolution 1373 and its implications for counter-terrorism, see Eric Rosand, *Security Council Resolution 1373, the Counter-Terrorism Committee, and the Fight Against Terrorism*, 97 AM. J. INT'L L. 333–41 (2003); Eric Rosand, *Security Council Resolution 1373 and the Counter-Terrorism Committee: The Cornerstone of the United Nations Contribution to the Fight Against Terrorism*, in LEGAL INSTRUMENTS IN THE FIGHT AGAINST INTERNATIONAL TERRORISM: A TRANSATLANTIC DIALOGUE 603–32 (C. Fijnaut, J. Wouters, & F. Naert eds., Martinus Nijhoff Publishers, 2004).

124. *Id.* (emphasis added). These two documents have also paved the way for other Security Council Resolutions on the United States–Afghan relationship. *See, e.g.*, S.C. Res. 1383, U.N. SCOR, 4434th mtg., U.N. Doc. S/RES/1383 (2001); S.C. Res. 1386, U.N. SCOR, 4443d mtg., U.N. Doc. S/RES/1386 (2001). Most importantly, the UN Security Council adopted Resolution 1378, which expressly embraces the new indirect responsibility paradigm by condemning "the Taliban for *allowing Afghanistan to be used as a base for the export of terrorism* by the Al-Qaida network and other terrorist groups and for *providing safe haven* to Usama Bin Laden, Al-Qaida and others associated with them." S.C. 1378, U.N. SCOR, 4415th mtg., U.N. Doc. S/RES/1378 (2001) (emphasis added).

125. For example, the Security Council did not recognize a right to self-defense in favor of the United States following the 1998 bombing of the embassies in Tanzania and Kenya. *See* Jinks, *supra* note 55, at 85–86. In response to 9/11, Jinks argued that "the Security Council impliedly endorsed, without expressly authorizing, the use of force against Afghanistan." *Id.* at 86. *See also* Nicholas Rostow, *Before and After: The Changed UN Response to Terrorism Since September 11th*, 35 CORNELL INT'L L. J. 475–90 (2002). On the Security Council's role in combating international terrorism, *see* Curtis A. Ward, *Building Capacity to Combat International Terrorism: The Role of the United Nations Security Council*, 8 J. CONFLICT & SECURITY L. 289–305 (2003).

126. There are hints of this reasoning in a letter sent by the United States to the UN. Letter from the Permanent Representative of the United States of America to the United Nations (Oct. 7, 2001), U.N. Doc. No. S/2001/946 (2001) [hereinafter October 7 Letter] (stating that the United States had "clear and compelling information" that Al Qaeda, supported by the Taliban in that the Taliban gave it a "base of operation," had a "central role" in the 9/11 attacks).

127. S.C. Res. 1267, *supra* note 110. Similar concerns pertaining to the "use of Afghan territory" for the "sheltering and training of terrorists" have been expressed in Security Council Resolutions 1214 and 1363. S.C. Res. 1214, *supra* note 110; S.C. Res. 1363, *supra* note 110.

128. S.C. Res. 1267, *supra* note 110.

129. S.C. Res. 1373, *supra* note 123.

130. *Id.* (emphasis added).

131. Franck, *supra* note 4, at 54. This phenomenon had somewhat been recognized or discussed before 9/11. *See, e.g.*, Baker, *supra* note 29, at 40 ("The attacked state has the right to use force against both the terrorists and the government which harbors them."). *See also* Robert J. Beck & Anthony Clark Arend, *"Don't Tread on Us": International Law and Forcible State Responses to Terrorism*, 12 WIS. INT'L L. J. 153–221 (1994); Leah M. Campbell, *Defending Against Terrorism: A Legal Analysis of the Decision to Strike Sudan and Afghanistan*, 74 TUL. L. REV. 1067–96 (2000); William A. O'Brien, *Reprisals, Deterrence and Self-Defense in Counter Terror Operations*, 30 VA. J. INT'L L. 421–78 (1990); Oscar Schachter, *The Extraterritorial Use of Force Against Terrorist Bases*, 11 HOUS. J. INT'L L. 309–16 (1989); Oscar Schachter, *The Lawful Use of Force by a State Against Terrorists in Another Country*, in TERRORISM & POLITICAL VIOLENCE: LIMITS & POSSIBILITIES OF LEGAL CONTROL 241–66 (H. H. Han ed., Oceana, 1993). It is also interesting to note that Professor Bowett underlined a shift in argument from self-defense to reprisals in the context of terrorist strikes and Israeli responses in the 1960s. Bowett, *supra* note 7, at 10.

132. The fact that the UN Security Council has never recognized the Taliban as a legitimate government, coupled with its insistence on having Osama Bin Laden brought to justice, contributes to establishing an overall relationship between the Taliban and al Qaeda, making the U.S.-Afghanistan record somewhat similar to the Arab-Israeli situation. The fact that the Taliban has always ignored the international community's plea to stop harboring members of al Qaeda also indicates a continued adversarial relationship between the United States and Afghanistan. On the refusal of the Taliban to revise its policy on harboring terrorists, see October 7 Letter, *supra* note 126. These considerations will become even more relevant in light of Article 14 of the *Draft Articles*, which expressly provides for the extended breach of an obligation when premised on an obligation to prevent: "The breach of an international obligation requiring a State *to prevent a given event* occurs when the event occurs and extends over the entire period during which the event continues and remains not in conformity with that obligation." *Draft Articles, supra* note 11 (emphasis added). I will discuss the obligation to prevent terrorist attacks below, but a few preliminary remarks are helpful.

A case can be made that Afghanistan has repeatedly failed to fulfill its obligation to prevent a terrorist attack emanating from its territory when considering the bombing of the embassies in Africa, the U.S.S. Cole, and so forth. Hence, there is a continuing breach by Afghanistan in not conforming to its international obligations. Based on that logic, Afghanistan would be indirectly responsible for an internationally wrongful act. Article 14 of the *Draft Articles*, coupled with the *Tehran* decision, which mentions "successive and still continuing breaches by Iran of its obligations to the United States under the Vienna Conventions of 1961 and 1963," *Tehran, supra* note 10, at 36–37, makes a compelling case for a finding of indirect responsibility in the U.S.-Afghan scenario. The mechanism of Article 14 is probably better tailored to govern a lasting relationship, albeit punctuated by attacks and reprisals, between two or more states. On the distinction between instantaneous and continuing breaches, *see* Rainbow Warrior (N.Z.-Fr.), 20 R.I.A.A. 217, 264 (1990). On the question of continuing breaches, generally, *see* Joost Pauwelyn, *The Concept of a "Continuing Violation" of an International Obligation: Selected Problems*, 66 BRIT. Y.B. INT'L L. 415 (1995).

133. In the context of the 1982 incident, Thomas Franck's RECOURSE TO FORCE explores the responsibility of the third-party host state through the lens of self-defense. Franck, *supra* note 4, at 59. ("In that light, Israel's claim to be acting in self-defense precisely poses the question whether such a right arises *against a state which harbors infiltrators and permits transborder subversion, yet has not itself participated in these armed attacks*.") (emphasis added). Based on the 2001 U.S.-Afghan precedent, the answer to this question seems to be affirmative.

134. Some scholars also opine that Israel's claim to self-defense is barred by the illegal occupation of certain territories. *See, e.g.*, Gray, *supra* note 4, at 102 ("the mere fact that many states regarded Israel's occupation of the West Bank and Gaza, the Golan and (until 2000) areas of South Lebanon as illegal was enough for them to condemn Israel's use of force against cross-border attacks by irregulars"). This proposition seems to distinguish the Israeli case from the U.S.-Afghan example because, before attacking Afghanistan in 2001, the United States did not occupy the Afghan territory illegally.

135. Franck, *supra* note 4, at 59.

136. S.C. Res. 1368, *supra* note 122.

137. This argument must be appreciated with caution. One could claim that the history of Palestinian attacks on Israeli targets, dating back to the Sinai incident and before, further distinguishes it from the U.S.-Afghanistan precedent. In fact, Israel made that argument, asking "how many Israelis have to be killed by the PLO terrorists for the Council to be persuaded that the limits of our endurance have been reached?" 1982 Let-

ter, *supra* note 95. As Professor Bowett noted, following the Qibya raid in 1953, Israel shifted from a narrow view of self-defense and, "for the first time, argued that its action was justified in the whole context of repeated theft, pillaging, border raids, sabotage and injury to Israeli property and life." Bowett, *supra* note 7, at 5. It is true that, when considered on its face, the U.S. attack on Afghanistan does not appear to be fueled by decades of terrorist incursions into the United States but rather by the horrendous acts of 9/11. However, one could also argue that the attacks on the Khobar Towers in 1996, the U.S. embassies in Kenya and Tanzania in 1998, and the *U.S.S. Cole* in 2000 have all contributed to establishing a similar situation to that of Israel, albeit shorter in duration and potentially engaging the international responsibility of several states. In sum, the United States has maintained an adversarial posture vis-à-vis Afghanistan following several terrorist acts substantially linked with the Afghan territory. From that perspective, it appears that the U.S.-Afghan situation could easily fit under the "continuing relationship" paradigm, as inspired by Israeli-Palestinian reprisals or under the "single event/chain of events" model, for which the 9/11 military campaign seems to stand. These concerns were central to Professor Bowett's thesis in the post-Beirut Raid days, when he asked, "Is the legality of the action to be determined *solely by reference to the prior illegal act* which brought it about or by reference to the *whole context of the relationship between the two states*?" *Id.* at 4 (emphasis added). The disproportionate nature of the Israeli response constitutes another important reason why states felt compelled to denounce the Israeli reprisals generally. *See* Franck, *supra* note 4, at 65.

138. *See* Press Release, North Atlantic Council, Statement by the North Atlantic Council (Sept. 12, 2001), *at* www.nato.int/docu/pr/2001/p01–124e.htm. It is interesting to note that, in characterizing the attack of 9/11, the Council specified that said attack "was directed from *abroad* against the United States," *id.* (emphasis added), thereby fitting the attack within my model of "international terrorism." *See supra* note 27. Based on that finding, the Council invoked Article 5 of the Washington Treaty in dealing with the armed attack. *See* Press Release, North Atlantic Council, Invocation of Article 5 Confirmed (Oct. 2, 2001), *at* www.nato.int/docu/update/2001/1001/e1002a.htm.

139. *See* Statement of Lord Robertson, NATO Secretary-General (Oct. 2, 2001), *available at* www.nato.int/docu/speech/2001/s011002a.htm ("We know that the individuals who carried out these attacks were part of the world-wide terrorist network of Al-Qaida, headed by Osama bin Laden and his key lieutenants and protected by the Taleban.").

140. OAS RC.24/RES.1/01, Terrorist Threat to the Americas, 1st Sess., 24th mtg., OAS Doc. No. OEA/

Ser.F/II.24 (Sept. 21, 2001), *available at* www.oas.org/OASpage/crisis/RC.24e.htm.

141. *See, e.g.*, Jinks, *supra* note 55, at 90–91.

142. It is helpful to recall that, in the context of the 1982 incident, a few days after Israel declared a cease-fire, the UN General Assembly sought to consecrate Lebanon's "sovereignty, territorial integrity, unity and political independence." *See* G.A. Res. 7/5, U.N. GAOR, 7th Emerg. Sess., U.N. Doc. A/RES/ES-7/5 (1982), *available at* http://domino.un.org. On the question of Israel's unilateral cease-fire, see 1982 U.N.Y.B. 440.

143. This tension also came to life in the 1995 Turkey-Iraq crisis. Turkish forces invaded the north-western portion of the Iraqi territory, as it was used as a frequent launch pad for attacks against Turkey by Kurdish irregulars. Iraq made the usual claim as to the violation of its territorial integrity and sovereignty. *See* 1995 U.N.Y.B. 494, U.N. Doc. S/1995/272. Although Iraq persisted in making claims against the Turkish invasion, the Security Council remained unmoved by the Iraqi plea. *See* U.N. Doc. S/1996/401; U.N. Doc. S/1996/762; U.N. Doc. S/1996/860; U.N. Doc. S/1996/1018; 1996 U.N.Y.B. 236–37. This type of in-action by the Security Council would foreshadow the new indirect responsibility paradigm: A state could now attempt to repress transborder subversion into a neigh-boring country where terrorist launch pads and bases of operation are located. The guiding principle seemed to hinge on the proportionality of the response to the cross-border insurgency. For an application of this prin-ciple to the post-9/11 era and other guidelines pur-porting to regularize recourse to force against terrorism, see Michael C. Bonafede, *Here, There, and Everywhere*: *Assessing the Proportionality Doctrine and U.S. Uses of Force in Response to Terrorism after the September 11 At-tacks*, 88 CORNELL L. REV. 155–214 (2002); Sage R. Knauft, *Proposed Guidelines for Measuring the Propriety of Armed State Responses to Terrorist Attacks*, 19 HAST-INGS INT'L & COMP. L. REV. 763–88 (1996). On the Turkey-Iraq situation, see Franck, *supra* note 5, at 63–64. It is also interesting to note that, prior to 9/11, some commentators expressed that the harboring of terrorists by a host state should in fact preempt any claim of sov-ereignty. *See, e.g.*, Baker, *supra* note 29, at 40 ("The right of self-defense trumps the claim of sovereignty. Allowing terrorist groups to wage war from one's territory is a clear act of aggression and not one of the privileges of sovereignty.").

144. Bowett, *supra* note 7, at 14.

145. *See* Reisman, *supra* note 2, at 50–51 (noting that international law has been reluctant to limit state sover-eignty and asking whether it might be appropriate to do so when a state is a "launch pad" for terrorist activities and the target state of those activities wants to "destroy the terrorist infrastructure").

146. *Id.* at 91. *See also* Robert O. Keohane, *The Glob-alization of Informal Violence, Theories of World Politics, and the "Liberalism of Fear,"* DIALOGUE I-O 29–43 (2002), *available at* http://mitpress.mit.edu/journals/INOR/Dialogue_IO/keohane.pdf. The prospect of gov-ernments waging surrogate warfare through private in-dividuals poses a significant challenge to the mechanism of attribution. Christenson, *supra* note 45, at 313 ("The tendency for those in power to achieve their ends through private or non-State actors, thereby avoiding at-tribution, engenders a wide range of conduct by inac-tion where both deniability and non-attribution serve to enhance the power of those in control of a State, if they in fact have control.").

147. Bowett, *supra* note 7, at 13 ("The Beirut raid also illustrates the Security Council's tendency to reject any notion of 'collective guilt' which might justify a reprisal against an Arab state irrespective of the origin of the injury which is the immediate cause of the reprisal action."); *see also id.* at 15 n.61.

148. *Id.* at 20.

149. *Id.* at 14.

150. *See supra* note 143.

151. *See, e.g.*, BINYAMIN NETANYAHU, TERRORISM: HOW THE WEST CAN WIN 220 (1986); Jordan J. Paust, *Federal Jurisdiction Over Extraterritorial Acts of Terrorism and Non-immunity for Foreign Violators Under the FSIA and the Act of State Doctrine*, 23 VA. J. INT'L L. 191, 221–25 (1983).

152. In *International Legal Responses to International Terrorism*, Reisman delivered a quintessential formula-tion of the problem at hand, stating, "We are concerned here with the policies that have been prescribed in con-temporary international law with respect to a state in whose territory terrorist acts are planned when the state has the capacity to prohibit such action." Reisman, *supra* note 2, at 42.

153. In *Attributing Acts of Omission to the State*, Christenson raised the possibility of rethinking attribu-tion in order to better reflect modern reality with regard to the current debate on state responsibility. Christen-son, *supra* note 45, at 369 ("The tradition of civil soci-ety with intermediate institutions that are neither market nor State offers a form of pluralism to rethink the international legal order's attention to attribution theory. Allocating supervisory responsibility and control to conduct of modern States in relation to non-State ac-tors in an exclusive system of territorial States will revise attribution theory to reflect the new realities of power.").

154. *See, e.g.*, Luigi Condorelli, *The Imputability to States of Acts of International Terrorism*, 19 ISR. Y.B. HUM. RTS. 233 (1989); YORAM DINSTEIN, WAR, AG-GRESSION AND SELF-DEFENSE 182–83 (2d ed. 2001) ("armed attack is not extenuated by the subterfuge of indirect aggression or by reliance on a surrogate. There

is no real difference between the activation of a country's regular armed forces and a military operation carried out at one remove, pulling the strings of a terrorist organization (not formally associated with the governmental apparatus)."); Reisman, *supra* note 2, at 39 ("State-sponsored terrorism is the most noxious and dangerous of its species, yet its authors and architects evade all deterrence and prospect of punishment if the fiction is that states are not involved and only their agents are deemed responsible for the terrorism."); Slaughter & Burke-White, *supra* note 117, at 20 ("The traditional 'effective control' test for attributing an act to a state seems insufficient to address the threats posed by global criminals and the states that harbor them."); *see also* Ian Brownlie, *International Law and the Activities of Armed Bands*, 7 INT'L & COMP. L. Q. 712, 718 (1958) (inferring that supporting or tolerating terrorist activities by a host state amounts to aggression).

155. *See, e.g.*, Jinks, *supra* note 55, at 83 ("the revision of trans-substantive secondary rules is a clumsy, and typically ineffective, device for vindicating specific policy objectives").

156. *See, e.g.*, Mohammed Bedjaoui, *Responsibility of States, Fault and Strict Liability*, 10 ENCYCLOPEDIA PUB. INT'L L. 358 (1987); Andrea Gattini, *La Notion de faute à la lumière du projet de convention de la Commission du Droit International sur la responsabilité internationale*, 3 EUR. J. INT'L L. 253–84 (1992). On the question of attributing warlike acts to the host state, *see* Frits Kalshoven, *State Responsibility for Warlike Acts of the Armed Forces*, 40 INT'L & COMP. L. Q. 827 (1991).

157. *See* IMMANUEL KANT, FOUNDATIONS OF THE METAPHYSICS OF MORALS WITH CRITICAL ESSAYS 52 (Robert Paul Wolff ed., Lewis White Beck trans., Bobbs-Merrill Co., 1969) (1785) ("Now, I say, man and, in general, every rational being exists as an end in himself and not merely as a means to be arbitrarily used by this or that will. In all his actions, whether they are directed to himself or to other rational beings, he must always be regarded at the same time as an end."); *see also id.* at 54 ("The practical imperative, therefore, is the following: Act so that you treat humanity, whether in your own person or in that of another, always as an end and never as a means only."). On the question of Kantian elements as found in the law of state responsibility, *see* Christenson, *supra* note 45, at 319–20 and the authorities cited therein. This phenomenon has carried over to other areas of the war on terrorism, especially in national jurisdictions, where various executives and judiciaries are called upon to balance security and civil liberties concerns. For hints of Kantian elements in these arenas, *see* Alan Gewirth, *Are There Any Absolute Rights?* 31 PHIL. Q. 1, 8–16 (1981); and Ronald Dworkin, *Terror & the Attack on Civil Liberties*, 50 NEW YORK REVIEW OF

BOOKS 37 (Nov. 6, 2003), *available at* www.nybooks.com/articles/article-preview?article_id=16738.

158. It is interesting to note that, in the context of the Armistice Agreements in Arab-Israeli relations, the parties expressed the wish to implement a mechanism of indirect responsibility, namely to make the territorial state accountable for the excursions of irregular forces outside its territory.

159. *Nicaragua*, *supra* note 8, 1986 I.C.J., at 65 (emphasis added); *see also* Crawford, *supra* note 29, at 110–11 (confirming that this question "was analyzed by the Court in terms of the notion of 'control'").

160. *See, e.g.*, Slaughter & Burke-White, *supra* note 117, at 2 ("The goal of this war is not economic advantage, territorial gain, or the submission of another state. It is to bring individual terrorists to justice and to punish and to deter the states that harbor them. To respond adequately and effectively to the threats and challenges that are emerging in this new paradigm, we need new rules.").

161. *Draft Articles*, *supra* note 11.

162. *Id.*

163. *See supra* note 83.

164. Crawford, *supra* note 29, at 110.

165. *Id.*

166. Jinks, *supra* note 55, at 88 (internal quotation marks omitted).

167. *Draft Articles*, *supra* note 11, at art. 11. On the question of responsibility by endorsement, see my comments, *supra* note 25 and accompanying text, and Brown, *supra* note 15, at 10–13. On the specific question of the endorsement of the 9/11 attacks, Brown argued that "the Taliban do not appear to have endorsed the attack. . . . [T]hey denied that bin Laden had anything to do with the attacks, asserting that 'bin Laden lacked the capability to pull off large-scale attacks,' . . . and proclaiming their confidence that a U.S. investigation would find him innocent." *Id.* at 11; *see also* Baker, *supra* note 29, at 36 ("But the state may not be as innocent as it appears. Terrorism is often carried out with the encouragement or approval of the sanctuary state.").

168. Crawford, *supra* note 29, at 110 ("conduct will be attributable to the State only if it directed or controlled the specific operation and the conduct complained of was an integral part of that operation. The principle does not extend to conduct which was only incidentally or peripherally associated with an operation and which escaped from the State's direction or control.").

169. On the difficulty of defining terrorism, see *supra* note 27; *see also* Reisman, *supra* note 2, at 9–13. Particularly strong resistance to formulating an international definition has come from several Arab states.

170. Bowett, *supra* note 7, at 17.

171. *See* CLYDE EAGLETON, THE RESPONSIBILITY OF STATES IN INTERNATIONAL LAW 80 (1928) ("A State

owes at all times a duty to protect other States against injurious acts by individuals from within its jurisdiction.").

172. Crawford, *supra* note 29, at 135. On the concept of time in the context of international state responsibility, *see* Wolfram Karl, *The Time Factor in the Law of State Responsibility*, in UNITED NATIONS CODIFICATION OF STATE RESPONSIBILITY 95–114 (Marina Spinedi & Bruno Simma eds., Oceana, 1987); Eric Wyler, *Quelques réflexions sur la réalisation dans le temps du fait internationalement illicite*, 95 REVUE GÉNÉRALE DE DROIT INTERNATIONAL PUBLIC 881–914 (1991). On time and the law, generally, *see* Rosalyn Higgins, *Time and the Law*, 46 INT'L & COMP. L. Q. 501 (1997).

173. Rainbow Warrior (N.Z.-Fr.), 20 R.I.A.A. 217 (1990).

174. *Id.* at 264.

175. *See, e.g., id.* at 265–66, 279–84 (Sir Kenneth Keith, dissenting); *see also Gabcíkovo-Nagymaros, supra* note 34, at 54.

176. *See, e.g., Blake v. Guatemala*, Inter-Am. Ct. H.R., Ser. C, No. 36, at para. 67 (Jan. 24, 1998).

177. *See, e.g., Papamichalopoulos v. Greece*, E.C.H.R., Ser. A, No. 260-B (Jun. 24, 1993); and *Loizidou v. Turkey*, 6 E.C.H.R. Rpts. 2216 (Dec. 18, 1996).

178. *See, e.g., Tehran, supra* note 10, at 145.

179. *See, e.g., Papamichalopoulos, supra* note 177; and *Loizidou, supra* note 177, at 2216.

180. *See, e.g., Lovelace v. Canada*, Communication No. R.6/24, U.N. Doc. A/36/40, at 172 (Jul. 30, 1981).

181. *Draft Articles, supra* note 11.

182. *See, e.g.,* Reisman, *supra* note 2, at 6–7 (noting that terrorism not only affects those who are killed or injured, it also intimidates others, "influencing their political behavior and that of their government" and "undermining inclusive public order").

183. The contractual doctrine of efficient breach is widely thought to have originated in Oliver Wendell Holmes's statement in *The Path of the Law* that "the duty to keep a contract at common law means a prediction that you must pay damages if you do not keep it—and nothing else." Oliver Wendell Holmes, *The Path of the Law*, 10 HARV. L. REV. 457, 462 (1897). In essence, this proposition entails that a contractual party might opt to breach a contract, should unforeseen or more advantageous circumstances arise, where the profits of the breach exceed the costs of damages. *See* William R. Corbett, *A Somewhat Modest Proposal to Prevent Adultery and Save Families: Two Old Torts Looking for a New Career*, 33 ARIZ. ST. L. J. 985, 1031 (2001) ("Proponents of efficient breach theory thus argue that there is nothing wrongful about a breach, and that by permitting efficient breaches, the law facilitates movement of resources to their most valuable use."); Lee Shidlofsky, *The Changing Face of First-Party Bad Faith Claims in Texas*, 50 S.M.U. L. Rev. 867, 893 (1997) ("Under the efficient breach doctrine, if it is economically advantageous for one party to breach the contract, the law should not deter the breach."). *See also supra* note 157 (commenting on the Kantian roots of the war on terror).

184. *Draft Articles, supra* note 11, art. 48(1)(b) (allowing any state to invoke another state's responsibility when that state breached an obligation "owed to the international community as a whole"). Should this position be endorsed, the obligation of preventing terrorist attacks would fit within the framework and reasoning of *Barcelona Traction, Light and Power Company*, which states that "an essential distinction should be drawn between the obligations of a State towards the international community as a whole, and those arising vis-à-vis another State in the field of diplomatic protection. By their very nature the former are the concern of all States. In view of the importance of the rights involved, all States can be held to have a legal interest in their protection; they are obligations *erga omnes*." Barcelona Traction, Light & Power Co. (Belg.-Spain) (Second Phase), 1970 I.C.J. Rep. 3, 32 (Feb. 5, 1970). For more background on the interplay between Article 48(1)(b) and obligations *erga omnes*, *see* Crawford, *supra* note 29, at 278; Pierre-Marie Dupuy, *A General Stocktaking of the Connections Between the Multilateral Dimension of Obligations and Codification of the Law of Responsibility*, 13 EUR. J. INT'L L. 1053, 1069–76 (2002); Linos-Alexander Sicilianos, *The Classification of Obligations and the Multilateral Dimension of the Relations of International Responsibility*, 13 EUR. J. INT'L L. 1127, 1136–38 (2002); Marina Spinedi, *From One Codification to Another: Bilateralism and Multilateralism in the Genesis of the Codification of the Law of Treaties and the Law of State Responsibility*, 13 EUR. J. INT'L L. 1099, 1113–14 (2002). Some commentators assert that *jus cogens* obligations also fall within the ambit of Article 48 of the *Draft Articles* in that they are "owed to the international community as a whole." Dupuy, *supra*, at 1061. On the mechanism of Article 48 generally and the invocation of international state responsibility, *see* Daniel Bodansky, John R. Crook, & Edith Brown Weiss, *Invoking State Responsibility in the Twenty-First Century*, 96 AM. J. INT'L L. 798, 803–6 (2002).

185. *See* Crawford, *supra* note 29, at 140 ("The breach of an obligation of prevention may well be a continuing wrongful act, although, as for other continuing wrongful acts, the effect of article 13 is that the breach only continues if the State is bound by the obligation for the period during which the event continues and remains not in conformity with what is required by the obligation.").

186. *Id.* (emphasis added).

187. The protection of civilians is paramount in the context of the laws of war. *See, e.g.,* International Committee of the Red Cross, Basic Rules of the Geneva

Conventions and Their Additional Protocols (1988), *available at* www.icrc.org/WEB/ENG/siteeng0.nsf/htmlall/p0365?OpenDocument&style=Custo_Final.4&View=defaultBody2; Advisory Opinion on the Legality of the Threat or Use of Nuclear Weapons, 35 I.L.M. 809, 827 (Jul. 8, 1996) (classifying the nontargeting of civilians as one of the "cardinal principles" of humanitarian law).

188. *See* Crawford, *supra* note 29, at n.270 ("An example might be an obligation by State A to prevent certain information from being published. The breach of such an obligation will not necessarily be of a continuing character, since it may be that once the information is published, *the whole point of the obligation is defeated*.") (emphasis added).

189. *See, e.g.*, Andrea Gattini, *Smoking/No Smoking: Some Remarks on the Current Place of Fault in the ILC Draft Articles on State Responsibility*, 10 EUR. J. INT'L L. 397–404 (1999); James Crawford, *Revising the Draft Articles on State Responsibility*, 10 EUR. J. INT'L L. 435, 438 (1999) (agreeing that "it is a serious error to think that it is possible to eliminate the significance of fault from the Draft Articles"). However, Crawford opened the door to the possible implementation of a mechanism of strict liability, stating that "different primary rules of international law impose different standards, ranging from 'due diligence' to strict liability, and that all of those standards are capable of giving rise to responsibility in the event of a breach. . . . [I]t depends on the interpretation of that rule in the light of its object or purpose." Crawford, *supra*, at 438. It inevitably follows from this proposition that, given the urgency of combating terrorism, coupled with the purpose of actually preventing terrorist attacks, the regime of indirect responsibility could reasonably transform into a mechanism of strict liability.

190. It should be noted that some commentators contest the importation of domestic law concepts into the international law of state responsibility. *See, e.g.*, Brownlie, *supra* note 14, at 37–38, 40–47.

191. The legal regime set forth by the *Draft Articles* is ripe for analogizing or importing domestic law principles into the realm of international state responsibility. Even though notions extracted from the national products liability paradigm inform analysis under international law, these notions may be, themselves, subsequently altered by the process of importation. *See, e.g.*, Crawford, *supra* note 29, at 21 ("It is not unusual for domestic analogies to be modified in the course of transplantation to international law. Indeed it is unusual for them not to be."); Daniel Bodansky et al., *The ILC's Articles on Responsibility of States for Internationally Wrongful Acts: A Retrospect*, 96 AM. J. INT'L L. 874, 878 (2002) (arguing that "the international law of responsibility is applied across the field of international obligations" and that it "comprises areas that—in terms of domestic

analogies—may be seen as like those of contract and tort, and others that might be seen as analogous to public law"). It is interesting to note that terrorism has sometimes been construed as a tort under the global legal order. For support of this proposition, *see* Eileen Rose Pollock, *Terrorism As a Tort in Violation of the Law of Nations*, 6 Fordham INT'L L. J. 236–60 (1982–83).

192. *See, e.g.*, Steven Shavell, *Strict Liability versus Negligence*, 9 J. LEGAL. STUD. 1–25 (1980).

193. For the underlying policy considerations of strict liability in products liability cases, *see* Justice Traynor's concurring opinion in *Escola v. Coca Cola Bottling Company*, 150 P.2d 436 (Cal. 1944), which likely represents the beginning of modern strict products liability in U.S. law.

194. *See Greenman v. Yuba Power Prods., Inc.*, 377 P.2d 897, 901 (Cal. 1962); *see also* Michael L. Rustad & Thomas H. Koenig, *Taming the Tort Monster: The American Civil Justice System as a Battleground of Social Theory*, 68 BROOKLYN L. REV. 1, 89 (2002) ("The underlying rationale of strict liability is to place the burden of precaution on the manufacturers because they have superior information about the product that makes them the 'cheapest cost avoider.'").

195. *See generally* Bowett, *supra* note 7, at 20–21 (addressing the Security Council's partial acceptance of "reasonable" reprisals). Professor Bowett also raised an interesting question, somewhat akin to the tort concept of contributory negligence, with regard to the aggrieved state's own conduct: "Why could not the state have defended itself against these guerilla activities by measures of defense adopted on its own territory?" *Id.* On the question of contributory negligence as it pertains to state responsibility, *see generally* David J. Bederman, *Contributory Fault and State Responsibility*, 30 VA. J. INT'L L. 335 (1990). On the question of due diligence as it pertains to state responsibility, *see generally* Ricccardo Pisillo-Mazzeschi, *The Due Diligence Rule and the Nature of International Responsibility of States*, 35 GERMAN Y.B. INT'L L. 9 (1992).

196. On the role of fault in a host state's failure to act in conformity with an international obligation, *see* Christenson, *supra* note 45, at 315–16; and Pierre-Marie Dupuy, *The International Law of State Responsibility: Revolution or Evolution?* 11 MICH. J. INT'L L. 105, 110 (1989).

197. *See infra* note 238.

198. *See* Kittichaisaree, *supra* note 79, at 227 ("International terrorism is one of the most heinous crimes that strike at the heart of peoples in virtually every corner of the globe.").

199. *See* Crawford, *supra* note 29, at 127–28 ("Moreover, obligations imposed on States by peremptory norms necessarily affect the vital interests of the international community as a whole and may entail a stricter

régime of responsibility than that applied to other internationally wrongful acts.").

200. *See, e.g.*, Carla Ann Clark, *Howard v. Allstate Insurance Co.—Louisiana's Attempt at Comparative Causation*, 49 La. L. Rev. 1163, 1166 (1989).

201. On the distinction between obligations of means and result, as applicable to the *Draft Articles, see* Pierre-Marie Dupuy, *Reviewing the Difficulties of Codification: On Ago's Classification of Obligations of Means and Obligations of Result in Relation to State Responsibility*, 10 Eur. J. Int'l L. 371 (1999). Dupuy argued that this distinction should be imposed on international law because certain situations must be avoided, such as "private activities which take place on national territory causing damage to another state." *Id.* at 375.

202. *See, e.g., id.*; David G. Owen, *Products Liability: User Misconduct Defenses*, 52 S.C. L. Rev. 1 (2000).

203. *See, e.g.*, Lee Feinstein & Anne-Marie Slaughter, *A Duty to Prevent*, Foreign Affairs (Jan./Feb. 2004), *available at* www.foreignaffairs.org/20040101 faessay83113-p0/lee-feinstein-anne-marie-slaughter/ a-duty-to-prevent.html ("The unprecedented threat posed by terrorists and rogue states armed with weapons of mass destruction cannot be handled by an outdated and poorly enforced nonproliferation regime. The international community has a duty to prevent security disasters as well as humanitarian ones—even at the price of violating sovereignty.").

204. *See also* Dupuy, *supra* note 201, at 381 (arguing that, "even in cases in which the situation to be prevented is defined in terms of the occurrence of damage, obligations of prevention *are* a sub-category, but a subcategory of 'obligations to endeavour' (i.e., 'obligations of conduct' in the civil law sense), not of 'obligations of result'").

205. Those belonging to the first school of thought have also argued that preemptive strikes are a useful tool against terrorist threats. *See, e.g.*, Posteraro, *supra* note 79. For recent accounts on the debate surrounding preemptive action and self-defense, *see, e.g.*, Michael Bothe, *Terrorism and the Legality of Pre-emptive Force*, 14 Eur. J. Int'l L. 227–40 (2003); Michael J. Glennon, *The Fog of Law: Self-Defense, Inherence, and Incoherence in Article 51 of the United Nations Charter*, 25 Harv. J. L. & Pub. Pol'y 539, 546–49 (2002); Christopher Greenwood, *International Law and the Pre-emptive Use of Force: Afghanistan, Al-Qaida, and Iraq*, 4 San Diego J. Int'l L. 7 (2003); Miriam Shapiro, *Iraq: The Shifting Sands of Preemptive Self-Defense*, 97 Am. J. Int'l L. 599 (2003); Michael N. Schmitt, *Preemptive Strategies in International Law*, 24 Mich. J. Int'l L. 513 (2003); and William H. Taft IV & Todd F. Buchwald, *Preemption, Iraq, and International Law*, 97 Am. J. Int'l L. 557 (2003).

206. *See* Dinah Shelton, *Judicial Review of State Action by International Courts*, 12 Fordham Int'l L. J.

361 (1989) (reviewing evidentiary concerns related to omissions); *see generally* Kevin A. Bove, *Attribution Issues in State Responsibility*, 84 Am. Soc'y Int'l L. Proc. 51 (1990).

207. On the difficulties of proving that a host state had the means to prevent a terrorist attack, *see* Christenson, *supra* note 45, at n.14. *See also* Condorelli, *supra* note 154. Proving a host state had the means to prevent a terrorist attack becomes particularly difficult when the host state wields exclusive control over the relevant facts. *See, e.g.*, Christenson, *supra* note 45, at 315 ("[P]rocedural questions giving practical effect to expectations of the international community are equally, if not more, important to international legitimacy and the recognition of arrangements of control within a State when a State has exclusive control over internal events, information and communications.").

208. Christenson, *supra* note 45, at 368 (arguing that, in a totalitarian state where the state controls every aspect of human action, the state would be responsible for any acts of international terrorism conducted by its citizens). Nor is the objective to encourage state sponsorship of terrorism by imposing multilateral structures. Although not directly on point, *consider* Evan Stephenson, *Does United Nations War Prevention Encourage State-Sponsorship of International Terrorism? An Economic Analysis*, 44 Va. J. Int'l L. 1197–1230 (2004).

209. Bowett had not completely ruled out the possible crafting of a rule of absolute liability in the context of indirect state responsibility. Bowett, *supra* note 7, at 19–20 ("The question of the illegality of guerilla activities (and, correspondingly, the reasonableness of reprisals against them) is inevitably linked to that of the responsibility of the state on whose territory these activities are organized. . . . [I]*nternational law has not developed any notion of absolute liability in this field* and the basic assumption has been that the territorial state assumed responsibility because it had the power to prevent these activities.") (emphasis added). *See also* Baker, *supra* note 29, at 48 ("[T]errorism may be the functional equivalent of an armed attack for which the perpetrators and their sanctuary states are *absolutely liable*.") (emphasis added).

210. *See, e.g.*, Byers, *supra* note 105, at 408 ("Even today, most States would not support a rule that opened them up to attack whenever terrorists were thought to operate within their territory."). Some commentators caution against being selective in the transplantation process in order to avoid importing a private law analogy without the corresponding procedural and evidentiary safeguards, especially in the context of the war on terror. *See, e.g.*, Jules Lobel, *The Use of Force to Respond to Terrorist Attacks: The Bombing of Sudan and Afghanistan*, 24 Yale J. Int'l L. 537, 550–51 (1999). The problems associated with imposing Western-derived legal transplants

have also been raised in a variety of contexts, with particular emphasis on the possible ensuing hegemonic thrust of the West. *See, e.g.*, Mark A. Drumbl, *Toward a Criminology of International Crime*, 19 OHIO ST. J. ON DISP. RESOL. 263, 271–72 (2003); Benedict Kingsbury, *"Indigenous Peoples" in International Law: A Constructivist Approach to the Asian Controversy*, 92 AM. J. INT'L L. 414, 455 (1998); and Makauwa Mutua, *Politics and Human Rights: An Essential Symbiosis*, in THE ROLE OF LAW IN INTERNATIONAL POLITICS 150 (Michael Byers ed., 2000).

211. In the context of the *Draft Articles*, any international obligation will necessitate the evaluation of several factors, including the conduct/result dichotomy. *See* Crawford, *supra* note 29, at 125 (noting that a prohibition may involve "an act or an omission or a combination of acts and omissions; it may involve the passage of legislation, or specific administrative or other action in a given case, or even a threat of such action, whether or not the threat is carried out, or a final judicial decision. It may require the provision of facilities, or the taking of precautions or the enforcement of a prohibition.").

212. The concept of fairness is undeniably one of the cardinal points of strict liability in U.S. law. *See, e.g.*, James A. Henderson, *Coping with the Time Dimension in Products Liability*, 69 CAL. L. REV. 919, 931–39 (1981). On the moral philosophy underlying products liability law, *see* David G. Owen, *The Moral Foundations of Products Liability Law: Toward First Principles*, 68 NOTRE DAME L. REV. 427 (1993).

213. *See, e.g.*, Posteraro, *supra* note 79, at 205 (arguing that, before taking unilateral action to defend themselves from terrorist threats, states should first seek to work with international institutions and then with coalition partners); Dove Waxman, *Terrorism: The War of the Future*, 23 FLETCHER F. WORLD AFF. 201, 205 (1999) ("The United States may be the world's only superpower, but even a superpower cannot fight terrorism alone. The increasingly transnational nature of terrorism means that it can only be tackled transnationally, requiring the cooperation of many states, all of whom jealously guard their national sovereignty."); *see also* Quigley, *supra* note 103.

214. This is another important tenet of domestic strict products liability.

215. Terrorist fund-raising is another significant dimension of indirect responsibility, one that extends beyond the scope of this chapter. *See* William Wechsler, *Strangling the Hydra: Targeting Al-Qaeda's Finances*, in HOW DID THIS HAPPEN? TERRORISM AND THE NEW WAR 121–43 (J. Hogue & R. Gideon eds., 2001); Bruce Zagaris, *The Merging of the Anti-Money Laundering and Counter-Terrorism Financial Enforcement Regimes After September 11, 2001*, 22 BERKELEY J. INT'L L. 123–57 (2004).

216. A similar case arose within the context of the World Trade Organization in the *Asbestos Case. European Communities—Measures Affecting Asbestos and Asbestos-Containing Products*, WTO Doc. WT/DS135/R (2000) (Dispute Settlement Panel) and WTO Doc. WT/DS135/AB/R (2001) (Appellate Body). In that litigation, France was called upon to justify its ban on asbestos and asbestos-containing products under Article XX of the General Agreement on Tariffs and Trade. The dispute settlement panel concluded that, although France's ban discriminated against other types of carcinogens, that discrimination could be justified under Article XX. Although France "won" before the panel, it appealed the case to the appellate body, which rejected the panel's discrimination rationale and instead focused on the likeness of the products at hand. In short, the appellate body recognized the right of France to afford different treatment to hazardous products without being labeled violators of the national treatment principle. *See, e.g., European Communities—Measures Affecting Asbestos and Asbestos-Containing Products*, in THE WTO CASE LAW OF 2001: THE AMERICAN LAW INSTITUTE REPORTERS' STUDIES 38 (Henrik Horn & Petros C. Mavroidis eds., 2004). Thus, it appears that, in this instance, the Appellate Body was aware of the social stigma involved in declaring that a state had violated international law (even if that violation was nullified on technical grounds). It is interesting to note that the rules of state responsibility have sometimes been extended to the WTO system. *See* Santiago M. Villalpando, *Attribution of Conduct to the State: How the Rules of State Responsibility May Be Applied Within the WTO Dispute Settlement System*, 5 J. INT'L ECON. L. 393–429 (2002). Finally, an argument may also be advanced to the fact that the prospect of incurring liability might prompt states to better thwart terrorist activities. For a recent account on similar issues, *see* Karl Zemanek, *Does the Prospect of Incurring Responsibility Improve the Observance of International Law?* in INTERNATIONAL RESPONSIBILITY TODAY: ESSAYS IN MEMORY OF OSCAR SCHACHTER 125–36 (Maurizio Ragazzi ed., Martinus Nijhoff Publishers, 2005).

217. *See* Trail Smelter Case (*U.S. v. Can.*), *reprinted in* 35 AM. J. INT'L L. 716 (1941); *see also Corfu Channel*, *supra* note 35, at 22–23 (not allowing a territory "knowingly" to be used to harm another state). *See generally* RENÉ LEFEBER, TRANSBOUNDARY ENVIRONMENTAL INTERFERENCE AND THE ORIGIN OF STATE LIABILITY 19–47 (1996). A third decision, taken in its whole, is sometimes invoked in scholarship to defend this position. *See, e.g.*, Lake Lanoux Case (*Fr. v. Spain*), 12 R.I.A.A. 281 (1957). It should be noted that some academics call into question the persuasiveness of this line of cases. *See, e.g.*, BENEDETTO CONFORTI, INTERNATIONAL LAW AND THE ROLE OF THE DOMESTIC

LEGAL SYSTEMS 170 (1993) (arguing that *Corfu Channel* and *Trail Smelter* do not prove the existence of an obligation to prevent ultra-hazardous and highly polluting activities).

218. Many commentators have recognized this obligation. *See, e.g.*, Brown, *supra* note 15, at 4–5, 13–18; Lippman, *supra* note 6; Feinstein & Slaughter, *supra* note 203.

219. *See, e.g.*, Declaration on Friendly Relations, *supra* note 73. The Declaration on Friendly Relations is repeated almost verbatim in the Declaration on Measures to Eliminate International Terrorism, which requires states, as customary international law, to take "effective and resolute measures" to end international terrorism. Declaration on Measures to Eliminate International Terrorism, Annex to G.A. Res. 49/60, U.N. GAOR, 84th mtg., U.N. Doc. A/RES/49/60, at 5(a) (1994).

220. Several Security Council resolutions stand for the principle that international terrorism should be eradicated. *See, e.g.*, S.C. Res. 883, U.N. SCOR, 3312th mtg., U.N. Doc. S/RES/883 (1993) (declaring "that the suppression of international terrorism . . . is essential for the maintenance of peace and security"); S.C. Res. 1044, U.N. SCOR, 3627th mtg., U.N. Doc. S/RES/1044 (1996) (declaring that the Security Council is "Deeply disturbed by the world-wide persistence of acts of international terrorism in all its forms which endanger or take innocent lives, have a deleterious effect on international relations and jeopardize the security of States"); S.C. Res. 1189, U.N. SCOR, 3915th mtg., U.N. Doc. S/RES/1189 (1998) ("reaffirming the determination of the international community to eliminate international terrorism in all its forms and manifestations"); S.C. Res. 1269, U.N. SCOR, 4053d mtg., U.N. Doc. S/RES/1269 (1999) (calling upon "all States to implement fully the international anti-terrorist conventions to which they are parties" and encouraging them "to consider as a matter of priority adhering to those to which they are not parties"); S.C. Res. 1267, *supra* note 110 ("reaffirming its conviction that the suppression of international terrorism is essential for the maintenance of international peace and security"); S.C. Res. 1333, U.N. SCOR, 4251st mtg., U.N. Doc. S/RES/1333 (2000).

221. Several multilateral treaties on combating international terrorism are currently in effect, thereby strengthening the will of the international community to recognize an affirmative obligation to prevent acts of terror. For an exhaustive list of multilateral treaties and UN resolutions, *see* Proulx, *supra* note 27, at n. 91.

222. The obligation of preventing terrorist acts has also been affirmed through judiciaries. *See supra* notes 61–66 and accompanying text.

223. *See, e.g.*, Feinstein & Slaughter, *supra* note 203, at 2 (citing a report of the Evans-Sahnoun Commission to argue that sovereignty implies responsibilities, such as the protection of citizens and their welfare, as well as rights, and that national leaders are responsible for their actions to international tribunals). On the mutual respect of sovereignty, *see* CLAUDE EMANUELLI, DROIT INTERNATIONAL PUBLIC: CONTRIBUTION À L'ÉTUDE DU DROIT INTERNATIONAL SELON UNE PERSPECTIVE CANADIENNE 411 (1998).

224. *See, e.g.*, Declaration on Friendly Relations, *supra* note 73; I OPPENHEIM'S INTERNATIONAL LAW, *supra* note 4, at 385; Emanuelli, *supra* note 223, at 216–18, 411.

225. *See* Brown, *supra* note 15, at 4.

226. *See, e.g.*, Baker, *supra* note 29, at 42 ("Terrorist acts carried out by armed bands with the support or encouragement of a foreign state is, in a literal sense, an armed attack."); *see also id.* at 48 ("Terrorism may be the functional equivalent of an armed attack for which the perpetrators and their sanctuary states are absolutely liable.").

227. The transplantation of these civil law concepts into international law has also engendered significant difficulties. *See* Crawford, *supra* note 29, at 21.

228. *Id.* at 140.

229. *Id.* at 129.

230. *Cf. Colozza and Rubinat v. Italy*, 85 Eur. Ct. H.R., Ser. A (1985) *with Iran v. U.S.A.* (Cases A15 (IV) and A24), 32 Iran-U.S. Cl. Trib. Rep. 115 (1996).

231. *See* Crawford, *supra* note 29, at 130.

232. Certain commentators have taken issue with Ago and Crawford's respective characterizations of obligations to prevent and obligations of result. *See supra* note 201. For the distinction between obligations of means and obligations of result, *see* Jean Combacau, *Obligations de résultat et obligations de comportement: quelques questions et pas de réponse*, in MÉLANGES OFFERTS À PAUL REUTER: LE DROIT INTERNATIONAL: UNITÉ ET DIVERSITÉ 181–204 (Daniel Bardonnet et al. eds., Pedone, 1981); Pierre-Marie Dupuy, *Le fait générateur de la responsabilité internationale des Etats*, 188 RECUEIL DES COURS DE L'ACADÉMIE DE DROIT INTERNATIONAL 9, 44 (1984); and Pauwelyn, *supra* note 132, at 415.

233. Some scholars hint at the idea of a variable model of state responsibility, albeit through the lens of armed reprisals. However, because much of the literature was written before 9/11, most of the relevant considerations hinge on *Nicaragua*-and-*Tadić*-inspired notions of control or knowledge. *See, e.g.*, Baker, *supra* note 29, at 36–37 (noting that a state's right of self-defense against a terrorist sanctuary state increases the more the sanctuary state is involved with, or has leverage over, the terrorists).

234. The proposed model of strict liability has, up to now, precluded applying *Corfu Channel* to host states.

The issue of constructive knowledge becomes paramount in the second tier of the strict liability approach, and given the importance of combating international terrorism, a host state will no longer be able to hide behind "willful blindness" to avoid responsibility. *See* Crawford, *supra* note 29, at 82 ("For example in the *Corfu Channel* case, the International Court of Justice held that it was a sufficient basis for Albanian responsibility that it knew, or must have known, of the presence of the mines in its territorial waters and did nothing to warn third States of their presence."). This finding is directly transferable to the current framework, as the amount of information a host state had or *ought* to have had is directly proportional to its level of responsibility.

235. *See supra* note 39 and accompanying text.

236. This element was also explored by Bowett when he assessed the reasonableness of reprisals against a host state for terrorist activity emanating from its territory. Bowett, *supra* note 7, at 27 (noting "That the appraisal of the retaliatory use of force [must] take account of the *duration and quality of support*, if any, that the target government has *given to terroristic enterprises*") (emphasis added).

237. This would be the case of the Taliban, which ignored several pleas by the Security Council to cease harboring members of al Qaeda. *See supra* notes 127–130 and accompanying text.

238. It is important to recall that the whole campaign against terrorism is an exercise in risk assessment. In this particular case, although the host state failed to prevent one terrorist attack, it should not exacerbate passions and, through an overactive zeal, instigate further terrorist attacks. Proportionality and reasonableness should govern this analysis. In fact, Bowett raised this problematic aspect of state responsibility through the lens of reprisals aimed at enticing host states to prevent terrorist activities. Bowett, *supra* note 7, at 20 ("No Arab Government, given the enormous popular support for the guerrilla activities amongst its own population, appeared able to risk an intensive campaign to stamp out these activities. . . . Reprisals are not likely to affect the toleration shown by a government to guerilla activities when a show of intolerance would bring the downfall of the government."). Although not directly on point, *consider* T. S. Rama Rao, *State Terror as a Response to Terrorism and Vice Versa: National and International Dimensions*, 27 IND. J. INT'L L. 183–93 (1987).

239. It is imperative to recall that the Taliban was, in fact, the de facto government in most of Afghanistan and, at the least, provided sanctuary to al Qaeda. *See* George H. Aldrich, *The Taliban, Al Qaeda, and the Determination of Illegal Combatants*, 96 AM. J. INT'L L. 891, 893 (2002); Antonio Cassese, *Terrorism Is Also Disrupting Some Crucial Legal Categories of International Law*, 12 EUR. J. INT'L L. 993, 999 (2001); RICHARD

FALK, THE GREAT TERROR WAR 101 (2003); Christopher Greenwood, *International Law and the "War Against Terrorism,"* 78 INT'L AFF. 301, 314 (2002); Mary Ellen O'Connell, *To Kill or Capture Suspects in the Global War on Terror*, 35 CASE W. RES. J. INT'L L. 325 (2003); Mofidi & Eckert, *supra* note 113, at 81–85. *But see* John C. Yoo & James C. Ho, *The Status of Terrorists*, 44 VA. J. INT'L L. 207, 218–20 (2003) (arguing that the Taliban was not a state actor). It is probably fair to assume that the United States' refusal to recognize the Taliban as the legitimate government of Afghanistan is attributable to its disapproval of the Taliban's oppressive regime. *See, e.g.*, Azubuike, *supra* note 27, at 131–34.

240. *See* Byers, *supra* note 3 (arguing, under the heading "Exceptional Illegality," that "The right to intervene by invitation is based on the undisputed fact that a state can freely consent to having foreign armed forces on its territory.").

241. This phenomenon also implies that economically weaker states might be called upon to sacrifice their sovereignty more readily. On the value of combating terrorism through multilateral channels, *see* John W. Head, *Essay: What Has Not Changed Since September 11—The Benefits of Multilateralism*, 12 KAN. J. L. & PUB. POL'Y 1–12 (2002); Fred C. Pedersen, *Controlling International Terrorism: An Analysis of Unilateral Force and Proposals for Multilateral Cooperation: Comment*, 8 TOL. L. REV. 209–50 (1976); Eric Remacle, *Vers un multilatéralisme en réseau comme instrument de la lutte contre le terrorisme?* in LE DROIT INTERNATIONAL FACE AU TERRORISME: APRÈS LE 11 SEPTEMBRE 2001 331–44 (K. Bannelier, O. Corten, T. Christakis, & B. Delcourt eds., 2002); Volker Röben, *The Role of International Conventions and General International Law in the Fight Against International Terrorism*, in TERRORISM AS A CHALLENGE FOR NATIONAL AND INTERNATIONAL LAW: SECURITY VERSUS LIBERTY? 789–821 (Christian Walter et al. eds., 2004).

242. This is consistent with the logic of *Colozza and Rubinat*, *supra* note 230. *See* Crawford, *supra* note 29, at 129 (noting that the European Court of Human Rights not only examined Italy's failure to afford an accused the right to a trial but also "what more Italy could have done to make the applicant's right 'effective.'").

243. It is interesting to note that international law has generally recognized the *jus cogens* character of the prohibition of the use of force in Article 2(4) of the UN Charter. *See Nicaragua*, *supra* note 8, at 100 ("[T]he law of the Charter concerning the prohibition of the use of force in itself constitutes a conspicuous example of a rule in international law having the character of jus cogens."); JAMES CRAWFORD, THE CREATION OF STATES IN INTERNATIONAL LAW 106 (1979); Alfred Vendross, *Jus Dispositivum and Jus Cogens in International Law*, 60 AM. J. INT'L L. 55 (1966); Michel Virally, *Réflexions sur*

le Jus Cogens, 12 ANNUAIRE FRANÇAIS DE DROIT INT'L 28 (1966). This would seem to put the whole debate surrounding direct responsibility to rest. In sum, if a host state directly participates in a terrorist attack, it fails to fulfill its *jus cogens* obligation pertaining to the prohibition of the use of force. As I discuss below, *jus cogens* obligations usually attract a stricter regime of state responsibility. In such cases, the responsibility of the host state would be easily established. For a background discussion on the role of Article 2(4) of the UN Charter in international relations, *see* Thomas Franck, *Who Killed Article 2(4)? Or: Changing Norms Governing the Use of Force by States*, 64 AM. J. INT'L L. 809 (1970); and Oscar Schachter, *The Right of States to Use Armed Force*, 82 MICH. L. REV. 1620 (1984).

244. As with obligations *erga omnes*, *jus cogens* obligations attract a stricter regime of state responsibility. *See, e.g.*, Crawford, *supra* note 29, at 132 ("State responsibility can extend to acts of the utmost seriousness, and the regime of responsibility in such cases will be correspondingly stringent. But even when a new peremptory norm of general international law comes into existence . . . this does not entail any retrospective assumption of responsibility."). However, it has sometimes been asserted that *jus cogens* rules are, in fact, narrower than *erga omnes* obligations. *See, e.g.*, Ronald St. J. Mac-

donald, *Fundamental Norms in Contemporary International Law*, 25 CAN. Y.B. INT'L L. 138 (1987); THEODOR MERON, HUMAN RIGHTS LAW-MAKING IN THE UNITED NATIONS 187 (1986). Other scholars expound that *jus cogens* and *erga omnes* rules are essentially equivalent because both deal with different facets of the same norms. *See, e.g.*, Michael Byers, *The Relationship Between Jus Cogens and Erga Omnes Rules*, 66 NORDIC J. INT'L L. 211, 230 (1997).

245. *See* Byers, *supra* note 244, at 228 ("The principal source of *jus cogens* rules may thus be identified as the process of customary international law.").

246. Baker warned about the inherent dangers of attempting to mount a military response against a terrorist attack, a caveat that is rightly concerned with potential harm to civilians. Baker, *supra* note 29, at 47 ("The problem is that the form of response to a terrorist attack often appears to be disproportionate to the actions which prompted it. . . . Such action is typically large scale and overt when compared to the small, covert actions of the terrorists.").

247. It is interesting to note that this obligation had also been recognized prior to 9/11. *See, e.g.*, *id.* at 40 ("A state has a categorical legal obligation to prevent its territory from being used to support or harbor terrorist groups.").

21

Force Qua Terrorism
International Law in the Wake of 9/11 *

ANNA OEHMICHEN

What we cannot but see outside the courtroom is that, more and more, legal justification of use of force within the system of the United Nations Charter is discarded even as a fig leaf, while an increasing number of writers appear to prepare for the outright funeral of international legal limitations on the use of force.

—Separate Opinion of Judge Simma [6] in the *Oil Platforms* case[1]

I. Introduction

The events of September 11, 2001, and the U.S. response to it triggered one of the most topical recent developments in international law. In the morning hours of this day, four aircraft were hijacked, and two were driven into the World Trade Center Twin Towers in New York City and the other two were aimed at the Pentagon in Washington, D.C., causing the deaths of approximately three thousand people.[2] Never before had a terrorist attack reached a similar scale of destruction. The United States very quickly attributed the attacks to an Islamist network called al Qaeda, led by Osama bin Laden, who was known to be installed with his network in Afghanistan. With the support of the United Kingdom and other states, the United States re-

acted to the events of 9/11 by declaring the "war on terrorism" and then launching a war against Afghanistan less than one month after the attacks (Operation Enduring Freedom). The United States justified the resort to force by invoking their right to self-defense, as provided for by Article 51 of the UN Charter (the Charter).[3] The question of legality of this war has raised lively debates among international legal scholars, with the two core issues being: Could the terrorist attacks of 9/11 qualify as an "armed attack" within the meaning of article 51 of the Charter? And if yes, did the attack justify the use of force against Afghanistan, even though it was not Afghanistan but rather international terrorists who were identified as responsible for the attack?[4]

Two years later, the United States, again with the support of other allies, invaded Iraq (Oper-

*The author would like to thank Olivier Corten, Christophe Marchand, and Aurélien Nicolet for their kind support.

ation Iraqi Freedom). This time, the justification was even more questionable: U.S. President George W. Bush stated, "And our mission is clear, to disarm Iraq of weapons of mass destruction, to end Saddam Hussein's support for terrorism, and to free the Iraqi people."[5] Was it again the right to self-defense, though this time preemptive self-defense against the threat of (imaginary) weapons of mass destruction or against presumed terrorist attacks prepared on the territory of a terrorist-supporting government, or was it rather humanitarian intervention, directed at protecting the human rights of the Iraqi people?[6]

These developments have brought about changes to international law that again were widely discussed in international legal literature.[7] The then UN Secretary-General Kofi Annan noted, "We have come to a fork in the road. This may be a moment no less decisive than in 1945 itself, when the United Nations was founded."[8]

In view of the already existing countless publications on these questions, the purpose of this chapter can only be modest. It attempts to find a normative answer to the question of whether—and if yes, under which circumstances—the use of armed force can be justified in response to international terrorist acts. In order to explore this, part II analyzes the existing international legal framework governing terrorism, and part III addresses the use of force and the right to self-defense. From this, we will attempt to formulate the desirable legal requirements—if any—for a potential right to force against terrorist acts.

II. Terrorism in International Law

1. Ambiguity of the Term

The notion of "terrorism" is extremely ambiguous. The term has been applied to a large number of diverging movements. It has been used to describe totalitarian methods in several dictatorships ("state terrorism") as well as guerilla warfare in colonial struggles for independence (thus the famous saying "One person's terrorism is another person's freedom fighter"). The term has also been attributed to religious groups, such as the AUM sect that lodged a Sarine attack in Tokyo's subway, the Christian Ku-Klux-Klan and anti-abortion movements, and Jewish groups like the Irgun in Israel in the 1930s. Throughout history, identifying these respective groups as state enemies has conveniently served governments well.[9] Moreover, the existing asymmetries of power have always shadowed the label of "terrorism." As M. Cherif Bassiouni put it: "No matter what the debate is about, it is always those with dominant power who control the characterization of their opponents' violence."[10]

2. The International Society's Attempts to Define Terrorism

The term terrorism is thus highly (if not exclusively) political.[11] It is, therefore, not surprising that the international community was incapable of defining it comprehensively, in spite of its multiple attempts in that direction. It is, however, notable that after the attacks of September 11, international actions to combat terrorism have intensified considerably.

The efforts of the international community to combat terrorism collectively date back as far as the 1930s. Thus, already in 1937, the League of Nations attempted a first, rather broad definition of terrorism in the Convention on the Prevention and Punishment of Terrorism, but only one country (India) ratified this Convention, so it never entered into force. In the late 1960s and 1970s a wave of hijackings and other international terrorist incidents triggered the United Nations to address the problem again. In 1972 the UN General Assembly created an ad hoc Committee on International Terrorism to draft a convention, but it was impossible to reach an agreement on the definition of terrorism.[12] The main problem was that opinions within the United Nations were divided as to whether national liberation movements should be excluded from the definition of terrorism.[13] As this conflict seemed difficult to resolve, attention shifted from the attempt to agree on a definition of terrorism to a more functional approach, that is, addressing specific acts of violence committed with a specific terrorist intent.[14] In this manner, from 1963 until 2005 thirteen conventions have been adopted in the framework of the UN, each of them addressing specific manifestations of terrorism but avoiding to define terrorism as such. These treaties covered a range of different actions, including aircraft security,[15] protection of diplomatic agents,[16] the taking of hostages,[17] protection of nuclear material,[18] acts of violence at airports,[19] maritime safety,[20] the safety of fixed platforms located on the continental shelf,[21] plastic explosives,[22] terrorist bombing,[23] terrorist financing,[24] and nuclear terrorism.[25] In addition, the General Assembly condemned acts of terrorism in a number of resolutions, again without defining the term.[26] Furthermore, in 1996 the General Assembly, in resolution 51/210 of December 17, established an ad hoc committee to elaborate two more international conventions concerning terrorist bombings and nuclear terrorism and, thereafter, to address means of further developing a comprehensive legal framework of conventions dealing with international terrorism. This committee is still busy drafting a comprehensive convention on international terrorism.[27] Whether a definition will be developed remains to be seen.

After 2001 terrorism became a priority on the UN's agenda. Although before 2001 terrorism was mainly addressed by the General Assembly, after September 11 the Security Council "weighed in on terrorism."[28] On September 12, 2001, it condemned the terrorist attacks of the previous day and called on all states to "work together urgently to bring to justice the perpetrators, organizers and sponsors" of the attacks and also called on the international community to "redouble their efforts to prevent and suppress terrorist acts including by increased cooperation and full implementation of the relevant international anti-terrorist conventions and Security Council resolutions."[29] Subsequently, the Security Council adopted Resolution 1373, which imposed a number of binding obligations on states. The Resolution is considered very far reaching, as it encompasses positive obligations that usually are only contained in treaties developed through the normal treaty-making process.[30] By imposing on all states certain obligations deriving from the 1999 Convention for the Suppression of the Financing of Terrorism, which at that time was not yet in force, the Council "rendered certain purely treaty rules binding on all Member States of the United Nations and thus assumed the role of a true international legislator."[31] Furthermore, on the basis of the Resolution 1373, the Counter-Terrorism Committee (CTC) was established, to which member states are obliged to report regularly on their implementation of the Resolution.

Moreover, it was only after the events of 9/11 that the first international agreement on defining terrorism could be reached, though solely at a regional level. Thus, the European Council adopted the European Framework Decision of June 13, 2002 on combating terrorism in order to approximate the definition of terrorism in all member states of the European Union.[32] It contained detailed provisions as to which offences member states should qualify as terrorism and also gave indications concerning the sentencing.[33] Furthermore, on the same date the Council Framework Decision on the European arrest warrant and the surrender procedures between member states was adopted, in which terrorism was included among the offences for which a European arrest warrant could be issued.[34]

It may be concluded that, apart from regional instruments such as the Council Framework Decision of 2002, terrorist offences have not been defined in a comprehensive manner internationally, despite increasing international efforts to collaborate in this matter. In view of the very political nature of the term, it remains doubtful whether the international community will ever be able to come up with a comprehensive definition. One could argue that a comprehensive definition was not really necessary, as most if not all potential terrorist acts would probably be covered by one or another of the multiple existing international treaties anyway. For instance, the attacks of 9/11 qualify as aircraft hijacking and hostage taking (both criminalized under the UN Conventions of 1979 and 1988), so that there will be no debate that these attacks can be characterized as terrorist. Moreover, the risk of a comprehensive definition will always be that it may be formulated too vaguely to be useful for criminal purposes, thereby violating the principles of clarity and certainty of the law.[35] The risk of nebulosity is even higher in the area of international law, which is always compromised by the search for diplomatic consensus.[36] In spite of these obstacles, a comprehensive definition, agreed upon by the international community, is strongly desirable because otherwise states can choose to only criminalize certain acts and not others, according to their political preferences, by ratifying only selectively some international instruments. Moreover, a comprehensive international convention on terrorism is necessary as the basis for international police and judicial cooperation. Without it, the international community is unable to effectively fight terrorism. Without defining precisely the acts that should be condemned, we are fighting only a ghost of "terrorism" in the darkness. Then our real target may easily evade our attacks and innocent victims may suffer from our own blind attacks. It is, therefore, important to define terrorism, but it is equally important to choose a politically neutral definition[37] by avoiding criminalizing ideas or opinions and, instead, strictly focusing on the specific violent acts.

III. The Use of Force Under International Law and the Right to Self-Defense

1. The Principle of Peace

Perhaps the most important principle governing the use of force in international law is actually its general prohibition, which constitutes the basis for international peace and security. Thus, the Preamble of the Charter states that the United Nations agree

by the acceptance of principles and the institution of methods, that armed force shall not be used, save in the common interest. Moreover, art. 2(4) of the Charter establishes that All Members shall refrain in their international relations from the threat or use of force against the territorial integrity or political independence of any state, or in any other manner inconsistent with the Purposes of the United Nations.

The drafting history of the Charter reveals the core importance of that principle, which was established in 1945 after the international community had experienced two devastating world wars from which it had yet to recover. Thus, preserving peace was at the heart of the international community's goals. At the San Francisco Conference (where the Charter was drafted and ultimately adopted), the president of the Committee stated, "With regard to peace we feel the need to emphasize that our first object was to be strong to maintain peace, to maintain peace by our common effort and at all costs, at all costs with one exception—not the cost of justice."[38] The Preamble of the Charter also reflects this purpose of creating the United Nations: the establishment of peace and security worldwide.[39]

2. The Recognized Exceptions

The text of the Charter, its drafting history, and the writings of eminent jurists show the drafters' intention that the Charter should be comprehensive, subject only to the express exceptions provided for in the Charter itself.[40] Under these premises, there are three recognized exceptions to the principle of the prohibition of force. First, military actions authorized by the Security Council under Chapter VII of the Charter (Article 42 of the Charter) are permitted in response to "any threat to the peace, breach of the peace, or act of aggression" (Article 39 of the Charter). Second, humanitarian intervention is permitted. Although it is not rooted in any provision of the Charter, it has been implicit in certain findings of and responses to "threats to international peace and security" under Chapter

VII.[41] Finally, the resort to force may be justified in the wake of an armed attack, as the "inherent right of individual or collective self-defense" (Article 51 of the UN Charter). The United States invoked this latter right when it launched the war in Afghanistan. As such, we need to explore whether this right indeed justifies the use of force in response to terrorist attacks.

3. The Right to Self-Defense as an Exception to the Prohibition of Force

Article 51 of the Charter allows states to invoke the inherent right of individual or collective self-defense if an armed attack occurs against a member of the United Nations. The legal issue to be addressed, in the aftermath of 9/11, is whether—and if yes, when—terrorist acts may qualify as "armed attacks" within the meaning of the cited provision.

Concerning the scope of force permitted, the question arises of against whom the force may be applied, and to what extent. In this context, it is necessary to explore what level of connection must be established between the terrorists who committed the act and the "harboring" state that is to be attacked in self-defense.

Finally, we will explore whether the notion of "armed attack" should also comprise the imminent threat of an attack that has not yet occurred but might, and if it did occur, would have such devastating effects that preemptive action is considered necessary.

a. Terrorist Acts as "Armed Attacks"?

Before September 11, 2001, resort to force was only justified under narrow circumstances. Although Article 51 of the Charter explicitly recognizes the right to self-defense, this right is not clearly defined in the Charter. Only customary international law provides a definition.[42] Considering its historical origins, it seems defendable that terrorist acts may give rise to citing self-defense, as the very first case in which this right was invoked was by states concerned about attacks carried out by rebels. The right to self-defense emerged in 1837 in the *Caroline* case. In

this case, the British were combatting a rebellion in Upper Canada, which was supported by U.S. citizens. The British set fire to the boat that the rebels used for transporting weapons and sent it over Niagara Falls. The British justified their act by invoking their "right to self-defense and self-preservation." U.S. Secretary of State Daniel Webster responded by recognizing, further defining, and thus limiting the right to self-defense. He created the formula that the necessity of self-defense had to be "instant, overwhelming, leaving no choice of means, and no moment for deliberation" and that this necessity implied that "nothing unreasonable or excessive" was done.[43] Thus, an international law concept was established that has governed the interpretation of Article 51 of the Charter since its drafting.

Until the incidents of September 11, resort to force was further limited by the following conditions:

- it had to be exclusively directed to repel the armed attack of the aggressor state;
- it had to be proportionate to this purpose of driving back aggression;
- it had to be of temporary nature, ending as soon as the aggression had come to an end or the Security Council had taken the necessary measures;[44] and
- its exercise had to comply with the fundamental principles of humanitarian law.[45]

There have been cases in which states invoked the right to self-defense in response to terrorist attacks (in particular, Israel and the United States), but the majority of states disapproved of these actions.[46]

Moreover, in the International Court of Justice's Advisory Opinion in the Israel/Palestine case, the court held that Article 51 recognized "the existence of an inherent right of self-defence in the case of armed attack by one State against *another State*."[47] This means that, at least according to the International Court of Justice, terrorist acts, by themselves, still do not qualify as an "armed attack" within the framework of Article 51. They may only qualify as such if a state engaged in them and, as a consequence, the action can be attributed not only to the individual actor but also to a particular state.[48] The core question is, therefore, what level of state engagement is needed for Article 51's purposes.

b. Self-Defense Against States Supporting or Harboring Terrorists?

The paradox in the case of the Afghanistan war is that although the attacks had been performed by nonstate actors outside the control of states, they were combatted by the oldest form of international response—war. Furthermore, the war did not target primarily the terrorists but rather another state.[49]

It is questionable whether Article 51 also allows self-defense against a state whose only responsibility for an armed attack lies in the fact that the actors of the attack prepared the attack on its territory. Article 51 is silent about the question of against whom the right to self-defense may be exercised. The question of whether self-defense can be used against a state that has actively supported terrorist attacks has been previously addressed by the International Court of Justice. In the Nicaragua case, the International Court of Justice had to consider the question of whether the United States, by training and providing arms to the Nicaraguan *contras*, were imputable to the acts the contras committed. The Court rejected the United States' position that the provision of arms constituted an armed attack by the Nicaraguan government justifying the right to self-defense. Instead, it demanded a strong nexus between the rebel groups launching the attack and the state supporting them.[50] The same approach is followed in the law governing state responsibility,[51] as it was also outlined by the ICJ in the same case with regard to the United States' responsibility for violations of humanitarian law committed by the Nicaraguan contras. The ICJ developed the "effective control test," requiring that a party had to be not only in effective control of a military or paramilitary group but also that the control had to be exercised with respect to the specific operation in the course of which breaches of in-

ternational humanitarian law might have been committed.[52] The International Law Commission has adopted the same test in its Articles on State Responsibility.[53]

This principle, the requirement of a close link between the actor of the armed attack and the state subject to the invocation of self-defense, has been practically overruled after September 11, when the United States invaded Afghanistan in reaction to the attacks in New York and Washington.[54] The United States justified invading Afghanistan by arguing that

> the attacks on 11 September 2001 and the ongoing threat to the United States and its nationals posed by the al-Qaeda organization have been made possible by the decision of the Taliban regime to allow the parts of Afghanistan that it controls to be used by this organization as a base of operation. Despite every effort by the United States and the international community, the Taliban regime has refused to change its policy. From the territory of Afghanistan, the al-Qaeda organization continues to train and support agents of terror who attack innocent people throughout the world and target United States nationals and interests in the United States and abroad.[55]

Thus, the United States argued that because the Taliban had allowed the organization of al Qaeda to use parts of its territory as a base of operation, this sufficed to establish that the Taliban had supported the armed attack and consequently could be attacked.

The United States received prompt support for this war from many nations. The North Atlantic Council unanimously adopted a statement on September 12, 2001, in which it agreed that an armed attack within the meaning of Article 5 of the Washington Treaty[56] was present.[57] Thus, the nineteen members of the Alliance considered the attacks of 9/11 to be an "armed attack" within the meaning of Article 51 of the Charter. Similarly, the members of the Organization of American States identified the 9/11 incidents as an "armed attack."[58] The worldwide support for the Afghanistan War, coupled with unprecedented offers of airspace and landing rights,[59] brought about a modification of customary international law.[60]

The general acceptance of U.S. actions led to the establishment that the right to self-defense also applies against states that actively support or willingly harbor terrorist groups.[61] However, this approach goes too far. The harboring as such cannot suffice to establish the required link between the state and terrorist action; rather, the harboring state must, at the very least, tacitly approve the terrorist action.[62] This implies that the state must have positive knowledge of the concrete terrorist activity, and this requires international consensus as to what is considered to be terrorism. As long as such consensus has not been reached, military force cannot be justified on the grounds of Article 51 against states "harboring terrorists." Any other view could (and probably would) lead, ultimately, to the most perverse situation. Let's imagine that totalitarian State A might consider certain persons to be terrorists due to their opposite views and resistance toward the government of State A. As a result of the "harboring doctrine," these persons would not be able to find any refuge anywhere in the world because all the other states would fear an armed attack from the "rogue" state A—justified, ironically, by the right to self-defense.

An additional problem of the harboring doctrine is the potential overlap with the law of judicial cooperation, especially with respect to extradition. As Michael Byers pointed out, it would be unclear at what point a state's right to choose between prosecuting or extraditing (*aut dedere aut judicare*) an accused terrorist could be superseded by another state's right to use force in self-defense.[63]

In view of these considerations, it seems highly problematic to allow the resort to self-defense against a state in cases in which the attack has been committed by nonstate actors, unless it is clearly established that the nonstate actor is "acting on the instructions of, or under the direction or control of, that State," as demanded by Article 8 of the International Law Commission's Articles on State Responsibility. I see no reason why the justification for self-defense, which effectively grants permission to go to war, could require any lower level of state responsibility.

c. Preemptive Self-Defense?

It is important to note that unlike military interventions in response to terrorist attacks, the United States had never engaged in a preemptive use of force against another state prior to invading Iraq in 2003.[64] The only state that did so in the past was Israel in June 1981, when it bombed the Iraqi Sirak nuclear reactor near Baghdad. Israel was subsequently unanimously condemned by the Security Council and by over one hundred states in the General Assembly.[65] Nonetheless, the National Security Strategy of the United States, adopted in 2002, provides for such a right, "even if uncertainty remains as to the time and place of the enemy's attack."[66] Whether such a view is compatible with contemporary international law is questionable.

Legal doctrine is divided with respect to this issue. Some authors recognize "preventive self-defense" under certain circumstances,[67] whereas according to others, contemporary international law is opposed to so wide an approach.[68] The latter view seems convincing. First of all, reconciling the idea of preemptive self-defense with the wording of Article 51 of the Charter is difficult. The term "armed attack," and not just "attack" or "imminent threat" rather suggests that a concrete armed attack has already occurred or is presently occurring.[69] Second, the objective of Article 51 is to recognize the right to resort to force without authorization of the Security Council only in exceptional cases and only for a limited period of time—"until the Security Council has taken measures necessary to maintain international peace and security." The general rule of the Charter is, therefore, to reserve the power to resort to force to the Security Council.[70] Only as s a rule of exception may a state resort to force for the purpose of self-defense. As always is the case with legal exceptions, they ought to be interpreted rather narrowly. The same follows also from a contextual interpretation. Considering its allocation at the end of Chapter VII of the UN Charter, the right to self-defense needs to be considered as subsidiary to actions authorized by the Security Council under Chapter VII.

However, after the events of September 11, 2001, some argued that because of the imminence of a certain threat, states had to be permitted to use force without having to wait for the Security Council's consent. Otherwise the Charter of the United Nations would force them to wait to be irreparably attacked, and this would turn the Charter into a sort of "suicide pact."[71] The problem with this view is that it opens the door to deliberate abuse, whereas the obvious purpose of the Charter, designed in the wake of two world wars, was actually to eradicate such potential abuse.[72] Acting on this view would "open the floodgates to the cycle of violence the Charter was enacted to prevent."[73] Allowing preventive self-defense would enable states to "defend" themselves whenever they subjectively feel threatened or, to put it even more bluntly, whenever they consider it convenient to say they feel threatened.

State practice following the drafting of the UN Charter confirms this point of view.[74]

The practical problem is the *establishment* of this imminent threat. How much evidence would be needed or, better, how little might the international community accept to establish the imminence and necessity? And who would decide the matter? A potential future threat feared by one country but has not yet materialized should not allow preventive action. An exception to this rule could only be justified, theoretically, if one knew *with certainty* of the existence of such a threat, its precise scope, its imminent realization, and if the state could not afford to wait for Security Council authorization because doing so would fail to prevent irreparable and severe harm. Additionally, we must presume that the person deciding on the use of force is competent to judge the situation, a person incapable of both human error and abuse. These conditions, I am afraid, can never be met. As long as we let the very country that seeks to resort to self-defense decide on whether self-defense is the appropriate reaction, we must require this country, at least, to apply a strict and narrow test when making such a far-reaching decision. In consideration of the potential fatal consequences of the resort to force, no broader application of the right to self-defense can be permitted.

IV. Conclusions

After the terrorist attacks of September 11 and the subsequent invasion of Afghanistan, international terrorism has reached a dimension that has invited international scholars to consider the resort to force against attacks similar to the ones of 2001. However, one basic problem in addressing this question is the definition of terrorism. Although, with respect to the events of 9/11, there was a broad consensus that these attacks did qualify as an "armed attack," the abstract question of whether terrorist acts as such constitute an "armed attack," has not been answered—and cannot be answered—in international law unless terrorism is comprehensively defined. Although the international community has attempted since 1937 to reach a consensus on the definition of terrorism, it has, up to today, not reached that goal. As long as the world does not have a united view on which acts carry the label of "terrorism," the question of whether resorting to force against terrorism is legitimate under international law lacks any foundation because we must always ask: Whose terrorism? An international definition is needed before any other question can satisfactorily be addressed. Moreover, when drafting such a comprehensive legal definition, we should restrict it to the criminalization of certain clearly defined terrorist acts and avoid any vague or ambiguous terms. To this end, only certain—physical—acts should be considered to be terrorism, not mere thoughts or ideas, because criminalizing ideas is deemed to be politically abused.

Moreover, we should recall once more that resorting to force is never the principle but rather the exception under international law. There are only a few exceptions to the prohibition of the use of force, one of them being the right to self-defense under Article 51 of the UN Charter. The right to self-defense, as a principle of international law governing interstate relations, should only be invoked in response to armed attacks committed by other states. An attack may, however, be attributed to a state, even when directly committed by nonstate actors, if it is established that the nonstate actor is "acting on the instructions of, or under the direction or control of, that State." The mere "harboring" of the nonstate actor should not suffice to trigger a right to self-defense. In that case, the attacked state should resort to other means, such as requesting extradition. Whether the nonstate actor was controlled by another state or not should be established with certainty, on the basis of sound evidence. Leaving the assessment of this question to the very state that was attacked is not satisfactory, as this state could then use any terrorist act as a pretext to invade another country. The question of which state is responsible for the act should, therefore, rather be answered by an external actor, for example, the UN Security Council. With respect to acts that can only be attributed to individuals "harbored" by another state, the use of force should not be permitted. In very extreme cases, for example, when the harboring state refuses any collaboration and the attack has been of considerable gravity, an action under Chapter VII with the authorization of the Security Council might be also envisaged, but there should be no place for the right to self-defense. This view is backed by the general principle reigning in international law, which is—let us recall it once more—the pursuit of peace and refraining as much as possible from violence.[75] Thus, preemptive self-defense should be rejected in its entirety, as it is neither recognized in international law nor desirable from a practical point of view. The devastating effects of resorting to force leaves no room for such a broad interpretation of Article 51 of the Charter. The risk that countries might use "preemptive self-defense" as a pretext to resort to war when it is opportune for them for quite different reasons is too great.

In conclusion, there may be very exceptional cases in which resorting to force against terrorism may be justified under international law, but it must be stressed that the use of force should always remain the very last resort—the *ultima ratio* a state should apply—and force should be applied always with respect for the principles of necessity and proportionality. The fact that a few suicide bombers were able in one concerted action to kill about 3,000 people does not make every criminal a potential 9/11 bomber. In most cases, criminal acts, including "terrorist" ones, will not reach the dimension of war. As a general rule, states should not respond to them with war either.

NOTES

1. *Islamic Republic of Iran v. United States of America*, (Merits), ICJ Rep 1 (2003).

2. In the judgment of the German Federal Court of Justice (*Bundesgerichtshof*) concerning Motassadeq, the latter had been accused of aiding and abetting to murder in 3,066 cases (BGH, case no. 3 StR 139/06, of Nov. 16, 2006, p. 4).

3. Article 51 of the UN Charter reads as follows: "Nothing in the present Charter shall impair the inherent right of individual or collective self defence if an armed attack occurs against a Member of the United Nations, until the Security Council has taken measures necessary to maintain international peace and security. Measures taken by Members in the exercise of this right of self-defence shall be immediately reported to the Security Council and shall not in any way affect the authority and responsibility of the Security Council under the present Charter to take at any time such action as it deems necessary in order to maintain or restore international peace and security."

4. On these questions, *see, e.g.,* Carsten Stahn, *"Nicaragua is dead, long live Nicaragua"—the Right to Self-Defence Under Art. 51 UN Charter and International Terrorism*, in TERRORISM AS A CHALLENGE FOR NATIONAL AND INTERNATIONAL LAW: SECURITY VERSUS LIBERTY? 827 (Christian Walter et al. eds., 2004); Carsten Stahn, *Terrorist Acts as "Armed Attack": The Right to Self-Defense, Article 51 (1/2) of the UN Charter, and International Terrorism*, 27 FLETCHER FORUM WORLD AFF. 35 (2003); Michael Byers, *Terrorism, the Use of Force and International Law after 11 September*, 16 INT'L RELS. 155 (2002); Devika Hovell, *Chinks in the Armour:*

International Law, Terrorism and the Use of Force, 27 U. NEW SOUTH WALES L. J. 398 (2004); Geir Ulfstein, *Terrorism and the Use of Force*, 34 SEC. DIALOGUE 153 (2003); Sean D. Murphy, *Terrorism and the Concept of "Armed Attack" in Article 51 of the U.N. Charter*, 43 HARV. INT'L L. J. 41–51 (2002).

5. President Discusses Beginning of Operation Iraqi Freedom, President's Radio Address of Mar. 22, 2003, published online by the White House, *at* http://george wbush-whitehouse.archives.gov/news/releases/2003/03/20030322.html.

6. On the legality of the Iraq war, *see, e.g.*, THE IRAQ CRISIS AND WORLD ORDER: STRUCTURAL, INSTITUTIONAL AND NORMATIVE CHALLENGES (Ramesh Thakur & Waheguru Pal Singh Sidhu eds., 2006); Radhika Satkunanathan, *The US Invasion of Iraq : "Neoconned" into an Illegal War?* 16 SRI LANKA J. INT'L L. 65 (2004); Jutta Brunnée & Stephen J. Toope, *The Use of Force: International Law After Iraq*, 52 INT'L & COMP. L. Q. 785 (2004); Michael N. Schmitt, *The Legality of Operation Iraq Freedom Under International Law*, in INTERNATIONAL LAW CHALLENGES: HOMELAND SECURITY AND COMBATING TERRORISM 367–394 (Thomas McK. Sparks & Glenn M. Sulmasy eds., 2006).

7. *See e.g.*, Antonio Cassese, *Terrorism Is Also Disrupting Some Crucial Legal Categories of International Law*, 12 EUR. J. INT'L L. 993 (2001); Rüdiger Wolfrum, *The Attack of September 11, 2001, the Wars Against the Taliban and Iraq: Is There a Need to Reconsider International Law on the Recourse to Force and the Rules in Armed Conflict?* 7 MAX PLANCK Y.B. U.N. L. 1–78 (2003); Mark B. Baker, *Terrorism and the Inherent Right of Self-Defense : A Call to Amend Article 51 of the United Nations Charter*, 10 HOUS. J. INT'L L. 25–49 (1987); TARCISIO GAZZINI, THE CHANGING RULES ON THE USE OF FORCE IN INTERNATIONAL LAW (2005).

8. Speech delivered at the General Assembly, 58th sess., 7th plen. mtg., Sept. 23, 2003 [3], U.N. Doc. A/58/PV.7 (2003).

9. For a comprehensive historical overview on movements that were labeled by some authors as terrorism, *see, e.g.*, ANNA OEHMICHEN, TERRORISM AND ANTI-TERRORISM LEGISLATION: THE TERRORIZED LEGISLATOR? 49–133 (2009).

10. M. Cherif Bassiouni, *Terrorism: The Persistent Dilemma of Legitimacy*, 36 CASE W. RES. J. INT'L L. 299–306 (2004).

11. Judge Rosalyn Higgins pointed out in 1997 that "Terrorism is a term without any legal significance. It is merely a convenient way of alluding to activities, whether of States or of individuals, widely disapproved of and in which either the methods used are unlawful, or the targets protected, or both." Rosalyn Higgins, *The General International Law of Terrorism*, in INTERNATIONAL LAW AND TERRORISM 28 (Rosalyn Higgins & M. Flory eds., 1997).

12. Gilbert Guillaume, *Terrorism and International Law*, 53 INT'L & COMP. L. Q. 537, 539 (2004).

13. Christopher J. Greenwood, *War, Terrorism and International Law*, in ESSAYS ON WAR IN INTERNATIONAL LAW 409–10 (Christopher J. Greenwood ed., 2006).

14. *Id.* at 411.

15. Convention on Offences and Certain Other Acts Committed on Board Aircraft, 20 UST 2941; TIAS 6768; 704 UNTS 219; Hague Convention for the Suppression of Unlawful Seizure of Aircraft, 22 UST 1641, TIAS 7192; and the Montreal Convention for the Suppression of Unlawful Acts against the Safety of Civil Aviation, 24 UST 564; TIAS 7570.

16. Convention on the Prevention and Punishment of Crimes Against Internationally Protected Persons, 28 UST 1975; TIAS 8532; 1035 UNTS 167.

17. International Convention against the Taking of Hostages, U.N. GA Res. 34/146 (XXXIV), 34 U.N. GAOR Supp. (No. 46) at 245, UN. Doc. A/34/46 (1979); TIAS 11081; 1316 UNTS 205; 18 ILM 1456 (1979).

18. Convention on the Physical Protection of Nuclear Material, TIAS 11080; 1456 UNTS 1101; 18 ILM 1419 (1979).

19. Protocol for the Suppression of Unlawful Acts of Violence at Airports Serving International Civil Aviation, supplementary to the Convention for the Suppression of Unlawful Acts Against the Safety of Civil Aviation, 974 UNTS 177; 24 UST 564; 10 ILM 1151 (1971).

20. Convention for the Suppression of Unlawful Acts against the Safety of Maritime Navigation and Protocol to the Convention for the Suppression of Unlawful Acts against the Safety of Maritime Navigation, 27 ILM 668 (1988); 1678 UNTS 221.

21. Protocol for the Suppression of Unlawful Acts Against the Safety of Fixed Platforms Located on the Continental Shelf, and the 2005 Protocol to the Protocol for the Suppression of Unlawful Acts Against the Safety of Fixed Platforms Located on the Continental Shelf, 1678 UNTS 304; 27 ILM 685 (1988).

22. Convention on the Marking of Plastic Explosives for the Purpose of Detection, 30 ILM 721 (1991).

23. International Convention for the Suppression of Terrorist Bombings, U.N. Doc. A/RES/52/164; 2149 UNTS 256; 37 ILM 249 (1998).

24. International Convention for the Suppression of the Financing of Terrorism, U.N. Doc. A/RES/54/109; TIAS No. 13075; 39 ILM 270 (2000).

25. International Convention for the Suppression of Acts of Nuclear Terrorism, U.N. Doc. A/RES/59/290 (2005).

26. *See, e.g.*, in the Declaration on Principles of International Law concerning Friendly Relations between States (U.N. G.A. res. 2625 (1970)), it was provided

that every state had the "duty to refrain from organizing, instigating, assisting or participating in acts of civil strife or terrorist acts in another State." *See, e.g., also* G.A. res. 34/175, 38/130, 40/61, 42/22, 42/159, 44/29, 46/51, and 49/60.

27. The current actions of the Committee can be consulted *at* www.un.org/law/terrorism/.

28. Nicholas Rostow, *Before and After: The Changed UN Response to Terrorism Since September 11th*, 35 COR-NELL INT'L L. J. 475–81 (2002).

29. S.C. Res. 1368 (2001).

30. *Supra* note 27, at 482.

31. Gilbert Guillaume, *Terrorism and International Law*, 53 INT'L & COMP. L. Q. 537–43 (2004).

32. Council Framework Decision No. 2002/475/JHA. Indent 6 of the Preamble reads as follows: "The definition of terrorist offences should be approximated in all Member States, including those offences relating to terrorist groups. Furthermore, penalties and sanctions should be provided for natural and legal persons having committed or being liable for such offences, which reflect the seriousness of such offences."

33. Thus, Article 1 defines terrorist offences as follows:

(a) attacks upon a person's life which may cause death;

(b) attacks upon the physical integrity of a person;

(c) kidnapping or hostage taking;

(d) causing extensive destruction to a Government or public facility, a transport system, an infrastructure facility, including an information system, a fixed platform located on the continental shelf, a public place or private property likely to endanger human life or result in major economic loss;

(e) seizure of aircraft, ships or other means of public or goods transport;

(f) manufacture, possession, acquisition, transport, supply or use of weapons, explosives or of nuclear, biological or chemical weapons, as well as research into, and development of, biological and chemical weapons;

(g) release of dangerous substances, or causing fires, floods or explosions the effect of which is to endanger human life;

(h) interfering with or disrupting the supply of water, power or any other fundamental natural resource the effect of which is to endanger human life;

(i) threatening to commit any of the acts listed in (a) to (h).

34. Council Framework Decision No. 2002/584/JHA.

35. *See, e.g.,* PIERRE KLEIN, LE DROIT INTERNATIONAL Á L'ÉPREUVE DU TERRORISME 261 (2007).

36. This observation is confirmed by the definition proposed in the European Council Framework Decision, which was the result of European-wide discussions.

The decision defines a terrorist group as a "structured group," specifying, to be sure, that "structured" means a group "that does not need to have formally defined roles for its members, continuity of its membership or a developed structure" (Art. 2(1) of the Decision). If the group does not have to dispose of a developed structure, how do the European legislators understand the very term "structured"?

37. *See, e.g.,* Christopher Blakesley's reflections on this question in TERROR AND ANTI-TERRORISM–A NORMATIVE AND PRACTICAL ASSESSMENT (2006).

38. Documents of the UN Conference on International Organization, San Francisco, UNCIO 1006 I/6, 2. At first sight, this statement appears noble and beautiful. However, considering the subjectivity of the term "justice" in political contexts, this permitted exception to the maintenance of peace actually deprives the statement of its main meaning.

39. The preamble reads as follows: "WE THE PEOPLES OF THE UNITED NATIONS DETERMINED to save succeeding generations from the scourge of war, which twice in our lifetime has brought untold sorrow to mankind, and to reaffirm faith in fundamental human rights, in the dignity and worth of the human person, in the equal rights of men and women and of nations large and small, and to establish conditions under which justice and respect for the obligations arising from treaties and other sources of international law can be maintained, and to promote social progress and better standards of life in larger freedom, AND FOR THESE ENDS to practice tolerance and live together in peace with one another as good neighbours, and to unite our strength to maintain international peace and security, and to ensure, by the acceptance of principles and the institution of methods, that armed force shall not be used, save in the common interest, and to employ international machinery for the promotion of the economic and social advancement of all peoples, HAVE RESOLVED TO COMBINE OUR EFFORTS TO ACCOMPLISH THESE AIMS."

40. Hovell, *supra* note 4, at 400.

41. Brunnée and Toope, *supra* note 6, at 800.

42. *See, e.g.,* Case Concerning Military and Paramilitary Activities in and against Nicaragua (*Nicaragua v. United States of America*) (Merits), Judgment of Jun. 27, 1986, ICJ Reports 14, 102–6, 110, 122–3, paras. 193–201, 210–11, 236–37.

43. *The Caroline and McLeod Cases*, 32 AMER. J. INT'L L. 82 (1938).

44. This condition is also confirmed by the wording of Article 51, which grants the right to self-defense only "until the Security Council has taken measures necessary to maintain international peace and security."

45. Cassese, *supra* note 7, at 995.

46. Israel used counter-terrorist force against Egypt in 1956, against Lebanon in 1968 and 1982, against an Iraqi aircraft in 1973, against Uganda in 1976, against Tunisia in 1985, and against a Libyan aircraft in 1986. These attacks were considered unlawful by a unanimous Security Council. By contrast, counter-terrorist force applied by the United States in more recent times has met considerably less opposition. The United States undertook counter-terrorist military action against Libya in 1986, against Iraq in 1993, and against Sudan and Afghanistan in 1998. The cruise missiles fired at targets in Sudan and Afghanistan responded to bombings of American embassies in Kenya and Tanzania. Many governments were concerned about the fact that the territorial integrity of sovereign states was violated by targeting, not the states themselves, but terrorists believed to be present there. For details, *see, e.g.,* Hovell, *supra* note 3, at 412, and Byers, *supra* note 3, at 159. *See also* Cassese, *supra* note 6, at 996.

47. Legal Consequences of the Construction of a Wall in the Occupied Palestinian Territory (Advisory Opinion) [2004] ICJ Rep p. 194, para. 139 (emphasis added).

48. *See also* Hovell, *supra* note 4, at 410.

49. Brunée and Toope, *supra* note 6, at 789.

50. Nicaragua Case, *supra* note 42, at para. 195: "The Court sees no reason to deny that, in customary law, the prohibition of armed attacks may apply to the sending by a State of armed bands to the territory of another State, if such an operation, because of its scale and effects, would have been classified as an armed attack rather than as a mere frontier incident had it been carried out by regular armed forces. But the Court does not believe that the concept of 'armed attack' includes not only acts by armed bands where such acts occur on a significant scale but also assistance to rebels in the form of the provision of weapons or logistical or other support."

51. *Cf.* Article 8 of the International Law Commission's Articles on State Responsibility: "The conduct of a person or group of persons shall be considered an act of a State under international law if the person or group of persons is in fact acting on the instructions of, or under the direction or control of, that State in carrying out the conduct." *See, e.g., also* Byers *supra* note 3, at 160 with further references.

52. Nicaragua Case, *supra*, note 42, at para. 115.

53. Article 8. However, this approach has been criticized by the International Criminal Tribunal for the Former Yugoslavia in its second decision in Tadić (*Prosecutor v. Tadić* (1999) 124 ILR 61, 108 *et seq*).

54. *See e.g.,* for details, Stahn, *supra* note 4.

55. Letter from John Negroponte, U.S. Permanent Representative to the UN, to the President of the Security Council on Oct. 7, 2001, U.N. Doc. S/2001/946.

56. Article 5(1) of the North Atlantic Treaty of 1949 provides, "The Parties agree that an armed attack against one or more of them in Europe or North America shall be considered an attack against them all and consequently they agree that, if such an armed attack occurs, each of them, in exercise of the right of individual or collective self-defence recognised by Article 51 of the Charter of the United Nations, will assist the Party or Parties so attacked by taking forthwith, individually and in concert with the other Parties, such action as it deems necessary, including the use of armed force, to restore and maintain the security of the North Atlantic area."

57. NATO, press release 124 of 2001 ("The Council agreed that if it is determined that this attack was directed from abroad against the United States, it shall be regarded as an action covered by Article 5 of the Washington Treaty, which states that an armed attack against one or more of the Allies in Europe or North America shall be considered an attack against them all.").

58. Byers, *supra* note 4, at 161, with further references.

59. *See, e.g.,* Stahn, *supra* note 4, at 35.

60. Hovell, *supra* note 4, at 414.

61. Byers, *supra* note 4, at 161.

62. Brunnée and Toope, *supra* note 6, at 795.

63. Byers, *supra* note 4, at164.

64. Hovell, *supra* note 4, at 415.

65. Hovell, *supra* note 4, at 416.

66. National Security Council, National Security Strategy of the United States of America, Sept. 17, 2002, *available at* www.globalsecurity.org/military/library/policy/national/nss-020920.pdf 15.

67. *See, e.g.,* Jutta Brunnée & Stephen J. Toope, *Slouching Towards New "Just" Wars: International Law and the Use of Force After September 11th*, 51 NETH. INT'L L. REV. 373 (2004).

68. *See, e.g.,* OLIVIER CORTEN, LE DROIT CONTRE LA GUERRE, L'INTERDICTION DU RECOURS Á LA FORCE EN DROIT INTERNATIONAL CONTEMPORAIN 619 (2008).

69. *Id.* at 619.

70. *Id.* at 624.

71. *See, e.g.,* Martti Koskenniemi, *Irak and the "Bush Doctrine" of Pre-Emptive Self-Defense*, CRIMES OF WAR PROJECT, expert analysis, Aug. 20, 2002.

72. Corten, *supra* note 68, at 625, with further references.

73. Hovell, *supra* note 4, at 418.

74. For details, *see* Corten, *supra* note 68, at 630, with further references.

75. *See* Cassese, *supra* note 7, at 998.

22

Exceptional Engagement

Protocol I and a World United Against Terrorism

MICHAEL A. NEWTON[1]

This chapter challenges the prevailing view that U.S. "exceptionalism" provides the strongest narrative for the U.S. rejection of Additional Protocol I to the 1949 Geneva Conventions. The United States chose not to adopt the Protocol in the face of intense international criticism because of its policy conclusions that the text contained overly expansive provisions resulting from politicized pressure to accord protection to terrorists who elected to conduct hostile military operations outside the established legal framework. The United States concluded that the commingling of the regime criminalizing terrorist acts with the *jus in bello* rules of humanitarian law would be untenable and inappropriate. In effect, the United States concluded that key provisions of Protocol I actually undermine the core values that spawned the entire corpus of humanitarian law. Whether or not the U.S. position was completely accurate, it was far more than rejectionist unilateralism because it provided the impetus for subsequent reservations by other NATO allies. More than two decades after the debates regarding Protocol I, the U.S. position provided the normative benchmark for the subsequent rejection of some states' efforts to shield terrorists from criminal accountability mechanisms required by multilateral terrorism treaties. This article demonstrates that the U.S. policy stance

regarding Protocol I helped to prevent the commingling of the laws and customs of war in the context of the multilateral framework for responding to transnational terrorist acts in the aftermath of September 11. In hindsight, other nations emulated the "exceptional" U.S. position as they reacted to reservations designed to blur the distinctions between terrorists and privileged combatants. U.S. "exceptionalism" in actuality paved the way for sustained engagement that substantially shaped the international response to terrorist acts. This chapter suggests that reservations provide an important mechanism for states to engage in second-order dialogue over the true meaning and import of treaties, which in turn fosters the clarity and enforceability of the text.

I. Introduction

The United States was one of the influential drivers in promulgating the principles regulating hostilities that define the lawful scope of participation in armed conflicts. This line of treaties, derived from the strong political and military support of the United States, ended during the negotiations for the 1977 Protocols to the 1949 Geneva Conventions.[2] Protocol I is applicable to armed conflicts of an international character, but the final text incorporated highly controversial changes to the types of conflicts that could legally be characterized as interstate wars, with the attendant consequence of conveying combatant immunity to a far broader class of persons. This occurred because many Third World nations, supported by the negotiating muscle of socialist states, hijacked the Protocol to achieve explicitly political objectives. This treaty is accordingly unique in having been described as "law in the service of terror."[3] The United States concluded that the most controversial aspects of Protocol I represented an impermissible altering of the cornerstone concepts of combatancy rather than a natural and warranted evolution of the laws of war. The U.S. rejection of Protocol I represented far more than hypocritical "exceptionalism," however, as the underlying policy position provided the template for sustained engagement with other nations. The overwhelming solidarity of states sharing the U.S. position that international law should afford no protection for the criminal acts of terrorists became clear over the course of more than two decades and was revalidated following the shock of September 11.

Terrorism in all its forms and manifestations constitutes one of the most serious threats to international peace and security as well as perhaps the most pernicious threat to the fundamental human rights of private, peace-loving citizens. There is universal and strongly articulated support for the positivist legal premise that "any acts of terrorism are criminal and unjustifiable, regardless of their motivation, whenever and by whomsoever committed and are to be unequivocally condemned."[4] The UN General Assembly reaffirms that "no terrorist act can be justified in any circumstances."[5] By extension, this dominant consensus led to the modern framework of multilateral conventions that obligate states to cooperate together to eradicate terrorism and to use their domestic legal systems to the fullest extent possible in detecting and prosecuting persons involved with perpetrating or supporting terrorist activities. Article 6 of the International Convention for the Suppression of the Financing of Terrorism, inter alia, requires acceding states (169 at the time of this writing[6]) to "adopt such measures as may be necessary, including, where appropriate, domestic legislation, to ensure that criminal acts within the scope of this Convention are under no circumstances justifiable by considerations of a political, philosophical, ideological, racial, ethnic, religious or other similar nature."[7] This bright-line bar is replicated in every major multilateral terrorism convention. Furthermore, the modern conventions seeking to prevent and punish terrorist acts embody the broadest possible jurisdictional authority for domestic courts[8] as well as expressly remove terrorist acts from the class of political offenses that might otherwise hinder extradition or requests for mutual legal assistance.[9]

The clarity with which international law categorizes and condemns discrete manifestations of terrorism actually masks the indeterminacy of the underlying definitional framework. "Terrorism" is a concept caught in a kaleidoscope of conflicting sociological, political, psychological, moral, and, yes, legal perspectives. The claim that "what looks, smells and kills like terrorism is terrorism"[10] belies the reality that the international community has unsuccessfully sought to agree on a comprehensive definition of the term for more than a century.[11] No comprehensive definition has achieved universal acceptance, whether approached from a moral,[12] psychological,[13] or historical[14] perspective. Despite the fact that nonstate participants in a Common Article 3 conflict are fully subject to prosecution for their warlike acts[15] and will often be simultaneously subject to the jurisdiction of courts with substantive authority over terrorism, criminal law generally disfavors reliance on terms such as "terrorism" that are perceived to lack objectivity, precision, and emotive neutrality.[16] Some have even argued that applying the label "terrorist" to a nonstate actor in a noninternational armed conflict carries a pejorative taint that creates an undesirable disincentive to abide by the laws and customs of war.[17] The paradox in a post-9/11 world is that the UN Security Council *requires* nations to "accept and carry out"[18] resolutions that oblige them to act against "terrorists" and "terrorism."[19] Giving operative legal significance to vaguely defined terms could be seen as undermining the world's "normative and moral stance against terrorism."[20] As a result, rather than relying on an overarching definitional framework with uncertain pedigree and feigned international acceptance, the international community developed a patchwork of norms and conventions that seeks to prevent and punish specific manifestations of terrorist activities.[21] By breaking down the macro problem of terrorism into identifiable manifestations, nation-states have negotiated and ratified a web of occasionally overlapping multilateral conventions built on the cornerstone of sovereign enforcement of applicable norms. The persistence of transnational terrorism as a feature of the international community shows that the plethora of conventional approaches is no panacea.[22] September 11 highlighted this striking systematic failure.

International law restricts the class of persons against whom violence may be applied during armed conflicts even as it bestows affirmative rights to wage war in accordance with accepted legal restraints.[23] Because of the central importance of these categorizations, the standards for ascertaining the legal line between lawful and unlawful participants in conflict provided the intellectual impetus for the evolution of the entire field of law relevant to the conduct of hostilities.[24] From the outset, states sought to prescribe the conditions under which they owed particular persons affirmative legal protections derived from the laws and customs of war.[25] The recurring refrain in negotiations can be described as "to whom do we owe such protections?" The constant effort to be as precise as possible in describing the classes of persons entitled to those protections was essential because the same criteria prescribe the select class who may lawfully conduct hostilities with an expectation of immunity. Conversely, terrorists commit criminal acts and are liable for those acts; they cannot hide behind a shield of combatant immunity in the same manner as lawful combatants.

The declarative norm that the "right of belligerents to adopt means of injuring the enemy is not unlimited"[26] is one of the organizing principles that unifies the framework of the law of armed conflict. Persons outside the framework of international humanitarian law who commit warlike acts do not enjoy combatant immunity and are, therefore, common criminals subject to prosecution for their actions.[27] The imperative that logically follows is that the right of *nonbelligerents* to adopt means of injuring the enemy is *nonexistent*. Those persons governed by the law of armed conflict derive rights and benefits but are also subject to bright-line obligations. Prisoners of war, for example, enjoy legal protection vis-á-vis their captors; because they are legally protected, they have no right to commit "violence against life and limb."[28] Conversely, lawful combatants become "war criminals" only when their actions transgress the established boundaries of the laws and customs of war.[29] Taken together, these principles form the backbone of the law of armed conflict, and terrorist acts represent the precise point of tension between the law of armed conflict and the default norms of international criminality. Lawful combatants use violence to achieve sociologically and legally permissible ends, whereas terrorists use some of the same techniques impermissibly in violation of established criminal norms.

Nevertheless, the lack of a specific and all-encompassing definition of the term "terrorism" has a sinister potential that could allow states to exploit the existing norms of treaty interpretation, thereby endangering civilian lives and objects by creating legal confusion over agreed treaty terms and thus preventing effective and timely prosecution of terrorists. As noted above, the United States chose not to adopt the Protocol based on policy conclusions that its provisions were the result of politicized pressure to accord protection to terrorists who elected to conduct hostile military operations beyond the accepted legal framework. In effect, the United States concluded that Protocol I actually undermined the humanitarian goal of protecting innocent civilian lives and property because its most contentious provisions could provide a legal smokescreen behind which transnational terrorists could kill with impunity. Every commander-in-chief since 1977 has shared this assessment. Whether the U.S. position was based on an accurate assessment of Protocol I, U.S. opposition to the treaty framed the debate regarding the relative status of the new categories of conflict and of combatants.

This chapter challenges the prevailing view that American exceptionalism provides the strongest rationale for the posture taken regarding U.S. accession to Protocol I to the 1949 Geneva Conventions. The United States endured scathing criticism for these positions, which has waned only marginally with the passage of time. U.S. opposition to Protocol I served as the catalyst for subsequent reservations taken by other NATO allies, which in turn provided a vital impetus for clarifying those norms as newly prescribed treaty provisions rather than preexisting customary international law. Rather than representing a rejection and withdrawal of the international legal regime, the U.S. position provided the normative benchmark against which other states measured later attempts to deliberately shield terrorists from criminal accountability mechanisms in the aftermath of September 11.

This chapter puts this instance of so-called "exceptionalism" into proper perspective by identifying the substantively identical positions that became manifest in the wake of September 11 as several of the most important multilateral terrorism treaties entered into force on the heels of a wave of state accessions. Several states used the pretext that Protocol I had established expansive protections for nonstate actors engaged in hostilities to propose reservations effectuating that same language in the multilateral terrorism conventions. Nearly thirty years after the United States rejected Protocol I, many other nations reacted decisively to reject the attempts to redefine the treaty definition of "terrorism." The U.S. policy stance regarding Protocol I pre-

saged the line drawn by many other nations to prevent the commingling of the laws and customs of war with the multilateral framework for responding to terrorist acts. U.S. "exceptionalism" represented a principled policy decision based on national interests that provided the impetus for deeper engagement in shaping the legal norms applicable to terrorist acts. The U.S. position accurately reflected underlying community interests of states engaged in a struggle against terrorists and, thus, established the normative standards that prevented later attempts to blur the distinctions between terrorists and privileged combatants.

In the case of Protocol I, what has been framed as U.S. "exceptionalism" was in fact proven over time to represent the overwhelming policy consensus of states. The mosaic of other states' reservations and reactions demonstrated a substantive solidarity with the underlying U.S. concerns. The experience with the attempt to define terrorist acts demonstrates that an a priori reliance on the process of diplomacy during negotiations would place the weight of multilateral enforcement on an uncertain and perhaps shifting fulcrum. Rather than accepting a treaty definition that is the product of compromise and consensus, the patterns of state practice, reactions to the diplomatic forays of other states, and the context of real world events provides a far more reliable gauge to measure the real depth of international agreement and the real meaning of otherwise vague treaty terms. This chapter concludes by suggesting that eliminating the opportunity for states to make reservations as the tools of a second order dialogue over the true meaning and import of treaty provisions endangers the utility of multilateral treaties. An ex ante preference for prohibiting reservations serves to short circuit healthy dialogue of diplomatic perspectives that minimizes uncertainty when adopting and applying multilateral treaties. Rather than sole reliance on the words accepted by the negotiators, subsequent state practice based on overarching objectives is the best measure for the true agreement of states. The United States paved the way for this process through the politically disadvantageous steps taken in reaction to the objectionable provisions found in Protocol I.

Part II of this chapter will review the development of the law related to belligerent status in order to provide the necessary predicate to understanding the revolutionary developments enshrined in Protocol I. Part II will also review the actions of the United States in response to Protocol I and examine the responses of other states as well as briefly consider the counterarguments that potentially undercut the U.S. position. Part III suggests that some exceptionalism is a necessary and healthy component of lawmaking between sovereign states. In retrospect, the U.S. response to Protocol I provided the platform for an extended international dialogue and accurately predicted the larger global priorities that manifested themselves in the wake of September 11. Part IV documents the attempts to redefine terrorism and states' reactions from around the world. In the final analysis, the rigid distinction between the laws and customs of armed conflict and terrorist acts has been solidified and clarified. Protocol I provides an example of global engagement in the guise of American exceptionalism.

II. Framing the Problem of Unlawful Belligerency

A. The Pragmatic Context

Military commanders and their lawyers do not approach the law of armed conflict as an esoteric intellectual exercise. The foundational principle of military necessity defines the necessary predicate for the lawful application of force in pursuit of the military mission, but it cannot concurrently serve as a convenient rationale for any level of unrestrained violence in the midst of an operation.[30] The law of armed conflict developed as a restraining and humanizing necessity to facilitate commanders' ability to accomplish the military mission even in the midst of fear, moral ambiguity, and horrific scenes of violence.[31] The incremental develop-

ment of what became a complex body of law from the baseline of foundational necessity prompted one of the Nuremberg prosecutors to muse that "the law of war owes more to Darwin than to Newton."[32] In fact, the laws and customs of war originated from the unyielding demands of military discipline under the authority of the commander or king whose orders must be obeyed. Writing in 1625, Hugo Grotius documented the Roman practice that "it is not right for one who is not a soldier to fight with an enemy" because "one who had fought an enemy outside the ranks: and without the command of the general was understood to have disobeyed orders," an offense that "should be punished with death."[33] The modern law of armed conflict is nothing more than a web of interlocking protections and legal obligations held together by the thread of respect for humankind and a reciprocal expectation that the same normative constraints bind other participants in armed conflict. This explains its historical roots in conflicts between states and those acting under the authority of states.

Nevertheless, the detailed provisions of the laws and customs of war relate back to the basic distinction between persons who can legally participate in conflict and the corresponding rights and obligations they assume. The courts of many ancient nations punished those who violated these norms, and the king's right to punish those who "excessively violate the law of nature or of nations in regard to any persons whatsoever" was well established.[34] Beginning in 1874, states accepted the principle that "the laws of war do not recognize in belligerents an unlimited power in the adoption of means of injuring the enemy."[35] During the Thirty Years' War, the Swedish king mandated that "no Colonel or Captain shall command his soldiers to do any unlawful thing; which who so does, shall be punished according to the discretion of the Judge."[36] By 1907 this concept morphed into the phrase "the right of belligerents to adopt means of injuring the enemy is not unlimited."[37] The modern formulation of this foundational principle is captured in Article 35 of Protocol I as follows: "In any armed conflict, the right of the Parties to the conflict to choose methods or means of warfare is not unlimited."[38] Military codes and manuals across the planet communicate the gravity and importance of such behavioral norms.[39]

The law of armed conflict emerged as the benchmark for military professionalism because its precepts are intended to restrain the application of raw power and bloodlust even in the midst of chaos, mind-numbing fear, and overwhelming uncertainty. Hence, the law of war is integral to the very notion of professionalism because it defines the class of persons against whom professional military forces can lawfully apply violence based on principles of military necessity and reciprocity.[40] Each individual military actor remains an autonomous moral figure with personal responsibility, and there is accordingly no defense of superior orders in response to allegations of war crimes.[41] The current context of armed conflict presents commanders with the challenge of implementing humanitarian restraints in an environment marked by an adversary's utter disregard for those bounds.[42] The overall mission will often be intertwined with political, legal, and strategic imperatives that cannot be accomplished in a legal vacuum or by undermining the threads of legality that bind together diverse aspects of a complex operation. The U.S. doctrine for counterinsurgency operations makes this clear in its opening section:[43]

> Globalization, technological advancement, urbanization, and extremists who conduct suicide attacks for their cause have certainly influenced contemporary conflict; however, warfare in the 21st century retains many of the characteristics it has exhibited since ancient times. Warfare remains a violent clash of interests between organized groups characterized by the use of force. Achieving victory still depends on a group's ability to mobilize support for its political interests (often religiously or ethnically based) and to generate enough violence to achieve political consequences. Means to achieve these goals are not limited to conventional forces employed by nation-states.

The objective of asymmetric warfare is achieved when professionalized military forces confront an enemy who seeks to gain an otherwise impossible military parity through a deliberate disregard for humanitarian law.[44] Even against a lawless enemy, there are two essential questions professional military forces must ask in this new style of conflict:

1. How may we properly apply military force?
2. If lawful means of conducting conflict are available, against whom may we properly apply military force?

The centrality of these themes in the development of the laws and customs of war cannot be overlooked when explaining the competing state interests embedded in the multilateral conventions that regulate conflicts. These themes also provide the golden thread of insight that is essential to understanding that the modern law of terrorism and the most fundamental aspects of humanitarian law are interrelated but distinct.

B. Early U.S. Leadership in Distilling the Law

Because only states enjoyed the historical prerogative of conducting warfare, the principles of lawful combatancy developed from the premise that only states had the authority to sanction the lawful conduct of hostilities.[45] Propelled by the classic view that "the contention must be between States" to give rise to the right to use military force,[46] the concept of combatant status developed to describe the class of persons operating under the authority of a sovereign state to wage war.[47] The intellectual roots of combatant immunity are thus grounded in the soil of state sovereignty. Then, as now, there was a stigma attached to being an unlawful combatant because the term carried implicit recognition that the sovereign power of the state was being thwarted without legal cause. For example, from 1777 to 1782 the British Parliament passed an annual act declaring that privateers operating under the license of the Continental Congress were pirates, *hosti humanis generis*, and as such could be prosecuted for their acts against the Crown.[48]

Combatant status conveys the necessary implication that lawful combatants enjoy protection under the laws of war to commit acts that would be otherwise be unlawful, such as killing persons and destroying property. Two essential implications follow from the conceptual foundation of combatant immunity as an offshoot of state sovereignty. First, although the application of international humanitarian law has expanded from international to noninternational armed conflicts,[49] the concept of "combatancy" has been strictly confined to international armed conflicts. Even as the law expanded to grant combatant immunity for irregular forces that do not line up in military uniforms on a parade field, participants in noninternational armed conflicts remain completely subject to domestic criminal prosecution for their warlike acts. Protections found in domestic law are grounded not on the status of a person but instead on the basis of actual activities because no one has an international law "right to participate in hostilities" in a noninternational armed conflict.[50]

Even during the Civil War era, the tactical uncertainty faced by Union forces waging a campaign against rebel forces thrust lawyers and the importance of sound legal analysis into the spotlight. The first comprehensive effort to describe the law of war in a written code, the Lieber Code, began as a request from the General-in-Chief of the Union Armies based on his confusion over the distinction between lawful and unlawful combatants.[51] General Henry Wager Halleck recognized that the law of armed conflict never accorded combatant immunity to every person who conducted hostilities and also could not provide pragmatic guidance to adapting to the changing tactics of war.[52] He knew, however, that the war could not be won without clear delineation to the forces in the field regarding the proper targeting of combatants and a correlative standard for the treatment of persons captured on the battlefield based on the legal characterization of their status. On August 6, 1862, General Halleck wrote to Dr. Francis Lieber, a highly regarded law professor at Columbia College in New York, to request his assistance in defining guerrilla warfare.[53]

This request, which can be described as the catalyst that precipitated more than one hundred years of legal effort resulting in the modern web of international agreements regulating the conduct of hostilities, read as follows:

My Dear Doctor: Having heard that you have given much attention to the usages and customs of war as practiced in the present age, and especially to the matter of guerrilla war, I hope you may find it convenient to give to the public your views on that subject. The rebel authorities claim the right to send men, in the garb of peaceful citizens, to waylay and attack our troops, to burn bridges and houses and to destroy property and persons within our lines. They demand that such persons be treated as ordinary belligerents, and that when captured they have extended to them the same rights as other prisoners of war; they also threaten that if such persons be punished as marauders and spies they will retaliate by executing our prisoners of war in their possession. I particularly request your views on these questions.[54]

The Union Army issued a disciplinary code governing the conduct of hostilities, known worldwide as the Lieber Code, as "General Orders 100 Instructions for the Government of the Armies of the United States in the Field" in April 1863.[55] General Orders 100 was the first comprehensive military code of discipline that sought to define the precise parameters of permissible conduct during conflict.[56] From this baseline, the principle endures in the law today that persons who do not enjoy lawful combatant status are not entitled to the benefits of legal protections derived from the laws of war, including prisoner of war status,[57] and are thus subject to punishment for their warlike acts.[58]

Lieber's description of unlawful combatancy is notable in light of operational uncertainties that have been prominent in current antiterrorist operations. Though this language is dated, it suggests the al Qaeda tactics in evocative terms:

> Men, or squads of men, who commit hostilities, whether by fighting, or inroads for destruction or plunder, or by raids of any kind, without commission, without being part and portion of the organized hostile army, and without sharing continuously in the war, but who do so with intermitting returns to their homes and avocations, or with the occasional assumption of the semblance of peaceful pursuits, divesting themselves of the character or appearance of soldiers—such men, or squads of men, are not public enemies, and therefore, if captured, are not entitled to the privileges of prisoners of war, but shall be treated summarily as highway robbers or pirates.[59]

Although the military forces serving sovereign states enjoyed combatant status as an indisputable right, treaty provisions later developed in response to the changing face of warfare. There have been over sixty conventions regulating various aspects of armed conflict, and a recognizable body of international humanitarian law has emerged from this complex mesh of conventions and custom.[60] In embarking on the age of positivist legal development, states attempted to clarify the line between lawful combatants and unlawful criminals when they perceived gaps between humanitarian goals and the operational realities; as a result, the legal framework appeared unresponsive to changing military requirements.

C. The 1949 Geneva Conventions

The provisions for according combatant status and for treating those entitled to combatant immunity must be followed unless states voluntarily expand the normative boundaries of the law. The Lieber Code provided the core around which the law developed, much like the grit around which a pearl is created layer by layer. The *franc-tireur* resistance during the Franco-Prussian War forced a reexamination of the line between legally protected civilians and partisan combatants.[61] The topic of belligerency conducted by private citizens in occupied territory was much debated but little settled during the period, and the subject was, therefore, omitted from the Brussels Declaration of 1874, the Oxford Manual of 1880, and the 1907 Hague Regulations.[62]

As of 1907 the scope of lawful combatancy included the so-called *levée en masse*, when the populace spontaneously organized to fight against an oncoming enemy.[63] Once the occupation was successfully effected, however, local civilians in occupied territory no longer enjoyed a de jure right to fight the enemy occupier.[64] Otherwise, lawful combatancy applied only to forces fighting for a state. The Hague Regulations embodied this legal regime as follows:

> Article 1. The laws, rights, and duties of war apply not only to armies, but also to militia and volunteer corps fulfilling the following conditions:
>
> 1. To be commanded by a person responsible for his subordinates;
> 2. To have a fixed distinctive emblem recognizable at a distance;
> 3. To carry arms openly; and
> 4. To conduct their operations in accordance with the laws and customs of war.
>
> In countries where militia or volunteer corps constitute the army, or form part of it, they are included under the denomination "army."[65]

This formulation enshrined the traditional linkage of the armed forces to the sovereign power of the state and included affiliated militia units that met the established criteria derived from customary international law. This language survived in essentially the same form until the 1977 Additional Protocols to the Geneva Conventions of 1949.

Because Hague Regulations extended protected status only to a defined subset of militia and volunteer forces but not to other irregular forces, the provision of the Lieber Code stating that unlawful combatants could be executed survived both in the letter of the law[66] and in the practice of courts[67] until after World War II. Private citizens in occupied territory, therefore, had no legally protected rights to rise up and oppose the forces of the occupying power.[68] Hence, rather than presuming that they represented the sovereign authority of the occupied state, private citizens were categorized as unlawful combatants subject to the penalty of death.[69]

The 1907 Hague delineations remained with only slight modifications until 1977, despite the wholesale evolution of warfare.[70] However, partisan fighters' patriotic resistance of the German occupations in World War II and the horrific crimes committed by German forces against the civilian populace in response[71] forced states to update the legal standards for obtaining combatant status during occupation. The fact that the provisions for regulating the status of irregular fighters did not become part of the 1949 Fourth Geneva Convention (designed to protect the civilian population) is itself legally significant. As one eminent commentator noted,

> The whole point about the lawful guerrilla fighter, so far as he could be identified and described, was that he was not a civilian. The Civilians Convention was for protecting civilians who remained civilians and whose gestures of resistance, therefore, would be punished as crimes, just as would any acts of guerrilla warfare which lay outside whatever lawful scope could be defined.[72]

Accordingly, the 1949 Geneva Conventions restated and updated the law of combatant status within the Third Geneva Convention on Prisoners of War. Under the Third Convention, the class of civilians entitled to prisoner of war status was described inter alia as

> Members of other militias and members of other volunteer corps, including those of organized resistance movements, belonging to a Party to the conflict and operating in or outside their own territory, even if this territory is occupied, provided that such militias or volunteer

corps, including such organized resistance movements, fulfil the following conditions:

> (a) That of being commanded by a person responsible for his subordinates;
> (b) That of having a fixed distinctive sign recognizable at a distance;
> (c) That of carrying arms openly;
> (d) That of conducting their operations in accordance with the laws and customs of war.[73]

This language reproduced the qualifications drawn from the 1907 Regulations, with the express addition of those operating on behalf of the displaced sovereign. The treaty also added a requirement for the detaining state to convene a "competent tribunal" to consider the facts relevant to a particular person's status when that status is in doubt.[74] This provision was intended to "avoid arbitrary decisions by a local commander"[75] and in practice may be accomplished by three officers with expeditious thoroughness.[76]

The addition of an entirely new international convention in 1949, designed to create legal entitlements on behalf of the civilian population, gave rise to the dualistic view of status that persists in some quarters to this day. The International Committee of the Red Cross (ICRC) took the position in its official commentary that because there "is no intermediate status" between combatant and civilian, every person in enemy hands "must have some status under international law."[77] Though the ICRC explicitly recognized that "Members of resistance movements must fulfill certain stated conditions before they can be regarded as prisoners of war,"[78] its dualist position was premised on an unstated assumption that the civilian unlawfully participating in the conflict lived in the territory occupied by another sovereign state. Modern transnational terrorist acts by definition belie this assumption, even if the ICRC premise reflected an accurate view of the law shortly after the Geneva Conventions concluded in 1949.[79]

Despite overturning several centuries of legal development and judicial practice,[80] the ICRC noted that this dualism would be "satisfying to the mind" because of its simplicity and humanitarian scope.[81] Insofar as it applied to the legal status of civilians under the occupation of a foreign power, the ICRC view accurately reflected the law. However, extrapolating this simple dualism beyond the narrow question of legal duties owed by an occupier to the citizens under its occupation reduces to obsolescence the historic practice of considering unlawful belligerents as unprotected participants in combat and, therefore, beyond the reach of international law. However, the dualist ICRC view did not accurately reflect the negotiating record of the 1949 Geneva Conventions nor the practice of states in applying its provisions.

For example, the plain reading of the legal criteria ultimately accepted by delegates during the 1949 Diplomatic conference reveals that although the two conventions might appear to cover all the categories concerned, irregular belligerents were not actually protected.[82] As a matter of pure logic, extending the protection of international law to all civilians who take up arms in violation of international law would undermine the legitimacy and enforcement of such law. Granting legal protection to any civilian who takes up arms would create a perverse incentive to defy the conventions regulating conduct and to deliberately conduct hostilities outside the bounds of the law all the while relying on the good will of the enemy to apply that same body of law. Some delegates pushed for a broader interpretation of the textual provisions that would have protected illegal combatants based on the understanding that the "categories named in Article 3 [the present Article 4 of the Third Geneva Convention] cannot be regarded as exhaustive, and it should not be inferred that other persons would not also have the right to be treated as prisoners of war."[83] The delegates politely but firmly rejected this position in favor of the view that the text itself is the exclusive source to "define what persons are to have the protection of the Convention."[84]

A number of other delegations explicitly confirmed that the text of the Geneva Conventions did not foreclose the traditional category of unlawful combatants. The Dutch delegate pointed

out that a summary conclusion to the effect that combatants who did not meet the criteria for prisoner of war status "are automatically protected by other Conventions is certainly untrue."[85] The ICRC dualist view is not warranted based on the view of the delegates who negotiated the provisions that convey combatant status. The Dutch delegate further clarified, with no evidence of disagreement from any national delegation, that the Fourth Geneva Convention (the Civilians Convention) "deals only with civilians under certain circumstances; such as civilians in an occupied country or civilians who are living in a belligerent country, *but it certainly does not protect civilians who are in the battlefield, taking up arms against the adverse party.*"[86] Furthermore, the UK delegate observed that "the whole conception of the Civilians Convention was the protection of civilian victims of war and not the protection of illegitimate bearers of arms, who could not expect full protection under rules of war to which they did not conform."[87]

Rather than simply extending blanket protections to every person, the drafters established some fundamental protections that are applicable to all individuals in times of armed conflict, even as they carefully crafted definitions for the categories of persons entitled to receive specific rights and protections.[88] Thus, the position of unlawful combatants as unprotected participants in conflict remained unchanged by the 1949 Geneva Conventions, with the narrow caveat that the Fourth Geneva Convention did provide residual protection for the citizens of occupied territory vis-á-vis the occupying power. This state of legal development became particularly important in light of the national responses to the purported expansion of combatant status to unprivileged belligerents in the textual provisions adopted as part of Protocol I, as will shortly be demonstrated.

D. Protocol I as an Evolutionary Vehicle

The ink was hardly dry on the texts of the 1949 Geneva Conventions when the ICRC began to advocate a further expansion of the law. As noted above, the law of war continually evolves in response to the needs of states conducting conflict. Although the 1949 Conventions regulate armed conflicts conducted between "two or more of the High Contracting Parties," the law applicable to noninternational armed conflicts does not provide for combatant status nor does it define combatants or specify a series of obligations inherent in combatant status.[89] Under the Geneva principles, anyone operating outside the authority of a state who participates in hostile activities can expect no form of automatic legal license or protection from prosecution.[90] Indeed, introducing the concept of "combatant immunity" in the context of noninternational armed conflicts would grant immunity for acts that would be perfectly permissible when conducted by combatants in an international armed conflict, such as attacks directed at military personnel or property.[91] This striking silence in the law applicable to noninternational armed conflicts means that any effort to describe a "combatant engaged in a non-international armed conflict" is an oxymoron. There simply is no legal category of "combatant" in a noninternational armed conflict, irrespective of the moral imperatives a party may claim so as to warrant hostile activities.[92] This premise remains valid even when nonstate actors perpetrate violence when seeking to accomplish goals similar to those of the sovereign state.[93]

These perceived inadequacies in the law of armed conflict began to surface in the context of the colonialist struggles of the 1960s. The ICRC convened a conference of government experts in 1971 to consider two draft Protocols ostensibly designed to reaffirm and develop the corpus of the laws and customs of war.[94] In the political sphere, the UN General Assembly adopted language that strikingly foreshadowed the international consensus against terrorism in the wake of September 11 by declaring that continuing colonialism "in all its forms and manifestations . . . is a crime and that colonial peoples have the inherent right to struggle by all necessary means at their disposal against colo-

nial Powers and alien domination in exercise of their right of self-determination."[95]

By a vote of eighty-three to thirteen, with nineteen abstentions, the General Assembly admonished the colonial powers that the moral basis for partisan struggles by civilians to reclaim their freedom from foreign powers warranted the application of the full array of rights under the 1949 Geneva Conventions:

> The armed conflicts involving the struggle of peoples against colonial and alien domination and racist régimes are to be regarded as international armed conflicts in the sense of the 1949 Geneva Conventions, and the legal status envisaged to apply to the combatants in the 1949 Geneva Conventions and other international instruments is to apply to the persons engaged in armed struggle against colonial and alien domination and racist régimes.
>
> The combatants struggling against colonial and alien domination and racist régimes captured as prisoners are to be accorded the status of prisoners of war and their treatment should be in accordance with the provisions of the Geneva Convention relative to the Treatment of Prisoners of War, of 12 August 1949.[96]

This position assumed a moral equivalence between private citizens fighting to free a people from colonial dominance and those who fought to restore the sovereign authority of an occupied sovereign state. The General Assembly urged that the 1949 Conventions be extended in order to achieve the protections of combatant immunity along with the corollary status as prisoners of war for the local population in the context of internal armed conflicts in Southern Rhodesia, Angola and Mozambique, South Africa, and Namibia.[97] This, in turn, buttressed the efforts of the ICRC to gain the widest possible applicability for the principles of Geneva Law.[98] The effort to extend these political positions into binding textual provisions proved to be far more contentious and problematic during the negotiations of Protocol I.[99] The Protocols Additional to the Geneva Conventions resulted from four widely attended diplomatic conferences held from 1974 to 1977. The Protocols culminated the efforts to provide textual application of the Geneva Conventions even in the context of armed conflicts between a High Contracting Party and nonstate actors (guerrillas, insurgents, and so-called freedom fighters). These fundamental modifications to the well-established law of combatant immunity would have arguably been impossible without the backdrop and international division caused by the Cold War. However, as in previous efforts to shape the law of war around the reality of ongoing military and political realities, the effort to draw sharp legal distinctions between protected civilians and persons who could be lawfully targeted was the driving concern behind the modern evolution embodied in the 1977 Protocols.[100]

Protocol I was intended to be an all-encompassing source of updated rules for determining combatant status, as it was meant to govern international armed conflicts and to supplement the 1949 Geneva Conventions.[101] Protocol I combined the Hague strand of international humanitarian law (dealing with constraints on the means and methods for conducting hostilities) with the Geneva strand (primarily focused on achieving humanitarian goals). It represented the end state of the law of combatancy by attempting to reduce the combatant category to its irreducible minimum while maximizing the class of protected civilians.[102]

In perhaps its most controversial provision, the Protocol amended the concept of an international armed conflict beyond its previously clear application of only to conflicts between two or more High Contracting Parties in its very first article. Article 1(4) of Protocol I purports to redefine international armed conflicts to

include armed conflicts in which peoples are fighting against colonial domination and alien occupation and against racist regimes in the exercise of their right of self-determination, as enshrined in the Charter of the United Nations and the Declaration on Principles of Interna-

tional Law concerning Friendly Relations and Co-operation among States in accordance with the Charter of the United Nations.[103]

The effect of this language would be to internationalize the actions of nonstate actors, thereby conveying combatant immunity and immunity from prosecution for crimes committed against the military and police forces of the sovereign state or colonial power. This provision in turn spawned two other controversial and key texts in order for the Protocol to maintain intellectual consistency.

On its surface, Protocol I appeared to protect previously unlawful combatants with two innovations. The era of colonial wars in no way eliminated the undercurrent of deep unease felt by states whose professional military forces require a clear articulation of the grounds for achieving combatant status, as those principles remain the backbone of military discipline and professionalism. However, by undermining the clarity of its application, the Protocol created textual uncertainty over the circumstances in which the laws of war operate to protect civilians and their property from the effects of hostilities. In the first place, Article 44 eroded the traditional qualifications for achieving combatant status by accepting the notion that there may be some circumstances "owing to the nature of the hostilities" in which combatants cannot distinguish themselves from the civilian population.[104] In such circumstances, the duty to distinguish may be watered down to the point that the combatant need only carry his arms openly "During each military engagement" or when "During such time as he is visible to the adversary while he is engaged in a military deployment preceding the launching of an attack in which he is to participate."[105]

This text appears to pave the way for any person, irrespective of an organized chain of command or manifestation of state authorization, to take up arms whenever the fancy strikes. Technically, any nonstate actor could claim combatant status (and accompanying immunity from criminal prosecution) based on a declaration by an "authority representing a people engaged against a High Contracting Party."[106] A literal reading of these provisions leads one to suppose that a person could engage in hostilities, put down his or her weapons, hide among the innocent civilian populace, strike at will, and yet claim combatant status for those warlike acts provided that a weapon is visible to an enemy at the precise moment it is used. This on/off combatant status, akin to the proverbial revolving door, would corrode the law of unlawful combatancy to its vanishing point.

Protocol I employed a second, somewhat more subtle means of appearing to define away the principle of unlawful combatancy. In attempting to gain the broadest possible protections for civilians, the text implicitly eroded the 1949 notions of combatancy by virtue of an exclusive dualist definition. For the first time in international law, Protocol I attempts to define the term civilian purely in contradistinction to the opposing status of combatant. Article 50 embodied the ICRC dualist view by defining a civilian as "any person who does not belong" to one of the specified categories of combatant.[107] This provision was intentionally inclusive in contrast to the categories of protected persons defined in the Fourth Geneva Convention of 1949. Thus, a literal reading of the plain text means that a civilian is anyone who is not a combatant. An unlawful combatant would, therefore, be legally equated to a civilian and hence entitled to the panoply of protections accorded to that class of persons.

In theory, the ICRC dualist view enshrined in Protocol I would protect any nonstate actor who elected to participate in hostilities from the effects of their misconduct. By definition, an unlawful combatant falls outside the traditional characterizations that would otherwise entitle him or her to prisoner of war status. Article 50 seems to embody a system in which there is no theoretical gap; a person is either a combatant or a civilian. This leads to the ineluctable presumption that an unlawful combatant who fails to qualify as a prisoner of war must be a civilian entitled to protection. Being legally classified as

a civilian puts the military forces opposing terrorist activities into the quandary of either supinely permitting the planning and conduct of terrorist activities or violating the clear legal norm that the "civilian population as such, as well as individual civilians, shall not be the object of attack."[108]

1. The U.S. Response

The United States joined the consensus on the final texts and signed both Protocols on December 12, 1977, the day they were opened for signature[109] (though the U.S. delegation narrowly missed being forced to walk out of the conference in 1975).[110] With respect to Protocol I, the United States stated at the time that

> 1. It is the understanding of the United States of America that the rules established by this protocol were not intended to have any effect on and do not regulate or prohibit the use of nuclear weapons.
>
> 2. It is the understanding of the United States of America that the phrase "military deployment preceding the launching of an attack" in Article 44, Paragraph 3, means any movement towards a place from which an attack is to be launched.[111]

The second of these understandings was clearly intended, even from the outset, to demonstrate the strong U.S. view that Article 44 could provide excessive protection to terrorists that would actually facilitate their criminal acts.[112] The wave of terrorist acts that provided the context for the negotiation of the 1977 Additional Protocols was conducted by "the alphabet-soup terrorists of the past, the IRA, ETA, PLO, RAF, and others [that] were essentially political organizations with political goals."[113]

Nevertheless, apologists for Protocol I point out that the provisions of Article 44 are contingent on the actors attaining the previous status as a lawful combatant.[114] In addition, the prerequisite combatant status envisaged by Article 44 remains contingent on "being under a command responsible" to a state party to the conflict.[115] Professor Yoram Dinstein has observed, "one cannot fight the enemy and remain a civilian."[116] Just as it is possible to lose combatant status (by becoming a prisoner of war, for example) and the immunity that goes with it (by failing to comply with the law of war), the terrorist cannot properly be termed a civilian in the same sense as those innocents who huddle in their homes while combat rages round them. By choosing to participate in hostilities, particularly in a manner that defies the very notions of human decency and compassion, modern terrorists should not be protected by a shield of combatant immunity derived from the very body of law that they deliberately flout.

Though the textual changes in Protocol I introduced new elements of ambiguity in defining the line between protected civilians and unlawful combatancy, they by no means eliminated the distinction. Even as these new provisions remain practically inapplicable in the real world of state practice, they do not vitiate the other requirements for lawful combatant status set forth in the Hague Regulations and Article 4 of the Geneva Convention on Prisoners of War 1949 (i.e., the Third Convention). Consequently, the official ICRC commentary to Protocol I specified that "anyone who participates directly in hostilities without being subordinate to an organized movement under a Party to the conflict, and enforcing compliance with these rules, *is a civilian who can be punished for the sole fact that he has taken up arms*."[117] The official ICRC Commentary further restates the long-established principle that "anyone who takes up arms without being able to claim this status [of a "lawful combatant"] will be left to be dealt with by the enemy and its military tribunals in the event that he is captured."[118]

Despite its apparent clarity, Protocol I preserves the principle of unlawful combatancy because it implicitly accepts the limitations inherent in civilian status. The Protocol emphasizes the limits of the traditional principle of combatant immunity by restating the traditional rule that only combatants "have the right to participate directly in hostilities."[119] In addition, the definition of combatant status incorporates the accepted categories from Article 4 of the Third Geneva Convention by reference.[120] Hence, the ICRC commentary correctly observed that the uncontroversial "provisions of Article 4 of the Third Convention are fully preserved."[121]

Finally, in one backhanded but extremely important provision, Protocol I sustained the existing law of unlawful combatancy by specifying that civilians enjoy the protections embodied in the Protocol "unless and for such time as they take a direct part in hostilities."[122] The simplistic dualist position becomes unsustainable in light of this language because by definition a person who takes part in hostilities is not a civilian but at the same time is not automatically entitled to prisoner of war status.[123] Accepting the reality that such persons are unlawful belligerents who may be prosecuted for their warlike acts, Protocol I describes a minimum set of due process obligations applicable to such prosecutions.[124] Article 45(3) provides that "Any person who has taken part in hostilities, who is not entitled to prisoner-of-war status and who does not benefit from more favourable treatment in accordance with the Fourth Convention shall have the right at all times to the protection of Article 75 of this Protocol."[125]

Eschewing these fine-grained technical distinctions, the United States categorically refused to accept the expanded classifications of combatancy promulgated in Protocol I.[126] From the U.S. perspective, the many positive developments in Protocol I failed to outweigh its "fundamentally and irreconcilably flawed" revisions to the classic law of combatancy.[127] President Reagan concluded that Article 1(4) and Article 44(3) would actually undermine the very purposes of the Protocol and unnecessarily endanger civilians during armed conflicts.[128] The Department of State Legal Advisor declared that, regardless of the time and diplomatic energy spent negotiating a major multilateral instrument, U.S. approval "should never be taken for granted, especially when an agreement deals with national security, the conduct of military operations and the protection of victims of war."[129] The Joint Chiefs of Staff unanimously opined that Protocol I would further endanger the lives of U.S. military personnel, even as its provisions would increase the danger to innocent civilians (in whose midst terrorist combatants could hide until the opportune moment to strike).[130]

In political terms, Protocol I was achieved only because Third World states ignored the views of the United States and its European allies in order to grant combatant status (and the lawful right to claim the benefits of the Third Convention) to terrorist groups fighting for the causes subjectively deemed to represent a moral imperative.[131] The Third World political agenda caused the conference to drag on for four years rather than one and revealed the naïveté of the ICRC and the Swiss government, which failed to anticipate the hijacking of the agenda.[132] The diplomatic dialogue from 1974–1977 was a "political event as well as a legal and humanitarian one" that was different from other multilateral negotiations in "the nakedness of its political pursuits and the grossness of its General Assembly–style conduct."[133] The ICRC and Swiss government faced the dilemma of whether to lock in the many positive legal developments in the text at the cost of agreeing to the more malodorous aspects. The United States, however, simply could not accept that grievous war crimes and offenses against law and order could be both justified and immunized based on the moral imperatives of self-determination marshaled by other states that advocated extending combatant status even to a nonstate actor who "displays a callous and systematic disregard for the law."[134]

Because of the political climate surrounding the negotiations, it was quite plausible for the United States to conclude that the real agenda behind the Protocol was to permit a one-sided extrapolation of combatant immunity. Thus, terrorists could be expected to derive the benefits from the laws and customs of war without also assuming the concomitant obligations under that body of law. In fact, in 1987 the U.S. Department of State Legal Advisor wrote,

The experience of the last decade confirms the hypocrisy of the regime established by Article l(4). Having achieved a political victory by "internationalizing" their own internal conflicts, so-called liberation groups have shown little interest in following through on the obligations of the Protocol. They have not acted in accordance with the existing requirements of customary international law, nor have they even bothered to file declarations with the Swiss Government accepting the obligations of the Protocol (as contemplated in Article 96). They have been content to cite the Protocol (e.g., in the United Nations) for the proposition that they must be accorded the benefits of humanitarian law (e.g., prisoner-of-war status) without fulfilling the duties expected. In practice, they have continued to make indiscriminate attacks on innocent civilians.[135]

Although the head of the U.S. delegation later wrote that neither Article 1 nor Article 44 would "provide any solace or support for terrorists,"[136] President Reagan concluded that succumbing to pressure from other nations to accept Protocol I would extract "an unacceptable and thoroughly distasteful price."[137] The commander-in-chief accordingly declared that the United States "must not, and need not, give recognition and protection to terrorist groups as a price for progress in humanitarian law."[138] Some states, such as Argentina, attempted to ameliorate the same concerns using interpretive declarations:

With reference to Article 44, paragraphs 2, 3 and 4, of the same Protocol, the Argentine Republic considers that these provisions cannot be interpreted:

a) as conferring on persons who violate the rules of international law applicable in armed conflicts any kind of immunity exempting them from the system of sanctions which apply to each case;

b) as specifically favouring anyone who violates the rules the aim of which is the distinction between combatants and the civilian population;

c) as weakening respect for the fundamental principle of the international law of war which requires that a distinction be made between combatants and the civilian population, with the prime purpose of protecting the latter.[139]

President Reagan nevertheless concluded that the problems with Protocol I "are so fundamental in character that they cannot be remedied through reservations, and I have therefore decided not to submit the Protocol to the Senate in any form."[140] He sent Protocol II to the Senate for its advice and consent on the basis of its "expansion of the fundamental humanitarian provisions contained in the 1949 Geneva Conventions."[141]

2. The National Reservations of NATO Partners

For a period of some years following the adoption of the text in 1977, the United States deliberated internally over the relative merits of reservations, understandings, or declarations in remedying the attempt to expand international protections to insurgents seeking self-determination.[142] The second sentence of Article 44(3), which has been the subject of so much debate through the decades, has been described by one of the most eminent international lawyers as a last-minute compromise that proves the truism that a treaty is "a disagreement reduced to writing."[143] As noted above, the rejection of Protocol I was based on the assessment that its expansive text could provide a pretext for terrorist acts and that the legal links of national reservations and understandings would be insufficient protection against the temptation of many states to protect terrorist acts under the rhetoric of lawful combatancy.[144] Phrased another way, the United States concluded that adhering to Protocol I in any form would serve to legitimize the subjective assessments of terrorists seeking public support for otherwise criminal acts.[145]

However, the articulated rationale for rejecting Protocol I provided the template for sustained U.S. engagement with other nations. U.S. diplomats met regularly with NATO members in Brussels in attempts to formulate appropriate diplomatic responses so as to preserve the humanitarian benefits of the Protocol while minimizing its potentially corrosive effects on military equities.[146] NATO allies of the United States shared a common sense of disappointment at the disingenuous manner that Protocol I purported to protect unlawful acts committed by nonstate actors, but they also sought to preserve its genuinely progressive measures.[147] Despite a common abhorrence for terrorist acts, the NATO allies ultimately disagreed with the U.S. decision to abstain from the Protocol based on their different assessment of the modalities for achieving that desired end state.[148] Pursuant to their commitment to the multilateral instrument in its own right, they issued authoritative diplomatic statements that comported with the humanitarian goals of the Protocol but would serve to limit future interpretations of its most contentious provisions should disputes arise over their meaning and normative import.[149] Rather than simple rejectionist "exceptionalism," the U.S. position vis-à-vis Protocol I framed the debate with key allies that, in turn, engaged in a second-order style of diplomacy to attempt to limit the deleterious effects of Article 44 in their own manner.[150]

At the time of this writing, 168 nations have ratified or acceded to Protocol I.[151] In the wake of extensive discussions with the United States, NATO allies Belgium, Canada, France, Germany, Ireland, Italy, the Netherlands, Spain, and the United Kingdom all ratified Protocol I subject to the following reservations[152] (using the example of the United Kingdom reservation):

> It is the understanding of the United Kingdom that:
> The situation in the second sentence of paragraph 3 can only exist in occupied territory or in armed conflicts covered by paragraph 4 of Article 1;
> "Deployment" in paragraph 3(b) means any movement towards a place from which an attack is to be launched.[153]

This language sought to inhibit terrorist operations by making the duty to carry one's arms openly as broad as possible[154] (deliberately para-phrasing the U.S. definition of "deployment" from December 1977[155]). At the same time, the NATO allies sought to restrict the coverage of Article 44 to a very limited context[156] (arguably no more extensive than the *levée en masse* provisions previously found in Article 4 of the 1949 Geneva Convention on Prisoners of War[157]). This narrow construction would protect an authentic struggle for self-determination to reclaim sovereignty from an occupying power that temporarily displaced sovereignty.[158] Conversely, the subjective assessments of nonstate actors who merely rebelled against the legitimate authorities of a sovereign state would be excluded from the umbrella of lawful combatancy on the basis of this interpretation.[159] The NATO allies sought to ensure that the provisions of Article 44 could not be extended by analogy to provide legal coverage that could otherwise serve to facilitate the commission of terrorist acts.[160] Other major non-NATO allies, such as Australia,[161] Japan,[162] Korea,[163] and New Zealand,[164] reached substantively identical conclusions and made nearly identical statements at the time of ratification.[165] The NATO allies and the United States simply selected different pathways to manifest identical substantive concerns.

In the wake of these diplomatic demarches, the drumbeat of criticism of the U.S. position intensified.[166] The legal advisor to the ICRC assailed President Reagan's determination as a "political" and "partisan" position that would deprive the world community of a "common framework" and "hinder the development and acceptance of universal standards in a field where they are particularly needed."[167] This criticism ignored the explicit language of the presidential statement rejecting Protocol I, which was intended to represent

a significant step in defense of traditional humanitarian law and in opposition to the intense efforts of terrorist organizations and their supporters to promote the legitimacy of their aims and practices. The repudiation of Protocol I is one additional step, at the ideological level so

important to terrorist organizations, to deny these groups legitimacy as international actors.[168]

The message from within the ICRC hierarchy was that the U.S. position was merely a pretext for a predetermined desire to avoid commitment to a multilateral treaty.[169] The presumption seemed to be that Protocol I embodied an inherent multilateral correctness based only on the twin realities that its text had been agreed upon under the sponsorship of the ICRC and because that text later entered into force based on the ratification of a number of states.[170] In other words, the very *fact* of the multilateral treaty created a logical and legal imperative for states to consent to the entire treaty regime, irrespective of their fundamental policy goals.

Echoing this political correctness, the UN General Assembly became a recurring forum for a reflexive reaffirmation that the United States' refusal to ratify Protocol I served to undermine both respect for humanitarian principles and international law. In 2006 the delegate from Kenya noted that accession of states to Protocol I is of "paramount importance in ensuring the safety of civilians" and proceeded to commend the work of the ICRC in its efforts to "consolidate a legal reading of the complex questions bound up with the fight against terrorism, including the development of guidelines on the detention of persons."[171] Many resolutions in the years following the Reagan decision implicitly attacked the U.S. position by calling on "all States parties to the Geneva Conventions that have not yet done so to consider becoming parties to the Additional Protocols at the earliest possible date."[172] The Organization of American States and the European Union used slightly softer language to make the same point: Opposition to Protocol I is couched internationally as a divisive point that continues to hinder international unity of purpose on the basis of common values.[173]

Despite the fact that the United States and its NATO allies shared an identical concern that terrorist acts should not be commingled within the rubric of protected combatant activities (though they may have selected differing methodologies for expressing it), UN Member States have not engaged publicly and substantively in UN debates to examine the relative merits of the U.S. policy perspective with respect to Protocol I. Rather, the flood of resolutions from UN organs simply assumed that the U.S. stance against terrorism in the context of Protocol I was misplaced and based on a misapprehension of the underlying utility of Protocol I. Protocol I, therefore, became one of the litany of commonly cited examples of American exceptionalism and resistance to a multilateral world based on a commonality of values and consensus lawmaking. These arguments, however, overlook the reality that the United States and its NATO allies were in fact engaged in sustained diplomatic efforts to achieve the precise purposes articulated in the letter of transmittal.

III. The Practice of Principled Exceptionalism

Alexis de Tocqueville was the first observer to note the distinctiveness in the U.S. approach to the world. Writing in 1830, Tocqueville referred to the United States as exceptional in a sense "that is, qualitatively different from all other countries."[174] The U.S ethos of rugged individualism in some sense originated with the rejection of European social structures and value systems as well as the success of colonists against the greatest military and economic power on the planet. The American Revolution spawned an enduring sense that the U.S. institutions, values, and intentions are unique and, thus, immune from an automatic assimilation within international discourse that is based on a presumed homogeneity. George Washington, for example, warned against "the insidious wiles of foreign influence" in his farewell address to the nation on September 19, 1796.[175] U.S. political and legal debate has since been inescapably affected by this enduring sense of uniqueness and national destiny.

The debate over the reasoning and implications of what has been labeled "American exceptionalism" has spawned a vast literature.[176] A search of English-language law review articles published between 1990 and 2006 identified nearly 1,300 articles referencing American "exceptionalism" or "unilateralism," a glut of writing that compares to fewer than ten pieces identified as addressing the reluctance of European nations to accept multilateral legal instruments.[177] The predominant academic argument denounces U.S. resistance to immersion and adherence to internationalized norms and legal institutions; such "exceptionalism" is often postulated to arise from American hypocrisy.[178] The U.S. stance toward Protocol I is frequently noted in this regard but is accompanied by a substantial list of other examples such as the U.S. refusal to join the International Criminal Court, the Kyoto Protocol on Climate Change, the Ottawa Convention on Anti-Personnel Landmines, the UN Convention on the Rights of the Child, and other international human rights agreements.[179] Indeed, awareness of a global audience that carries a keenly critical predisposition has affected U.S. jurisprudence, as judges address charges of "exceptionalism" in both explicit and implicit ways.[180]

Most scholarship on legal exceptionalism accepts a binary approach: Has a country acceded to a convention, or in the alternative, has it refused to join or joined but sought to evade core treaty norms by using reservations? In the human rights context, international criticism has centered on the "number and far-reaching nature of reservations taken by the United States."[181] The Human Rights Committee, for example, expressed regret at the number of U.S. reservations to the International Covenant on Civil and Political Rights and expressed its belief that "taken together, they intended to ensure that the United States has accepted only what is already the law of the United States."[182] Dean Koh described this approach as a sort of "flying buttress" mentality in that America attempts to support the cathedral of international human rights from the outside based on incomplete adherence and adoption rather than as a strong supporting pillar fully embedded within the multilateral treaty regime.[183] From a superficial perspective, this could describe the U.S. attitude toward Protocol I whereby other nations perceived the United States to express glibly that humanitarian law should be expanded and enforced, although the U.S. policy was in fact intended to avoid the application of those norms to its own forces.[184]

The U.S. position toward Protocol I did presage a litany of multilateral instruments that a succession of U.S. presidents, from all points of the political spectrum,[185] would later term "fatally flawed"[186] or "fundamentally flawed."[187] It is also no coincidence that many of the treaties that the United States has rejected outright have been accompanied by a clause prohibiting reservations.[188] Reflexive acceptance of the proposition that U.S. resistance to multilateral instruments flows primarily from a hypocritical desire to enjoy differing standards from the rest of the world is accordingly misplaced and superficial. By way of illustration, U.S. delegates to the negotiations leading up to the 1997 Ottawa Convention on the Prohibition of the Use, Stockpiling, Production and Transfer of Anti-Personnel Mines and on Their Destruction[189] sought agreement on a regime that would preserve the U.S. obligations to deter armed conflict along the Korean demilitarized zone while also advancing the stated purpose of preventing the loss of innocent life caused by unrecovered landmines globally.[190]

The United States refrained from joining both Protocol I and the Ottawa Convention not because of a knee-jerk exceptionalist mantra or a visceral distrust of multilateral instruments but rather because delegates adopted a treaty that disregarded the legitimate equities of the United States.[191] The Ottawa Convention does not allow reservations[192] and completely ignores the special military interests of a major military power with a substantial troop presence deployed to prevent a numerically superior enemy from crossing an international border clearly marked by the high fences, guard towers, and emplaced minefields.[193]

Commenting on the unfortunate choice required by a treaty that does not permit reserva-

tions yet undermines U.S. interests, President Clinton remarked that

One of the biggest disappointments I've had as President, a bitter disappointment for me, is that I could not sign in good conscience the treaty banning land mines, because we have done more since I've been President to get rid of land mines than any country in the world by far. We spend half of the money the world spends on de-mining. We have destroyed over a million of our own mines.

I couldn't do it because the way the treaty was worded was unfair to the United States and to our Korean allies in meeting our responsibilities along the DMZ in South Korea, and because it outlawed our anti-tank mines while leaving every other country intact. And I thought it was unfair.

But it just killed me. But all of us who are in charge of the nation's security engage our heads, as well as our hearts.[194]

Just as in the Ottawa Convention context, the United States exercised principled exceptionalism in rejecting Protocol I. Protocol I blurred the lines circumscribing lawful combatants by creating new legal rules without rigorously articulating the rationale for why such protections should flow to "A category of persons who are not entitled to treatment either as peaceful civilians or as prisoners of war by reason of the fact that they have engaged in hostile conduct without meeting the qualifications."[195] As the International Court of Justice noted in the *Nuclear Weapons* case, the law of war is *lex specialis* that takes precedence over some otherwise applicable human rights provisions during an armed conflict.[196] Thus, the corpus of humanitarian law cannot be said to necessarily subsume the most important aspects of the international law related to terrorist acts.

The United States concluded that commingling the regime criminalizing terrorist acts with the *jus in bello* rules of humanitarian law would be untenable and inappropriate.[197] Rather than accepting the veiled assertion repeated through the years throughout UN channels that the only appropriate approach to Protocol I is complete adherence to its principles,[198] the U.S. perspective was that a technical and lawyerly approach based on discrete reservations and interpretive instruments between sovereign states would be both inadvisable and ultimately impossible.[199] The very act of accepting the principles enshrined in Articles 1(4) and 44(3) would, in the U.S. view, grant terrorists a psychological and legal victory that would later be used to undermine the peace and security of innocent and peace-loving citizens.[200] In other words, even a partial acknowledgment of the propriety of terrorists' claims to combatant status presented an unnecessary risk to innocent lives and property.

American exceptionalism with regard to Protocol I was in fact a policy determination based on national self-interests that reflected the underlying community interests of states engaged in a struggle against terrorists. Governments across the globe share the duty and desire to protect innocent citizens from threats to their lives and liberty posed by terrorist acts. The NATO allies concurred completely with the substance of the U.S. desire to withhold any recognition of privileged status to terrorists or to accord their crimes any sphere of legal protection.[201] Rather than establishing an exceptionalist rejection of internationalist rhetoric, however, the U.S. position formed the benchmark for continued engagement with other nations in addressing common concerns. The U.S. rejection of Protocol I was a principled position that took political courage in the face of nearly unrelenting criticism in subsequent decades, although in fact the NATO position differed only in form and modality. U.S. leadership, in shaping this normative framework, became clear as states around the world hurried to ratify the most modern terrorism conventions in the aftermath of September 11.

IV. The Post-9/11 Legal Context

As shown above, the U.S. policy stance regarding Protocol I helped to prevent the commin-

gling of the laws and customs of war. In the aftermath of September 11, the "exceptional" U.S. position formed the substantive benchmark around which other nations rallied in reaction to reservations designed to blur the distinctions between terrorists and privileged combatants. September 11 destroyed the naïve notion that there is a bright legal line that neatly divides a combat zone into innocent civilians (who are legally protected from deliberate hostilities) and combatants who may lawfully be targeted and killed.[202] The attacks transformed an esoteric problem that was important only to specialists in the law of armed conflict into a tactical and legal problem highly relevant to current operations. The dualistic ICRC view of legal status noted above simply does not square with the facts related to the war against transnational terrorist operations. Al Qaeda and its supporters acted as private citizens in declaring war on U.S. citizens and values,[203] and they carried out their attacks with a purposeful intensity that rises to the level of armed conflict by any common-sense definition. Moreover, the conflict against al Qaeda and its supporters is an armed conflict governed by the law of armed conflict as defined by the International Criminal Tribunal for the Former Yugoslavia.[204] Invoking the mutual defense obligations of Article 5 for the first time in NATO history, NATO accepted the legal conclusion that al Qaeda committed an armed attack on the United States.[205] Despite al Qaeda rhetoric alluding to a struggle for liberation and self-determination, no nation would ever accept the normative proposition that the private group of terrorists acted with a legally cognizable expectation of combatant immunity. Al Qaeda and its supporters forfeited the rights that would normally accrue to civilian persons caught in the midst of hostilities, chief among them the right to be free from deliberate efforts at targeting them.[206]

Above all, September 11 proved that some private terrorist groups are undeterred by existing criminal law prohibitions and treaty obligations designed to apply to sovereign states in a world governed by respect for the rule of law.

The United States took the view that the inherent right of self-defense permits the United States to seek "justice" using its military power.[207] The attacks provided graphic affirmation of Justice Jackson's famous truism from the Nuremberg Tribunal that "wars are started only on the theory and in the confidence that they can be won. Personal punishment . . . will probably not be a sufficient deterrent to prevent a war where the warmaker feels the chances of defeat to be negligible."[208] Transnational terrorism challenges the community of civilized nations precisely because a group of private persons linked by shared ideology is now waging war in direct defiance of international law. The classic style of terrorist sought short-term political gain through revolution, national liberation, or secession;[209] the new terrorist, however, seeks to transform the world and is motivated by religious and ideological imperatives under the influence of a larger transcendental mythology.[210] This approach is a far cry from the anticolonial efforts against a specific government conducted by organized gangs that provided the impetus for Protocol I.

The U.S. response to the terrorist attacks reshaped the paradigm for dealing with terrorists from an exclusive reliance on judicial mechanisms to address criminal conduct to a war-fighting model. International terrorism constitutes a national security problem as well as a law enforcement problem because it is a unique form of transnational crime in which private actors seek to unravel the fabric of civilized society and thereby undermine state, regional, and global security.[211] This new paradigm required an interface between established law of armed conflict norms and existing judicial mechanisms capable of prosecuting those perpetrators who are not eliminated or emasculated by the application of military power.[212]

In that sense the war on terrorism is more than a politically convenient concept. Without applying the law of armed conflict to transnational terrorists, it would be a non sequitur to even consider whether they are entitled to combatant immunity for their warlike acts. Despite the widespread ratifications of Protocol I, no domestic court in the world has accepted the claims of terrorists to immunity that are unwarranted under existing international law.[213] Al Qaeda and its operatives scattered across the world cannot meet the Geneva Convention requirements for treatment as prisoners of war under any scenario.[214] The European Parliament accepted that reality by adopting a resolution recognizing that the terrorists "do not fall precisely within the definitions of the Geneva Convention."[215] By the accepted definition, also found in Protocol I, they became lawful targets for military action because the "destruction, capture or neutralization" of al Qaeda and its supporters "offers a definite military advantage."[216] They relinquished the protections afforded innocent civilians, who are protected from being targeted, and simultaneously forfeited the legal protections enjoyed by lawful combatants who fall into the hands of the enemy.

A. The Changing Face of Terror

Following September 11, the European Parliament opined that the law of armed conflict must "be revised to respond to the new situations created by the development of international terrorism."[217] In hindsight, Protocol I failed to bring closure to the persistent international efforts to define the boundaries of the class of "unprivileged belligerents"[218] who forfeit their protection from attack by conducting hostile activities without the privileges accruing to "combatants" under the established laws of war. If Protocol I embedded the meanings intended by its most progressive supporters, then such evolution would be unnecessary because the law would already establish an accepted legal right for al Qaeda to claim combatant status. However, the United States' reliance on the *jus in bello* paradigm necessitated discussion of combatant status as debates swirled around the proper categorization of terrorist acts and of captured terrorists.[219] Some international law scholars would argue that lawyers interpreting and applying the treaties governing the conduct of hostilities must extrapolate from the text to fashion legal advice that focuses on the "high purposes which are the raison d'être of the convention."[220] From this vantage point, Protocol I would provide the baseline from which the law would evolve in response to new forms of transnational terrorism.

In practice, September 11 provided the impetus for precisely the opposite legal development. The international community refocused on the matrix of existing terrorism conventions as the acceptable starting point for analysis when assessing the conduct and status of suspects accused of terrorist acts.[221] Only 3 states had become parties to the Convention for the Suppression of Terrorist Financing at the time of the attacks, in contrast to the 171 parties at the time of this writing.[222] Likewise, though the Terrorist Bombing Convention entered into force on May 23, 2001, it boasted only 24 participating states as opposed to 164 at the time of this writing.[223] September 11 caused a reevaluation of the multilateral framework for criminalizing terrorist acts, which in turn resulted in emphatic international rejection of arguments that the legal accountability for terrorist acts can be shrouded by resorting to subjective and shifting justifications or to arguments based on moral equivalency.[224]

The U.S. position vis-à-vis Protocol I that there must be a bright line between the applicable *jus in bello* and the status accorded to terrorist suspects has been emphatically validated in the diplomatic dialogues accompanying state ratification of the key post-9/11 terrorism conventions.[225] International law is clear that terrorist acts will *always* be punishable under the criminal codes of one or more domestic states.[226] Although the U.S. rejection of Protocol I has been portrayed as exceptionalist and hypocritical, all nations shared the underlying substantive assessment that terrorists could expect no immunity for acts that undermine the protection of human life and the goal of minimizing damage to civilian property.[227] These common concerns are the source of humanitarian law,

and states have resoundingly rejected challenges to this shared conception of the international legal order.[228]

Conversely, Protocol I provides an articulable textual basis purporting to legitimize acts of nonstate actors seeking self-determination or conducting hostilities against domination by foreign sovereigns. Some states sought to extrapolate from its provisions by analogy in an attempt to redefine terrorism in the context of the Terrorism Financing Convention and the Terrorist Bombing Convention. Sovereign states overwhelmingly rejected Egypt's, Syria's, and Jordan's attempts to introduce subjective elements drawn from Protocol I into the definition of terrorism. In so doing, they followed the example that the United States had provided nearly thirty years previously in the context of its rejection of Protocol I.[229] The United States was prescient in its position that the law of terrorism and the *jus in bello* applicable to status determinations cannot be commingled. The rejection of reservations that sought to weave the Protocol I standards into the law of terrorism marked the definitive adoption of the U.S. position.

B. Evolution of the Multilateral Framework Regulating Terrorism

1. Reservations to the Terrorism Financing Convention

The essence of the Terrorism Financing Convention is its core criminal prohibition found in Article 2:

> Any person commits an offence within the meaning of this Convention if that person by any means, directly or indirectly, unlawfully and willfully, provides or collects funds with the intention that they should be used or in the knowledge that they are to be used, in full or in part, in order to carry out:
>
> (a) An act which constitutes an offence within the scope of and as defined in one of the treaties listed in the annex; or
>
> (b) Any other act intended to cause death or serious bodily injury to a civilian, or to any

other person not taking an active part in the hostilities in a situation of armed conflict, when the purpose of such act, by its nature or context, is to intimidate a population, or to compel a government or an international organization to do or to abstain from doing any act. [230]

The object and purpose of the Terrorism Financing Convention is to hinder *all* acts of terrorism by holding *all* persons[231] and legal entities liable using the broadest range of remedies available.[232] These remedies include criminal sanctions for persons as well as civil, criminal, and administrative sanctions for legal entities that collect or provide funds to be used in terrorist acts defined in Article 2 of the Convention.[233] Like other multilateral terrorism conventions, the Terrorism Financing Convention specifically provides that none of the defined offenses "shall be regarded for the purposes of extradition or mutual legal assistance as a political offence or as an offence connected with a political offence or as an offence inspired by political motives."[234] Finally, in the clearest possible language, the Convention sweeps broadly in attempting to eliminate any room for affirmative defenses based on justification.[235] Article 6 of the Convention requires ratifying states to "adopt such measures as may be necessary, including, where appropriate, domestic legislation, to ensure that criminal acts within the scope of this Convention are under no circumstances justifiable by considerations of a political, philosophical, ideological, racial, ethnic, religious or other similar nature."[236]

Some states attempted to erode the manifest intent of the Terrorist Financing Convention through the use of reservations and declarations. A reservation is "a unilateral statement . . . made by a State, when signing, ratifying, accepting, approving, or acceding to a treaty, whereby it purports to exclude or to modify the legal effect of certain provisions of the treaty in their application to that State."[237] Egypt's "explanatory declaration" is a unilateral statement made at the time of ratification of the Convention that purports to exclude or modify the legal effect of the

Convention. Drawn from the substantive soil of Protocol I, article 1, paragraph 4, the "explanatory declaration" states,

> Without prejudice to the principles and norms of general international law and the relevant United Nations resolutions, the Arab Republic of Egypt does not consider acts of national resistance in all its forms, including armed resistance against foreign occupation and aggression with a view to liberation and self-determination, as terrorist acts within the meaning of article 2, [paragraph 1] subparagraph (b), of the Convention.[238]

Article 3 of the Terrorism Financing Convention limits its applicability in situations in which "the offence is committed within a single State, the alleged offender is a national of that State and is present in the territory of that State and no other State has a basis under article 7, paragraph 1, or article 7, paragraph 2, to exercise jurisdiction."[239] Hence, if the Egyptian declaration represents a valid interpretation of the Convention, Egypt would become a sanctuary state for terrorists who sought to plan, finance, and conduct operations around the world. The declaration states that Egypt does not consider all acts of national resistance as terrorism, which can be seen as permitting funding from within Egypt with the objective of bankrolling Taliban operations in Afghanistan, the murderous Badr brigades in Iraq, Palestinian activities, or even Hezbollah activities in Lebanon and northern Israel. The "explanatory declaration" also purported to limit the definition of acts for which Egypt would have to hold accountable under Article 4 of the Convention any person who committed such acts, which may be seen as undercutting the universality of international cooperation in the fight against terrorist acts.[240] The explanatory declaration would modify Article 6 of the Convention by creating a defense of political and ideological justification derived from the subjective assessments of the terrorist for acts that would otherwise fall within the definition of Article 2 of the Convention.

Echoing the U.S. position from the Protocol I debates, at the time of this writing twenty-one states have opposed such an extrapolation into the Terrorist Financing context using virtually identical language and reasoning to emphatically and unequivocally reject Egypt's position.[241] The German response is typical and follows in its entirety.

With regard to Egypt's explanatory declaration upon ratification:

The Government of the Federal Republic of Germany has carefully examined the declaration made by the Arab Republic of Egypt to the International Convention for the Suppression of the Financing of Terrorism upon ratification of the Convention relating to Article 2 paragraph 1 (b) thereof. It is of the opinion that this declaration amounts to a reservation, since its purpose is to unilaterally limit the scope of the Convention. The Government of the Federal Republic of Germany is furthermore of the opinion that the declaration is in contradiction to the object and purpose of the Convention, in particular the object of suppressing the financing of terrorist acts wherever and by whomever they may be committed.

The declaration is further contrary to the terms of Article 6 of the Convention, according to which States Parties commit themselves to adopt such measures as may be necessary, including, where appropriate, domestic legislation, to ensure that criminal acts within the scope of this Convention are under no circumstances justifiable by considerations of a political, philosophical, ideological, racial, ethnic, religious or other similar nature.

The Government of the Federal Republic of Germany recalls that, according to customary international law as codified in the Vienna Convention on the Law of Treaties, reservations that are incompatible with the object and purpose of a convention are not permissible.

The Government of the Federal Republic of Germany therefore objects to the above-mentioned declaration by the Arab Republic of Egypt to the International Convention for the Suppression of the Financing of Terrorism. This objection shall not preclude the entry into force of the Convention as between the Federal Republic of Germany and the Arab Republic of Egypt.[242]

Joining the Germans, the following states objected to Egypt's declaration on the same legal basis, including Austria, Belgium, Canada, the Czech Republic, Denmark, Estonia, Finland, France, Hungary, Ireland, Italy, Latvia, the Netherlands, Poland, Portugal, Spain, Sweden, the United Kingdom, and, of course, the United States.[243] Some states added their own insights supporting their position. Argentina, for example, added with respect to the Egyptian declaration, or any future such pronouncement by any other state that "the Government of the Argentine Republic considers that all acts of terrorism are criminal, regardless of their motives, and that all States must strengthen their cooperation in their efforts to combat such acts and bring to justice those responsible for them."[244] Ireland admonished that it is "in the common interest of States that treaties to which they have chosen to become party are respected as to their object and purpose and that States are prepared to undertake any legislative changes necessary to comply with their obligations under these treaties."[245]

Against this array of diplomatic solidarity, only Syria and Jordan entered reservations that could even be remotely construed as ideologically similar.[246] The Syrian Arab Republic wrote that "acts of resistance to foreign occupation are not included under acts of terrorism."[247] Other than Argentina and Ireland, every nation that rejected the Egyptian declaration used very similar language to reject the Syrian effort, with the additions of Japan and Norway.[248] Finally, the Jordanian declaration read as follows: "The Government of the Hashemite Kingdom of Jordan does not consider acts of national armed struggle and fighting foreign occupation in the exercise of people's right to self-determination as terrorist acts within the context of paragraph 1 (b) of article 2 of the Convention."[249]

Predictably, this declaration was rejected by twenty states—those listed above with the notable addition of the Russian Federation.[250]

In the context of Protocol I, all NATO allies, except the United States (for the policy reasons noted above), attempted to constrain a lawful right to internationalize an armed conflict on behalf of nonstate participants in the context of occupation.[251] By rejecting the Egyptian, Syrian, and Jordanian declarations, they echoed the position that the United States had proclaimed nearly three decades prior. Hence, apart from three states, whose feeble attempts were scattered like the detritus of the World Trade Towers, international law is clear as a matter of both *opinio juris* and conventional text in that there is simply no articulable justification for the financially facilitating terrorist acts. In hindsight, the world reacted to validate and reinforce the U.S. effort to prevent commingling the *jus in bello* protections afforded to lawful combatants with the bright-line international condemnation of terrorist acts irrespective of their context or subjective motivations.

2. Reservations to the Terrorist Bombing Convention

The International Convention for the Suppression of Terrorist Bombings presents an even more striking example of the prescience of the U.S. position at the time of Protocol I. The material penal provision in Article 2 provides that

1. Any person commits an offence within the meaning of this Convention if that person unlawfully and intentionally delivers, places, discharges or detonates an explosive or other lethal device in, into or against a place of public use, a State or government facility, a public transportation system or an infrastructure facility:

a. With the intent to cause death or serious bodily injury; or

b. With the intent to cause extensive destruction of such a place, facility or system, where such destruction results in or is likely to result in major economic loss.

2. Any person also commits an offence if that person attempts to commit an offence as set forth in paragraph 1 of the present article.

3. Any person also commits an offence if that person:

a. Participates as an accomplice in an offence as set forth in paragraph 1 or 2 of the present article; or

b. Organizes or directs others to commit an offence as set forth in paragraph 1 or 2 of the present article; or

c. In any other way contributes to the commission of one or more offences as set forth in paragraph 1 or 2 of the present article by a group of persons acting with a common purpose; such contribution shall be intentional and either be made with the aim of furthering the general criminal activity or purpose of the group or be made in the knowledge of the intention of the group to commit the offence or offences concerned.[252]

The Convention was originally intended to fill lacunae in the normative structure, but even in its preamble it reinforces the dichotomous approach to preventing and prosecuting terrorist acts. It specifically notes "that the activities of military forces of States are governed by rules of international law outside the framework of this Convention and that the exclusion of certain actions from the coverage of this Convention does not condone or make lawful otherwise unlawful acts, or preclude prosecution under other laws."[253] The object and purpose of the Terrorist Bombing Convention is to regulate terrorist bombings,[254] it does *not* aim to provide a basis for invoking a moral equivalency between terrorist acts and the conduct of operations by armed forces.

One of the most important and widely agreed upon provisions, Article 19(2) of the Terrorist Bombing Convention, reinforces the division between the law of terrorism and the *jus in bello* applicable to armed conflicts:

The activities of armed forces during an armed conflict, as those terms are understood under international humanitarian law, which are governed by that law, are not governed by this Convention, and the activities undertaken by military forces of a State in the exercise of their official duties, inasmuch as they are governed by other rules of international law, are not governed by this Convention.[255]

Recent international practice has reinforced the notion that the deliberate use of terror as a military tactic would violate international law. Both Protocol I and Protocol II prohibit acts or threats of violence whose primary purpose is to "spread terror among the civilian population."[256] The International Criminal Tribunal for the Former Yugoslavia opined that "the prohibition against terror is a specific prohibition within the general prohibition of attack on civilians," the latter of which constitutes a "peremptory norm of customary international law."[257] The ICRC Commentary notes that military operations that seek to inflict terror "are particularly reprehensible, . . . occur frequently, and inflict particularly cruel suffering on the civilian population."[258] More recently, in upholding the convictions in the AFRC Case, the Appeals Chamber of the Special Court for Sierra Leone accepted that convictions for "acts of terrorism" could result for the three appellants who engaged in a "common plan to carry out a campaign of terrorizing and collectively punishing the civilian population of Sierra Leone . . . in order to achieve the ultimate objective of gaining and exercising political power and control over the territory of Sierra Leone."[259] Furthermore, as this chapter goes to press, Bosnian Serb leader Radovan Karadžić is being tried at The Hague, inter alia, on the charge of unlawfully inflicting terror on civilians.[260]

Just as it did in the context of the Terrorism Financing Convention, Egypt attempted to blur the lines separating differing legal regimes. One of its reservations stated that "The Government of the Arab Republic of Egypt declares that it is bound by Article 19, paragraph 2, of the Convention insofar as the military forces of the State, in the exercise of their duties do not violate the rules and principles of international law."[261] The response of the United Kingdom exemplifies the language and approach other states have taken (which included Canada, France, Germany, Italy, the Netherlands, the Russian Federation, Spain, and the United States) in opposing the Egyptian effort.

With regard to Egypt's reservation made upon ratification,

The Government of the United Kingdom of Great Britain and Northern Ireland have examined the declaration, described as a reservation, relating to article 19, paragraph 2 of the International Convention for the Suppression of Terrorist Bombings made by the Government of the Arab Republic of Egypt at the time of its ratification of the Convention.

The declaration appears to purport to extend the scope of application of the Convention to include the armed forces of a State to the extent that they fail to meet the test that they "do not violate the rules and principles of international law." Such activities would otherwise be excluded from the application of the Convention by virtue of article 19, paragraph 2. It is the opinion of the United Kingdom that the Government of Egypt is entitled to make such a declaration only insofar as the declaration constitutes a unilateral declaration by the Government of Egypt that Egypt will apply the terms of the Convention in circumstances going beyond those required by the Convention to their own armed forces on a unilateral basis. The United Kingdom considers this to be the effect of the declaration made by Egypt.

However, in the view of the United Kingdom, Egypt cannot by a unilateral declaration extend the obligations of the United Kingdom under the Convention beyond those set out in the Convention without the express consent of the United Kingdom. For the avoidance of any doubt, the United Kingdom wishes to make clear that it does not so consent. Moreover, the United Kingdom does not consider the declaration made by the Government of Egypt to have any effect in respect of the obligations of the United Kingdom under the Convention or in respect of the application of the Convention to the armed forces of the United Kingdom.

The United Kingdom thus regards the Convention as entering into force between the United Kingdom and Egypt subject to a unilateral declaration made by the Government of Egypt, which applies only to the obligations of Egypt under the Convention and only in respect of the armed forces of Egypt.[262]

The French added that "the effect of the reservation made by the Government of the Arab Republic of Egypt is to bring within the scope of the Convention activities undertaken by a State's armed forces which do not belong there because they are covered by other provisions of international law. As a result, the reservation substantially alters the meaning and scope of article 19, paragraph 2 of the Convention."[263]

The net effect of these consular notifications is to reinforce the bright-line distinction between the relevant bodies of law. The military forces representing sovereign states are subject to the limitations of the laws and customs of war: They cannot be demeaned as terrorists because they are not operationally or legally equivalent to terrorists.[264] This principle in no way undermines the right of states to prosecute as war criminals those combatants who transgressed the boundaries of the law of war.[265] Terrorists, however, are subject to the criminal sanctions of domestic laws,[266] especially those deriving from the definitions and condemnations enshrined in the plethora of multilateral conventions that proscribe their tactics. States are absolutely united in opposing any efforts to erode the core prohibition that all acts of terrorism are—and ought to be—criminalized and that any attendant claim to combatant immunity is unfounded and ill advised.[267]

V. Conclusion

In the modern vernacular, those who commit acts that contravene the applicable conventions

are termed terrorists, regardless of their ideological or religious motivations.[268] State practice since 1977 reinforces the clarity and enforceability of the agreed prohibitions against the diverse manifestations of terrorist ideology.[269] Protocol I attempted to elevate nonstate actors to the status of lawful combatants, but the efficacy of those textual promises has been eroded to a vanishing point by states' unified and repeated opposition.[270] In the real world, the effort to decriminalize terrorists' conduct—so long as it complied with applicable *jus in bello* constraints in the context of wars of national liberation—has run aground on the shoals of sovereign survival. In practical terms, the Protocol I provisions mean little because they have never been applied or accepted, and their only residual value is as "agitational or rhetorical" tools.[271]

The core problem in defining and proscribing transnational terrorism is that residual uncertainty over the lawful scope of violence to achieve political ends would have the inevitable result of inducing more individuals to commit more terrorist acts. This danger becomes exponentially greater if such politicized violence were conducted with state sponsorship or umbrella authorization. Persons who employ violence amounting to the conduct of hostilities governed by the law of war do so unlawfully unless they can find affirmative legal authority for their acts under international law. Under the law of armed conflict, individuals acting with the requisite legal authority have historically been termed belligerents or combatants. Persons who have no legal right to wage war or adopt means of inflicting injury on their enemies have been described synonymously as nonbelligerents, unprivileged belligerents, unlawful combatants, or unlawful belligerents.[272] Terrorists remain in this class notwithstanding the efforts of some states to extend the protections derived from the laws and customs of war. This chapter has demonstrated that the U.S. engagement in these essential debates began with the decision to oppose Protocol I in its entirety. In the intervening thirty years, states have overwhelmingly adhered to the United States' substantive preference to oppose all reservations that seek to blur the line between criminal acts of terrorism and lawful acts inherent in the conduct of hostilities.

The law of armed conflict was never intended to provide a shield behind which terrorists would be free to gnaw away at the values of freedom and peace. Private efforts to wage war fall outside the structure of law that binds sovereign states together on the basis of reciprocity and shared community interests.[273] Thus, as noted above, no state in the world willingly accepts the normative proposition that international law bestows upon private citizens an affirmative right to become combatants whose warlike activities are recognized and protected. This is more than a residual appendage of sovereignty. It reflects the very essence of sovereign survival and respect for the dignity and individual worth of humans in the context of civilized society.

Words matter, particularly when they are charged with legal significance and purport to convey legal rights and obligations. Elevating to the status of combatants those non-state actors whose warlike activities indiscriminately target and terrorize innocent civilians would discredit the law of armed conflict even further in the eyes of a cynical world. Though incomplete compliance with the *jus in bello* is the regrettable norm, knowledge of the law and an accompanying professional awareness that the law is binding remains central to the professional ethos of military forces around our planet.[274] For example, entitlement to prisoner of war status was limited to persons "captured by the enemy" under the 1929 Geneva Conventions.[275] Based on the text of the convention, the thousands of Germans who surrendered during World War II were categorized as "Surrendered Enemy Persons" not automatically entitled to the rights and privileges accorded to prisoners of war.[276]

Unless the world is prepared to accept terrorist acts justified wholly on the subjective, political, or religious motivations of the perpetrator, there must be a strict bulwark between the laws and customs of war regulating the authorization to conduct military operations and the legal framework regulating terrorism. The semantic label applied to captured Germans made little difference in their treatment or their attitudes. In the context of transnational terrorism, even a partial acknowledgment of the propriety of terrorist claims to combatant status presents an unnecessary and ill-advised risk to innocent lives and property. The legal regime governing terrorist conduct should remain fixed in its clarity of purpose and principle rather than being reduced to a subjective and indeterminate mass of text and pretext. U.S. exceptionalism in the context of Protocol I represented an act of leadership based on national self-interest that in reality reflected the underlying community interests of states engaged in the larger struggle for the international rule of law. The United States concluded that the commingling of the regime that criminalizes terrorist acts with the *jus in bello* rules of humanitarian law would be untenable and inappropriate. Though no state has formally acknowledged the wisdom of the U.S. rejection of the most politicized provisions of Protocol I, states' actions in demonstrating a cohesive legal front to deflect efforts to protect terrorists from prosecution provide implicit acceptance and accolade. By rejecting the principles embodied in Articles 1(4) and 44(3), the United States led the world and, thereby, denied terrorists a psychological and legal victory, and the international cohesiveness against efforts to undermine the multilateral terrorism conventions further reinforced this victory.

NOTES

1. Professor of the Practice of Law, Vanderbilt University Law School. I am grateful to the participants in the Terrorism and Humanitarian Law Roundtable held at Vanderbilt University Law School for their insights and assistance in refining and reframing the arguments herein. In particular, Larry Helfer, Ingrid Wuerth, Charles Garraway, Mark Osiel, Linda Malone, Mark Drumbl, Greg McNeal, Michael Scharf, Elies van Sliedregt, Roger Alford, Laura Olson, Laura Dickinson, Jelena Pejic, Richard Jackson, Gary Solis, Eve La Haye, Rachel Gore, and Chris Cunico have been instrumental in bringing this article to fruition.

2. Protocol Additional to the Geneva Conventions of Aug. 12, 1949, and relating to the Protection of Victims

of International Armed Conflicts (Protocol I) Annex I, Dec. 7, 1979, 1125 U.N.T.S. 3 [hereinafter Protocol I]; *see also* Douglas J. Feith, *Law in the Service of Terror*, 1 NAT'L INT. 36, 39–41 (1985) (discussing differences of opinion held by "Westerners" and "socialists" during the negotiations for Protocol I and how the United States' arguments ultimately did not prevail, thereby leading to their abstention from voting).

3. Feith, *supra* note 1, at 36–37; *see also* Abraham Sofaer, *Terrorism and the Law*, 64 FOR. AFF. 901, 901–3 (1986) ("At its worst the [international] law [applicable to terrorism] has in important ways actually served to legitimize international terror, and to protect terrorists from punishment as criminals.").

4. S.C. Res. 14565, Annex, U.N. Doc. S/RES/1456 (Jan. 20, 2003). The UN Global Counterterrorism Strategy expresses "strong condemnation of terrorism in all its forms and manifestations, committed by whomever, wherever and for whatever purposes." G.A. Res. 60/228, para. 2, U.N. Doc. A/RES/60/288 (Sept. 20, 2006).

5. Measures to Eliminate International Terrorism, G.A. Draft Res., at 3, U.N. Doc. A/C.6/62/L.14 (Nov. 13, 2007).

6. Status Report on International Convention for the Suppression of the Financing of Terrorism, *available at* http://treaties.un.org/Pages/ViewDetails.aspx?src=IND &mtdsg_no=XVIII-11&chapter=18& lang=en.

7. International Convention for the Suppression of the Financing of Terrorism, 2175 U.N.T.S. 197, art. 6, U.N. Doc. A/RES/54/109 (Dec. 9, 1999) [hereinafter Terrorism Financing Convention].

8. *See, e.g.*, *id.* at art. 7, stating,

1. Each State Party shall take such measures as may be necessary to establish its jurisdiction over the offences set forth in article 2 when:

(a) The offence is committed in the territory of that State;

(b) The offence is committed on board a vessel flying the flag of that State or an aircraft registered under the laws of that State at the time the offence is committed;

(c) The offence is committed by a national of that State.

2. A State Party may also establish its jurisdiction over any such offence when:

(a) The offence was directed towards or resulted in the carrying out of an offence referred to in article 2, paragraph 1, subparagraph (a) or (b), in the territory of or against a national of that State;

(b) The offence was directed towards or resulted in the carrying out of an offence referred to in article 2, paragraph 1, subparagraph (a) or (b), against a State or government facility of that State abroad, including diplomatic or consular premises of that State;

(c) The offence was directed towards or resulted in an offence referred to in article 2, paragraph 1, subparagraph (a) or (b), committed in an attempt to compel that State to do or abstain from doing any act;

(d) The offence is committed by a stateless person who has his or her habitual residence in the territory of that State;

(e) The offence is committed on board an aircraft which is operated by the Government of that State.

3. Upon ratifying, accepting, approving or acceding to this Convention, each State Party shall notify the Secretary-General of the United Nations of the jurisdiction it has established in accordance with paragraph 2. Should any change take place, the State Party concerned shall immediately notify the Secretary-General.

4. Each State Party shall likewise take such measures as may be necessary to establish its jurisdiction over the offences set forth in article 2 in cases where the alleged offender is present in its territory and it does not extradite that person to any of the States Parties that have established their jurisdiction in accordance with paragraphs 1 or 2.

5. When more than one State Party claims jurisdiction over the offences set forth in article 2, the relevant States Parties shall strive to coordinate their actions appropriately, in particular concerning the conditions for prosecution and the modalities for mutual legal assistance.

6. Without prejudice to the norms of general international law, this Convention does not exclude the exercise of any criminal jurisdiction established by a State Party in accordance with its domestic law.

9. *Id.* at art 14.

10. U.N. GAOR, 56th Sess., 12th plen. mtg., at 18, U.N. Doc. A/56/PV.12 (Oct. 1, 2001).

11. *See* Thomas M. Franck & Bert B. Lockwood Jr., *Preliminary Thoughts Towards an International Convention on Terrorism*, 68 AM. J. INT'L L. 69, 72–82 (1974) (tracing historical definitions of "terrorism" from the French Revolution to 1974).

12. *See* C. A. J. Coady, *The Morality of Terrorism*, 60 PHIL. 47, 52 (1985) ("As amended then, the definition of a terrorist act would go as follows: 'A political act, ordinarily committed by an organized group, which involves the intentional killing or other severe harming of non-combatants or the threat of the same or intentional severe damage to the property of non-combatants or the threat of the same.' The term 'terrorism' can then be defined as the tactic or policy of engaging in terrorist acts.").

13. Martha Crenshaw, *The Psychology of Terrorism: An Agenda for the 21st Century*, 21 POL. PSYCHOL. 405, 406 (2000) ("The problem of defining terrorism has hindered analysis since the inception of studies of terrorism in the early 1970s. One set of problems is due to the fact that the concept of terrorism is deeply contested. The use of the term is often polemical and rhetorical. It can be a pejorative label, meant to condemn an opponent's cause as illegitimate rather than describe behavior. Moreover, even if the term is used objectively as an analytical tool, it is still difficult to arrive at a satisfactory definition that distinguishes terrorism from other violent phenomena. In principle, terrorism is deliberate and systematic violence performed by small numbers of people, whereas communal violence is spontaneous, sporadic, and requires mass participation. The purpose of terrorism is to intimidate a watching popular audience by harming only a few, whereas genocide is the elimination of entire communities. Terrorism is meant to hurt, not to destroy. Terrorism is preeminently political and symbolic, whereas guerilla warfare is a military activity. Repressive "terror" from above is the action of those in power, whereas terrorism is a clandestine resistance to authority. Yet in practice, events cannot always be precisely categorized.").

14. Gilbert Guillaume, *Terrorism and International Law*, 53 INT'L & COMP. L. Q. 537, 540 (2004) ("In the context of international law, it would appear to me that the adjective 'terrorist' may be applied to any criminal activity involving the use of violence in circumstances likely to cause bodily harm or a threat to human life, in connection with an enterprise whose aim is to provoke terror. Three conditions thus have to be met: (a) the perpetration of certain acts of violence capable of causing death, or at the very least severe physical injury. Certain texts of domestic and European law go further than this, however, and consider that the destruction of property even without any danger for human life may also constitute a terrorist act; (b) an individual or collective enterprise that is not simply improvised, in other words an organized operation or concerted plan reflected in coordinated efforts to achieve a specific goal (which, for example, excludes the case of the deranged killer who shoots at everyone in sight); (c) the pursuit of an objective: to create terror among certain predetermined persons, groups or, more commonly, the public at large (thus differentiating terrorism from the political assassination of a single personality, such as that of Julius Caesar by Brutus).").

15. *See* YORAM DINSTEIN, THE CONDUCT OF HOSTILITIES UNDER THE LAW OF INTERNATIONAL ARMED CONFLICT 31 (2d ed. 2004) (clarifying that *jus in bello* merely prescribes the offenses under which lawful combatants can be brought to trial. With regard to unlawful combatants, *jus in bello* "merely takes off a mantle of immunity from the defendant, who is therefore accessible to penal charges for any offence committed against the domestic legal system.").

16. M. CHERIF BASSIOUNI, INTERNATIONAL TERRORISM: MULTILATERAL CONVENTIONS (1937–2001) 3 (2001).

17. M. Cherif Bassiouni, *The New Wars and the Crisis of Compliance with the Law of Armed Conflict by Non-State Actors*, 98 J. CRIM. L. & CRIMINOLOGY 711, 739 (2008).

18. U.N. Charter, art. 25.

19. S.C. Res. 1377, Annex, U.N. Doc. S/RES/1377 (Nov. 12, 2001).

20. The Secretary-General, *A More Secure World: Our Shared Responsibility: Report of the Secretary-General's High-Level Panel on Threats, Challenges, and Change*, para. 159 (2004), *available at* www.un.org/secureworld/.

21. *See* Convention on Offenses and Certain Other Acts Committed on Board Aircraft, Sept. 14, 1963, 20 U.S.T. 2941, 704 U.N.T.S. 219 [hereinafter Tokyo Hijacking Convention]; Hague Convention for the Suppression of Unlawful Seizure of Aircraft, Dec. 16, 1970, 22 U.S.T. 1641, 860 U.N.T.S. 105 [hereinafter Hague Hijacking Convention]; Convention for the Suppression of Unlawful Acts Against the Safety of Civil Aviation, Sept. 23, 1971, 24 U.S.T. 565, 974 U.N.T.S. 177 [hereinafter Montreal Hijacking Convention]; Protocol on the Suppression of Unlawful Acts of Violence at Airports Serving International Civil Aviation, Feb. 24, 1988, 1589 U.N.T.S. 474 [hereinafter Montreal Protocol]; Convention on the High Seas, Apr. 29, 1958, 13 U.S.T. 2312, 450 U.N.T.S. 82; United Nations Convention on the Law of the Sea, Dec. 10, 1982, 1833 U.N.T.S. 396; Convention on the Prevention and Punishment of Crimes Against Internationally Protected Persons, Including Diplomatic Agents, Dec. 14, 1973, 28 U.S.T. 1975, 1035 U.N.T.S. 167 [hereinafter Diplomats Convention]; Convention on the Safety of United Nations and Associated Personnel, Dec. 9, 1994, 2051 U.N.T.S. 363 [hereinafter UN Personnel Convention]; Convention for the Suppression of Unlawful Acts Against the Safety of Maritime Navigation, Mar. 10, 1988, 1678 U.N.T.S. 221; Protocol for the Suppression of Unlawful Acts Against the Safety of Fixed Platforms Located on the Continental Shelf, Mar. 10, 1988, 1678 U.N.T.S. 304; International Convention Against the Taking of Hostages, Dec. 17, 1979, 1316 U.N.T.S. 205 [hereinafter Hostage-Taking Convention]; International Convention for the Suppression of Terrorist Bombings, Dec. 15, 1997, 2149 U.N.T.S. 256 [hereinafter Terrorist Bombing Convention]; Terrorism Financing Convention, *supra* note 7, at art. 7.

22. BASSIOUNI, *supra* note 16, at 6; M. Cherif Bassiouni, *Legal Control of International Terrorism: A Policy-Oriented Assessment*, 43 HARV. INT. L. J. 83, 90–91 (2001).

23. Bassiouni, *supra* note 17, at 720.

24. The field is frequently described as international humanitarian law. This vague rubric is increasingly used as shorthand to refer to the body of treaty norms that apply in the context of armed conflict as well as the less distinct internationally accepted customs related to the treatment of persons. The core of the international law of war includes the Geneva Convention for the Amelioration of the Condition of the Wounded and Sick in Armed Forces in the Field, Aug. 12, 1949, 6 U.S.T. 3114, 75 U.N.T.S. 31 (replacing previous Geneva Wounded and Sick Conventions of Aug. 22, 1864, Jul. 6, 1906, and Jul. 27, 1929 by virtue of Article 59); Geneva Convention for the Amelioration of the Condition of Wounded, Sick, and Shipwrecked Members of Armed Forces at Sea, Aug. 12, 1949, 6 U.S.T. 3217, 75 U.N.T.S. 85 (replacing Hague Convention of Oct. 18, 1907, 36 Stat. 2371); Geneva Convention Relative to the Treatment of Prisoners of War, Aug. 12, 1949, 6 U.S.T. 3316, 75 U.N.T.S. 135 (replacing the Geneva Convention Relative to the Protection of Prisoners of War of Jul. 27, 1929, 47 Stat. 2021); Geneva Convention Relative to the Protection of Civilians in Time of War, Aug. 12, 1949, 6 U.S.T. 3516, 75 U.N.T.S. 287 [hereinafter Civilians Convention].

25. GEOFFREY BEST, WAR AND LAW SINCE 1945, 128–33 (1994).

26. Hague Convention IV Respecting the Laws and Customs of War on Land, 1907, Annex art. 22, Jan. 26, 1910, *reprinted in* ADAM ROBERTS & RICHARD GUELFF, DOCUMENTS ON THE LAWS OF WAR 73, 77 (3d ed. 2000) [hereinafter 1907 Hague Regulations].

27. In a classic treatise, Professor Julius Stone described the line between lawful participants in conflict and unprivileged or "unprotected" combatants as follows: "The . . . distinction draws the line between those personnel who, on capture, are entitled under international law to certain minimal treatment as prisoners of war, and those not entitled to such protection. 'Non-combatants' who engage in hostilities are one of the classes deprived of such protection. . . . Such unprivileged belligerents, though not *condemned* by international law, are not protected by it, but are left to the discretion of the belligerent threatened by their activities." JULIUS STONE, LEGAL CONTROLS ON INTERNATIONAL CONFLICT 549 (1954).

28. *See* Geneva Convention Relative to the Treatment of Prisoners of War, *supra* note 24, at art. 93.

29. 42 INTERNATIONAL LAW REPORTS 481 (E. Lauterpacht ed., 1971) ("Similarly, combatants who are members of the armed forces, but do not comply with the minimum qualifications of belligerents or are proved to have broken other rules of warfare, are war criminals as such."); Protocol I, *supra* note 1, at art. 85 ("Without prejudice to the application of the Conventions and of this Protocol, grave breaches of these instruments shall be regarded as war crimes.").

30. *See* FRANCIS LIEBER, WAR DEP'T., ADJT. GEN. OFFICE: INSTRUCTIONS FOR THE GOVERNMENT OF ARMIES OF THE UNITED STATES IN THE FIELD (1863), *reprinted in* THE LAWS OF ARMED CONFLICTS: A COLLECTION OF CONVENTIONS, RESOLUTIONS, AND OTHER DOCUMENTS 6, art. 16 (Dietrich Schindler & Jiri Toman eds., 2004) [hereinafter Lieber Code] (a reproduction of texts on armed conflicts and the law as it applies to U.S. armies).

31. *See* Lieber Code, *supra* note 30, at vi ("During the second half of the nineteenth century, a growing conviction spread over the Western world that civilization was rapidly advancing and that it was therefore imperative 'to restrain the destructive forces of war.'").

32. Thomas F. Lambert, *Recalling the War Crimes Trials of World War II*, 149 MIL. L. REV. 15, 23 (1995).

33. 3 HUGO GROTIUS, DE JURE BELLI AC PACIS, ch. 18 (1625), available at www.lonang.com/exlibris/grotius/gro-318.htm. Grotius explained the necessity for such rigid discipline as follows: "The reason is that, if such disobedience were rashly permitted, either the outposts might be abandoned or, with increase of lawlessness, the army or a part of it might even become involved in ill-considered battles, a condition which ought absolutely to be avoided." *Id.*

34. EVE LA HAYE, WAR CRIMES IN INTERNAL ARMED CONFLICTS 105 (2008) (quoting 2 HUGO GROTIUS, DE JURE BELLI AC PACIS 504 (F. Kelsey trans., 1925) (1625)).

35. The Brussels Project of an International Declaration Concerning the Laws and Customs of War, art. 12, *reprinted in* DIETRICH SCHINDLER & JIRI TOMAN, THE LAWS OF ARMED CONFLICTS 21–28 (2d ed. 1981) [hereinafter Brussels Declaration].

36. M. CHERIF BASSIOUNI, CRIMES AGAINST HUMANITY IN INTERNATIONAL CRIMINAL LAW 59 (2d. ed. 1999) (quoting GUSTAVUS ADOLPHUS, ARTICLES OF WAR TO BE OBSERVED IN THE WARS (1621)).

37. 1907 Hague Regulations, *supra* note 26, at art. 22 and accompanying text.

38. Protocol I, *supra* note 2, at art. 35.

39. W. Michael Reisman & William K. Leitzau, *Moving International Law from Theory to Practice: The Role of Military Manuals in Effectuating the Laws of Armed Conflict*, THE LAW OF NAVAL OPERATIONS, 64 NAVAL WAR COL. INT'L. L. STUD. 1, 5–6 (Horace B. Robertson, Jr. ed., 1991).

40. *See generally* Leslie C. Green, *What Is—Why Is There—The Law of War?* in ESSAYS ON THE MODERN

LAW OF WAR (2d. ed. 1999) (providing a historical account of how and why the law of war developed).

41. Report of the International Law Commission Covering its Second Session, June 5–July 29, 1950, U.N. GAOR, 5th Sess., Supp. No. 12, U.N. Doc. A/1316, *reprinted in* THE LAWS OF ARMED CONFLICTS: A COLLECTION OF CONVENTIONS, RESOLUTIONS, AND OTHER DOCUMENTS 1265–66 (Dietrich Schindler & Jiri Toman eds., 1988).

42. *See, e.g.*, Letter from Gen. David H. Petraeus, Commanding Officer of Multi-National Force-Iraq, to Multi-National Force-Iraq (May 10, 2007), *available at* www.humanrightsfirst.org/blog/torture/2009/02/general-petraeus-what-sets-us-apart.asp (addressing a letter to all coalition forces serving in Iraq, "Soldiers, Sailors, Airmen, Marines, and Coast Guardsmen serving in Multi-National Force-Iraq: Our values and the laws governing warfare teach us to respect human dignity, maintain our integrity, and do what is right. Adherence to our values distinguishes us from our enemy. This fight depends on securing the population, which must understand that we—not our enemies—occupy the moral high ground. This strategy has shown results in recent months. Al Qaeda's indiscriminate attacks, for example, have finally started to turn a substantial proportion of the Iraqi population against it.").

43. 42 DEPARTMENT OF THE ARMY, FIELD MANUAL NO. 3–24, MARINE CORPS WARFIGHTING PUBLICATION NO. 3–33.5, COUNTERINSURGENCY 1 (2007).

44. Walter Laquer, *The Terrorism to Come*, 126 POL'Y REV. 58–59 (Aug.–Sept. 2004) ("When regular soldiers do not stick to the rules of warfare, killing or maiming prisoners, carrying out massacres, taking hostages or committing crimes against the civilian population, they will be treated as war criminals. . . . If terrorists behaved according to these norms they would have little if any chance of success; the essence of terrorist operations now is indiscriminate attacks against civilians. But governments defending themselves against terrorism are widely expected not to behave in a similar way but to adhere to international law as it developed in conditions quite different from those prevailing today. . . . Terrorism does not accept laws and rules, whereas governments are bound by them; this, in briefest outline, is asymmetric warfare. If governments were to behave in a similar way, not feeling bound by existing rules and laws such as those against the killing of prisoners, this would be bitterly denounced.")

45. L. OPPENHEIM, INTERNATIONAL LAW: A TREATISE 203 (H. Lauterpacht ed., 7th ed. 1952).

46. *Id.*

47. *See* Geneva Convention Relative to the Treatment of Prisoners of War, *supra* note 24.

48. ALFRED P. RUBIN, THE LAW OF PIRACY 154 (1988).

49. *See, e.g.*, Rome Statute of the International Criminal Court, art. 8(2)(e), July 1, 2002, 2187 U.N.T.S. 90, 139 [hereinafter Rome Statute].

50. MARCO SASSOLI & ANTOINE BOUVIER, HOW DOES LAW PROTECT IN WAR? 208 (Int'l Comm. of the Red Cross, 1999).

51. Letter from General Halleck to Dr. Francis Lieber, Aug. 6. 1862, *reprinted in* FRANCIS LIEBER, LIEBER'S CODE AND THE LAW OF WAR 2 (Richard Shelly Hartigan ed., 1983).

52. *Id.*

53. *Id.*

54. *Id.*

55. Lieber Code, *supra* note 30, at 3. For descriptions of the process leading to General Orders 100 and the legal effect it had on subsequent efforts, *see generally* Grant R. Doty, *The United States and the Development of the Laws of Land Warfare*, 156 MIL. L. REV. 224 (1998); George B. Davis, *Doctor Francis Lieber's Instructions for the Government of Armies in the Field*, 1 AM. J. INT'L L. 13 (1907).

56. Lieber Code, *supra* note 30, at 3.

57. This statement is true subject to the linguistic oddity introduced by Article 3 of the 1907 Hague Regulations, which makes clear that the armed forces of a state can include both combatants and noncombatants (meaning chaplains and medical personnel) and that both classes of military personnel are entitled to prisoner of war status if captured. *See* 1907 Hague Regulations, *supra* note 24, at art. 3 ("The armed forces of the belligerent parties may consist of combatants and noncombatants. In the case of capture by the enemy, both have a right to be treated as prisoners of war.").

58. *See infra* note 67 (discussing the U.S. Military tribunal at Nuremberg's finding that resistance groups were not entitled to be treated as prisoners of war).

59. Lieber Code, *supra* note 30, art. 82.

60. *See generally* M. CHERIF BASSIOUNI, CRIMES AGAINST HUMANITY IN INTERNATIONAL CRIMINAL LAW (Kluwer Law Int'l, 2d ed. 1999) (offering discussions of sources for the law of armed conflicts, the world's major criminal justice systems, and the Charter of the International Military Tribunal for the Prosecution of the Major War Criminals of the European Theater).

61. *See generally* Major R. R. Baxter, *So-Called Unprivileged Belligerency: Spies, Guerillas, and Saboteurs*, 28 BRIT. Y.B. INT'L L. 323 (1951) [hereinafter Baxter] (examining acts of "unlawful belligerents operating in areas which are not under belligerent occupation").

62. DORIS APPEL GRABER, THE DEVELOPMENT OF THE LAW OF BELLIGERENT OCCUPATION 1863–1914, 79 (Columbia Univ. Press, 1949).

63. This concept brings to mind the uprising of Russian peasants in opposition to Napoleonic invaders. It was enshrined in Article 2 of the Hague Regulations and

remains unchanged. 1907 Hague Regulations, *supra* note 24, at art. 2 ("The inhabitants of a territory which has not been occupied, who, on the approach of the enemy, spontaneously take up arms to resist the invading troops without having had time to organize themselves in accordance with Article 1, shall be regarded as belligerents if they carry arms openly and if they respect the laws and customs of war.").

64. *See* 1907 Hague Regulations, *supra* note 26, at arts. 1–2 (stating that inhabitants not covered by Article 2 are governed by the text of Article 1 and are no longer considered lawful combatants).

65. *Id.*

66. Lieber Code, *supra* note 30, at art. 85 ("War-rebels are persons within an occupied territory who rise in arms against the occupying or conquering army, or against the authorities established by the same. If captured, they may suffer death, whether they rise singly, in small or large bands, and whether called upon to do so by their own, but expelled, government or not. They are not prisoners of war; nor are they if discovered and secured before their conspiracy has matured to an actual rising or to armed violence.").

67. For example, the U.S. Military tribunal at Nuremberg stated, "The evidence shows that the bands were sometimes designated as units common to military organization. They, however, had no common uniform. They generally wore civilian clothes although parts of German, Italian and Serbian uniforms were used to the extent they could be obtained. The Soviet Star was generally worn as insignia. The evidence will not sustain a finding that it was such that it could be seen at a distance. Neither did they carry their arms openly except when it was to their advantage to do so. There is some evidence that various groups of the resistance forces were commanded by a centralized command, such as the partisans of Marshal Tito, the Chetniks of Draja Mihailovitch and the Edes of General Zervas. It is evident also that a few partisan bands met the requirements of lawful belligerency. The bands, however, with which we are dealing in this case were not shown by satisfactory evidence to have met the requirements. This means, of course, that captured members of these unlawful groups were not entitled to be treated as prisoners of war. *No crime can be properly charged against the defendants for the killing of such captured members of the resistance forces, they being franc-tireurs.*" The Hostages Trial (Trial of Wilhelm List and Others) (U.S. Military Trib., Nuremberg July 8, 1947–Feb. 19, 1948), *reprinted in* 8 THE UNITED NATIONS WAR CRIMES COMMISSION, LAW REPORTS OF TRIALS OF WAR CRIMINALS 34, 57 (emphasis added) [hereinafter The Hostages Trial].

68. *See* 1907 Hague Regulations, *supra* note 24, at arts. 1–2 (stating that inhabitants not covered by Article

2 are governed by the text of Article 1 and are no longer considered lawful combatants).

69. A. PEARCE HIGGINS, WAR AND THE PRIVATE CITIZEN: STUDIES IN INTERNATIONAL LAW 42 (P. S. King & Son, 1912).

70. *See* 1907 Hague Regulations, *supra* note 26; Protocol I, *supra* note 2 (presenting the 1977 changes); Protocol Additional to the Geneva Conventions of 12 Aug. 1949, and relating to the Protection of Victims of Non-International Armed Conflicts (Protocol II), art. 13, para. 2, 1125 U.N.T.S. 1 [hereinafter Protocol II] (presenting more 1977 changes).

71. *See, e.g.*, *United States v. Otto Ohlendorf* (The Einsatzgruppen Case), 4 TRIALS OF WAR CRIMINALS BEFORE THE NUREMBERG MILITARY TRIBUNALS UNDER CONTROL COUNCIL LAW, NO. 10 (Military Tribunal II-A, Nuremberg, Germany, Jul. 8, 1947–Feb. 19, 1948), *reprinted in* HOWARD LEVIE, DOCUMENTS ON PRISONERS OF WAR 408 (1979) (describing directives that ordered the imprisonment and mass-murder of civilians); *Italy, Sansoli and Others v. Bentivegna and Others*, Court of Cassation, 24 INT. L. REP. 986 (1958), *reprinted in* SASSOLI & BOUVIER, *supra* note 50, at 701 (upholding the legal status of Italian irregulars in fighting against German occupation).

72. GEOFFREY BEST, WAR AND LAW SINCE 1945, 127–28 (Oxford Univ. Press, 2002).

73. Geneva Convention Relative to the Treatment of Prisoners of War, *supra* note 24, at art. 4. This is only a partial listing of the provisions most relevant for determining the status of terrorists and their supporters.

74. *Id.* at art. 5.

75. Final Record of the Diplomatic Conference of Geneva of 1949 Vol. II-B 270 (Fed. Political Dep't, 1949).

76. DEPARTMENT OF THE ARMY, FM 27–10: DEPARTMENT OF THE ARMY FIELD MANUAL: THE LAW OF LAND WARFARE 30 (1956).

77. INTERNATIONAL COMMISSION OF THE RED CROSS, COMMENTARY ON THE GENEVA CONVENTIONS OF 12 AUGUST 1949: VOLUME 4, 51 (Int'l Comm. of the Red Cross, 1958) [hereinafter ICRC COMMENTARY ON GENEVA CONVENTION] ("Every person in enemy hands must have some status under international law: he is either a prisoner of war and, as such, covered by the Third Convention, a civilian covered by the Fourth Convention, or again, a member of the medical personnel of the armed forces who is covered by the First Convention. There is no intermediate status; nobody in enemy hands can be outside the law.").

78. *Id.* at 50 ("resistance movements must fulfill certain stated conditions before they can be regarded as prisoners of war. If members of a resistance movement who have fallen into enemy hands do not fulfill those conditions, they must be considered to be protected per-

sons within the meaning of the present Convention. That does not mean that they cannot be punished for their acts, but the trial and sentence must take place in accordance with the provisions of Article 64 and the Articles which follow it.").

79. Kristopher K. Robinson, Edward M. Crenshaw, & J. Craig Jenkins, *Ideologies of Violence: The Social Origins of Islamist and Leftist Transnational Terrorism*, 84 Soc. F. 2009, 2013 (2005) ("To qualify as a *transnational* terrorist attack, the attack must involve multiple nationalities (defined in terms of country of origin) in terms of its victims, the primary actors, and/or the location of the attack relative to the actor and target. They must also be conducted by an autonomous non-state actor (i.e., a group that is not directly controlled by a sovereign state), have political goals, make use of extra-normal violence, and at least ostensibly be designed so as to induce anxiety among various targets, including the general public.").

80. *See, e.g.*, The Hostages Trial, *supra* note 67, at 57–58 ("Guerilla warfare is said to exist where, after the capitulation of the main part of the armed forces, the surrender of the government and the occupation of its territory, the remnant of the defeated army or the inhabitants themselves continue hostilities by harassing the enemy with unorganised forces ordinarily not strong enough to meet the enemy in pitched battle. They are placed much in the same position as a spy. By the law of war it is lawful to use spies. Nevertheless, a spy when captured, may be shot because the belligerent has the right, by means of an effective deterrent punishment, to defend against the grave dangers of enemy spying. The principle therein involved applied to guerrillas who are not lawful belligerents. Just as the spy may act lawfully for his country and at the same time be a war criminal to the enemy, so guerrillas may render great service to their country and, in the event of success, become heroes even, still they remain war criminals in the eyes of the enemy and may be treated as such. In no other way can an army guard and protect itself from the gadfly tactics of such armed resistance. And, on the other hand, members of such resistance forces must accept the increased risks involved in this mode of fighting. Such forces are technically not lawful belligerents and are not entitled to protection as prisoners of war when captured.").

81. ICRC COMMENTARY ON GENEVA CONVENTION, *supra* note 77, at 49; *see also supra* text in note 73.

82. Geneva Convention Relative to the Treatment of Prisoners of War, *supra* note 24, at art. 4.

83. Final Record of the Diplomatic Conference of Geneva of 1949: Vol. II-B, *supra* note 75, at 268 (quoting the Danish delegate who argued that "the cases not provided for by Article 3 must be treated separately and in accordance with present-day international law").

84. *Id.*

85. *Id.* at 271.

86. *Id.* (emphasis added).

87. *Id.* at 621. Brigadier Page noted that illegal combatants "should no doubt be accorded certain standards of treatment, but should not be entitled to all the benefits of the convention." *Id.* The Swiss delegate expressed an almost identical view that "in regard to the legal status of those who violated the laws of war, the Convention could not of course cover criminals or saboteurs." *Id.*

88. FRANCOISE BOUCHET-SAULNIER, THE PRACTICAL GUIDE TO HUMANITARIAN LAW 302 (Laura Brav ed. & trans., 2002).

89. Geneva Convention Relative to the Treatment of Prisoners of War, *supra* note 24, at art. 2.

90. *Id.*

91. In light of the current military operations in the Gaza strip at the time of this writing, it is apropos to note that Professor Bassiouni posited that "It is almost always the case that an attack by Israeli armed forces against Palestinian targets is presented in the public discourse as being legitimate both in purpose and in means, while a Palestinian attack upon on [sic] Israeli targets is almost invariably described in opposite terms. An attack upon military targets is permissible under IHL. Thus, if the Palestinians attack Israeli armed forces, they are legitimate targets. However, Israel always describes such attacks as terrorist attacks. For Israel to recognize the legitimacy of such attacks upon its armed forces would be a major political concession to Palestinian nationalistic claims and would add significantly to the legitimacy of their conflict against Israel as being a war of national liberation. Geneva Convention Protocol I would apply to such a conflict, thus giving the Palestinian combatants the status of POWs, which Israel has denied to date. The analogy in this case extends only with respect to Israeli armed forces. With respect to Israeli attacks on Palestinian targets, the target may be a civilian one, which is not authorized under IHL, or a legitimate military target, but attacked with disproportionate use of force that causes civilian casualties and destruction of private property, which would be prohibited by IHL. In both of these cases, the attack would be a violation of IHL, but is almost always presented as justified. Conversely, when the Palestinians attack a legitimate military target, it is almost always labeled an act of terrorism. Without question, if Palestinians attack a civilian target, that violates IHL." Bassiouni, *supra* note 17, at 786 n.307 (2008).

92. In fact, a wide range of states coalesced around the effort to defeat the diplomatic draft applicable to noninternational armed conflicts that was tabled in 1975 by the ICRC and supported by the United States and other Western European nations. The group of

states, which included Argentina, Honduras, Brazil, Mexico, Nigeria, Pakistan, Indonesia, India, Romania, and the Soviet Union, succeeded in raising the threshold for applying Protocol II (designed to regulate noninternational armed conflicts) precisely because of fears that extending humanitarian protections to guerillas and irregular forces might elevate the status of rebel groups during such conflicts. David P. Forsythe, *Legal Management of Internal War: The 1977 Protocol on Non-International Armed Conflicts,* 72 AM. J. INT'L L. 272, 284 (1978). *See also* ELEANOR C. MCDOWELL, 1976 DIGEST OF UNITED STATES PRACTICE IN INTERNATIONAL LAW 697 (1976) (documenting the U.S. success in eliminating subjective qualifiers such as "significant" or "important" that might have permitted some states to selectively apply the provisions of Protocol II).

93. This article defines terrorism as the use or threat of use of anxiety-inducing extranormal violence for political purposes by any individual or group, whether acting for or in opposition to established governmental authority, where such action is intended to influence the attitudes and behavior of a target group wider than the victims. EDWARD F. MICKOLUS ET AL., INTERNATIONAL TERRORISM IN THE 1980S: VOLUME II 1984–1987 xiii (1989). For the purposes of this work, "terrorist incidents are restricted to actions that purposely seek to spread terror in the population either by directly targeting noncombatants or by destroying infrastructures that may affect the life and well-being of the civilian population at large. . . . Insurgent, revolutionary, and right-wing terrorism are generally included under the terrorism rubric. Insurgent terrorism refers to violent acts perpetrated by identifiable groups that attack governmental or other targets for short-term goals aimed at sparking widespread discontent toward the existing government. This kind of terrorism is often grounded on a defined ideology, and it seeks to unleash a process of revolution. Revolutionary terrorism defines terrorist actions that take place during existing struggles against a determined regime and develop as a guerrilla tactic. Right-wing terrorism refers to acts perpetrated by outlawed groups that do not seek a social revolution but resort to violence as a way to express and advance their political goals, such as ultranationalism and anticommunism." Andreas E. Feldmann & Maiju Perala, *Reassessing the Causes of Nongovernmental Terrorism in Latin America,* 46 LAT. AM. POL. & SOC'Y 101, 104 (2004).

94. ADAM ROBERTS & RICHARD GUELFF, DOCUMENTS ON THE LAWS OF WAR 387 (3d ed. 2000).

95. Basic Principles of the Legal Status of the Combatants Struggling Against Colonial and Alien Domination and Racist Regimes, G.A. Res. 3103 (XXVII), U.N. Doc. A/RES/3103 (XXVIII) (Dec. 12, 1973).

96. *Id.* at paras. 3 & 4.

97. *See, e.g.*, U.K. MINISTRY OF DEFENSE, THE MANUAL OF THE LAW OF ARMED CONFLICT, para. 15.2.3 (2004) (explaining that the background to this development was the emergence of a large number of postcolonial states, many of which gained independence from their former colonial rulers after long struggles and wished to see some ongoing struggles recognized as essentially international in character).

98. BEST, WAR AND LAW, *supra* note 72, 331–43.

99. *See* MCDOWELL, *supra* note 92, at 695–96 (indicating that the issue of prisoner of war status for guerilla fighters or irregular fighters was not quickly solved at the beginning of the series of diplomatic conferences).

100. BEST, *supra* note 72, at 257.

101. Protocol I, *supra* note 2, at art. 1, para. 3.

102. *See* Civilians Convention, *supra* note 24, at art. 4. The legal category of protected persons is not intended to be an all-inclusive category of civilians even on the face of the Convention. Article 4 provides a definition of the legal term of art, protected persons, that limits the applicability of the protections afforded by the other provisions of the Convention as follows (using admittedly odd grammar): "Art. 4. Persons protected by the Convention are those who, at a given moment and in any manner whatsoever, find themselves, in case of a conflict or occupation, in the hands of a Party to the conflict or Occupying Power of which they are not nationals. . . . Nationals of a State which is not bound by the Convention are not protected by it. Nationals of a neutral State who find themselves in the territory of a belligerent State, and nationals of a co-belligerent State, shall not be regarded as protected persons while the State of which they are nationals has normal diplomatic representation in the State in whose hands they are." Civilians Convention, *supra* note 24, at art. 4.

103. Protocol I, *supra* note 2, at art. 1, para 4.

104. *Id.* at art. 44, para. 3. The text does contain some qualifiers by which Protocol I proponents sought to legitimize this erosion of traditional principles. For example, Article 44, para. 7 specifies that "This Article is not intended to change the generally accepted practice of States with respect to the wearing of the uniform by combatants assigned to the regular, uniformed armed units of a Party to the conflict."

105. *Id.* at art. 44, para. 3.

106. *Id.* at art. 96, para. 3:

The authority representing a people engaged against a High Contracting Party in an armed conflict of the type referred to in Article 1, paragraph 4, may undertake to apply the Conventions and this Protocol in relation to that conflict by means of a unilateral declaration addressed to the depositary. Such declaration shall, upon its receipt by the depositary, have in relation to that conflict the following effects:

(a) The Conventions and this Protocol are brought into force for the said authority as a Party to the conflict with immediate effect;

(b) The said authority assumes the same rights and obligations as those which have been assumed by a High Contracting Party to the Conventions and this Protocol; and

(c) The Conventions and this Protocol are equally binding upon all Parties to the conflict.

107. *Id.* at art. 50, para. 1.

108. *Id.* at art. 51, para. 2.

109. International Committee of the Red Cross, International Humanitarian Law—State Parties/Signatories to Protocol I, *available at* www.icrc.org/ihl.nsf/WebSign?ReadForm&id=470&ps=S.

110. *See* George Aldrich, *Prospects for United States Ratification of Additional Protocol I to the 1949 Geneva Conventions*, 85 Am. J. Int'l L. 1, 4 n.11 (1991) (explaining that Secretary of State Kissinger had ordered the U.S. delegation to leave if the National Liberation Front of South Vietnam (the Vietcong) were admitted to the conference and that their admission was defeated by a tie vote).

111. Roberts & Guelff, *supra* note 94, at 512.

112. *See id.*

113. Ralph Peters, New Glory: Expanding America's Global Supremacy 155 (2005) ("No matter how brutal their actions or unrealistic their hopes, their common intent was to . . . gain a people's independence or to force their ideology on society.").

114. Christopher Greenwood, *Terrorism and Humanitarian Law: The Debate over API*, 19 Isr. Y.B. Hum. Rts. 187, 203–04 (1989); George H. Aldrich, *New Life for the Laws of War*, 75 Am. J. Int'l L. 764 (1983).

115. Protocol I, *supra* note 2, at art. 43, para. 1. This provision does contain a moderate victory for the Third World states that sought expanded legal protections through Protocol I in that the government need not be recognized by the opposing state party in order for its forces to achieve combatant status.

116. Yoram Dinstein, *Unlawful Combatants*, 32 Isr. Y.B. Hum. Rts. 247, 248 (2002).

117. International Commission of the Red Cross, Commentary on the Additional Protocols of 8 June 1977 to the Geneva Conventions of 12 August 1949, 514 (Yves Sandoz et al. eds., 1987) (emphasis added) [hereinafter ICRC Commentary on Protocols].

118. *Id.* at 510.

119. Protocol I, *supra* note 2, at art. 43, para. 2 ("Members of the armed forces of a Party to a conflict (other than medical personnel and chaplains . . .) are combatants, that is to say, they have the right to participate directly in hostilities.").

120. *See id.* at art. 44, para. 6 (discussing the status of combatants and prisoners of war) ("This Article is without prejudice to the right of any person to be a prisoner of war pursuant to Article 4 of the Third Convention.").

121. ICRC Commentary on Protocols, *supra* note 117, at 522.

122. Protocol I, *supra* note 2, at art. 51, para. 3.

123. *See id.* at art. 50, para. 1 (defining civilian in a way that excludes all definitions in art. 43 of Protocol I and Article 4 of the Third Convention). At the same time that an individual engaged in combat is not a civilian, however, this individual's conduct must also meet certain conditions to qualify him or her for prisoner of war status, if captured. *See id.* at art. 44, para. 3 (specifying guidelines of combatant conduct that, if met, will qualify one for prisoner of war status, if captured).

124. *Id.* at art. 45, para. 3.

125. *Id.*

126. Letter of Transmittal from President Ronald Reagan, Protocol II Additional to the 1949 Geneva Conventions and Relating to the Protection of Victims of Noninternational Armed Conflicts, S. Treaty Doc. No. 2, 100th Cong., 1st Sess., III (1987), *reprinted in* 81 Am. J. Int'l L. 910, 911 (1987) [hereinafter Reagan Protocols Letter of Transmittal].

127. *Id.*; *see also* Marco Sassoli & Antoine Bouvier, How Does Law Protect in War? 603, 604 (Int'l Comm. of the Red Cross, 1999) (discussing flaws in the Protocol, justifying it should not be forwarded to the Senate for consideration).

128. *See* Reagan Protocols Letter of Transmittal, *supra* note 126.

129. Abraham D. Sofaer, *The Rationale for the United States Decision*, 82 Am. J. Int'l L. 784, 787 (1988).

130. *Id.* at 785–86.

131. *Id.* at 784–86.

132. Christopher Greenwood, Essays on War in International Law 206 (2006). Apart from the victories in Article 1(4) and Article 44, Third World states also secured a provision that banned mercenaries from participating in armed conflict. Protocol I, *supra* note 2, at art. 47.

133. Best, *supra* note 72, at 406, 415–16.

134. *Id.* at 486.

135. Sofaer, *supra* note 129, at 786.

136. Aldrich, *supra* note 110, at 10: "Finally, it should be obvious that neither the provisions of Article 1, paragraph 4, nor those of Article 44, nor those of the two in combination provide any solace or support for terrorists. Failure by combatants to distinguish themselves from the civilian population throughout their military operations is a punishable offense. Terrorist acts are all punishable crimes, including attacks on civilians, the taking of hostages, and disguised, perfidious attacks on

military personnel, whether committed by combatants or by noncombatants, and whether the perpetrator is entitled to POW status or not. Assertions that ratification of Protocol I would give aid to, or enhance the status of, the PLO or of any terrorist group are totally unfounded. That such assertions should have been made by a President of the United States and those who advised him is regrettable."

137. Reagan Protocols Letter of Transmittal, *supra* note 126, at 911.

138. *Id.*

139. Protocol I, Argentina: Interpretive Declarations Made at the Time of Accession, Nov. 26, 1986, *available at* www.icrc.org/ihl.nsf/NORM/1F3EE768E1F92B5FC1256402003FB24B?OpenDocument.

140. Reagan Protocols Letter of Transmittal, *supra* note 126, at 911.

141. *Id.* at 910.

142. Aldrich, *supra* note 110, at 2.

143. GREENWOOD, *supra* note 132, at 217.

144. Reagan Protocols Letter of Transmittal, *supra* note 126, at 911.

145. *Id.* at 911–12.

146. Aldrich, *supra* note 110, at 2–3: "The only contentious issue at that time within the U.S. Government was whether we should reserve certain rights of reprisal that would otherwise be prohibited by the Protocol. When I left Washington in May 1981, the ultimate submission of Protocol I to the Senate for advice and consent to ratification seemed merely a matter of time. It also seemed entirely probable that, like the 1949 Geneva Conventions, Protocol I would eventually achieve nearly universal acceptance, with only a few exceptions."

147. *See* Theodor Meron, *The Time Has Come for the United States to Ratify Geneva Protocol I*, 88 AM. J. INT'L L. 678, 680–81 (1994) (explaining that although some NATO members shared U.S. concerns with Protocol I, they felt it was not fundamentally flawed).

148. *Id.* at 680–81.

149. *See id.* at 681 (stating that NATO allies produced interpretive statements and reservations limiting the Protocol).

150. *See* Hans-Peter Gasser, *An Appeal for Ratification by the United States*, 81 AM. J. INT'L L. 912, 920–21 (1987) (providing a description of how various nations issued understandings to provisions of Article 44).

151. International Committee of the Red Cross, International Humanitarian Law—State Parties/Signatories, *available at* www.icrc.org/ihl.nsf/WebSign?ReadForm&id=470&ps=P#ratif. With the caveat that though the Swiss government received a letter on June 21, 1989 to the effect that the Executive Committee of the Palestine Liberation Organization had decided on

May 4, 1989, "to adhere to the Four Geneva Conventions of August 12, 1949, and the two Protocols additional thereto," the Swiss Federal Council was not in a position to decide whether the letter constituted an instrument of accession "due to the uncertainty within the international community as to the existence or non-existence of a State of Palestine." *Id.*

152. Julie Gaudreau, *The Reservations to the Protocols Additional to the Geneva Conventions for the Protection of War Victims*, 849 INT'L REV. RED CROSS 143 (2003).

153. Ratification of Protocol I by the United Kingdom of Great Britain and Northern Ireland, Jan. 29, 1998, 2020 U.N.T.S. 75, 76–77.

154. *See* Rene Kosirnik, *The 1977 Protocols: A Landmark in the Development of International Humanitarian Law*, 320 INT'L REV. RED CROSS 483 (1997), *available at* www.cicr.org/web/eng/siteeng0.nsf/htmlall/57jnuz?opendocument.

155. *See* Aldrich, *supra* note 110, at 2.

156. *See* ICRC Commentary on Protocols, *supra* note 117, at 530 n.43 (providing a statement by the United Kingdom and a summary of considerations by other countries).

157. *See id.* at 526 n.21 (explaining that one of the *levée en masse* provisions requires members of a *levée en masse* to act in accordance with the laws and customs of war in their operations).

158. *Id.* at 529–31.

159. *See id.*

160. *See* Aldrich, *supra* note 110, at 10.

161. Ratification of Protocol I by Australia, June 21, 1991, 1642 U.N.T.S. 473 ("It is the understanding of Australia that in relation to Article 44, the situation described in the second sentence of paragraph 3 can exist only in occupied territory or in armed conflicts covered by paragraph 4 of Article 1. Australia will interpret the word 'deployment' in paragraph 3(b) of the Article as meaning any movement towards a place from which an attack is to be launched. It will interpret the words 'visible to the adversary' in the same paragraph as including visible with the aid of binoculars, or by infra-red or image intensification devices.").

162. Ratification of Protocol I by Japan, Aug. 31, 2004, 2283 U.N.T.S. 265 ("The Government of Japan declares that it is its understanding that the situation described in the second sentence of paragraph 3 of Article 44 can exist only in occupied territory or in armed conflicts covered by paragraph 4 of Article 1. The Government of Japan also declares that the term 'deployment' in paragraph 3 (b) of Article 44 is interpreted as meaning any movement towards a place from which an attack is to be launched.").

163. Ratification of Protocol I by South Korea, Jan. 15, 1982, 1271 U.N.T.S. 408 ("In relation to Article 44

of Protocol I, the situation described in the second sentence of paragraph 3 of the Article can exist only in occupied territory or in armed conflicts covered by paragraph 4 of Article 1, and the Government of the Republic of Korea will interpret the word deployment in paragraph 3 (b) of the Article as meaning any movement towards a place from which an attack is to be launched.").

164. Ratification of Protocol I by New Zealand, Feb. 8, 1988, 1499 U.N.T.S. 358 ("The government of New Zealand will interpret the word 'deployment' in paragraph 3 (b) of the Article as meaning any movement towards a place from which an attack is to be launched. It will interpret the words 'visible to the adversary' in the same paragraph as including visible with the aid of any form of surveillance, electronic or otherwise, available to help keep a member of the armed forces of the adversary under observation.").

165. *Compare* Ratification of Protocol I by the United Kingdom of Great Britain and Northern Ireland, *supra* note 153, *with* Ratification of Protocol I by Australia, *supra* note 161, Ratification of Protocol I by Japan, *supra* note 162, Ratification of Protocol I by South Korea, *supra* note 163, *and* Ratification of Protocol I by New Zealand, *supra* note 164.

166. *See, e.g.*, Gasser, *supra* note 150.

167. *Id.* at 924.

168. Reagan Protocols Letter of Transmittal, *supra* note 126, at 912.

169. *See* Sofaer, *supra* note 129, at 784 (restating the ICRC's belief that the U.S. position on Protocol I was politically motivated).

170. *See* Organization of American States, Promotion and Respect for International Humanitarian Law, June 5, 2001, O.A.S.T.S. AG/RES. 1771 (stating that for international treaties like Protocol I to work, all the states involved have to consent).

171. U.N. GAOR, 61st Sess., 8th mtg., para. 67, U.N. Doc. A/C.6/61/SR.8 (Nov. 15, 2006).

172. G.A. Res. 66/1, para. 2, U.N. Doc. A/C.6/61/L.9 (Nov. 2, 2006).

173. Organization of American States, *supra* note 170; Ceta Noland, Legal Counsel, Permanent Mission of the Kingdom of the Netherlands, EU Presidency Statement: Status of Protocols Additional to the Geneva Conventions (Oct. 18, 2006), *available at* www.europa-eu-un.org/articles/en/ article_3902_en.htm.

174. SEYMOUR MARTIN LIPSET, AMERICAN EXCEPTIONALISM: A DOUBLE-EDGED SWORD 18 (1996); *see also* Harold Hongju Koh, *On American Exceptionalism*, 55 STAN. L. REV. 1479, 1481 n.4 (2003) (describing historic basis of American exceptionalism).

175. George Washington, *Farewell Address*, in GEORGE WASHINGTON: WRITINGS 962, 974 (John Rhodehamel ed., 1997) (concluding that the primary interests of Europe would cause "frequent controversies" and that "it must be unwise in us to implicate ourselves, by artificial ties, in the ordinary vicissitudes of her politics or the ordinary combinations and collisions of her friendships or enmities").

176. *See, e.g.*, Stephen Gardbaum, *The Myth and the Reality of American Constitutional Exceptionalism*, 107 MICH. L. REV. 391 (2008); MICHAEL IGNATIEFF, THE LESSER EVIL: POLITICAL ETHICS IN AN AGE OF TERROR (2004). PETER HUCHTHAUSEN, AMERICA'S SPLENDID LITTLE WARS: A SHORT HISTORY OF U.S. MILITARY ENGAGEMENTS, 1975–2000 (2003).

177. Sabrina Safrin, *The Un-Exceptionalism of U.S. Exceptionalism*, 41 VAND. J. TRANSNAT'L L. 1307, 1309–10 (2008).

178. *Id.* at 1310–14.

179. *Id.* at 1310; *see also* Michael Ignatieff, *Introduction: American Exceptionalism and Human Rights*, in AMERICAN EXCEPTIONALISM AND HUMAN RIGHTS 1, 4–5 (Michael Ignatieff ed., 2005); Koh, *supra* note 174, at 1485–86. As an example of the difficulties posed by the federalist structure of our Republic with regard to multilateral instruments, the much-criticized U.S. refusal to join the Convention on the Rights of the Child can be rationally explained by examining the Convention's applicability to numerous issues usually left to the states. These include many aspects of family law and juvenile justice, such as family separation and reunification, child custody, and child abuse and neglect. Lainie Rutkow & Joshua T. Lozman, *Suffer the Children?: A Call for United States Ratification of the United Nations Convention on the Rights of the Child*, 19 HARV. HUM. RTS. J. 161, 175–77 (2006).

180. *See generally* Margaret E. McGuinness, *Sanchez-Llamas, American Human Rights Exceptionalism and the VCCR Norm Portal*, 11 LEWIS & CLARK L. REV. 47 (2007) (explaining how "judges—implicitly and explicitly—respond to arguments for and against exceptionalism").

181. Martin Scheinin, *Reservations by States Under The International Covenant on Civil and Political Rights and Its Optional Protocols, and the Practice of the Human Rights Committee*, in RESERVATIONS TO THE HUMAN RIGHTS TREATIES AND THE VIENNA CONVENTION REGIME: CONFLICT, HARMONY, OR RECONCILIATION 41, 46 (Ineta Ziemele ed., 2004) (noting that the U.S. report to the Human Rights Committee came some six months following the adoption of its General Comment 24 and was, therefore, "the first test for the practical application of the Committee's approach as presented in the General Comment").

182. *Report of the Human Rights Committee*, U.N. Doc. CCPR/C/79/Add.50, *reprinted in* Human Rights Committee, Annual Report of the Human Rights Committee, para. 279, U.N. Doc. A/50/40 (Oct. 3, 1995).

183. Koh, *supra* note 174, at 1484–85.

184. *Id.* at 1485–87.

185. On December 31, 2000, the last day that the Rome Statute was open for signature, Ambassador David Scheffer signed the Rome Statute of the International Criminal Court, but President Clinton's signing statement expressed the U.S. resistance to accession as follows: "In signing, however, we are not abandoning our concerns about significant flaws in the treaty. In particular, we are concerned that when the court comes into existence, it will not only exercise authority over personnel of states that have ratified the treaty but also claim jurisdiction over personnel of states that have not. . . . Given these concerns, I will not, and do not recommend that my successor, submit the treaty to the Senate for advice and consent until our fundamental concerns are satisfied." President Clinton, *Statement on the Rome Treaty on the International Criminal Court*, 37 WEEKLY COMP. PRES. DOC. 4 (Jan. 8, 2001), *reprinted in* SEAN D. MURPHY, UNITED STATES PRACTICE IN INTERNATIONAL LAW, VOLUME 1: 1999–2001 381–85 (2002).

186. *See, e.g.*, Jonathan Weisman, *Ex-Clinton Aides Admit Kyoto Treaty Flawed*, USA TODAY, June 11, 2001, at 7A.

187. JANET R. HUNTER & ZACHARY ALDEN SMITH, PROTECTING OUR ENVIRONMENT: LESSONS FROM THE EUROPEAN UNION 101 (2005); *see also* Reagan Protocols Letter of Transmittal, *supra* note 126 (arguing that "Protocol I is fundamentally and irreconcilably flawed").

188. *See., e.g.*, Rome Statute, *supra* note 48, at art. 120 (providing that "No reservations may be made to this Statute").

189. The meeting resulted in the Convention on the Prohibition of the Use, Stockpiling, Production and Transfer of Anti-Personnel Mines and on their Destruction, Mar. 1, 1999, 2056 U.N.T.S. 211 [hereinafter Ottawa Convention].

190. *See* Andrew C. S. Efaw, *The United States Refusal to Ban Landmines: The Intersection Between Tactics, Strategy, Policy, and International Law*, 159 MIL. L. REV. 87, 98–102 (1999) (discussing the dilemma of "balancing military needs against humanitarian consideration" and mentioning the potential benefit of U.S. landmines on the demilitarized zone of the Korean peninsula).

191. *Id.* at 149–51.

192. Ottawa Convention, *supra* note 189, at art. 19.

193. Efaw, *supra* note 190, at 101; Phillip Bobbit, *American Exceptionalism: The Exception Proves the Rule*, 3 U. ST. THOMAS L. J. 328, 330 (2005) (concluding that "No realistic conventional force could be protected from such a huge North Korean force without mines."); *National Defense Authorization Act for Fiscal Year 1999: Hearing Before the H. Comm. on National Security*, 105th

Cong. (1998) (statement of Gen. Henry H. Shelton, Chairman, Joint Chiefs of Staff), *available at* www.globalsecurity.org/military/library/congress/1998_hr/2-5-98shelton.htm (testifying that "In Korea . . . where we stand face-to-face with one of the largest hostile armies in the world, we rely upon anti-personnel landmines to protect our troops").

194. *See* Press Release, The White House, Office of the Press Secretary, Clinton Remarks on Comprehensive Test Ban Treaty (Oct. 6, 1999), *available at* www.fas.org/nuke/control/ctbt/news/991006-ctbt-usia1.htm.

195. Baxter, *supra* note 61, at 328.

196. *See* Michael J. Matheson, *The Opinion of the International Court of Justice on the Threat or Use of Nuclear Weapons*, 91 AM. J. INT'L. L. 417, 422 (1997) ("the test of what is an arbitrary deprivation of life, however, fails to be determined by the applicable lex specialis, namely, the law applicable in armed conflict which is designed to regulate the conduct of hostilities"); *see also* Osman Bin Haji Mohamed Ali and Another Appellant and the Public Prosecutor, (1969) 1 Law Rep. 430 (P.C.) (appeal taken from the Fed. Ct. of Malay), *reprinted in* MARCO SASSOLI & ANTOINE BOUVIER, HOW DOES LAW PROTECT IN WAR? 767, 771–73 (Int'l Comm. of the Red Cross, 1999) (rejecting combatant status for members of the Indonesian armed forces who failed to comply with the four criteria laid out in Article 4 of the Geneva Convention).

197. *See* Matheson, *supra* note 196, at 421–22 (the United States argued that the law of armed conflict, rather than peacetime human rights law, should determine what constitutes an "'arbitrary' deprivation of life").

198. *See* GREENWOOD, *supra* note 132, at 209 (stating that Protocol I is firmly embedded in international law).

199. *Id.* at 202.

200. *See id.* (quoting a U.S. government official calling Protocol I "law in the service of terror"); *see also* Feith, *supra* note 2 (accusing the U.N. General Assembly of issuing a "pro-terrorist treaty masquerading as humanitarian law").

201. *See* Feith, *supra* note 2 (discussing Western European representatives' opposition to the Additional Protocols during the Diplomatic Conference debate).

202. This dualistic view of the law was privately expressed by the International Committee of the Red Cross and publicly expounded by a number of commentators on the law of armed conflict. Article 48 of Protocol I, *supra* note 2, reflects this simple dualism with the basic rule that parties to the conflict must distinguish "at all times" between civilians and protected civilian objects and "shall direct their operations only against military objectives."

203. Osama bin Laden has made more than fifty declarations of war against the United States (summary of

statements on file with author). In the official fatwa signed by bin Laden and four others on February 23, 1998, THE AL QAEDA READER 13 (Raymond Ibrahim, ed. and trans., 2007), he declared his objective:

The ruling to kill the Americans and their allies— civilians and military—is an individual duty for every Muslim who can do it in any country in which it is possible to do it, in order to liberate the al-Aqsa Mosque and the holy mosque [Mecca] from their grip, and in order for their armies to move out of all the lands of Islam, defeated and unable to threaten any Muslim. This is in accordance with the words of Almighty God, "and fight the pagans all together as they fight you all together," and "fight them until there is no more tumult or oppression, and there prevail justice and faith in God."

This is in addition to the words of Almighty God: "And why should ye not fight in the cause of God and of those who, being weak, are ill-treated (and oppressed)?—women and children, whose cry is: 'Our Lord, rescue us from this town, whose people are oppressors; and raise for us from thee one who will help!'"

We—with God's help—call on every Muslim who believes in God and wishes to be rewarded to comply with God's order to kill the Americans and plunder their money wherever and whenever they find it. We also call on Muslim ulema, leaders, youths, and soldiers to launch the raid on Satan's U.S. troops and the devil's supporters allying with them, and to displace those who are behind them so that they may learn a lesson.

204. *See Prosecutor v. Tadić*, Case No. IT-94–1, Decision on the Defence Motion for Interlocutory Appeal on Jurisdiction, para. 70 (Oct. 2, 1995) ("an armed conflict exists whenever there is a resort to armed force between States or protracted armed violence between governmental authorities and organized armed groups or between such groups within a State").

205. Lord Robertson, NATO Secretary General, Statement on September 11 Attacks (Oct. 2, 2001), *available at* www.nato.int/docu/speech/2001/s011002a .htm (announcing NATO's determination that the September 11 attack "shall therefore be regarded as an action covered by Article 5 of the Washington Treaty, which states that an armed attack on one or more of the Allies in Europe or North America shall be considered an attack against them all").

206. The law of armed conflict provides that lawful attacks may only be directed at military objectives (which includes enemy combatants). Civilians may not be deliberately attacked unless they directly participate in hostilities. *See* Protocol I, *supra* note 2, at art. 51, paras. 2–3. Celebrated in international law as the principle of distinction, the president of the ICRC opined that this principle is "crucial." Dr. Jakob Kellenberger, International Humanitarian Law at the Beginning of the 21st Century, The Two Additional Protocols to the Geneva Conventions: 25 Years Later—Challenges and Prospects, Statement at the 26th Round Table in San Remo on the Current Problems of International Humanitarian Law (Sept. 5, 2002), *available at* www.icrc.org/Web/Eng/siteeng0.nsf/iwpList74/EFC5A 1C8D8DD70B9C1256C36002EFC 1E.

207. *See generally* Jack M. Beard, *America's New War on Terror: The Case for Self-Defense Under International Law*, 25 HARV. J. L. & PUB. POL'Y 559, 559–60 (2002).

208. 2 Trial of the Major War Criminals Before the International Military Tribunal 153–54 (1947).

209. *See* Martha Crenshaw, *The Psychology of Terrorism: An Agenda for the 21st Century*, 21 POL. PSYCHOL. 405, 411 (2000) (describing "old" terrorism as it compares to "new" terrorism).

210. *Id.*; *see also* Michael J. Stevens, *What Is Terrorism and Can Psychology Do Anything to Prevent It?* 23 BEHAV. SCI. & L. 507, 508 (2005) (discussing the psychology of today's terrorism).

211. Stevens, *supra* note 210, at 517–18.

212. *See generally* William L. Waugh Jr. & Richard T. Sylves, *Organizing the War on Terrorism*, 62 PUB. ADMIN. REV. 145 (2002) (discussing the United States' efforts to redefine the relationship between law enforcement and national security agencies after September 11).

213. *See, e.g., Her Majesty the Queen v. Mohammed Momin Khawaja*, [2008] Ontario Superior Court of Justice 04-G30282; *see also* CrimA 6659/06, 1757/07, 8228/07, 3261/08, *A & B v. State of Israel* [2008]; *Munaf v. Geren*, 128 S.Ct. 2207, 553 U.S. (June 12, 2008); *The Military Prosecutor v. Omar Mahmud Kassem and Others*, 41 I.L.R. 470 (1971) (Israeli Military Court, Ramallah, April 13, 1969), *reprinted in* 60 HOWARD LEVIE, DOCUMENTS ON PRISONERS OF WAR, NAVAL WAR COL. INT. L. STUD. 771, 780 (1979) (rejecting the claim of combatant immunity raised by a member of the "Organization of the Popular Front for the Liberation of Palestine"); Osman Bin Haji Mohamed Ali and Another Appellant and the Public Prosecutor, *supra* note 196, at 767 (rejecting combatant status for members of the Indonesian armed forces who failed to comply with the provisions of Article 4 of the Geneva Conventions).

214. *See* George H. Aldrich, *The Taliban, Al Qaeda and the Determination of Illegal Combatants*, 96 AM. J. INT'L L. 891, 893 (Oct. 2002) ("Al Qaeda does not in any respect resemble a state, is not a subject of international law, and lacks international legal personality."). With respect to terrorists in the post-9/11 era, the Legal Advisor of the U.S. State Department mirrored the concerns voiced by previous administrations in the context of Protocol I by writing that "The purposes of the law of armed conflict are not advanced by granting illegitimate fighters immunity for their belligerent acts, for that

would undermine the law's fundamental purpose, bring the entire body of law into disrepute, and strip it of credibility. The positive incentives of the existing normative system require that soldiers follow the rules and, most importantly, distinguish combatants from civilians. To recognize terrorists as lawful combatants would upend the entire system and cause predictably grim humanitarian consequences." William H. Taft, *The Law of Armed Conflict After 9/11: Some Salient Features*, 28 YALE J. INT'L L. 319, 321 (2003).

215. Resolution on the Detainees in Guantanamo Bay, EUR. PARL. DOC. B5–0066 (2002) [hereinafter European Parliament Resolution].

216. Protocol I, *supra* note 2, at art. 52, para. 2.

217. European Parliament Resolution, *supra* note 215.

218. Baxter, *supra* note 61, at 343 ("The correct legal formulation is, it is submitted, that armed and unarmed hostilities, wherever occurring, committed by persons other than those entitled to be treated as prisoners of war or peaceful civilians merely deprive such individuals of a protection they might otherwise enjoy under international law and place them virtually at the power of the enemy. 'Unlawful belligerency' is actually 'unprivileged belligerency.'").

219. *See, e.g.*, Gilbert Guillaume, *Terrorism and International Law*, 53 INT'L. COMP. L. Q. 537, 547 (2004) (discussing the same issue and focusing on the status of captured terrorists).

220. Reservations to the Convention on the Prevention and Punishment of the Crime of Genocide, Advisory Opinion, 1951 I.C.J. 23 (May 28) ("The objects of such a convention must also be considered. The Convention was manifestly adopted for a purely humanitarian and civilizing purpose. It is indeed difficult to imagine a convention that might have this dual character to a greater degree, since its object on the one hand is to safeguard the very existence of certain human groups and on the other to confirm and endorse the most elementary principles of morality.").

221. *See, e.g.*, Terrorism Financing Convention, *supra* note 7; Terrorist Bombing Convention, *supra* note 21.

222. The Convention entered into force on April 10, 2002 in accordance with Article 26, which states:

1. This Convention shall enter into force on the thirtieth day following the date of the deposit of the twenty-second instrument of ratification, acceptance, approval or accession with the Secretary-General of the United Nations.

2. For each State ratifying, accepting, approving or acceding to the Convention after the deposit of the twenty-second instrument of ratification, acceptance, approval or accession, the Convention shall enter into force on the thirtieth day after deposit by such State of its instrument of ratification, acceptance, approval or accession.

Terrorism Financing Convention, *supra* note 7. The Convention entered into force for the United States on July 25, 2002, in accordance with Article 26, cited above. The United States deposited its instrument of ratification on June 25, 2002; the same day President Bush signed the Convention's implementing legislation, 18 U.S.C. § 2339C, into law. *See* Terrorist Bombings Convention Implementation Act of 2002, H.R. 3275, 107th Cong. (2d Sess. 2002) ("An Act to implement . . . the International Convention of the Suppression of the Financing of Terrorism, to combat terrorism and defend the Nation against terrorist acts").

223. *See* Terrorist Bombing Convention, *supra* note 21 (requiring twenty-two states to have ratified, accepted, approved, or acceded to the Convention for the treaty to enter into force).

224. *See, e.g.*, Crenshaw, *supra* note 13 and accompanying text.

225. *See, e.g.*, International Convention for the Suppression of the Financing of Terrorism, Argentina Communication Concerning the Declaration Made by Jordan Upon Ratification, Oct. 10, 2005, C.N.1034.2005. TREATIES-35 [hereinafter Argentina Communication Concerning Jordan] (providing an example of support for a bright-line declaration that all terrorist acts are criminal, regardless of motives).

226. *See, e.g.*, Terrorism Financing Convention, *supra* note 6, at art. 4.

227. *See, e.g.*, Argentina Communication Concerning Jordan, *supra* note 225.

228. *See* Lea Brilmayer & Geoffrey Chepiga, *Ownership or Use? Civilian Property Interests in International Humanitarian Law*, 49 HARV. INT'L. L. J. 413, 419 (2008) (stating that the protection of the civilian person and civilian property are principles "firmly embedded in modern international humanitarian law").

229. *See* Reagan Protocols Letter of Transmittal, *supra* note 126 (describing the need to distinguish international and noninternational conflicts in objective terms and avoid subjective terms that are ill defined and threaten to politicize humanitarian law).

230. Terrorist Financing Convention, *supra* note 7, at art. 2. The Annex referenced in subpart (a) sets forth the entire universe of applicable terrorist conventions: 1. Convention for the Suppression of Unlawful Seizure of Aircraft, 2. Convention for the Suppression of Unlawful Acts against the Safety of Civil Aviation, 3. Convention on the Prevention and Punishment of Crimes against Internationally Protected Persons, including Diplomatic Agents, 4. International Convention against the Taking of Hostages, 5. Convention on the Physical Protection of Nuclear Material, 6. Protocol for the Suppression of Unlawful Acts of Violence at Airports Serving International Civil Aviation, supplementary to the Convention

for the Suppression of Unlawful Acts against the Safety of Civil Aviation, 7. Convention for the Suppression of Unlawful Acts against the Safety of Maritime Navigation, 8. Protocol for the Suppression of Unlawful Acts against the Safety of Fixed Platforms located on the Continental Shelf, and 9. International Convention for the Suppression of Terrorist Bombings. *Id.* at annex.

231. The Convention adopts a broad construction of personal and subject-matter jurisdiction. Terrorism Financing Convention, *supra* note 7, at art. 7, para 2.

232. *See, e.g., id.* at art. 5, para. 1 ("Each State Party, in accordance with its domestic legal principles, shall take the necessary measures to enable a legal entity located in its territory or organized under its laws to be held liable when a person responsible for the management or control of that legal entity has, in that capacity, committed an offence set forth in article 2. Such liability may be criminal, civil or administrative.").

233. *See, e.g., id.* at art. 5, para. 3 ("Each State Party shall ensure, in particular, that legal entities liable in accordance with paragraph 1 above are subject to effective, proportionate and dissuasive criminal, civil or administrative sanctions. Such sanctions may include monetary sanctions.").

234. *Id.* at art. 14.

235. *Id.* at art. 6.

236. *Id.*

237. Vienna Convention on the Law of Treaties, art. 2, para. 1(d), May 23, 1969, 1155 U.N.T.S. 331.

238. International Convention for the Suppression of the Financing of Terrorism, Egypt: Ratification, Mar. 1, 2005, C.N.176.2005.TREATIES-3 [hereinafter Egypt Ratification].

239. Terrorism Financing Convention, *supra* note 7, at art. 3.

240. *See* Egypt Ratification, *supra* note 238 (limiting the definition of terrorist acts).

241. *See* UN Treaty Collection, *available at* http://treaties.un.org/Pages/ViewDetails.aspx?src=UNTSONLINE&tabid=2&mtdsg_no=XVIII-11&chapter=18&lang=en (listing the objecting states).

242. International Convention for the Suppression of Financing of Terrorism, Germany: Objection with Regard to the Explanatory Declaration Made by Egypt upon Ratification, Aug. 16, 2005, C.N.677.2005.TREATIES-24; *see* UN Treaty Collection, *supra* note 241.

243. UN Treaty Collection, *supra* note 241.

244. International Convention for the Suppression of the Financing of Terrorism, Argentina: Communication Concerning the Explanatory Declaration Made by Egypt upon Ratification, Aug. 22, 2005, C.N.1034.2005.TREATIES-35.

245. International Convention for the Suppression of the Financing of Terrorism, Ireland: Objection Relating to the Explanatory Declaration Made by Egypt

upon Ratification, June 23, 2006, C.N.555.2006.TREATIES-21.

246. *See* International Convention for the Suppression of the Financing of Terrorism, Syrian Arab Republic: Accession, Apr. 24, 2005, C.N.326.2005.TREATIES-6 [hereinafter Syrian Accession] (stating reservations similar to Egypt's); International Convention for the Suppression of Financing of Terrorism, Jordan: Ratification, Aug. 28, 2003, C.N.910.2003.TREATIES-32 [hereinafter Jordanian Accession] (stating reservations similar to Egypt's).

247. Syrian Accession, *supra* note 246.

248. *See* UN Treaty Collection, *supra* note 241.

249. Jordanian Accession, *supra* note 246.

250. *See* UN Treaty Collection, *supra* note 241.

251. Protocol I, *supra* note 2.

252. Terrorist Bombing Convention, *supra* note 21, at art. 2.

253. *Id.* at preamble.

254. *See id.*

255. *Id.* at art. 19(2).

256. Protocol I, *supra* note 2, at art. 51(2); Protocol II, *supra* note 70, at art. 13, para. 2.

257. *Prosecutor v. Galic*, Case No. IT-98–29-T, Judgment and Opinion, para. 98 (Dec. 5 2003), *available at* www.icty.org/x/cases/galic/tjug/en/gal-tj031205e.pdf.

258. ICRC Commentary on Protocols, *supra* note 117, at 1453.

259. *Prosecutor v. Alex Tamba Brima, et al.*, Case No. SCSL-2004–16-A, para. 70 (Feb. 22, 2008), *available at* www.sc-sl.org/CASES/ArmedForcesRevolutionaryCouncilAFRCComplete/AFRC Judgment/tabid/173/Default.aspx.

260. *The Prosecutor v. Radovan Karadzic*, Case No. IT-95–5, Amended Indictment, paras. 44–52 (Feb. 18, 2009), *available at* www.icty.org/x/cases/karadzic/ind/en/090218.pdf.

261. International Convention for the Suppression of Terrorist Bombings, Egypt: Ratification, Aug. 9, 2005, C.N.6 34.2005 TREATIES-1. The following articulation was made by Egypt at the time of ratification of the Terrorist Bombing Convention:

1. The Government of the Arab Republic of Egypt declares that it shall be bound by article 6, paragraph 5, of the Convention to the extent that the national legislation of States Parties is not incompatible with the relevant norms and principles of international law.

2. The Government of the Arab Republic of Egypt declares that it shall be bound by article 19, paragraph 2, of the Convention to the extent that the armed forces of a State, in the exercise of their duties, do not violate the norms and principles of international law.

262. International Convention for the Suppression of Terrorist Bombings, United Kingdom of Great Britain and Northern Ireland: Objection to the Reservation

Made by Egypt Upon Ratification, Aug. 3, 2006, C.N.655.2006.TREATIES-11.

263. International Convention for the Suppression of Terrorist Bombings, France: Objection to the Reservation Made by Egypt upon Ratification, Aug. 15, 2006, C.N.667.2006.TREATIES-13.

264. Geneva Convention Relative to the Treatment of Prisoners of War, *supra* note 24, at art. 4.

265. *See id.* at art. 85 (relating to prisoners of war who are prosecutable under the laws of the detaining authority).

266. Official Statement, International Committee of the Red Cross, The Relevance of IHL in the Context of Terrorism (Jul. 21, 2005), *available at* www.icrc.org/web/eng/siteeng0.nsf/html/terrorism-ihl-210705.

267. *See, e.g.*, Terrorist Financing Convention, *supra* note 7, at art. 6 (requiring acceding states to "adopt such measures as may be necessary, including, where appropriate, domestic legislation, to ensure that criminal acts within the scope of this Convention are under no circumstances justifiable by considerations of a political, philosophical, ideological, racial, ethnic, religious or other similar nature").

268. Coady, *supra* note 12, at 47 (stating that the "ism" in terrorism indicates "no more than a relatively systematic nature of a method or a tactic"; it is not itself an ideology).

269. *See, e.g.*, Terrorist Bombing Convention, *supra* note 21, at art. 2 (providing an example of the codification of state practice in opposition to terrorist acts post-1977).

270. *See, e.g.*, *Kasem*, 41 I.L.R. 470 (rejecting the claim of combatant immunity raised by a member of the "Organization of the Popular Front for the Liberation of Palestine"); *see generally* Aldrich, *supra* note 110.

271. BEN SAUL, DEFINING TERRORISM IN INTERNATIONAL LAW 76 (2006) (stating that "Protocol I provisions mean little as they have never been applied or accepted").

272. *See, e.g.*, Stone, *supra* note 27, at 549.

273. II OPPENHEIM'S INTERNATIONAL LAW, *supra* note 45, at 574 ("Private individuals who take up arms and commit hostilities against the enemy do not enjoy the privileges of armed forces, and the enemy has, according to a customary rule of International Law, the right to treat such individuals as war criminals.").

274. *See* W. Michael Reisman, *supra* note 39, at 5–6 (stating that military codes and manuals across the planet communicate the "gravity and importance" of such behavioral norms).

275. Geneva Convention Relative to the Treatment of Prisoners of War, *supra* note 24, at art. 1.

276. JAGK-CM 302791 (1946), *reprinted in* 8 BULL. OF THE JUDGE ADVOCATE GENERAL OF THE ARMY 262 (Sept.–Oct. 1946).

PART EIGHT

POSTCOLONIALISM

23

Terrorism as Postcolonialism

THOMAS R. O'CONNOR

In recent years a new, critical field of academic study has come about that mixes scholarly activism[1] with a strong dose of historical revisionism (e.g., Columbus never really "discovered" America). No, it's not Marxism nor is it the antiglobalization movement; rather it's *post*colonialism, and it's the hottest thing right now for any aspiring scholar in global or international studies. Once relegated to a backseat role in the field of international relations along with the likes of feminist theory, postcolonialism has now emerged into its own (yet its practitioners make a big deal out of whether the prefix "post" ought to be hyphenated or not, and they are also self-critical about whether the prefix "post" ought to be used at all). The field hasn't really taken off in the United States yet (practitioners wonder why there's no American postcolonialism school), but it is quite popular in Europe, Asia, Australia, Africa, the Caribbean, and the Middle East. It's popular among the reparations crowd, and it's popular among terrorist apologists and sympathizers (and some terrorists, too) as an intellectual ideology for the causes of terrorism. However, in all fairness, it's a complex field of study that few people are able to master, so terrorists probably adopt "crude" versions of it. No less than the foremost public intellectual Noam Chomsky himself said he finds it hard to understand postcolonialism—ironic, seeing that postcolo-

nialism owes a deep debt of gratitude to structural linguistics, Chomsky's original field of study. Structural linguist postcolonialists seem to favor Ferdinand de Saussure, who, even though a structuralist, admitted that binary oppositions in words (e.g., sun/moon; man/woman; birth/death; black/white) did *not* represent extreme differences but only arbitrary signifiers in people's minds.

In this chapter, I'll do my level best to explain what postcolonialism is all about. However, what's here is *not* intended as some all-encompassing overview of the field. For that, Robert Young[2] is recommended or, better yet, John McLeod[3] for the absolute beginner. Also, I admit that opinions vary regarding the connections or interrelationships between terrorism and postcolonialism. Novel connections are not made easily, and in no way do I suggest that postcolonialists are terrorists, terrorist supporters, or anything like that. It may be that postcolonialism ends up making the world a happier, more peaceful place; but it is also possible that postcolonialism might become the dominant twenty-first-century terrorist ideology.

Consider for a moment the underlying assumption of postcolonialism that the great European colonial powers screwed up the world between the sixteenth and nineteenth centuries—Spain and Portugal in Latin America; Britain in the Middle East; the Dutch and French in Asia;

Belgium and everyone else in Africa. They left a mess behind. There's no denying that colonialism played a large role in making the world as it is today. Borders were drawn up arbitrarily, people were forced to become bilingual, natural resources and raw materials were severely drained, and the European powers often pitted brother against brother in their quest to bring civilization to the savages. Small wonder, then, why it's so easy to jump on the notion that terrorism is the latest aftermath of colonialism. Perhaps it's all too easy to embrace this idea. There must be something that explains all the academic window dressing.

Philosophical Contributors

Edward Said, internationally renowned Columbia University professor, practically invented the field of postcolonial studies as a subfield of critical international relations theory. We know that Said's book, *Orientalism*,[4] was quite influential in this regard, arguing there's no way to fully get rid of that curious stereotype that Asians are somehow exotic, devious, and untrustworthy. And, even though Said's book was about Asians, there's no escaping the fact that his ideas are quite popular in the world of Islam and especially among Islamic terrorists. The full framework of his ideas can be traced to other writings and comments,[5] and one might even want to go further back to include certain anticolonialist tracts by Frantz Fanon.[6] Fanon (perhaps the father of African terrorism) is the one who advocated violence for the sake of psychological well-being.

One might want to go even further back to the late nineteenth and early twentieth centuries, when philosophers like Søren Kierkegaard, Friedrich Nietzsche, and Jean-Paul Sartre laid the groundwork for modern existentialism (the idea that there is no such thing as objective truth). Then, there are the deconstructionist philosophers like Martin Heidegger, Ludwig Wittgenstein, and Jacques Derrida who are frequently cited by postcolonialists. Deconstruction (or deconstructivism) is the belief that there

are no superior lifestyles or methods for achieving fundamental truths or principles—that is, that all modern methods of learning (epistemology) are antiquated. Deconstruction is closely related to postmodernism, and the main postmodernist philosophers of relevance are Michael Foucault, Richard Rorty, and Jean Baudrillard. Postmodernism, for all practical purposes, is synonymous with something called poststructuralism, which is a type of historical revisionism that looks at some past event *not* in terms of how it was experienced by people at the time but rather in terms of how it can be interpreted now, in the present, by the reader, with the most important variable being the identity of the reader. An example would be the work by Terry Eagleton,[7] which argues that there is something sacred (and inherently dangerous) about terrorism, and it is always here to stay in society because throughout history people have always needed to give into sprees of reckless self-abandonment and orgies of unreason. Postcolonialism, drawing heavily from poststructuralism, claims to involve theories of identity politics that study various forms of ethnic nationalisms and religious conflicts while at the same time being committed to doing away with social injustices of all kinds by organizing regional resistance movements that happen to have self-liberation or self-abandonment effects. This sounds a lot like liberation theology, but it is more academic in that the whole point seems to be to create new avenues for theoretical exploration. Undoubtedly, it is esoteric, nontraditional philosophy.

Some comment on identity politics as a current manifestation might be in order. From the *Encyclopedia of Gay, Lesbian, Bisexual, Transgender, and Queer Culture*, identity politics refers to activism, politics, theorizing, and other activities based on the shared experiences of members of a specific social group (often relying on shared experiences of oppression) that is organized around identities based on gender, race, ethnicity, nationality, religion, and disability. The most important and revolutionary element of identity politics is the demand that oppressed

---

The Terrorism Connection with Postcolonialism

The terrorism connection is this: "the radical Islamist ideology that has motivated terror over the past decade must be seen in large measure as a manifestation of modern identity politics rather than of traditional Muslim culture." Those are the words of Francis Fukuyama,[1] an esteemed international relations professor at Johns Hopkins who also wrote in 1992 that multiculturalism was "the game at the end of history" that tried to ornament the late stages of liberal pluralism with ethnic food, colorful dress, and traces of distinctive historical traditions from other cultures. Regardless of what one thinks of Fukuyama's end-of-history thesis, his basic idea that Islamic terrorism may be feeding on a growing, self-perpetuated movement toward Muslim resentment and outrage over all things that do not give them special privileges is sound. For example, Muslim immigrant groups have demanded special exemptions from family laws that apply to everyone else in society. Muslim groups have also demanded the right to exclude non-Muslims from certain types of events, to challenge free speech in the name of religion, and to be sworn into court or political office with the Koran instead of the Bible, and in some cases they have advocated the replacement of American criminal law with Sharia law. Fukuyama is not the only one to point out things like this. Oliver Roy said pretty much the same thing,[2] and the process called Islamification of a host country by Muslim migrants is well known. Homegrown Islamic extremism, riots, protests, and terrorism can be traced to an underswelling of Muslim impatience with Islamification, and postcolonialism plays right into that.

NOTES

1. Francis Fukuyama, *Identity and Migration*, PROSPECT 131 (Feb. 2007).
2. OLIVER ROY, GLOBALIZED ISLAM (2006).

---

groups be recognized not *in spite* of their differences but specifically *because* of their differences. Identity politics is the ideological underpinning of the current emphasis on multiculturalism and diversity. Along those lines, as Stanley Fish[8] put it, there is "boutique multiculturalism" and "strong multiculturalism." It's easy to be a boutique multiculturalist who respects cultures other than his/her own, but it's hard to be a strong multiculturalist in the face of an intolerant other culture that calls for some basic deprivation of human rights. For example, no matter how liberal one tries to be, it's hard to support Islamic holy men who issue fatwah assassination orders on those who exercise their free speech. Most multiculturalists today simply resort to identity politics—"speaking truth to power" or practicing "the personal is the political." When Senator Barbara Boxer in January 2007 suggested that Secretary of State Condoleezza Rice couldn't understand how mothers feel about the war in Iraq because Condi was childless, that was identity politics. Playing the victim card is identity politics. Annoying people in public by speaking a foreign language is identity politics. Pretending to be outraged over a cartoon of the prophet is identity politics. Excluding straight white males is identity politics. Thinking that the war on terror is some kind of hyper-masculinity strategy launched by privileged white males to bolster white male identity and discursively emasculate opponents is identity politics.

Toward a Definition of Postcolonialism

Postcolonialists don't like definitions. Anything you could think of to put in a definition would be biased anyway. Then, the simple act of defining (or describing) something (or someone) is simply the act of engaging in a (neo)colonialistic labeling process. One can either engage in a neocolonialist process (reinforcing the continuing influence of colonialism) or a postcolonialist process (trying to create a newly articulated identity). Postcolonialism, you see, is the study of the ideological and cultural aftermath of Western colonialism, and in order to escape the inevitable bias that is the profound experience of colonialism, one has to escape their own actual history and biography, much like how a former colonial nation must come to resent its given past and both paradoxically and ironically come up with a new national identity. It's unclear exactly how paradox and irony came to be components of postcolonialism, perhaps from Jean Baudrillard, who, like a typical practitioner in this field, says things like the 9/11 terrorist attacks on America were an example of destruction forced on a society by a society that created its own forces of destruction. Again, it is important not to think that all postcolonialists are terrorist sympathizers. They believe that image is everything and that if you just put something in the media in front of people long enough, it will become believable.

Postcolonialism avoids a material focus on the economics of a capitalist world order in favor of a focus on the psychological and sociological effects of colonization on cultures and societies. The shortest possible definition of the field called postcolonial studies is the study of the various cultural effects of colonization.[9] Culture can be defined as "the guidelines people inherit as members of a particular society which tells them how to view the world, how to experience it emotionally, and how to behave in it."[10] Postcolonial thinkers look at culture from two standpoints: a postmodernist approach (rejecting all that modern science has to offer), and (2) a poststructuralist approach (heavily criticizing all known historical facts). This basically means that postcolonial thinkers always look "behind" or "beyond" anything written or spoken to critically examine the construction of reality in "signifiers" and hidden meanings. They are quick to spot racism and sexism. They don't trust many theories, don't believe in any moral absolutes, and don't like fixed categories or labels, even when applied to themselves. Like antiglobalists, they are best understood by *what they reject* than what they are for. They are particularly rejecting

anything Eurocentric, especially anything involving the legacy of European colonizers such as the English, French, Dutch, and other Western European powers.

The Conceptual Vocabulary

Bill Ashcroft and his associates[11] are to be credited with putting together a good dictionary of postcolonialism, and several of their key concepts are also covered here. One interesting point they make, however, is that African American studies and Chicano studies don't usually qualify as being part of postcolonial studies because, among other reasons, such groups were particular victims of slavery and exile. (Exile is sometimes produced by colonialism, but not knowing the "home" for an exile group seems to create theoretical problems.) Study of diaspora groups also apparently isn't relevant. Native American studies might qualify for study because the defining characteristic of that group was invasive settlement. The most appropriate groups for study appear to be anticolonial "freedom fighters" who articulate some radical, revitalization discourse in the name of racial justice and/or ethnic nationalism and fight on their own territory. Postcolonialists are somewhat ambivalent about race because racial thinking has been such a powerful tool for imperialism, but the same could be said for nationalism. It is sometimes said that postcolonialists are critical Fanonists in this regard. They much prefer the concept of ethnicity or, better, the Kantian notion of "unchanging inner essence" as with the phrase "race of mankind." This shows how fluid the field of postcolonialism is, so it will be difficult to be precise with the conceptual vocabulary. And although there are many practitioners who could surely be cited, I have decided to focus on three main scholars in the field.[12] I will utilize these three individuals below to outline the key concepts of postcolonialism.

Prof. Homi Bhabha of Harvard is perhaps the most popular speaker and influential postcolonialism scholar. He is known for his extensive critique of binary opposites in language (e.g., rational vs. emotional, civilized vs. savage, etc.) However, all postcolonialists pretty much take for granted that poststructural and feminist theories have, once and for all, demonstrated the futility of binarism. In fact, the critique of binary opposition (polar opposites, or dichotomies) comprise an important part of many perspectives, such as postfeminism, postanarchism, and critical race theory. Such scholars firmly believe that such dichotomies have perpetuated and legitimized Western power structures favoring "civilized" white men. Bhabha[13] is best known for extending a subfield called colonial discourse theory, adding the concept of "ambivalence" (a psychological term meaning that, among colonized subjects, there is the simultaneous existence of a complicit and resistant state of mind). Bhabha[14] believes that ambivalence causes all colonialism and imperialism to carry the seed of its own destruction. Bhabha's theory holds that ambivalence causes colonized subjects to fluctuate between mimicry and mockery. Sometimes the colonized identify with their occupiers, and other times they make fun of them. An additional related term is perhaps the most often used concept in postcolonialism, hybridity, which refers to the creation of new, "transcultural" forms of speech and behavior. Most postcolonialists prefer nativism, or a return to indigenous practices and language. Hybridity occurs, for example, when occupied people create new words or phrases, mixing their native language with the occupier's language. Postcolonialists consider hybridity to be bad because it reinforces the exoticism of diversity and is nothing more than an example of assimilation depriving subjects of authenticity. Bhabha[15] also utilized the psychological concept of liminality (from "limen," or threshold, as between the sensate and subliminal) to refer to the constant identity conflicts that colonized subjects have, suggesting that the upper/lower dichotomy was particularly troublesome. Finally, Bhabha[16] is known for clarifying the postcolonialist distinction between "nation" and "nation-state." Postcolonialists think of nation in terms of local communities, domiciles, families, or

places of belonging, and they argue that for far too long imperialist rulers of nation-states have drummed up nationalism fever in order to confuse people and mythologize history.

Prof. Edward Said (who died in 2003) was a Columbia University professor, outspoken Palestinian activist, and, of course, a founding figure in postcolonialism. A colorful and popular figure, he is best known for his *Orientalism* thesis,[17] which described a subtle and persistent Eurocentric prejudice against Arab-Islamic peoples and their cultures. According to Said,[18] all existing written history of European colonial rule and political domination over the East is distorted and false, and he concluded that Western writers always depict the Orient as an irrational, weak, feminized "Other," as compared to the rational, strong, masculine West. He was a critic of the war on terror, saying it was stirred up by "experts" advocating a "devil theory of Islam." Said[19] is also known for his distinction between imperialism and colonialism. It goes like this: Imperialism refers to the practice, theory, and attitudes of a dominating metropolitan center ruling a distant territory, and colonialism, which is almost always a consequence of imperialism, refers to the implanting of settlements on distant territories. The concept of the "other" is key to colonial power, as colonizers always hold out the promise of uplifting or improving the inferior colonials so that at some future time they might be raised to the status of the colonizer; in practice, however, this never happens and is always endlessly deferred. If Said[20] specialized in anything, it was decolonization, which refers to the process of revealing and dismantling colonial power in all its forms, including the hidden aspects that remain after political independence is achieved. Some of his key concepts in this regard are the pair of terms known as filiation and affiliation.[21] Filiation is how English writers do things, making it seem like all the world's great literature is a seamless lineage of heritage or descent (almost as if blood lines), whereas third world literature is forced to be affiliative, or identifying with the world through cultural, social, or political institutions.

Globalization is then seen by postcolonialists as an example of this as well as a transcultural phenomenon that cannot be separated from the confluence of European imperialism, capitalism, and modernity.

Prof. Gayatri Chakravorty Spivak[22] is a Columbia professor and third world feminist who is best known for her work with concepts such as "subaltern" social groups, which refer to marginalized groups and lower classes who have been rendered without agency because of their social status. The word "subaltern" was originally a term for someone of inferior rank in a military hierarchy, but it came to be associated with oppressed minority groups in an elite-dominated landscape through the work of neo-Marxist Antonio Gramsci in his writings on hegemony. There are some complicated terms here, so let's explain them. Hegemony is an ancient Greek word for rule by threat of force (more by power to control thought), and Gramsci's ideas about it are Marxists' favorite explanation as to why capitalism never collapsed and the worldwide communist revolution never took place. Agency is a word used by sociologists and philosophers to refer to freedom of choice, not just in choosing simple actions, but actions that are designed to change the world or make your mark, as in the famous juxtaposition of agency and structure that permeates most social sciences as a meta-theoretic issue involving culture-structure debates. In any event, the subfield called subaltern studies is very popular among postcolonialists as the study of how nonelites (subalterns) become agents for political and social change. The basic Spivak message (if it can be said there is a basic message) is that Marxism and feminism can be brought together in ways to make postcolonialism more interdisciplinary. Of course, in all this, going back to Kant and Hegel is good philosophy, and it must always be remembered that colonialism is heterogeneous (i.e., it's not just one country imposing it's culture on another but rather a whole global system of class composition and social positionality—"worlding" she calls it). Furthermore, one must always be sus-

picious of "white boys doing postcolonialism" because that smacks of appropriation (the usurpation or exploitation of the cultural domains of the powerless).[23]

Patterns of Imperialism and Colonialism

It is essential to understand what postcolonialism is against. Two enemies exist: imperialism and colonialism. Imperialism is the formation of empire. It occurs when a powerful entity consciously and openly acquires colonies for economic, strategic, and political advantage. So-called "classic" imperialism is for expansionist purposes,[24] with the so-called "Scramble for Africa" between 1884 and 1914 serving as a classic example. Lenin's theory of imperialism[25] (which became the Communist Party line) holds that it is necessary for capitalism to expand by economically exploiting one region by another. Following Marx's labor theory of value, Lenin saw monopoly capital as synonymous with imperialism and being plagued by the law of the tendency for profit to fall, as the ratio of constant capital to variable capital increases. Because only variable capital creates profit in the form of surplus value, as the ratio of surplus value to the sum of constant and variable capital falls, so does the rate of profit on invested capital. It is a customary practice among graduate professors to have students attempt to critique the Marxist labor theory of value when, in fact, it is largely uncritiqueable and irrefutable unless one radically redefines some terms. Another significant figure in the conceptualization of imperialism is J. A. Hobson,[26] a prolific writer best known for his theory of underconsumption (when workers produce more than they can afford to buy). Hobson's ideas provided the intellectual foundation for all the so-called "crisis" (of capitalism) studies in political economy during the twentieth century. Also worthy of note is Immanuel Wallerstein,[27] who developed modern world-systems theory, which holds that all the nations in the world can be classified as core, periphery, or semiperiphery. Postcolonialists are somewhat ambivalent toward world-systems theory because Wallerstein said he isn't interested in the politics of colonialism. Postcolonialists argue that even humanitarian and philanthropic missions are examples of imperialism, although some call it hegemony.

Colonialism is the extension of sovereignty over the territory of another for the purpose of imposing "civilized" structures over a perceived "inferior" race or group of people. A phrase that accurately captures the essence of colonialism is "white man's burden," from an 1899 poem by Rudyard Kipling, although similar phrases include "manifest destiny" and "social Darwinism." Numerous debates exist about the perceived positive and negative impacts of colonialism as practiced by the great powers over the years, and needless to say, postcolonialists argue that the impacts were mostly negative. Historically, there were many different kinds of colonies. A basic type was the "settler" colony, where descendants of European settlers made up the majority of the population and the native inhabitants were almost all killed off by disease and civil war. The typical colonial technique for this was for the settlers to exploit long-standing ethnic divisions among the people, pitting one tribe against another. Also, the colonial powers tended to favor one ethnic group over another, recruiting such favored minorities into civil service jobs like police officers or government clerks. In some colonies, Western-style education was put in place, but in other colonies there were no opportunities provided because the colonists feared the dangers posed by college-educated natives. Mixed marriages or miscegenation were strictly disapproved of, this being an issue that postcolonialists often find extremely interesting to study for some reason. Social life in the colonies revolved around segregated "country clubs," where the natives were only allowed entry as servants. The colonists tried a variety of things to improve economic production in the colonies but generally found that native work habits were hard to change, and hence supervision became quite harsh, and the socioeconomic lot of the majority never improved. Railways and transportation lines were only built for the benefit of commerce, and in the end, colonialism fell apart due to its own shortcomings as much as due to the celebrated "liberation movements" that postcolonialists triumph. Postcolonialists today argue that practically all U.S. foreign intervention is a form of colonialism, although some call it imperialism.

Epilogue on Postcolonialism

There's nothing inherently wrong with the hundreds of English, history, and philosophy students pursuing doctoral study in postcolonialism these days. They hardly ever make any connection between their studies and terrorism, and they would likely never see a connection even if a terrorist told them they were inspired by postcolonialist ideas. The whole rage seems to be about making the study of literature "fun" again, so it's perfectly understandable why the folks in humanities are attracted to these things. After all, who wants to see a literature so ossified in the past that it consists of dusty tomes written by dead white men? One wonders exactly where or when this negative attitude toward the "classic" contributions to Western civilization came about. Perhaps it's some psychological disposition to hate the establishment or maybe some point is reached in one's academic study in which they get tired of reading so many "classic" thinkers. Regardless of these speculations on the motivation to become a postcolonialist, it is apparent they intend to swamp academe with their brand of scholarly activism,[28] and they intend to rewrite history from that new "theoretical space" carved out for modern multiculturalism. Whether or not postcolonialism becomes a dominant paradigm or model is a matter for time to tell.

NOTES

1. Robert Young, *Academic Activism and Knowledge Formation in Postcolonial Critique,* 2 POSTCOLONIAL STUD. 29–34 (1999).

2. ROBERT YOUNG, POSTCOLONIALISM: A VERY SHORT INTRODUCTION (2003).

3. JOHN MCLEOD, BEGINNING POSTCOLONIALISM (2000).

4. EDWARD SAID, ORIENTALISM (1978).

5. *Id.* and EDWARD SAID, CULTURE AND IMPERIALISM (1993).

6. FRANZ FANON, BLACK SKIN, WHITE MASKS (1952).

7. TERRY EAGLETON, HOLY TERROR (2005).

8. STANLEY FISH, PROFESSIONAL CORRECTNESS (1999).

9. BILL ASHCROFT ET AL., POST-COLONIAL STUDIES (2000).

10. CECIL G. HELMAN, CULTURE, HEALTH AND ILLNESS (1994).

11. *Supra* note 9.

12. *Supra* note 4, HOMI BHABA, THE LOCATION OF CULTURE (1994), and GAYATRI CHAKRAVORTY SPIVAK, IN OTHER WORLDS: ESSAYS IN CULTURAL POLITICS (1987).

13. *Id.* Bhaba.

14. *Id.*

15. *Id.*

16. NATION AND NARRATION (H. Bhabha ed., 1990).

17. *Supra* note 4.

18. *Id.*

19. CULTURE AND IMPERIALISM, *supra* note 5.

20. *Supra* note 5.

21. EDWARD SAID, THE WORLD, THE TEXT, AND THE CRITIC (1983).

22. Spivak, *supra* note 12.

23. For a good read on subaltern studies as a "history from below" project, *see* MAPPING SUBALTERN STUDIES AND THE POSTCOLONIAL (V. Chaturvedi ed., 2000). The best overview of Spivak's ideas is found in THE SPIVAK READER (G. Spivak et al. eds., 1995).

24. WOLFGANG BAUMBART, IMPERIALISM (1982).

25. V. I. LENIN, IMPERIALISM (1917).

26. JOHN A. HOBSON, IMPERIALISM (1902).

27. IMMANUEL WALLERSTEIN, THE MODERN WORLD SYSTEM (1989).

28. *Supra* note 1.

24

The Flawed Foundations of Post-Colonial State Borders

Uti Possidetis Juris *and Self-Determination*

ANDREW A. ROSEN

Introduction

If nation-states are to cooperate with each other, they must agree about where each begins and the others end. On a map, the answer is clear—the black line of a border. But the creation of these borders has left some difficult legacies, particularly in the post-colonial world. These border disputes continue to challenge international order. To resolve them efficiently, it would seem wise to rely on straightforward principles. *Uti possidetis juris* is one such principle; it is an idea dating back to the Roman Empire that holds that after a property dispute, the land stays with its possessor. In the context of newly independent post-colonial states, the international community has interpreted *uti possidetis* to mean that the new national borders should be the same as the administrative borders that they had under their colonial regime. The application of the rule has left clear black lines on the world map, but it has also preserved colonial-era legacies of questionable border agreements and shady arrangements by the Great Powers. In many instances, the application of *uti possidetis juris* has not resolved border disputes, and its core assumptions have invited the challenges of post-colonialist scholars to its most basic assumptions.

Uti possidetis juris was introduced to the modern world following the wars for Latin American independence between 1810 and 1824. The catalyst was the need of the region's former colonies to quickly transform into self-governing territories. In order to establish borders, European and Latin American officials invoked *uti possidetis juris*: The nation-states would be defined by their colonial-era administrative boundaries.[1] Spanish governmental instruments and treaties between Spain and Portugal provided the evidence needed to determine what those boundaries were.[2]

Two different rationales guided the application of *uti possidetis juris* in Latin America. First, Europeans sought to transfer the balance of power politics to Latin America, and the nation-state served as the foundation for this form of diplomacy. Second, *uti possidetis juris* protected the new countries both from European interference and from having border disputes with each other.[3]

Uti possidetis juris became a cornerstone of modern international law in 1946, after the end of World War II. It has driven the formation of the post-colonial world after new nations were forged from former colonies. The withdrawal of former Great Powers from territories in Asia, the

Middle East, and Africa left colonial-era administrative boundaries, which emerged into states over the course of the next fifty years: France's control over French Indochina ended with the Geneva Accords in 1954; a majority of African states reached independence in the 1960s; and, the independence of nations in the Middle East came at the end of World War II, in the 1950s, and in the 1970s.[4] Similarly, the Soviet Union's demise in the 1990s precipitated another wave of new states. *Uti possidetis juris* has served as the international legal backbone of these new states and is arguably the glue of international order in the twenty-first century.

This chapter will focus on the flawed application of *uti possidetis juris* under international law. First, it will discuss how the International Court of Justice has applied the rule to uphold borders despite convincing historical evidence to the contrary. Second, it will discuss how post-colonialist scholars have attacked the core assumptions of *uti possidetis juris* and, in having done so, have raised serious questions as to whether it should be applied at all. The result is that at the beginning of the twenty-first century, this cornerstone of modern international law has ultimately been disproven both in its application and by students of its consequences, with few proposed alternatives.

Part I: International Law and *Uti Possidetis*

Historically, *uti possidetis juris* implies a general agreement between former colonial powers and new states. This was reflected in the wide-scale border remapping that came after World War II, when Great Britain relinquished its rule in many parts of Africa. The Great Powers and post-colonial states seem to have implicitly agreed to apply *uti possidetis juris* under two conditions.

The first part of the agreement was that the borders will stay the same, even if problematic in application. In post-colonial Africa, borders derived initially from "spheres of influence"—arrangements between European colonial powers that provided for noninterference by each party in the sphere of interest of the other.[5]

These spheres ultimately evolved into administrative boundaries as colonial powers further secured control over their respective territories.[6] But these boundaries were rarely clear delineations; rather, they often marked protectorates, neutral and buffer zones, and suzerainties that had been set up to reflect "spheres of influence."[7] Moreover, these lines were often determined primarily with regard to latitude and longitude and with little knowledge of the topography of the terrain—geographic or demographic.

The second part of the agreement was that the adoption of the colonial borders is an act of self-determination. When these boundaries, despite their problems, were adopted by post-colonial African nation-states as borders, these were considered acts of self-determination. The adoption was officially affirmed in the Cairo Declaration (1943), a declaration by the Organization of African Unity (OAU) that the borders of Africa reflect a "tangible reality" and that all leaders of Africa were committed to respect the borders existing at the time of independence.[8] This declaration continues to uphold modern African borders and has been adopted by the OAU's newest reorganization as the African Union.[9] *Uti possidetis juris* has become the legal basis for upholding these borders today, whereas claims on ethnic, historic, or other entitlements do not have much standing.[10]

A. The International Court of Justice Applies *Uti Possidetis Juris*

The historical strength of the legal precedent of *uti possidetis juris* has laid in the simplicity of its application. The negotiated boundaries with vague underpinnings became clearly delineated black lines, and in turn, former colonies became nation-states.[11] But the weakness of the precedent is also evident in the simplicity of the application—beyond longitude and latitude, boundaries negotiated were not representative of demographic or geographic realities. For these reasons, newly independent nation-states have raised and challenged *uti possidetis juris* at the International Court of Justice.

The International Court of Justice (ICJ) first ruled on a post-colonial border dispute in 1986, in the Case Concerning the Frontier Dispute.[12] Both states, Burkina Faso and Mali, were former French colonies that had been part of a region called French West Africa. In deciding whether to rely on *uti possidetis*, the Court classified it as "not a special rule" but "a general principle, which is logically connected with the phenomenon of the obtaining of independence, wherever it occurs."[13] Its legal authority does not derive from agreements between states (in this case, arguably the Organization for African Unity's 1964 proclamation would be relevant) but rather from tradition.[14] Accordingly, the Court determined the administrative borders of Burkina Faso and Mali at the moment of their independence and then upheld them. This decision is now the conceptual basis for the application of *uti possidetis juris* in international law.

Since then, the logic of this ruling has been challenged, both by disputing parties and justices, in a series of cases involving post-colonial border disputes. The most common problem has been the historical challenge to post-colonial borders; specifically, the history of colonial management had left some ambiguities about border locations, and post-colonial states challenged their borders on that basis. Three cases are of particular note here: *Hawar Islands*, *Namibia v. Botswana*, and *Nigeria v. Cameroon*.

All three cases have two themes in common: First, the perceived ambiguity in the border, either historical (*Hawar Islands*) or argued (*Namibia v. Botswana* and *Nigeria v. Cameroon*), is preserved by *uti possidetis juris* but challenged by the parties purely on economic considerations. Second, the Court rules in all three cases to preserve the border, despite substantial evidence that they should not.

B. Hawar Islands Dispute

In 2001 a dispute between Qatar and Bahrain highlighted the problem of applying *uti possidetis juris* to an ambiguous colonial history.[15] Had colonial powers always set borders according to administrative considerations, or were they considering other factors? What if the colonial-era borders unjustly favored one indigenous people over another?

The Hawar Islands lie within three to twelve nautical miles of the coast of Qatar,[16] but the British Political Agent unofficially handed them to Bahrain in 1936, a decision the British government officially affirmed in 1939.[17] Qatar had objected to the decision since 1939, claiming that it had not been informed of the British decision of 1936 nor had it consented to it.[18] The ICJ intervened at the request of both parties, which had been in dispute over the islands since the 1939 award.

The Court ruled in favor of Bahrain, holding the British award as having had legal effect and, therefore, as binding on both parties.[19] Fundamental to its decision was the conclusion that despite the existence of treaties with the British Commonwealth for both nation-states dating back to the eighteenth century as well as evidence that the British Foreign Agent may have been directly involved in the decision to award the Hawar Islands to Bahrain, neither Qatar nor Bahrain was ever a protectorate of the British Empire.

The issue of whether both nation-states had been protectorates prior raises two uncertainties in the case that the dissent highlights. First, there is the historical uncertainty of Qatar and Bahrain's geographic and political identities from the eighteenth century onward—first under the Ottoman Empire and subsequently as independent sheikdoms with treaties of protection with the British Commonwealth. The multifaceted history of these states, as reconstructed by the Court, provides little foundation to pinpoint as to whether these states were independent before 1970[20] or if they could have ever been considered protectorates of the British Empire.[21]

Second, given the uncertainty of the identities of these states, it is unclear as to how the Hawar Island border between them should be conceptualized. If Qatar and Bahrain were protectorates of the British Commonwealth, then the border should be conceived of as a former administrative boundary of the British Commonwealth. In this case, *uti possidetis juris* would apply, and the British government's decision in 1939 would be considered an administrative decision. But if it was a border dispute between two independent countries resolved by a third party, *uti possidetis juris* by definition cannot apply.

These uncertainties are addressed by the dissent, which offers two interpretations of post-colonial borders as alternatives to *uti possidetis juris*: first, as the economic interest of the former colonial power, and second, borders as a co-operative arrangements between countries.

i. Hawar Dissent: Post-Colonial Borders as the Economic Interests of the Former Colonial Power

The dissent focuses on the history of the border and, consequently, is unwilling to use *uti possidetis juris* as "relevant title" for the basis of a decision. It regards the decision of the British government to award the Hawar Islands to Bahrain as an economic decision made for political reasons, and hence, "of questionable legal value."[22] The dissent relies on evidence stating that the British motives in awarding the islands to Bahrain in 1936 were to secure maximum oil concessions. This motive is suggested but not addressed in the Court's opinion, which chooses to avoid discussion of the relevant evidence.[23]

The dissent focuses on a confidential British memorandum that Great Britain had considered the Hawar Islands part of Qatar until 1936 but changed its consideration based on "the local policy of certain British representatives and the rush for oil with the advent of off-shore exploration."[24] The dissent presents the ruler of Bahrain as having needed more concessions to fulfill a promise to the British, and so he laid claim to the Hawar Islands.[25] In response, the British Political Resident—who in 1933 had stated "Hawar Island is clearly not one" of Bahrain's group—in 1936 agreed with the British Political Agent's assessment that "it might suit us politically to have as large an area as possible included under Bahrain."[26] It was this

decision that underlay the original 1936 British recognition of Bahraini sovereignty over the Hawar Islands, which then underlay the 1939 British award of the islands to Bahrain.[27]

The dissent's construction of events suggests that the Hawar Islands border was an administrative border between two British protectorates, but one established on economic considerations solely and not the administration of the polity. For this reason the dissent is unwilling to use *uti possidetis juris* as "relevant title" for the "real motives underlying the legal contrivance which was the British decision of 1939, directly inspired as it was by rival oil interests."[28] Thus, the dissent suggests that not only may the Hawar Islands border have been founded on the economic interests of the British but that such a determination is objectionable and a "contrivance."

ii. Hawar Dissent: Borders as Representing a Cooperative Arrangement Between Countries

The dissent proposes an alternative solution to *uti possidetis juris* for disputed post-colonial borders—borders as representing a cooperative arrangement between countries. It is proposed at the conclusion of the dissent's analysis of the claim of *effectivités* by Bahrain, but the majority chose not to explore it.[29] Effectivités, as defined by the ICJ in the Frontier Dispute (Faso v. Mali), are administrative activities that demonstrate jurisdiction over territory.[30] The dissent refutes Bahrain's claim, writing that Qatar's persistence in refusing to acquiesce quietly to Bahrain's claim to the islands prevented *effectivités*.[31] But the dissent concedes, given the majority's decision to base its ruling in the 1939 British award, that perhaps the islands should be shared between the two parties.[32]

The dissent bases a cooperative arrangement on three grounds: condominia, the sentiments of the polities, and the dissent's desire to rectify a perceptibly unjust decision. All three suggest a concern for the polities of both states in this proposition, but they are ultimately abstract. The international legal grounds are unclear.

Condominia is an actual international legal principle, but it is not directly proposed as a solution. The grounds of empathy may be considered to be genuine or a diplomatic gesture by the Court in an attempt to craft a just solution to a perceived historical injustice, but again, it is not a clear-cut solution. Last, the interpretation of a cooperative border is rooted in the identity of the polity, but this relationship is tenuous as it is unclear where one polity begins and the other ends, either historically or administratively.

Implicitly, then, the dissent has offered an alternative to *uti possidetis juris*.

iii. The Hawar Dissent's Interpretations Reflected in the Court's Opinion

In highlighting these two interpretations, the dissent highlights flaws in the application of *uti possidetis juris*. The majority chooses not to address *uti possidetis juris*, but notably, these two interpretations are present in the majority's decision in its handling of Qatar and Bahrain's historical status and in its choice not to address *uti possidetis juris*.

Fundamental to the majority's opinion is the conclusion that neither Qatar nor Bahrain was ever a protectorate of the British Commonwealth. It bases this opinion on both an Exclusive Protection Agreement of March 13, 1892, between the Sheikh of Bahrain and the British Political Resident in the Gulf, and an exclusive agreement between Great Britain and Qatar dated November 3, 1916, that, for all intents and purposes, rendered Qatar a protectorate of Great Britain.[33] But these treaties seem to indicate that both Qatar and Bahrain were protectorates of the British Commonwealth.[34]

Yet the majority does not label either state as former "protectorates" or "protected states."[35] Moreover, it is unclear in the majority's decision what the appropriate label for their colonial status should be. The decision suggests that both states were either post-Ottoman independent nation-states or protectorates of the British Commonwealth. But in having done so, the Court rules out the application of *uti possidetis juris* altogether; instead, the implication appears

to be that each party was an independent state at the time.[36] Thus, it seems that it is implicitly true that both states were protectorates, but explicitly, the Court carefully avoids not stating or defining this.[37]

The Court also seems to implicitly recognize the 1936 decision was a fundamentally economic one. It recognizes the communications that led to the decision were tied to the "negotiations then in progress for the grant of an oil concession."[38] However, it does not address the decision itself at all, except to say it stands,[39] and rather focuses only on the 1939 decision. Moreover, the Court's recitation of the facts suggests that the British Political Resident and British Political Agent both engaged in roles resembling an administrator more than a diplomat. Some indication of this point is evident in the fact that the Resident had to refer back to the India Office—the heart of Britain's colonial empire in the region—for an opinion on the matter.[40] Most indicative of this point is the failure of either the Agent or the Resident to contact Qatar regarding this decision.

Were the issue of *uti possidetis juris* not present or had there not been protectorate treaties in existence, perhaps the 1936 decision could have been regarded as an unfortunately unfair decision by the British government. It appears this is the angle that the majority hoped to adopt by ruling that the 1939 decision stands because both Bahrain and Qatar consented to it.[41] But because both issues are recognized in this case, the Court recognizes that a border determination by the administrators of a colonial power was solely for economic purposes and not for the polity, and it chooses to uphold that border nonetheless. The Court thus appears unwilling to undermine the fundamental assumption of *uti possidetis juris* that colonial borders were necessarily administrative.

The Hawar Islands dispute thus highlights some of the fundamental flaws of *uti possidetis juris* as a precedent in the post-colonial world. In particular, the simplicity of its application belies flawed colonial-era boundary decisions that were based solely on economic considerations.

C. Botswana v. Namibia

Another case decided around this time presents a challenge to post-colonial borders in a similar vein to the Hawar Islands case, but this time through present economic interests of the parties. The Court's decision also reflects its unwillingness to question *uti possidetis juris* despite evidence to the contrary.

Namibia and Botswana sought ICJ intervention in a dispute over the title to Kasikili/Sedudu Island in the Chobe River, which lies north of Botswana and South of Namibia. The island, about 3.9 square kilometers in area, creates a fork in the river before it meets with the Zambezi, resulting in a northern channel bordering Namibia and a southern channel bordering Botswana.[42] Botswana's Chobe National Park, a protected wildlife reserve, lies directly south of the island. To the north in Namibia lies a flood plain known as the Caprivi Strip.[43] The closest Namibian village is across the river from the island, whereas the closest village in Botswana is 1.5 km downstream.[44]

There is no question as to the post-independence status of either Namibia or Botswana— both were former colonies whose borders have been internationalized via *uti possidetis juris*. Nor is there any question that the border had been a colonial-era administrative border—the island formed part of the demarcation of the spheres of influence between Germany and Great Britain in Southwest Africa, embodied in the Anglo-German Agreement of 1890.[45] Additionally, there is no contention as to whether the treaty is binding on either party—both acknowledge that they are bound by the 1890 Agreement.[46] Thus, according to these three international legal standards, it is arguably indisputable to conclude the border was an administrative border for both Germany and Great Britain.

The similarity to the Qatar v. Bahrain dispute lies in the border itself, established by a colonial power largely for economic reasons—in this case the "transportation of commerce." But whereas in that dispute the Court had been asked to overturn a border determination that had been predicated on economic interests, here the Court has been asked to resolve a border dispute that is predicated on an economic interest of both parties. The economic interest is tourism, which for Botswana's economy is one of its "key sectors" and where Chobe National Park is an integral attraction.[47] By contrast, Namibia is heavily dependent on the minerals industry; tourism is not even considered a key source of income.[48] But it does possess a tourist industry and has an interest in developing it.[49]

Again, the Court shows discomfort with recognizing economic interests as determinative of a post-colonial state border, whereas the dissent explicitly regards economic interests as the determinative factor. Justice Weeramantry writes: "As Namibia informed the Court at the oral hearings, tens of thousands of tourists from all over the world come to Namibia to visit its game parks."[50] He notes additionally, "The use of the southern channel to observe the wildlife on Kasikili/Sedudu Island would be a natural and important part of the agenda of the tourists in both countries."[51] But Weeramantry is most sensitive to Botswana's interests in a favorable ruling: "The principal loss and inconvenience to Botswana would not be in regard to navigation, but in regard to the tourism and preservation of wildlife which would ensue from the fact that the teeming wildlife on the Botswana side has habitually crossed over to the Island and that the Island is in a sense an integral part of this wildlife preserve."[52]

The Court, however, only recognizes the importance of tourism to both countries when it notes the "economic importance" of "the use of the southern channel by flat-bottomed tourist boats."[53] It instead explicitly rests the decision on its interpretation of thalweg, which the Court states may mean: "'the most suitable channel for navigation' on the river, 'the line determined by the line of deepest soundings,' or 'the median line of the main channel followed by boatmen travelling downstream.'"[54] All three meanings laid out by the Court suggest an inherent commercial meaning to thalweg.[55]

But unlike in Qatar v. Bahrain, the Court is comfortable with this fact. The border was established on thalweg, but it also stood as an administrative division between the spheres of influence. Therefore, the Court resolves the ambiguity underlying thalweg, but it is unwilling to do otherwise.

The alternate ground for a holding was to have ruled in favor of a party based on the significance of the island to that party. However, given the descriptions of the island presented by both parties, this island and border has little use for either party, except for the tourist industry. Namibia argues that the Masubians, who inhabit the Caprivi Strip in Kasika village, have had "continuous, exclusive, and uninterrupted" occupation of the island, "in so far as the physical conditions of the Island allowed."[56] Namibia portrays the Masubians as moving "in accordance with the dictates of the annual flood."[57] By contrast, Botswana portrays the island as an occasional habitat for wildlife, to which Justice Weeramantry further adds: "[it is] a place where they meet and feed and breed."[58] Moreover, "The grazing on the island is excellent and there is a daily elephant migration to the island."[59] Namibia thus claims occupation of the island when there is no flooding, but recognizes the importance of the island to wildlife, whereas Botswana claims the significance of the island is only for wildlife.

Therefore, the Court does not have much ground for a decision based on the importance of the island to any particular interest of either side, except for tourism and thalweg. The Court appears to have rested the decision on thalweg and, thus, the former colonial administrative borders, because to do otherwise would be to determine a border based on the current economic interests of the state. As was suggested in the analysis of the Qatar v. Bahrain decision above, the Court appears uncomfortable with this latter course. Nonetheless, the Court's avoidance of the issue, especially in light of the facts presented by Judge Weeramantry's dissent opinion, suggests that the Court still recognizes that a border may represent economic interests for a state. However, it will not rule that such interests may be or have been determinative of that border.

D. Nigeria v. Cameroon

The border dispute in Cameroon v. Nigeria is also in the same vein as the Hawar Islands dispute, as it involves a disputed border that represents an economic interest of the state. Unlike the others, however, the disputed border represents a future economic interest of the parties to the dispute.

Nigeria's and Cameroon's borders rest on the spheres of influence established by a series of treaties between Germany, France, and Great Britain between 1906 and 1913.[60] The boundary of the Bakassi Peninsula specifically rests upon both a Treaty of Protection between Great Britain and the local kings and chiefs of the region (known as Old Calabar) from 1886, and upon two subsequent agreements reached between Great Britain and Germany in 1913 that established the "Frontier between Nigeria and the Cameroons, from Yola to the Sea."[61] The Milner-Simon Declaration of 1919 created the Lake Chad border, and it was clarified in subsequent agreements between the French and British during their period of control by mandate of the region.[62] The work of the Lake Chad Basin Commission has also subsequently clarified this border.[63] Thus, the roots of both the Lake Chad and Bakassi Peninsula borders are geopolitical arrangements and have been internationalized by *uti possidetis juris.* Neither border was established on necessarily economic or administrative grounds.[64]

There are three elements to the disagreement over these particular borders. As in the other two disputes discussed in this chapter, these borders represent economic interests. The Lake Chad border, a settlement for Nigerian fishermen,[65] represents a current economic interest of Nigeria, and the Bakassi Peninsula represents a future alternative to the Persian Gulf as a major supplier of oil to the United States and other major importers.[66] Second, like the Kasikili/Sedudu Island and Qatar v. Bahrain disputes, the treaties above do not necessarily define these borders.[67] Last, like the Kasikili/Sedudu Island dispute, the population of a party is involved, but to a much greater extent. There is a significant Nigerian population in both regions—over 150,000 Nigerians in the Bakassi Peninsula,[68] thirty-three Nigerian villages settled in the disputed Lake Chad territory,[69] and over three million Nigerians in Cameroon.[70] Nigeria's arguments thus confronted the Court with a novel problem: It has an economic and legal rationale for disputing these territories with the unprecedented additional rationale that Nigerians inhabit those territories.

The Court holds for both the Bakassi Peninsula and Lake Chad that the agreements cited above established the borders and, thus, cannot be altered as Nigeria had sought to alter them.[71] Although these holdings are not based on *uti possidetis juris*, they follow the same rationale. Yet the presence of Nigerian villages governed by the Nigerian government in the Lake Chad region and of Nigerians in the Bakassi Peninsula suggests that the Court's decision to uphold the border may be too simple a solution.

This is first evident in the Court's decision regarding Lake Chad. Nigeria argues that the Lake Chad region is a historically undefined territory, and the historical consolidation of the region by Nigerians is a consequence of this ambiguity.[72] The Court rejects these arguments, instead holding that Cameroon had original title to the land.[73] But the Court recognizes this title as problematic in the treaties that had established this border:

> Despite the uncertainties in regard to the longitudinal reading of the tripoint in Lake Chad and the location of the mouth of the Ebeji, and while no demarcation had taken place in Lake Chad before the independence of Nigeria and Cameroon, the Court is of the view that . . . , certainly by 1931, the frontier in the Lake Chad area was indeed delimited and agreed by Great Britain and France.[74]

Moreover, it makes this decision despite the fact that the thirty-three villages have been established on territory recently created by unprecedented environmental conditions: dried-up lakebed, islands perennially surrounded by water, or on locations that are islands in the wet season only.[75] Last, the villages appear to have been established with Cameroon's tacit consent: The existence of these villages had been challenged only once by Cameroon before it filed suit in 1994.[76] The above factors suggests shaky evidence of original title to the region for Cameroon and novel issues underlying the settlement of Nigerians in the region, but the Court still upholds the border as it was originally founded.

The Court takes a similar approach to the Bakassi Peninsula, where the history of historical title is similarly problematic, and the territory's inhabitants are Nigerian. Nigeria attempts to argue that there are ambiguities in the transfer of title in the historical treaties.[77] It argues that the treaty retained original title with the kings and chiefs of Old Calabar, and because Bakassi was a protectorate, Great Britain did not have the authority to give Bakassi to Germany in 1913.[78] The Court rejects both arguments, finding as to original title "no evidence of any protest in 1913 by the Kings and Chiefs of Old Calabar."[79] Moreover, the Court finds that the treaty may not have established an international protectorate, but it confirmed "British administration by indirect rule."[80] The Court thus rejects Nigeria's arguments that historical ambiguity may also open the door to a claim of title to this land.

Unlike the other cases discussed in this chapter, it is not the dissent who is aware of the questionable grounds of the Court's decision.[81] Rather, it is the Court itself, which rests original title to the region on a note verbale of 1962 from Nigeria to Cameroon regarding oil licensing blocks despite historical evidence that suggests otherwise. Although this note explicitly states that Nigeria recognized Bakassi as having belonged to Cameroon at one point in the 1960s,[82] it does little else to clarify historical ambiguities surrounding the question of original title. The Court also uses this evidence as grounds to refute Nigeria's claim of historical consolidation,[83] though Nigeria's arguments present a much more complex relationship with the region, including the establishment of health centers, community schools, and the collection of taxes from villages.[84] Nigeria uses these arguments to claim historical consolidation of the region since independence, claiming they collectively constitute independent and self-sufficient title to Bakassi.[85] But the Court holds that Cameroonian title had already been established in Bakassi, tenuous though it may be.[86]

Thus, with Cameroon's historically ambiguous title to the region and Nigeria's administrative and representative presence in both the Bakassi Peninsula and Lake Chad regions, there exist historical and representative grounds for Nigeria's claim to the region. But the Court does not accede to them, and it is explicitly unclear from the decision as to why. But it is implicitly clear that the economic interests of Nigeria in both regions—agrarian in Lake Chad and oil concessions in Bakassi—substantially affected the Court. The Court appears most troubled by Nigeria's intentions,[87] as Nigeria's acts constitute a naked challenge to border stability, if not an attempt to revive terra nullius.[88] The Court seems troubled enough that it would rest much of its decision on a note verbale while also spending much of its discussion avoiding the historical uncertainties that plague the region. Moreover, it does so despite the substantial Nigerian population present in Cameroon, specifically in the disputed territories. Thus, the ruling may be best regarded as an explicit rejection of Nigeria's treatment of post-colonial borders as terra nullius for the sake of potential future economic interests. Put in alternate terms, the Court is rejecting Nigeria's implicit interpretation of a border as a future economic interest for a state. In having done so, it has also rejected arguments for redrawing post-colonial borders for the interests of the polity.

E. Conclusion

Each dispute reflects the difference in neighboring states' subjective perceptions of post-colonial borders—past, present, and future. There are two consistent themes in all three cases that are worth highlighting here.

The first consistent theme is that the arguments of the parties in each case can be tied back to an economic interest. In Hawar Islands, the historical root of a border between Qatar and Bahrain was rooted in the past economic interests (oil) of the British foreign office. But this did little to sway the Court from diverging from *uti possidetis juris*. The parties in Botswana v. Namibia presented the Court with similar historical evidence and Namibia's claim to a current economic interest (tourism). Rather than defer to the economic interests of either party or envision an alternate solution (as proposed in the Weeramantry dissent), the Court defers to the flawed historical precedent of thalweg. Last, the Court refused to change a border despite evidence of historical and representative grounds for Nigeria's claim to the region, perhaps because Nigeria's claim is very much rooted in the future oil prospects for the Bakassi Peninsula.

Second, in each of the three cases, there is convincing evidence that the old borders are impractical as drawn. The ICJ has passed over this evidence and its supporting arguments, opting instead to rule based on precedent. This reflects how the application of *uti possidetis* conflicts with practical concerns. In the hands of the ICJ, a practical method of drawing borders has not evolved beyond its original application and has thus become a rigid ideology impervious to facts.

Part 2: Conceptual Flaws of *Uti Possidetis Juris*

The problems with *uti possidetis* are not only practical; they are also theoretical. In the past few decades, post-colonialist scholars have exposed the weaknesses in its conceptualization. They have not attacked the rule itself but rather have focused on its external (post-colonial borders) and internal legacies (post-colonial governance). Their attacks have exposed *uti possidetis* to be a flawed rule that perpetuates colonial-era injustices—not an innocuous rule designed to ease international order.

The external attack argues that borders signify an imposed identity on the polity, and, therefore, no connection exists between administrative borders and the polity of the post-colonial state.[89] Both Antony Anghie and Makau wa Mutua have laid out external attacks, but each author has a distinctly different approach. Anghie argues that sovereignty is a European concept, imposed on the colonies and protectorates of the colonial era and foreign to the non-Western world.[90] *Uti possidetis juris* and sovereignty are concepts that were imposed on the colonial polity and, therefore, the post-colonial polity should not inherit them. Mutua attacks statehood itself, labeling it "false statehood" and disassociating the term "nation-state" from post-colonial African identity.[91]

According to the internal attack, the post-colonial borders are not the problem; rather, the colonial administrative legacy within those borders is impeding the modern African state.[92] Mahmood Mamdani has posited this attack, arguing that post-colonial borders embody a self, but whether that self may be able to democratize will depend on rectifying the imbalance of political power between urban and rural that colonial administration fostered.[93]

Both the internal and external attacks on the post-colonial self are effective lenses for questioning the continued application of *uti possidetis juris*.

A. External Attack

The external attack's effects may be best understood by analyzing it against two interpretations of borders that presented themselves in the cases above: borders as the economic interests of the state and borders as a cooperative arrangement between states. In the first case, a border represents an economic interest only. In the second case, the border may be cooperatively governed by both bordering states.

i. Borders as the Economic Interests of the State

In the three cases analyzed above, there are three relationships suggested by an economic interpretation of borders: pre-independence borders

may not have represented the polity (Qatar v. Bahrain); post-independence borders may not currently represent the polity (Namibia v. Botswana; Cameroon v. Nigeria); and post-independence borders must be altered to represent the polity (Cameroon v. Nigeria). In other words, in all three cases the borders preserved by *uti possidetis juris* may not, in fact, represent a self.

The first proposition comes from Qatar v. Bahrain, in which the Hawar Islands border had been established based on the economic interests of Great Britain. Moreover, the decision to establish that border was made without the consent of the sheikh of Qatar and was finalized by Great Britain. The self that was created upon independence in 1970 was, therefore, an artificially imposed self, whereas for Bahrain it was an artificially created self. Thus, Mutua and Anghie would argue that the states' international identities and their sovereignty as defined by the Hawar Islands are false constructs. Qatar v. Bahrain is proof in the pudding for the external attacks.

Put in alternate terms, the inherited border never represented the polity. Moreover, the inherited border was not necessarily an administrative border at all but rather represented the interests of Great Britain. A pre-independence border had been established primarily, if not only, for the purpose of securing oil concessions for the British Commonwealth. Anghie and Mutua would argue that the Court has upheld an unjustly established colonial-era border by ruling in favor of Bahrain.

Although *uti possidetis juris* does not necessarily apply to Qatar and Bahrain as post-commonwealth independent states, the concept's implications are present. The decision betrays an attenuated relationship between *uti possidetis juris* and self-determination. Without intending to, the Court further attenuates this relationship by refusing to base the grounds of its decision on effectivités. Bahrain's arguments regarding the Dowasir were fundamental to this rationale, along with a wide variety of other forms of argued *effectivités*, whereas Qatar was unable to produce similar evidence of effectivités.[94]

Grounds suggesting that a self may exist on the disputed territory are not a factor in the Court's decision.[95] In avoiding these grounds as a basis for territorial delineation, the Court inadvertently confirms the external attack that post-colonial borders do not represent a self.

The second proposition comes from both Namibia v. Botswana and Cameroon v. Nigeria: disputed post-independence borders may currently represent an economic interest of the post-colonial state. This suggestion alone does not necessarily relate to the arguments of Mutua and Anghie; however, both cases add the complicating factor of members of the polity inhabiting the disputed territories. Put in alternate terms, then, a disputed territory traditionally inhabited by members of the polity represents a current economic interest of the post-independence state.

It is unclear what the external attack would argue as to a state seeking to alter a border based on present economic interests. Although the state is attempting to remedy an imposed identity, it is also arguably preying on its neighbor's resources. Namibia introduces the additional historical factor of Masubian habitation and migration on Kasikili/Sedudu Island, and Nigeria introduces the additional factors of Nigerian habitation on the Lake Chad and Bakassi regions. Therefore, it could be argued that the state is seeking to remedy an imposed post-colonial identity by seeking a more representative border. In such a case, the external attack supports the states' arguments. But as the implications of the economic motives of the state make such an argument unwieldy, so does the suggestion that the external attack supports such an argument. Nevertheless, the external attack suggests that to the extent that the border disputes are over the inhabitants in the disputed regions, the disputes are indicative of an imposed identity. This additionally makes it unclear whether Mutua and Anghie would necessarily attack the Court's holdings that do not alter the borders as unjust.[96]

The third proposition comes from Cameroon v. Nigeria, where a state seeks to alter its post-independence borders to represent the polity. Nigeria's arguments for original title to the Bakassi Peninsula support an adjustment of a colonial border for the interests of its polity. The Court's reasoning suggests that had this proposition been presented by Nigeria without the implication of its economic interests, then it would have applied the external attack on post-colonial borders in its purest form. However, arguments for original title and historical consolidation seem tainted by the reality of the future oil prospects on the Bakassi Peninsula. Assuming that the former argument had been presented as the only grounds for the Court's decision, Mutua and Anghie would probably support changing the border. As this argument shows that the border does not represent the polity, Nigeria should prevail. Mutua and Anghie would disagree with the Court's ruling, perhaps even critiquing it for having failed to rectify a historical falsehood.

In sum, these three cases reflect how the external attack exposes the weakness in the ICJ's application of *uti possidetis juris*—specifically, the application of *uti possidetis juris* has not resulted in outcomes that reflect the "self" of either party. Rather than solving problems, *uti possidetis juris* exposes and then preserves the flaws in a post-colonial border.

ii. Borders as a Cooperative Arrangement Between States

Interestingly, the external attack also highlights an alternative to applying *uti possidetis juris*. This alternative proposition may be found in both Qatar v. Bahrain and Botswana v. Namibia, and it argues that one remedy to a post-colonial border dispute is the establishment of a cooperative border. Put in the terms of the external attack, the post-colonial border is a lasting wound from the colonial era, and the best remedy is one that recognizes the interests of all injured parties. Such an argument is closest to Anghie's perspective, but may also reflect Mutua's.

For Anghie, sovereignty and statehood are foreign concepts that Europe imposed on the rest of the world.[97] Any model of statehood and/or borders that suggests that a region could be cooperatively governed and, therefore, transcend the identities of both states, could thereby transcend the European model of statehood. Perhaps the same conclusion could be reached for Mutua, but the answer is less clear, as he did not address the scenario, and both states would still exist as states beyond the shared border. Notably, neither theorist suggests that a border should be established in international law for the sake of an international treaty or the particular concerns of that treaty, as Weeramantry suggests.[98]

However, a cooperative border may also be a return to pre-colonial frontiers. For Anghie, a cooperative border may be a territory when sophisticated forms of political and social organization exist but do not constitute a state. In order for this to be acceptable, a polity must exist within this cooperative region. Perhaps, then, Kasikili/Sedudu Island would provide such an opportunity. But Weeramantry's exclusion of Masubian use of this island as a rationale for a cooperative regime suggests that he did not envision an alternative to sovereignty.

B. Internal Attack

The internal attack focuses on the state's internal self or, rather, its administrative structure. Mahmood Mamdani argues that the administrative structure preserved within the borders of the post-colonial state has preserved a political and economic structure not conducive to democracy.[99] In particular, a legacy of central government control over rural markets and economies (particularly the pastoral economy) has imposed restrictions on traditional agrarian life in postcolonial African states. This model has also concentrated nonagrarian power in the central government.[100] Through this model, the internal attack suggests that the self preserved by post-colonial borders is fundamentally flawed; it is divided between urban and rural, with the former preying on the latter.

In Botswana v. Namibia, the divided self within both states is present. First, it is present

in the ruling in favor of Botswana in the face of the supporting evidence of the Masubian pastoral culture. The decision further emphasizes the pastoral vs. central government dichotomy by restricting the Masubian's pastoral culture, already circumscribed by colonial-era borders.[101]

Second, according to Mamdani's dichotomy, a decision in favor of Botswana's tourist industry favors Botswana's central government. Botswana's rural vs. central government dichotomy is a colonial inheritance that Mamdani highlights: He notes Botswana's transfer of pastoral lands to the colonial government prior to its independence.[102] This transfer reflected the state's interests in building a tourist industry while dominating the pastoral farmer. The Court's decision in Botswana v. Namibia preserves this inequitable colonial-era legacy.

Last, this divide is present in Namibia's argument that were it to have been awarded Kasikili/Sedudu Island, the importance of the award would not have been for the Masubian people but for the development of its own tourist industry. In this instance, the Masubian rural economy is of little or no use to the Namibian government: It is secondary, if not subordinate to, Namibia's needs to build its tourist industry. All three flaws suggest that the interests of the rural economy are or would be subordinate reasons to the economic interests of the state.

Cameroon v. Nigeria reflects the internal attack in slightly different ways. First, the internal attack exposes how the Court's decision preserves post-colonial legacies. The Court's holding reinforces Mamdani's model by upholding a border that has divided the Nigerian people in the Bakassi region. The implication is that the central government of Cameroon has control over the rural, historically ethnic Nigerian people. The Nigerian self is left divided by the decision. Nigeria highlights, but the Court's decision does not recognize, the migratory settlements of Nigerian peoples in the Lake Chad region as legitimate claims to land there.[103] These migratory settlements are implicitly predatorial claims to rural land by the central government of Nigeria. The Court forces Nigeria to revert to a norm that preserves the divided Nigerian post-colonial state and the Cameroonian control over rural Nigerians in its territory.

However, the Court undermines the internal attack by refusing to allow Nigeria to consolidate its oil interests. Nigeria's moves in the Bakassi Peninsula are nakedly ambitious attempts to consolidate control over an oil-rich region. For the Court to have permitted Nigeria to do so, according to Mamdani's logic, it would permit a central government to perpetuate a colonial economic legacy at the expense of a traditional rural economy.

In sum, the internal attack is a helpful lens for looking at the implications of these cases. When applied to these cases, it suggests indirectly that *uti possidetis juris* has preserved structures internal to the state that are incompatible with self-determination. From here, we may conclude that the ICJ's consistent application of *uti possidetis juris* undermines the rationale for further application of the rule.

Conclusion

It is important to recall here that *uti possidetis juris* is considered to be an act of self-determination. As such, *uti possidetis juris* establishes that there is a self defined by the borders as previously drawn.

The external attack has sought to prove that the borders of the "self" do not in fact represent a self. In all three disputes, this is true: the application of *uti possidetis juris* has not resulted in outcomes that reflect the "self" of either party. Rather than becoming a solution, the application of *uti possidetis juris* exposes and then preserves the flaws in a post-colonial border.

The internal attack highlights the weakness of the self preserved within the borders by focusing on the administrative legacies of the colonial era. There is no "self" but rather a divided self between the central government of the state and the pastoral, and the Court's decisions in both Botswana v. Namibia and Cameroon v. Nigeria preserves these post-colonial dynamics within each state.

By attacking the "self," both attacks highlight, albeit indirectly, how *uti possidetis juris* is flawed at its definitional core. These attacks further imply that the Court's continued application of *uti possidetis juris* has preserved post-colonial legacies that are detrimental to the future of the state. In this light, the continued reliance on *uti possidetis juris* seems to create grounds for more problems for the post-colonial states seeking solutions.

Part 3: The Road Ahead for *Uti Possidetis Juris*

Looking ahead, the doctrine of *uti possidetis* is in trouble.

Despite its flaws, it continues to be applied. Upon the breakup of Yugoslavia, the European Economic Community set up a commission, known as the Badinter Commission, to answer legal questions that the dissolution raised. One of these was whether *uti possidetis* applied. The commission's conclusion that it did apply both widened the doctrine and increased confusion about it.

The Badinter Commission broadened *uti possidetis juris*. In determining whether to apply the doctrine to the new states, the Badinter Commission drew on the ICJ's only ruling on the subject up to that date (1992), the Frontier Dispute. But although that case came out of the decolonization process, the new states under consideration by the Badinter Commission were seceding. The commission has been accused of eliding these differences and willfully ignoring language in the Frontier Dispute that limited *uti possidetis* to the decolonization context.[104]

The Badinter Commission muddied *uti possidetis juris*; for this reason, dissolving states cannot be sure if the international community will apply it to them. On the one hand, the Badinter Commission was a powerful international body, so other bodies might adopt its interpretation; on the other hand, its logic was weak and it has been widely criticized.[105] Even if the international community accepts Opinion No. 2 as an accurate statement of law, its authority is explicitly limited to Europe.[106] So would *uti possidetis* apply to a dissolving nation in Asia, for example, or should the European situation be considered unique? This uncertainty about the law discourages parties from negotiating with each other because they do not know who has the legal advantage or whether the international community will respect their agreements.[107]

Put together, the ICJ decisions and Badinter Commission opinion create a lot of gray area around *uti possidetis*. The principle seems easy to apply at first, but it then emerges from these real-world tests seeming almost inoperable. In practice, it is not a functioning law: Citizens of disputed territories around the world are disregarding it. As a theory, scholars have dismantled all of its components to such a point that it seems useless to try to repair it. But what will replace it? When it comes to border disputes between emerging states, the international community has no other legal doctrines to implement instead.

Nations around the world are still struggling with unresolved colonial borders. Afghanistan and Somalia have degenerated into failed states; Pakistan, Sudan, and Georgia are struggling with their independence; Ethiopia is ensconced in a border dispute. Different mechanisms have emerged to deal with these conflicts. NATO has stepped in on occasion (Somalia, Darfur) and the U.S. military has of course played a major part in Afghanistan and Iraq. But nonmilitary solutions are hard to come by. The UN disfavors secession, and its management record is mixed. The ICJ works slowly and only hears disputes between pairs of sovereign states.[108] A principled, legalistic approach is desirable, but the only doctrine available is uti possidetis—a discredited and vague theory.

Where does *uti possidetis juris* stand now? Perhaps Stephen Ratner's assessment of *uti possidetis juris* as an idiot rule is the best assessment of that question. As an idiot rule, *uti possidetis juris* serves as the last barrier between terra nullius and order.[109] But it is evident above that to call *uti possidetis juris* a "rule" is to give it too much credibility, especially when the ICJ has actively avoided using it as grounds for a decision.[110]

Thus, *uti possidetis juris* is not an "idiot rule"; rather, it is a conceptual barrier increasingly unrelated to issues of democracy and increasingly challenged by economic development. Its only remaining justification for existence appears to be as the last wall between order and disorder in the post-colonial world.

Where will *uti possidetis juris* end up? Perhaps what is most apparent from the above is that post-colonial borders are increasingly under attack, both legally and diplomatically, over present or future economic interests. Nowhere is this more present than in Latin America, where *uti possidetis juris* has its roots.[111] These new disputes are not over polities nor are they over conflicting identities of the polities within post-colonial borders; rather, the disputes are over resources. The ultimate irony, then, is that the states that benefited from the stability afforded to them via *uti possidetis juris* are seeking to create instability in their hunt for natural resources and economic advantage.

Going forward, the question will be whether the Court will continue to rely on the logic of *uti possidetis juris* as a guiding concept for stability as states increasingly seek to undermine it. The Court's decisions in these three cases suggest that it will continue to uphold post-colonial borders in the face of increasingly complicated issues, including more challenges to the definition of the "self." Given the already tenuous link between post-colonial states and democracy, such an approach may only serve to further undermine prospects for democracy in the post-colonial world.

NOTES

1. Enver Hasani, *International Law Under Fire: Uti possidetis juris: From Rome to Kosovo*, 27 FLETCHER F. WORLD AFF. 5, 86 (2003).

2. *See* Steven R. Ratner, *Drawing a Better Line: Uti possidetis and the Borders of New States*, 90 AM. J. INT'L L.4 (1996) [hereinafter Ratner]. Similar problems occurred in post-colonial Asia. *See generally* Case Concerning the Temple of Preah Vihear *(Cambodia v. Thailand)* 1962 I.C.J. 6 (Jun. 15) [hereinafter Temple of Preah Vihear].

3. *See* Hasani, *supra* note 1 at 87.

4. WILLIAM R. KEYLOR, THE TWENTIETH-CENTURY WORLD: AN INTERNATIONAL HISTORY Asia map at 429, Middle East map at 343, Geneva Accords at 369 (3d ed. 1996).

5. *See* MALCOLM SHAW, TITLE TO TERRITORY IN AFRICA 48 (1986).

6. *Id.*

7. *See* Hasani, *supra* note 1, at 88.

8. "The view at the time was that Africa needed to settle down." Paul Reynolds, *African Union Replaces Dictators' Club*, BBC NEWS WORLD EDITION, July 8, 2002, *available at* http://news.bbc.co.uk/2/hi/africa/2115736.stm. As will be seen later on, the other problem is that self-determination as currently defined under international law does not include a right to secession. *See infra* note 22.

9. *Id.*

10. *See* Hasani, *supra* note 1, at 88.

11. Hasani quotes Jeffery Herbst, who argues "borders are always artificial because states are not natural creations." For this reason, Herbst argues, it is important to judge borders "on the basis of their usefulness to those who created them," and not on demographic, ethnographic, or topographic criteria. On this basis, Herbst believes African boundaries are not arbitrary. *See id.* at 94, quoting Jeffrey Herbst, *The Creation and Maintenance of National Boundaries in Africa*, 43 INT'L ORG. 692 (1989).

12. *See* Case Concerning the Frontier Dispute (*Burk. Faso v. Republic of Mali*) 1986 I.C.J. 554, 566–67 (Dec. 22) [hereinafter Frontier Dispute (*Faso v. Mali*)].

13. *Id.* at 565.

14. *Id.* at 567.

15. Case Concerning Maritime Delimitation and Territorial Questions between Qatar and Bahrain (*Qatar v. Bahrain*) 2001 I.C.J. 40 (March 16) [hereinafter *Qatar v. Bahrain*].

16. *Id.* at 70.

17. *Id.* at 73.

18. *Id.* at 59–60.

19. *Id.* at 85.

20. *Id.* at 62.

21. The majority substantially focuses on the details of both Qatar's and Bahrain's post-Ottoman history, and both countries' identities were established via their Treaties with Great Britain. Within this history, Qatar's status develops from Bahraini rule to independence to Ottoman rule and then ultimately to independence secured by a Treaty with Great Britain. Bahrain's status is portrayed as that of an independent state whose security is ensured by Great Britain. *See generally id.* at 55–58.

22. *See id.* at 154 (joint dissenting opinion).

23. *Id.* at 155 note 8. In the Court's decision, it briefly lays out a series of communications between the British Political Agent, the Adviser to the Government of Bahrain, and Petroleum Concessions Ltd. regarding ownership of the Hawar Islands.

24. *Qatar v. Bahrain, supra* note 15, at 155 n.9. The "confidential letter" is from 1964, but it explicitly confirms the motives that appear to have been determinative of the original 1936 award of the Hawar Islands to Bahrain.

25. *Id.* at 155 (joint dissenting opinion).

26. *Id.* at 155–56. For an understanding of this relationship, *see* 2001 I.L.M., at para. 38: "Representation of British interests in the region was entrusted to a British Political Resident in the Gulf, installed in Bushire (Persia), to whom British Political Agents were subsequently subordinated in various sheikhdoms with which Great Britain had concluded agreements." *Id.* at 54.

27. *Id.* at 156 (joint dissenting opinion).

28. *Qatar v. Bahrain, supra* note 15 (joint dissenting opinion), at 214.

29. *Qatar v. Bahrain, supra* note 15 (joint dissenting opinion), at 167–72.

30. Effectivités frequently include deed registration, tax collection, and licensing of professions. *See* Frontier Dispute (*Faso v. Mali*), *supra* note 12, at 586.

31. *Qatar v. Bahrain, supra* note 15 (joint dissenting opinion), at 168.

32. *Id.* (joint dissenting opinion), at 168.

33. *Qatar v. Bahrain, supra* note 15 (joint dissenting opinion), at 56, 57.

34. See IAN BROWNLIE, PRINCIPLES OF PUBLIC INTERNATIONAL LAW 113–14, 114 (6th ed. 2003); O. HOOD PHILLIPS, THE CONSTITUTIONAL LAW OF GREAT BRITAIN AND THE COMMONWEALTH (1952).

35. Interestingly, though the dissent conveys both Qatar and Bahrain as having been Protectorates, it also refuses to label both states as such. Rather the dissent states that, "the 'special relationship of protection' between the United Kingdom and the two States parties to the present dispute gave rise to a flexible division, evolving over time, of responsibilities between the protecting Power and the protected State, as a result of which the State retained its personality; this was not the case for most countries in Africa." *Qatar v. Bahrain, supra* note 15 (joint dissenting opinion), at 214.

36. This approach to *uti possidetis juris* by the Court is somewhat evident in its strategy for the ruling. The majority focuses on the nature and validity of the 1939 decision, rather than the three other legal issues it perceived to exist in the case: the existence of an original title to the islands for either side; effectivités; and, whether Bahrain's defense of *uti possidetis juris* was applicable to this dispute. All three issues all touch on both *uti possidetis juris* and the traditional assumption of administrative borders, but the Court ultimately addresses none of them. *Id.* at 75.

37. Ultimately, then, neither a concrete conceptualization of borders nor a ruling on the application of *uti possidetis juris* to this matter may be found in the majority's decision. Rather, it seems that the Court simply regards the states as they are today—independent members of the international community. The Court appears to create the fiction that Qatar and Bahrain were independent sheikhdoms who sought out the opinion of the British government as an independent third party. This is most evident where the majority writes, "the 1939 decision is not an arbitral award<el>. This does not, however, mean that it was devoid of all legal effect. Quite to the contrary, the pleadings, and in particular the Exchange of Letters referred to above<el>, show that Bahrain and Qatar consented to the British Government settling their dispute over the Hawar Islands. The 1939 decision must therefore be regarded as a decision that was binding from the outset on both States and continued to be binding on those same States after 1971, when they ceased to be British protected States." *Id.* at 83.

38. *Id.* at 58–59.

39. *Id.* at 84.

40. *Id.* at 59.

41. *Id.* at 83–84.

42. Case Concerning Kasikili/Sedudu Island (Botswana/Namibia) 1999 I.C.J. 1045, 1053 (Dec. 13) [hereinafter Botswana/Namibia.].

43. *Id.* at 1054.

44. *Id.* at 1057, Sketch-Map No. 3. The closest village in Namibia is Kasane, which lies inland on the northwestern bank of Chobe, and the closest village in Botswana is Kasika, which lies 1.5km downstream from the island.

45. *Id.* at 1059.

46. *Id.* Interestingly, under the Vienna Convention on the Law of Treaties of May 23, 1969, neither party would be considered a party to the original agreement as neither was a signatory to it. However, in addition to the express consent of the parties, the Court cites the OAU's Cairo Resolution and customary international law as bases for this treaty to apply to both Botswana and Namibia. Botswana/Namibia, *supra* note 42, at 1059.

47. *See* Botswana Tourism, Chobe National Park, *available at* www.botswana-tourism.gov.bw/attractions/chobe_n.html.

48. *Id.*

49. Botswana/Namibia (dissenting opinion of Judge Weeramantry), at 1177. An interesting perspective on the growing importance of the tourist industry to both parties may be found in Joseph R. Berger's article. He writes, "Although the 'buffalo fence' is not electric and is broken by elephants, the Botswana wildlife authorities use problem animal control techniques—scaring elephants with firecracker-type devices, shooting them if necessary—to try to keep them from crossing the fence on a regular basis (lions that jump over the fence are likewise a problem). To the north, the elephant population spreads through Namibia's Caprivi strip, then thins into war-torn Angola. To the north and east, it also spreads into Zambia and Zimbabwe. When I visited Botswana in December 1999, I was informed by a local naturalist about a decision of the International Court of Justice handed down days earlier, settling a decades old dispute between Botswana and Namibia over Sedudu Island in the Chobe River, which forms their border, awarding sovereignty over the island to Botswana. *See* Case Concerning Kasikili/Sedudu Island [Bots./Namib.], Dec. 13, 1999, 39 I.L.M. 310. I passed the island, and it appeared an empty grassland. But during the dry season (which is the southern hemisphere winter), the island teems with elephants, buffalo and other wildlife. Although wildlife was not a historical basis for the dispute, wildlife has made the island more valuable to both Botswana and Namibia, as tourism in the area has increased rapidly. Elephant populations frequently straddle international borders, and while this often causes disputes, particularly over ivory poaching, it may also form the basis for international cooperation, under the right circumstances." Joseph R. Berger, *The African Elephant, Human Economies, and International Law: A Great Rift for East and Southern Africa*, 13 GEO. INT'L ENVTL. L. REV. 417, 436 n.106 (2001).

50. Botswana/Namibia (dissenting opinion of Judge Weeramantry), *supra* note 42, at 1178. Namibia appears to have subtly attempted to convey the importance of wildlife to its tourist industry in its arguments regarding which channel should be considered the main channel. It did so by introducing evidence consisting of photographs of "a herd of elephants crossing the two channels of the Chobe." The Court took note of this evidence, but found it unconvincing. *See id.* at 1066.

51. *Id.* at 1178.

52. *Id.*

53. *Id.* at 1071. However, the Court refuses to use this as a basis for establishing the border as the southern channel, despite Namibia's argument in favor of such an interpretation.

54. Botswana/Namibia, *supra* note 42, at 1061–62. Akweenda offer an alternative way of stating these three different meanings. For Akweenda, thalweg marks the line that connects the deepest points in the river; the line that connects the deepest points in a channel; or the center of the normal principal navigation channel. *See* S. AKWEENDA, NAMIBIA: A CASE STUDY 56 (1997). For the purposes of this paper, however, I will follow the Court's definition, as its use of the terms "navigation" and "boatmen" inhere a more commercial meaning to the term thalweg. Additionally, how thalweg is translated in the English version of the treaty is a nonissue in the case. *See* Botswana/Namibia, *supra* note 42, at 1062.

55. Also, when determining navigability of the watercourses, it notes "Those conditions [of varying navigability] can prevent the use of the watercourse in question by large vessels carrying substantial cargoes, but permit light flat-bottomed vessels." *See id.* at 1071. The point here is that rather than focusing solely on the technical meaning of thalweg, the Court additionally focuses on the commercial implications of the proper interpretation of this term. Moreover, the Anglo-German Agreement of 1890 was very much a commercial treaty; it was signed both by the British to protect north-south trade routes in southwestern Africa, and by Germany to secure British recognition of its access to the Zambezi. *Id.* at 1054.

Hence, the problem with thalweg in this dispute is that the dividing line between the spheres of influence between Great Britain and Germany was agreed to be on the "main channel" of the Chobe River, and it is unclear whether the agreed main channel was the northern channel or the southern channel. The Court rules, based on three different surveys conducted between 1912 and 1985, that the northern channel is the main channel. *Id.* at 1072.

56. Botswana/Namibia, *supra* note 42, at 1093. This argument is part of Namibia's broader argument of prescriptive title to the island, which claims that the Masubia behavior "constituted a key component of the system of 'indirect rule' which prevailed in the region." *Id.* The Court dismisses this first ground for two different reasons. First, it does not see any evidence that the Masubians occupied the island *à titre de souverain*, but rather for their own needs, primarily agricultural but also in response to the flood season. Second, Botswana's predecessors never acquiesced to Caprivi claims of the border's location in the southern channel and, moreover, treated the issue of the Masubia as independent from the border issue. *Id.* at 1105–06. The Court additionally dismisses Namibia's argument by pointing out that it was not "uncommon for the inhabitants of border regions in Africa to traverse such borders for purposes of agriculture and grazing, without raising concern on the part of the authorities on either side of the border." *Id.* at 1094.

57. Botswana/Namibia, at 1093.

58. *Id.* at 1181 (dissenting opinion of Judge Weeramantry).

59. *Id.* (citing Counter-Memorial of Namibia, vol. III, p. 34, para. 11.9). In other words, this is a point that Botswana argued and Namibia reaffirmed.

60. Case Concerning the Land and Maritime Boundary Between Cameroon and Nigeria (*Cameroon v. Nigeria*; Eq. Guinea intervening) 2002 I.C.J. 303, 331 (Oct. 10) [hereinafter *Cameroon v. Nigeria*].

61. *Id.* at 333. This agreement placed the Bakassi Peninsula in German territory and, therefore, in modern-day Nigeria.

62. *Id.* at 344. This region did not have any border delimitations or demarcations derived from spheres of influence and, thus, had been left open under most pre–World War I agreements. Additionally, the Court turns to the work of the Lake Chad Basin Commission (LCBC), established in 1964 and given, among other tasks, the task of dealing with certain boundary and security issues.

63. *See id.* at 351.

64. There is discussion of demarcation versus delimitation, but as this is a related argument not integral to the decision, I will not explore it. *See Cameroon v. Nigeria*, *supra* note 60 at 334–35. *See also id.* (dissenting opinion of Ajibola), at 542–43.

65. *See id.* at 330.

66. *See U.N. ruling Favors Cameroon*, ANTHONY DEUTSCH AP ONLINE, Oct. 10, 2002.

67. With respect to the Lake Chad region, Nigeria claims that a subsequent agreement to the Milner-Simon Declaration (the Thomson-Marchand Declaration of 1929–1930) did not provide a final delimitation of the Anglo-French boundary at Lake Chad. *See Cameroon v. Nigeria*, *supra* note 60, at 334. The Court agrees to an extent, holding "the Declaration does have some technical imperfections and that certain details remain to be specified" but that the "Declaration provided for a delimitation that was sufficient in general for demarcation." *See id.* at 341.

68. *Id.* (dissenting opinion of Ajibola), at 539.

69. *Id.*

70. *Id.*

71. An additional argument was made by Cameroon that Nigeria was bound by the work of the LCBC in the 1980s and 1990s in the demarcation of the border, but the Court holds that Nigeria was not bound by that agreement. *See Cameroon v. Nigeria*, *supra* note 60, at 335–40.

72. Nigeria argues historical consolidation on three grounds: long occupation by Nigeria and Nigerian nationals constituting historical consolidation of title; effective administration by Nigeria, acting as sovereign and an absence of protest; and, manifestations of sovereignty by Nigeria together with the acquiescence by Cameroon in Nigerian sovereignty over Darak and the associated Lake Chad villages. *See id.* at 349.

73. The Court specifically holds that "there was no acquiescence by Cameroon in the abandonment of its title in the area in favour of Nigeria. Accordingly, the Court concludes that the situation was essentially one where the effectivités adduced by Nigeria did not correspond to the law," and cites Frontier Dispute (*Faso v. Mali*) as grounds for ruling in favor of Cameroon. *See id.* at 354–55.

74. *Id.* at 341.

75. *Id.* at 349. The dried-up lake bed presents a novel issue, as it is land newly created by an environmental problem and an ambiguous border.

76. *Cameroon v. Nigeria*, *supra* note 60, at 349–50. Moreover, Nigeria points out that Cameroon does not provide evidence of the settlement of "a substantial number of villages," thereby implying that Cameroon had implicitly allowed the settlement of those villages in the past. The implicit suggestion was that Cameroon did not perceive these settlements to be problematic until Nigeria's behavior became more aggressive along the border.

77. *Id.* at 366. *See also id.* (Nigeria had argued that the Agreement of 1913 was not put into effect and was invalid because, among other things, Great Britain did not possess title to the Bakassi.).

78. *See id.* at 400.

79. *Id.* at 406–7.

80. Additionally, the Court cites historical evidence that the British did not refer to Old Calabar in any British Orders of Council. *See id.* at 407.

81. There are two dissenting opinions in this case, Judge Ajibola's and Judge Koroma's. Judge Ajibola agrees with Nigeria's arguments as to the original title. *See generally id.* (Ajibola dissent), at 547–52. Judge Oda's dissent in Botswana/Namibia takes issue with the specificity of the Court's delineation of the Lake Chad region. *See* Botswana/Namibia (separate opinion of Judge Oda), *supra* note 42, at 1116.

82. *Cameroon v. Nigeria*, *supra* note 60, at 410.

83. *See id.* at 411–12.

84. *See id.* at 413.

85. *See id.* at 412–13.

86. *Id.* at 413–14.

87. For the Lake Chad region, the Court cites Cameroon's argument that Nigeria's border incursions at the Lake Chad region are "acts of conquest which cannot found a valid territorial title under international law." *Cameroon v. Nigeria*, *supra* note 60, at 351. Moreover, it is troubled enough to devote the last three pages of its decision to a discussion of the deployments of force by both sides in the disputed regions. *Id.* at 450–53.

88. *Terra nullius* is a Latin expression deriving from Roman law meaning "land belonging to no one" (or "no man's land"), which is used in international law to describe territory that has never been subject to the sovereignty of any state or over which any prior sovereign has expressly or implicitly relinquished sovereignty. *See* Wikipedia at http://en.wikipedia.org/wiki/Terra_nullius.

89. Frontiers had been a foreign concept before European colonization, as "frontiers were zones through which one clan or tribe passed from one region to another; and any borders depended solely on who would be paid tribute. When European powers drew borders, they did so "with only slight knowledge of or regard for local inhabitants or geography," instead making allocations "to reduce armed conflict among themselves." *See id.* at 595. "We have been engaged . . . in drawing lines upon maps where no white man's feet have ever trod; we

have been giving away mountains and rivers and lakes to each other, but we have only been hindered by the small impediment that we never knew exactly where those mountains and rivers and lakes were." Lord Salisbury, as quoted by Judge Adjibola in his Separate Opinion, Territorial Dispute (Libyan Arab Jamahiriya/Chad) 1990 I.C.J. (Feb. 13), *available at* www.icj-cij.org/icjwww/icases/idt/idt_ijudgments/idt_ijudgment_19940203_separateAjibola.pdf (at section 8, or p. 53).

90. *See generally* Antony Anghie, *Finding the Peripheries: Sovereignty and Colonialism in Nineteenth Century International Law*, 40 HARV. INT'L. L. J. 1 (1999); Antony Anghie, *Francisco De Vitoria and the Colonial Origins of International Law*, in 5:3 SOCIAL AND LEGAL STUDIES 321, 321–23, 331–33 (1996).

91. Mutua also has attacked the identity of the post-colonial polity, labeling it "a contrived and artificial citizenry." Makau wa Mutua, *Why Redraw the Map of Africa: A Moral and Legal Inquiry*, 16 MICH. J. INT'L L. 1113, 1142–45 (1995).

92. MAHMOOD MAMDANI, CITIZEN AND SUBJECT: CONTEMPORARY AFRICA AND THE LEGACY OF LATE COLONIALISM (Sherry B. Orner, Nicholas B. Dirks, & Geoff Eley eds., 1996). This is an Africa-specific argument and will be applied only to *Cameroon v. Nigeria* and *Botswana v. Namibia*.

93. *Id.* at 18.

94. *See Qatar v. Bahrain*, *supra* note 15, at 71. These effectivités include Bahraini passports issued to residents of the Hawar islands and former Hawar Islands residents who now live elsewhere in Bahrain.

95. Concededly, the grounds for self are arguably implicit in the Court's reliance on the 1939 decision, which highlights the Dawasir's historical use of the Hawar Islands as evidence of Bahraini occupation. *See id.* at 80–81. The point here, however, is that the Court explicitly avoids utilizing either *uti possidetis juris* or self-determination as grounds for this decision.

96. This dilemma presents an interesting issue: Should a state's borders be rectified to represent the polity, despite the loss of an economic advantage to the other country? This is an implicit issue in all three cases discussed above. The Dissent in *Qatar v. Bahrain* suggests a financial payment from one side to the other. *See Qatar v. Bahrain*, *supra* note 15, at 145 (joint dissenting opinion). But does a financial payment necessarily rectify a flawed representation of the polity?

97. *See* Anghie, *Finding the Peripheries*, *supra* note 89, at 71.

98. It is unclear where either Mutua or Anghie would stand on this issue. Anghie appears to be interested most in the mandate system and globalization. Mutua seems most interested in deconstructing the post-colonial legacy. Neither seems to have touched on this interesting middle ground. *Cf.* Malgosia Fitzmaurice, *Water Man-*

agement in the 21st Century, in LEGAL VISIONS OF THE 21ST CENTURY: ESSAYS IN HONOUR OF JUDGE CHRISTO-PHER WEERAMANTRY 428–36 (Antony Anghie & Garry Sturgess eds., 1998).

99. The model was a single model of customary authority in precolonial Africa: "That model was monarchical, patriarchal, and authoritarian. It presumed a king at the center of every polity, a chief on every piece of administrative ground, and a patriarch in every homestead or kraal. Whether in the homestead, the village, or the kingdom, authority was considered an attribute of personal despotism." Mamdani, *supra* note 91, at 39. Decentralized despotism is Mamdani's term for this structure of the post-colonial state (*id.* at 145), a divided world where "on one side free peasants closeted in separate ethnic containers, each with a customary [legal] shell guarded over by a Native Authority, on the other a civil society bounded by the modern laws of the modern state." *See id.* at 61. (The Native Authority was the administrative entity for the nonsettler parts of the colonies. *See id.* at 21–22.) This structure created a dual-faceted problem in post-colonial Africa: states that preserved decentralized despotism and states that created a much more centralized model. *Id.* at 170. The problem, Mamdani argues, is that efforts to reform one form ultimately results in the other. Mamdani, *supra* note 91, at 291.

100. Mamdani only implicitly attacks borders as having imposed fixed borders and identities on a pastoral culture where "Mobility was the precondition not only for the optimal utilization of resources, but also for their optimal conservation." *Id.* at 166. The result of these borders is the exacerbation of ethnic divisions, as tribes were allotted counties within borders. Therefore, Mamdani argue that decentralized despotism exacerbates ethnic tensions. Additionally, he argues that the alternative, centralized despotism, exacerbates the urban-rural division by establishing power within the city centers. He describes the result as a seesaw effect: Centralization resolves the ethnic tensions created by decentralization, but decentralization resolves the divide between urban and rural created by centralization. *Id.* at 291.

101. *See id.* at 165–66. It is unclear from Mamdani how environmental issues would factor into his argument.

102. Mamdani writes, "In Botswana it is estimated that if one added together the land set aside for commercial ranching, national parks, and game reserves (and the newly proposed Wildlife Management Areas), the sum would amount to 41 percent of Botswana's total land area!" *Id.* at 322 n.77.

103. As settlements in both regions had the support of the Nigerian state, it is unclear whether Mamdani would consider this a positive development. The positive spin would be that the state recognizes the migratory history of peoples in the region and, rather than delineate it as in the past, supports it. However, permitting migratory behavior amongst rural areas was characteristic of the indirect rule paradigm. *See, e.g.,* Mamdani, *supra* note 91, at 41.

104. Peter Radan, *Post-Secession International Borders: A Critical Analysis of the Opinions of the Badinter Arbitration Commission,* 24 MELB. U. L. REV. 50, 61–62 (2000).

105. *Id.*; *see also* Jochen A. Frowein, *Self-Determination as a Limit to Obligations Under International Law,* in MODERN LAW OF SELF-DETERMINATION 216–17 (Christian Tomuschat ed., 1993).

106. Conference on Yugoslavia Arbitration Commission, Opinions on Questions Arising from the Dissolution of Yugoslavia (1992).

107. Nathan Richardson, *Breaking Up Doesn't Need to Be So Hard: Default Rules for Partition and Succession,* 9 CHI. J. INT'L L. J. 685, 696 (2009).

108. Peter I. Belk & Andrew A. Rosen, *Let NATO Settle the Border Wars,* WALL STREET JOURNAL, Apr. 3, 2009.

109. *See* Steven R. Ratner, *Drawing a Better Line: Uti Possidetis and the Borders of New States,* 90 AM. J. INT'L L. 590, 594, 617 (1996). "*Uti possidetis* thus represents the classic example of what Thomas Franck has called an 'idiot rule'—a simple, clear norm that offers an acceptable outcome in most situations but whose very clarity undermines its legitimacy in others."

110. This is true even after the Frontier Dispute (Benin/Niger), where the principle was applied because both parties had signed a Special Agreement to refer the case to the ICJ, in which they stated they "are in agreement on the relevance of the principle of *uti possidetis juris* for the purposes of determining their common border." *See* Case Concerning the Frontier Dispute (Benin/Niger) 2005 ICJ (July 12), *available at* www.icj-cij.org/icjwww/idocket/ibn/ibnframe.htm (at para. 23). Therefore, it is arguable that the Court in this instance is only applying *uti possidetis juris* because both parties requested its application.

111. Jack Epstein sums up the current disputes in Latin America: "A dispute between Chile and Peru over a maritime dividing line persists despite a 1999 pact; Guyana and Surinam are fighting over an oil-rich marine area off the Corentyne River that separates the two nations; at least 1,000 Honduran fishermen have been arrested by Nicaragua during the past 10 years over sea rights in the shrimp-rich Gulf of Fonseca; and Venezuela claims Guyana's Florida-sized Essequibo area, home to gold, diamond and timber investments. Caracas argues that it was unfairly stripped of the region in a 19th-century arbitration decision." Jack Epstein, *Silicon Jack,* LATIN TRADE 24 (Jan. 2003).

25

Modernity and International Law

Mythological Materialism in the East-West Telos [*]

PRABHAKAR SINGH

I. Introduction

This chapter takes on modern art as the location of modernity. This subject, in my view, holds potential for a productive multilogue, rather than just a dialogue, between three binary sociocultural categories: child and adult, normal and mad, and colonisers and colonised. Modern art raises very interesting questions, and as an area that is often ignored in the analysis of law and science, it forms a powerful field for exploring both as well as their intersections. Exploring the psychology of colonisation/domination is an important objective of this chapter. In order to get at it, the chapter imbibes Arjun Appadurai, Michel Foucault, and Ashis Nandy as offering complementary stances on modernity and the subsequent globalisation of intra-European relations after the Industrial Revolution. In doing, I relate aspects of semiotic theory by looking at theories of myth. This chapter concludes by applying their relevance to the strategy of signification that international law/relations deploys.

There is nothing new about the discourse on art, myth, and modernity. Nonetheless, it is in-deed revealing. Such has been the pervasiveness of modernity that new facets emerge every time an author takes on modernity. Today a discourse of modernity must not remain the exclusive preserve of anthropologists and sociologists; instead, it should now also engage international lawyers, as a series of thinkers first from the West and then from the East have spoken about modernity and capitalism.

Michel Foucault,[1] Arjun Appadurai,[2] and Ashis Nandy,[3] among many others, are some of the names that I find stimulating. They have spoken about the relationship between modernity and colonisation and its effects in shaping our consciousness. Modernity has altered societal relations, thereby producing conflicts within and outside colonised societies—the content of postcolonial studies. In layman's terms, modernity evokes hesitation, often timorous, as human conscience around the world has shown a fetish for its past.

Appadurai's decisive discourse on modernity reveals its ability to create five kinds of pasts. These are history, tradition, evolution, antiquity, and civilisation.[4] India, Ashis Nandy analysed, has many pasts; depending on the needs of each

*This chapter is a version of the article published in 3:1 J. East Asia & Int'l. L 67 (2010); copyright Yijun Institute of International Law, 56 Migaro, Kwangjin-Gu, #302, Seoul, 143–825, South Korea. The section on "Foucault and International law" was presented at the BIARI (Towards Global Humanities), Brown University, 2010. I am particularly thankful to Shilpi Bhattacharya for her comments and Josephine Mariea for her detailed editorial help.

age, the nation brings a particular past into its consciousness.[5] Such choices of pasts are guided by two aspects of human psychology: a particular culture's obsession for particular mythology as the real history and cultures' abhorrence of science and technology that often creates conflicting social situations, new modes of interaction, and new behavioural changes that rekindle the old-new or modern-ancient debate.

The political and cultural sphere of India has witnessed a fierce battle between forces that are folk and *Sanskritic*. The Constitution of India and the political turmoil of the 1980s and the 1990s amply reflect this.[6] In its lived experience, humanity has shown marked love for one or the other kind of past at different times. Therefore, the coloniser and the colonised held to different choices: Of the types of past offered in Appadurai's analysis, coloniser chose civilisation, history, and evolution, whereas the colonised settled with tradition and antiquity as their authentic past.

The psychological pull behind choosing a type of past lies in its ability to distract people, Eastern or Western, and offer relaxing coordinates that direct their imagination to glory, prosperity, happiness, wealth, and good environment. Nonetheless, Appadurai identifies a minimal set of four formal constraints on all sets of norms about the past: authority, continuity, depth, and interdependence.[7] Nandy argued that colonisers saw history as reality as against myth, which,

> being a flawed, irrational fairy tale produced by "unconscious" history, [was] meant for savages and children. The core of such a concept of time-produced in the West for the first time after the demise of medievalism—consists in the emphasis on causes rather than on structures, on progress and evolution as opposed to self-realization-in-being, and on the rationality of adjustment to historical reality.[8]

Postmodernists and antimodernists have indulged in such enquiries before. Such an exercise has been primarily a task in the epistemology of myth, imaginations, capitalism, consciousness, and narratives of modernity. A sustained discussion on art as the location of modernity also informs the coloniser-colonised relation, for now it is widely evident that the East and West have different purposive intents behind their pastoral choices. The coloniser-colonised debate, by its nature, leads us to issues of racism, the imaginations of men as subhuman, native science as folk, knowledge as ignorance, and modernity of the Other being a Western myth. Postcolonial theories, thus, remain

> Wedded to ways of conceiving the relation of the non-West to the West, and of conceiving human motivation and political agency more generally, that emerged from a distinctively European mid twentieth-century intellectual climate in which non-Western peoples and societies were understood to be in principle incapable of historical emancipatory agency until jump-started by Western material and conceptual colonial violence.[9]

Throughout this chapter, the term "myth" will be used in a number of its guises: the Bartheanidentified framework of understanding, in which systems of knowledge are understood as "truth" within a cultural context; the label used in European discourses delegitimising other knowledge as lacking in scientific ground; and as the allegorical stories of folk and tribal cultures. This has been done to encapsulate myth in a comprehensive fashion. As the story of myth traverses different sections of this chapter, it will become evident which of the above meanings of myth has been applied. This composite nature of myth has a mutually exchangeable set of actors—as symbols that appear different on their face but emerge from similar psyche.

II. What Is Mythological Materialism?

Thus, a set of impromptu questions follow from the discussion in section I: What is the relation of myth/mythology, antiquity, history, and tradition with modern art and to the lived

TABLE 25.1 Distinctions between historical and mythological materialism

Historical materialism (Marx/Mainstream)	Mythological materialism (Current author/alternative)
Colonisers' chief tool of exploitation	Colonised's only way of resurrection
Starts by defining history	Pits mythology as true alternative to history
History as the story of class struggle	Mythology is the true history
Thesis, antithesis, and synthesis	No contradiction/antagonism
Deterministic and scientific	Accommodates ideas, imaginations, and role of psyche (allegedly nonscientific)
Inspired by Hegel and Kant and propounded by Karl Marx	Nietzsche, Foucault, Sartre, Said, and Nandy can be said to be its proponents
Conflict as the basis of historical development	Cohabitation and peaceful existence as the engine of growth
Progress as linear	Progress is circular
Ignores the role of emotions	Emotive aspects equally important
History here is sponsored and written (kings, chiefs, and colonisers)	Ahistoricals, historyless, and subalterners are the major agents of mythology (e.g., women, peasants, and children)
Enlightenment as the source of knowledge	Treats Enlightenment as an scandal
Noninterdisciplinary	Multidisciplinary vision
War, destruction, and fresh beginning	Continuity, eternity, and seamless progress
Preserved as written text	Found in folklore and oral traditions

Source: The author

experience of humans? Can we use art and myth to see history and perceive reality in the way Marx perceived his by using historical materialism? Can we see reality through the prism of what I call *mythological materialism*? Can modern art and myth become the explanatory coordinates of reality? In other words, can reality be the myth that colours art? Or is it the myth that colours realty by using art?

A European child and a colonised native, thus, will appear as two inseparable sides of a coin. Modern art will appear as violent and destructive as the forces of science. Colonisers will seemingly acquire a paedophile's face and an artist will become a ruthless cog in the dialectic of historical materialism. In such a narrative, international law becomes an unpopular and vicious project that endorses historical materialism as against more nuanced mythological materialism.[10] The table above has been prepared with

an aim to throw a comparative light on mythological materialism.

An attempt to define mythological materialism's phenomenology is an exercise in semiotics of both sociology and anthropology; as such, international law has understandably avoided myth for history. Mythological materialism signifies the struggle between various narratives of competing pasts that eventually characterise particular cultures' symbiotic semiotics. Mythology essentially is a kind of symbolism and thus semiotic in its appeal to both supporters and detractors of cultural relativism. I am often tempted to see Gandhi as the chief protagonist of mythological materialism. This will be discussed later via Nandy's narrative of Gandhi, though very briefly. Therefore, the following pages will engage the readers in a discussion about myth, history, art, and modernity. Modern art will be used to explain an industrialised modern view that was instrumental in the colonisers' claims of superiority.

III. Examples of Myth as History and History as Myth: The Case of Greek Alexander and Nazi Hitler

Our dreams and imaginations both, said Foucault, are seemingly made of the same matter.[11] Both offer soothing solutions to consciousness, albeit, mostly intangible. Yet consciousness has never been argued as constituting one of the types of past, partly because the discussion of history is not aimed at creating solutions. Ideology of Western intellectuals has made history as an offering to the nondominant, the subaltern, the uncivilised, the heathen, the folk, and the nonmodern possible.[12]

Ideology uses history as a device to explain world events politically. It sees history as a monolithic and homogeneous process; it does not offer history of the world as it is but rather world-as-history.[13] Therefore, Western historians wrote an ambitious and war-mongering Greek Alexander as *Alexander the Great* and not a villain of history. On the contrary, many war mongers from the East with similar ambitions were simply invaders who invaded the West. History is, therefore, simply an agenda of the dominant ideologue of a particular time. The untold sufferings that Alexander inflicted on India included

> Massacre, rapine, and plunder on a scale till then without a precedent in her annals, but [was] repeated in later days by more successful [Muslim] invaders like Sultan Mahmud, Tamerlane, and Nadir Shah. In spite of the halo of romance that Greek writers have woven round the name of Alexander, the historians of India can regard him only as the precursor of these recognized scourges of Mankind. This may be an extreme statement. But so is the statement that Alexander proclaimed for the first time the unity and brotherhood of mankind.[14]

Alexander's campaign in India was, therefore, certainly not a political success. It is also true that it left no permanent mark on the literature, life, or government of the people.[15] The name of Alexander is not found in Indian literature—folk or unwritten history. How can the oral traditions bypass an invasion of such magnitude as Alexander's? Oral folk traditions, which at the most paint and picture their narratives, cannot lie, as they are not state sponsored to create an official version of history.

Certainly, Alexander did not intend his conquests in India to be as meaningless as this. But it was so.[16] What we see today as history is a substantial signification of rather insignificant truths. Alexander's greatness and his conquests in India are but myths that have been written as history. It was this assigned valour that the Nazis tried to emulate along with the Greek tradition of art, discussed later in greater details. No wonder Hitler died as frustrated as Alexander, as both had their life shortened—Alexander's by a poisonous arrow through his chest and Hitler's by a bullet through his head. And yet Alexander is a hero and Hitler a villain of history. Why? Probably because Alexander waged a war on non-Greeks, non-Whites, the Semites, and coloured Asians whereas Hitler tortured the French, the Polish, and other ethnic communities victimising the Jews, who were whites, nonetheless.

IV. Semiotics of the Modern Art as Violent: Art, Myth, and Colonisation

During the early fourteenth and fifteenth centuries, when colonisation was more a fashion—a form of artistic expression—than a planned activity, the ideology of the French, English, Dutch, and the like was to see themselves helping in the development of the rest of the world. The Germans were late risers. In a world of nearly patented ideology of colonisation, the Germans encountered a destabilising inferiority complex. The lack of a grand art, as many suggest, was part of this inferiority complex for a nation that saw itself as a pure Aryan race.

In a work published in 1869, J. W. Jackson tells us how Aryans are different from Semites:

Influenced by his predominant moral principles, the Semite believes and worships, whereas the Aryan, guided by his preponderating intellectual faculties, investigates facts and deduces a conclusion.[17] The Germans imitated myth as an exercise in acquiring art. Translations of Europe's overall disenchantments, together with a particular section of European population that subsequently is identified as the father of the middle class, with its own life into theories of natural and social science, has been possible through the birth of various disciplines, including avant-garde modern art.

The absence of art in a political culture can be suicidal if seen semantically. We have seen Germans' insecurity about their lack of a grand art in their consciousness forced them to embrace Nazism; psychologically, Nazism can actually be interpreted as a movement of racial purification through the symbolism of the swastika, exhibiting a high degree of psychosocial manifestation of politicocultural semiotics.

A. Violent Modern Art and Childhood

In his book *Philosophy of History*, Hegel recalled comparing the Greek world with a period of adolescence and how individuality was aesthetically conditioned.[18] And yet this was not for the first time that a section of European consciousness had shown how an absence of art could become violent while discarding mythology. The Greek political thoughts, later idealised in Germanic imaginations, showed a fear of mythology when philosophers like Plato called for banishing myth for a modern political history. Plato embraced historical materialism without speaking about it whereas Gandhi rejected it in practice. I will engage in a Plato-Gandhi discourse again in other sections. Nonetheless, I need not emphasize the limitation that I ought to respect in this chapter: If at all Hitler was motivated by any non-Germanic ideals, it was by the (mis)givings of the Greeks.[19]

What this misgiving eventually produced was ugly and despicable—that, too, in a bid to acquire an authentic art. Thus, not only can the struggle for art turn ugly, bloody, and cruel, but it can also induce cultures and societies into violence and brutality. It can poison the vision of an entire community like the Nazis, who, angered by the absence of remaining territory for colonisation, took to the idea of punishing European nations. Colonisation, as an avenue for development as Marx had expressly prescribed, from now on should be seen as the natural fallout of an artistic regression of modern Europe. Some scholars have, to an extent, rightly grasped this psychological waning of Nazi Germany in its search for a grand art.[20]

What Germany lacked, therefore, in practical terms, was its subject. Consequently, what Germany wanted to create was such a subject, its own subject. This explains its intellectual and aesthetic voluntarism as a will to art. If the Germans' obsession or fear was always that of failing to become artists, of not being able to accede to great Art; if in their art or their practice there was often such an effort, and so many theoretical expectations, it is because what was at stake was their identity (or the vertigo of an absence of identity).[21]

Art is often seen as beautiful, childlike, non-violent, poetic, aesthetic, meek, and passive. This conception, as discussed above, is not true. A non-Western alternative vision of modern art, therefore, sees art as a major culprit of violence against the non-West. The colonial scheme of the Europeans is an antithesis of the attributed innocence to art. Consequently, I wonder whether art is what has caused colonisation on a psychological level? This psychological change did not go unnoticed in European societies. Before Europe went on a colonising spree, they colonised the European childhood only to see its alter ego in the natives later. There is no better example of a racist text than the scholarship of Jackson, who claimed to utter no prejudice but rather to simply state the facts.[22] This is one of the most unscientific and narcissistic of literatures that we might come across in any academic journal.[23] He testified that

In the Negroid type, the brain lacks volume; the nervous system is not adequately centralised: and this brain, thus deficient in quantity, is equally wanting in quality . . . the Aryan of the Europe is, and—to the remotest verge of history—always has been, the perfection of his type, whether we regard strength, stature, beauty, or longevity.[24]

After dismantling the Negroid races on the basis of their appearance, he brought down the Indian-Aryans for its primitivism. The truth, indeed, is—as he continued—that the Aryan patriarchs, who celebrated their simple sacrifices to the sacred chants of the Vedic hymns, were isolated strangers maintaining themselves against the incessant attacks of the alien races only through the utmost efforts.[25] What if such a perception about the colonised native influenced how the colonisers saw their own children; colonisation corrupted the colonisers as much as it harmed the colonised. The colonisers treated people of the Negroid race, children, and colonised as one and the same. Thus, international law, as an instrument of its own proliferation, cannot be assumed to be free of such sentiments. Colonialism dutifully picked up these ideas of growth and development and drew parallels, as discussed next, between primitivism and childhood.

B. Childhood in the Wake of Industrialisation and Colonisation

Nandy, after conducting extensive research, argued that the modern concept of childhood is a product of seventeenth-century Europe.[26] Earlier, Foucault had already said that man was an invention of the eighteenth century.[27] There is, then, no option but to conclude that both manhood and childhood are recent inventions. Regnant in Europe, the new concept of childhood bears a direct relationship to the doctrine of progress.[28] Nandy went on to say that

Child was not seen as beginner of life but as someone opposed to an adult, for example—an inferior version of maturity, less productive and

ethical, and badly contaminated by the playful, irresponsible and spontaneous aspects of human nature . . . it became the responsibility of the adult to "save" the child from a state of unrepentant, reprobate sinfulness through proper socialisation, and help the child grow towards a Calvinist ideal of adulthood and maturity.[29]

This paradigm shift in Europeans' perceptions of childhood alone pushed the innocence of European childhood into factories. Exploiting children in Britain during the early phase of industrial revolution was a natural corollary of fabricating such fictional childhood. Capitalist modernity planned and orchestrated this change in perception. It served to justify child labour; a child, as a vile adult in disguise, had to be reformed so that s/he becomes a civilised adult when an adult. Factories, as new avenues for child labour, were new schools that corrupt and selfish modernity had gifted to childhood. Factories were new houses of correction for the children who, for the capitalist, formed a soft fleet of workers demanding meagre wages and supplying undemanding labour. They came as a bonus with working women who, in the changed industrialised society, had to divide their motherhood between factory hours and home time.

Thus, childhood, as an important aspect of a women's motherhood, drastically transformed modern art in the industrial sociology of modernising Europe. This is what I intend to convey when I say that the new art saw the child as an undergrown adult, though I am not the first to write about it. Furthermore, famous men of creativity—artists and sculptures of modern times—had indulged in paedophilic activities.[30] Molesting childhood—whether it be mental, emotional, psychological, sexual, and/or industrial—was another violence that art had inflicted on the society, encouraged by lusty modernisation. Later, the colonisers saw the same opportunity to molest when they found the coloured and so-called heathen natives of the non-West. Like childhood, the natives presented them an opportunity to exploit at a very a high market value.

TABLE 25.2 Parallels between primitivism of colonised and the conception of childhood by the colonisers

Colonisation	Childhood
Colonisers	Artists, industrialists
Natives (ugly, uncivilized, primitive)	Children (foolish, needing discipline, childish/childlike)
Funded by capitalists for trade	Exploited through art, expression, and paedophilic activities
Masculine, adult	Feminine, vile-adult/inferior adult needing correction
Calvinistic ideal of maturity	No more a blissful prototype of beatific angels
Ahisorical, cultureless subhumans needing enlightenment	Blank slate on which adult must write moral code
Duty of colonizers to save children from a state of unrepentant, reprobate sinfulness through imparting civilization	Rural, sinful, and spare the rod and spoil the child

Source: The author (based on the text by Nandy, *supra* note 3, at 14–15)

The colonised, like the European children, could be turned into almost rightless labourers who would aid the colonisers in exploiting their very own natural resources while at the same time mutilating their culture through the psychological forces that colonial encounters released. Therefore, colonisers' psyche of spreading modernity saw the non-European natives in a way similar to European children—as a soft bunch of underdeveloped humanity waiting to be corrected by industrialisation and Calvanisation.

The elitist historiography was always a useful tool to control artistic expressions through private sponsorship, thereby subverting any objections to behavioural changes under capitalist aesthetics. This new capitalist aesthetics coloured the modern art as well. Because of the salient priorities of capitalism—seed-money, cheap labour, racial division, and colonial influences—new subjects, images, moralism, and ideals prioritised art. Modern art is often associated with invoking realism and restoring prudence—but at the cost of beauty. Modern art, indeed, brought existing sociology and the changing location of anthropology to the canvas. But what is often ignored is that this new painting on canvas was not automatic; rather, capitalists who were legitimising modernity's priorities sponsored it. The industrial sociology of womanhood, motherhood, and childhood in

seventeenth-century Europe was a crystal ball of a future yet to unfold.

V. Politics, Art, and Modernity: The Vision of Mythological Materialism

A. Kant and Beauty

In *Critique of Aesthetic Judgement*, Kant defined concepts like taste, beauty, aesthetics, types of delight, and judgement.[31] For him, the antonym for aesthetic is logic.[32] The beautiful is, Kant said, that which, apart from the concept, pleases universally.[33] One of the most important tasks for a transcendental philosopher, he continued—and I presume he counts himself as one of them—is to ascertain the universality of aesthetics.[34]

A judgement of taste by which an object is described as beautiful, under the condition of a definite concept, is not pure. There are two kinds of beauty: free beauty (*pulchritude vaga*), or beauty which is merely dependent (*pulchritude adhaerens*). The first presupposes no concepts of what the object should be; the second does presuppose such a concept, with it, an answering perfection of the object. . . . Beauty of man (including under this head that of a man, woman, or child), the beauty of a horse, or of a building (such as a church, palace, arsenal, or summer house), presupposes a concept of the end that defines what the thing has to be, and consequently a concept of its perfection; and is therefore merely appendant beauty.[35]

By deduction, the men of cultures other than his own are a subject of Kantian inquiry under *pulchritude adhaerenes*, that is, a breed constantly looking for example from which to copy. For Kant to believe that a work is a work of art, indeed some work of man is always necessary.[36] A later variant of racial and cultural superiority known as National Socialism should, therefore, not come as a surprise: It did not lead to the aestheticisation of politics or politicisation of art, but rather a fusion of politics and art, the production of the political as a work of art.[37] As early as Hegel, the Greek world saw cities as a work of art.[38]

Plato apprehended a dangerous liaison between myth and art. He feared myth so much so that he argued for purging it out of the history of the Greeks. Myth, as he saw it, had the function of exemplarity and the ability to fashion plastic art.[39] Conversely, for Levi-Strauss, what gives the myth an operative value is that the specific pattern described is everlasting.[40] However, unlike sciences, whether natural and social, art could not be harnessed directly, that is, industrially, to bolster imperialism.

The semiotic understanding of modern art as boosting violence is collateral and psychological. The construction of the modern myth or the modern work of art, therefore, is the result of a dialectical process. And that is exactly why what we called the "aesthetic solution" is inseparable from the philosophical and theoretical solution.[41] Often West accuses the non-West of eulogising its mythological superiority. Arguably, Levi-Strauss defended this through his observation that for cultures and societies, repetition functions to make the superstructure of the myth apparent.[42]

Modernity has obscured myth for a history that was nonrepetitive. Modern art, one of the visages of modernity, is what bespectacled modernity to see men as ancient and modern, folk and classic, scientific and unscientific, methodical and wayward, calculative and naïve, cultured and barbaric, historical and mythological, prudent and imaginative, and provider and needy. Modern art, as against fine art, is a product of a paradigm shift in the worldview on aesthetics and usefulness. Picasso's famous cubism, therefore, viewing the world from a rectangular window, is no wonder one of the most celebrated ideas of modern art. Modernity has, therefore, replaced symmetry, an idea based on aesthetics, with geometry, an accurate science that uses mathematics.

B. Tragedy, Art, and War: From Plato to Nietzsche

[If] it is proved that a superior race is to annihilate races and peoples that are considered inferior and decadent, incapable of living a life as it should be lived, before what means of extermination will they recoil? This is the ethics of immorality, the result of the most authentic Nietzscheism, which considers that the destruction of all conventional ethics is the supreme duty of man.[43]

This was argued on January 17, 1946, before the Nuremberg Trial. Nietzsche's *The Birth of Tragedy* establishes a parallel between (a) the victory of the Greeks over the Persians and (b) the victory of the Germans over the French. In other words, it draws a parallel between: (c) the cult of Dionysus in Greece and (d) the revolutionary sweep in Europe. Thus, by the same analogy, as the fifth-century Greeks were forced to make a difficult choice and so they found Aeschylus, so did Europe, according to Nietzsche, find Wagner, the genius of music-drama.

Through the Appolline drama, what happened on stage gave pleasure to the audience because the heroes take on the audience's suffering. Suffering then becomes enjoyment. Wagner (1813–1883), a famous dramatist-musician, enjoyed the reputation of being a revolutionary one.[44] As we can already see, Nietzsche was quoted in the Nurembourg Trial of war criminals, a price that he paid posthumously—he died in 1900—when his works were closely associated with Nazi ideology.[45]

The colossal of modernity stands on geometric pillars mapped by disenchanted capitalists—the famous conclusion of postmodernism.[46] The early capitalists were both producers and consumers of modernity. It only made sense for them to exploit modernity's economies of scale. What lay before them was an idea that, if translated into action, would redeem Europe politically, economically, and historically. Europe that was now in the grips of unemployment, wars, and poverty, candidly accepted the logic of scale economies. But this logic had an adverse side effect, which even its detractors did not want to point out.

Therefore, for an antimodern Nietzsche, the total character of the world is, in all eternity, a chaos. His world is defined by a lack of order, arrangement, form, beauty, wisdom, and whatever other names there are for our aesthetic anthropomorphisms. Such arguments did not help those who were to become debtors of modernity. The non-West had to buy modernity from its sellers, whose merchandise had high discursive aftermaths. The recipe of modernity was sold as a cure to obscurantism, ignorance, and the lack of secular hierarchies in India. Instantly, it befriended the aristocracy of the new land: a breed of third world aristocracy that sought to align its history with the feudal history of Europe, an act of identification with the aggressor, as Nandy put it.[47] Thus, it immediately traded myth for history.

In return, the impotent aristocracy, princely states, and decaying monarchy of the colonised world received a fresh lease on life at the cost of the subaltern, the tribal, and the folk. Postmodernists' anti-science links the aesthetics of the East to the West's disenchantment with modernity. However, the Eastern epistemology never produced knowledge that saw the cosmos as schemeless. Mythology, at its cognitive best, links mass emotion to concepts—concepts that are revolutionary, nonrevolutionary, or none of these. In Oriental cultures, scientific discourses and inventions are often the preserve of tradition, mostly oral.

Thus, what it mostly contains is the end result: A detailed formulation of any invention cannot possibly be transferred to semiotics. Science, as a thankless imitation, can also be defined as a process of materialising the semiotics of mythology. In fact, this is what science has done. Concepts of progress (like spreading civilisation, the burden of enlightening, conquering the entire world, and modernising the nonmodern) and Nazism were both seen as scientific: Both Nazism and the science are exposed as an effort to imitate. However, unlike Nietzsche's frustration, the East witnessed a political decline before intellectual disenchantment, and therefore, the East is marked by an absence of chaos theories.

C. Myth, Colonisation, and Gandhi: Ideological Transplant

International law's intellectual borrowings from modernity have disregarded the aboriginal and village worldview as nonmodern and heathen. Supposedly, the Greeks were the Aryans of antiquity who produced myth as art.[48] Since their era of imperial city-states, art has been an end in itself for Europeans.[49] When Europeans, en masses, turned into colonisers, from the start, their artistic buds rejected foreign myth and failed to appreciate any other flavour of cultures that had their own aesthetics, often as village and tribal cultures.

Later, science and technology perverted colonisers taste even more. Plato constructed the political, by the same token delimiting the philosophic as such by excluding myth—as well as major art forms linked to myth—from the pedagogy of the citizen and more generally from the symbolic space of the city.[50] Ancient Plato can be pitted against modern Gandhi by using Nandy's psychoanalysis of Gandhi.[51] Gandhi rejected history for a mythology of the subaltern, the tribal, the rural, and the women of India.

Thus, Plato's politics discarded myth for history, whereas Gandhi's politics discarded history for myth. This constitutes an enchanting discourse. History will decide who, between Gandhi and Plato, was decisive as a liberating force in the struggle against colonialism. Gandhi's choice of myth does not render him ineffective; he rejected a chronicled past in his self-styled resistance to colonialism. History, as he saw it, was a narrative of the elite, both in the West and the East. His mythology gave history to women, folk, subaltern, and tribal cultures that constitute the majority of Oriental population and, therefore, the majority of semiotic imaginations, mostly unrecorded in history. Nandy reminded us that Gandhi, for example, "Never cared for chronologies of past events. History to him was a contemporary myth which had to be interpreted and reinterpreted in terms of contemporary needs."[52] Gandhi's mythological devices of *ahimsa* (nonviolence) and *satyagrah* (truthful request/civil disobedience) are not only the most original devices of international relations for cultural defence invented in the twentieth century, but they also prove beyond doubt the relevance of mythology over history and science. Arguably, they are two components of this mythological materialism. Gandhi's success when seeking India's liberation can be attributed to his ability to create a political tool out of India's memories and to what Habermas agreed was future-oriented memories.[53]

History is, arguably, always constructed by the authorship of elites, whereas mythology still always exists, albeit in the imaginations of the non-elites and in texts that are called religious and superstitious. Gandhi demonstrated that those who seek liberation and freedom must learn that history can sometimes be made to follow from myths.[54] In a way, then, India fashioned, in Gandhi, a discourse of science versus mythology.

Only now have we begun to assign rights to the tribal people under international law. However, they are far from getting justice. History has not been able to save them, but mythology

can. History, unfortunately, reduces people and incidents to data and statistics, whereas mythology sees them as lucid and emotional entities capable of establishing dialogues thus far unrecorded in history. History neutralises any emotion that may be associated with the non-dominant actors such as the folk, the tribal, and the subaltern, whereas myth imbues them with flesh and blood. Kantian cosmopolitanism added a functional variant to so-called law, made international by consequential rather than accidental ventures, for the sympathetic modernisation of colonies.[55] Because something that is beautiful is not always systematic and productive, science used this as an excuse to create an antipathy for Oriental aesthetics and civilisation.

Capitalism relied only on productivity, system, process, market, and management. It justified violent revolution and legitimised the eradication of nonmodern and nonindustrialised societies through colonial interventions. It was rewarded with raw materials, cheap labour, slaves, new masses of land, and land-induced prosperity. This prosperity, in turn, gave capitalists wealth to purchase political power in democratic systems back home. This vicious circle was profitable for the coloniser and degrading for the colonised. The meeting of the West and the East, therefore, led to a capitalist consensus that the Orient was beautifully ugly, logically illogical, systematically unsystematic, articulately subtle, and dysfunctionally functional.[56]

Many claim, Marx among them, that the non-West should accept the debt of the colonisers as the harbinger of modernity, knowledge, science, medicine, wealth, and light. What I fail to understand is if colonisation intended charity, why was it so ugly? An ugly charity is no charity. Claims that the non-West did not have enough intellectual force to affect its own rise often come from arguments of historical materialism. As such, why not reject it for mythological materialism?

This brings us back to the issue of choices that modernity made. Mythology, I propose, is the sixth past that modernity has overlooked for its own survival. One of the major distinctions between myth and history is that the former is continuous, encapsulating the past, present, and future, whereas the latter is fractured. Mythology has the inertia of motion that does not need ignition, whereas history has to be woken out of slumber, which results in revolution, often justifying violence as a means to modernity's end. And when I say violence, I mean all kinds of violence: violence of act, violence of words, and violence of thought—all of which result in the violence of art. By the early second half of the twentieth century, probably due to the vagaries of two world wars, Western scholarship had recognised the truth of myth. Levi-Strauss, thus, commented that the "Same logical processes are put to use in myth as in science, and . . . man has always been thinking equally well; the improvement lies, not in an alleged progress of man's conscience, but in the discovery of new things to which it may apply its unchangeable abilities."[57] The kind of logic mythological thought uses is as rigorous as that of modern science, and the difference lies not in the quality of the intellectual process but in the nature of the things to which it is applied.[58] Thus, the choice of historical materialism over mythological materialism seems suspect. This is understandable. History is a contested narrative of progress; myth is not. For modernity to justify true past as evolution, myth must not have any place. Accepting myth would immediately lead to embracing that we have never been modern. Myth proves that men have always been intellectual; all cultures in the world—Indian, Chinese, Egyptian, Mayans, and others—have produced similar myths. This rejects any anthropological theory of a superior race, which also discards the evolution of races, with whites at the top followed by browns, Arabs, yellows, and blacks stranded at different levels of evolution.

VI. Coloniser Versus Colonised's Knowledge: Architecture as Art

Appadurai argued that hierarchy is one of an anthology of images in and through which anthropologists have frozen the contribution of specific cultures to our understanding of the human condition.[59] Such metonymic freezing has its roots, he continued, in a deeper assumption of anthropological thought regarding the boundedness of cultural units and the confinement of the varieties of human consciousness within these boundaries.[60] Very interestingly, tribal existence is one of the dimensions that claim to redefine modernity from an anthropological standpoint, conceding that anthropology, history, archaeology, and other disciplines jostle one another to lay authoritative claims to the pasts of modernity:[61]

Although the term native has a respectable antiquity in Western thought and has often been used in positive and self-referential ways, it has gradually become the technical preserve of anthropologists. Although some other words taken from the vocabulary of missionaries, explorers, and colonial administrators have been expunged from anthropological usage, the term native has retained its currency, serving as a respectable substitute for terms like primitive, about which we now feel some embarrassment.[62]

Western science has progressed with an imagined animosity toward the so-called primitiveness and irrationality of the Orient. Premodern reason, rationality, and non-Western conceptions of beauty and aesthetics collectively constituted an antithesis to the new Western science. But this science failed to appreciate that every culture produces its own science, just as each scientific achievement produces new cultural realities. Western science symbolised disciplines like architecture as worth pursuing.

Houses and palaces were soon to become more geometrical, with spheres, domes, cylindrical Roman pillars, and rectangular windows, as against previous symmetries of pregeometrical sculptures and designs of flora and fauna. Mathematics formed the root of architecture, as though it was the base of all the sciences as August Comte liked to believe.[63] Architecture also fundamentally altered the ratio of labour and raw materials in a rapidly industrialising Europe.

This is the mathematics of colonisation, pure and simple. This new mathematical formulae used non-West natives as the catalytic coefficient of modernity's expansions. Physical labour, raw materials, and more cartography skills were required now. Artists, therefore, turned into engineers. Thus, old art ushered in modern art. Engineers were now the new artists, who colonised labourers ably supported. This heralded the birth of technology. Myth as a language exposes the vulnerability of poetry to translations and transportations to foreign cultures, whereas technology travels well even in its translations.

This also is a reason why technology is quickly taking root away from its Western headquarters, with its burgeoning followers among its slaves. Furthermore, unlike poetry, myth has, in a way, universality at its core, as its substance does not lie in the style of narration but rather in the story it tells.[64] As such, technology transplanted its universality into modern art and its latent cultural violence manifested as fashion. Thus, what we often see among the fashion-conscious people is the violence of art. Fashion, an offspring of modernity, is the cultural violence of modern art. Arguably, archaeology, architecture, and fashion thus have a common father: technology.

Few have noted that the art of the non-West, like science, has manifestly been tied to the voyage elsewhere. However, enquiries about such artistic location are linked in complicated ways to the history of European expansion, the vagaries of colonial and postcolonial pragmatics, and the shifting tastes of Western men of letters.[65] Though all anthropologists traffic in Otherness, some Others, according to Appadurai, are more Other than others. The plea of the small, the simple, the elementary, and the face-to-face has driven the culture of anthropology.[66] The anthropology of composite non-Western societies has, until recently, been a second-class citizen in anthropological discourse. This engages a kind of repeal of non-Westernism, whereby complexity, literacy, historical depth, and structural messiness[67] function as exclusions in the struggle of places in a metropolis. Yet this classification of the responsibility of multifarious time-honoured civilisations in anthropological theory is too simple and conspiratorial.[68]

Neither the West nor the colonisers ever accepted idioms as capsules of knowledge, which originated in the East. Such capsules have remained limited in their appeal to the international community, whereas the domestic idioms of the West as expressed in Latin, French, and German maxims have been made fairly international first through colonisation and then through advocacy, scholarship, politics of knowledge creation, and cultural domination. Thus, knowledge is not a singular unit of global wisdom but rather a category constructed with a fair bit of elitism, discrimination, Eurocentricism, and anti-Orientalism. The rejection of mythology is its immediate effect.

Bringing the insights of botany, zoology, and *Darshan* (philosophy) together, Vidyanath Jha and D. N. Tiwari have made certain scientific observations about ancient Indian philosophy. Elaborately expressed in the pristine Sanskrit maxim, *laukik nyaya sutras* (idioms of earthly, material, and practical justice), these are specimens of a cordial cohabitation of both the natural and social sciences in Indian philosophical mythology.[69] These idioms have brought science closer even to laymans, and today, in India, they are a part of the vernacular knowledge system of over fifty languages and one thousand dialects. In a semantic antagonism today, all that is history in the East is mythology to the West and all that is history to the West is a myth to the East. Mythology, in one of my conceptions, is nothing but fossilised history.[70] The disenchanted industrialised bourgeois harnessed and funded history for colonial conquests.

VII. International Law as Foucault's Psychology

The parallel of international law and Foucault's critiques of psychology is a fascinating discussion. Woven throughout my overall argument, such an approach would strengthen the argument paralleling the madness/unreason that

TABLE 25.3 Madmen versus colonised

Mad people in Europe	Colonised natives
Madness/poverty (Calvinism)	Cultural and material destitution
Caged in houses of correction	Confined in their own native land
Provided unpaid/free labour	Free labour
Labourhood as prescribed medical treatment	Civilizing though punishment, rules, and institutions
Used as a tool to come out of financial crisis	Producing raw materials and as market both
Confinement hid away unreason	Labourhood produced market
Classicism deemed madness as hidden animality as return to kindness of nature	Natives a prototype of madmen
Question of philosophy/psychology	Subject of anthropology

Source: The author

Foucault traced in the European asylum with the unreason that colonial discourses have ascribed to indigenous knowledge systems. This narrative seeks to create a clearer path to help guide the reader through the complexity of the greater argument, as international law is as psychological, sociological, and political as it is legal. Sympathising with the victims of modernity and science, who fall outside the periphery of the civilised world, I shall, thus, offset myth against the science and history of international law.[71]

Classic international law is an expression of the Western attitude similar to the one harboured for madness, the theorization of which Foucault gained fame. Non-Western man is the classic international law's madman. Views about madness led the West to confine madmen within the walls of lunatic asylums. By the same logic, international law's madmen were supposed to be confined within the walls of corrupt science and plastic modernity. The Oriental madmen of international law had to be confined, policed, and cured. Madness was unscientific,

which in the eyes of history must appear as the reduction of the classical experience of unreason to a strictly moral perception of madness, which would secretly serve as a nucleus for all the concepts that the nineteenth century would

subsequently vindicate as scientific, positive and experimental.[72]

The madman was savage, and industries needed labourers. The classic period in Europe hailed a labourer as someone whose world was suffused with wisdom, which cures madness.[73] Madness, therefore, had to be cured with the punishment of labourhood. The conception of punishment draws its power from the contractual exchange relation between creditor and debtor, which is an idea as old as legal subjects.

The fundamental forms of buying, selling, bartering, trading, and trafficking could be ensured through labourhood. Labourhood, either in field or in industry, looped labourers in the cycle of work, that is, to produce, buy, and consume. Thus, all those outside the vicious circle of industrialisation and modernity risked being called mad and, as such, policed into confinement. They had, therefore, the responsibility of proving otherwise through their labourhood. The ideas of contractual obligation and repudiation of contract leading to punishment were soon to follow:

The original instinctual artists who formed man exchanged the creditor's psychological pleasure in inflicting physical pain for the debtor's infraction of the communal contract. Later, theologians and moralists spiritualized punishment; they replaced physical with psychic pain. The history of culture is the spiritualization of cruelty.[74]

Foucault's *The Archaeology of Knowledge*—wherein, for him, archaeology is a discipline about silent monuments and inert remains of the past—hides the narratives of modernity. Thus, if archaeology is a seed of modernity, then the megacity is the tree that germinates out of it. Modernity here becomes a project of producing a megacity of super structures. But Foucault did change between *Archaeology* and *Discipline and Punish* in his conception of history. With the growth of megacities in modern Europe, the rural came to be condemned as backward and the poor as immoral, deprived of the fruits of labour and doomed to live in slums. In *Madness and Civilisation*, Foucault pointed to the mode of perception that we must investigate in order to discover the form of sensibility to madness.[75]

The sensibilities about madness organises into a complex unity a new sensibility to poverty and to the duties of assistance, new forms of reaction to the economic problems of unemployment and idleness, a new ethic of work, and the dream of a city where moral obligation was joined to civil law within the authoritarian forms of constraint.[76] Foucault's next observation is rather direct: Have you not yet discovered the secret of forcing all the rich to make all the poor work? Are you still ignorant of the first principles of police?[77] Hidden in the attitude towards the madmen and the poor and its professed cure in confinement lies the corrupt sympathy of the rich West for the poor of the non-West, as manifested in the international overtures of transnational law.

Driving both the mad and the poor into confinement while heralding the birth of policing, seventeenth-century Europe endeavoured to solve the problems of unemployment. *De novo* corrupt scientific prescriptions for curing both madness and poverty was confinement. We see the reflection of this antipathy to poverty in England as well through its Poor Law.[78] A dream city of the rich bourgeois was designed by driving the poor out of cities.[79] Such pathologies of seventeenth-century Europe regards slums closer to village life even though there are marked differences between both. Conversely, in the culture of Vedic India, the village was as modern a thought as the megacity of science. This is another way of stating what Levi-Strauss means when he says both myth and science are intellectual work of equal merits.[80]

Western narratives of linear modernity, exposed by Foucault, are guilty of ignoring non-Western ethos, for which modernity is a circular path of both mega- and minimal structures. Confinement constituted seventeenth-century Europe's sole possible answer to an economic crisis that affected the entire Western world: the reduction of wages, unemployment, and scarcity of coins.[81] This attitude of confinement translated into the spirit of colonisation under the pressure of market, modernity, and science.

Thus, Alexander's greatness, Nazis' passion for blood-curdling art, and Foucault's vision of madness all align, though psychologically, with the regression of art and science. As if this was not enough, colonisation assumed a role of a teacher in India to subject its people to an alien sets of norms, rules, and laws. The history of Europe overran Indian myth and shamelessly justified its aggression as benevolence. One should not forget that Alexander did try to colonise India by leaving his satraps—Seleucus was the most famous of all—to manage his conquered territories on his behalf. This bid of colonisation was averted only through a powerful uprising led by Chandragupta and Kautilya, *Arthashastra*'s author.

VIII. Critical Debate Between the Orientalist and the Anglicists: The Utilitarian Universalists

Edward Said's *Orientalism* has done a great deal of service to the cause of the non-West.[82] His brilliant work exposed the formation of the political knowledge and the making of the East. The construction of the Occident, he argued, was piled on the base of the Orient.[83] It is precisely because of this image making that Max Müller advised his students not to visit India despite his works on Indology. The India of ancient times, he believed, was dead, and what was left during the British rule was not the true India.[84] Yet a discussion about this, however repetitive it might appear, is necessary.

The major difference between those living in history and those living outside it, especially in societies where myths are the predominant mode of organizing experiences of the past, is the principle of principled forgetfulness. All myths are morality tales. Mythologization is also moralization; it involves a refusal to separate the remembered past from its ethical meaning in the present. For this refusal, it is often important not to remember the past, objectively, clearly, or in its entirety. Mythic societies sense the power of myths and the nature of human frailties; they are more fearful than the modern ones—forgive the anthropomorphism—of the perils of mythic use of amoral certitudes about the past.[85]

Jeremy Bentham's hedonist calculus at once recognised the historical potential of his idea about the ahistorical Indians. The Orientalists supporting the ahistoricity of India wilted and gave up under the pressure of Anglicists' advocacy. Thus, utilitarianism rejected the Orientalist respect for indigenous knowledge. The 1857 Mutiny offered the justification for the British project of reforming India through utilitarianism. Bentham, the key architect of its administrative colonisation, then planned the administrative and judicial process of civilising India. The East India Company, the most powerful coloniser and capitalist of those times, employed his services. Eric Stokes has demonstrated the striking influence of Bentham in Indian affairs, particularly in the field of legal reform. The new agenda of civilisation through legalisation began by wiping out all of Mugal and pre-Mugal ahistorical administrative systems for a historically accented British mode of governance.

Utilitarianism ushered in an era of paper planning and routine law codes: The sword was exchanged for the pen and the soldier-diplomat gave way to the administrator-judge.[86] The Indian Legislative Council, inspired by Bentham, initiated a series of acts in the mid-nineteenth century designed to facilitate the efficient administration of justice. The Civil Procedure Act of 1859 promised to secure—so far as judicial institutions can secure that blessing—as good and accessible an administration of civil justice as the lights of the age were capable of conferring on it.[87] The Penal Code of 1860 and the Code of Criminal Procedure of 1861 brought changes to criminal jurisdiction. These are some of the events that amply demonstrate the British efforts to introduce modernity into the ahistorical India. Similar to the discussion about Foucault and international law:

Every society has a mythology surrounding the origins of rules of conduct and systems of law, revealing that law is not based on experimental data. Such myths most often begin with a postulated relationship to a sacred presence or personage in the universe that might be viewed as contractual. Cultural groups may or may not have sacred places and objects, but in all of them the foundations of rules of conduct and proper relationships to persons, animals and things cultural or natural, reside in the contract with the sacred power. The contract includes agreement about good and evil (crime and punishment), group membership (allowed and disallowed, with exclusionary provisions), marriage rules, sexual taboos, sexual access and denial, punitive measures meted out through illness, death, or the many forms of loss, as well as some advice for conflict resolution.[88]

A proficient legal system was also central to the idea of administrative superiority that was asserted ruthlessly. Both an efficient legal system and a strong government were pivotal for this much sought-after growth spurt toward maximizing happiness: Law should provide a rational and convenient framework in which the new state of things may prosper.[89] It carried out its agenda largely so that the rule of law might complete its civilising mission.[90] As such, the principle of pleasure is defined in the negative by what it excludes.[91] The way in which the success of an administrative, executive, or judicial system is measured is according to whether or not it mitigates against evil hindrances rather than in terms of a happiness effect.[92]

This was certainly true of the Benthamite reforms implemented in British India.[93] To continue the earlier discussion, the utilitarianism was modernity in disguise, its colonial architecture planned in accordance with the erstwhile biggest capitalist, the East India Company. This reform was marked by a new cultural relativism, which saw Indian culture as "infantile" and "immoral" against the British culture that was promoted through British public schools. The Westernised Indians were declared austere, courageous, self-controlled adult men as against the illiterate, superstitious, and infantile natives.[94] This political and cultural adulthood assigned to the educated Indians is what Gandhi rejected; instead, he chose myth over manufactured history.

IX. Indian Subaltern Studies

In the *Panopticon*, Bentham says in the preface of his work that

> Morals reformed—health preserved—industry invigorated—instruction diffused—public burdens lightened—Economy seated, as it were, upon a rock—the Gordian knot of the poor-laws not cut, but untied—all by a simple idea in architecture! [Foucault thus maintains that] Bentham envisioned the same basic concept of factories, schools, barracks, hospitals, madhouses. . . . The prison succeeded disciplining a man into a docile worker who does as ordered without question—and automation, the perfect fodder for Capitalist factory.[95]

Now if Bentham saw his own people as those needing correction, as discussed above, does it surprise the reader that his policies of colonial management of the Other were so harsh? The preface to his work is a crystal ball of his hedonistic calculus. The elite historiography pursued in India after independence only continued the tradition of Bentham without any epistemological break. This historiography wrote away subaltern reality of India as a myth.

An effort to expose the falsity of Indian elite is also called the subaltern studies. Gayatri Chakravorty Spivak has admitted that South Asian model postcolonialists have not come to grips with the fact that India, with its ninety million Aboriginals, is a precapitalist, precolonial, non-European settler colony, whereas the postcolonial Hindu majority of India is, roughly speaking, the first settler—and even this formulation is mired in Aryanist nonsense.[96] No wonder that scholars' work in the 1960s raised controversial questions regarding the nature and results of the colonial rule in India. Did the imperialist British deserve credit, they asked, after all for making India into a developing, modern, and united country? Better than anyone else, Dipesh Chakrabarty summed up the spirit of enquiry among rebelling historians who discarded the Cambridge school of historiography when he wrote,

> Official documents of the British government of India—and traditions of imperial history writing—always portrayed colonial rule as being beneficial to India and her people. They applauded the British for bringing to the subcontinent political unity, modern educational institutions, modern industries, modern nationalism, a rule of law, and so forth. Indian historians in the 1960s—many of whom had English degrees and most of whom belonged to a generation that grew up in the final years of British rule—challenged that view. They argued instead that colonialism had had deleterious effects on economic and cultural developments. Modernity and the nationalist desire for political unity, they claimed, were not so much British gifts to India as fruits of struggles undertaken by the Indians themselves.[97]

Ranajit Guha, the pioneer of the subaltern studies, insisted that instead of being a survivor in a modernising colonial world, the peasant was a real contemporary of colonialism and a fundamental part of the modernity to which colonial rule gave rise in India.[98] Comparatively, the peasants were more violent than the elites. However, history, unlike mythology, is authored, and the peasants cannot be expected to maintain written records like the intellectuals.

However, the absence of peasant autobiographies and the recognition of this absence forms the semiotic base of subaltern studies. A notion of resistance against the elitist history is vital to a subaltern motivation. The peasant uprisings in colonial India, Guha argued, reflected this separate and autonomous grammar of mobilization in its most comprehensive form.[99] Even in the cases of urban workers' resistance and protests, the figure of mobilization was one that was derived directly from peasant insurgency.[100]

Subaltern studies was in part a product of a metropolitan Marxist tradition of a history from below. But the nature of political modernity in colonial India made this project of history writing nothing short of an engaged critique of the academic discipline of history itself. The semiotic theories take signs or sign systems as their object of study. Subaltern studies is essentially a project of looking for indigenous signs of resistance to modernity—that is, peasant struggles in India, against the elitist historiography.

India's subaltern reality that was filed away by the officially documented history of British historians can be studied as a history of the communication of the signs that the regular peasant uprisings against colonial rule had produced, only to be rediscovered later. Afterward, the subalterners have examined areas belonging also to the natural sciences. Now we must turn to pragmatics—the branch of semiotics that deals with all the psychological and sociological phenomena that materialise in the functioning of signs. This chapter is a small step in that direction.

X. Signification of International Law

Myth can also be seen as a language that needs decoding.[101] Thus, what is needed is to apply the theory of signification. The theory of signification, if applied to international law, has an insightful potential. However, this chapter does not mandate a full-length deliberation on the grammar and dialectic of international law while signifying it. Yet there are many international law scholars, such as Martti Koskenniemi, who have expressed concerns about the grammar of international law, particularly its universality.[102] B. S. Chimni, however, felt that such a critique of international law from the West, identified as new approaches to international law (NAIL), does not offer solutions unlike third world approaches to international law (TWAIL).[103]

Nonetheless, this debate takes us to the issue of myth in international law. Koskenniemi thought that finding equitable solutions or knowing who the aggressor is or when to launch a humanitarian operation would not be impossible or even necessarily difficult.[104] But little about such a decision-making process can plausibly be seen in terms of employing a legal vocabulary of rules and principles, precedents or institutions.[105] Instead, the relevant considerations always seem to require technical expertise and calculations of the data produced in the context in order to figure out the best outcome.[106] Thus, the problem of science in Koskenniemi's characterisation is actually a problem of technicality:

> The power of myth must be reawakened, in opposition to the inconsistency of the abstract universals (of science, of democracy, of philosophy) and in the face of the collapse (fully realized in the war of 1914–18) of the two beliefs of the modern age: Christianity, and the belief in humanity.[107]

Mired in the interpolations and polemic of development, international law is essentially an exercise in semiotics. The aim of universalising international law contains the hidden agenda of capitalist avarice that, in turn, has a bearing on the grammar and dialectic of international law's language. The language of international law and its potential room for dialectic is indeed of prime importance for the subject who seeks to modernise and civilise. For example, the grammar and dialectic of this law justifies the project of exploiting the tribal peoples around the world, all in the name of development.

XI. Conclusion

While contextualising semiotics, development, and modernity in international law, we automatically come to constitutionalist discourses. Hidden in the symbolism produced beyond the text of a constitution, though similar in accent to the history texts authored by the elites, are signals of resistance offered by the textless, illiterate, and so-called backward non-Western sentiments. The semiotics of law must capture it. Acclaimed human rights scholar Upendra Baxi wrote that

> The history of evolution of modern constitutionalism is a narrative of growth of asymmetries in domination and resistance. Principles of constitutionalism were perfected in Europe at the very historic moment when colonialism flourished. In retrospect, the narrative of constitutional development in decolonized societies provides a massive indictment of accomplishments of liberal thought.[108]

An ideal type investigative methodology in social sciences, though serving the cause of a composite international law, is much more than simply paying lip service to its relationship with semiotics. Consequently, the task of the semiotic study of history is to observe numerous individual cases and, from these, abstract typical characteristics. Mine is such an exercise. An ideal investigation of various kinds of pasts to reveal the status of the present never really exists in reality; instead, it is a pure theoretical configuration. Semiotics helps to an extent in locating and interpreting the signals and signs hidden in mythological narrations, which, unlike history, are not authored.

Because true myth is unauthored, the chances of finding truth in its symbolism are very high. The Frankfurt School has long criticised the positivism of scientific studies that ignore the psychological aspect of value creation. As a consequence, we can see how myth was rejected for history that tried to subdue certain signals of equality and apathy for similar activities globally. It will now become clearer why Plato rejected myth in his politics and, as soon as the Second World War was over, the Frankfurt scholars went back to their agenda of antifascism.

Today, few people believe in the plurality of science. The mainstream view of science would not believe that there can be politics or culture in the content of science.[109] On the sociological level, one solution could be to understand the diverse moorings of diverse civilisations. For example, any attempt to align the tribes with today's selfish modernity is an act of aggression and expression of modernity's superior science over those who either fail to understand it or who do not wish to engage with it. The birth of disciplines has likewise obscured cultural and intellectual values from the point of view of defeated systems of knowledge and with the psychological costs of confronting an imperial system of knowledge outside the western world.[110] International law has been a language of colonisation and, therefore, modernisation.

On a theoretical level, therefore, we can debate whether international law is a science, natural or social, or simply an alleged servant of empire. International lawyers, like other social scientists, are the makers and managers of meaning in a much deeper way than most lawyers actually realise. They not only manage the meaning of law but are also managed by it. Thus, the question of authority and the source of knowledge is very important in attempting to understand international law on a semiotic plane. The sources of knowledge—not only legal—constitute long-standing discussion. The distinction between the East and the West has been its symbolic attachment with knowledge's semiotics. History has been the origin of Western knowledge, whereas myth has been the mother of Eastern knowledge.

Linguistic studies of myth have shown that structures of myth are as rigorous as that of science. Thus, what obscures myth against science is the paucity of semiotic vision in law. Unfortunately, not many scholars in international law have been able to appreciate semiotics as an important vehicle for a full-blown alternative vision of international law. Semiotics of international law should not be confused with myth-science animosity; rather, it should be seen as a possible bridge between them. Semiotics is the art of revealing symbolism hidden in the epistemology of myth. Thus, civilisations with their myths can potentially provide solutions not imagined before.

The search for an alternative vision of international law is such an exercise. The structural studies of myth carried in anthropology have not been adequately followed in international law. Foucault and other postmodernists have usefully used semiotics to employ myth for reality. Appadurai's discourse on the past and its boundaries is only a modicum of this alternative vision. An ounce of Foucault's and another from Nandy's mixed into Appadurai's could turn into a possible panacea of semiotic vision of modernity, myth, and the past.

A commissioned study for intellectual exploitation of this medicine can definitely cure some of the open wounds that the intellectual harangue against the non-Western knowledge systems have inflicted. My most serious concern is that the globalisation of prosperity is creating new elites and de-eliting some of the old members. The scene remains unchanged as new patterns of poverty, injustice, and exploitation are only changing geography and race. International law must capture these changing semiotics.

NOTES

1. It would be unfair to cite a single work of Foucault for the purposes of this chapter. All his works—*The Birth of the Clinic, The Order of Things, Discipline and Punish*, three volumes of *The History of Sexuality*, and *History of Madness* (an earlier abridged version was translated as *Madness and Civilization*, used here)—can all be read chronologically to get at his deductions. They have thus been cited as and when needed throughout the chapter. Between *The Archaeology of Knowledge* and *Discipline and Punish*, Foucault did change—a reading of Nietzsche's *Genealogy of Morals* shifted his model of history—from a layered view to directionless branches. This turned out to be boon for new studies that followed, and it is also true about this current chapter.

2. Arjun Appadurai, Modernity at Large: Cultural Dimensions of Globalization (1996).

3. Ashis Nandy, *The Intimate Enemy: Loss of Recovery of Self Under Colonialism, in* Exiled at Home v (Ashis Nandy ed., 2002).

4. Steney Shami, *Prehistories of Globalisation: Circassian Identity in Motion, in* Globalisation, 220–21(Arjun Appadurai ed., 2001).

5. Nandy, *supra* note 3, at 47–48.

6. A. G. Noorani, *The Constitution and the Course of Politics*, 17:7 Frontline, Apr. 1, 2000, *available at* www.hinduonnet.com/fline/fl1707/17070820.htm (reviewing Granville Austin, Working a Democratic Constitution: The Indian Experience (2000).

7. Arjun Appadurai, *The Past as a Scarce Resource*, 16 Man 203, 201–19 (1981).

8. Nandy, *supra* note 3, at 60.

9. Donald Wehrs, *Sartre's Legacy in Postcolonial Theory; Or, Who's Afraid of Non-Western Historiography and Cultural Studies?* 34 New Liter'y Hist. 763, 761–89 (2003).

10. I have discussed the role of myth, native knowledge, and international law's construction in Prabhakar Singh, *The Scandal of Enlightenment and the Birth of Discipline: Is International Law a Science?* 12 Int'l. Commun'y. L. Rev. 5–34 (2010).

11. Michel Foucault, Madness and Civilization: A History of Insanity in the Age of Reason, 96–100 (Richard Howard trans., 2003).

12. *See* Antonio Gramsci, *Intellectuals, in* Selections from the Prison Notebooks of A. Gramsci 5–23 (2010).

13. Philippe Lacoue-Labarthe & Jean-Luc Nancy, *The Nazi Myth*, 16 Crit. Inq. 293, 291–312 (Brian Holmes trans., 1990).

14. A. K. Narain, *Alexander and India*, 12 Greece & Rome, 162, 155–65 (1965).

15. *Id.*

16. *Id.*

17. J. W. Jackson, *The Aryan and the Semite*, 7 Anthropological Rev. 335, 333–65 (1869).

18. F. Hegel, *Philosophy of History, in* 43 Great Books of the Western World: A Chronology of Great Authors, 274–82 (Mortimer Adler ed., 2007).

19. Lacoue-Labarthe & Nancy, *supra* note 13, at 299.

20. *Id.*

21. *Id.*

22. Jackson, *supra note* 17, at 336.

23. *Id.* (emphasis added).

24. *Id.* at 336, 341.

25. *Id.* at 340 (emphasis added).

26. Nandy, *supra* note 3, at 14.

27. LYDIA ALIX FILLINGHAM, FOUCAULT FOR BEGINNERS 83 (2008).

28. Nandy, *supra* note 3, at 15.

29. *Id.* (emphasis supplied).

30. Nandy, *supra* note 3. This is not only a question worthy of academic debate. The regular print media have, after a number of very high-profiles cases, begun questioning the psychological violence of modern art that has issues with today's values and morality. *See* Stephen Glover, *A Paedophile Photograph. Polanski. Why On Earth Does the Arts World Think It Is Immune from Morality?* THE MAIL ONLINE (Oct. 1, 2009), *available at* www.dailymail.co.uk/debate/article-1217282/ STEPHEN-GLOVER-A-paedophile-photograph—Polanski—earth-does-arts-world-think immune-morality .html.

31. Kant, *Critique of Aesthetic Judgement, in* 39 GREAT BOOKS OF THE WESTERN WORLD: A CHRONOLOGY OF THE GREAT AUTHORS, 476–77 (Mortimer Adler ed., 2007).

32. *Id.* at 481.

33. *Id.* at 483.

34. *Id.* at 480.

35. *Id.* at 488.

36. *Id.* at 523.

37. Lacoue-Labarthe & Nancy, *supra* note 13, at 303.

38. *Id.*

39. *Id.* at 297.

40. Claude Levi-Strauss, *The Structural Study of Myth*, 68 J. AM. FOLKLORE 430, 428–444 (1955).

41. Lacoue-Labarthe & Nancy, *supra* note 13, at 309.

42. Levi-Strauss, *supra* note 41, at 443.

43. Nuremberg Trial Proceedings, Vol. 5, Thirty-Sixth Day, Thursday, Jan. 17, 1946, *Morning Session*, 422, *available at* http://avalon.law.yale.edu/imt/01–17 –46.asp.

44. MARC SAUTET, NIETZSCHE FOR BEGINNERS 52–58 (2010).

45. Nietzsche was cited thus: The culminating philosophy of Nietzsche was to exercise a dominant influence over people in this state of spiritual crisis and of negations of traditional values. In taking the will to power as a point of departure, Nietzsche preached certainly not inhumanity but rather superhumanity. For Nietzsche the Industrial Revolution necessarily entails the rule of the masses, the automatism and the shaping of the working multitudes. The state endures only by virtue of an elite of vigorous personalities who—by the methods so admirably defined by Machiavelli, which alone are in accord with the laws of life—will lead men by force and by ruse simultaneously, for men are and remain wicked and perverse. Without doubt, the late philosophy of Nietzsche cannot be identified with the brutal simplicity of National Socialism. Nevertheless, National Socialism was wont to glorify Nietzsche as one of its ancestors. And justly so, for he was the first to formulate in a coherent manner criticism of the traditional values of humanism; also, because his conception of the government of the masses by masters knowing no restraint is a preview of the Nazi regime. Besides, Nietzsche believed in the sovereign race and attributed primacy to Germany, whom he considered endowed with a youthful soul and unquenchable resources. *See* Nuremberg Trial Proceedings, *supra* note 43, at 375, 376.

46. JIM POWELL, POSTMODERNISM FOR BEGINNERS (2010).

47. Ashis Nandy, *The Psychology of Colonialism, in* Nandy, *supra* note 3, at 7. This is not to say that Gandhi did not have detractors. Naicker's dissent was not with Gandhi but rather with his own identity as a Tamil Hindu. Even though he bore the name of Rama, the most successful of all Hindu Gods, which is often highly politicised, Naicker claimed a non-Hindu Tamil identity. The Sri Lankan Singhal-Tamil disputes are an offshoot of a similar identity crisis. But what is important about Gandhi is that he was the first visionary national politician who appreciated the plight of the non-elites and demanded their emancipation. How can one forget the seminal work of Gandhi in socially and politically uplifting the untouchables, calling them the men of God (*Harijan*), and empowering women though cooperative, self-sufficient village economy? Thus, what he preached in India came from his South African experience with apartheid. *See* P. C. AGGARWAL, HALFWAY TO EQUALITY: THE HARIJANS OF INDIA (1983).

48. Levi-Strauss, *supra* note 40, at 309.

49. *Id.*

50. *Id.* at 297.

51. Nandy, *supra* note 3, at 83.

52. *Id.*

53. Jürgen Habermas, *Moral Development and Ego Identity, in* COMMUNICATION AND THE EVOLUTION OF SOCIETY 69 (Thomas McCarthy trans., 1979).

54. Nandy, *supra* note 3, at 63.

55. Peter Niesen, *Colonialism and Hospitality* 3 POL. & ETHICS REV. 90–108 (2007).

56. Singh, *supra* note 10, at 14–19.

57. Levi-Strauss, *supra* note 40, at 444.

58. *Id.*

59. Arjun Appadurai, *Putting Hierarchy in Its Place*, 3 CULTURAL ANTHROPOLOGY 36–49 (1988).

60. *Id.*

61. Shami, *supra* note 4, at 221.

62. A. APPAURAI, HIERARCHY IN ITS PLACE 36 (1988).

63. SOCIOLOGY: AN INTRODUCTION 6 (S. M. Dubey & Dinesh Sharma, eds., Susheela Dobhal trans., 1990).

64. Levi-Strauss, *supra* note 40, at 420.

65. Arjun Appadurai, *Theory in Anthropology: Center and Periphery*, 28 COMP. STUD. SOC'Y & HIST. 357, 356–61 (1986).

66. *Id.*

67. *Id.*

68. *Id.*

69. Vidyanath Jha & D. N. Tiwari, *Certain Scientific Observations as Depicted in Indian Philosophical Principles*, 2 INDIAN J. TRADITIONAL KNOWLEDGE 170–80 (2003).

70. For a powerful discourse on the science of mythology, *see* C. G. JUNG & C. KERÉNYI, ESSAYS ON A SCIENCE OF MYTHOLOGY: THE MYTH OF THE DIVINE CHILD AND THE MYSTERIES OF ELEUSIS (2001).

71. Nandy, *supra* note 3, at viii.

72. Foucault, *supra* note 11, at 187.

73. *Id.* at 184.

74. Nancy S. Love, *Epistemology and Exchange: Marx, Nietzsche, and Critical Theory*, 41 NEW GERMAN CRIT. 83, 71–94 (1987).

75. Foucault, *supra* note 11, at 42.

76. *Id.* at 42.

77. *Id.* at 43.

78. CHAIM WAXMAN, THE STIGMA OF POVERTY: A CRITIQUE OF POVERTY THEORIES AND POLICIES, 67 (2d. ed., 1983).

79. Foucault, *supra* note 11, at 42.

80. Levi-Strauss, *supra* note 40, at 444.

81. Foucault, *supra* note 11, at 45–45.

82. EDWARD SAID, ORIENTALISM (1979).

83. *Id.* at 5

84. Nandy, *supra* note 3, at 17.

85. Ashis Nandy, *History's Forgotten Doubles*, 34 HIST. & THEORY, 47, 44–66 (1995).

86. ERIC STOKES, THE ENGLISH UTILITARIANS AND INDIA 13 (1989).

87. *Id.* at 259.

88. LOLA ROMANUCCI-ROSS & LAURENCE TANCREDI, WHEN LAW AND MEDICINE MEET: A CULTURAL VIEW 21 (2004).

89. Piyel Haldar, *Utilitarianism and the Painful Orient*, 16 SOC. & LEGAL STUD. 577 (2007).

90. Stokes, *supra* note 86, at 279.

91. Haldar, *supra* note 89, at 279.

92. *Id.*

93. Stokes, *supra* note 86, at 367.

94. Nandy, *supra* note 3, at 6 n.8.

95. Fillingham, *supra* note 27, at 126, 129.

96. G. C. Spivak, *Foreword: Upon Reading the Companion to Postcolonial Studies*, in A COMPANION TO POSTCOLONIAL STUDIES, xvii, xv–xxii (Henry Schwarz & Sangeeta Ray eds., 2000).

97. Dipesh Chakrabarty, *Subaltern Studies and Postcolonial Historiography*, 1 NEPANTLA: VIEWS FROM SOUTH 11, 9–32 (2000).

98. *Id.* at 17.

99. *Id.* at 16.

100. *Id.*

101. Levi-Strauss, *supra* note 40, at 430.

102. MARTTI KOSKENNIEMI, FROM APOLOGY TO UTOPIA: THE STRUCTURE OF INTERNATIONAL LEGAL ARGUMENT (2005).

103. B. S. Chimni, *Towards a Radical Third World Approach to International Law*, 5 ICCLP REVIEW 1, 4–26 (2002).

104. Martti Koskenniemi, *The Fate of Public International Law: Between Technique and Politics*, 70 MOD. L. REV. 10, 1–30 (2007).

105. *Id.*

106. *Id.*

107. Lacoue-Labarthe & Nancy, *supra* note 13, at 307.

108. Upendra Baxi, *Postcolonial Legality*, in A COMPANION TO POSTCOLONIAL STUDIES 540 (Henry Schwarz & Sangeeta Ray eds., 2005).

109. ASHIS NANDY, ALTERNATIVE SCIENCES: CREATIVITY AND AUTHENTICITY IN TWO INDIAN SCIENTISTS viii (2d ed. 2001).

110. *Id.* at ix.

26

The Postcoloniality of International Law

SUNDHYA PAHUJA

How are we to understand the relationship between international law and imperialism? What bearing might that have on how we see contemporary international law? According to one view, international law is simply a "cloak of legality" thrown over the subjugation of colonized peoples by the imperial powers in a distortion of international law's true spirit.[1] According to this understanding, the contemporary task is to rid international law of the vestiges of that misappropriation. We must accept decolonization at face value and continue to broaden the scope and content of international law in a culturally sensitive way. If we were to set ourselves this task of "envisioning new orders," we would, therefore, be required to rescue international law from the corruption of power to make good international law's explicit promise of universality and sovereign equality.[2]

At the other end of the spectrum is the belief that international law has always been encompassed by and in service to empire. At this pole, the very doctrines and institutions of international law are understood to have been molded by the powerful in order to serve their interests. Those who hold power in the contemporary setting maintain the capacity to create and deploy international law, in turn facilitating practices of (neo)colonialism.

However, most scholars engaged with the "postcolonial" in some form or other would hesitate to embrace either of these two polar positions. On the one hand, the perception of international law as an innocent victim waiting to be rescued from the corruptions of imperialism is untenable. On the other hand, the view that international law abjectly serves empire is equally unpopular with those so engaged. They are generally unwilling to accept such an encompassing frame and its attendant demand to abandon international law as a site of contestation, both historically and presently. And, thus, there is an irresolution that disrupts any attempt to characterize international law neatly as either on the side of the angels or in devilish league with imperialism.

Rather than simply attributing this to the indeterminacy of language or to the formal nature of law, it is important to inquire into the quality of this irresolution and to ask whether it is *itself* significant.[3] Arguably there is something distinctive about the relation implied in the "postcolonial"—both a break from and a continuity with past forms of domination—and something particular about the capacity of law to be both appropriated to imperial ends and used as a force for liberation.[4]

With this in mind, I argue that the quality of this irresolution suggests that *international law is itself already postcolonial* in that it both sustains and contains within it what we might call the condition of the postcolonial. Succinctly stated, this can be understood not only as the circular self-constitution of self and Other but also as the paradoxical inclusion of the excluded necessitated by the claim to universality of this constitution. This dynamic accounts for both international law's imperializing effect and its anti-imperial tendency. Crucially, whether or not this dynamic is in some way addressed would seem to indicate whether an approach to international law is likely to have any critical purchase or will instead be drawn back into reproducing colonial relations of power.

In the rest of this chapter, I will outline the dimensions of this postcoloniality and its implications with reference to two examples. The first is the universalization of international law through decolonization, and the second is the limited success of recent attempts to "decolonize" human rights by refounding them on more "truly" universal grounds.

I. The Postcoloniality of International Law

Let us begin with the near truism of postcolonial literature: "that European or Western identity is constituted in opposition to an alterity that it has itself constructed."[5] In other words, the formation of the West depends on the construction of an "Other" by reference to which the West defines itself. To this Other are attributed characteristics the West both rejects and ostensibly lacks—the Other is crucially what the West is *not*. This Other does not exist as such in that it is not a being with any quiddity before this circular self-constitution of the West. Nonetheless, the construction has real consequences and effects for those who people the construction, those who are variously understood to be "savages and barbarians, or even those of the West less occidental than they should be."[6] Significantly, this self-constitution forms identity in a "defining exclusion of certain existent peoples accorded characteristics ostensibly opposed to that identity."[7] The "defining exclusion" arises when the characteristics attributed to the Other are ostensibly driven out but become essential to the identity of the West by the process of negative definition.

What is less frequently observed, and what could be said to "initiate the defining moment of postcolonialism," is that "the exclusion of these others is intrinsically antithetical to the West's arrogation of the universal to itself since this arrogation would require the inclusion within the West of those very Others excluded in its constitution."[8] In other words, the West claims to itself the character of the "universal." Its reason may be applied to the many. Its knowledge of the world is defining, and the world is made (one) within it. But for this claim to be true, for the values of the West to *be* universal, it would require that what is excluded in the very act of self-constitution be included. Those who populate the Other, those subjected in this process, are thus "torn between exclusion as something radically different to the West and the demand to join and become the same as it."[9]

This paradox—of the circular self-constitution of Other and self combined with the universal applicability of that claim—explains, at least in part, the impelling dynamic of international law and its puzzling containment of both liberatory promise and imperializing peril. Furthermore, it also explains why strategies that are based on producing "genuine" universality, or revalorizing the Other, or even projects that are directed at revealing the politics of international law in a nonspecific way are destined to reproduce the imperializing urge. Let us turn briefly to two examples to explore this idea further.

II. Decolonization as the "Universalization" of International Law

It is commonplace in standard texts of international law to observe that after decolonization took place, international law became truly universal and a real community of states came into being. This universality lay in the fact that those who had been excluded from the realm of sovereignty were now included and could participate in the international system on the footing of sovereign equals.[10]

It could be argued, though, that given the fact that international law had already become *uni-*

versally applicable during the period of colonization as the determinative system of law governing relations over the whole of the globe, this shift was not a shift toward universality as such but instead from one universalism to another. This shift would then illustrate the postcoloniality of international law.

Wherever international law goes, it claims to already have the jurisdiction to act as the law and to extend to everyone. At the same time as international law claims to extend to everyone, there is a formation of and differentiation between the self who is the subject of law, and the Other who is encompassed by this speaking of the law but not able to claim subjecthood within it.

Indeed, from the very beginning, international law had to posit, contain, and differentiate between selves and Others. As Antony Anghie has shown in relation to Francisco de Vitoria and his ostensible defense of the Indian, the law had to be universal in that it had to apply *to* the Indians. Nevertheless, Indians still had to be differentiated; otherwise how could their land justifiably be appropriated?[11]

When it comes to the subject proper of international law, the nation-state, a similar constitution of law and subject exists. Indeed, as John Strawson has aptly observed, the Peace of Westphalia in 1648 can be understood as having "granted a monopoly of legal personality to the European powers" rather than as having established the doctrine of state sovereignty as such.[12] This unavoidable circularity is still apparent in international law's doctrinal relation to the nation-state. For instance, it is evident in international law's tendency to oscillate (in)decisively between recognizing a preexisting nation-state and declaring that a nascent state shall hereinafter exist, revealing a law that declares itself to be founded on the consent of states, the very juridical entities it defines.

The circular inauguration of law and subject and the capture of legal personality by the nation-state are accompanied by a universal claim of nation made in both spatial and temporal terms. The "modern" nation covers the earth. The terms of international "comity" then "society" and now "community" "effect a closure around nation [and] confirm its universal reach" because those terms are "secured in the pervasion of nation . . . leav[ing] no space that is not national space."[13]

But the nation also makes a universal claim in the temporal dimension. It presents itself as the axiomatic form of "modern" social organization. Peoples who were not nations were not *yet* nations. Although they existed in the same moment in fact, they were organized conceptually as existing in the past. The present of the nation was the future of the non-nation. That is, for the nation to be universal, there had to be some way of securing this reality. Non-national forms of social and political organization had to be maintained in their particularity, or *non*universality, both to enable their domination and maintain their inclusion as nonsubjects within the realm of the law. And this was where that remarkable conceptual arsenal came into play, quilting around historicism—"the idea that to understand anything it has to be seen both as a unity and in its historical development."[14] Thus, a distinction could be posited between the "civilized" and "uncivilized" parts of the world through which colonization and the appropriation of land were facilitated and justified.

Therefore, the self-founding—of international law and its national subjects—entails what we might call a "cut" between self and Other. This cut has the effect of constituting both that which is brought into being—or founded—and its opposite, that which is not. But the constitution of and differentiation between that which is ostensibly being founded and that which is not—here the nation—must also make a claim to be universal. The paradoxical effect of this encompassing is to secure the fixity of the cut while erasing its occurrence and, thereby, rendering it authoritative and so seemingly universally true.[15]

To summarize briefly, it is the putative universality of the nation that made it open to appropriation by proto-national liberation movements. The non-nation is also peopled—and by people

who cannot be constituted in a complete or finite way. This excess is evidenced by the fact
that colonized nationalists opposed the "not yet"
of the historicist response to the claim for national liberation with an insistent "now."[16] And
so those unwilling to accept that they were incapable of self-rule challenged the "waiting
room" version of history.[17]

For present purposes, it is significant that the
struggles that were successful took the form of
national liberation struggles rather than struggles
for decolonization in some other form. Although some have attributed this continuity to
the subsumption by the decolonizing elites of
imperial structures of rule or to the acceptance
(often through education) of the colonizer's
episteme,[18] in international legal terms, the only
way to decolonize was through self-determination as a nation-state.[19] Indeed, several mutually
supportive doctrines of international law existed
to ensure this. These included the rules surrounding statehood and the investiture of international legal personality exclusively in the
nation-state—reinforced by doctrines such as *uti
possedetis*—which ensured not only that the
nation-state form was "the only way to enter the
world beyond and be recognized as a rightful
player in it,"[20] but also that the territorial definition of the new state remained the one be-
queathed to it by the colonial powers.[21]
Therefore, although the universal claim of nation contained the dangerously emancipatory
possibility of universality—that is, of applying
to everyone—adopting the particular form of
the nation-state was the only way to become
"someone" and to enter the community of nations. That is, the achievement of "self-determination" took place through a contradictory
relationship to the categories of international
law that became "truly" universal only by granting formal legal status to new subjects by rendering them commensurable with its forms.

But this containment within was not the end
of the story because although (almost) all of the
newly decolonized territories received formal
legal recognition as nation-states sooner or later,
they still could not overcome their particularity.

Just because the newly independent states had
rejected the historicist injunction that they were
not ready for independence, that did not mean
that the West had wholly accepted that rejection
and abandoned historicist assumptions or understandings of the world. Indeed, in some ways
this responsive adaptation of international law
to national liberation struggles brought the savage Other into an even more proximate relation
with the West, thus necessitating a new form of
containment. Even as the promise of universality was captured to the extent of ascribing the
juridical form of nation to these entities, other
conceptual mechanisms were engendered to effect the ongoing containment of the savage
Other while its endless transformation into the
modern, or universal, nation was continually
re-enacted.

Thus, it is no coincidence that the notions of
"development" and "underdevelopment" were
born at the same moment that decolonization
was underway.[22] According to this deeply historicist account, the nonuniversality of the
newly formed nations was understood in contradistinction to the universal (Western) nations
and was maintained once again through the idea
that nonmodern forms of social organization existed in the historical past and that the present
Western nations were exemplars of the future for
those nonmodern nations. Thus, instead of different kinds of entities, potentially both national
and non-national and existing heteronomously
side by side, the modern nation existed in "ho-
mogenous empty time."[23] As Chatterjee put it,
"by imagining . . . modernity . . . as an attribute
of time itself, this view succeeds not only in
branding the resistances to it as archaic and
backward, but also in securing for capital and
modernity their ultimate triumph, regardless of
what some people may believe or hope, because
after all, time does not stand still."[24]

This understanding of the world authorized—
indeed necessitated—ongoing interventions to
make the Third World "modern." From the
Trusteeship and Mandate system[25] to the contemporary interventions of the International
Monetary Fund and World Bank as well as

countless other development institutions and aid organizations, the savage, primitive, backward, and, finally, underdeveloped peoples of the world were reconstituted as Other to the West. An international community founded on "universal values" replaced the notion of the comity of (civilized) nations. These values provided the ground on which interventions took place, based on the notion that these values are, and should be, universally acknowledged. Such putative grounding permits the notion of international community to contain and cohere a scalar progression of nations "from the most 'advanced' liberal democracies to barely coherent nations always about to slip into the abyss of an ultimate savage alterity that still remains . . . and has to be transcended to achieve fullness as a nation."[26] These "universal values" become a sort of generative matrix out of which we can see the production of a particular sort of (universal) nation.[27] Not only is "nation" produced by this matrix, but the international community is generated as well. In many documents justifying interventions of various kinds,[28] the international community is imagined as being composed of the aggregate of particular nations but is also posited at the same time as the source of "universal" values on which international institutions draw to justify their characterization of these particular values as universal.[29] Thus, there is a circular relation of nation and international community in which each reinforces the Other's claim to universality. At the same time, though, the matrix of possibility excludes those kinds of nations that fail to meet the test of a particular kind of universalized nation.

Therefore, the universalization of international law after decolonization can be seen on the one hand to mark the newly decolonized peoples' capture of the promise of a generally applicable law, and on the other hand to show the way this promise could only be made good through adopting legal forms already commensurable with international law. This demand for commensurability is produced by the way in which universalization is a definite process that requires a specific form to *be* universalized but

that depends on the paradoxical claim that what is being universalized is *already* universal. And so the process secures its occurrence. This dynamic is also visible in the instance of human rights, where contemporary attempts to render those rights "truly" universal can be seen as almost an inverse example of the foregoing. Indeed, as if to intensify the echo, some have even referred to this process as the "decolonization" of human rights.[30]

III. Refounding Human Rights

Among postcolonial approaches to international law there have been several attempts to move toward a new concept of human rights, one that is more concordant with the times. Such approaches laudably attempt to bring different perspectives to bear on human rights or to incorporate different voices among those who speak the law. Scholars working in this vein acknowledge that it is no longer possible to deny the cultural specificity of the human rights regime and that it is increasingly untenable to embrace a vision of human rights that ignores the colonial origins of international law. They draw on a persuasive array of examples of the exclusionary effects of contemporary human rights, especially in relation to indigenous peoples.[31] In such work, there is also sometimes a useful emphasis on the ways in which the hierarchization of civil and political rights on the one hand and economic, social, and cultural rights on the other perpetuates the continuation of colonial structures of oppression.[32] The concomitant privileging of the individual over the collective exacerbates this perpetuation.[33]

Often these approaches draw a connection between the limitations of human rights and their putative universality. Universality is taken to have been temporarily appropriated by the "Euro-American meaning of universality" that "it is necessary to give up . . . If international human rights are to continue to have universal relevance."[34] When the problem is cast this way, what seems necessary is the production of more inclusive standards of behavior that cut across different cultures so as to find values that are shared and that transform a culturally specific universality into a real universality.

Approaches in this vein follow in the footsteps of radical Third World international lawyers who tried to take advantage of the universalization of international law through decolonization and refound international law on more genuinely universal grounds, both through mechanisms such as the voting power acquired in the UN General Assembly and in scholarship and writing.[35] Such a universalizing process would require that "many more universal perspectives drawn from all the world's cultural traditions can and must be fed into [international law] as it develops to suit the needs of the twenty-first century."[36] In a more self-consciously postcolonial vein, human rights law scholars reveal the hidden sources of positive value in the ostensibly occidental universal values by acknowledging the exchange of values between colonized and colonizer.[37] In other words, such approaches justify the universality of international law and/or human rights on the grounds that non-European cultural values are equally entitled to inform universal values or, indeed, already have shaped universal values through colonial exchange.

This of course brings us back to the universal, for if the argument is that human rights would be better if they were genuinely universal, if they were truly "applicable to everyone," then arguably it is necessary to explore the relationship between the concept of universality itself and the "byzantine reinforcements of colonial power and knowledge,"[38] not to mention its relationship to Christianity.[39] Similarly, the project of refounding human rights in different or other cultures leaves unexamined the way in which modern law marks its authority precisely through originary gestures.[40] Arguably, no matter a system's normative content or its philosophical foundations, the search for foundations is itself a search for authority. It is an act of "discovering" and narrating an origin that draws a limit by saying "this is our beginning," and it is from here that we exist and have meaning. The effect is thus au-

thoritative and authorizing. By founding authority, the narrative of origin erases the possibility of being otherwise. Moreover, it prevents the subject of narration from being more than the origin allows. The subject is fixed: It is always that which is born of its origin. Theories and narrations of self-determination and sovereignty are inextricably bound up with narratives of law's authority as well as that of the state and its claim to legitimate power and violence.[41]

It is, therefore, doubtful whether refounding human rights, even on unacknowledged and richly diverse sources, would ultimately be capable of escaping the originary violence of the creation of the subject of law and, therefore, of the Other—even if now the self is recast. Indeed such refounding may play into international law's imperializing urges, this time powerfully delineating what it means to be human.

Thus, in effect, projects directed at refounding seem to grant too solid an existence to the Other by attempting, for instance, to revalorize cultures that have been devalorized. In this, there is a subtle underlying acceptance of certain essences or fixable identities and a concomitant slippage into certain of the "anthropological vision[s] that conferred cultural explanations on the colonized world."[42] For although it is indeed central to analyze practices of knowledge creation such that an Other to Europe was constructed, it is likewise crucial to explore the construction of the Other in terms of its necessity for constructing the self. This exploration could entail a consideration of the need for the self to be "whole"[43] or to have an identity that can be fixed. Such an interpretation would stand in contrast to understanding that construction as revealing facts about the Other as a being.

Rather than feeling the angst that many contemporary human rights scholars bear toward the familiar conundrum of the seeming choice, we must decide between the myth of universality and the nihilism of cultural relativism; the oscillation should be understood and embraced as symptomatic of the postcolonial quality of law and the radical impossibility of closure it generates. In an attempt to "decolonize" human rights, it is important to recognize that the split between self and Other is not so much "*within* the foundations of Enlightenment civilisation"[44] as it *is* the foundation itself. It is the "cut" that makes the categories that are the foundation of such thought. A recognition of the same might bring us to a more relational understanding in which we are forced to take account of the impossibility of fixed and determinate being—both for our selves and for our Others—in ways that open up, rather than broaden, reorganize, or even revalorize, the categorizations on which colonialism and imperialism depended and, arguably, on which human rights still depend.[45]

IV. Conclusion

The "post" in postcolonial designates a state neither clearly beyond nor after the colonial. Instead it denotes a "continuation of colonialism in the consciousness of the formerly colonized people, and in the institutions which were imposed in the process of colonization."[46] Key amongst those institutions is international law, which in some senses was formed out of the exigencies of imperialism. But if international law was the child of imperialism, "it is not only . . . a dutiful child but also . . . a child with oedipal inclinations."[47] And although international law is susceptible to power, it also maintains an oppositional relation to power. This irresolution can be understood as symptomatic of the "postcoloniality" of international law. This postcoloniality, in part, describes the way in which international law must continually effect a cut between "self" and "Other," rendering that which is excluded crucial to the formation of the included, but it also makes a claim to universality antithetical to this exclusion and that, in its encompassing, brings this productive instability to the heart of international law.

NOTES

1. CHRISTOPHER WEERAMANTRY, UNIVERSALISING INTERNATIONAL LAW 4 (2004). This is the mainstream view, if only because of colonialism's conspicuous absence from the dominant discourse.

2. For an exposition of this idea (not an espousal of the position), *see* John Strawson, *Book Review*, 5 MELB. UNIV. L. REV. 513 (2004) (reviewing CHRISTOPHER WEERAMANTRY, UNIVERSALISING INTERNATIONAL LAW (2004)).

3. For an eloquent take on the ambivalences of international law in relation to empire and its legacies, *see* Nathaniel Bermann, *In the Wake of Empire*, 14 AM. UNIV. INT'L L. REV. 1521 (1999).

4. *See generally* Peter Fitzpatrick, "*Gods Would be Needed . . .*" *American Empire and the Rule of (International) Law*, 16 LEIDEN J. INT'L L. 429 (2003); Peter Fitzpatrick, *Latin Roots: Imperialism and the Formation of Modern Law*, in CLAVE: COUNTERDISCIPLINARY NOTES ON RACE, NATION AND THE STATE (2005) [hereinafter Fitzpatrick, *Latin Roots*] (manuscript on file with the HARVARD INTERNATIONAL LAW JOURNAL).

5. Eve Darian-Smith & Peter Fitzpatrick, *Laws of the Postcolonial: An Insistent Introduction*, in LAWS OF THE POSTCOLONIAL 1 (1999). As Kumar has observed, it is appropriate to eschew an identification of the inaugural moment of postcolonial theory. Although this insight about the relationship between colonialism and the production of occidental knowledge, particularly knowledge about the "Orient," is usually said to have been inaugurated by Edward Said, even Said would agree that the lineage stretches back further than himself "in light of his numerous (relatively less-prominent) precursors, which include, among others, Franz Fanon, C. L. R. James, Chinua Achebe, Anta Diop, W. E. B. Du Bois, Romila Thapar, Aime Cesaire, not to mention the spate of 'Commonwealth literature' authors writing in the 1960s and 1970s." Vidya S. A. Kumar, *A Proleptic Approach to Postcolonial Legal Studies? A Brief Look at the Relationship Between Legal Theory and Intellectual History*, 2 LAW SOC. JUST. & GLOBAL DEV. J. (2003), *available at* www2.warwick.ac.uk/fac/soc/law/elj/lgd/2003_2/kumar/.

6. Darian-Smith & Fitzpatrick, *supra* note 5, at 1.

7. *Id.*

8. *Id.* at 1–2.

9. *Id.* at 2.

10. *See* ANTONY ANGHIE, IMPERIALISM, SOVEREIGNTY AND THE MAKING OF INTERNATIONAL LAW 197 (2004).

11. *Id.* at ch. 1.

12. Strawson, *supra* note 2, at 516.

13. *See* Sundhya Pahuja & Ruth Buchanan, *Law, Nation and (Imagined) International Communities*, 8 LAW TEXT CULTURE 137 (2004). *See also* PETER FITZPATRICK, MODERNISM AND THE GROUNDS OF LAW 121 (2001); Antony Anghie, *Finding the Peripheries: Sovereignty and Colonialism in Nineteenth Century International Law*, 40 HARV. INT'L L. J. 1 (1999).

14. DIPESH CHAKRABARTY, PROVINCIALIZING EUROPE 6 (2000).

15. This securing lasts only for an instant and so must constantly be reiterated.

16. Chakrabarty, *supra* note 14, at 9.

17. *Id.*

18. *See, e.g.*, Ranajit Guha, *On Some Aspects of the Historiography of Colonial India*, in SELECTED SUBALTERN STUDIES 37 (Ranajit Guha & Gayatri Chravorty Spivak eds., 1988).

19. *See, e.g.*, Dianne Otto, *Subalternity and International Law: The Problems of Global Community and the Incommensurability of Difference*, 5 SOC. & LEGAL STUD. 337, 339 (1996).

20. Fitzpatrick, *supra* note 13, at 127.

21. *Uti Possedetis Jure*: "you will have sovereignty over those territories you possess as of law." On this point and whether it is a rule of customary international law, a general principle of law, or a "simple practice," *see* ANTONIO CASSESE, INTERNATIONAL LAW 57 (2001).

22. *See* ARTURO ESCOBAR, ENCOUNTERING DEVELOPMENT: THE MAKING AND UNMAKING OF THE THIRD WORLD (1995); Gustavo Esteva, *Development, in* THE DEVELOPMENT DICTIONARY: A GUIDE TO KNOWLEDGE AS POWER 6 (Wolfgang Sachs ed., 1992).

23. BENEDICT ANDERSON, IMAGINED COMMUNITIES: REFLECTIONS ON THE ORIGIN AND SPREAD OF NATIONALISM (1983).

24. PARTHA CHATTERJEE, THE POLITICS OF THE GOVERNED 5 (2004).

25. *See, e.g.*, Anghie, *supra* note 10, at ch. 3; BALAKRISHNAN RAJAGOPAL, INTERNATIONAL LAW FROM BELOW: DEVELOPMENT, SOCIAL MOVEMENTS AND THIRD WORLD RESISTANCE ch. 3 (2003).

26. Fitzpatrick, *supra* note 13, at 127–28.

27. *See* Sundhya Pahuja & Ruth Buchanan, Difference Without Plurality: Nation-Building and the Imperializing Logic of International Law, International Law and Imperialism, Paper Presented at the Second Joint Workshop of Birkbeck and the Foundation for New Research in International Law, London (May 11, 2004).

28. *See, e.g.*, WORLD COMMISSION ON THE SOCIAL DIMENSION OF GLOBALIZATION, A FAIR GLOBALIZATION: CREATING OPPORTUNITIES FOR ALL (2004), *available at* www.ilo.org/public/english/wcsdg/docs/report.pdf.

29. *See* Pahuja & Buchanan, *supra* note 13.

30. *See, e.g.*, SHELLY WRIGHT, INTERNATIONAL HUMAN RIGHTS, DECOLONIZATION AND GLOBALIZATION: BECOMING HUMAN (2001).

31. *Id.*

32. *See, e.g., id.* at 190.

33. *See, e.g., id.* at 67.

34. *Id.* at 131.

35. Examples include the attempt to establish a new international economic order as well as the establishment of the UN Conference on Trade and Development. For a very useful background to these developments, *see* PETER KÖRNER ET AL., THE IMF AND THE DEBT CRISIS 5–73, 128–61 (Paul Knight trans., 1986).

36. Weeramantry, *supra* note 1, at 2–3.

37. *See, e.g.*, Wright, *supra* note 30.

38. NICHOLAS B. DIRKS, CASTES OF MIND: COLONIALISM AND THE MAKING OF MODERN INDIA 10 (2001).

39. One entry for "universality" in the *Oxford English Dictionary* defines it as Roman Catholicism's "extension to the whole world." 19 THE OXFORD ENGLISH DICTIONARY 85 (2d ed. 1989). Indeed, the Christian origins of human rights law as well as the replacement of sacred by secular orthodoxies for the foundations and ongoing project of human rights is a closely related and underexplored project in international law. *See generally* Jennifer Beard, *Understanding International Development Programs as a Modern Phenomenon of Early and Medieval Christian Theology*, 18 AUSTL. FEMINIST L. J. 27 (2003) (discussing the Christian origins of international law).

40. Fitzpatrick, *supra* note 13. *See also Special Issue, Divining the Source: Law's Foundation and the Question of Authority*, 19 AUSTL. FEMINIST L. J. (Jennifer Beard & Sundhya Pahuja eds., 2003).

41. Jacques Derrida, *Force of Law: The "Mystical Foundation of Authority," in* ACTS OF RELIGION 231 (Gil Anidjar ed., 2002). *See also* BARRY HINDESS, DISCOURSES OF POWER: FROM HOBBES TO FOUCAULT (1996).

42. Dirks, *supra* note 38, at 303.

43. *See* JENNIFER BEARD, THE POLITICAL ECONOMY OF DESIRE: LAW, DEVELOPMENT AND THE NATION STATE (2005); Jennifer Beard, *Representations of the Liberal State in the Art of Development*, 10 GRIFFITH L. REV. 6 (2002).

44. Wright, *supra* note 30, at 186.

45. This idea of thinking through relationality is inspired by my readings of Jean-Luc Nancy. *See* JEAN-LUC NANCY, THE INOPERATIVE COMMUNITY (1991); JEAN-LUC NANCY, SENSE OF THE WORLD (1997); Jean-Luc Nancy, *Finite History, in* THE BIRTH TO PRESENCE 143 (1993). These provocations do not come in any way close to indicating Nancy's argument but rather provoke the reader to explore them further.

46. MARGARET DAVIES, ASKING THE LAW QUESTION 278 (2d ed. 2002).

47. Fitzpatrick, *Latin Roots, supra* note 4, at 3.

PART NINE

INTERNATIONAL POLITICAL INTERACTION

27

The Evolution of Core Legal Principles

JEFFREY S. MORTON

Introduction

International law is "that body of principles, customs, and rules recognized as effectively binding obligations by sovereign states and such other entities as have been granted international personality."[1] The "other entities" referenced above include individuals, international organizations, and, to some extent, multinational corporations and even terrorist groups. One century earlier, Lassa Oppenheim provided a much more restrictive definition in the second volume of the *American Journal of International Law*: "International law is a law between states, which concerns states only and exclusively."[2] However, the expansion of international law subjects since 1908 represents a significant evolution of international law in response to the changed global political environment. A review of the evolution of international law since its modern inception in 1648 reveals several similar revisions of key underlying principles made necessary by the changing demands of international relations.

An integral part of world politics, international law both conditions and is conditioned by the international system within which it functions. Major events in world politics, ranging from world wars to changes in the power hierarchy of states, frequently result in revisions in the international legal order. At times, the major event reveals a weakness in international law that is addressed afterward. Other times, major wars or structural shifts are vehicles for eliminating key international rules and replacing them with others. Just as world politics has unfolded in definitive eras, international law has evolved over the course of modern history.

The purpose of this chapter is to gain a sense of the trajectory of international law into the twenty-first century. Such a task cannot be effectively undertaken by an empirical measure of the volume of rules, institutions, and court rulings that make up the corpus of international law. Nor can the evolving international legal system be understood by estimating compliance with existing limitations placed on states and other legal persons. Although the volume and compliance questions are critically important intellectual pursuits, they provide only a partial understanding of the direction that international law is taking in the unfolding century. In order to ascertain the trajectory of international law as the global system of actors evolves, one must examine the current system of rules within the context of modern international law's evolution since its inception in the seventeenth century. To do so, my emphasis is less on the process and application of international law and more on the establishment of core principles that came to define the international legal system at various points of its evolution.

Since its emergence following the Thirty Years' War (1618–1648), international law has evolved in three broad eras, each reflecting a legal order both similar to and distinct from its predecessor era. Eras can be compared by evaluating their most important or core principles. Core principles of international law are defined as those rules so fundamental that they provide a structural basis for international law and world politics. The core principles of international law provide the foundation on which secondary rules of engagement are based and understood. As such, core principles are considered foundational in that they provide the legal and political underpinnings of an era. This chapter examines the core principles of international law in three distinct eras: the classic system (1648–1945), the contemporary system (1945–1999), and the emerging twenty-first century (1999–).

The Classic System: Westphalia to World War II

Legal scholars, notably Malcolm Shaw, Antonio Cassese, and Gerhard von Glahn and James Larry Taulbee, have formed a general consensus that modern international law dates to the conclusion of the Thirty Years' War (1618–1648) and the drafting of the Treaties of Westphalia (1648).[3] In addition to ending the conflict, the Treaties of Westphalia established the nation-state as the primary actor in world politics. The decline of the Catholic Church as a rule-setting institution left sovereign nation-states to determine the permissibility of their foreign relations with other sovereign states. The development of international law from the end of the Thirty Years' War until the onset of the Second World War involved the establishment of a significant number of secondary principles of international law, ranging from the removal of religious differences among states as a legal recourse to war to protections afforded to diplomats and other state representatives in the conduct of their profession. What is of central importance for the purpose of understanding the trajectory of international law across several centuries, however, are the core principles that came to define the

era and provide the jurisprudence foundation for all international rules.

The Classic Legal System (1648–1945) produced a series of core principles—legal positivism, the state as the primary legal person, a doctrine of intervention, and neutrality—that provided the foundation of modern international law for three centuries.

Legal Positivism

In the immediate aftermath of the Thirty Years' War and the onset of the Classic Legal Order, a vibrant debate emerged over the principal source of international rules. Two schools of thought, Natural Law and Legal Positivism, engaged in a struggle for supremacy that would not be fully concluded for more than a century. Advocates of Natural Law contended that laws, both international and domestic, were the product of nature. Laws were arrived at through logical reason rather than diplomatic negotiations. The line that separated municipal law from international law was vague, as nature provided the rules that governed internal as well as international policies. Leading naturalist writers, according to Peter Malanczuk, include Hugo Grotius, Francisco de Vitoria, Francisco Suárez, Alberico Gentili, and Richard Zouche.[4] Although differences on specific principles can be noted among these legal scholars, Malanczuk observed that "all these writers agreed that the basic principles of all law (national as well as international) were derived, not from any deliberate human choice or decision, but from principles of justice which had a universal and eternal validity and which could be discovered by pure reason; law was to be found, not made."[5] Within the Natural Law School, a significant schism existed between those who believed law to have a divine origin and those who countered that law's existence was not contingent on religion. The secular naturalists, such as Grotius, based their position, in part, on the reality that differing societies believed in different gods. To achieve a universally applicable law, the secularists removed god from the equation.

Conversely, legal positivism removed both god and nature from the process through which law was established. Their contention was that law, both domestic and international, was made by individuals without the natural law pretext that law was anchored in justice. International law, therefore, was to result from the diplomatic negotiations of states that produced binding agreements or through the pattern of their actions that resulted in custom. By the nineteenth century, treaty and custom were acknowledged as the primary sources of international law. The common element of these two sources of international law is state consent—not nature, god, or justice. The general acceptance of legal positivism as a doctrine of international law, therefore, represents a core principle of the legal order during the Classic Legal Order.

State System

As the building blocks of world politics since at least the Treaties of Westphalia, states are acknowledged to enjoy a significant degree of independence from other states and actors. In legal terms, this independence is based on the principle of state sovereignty. The sovereignty of states is considered a core, or foundational, principle of international law because it ensures that international law remains at, if not below, the nation-state. Due to state sovereignty, the state is subject to no higher authority. Whereas legal positivism determines that states make international law, state sovereignty ensures that states retain their independence of action in areas not specifically limited by international agreements. Sovereignty provides states with the means of entering into binding legal agreements and is an essential element of legal personality, or subject status, in international law. The domination of nation-states over international law, however, has its limits. Although states enjoy the full legal capacity to either enter into binding international law or remain outside of international treaties, the principle of *pacta sunt servanda* dictates that treaties signed must be respected.

Doctrine of Intervention

The relationship between international law and armed conflict among nations is undeniable. A primary objective of international law is to reduce the frequency of armed conflict and, failing that, to regulate the behavior of belligerents in times of war. At the onset of modern international law, there existed few restrictions on the sovereign, independent nation-state in terms of its right to engage in armed conflict. Grotius's attempts to limit the recourse to war through requirements of public declarations or by limiting "just" war to instances of self-defense largely failed to impress states to accede to restrictions of their *competence de guerre*.[6] By the late 1500s the distinction between just and unjust war began to break down, and by the eighteenth century there occurred an almost complete abandonment of the distinction between legal and illegal wars. According to Malanczuk, "Wars were said to be justified if they were fought for the defense of certain vital interests, but each state remained the sole judge of its vital interests, which were never defined with any attempt at precision."[7] Thus, a defining element of the classic legal order was the inherent right of states to engage in armed conflict, with few meaningful restrictions placed on their *competence de guerre*.

Neutrality

Louis Henkin and his associates noted that the laws of neutrality, with roots in the fourteenth century, became an integral part of international law in the sixteenth century.[8] In times of armed conflict, nonbelligerent states enjoyed the right to proclaim neutrality, resulting in the requirement to show impartiality toward belligerents. In return for its impartial status, the neutral state was guaranteed the inviolability of its territory from belligerent actions. States claiming the status of neutrals were obligated not to allow their territory to be used for either training or passage of belligerent forces, nor could belligerents use their ports and territorial waters.

TABLE 27.1 Core legal principles of the Classic Legal order

Era	Core principles			
1648–1945	Legal positivism	State system	Doctrine of intervention	Right of neutrality

The onset of the twentieth century marked the early stages of the decline of the classic legal order. Since its inception, international law had principally been a European endeavor, a reflection of the geographic concentration of great powers on the continent. The internationalization of international law, which dates to the late nineteenth century, resulted from including non-European states in the law-making process. The rise of the United States and Japan as great powers, each demanding a role in constructing rules, and the direct participation of non-European, non-great powers in international conferences gave rise to challenges to the existing order. The first Hague Convention (1899), for example, was attended by twenty-seven states, and the second Hague Convention (1907) involved forty-three states, many of which were previously excluded from the process of creating international laws. The broader array of participating states along with the historic level of destruction associated with the First World War created the impetus for reconsidering the core principles that had come to define international law since 1648. Although the Classic System would survive World War I, by the onset of World War II, challenges to the doctrine of intervention and the utility of neutrality as a legal concept mounted. The emerging contemporary system (1945–1999), though maintaining the legal positivist approach and the prominence of the nation-state, incorporated new core principles in order to better address the needs of the nuclear era.

The Contemporary System: World War II to 1999

In many ways, the Second World War represents a *sui generis* event in human history. The level of human and physical destruction caused by the war, the rearrangement of the global structural order resulting from the war, and the advent and use during the conflict of the most destructive military weapon ever invented impacted the international system in ways not previously experienced. Although two of the core legal principles developed during the Classic System—legal positivism, state system—were retained as foundational elements of the new legal order, two of the era's core principles—doctrine of intervention, neutrality—were either replaced in their entirety or allowed to significantly erode. Rather than contracting, however, with the loss of two core principles, the international legal order expanded during the contemporary era with the addition of alternative core principles.

During the post–World War II–era legal order, the system's most powerful and leading state, the United States, introduced three additional core principles—nonintervention, free trade, and human rights. Although it is debatable as to whether the United States enjoyed the mantle of hegemon in the immediate aftermath of World War II, given the size and power of its rival, the Soviet Union, by the end of the Contemporary System there was no doubt that the United States was the unparalleled leading state, or hegemon, in the international system. Through American leadership, the primary global institutions—the United Nations, the International Monetary Fund, the International Bank of Reconstruction and Development, and the World Trade Organization—were established both to institutionalize the global status and influence of the United States as well as to serve as vehicles for establishing and maintaining the core principles that would come to define international relations and international law in the Contemporary System.

State System

One of the more intriguing revisions of a core principle in the transition from the classic to the contemporary legal era is the expansion of subjects, or legal persons, in international law. During the classic era, states constituted the sole entity endowed with legal personality. Nonstate actors were considered mere objects of international law. The decision to limit the jurisdiction of the Permanent Court of Justice (PCIJ) to states in the aftermath of World War I reflects the state-centric nature of world politics and the supremacy of the state in international law. Although the International Court of Justice (ICJ) similarly restricts its jurisdiction to states, as an extension of its predecessor, the ICJ is more a reflection of the previous classic era than the contemporary era in which it was created.

Considering key nonstate actors, such as international organizations and individuals, as legal persons greatly expanded the scope of international law in the post–World War II era. Precedent-setting rulings by international courts, most notably the 1948 Reparations for Injuries Case and the 1961 Lawless Case, expanded the range of actors considered subjects in international law and paved the way for, among others, the field of human rights.[9]

Nonintervention

As a leading state in the post–World War II system, the United States calculated that a global order in which war among states was kept to a minimum would further its vested interests. The dangers presented by the advent of the atomic and, later, nuclear bomb, the desire to restrict the number of conflicts that it engaged in for strategic and economic reasons, and its interest in overseeing a global economy based on the free trade model resulted in a U.S. effort to legally render wars of aggression impermissible. Up until 1945, states were considered to enjoy a nearly complete *competence de guerre*, or legal right to go to war. *Jus ad bellum* principles, which determined the *competence de guerre* of states during the Classic era, had only narrowly restricted the legal ability of sovereign states to engage in armed conflict. The laws restricting the right of states to wage war provided only weak restraints on sovereigns. The Just War Doctrine that encompassed restrictions

on the right to initiate or respond to war possessed a moral, not legal, basis. As such, throughout the classic era, nation-states operated on the premise that war waging was a sovereign right that was determined internally. International law, therefore, placed few restrictions on the *competence de guerre* of states.

The nonintervention principle was a revolutionary idea espoused by the leading states that negotiated the UN Charter in 1945. Seeking to dramatically limit the rights of states to engage in armed conflict, the major powers, led by the United States, reduced the *competence de guerre* of states to three conditions—self-defense, collective self-defense, and Security Council authorization. By greatly narrowing the legal rights of states to go to war, the nonintervention principle fundamentally altered international law and world politics. Article 2, paragraph 4, of the UN Charter represents the explicit limitation on the right of states to enter into armed conflict and represents a core principle of the Contemporary legal system. Further, by deeming armed intervention in most instances to be contrary to prevailing international law and an offense against all nations, the UN Charter effectively undermined the principle of neutrality. The global collective security system that the Charter attempted to create rendered the Classic era's core principle of neutrality significantly less relevant in the Contemporary era.

Free Trade

The intensification of trade in the post-Westphalian period gave rise to the conclusion of an increasing number of commercial agreements among states. During the classic era, however, treaties dealing with economic trade were primarily on technical aspects of the field, such as the convertibility of currencies and the gold standard. The global economic collapse in the 1920s then caused a decline in state interest in international economic agreements, as protectionist policies and currency instability reflected an inward-looking economic focus. In the aftermath of the Second World War, however, the

United States sought to create an international legal economic regime that reflected a classic liberal economic philosophy based on the principles found in Adam Smith and David Ricardo. Not only were agreements reached with the intent to establish free trade as the only legitimate economic strategy, but institutions were created to internationalize the liberal capitalist economic philosophy. The ad hoc trade negotiation framework provided by the General Agreement on Tariffs and Trade (GATT) complemented the International Monetary Fund (IMF) and International Bank of Reconstruction and Development (IBRD), or the World Bank. The GATT system was adopted after a failed attempt to create the International Trade Organization (ITO) shortly after World War II; that missing institutional element of the international economic system was filled by the World Trade Organization (WTO), which came into existence in the mid-1990s.

Human Rights

During the Classic Era of international law, the state principally determined the rights of individuals. In a setting characterized by legal positivism and state sovereignty, the general absence of human rights as a part of international law is expected. International law was considered to be the product of negotiations among sovereign and equal states, without a required underlying context of justice. Individuals in some states enjoyed significant rights, or civil liberties, whereas those in other states enjoyed few if any such liberties. Individual rights and liberties were the exclusive domain of the state, with its sovereignty shielding its internal affairs from international regulation. Even after the First World War, there was little movement toward recognizing the rights of individuals in international relations; human rights were not referenced in the League of Nations Covenant even though the League later pursued protections for certain minority groups in Europe. As Jack Donnelly noted, "Before World War II, human rights were rarely discussed in international politics. Most states violated human rights systematically."[10]

In the post–World War II era, due to a strong impetus from the United States, protections for individuals became a part of international law. It is not abundantly clear why the United States sought to establish human rights as a core principle of international law after World War II—whether as a desire to internationalize the norms found in its founding constitution or as a response to the catastrophic human loss resulting from the Holocaust. Regardless of the impetus, the decision to promote individual rights through the establishment of universal protections created a novel core principle of international law.

Unlike the League of Nations Covenant, the UN Charter explicitly references human rights on several occasions. The preamble reaffirms "faith in fundamental human rights," and Article 1 promotes and encourages "respect for human rights and fundamental freedoms," a proposition that is restated in Article 55. Key international legal instruments, including the 1948 Universal Declaration of Human Rights, the 1948 Genocide Convention, the 1966 International Covenants on Civil and Political Rights (ICCPR), and Economic, Social and Cultural Rights (ICESCR), further established human rights as a core principle in the post–World War II legal order.

The Twenty-First Century: 2000–

The end of the Cold War represented one of the most impressive and peaceful transitions of global order in modern times. Historically, changes to the structure of the international system were preceded by major conflicts (e.g., 1618, 1914, 1945). The events of the late 1980s and early 1990s, however, were effectively managed such that the transition from a bipolar international system to a unipolar international system occurred without a major war. The result was an international order that was characterized by American power and unparalleled leadership, which was a quintessential victory for the United States and the core legal, social, and political principles that it had espoused during the post–World War II era. The decade following the Cold War's end provided the United States with the opportunity to reassess the core

TABLE 27.2 Core Principles of the Classic and Contemporary eras

Era	Classic	Contemporary
Dates	1648–1945	1945–1999
Core principles	Legal positivism	Legal positivism
	State supremacy	States & Nonstates
	Intervention	Nonintervention
	Neutrality	Free trade
		Human rights

principles—nonintervention, free trade, human rights—that it had articulated in the period following World War II. Since the end of the twentieth century, actions taken by the United States in particular have served to fundamentally alter one of the core legal principles—nonintervention—that it drafted after World War II.

Preemption

The nonintervention principle espoused by the United States after World War II was problematic on several levels. The first problem with the nonintervention principle is legal. Although deeming aggression to be in contradiction to the UN Charter, a legal definition of what constitutes aggression was not drafted for nearly three decades after 1945. Article 1 of General Assembly Resolution 3314 (1974) defines aggression as "the use of armed force by a state against the sovereignty, territorial integrity or political independence of another state, or in any other manner inconsistent with the Charter of the United Nations." The legal quandary this definition creates is obvious in two ways. First, the use of armed force by one state against another fails to take into account the three permissible recourses to war allowed for in Article 2, paragraph 4, namely, self-defense, collective self-defense, and Security Council authorization. Second, prohibiting the use of armed force in any manner inconsistent with the UN Charter invites a subjective interpretation of the Charter and state action that renders the rule extraordinarily difficult to apply. The second problem with the nonintervention principle flows from the first, namely, the fact that the UN Security Council was a highly politicized body that

subjectively authorized, or failed to authorize, armed intervention in response to aggression. Despite several opportunities to authorize the use of force during the Cold War era, the Council did so only twice—in 1950 in response to North Korea's invasion of South Korea and in 1990 in response to Iraq's invasion of Kuwait. Despite those limitations, however, the nonintervention principle created a new, if not always respected, norm of international relations.

Since 1999, however, the principle of nonintervention has come under intense assault by the calculated actions of the major powers. In 1999, when violence in the Serbian province of Kosovo reached unacceptable levels, the United States led a ten-nation armed attack against the former Yugoslavia. Because Serbia's actions were not directed at any of the intervening states, the legal right of self-defense could not be invoked, and because Kosovo was a province of a state, and not an independent, sovereign state, the legal right of collective self-defense was not applicable. As such, only with Security Council authorization could the United States and its NATO allies legally intervene in the conflict. Three times in the fall of 1998 the UN Security Council considered the deteriorating situation in Serbia. While evoking Chapter VII language, each of the three resolutions reasserted the territorial integrity of the former Yugoslavia. The Council made no explicit authorization of armed intervention, and the resulting intervention signaled a reduction of respect for the nonintervention principle.

Four years later the United States militarily intervened in Iraq. As was the case with Serbia in 1999, none of the three permissible conditions for the use of force was met. U.S. effort to generate sufficient Security Council support for an authorization for war fell short, and the result was that the United States withdrew the draft resolution prior to a vote. As a foundational principle of the contemporary legal era, the nonintervention principle was designed to prevent states from arbitrarily using power. It should be noted that the use of force against the former Yugoslavia in 1999 and Iraq in 2003 were, by no means, the first instances of armed force by a major power since 1945 in violation of the UN nonintervention principle. Among others, U.S. Cold War interventions in Vietnam, Grenada, and Panama, along with the Soviet invasion of Afghanistan, represent uses of force that were not authorized by the Security Council or constituted self-defense. The Kosovo and Iraq wars stand out, however, because in both of those instances the United States sought authorization from the Security Council, only to be denied. The U.S. interventions in Vietnam, Grenada, and Panama as well as the Soviet invasion of Afghanistan were conducted without efforts to gain Security Council authorization. Thus, the U.S. invasions of the former Yugoslavia and Iraq constitute direct assaults on the nonintervention principle. Through its actions in 1999 and 2003, the United States not only used arbitrary power in the form of armed intervention but also severely weakened a core principle of the era. In 2008 the Russian intervention in Georgia in the absence of self-defense or Security Council authorization reflected the precedent set by the United States and further undermined the nonintervention principle.

An opportunity to reaffirm the principle of nonintervention presented itself during the 1999 Kosovo War. The Federal Republic of Yugoslavia (FRY), the target of the NATO aerial bombardment, filed suit on April 29, 1999, against the ten nation-states that participated in the intervention.[11] Yugoslavia requested provisional measures requiring each of the attacking states to cease their military operations and to refrain from any act of threat or use of force against the FRY. On jurisdictional grounds, the International Court of Justice initially dismissed the cases against Spain and the United States, as each of those states were shielded from the Court's compulsory by reservations. In each of the remaining cases, however, the Court subsequently found that it had no "prima facie jurisdiction to entertain Yugoslavia's application and thus was unable to indicate provisional measures."[12] The Court's failure to issue a ruling on a case that held the prospect of reasserting the nonintervention principle contributed to eroding that core principle that had served as a foundational limitation on the use of force during the Contemporary era. Although not explicitly endorsing a legal right of intervention, the Court's action in *Yugoslavia v. NATO* engendered a sense that the protections from outside intervention built into the foundation of international law in 1945 were giving way to an era when intervention on humanitarian grounds was acceptable.

Humanitarian Intervention

As a result of the erosion of the principle of nonintervention, an emerging principle of international law in the twenty-first-century legal order is humanitarian intervention. The notion of military intervention in response to a humanitarian catastrophe in a foreign state, without explicit authorization by the target state, has long been a subject of legal and moral debate. Grotius listed cannibalism, piracy, abuse of the elderly, rape, and castration of male subjects as examples of just causes for humanitarian intervention.[13] More recently, Michael Waltzer contended that humanitarian intervention justifies the use of force under extreme instances of human rights violations.[14] Under Charter Law (1945–), there appears to be sufficient limitation placed on the right of states to militarily intervene for humanitarian purposes without explicit authorization. Article 2, paragraph 7, states, "Nothing contained in the present Charter shall authorize the United Nations to intervene in matters which are essentially within the domestic jurisdiction of any state." The above limitation on state intervention for humanitarian purposes appears absolute, with the exception of an intervention authorized by the Security Council, as provided for later in the same paragraph.[15]

TABLE 27.3 Core Principles of the Classic and Contemporary Eras

Era	Classic	Contemporary	Twenty-first century
Dates	1648–1945	1945–1999	2000–
Core principles	Legal positivism	Legal positivism	Legal positivism
	State supremacy	States & Nonstates	States & Nonstates
	Intervention	Nonintervention	Humanitarian intervention
	Neutrality	Free trade	Free trade
		Human rights	Human rights

The failure of the ICJ to fully refute Belgium's humanitarian intervention justification defense in the *Yugoslavia v. NATO* case along with the Security Council's postwar endorsement of the outcome of that conflict signal that the international community is in the process of reconsidering the Charter's prohibition on unauthorized intervention for humanitarian purposes.

Reflecting an interest in endorsing the right of states to intervene on humanitarian grounds is the emerging Responsibility to Protect (R2P) principle. In September 2000, at the onset of the current international legal era, Canada announced the creation of the International Commission on Intervention and State Sovereignty (ICISS). As discussed in chapter three of this volume, R2P acknowledges a primary responsibility of states to protect their own citizens. In the event of a failure to do so, the Responsibility to Protect reverts to the international community. The December 2001 ICISS Report embraces three specific responsibilities:

1. The responsibility to prevent the root causes and direct causes of internal conflict and other man-made crises putting populations at risk.
2. The responsibility to react to situations of compelling human need with appropriate measures, which may include coercive measures like sanctions and international prosecution and, in extreme cases, military intervention.
3. The responsibility to rebuild, particularly after a military intervention.[16]

Although the ICISS Report calls on states to seek approval for military intervention from the UN Security Council, it leaves ample room for extra-Council authorization for military intervention in the event that the Security Council fails to address the issue. Accordingly, such alternative authorizations include the General Assembly of the United Nations and authorization from subregional organizations.[17] The clear implication of the report is that state sovereignty is being further eroded and the nonintervention principle that constituted a core and defining principle of the Contemporary legal era is weakening.

Conclusion

As an integral part of world politics, international law is a fluid set of principles and rules that are altered over the course of time as the legal and political disposition of states change. International law, in its most fundamental sense, provides the parameters of acceptable, or legal, behavior of states and other legal persons. What constitutes a legal course of action in one era is considered illegal in another, as new international rules are developed or existing rules erode. By undertaking a historical evaluation of international law with a primary focus on the key foundational, or core, legal principles identified in three distinct eras, this chapter gives the reader a sense of the fluidity of international law and its continued evolution into the twenty-first century.

During the Classic Legal era (1648–1945), four core principles of international law were identified: legal positivism, the centrality of states, the doctrine of intervention, and neutrality. By the onset of the Contemporary era (1945–1999), the doctrine of intervention and the right of neutrality had disappeared as core legal principles, and the state-centric system gave way to a legal system in which both states and nonstate actors were considered subjects of international law. Additional core principles, including nonintervention, human rights, and free trade, emerged and became influential foundational principles of the legal order. The twenty-first-century era, only in its first decade, is characterized by the erosion of the nonintervention principle and, with the emergence of the responsibility to protect, a decline in the legal sanctity of the state to control its domestic affairs free of outside interference. Because the R2P concept bases its legitimacy in promoting the rights of individuals, the core principle of human rights remains a defining feature of the current legal order. It is too soon to tell if the free trade principle will be retained in the twenty-first century; global economic turbulence as witnessed since 2008 may serve to reinforce the principle or may cause its erosion if leading states abandon open markets and free trade as strategies for dealing with the implications of grave levels of indebtedness.

How international law in the twenty-first century ultimately evolves is a matter of great conjecture and importance. Based on an evaluation of the core, or defining, principles of the international legal order since 1648, there has evolved a struggle between efforts to empower the state, on the one hand, and attempts to restrict state action, on the other. During the Classic era (1648–1945) states increasingly enjoyed the right to control both their internal and external affairs with only limited legal restrictions found in international law. The rise of human rights, the principle of nonintervention, and the free trade mandate after World War II effectively curtailed what states could legally do at home and abroad. The twenty-first-century legal order, which dates to 1999, appears to be further limiting states by requiring good governance at home. Accordingly, failure to protect one's citizens can result in humanitarian intervention justified under the Responsibility to Protect principle.

What is certain is that the international legal system continues, as it has since its inception, to evolve. Where that evolution ultimately arrives

before the current legal era ends and is replaced by another remains to be seen. This chapter posits that the most appropriate means of evaluating the international legal order is through a focus on the core, or foundational, legal principles that give definition to any era.

NOTES

1. GERHARD VON GLAHN & JAMES LARRY TAULBEE, LAW AMONG NATIONS: AN INTRODUCTION TO PUBLIC INTERNATIONAL LAW 3 (9th ed. 2010).

2. Lassa Oppenheim, *The Science of International Law: Its Task and Method*, 2 AM. J. INT'L L. 340 (1908).

3. *See* ANTONIO CASSESE, INTERNATIONAL LAW (2001); MALCOLM N. SHAW, INTERNATIONAL LAW (2008); and VON GLAHN & TAULBEE, *supra* note 1.

4. PETER MALANCZUK, AKEHURST'S MODERN INTRODUCTION TO INTERNATIONAL LAW (7th ed. 1997).

5. *Id.* at 15.

6. HUGO GROTIUS, THE LAW OF WAR AND PEACE (Francis W. Kelsey trans., The Bobbs-Merrill Company, 1962) (1625).

7. *Supra* note 4, at 307.

8. LOUIS HENKIN ET AL., INTERNATIONAL LAW: CASES AND MATERIALS (1980).

9. Reparations for Injuries Suffered in the Service of the United Nations, Advisory Opinion, 1948 I.C.J. 174; *Lawless v. Ireland*, 332/57 Eur. Ct. H.R.1 (1961).

10. JACK DONNELLY, INTERNATIONAL HUMAN RIGHTS 3 (2d ed. 1998).

11. *See* Application of Yugoslavia, Legality of Use of Force, 1999 I.C.J. Ten individual cases were brought by the FRY, one against each of the ten participating NATO states.

12. Aaron Schwabach, *Yugoslavia v. NATO, Security Council Resolution 1244, and the Law of Humanitarian Intervention*, 77 SYRACUSE J. INT'L L. & COM. 93 (2000).

13. GROTIUS, *supra* note 6, at Bks. II, III, XIX, XL.

14. MICHAEL WALZER, JUST AND UNJUST WARS (2d ed. 1992).

15. U.N. Charter, art. 2, para. 7.

16. Report by the International Commission on Intervention and State Sovereignty (ICISS), Dec. 2001.

17. According to the ICISS Report, the General Assembly enjoys the legal capacity to authorize armed intervention for humanitarian purposes in the event that the Security Council fails to act based upon the 1950 Uniting for Peace Resolution. That resolution, however, has no legal validity because the powers that it grants to the General Assembly require a revision of the UN Charter.

28

International Law and Politics

JAMES LARRY TAULBEE

Some Preliminary Thoughts

The relationship between international law and politics has always generated much debate. As many have pointed out, positions range from those who regard international law as little more than a form of rhetorical justification for what states wish to do to those who see an evolving world order based on the rule of law at the international level.[1] Needless to say, political realists, liberal internationalists, Marxists, and constructivists have very different views.[2] To state an obvious proposition, the evaluation of the "political" nature of international law depends on the premises from which the analyst begins. Yet the reader needs to keep this proposition firmly in mind as we explore the relationship between law and politics at the international level.

In this chapter I will discuss the extent to which international law guides statesmen in making decisions. Rather than a systematic discussion and critique of various theoretical approaches, let me begin by stating my assumptions regarding how analysts have failed to address critical questions about how politics and law intersect at the international level. Most of these misconceptions involve comparisons of international law with idealized conceptions of domestic law as it *ought* to operate within advanced industrial democracies.

- First, in the paragraph above, I have deliberately used the word guide because international law will *seldom* constitute the sole determining factor in any decision process.
- Second, most comparisons of international law with domestic law tend to overestimate the efficacy of domestic law and underestimate the role and impact of international law.
- Third, comparisons often underestimate or misconstrue the relationship between law and politics because analysts tend to focus on criminal law and procedure as the model, when actually domestic civil (private) law and procedure form a better analog to the legal process at the international level.
- Fourth, comparisons tend to ignore the fact that the international decision-making process has different participants and goals when compared to the domestic process.
- Fifth, comparisons often dismiss areas in which international law seems an important consideration as merely "low politics."
- Sixth, given points four and five, the international legal process does have a higher political content than the ideal domestic process.
- Seventh, defenders tend to overestimate the coherence of the international legal order.

Perspectives on Law and Politics

David Easton's classic definition of politics—the authoritative allocation of values *for a society*—provides a useful point of departure.[3] Easton's definition reminds us that politics involves decisions about how values and scarce resources are distributed within human societies. Although some (in particular, structural realists) may quibble over whether an international "society" exists, I will adopt the characterization used by Hugo Grotius and the English School.[4] This position has the utility of acknowledging and emphasizing the role of sovereignty as a fundamental element of contemporary international politics while also acknowledging the possibility that rational actors may find and act on common interests to create binding rules of behavior.[5]

Law may be defined as a mechanism that guides the actions of rational egoists (states/governments and individuals) toward collective goals based on enlightened self-interest rather than individual goals based on self-interest narrowly defined. As such, it constitutes only one method of determining the distribution of resources and values and only one technique of dispute resolution within the broader political process. It does not form the sole method, nor does law necessarily provide a solution to all disputes. Nonetheless, many perceive law as a set of techniques superior to politics, ignoring the fact that the law embodies a set of choices that result from political bargaining. Note that "law" in the United States has at one time permitted slavery and segregation. Judith Shklar argued that "those . . . adherents who, in their determination to preserve law from politics, fail to recognize that they too have made a choice among political values."[6] We find this particularly reflected in discourses about international law. Marti Koskenniemi observed that

> Throughout the present century, reconstructive doctrines have claimed that what merits criticism is the corruption of the Rule of Law either in the narrow chauvinism of diplomats or the speculative utopias of an academic elite. If only the Rule of Law can be fortified to exclude these contrasting distortions, then at least the jurist's part in the construction of a just world order has been adequately executed . . . [O]ur inherited ideal of a World Order based on the Rule of Law thinly hides from sight the fact that social conflict must still be solved by political means and that even though there may exist a common legal rhetoric among international lawyers, that rhetoric must, for reasons internal to the ideal itself, rely on essentially contested political principles to justify outcomes to international disputes.[7]

From this perspective, the question then becomes: What role(s) does law play in the broader political process? Understanding the relationship between international law and international political processes requires a brief examination of the roles law presumably plays in organizing human society. The content of any legal obligation, whether international or domestic, always involves some specified human action/behavior either in terms of positive requirements or permissions to perform certain duties under certain circumstances or in terms of prohibitions, that is, a duty to refrain from certain actions under certain circumstances. John Locke argued that the principal function of law is to build fences. He identified two essential fences—one that defines and governs the relationship between the government and its citizens, and one that defines and governs the relationships between individual citizens.[8] Locke's dichotomy roughly corresponds to the modern distinction between public and private (civil) law. When discussing international law, the tendency is to focus on Locke's first category because clearly the lack of an overarching international political authority immediately calls into question the possibility of an international *public* law. The simple fact that no set of centralized institutions exist at the international level has always bedeviled jurisprudence. Indeed, Nicholas Onuf, noting the problematic sources of authority at the international level, has characterized international law as the vanishing point of jurisprudence.[9]

The concentration on the first category, however, can lead analysts astray because it tends to overemphasize the criminal law model of prohibitions and punishments. This embodies a "cop on the corner" view that focuses on enforcement and punishment—"you do the crime, you do the time"—but ignores the broader roles that law plays in society. It also emphasizes the idea of *violating* the law, which simply reinforces the idea that all law involves sanctions. As H. L. A. Hart noted, to focus on the lack of centralized, organized sanctions means that one tacitly accepts the rather narrow conception that "law is essentially a matter of orders backed by threats."[10] The criminal code forms only one part of a broader category of regulation. Locke's first category also includes constitutional law[11] and administrative law.[12] The focus on criminal law also ignores Locke's second category, private or civil law that governs the relationships among individuals as well as among other entities such as corporations that have a "legal or *juristic* personality."[13]

Criminal law, as a collective security regime,[14] depends on a centralized enforcement system. Although individuals may initiate a complaint—an allegation of rape, assault, or battery for example—agents of the state then control the process from start to finish. The individual who initiated the complaint may have little or no say in the process except to tell his or her story at times mandated by the process but designated by the agents involved (police interview, formal deposition, court testimony). The goal is punishment for the violation if the accused is found guilty of the offense.

Administrative and constitutional law utilize a very different pattern from criminal law with respect to procedure and goals. The issues revolve around compliance, dispute resolution, and/or redress of the situation more so than with punishment. The idea of compliance/noncompliance better captures the process because noncompliance with constitutional and administrative law seldom involves physical (criminal) sanctions, although penalties in the form of fines or monetary compensation (compensatory and/or punitive damages) may result. For example, failures to read defendants their Miranda rights usually result in a new trial, not a sanction. If a state or local government passes legislation that exceeds their authority under the federal or relevant state constitution, the result is not a sanction but rather nullification of the statute or ordinance. Other examples of public law come from laws/regulations aimed at eliminating discrimination (race, gender, disability) or those dealing with safety in the workplace (OSHA). Noncompliance with the obligations imposed by these laws again does not normally entail criminal penalties.

Moreover, as noted above, public law constitutes only one part of modern legal codes. The bulk of all modern legal codes consists of *private law*—in the United States and Canada often termed civil law—that regulates relationships among individuals and, between individuals and entities such as corporations that have juristic personality.[15] Wills, contracts, property transfers, marriage, corporate law, and divorce fall into this category. Noncompliance with a legal contract or a suit involving willful damage done to one's property (i.e., a tort or a wrongful civil act[16]) or product liability normally involves a demand for compliance (enforcement), redress, and/or damages, not incarceration. Settlement of many of these disputes occurs through other than formal judicial processes (mediation, arbitration, direct negotiation). In sum, the greatest part of the legal code in modern states consists of noncriminal rules in which "you do the crime, you do the time" does not apply.

Looking at the question of enforcement, unlike the criminal law in which the primary responsibility for enforcement in the sense of arrest and prosecution for violations/noncompliance lies with the appropriate organs of the state (government), the primary responsibility for initiating a complaint in administrative, constitutional, and civil law lies with the individual. "Contracts must be observed" forms a fundamental rule of civil law. But enforcement of the norm if one party to the contract feels that a breach has occurred depends on the party alleging noncompliance taking the first step to deal with the alleged failure to perform the contractual obligations. The element of self-help in the domestic system is often overlooked. For example, if you own rental property, civil law governs the contractual relationship between you and your tenants. If your tenants fail to pay the rent on time, *you* must initiate the appropriate procedures to collect or evict. No government (public) agency will automatically step in to assume the burden of "enforcement." Even if your tenants fail in their obligations, whether willful or not, they will not incur criminal penalties. The "debtor's prison" of Dickens does not exist in contemporary advanced industrial societies. You have a right to demand redress or restitution in the form of compensation owed for rent and damages to the property, but not "jail time." Moreover, you may never receive the compensation owed even if you have successfully pressed your case in the relevant court because the process to recoup the back rents and fees may entail costs that outweigh the monies gained.

In constitutional, administrative, and civil law, criminal penalties in the sense of personal physical sanctions will come into play *only* if the individual has committed a criminal act such as perjury (lying under oath) or criminal fraud (a deliberate deception to acquire something of value without appropriate compensation or through misrepresentation of the facts—e.g., theft by deception, a scam, or a false insurance claim). In the Howard Hughes biography hoax perpetrated by Clifford Irving, Irving and his wife were indicted and convicted of criminal offenses associated with the hoax that included mail fraud, perjury, and grand larceny.[17] Conversely, copyright infringement, representing the work of others as your own, popularly referred to as "plagiarism," or other intellectual property theft such as patent infringement (profiting from the ideas of others) normally results in demands for damages (redress, restitution), not a criminal prosecution for "theft." Thus, the American Trust Company Bank, which owned

the rights to *Gone with the Wind*, sued author Regine Deforges for copyright infringement, claiming that her best-selling book, *The Blue Bicycle* clearly drew its story line from the earlier work.[18] The suit asked for US$330,000 in damages. Similarly, the BlackBerry case involving accusations of patent infringement against Research in Motion (RIM) by NTP, Inc. stands as a good contemporary illustration as well.[19] NTP sued RIM, alleging that the text transmission feature of the BlackBerry wireless network required a royalty payment because NTP held the patent rights to any such use. RIM settled the case through negotiation among the parties. Although negotiation does clearly exist in the American criminal justice system in the form of the plea bargain, note the difference. The negotiation centered on appropriate compensation, not appropriate punishment. RIM did "pay" for the alleged violation, but no RIM official faced any time in jail. In the Deforges case, the appeals court found no merit to American Trust's claim after the lower court had awarded the damages asked. The Deforges case did utilize a court, but the RIM settlement did not.

Note the parallels to international legal process. In constitutional, administrative, and civil law, individual plaintiffs must initiate complaints. The one exception here is the ability of the prosecutor of the newly formed International Criminal Court to initiate cases *proprio motu* (on his or her own authority). Otherwise, states have a choice of means to resolve the complaint. Article 33 of the UN Charter lists the possible methods of peaceful settlement. The criminal law permits no such choice. In public (and private) international law, individual states must initiate the process of enforcing compliance if they perceive an infraction.[20] The goals seldom involve punishment; more often they involve demands for compliance or redress.

During the conflict between Ethiopia and Eritrea (1998–2000), Ethiopia failed to prevent the seizure and sack of the Eritrean Embassy in Addis Ababa and the alleged harassment of diplomats as they exited Ethiopia. The Ethiopia-Eritrean Claims Commission[21] held that Eritrea was "entitled to satisfaction in the form of a declaration of the serious wrongfulness of Ethiopia's actions in entering, ransacking, searching and seizing personal property."[22] The panel also awarded US$155,000 in compensation for the contents of the building. During the Cold War, the United States and the Soviet Union regularly traded accusations of noncompliance with the ABM Treaty. The Treaty had established a Standing Consultative Commission to deal with the issues raised. Neither side demanded penalties for alleged infractions. On the one hand the verbal sparring, the allegations of cheating, formed an expected Cold War exercise with regard to a highly sensitive topic. On the other hand, they were also a constant reminder of the common interest in compliance shared by the two parties to the agreement.

Politics and Law: The Domestic Level

As noted above, emphasizing the difference between "law" and politics often implies a relative absence of political considerations at the domestic level. I will concede that, because of the absence of centralized institutions, many applications of law at the international level *are* likely to have a much higher political content than those within states. Nonetheless, this does not mean that political considerations are totally absent from domestic legal systems. To the contrary, most law at the domestic level results from the highly politicized process associated with legislatures. Although at their core all domestic legal codes seem to share some common rules such as prohibitions against murder, theft, and violent assault against persons, others depend on the attitudes of those subject to the specific law code. To give but one quick example, the standards that separate fraud from just a "sharp business practice" not only differ from society to society but also often vary even within societies with respect to specific techniques and procedures. What *is* the line between false advertising and good promotion of a product?

Moreover, rules may become the target of challenge or change because of shifts in public opinion or political ideology. We can point both to quantum shifts such as the abolition of the "separate but equal" doctrine in U.S. law as unconstitutional and to the ongoing controversies over abortion, gay and lesbian rights, and the definition of pornography to emphasize the connection. Similarly, issues relating to immigration—who deserves entry and the status and rights of illegal immigrants once here—form the core of a continuing and contentious debate. Certain rules may simply be unenforceable or go unenforced. Those who enforce the law have considerable discretion in many areas. For example, many states still have laws on their books prohibiting adultery, but these go unenforced.

Additionally, within the United States, district attorneys, state attorneys general, solicitors, sheriffs, and judges are elected officials in many jurisdictions. At the local level, the decision to charge an individual with a specific crime or the recommendation of a specific sentence such as the death penalty may depend on the district attorney's reading of public sentiment (or available prison space). Nor does the appointment of officials cancel out politics. Appointment merely shifts the venue in which politics applies. Politicians still participate in and define the criteria for the selection process. In a change of administrations, a newly elected U.S. president can appoint U.S. attorneys for various jurisdictions. Every judicial appointment at the federal level revolves around political issues.[23] Clearly, those involved in the appointment process have political agendas they feel can be either protected or accomplished with the appointment of like-minded individuals to the bench.

Domestic Politics and International Law

Robert Putnam has argued that many aspects of international politics resemble a two-level game.[24] On the first level, decision makers conclude bargains, but then these must be ratified by appropriate institutions at the domestic level. In actual fact, this applies in full only to states where legislatures and public opinion have real power. For nondemocratic governments, pressure from alliances, trade, financial dependence, or other relationships may influence governments' decisions to participate in regimes they might find intrusive and somewhat inconvenient. For illustration, I will use the record of U.S. response to human rights treaties. The United States, as a very powerful state, has more latitude in shaping the law than most states. This does not mean, however, that the United States will always have its way. The rejection of several U.S. proposals for amendments to the Rome Statute of the International Criminal Court shows this clearly. The following section examines the internal considerations that have governed the U.S. response to ratifying several major human rights treaties.

The response has involved a mix of technical considerations, emotional appeals, and special pleadings based on perceptions of internal political imperatives. The arguments reflect five major themes or concerns, which first appeared in the U.S. Senate debates surrounding the initial discussions associated with the ratification of the Genocide Convention and the introduction of the Bricker Amendment in the early 1950s.[25] Though modified in committee and by Bricker himself over time, the amendment, in its various forms, sets the initial tone for the human rights debate in Congress and has since cast a long shadow over subsequent efforts by the U.S. Senate to seek ratification and implementation of international conventions. Critics fear that under the guise of setting an international standard,

1. The treaties could abridge or deny rights currently guaranteed to U.S. citizens under the Constitution, such as freedom of speech and press as well as trial by jury.
2. The treaties could radically alter the balance of rights between the states and the federal government by giving powers to the federal government that by law and usage belong to the states. Self-executing treaties, in particular, embody this risk.
3. The treaties would erode U.S. sovereignty and promote world government.

4. The treaties would create perennial opportunities for those inimical to the policies and practices of the United States to criticize and create embarrassing situations.
5. Some treaties contain provisions that both undermine values fundamental to the free enterprise system and promote socialism/communism.

Note that it took the United States forty years to ratify the Genocide Convention. Beginning with the serious debate over its ratification in the late 1980s, the U.S. Senate, as a condition of its consent, has systematically appended a number of reservations, understandings, and declarations (RUDs) to each human rights treaty, the intent of which is to limit the impact of certain provisions on domestic law and practice.[26] Each set of RUDs bears the imprint of the Bricker legacy. The five traditional themes have translated into four axioms of contemporary political wisdom:

1. The United States will not commit to any treaty obligation deemed inconsistent with the U.S. Constitution.
2. The United States will not submit to the jurisdiction of the International Court of Justice with regard to application or interpretation of any human rights convention.[27]
3. The United States will not regard any human rights treaty as self-executing; all treaties will require enabling legislation.[28]
4. The United States will not undertake any treaty obligation that might change the balance of rights between the federal government and the states.

The question as to the extent to which these RUDs may actually mute the potential international responsibility of the United States lies beyond the scope of this chapter, but their general tenor and purpose form an important part of the context in any analysis of the position of the United States with respect to the Rome Statute.[29] The impact of past practice seems very much evident in the American negotiating positions and justifications for opposing the Statute as adopted.

International Legal Process and Politics I: Incentives, Participants, and Goals

When disputes between states involve fundamental principles, the key players here will not be judges (although lawyers may be involved at some point) but instead political officials who have quite different modes of search, discovery, and application with respect to applicable rules and acceptable outcomes. Many courses of action will affect others' as well as the decision makers' own state. Political advisers must take into account the attitudes of allies, adversaries, internal constituencies, and onlookers about what constitutes permissible conduct within the parameters of a specific incident. Will a particular course of action incur approval, acquiescence, or resistance from other states, and which states will utilize the foregoing judgments and in what manner? State officials seldom have the luxury of considering a high-profile incident in strictly legal terms because it will have other repercussions or consequences depending on the response. Many high-profile diplomats see law as a factor that inhibits creativity and flexibility in diplomacy.[30]

Sovereignty and the norms associated with it militate against action. The sovereign state still forms the most important element in any effort to enforce international law. The "hard shell" idea of sovereignty, often reinforced by strong feelings of nationalism, still exerts a powerful pull. For example, there exists a fundamental tension between evolving human rights regimes that assert that all human beings have certain minimum rights and the idea that the relationship between a government and its subjects/citizens is solely a matter of domestic, not international, concern. Statesmen intuitively understand the idea expressed in the old adage, "What is sauce for the goose is sauce for the gander." Vattel expressed this sentiment in his Golden Rule for sovereigns: One cannot complain when one is treated as one treats others. Intervention

into the internal affairs of others might invite criticism and, in turn, justify intervention by others into one's own affairs. A century and a half ago, in a remarkably prescient statement directed at the avidness with which certain congressmen advocated overt support for Louis Kossuth, the leader of the Hungarian revolution, Henry Clay eloquently pointed out the dilemmas involved in an active interventionist human rights policy. He noted that in undertaking such ventures, the United States would expose itself "to the reaction of foreign Powers, who, when they see us assuming to judge of their conduct, will undertake in their turn to judge of our conduct."[31]

Enforcement requires expenditures of resources, both tangible in the form of manpower, materiel, and money, and intangible in the sense of reputation and public support. For governments, immediate self-interest will tend to override arguments based on the good of the international community. Accordingly, one expects appropriate action when the issues directly affect a state, but generating support for taking action against noncompliance in instances in which a state does not have an immediate substantive interest becomes problematic. For example, rhetorical support for peace, nondiscrimination, and other human rights values comes easily, but, rhetoric and reality often clash when circumstances require intervention to address a major breach of "community" obligations, such as the ongoing situation in Darfur (Sudan). A response here would necessitate a major commitment of resources to a problem that does not directly affect the self-interest of states outside the immediate area. This explains the reluctance of states to engage in Bosnia, Sierra Leone, and Rwanda in a timely fashion. Judge Antonio Cassese concluded that "A strong reaction by States to these breaches presupposes the existence of a community interest to put a stop to them. However, the community interest in their fulfillment remains potential rather than real."[32] Action based on enlightened self-interest rather than immediate self-interest narrowly defined entails real costs without any perceived real gains for the expenditure. This does not necessarily mean action in response to perceived breaches will not happen, but it does mean that the nature of the breach must be perceived as extraordinarily egregious to trigger a collective (community) move for action.

Dispute Resolution

Dealing with disputes, either to prevent or to settle them satisfactorily, constitutes one of the major purposes of law at any level. Dispute settlement at the international level has many different facets. States make demands for redress in the form of a claim or formal demand for action to address the breach of obligation. States may resolve claims in many different ways, ranging from direct negotiation to submission to an international tribunal. The cases we shall discuss below illustrate diplomatic correspondence (direct negotiation), mediation, and arbitration, and then will focus on the strengths and weaknesses of adjudication by international arbitral tribunals and international courts. States tend toward negotiation (diplomatic correspondence) and mediation. These techniques do not necessarily produce legally binding decisions (unless the agreement results in a treaty) and do not necessarily reflect principles of law. International adjudication as a method involves the use of a third-party tribunal, arbitration panel, or court that will issue a binding decision based on law. For reasons discussed below, formal legal proceedings form a minor method of dispute resolution at the international level. However, states may still prefer negotiation and mediation because they remain in control of the process. From this perspective, keep in mind the earlier discussion concerning participants and their goals.[33]

Expectations about what an effective "rule of law" at the international level would require inevitably reflects the vision of the perceived central role of courts in the domestic legal order, where adjudication by permanent courts with standard rules of procedure, forms the ideal method of dispute settlement. Needless to say,

if this is the true measure, given the relatively limited scope accorded adjudication in contemporary practice, the current system falls far short of the ideal. Simply stated, states have seldom submitted disputes involving important interests to arbitral tribunals or courts. Yet one needs to remember the earlier discussion about reparations and redress and that adjudication forms but one method of dispute settlement, even in domestic societies. Remember as well that techniques of dispute resolution are not mutually exclusive exercises. To start, negotiation will almost always play a role in any dispute resolution effort no matter what method(s) states eventually choose for final resolution.[34]

Indeed, at least in the United States, mediation and other forms of alternative dispute resolution have become the preferred techniques for many varieties of disputes involving civil law.[35] Note as well the following advice from the U.S. Department of Commerce about settling commercial disputes in China: "Simple negotiation with your partner is usually the best method of dispute resolution. It is the least expensive and *it can preserve the working relationship of the parties involved*."[36] Add to this the following advice from another source: "The best approach in dealing with individual disputes varies from case to case."[37]

The Politics of Adjudication

Earlier I noted that "law" may not provide an adequate solution to every dispute. Here, even if law has relevance, adjudication may not be the best method of dealing with the issues. As with every technique of dispute resolution, adjudication has advantages and disadvantages. State decision makers will weigh these in electing a course of action. States resort to adjudication because they see it as impartial, impersonal, principled, and authoritative.[38] As a strategy it may buy time and defuse the situation. It can help develop international law. At least in theory, the ideas of impartiality and neutral principle underlie all adjudication by third parties. Arbitrators or judges presumably apply the rules of relevant law or other agreed upon principles rather than relying on personal preference or political factors associated with the dispute. This also embodies the idea of an impersonal process in that presumably neither party can influence the decision except through persuasive argument based on facts and law. The process of having to frame opposing claims within a legal framework may clarify the facts and issues in dispute. Decisions of impartial tribunals convey strong claims for legitimacy to other states. This bolsters legal development in reinforcing the authority of the principles and the process.

To understand why judicial settlement may not be appropriate to all cases, one must address several main problems: expense, lack of control, possible delay, limitation on relevant issues, limitation on possible solutions, the winner-loser context, and possible effects on the parties. These issues are interrelated. Litigation is very expensive and time consuming; plus, to a great extent, control moves from the parties to the lawyers and judges actively involved in the case (the experts). The costs of preparing and hearing the case flow from the necessity of framing all of the issues in terms of the law perceived to be relevant law *even if* doing so does not adequately capture the underlying issues in the case or address longer-term considerations. As one commentary has noted, issues in litigation often become couched in terms of money when the real questions revolve around trust, respect, or other emotional issues.[39] Having to frame any solution in terms of relevant law limits the possibility of the parties finding common ground for solution other than that dictated by applying the law. The winner-loser framework adds to the possible psychological costs and impact over time. Add to this the nature of the adversarial process, which requires each side to present its case in the strongest possible terms while critiquing the case/conduct of its opponent. One need look no further than the process and outcomes of high-profile divorce cases (or perhaps divorce litigation, high-profile or not) to understand the potential problems. Adjudication is also a conservative

technique in that it tends to look for principles of existing law rather than for principles to develop the law if needed. States may in theory enable tribunals to decide on the basis of "reasonable and fair" (*ex aequo et bono*) but have seldom done so. Finally, some have argued that a principal focus on adjudication reflects a Western bias toward adversarial methods and ignores the long practice of many non-Western societies for nonadversarial methods that emphasize mediation and accommodation.[40]

On balance, the argument cannot be resolved in the abstract. As Richard Bilder has pointed out, even if a relatively few international disputes are resolved through judicial methods, this does not mean that adjudication can be relegated to a shadowy corner of the dispute resolution landscape. A number of situations lend themselves to resolution through adjudication. Among these are disputes that do not involve a significant interest but governments may still feel unable to make concessions in direct negotiations because they involve highly charged emotional issues such as borders or maritime boundaries or disputes that involve difficult factual or technical questions.[41] A quick perusal of ICJ cases quickly establishes that territorial and maritime questions have formed a great part of the workload of the Court. Since 2000 six of the twelve contentious cases heard by the Court have involved territorial or maritime questions.

Generally, adjudication has played a relatively minor role in dispute settlement at the international level. The jurisdiction of all international courts relies on formal state consent. Unless a treaty or other agreement designates a specific court or arbitration as the process for dispute settlement, no rule of customary law mandates a compulsory rule for dispute settlement. Certainly, no rule of customary law mandates that states submit disputes to judicial determination. An international court or arbitration panel may render a binding decision *if and only* if the states involved have given their consent in some form to the proceedings. Many treaties specify the International Court of Justice as the method of resolving disputes over disputes (or interpretations), but obviously treaties require consent. Some treaties, like that setting up the World Trade Organization or the regime of UNCLOS III, have their own dispute resolution mechanisms that may employ a form of adjudication. Others require states to negotiate in good faith.

The Rainbow Warrior[42]

Acting on the basis of an anonymous tip in the wake of the explosion that destroyed the *Rainbow Warrior*, New Zealand authorities detained a couple traveling on Swiss passports on the charge of violating immigration laws. New Zealand authorities also traced the explosives used to a chartered yacht, the *Ouvea*, which had a crew of French nationals. Before authorities could arrest the crew, the *Ouvea* sailed and was never seen again. Soon the French media began to suggest a link between the French secret service (DGSE) and the bombing, an allegation that French President François Mitterand openly and categorically denied. President Mitterand promised full cooperation and punishment of those involved if the allegations proved to be true.

The Swiss couple proved to be two high-ranking agents of DGSE as members of the crew of the *Ouvea*. Two months after the bombing, the French government admitted complicity. Direct talks between the two governments failed to produce a satisfactory agreement. The Secretary-General of the United Nations (Javier Pérez de Cuéllar) then agreed to mediate the dispute. Eventually, the French agreed to pay New Zealand NZ$13 million dollars, Greenpeace US$8 million dollars, and issued a public apology.

The story does not end here. The two French agents in custody pled guilty to manslaughter and arson charges. They received sentences of ten years for manslaughter and seven years for arson, with the sentences to run concurrently. Responding to pressure from the French public, the French government demanded the return of the two agents to France. When New Zealand refused, the French instituted an embargo against a wide range of New Zealand products.

As part of the mediated agreement, the two convicted agents were transferred to the island of Hao (under French control) with the understanding that they would serve a minimum of three years. Within a year, one agent returned to France, ostensibly for medical treatment, and the other returned to France less than a year later, presumably because her father was terminally ill. France ignored all protests from New Zealand. When, in 1991, New Zealand attempted to extradite from Switzerland another French agent involved in the plot, France again applied economic pressure until New Zealand dropped the effort.

Reparations/Redress

What does this case say about reparation and redress of the breach that occurred? Several points need elaboration to illustrate the complexity of the problem. First, perception based on the assumptions we make about appropriate punishment play a great role here in assessing the outcome. Instinctively, because of the nature of the act, the assumptions and processes associated with municipal criminal law spring to mind. Yet the reader needs to keep one important point in mind here. This case, because of its high profile and connection to vital interests, was not resolved through an independent court using legal methods of search, discovery, and application.

Second, because we do tend to focus on the domestic criminal law paradigm in cases such as the *Rainbow Warrior* and because the incident certainly involved criminal acts, we do tend to overlook the fact that in many cases involving breach of contract in municipal law, the solution relies on what the parties negotiate and are willing to accept in terms of satisfaction. Abstract standards of justice give way to pragmatic concerns of what is possible. Third, even if we do rely on domestic criminal law as our model, consider the mediation effort as the equivalent of an international plea bargain: France publicly acknowledged guilt, allocuted to the circumstances, and paid compensation. Even so, from a criminal law viewpoint and from a subjective point of view, the seeming lack of punishment for the individuals involved raises questions. In the end, however, France did not honor the bargain in full and used the power of the state to pressure New Zealand to return the agents to France.

International Legal Process and Politics II: The Constitutive and Regulative Functions

We clearly see the constitutive factor at work as a major component of contemporary international law in the number of intergovernmental international organizations (IGOs). This alone separates the contemporary era from any other era in human history—from the overarching United Nations, whose membership includes almost every recognized state, to the specialized agencies such as the World Trade Organization, the World Health Organization, the International Bank for Reconstruction and Development (World Bank), and the Universal Postal Union. Most IGOs, the UN included, have the authority to legislate for themselves in terms of internal rules and operating procedures not specified in the constitutive document, but it is the role of these organizations in the global policy-making process that is of concern here. They have made rules and regulations for international mail delivery, telephone calls, and travel. It is easy to dismiss this contribution to order as "low politics." Still, one needs to think of how much more complex life might be without these arrangements. How difficult would international travel be without the standardization of items that constitute valid travel documents for entry into another country?

The creation of new rules, regulations, and policies involves politics. J. Martin Rochester noted that policy making has four components: 1) agenda setting (identifying problems and issues); 2) policy formulation (proposals for appropriate rules and regulations); 3) policy adoption (selection of particular rules and regulations); and 4) policy implementation.[43] Intuitively, one can see where politics plays a role in addressing any problem that may arise. Moving from identifying and specifying a problem to finding a final solution will require much negotiation and exchange between those interested. Moreover, one should note the comments relating to the politics of enforcement earlier in this chapter. Just because a problem has been identified does not mean states will move to remedy it. As with enforcement, addressing new problems requires a commitment of resources in terms of reputation, time, money, and manpower. Solutions to problems are certainly not cost free. Moreover, given the nature and number of problems and potential commitments, most states will have to set priorities. Accordingly, a fairly widespread consensus with regard to a particular issue does not mean that states will necessarily initiate action to address it through collective action. Lack of funding can inhibit action as well. If states do choose to act, this does not mean that they will, out of necessity, provide resources adequate to ensure the success of the venture. For example, only 11 percent of the budget for the UN Human Rights Council is funded from the regular UN budget.[44] The Council must rely on voluntary contributions for the rest. Because many lesser-developed states, pleading poverty, have not paid the United Nations their dues and assessments, it suffers from a chronic budget crisis.

A second consideration comes into play here. The treaties establishing each organization will define a specifically defined sphere of competence. Problems at the international level often cut across several areas of functional competence. As a consequence, appropriate action may require coordination among a number of IGOs, nongovernmental organizations (NGOs), and other players. Indeed, the involvement of an IGO will mean an expansion of the number and diversity of actors involved.[45] This means that, even when states and organizations have decided that an issue needs attention and the preparatory work begins, the process may appear glacial. In the wake of the *Achille Lauro* incident in 1985, it took seven years before the Convention for the Suppression of Unlawful Acts Against the Safety of Maritime Navigation entered into effect (see discussion below).

Third, when states choose IGOs as the appropriate forum to address an issue, they often do so because they prefer a venue that has "sunk costs" and familiar operational parameters rather than an ad hoc conference. Moreover, given the possibilities among bilateral negotiations, regional organizations, the UN, or the various functional organizations, states have many choices of venues to develop an appropriate treaty. This stands apart from the actual consideration of issues. Each venue offers opportunities and constraints. The choice of IGO will determine whether the negotiations will be more or less transparent or open to input beyond governments. Consider, for example, what is the appropriate venue to discuss and develop further constraints on nuclear weapons proliferation? Is it the IAEA or the UN General Assembly?[46] Or is it more appropriate to cast the discussion at regional levels to develop nuclear-free zones? As José Alvarez noted, "The choice of organizational venue speaks volumes concerning the interest of principal treaty backers."[47]

Fourth, interest-group politics operate at the international level. In many negotiations, power still counts, though it does not necessarily dictate outcomes. At the Rome Conference that approved the ICC Statute for signature, the rejections of amendments the United States considered crucial for its participation provides a clear signal that the politically powerful do not always get their way. In modern negotiations, new interests may emerge as the negotiations proceed. This will complicate the negotiating process and slow progress toward mutually acceptable rules. Within IGOs and other venues, the processes of coalition building and negotiating differences is an important process. We take this for granted at the domestic level but seem to find it as an aberration that needs fixing at the international level.

International Legal Process and Politics III: Ambiguity and Incoherence

The international legal order does not have a unified, universal, coherent legal code; rather, it is a patchwork of treaties and customary rules that have evolved over time through state practice. It has not evolved in a logical or consistent way; rather, it has developed in bits and pieces through different experiences that may or may not be linked to one another. Moreover, treaties and customary law are often vague and incomplete. Without going too far into technical explanations, simply making certain actions an offense under international law marks only the first step. Treaties and customary law may contain prohibitions against certain battlefield actions, such as deliberate attacks on civilians, but fail to define other essential elements necessary to turn a prohibition into an enforceable rule. Further, the relevant law may fail to define what consequences should follow from specific violations. Many treaties lack any provisions for enforcement at all, leaving it to states essentially to "fill in the blanks" if they choose to do so. States are bound only by those treaties and customary rules that they choose to accept. Although a category of customary law, *jus cogens*, presumably binds all regardless of consent, one finds little agreement on what rules enjoy this status.[48] Because of nearly universal membership, one can argue that the principles and obligations embodied in the UN Charter are binding on all, including those few who have not opted to join the organization.

Recognition

Recognition (both state and government) forms a fundamental legal process in that it determines the structure of the international legal system.[49] Yet no explicit rules, other than that each state has the right to identify those whom it sees as legitimate actors, exist. Hard questions arise with secessionist movements. The struggle of the Former Yugoslav Republic of Macedonia (FYROM) to achieve recognition forms the quintessential example. When Macedonia announced its independence from Yugoslavia in September 1991, Greece opposed recognition because it felt the new state had aspirations to annex the historic Macedonia (home of Alexander the Great), which formed part of Greece.[50] Conversely, consider the status of "failed states." Logic would dictate that other states might withdraw recognition. This has not happened. As we will discuss below, Somalia has no effective central government. It no longer meets the most fundamental requirements for a "state," but other states have not withdrawn recognition even though the "state" of Somalia does not have an effective central government in control within the borders recognized as Somalian territory. Russia supports a South Ossetian secessionist movement, although no other state does. During the Nigerian civil war (1967–1971), several states recognized the state of Biafra, but many did not.

When an unconstitutional change occurs in a government, states have the option of choosing whether they will deal with the new government or not. Recognition of government decides which group among competing factions another state will deal with as the official representatives of a state.[51] As example, the continuing controversy over Taiwan is actually a question of recognition of the government. Both the government in Taipei and the government in Beijing claim to control all of China. This underlies the stance of the Beijing government that other states may not have a "two Chinas" policy. Similarly, only three states recognized the Taliban government of Afghanistan.

Piracy and Politics

Writers tend to agree that the ban on piracy stands as one of the oldest rules of international law and can be considered *jus cogens*.[52] In theory, all states have the right to seize ships and individuals engaged in piracy (universal jurisdiction). Yet the problems associated with dealing with contemporary piracy provide cogent examples of many of the themes in this chapter.[53] Differences exist between the traditional definition of piracy and that contained within UNCLOS III.[54] Piratical acts also fall under the Convention for the Suppression of Unlawful Acts against the Safety of Maritime Navigation

(SUA Convention), even though the main purpose of the Convention is to combat terrorism.[55] The SUA Convention does not contain a definition of piracy, but it does include piratical acts as part of a larger category of offenses against ships. To complicate matters further, because no international court has jurisdiction to try piracy cases, the treaties authorize each state to pass appropriate legislation.

Beyond the obvious variations that may arise from two hundred–plus states enacting their own legislation, the current law has several problems. The UNCLOS III definition limits piracy to acts committed on the high seas. It does not specify punishment but rather leaves enforcement to domestic legislation. The SUA Convention has an extradite-or-try provision with respect to offenses covered by the treaty. Neither convention permits states to enter the jurisdiction of another state for the purposes of arrest or enforcement.

Somalia has signed and ratified UNCLOS III but not the SUA Convention. Typically, the recent pirate attacks occurred either within Somalia's territorial seas or when the pirates captured a ship on the high seas and then retreated into Somalia's territorial sea. Much of the problem stems from the lack of Somali capacity to take effective action against the pirates within its jurisdiction because the state has no functioning central government. Even if it did have a central government reasonably in control of the territory, the effort to control piracy would be hampered by a lack of money and trained manpower.

Under the SUA Convention, a capturing state has three ways to establish jurisdiction over pirates: if the pirates operate in the territorial waters of a state party; if a ship flies the flag of the arresting state; or if the pirates are nationals of a state party.[56] The first possibility does not apply because the pirates are not operating in the territorial seas of any state party. The pirates ply their trade in Somalia's territorial seas or the Gulf of Aden. Second, a majority of the hijacked ships fly flags of convenience. Many of the naval ships in the area are from the United States, the

European Union, Denmark, Russia, India, and Canada. If a U.S. ship captured pirates attacking a Liberian ship, it would have no jurisdiction to prosecute them under the SUA Convention because the pirates did not attack a U.S. ship. Finally, the third jurisdiction option does not apply because the pirates are from Somalia; they are not nationals from any state party.

The UN Security Council has attempted to shore up authority to deal with the Somali pirates through a number of temporary resolutions that permit interested states to enter the territorial waters of Somalia to capture suspected pirates.[57] Even if states do so, they may not have the requisite authority to prosecute because their laws reflect the "high seas" definition. Extradition to Somalia is not an option because clearly Somalia does not have the ability to carry out effective prosecutions. More to the point, many states may not have an extradition treaty with Somalia. Other states find themselves burdened. Kenya and the Seychelles had agreed to take several of the pirates but now find their judicial systems overburdened.[58] In part this is a question of funding, but it also involves appropriate manpower—the states lack sufficient judges, prosecutors, and defense lawyers.

The UN recently stepped in again. The Security Council unanimously adopted a Russian-sponsored resolution requiring the Secretary-General to report on options for dealing with the situation, including the possibility of setting up international piracy courts.[59] The Secretary-General has three months to produce the report, but action may still be several years away. This will depend on sustaining the political will to do something. Questions of funding will also play a central role. International courts are expensive. The International Criminal Tribunal for the former Yugoslavia alone will expend US$644.3 million for the period 2008–2010.[60]

International Legal Process and Politics IV: Soft Law[61]

Soft law, an apparent contradiction in terms, has two different meanings in international law lit-erature. Some analysts use the term to refer to treaty provisions that cannot be implemented because they lack specificity.[62] More recently, the term has come to describe the fluctuating borderline between the politics of policy making and customary law. Not all international agreements come in treaty form. Declarations and joint statements of policy or intention signify agreements and establish commitments but not binding legal obligations. Statesmen may prefer nontreaty arrangements for many reasons. The following list is meant to be suggestive, not exhaustive, and many of the reasons may overlap or complement one another: confidence building, impetus for coordinated national legislation, avoidance of cumbersome domestic approval procedures, or the creation of a preliminary regime with hope for development. As with comity, Professor David Bederman argued that this last reason, the possibility of evolution (or devolution), should be highlighted:

> When international actors develop a standard of conduct, and even when it is expressly couched in the idiom of aspiration or informality, the inevitable trend is that soft law hardens into legal obligation. I believe that in any rules, standards, or typology for norms, there is an asymmetric dynamic at work. Rules rarely dissolve into standards, but standards (my surrogate for soft law in an international context) will usually solidify into legal rules.[63] Thus, in many cases we might regard soft law as *de lege ferenda*, that is, as law in development or as an aspirational goal. In particular, this seems to hold true with respect to economic and environmental agreements.

Advocates often cite the Helsinki Final Act of the 1975 Conference on Security and Cooperation in Europe (CSCE) as a prime example of soft law. Article X of the Final Act[64] declares that the parties had agreed to "pay due regard to, and implement the provisions in the Final Act" and expressed "their determination fully to respect and apply these principles . . . in all aspect to their mutual relations." A follow-up memorandum of understanding instructed the government of Finland to transmit the document to the Secretary-General of the United Nations but also declared that the document did not qualify as a treaty and, therefore, did not have to be registered (see Article 102 of the Charter). Although not regarded as a treaty, the document still had an enormous impact because of its publication and dissemination within Eastern Europe and the very public commitments made by the governments that signed the agreement.

Pragmatically, the political difference between the binding power of treaty and nontreaty arrangements may be minimal. There is little evidence to suggest that states regard soft law agreements less seriously than formal treaty obligations. Both treaties and nonlegal agreements depend on continuing cooperation between or among the parties to secure the benefits. If that willingness to cooperate erodes or disappears, then neither treaty nor "soft law" agreement will remain viable. As we have discussed above, in theory, the aggrieved state may seek redress for the nonperformance of a treaty obligation; in practice, the possible political and material costs may outweigh the desire for redress or punishment.

NOTES

1. The classic discussion, though now somewhat dated, still remains John H. E. Fried, *How Efficient Is International Law*, in THE RELEVANCE OF INTERNATIONAL LAW 93–132 (Karl W. Deutsch & Stanley Hoffmann eds., 1968).

2. For a systematic analysis of various paradigms and the consequent place of international law, *see* J. MARTIN ROCHESTER, BETWEEN PERIL AND PROMISE: THE POLITICS OF INTERNATIONAL LAW 3–31 (2006).

3. DAVID A. EASTON, THE POLITICAL SYSTEM: AN INQUIRY INTO THE STATE OF POLITICAL SCIENCE (1953).

4. *See* HEDLEY BULL, THE ANARCHICAL SOCIETY (2002).

5. For a defense of sovereignty as a necessary element of the contemporary legal regime, *see* LARRY MAY, CRIMES AGAINST HUMANITY: A NORMATIVE ACCOUNT (2005).

6. JUDITH N. SHKLAR, LEGALISM: LAW, MORALS, AND POLITICAL TRIALS 10 (1964).

7. Marti Koskenniemi, *The Politics of International Law*, 1 EUR. J. INT'L L. 1 (1989). *See also* MARTI KOSKENNIEMI, FROM APOLOGY TO UTOPIA: THE STRUCTURE OF INTERNATIONAL LEGAL ARGUMENTS (2005). Koskenniemi again addresses the topic in *The Politics of International Law—20 Years Later*, 20 EUR. J. INT'L L. 7–19 (1999).

8. JOHN LOCKE, TWO TREATISES OF GOVERNMENT; THE SECOND TREATISE OF GOVERNMENT §222 (Peter Laslett ed., Cambridge University Press, 1988) (1681–1682).

9. Nicholas Greenwood Onuf, *The International Legal Order as an Idea*, 73 AM. J. INT'L L. 244 (1979).

10. H. L. A. HART, THE CONCEPT OF LAW (1961).

11. *See* PHILIP J. PRYGOSKI, CONSTITUTIONAL LAW (12th ed. 2007).

12. *See* JACK M. BEERMAN, ADMINISTRATIVE LAW (2006).

13. An entity that has juristic personality is treated as an *artificial person* who has the capacity to enter into contracts and sue or be sued. For its application in international law, *see* JANNE ELISABETH NIJMAN, THE CONCEPT OF INTERNATIONAL LEGAL PERSONALITY: AN INQUIRY INTO THE HISTORY AND THEORY OF INTERNATIONAL LAW (2004).

14. Simply, the criminal law system embodies the idea of the community versus the offender/violator—all against one. We have seen this in case designations such as the *U.S. v. John Doe*, or *The People v. Jane Doe*.

15. *See* JAMES GORDLEY & ARTHUR TAYLOR VON MEHRAN, AN INTRODUCTION TO THE COMPARATIVE STUDY OF PRIVATE LAW: READINGS, CASES, MATERIALS (2006).

16. Torts involve wrongful acts other than breach of contract. While *some* torts may be crimes punishable with imprisonment, the *primary* purpose of tort law is to provide relief for the *damages* incurred and deter others from committing the same harms. *See* www.law.cornell .edu/wex/index.php/Tort#definition.

17. *See* STEPHEN FAY, LEWIS CHESTER, & MAGNUS LINKLATER, HOAX: THE INSIDE STORY OF THE HOWARD HUGHES-CLIFFORD IRVING AFFAIR (1972).

18. Newspaper accounts described this as a case of "plagiarism," but plagiarism is not a *legal* doctrine. The term as such cannot be found in any copyright or author's rights act. Lawyers may generally speak of plagiarism for cases in which the unauthorized use of a work coupled with a false attribution of authorship infringes on the copyrights of the original author. Although both concepts may appear to the lay person as being the same, copyright infringement has a much narrower definition, and therefore, acts of plagiarism may constitute copyright infringement only in very precise cases. *See* Francisco Javier Cabrera Blázquez, *Plagiarism: An Original Sin? available at*: www.obs.coe.int/online_publication/

expert/plagiarism.pdf.en; Justine Pila, *Copyright and its Categories of Original Works*, 30 OXFORD J. LEGAL STUD. 229–54 (2010).

19. *See* BlackBerry Lawsuit FAQ: What You Need to Know, *available at* www.computerworld.com/newsletter/0,4902,108445,00.html?nlid=MW2.

20. Rome Statute of the International Criminal Court, Article 15, circulated as document A/CONF .183/9 of Jul. 17, 1998 and corrected by *process-verbaux* of Nov. 10, 1998, Jul. 12, 1999, Nov. 30, 1999, May 8, 2000, Jan. 17, 2001, and Jan. 16, 2002. The Statute entered into force on Jul. 1, 2002, 37 I.L.M. 1002 (1998), 2187 U.N.T.S. 90.

21. Set up under the auspices of the Permanent Court of International Arbitration.

22. PERMANENT COURT OF ARBITRATION SUMMARIES OF AWARDS 1999–2000, at 275 (Belinda Macmahon & Fedelma Claire Smith eds., 2010).

23. *See* Bob Tarantino, *Face It: Judging Is Political*, NAT'L POST (Canada), Jun. 11, 2009, at A22; Rupert Cornwell, *A Small Nudge Toward Breaking the Conservative Grip on the Judiciary*, THE INDEPENDENT (London), May 11, 2010, at 22; Wes Allison, *Direction of High Court Depends upon Election*, ST. PETERSBURG TIMES, Nov. 2, 2008, at 7A.

24. Robert D. Putnam. *Diplomacy and Domestic Politics: The Logic of Two-Level Games*, 42 INT'L ORG. 427–60 (1988).

25. Between 1950 and 1955 Senator John W. Bricker of Ohio led a movement to amend the Constitution in ways designed to make it impossible for the United States to ratify human rights treaties without modifying it to suit American preferences. The campaign for the Bricker Amendment represented a move by anti-civil rights and "states' rights" forces to prevent bringing an end to racial discrimination and segregation by international treaty. On January 7, 1953, Senator Bricker introduced a joint resolution calling for an amendment to the U.S. Constitution. The Bricker Amendment, clearly fashioned to restrict the power of the president to commit the United States through treaty or executive agreement, had five important sections:

Section 1. A provision of a treaty which denies or abridges any right enumerated in this Constitution shall not be of any force or effect.

Section 2. No treaty shall authorize or permit any foreign power or any international organization to supervise, control, or adjudicate rights of citizens of the United States within the United States enumerated in this Constitution or any other matter essentially within the domestic jurisdiction of the United States.

Section 3. A treaty shall become effective as internal law in the United States only through the enactment of appropriate legislation by the Congress.

Section 4. All executive and other agreements between the President and any international organization, foreign power, or official thereof shall be made only in the manner and the extent to be prescribed by law. Such agreements shall be subject to the limitations imposed on treaties, or the making of treaties, by this article.

Section 5. The Congress shall have power to enforce this article by appropriate legislation.

Amendment of Constitution Relating to Treaties and Executive Agreements, S.J. Res. 1-A, 83d Cong. (1953) is the most often cited, but *see also* S.J. Res 102, 82d Cong. (1951); S.J. Res. 130, 82d Cong. (1952); S.J. Res. 181, 83d Cong. (1954). *See generally* DUANE TANNABAUM, THE BRICKER AMENDMENT CONTROVERSY: A TEST OF EISENHOWER'S POLITICAL LEADERSHIP 1–15 (1988); Cathal J. Nolan, *The Last Hurrah of Conservative Isolationism: Eisenhower, Congress and the Bricker Amendment*, 22 PRES. STUD. Q. 337–44 (1992).

26. Louis Henkin, *U.S. Ratification of Human Rights Conventions: The Ghost of Senator Bricker*, 89 AM. J. INT'L L. 341 (1995), 341; *see also* Genocide Convention, S. Rep. No. 99–2, at 26–27 (1985); International Covenant on Civil and Political Rights, S. Rep. No. 102–23, at 10–20 (1992); International Convention on the Elimination of All Forms of Racial Discrimination, S. Rep. No. 103–29, at 9 (1994). *See also* David P. Stewart, *United States Ratification of the Covenant on Civil and Political Rights: The Significance of the Reservations, Understandings, and Declarations*, 42 DE PAUL L. REV. 1183 (1993). For a discussion of the reasoning behind the reservations to the Racial Discrimination Convention, *see* Marian Nash (Leich), *Contemporary Practice of the United States Relating to International Law*, 88 AM. J. INT'L L. 721 (1994).

27. *See, e.g.,* the statement and answers to questions of Conrad K. Harper, Legal Adviser, U.S. Department of State, during the ratification of the Racial Discrimination Convention. International Convention on the Elimination of All Forms of Racial Discrimination: Hearings Before the Senate Committee on Foreign Relations, 103d Cong. 13, 21 (1994) (statement of Conrad K. Harper, Legal Advisor, U.S. Department of State).

28. For the legislation accompanying the Genocide Convention, *see* 18 U.S.C. 1091–93 (1998). For material relevant to the Torture Convention, *see* the Torture Victim Protection Act, 28 U.S.CA. 1350 (1998).

29. At present, Congress has not enacted any implementing legislation for the Racial Discrimination Convention. Of course the effect, if not the intention, of the RUDs attached by the United States is to preclude other countries' judgments regarding interpretation and also to deny that international norms set a more demanding standard. *See* The Vienna Convention on the Law of

Treaties, May 23, 1969, arts. 19(c), 27, 1155 U.N.T.S. 331; 8 I.L.M. 679 (1969). *See also* Oscar Schacter, *The Obligation of the Parties to Give Effect to the Covenant on Civil and Political Rights*, 73 AM. J. INT'L L. 462 (1979).

30. *See, e.g.*, Henry A. Kissinger, *The Pitfalls of Universal Jurisdiction*, 80 FOR. AFF. 86–96 (2001).

31. CONG. GLOBE, 31st Cong., 1st Sess. 116 (1850).

32. ANTONIO CASSESE, INTERNATIONAL CRIMINAL LAW 5 (2003).

33. *See* Richard A. Bilder, *Adjudication: International Arbitral Tribunals and Courts*, in PEACEMAKING IN INTERNATIONAL CONFLICT: METHODS AND TECHNIQUES 155 (I. William Zartman & J. Lewis Rasmussen eds., 1997). For a concise discussion, *see also* Brad Spangler, *Adjudication*, in BEYOND INTRACTABILITY (Guy Burgess & Heidi Burgess eds., 2003), *available at* www.beyondintractability.org/essay/adjudication/; and J. G. MERRILLS, INTERNATIONAL DISPUTE SETTLEMENT (4th ed. 2005).

34. Bilder, *id.* at 157. Bilder also suggested that the unique characteristics of international politics—a relatively small group in continuous interaction—may require institutions and techniques very different from those designed to deal with domestic problems. *Id.*

35. *See* ADR, Cornell Law School, *available at* www.law.cornell.edu/wex/index.php/ADR. Note that at the domestic level, most lists of alternative dispute resolution (ADR) methods will include arbitration as distinguished from litigation in any list of alternative methods. The reason flows from the broad definition given to ADR on this website: "any means of settling a dispute outside the courtroom." Note also the following advice from the International Trade Forum: "Competition means conflict, but the courts are rarely the best way to settle disputes in business. Trials can be expensive, lengthy and sometimes embarrassingly public." *Dispute Resolution: Bridge Building in a New World*, INT'L TRADE FORUM, Apr. 2004, *available at* www.tradeforum.org/news/fullstory.php/aid/770/Dispute_Resolution:_Bridge-building_in_a_New_World.html.

36. Dispute Avoidance and Dispute Resolution in China, *available at* http://library.findlaw.com/ 2002/Nov/1/132533.html (emphasis added).

37. Dispute Avoidance and Dispute Resolution, *available at* www.export.gov/china/ exporting_to_china/disputeavoidanceandresolution.pdf.

38. Based on Bilder, *supra* note 33, 174–75.

39. Spangler, *supra* note 33.

40. *See, e.g.*, the discussion in INTERNATIONAL ARBITRATION AND MEDIATION—FROM THE PROFESSIONAL'S PERSPECTIVE 66–67 (Anita Alibekova & Robert Carrow eds., 2007).

41. Bilder, *supra* note 33, at 179.

42. For a narrative and chronology, *see* www.greenpeace.org/international/rainbowwarriorbombing/

spystory/spystory2/spystory3/spystory4; and http://www.kauricoast.co.nz/Feature.cfm?WPID=70.

43. J. Martin Rochester, *supra* note 2, at 35–36.

44. *See* Funding and Budget, *available at* www.ohchr.org/EN/AboutUs/Pages/FundingBudget.aspx.

45. JOSÉ E. ALVAREZ, INTERNATIONAL ORGANIZATIONS AS LAW-MAKERS 283 (2005).

46. *Id.* at 285.

47. *Id.* at 286.

48. *Jus cogens* (peremptory norms) is a category of rules of customary law considered so fundamental and significant to the structure and functioning of the international community that they bind states even if the state has not given formal consent. As one might expect, considerable controversy surrounds the question of what norms do and do not have peremptory status. Besides Charter norms, the following sets of rules have been suggested: (1) the traditional rule of the inviolability of diplomatic agents; (2) the prohibition on the use of aggressive force between states; (3) respect for the self-determination of peoples; (4) respect for basic human rights; (5) respect for the rules guaranteeing the international status of sea, air, and space beyond the limits of national jurisdiction; and (6) respect for the basic international rules governing armed conflicts. *See* LAURI HANNIKAINEN, PREEMPTORY NORMS (JUS COGENS) IN INTERNATIONAL LAW: HISTORICAL DEVELOPMENT, CRITERIA, PRESENT STATUS 21 (1988).

49. For the definitive treatment, *see* JAMES CRAWFORD, THE CREATION OF STATES IN INTERNATIONAL LAW (2nd ed. 2006).

50. *See* The Macedonian Issue, *available at* web.mit.edu/hellenic/www/macedonia.html.

51. For an extended discussion, *see* GERHARD VON GLAHN & JAMES LARRY TAULBEE, LAW AMONG NATIONS ch. 8 (9th ed. 2009).

52. Alfred P. Rubin has challenged the assertion that pirates have been considered outlaws since "time immemorial." He has argued that raiding formed part of the culture around the ancient Mediterranean. Moreover, Sir Frances Drake and Sir Henry Morgan, among others, made their fortunes by piracy against the Spanish. *See* ALFRED P. RUBIN, THE LAW OF PIRACY (1998).

53. *See* Jill Harrison, *Blackbeard Meets Blackwater: An Analysis of International Conventions That Address Piracy and the Use of Private Security Companies to Protect the Shipping Industry*, 25 AMER. U. INT'L L. 283–312 (2010).

54. *See* UN Convention on the Law of the Sea, Dec. 10, 1982, Articles 100–106, 1833 U.N.T.S. 3, 397; 21 I.L.M. 1261 (1982). The International Maritime Bureau (IMB) has a broader definition of piracy that it uses to track incidents. *See* INTERNATIONAL CHAMBER OF COMMERCE, INTERNATIONAL MAR. BUR. PIRACY AND ARMED ROBBERY AGAINST SHIPS, REPT. FOR THE

PERIOD 1 JANUARY–30 SEPTEMBER 2008, at 32 (2008). This established the International Maritime Bureau (IMB) as a division of the International Chamber of Commerce. It is designed to be the central point for combating all maritime crime. The IMB REPORT defines piracy as "An act of boarding or attempting to board any ship with the apparent intent to commit theft or any other crime and with the apparent intent or capability to use force in the furtherance of that act." *Id.* at 4.

55. Convention for the Suppression of Unlawful Acts against the Safety of Maritime Navigation, Mar. 10, 1988, 1678 U.N.T.S. 222.

56. *Id.*

57. *See, e.g.,* S.C. Res. 1846, U.N. Doc. S/RES/1846 (Dec. 2, 1008) (authorizing the states to treat Somalia's territorial seas as high seas for the purpose of combating piracy). This resolution expired on December 2, 2009. *Id.*

58. J. Peter Pham, *Lawyers vs. Pirates*, FOR. POL'Y (Apr. 20, 2010), *available at* www.foreignpolicy.com/aricles/2010/04/30/Lawyers-vs.-pirates.

59. S.C. Res. 1918, U.N. Doc. S/RES/1918 (Apr. 27, 2010).

60. ICTY, The Cost of Justice, *available at* www.icty.org/sid/325.

61. For a concise but perceptive discussion, *see* Hartmut Hilgenberg, *A Fresh Look at Soft Law*, 10 EUR. J. INT'L L. 499–515 (1999); *see also* C. M. Chinkin, *The Challenge of Soft Law*, 38 INT'L & COMP. L. Q. 850–66 (1989).

62. *See, e.g.,* Prosper Weil, *Towards Relative Normativity in International Law?* 77 AM. J. INT'L L. 414 (1983).

63. David J. Bederman, *Constructivism, Positivism, and Empiricism in International Law*, 89 GEO. L. J. 490 (2001).

64. 14 I.L.M. 1292 (1975).

29

Law Versus Justice in International Negotiations

The Israeli-Palestinian Conflict-Resolution (Management) Process*

SANFORD R. SILVERBURG

> *C'est sur cette définition des règles que réside le plus grand obstacle à cette démocratisation qui est la voie pour que l'ordre ne soit pas synonyme d'injustice et pour que la quête de justice ne se traduise pas par des désordres qui mettent en péril l'existence de la nation.*[1]
>
> —Djaaffer Saïd

> *It may be unjust but not illegal. Injustice and illegality are not the same thing. What is legal is not necessarily just.*[2]
>
> —Avi Shlaim

Introduction

The purpose of this essay is to provide a prolegomenon to a two-level model[3] employing drama theory[4] that will set the stage for still another appreciation of the difficulty in managing the Arab-Israeli conflict[5] to a lower intensity that could be subject to diplomatic negotiation. The contention presented here is that there is a set of incongruous maximum goals (IMG) maintained by Israel and the Palestinians that cannot be mitigated unless the asymmetric diplomatic space between the two can be reduced to allow for acceptance of an agreement by respective governments as well as their domestic populations. Additionally, the difference in the set of issues that either party has prioritized makes convergence in any negotiating sequence more protracted because the preferences cannot easily be equated or compared. Perhaps most important is a precautionary note to avoid any assumption of irreconcilable political differences;

---

*Initially prepared for "Looking to the Future: New Paradigms and Perspectives on the Middle East," Santa Barbara Community College, Santa Barbara, CA, Apr. 16–18, 2008 and subsequently adapted to its present version.

rather, the argument offered here is a nuanced adaptation of the work presented by Shaul Mishal and Nadav Morag, who focused on the differences in the negotiation process between two dyads, Israel and Egypt and Israel and Jordan. With the former, Egypt, the context is one of hierarchy versus networking, with Egypt representing a state with a geographical distinctiveness, a pre-Arab culture, and an etatist national identity that was conducting a formal agreement with Israel. Conversely, the case with Jordan finds Israel dealing with a context of contract versus trust. In Jordan the authority structure is based more on a networked system ensconced in a multilayered system, diverse relations, and identity based more on communities that were informal and trust-based.[6]

Hence, for our purposes, Israel tends to focus on the legalities of political positions that are equated with notions of security, both national and personal,[7] embedded in a bounded legal structure, whereas the Palestinians demand some interpreted notion of justice. It should not be surprising that Israelis and Palestinians have a divergent perspective on the conflict that engulfs each of their collective lives. Both people have a widely dissimilar cultural ethos, separate identity, value system, and divergent national narratives. Both disputants have frequently engaged one another in traditional diplomatic fora but have yet to produce measures that would either provide Israel greater security or Palestinians a more sustainable lifestyle. There have been occasions when agreements were reached, rarely though they may have been. Negotiators, at the end of the day go home and translate agreements written in diplomatic lingo into what the respective domestic audiences can understand as satisfaction for their personal interests. This condition is what the two-level game recognizes as the relationship between the international and the national. In this particular case, there is the additional issue of cross-cultural communication, which has never been fully satisfied, either among Israelis and Palestinians or other intercultural conflict contacts. This difficulty has been pointed out by Harald Müller, who em-ployed communicative action theory to explain the phenomenon.[8]

Although law and justice are frequently understood as interchangeable among many legalists, legal activists—as opposed to legal advocates—to be sure, are wont to declare that there cannot be law without justice or that justice stands on a higher plain of aspiration and thus requires law to continuously work toward this end. The fact that both parties to this dispute have deconstructed this supposed connection, however, is but one indicator of the separateness of the concepts.[9]

The wide variance in approach taken by the parties has underscored the failure to reach a substantive agreement between Israel and the Palestinians. But notice that this situation does not necessarily have to be the case, and here we refer to evidence of agreements, admittedly involving full-fledged states. Treaty relations have been established, albeit fragile at times, between Israel and Egypt and Jordan, respectively. The Arab League states, Egypt, Jordan, and Mauritania have full diplomatic relations with Israel, and Israeli and Omani foreign ministers have met in the latter's capital. It should also be noted that the Israeli foreign minister has conducted *sub rosa* meetings with her Bahraini and United Arab Emirate counterparts either in European capitals or pursuant to other occasions in the UN General Assembly. True, diplomatic relations traditionally are conducted at an official level between governments, but contemporary international politics has expanded the avenues of interchange and is now expressive along far more creative dimensions. Representatives of disputant parties, it can be demonstrated, need not be official government spokespersons. Nevertheless, it is also recognized that any concrete implementation of an agreement must, in the end, come from an official source. Although we focus here on the two principal agents to a dispute on two levels, an international and a domestic one, there is still another alternative. It should be appreciated that "peace plans" need not be reserved for negotiated positions by governments that require support from a domestic audience. An agreement reached by Yossi Beilin, a former Israeli Knesset member, and Yasser Abed Rabbo, a former Palestinian Authority (PA) minister together created what became known as the Geneva Accord (October 20, 2003).[10] Although many peace activists met the proposal with favor, it fell on deaf ears and both Israelis and Palestinians ultimately rejected it. Reaching an agreement over widely disparate objectives between groups with little mutual trust can be a Herculean task. A people's needs require representation by agencies that can ultimately provide satisfaction, thus creating a situation of codependency. Again, it must be repeated: The difficulty here is the incompatibility of two peoples' demands that they have created for themselves and that have to be satisfied by their respective governments.

Israel: Law & Order

Arab-Israeli Context

The success of Zionism cannot be understated when one considers the establishment of the state of Israel as the first new Western-styled democracy in the post–World War II era. An integral part of this political institution was an appreciation of structure and order based on a firm legal system that was inherited from the state's founder's cultural heritage, largely British, borrowing some from the former Ottoman code that operated in the region. But the implacable importance of law made a definite imprint on all aspects of the state's development and outlook.[11]

One of the more important components of Israel's ideology is its emphasis on its territorial integrity, which has historically been inexorably attached to the ever-evolving understanding of national security.[12] The current context retains the notion of strategic depth with the displacement of threat from its eastern and southern Arab neighbors via peace treaties, supplanted by terrorist incursions and violence from Hizbullah in the north and Hamas from Gaza in the south and to a lesser extent the West Bank.

Hence, an Israeli official from the Foreign Affairs Ministry spelled out the position in the following terms: "Once Israel can be assured that its right of existence amongst its neighbors in the region will be recognized, once Israel can be confident of its right to self-defense against existential threats and mass terrorism, then the country can be more flexible regarding issues that still divide it from Arab and Palestinian neighbors."[13] The national security agenda for Israel has evolved to include the issue of communal housing settlements in the Occupied Territories, which are understood to support defensible borders to be precise, and that from the Israeli perspective is integral but is also especially grievous to the Palestinians. Thus, soon after the 1967 Arab-Israeli conflict, Israel, in its newly configured strategic position, made a decision to unify Jerusalem and reaffirm it as the nation's capital in its new historic condition. Plans for protecting the area included the creation of a "security barrier" around the city. More currently and in line with this policy position, Prime Minister Ehud Olmert has spelled out an official position that represents both a maximum and minimum position that housing settlements in eastern Jerusalem should *not* be abandoned;[14] settlements have also been placed in an overall strategic pattern throughout the West Bank. The Israelis, with their western border on the Mediterranean Sea and the remaining borders abutting potential hostile Arab states, believe they are confronted with a serious threat. The Israeli demand for settlement blocs in the West Bank and around Jerusalem as well as a special security arrangement on the mountain range east of the Ben Gurion Airport necessarily creates a conflict over a core issue of the negotiation process—borders for a proposed Palestinian state—so the Palestinians have strongly contested it.[15]

The significance of the settlements issue has also become an interest to various U.S. administrations.[16] The external involvement becomes credible because of its superpower status at a cost of infusing confusion into bargaining points with the insertion of a nonregional actor's interests. The "special relationship" that the United States maintains with Israel has caused the Palestinians to demand that they place pressure on the Israelis to halt settlement expansion and, ultimately, remove the settlements. But in an American presidential communication to the then Israeli Prime Minister Ariel Sharon, and speaking to the issue of the future borders of Israel and a Palestinian state, a particular implication was given as a result of the statement that

> In light of new realities on the ground, including already existing *major Israeli population centers*, it is unrealistic to expect that the outcome of final status negotiations will be a full and complete return to the armistice lines of 1949, and all previous efforts to negotiate a two-state solution have reached the same conclusion. It is unrealistic to expect that any final status agreement will only be achieved on the basis of mutually agreed changes that reflect these realities.[17]

Thus, the Israelis believed that territorial adjustments, which would be a part of any U.S.-initiated effort, would allow for the permanent acceptance of many of the already established settlement blocs. In fact, Sharon felt sufficiently confident to allow him to announce to the Israeli Knesset that

> There is American acknowledgment that in any final status agreement there will be no Israeli withdrawal to the 1967 lines. . . . This acknowledgment appears in two ways: Understanding the facts determined by the large Israeli settlement blocs such as making it impossible to return to the 1967 lines, and implementation of the concept of "defensible borders."[18]

What, then, will ultimately complicate matters is a confirmation letter sent by Dov Weinglass, Sharon's chief of staff, to Condoleezza Rice, the then-serving National Security Advisor, interpreting the American commitment as any limitation on settlement expansion would follow a policy made "within the agreed principles of set-

tlement activities . . . to have a better definition of the *construction line of settlements* in Judea and Samaria."[19] But diplomatic parlance, being what it is, allowed Secretary of State Rice to qualify these remarks later, acknowledging that "there are current realities and new realities since 1949 and 1967 for both sides . . . the President's letter talked about realities at that time."[20]

The extent to which the Israeli government has committed itself to reinforce long-held goals in so many areas of its communal life is a testimony to how strongly the supporting values are. Having said this, it is to be expected in a democracy that there be opposing viewpoints expressed particularly on the most essential matters. Issues of conflict between national security and civil liberties are generally the most contentious. This is frequently the case when it comes to national security; a nation's judiciary tends to show the maximum degree of deference to the government's efforts to defend the state. In Israel, however, this has not necessarily been the absolute case. The most erudite and critical examination of Israeli administrative policies affecting Palestinian lives has emerged from the Israeli Supreme Court, which on numerous occasions has taken strong positions opposite to official policy, especially with reference to administrative detentions, house demolitions, and settlements.[21] What this has meant is that the Israeli government's negotiating position has been blunted by elements of its own organization.

Domestic Audience

The most recent phase of the peace process is arbitrarily dated from the signing of the Oslo accords, an agreement the Israeli Labor government engaged in signing that was clouded by the secret process in which it was conducted. When announced, the diplomatic effort was met with strong resistance from the oppositional Likud party and the Jewish settler movement. Voting in the Knesset resulted in only 61 of the 120 members voting to ratify the agreement and was brought about only with the connivance of the Israeli Arab members of the parliamentary body.[22] The Israeli body politic is largely divided along a bifurcated ideological scale, the Left and the Right. In a parliamentary democracy at the time of elections, unless either bloc can sustain a simple majority, a coalition of sorts is in order, thereby requiring some number of political parties to cross the ideological line, even if temporarily, so as to create a government. Public opinion in these cases can play an important role and did prior to the 1992 Israeli elections, allowing for a bounce in favor of Labor over Likud and the acceptance of the Oslo Accords.[23] However, every opportunity to break the cycle of violence—provocation ⟶ violent acts ⟶ retaliation—is offset when the Israeli public confidence is shaken as a result of a perception of a lack of resolve to deal adequately with the threat of a terrorist attack. When the government, on its own or under pressure from external actors like the United States, offers concessions to the Palestinians, Likud has made its opposition known in no uncertain terms. From the perspective of the Right in Israel, not only is Hamas a threat, but increasingly Iran has become a *bête noire*.[24] Perceived threat need not take into consideration whatever condition gave rise to the action that caused the perception to be held. But the government, which is influenced to no small degree by the agency of the military, must respond to perceived threats in order to maintain the necessary level of domestic support so as to allow the government to operate effectively.[25]

In a similar regard, the religious component in Israeli politics cannot be underestimated. Religious political parties can be, for example, the linchpin in an Israeli Prime Minister's ability to form a government. Consequently, policies that religious parties find unacceptable can mean that the parties will withdraw their support from a coalition to bring about the dissolution of the government.[26] In the context of the Arab-Israeli conflict, religious parties can push for policies that make it difficult for a government to alter its maximum demands. Such is the case, for example, of settlement expansion—as distinct

from dismantling illegal "outposts"—on the West Bank. The religious party Shas, supported by Moetzet Yesha (the Council of Jewish Communities in Judea, Samaria, and Gaza), which is the organization that represents West Bank settlers, has consistently demanded the government allow settlements based on some divinely inspired notion and, as a result, provided sharp opposition to announced moves to freeze plans for expanded building.[27] This domestic pressure perforce places impediments in the government's negotiating space.

The settlement issue is of course, as stated above, a major potential deal breaker not only with the Palestinians but also with the United States. The matter is a complex one, involving settlements, their establishment or expansion in the area of the Jerusalem municipality and in the West Bank, and "outposts" in the West Bank. Opposition to increasing the Israeli presence is certainly in the forefront of Palestinian demands, but also with Israeli peace activist organizations such as Peace Now, which monitors these activities.[28]

Still another component of the Israeli body politic that requires mention is the Israeli Arab sector, which when the ethnic factor is included into the political dimension clearly clouds any notion of democracy. Israeli Arabs are active political participants in the Israeli Knesset, but they must tread a very thin line between supporting terrorism and impermissible support of terrorist organizations while simultaneously voicing representative opinions of their Palestinian Arab brethren.[29] Their voice in the legislature or as an element of Israeli public opinion can play an important role.

Palestine: Justice ⟶ Peace

Justice is an idea that has a noble history and has had multiple definitions bandied about. Although frequently lacking expressed statutory or codified effect, justice has an almost universal appeal among peoples who consider themselves civilized. As contextualized by international legal specialists concerned with ending violent conflicts, the content is most frequently consigned to the notion of redistributive justice, or a reallocation of some set of goods following the negotiating phase of the conflict. Palestinians have frequently connected this concept to their historic plight in an attempt to concretize their national identity, provide an essential life support system for their folk, and readjust an asymmetric power position vis-à-vis the perceived force impeding this goal, Israel. The theme of justice is also frequently placed in an historical perspective, which has developed from the singular historic trauma of the first open Israeli-Palestinian conflict in 1948, characterized by Palestinians as *an-Nakba* (the Catastrophe). From this point in time and even before, to include the taciturn social relations between Zionist settlers and Palestinian *fellahin* that preceded the establishment of Israel and the forestalling of Palestinian political self-determination, the denial of some set of "rights" becomes a tale of wrongdoing that must be undone.[30] That initial experience of acting as a non-Western, national folk confronting an institutionalized Western community set into motion a self-debilitating cultural motif that continues to frame Palestinian objectives and approaches when dealing with the Israelis. As one Palestinian observer has noted as a measure creating the context for the Palestinian negotiating position: "The experience of dispossession, exile, and military occupation have deprived Palestinians not only of living together as a nation but also of the opportunity to build a unified national narrative and tradition."[31] This angst was similarly voiced by another Palestinian thusly:

> The claim for justice in the Palestinian context is the demand to acknowledge the "event" of 1948 as a boundary marking the end of an unreflective existence and the beginning of the making of a particular people, and the construction of a particular identity. It produced a disruption of an organic place/time, a rupture between a before and after that makes the emergence of a national narrative.[32]

Is justice considered an alternate goal, achievable through a strategy at the international or regional level? Or is it a means to gain a momentum toward political success? Can the condition be rightfully assigned to more than one conflicted party?

The most current version of a Constitution for Palestine indicates the primacy of justice, as it is found in Article 2, the first humanistic principle listed among four, the others being liberty, equality, and human dignity. The other political principle evinced is the "right to practice self-determination and sovereignty over their land."[33]

In perhaps what is the most eloquent and simultaneously concise treatment of this idea, the Palestinian political philosopher Sari Nusseibeh set out the parameters of the argument,[34] to wit:

Justice is generally understood to be

1. recognition as national people, presumably as a Muslim or Christian community; and
2. "the option of returning to their homeland" commonly referred to the Right of Return[35]

The demand for control over the entire historic Palestine as a geographic entity preserved by national memory stands in clear and unambiguous opposition to those who suggest some further diminution.[36]

The emphasis on land when related to a state necessarily is defined in the political terms of territory. But for Palestinians, whether the referent is land or territory, the historic patrimony is understood by communal memory, although there is little if any historical empirical experience that can be used for support. But with the past in mind, whatever Arab Palestine can be must at best be superimposed on territory already part of an existing sovereign state. The relevance may be logical but has little functional practicality for Palestinians to demand a means of providing the essentials of life within a cultural setting.

Interestingly, this understanding of the right of Palestinians to justice is based, *inter alia*, on the character of equality between the two parties. However, when the religious component of either society is inserted, there is some hesitancy to fully accept that which is demanded. At one point in the ongoing negotiating process, when the Israelis demanded the PA recognize Israel as a "Jewish" state, Mahmoud Abbas immediately rejected the idea.[37] But at the same time the Constitution of the [Proposed] State of Palestine categorically announces Islam as the state religion.[38] The unacceptability of the Jewish character of Israel as distinct from diplomatic recognition of the state is something that evolved from the onset of contacts between Palestinian Arab Muslims and Christians with Jewish Zionists, both secular and religious. Subsequently, Israel on occasion has legislated with a discriminatory bent favoring its Jewish citizens over non-Jewish citizens, that is, rules regarding land purchase. Some in the Arab world see this hostility as a lack of sensitivity, which in turn creates conditions on the domestic front that reduces Israel's negotiating team's ability to gain greater latitude.[39] For other Palestinian political analysts, justice is an umbrella term that covers the lack of support that a people without political or military power have in the asymmetric battle with Israel. Thus, the second *intifada* was a Palestinian popular demand, as distinct from their leadership, to satisfy some of their most basic requirements for survival.[40]

The Palestinian demand for "justice" as the critical component of their gravamen with Israel obfuscates the perceived conflation of law and justice within the internal operation of the Palestinian polity, such as it is.[41] When considered as synonymous concepts, "the embrace of legal justice is, at best, a rhetorically appealing device for quieting alarm for the excesses and inequities social and economic arrangements inevitably arouse."[42] Although justice is an overarching theme that sets the publicly stated goals in their proper setting, one cannot lose sight of what the Palestinian negotiating team has as their maximum agenda.[43] According to Abbas, there are six issues for which Palestinians seek resolution: 1) Jerusalem, 2) Jewish settlements on the West Bank, 3) repatriation of Palestinian refugees, 4) borders that would outline a Palestinian state, 5) certain security issues, and 6) water resources.[44] Later Abbas would set out another goal: the release of Palestinian prisoners in Israeli jails. This issue, Abbas insisted, was a part of the *sine qua non* for any sort of a final agreement to be reached—in other words, a maximum demand.[45] Hamas's "foreign minister," Mahmoud al-Zuhar, somewhat mirrored the mainline position of Fatah in the PA in the following words:

A "peace process" with Palestinians cannot take even its first tiny step until Israel first withdraws to the borders of 1967; dismantle all settlements; remove all soldiers from Gaza and the West Bank; repudiates its illegal annexation of Jerusalem; releases all prisoners; and ends its blockade of our international borders, our coastline and our airspace permanently.

This was meant not only to be the maximum demand but, some might say, that position plus, when he added "This would provide the starting point for just negotiations and would lay the groundwork for the return of millions of refugees."[46] The interest in Hamas's position creates the condition that provides that group with implicit support for its independence or at least its separateness from Fatah's dominance. Without some kind of rapprochement between the two main factions, it is difficult to grant the Palestinians any ability to negotiate with Israel with organizational unity; rather, the demand to recognize Hamas in some way necessarily diminishes the PA's credulity and its authority. Far more pressing is the condition that without a uniform position taken by all organizational segments of the PA, including acceptance across the board of the state of Israel—as Jewish political entity—and recognizing it diplomatically, what is the incentive for Israel to negotiate with the PA even if it were functional?

Hamas's political leader Khaled Mashaal, in a news conference following a visit in Damascus from ex-president Jimmy Carter, reiterated the organization's acceptance of a two-state solution,[47] combined with a ten-year *hudna* (truce)—as distinct from a *tahdi'a* (a period of calm/cease-fire)—and without, however, any formal recognition of Israel, thus falling back to its formal position in the organization's Charter.[48] At one previous point, Hamas's prime minister, Isma'il Haniyeh, did indicate that recognition would be forthcoming "If Israel declares that it will give the Palestinian people a state and give them back all their rights."[49] The alternative of Hamas's ultimate goal can be characterized achieving tactical advantage without an explicit statement of an ideological shift. Hamas's religious heritage led it to oppose Fatah's secular orientation in order to create a Muslim Palestine (*Filastin al-Muslima*). But can it set aside, as has Fatah, its position of representing a revolutionary Palestine (*Filastin al-Thawra*) so the latter is the means to gain the former? In either case, whether each is a maximum or a minimum demand, neither can be countenanced by Israel with a reasonable expectation because its religious orientation always places the Palestinian cause within a conservative value Islamic essence (*Islamiyat al-qadiyya al-Filastiniyya*).[50] Under these circumstances the conflict becomes more than competing nationalisms; it becomes one of different absolute belief systems.

Nationalist Response

The origin of Palestinian nationalism is necessarily connected to the appearance of a national Palestinian identity and some sort of recognition of a Palestinian polity. All these components are mired in controversial historical perspective and objectification. There is no widely accepted account of when Arabs in "historic Palestine" made the connection, but certainly at some point in the early part of the twentieth century, Arabs of *bilad al-sham*, denied the opportunity for an independent Arab state as promised by European imperial powers, publicly assumed the collective identity of Palestinians. When exactly this condition can be dated from or the conditions under which it

evolved, for all practical purposes, is an academic exercise that is best pursued by a college of experts.[51] Indeed, the connection between "peoplehood" and the juridical state has been viewed for so long through a Western-oriented prism that our appreciation of an alternative social statement may be lacking.[52]

Contemporary geographic Palestine is the West Bank and the Gaza Strip, with the official operating government under the control of the PA's political representative, Fatah (*Harakat al-Tahrir al-Watani al-Filastin*, the Palestinian National Liberation Movement), its de facto capital in Ramallah, in the West Bank, with significant political opposition and a competing governing body, Hamas (zeal, *Harakat al-Muqawamah al-Islamiyya*, Islamic Resistance Movement) in de facto control of the Gaza Strip. The behavior of either political element toward Israel is considerably different. Through Fatah, the PA engages Israel with formalized, diplomatic contacts, perhaps not to the extent of everyone's satisfaction. Hamas, although it achieved domestic recognition through a truly democratic election, was marginalized and denied access to governing. In any case, its reliance on a revolutionary program has meant that it participates in active armed conflict, labeled by Israel as terrorist because civilians are regularly and systematically targeted. The ability of the PA as the official governing body to contain and constrain elements within its political umbrella is conditioned by 1) the organizational ability of its domestic security apparatus, 2) the continued support from Palestinians for their efforts, and 3) the level of satisfaction by the Israeli government for not only the efforts of the Palestinian forces, but also and more importantly, the continuation of terrorist incidents.[53]

Although many political observers watched with enthusiasm the democratic election of the Palestinian Legislative Council on January 25, 2006, the outcome that brought overwhelming success to Hamas was not greeted with commensurate cheer. Reiterating for emphasis, the subsequent isolation, marginalization, and nonacceptance of Hamas's victory led it to assume a separate political life of its own.[54] The takeover and effective control of the Gaza Strip by Hamas in June 2007, for all practical purposes, destroyed the notion of a Unity Government that the "Mecca agreement" had engineered (February 8, 2007),[55] bringing together the two main elements. Acting independently, Hamas continues to demonstrate not only its military prowess, albeit employing terrorist tactics, but also its ability to operate as a shadow political movement to Fatah, thereby reducing the PA's legitimacy and its credibility as a logical and legitimate negotiating party with Israel. After Hamas's takeover of Gaza, PA President Abbas removed the breakaway faction from the government and appointed Salam Fayyid as Prime Minister of what would be a caretaker government deposing Isma'il Haniyeh. As a competitor to Fatah's leadership, Hamas's defiance may, in fact, be a tactic to outshine the legitimate leader's recognized nationalistic position. The desperate condition of life for the Palestinians has meant that if either group were to concede anything to the Israelis, it would be seen as compromise in the Palestinian community and a sign of weakness,[56] but, in turn, it also has the effect of reducing the presence of a cohesive governing body.[57]

Often lacking in any discussion of the Palestinian diplomatic position is the role of that community's public opinion as it emerges in either the West Bank or Gaza. As pointed out by a Palestinian specialist in this area, Palestinian public opinion has been effective "in several ways." Khalil Shikaki went on to illustrate his point by showing that Palestinian public opinion has lent legitimacy to the PA's leadership and institutions as well as allowing it to reduce the level of violence by "cracking down" on those elements that were prone to disruptive behavior, albeit minimally. Nevertheless, the business of peacemaking is left to the elites as, in the end, Palestinian public opinion toward Israelis is framed by those Israelis with whom most Palestinians have some kind of contact—soldiers and armed settlers—and it is shaped, to no small degree, by the framing process initiated by the national leadership.[58] The difficulties are, to say the least, complicated. One researcher with an Arab cultural appreciation noted,

> The problem finding a solution to this complex conflict has been by [a] set of strategic, military, political and religious overtones. The parties involved are mired in global and regional rivalries. Thus, the Israeli-Palestinian conflict, unlike Israel's conflicts with Egypt and Jordan, is not a simple bi-lateral issue between Israel and the PNA because it involves several layers of influence on the Palestinian side which hampers the possibility of reaching a stable and workable agreement with Israel.[59]

Arab-Islamic World

The Palestinian predicament is never placed too far from the formulation of public diplomacy in either the Arab or Muslim states' decision-making arena. Whether or not it is a cynical or a pragmatic filter that is employed to determine the affinity that diplomats in the Arab or Islamic world have for their brethren, the divide can be as wide or narrow as the goal of the analyst wants it to be; nevertheless, the interest remains. The most pronounced effort, at least recently, was made public when Saudi Crown Prince Abdallah presented a proposal at the 18th Arab summit held in Beirut in March 2002, later colloquially referred to as the Arab Peace Initiative.[60] Initially, little support was given to the effort; it was, in any case, reactivated at the 19th Arab summit in Riyadh in March 2007. The importance of this declaration, when supported by the Arab League, is that it was a regional support system for Palestinian demands taking the conflict to a higher level of concern and involvement.[61] The dynamic, if indeed that is how it is to be, was maintained with the support of a full range of Arab and Muslim dignitaries who attended the Annapolis Conference for Peace in the Middle East in November 2007. Even more recently, Yemen has been actively involved in resolving the differences between Fatah and

Hamas that led to internecine conflict. Its success was in obtaining an agreement, the Sanaa Declaration, for both organizations to engage in a dialogue. Hamas did subsequently note that it was "resuming talks rather than accepting any demands by either side."[62] Similarly, Egypt has been serving as an interlocutor between both Hamas and Islamic Jihad and Israel, attempting to introduce a truce between the parties, calling for Hamas to halt its rocket attacks on southern Israel in return for Israel limiting its defensive incursions into Gaza. However, both Palestinian groups rejected the truce because it was limited to the Gaza Strip.[63] While in the Gulf region, the Qatari Prime Minister used the occasion of the 8th Doha Forum on Democracy, Development, and Free Trade, held in April 2008, to which the Israeli Foreign Minister had been invited, to raise the issue of the severe hardship that the Israeli-imposed blockade creates for Gazans.[64]

But regional involvement may not necessarily produce any positive Palestinian end. What must also be included in this wide geographic and political swath is the cost of the destructive actions on the part of Syria and Iran, whose material and political support to its proxies, Hizbullah and Islamic Jihad, adds to increasing tensions and continued provocations. In fact, their actions have the effect of heightening the Israeli threat perception and the overall danger of increasing hostile behavior on all sides.

Negotiating Difficulties

In a negotiation process, though not inevitable, cases involving a bilateral setting involve the high probability that one party may dominate by virtue of ante-existing conditions, especially with the condition of political and military imbalance. Such is the case with Israel and the Palestinians, in which the former already enjoys the character of territorial sovereignty. For Israelis, the territory— "historic Israel"—or whatever permutations have evolved, permits the condition of a clear

advantage. Although the Palestinians are tied to the land[65] regardless of the relative meaninglessness of territory, in terms of defending territory in the context of a modern security environment, they have little to no leverage over the dominating Israelis, who occupy much of the proposed state. Hamas, as a proponent of Islamic-based Palestinian nationalism, regards Palestine as *waqf* (religious endowment) because they hold the position that it is Muslim territory.[66] Territory can be the primary factor in conflict when tied to nationalistic symbolism and religious fervor, which is the case in the Arab-Israeli conflict.[67]

In the negotiating phase of conflict management, the Israeli parliamentary system, as already stated, is vulnerable to coalition dissolution subject to political but also religious considerations. Whereas amongst Palestinians, the question remains: What constitutes the substantive nature of the PA? Prominent today is the split organization of the PA, including as a spoiler the violence-oriented and operationally capable Hamas, which holds out its support for the more widely recognized and legitimate Fatah. Can there be a singularly representative negotiating party? Is there a requirement for an allowance to substitute some compromising method of contact with Hamas in order to realize the reality of that organization's presence? Although the state's existence is considered to be the goal of the bargainer's position, negotiation over this element is considered to be, in negotiating logic, a benefit to a staunch position by the underdog in an asymmetric situation. In this case, the dominant party's position is less likely to diminish.[68] It is presumptive to expect the Israelis to be embarrassed by their political and military preponderance or to offer apologies. Nor should the Israelis think that continuing policies that restrict Palestinian lifestyle to some level that countenances resistance will break their will to resist the occupation or their resoluteness.

Although our thesis is that the two parties' goals are incongruous, that doesn't detract from the fact that each side does have a set of goals that are consciously sought. Now the issue raised is: What does each have to offer the other as a form of exchange, regardless of the divergence of interest? Each party might not necessarily have to give up something in order to satisfy the minimally acceptable demand of the other, which can also be the cumulative benefit when there are multiple goals or, in this case, more than one "core" issue.

The Israeli primary negotiating position, that is, its maximum bargaining point, is the territorial integrity of the state and, more importantly, the protection of its citizens. Its backup position, subject to a negotiated settlement of issues, is the acceptance of a sovereign Palestinian state *within* the West Bank and Gaza Strip, thus allowing for some territorial adjustment of those territories occupied as a result of the June 1967 conflict. The Israelis' demand *de minimus* of the Palestinians is the cessation of armed attacks on its citizens and their property as well as recognition of the Jewish character of the state of Israel, in conjunction with diplomatic recognition, the second part of which has, in effect, been in place. Thus, it can be asserted that an implicit acceptance of Palestinian resistance efforts against occupation authorities or the Israeli military exists, but beyond those limits will bring a harsh response.[69]

Conversely, the Palestinian set of maximum demands is the establishment of a sovereign state within the Occupied Territories as closely as possible to the 1948 armistice lines, which in sequence implies control over its territory and, ergo, the removal of Jewish settlements and outposts that are viewed as a component of an Israeli strategy of creating facts on the ground. Additionally, Palestinians strongly demand the cessation of the Israeli seizure of Palestinian land, especially for the purpose of establishing Jewish settlements, the repatriation of Palestinian refugees, and the establishment of a newly created state capital in Jerusalem. The minimal position is relatively similar to the firm establishment of the state within the pre-1967 boundaries without the presence of Israeli settlements and outposts, restitution for the Palestinian *diasporate*, and Jerusalem as the state's capital.

Analysis

In order to analyze our set of conditions, let us assume the following operational codes:

MDI_g = Maximum demand set by the government of Israel

$MDPA_g$ = Maximum demand set by the Palestinian Authority

MDI_p = Maximum set of demands held by some important portion of the domestic Israeli population

$MDPA_p$ = Maximum set of demands held by some important portion of the domestic Palestinian population

MAI_g = Minimally accepted position to be taken by the government of Israel, subject to the negotiation process

$MAPA_g$ = Minimally accepted position to be taken by the Palestinian Authority, subject to the negotiating process

$(MD_g)I$ = Conditioned by a parliamentary system, and by religious nationalists

$(MD_g)PA$ = Conditioned by political-religious opposition, in part by religious nationalists

Given the persistent condition of MDI_g and $MDPA_g$ there can be no movement because there is nothing to compromise. Thus, one party or the other must reduce the value they place on their respective demands. A changed condition can only be reasonably assumed to emerge if the party initiating the change can anticipate reciprocity.[70] In turn, reciprocity only provides a payoff if the moves continue and lead to similarly mutually advantageous expectations. The key to this series is to change the nature of the incongruity between the party's conditional demands—hence, a two-level system.

The negotiating space with local populations between the parties becomes important. Conflict abatement occurs when the MDI_g coincides with the MAI_g. The alternative occurs

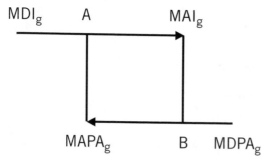

when the distance between Point A and MAI_g increases and is conflict management or reduction. The movement from MDI_g to $MDPA_g$, and vice versa, $MDPA_g$ to MDI_g, is pursuant to domestic pressure on national decision makers. Again, our thesis is that the Israeli MAI_g is beyond Point A and closer to MDI_g than the distance between A and MAI_g. Similarly, the Palestinian Point B is beyond $MAPG_g$ and closer to $MDPA_g$ than the distance between MAI_g and A.[71]

To be sure, the negotiating representatives of both the Israeli government and the PA must be cognizant of what they believe their respective domestic audiences will find acceptable. The ability to gauge that audience's response is far from an exact science and can take a devastating toll if miscalculated, more so for the Palestinians than the Israelis. Hereto the record of what has happened to compromising Arab leaders is far more sanguine than the lost political careers of some Israelis. In the end, therefore, the following conditions are a given:

(1) MAI_g-(MD_g)I
(2) $MAPA_g$-(MD_g)PA $\rightarrow$

When (1) is combined with (2) and delivered in a calculated manner, the result should be an expected outcome that is, to some degree, one of relative success.

In order to reduce the spatial demand gap between the Israelis and the Palestinians, they first must have an understanding and an appreciation of the other's primary goal and be willing to offer some form of satisfaction that would be acceptable to the other. Another point to contemplate is the need for either party to be aware of that point in the negotiation process when it is "ripe" to seize an opportunity, either to compromise or to accept an offer.[72] At the Annapolis Conference, PA President Abbas fully displayed the panoply of Palestinian demands along with a litany of its perceived Israeli-initiated abuses. He addressed Israel's concerns with his comment that "I would like to emphasize that we will continue to carry out our responsibilities in accordance with the Roadmap in fighting lawlessness, violence and terrorism and in restoring law and order."[73] Thus, following the international meeting at Annapolis, Maryland, a Donors Conference was convened in Paris to provide economic assistance to the PA for the dire needs of Palestinians in both Gaza and the West Bank. At this meeting, the Israeli Vice Prime Minister and Minister for Foreign Affairs Tzipi Livni acknowledged the inevitability of the establishment of a Palestinian state. However, her remarks were couched in such a way as to equate that goal with Israel's prime interest. Hence, she told the assemblage that "I am here because the establishment of a peaceful and prosperous Palestinian state *that respects laws and order* and fulfills the legitimate national aspirations of its people is not just a Palestinian dream—it is also an Israeli interest."[74] The issue of the establishment of an independent Palestinian state is not insoluble, although the extent of any future sovereignty might be. The issues that emerge pursuant to state creation, however, are those that are meant to satisfy the Palestinian need to compensate to some degree for their historical past and to which a perceived threat by the Israelis is linked to its formally established political system.

Conclusion

The incongruous level of demands makes an agreement *ceteris paribus* most unlikely because neither party has prioritized the other's maximum goal as sufficiently important but simply at a different level of interest. Is justice an ultimate goal, achievable through a strategy at the international or regional level, or is it a means to gain momentum toward political success? The value orientation of either party is not a symmetrical condition with legal existence of a state that may, in part, help to explain the differences in approaches. Israel is a state *in situ* facing an opponent that is a state *in statu nascendi*. Perhaps the intractability of negotiating between the Israelis and the Palestinians is the position of the parties that is not at the same state level, and therefore, respect for one another is unequal. The decision-making processes operating in each system are different, with a distinctive relationship between the governing authority and the responsive domestic audience. Additionally, the democratic nature of the Israeli polity, with its established system of political opposition, places a burden on its leadership to satisfy a wide array of separate constituent demands. With the PA, not only is there a strong opposition in the form of Hamas but also that Hamas's stated goals and objectives with regard to Israel, combined with its predilection for violence toward the PA and Israel, seriously reduces any credibility the PA could muster as a negotiating party, particularly considering Israel's minimum position.

In order to achieve any sort of agreement given the condition that conflict keeps both parties apart, there needs to be movement on both sides in order to reduce the tension that IMG provide. Two problems immediately come to the fore: First, who initiates the trust-building effort, based on the ability to do so, to incorporate a domestic political support system? Secondly, how does one ensure that reciprocity ensues, which, it should be understood, does not necessarily lead to a condition of cooperation?[75] As shown by Chae-Han Kim, reciprocity must be linked to the perceived payoff as it relates to preferences.[76]

Whatever impasses that existed in the past were conditioned by temporal factors that, when prioritized by each act of national decision makers, simply did not allow for acceptable compromise.[77] Expediency as a principle,

whether imposed by external actors or serving the interests of either of the negotiating teams to gain an early acceptance at home may make achieving a formal agreement more difficult.[78] According to Israeli Prime Minister Ehud Olmert, the progress of negotiations is, in fact, moving in the direction of accepting a set of principles in accordance with what was agreed to at the Annapolis conference, which would lead to implementation at some undisclosed and later date.[79] Nevertheless, we would argue that conflict resolution, if understood to mean conflict abatement, is probably an unrealistic expectation, indeed an ideal that leads to continuing suffering. Rather, we propose conflict management as an alternative. Conflict management is a condition we propose can occur to reduce levels of violence. To this end, we find ourselves in general agreement with the strategic policy thinker Efraim Inbar, who opined, cogently, that:

> The inescapable conclusion is that the "peace process" has probably ended when Hamas catapulted to a leading position in the Palestinian political system. Many will continue to pay lip service to the "peace process" but efforts for gradual conflict resolution such as the "Road Map" are likely to fall in the near future. An attempt to skip the built in gradualism of the "Road Map" and to negotiate a comprehensive agreement has even less chance of success due to the unbridgeable differences between the demands of the two parties.[80]

Noting that the initial position of both parties is a set at the level of maximum demands is certainly not surprising and fulfills, generally, a complete information system. What complicates matters significantly is the match up of either party's fallback position. When the fallback position is unacceptable to opponents, a deadlock occurs. Why must there be a point beyond which there is a not only a different but also significantly divergent view to not permit confluence? In the situation at hand, not only is there a cultural divide between the Israelis and

Palestinians but also the basis for the establishment of their respective goals, and the motivation thereto is so wide as to defy bridging. We also cannot minimize the level of misperception that each has of the other's acceptable goals—in this instance, the fallback position—regardless of official statements.[81] Israel more than likely will not reduce its maximum goal of national security, understood to be a Jewish state with reasonably protective borders, Jerusalem as its symbolic centerpiece capital, and the ability to ensure a cultural heritage. This goal is clearly dependent on the structural order bounded by legal arrangements, preferably codified. The Palestinians, long denied what they consider even a semblance of an opportunity to political identification and without a documented political testimony to support a claim to a Western-styled state, tend to rely, therefore, on a construed memory, calling for justice. The argument is imbued with acceptance, as if it was an already delineated concept equitable in diplomatic parlance with political practice. Although Palestine, at present, is a state *in statu nascendi*, it relies heavily on not only the ability to institutionalize measures that would support the operation of the polity but also an agreement from an adversary, Israel. There are clearly elements within the Palestinian social and political complex that not only contemplate the creation of a sovereign Palestinian state but also seek the dissolution of Israel. Without an outward and formal renunciation of this ideological component, the Israelis cannot reduce their maximum demand or fallback position for a unified Palestinian position that is pacific in nature. There also are, in fact, elements in Israel that pronounce extremely destructive sentiments toward the Palestinians and have irregularly acted on these sentiments. But the extreme elements of either party cannot be equated because there is no Israeli government sanction for such measures or actions.

As we have shown, Palestinian objectives are largely established on the normative principle of justice, an appealing call. But as Cecilia Albin has concluded from serious study, when Israeli and Palestinian negotiators have met, "Principles which failed to address the concerns of parties and to benefit them in a balanced way seldom became influential."[82] We might also add here that we presented the argument that the core difficulty in the negotiating process has been incongruous goals that may, in fact, be attributed to the differences in a cultural orientation. If this is indeed the case, then it is what Alan Page Fiske and Philip Tetlock suggested, namely that "People take their shared implementation paradigms for granted as right and natural, without realizing their cultural relativity" and, thus, hardening their relative positions, making movement away from the maximum position more difficult.[83]

Resolution of the conflict may not be a viable option nor may it be a reasonable expectation. It was the reasoned, if not politically motivated, opinion of Secretary Rice that "if the parties want to do this and will put the energy and the will into it, I think they can do it . . . nothing's really impossible. It might be improbable but it's not impossible."[84] As we have argued above, resolution is but one approach, whereas our preference is to manage a reasonably mutually agreed upon level of acceptance. This does not mean, however, that the frequency or the intensity of violent incidents cannot be reduced or the level of animosity or distrust be limited to a tolerable range.[85] Hence, negotiations offer an opportunity to arrange a relationship of shared mistrust with, perhaps, minimal cooperation but short of openly defined violent conflict over a protracted period of time.

NOTES

1. Djaaffer Saïd, *Islamisme: Le conflit entre l'ordre et la justice*, in ALGÉRIE: COMPRENDRE LA CRISE 174 (Gilles Manceron ed., 1996).

2. AVI SHLAIM, ISRAEL AND PALESTINE: REAPPRAISALS, REVISIONS, REFUTATIONS xi (2009).

3. We owe a debt of gratitude to Robert Putnam for an appreciation of linkage politics applied to a game theoretic environment. Robert D. Putnam, *Diplomacy and Domestic Politics: The Logic of Two-Level Games*, 42 INT'L ORG. 427–60 (1988). The discussion was subsequently expanded in DOUBLE-EDGED DIPLOMACY: INTERNA-

TIONAL BARGAINING AND DOMESTIC POLITICS (Peter B. Evans et al. eds., 1993) and updated in Mark A. Boyer, *Issue Definition and Two-Level Negotiations: An Application to the American Foreign Policy Process*, 11 DIPL. & STATECRAFT 185–212 (2000).

4. Drama theory is a relatively new approach to the study of conflict as an adaptation to game theory allowing for the introduction of emotion and nonrational behavior in interstate relations. Much of our understanding comes from the effort of Nigel Howard. For a fuller discussion, the reader should consult Nigel Howard et al., *Manifesto for a Theory of Drama and Irrational Choice*, 44 J. OPERATIONAL RES. SOC'Y 99–103 (1993); Nigel Howard, *Drama Theory and Its Relation to Game Theory. Part I: Dramatic Resolution vs. Rational Solution*, 3 GROUP DECISIONS & NEGOTIATIONS 187–206 (1994); and *Id. Part 2: Formal Model of the Resolution Process*, 207–35; Peter G. Bennett, *Games and Dramas: Rationality and Emotion*, 40 MERSHON INT'L STUD. REV. 171–75; Nigel Howard & Andrew Tait, "Analytic Approaches to Studying Power and Influence in Contemporary Public/Military Affairs (CDERA), Farnborough, England, October 1998; Nigel Howard, "Resolving Conflicts in a Tree: Drama Theory in the Extensive Form," a paper presented at the IMA (Institute of Mathematics and its Applications) Analyzing Conflict and Its Resolution, Oxford, England, Jun. 28–30, 2004; Peter Bennett et al., *Drama Theory and Confrontational Analysis*, in RATIONAL ANALYSIS FOR A PROBLEMATIC WORLD REVISITED: PROBLEM STRUCTURING METHODS FOR COMPLEXITY, UNCERTAINTY AND CONFLICT 225–48 (Jonathan Rosenhead & John Mingers eds., 2d ed. 2001).

5. The notion of conflict management as distinct from conflict resolution here is intentional as can be gleaned from a previously argued position in Sanford R. Silverburg, *Procedural Conflict Resolution (Management)*, 30 CHITTY'S L. J. 144–49 (1982). This approach is reiterated by Moshe Amirav, *Conflict Management, Not Overall Solution*, 13 PALESTINE-ISRAEL J. 6–9 (2006); and George Emile Irani, *Acknowledgment, Forgiveness, and Reconciliation in Conflict Resolution: Perspectives from Lebanon*, 5 CHRONOS 195–220 (2002). Stated in a somewhat different manner: "The utter lack of trust between the two sides and the depth of their enmity dictate against the wisdom of a single all-encompassing solution." LAURA ZITTRAIN & NEIL CAPLAN, NEGOTIATING ARAB-ISRAELI PEACE: PATTERNS, PROBLEMS, POSSIBILITIES 128 (1998).

6. Shaul Mishal & Nadav Morag, *Trust or Contract? Negotiating Formal and Informal Agreements in the Arab-Israeli Peace Process*, 5 INT'L NEGOTIATION 525 (2000).

7. Perhaps the most succinct statement capturing the importance of law as a national priority can be found in a judgment by Israeli Chief Justice Aharon Barak, who wrote, "There is no security without law." HCJ 2056/04 *Beit Sourik Village Council v. The Government of Israel* (2004) P.D. 46 (2), para. 86. For a discussion of Israeli national security as it relates to a "rule of law" as characteristic of a predominant value in Israeli foreign policy making, *see* MENACHEM HOFNUNG, DEMOCRACY, LAW & NATIONAL SECURITY IN ISRAEL 4–10 (1996).

8. *International Relations as Communicative Action*, in CONSTRUCTING INTERNATIONAL RELATIONS: THE NEXT GENERATION 165 (Karin M. Fierke & Knud Erik Jørgensen eds., 2001).

9. The theoretical connection between the two concepts is contextualized in Thomas R. Kearns & Austin Sarat, *Legal Justice and Injustice: Toward a Situated Perspective*, in JUSTICE AND INJUSTICE IN LAW AND LEGAL THEORY 1–17 (Austin Sarat & Thomas R. Kearns eds., 1996). The position taken here is in between two legal scholars: John Quigley, *The Role of Law in a Palestinian-Israeli Accommodation*, 31 CASE W. RES. J. INT'L L. 351–81 (1999), and Perry Dane, *Pluralities of Justice, Modalities of Peace: The Rule of Law(s) in a Palestinian-Israeli Accommodation, Id.* at 273–85 (Special Supplement 2000).

10. *See* www.heskem.org.il/Heskem_en.asp. *See generally* MENACHEM KLEIN, A POSSIBLE PEACE BETWEEN ISRAEL & PALESTINE: AN INSIDER'S ACCOUNT OF THE GENEVA INITIATIVE (2007). The conditions set out in this private diplomacy were later publicly supported by former President Jimmy Carter. The Carter Center, "Peace With Justice in the Middle East," Remarks made at the Mansfield College, Oxford, "Hands Lecture" on Jun. 21, 2007, *available at* www.cartercenter.org/news/editiorials_speeches/oxford_062107.html. Actually, this condition was preceded by the Ayalon-Nusseibeh Plan (The People's Choice) (Jul. 27, 2002) and met with a similar response, *available at* www.bitterlemons.org/docs/ayalon.html.

11. Aharon Barak, *Begin and the Rule of Law*, 10 ISRAEL STUD. 1–28 (2005).

12. Arye Naor, *The Security Argument in the Territorial Debate: Rhetoric and Policy*, 4 ISRAEL STUD. 150–177 (1999); Daniel Bar-Tal & Dan Jacobson, *The Elusive Concept, and Pursuit of Security*, in SECURITY CONCERNS: INSIGHTS FROM THE ISRAELI EXPERIENCE 15–36 (Daniel Bar-Tal et al. eds., 1988); HOFNUNG, *supra* note 7.

13. Ambassador Yaacov Levy, Director of Policy Planning, Israel, Ministry of Foreign Affairs. "Israel's Security in a Changing Strategic Environment," before an Atlantic Community Policy Workshop, Oct. 10, 2007, *available at* www.atlantic-community.org/indes/articles/views/Israel's_Security_in_a_Changing_Strategic_Environment.

14. *No Chance Israel Will Cede E. Jerusalem Areas Like Har Homa*, HA'ARETZ, Mar. 17, 2008, *available at*

http://haaretz.com/hasen/spages/965116.html. As an indication of the distance between the two parties, Saeb Erekat responded to Foreign Minister Livni that this position was "absolutely unacceptable." *Id.*

15. Roni Sofer & Ali Waked, Mar. 29, 2008, *available at* www.ynetnews.com/articles/0,7340,L-3537537,00.html. At one time, Sharon conceived of Israel's eastern defensible border as the Jordan River. Aluf Benn & Yossi Verter, *Even King Solomon Ceded Territories*, HA'ARETZ, Apr. 22, 2005, at 1.

16. A current picture of the involvement of all relevant actors can be gleaned from MARK MATTHEWS, LOST YEARS: BUSH, SHARON AND FAILURE IN THE MIDDLE EAST (2007).

17. The White House, Letter From President Bush to Prime Minister Sharon. Apr. 14, 2004, *available at* www.whitehouse.gov/news/release/2004/04/print/20040414-3.html (emphasis added).

18. Prime Minister Ariel Sharon's Speech at the Knesset, Apr. 22, 2004, *available at* www.pmo.gov.il/PMO-Eng/Communication/PMSpeaks/speech2204.htm.

19. *See* www.imra.org.il/story.php3?id=20479 (emphasis added). A more complete discussion of the controversy can be gleaned from Glenn Kessler, *Israelis Claim Secret Agreement with U.S.: American Insist No Deal Made on Settlement Growth*, WASHINGTON POST, Apr. 24, 2008, at A14, and the State Department's daily press briefing, *available at* www.state.gov/r/pa/prs/dpb/2004/35296.htm. Although "population centers" and "settlement blocs" may appear as separate entities, American diplomats from the Secretary of State to the American Ambassador to Israel have publicly stated that they are synonymous. Secretary of State Rice with Yaron Dekel on Israel Radio, Mar. 27, 2005, in Aluf Benn, *PM: Understanding with U.S. About West Bank Settlement Blocs Holds Firm*, HA'ARETZ, Mar. 27, 2005, *available at* www.usembassy-israel.org.il/publish/mission/amb/03205b.html.

20. U.S. Department of State, Press Availability en route Shannon, Ireland. May 5, 2008, *available at* www.state.gov/secretary/rm/2008/05/104393.htm.

21. *See generally* DAVID KRETZMER, THE OCCUPATION OF JUSTICE: THE SUPREME COURT OF ISRAEL AND THE OCCUPIED TERRITORIES (2002).

22. YAACOV BAR-SIMON-TOV, PEACE POLICY AS DOMESTIC AND AS FOREIGN POLICY 22 (1998).

23. A general discussion on mood shifts in Israel that led to political change is analyzed in Jonathan Rynhold, *Cultural Shift and Foreign Policy Change: Israel and the Making of the Oslo Accords*, 42 COOPERATION & CONFLICT 419–40 (2007).

24. *Concessions Will Strengthen Hamas*, JERUSALEM POST, Mar. 30, 2008, *available at* www.jpost.com/servlet/Satellite?cid=1206632369093&pagename=JPost%2FJPArticle%2FShowFull.

25. Christopher Sprechler & Karl DeRouen Jr., *Military Actions and Internalization-Externalization Process*, 46 J. CONFLICT RESOLUTION 244–59 (2002).

26. Juliet Kaarbo, *Influencing Peace: Junior Partners in Israeli Coalition Cabinets*, 31 COOPERATION & CONFLICT 243–84 (1996) and her *Power and Influence in Foreign Policy: The Role of Junior Coalition Partners in German and Israeli Foreign Policy*, 40 INT'L STUD. Q. 501–30 (1996).

27. Ilere Prusher, *Israel's "Religious Right" Gains Clout, Complicating Peace with Palestinians*, CHRISTIAN SCIENCE MONITOR, Mar. 18, 2008, *available at* www.csmonitor.com/2008/0318/p04s06-wome.html. Yesha did, however, agree to evacuate the illegal outpost of Mevo Horon North. *Yesha Council Evacuates Outpost Near Modi'in as Part of Deal*, JERUSALEM POST, Apr. 15, 2008, *available at* www.jpost.com/servlet/Satellite?cid=1208179716203&pagename=JPost%2FJPArticle%FShowFull.

28. Tovah Lazaroff & Rebecca Anna Stoil, *PM Olmert: "We'll Build in Major Settlement Blocs*," JERUSALEM POST, Mar. 31, 2008, *available at* www.jpost.com/servlet/Satellite?cid=1206632375576&pagename=JPost%2FJPArticle%2FShowFull.

29. Nancy L. Rosenblum, *Banning Parties: Religious and Ethnic Partisanship in Multicultural Democracies*, 1 L. & HUM. ETHICS 47–49 (2007).

30. A general treatment of this phenomenon is found in Jeff Spinner-Halev, *From Historical to Enduring Justice*, 35 POL. THEORY 574–97 (2007), and George Sher, *Ancient Wrongs and Modern Rights*, 10 PHIL. & PUB. AFF 11–13 (1981).

31. Omar M. Dajani, *Surviving Opportunities: Palestinian Negotiating Patterns in Peace Talks with Israel*, in HOW ISRAELIS AND PALESTINIANS NEGOTIATE: A CROSS-CULTURAL ANALYSIS OF THE OSLO PEACE PROCESS 41 (Tamara Cofman Wittes ed., 2005).

32. May Jayyusi, *Justice, Narrative and the Occlusion of Particularity*, THE PALESTINIAN INSTITUTE FOR THE STUDY OF DEMOCRACY (n.d.), *available at* www.muwatin.org/staff/May_thesis.html.

33. Palestine Center for Policy and Survey Research (PSR), The Constitution Committee, The DRAFT of the Palestinian Constitution (2001), *available at* www.pcpsr.org/domestic/2001/constel.html.

34. Sari Nusseibeh, Palestinians Demand Justice! paper presented at the 1st International Conference on Ethics and Politics, Crete, May 2006, *available at* http://sari.alquds.edu/PALESTINIANS_DEMAND_JUSTICE.htm.

35. *Id.*

36. Ezzedin Al-Qassem Brigades, *Hamas. We Won't Waive an Inch of Palestinian Lands*, Dec. 9, 2007, *available at* www.alqassam.ps/english/?action=showdetail&fid=758. This view was similarly evinced by the de-

posed Palestinian Prime Minister Isma'il Haniyeh. *Haniyeh: We Will Not Accept a Dwarfed Palestinian State*, MAAN NEWS, Jan. 12, 2008, *available at* www.maannews .net/en/index.php?opr=ShowDetails&ID=27171.

37. Samih Khalidi, *Thanks, But No Thanks*, GUARDIAN, Dec. 13, 2007, *available at* www.guardian .co.uk/israel/Story/0 . . . 2226615.00.html. It is considered here, that the creation of a Palestinian state is an attempt to further constrain the just creation of the ultimate historic Palestine.

38. For at the Annapolis Middle East Conference in Nov. 2007, where there was a general agreement on a two-state "solution," Israel Prime Minister Ehud Olmert qualified the conditions as one state, Israel, being Jewish, *see* Address by PM Olmert at the Annapolis Conference, Nov. 27, 2007, *available at* http://mfa.gov.il. For U.S. President George Bush reemphasizing the American commitment to the security of Israel as a Jewish state, *see* President Bush Attends Annapolis Conference, Nov. 27, 2007, *available at* http://whitehouse.gov.news/ release/2007/11/20071127–2.htm. For Abbas, again at Annapolis and when the subsequent Paris Donors Conference refused to accept this characterization, but rather focused on Palestinian core demands, *see* President Abbas in Annapolis: Israel Should End Its Occupation of All Territories Occupied in 1967, Nov. 27, 2007, *available at* www.wafa.ps/english/body.asp?id=10677. The message was echoed by Saeb Eerkat, the Palestinian Chief Negotiator at Annapolis. Barak Ravid, Erekat: Palestinians Will Not Accept Israel as a "Jewish State," HA'ARETZ, *available at* www.haaretzcom/hasen/spages/ 923076.html. Interestingly, the Roman Catholic Patriarch of the Holy Land, a Palestinian, Michel Sabbah, in his Christmas 2007 message, rejected the notion of a "State that would exclude or discriminate against other relations." Latin Patriarch, *Christmas Message 2007*, *available at* www.lpj.org/newsite2006/patriarch/archives/ 2007/12/christmas-message-en.html.

39. Article 6 declares that "Islam shall be the official religion of the state. The monotheistic religions shall be respected." One may also question the substance of the objection if we consider the religious essence of Fatah. Ido Zelkowitz, *Fatah's Embrace of Islamism*, MIDDLE EAST Q. 19–26 (2008), *available at* www.meforum .org/article/1874.

40. *No Peace Without Justice*, JORDAN TIMES, Dec. 13, 2007, *available at* www.jordantimes.com/?news=43432.

41. Kearns & Sarat, *supra* note 9, p. 10. Raef Zreik, *The Palestinian Question: Themes of Justice and Power. Part I: The Palestinians of the Occupied Territories*, 32 J. PALESTINE STUD. 45 (2003). A similar diplomatic standoff occurred subsequent to the CIA initiated coup d'état in Iran when the British and the Americans attempted to negotiate with the Iranians and the latter demanded justice. Indeed, one American diplomat thoroughly fa-

miliar with Persian political culture commented on the situation, noting that "It was too imprecise for Western lawyers and accountants." JOHN W. LIBERT, NEGOTIATING WITH IRAN: WRESTLING THE GHOSTS OF HISTORY 84 (2009).

42. For a general discussion of my point here, *see* Hillel Hirsch & Menachem Hofnung, *Power or Justice? Rule and Law in the Palestine Authority*, 44 J. PEACE RES. 331–48 (2007), and Seth G. Jones & K. Jack Riley, *Law and Order in Palestine*, 46 SURVIVAL 157–78 (2004–05).

43. A maximalist position, as a strategy, served to prolong the negotiating structure and process of the North Vietnamese so as to gain the withdrawal of U.S. military forces from South Vietnam during the Paris peace talks, although they ultimately gained their objective. The strategy was successful, however, only with the sustained military assistance from China and the Soviet Union. This argument is forcefully examined by Lorenz M. Lüthi, *Beyond Betrayal: Beijing, Moscow, and the Paris Negotiations, 1971–1973*, 11 J. COLD WAR STUD. 72, 73, 76, 94, 97, 107 (2009).

44. *Abbas: Negotiations on Core Issues to Begin Monday*, JERUSALEM POST, Jan. 13, 2008, *available at* www.jpost.com/servlet/Satellite?cit=119996491312&pa gename=JPost%2FJPArticle%2FShowFull. It should be pointed out that poll data obtained after the Annapolis Peace Conference indicate that these goals are supported by a wide range of Palestinians. Palestine Center for Public Opinion (PCPO). Poll No. 163, Nov. 25, 2007, *available at* www.pcpo.ps.

45. WAFA-PLO News Agency, *No Peace Deal Will Be Signed as Long as Palestinian Prisoners Held in Israeli Jails*, Mar. 8, 2008, *available at* www.wafa.ps/english/body .asp?id=11292. In the past, when this demand was proffered by Hamas, the Israeli government rejected it. Amos Harel & Barak Ravid, *Israel Won't Free 85% of Prisoners Hamas Wants Released*, HA'ARETZ, Jan. 21, 2008, *available at* http://haaretz.com/hasen/spages/ 946725.html.

46. Mahmoud al-Zuhar, *No Peace Without Hamas*, WASHINGTON POST, Apr. 17, 2008, at A23.

47. In May 2006 a representative from each of the Palestinian resistance groups being held as a political prisoner in Israel's Hadarim prison signed a document known as the "Prisoners Agreement," accepting a two-state solution. This was followed on June 25 with all Palestinian groups except Islamic Jihad signing the National Conciliation Document, reflecting the prisoner's initiative. Although Hamas rejected PA President Abbas's call for a referendum on the document, it did agree some weeks later on its major points. In particular, *see* Article 11, which holds that "the land of Palestine is . . . consecrated for future Muslim generations until Judgment Day. It, or any part of it, should not be squandered . . . or . . . given up." Further along in Article 34,

there is an ominous warning that Palestine can "only be liberated by *jihad*." *See* www.mideastweb.org.

48. The Covenant, or officially known as the Charter of Allah: The Platform of the Islamic Resistance Movement (Aug. 1988). *Hamas Agrees to Palestinian State but Will Not Recognize Israel, available at* www.maannews.net/en/index.php?opr=ShowDetails&ID=28875.

49. Lally Weymouth, *"We Do Not Wish to Throw Them into the Sea,"* WASHINGTON POST, Feb. 26, 2006, at B02. A nuanced perspective was offered by Mohamed Ghazal, who thought that Hamas's recognition was premature "while Israel doesn't recognize me as a victim," and the basic set of demands followed. *Hamas: We'll Rethink Call to Destroy Israel*, Sept. 21, 2005, YNETNEWS.COM, *available at* www.ynetnews.com/articles/0,7340,L-3145475,00.html.

50. Differing views on Hamas's ideology as it reflects either principles of Islamic theology or political pragmatism can be gleaned from the following: Mohammed S. Dajani Daoudi, *Hamas and Palestinian Religious Moderation*, 13 PALESTINE-ISRAEL J. 10–15 (2006); Shai Gruber, *Hamas: Pragmatic Ideology*, AL NAKHLAH 1–10 (2007); Michael Herzog, *Can Hamas Be Tamed?* 85 FOR. AFF. 83–94 (2006); Haim Malka, *Forcing Choices: Testing the Transformation of Hamas*, 28 WASHINGTON QUARTERLY 37–54 (2005); Henry Siegman, *Hamas: The Last Chance for Peace?* 53 NY REV. BOOKS 42–48 (2006).

51. For an intellectual *tour d'force* discussion of the point, *see* Glenn Bowman, *Tales of the Lost Land: Nationalist Consciousness*, in SPACE AND PLACE: THEORIES OF IDENTITY AND LOCATION 73–99 (Erica Carter et al. eds., 1993).

52. The recognition of the failure of both Western and Palestinian historians to determine in an adequate manner the earliest era of "Palestinianism" can be found in Beshara B. Doumani, *Rediscovering Ottoman Palestine: Writing Palestinians into History*, in THE ISRAEL/PALESTINE QUESTION 11–40 (Ilan Pappé ed., 1999), and Maurus Reinkowski, *Late Ottoman Rule Over Palestine: Its Evaluation in Arab, Turkish and Israeli Histories, 1970–90*, 35 MIDDLE EASTERN STUD. 66–97 (1999). Some general historical treatments on the geography of Palestine are found in MODERN HISTORY OF PALESTINE & ISRAEL: HISTORICAL DOCUMENT COLLECTIONS (various years); SUSAN HATTIS ROLEF, THE POLITICAL GEOGRAPHY OF PALESTINE: A HISTORY AND DEFINITION, Middle East Review Special Studies, No. 3 (1983); Louis H. Feldman, *Some Observations on the Name of Palestine*, 61 HEBREW UNION COLLEGE ANN. 1–23 (1990); Bernard Lewis, *Palestine: On the History and Geography of a Name*, 2 INT'L HIST. REV. 1–12 (1980); and Yitzhak Gil-Har, *The Separation of Trans-Jordan from Palestine*, in 1 THE JERUSALEM CATHEDRA 284–310 (Lee I. Levine ed., 1981).

53. This is discussed more fully with Africa in mind *in* Robert H. Jackson & Carl G. Rosberg, *Sovereignty and Underdevelopment: Juridical Statehood in the African Crisis*, 24 J. MOD. AFR. STUD. 1–31 (1986).

54. Although the PA, the United States, and the Quartet expressed strong opposition to Hamas's electoral success, the Organisation of the Islamic Conference (OIC), in Its Istanbul Declaration (Apr. 13, 2006) welcomed the outcome. *See* www.puoic.com/english/PressRelease/InstanbulDeclaration.htm.

55. *See* www.pnic.gov.ps/arabic/palestine/pal-maka.html.

56. A declaration that Hamas would not recognize any effort that reduced Palestinian demands in talks with the Israelis was issued by Dr. Khalil Al Haiya, a leader of the Ezzedine Al-Qassem Brigades, the armed branch of Hamas, announced at a religious festival. *No Free Calm With the Zionist Entity*, Mar. 23, 2008, *available at* www.alqassam.ps/english/?action=showdetail&fid=923.

57. Echoed by Amin M. Hussain, who also argues that Hamas's emphasis on violence tends to forestall the achievement of the legitimate right of Palestinian self-determination. *Who Is the Legitimate Representative of the Palestinian People?* 24 CHINESE J. INT'L L. 223–24 (2003).

58. *Willing to Compromise: Palestinian Public Opinion and the Peace Process*, Special Report 158, at 12–14 (U.S. Institute of Peace, 2006).

59. RIAD A. ATTAR, ARMS AND CONFLICT IN THE MIDDLE EAST 59 (2009).

60. *Arab Peace Initiative, available at* www.nad-plo.org/news-updates/MOBADARA4%20E.pdf. For a general discussion of this effort, *see* Naomi Weinberger, *The Palestinian National Security Debate*, 24 J. PALESTINE STUD. 16–30 (1995).

61. Poll data indicate that Palestinians strongly agree with the Saudi plan, with slightly fewer Israelis opposing the initiative. Harry S. Truman Research Institute for the Advancement of Peace and Palestinian Center for Policy and Survey Research, PSR Poll of Palestinians Show Support Terror, PSR Poll No. 27, Mar. 13–15, 2008, *available at* www.pcpsr.org/survey/polls/2008/p27el.html.

62. *Hamas and Fatah Agree to Resume Dialogue*, MAAN NEWS AGENCY, *Available at* www.maannews.net/en/index.php?opr=ShowDetails&ID=28435; *Hamas, Fateh Sign Reconciliation Deal*, JORDAN TIMES, Mar. 24, 2008, *available at* www.jordantimes.com/priont.html; and Raphael Anderson, *Fatah Backpedals*, MAAN NEWS AGENCY, *available at* www.maannews.net/en/index.php?opr=ShowDetails&Do=Print&ID=28482.

63. *Hamas, Islamic Jihad Reject Egypt Truce*, JORDAN TIMES, Mar. 28, 2008, *available at* http://jordantimes.com/?news=6769. The full text can be read in English in 14 PALESTINE-ISRAEL J. 121–22 (2007).

64. Agence France-Presse, *Qatar Insists It Will Raise Gaza with Israel FM*, Apr. 14, 2008, *available at* www.gulfinthemedia.com/index.php?id=395038&news_typwe=Top&lang=en&PHPSESSID=14618b6ecfa64e03880325b5747b3edf().

65. David Newman, *Real-Spaces, Symbolic Spaces: International Notions of Territory in the Arab-Israeli Conflict*, in A Road Map to War: Territorial Dimensions of International Conflict 3–36 (Paul F. Diehl ed., 1998). In a more general setting, Mira Sucharov, Regional Identity and the Sovereignty Principle: Explaining Israeli-Palestinian Peacemaking Boundaries, Territory and Postmodernity 177–96 (1999).

66. For a general discussion as well as specific references to Palestine, *see* Andrew Grossman, *Islamic Land: Group Rights, National Identity and Law*, 3 UCLA J. Islamic & Near Eastern L. 53–89 (2003–2004).

67. The importance of land to Palestinians can be appreciated in an Israeli Supreme Court case, H.C. 6698/95, *Qa'dan v. Israel Lands Administration, et al.*, P.D. 54 (1) 258. *See also* the entire issue of Adalah's Review 2 (Fall 2000), which focuses on the concept of land.

68. This condition is noted by Timo Kivimäki, Distribution of Benefits in Bargaining Between a Superpower and a Developing Country: A Study in Negotiating Processes Between the United States and Indonesia, Commentationes Scientiarum Socialium 45, 198 (1993).

69. A brief discussion of this point was handled by Lt. Col. (Res.) Jonathan Dahoah Halevi (IDF), *Does B'Tselem Justify Killing Soldiers*, Israeli Newswire News First Class (NFC), *available at* www.nfc.co.il/Archive/003-D-28707–00.html?tag=15–41–44 (in Hebrew).

70. As was pointed out earlier by the work of Lüthi, the North Vietnamese could afford to hold onto a maximalist strategy only with the assurance of external assistance, in this case from the Chinese and the Soviet Union, all the while gambling on the outcome of the American presidential election. *Supra* note 43.

71. What is proposed here mirrors "the Bargaining Zone" set out by Russell Korobkin & Jonathan Zasloff, *Roadblocks to the Road Map: A Negotiation Theory Perspective on the Israeli-Palestinian Conflict After Yasser Arafat*, 30 Yale J. Int'l L. 6–10 (2005). A far more sophisticated, mathematically based exposition of this model as an extended discussion of "fallback bargaining" is presented by Steven J. Brams et al., *A Minimax Procedure for Negotiating Multilateral Treaties*, in Diplomatic Games: Formal Models and International Negotiations 265–82 (Rudolf Avenhaus & I. William Zartman eds., 2007).

72. I. William Zartman, *The Timing of Peace Initiatives: Hurting Stalemates and Ripe Moments*, 1 Global Rev. Ethnopol. 8–18 (2001).

73. His Excellency President Mahmoud Abbas, Chairman of the Executive Committee of the Palestine Liberation Organization and the President of the Palestine National Authority, Annapolis Conference, United States, Annapolis, Nov. 27, 2007, *available at* www.nad-plo.org/news-updates/Engliush%20/Annapolis%20Speech%20Final.pdf.

74. Israel, Ministry of Foreign Affairs. Address by FM Livni to the Paris Donors Conference, Dec. 17, 2007, *available at* www.mfa.gov.il (emphasis added). There is ample evidence that Israeli official as well as popular sentiment to support the acceptability of a sovereign Palestinian state. Shlomo Bron, From Rejection to Acceptance: Israeli National Security Thinking and Palestinian Statehood, Special Report 177 (U.S. Institute of Peace, 2007).

75. Joshua Goldstein et al., *Reciprocity, Triangulation and Cooperation in the Middle East, 1979–1997*, 45 J. Conflict Resolution 594–620 (2001).

76. Chae-Han Kim, *Reciprocity in Asymmetry: When Does Reciprocity Work?* 31 Int'l Interactions 13 (2005).

77. A similar conclusion was reached with regard to American foreign policy and Secretary of State Rice's introduction of a "shelf agreement" concept or a "parallel process." Secretary Rice Remarks with PA President Abbas, *available at* www.state.gov/secretary/rm/2007/mar/82165.htm. There is further analysis in David M. Weinberg, Shelve the Shelf Agreement, *Perspective Papers No. 40*, Mar. 26, 2008, BESA (The Begin-Sadat Center for Strategic Studies), *available at* www.biu.ac.il/SOC/besa/perspectives40.html.

78. An analysis of the pros and cons of negotiating a "shelf" agreement rather than a permanent arrangement, from an admittedly Israeli perspective, although the logic could as easily be applied to the Palestinian position, is Shmuel Even, Israel's Policy Options, INSS Policy Brief No. 12 (Institute for National Security Studies, 2008), *available at* www.inss.org.il:80/publications.php?cat=21&incat=&read=1814.

79. The announcement was at the Israeli Presidential Conference "Facing Tomorrow," May 2008. Aluf Benn, *The Israeli-Palestinian Negotiations: What Was—and Was Not—Agreed On*, INSS Insight No. 56 (The Institute for National Security Studies, 2008), *available at* www.inss.org.il:80/research.php?cat=45&incat=&read=1816. *Prime Minister Ehud Olmert's Speech at the "Facing Tomorrow" Presidential Conference*, May 13, 2008, *available at* www.pmo.gov.il/PMOEng/Communication/PMSpeaks/speechtomorrow130508.htm.

80. Efraim Inbar, *Israel's Palestinian Challenge*, in Israel's Strategic Agenda 213 (Efraim Inbar ed., 2007).

81. Arie M. Kacowicz, after interviewing many of the key actors in the Oslo negotiation process, found this to be the case from the Israeli perspective. *Rashomon in the Middle East: Clashing Narratives, Images and Frames in the Israeli-Palestinian Conflict*, 40 COOPERATION & CONFLICT 343–60 (2005).

82. CECILIA ALBIN, JUSTICE AND FAIRNESS IN INTERNATIONAL NEGOTIATIONS 225 (2001).

83. Alan Page Fiske & Philip E. Tetlock, *Taboo Trade-offs: Reactions to Transactions That Transpire the Spheres of Justice*, 18 POL. PSYCHOL. 274 (1999).

84. Interview with Maggie Rodriguez of CBS's *The Early Show*, May 12, 2008, *available at* www.state.gov/secretary/rm/2008/05/104669.htm.

85. The cultural divide in the conflict must also appreciate the Palestinian employment of suicide to achieve martyrdom (*amaliyyat istishhadiyya*) simply cannot be matched by Israeli culture. The particular Palestinian cultural understanding and approach is best discussed in NASSER ABUFARHA, THE MAKING OF A HUMAN BOMB: AN ETHNOGRAPHY OF PALESTINIAN RESISTANCE (2009).

SELECTED BIBLIOGRAPHY

A bibliography on international law could easily fill a library. Indeed, there are libraries completely devoted to the subject as well as subtopics. Hence, what is offered here is, as the term employed, a selected guide for further reading that is a sample of materials geared to, first, the subjects covered in this reader and, second, items that can be employed for pedagogical support.

There was no attempt to post sources used by the contributors but rather to supplement in a most general manner the subject matter covered, particularly traditional subjects as well as developing themes in international law.

GENERAL REFERENCE WORKS

Legal Portals

American Society of International Law (ASIL). *ASIL Guide to Electronic Resources for International Law.* www.asil.org/ergintr1.cfm.

ASIL. *Foreign, Comparative and International Law Special Interest Section, FCIL Newsletter.* www.aalnet .org/sis/fcilsis/newsletter.html.

ASIL. *The International Legal Research Interest Group (ILRIG).* www.asil.org/interest-groups-view.cfm ?groupid=62.

Citizen Law Media Law Project. *Legal Threats Database.* www.citmedialaw.org/database.

Electronic Information Systems for International Law (EISIL). *Treaty Index.* www.eisl.org/index .php?cat=705&t=sub_pages

Engsberg, Mark. "An Introduction to Sources for Treaty Research." NYU Law. www.nyulawglobal.org/ globalex/Treaty-Research.htm.

Feliú, Vincenç. "Introduction to Public International Law." NYU Law. www.nyulawglobal.org/globalex/ Public_International_Law_Research.htm.

Foreign and International Law on DVD and on the Web. http://lib.typepad.com/dangelo/2010/08/ foreign-and-international-law-on-dvd-and-on-the-web.html.

Foreign Law Guide. http://foreignlawguide.com/.

Global Legal Info-Network (GLIN). www.glin.gov/search.action.

Greenleaf, Graham. "The Global Development of Free Access to Legal Information." *European Journal of Law and Technology* 1, no. 1 (2010): http://ejlt.org//article/view/Article/17/39.

Hauser Global Law School Program. *GlobaLex.* www.nyulawglobal.org/globalex/about.htm.

ICC. *Basic Legal Texts* (Legal tools database). www.icc-cpi.int/Menus/ICC/Legal+Texts+and+Tools/.

International Center for Transitional Justice. www.ictj.org/static/Publications.

International Committee of the Red Cross, Customary International Humanitarian Law. www.icrc .org/customary-ihl/eng/docs/home.

Justis. *The International Law Reports on the Internet.* http://www.justis.com/ilr.

KULeuven. *Guide to Western European Legal Abbreviations and Other Online Legal Abbreviation Legal Databases.* www.law.kuleuven.be/rechtsaf/.

Law Library Resource Xchange. www.llrx.com/.

Library of Congress. *Global Legal Information Catalog (GLIC).* www.loc.gov/lawweb/servlet/Glic?home.

Library of Congress. *Guide to Law Online.* www.loc.gov/law/help/guide.html.

Lyonette, Louis-Jacques. "The State of Digitization of United Nations Documents." Slaw.ca, June 29, 2010. www.slaw.ca/2010/06/29/the-state-of-digitation-of-united-nations-documents.

Max Planck Encyclopedia of Public International Law. www.mpepil.com/.

News Bank Colleges. *AccessUN*. www.newsbankcolleges.com/colleges/prodiuct.cfm?product=91.

Oxford University Press. *Constitutions of the Countries of the World Online*. www.oup.com/online/oceanalaw/ccwo/.

Oxford University Press. *Oxford Reports on International Law*. http://ildc.oxfordlawreports.com.

Rumsey, Mary. "Frequently-Cited Treaties and Other International Instruments." University of Minnesota Law School. http://library.law.umn.edu/researchguides/most-cited.html.

Sabinet. *African Journal Archive*. www.sabinet.co.za/?page=african-journal-archive.

Terrorism. http://www.history.navy.mil/library/guides/terrorism.htm.

United Nations. *Documentation* (UN documents in PDF format from 1993 to date, from the NY and Geneva offices; the Vienna office from 1997 to date; all resolutions from 1946 to date). http://untreaty.un.org/ilc/documentation/documentation.htm.

United Nations. *Official Documents of the United Nations*. http://documents.un.org/.

United Nations. *UNBisNet*. (UN documents online can be found using the UN library catalog with a direct link to PDF formats).

United Nations. *United Nations Audiovisual Library of International Law*. www.un.org/law/avl/.

United Nations. *United Nations Data, Internet Resources*. http://data.un.org.

United Nations. *United Nations Resolutions' Voting Records*. http://unbisnet.un.org:8080/ipac.jsp?profile=voting&menu=searchpower#focus.

United Nations. *United Nations Treaty Collection*. http://untreaty.un.org/English/treaty.asp.

United Nations. (UN International Law Commission's documents in PDF format from 1949 to date). http://unbisnet.un.org.

University of Chicago. *Legal Research on International Law Issues Using the Internet*. www2.lib.uchicago.edu/~llou/forintlaw.

WashLaw Web. *Legal Research on the Web*. http://www.washlaw.edu/.

Weigmann, Stephanie. Features—Researching Non-U.S. Treaties and Agreements. www.llrx.com/features/non-ustreaty.htm; www.llrx.com/features/non_ustreaties.htm.

World Legal Information Institute. www.worldlii.org

Books

Armstrong, J. D., and Jutta Brunée, eds. *Routledge Handbook of International Law*. New York: Routledge, 2009.

Aust, Anthony. *Handbook of International Law*. New York: Cambridge University Press, 2005.

Boczek, Boleslaw Adam. *International Law: A Dictionary*. Lanham, MD: Scarecrow Press, 2005.

Grant, John P., and J. Craig Barker, eds. *Parry & Grant Encyclopædic Dictionary of International Law*. 3rd ed. New York: Oxford University Press, 2009.

Hoffman, Marci, and Mary Rumsey. *International and Foreign Legal Research: A Coursebook*. Leiden and Boston: Martinus Nijhoff, 2007.

Langford, Malcolm, ed. *Social Rights Jurisprudence: Emerging Trends in International and Comparative Law*. New York: Cambridge University Press, 2009.

Articles

Bernal, Marie-Louise H. "Reference Sources in International Law." *Law Library Journal* 76, no. 3 (Summer 1983): 427–35.

O'Connor, Linda Karr. "International and Foreign Legal Research: Tips, Tricks and Sources." *Cornell International Law Journal* 28, no. 2 (1995): 417–51.

Williams, John W. "Research Tips in International Law." *The Journal of International Law and Economics* 15, no. 1 (1981): 1–321.

NORMS

Books

Buchanan, Allen E. *Justice, Legitimacy, and Self-Determination: Moral Foundations for International Law*. New York: Oxford University Press, 2004.

Charlesworth, Hilary, and Jean-Marc Coicaud, eds. *Fault Lines of International Legitimacy*. New York: Cambridge University Press, 2009.

Christie, George C. *Law, Norms and Authority*. London: Duckworth, 1982.

de Casadevante y Romani, Carlos Fernández. *Sovereignty and Interpretation of International Norms*. Berlin: Springer Verlag, 2007.

Drobak, John N., ed. *Norms and the Law*. New York: Cambridge University Press, 2006.

Franck, Thomas. *The Power of Legitimacy Among Nations*. New York: Oxford University Press, 1990.

Joyner, Christopher C. *International Law in the 21st Century: Rules for Global Governance*. Lanham, MD: Rowman & Littlefield, 2005.

Kelsen, Hans. *General Theory of Norms*. New York: Clarendon Press, 1991.

Nasser, Salem Hikmat. *Sources and Norms of International Law: A Study on Soft Law*. Berlin: Galda + Wilch Verlag, 2008.

Proukaki, Elena Katselli. *The Problem of Enforcement in International Law: Countermeasures, the Non-Injured State and the Idea of International Community*. New York: Routledge, 2010.

Shelton, Dinah. *Commitment and Compliance: The Role of Non-Binding Norms in the International Legal System*. New York: Oxford University Press, 2000.

Standholtz, Wayne, and Kendall W. Stiles. *International Norms and Cycles of Change*. New York: Oxford University Press, 2008.

Articles

Allen, Michael H. "Globalization and Peremptory Norms in International Law: From Westphalian to Global Constitutionalism?" *International Politics* 41, no. 3 (September 2004): 341–53.

Deli, Armanda. "International Norms and *lex mercatoria*: A Perspective on Consumer Protection in Information Technology." *The Indian Journal of International Law* 41, no. 2 (April–June 2001): 257–74.

Finnemore, Martha. "Are Legal Norms Distinctive?" *New York University Journal of International Law & Politics* 32, no. 3 (Spring 2000): 699–705.

Keenan, Patrick J. "Do Norms Matter? The Corrosive Effects of Globalization on the Vitality of Norms." *Vanderbilt Journal of Transnational Law* 41, no. 2 (March 2008): 327–79.

McAdams, Richard H. "The Origin, Development, and Regulation of Norms." *Michigan Law Review* 96, no. 2 (November 1997): 338–433.

Navarro, Pablo E. "Applicability of Legal Norms." *The Canadian Journal of Law and Jurisprudence* 17, no. 2 (July 2004): 337–59.

Orchard, Phil. "Protection of Internally Displaced Persons: Soft Law as a Norm-Generating Mechanism." *Review of International Affairs* 36, no. 2 (April 2010): 281–304.

Steele, David B. "Embedding UN Norms." *International Journal of Human Rights* 3, no. 3 (Autumn 1999): 62–96.

Tahvanainen, Annika. "Hierarchy of Norms in International and Human Rights Law." *Nordisk tidsskrift for menneskerettigheter* 24, no. 3 (2006): 191–205.

Tarzi, Shah M. "The Role of Norms and Regimes in World Affairs." *International Relations* 14, no. 3 (September 1998): 71–84.

RESPONSIBILITY TO PROTECT (R2P)

Internet Portal

UNRIC Library. "Information on 'Responsibility to Protect' ('RtoP' or 'R2P')." www.unric.org/html/english/library/backgrounders/R2P_eng.pdf.

Books

Cooper, Richard H., and Juliette Voïnov Kohler, eds. *Responsibility to Protect: The Global Moral Compact for the 21st Century*. New York: Palgrave Macmillan, 2008.

Evans, Gareth J. *The Responsibility to Protect: Ending Mass Atrocity Crimes Once and for All*. Washington DC: Brookings Institution Press, 2008.

Pattison, James. *Humanitarian Intervention and the Responsibility to Protect: Who Should Intervene?* New York: Oxford University Press, 2010.

Strauss, Ekkehard. *The Emperor's New Clothes? The United Nations and the Implementation of the Responsibility to Protect.* Portland, OR: Nomos Publishers, 2009.

Thakur, Ramesh Chandra. *The United Nations, Peace and Security: From Collective Security to the Responsibility to Protect.* New York: Cambridge University Press, 2006.

Waxman, Matthew C. *Intervention to Stop Genocide and Mass Atrocities: International Norms and U.S. Policy.* Washington, DC: Council on Foreign Relations, 2009.

Weiss, Thomas G. *Military-Civilian Relations: Humanitarian Crisis and the Responsibility to Protect.* 2nd ed. Lanham, MD: Rowman & Littlefield, 2005.

Essays

Brunnée, Jutta. "International Law and Collective Concerns: Reflections on the Responsibility to Protect." In *Law of the Sea, Environmental Law, and Settlement of Disputes:* Liber Amicorum *Judge Thomas A. Mensah,* ed. Tafsir Malick Ndiaye and Rüdiger Wolfrum, 35–51. Leiden: Martinus Nijhoff, 2007.

Articles

Barbour, Brian M., and Brian Gorlick. "Embracing the 'Responsibility to Protect': A Repertoire of Measures Including Asylum for Potential Victims." *International Journal of Refugee Law* 20, no. 4 (December 2008): 533–66.

Bellamy, Alex J. "Whither the Responsibility to Protect? Humanitarian Intervention and the 2005 World Summit." *Ethics and International Affairs* 20, no. 2 (Summer 2006): 143–69.

Breau, Susan C. "The Impact of the Responsibility to Protect on Peacekeeping." *Journal of Conflict and Security Law* 11, no. 3 (Winter 2006): 429–64.

Dorr, Noel. "The Responsibility to Protect—an Emerging Norm?" *Irish Studies in International Affairs* 19 (2008): 189–207.

Evans, Gareth. "From Humanitarian Intervention to Responsibility to Protect." *Wisconsin International Law Journal* 24, no. 3 (Fall 2006): 703–22.

Focarelli, Carlo. "The Responsibility to Protect Doctrine and Humanitarian Intervention: Too Many Ambiguities for a Working Doctrine." *Journal of Conflict and Security Law* 13, no. 2 (Summer 2008): 191–213.

Hamilton, Rebecca J. "The Responsibility to Protect: From Document to Doctrine—But What of Implementation?" *Harvard Human Rights Journal* 19 (Spring 2006): 289–97.

Koivurova, Timo. "International Legal Avenues to Address the Flight of Victims of Climate Change Problems and Prospects." *Journal of Environmental Law and Litigation* 22 (2007): 267–99.

Levitt, Jeremy I. "The Responsibility to Protect: A Beaver Without a Dam?" *Michigan Journal of International Law* 25, no. 1 (Fall 2003): 153–77.

Magnuson, William. "The Responsibility to Protect and the Decline of Sovereignty: Free Speech Protection under International Law." *Vanderbilt Journal of Transnational Law* 43, no. 2 (March 2010): 255–312.

McClean, Emma. "The Responsibility to Protect: The Role of International Human Rights Law." *Journal of Conflict and Security Law* 13, no. 1 (Spring 2008): 123–52.

Orford, Anne. "Jurisdiction Without Territory: From the Holy Roman Empire to the Responsibility to Protect." *Michigan Journal of International Law* 30, no. 3 (Spring 2009): 981–1015.

Stahn, Carsten. "Responsibility to Protect: Political Rhetoric or Emerging Legal Norm?" *American Journal of International Law* 101, no. 1 (January 2007): 99–120.

UNIVERSAL JURISDICTION

Books

Kaleck, Wolfgang et al., eds. *International Prosecution of Human Rights Crimes.* New York: Springer, 2006.

King-Irani, Laurie. *Universal Jurisdiction for Humanitarian Crimes.* London: Glass House, 2006.

Macedo, Stephen, ed. *Universal Jurisdiction: National Courts and the Prosecution of Serious Crimes Under International Law.* Philadelphia: University of Pennsylvania Press, 2004.

Reydams, Luc. *Universal Jurisdiction: International and Municipal Legal Perspectives.* New York: Oxford University Press, 2004.

Articles

Abass, Ademola. "The International Criminal Court and Universal Jurisdiction." *International Criminal Law Review* 6, no. 3 (2006): 349–85.

Abi-Saab, Georges. "The Proper Role of Universal Jurisdiction." *Journal of International Criminal Justice* 1, no. 3 (2003): 596–602.

Bassiouni, M. Cherif. "Universal Jurisdiction for International Crimes: Historical Perspectives and Contemporary Practice." *Virginia Journal of International Law* 42, no. 1 (Fall 2001): 81–162.

Becker, Steven W. "Universal Jurisdiction: How Universal Is It?" *The Palestine Yearbook of International Law* 12 (2002/2003): 49–75.

Bekou, Olympia, and Robert Cryer. "The International Criminal Court and Universal Jurisdiction: A Close Encounter?" *International and Comparative Law Quarterly* 56, no. 1 (January 2007): 49–68.

Benavides, Luis. "The Universal Jurisdiction Principle: Nature and Scope." *Annuario Mexicano de Derecho Internacional* 1 (2001): 19–96.

Boyd, Kathyrn Lee. "Universal Jurisdiction and Structural Reasonableness." *Texas International Law Journal* 40, no. 1 (Summer 2004): 1–58.

Brown, Bertram S. "The Evolving Concept of Universal Jurisdiction." *New England Law Review* 35, no. 2 (Winter 2000/2001): 383–97.

Broomhall, Bruce. "Towards the Development of an Effective System of Universal Jurisdiction for Crimes under International Law." *New England Law Review* 35, no. 2 (Winter 2000/2001): 399–420.

Colangelo, Anthony J. "The New Universal Jurisdiction: in absentia: Signaling Over Clearly Defined Crimes." *Georgetown Journal of International Law* 36, no. 2 (Winter 2005): 537–603.

Kissinger, Henry A. "The Pitfalls of Universal Jurisdiction." *Foreign Affairs* 80, no. 4 (July–August 2001): 86–96.

Ongena, Tom, and Ignace van Daele. "Universal Jurisdiction for International Core Crimes." *Leiden Journal of International Law* 15, no. 3 (September 2002): 687–701.

Roth, Kenneth. "The Case for Universal Jurisdiction." *Foreign Affairs* 80, no. 5 (September–October 2001): 150–64.

Sriram, Chandra Lekha. "Exercising Universal Jurisdiction." *International Journal of Human Rights* 6, no. 4 (Winter 2002): 49–76.

NONTERRITORIALISM

Internet Portal

World Bank. *Uncivil Societies—A Theory of Sociopolitical Change.* http://econ.worldbank.org/external/default/main?pagePK=64165259&theSitePK=469372&piK=64165421&menuPK=64166093&entityID=000158349_20090519151120.

Books

Andreopoulos, George J., ed. *Non-State Actors in the Human Rights Universe.* Bloomfield, CT: Kumarian Press, 2006.

Bianchi, Andrea. *Non-State Actors and International Law.* Burlington, VT: Ashgate, 2009.

Dupuy, Pierre-Marie, and Lusia Vierucci, eds. *NGOs in International Law: Efficiency in Flexibility?* Northamton, MA: Edwin Elgar, 2008.

Higgott, Richard A. *Non-State Actors and Authority in the Global System.* New York: Routledge, 2000.

Hofmann, Rainer, ed. *Non-State Actors as New Subjects of International Law: International Law—From the Traditional State Order Towards the Law of the Global Community: Proceedings of an International Symposium of the Kiel Walther-Schücking-Institute of International Law, March 25–28, 1998.* Berlin: Duncker & Humblot, 1999.

Lubell, Noam. *Extraterritorial Use of Force Against Non-State Actors.* New York: Oxford University Press, 2010.

Articles

Carpenter, Chad. "Business, Green Groups and the Media: The Role of Non-Governmental Organizations in the Climate Change Debate." *International Affairs* 77, no. 2 (April 2001): 313–28.

Cawley, Jared B. "Friend of the Court: How the WTO Justifies the Acceptance of the Amicus Curiae Brief from Non-Governmental Organizations." *Penn State International Law Review* 23, no. 3 (Summer 2004): 47–78.

Dieng, Adama. "The Value of Customary International Law in the Light of the Recent Emergence of Non-State Actors as Subjects of International Law." *African Yearbook on International Humanitarian Law* (2007): 166–71.

George, Barbara Crutchfield. "A Coalition of Industrial Nations, Developing Nations, Multilateral Development Banks, and Non-Governmental Organizations." *Cornell International Law Journal* 33, no. 3 (2000): 547–92.

Hartwick, Jeffrey Andrew. "Non-Governmental Organizations at United Nations Sponsored World Conferences." *Loyola of Los Angeles International and Comparative Law Review* 26, no. 2 (Spring 2003): 217–80.

Kammerhofer, Jörg. "The Armed Activities Case and Non-State Actors in Self-Defence Law." *Leiden Journal of International Law* 20, no. 1 (March 2007): 89–113.

Marshall, Jill. "Torture Committed by Non-State Actors." *Non-State Actors and International Law* 5, no. 3 (2005): 171–82.

Oliounine, Iouri. "Response of Governmental and Non-Governmental Organizations to Marine Natural Disasters." *Ocean Yearbook* 20 (2006): 7–19.

Pariotti, Elena. "International Soft Law, Human Rights and Non-State Actors: Towards the Accountability of Transnational Corporations?" *Human Rights Review* 10, no. 2 (June 2009): 139–55.

Pearson, Zoe. "Non-Governmental Organizations and the International Criminal Court: Changing Landscapes of International Law." *Cornell International Law Journal* 39, no. 2 (2006): 243–84.

PoKempner, Dinah. "The 'New' Non-State Actors in International Humanitarian Law." *The George Washington International Law Review* 38, no. 3 (2006): 551–60.

Quiroz, Diego. "Expanding International Law to Non-State Actors." *South African Yearbook of International Law* 32 (2007): 66–84.

Simon, Karla W. "International Non-Governmental Organizations." *International Lawyer* 41, no. 2 (Summer 2007): 525–39.

Srivastava, Jayati. "Non-Governmental Organizations as Negotiators at the World Trade Organization." *International Studies* 39, no. 3 (July/September 2002): 245–57.

Ssenyonjo, Manisuli. "The Applicability of International Human Rights Law to Non-State Actors: What Relevance to Economic, Social and Cultural Rights?" *International Journal of Human Rights* 12, no. 5 (October 2008): 725–60.

ECONOMIC INSTRUMENTS

Legal Portals

Global Trade Alert. www.globaltradealert.org/.

International Chamber of Commerce (ICC). *International Court of Commercial Arbitration*. http://iccwbo.org/court/arbitration/id4096/index.html.

NYU Law. *A Guide on the Harmonization of International Commercial Law*. /www.nyulawglobal.org/globalex/Unification_Harmonization1.htm.

Regional Trade Agreements Information System. http://rtais.wto.org/UI/PublicMaintainRTAHome.aspx.

Trans-LEX.org. *Transnational Commercial Law*. www.trans-lex.org.

Reference

Bhan, Meenakshi. "Select Bibliography on International Economic & Trade Law, Arbitration, and the Law of the Sea." *Indian Journal of International Law* 47, no. 2 (2007): 340–53.

Browndorf, Eric, and Scott Riemer. *Bibliography of Multinational Corporations and Foreign Direct Investment*. Dobbs Ferry, NY: Oceana Publications, 1980.

Books

Ala'l, Padideh, Tomer Broude, and Colin Picker, eds. *Trade as the Guarantor of Peace, Liberty and Security? Critical, Historical and Empirical Perspectives*. Washington, DC: ASIL Press, 2006.

Anghie, Antony, ed. *The Third World and International Order: Law, Politics, and Globalization.* Leiden: Martinus Nijhoff Publishers, 2003.

Basedow, Jürgen, ed. *Legal Aspects of Globalization: Conflict of Laws, Internet, Capital Markets an Insolvency in a Global Economy.* The Hague: Kluwer Law International, 2000.

Bederman, David J. *Globalization and International Law.* New York: Palgrave, 2008.

Berman, Paul Schiff, ed. *The Globalization of International Law.* Burlington, VT: Ashgate, 2005.

Bernasconi-Osterwalder, Nathalie et al. *Environment and Trade: A Guide to WTO Jurisprudence.* Sterling, VA: Earthscan Publications, Ltd., 2006.

Beveridge, Fiona, ed. *Globalization and International Investment.* Burlington, VT: Ashgate, 2005.

Broude, Tomer, Amy Porges, and Marc L. Busch, eds. *The Politics of International Economic Law.* New York: Cambridge University Press, 2010.

de Sousa Santos, Boaventura, ed. *Law and Globalization from Below: Towards a Cosmopolitan Legality.* New York: Cambridge University Press, 2005.

Griller, Stefan, ed. *International Economic Governance and Non-Economic Concerns: New Challenges for the International Legal Order.* New York: SpringerWien, 2003.

Grote, Rainer, and Thilo Marauhn, eds. *The Regulation of International Financial Markets: Perspectives and Reform.* New York: Cambridge University Press, 2006.

Jackson, John H. et al. *New Directions in International Economic Law: Essays in Honour of John H. Jackson.* The Hague: Kluwer Law International, 2000.

Kehl, Jenny Rebecca. *Foreign Investment and Domestic Development: Multinationals and the State.* Boulder, CO: Lynne Rienner Publishers, 2009.

Kiss, Alexandre C., ed. *Economic Globalization and Compliance with International Environmental Agreements.* The Hague: Kluwer Law International, 2003.

Kohona, Palitha Tikiri Bandara. *The Regulation of International Economic Relations Through Law.* Boston: Martinus Nijhoff, 1985.

Lee, Yong-Shik. *Reclaiming Development in the World Trading System.* New York: Cambridge University Press, 2006.

Picker, Colin B., Isabela D. Bunn, and Douglas W. Arner, eds. *International Economic Law: The State and Future of the Discipline.* Oxford: Hart Publishing, 2008.

Qureshi, Asif H., and Andreas R. Ziegler. *International Economic Law.* 2nd ed. London: Sweet & Maxwell, 2007.

Schneiderman, David. *Constitutionalizing Economic Globalization: Investment Rules and Democracy's Promise.* New York: Cambridge University Press, 2008.

Seid, Sherif H. *Global Regulation of Foreign Direct Investment.* Burlington, VT: Ashgate Dartmouth, 2002.

Shan, Wenhua, Penelope Simons, and Dalvinder Singh, eds. *Redefining Sovereignty in International Economic Law.* Oxford: Hart, 2008.

Shihata, Ibrahim Fahmi Ibrahim. *Legal Treatment of Foreign Investment: "The World Bank Guidelines."* Dordrecht: Martinus Nijhoff Publishers, 1993.

Sumner, Andrew et al., eds. *Transnational Corporations and Development Policy.* New York: Palgrave Macmillan, 2008.

Tarullo, Daniel K. *Banking on Basel: The Future of International Financial Regulations.* Washington, DC: Peterson Institute for International Economics, 2008.

Trachtman, Joel P. *The Economic Structure of International Law.* Cambridge, MA: Harvard University Press, 2008.

Trubek, David M., and Alvaro Santos. *The New Law and Economic Development: A Critical Appraisal.* New York: Cambridge University Press, 2006.

Yueh, Linda, ed. *The Law and Economics of Globalisation: New Challenges for a World in Flux.* Northhamton, MA: Edward Elgar, 2010.

Articles

Barr, Michael S., and Reuven S. Avi-Yonah. "Globalization, Law & Development: Introduction and Overview." *Michigan Journal of International Law* 26, no. 1 (Fall 2004): 1–12.

Baudenbacher, Carl. "Judicial Globalization: New Development or Old Wine in New Bottles?" *Texas International Law Journal* 38, no. 3 (Spring 2003): 505–26.

Dupuy, Pierre-Marie. "International Law: Torn Between Coexistence, Cooperation and Globalization: General Conclusions." *European Journal of International Law* 9, no. 2 (1998): 278–86.

Franck, Susan D. "Foreign Direct Investment, Investment Treaty Arbitration, and the Rule of Law." *Pacific McGeorge Global Business & Development Law Journal* 19, no. 2 (2007): 337–73.

Garcia, Frank J. "Globalization and the Theory of International Law." *International Legal Theory* 11 (Fall 2005): 9–26.

Hunter, Richard J. et al. "Legal Considerations in Foreign Direct Investment." *Oklahoma City University Law Review* 28, nos. 2/3 (Summer/Fall 2003): 851–74.

Lee, Yong-Shik. "Foreign Direct Investment and Regional Trade Liberalization: A Viable Answer for Economic Development." *Journal of World Trade* 39, no. 4 (August 2005): 701–17.

Lewis, Douglas. "Law and Globalization: An Opportunity for Europe and Its Partners and the Legal Scholars." *European Public Law* 8, no. 2 (June 2002): 219–39.

Masser, Adam L. "The Nexus of Public and Private in Foreign Direct Investment: An Analysis of IFC, MIGA, and OPIC." *Fordham International Law Journal* 32, no. 5 (May 2009): 1698–1743.

Paulus, Andreas L. "Law and Politics in the Age of Globalization." *European Journal of International Law* 11, no. 2 (2000): 465–72.

Reitz, Curtis R. "Globalization, International Legal Developments, and Uniform State Laws." *Loyola Law Review* 51, no. 2 (Summer 2005): 301–27.

Roberts, Anthea. "Power and Persuasion in Investment Treaty Interpretation: The Dual Role of States." *American Journal of International Law* 104, no. 2 (April 2010): 179–225.

Salacuse, Jeswald W. "Direct Foreign Investment and the Law in Developing Countries." *ICSID Review* 15, no. 1 (Spring 2000): 382–400.

Spiro, Peter J. "Globalization, International Law, and the Academy." *New York University Journal of International Law & Politics* 32, no. 2 (Winter 2000): 567–90.

Williams, David. "Courts and Globalization." *Indiana Journal of Global Legal Studies* 11, no. 1 (Winter 2004): 57–69.

INTERNATIONAL COURTS AND TRIBUNALS

Books

Baudenbacher, Carl, and Erhard Busek, eds. *The Role of International Courts*. Frankfurt-am-Main: German Law Publications, 2008.

Goldstone, Richard J., and Adam M. Smith. *International Judicial Institutions: The Architecture of International Justice at Home and Abroad*. New York: Routledge, 2009.

REGIONAL COURTS

African Court of Justice

Articles

Kidiki, Kithure. "The Proposed Integration of the African Court of Justice and the African Court of Human and Peoples' Rights." *African Journal of International and Comparative Law* 15, no. 1 (2007): 138–46.

African Court of Justice of the African Union

Books

Du Plessis, Max, ed. *African Guide to International Criminal Justice*. Tswane, SA: Institute for Security Studies, 2008.

Articles

Magliveras, Konstantinos D. "The African Court of Justice." *Zeitschrift für ausländisches öffentliches Recht und Völkerrecht* 66, no. 1 (2006): 187–213.

African Court on Human Rights

Articles

Bekker, Gina. "The African Court on Human and Peoples' Rights: Safeguarding the Interests of African States." *Journal of African Law* 51, no. 1 (April 2007): 151–72.

Ebobrah, Solomon T. "Litigating Human Rights Before Sub-Regional Courts in Africa: Prospects and Challenges." *African Journal of International and Comparative Law* 17, no. 1 (March 2009): 79–101.

Eno, Robert Wundeh. "The Jurisdiction of the African Court on Human and Peoples' Rights." *African Human Rights Law Journal* 2, no. 2 (2002): 223–33.

Krisch, Nico. "The Establishment of an African Court on Human and Peoples' Rights." *Zeitschrift für ausländisches öffentliches Recht und Völkerrecht* 58, no. 3 (September 1998): 713–32.

Nmehielle, Vincent Obisienunwo Orlu. "Towards an African Court of Human Rights: Structuring and the Court." *Annual Survey of International & Comparative Law* 6, no. 1 (Spring 2000): 27–60.

van der Mei, Anne Pieter. "The Advisory Jurisdiction of the African Court on Human and Peoples' Rights." *African Human Rights Law Journal* 5, no. 1 (2005): 27–46.

Viljoen, Frans, and Evarist Baimu. "Courts for Africa: Considering the Co-existence of the African Court on Human and Peoples' Rights and the African Court of Justice." *Netherlands Quarterly of Human Rights* 22, no. 2 (2004): 242–67.

Caribbean Court of Human Rights
Articles

Bascombe, Dominic. "The Introduction of the Caribbean Court of Justice and the Likely Impact on Human Rights Standards in the Caribbean Commonwealth." *Commonwealth Law Bulletin* 31, no. 2 (2005): 117–25.

Caribbean Court of Justice
Books

Pollard, Duke E. *The Caribbean Court of Justice: Closing the Circle of Independence.* Kingston, Jamaica: The Caribbean Law Publishers, 2004.

Articles

Birdsong, Leonard E. "The Formation of the Caribbean Court of Justice: The Sunset of British Colonial Rule in the English Speaking Caribbean." *The University of Miami Inter-American Law Review* 36, nos. 2/3 (Winter/Spring 2005): 197–227.

Hamilton, Rhea P. "A Guide to Researching the Caribbean Court of Justice." *Brooklyn Journal of International Law* 27, no. 2 (2002): 531–42.

McDonald, Sheldon A. "The Caribbean Court of Justice: Enhancing the Law of International Organizations." *Fordham International Law Journal* 27, no. 3 (February 2004): 930–1016.

Nicholson, A. J. "The Caribbean Court of Justice: A Developmental Tool." *West Indian Law Journal* 28, no. 2 (October 2003): 1–15.

Simmons, David. "The Caribbean Court of Justice." *Commonwealth Law Bulletin* 31, no. 1 (2005): 71–90.

East African Court of Justice
Articles

Ojienda, Tom O. "'Alice's Adventures in Wonderland': Preliminary Reflections on the Jurisdiction of the East African Court of Justice." *The East African Journal of Human Rights and Democracy* 2, no. 2 (June 2004): 94–103.

———. "The East African Court of Justice in the Reestablished East African Community: Institutional Structure and Function in the Integration Process." *East African Journal of Peace & Human Rights* 11, no. 2 (2005): 220–40.

Economic Community of West Africa States (ECOWAS) Community Court of Justice
Articles

Allain, Jean. "Hadijatou Mani Koraou v. Republic of Niger, Judgment No. ECW/CCJ/JUD/06/08." *American Journal of International Law* 103, no. 2 (April 2009): 311–17.

Ebobrah, Solomon T. "A Rights-Protection Goldmine or a Waiting Volcanic Eruption? Competence of, and Access to, the Human Rights Jurisdiction of the ECOWAS Community Court of Justice." *African Human Rights Journal* 7, no. 2 (2007): 307–29.

van der Mei, Anne Piegter. "Regional Integration: The Contribution of the Court of Justice of the East African Community." *Zeitschrift für öffentliches Recht und Völkerrecht* 69, no. 2 (2009): 403–25.

European Court of Human Rights
Books

Anagnostou, Dia, and Evangelia Psychogiopoulou, eds. *The European Court of Human Rights and the Rights of Marginalised Individuals and Minorities in National Context*. Leiden and Boston: Martinus Nijhoff Publishers, 2009.

Arold, Nina-Louisa. *The Legal Culture of the European Court of Human Rights*. Leiden: Martinus Nijhoff Publishers, 2007.

Bates, Ed. *The Evolution of the European Convention on Human Rights: From Its Inception to the Creation of a Permanent Court of Human Rights*. New York: Oxford University Press, 2010.

Goldhaber, Michael D. *A People's History of the European Court of Human Rights*. New Brunswick, NJ: Rutgers University Press, 2007.

Reid, Karen. *A Practitioner's Guide to the European Convention on Human Rights*. 3rd ed. London: Sweet & Maxwell, 2008.

Šikuta, Ján, and Eva Hubálková. *European Court of Human Rights: Case-Law of the Grand Chamber 1998–2006*. The Hague: Asser Press, 2007.

Tochilovsky, Vladimir. *Jurisprudence of the International Criminal Courts and the European Court of Human Rights*. Leiden: Martinus Nijhoff Publishers, 2008.

Wildhaber, Luzius. *The European Court of Human Rights*. Kehl, Germany: N. P. Engel, 2006.

Articles

Evans, Carolyn. "The 'Islamic Scarf' in the European Court of Human Rights." *Melbourne Journal of International Law* 7, no. 1 (May 2006): 52–73.

Lambert-Abdeigawad, Elisabeth. "The Execution of the Judgments of the European Court of Human Rights: Towards a Non-Coercive and Participatory Model of Accountability." *Zeitschrift für öffentliches Recht* 69, no. 3 (September 2009): 471–506.

Lebeck, Carl. "The European Court of Human Rights on the Relation Between ECHR and EC-Law: The Limits of Constitutionalisation of Public International Law." *Zeitschrift für öffentliches Recht* 62, no. 2 (June 2007): 195–236.

Marmo, Marinella. "The Execution of Judgments of the European Court of Human Rights: A Political Battle." *Maastricht Journal of European and Comparative Law* 15, no. 2 (2008): 235–58.

McKaskie, Paul L. "The European Court of Human Rights: What Is It, How It Works, and Its Future." *University of San Francisco Law Review* 40, no. 1 (Summer 2005): 1–84.

Orakhelashvili, Alexander. "State Immunity in National and International Law: Three Recent Cases Before the European Court of Human Rights." *Leiden Journal of International Law* 15, no. 3 (September 2002): 703–14.

Pierini, Jean Paul. "The Jurisprudence of the European Court of Human Rights in Respect of Conduct of a Foreign State or an International Organization in the Territory of a Contracting State and the Extraterritorial Effect of Foreign Acts." *Revue de droit militaire et de droit de le guerre* 45, nos. 3/4 (2006): 389–435.

European Court of Justice
Books

Arnull, Anthony. *The European Union and Its Court of Justice*. New York: Oxford University Press, 1999.

Bengoetxea, Joxerramon. *The Justification of Decisions by the European Court of Justice*. Saarbrücken: Europa-Institut, 1989.

Brown, Lionel Neville, and Tom Kennedy. *The Court of Justice of the European Communities*. London: Sweet & Maxwell, 2000.

Dashwood, Alan, and Marc Maresceau, eds. *Law and Practice of EU External Relations: Salient Features of a Changing Landscape*. New York: Cambridge University Press, 2008.

De Búrca, Gráinne, ed. *The European Court of Justice*. New York: Oxford University Press, 2001.

Dehousse, Renaud. *The European Court of Justice: The Politics of Judicial Integration*. Basingstoke: Macmillan, 1998.

Dougan, Michael. *National Remedies Before the Court of Justice*. Oxford: Hart, 2004.

Guild, Elspeth, and Guillaume Lesieur, eds. *The European Court of Justice on the European Convention on Human Rights: Who Said What, When?* London: Kluwer Law International, 1998.

Parga, Alicia Hinarejos. *Judicial Control in the European Union: Reforming Jurisdiction in the Intergovernmental Pillars.* New York: Oxford University Press, 2010.

Talmon, Stefan. *The Jurisprudence of the European Court of Justice in Matters of International Law.* Oxford: Hart, 2010.

Tridimas, Takis. *The European Court of Justice and the EU Constitutional Order: Essays in Judicial Protection.* Oxford: Hart, 2009.

Volcansek, Mary L. *Courts Crossing Borders: Blurring the Lines of Sovereignty.* Durham, NC: Carolina Academic Press, 2005.

Articles

Allain, Jean. "The European Court of Justice Is an International Court." *Nordic Journal of International Law* 68, no. 3 (1999): 249–74.

Becker, Sebastian. "European Court of Justice Secures Fundamental Rights from UN Security Council Resolutions." *Göttingen Journal of International Law* 1, no. 1 (2009): 159–78.

Boelaert-Suominen, Sonja. "The European Community, the European Court of Justice and the Law of the Sea." *International Journal of Marine and Coastal Law* 23, no. 4 (2008): 643–714.

Crossen, Teall, and Veronique Niessen. "NGO Standing in the European Court of Justice: Does the Aahus Regulation Open the Door?" *Review of European Community & International Environmental Law* 16, no. 3 (November 2007): 332–40.

Defeis, Elizabeth F. "Human Rights and the European Union: Who Decides? Possible Conflicts Between the European Court of Justice and the European Court of Human Rights." *Dickinson Journal of International Law* 19, no. 2 (Winter 2001): 301–31.

Fennelly, Nial. "Legal Interpretation at the European Court of Justice." *Fordham International Law Journal* 20, no. 3 (February 1997): 656–79.

Harby, Catharina. "The Changing Nature of Interim Measures Before the European Court of Human Rights." *European Human Rights Law Review* no. 1 (2010): 73–84.

Harpaz, Guy. "The European Court of Justice and Its Relations with the European Court of Human Rights." *Common Market Law Review* 46, no. 1 (February 2009): 105–41.

Henkel, Christoph. "Constitutionalism of the European Union: Judicial Legislation and Political Decision-Making by the European Court of Justice." *Wisconsin International Law Journal* 19, no. 2 (2001): 153–80.

Jacobs, Francis. "The Role of the European Court of Justice in the Protection of the Environment." *Journal of Environmental Law* 18, no. 2 (2006): 185–205.

Lavranos, Nikolaos. "Judicial Review of UN Sanctions by the European Court of Justice." *Nordic Journal of International Law* 78, no. 3 (2009): 343–59.

O'Boyle, Michael. "On Reforming the Operation of the European Court of Human Rights." *European Human Rights Law Review* no. 1 (2008): 1–11.

Perju, Vlad F. "Reason and Authority in the European Court of Justice." *Virginia Journal of International Law* 49, no. 2 (Winter 2009): 307–77.

Rieder, Clemens. "Protecting Human Rights Within the European Union: Who Is Better Qualified to Do the Job—The European Court of Justice or the European Court of Human Rights?" *The Tulane European and Civil Law Forum* 20 (2005): 73–107.

Skouris, Wassilios. "The Position of the European Court of Justice in the EU Legal Order and Its Relationship with National Constitutional Courts." *Zeitschrift für öffentliches Recht* 60, no. 3 (September 2005): 323–33.

Solan, Lawrence M. "The Interpretation of Multilingual Statutes by the European Court of Justice." *Brooklyn Journal of International Law* 34, no. 2 (2009): 277–302.

Solanke, Iyiola. "Diversity and Independence in the European Court of Justice." *The Columbia Journal of European Law* 15, no. 1 (Fall 2008): 89–121.

Inter-American Court of Human Rights

Books

Davidson, Scott. *The Inter-American Court of Human Rights.* Aldershot: Dartmouth, 1992.

Pasqualucci, Jo M. *The Practice and Procedure of the Inter-American Court of Human Rights.* New York: Cambridge University Press, 2003.

Articles

Basch, Fernando Felipe. "The Doctrine of the Inter-American Court of Human Rights Regarding States' Duty to Punish Human Rights Violations and Its Dangers." *American University International Law Review* 23, no. 1 (2007/08): 195–229.

Bertoni, Eduardo Andrés. "The Inter-American Court of Human Rights and the European Court of Human Rights: A Dialogue on Freedom of Expression Standards." *European Human Rights Review* no. 3 (2009): 332–52.

Brunner, Lisi. "The Rise of Peoples Rights in the Americas: The Saramaka People Decision of the Inter-American Court of Human Rights." *Chinese Journal of International Law* 7, no. 3 (November 2008): 699–711.

Cavallaro, James L., and Stephanie Erin Brewer. "Reevaluating Regional Human Rights Litigation in the Twenty-First Century: The Case of the Inter-American Court." *American Journal of International Law* 102, no. 4 (October 2008): 768–827.

Delgado, Jorge Luis. "The Inter-American Court of Human Rights." *ILSA Journal of International & Comparative Law* 5, no. 3 (Summer 1999): 541–49.

Osuna, Karla Irasema Quintana. "Recognition of Women's Rights Before the Inter-American Court of Human Rights." *Harvard Human Rights Journal* 21, no. 2 (Summer 2008): 301–12.

INTERNATIONAL HUMANITARIAN LAW

Internet Portals

Human Rights/Constitutional Rights at Columbia University. www.hrcr.org/.

Human Rights Guide at the University of Toronto. www.law-lib.utoronto.ca/resguide/humrtsgu.htm.

Rights International Research Guide for International Human Rights Lawyers. http://rightsinternational .org/guide.html.

Reference

Joseph, Sarah, and Adam McBeth. *Research Handbook on International Human Rights Law*. Northhampton, MA: Edward Elgar, 2010.

Books

Arnold, Roberta, and Noëlle Quénivet, eds. *International Humanitarian Law and Human Rights Law: Towards a New Merger in International Law*. Leiden and Boston: Martinus Nijhoff, 2008.

Askin, Kelly Dawn, and Dorean M. Koenig. *Women and International Human Rights Law*. Vols. 1–3. Ardsley, NY: Transnational, 1999–2001.

Bouchet-Saulnier, François. *The Practical Guide to Humanitarian Law*. 2nd Eng. ed. Lanham, MD: Rowman & Littlefield Publishers, 2007.

Gibney, Mark. *International Human Rights Law: Returning to Universal Principles*. Lanham, MD: Rowman & Littlefield Publishers, 2008.

Gibson, John S. *Dictionary of International Human Rights Law*. Lanham, MD: Scarecrow Press, 1996.

Gondek, Michal. *The Reach of Human Rights in a Globalizing World: Extraterritorial Application of Human Rights Treaties*. Antwerp: Intersentia, 2009.

Halshoven, Frits, and Peter Macalister-Smith. *The Implementation of International Humanitarian Law*. Boston: Martinus Nijhoff, 1989.

Heinze, Eric. *Waging Humanitarian War: The Ethics, Law, and Politics of Humanitarian Intervention*. Albany: State University of New York Press, 2009.

Humphrey, John P. *No Distant Millennium: The International Law of Human Rights*. Paris: Unesco, 1989.

Ibhawoh, Bonny. *Imperialism and Human Rights: Colonial Discourses of Rights and Liberties in African History*. Albany: State University of New York Press, 2007.

James, Stephen. *Universal Human Rights: Origins and Development*. New York: LFB Scholarly Publishers, 2007.

Kaleck, Wolfgang et al. *International Prosecution of Human Rights Crimes*. New York: Springer, 2007.

McBeth, Adam. *International Economic Actors and Human Rights*. New York: Routledge, 2009.

Normand, Roger, and Sarah Zaidi. *Human Rights at the UN: The Political History of Universal Justice*. Bloomington: Indiana University Press, 2008.

Seibert-Fohr, Anja. *Prosecuting Serious Human Rights Violations*. New York: Oxford University Press, 2009.

White, James D., and Anthony J. Marsella, eds. *Fear of Persecution: Global Human Rights, International Law, and Human Well-Being*. Lanham, MD: Lexington Books, 2007.

Articles

Duxbury, Alison. "Drawing Lines in the Sand—Characterising Conflicts for the Purpose of Teaching International Humanitarian Law." *Melbourne Journal of International Law* 8, no. 2 (October 2007): 259–72.

Reisman, W. Michael. "The Lessons of Qana." *Yale Journal of International Law* 22, no. 2 (Summer 1997): 381–99.

Sassòli, Marco. "The Implementation of International Humanitarian Law: Current and Inherent Challenges." *Yearbook of International Humanitarian Law* 10 (2007): 45–73.

INTERNATIONAL ENVIRONMENTAL LAW

Internet Portals

BNA. *Daily Environmental Report*. www.bna.com/products/ens/bder.htm.

BNA. *International Environment Daily*. www.bna.com/products/ens/iedm.htm.

BNA. *World Climate Change Report*. www.bna.com/product/ens/wccr.htm.

Center for International Environmental Law (CIEL). www.ciel.org/.

Climate Wire. www.eenews.net/cw/.

CRS Reports on the Environment. http://ncseonline.org/NLE/CRs/.

EcoLex. www.ecolex.org/.

Electronic Information System for International Law (EISIL). www.eisil.org/.

Environmental Law Reporter. www.elr.info/index.cfm.

Environmental Treaties and Resource Indicators (ENTRI). http://sedac.ciesin.columbia.edu/entri.

Green Wire. www.greenwire.com/.

National University of Singapore. *APCEL (Asia Pacific Centre for Environmental Law)*. http://law.nus.edu.sg/apcel/.

Pacific Regional Environment Programme. www.sprep.org/.

Reference

Fitzmaurice, Malgosia et al., eds. *Research Handbook on International Environmental Law*. Northhampton, MA: Edward Elgar, 2010.

Books

Andresen, Steiner et al. *Science and Politics in International Environmental Regimes: Between Integrity and Involvement*. New York: Manchester University Press, 2000.

Birnie, Patricia et al. *International Law and the Environment*. 3rd ed. New York: Oxford University Press, 2009.

Bodansky, Dan. *The Art and Craft of International Environmental Law*. Cambridge, MA: Harvard University Press, 2010.

Breitmeier, Helmut et al. *Analyzing International Environmental Regimes: From Case Study to Database*. Cambridge, MA: MIT Press, 2006.

Ebbesson, Jonas, and Phoebe Okowa, eds. *Environmental Law and Justice in Context*. New York: Cambridge University Press, 2009.

Haas, Peter M. et al., eds. *Institutions for the Earth: Sources of Effective International Environmental Protection*. Cambridge, MA: MIT Press, 1993.

Miles, Edward L. *Environmental Regime Effectiveness: Confronting Theory with Evidence*. Cambridge, MA: MIT Press, 2002.

Paddock, Lee et al., eds. *Compliance and Enforcement in Environmental Law*. Northhampton, MA: Edward Elgar, 2010.

Stephens, Tim. *International Courts and Environmental Protection*. New York: Cambridge University Press, 2009.

Essays

Haas, Peter M. "Epistemic Communities." In *The Oxford Handbook of International Environmental Law*, ed. Dan Bodansky et al., 791–806. New York: Oxford University Press, 2007.

Articles

Barrett, Scott. "The Incredible Economics of Geoengineering." *Environmental and Resource Economics* 39, no. 1 (January 2008): 45–54.

Downs, George W. et al. "The Transformational Model of International Regime Design: Triumph or Experience?" *Columbia Journal of Transnational Law* 38, no. 3 (2000): 465–514.

Weiss, Edith Brown. "International Environmental Law: Contemporary Issues and the Emergence of a New World Order." *Georgetown Law Journal* 81, no. 3 (March 1993): 675–710.

THE ENVIRONMENT: AIR LAW

Reference

Heere, Wybo P. "Bibliography of Air Law 2000." *Air and Space Law* 26, nos. 4/5 (September 2001): 236–87.

Books

Ashford, Nicholas A., and Charles C. Caldart. *Environmental Law, Policy, and Economics: Reclaiming the Environmental Agenda*. Cambridge, MA: The MIT Press, 2008.

Bankö, Marietta, and Kai Uwe-Schrogl, eds. *Space Law: Current Problems and Perspectives for Future Regulation*. Utrecht: Eleven International Publications, 2005.

Banner, Stuart. *Who Owns the Sky? The Struggle to Control Airspace from the Wright Brothers On*. Cambridge, MA: Harvard University Press, 2008.

Cheng, Chia-Jui. *The Use of Airspace and Outer Space for All Mankind in the 21st Century*. The Hague and London: Kluwer Law International, 1995.

Gangale, Thomas. *The Development of Outer Space: Sovereignty and Property Rights in International Space Law*. Santa Barbara, CA: Praeger, 2009.

Haanappel, P. P. C. *Law and Policy of Air, Space and Outer Space*. Boston: Kluwer Law International, 2009.

Lyall, Francis, and Paul B. Larsen. *Space Law: A Treatise*. Burlington, VT: Ashgate Publishing, 2009.

Okowa, Phoebe. *State Responsibility for Transboundary Air Pollution in International Law*. New York: Oxford University Press, 2000.

Reitze, Arnold W. *Air Pollution Control Law*. Washington, DC: Environmental Law Institute, 2001.

Stokes, Paul. *A Practical Approach to Environmental Law*. New York: Oxford University Press, 2009

Vietzen, Laurel A. *Practical Environmental Law*. New York: Aspen Publications, 2008.

Articles

Bentivoglio, Ludovico Matteo. "Conflicts Problems in Air Law." *Recueil des Cours* 119, no. 3 (1966): 73–180.

Cheng, Bin. "A New Era in the Law of International Carriage by Air from Warsaw (1929) to Montreal (1999)." *The International and Comparative Law Quarterly* 53, no. 4 (October 2004): 833–59.

———. "The Labyrinth of the Law of International Carriage by Air: Has the Montreal Convention 1999 Slain the Minotaur?" *Zeitschrift für Luft-und Weltraumrecht* 50, no. 2 (2001): 155–72.

Dempsey, Paul Stephen. "Accidents and Injuries in International Air Law." *Annals of Air and Space Law* 34 (2009): 285–310.

Haanappel, Peter P. C. "The Impact of Changing Air Transport Economics on Air Law and Policy: A Short Commentary." *Annals of Air and Space Law* 34 (2009): 519–27.

Huston, James W., and Bill O'Connor. "Admiralty Law and Jurisdiction in Air Crash Cases." *The Journal of Air Law and Commerce* 69, no. 2 (Spring 2004): 299–317.

Milde, Michael. "'Rendition Flights' and International Air Law." *Zeitschrift für Luft-und Weltraumrecht* 57, no. 4 (2008): 477–86.

Moore, Larry. "The New Montreal Liability Convention, Major Changes in International Air Law: An End to the Warsaw Convention." *Tulane Journal of International and Comparative Law* 9 (Spring 2001): 223–32.

Oduntan, Gbenga. "The Generational-Technological Gap in Air and Space Law." *Journal of Space Law* 29, nos. 1/2 (Spring/Fall 2003): 185–204.

Polkowska, Małgorzata. "The Development of Air Law: From the Paris Conference of 1910 to the Chicago Convention of 1944." *Annals of Air and Space Law* 33 (2008): 59–90.

Sachdeva, G. S. "Challenges in Air Law." *The Indian Journal of International Law* 47, no. 2 (April–June 2007): 200–24.

THE ENVIRONMENT: MARITIME LAW

Internet Portals

International Fisheries Law and Policy Portal. www.intfish.net

United Nations. *Division of Ocean Affairs and the Law of the Sea, Office of Legal Affairs.* www.un.org/depts/los

Reference

Lowe, Vaughn, and Stefan Talmon, eds. *The Legal Order of the Oceans: Basic Documents on Law of the Sea.* Oxford: Hart Publications, 2009.

Books

Anderson, David. *Modern Law of the Sea.* Leiden: Martinus Nijhoff Publishers, 2007.

Cainos, Hugo. *Law of the Sea.* Aldershot: Dartmouth, 2001.

Elferink, Alex G. Oude, ed. *Stability and Change in the Law of the Sea: The Role of the LOS Convention.* Leiden: Martinus Nijhoff Publishers, 2005.

Juda, Lawrence. *International Law and Ocean Use Management: The Evidence of Ocean Governance.* New York: Routledge, 1996.

Koivurova, Timo et al., eds. *Climate Governance in the Arctic.* New York: Springer, 2009.

Mandaraka-Sheppard, Alexandra. *Modern Maritime Law and Risk Management.* London: Informa Publishing, 2008.

Nordquist, Myron H., ed. *Freedom of Seas, Passage Rights and the 1982 Law of the Sea Convention.* Leiden: Martinus Nijhoff Publishers, 2009.

Ringborn, Henrik, ed. *Competing Norms in the Law of Marine Environmental Protection: Focus on Ship Safety and Pollution Prevention.* London: Kluwer Law International, 1997.

Symmons, Clive Ralph. *Historic Waters in the Law of the Sea: A Modern Re-Appraisal.* Leiden: Martinus Nijhoff Publishers, 2008.

Vidas, Davor, ed. *Law, Technology and Science for Oceans in Globalisation.* Boston: Martinus Nihoff Publishers, 2010.

Articles

Becker, Michael A. "International Law of the Sea." *International Lawyer* 43, no. 2 (Summer 2009): 915–28.

Blanco-Bazán, Agustin. "Peace and the Law of the Sea." *Ocean Yearbook* 18 (2004): 88–97.

de la Fayette, Louise. "The Marine Environment Protection Committee: The Conjunction of the Law of the Sea and International Environmental Law." *International Journal of Marine and Coastal Law* 16, no. 2 (June 2001): 155–238.

Dubner, Barry. "On the Interplay of International Law of the Sea and the Prevention of Maritime Pollution: How Far Can a State Proceed in Protecting Itself from Conflicting Norms in International Law." *Georgetown International Environmental Law Review* 11, no. 1 (Fall 1998): 137–61.

Dzidzornu, David M. "Marine Environment Protection Under Regional Conventions: Limits to the Contribution of Procedural Norms." *Ocean Development and International Law* 33, nos. 3/4 (2002): 263–316.

Hafetz, Jonathan L. "Fostering Protection of the Marine Environment and Economic Development: Article 121(3) of the Third Law of the Sea Convention." *American University International Law Review* 12, no. 3 (2000): 583–637.

Koivurova, Timo, and Leena Mäläki. "The Participation of Indigenous Peoples in International Norm-Making in the Arctic." *Polar Record* 42, no. 221 (April 2006): 101–9.

Randeniya, Chatura. "Sharing the World's Resources: Equitable Distribution and the North-South Dialogue in the New Law of the Sea." *Sri Lanka Journal of International Law* 15 (2003): 149–70.

Schwarte, Christoph. "Environmental Concerns in the Adjudication of the International Tribunal for the Law of the Sea." *Georgetown International Environmental Law Review* 16, no. 3 (Spring 2004): 421–39.

Scovazzi, Tullio. "The Evolution of International Law of the Sea." *Recueil des Cours* 286 (2001): 39–244.

Stiles, Kendall. "Who Is Keeping the Seas Safe? Testing Theories of International Law Compliance." *Cooperation and Conflict* 45, no. 2 (June 2010): 139–61.

Treves, Tullio. "Human Rights and the Law of the Sea." *Berkeley Journal of International Law* 28, no. 1 (2010): 1–14.

Weeks, Edythe E. "After Interdependence: Aren't We Back to Hegemony?: Revisiting Interdependence and the Law of the Sea, in a Unipolar Era." *Revue de Droit International de Sciences Diplomatique et Politiques* 81, no. 2 (2003): 117–48.

FORCE QUA TERRORISM

Internet Portals

Grossman, Andrew. "A Research Guide to Cases and Materials on Terrorism." www.nyulawglobal.org/globalex/Terrorism.htm.

Maja, Innocent. "Defining International Terrorism in Light of Liberation Movements." www.nyulawglobal.org/globalex/International_terrorism&Liberation_movements.htm.

Reference Works

Mehta, Raj K., ed. *International Encyclopædia of Terrorism Laws*. New Delhi: Pentagon Press, 2007.

Books

Barnidge, Robert P., Jr. *Non-State Actors and Terrorism: Applying the Law of State Responsibility and the Due Diligence Principle*. The Hague: Asser Press, 2007.

Blakesley, Christopher L. *Terrorism and Anti-Terrorism: A Normative and Practical Assessment*. Ardsley, NY: Transnational Publishers, 2006.

Chainoglou, Kalliopi. *International Terrorism and Changes in International Law*. Cizur Menor, Spain: Thomson/Aranzadi, 2007.

Duffy, Helen. *The "War on Terror" and the Framework of International Law*. New York: Cambridge University Press, 2005.

Ginbar, Yuval. *Why Not Torture Terrorists?: Moral, Practical, and Legal Aspects of the "Ticking Bomb" Justification for Torture*. New York: Oxford University Press, 2008.

Guelke, Adrian. *Terrorism and Global Disorder: Political Violence in the Contemporary World*. New York: I. B. Tauris, 2006.

Imre, Robert et al. *Responding to Terrorism: Political, Philosophical and Legal Perspectives*. Burlington, VT: Ashgate, 2008.

Koufa, Kalliopi, ed. *International Law at the Turn of the Century*. Athens: Sakkoulas, 1998.

Ku, Charlotte, and Harold K. Jacobson, eds. *Democratic Accountability and the Use of Force in International Law*. New York: Cambridge University Press, 2003.

Lang, Anthony F., ed. *War, Torture, and Terrorism: Rethinking the Rules of International Security*. New York: Routledge, 2009.

Lubell, Noam. *Extraterritorial Use of Force Against Non-State Actors (Oxford Monographs in International Law)*. New York: Oxford University Press, 2010.

May, Larry. *War Crimes and Just War*. New York: Cambridge University Press, 2007.

Pati, Rosa. *Due Process and International Terrorism: An International Legal Analysis*. Boston: Martinus Nijhoff Publishers, 2009.

Sánchez, Pablo Antonio Fernández, ed. *International Legal Dimension of Terrorism*. Leiden: Martinus Nijhoff Publishers, 2009.

Saul, Ben. *Defining Terrorism in International Law*. New York: Oxford University Press, 2006.

van Krieken, Peter J., ed. *Terrorism and the International Legal Order: With Special Reference to the UN, the EU and Cross-Border Aspects*. The Hague: TMC Asser, 2002.

Weinbert, Leonard, ed. *Democratic Responses to Terrorism*. New York: Routledge, 2008.

Articles

Abi-Saab, Georges. "The Proper Role of International Law in Combating Terrorism." *Chinese Journal of International Law* 1, no. 1 (2002): 305–13.

Ackerman, Bruce A. "Terrorism and the Constitutional Order." *Fordham Law Review* 75, no. 2 (November 2006): 475–88.

Barna, Christian. "Multilateral Engagement in Fighting Terrorism." *Romanian Journal of International Affairs* 9, nos. 2/3 (2003): 135–51.

Bassiouni, M. Cherif. "Terrorism: The Persistent Dilemma of Legitimacy." *Case Western Journal of International Law* 36, nos. 2/3 (2004): 299–306.

Cassese, Antonio. "Terrorism Is Also Disrupting Some Crucial Legal Categories of International Law." *European Journal of International Law* 12, no. 5 (December 2001): 993–1001.

Charney, Jonathan I. "The Use of Force Against Terrorism and International Law." *American Journal of International Law* 95, no. 4 (October 2001): 835–39.

Fletcher, George P. "The Indefinable Concept of Terrorism." *Journal of International Criminal Justice* 4, no. 5 (November 2006): 894–911.

Greenwood, Christopher. "War, Terrorism, and International Law." *Current Legal Problems* 56 (2003): 505–30.

Guillaume, Gilbert. "Terrorism and International Law." *The International and Comparative Law Quarterly* 53, no. 3 (July 2004): 537–48.

Liese, Andrea. "Exceptional Necessity: How Liberal Democracies Contest the Prohibition of Torture and Ill-Treatment When Countering Terrorism." *Journal of International Law & International Relations* 5, no. 1 (Winter 2009): 17–47.

Lippman, Matthew. "The New Terrorism and International Law." *Tulsa Journal of Comparative & International Law* 10, no. 2 (Spring 2002): 297–368.

Mani, V. S. "International Terrorism and the Quest for Legal Controls." *International Studies* 40, no. 1 (February 2003): 41–67.

Möckli, Daniel. "The Emergence of Terrorism as a Distinct Category of International Law." *Texas International Law Journal* 44, no. 1 (Fall/Winter 2008): 157–83.

Rona, Gabor. "Legal Frameworks to Combat Terrorism: An Abundant Inventory of Existing Tools." *Chicago Journal of International Law* 5, no. 2 (Winter 2005): 499–509.

Rostow, Nicholas. "Before and After: The Changed UN Response to Terrorism Since September 11th." *Cornell International Law Journal* 35, no. 3 (Winter 2002): 475–90.

Schmid, Alex. "Terrorism—The Definitional Problem." *Case Western Reserve Journal of International Law* 36, nos. 2/3 (2004): 375–419.

Sloane, Robert D. "The Cost of Conflation: Preserving the Dualism of *Jus ad Bellum* and *Jus in Bello* in the Contemporary Law of War." *The Yale Journal of International Law* 34, no. 1 (Winter 2009): 47–112.

Stahn, Carsten. "Terrorist Acts as 'Armed Attack': The Right to Self-Defense, Article 51 (1/2) of the UN Charter and International Terrorism." *The Fletcher Forum of World Affairs* 27, no. 2 (Summer 2003): 35–54.

Sultan, Maria. "Biological Terrorism: The Threat of the 21st Century." *Strategic Studies* 21, no. 4 (Winter 2001): 116–40.

Wattellier, Jeremie J. "Comparative Legal Response to Terrorism: Lessons From Europe." *Hastings International and Comparative Law Review* 27, no. 2 (Winter 2004): 397–419.

Young, Reuven. "Defining Terrorism: The Evolution of Terrorism as a Legal Concept in International Law and Its Influence on Definition in Domestic Legislation." *Boston College International and Comparative Law Review* 29, no. 1 (Winter 2006): 23–105.

POSTCOLONIALISM

Books

Afzal-Khan, Fawzia, and Kalpana Sheshadri-Crooks, eds. *The Pre-Occupation of Post-Colonial Studies*. Durham, NC: Duke University Press, 2000.

Anghie, Antony. *Imperialism, Sovereignty and the Making of International Law*. New York: Cambridge University Press, 2005.

Ashcroft, Bill, Gareth Griffiths, and Helen Tiffin. *The Post-Colonial Studies Reader*. New York: Routledge, 2006.

Benton, Lauren A. *Law and Colonial Cultures: Legal Regimes in World History, 1400–1900*. New York: Cambridge University Press, 2002.

Césaire, Aime. *Discourse on Colonialism*. New York: Monthly Review Press, 1972.

Darian-Smith, Eve, and Peter Fitzpatrick, eds. *Laws of the Postcolonial*. Ann Arbor: University of Michigan Press, 1999.

Fautsmann, Hubert, and Nicos Peristianis, eds. *Britain in Cyprus: Colonialism and Post-Colonialism 1878–2006*. Mannheim: Bibliopolis, 2006.

Young, Robert J. C. *Post-Colonialism: A Very Short Introduction*. New York: Oxford University Press, 2003.

Articles

Anghie, Antony. "The Evolution of International Law: Colonial and Postcolonial Realities." *Third World Quarterly* 27, no. 5 (July 2006): 739–53.

Harris, Cole. "How Did Colonialism Dispossess? Comments from an Edge of Empire." *Annals of the Association of Geographers* 94, no. 1 (2004): 165–82.

Harzenski, Sharon. "Post-Colonial Studies: Terrorism, a History, Stage Two." *Temple International and Comparative Law Journal* 17, no. 2 (Fall 2003): 351–407.

Kennedy, Dane. "Imperial History and Post-Colonial Theory." *The Journal of Imperial and Commonwealth History* 24, no. 3 (1996): 345–63.

Lyon, Beth. "Discourse in Development: A Post-Colonial Theory 'Agenda' for the UN Committee on Economic, Social and Cultural Rights Through the Post-Colonial Lens." *Journal of Gender, Social Policy & the Law* 10, no. 3 (2002): 536–79.

INTERNATIONAL POLITICAL INTERACTION

Reference Works

Gill, Terry, and Dieter Fieck, eds. *Handbook of the International Law of Military Operations*. New York: Oxford University Press, 2010.

Journal of International Law & International Relations 1, nos. 1–2 (December 2005).

Books

Armstrong, James D., Theo Farrell, and Hélène Lambert. *International Law and International Relations*. New York: Cambridge University Press, 2007.

Biersteker, Thomas et al., eds. *International Law and International Relations: Bridging Theory and Practice*. New York: Routledge, 2006.

Bolewski, Wilfried M. *Diplomacy and International Law in Globalized Relations*. Berlin: Springer Verlag, 2007.

Brütsch, Christian, ed. *Law and Legalization in Transnational Relations*. New York: Routledge, 2007.

Byers, Michael. *The Role of Law in International Politics*. New York: Oxford University Press, 2000.

Çali, Basak. *International Law for International Relations*. New York: Oxford University Press, 2010.

Covell, Charles. *Kant and the Law of Peace: A Study in the Philosophy of International Law and International Relations*. New York: Macmillan, 1998.

Dekker, Ige F., and Wouter G. Werner, eds. *Governance and International Legal Theory*. Boston: M. Martinus Nijhoff Publishers, 2004.

Frick, Marie-Luisa, and Andreas Oberprantacher. *Power and Justice in International Relations: Interdisciplinary Approaches to Global Challenges*. Burlington, VT: Ashgate Publishing Co., 2010.

Giorgetti, Chiara. *A Principled Approach to State Failure: International Community Actions in Emergency Situations*. Boston: Martinus Nijhoff Publishers, 2010.

Hill, Norman. *Claims to Territory in International Law and Relations*. New York: Oxford University Press, 1945.

Kaufmann, Johan. *The Diplomacy of International Relations: Selected Writings*. The Hague: Kluwer Law International, 1998.

Kratochwil, Friedrich. *Rules, Norms and Decisions on the Conditions of Practical and Legal Reasoning in International Relations and Domestic Affairs.* New York: Cambridge University Press, 1989.

Meyer, Lukas H., ed. *Legitimacy, Justice and Public International Law.* New York: Cambridge University Press, 2009.

Onuf, Nicholas Greenwood. *International Legal Theory: Essays and Engagements, 1966–2006.* London: Routledge-Cavendish, 2008.

Reus-Smit, Christian, ed. *The Politics of International Law.* New York: Cambridge University Press, 2004.

Stumpf, Christoph A. *The Grotian Theology of International Law: Hugo Grotius and the Moral Foundations of International Relations.* New York: Walter de Gruyter, 2006.

Articles

Carty, Anthony. "International Legal Personality and the End of the Subject: Natural Law and Phenomenological Responses to New Approaches to International Law." *Melbourne Journal of International Law* 6, no. 2 (October 2005): 534–52.

Cullet, Philippe. "Differential Treatment in International Law: Towards a New Paradigm of Interstate Relations." *European Journal of International Law* 10, no. 3 (1999): 549–82.

Duruigbo, Emeka. "International Relations, Economics and Compliance with International Law: Harnessing Common Resources to Protect the Environment and Solve Global Problems." *California Western International Law Journal* 31, no. 2 (Spring 2000): 177–213.

Ecobescu, Nicolae. "Sovereignty as the Foundation and Basic Principle of International Law." *Romanian Journal of International Affairs* 4, nos. 3/4 (1998): 40–64.

Ferreira-Snyman, Anél. "Sovereignty and the Changing Nature of Public International Law: Toward a World Law?" *The Comparative and International Law Journal of Southern Africa* 40, no. 3 (November 2007): 395–424.

Krasner, Stephen D. "International Law and International Relations: Together, Apart, Together?" *Chicago Journal of International Law* 1, no. 1 (Spring 2000): 93–99.

Nagan, Winston P., and Craig Hammer. "The Changing Character of Sovereignty in International Law and International Relations." *Columbia Journal of Transnational Law* 43, no. 1 (2004): 141–87.

Nagy, Boldizsár. "The Theory of International Relations and the Science of International Law." *Annales Universitatis Scientiarum Budapestinensis de Rolando Eötvös Nominatae* 29 (1988): 112–26.

Nirmal, B. C. "Sovereignty in International Law." *Soochow Law Journal* 3, no. 2 (July 2006): 1–51.

Palmer, Matthew S. R. "International Law/Intercultural Relations." *Chicago Journal of International Law* 1, no. 1 (Spring 2000): 159–65.

Simpson, Gerry. "Dueling Agendas: International Relations and International Law (Again)." *Journal of International Law & International Relations* 1, nos. 1–2 (December 2005): 61–73.

Vagts, Detlev F. "International Relations Looks at Customary International Law: A Traditionalist's View." *European Journal of International Law* 15, no. 5 (2004): 1031–40.

Walker, Jeffrey K. "Law & International Relations." *University of Kansas Law Review* 51, no. 2 (February 2003): 297–301.

Yannis, Alexandros. "The Concept of Suspended Sovereignty in International Law and Its Implications in International Politics." *European Journal of International Law* 13, no. 5 (December 2002): 1037–52.

REPRINT PERMISSIONS

CHAPTER 5

Originally appearing in *The Michigan Journal of International Law*, Forthcoming; SMU Dedman School of Law Legal Studies Research Paper No. 00–35.

CHAPTER 14

Originally appearing in *The Journal of Air Law and Commerce*, vol. 73, no. 1. Reprinted with permission of the SMU Law Review Association and the Dedman School of Law at Southern Methodist University.

CHAPTER 16

Originally appearing in *The International Journal of Marine and Coastal Law*, vol. 24, no. 1, March 2009, pp. 1–66. Reprinted with permission.

CHAPTER 20

Copyright 2005 by the Regents of the University of California. Reprinted in the *Berkeley Journal of International Law*, vol. 23, no. 3, by permission of the Regents of the University of California.

CHAPTER 22

Originally appearing in the *Texas International Law Journal*, vol. 45, no. 2, 2009. Reprinted with permission.

CHAPTER 24

Originally appearing in the *Penn State International Law Review*, vol. 25, no. 1, 2007. Reprinted with permission.

CHAPTER 25

Originally appearing in The *Journal of East Asia and International Law*, vol. 3, no. 1, 2010. Reprinted with permission.

INDEX